A LINGUISTIC KEY TO THE GREEK NEW TESTAMENT

Fritz Rienecker

Translated, with additions and revisions, from the German
SPRACHLICHER SCHLUESSEL ZUM GRIECHISCHEN NEUEN
TESTAMENT
edited by Cleon L. Rogers, Jr.

ZondervanPublishingHouse
Grand Rapids, Michigan

A Division of HarperCollins*Publishers*

A Linguistic Key to the Greek New Testament
Copyright © 1976, 1980 by The Zondervan Corporation
Grand Rapids, Michigan

Requests for information should be addressed to:
Zondervan Publishing House
Grand Rapids, Michigan 49530

This book was first published in Germany under the title Sprachlicher Schluessel
Zum Griechischen Neuen Testament © 1970 by Brunnen-Verlag, Giessen

The Greek text used in this book is that of The Greek New Testament edited by Kurt Aland,
Matthew Black, Carlo M. Martini, Bruce M. Metzger and Allen Wikgren. Copyright © 1966,
1968 by the American Bible Society, British and Foreign Bible Society, National Bible Society
of Scotland, Netherlands Bible Society, Württemberg Bible Society. This text was checked
against Novum Testamentum Graece edited by Eberhard Nestle.

Library of Congress Cataloging in Publication Data

Reinecker, Fritz.
    A linguistic key to the Greek New Testament.

    CONTENTS: v. 1. Matthew through Acts.—
v. 2. Romans through Revelation.
    1. Bible.   N.T.—Criticism, Textual.   2. Bible.
N.T.   Greek-Versions.   I. Rogers, Cleon L.
II. Title.
BS1938.R513   225.4'8   75-45486
ISBN 0-310-32050-X

Edited by Edward Viening

Printed in the United States of America

95 96 97 98 99 00 / DP / 20 19 18 17 16 15

This edition is printed on acid-free paper and meets the American National Standards Institute
Z39.48 standard.

CONTENTS

FOREWORD TO THE ENGLISH REVISION

The *Sprachlicher Schlüssel* has undergone numerous German editions and has proven to be a real help to students of God's holy Word. All who have used it with immense profit are deeply indebted to the scholar and man of God, Fritz Rienecker.

On August 15, 1965, the earthly work of Fritz Rienecker came to an end. The Lord whom he so loved called him home after a fruitful ministry here on earth. His many literary works live on and continue to be used by those seeking to study the Bible.

Mr. Rienecker had intended to write two other books which were to supplement the *Linguistic Key*. One was to cover the theological concepts of the Scriptures and the other was to provide a historical background explaining the world of the New Testament. The realization of this vision was cut short by his death.

The translation and revision of the *Linguistic Key* has attempted in a limited way to achieve the purpose intended by the two proposed works of Rienecker. Explanations have been given not only regarding the grammatical forms, but there are also numerous new references to other works where the background material may be found. The revision includes a wider range of references to grammatical works, commentaries, journal articles, and historical works, and these are especially adapted to the English reader. The citation of a work does not mean that the theological position of its author is endorsed, but only that the particular quote was deemed valuable in reference to its historical or grammatical insight.

A word of thanks is due to my family, relatives and friends for their patient endurance during the long hours of work with Rienecker. A special word of thanks is due to Dr. Robert De Vries and The Zondervan Corporation for their kindness and patience. The faithful work of the typists, Mrs. Linda Hutchinson, Mrs. Barbara Capps and Miss Aileen Dunn has also been deeply appreciated. It would also be in order to thank my son, Cleon III, for his untiring work in copying the Greek words and proofreading the manuscript.

May the Spirit of God use these efforts to increase an interest in and an understanding of His holy Word.

Cleon Rogers,
Seeheim, Germany

FROM THE FOREWORD OF THE FIRST EDITION

A renewed struggle for a deeper understanding of God's Word is present in the ranks of all who earnestly want to live as Christians. There is a stronger desire to be clothed with the "whole armor of God." Where do we find the whole armor of God? It is not in the polemic, not in the apologetic, not in speculations, not in the mystical, and not in philosophy, but rather in the Word, the Holy Scriptures alone. This is where God has revealed Himself. This is where we must be at home. This is what matters, to grasp and learn the Word in all its weight and reality.

In order for this to be accomplished three tools are designed to help us. These are "Keys" which are to open the door of the New Testament for us, especially the door of the original text. Three "Keys" are designed to be our servants: *A Linguistic Key; A Key to the Concepts of the New Testament; A Key to the Background of the New Testament.*

Exactly what these three "Keys" mean, and the special duty of each will be presented in an introduction to each and references will be made to each of these three keys.

However, above everything else, this thesis remains absolute and certain: the Holy Spirit is the only true Key to the Word of God. Nevertheless, the petition for the Holy Spirit does not exclude earnest and energetic study.

Introduction to the *Linguistic Key to the New Testament.*

In 1524 Luther wrote this concerning the value of the Greek language: "In the measure that we love the Gospel, so let us place a strong emphasis on the languages. For it was not without reason that God wrote the Scriptures in two languages, the Old Testament in Hebrew and the New Testament in Greek. That language which God did not despise but rather chose above all others for His Word is the language which we also should honor above all others. It is a sin and shame that we do not learn this language of our Book, especially since God has now provided us people and books, and gives us all kinds of things which both help us with this task and at the same time stimulates us to do this." There is nothing more to add to these words of Luther.

The user of the *Linguistic Key* will find in this work an exact explanation of the verb forms. The substantives and adjectives are given in the nominative. When it is necessary, the root of both the verbs and substantives will be presented; that is when it appears important to the author that it serves a practical purpose, but not however as an extra philological burden just for the sake of philology. The results of the newest commentaries will conscientiously be considered. The concern is that the reader and the exegete will be given an abundance of points of contact which the scientific student can only receive from the original text. Every chapter is complete in itself and even every section is understandable in itself.

It will often be seen in the *Linguistic Key* how important it is for the seeking reader and the practical exegete to take into consideration the grammatical side of the text investigation. He must do this through the exact examination of what may perhaps appear to be an unimportant "but" or "for." It is intended to sharpen his vision for the world of the little and the least. By this careful detail work it can, under circumstances, happen that a totally unimportant appearing word turns out to have a decisive meaning. It can even be that without this, a true understanding of the text is not possible. The *Linguistic Key* is intended also to be an initial and quick introduction to the understanding of the original text. Born out of the practical need, the *Key* is to serve the practical. It is intended to make possible a constant and living relation to the original text, to encourage a reflective reading of the text, to produce joy in the study of the Bible, both in family and private devotions, and to provide a personal adherence and careful attention to the Word. May the *Linguistic Key* often give new light through the grammatical usage to many a well-worn and threadbare word. May many words regain new life and new love.

In regard to the external feature, the *Linguistic Key* is further intended to be an aid in learning the New Testament vocabulary. Then, it is to build a first bridge to the use of the scholarly New Testament Greek grammar of Blass and Debrunner and to make reference to the great and valuable *Lexica* of Menge-Güthling, Bauer, and above all to Kittel's great *Theological Dictionary*. May the *Key* give a greater incentive to the useful study of the commentaries.

Fritz Rienecker

FOREWORD TO THE 7TH EDITION

No one would ever have thought that with the first edition of the *Linguistic Key* there would have been such a surprisingly large demand for it and that this demand would have continued. From 1938 to the first years of the war there were already 17,000 copies in 6 editions sold. The growing distress of war and the ever-increasing pressure of anti-Christian tendencies which were opposed to everything biblical made another new edition impossible. Since the end of the war the request for a new edition has been continually present. The interest for the *Linguistic Key* has started and continues so strongly that is has put the earlier demands in the shadows. The Brunnen Publishers, Giessen, have graciously undertaken the new edition. May God's goodness guide this new edition and may He use the 7th edition to deepen the study of the original text of the New Testament!

FOREWORD TO THE 8TH EDITION

The editors and the publishers thankfully rejoice that already, nine months after the appearance of the 7th edition, a new printing of the *Linguistic Key* is necessary. The fact that this edition is printed on India paper is welcomed with joy. May the Lord of the Word grant through His Spirit His blessed presence to this aid to the study of the Scriptures!

FOREWORD TO THE 9TH EDITION

In this edition of the *Linguistic Key* there are a few corrections. They have to do with corrections of some grammatical explanations (in the earlier editions there were always some typographical errors which kept creeping in). There are also some better styled expressions related to matters found in the latest commentaries.

The fact that 45,000 copies have been printed has filled our hearts with joy, especially since this is a work which is not designed to edify, but rather to give a purely linguistic help. It is a new proof showing how strong the desire is among earnest students of the Word and energetic readers to penetrate to a deeper understanding of God's Word with the help of the original text. May the Lord of the Word bless all of these dear friends and students of our faithful Bible!

Fritz Rienecker

ABBREVIATIONS

BOOKS AND JOURNALS

Abbott   Edwin A. Abbott, *Johannine Grammar* (London: Adam and Charles Black, 1906).

Abbott   T. K. Abbott, *A Critical and Exegetical Commentary on the Epistles to the Ephesians and the Colossians. The International Critical Commentary* (Edinburgh: T. & T. Clark, 1956).

Adamson   James Adamson, *The Epistle of James. The New International Commentary on the New Testament* (Grand Rapids: Eerdmans, 1977).

Alex   Joseph Addison Alexander, *Commentary on the Acts of the Apostles* (Grand Rapids: Zondervan, 1956).

Alford   Henry Alford, *The Greek Testament,* 5 vols. (London: Rivingtons, 1855).

Allen   Willoughby C. Allen, *A Critical and Exegetical Commentary on the Gospel According to St. Matthew. The International Critical Commentary* (Edinburgh: T. & T. Clark, 1965).

AM   W. F. Albright and C. S. Mann, *The Anchor Bible: Matthew* (Garden City, N.Y.: Doubleday, 1971).

ANET   James B. Pritchard (ed.), *Ancient Near Eastern Texts* (Princeton: Princeton University Press, 1955).

APC   Leon Morris, *The Apostolic Preaching of the Cross* (Grand Rapids: Eerdmans, 1956).

Arndt   W. F. Arndt, *Bible Commentary, The Gospel According to St. Luke* (St. Louis: Concorida, 1956).

AS   G. Abbott-Smith, *A Manual Greek Lexicon of the New Testament* (Edinburgh: T. & T. Clark, 1936).

BA   *Biblical Archaeologist.*

BAG   Walter Bauer, *A Greek-English Lexicon of the New Testament.* Translated by William F. Arndt and F. Wilbur Gingrich (Chicago: University of Chicago Press, 1957).

Bakker   W. F. Bakker, *The Greek Imperative* (Amsterdam: Adolf M. Hakkert, 1966).

Barrett   C. K. Barrett, *The Gospel According to St. John, An Introduction With Commentary and Notes on the Greek Text* (London: SPCK, 1958).

Barrett	C. K. Barrett, *The Epistle to the Romans* (New York: Harper, 1957).
Barrett	C. K. Barrett, *A Commentary on the First Epistle to the Corinthians* (London: Adam and Charles Black, 1968).
Barrett	C. K. Barrett, *The Second Epistle to the Corinthians* (London: Adam and Charles Black, 1973).
Barth	Marcus Barth, *The Anchor Bible: Ephesians,* 2 vols. (Garden City, N.Y.: Doubleday, 1974).
BC	F. J. Foakes Jackson and Kirsopp Lake, *The Beginnings of Christianity,* 5 vols. (London: Macmillan, 1920).
BD	F. Blass and A. Debrunner, *A Greek Grammar of the New Testament.* Translated and Revised by R. W. Funk (Chicago: University of Chicago Press, 1957).
BE	Richard Longenecker, *Biblical Exegesis in the Apostolic Period* (Grand Rapids: Eerdmans, 1975).
Beare	F. W. Beare, *The Epistles to the Philippians* (London: Adam and Charles Black, 1969).
Beare	F. W. Beare, *The First Epistle of Peter* (Oxford: Basil Blackwell, 1958).
Bengel	John Albert Bengel, *Gnomon of the New Testament,* 5 vols. (Edinburgh: T. & T. Clark, 1857).
Bernard	J. H. Bernard, *A Critical and Exegetical Commentary on the Gospel According to St. John. The International Critical Commentary,* 2 vols. (Edinburgh: T. & T. Clark, 1969).
Best	Ernest Best, *A Commentary on the First and Second Epistles to the Thessalonians* (London: Adam and Charles Black, 1972).
Best	Ernest Best, *First Peter. The New Century Bible* (London: Oliphants, 1971).
Beyer	Klaus Beyer, *Semitische Syntax im Neuen Testament* (Gottingen: Vandenhoeck & Ruprecht, 1968).
BG	Maximillian Zerwick, *Biblica Greek* (Rome: Scripta Pontificii Instituti Biblici, 1963).
BHS	James D. G. Dunn, *Baptism in the Holy Spirit* (London: SCM Press, 1974).
Bib Sac	*Bibliotheca Sacra.*

Bigg	Charles Bigg, *A Critical and Exegetical Commentary on the Epistles of St. Peter and St. Jude. The International Critical Commentary* (Edinburgh: T. & T. Clark, 1902).
Blinzler	Josef Blinzler, *The Trial of Jesus,* translated by Isabel and Florence McHugh (Westminster: Newman Press, 1959).
Blomqvist	Jerker Blomqvist, *Greek Particles in Hellenistic Prose* (Lund, Sweden: C. W. K. Gleerup, 1969).
Bousset	Wilhelm Bousset, *Die Offenbarung Johannis* (Gottingen: Vandenhoeck & Ruprecht, 1906).
BRD	William Ramsay, *The Bearing of Recent Discovery on the Trustworthiness of the New Testament* (Grand Rapids: Baker, 1953).
Brooke	A. E. Brooke, *A Critical and Exegetical Commentary on the Johannine Epistles. The International Critical Commentary* (Edinburgh: T. & T. Clark, 1912).
Brown	Raymond E. Brown, *The Anchor Bible: The Gospel According to John,* 2 vols. (London: Geoffrey Chapman, 1972, 1972).
Bruce	F. F. Bruce, *The Acts of the Apostles: The Greek Text With Introduction and Commentary* (Grand Rapids: Eerdmans, 1953).
Bruce-ET	F. F. Bruce, *Commentary on the Book of Acts: The English Text With Introduction, Exposition and Notes* (Grand Rapids: Eerdmans, 1960).
Bruce	F. F. Bruce, *I and II Corinthians. The New Century Bible* (London: Oliphants, 1971).
Bruce	F. F. Bruce, *Commentary on the Epistle to the Hebrews* (Grand Rapids: Eerdmans, 1977).
Bruner	Frederick Dale Bruner, *A Theology of the Holy Spirit; Pentecostal Experience and the New Testament Witness* (London: Hodder & Stoughton, 1971).
BS	Adolph Deissmann, *Bible Studies,* 2nd edition. Translated by Alexander Grieve (Edinburgh: T. & T. Clark, 1903).
Buchanan	George Wesley Buchanan, *The Anchor Bible: To the Hebrews* (Garden City, N.Y.: Doubleday, 1972).
Buckland	W. W. Buckland, *A Textbook of Roman Law* (Cambridge: Cambridge University Press, 1932).

Bultmann	Rudolph Bultmann, *The Gospel of St. John* (Philadelphia: Fortress Press, 1971).
Bultmann	Rudolf Bultmann, *Der zweite Brief an die Korinther; Kritschexegetischer Kommentar über das Neue Testament* (Gottingen: Vandenhoeck & Ruprecht, 1976).
Bultmann	Rudolf Bultmann, *Die drei Johannesbriefe. Kritschexegetischer Kommentar über das Neue Testament* (Gottingen: Vandenhoeck & Ruprecht, 1967).
Burton	Ernest DeWitt Burton, *A Critical and Exegetical Commentary on the Galatians. The International Critical Commentary* (Edinburgh: T. & T. Clark, 1956).
CAC	Fred O. Francis and Wayne A. Meeks (Editors), *Conflicts at Colossae: A Problem in the Interpretation of Early Christianity Illustrated by Selected Modern Studies*. Revised Edition (Missoula, Mont.: Scholars Press, 1975).
CAH	*The Cambridge Ancient History,* 12 vols. (Cambridge: At the University Press, 1927–1975).
Caird	G. B. Caird, *The Gospel of Luke* (London: Penguin Books, 1963).
Caird	G. B. Caird, *The Revelation of St. John the Divine. Black's New Testament Commentaries* (London: Adam and Charles Black, 1966).
Carrington	Philip Carrington, *According to Mark: A Running Commentary on the Oldest Gospel* (Cambridge: At the University Press, 1960).
Catchpole	David R. Catchpole, *The Trial of Jesus* (Leiden: E. J. Brill, 1971).
CBB	L. Coenen, E. Beyreuther, H. Bietenhard, *Theologisches Begriffslexicon zum Neuen Testament,* 3 vols. (Wuppertal: Brockhaus, 1971). English Edition; Colin Brown (ed.), *The New International Dictionary of New Testament Theology* (Grand Rapids: Zondervan, 1975).
CC	Stephen Benko and John J. O'Rourke, *The Catacombs and the Colosseum* (Valley Forge: Judson Press, 1971).
CD	*Cairo Damascus Covenant.*
CEC	Richard Longenecker, *The Christology of Early Jewish Christianity. Studies in Biblical Theology.* Second series 17 (London: SCM Press, 1970).

CEJC   Richard N. Longenecker, *The Christology of Early Jewish Christianity. Studies in Biblical Theology* (London: SCM Press, 1970).

CH   W. J. Conybeare and J. S. Howson, *The Life and Epistles of St. Paul* (Grand Rapids: Eerdmans, 1953).

Charles   R. H. Charles, *A Critical and Exegetical Commentary on the Revelation of St. John. The International Critical Commentary,* 2 vols. (Edinburgh: T. & T. Clark, 1920).

CNT   Leon Morris, *The Cross in the New Testament* (Grand Rapids: Eerdmans, 1965).

Conzelmann Hans Conzelmann, *Der erste Brief an die Korinther. Kritsch-exegetischer Kommentar über das Neue Testament,* von H. A. W. Meyer (Gottingen: Vandenhoeck & Ruprecht, 1969).

CPJ   Victor A. Tcherikover and Alexander Fuks (eds.), *Corpus Papyrorum Judaicarum* (Cambridge, Mass.: Harvard University Press, 1957-1964).

Cranfield   C.E. B. Cranfield, *The Gospel According to St. Mark. The Cambridge Greek Testament Commentary* (Cambridge: At the University Press, 1972).

Carnfield   Charles E. Cranfield, *Epistle to the Romans* (Naperville, Ill.: Allenson, 1979).

Cremer   Hermann Cremer, *Biblico-Theological Lexicon of the New Testament Greek,* Translated by William Urwick (Edinburgh: T. & T. Clark, 1954).

Crouch   James E. Crouch, *The Origin and Intention of the Colossian Haustafel* (Gottingen: Vandenhoeck & Ruprecht, 1972).

DC   Dio Chrysostom.

DCNT   G. Mussies, *Dio Chrysostom and the New Testament* (Leiden: E. J. Brill, 1972).

Delitzsch   Frank Delitzsch, *Commentary on the Epistle to the Hebrews.* Translated from the German by Thomas L. Kingsbury, 2 vols. (Grand Rapids: Eerdmans, 1952).

DGRA   William Smith, *A Dictionary of Greek & Roman Antiquities* (London: John Murray, 1872).

Dibelius   Martin Dibelius, *An Die Kolosser Epheser An Philemon. Handbuch zum Neuen Testament. Dritte Auflage; Neu Bearbeitet von Heinrich Greeven* (Tübingen: J. C. B. Mohr, 1953).

Dibelius	Martin Debelius, *Die Pastoralbriefe; Handbuch zum Neuen Testament* Vierte, ergäntze Auflage von Hans Conzelmann (Tübingen: J. C. B. Mohr, 1966).
Dibelius	Martin Dibelius and Heinrich Greeven, *A Commentary on the Epistle of James. Hermeneia.* Translated by Michael A. Williams (Philadelphia: Fortress Press, 1976).
DM	H. E. Dana and J. R. Mantey, *A Manual Grammar of the Greek New Testament* (New York: Macmillan, 1950).
Dodd	C. H. Dodd, *The Interpretation of the Fourth Gospel* (Cambridge: At the University Press, 1958).
Dodd	C. H. Dodd, *The Epistle of Paul to the Romans* (London: Hodder & Stoughton, 1932).
DSS	*Dead Sea Scrolls.*
Eadie	John Eadie, *Commentary on the Epistle of Paul to the Galatians* (Minneapolis: James and Klock Christian Publishing Co., 1977).
Eadie	John Eadie, *Commentary on the Epistle to the Ephesians* (Grand Rapids: Zondervan, 1956).
Eadie	John Eadie, *Commentary on the Epistle of Paul to the Colossians* (Minneapolis: James and Klock Christian Publishing Co., 1977).
EBC	Frank E. Gaebelein (Gen. ed.), *The Expositor's Bible Commentary* (Grand Rapids: Zondervan, 1976).
ECC	Vernon H. Neufeld, *The Earliest Christian Confessions* (Grand Rapids: Eerdmans, 1963).
Edersheim, Temple	Alfred Edersheim, *The Temple: Its Ministry and Services* (Grand Rapids: Eerdmans, 1954).
EGT	W. Robertson Nicol (ed.), *The Expositor's Greek Testament,* 5 vols. (Grand Rapids: Eerdmans, 1956).
Ellicott	Charles J. Ellicott, *A Critical and Grammatical Commentary on St. Paul's Epistle to the Galatians* (Boston: Draper and Halliday, 1867).
Ellicott	Charles J. Ellicott, *St. Paul's Epistle to the Ephesians:* With a Critical and Grammatical Commentary, and a Revised Translation, 4th Edition (London: Longman, Green, Reader and Dyer, 1868).

Ellicott	Charles J. Ellicott, *St. Paul's Epistle to the Philippians, the Colossians and Philemon* (London: Longman, Green, Longman, Roberts and Green, 1865).
Ellicott	Charles J. Ellicott, *A Critical and Grammatical Commentary on St. Paul's Epistles to the Thessalonians* (Andover: Warren F. Draper, 1865).
Ellicott	Charles J. Ellicott, *The Pastoral Epistles of St. Paul.* 5th ed. corrected (London: Longmans, Green and Co., 1883).
Ellis	E. Earle Ellis, *The Gospel of Luke. The New Century Bible* (London: Nelson, 1966).
EWNT	Horst Balz and Gerhard Schneider, *Exegetisches Wörterbuch Zum Neuen Testament* (Stuttgart: Kohlhammer, 1978).
ELR	H. A. Trebel and K. M. King, *Everyday Life in Rome* (Oxford, Oxford University Press, 1958).
Fairbairn	Patrick Fairbairn, *Commentary on the Pastoral Epistles, First and Second Timothy, Titus* (Grand Rapids: Zondervan, 1956).
Fascher	Erich Fascher, *Der Erste Brief des Paulus An die Korinther* (Berlin: Evangelische Verlagsanstalt, 1975).
FCS	S. Scott Bartchy, *First Century Slavery & First Corinthians 7:21* (Missoula, Mont.: The Society of Biblical Literature, 1973).
FFB	*Fauna and Flora of the Bible. Helps for Translators,* vol. XI (United Bible Societies, 1972).
Filson	Floyd V. Filson, *The Gospel According to St. Matthew* (London: Adam and Charles Black, 1971).
Fitzmyer	Joseph A. Fitzmyer, *Essays on the Semitic Background of the New Testament* (Missoula, Mont.: Scholars Press, 1974).
Ford	J. Massynberde Ford, *Revelation. The Anchor Bible* (Garden City, N.Y.: Doubleday, 1975).
Frame	James Everett Frame, *A Critical and Exegetical Commentary on the Epistles of St. Paul to the Thessalonians. The International Critical Commentary* (Edinburgh: T. & T. Clark, 1953).
Funk	Robert W. Funk, *A Beginning-Intermediate Grammar of Hellenistic Greek,* 3 vols. (Missoula, Mont.: Society of Biblical Literature, 1973).
GAM	William M. Ramsay, *The Historical Geography of Asia Minor* (Amsterdam: Adolf M. Hakkert, 1962).

Gaugler   Ernst Gaugler, *Der Epheserbrief: Auslegung Netutestamentlischer Schriften* (Zurich: EVZ—Verlag, 1966).

Gaugler   Ernst Gaugler, *Die Johannesbrief. Auslegung Neutestamentlicher Schriften* (Zurich: EVZ—Verlag, 1964).

Geldenhuys   J. Norval Geldenhuys, *Commentary on the Gospel of Luke* (London: Marshall, Morgan & Scott, 1971).

GELS   H. G. Liddell, Robert Scott, H. Stuart Jones, *A Greek-English Lexicon. A Supplement*. Edited by E. A. Barber with the assistance of P. Mass, M. Scheller and M. L. West (Oxford: At the Clarendon Press, 1968).

GEW   Hjalmar Frisk, *Griechisches Etymologisches Wörterbuch* (Heidelberg: Carl Winter, 1973).

GI   Nigel Turner, *Grammatical Insights Into the New Testament* (Edinburgh: T. & T. Clark, 1965).

Gifford   E. H. Gifford, *The Epistle of St. Paul to the Romans* (London: John Murray, 1886).

Gnilka   Joachim Gnilka, *Der Epheserbrief. Herders Theologischer Kommentar zum Neuen Testament* (Basel: Herder, 1971).

Gnilka   Joachim Gnilka, *Der Philipperbrief. Herders Theologischer Kommentar zum Neuen Testament* (Freiburg: Herder, 1976).

GNT   James Moffatt, *Grace in the New Testament* (New York: Ray Long and Richard R. Smith, Inc., 1932).

Godet   Frederick L. Godet, *A Commentary on the Gospel of St. Luke*, 2 vols. (Grand Rapids: Zondervan, 1969).

Godet, John   Frederick L. Godet, *Commentary on the Gospel of John* (Grand Rapids: Zondervan, 1969).

Godet   Frederick L. Godet, *The Commentary on the Epistle to the Romans*. Translated by A. Cusin and Talbot W. Chambers (Grand Rapids: Zondervan, 1956).

Godet   Frederick L. Godet, *Commentary on the First Epistle of St. Paul to the Corinthians*. Translated by A. Cusin, 2 vols. (Grand Rapids: Zondervan, 1957).

Goppelt   Leonhard Goppelt, *Der erste Petrusbrief. Kritschexegetischer Kommentar über das Neue Testament*. Herausgegeben von Ferdinand Han (Gottingen: Vandenhoeck & Ruprecht, 1977).

Gould   Ezra E. Gould, *A Critical and Exegetical Commentary on the*

	Gospel According to Mark. The International Critical Commentary (Edinburgh: T. & T. Clark, 1896).
Govett	Robert Govett, *The Apocalypse Expounded by Scripture,* abridged from the 4 vol. ed. 1864 (London: Charles J. Thynne, 1920).
GPT	F. E. Peters, *Greek Philosophical Terms: A Historical Lexicon* (New York: New York University Press, 1967).
Green	Michael Green, *The Second Epistle General of Peter and the General Epistle of Jude. Tyndale New Testament Commentaries* (London: The Tyndale Press, 1970).
Grosheide	Frederick Grosheide, *Commentary on First Corinthians, New International Commentary on the New Testament* (Grand Rapids: Eerdmans, 1953).
Guthrie	Donald Guthrie, *Galatians. The New Century Bible* (London: Oliphants, 1969).
Guthrie	Donald Guthrie, *The Pastoral Epistles* (London: Tyndale Press, 1969).
GW	David Hill, *Greek Words and Hebrew Meanings; Studies in the Semantics of Soteriological Terms* (Cambridge: At the University Press, 1967).
HA	Harold Hoehner, *Herod Antipas* (Cambridge: At the University Press, 1972).
Haenchen	Ernst Haenchen, *The Acts of the Apostles: A Commentary* (Philadelphia: Westminster Press, 1971).
Harner	Philip B. Harner, *"Qualitative Anarthrous Predicate Nouns,"* JBL 92 (March, 1973), 75-78.
HDB	James Hastings (ed.), *A Dictionary of the Bible,* 5 vols. (Edinburgh: T. & T. Clark, 1901).
HDCG	James Hastings (ed.), *A Dictionary of Christ and the Gospels,* 2 vols. (Edinburgh: T. & T. Clark, 1906).
Hendriksen	William Hendriksen, *New Testament Commentary: Colossians and Philemon* (Edinburgh: The Banner of Truth Trust, 1974).
Hering	Jean Hering, *The First Epistle of St. Paul to the Corinthians.* Translated by A. W. Heathcote & P. J. Allcock (London: Epworth Press, 1969).
Hering	Jean Hering, *The Second Epistle of St. Paul to the Corinthians.* Translated by A. W. Heathcote and P. J. Allcock (London: Epworth Press, 1967).

Hewitt   Thomas Hewitt, *The Epistle to the Hebrews. An Introduction and Commentary. Tyndale New Testament Commentary* (Grand Rapids: Eerdmans, 1960).

Hill   David Hill, *The Gospel of Matthew. The New Century Bible* (London: Oliphants, 1972).

HJP   Emil Schürer, *A History of the Jewish People in the Time of Jesus Christ,* two divisions, translated by John Macpherson (Edinburgh: T. & T. Clark, 1910).

HJP (NEE)   Emil Schürer, *The History of the Jewish People in the Age of Jesus Christ* (175 B.C.–A.D. 135), new English edition revised and edited by Geza Vermes and Fergus Millar, vol. 1 (Edinburgh: T. & T. Clark, 1973).

Hodge   Charles Hodge, *Commentary on the Epistle to the Romans* (Grand Rapids: Eerdmans, 1953).

Hodge   Charles Hodge, *Commentary on the First Epistle to the Corinthians* (Grand Rapids: Eerdmans, 1953).

Hodge   Charles Hodge, *Commentary on the Second Epistle to the Corinthians* (Grand Rapids: Eerdmans, 1953).

Hodge   Charles Hodge, *A Commentary on the Epistle to the Ephesians* (Grand Rapids: Eerdmans, 1950).

Hofius   Otfried Hofius, *Der Christushymnus Philipper 2, 6-11* (Tübingen: J. C. B. Mohr, 1977).

Hort   F. J. A. Hort, *The First Epistle of St. Peter I.1-II.17* (London: Macmillan, 1898; reprint Minneapolis: James and Klock Publishing Co., 1976).

Hort   F. J. A. Hort, *The Apocalypse of St. John I–III* (London: Macmillan, 1908; reprint Minneapolis: James and Klock Publishing Co., 1976).

Hoskyns   Edwyn Clement Hoskyns, *The Fourth Gospel,* edited by Francis Noel Davey (London: Oxford University Press, 1972).

Houlden   J. L. Houlden, *A Commentary on the Johannine Epistles. Black's New Testament Commentary* (London: Adam and Charles Black, 1973).

Hughes   Philip E. Hughes, *Commentary on the Second Epistle to the Corinthians* (Grand Rapids, Eerdmans, 1971).

Hughes   Philip Edgcumbe Hughes, *A Commentary on the Epistle to the Hebrews* (Grand Rapids: Eerdmans, 1977).

Huther	Joh. Ed. Huther, *Critical and Exegetical Handbook to the Epistles of St. Paul to Timothy and Titus. Critical and Exegetical Commentary on the New Testament* (Edinburgh: T. & T. Clark, 1881).
Huther	J. E. Huther, *Critical and Exegetical Handbook to the General Epistles of Peter and Jude. Critical and Exegetical Commentary on the New Testament* (Edinburgh: T. & T. Clark, 1881).
IB	George Arthur Buttrick (ed.). *The Interpreter's Bible,* vol. 10 (Nashville: Abingdon Press, 1952).
IBG	C.F.D. Moule, *An Idiom Book of New Testament Greek* (Cambridge: University Press, 1959).
IDB	George Arthur Buttrick (ed.). *The Interpreter's Dictionary of the Bible,* 4 vols. (Nashville: Abingdon Press, 1962).
Interp.	*Interpretation.*
Jastrow	Marcus Jastrow, *Dictionary of the Targumim, The Talmud Babli and Yerushalmi, and the Midrashic Literature,* 2 vols. (New York: Pardes, 1950).
JBL	*Journal of Biblical Literature.*
Jeremias, Parables	Joachim Jeremias, *The Parables of Jesus* (London: SCM Press, 1962).
Jeremias	Joachim Jeremias, *Die Briefe an Timotheus und Titus: Das Neue Testament* Deutsch (Gottingen: Vandenhoeck & Ruprecht, 1963).
JETS	*The Journal of the Evangelical Theological Society.*
JNP	G. N. Stanton, *Jesus of Nazareth in the New Testament Preaching* (Cambridge: Cambridge University Press, 1974).
Johnson	Alan F. Johnson, *The Freedom Letter* (Chicago: Moody Press, 1974).
Jones	A. H. M. Jones, *The Roman Economy. Studies in Ancient Economy and Administrative History.* Edited by P. A. Brunt (Oxford: Blackwell, 1974).
JPF	S. Safrai and M. Stern (eds.), *The Jewish People in the First Century: Historical Geography, Political History, Social, Cultural and Religious Life and Institutions,* vol. 1 (Assen, Holland: Van Gorcum & Comp. B.V., 1974).

JS   Otto Betz, Klaus Haacker, Martin Hengel (eds.) *Josephus-Studien. Untersechenven zu Josephus, dem antiqun Judentum und den Neuen Testament*. Sustschrift sur Otto Michel (Gottingen: Vandenhoeck & Ruprecht, 1974).

JTJ   Joachim Jeremias, *Jerusalem in the Times of Jesus* (London: SCM Press, 1969).

JTS   *Journal of Theological Studies*. N.S. (New Series).

Käsemann   Ernst Käsemann, *An Die Römer Handbuch Zum Neuen Testament* (Tübingen: J. C. B. Mohr, 1974).

Kelly   J. N. D. Kelly, *A Commentary on the Pastoral Epistles* (London: Adam and Charles Black, 1972).

Kelly   J. N. D. Kelly, *A Commentary on the Epistles of Peter and Jude. Black's New Testament Commentaries* (London: Adam and Charles Black, 1969).

Kent   Homer A. Kent, Jr., *The Epistle to the Hebrews: A Commentary* (Winona Lake, Ind.: B. M. H. Books, 1974).

Knowling   R. J. Knowling, *The Epistle of St. James. Westminster Commentaries* (London: Methuen and Co., 1904).

KP   Konrat Ziegler & Walther Sontheimer (eds.), *Der Kleine Pauly: Lexikon der Antike* (Munich: Alfred Druckenmüller, 1975).

Kuss   Otto Kuss, *Der Romer Brief* (Regensburg: Friedrick Pustet, 1963).

Ladd   George Eldon Ladd, *A Theology of the New Testament* (Grand Rapids: Eerdmans, 1974).

LAE   Adolf Deissmann, *Light From the Ancient East*. Translated by Lionel R. M. Strachan (London: Hodder & Stoughton, 1927).

Lane   William L. Lane, *The Gospel of Mark* (Grand Rapids: Eerdmans, 1974).

LC   Kirsopp Lake and Henry L. Cadbury, *The Beginnings of Christianity*, vol. 4 (London: Macmillan, 1933).

Leaney   A.R.C. Leaney, *The Gospel According to St. John*, 2nd ed. (London: Adam and Charles Black, 1966).

Lenski   R. C. H. Lenski, *The Interpretation of the Epistle to the Hebrews and the Epistle of James* (Minneapolis: Augsburg, 1966).

Lenski   R. C. H. Lenski, *The Interpretation of St. Paul's I & II Epistles to the Corinthians* (Columbus, Ohio: Wartburg Press, 1956).

Lietzmann   Hans Lietzmann, *An die Korinther I-II: Handbuch zum Neuen Testament* (Tübingen: J. C. B. Mohr, 1969).

Lightfoot   R. H. Lightfoot, *St. John's Gospel, A Commentary,* edited by C. F. Evans (London: Oxford University Press, 1972).

Lightfoot   J. B. Lightfoot, *St. Paul's Epistle to the Colossians and to Philemon* (Grand Rapids: Zondervan, reprint of 1879 edition).

Lightfoot   Joseph Barber Lightfoot, *The Epistle of St. Paul to the Galatians* (Grand Rapids: Zondervan, 1956).

Lightfoot   J. B. Lightfoot, *St. Paul's Epistle to the Philippians* (Grand Rapids: Zondervan, 1953).

Lightfoot,   J. B. Lightfoot, *Notes on the Epistles of St. Paul* (I & II
Notes   Thessalonians, I Corinthians 1-7, Romans 1-7, Ephesians 1:1-14) (Grand Rapids: Zondervan, 1957).

N. Lightfoot Neil R. Lightfoot, *Jesus Christ Today, A Commentary on the Book to the Hebrews* (Grand Rapids: Baker, 1976).

Lindars   Barnabas Lindars, *The Gospel of John. The New Century Bible* (London: Oliphants, 1972).

LNT   J. Duncan and M. Derrett, *Law in the New Testament* (London: Darton, Longman & Todd, 1970).

Lock   Walter Lock, *A Critical and Exegetical Commentary on the Pastoral Epistles. The International Critical Commentary* (Edinburgh: T. & T. Clark, 1966).

Lohmeyer   Ernst Lohmeyer, *Die Briefe an die Philipper, and die Kolosser und an Philemon. Kritschexegetischer Kommentar über das Neue Testament* (Gottingen: Vandenhoeck & Ruprecht, 1964).

Lohse   Eduard Lohse, *Die Offenbarung Des Johannes. Das Neue Testament Deutsch* (Gottingen: Vandenhoeck & Ruprecht, 1971).

Lohse   Eduard Lohse, *Hermeneia. A Critical and Historical Commentary on the Bible: Colossians and Philemon* (Philadelphia: Fortress Press, 1976).

LP   William M. Ramsay, *Luke the Physician and Other Studies in the History of Religion* (Grand Rapids: Baker, 1956).

LS	Henry George Liddell and Robert Scott, *A Greek English Lexicon,* A new edition revised and augmented throughout by Henry Stewart Jones and Roderick McKenzie (Oxford: Oxford University Press, 1953).
LSC	William M. Ramsay, *The Letters to the Seven Churches of Asia* (London: Hodder & Stoughton, 1904).
LT	Alfred Edersheim, *The Life and Times of Jesus the Messiah,* 2 vols. (Grand Rapids: Eerdmans, 1956).
Lünemann	Gottlieb Lünemann, *Critical and Exegetical Commentary on the New Testament.* Edited by H. A. W. Meyer (Edinburgh: T. & T. Clark, 1880).
M	James Hope Moulton, *A Grammar of New Testament Greek: Prolegomena,* I (Edinburgh: T. & T. Clark, 1957).
M	(f. by the name of the tractate) *The Mishnah,* translated by Herbert Danby (London: Oxford University Press, 1967).
Marshall	I. Howard Marshall, *The Epistles of John. The New International Commentary on the New Testament* (Grand Rapids: Eerdmans, 1978).
Martin	Ralph Martin, *Colossians: The Church's Lord and the Christian's Liberty* (Grand Rapids: Zondervan, 1973).
Martin	R. P. Martin, *Carmen Christi. Philippians 2.5-11.* In recent interpretation and in the setting of early Christian worship (Cambridge: At the University Press, 1967).
Martin, NCB	Ralph Martin, *Colossians and Philemon. The New Century Bible* (London: Oliphants, 1974).
Mayor	Joseph B. Mayor, *The Epistles of St. James* (Grand Rapids: Zondervan, 1954).
Mayor	Joseph B. Mayor, *The Epistle of St. Jude and the Second Epistle of St. Peter* (Grand Rapids: Baker, 1965).
McKay	K. L. McKay, "The Use of the Perfect Down to the 2nd Century A.D.,"*Bulletin of the Institute of Classical Studies of the University of London,* 12 (1865), 1-21.
McNeile	A. H. McNeile, *The Gospel According to St. Matthew* (New York: Macmillan, 1955).
Meeks	Wayne A. Meeks, *The Prophet-King* (Leiden: E. J. Brill, 1967).
Meyer	Heinrich August Wilhelm Meyer, *Critical and Exegetical Commentary on the New Testament.* Translation revised and

edited by William P. Dickson and Frederick Crombie, 20 vols. (Edinburgh: T. & T. Clark, 1891).

MH   James Hope Moulton and William Francis Howard, *A Grammar of New Testament Greek: Accidence and Word-Formation,* II (Edinburgh: T. & T. Clark, 1956).

Michel   Otto Michel, *Der Brief an die Romer, Kritschexegetischer Kommentar über das Neue Testament* (Gottingen: Vandenhoeck & Ruprecht, 1966).

Michel   Otto Michel, *Der Brief an die Hebräer. Kritschexegetischer Kommentar über das Neue Testament* (Gottingen: Vandenhoeck & Ruprecht, 1966).

Milligan   George Milligan, *St. Paul's Epistles to the Thessalonians* (Grand Rapids: Eerdmans, 1953).

MKG   G. Mussies, *The Morphology of Koine Greek, As Used in The Apocalypse of St. John: A Study in Bilingualism* (Leiden: E. J. Brill, 1971).

MLL   William K. Hobart, *The Medical Languages of St. Luke* (Grand Rapids: Baker, 1954).

MM   James Hope Moulton and George Milligan, *The Vocabulary of the Greek Testament* (London: Hodder & Stoughton, 1952).

MNTW   William Barclay, *More New Testament Words* (London: SCM Press, 1958).

Moffatt   James Moffatt, *A Critical and Exegetical Commentary on the Epistle to the Hebrews. The International Critical Commentary* (Edinburgh: T. & T. Clark, 1968).

Montefiore   Claude Joseph Goldsmith Montefiore and Herbert Martin James Loewe, *A Rabbinic Anthology* (New York: Meridian Books, Inc. [n.d.]).

Montefiore   Hugh Montefiore, *A Commentary on the Epistle to the Hebrews* (London: Adam and Charles Black, 1964).

Moore   A. L. Moore, *The First and Second Thessalonians. The Century Bible* (London: Thomas Nelson and Sons, 1969).

Moore, Judaism   George Foot Moore, *Judaism in the First Centuries of the Christian Era the Age of Tannaim,* 3 vols. (Cambridge: Harvard University Press, 1958).

Moorhouse   A. C. Moorhouse, *Studies in the Greek Negatives* (Cardiff: University of Wales Press, 1959).

Morris	Leon Morris, *The Gospel According to John* (London: Marshall, Morgan & Scott, 1972).
Morris, Studies	Leon Morris, *Studies in the Fourth Gospel* (Grand Rapids: Eerdmans, 1969).
Morris	Leon Morris, *The First and Second Epistles to the Thessalonians. The New International Commentary on the New Testament* (Grand Rapids: Eerdmans, 1959).
Morris	Leon Morris. *The First Epistle of Paul to the Corinthians* (Grand Rapids: Eerdmans, 1958).
Moule	C. F. D. Moule, *The Epistles to the Colossians and to Philemon. The Cambridge Greek Testament Commentary* (Cambridge: At the University Press, 1958).
Mounce	Robert H. Mounce, *The Book of Revelation. The New International Commentary on the New Testament* (Grand Rapids: Eerdmans, 1977).
MRP	J. A. Ziesler, *The Meaning of Righteousness in Paul* (Cambridge: Cambridge University Press, 1972).
MS	C. H. Dodd, *More New Testament Studies* (Grand Rapids: Eerdmans, 1968).
MT	James Hope Moulton and Nigel Turner, *A Grammar of New Testament Greek: Syntax* vol. III (Edinburgh: T. & T. Clark, 1963).
MT Style	James Hope Moulton and Nigel Turner, *A Grammar of New Testament Greek: Style* vol. IV (Edinburgh: T. & T. Clark, 1976).
Munck	Johannes Munck, *Christ and Israel, An Interpretation of Romans 9-11* (Philadelphia: Fortress Press, 1967).
Murray	John Murray, *The Epistle to the Romans,* 2 vols. (Grand Rapids: Eerdmans, 1971).
Mussner	Franz Mussner, *Der Galaterbrief. Herders Theologischer Kommentar zum Neuen Testament* (Basel: Herder, 1974).
Mussner	Franz Mussner, *Der Jakobusbrief. Herders Theologischer Kommentar zum Neuen Testament* (Freiburg: Herder, 1975).
NBD	J. D. Douglas (ed.), *The New Bible Dictionary* (Grand Rapids: Eerdmans, 1962).
ND	Richard N. Longenecker and Merrill C. Tenney (eds.), *New Dimensions in New Testament Study* (Grand Rapids: Zondervan, 1974).

Nov T	*Novum Testamentum.*
NTCW	Allison A. Trites, *The New Testament Concept of Witness* (Cambridge: Cambridge University Press, 1977).
NTRJ	David Daube, *The New Testament and Rabbinic Judaism* (New York: Arno Press, 1973).
NTS	*New Testament Studies.*
NTW	William Barclay, *A New Testament Wordbook* (London: SCM Press, 1955).
Nygren	Anders Nygren, *Commentary on Romans.* Translated by Carl C. Rasmussen (Philadelphia: Fortress Press, 1949).
OCD	H. G. L. Hammond and H. H. Scullard (eds.), *Oxford Classical Dictionary,* 2nd ed. (Oxford: University Press, 1972).
PAA	John Howard Schütz, *Paul and the Anatomy of Apostolic Authority* (Cambridge: Cambridge University Press, 1975).
PAM	Victor C. Pfitzner, *Paul and the Agon Motif. Tratitional Athletic Imagery in the Pauline Literature* (Leiden: E. J. Brill, 1967).
PAT	Robert Jewett, *Paul's Anthropological Terms* (Leiden: E. J. Brill, 1971).
PCG	Edwin M. Yamauchi, *Pre-Christian Gnosticism* (London: Tyndale Press, 1973).
Pearson	Birger Albert Pearson, *The Pneumatikos-Psychikos Terminology* (Missoula, Mont.: The Society of Biblical Literature, 1973).
PGL	G. W. H. Lampe, *A Patristic Greek Lexicon* (Oxford: Clarendon Press, 1968).
PIP	Gordon P. Wiles, *Paul's Intercessory Prayers: The Significance of the Intercessory Prayer Passages in the Letters of Paul* (Cambridge: Cambridge University Press, 1974).
Plummer	Alfred Plummer, *A Critical and Exegetical Commentary on the Gospel According to St. Luke. The International Critical Commentary,* 5th ed. (Edinburgh: T. & T. Clark, 1952).
Plummer	Alfred Plummer, *An Exegetical Commentary on the Gospel of Matthew* (Grand Rapids: Eerdmans, 1956).

Plummer	Alfred Plummer, *The Epistles of St. John. The Cambridge Bible for Schools and Colleges* (Cambridge: At the University Press, 1894).
Plummer	Alfred Plummer, *A Critical and Exegetical Commentary on the Second Epistle of St. Paul to the Corinthians. The International Critical Commentary* (Edinburgh: T. & T. Clark, 1956).
Preisigke	Friedrich Priesigke, *Wörterbuch der griechischen Papyrus-surkunden* (Heidelberg-Berlin, 1924-31).
PRJ	W. D. Davies, *Paul and Rabbinic Judaism: Some Rabbinic Elements in Pauline Theology* (London: SPCK, 1965).
PS	J. N. Sevenster, *Paul and Seneca* (Leiden: E. J. Brill, 1961).
PTR	W. M. Ramsay, *St. Paul the Traveller and Roman Citizen* (London: Hodder & Stoughton, 1895).
PTW	Hans Dieter Betz, *Plutarch's Theological Writings and Early Christian Literature* (Leiden: E. J. Brill, 1975).
PW	R. G. Hamerton-Kelly, *Pre-existence Wisdom and the Son of Man* (Cambridge: Cambridge University Press, 1973).
PWC	Charles Caldwell Ryrie, *The Place of Women in the Church* (New York: Macmillan, 1958).
IQS	*The Manual of Discipline.*
IQH	*Hymns of Thanksgiving.*
IQM	*War of the Sons of Light Against the Sons of Darkness.*
IQ Gen Ap	*The Genesis Apocryphon*
4QFlor	*Florilegium*—comments on various portions.
1QPHab	*Commentary on Habakkuk.*
R	Johannes Friedrich, Wolfgang Pohlmann, Peter Stuhlmacher (eds.) *Rechtfertigung: Festschrift für Ernst Käsemann* (Tübingen: J. C. B. Mohr, 1976).
RAC	Theodor Klauser (ed.), *Reallexikon für Antike und Christentum* (Stuttgart: Anton Hierseman, 1950-76).
Rackham	Richard Belward Rackham, *The Acts of the Apostles. Westminster Commentaries* (London: Methuen, 1957).
Ramsay	William M. Ramsay, *A Historical Commentary of St. Paul's Epistle to the Galatians* (Grand Rapids: Baker, 1965).

Ramsay, LP	William M. Ramsay, *Luke the Physician and other Studies in the History of Religion* (Grand Rapids: Baker, 1956).
Reicke	Bo Ivar Reicke, *The Anchor Bible. The Epistles of James, Peter, and Jude* (Garden City, N.Y.: Doubleday, 1964).
RG	A. T. Robertson, *A Grammar of the Greek New Testament in the Light of Historical Research* (Nashville: Broadman, 1934).
RH	Robert Banks (ed.), *Reconciliation and Hope: New Testament Essays on Atonement and Eschatology* (Grand Rapids: Eerdmans, 1974).
Ridderbos	Herman N. Ridderbos, *The Epistle of Paul to the Churches of Galatia. The New International Commentary on the New Testament* (Grand Rapids: Eerdmans, 1970).
Riggenbach	Edward Riggenbach, *Der Brief an die Hebräer* (Leipsig: A. Deichert, 1913).
Robinson	J. Armitage Robinson, *St. Paul's Epistle to the Ephesians* (London: Macmillan & Co., 1914).
Ropes	James Hardy Ropes, *A Critical and Exegetical Commentary on the Epistle of St. James. The International Cricitcal Commentary* (Edinburgh: T. & T. Clark, 1916).
RP	Archibald Robertson and Alfred Plummer, *A Critical and Exegetical Commentary on the First Epistle of St. Paul to the Corinthians. The International Critical Commentary,* 2nd ed. (Edinburgh: T. & T. Clark, 1955).
RWP	A. T. Robertson, *Word Pictures in the New Testament,* 6 vols. (New York: Harper & Brothers, 1930).
Sanders	J. N. Sanders and B. A. Mastin, *The Gospel According to St. John* (London: Adam and Charles Black, 1968).
SB	H. L. Strack and P. Billerbeck, *Kommentar zum Neuen Testament aus Talmud und Midrasch,* 6 vols. (Munich: C. H. Beck, 1965).
SBT	Robert H. Gundry, *Soma in Biblical Theology With An Emphasis on Pauline Anthropology* (Cambridge: Cambridge University Press, 1976).
SCA	Richard C. Trench, *Commentary on the Epistles to the Seven Churches in Asia–Revelation II–III,* 6th ed. (Minneapolis: Klock and Klock, 1978, originally published in 1897).

Schelkle   Karl Hermann Schelkle, *Die Petursbriefe, Der Judasbrief. Herders Theologischer Kommentar zum Neuen Testament.* Dritte Auflage (Freiburg: Herder, 1970).

Schl.   Adolf Schlatter, *Der Evangelist Matthäus* (Stuttgart: Calwer Verlag, 1963).

Schlatter   Adolf Schlatter, *Die Kirche der Griechen im Urteil des Paulus. Eine Auslegung seiner Briefe an Timotheus und Titus* (Stuttgart: Calwer Verlag, 1958).

Schlier   Heinrich Schlier, *Der Brief an die Galater. Kritschexegetischer Kommentar über Das Neue Testament* (Gottingen: Vandenhoeck & Ruprecht, 1965).

Schlier   Heinrich Schlier, *Der Brief an die Epheser* (Düsseldorf: Patmosverlag, 1968).

Schnackenburg   Rudolf Schnackenburg, *Das Johannesevangelium. Herders Theologischer Kommentar zum Neuen Testament,* 2 vols. (Joh. 1-12) (Freiburg: Herder, 1971).

Schnackenburg   Rudolf Schnackenburg, *Die Johannesbriefe. Herders Theologischer Kommentar zum Neuen Testament* (Basil: Herder, 1965).

Schweizer   Eduard Schweizer, *Der Brief an die Kolosser: Evangelisch-Katholischer Kommentar zum Neuen Testament* (Zürich: Benziger Verlag, 1976).

Scott   Walter Scott, *Exposition of the Revelation of Jesus Christ* (London: Pickering and Inglis [n.d.]).

SEH   M. Rosteovtzeff, *The Social & Economic History of the Roman Empire,* 2nd ed., 2 vols. (Oxford: Oxford University Press, 1960, 1963).

Seiss   Joseph Augustus Seiss, *The Apocalypse. Lectures on the Book of Revelation* (Grand Rapids: Zondervan, 1957).

Selwyn   Edward Gordon Selwyn, *The First Epistle of St. Peter* (London: Macmillan, 1958).

SH   William Sanday and Arthur C. Headlam, *A Critical and Exegetical Commentary on the Epistle to the Romans. The International Critical Commentary* (Edinburgh: T. & T. Clark, 1955).

Sherwin-White   A. N. Sherwin-White, *Roman Society and Roman Law in the New Testament* (Oxford: Oxford University Press, 1965).

| Simpson | E. K. Simpson and F. F. Bruce, *Commentary on Ephesians and Colossians. The New International Commentary on the New Testament* (Grand Rapids: Eerdmans, 1975). |

| SL | Robert A. Kraft, *Septuagintal Lexicography* (Missoula, Mont.: Scholars Press, 1975). |

| SMT | Ernest DeWitt Burton, *Syntax of the Moods and Tenses in New Testament Greek,* 3rd ed. (Edinburgh: T. & T. Clark, 1955). |

| SP | A. S. Hunt and C. C. Edgar (eds.) *Selected Papyri,* 2 vols. *The Loeb Classical Library* (Cambridge, Mass.: Harvard University Press, 1932). |

| Spicq | C. Spicq, *L, Èpitre Aux Hebreux,* 2 vols. (Paris: J. Gabalda, 1952-53). |

| SSM | W. D. Davies, *The Setting of the Sermon on the Mount* (Cambridge: At the University Press, 1966). |

| Stibbs | Alan M. Stibbs and Andrew F. Walls, *The First Epistle General of Peter. Tyndale New Testament Commentaries* (London: Tyndale Press, 1971). |

| Stonehouse | N. B. Stonehouse, *Origins of the Synoptic Gospels: Some Basic Questions* (London: Tyndale Press, 1964). |

| Stott | John R. W. Stott, *The Epistles of John. Tyndale New Testament Commentaries* (London: Tyndale Press, 1969). |

| Stuhlmacher | Peter Stuhlmacher, *Der Brief an Philemon: Evangelisch-Katholisher Kommentar zum Neuen Testament* (Zürich: Benziger Verlag, 1975). |

| Swete | Henry Barclay Swete, *The Gospel According to St. Mark* (Grand Rapids: Eerdmans, 1952). |

| Swete | Henry Barclay Swete, *The Apocalypse of St. John* (London: Macmillan, 1907). |

| T | Joseph Henry Thayer, *A Greek-English Lexicon of the New Testament* (New York: American Book Company, 1889). |

| Tasker | R. V. G. Tasker, *The Gospel According to St. John* (London: Tyndale Press, 1970). |

| Tasker | R. V. G. Tasker, *The Gospel According to St. Matthew. Tyndale New Testament Commentaries* (London: Tyndale Press, 1969). |

| Tasker | R. V. G. Tasker, *The General Epistle of James. Tyndale New Testament Commentaries* (Grand Rapids: Eerdmans, 1956). |

Taylor   Vincent Taylor, *The Gospel According to St. Mark* (London: Macmillan, 1957).

TB   *Tyndale Bulletin.*

TC   Bruce M. Metzger, *A Textual Commentary on the Greek New Testament* (London: United Bible Societies, 1971).

TDNT   Gerhard Kittel and Gerhard Friedrich (eds.), *Theological Dictionary of the New Testament,* 9 vols. (Grand Rapids: Eerdmans, 1973).

TDOT   G. J. Botterweck and Helmer Ringgren, *Theological Dictionary of the Old Testament* (Grand Rapids: Eerdmans, 1973).

Thrall   Margaret E. Thrall, *Greek Particles in the New Testament* (Leiden: E. J. Brill, 1962).

Trench,   R. C. Trench, *Synonyms of the New Testament* (Grand
Synonyms   Rapids: Eerdmans, 1953).

TT   Martin MacNamara, *Targum and Testament, Aramaic Paraphrases of the Hebrew Bible: A Light on the New Testament* (Grand Rapids: Eerdmans, 1972).

UBD   Merril F. Unger, *Unger's Bible Dictionary* (Chicago: Moody Press, 1957).

Vincent   Marvin R. Vincent, *A Critical and Exegetical Commentary on the Epistles to the Philippians and to Philemon. The International Critical Commentary* (Edinburgh: T. & T. Clark, 1955).

von Dobschütz   Ernst von Dobschütz, *Die Thessalonickerbriefe* (Gottingen: Vandenhoeck & Ruprecht, 1974).

Walvoord   John F. Walvoord, *The Revelation of Jesus Christ* (Chicago: Moody Press, 1966).

Weiss   Johannes Weiss, *Der erste Korinther Brief* (Gottingen: Vandenhoeck & Ruprecht, 1910).

Westcott   Brooke Foss Westcott, *The Gospel According to St. John, The Greek Text With Introduction and Notes* (Grand Rapids: Eerdmans, 1954).

Westcott   Brooke Foss Westcott, *The Epistles of John* (Cambridge: Macmillan, 1892).

Westcott   Brooke Foss Westcott, *The Epistle to the Hebrews* (Grand Rapids: Eerdmans, n.d.).

Westcott   Brooke Foss Westcott, *St. Paul's Epistle to the Ephesians* (Grand Rapids: Eerdmans, 1952).

Wiesinger   August Wiesinger, *Biblical Commentary on St. Paul's Epistles to the Philippians, to Titus, and the First to Timothy* (In Continuation of the work of Olshausen) (Edinburgh: T. & T. Clark, 1861).

Williams   C. S. C. Williams, *The Acts of the Apostles. Black's New Testament Commentaries* (London: Adam and Charles Black, 1964).

Windisch   Hans Windisch, *Der zweite Korintherbrief. Kritschexegetischer Kommentar über das Neue Testament* (Gottingen: Vandenhoeck & Ruprecht, 1970).

Wuest   Kenneth S. Wuest, *Galatians in the Greek New Testament* (Grand Rapids: Eerdmans, 1951).

ZNW   *Zeitschrift für die Neutestamentliche Wissenschaft*

ZPEB   Merrill C. Tenney (gen. ed.), *The Zondervan Pictorial Encyclopedia of the Bible* (Grand Rapids: Zondervan, 1975).

GENERAL ABBREVIATIONS

abs	absolute	n	neuter
acc	accusative	neg	negative
adj	adjective	nom	nominative
aor	aorist	obj	object
adv	adverb	obj. gen	objective genitive
cf	confer (compare)	opt	optative
comp	comparative	org	original
conj	conjunctive	p. pp	page (s)
dat	dative	part	participle
dep	deponent	pass	passive
dimin	diminutive	perf	perfect
e.g.	exempli gratia	pers	person
	(for example)	pl	plural
esp	especially	plperf	pluperfect
f, ff	following	poss	possessive
fem	feminine	pred	predicate
fig	figuratively	pref	prefix
fut	future	prep	preposition
gen	genitive	pres	present
Gr	Greek	pron	pronoun
imp	imperative	refl	reflexive
Heb	Hebrew	rel	relative
impf	imperfect	s	see
indef	indefinite	sing	singular
ind	indicative	subj	subjunctive
indir	indirect	subst	substantive
inf	infinitive	suf	suffix
instr	instrumental	superl	superlative
intr	intransitive	synon	synonymous
interat	interative	t.t.	technical term
masc	masculine	temp	temporal
mid	middle	trans	transitive
Lat	Latin	voc	vocative
lit	literally	Vulg	Vulgate
LXX	Septuagint	w	with

THE GOSPEL OF MATTHEW

βίβλος book, different from βιβλίον, has a connotation of 1
sacredness and veneration (AS). γένεσις origin, birth, genealogy (BAG). Χριστός s. 16:16.

■ ἐγέννησεν aor. γεννάω to beget (not necessarily im- 2
mediate parentage but merely direct descent, RWP). ἀδελφός
brother. ■ βασιλεύς king. Strikes the keynote of the book of 6
Matthew. Jesus Christ as son of David is king. ■ ἐπί w. gen. "At 11
the time of " (MT, III, 271). μετοικεσία removal to another
place of habitation, deportation (BAG).

■ μετά after. ■ In addition to Μαρία the NT also has 12/16
Μαριάμ. ἐγεννήθη aor. pass. γεννάω. λεγόμενος part. pass.
λέγω to say, to name.

■ πᾶς every, whole, pl. all. γενεά generation. ἀπό from. 17
ἕως until. μετοικεσία s.v.11.

■ οὕτως so, thus (BD, 224). ἦν impf. εἰμί to be. 18
μνηστευθείσης aor. part. pass. gen. abs. after his mother . . . (s.
BD, 218; RG, 514). μνηστεύω to woo and win, betroth, pass.
to be betrothed, to become engaged (BAG). The aor. part. begins
the sentence, the subject is first, and the pres. part. follows. It
means that the action indicated by the part. accompanies the
action of the main clause (Schl., 11). (For the custom of betroth-
al, marriage, and divorces. M, Kiddushin; M, Gittin; Moore,
Judaism I, 119-126.) μήτηρ mother. πρὶν ἤ for (w. acc., w. inf.).
συνελθεῖν aor. inf. συνέρχομαι to go together, to come together (used of sexual intercourse). εὑρέθη aor. pass. εὑρίσκω
to find (BD, 215). γαστήρ stomach, womb. ἔχουσα part. ἔχω
to have. ἐν γαστρὶ ἔχειν to be pregnant. ἐκ indicates the source
of cause from which something arises. πνεῦμα Spirit refers to
the Holy Spirit. The article omitted owing to the prep.
(McNeile). ἅγιος holy. ■ ὤν part. εἰμί to be. θέλων part. θέλω 19
to will. δειγματίσαι aor. inf. δειγματίζω to expose publicly,
to humiliate publicly (s. TDNT). ἐβουλήθη aor. βούλομαι to
will. λάθρα secretly. It was a private arrangement (McNeile).
ἀπολῦσαι aor. inf. ἀπολύω to release, to dismiss, to divorce,
to send away one's wife or betrothed (BAG). ■ ταῦτα τοῦτο 20

1

these things. ἐνθυμηθέντος aor. part. gen. abs. "after he . . . ."
ἐνθυμέομαι to consider, to think about. The gen. abs. indicates
the time of the vision and the verb the state of mind: revolving
the matter in thought without clear perception of outlet (EGT).
ἰδού behold. Points to the surprising, unexpected type of action
(Schl.). ἄγγελος messenger, angel. κύριος lord, ruler. Used in
the OT sense for *Yahweh* especially when it is in the gen. (CBB).
κατ᾿= κατά in a dream (BD, 27). ἐφάνη aor. φαίνομαι to
appear, to show oneself. λέγων part. s.v.16. υἱός son. The form
of address summarizes the thought of the genealogy (McNeile).
(For the nom. instead of the voc. s. MT, 34.) φοβηθῇς aor. subj.
(+ μή = neg. imp.). φοβέομαι to be afraid, to fear someone or
something. παραλαβεῖν aor. inf. Something already existing is
to stop (BD, 172f.) παραλαμβάνω to take to oneself, to lead
home, of one's wife, to take her into one's home (BAG). γυνή,
γυναικός wife. γάρ for (cause). γεννηθέν aor. part. pass.
21 γεννάω s.v.2. ἐστίν pres. εἰμι. ■ τέξεται fut. τίκτω to give
birth. καλέσεις fut. καλέω to call, to name. (For the fut. to
express a command MT, 86.) ὄνομα name. σώσει fut. σῴζω to
save. (For linguistic study of the word s. TDNT and CBB; NTW,
114–121.) λαός people. ἀπό from. ἁμαρτία a missing the
mark, sin (AS). (For a study of the word s. TDNT; NTW; CBB.)
22 ■ ὅλος whole (BAG). γέγονεν perf. (BD, 177). γίνομαι to
become, to happen. ἵνα w. subj. that, in order that. πληρωθῇ
aor. pass. πληρόω to fulfill. ῥηθέν aor. part. pass. λέγω. ὑπό
23 by (w. pass.). διά through. ■ παρθένος virgin. ἕξει fut. ἔχω.
μεθερμηνευόμενον pass. part. μεθερμηνεύω to interpret, to
24 translate. μεθ᾿= μετά with (accompanying). ■ ἐγερθείς aor.
pass. part. When two actions are joined to one process, the aor.
part. is placed before the aor. of the main verb in order to prepare
for the action of the main verb (Schl. 23). ἐγείρω trans. to
awake, to arise, pass. to wake up, to awake (BAG). ὕπνος sleep.
ἐποίησεν aor. ποιέω to do. προσέταξεν aor. προστάσσω to
25 prescribe, to order. παρέλαβεν aor. ■ ἐγίνωσκεν impf.
γινώσκω to know (used in sexual sense). ἕως (οὗ) until. ἔτεκεν
aor. τίκτω. ἐκάλεσεν aor. καλέω.

Ch. 2

1   ■ γεννηθέντος aor. pass. part. [gen. abs. "after, when Joseph . . . "] γεννάω to beget, pass. to be born. ἡμέρα day.
βασιλεύς king. ἰδού behold (surprise) ἰδού is used by Matthew
62 times (s. M, I, 11; E.J. Pryke, "ΙΔΕ and ΙΔΟΥ," NTS, 14
[April, 1968], 418–424). μάγος person or Babylonian priest or
"wiseman" who is esp. acquainted with the interpretation of

2

stars and dreams as well as with other things (s. TDNT; HDCG, II, 97–101). ἀνατολή rising of stars, then sunrise, pl. (BD, 78). The word for east means "from the rising" of the sun (RWP). The geographical meaning is orient. παρεγένοντο aor. παραγίνομαι to come, to arrive, to be present (BAG). ■ 2 λέγοντες part. λέγω to say. ποῦ where? ἐστίν pres. εἰμί. τεχθείς aor. part. pass. τίκτω to give birth. εἴδομεν aor. ὁράω to see. γάρ for (explanatory). ἀστήρ, ἐρος star. (For the position of the poss. gen. αὐτοῦ s. BD, 148.) ἤλθομεν aor. ἔρχομαι to come. προσκυνῆσαι aor. inf. προσκυνέω to fall down and worship, to do obeisance to, to prostrate oneself before, used to designate the custom of prostrating oneself before a person and kissing his feet, the hem of his garment, the ground, and so forth (BAG). ■ ἀκούσας aor. part. ἀκούω to hear. ἐταράχθη aor. 3 pass. ταράσσω lit. to shake together, to stir up; fig. to stir up, to disturb, to unsettle, to throw into confusion (BAG). πᾶς each, whole, pl. all. μετ᾿= μετά with. ■ συναγαγών aor. part. temp. 4 usage συνάγω to bring or call together, to gather. ἀρχιερεύς chief or high priest. γραμματεύς scribe (γράμμα letter of the alphabet). (For chief priest and scribes s. Schürer HJP, II, i, 163–379.) λαός people. ἐπυνθάνετο imperf. πυνθάνομαι to inquire. The impf. tense suggests that Herod inquired repeatedly (RWP). παρ᾿= παρά w. gen. from the side of, from. γεννᾶται pres. ind. pass. γεννάω prophetic pres. (McNeile). ■ εἶπαν aor. 5 λέγω. οὕτως so. γέγραπται perf. pass. γράφω to write. "It stands written" refers to the regulative and authoritative character of the document referred to (MM; s. also Deissmann, BS 112–114, 249–250). διά through.

■ γῆ here land in a territorial sense. οὐδαμῶς certainly not, 6 not at all. ἐλάχιστος superl. μικρός small, least in honor (McNeile). εἶ pres. εἰμί. ἡγεμών leader, ruler. ἐξελεύσεται fut. ἐξέρχομαι to go out. ἡγούμενος part. ἡγέομαι to lead. Present part. used of men in any leading position (BAG). ὅστις general rel. pron. who. ποιμανεῖ fut. ποιμαίνω to herd, to tend, to lead to pasture. Figurative of activity that protects, rules, governs (BAG).

■ τότε then. λάθρα adv. secretly. καλέσας aor. part. 7 καλέω to call, part. used temporally. μάγος. s.v.1 ἠκρίβωσεν aor. ἀκριβόω to learn exactly or accurately (RWP). παρ᾿ s.v.4. χρόνος time. φαινομένου part. φαίνομαι to appear. ἀστήρ s.v.2. ■ πέμψας aor. part. πέμπω to send. εἶπεν aor. part. 8 λέγω. πορευθέντες aor. part. πορεύομαι to go, to proceed on one's way. Redundant part. here is attendant circumstance and can be translated as an imp. "go and inquire" (s. M, I, 230f.).

ἐξετάσατε aor. imp. ἐξετάζω to examine, to inquire. ἀκριβῶς adv. ἀκριβής exact. περί concerning. παιδίον child, dimin. from παῖς (TDNT). ἐπάν w. subj. when, as soon as. εὕρητε aor. subj. εὑρίσκω to find. ἀπαγγελατε aor. imp. ἀπαγγέλω to report, to make known. ὅπως w. subj. that, in order that. κἀγώ = καὶ ἐγώ. ἐλθών aor. part. ἔρχομαι coming, to come, to go.

9 προσκυνήσω aor. subj. s.v.2. ■ ἀκούσαντες aor. part. ἀκούω to hear (temp. use). The king ought rather to have heard and assisted them (Bengel). βασιλεύς king. ἐπορεύθησαν aor. s.v.8. ἰδού behold. ὅς s.v.6. εἶδον s.v.2. Here used as plperf. "They had seen" (Meyer). ἀνατολή s.v.1. προῆγεν impf. προάγω to lead ahead, to lead further, to go before. It kept on going before them until (ἕως) arriving at Bethlehem it took up its position (ἐστάθη aor. ἵστημι to stand still) right over the spot where the child was (EGT). ἐπάνω above, over (s. MT,

10 279). οὗ rel. where. ἦν impf. εἰμί to be. ■ ἰδόντες aor. part. ὁράω to see. ἐχάρησαν aor. χαίρω to rejoice, to be happy. χαρά joy. The cognate acc. or acc. of content repeating the content of the verb itself (IBG, 32). μέγας great. σφόδρα very.

11 ■ οἰκία house. εἶδον s.v.2. μετά s.v.3. μήτηρ mother. πεσόντες aor. part. πίπτω to fall down, part. of manner. προσεκύνησαν aor. ἀνοίξαντες aor. part. ἀνοίγω to open. θησαυρός casket, receptical for valuables (RWP). προσήνεγκαν aor. προσφέρω to bring to, to present. δῶρον gift, present. χρυσός gold. λίβανος frankincense, a white resinous gum obtained from several kinds of certain trees in Arabia (BAG). σμύρνα myrrh. (For the use of frankincense and myrrh s. Gus. W. Van Beek, "Frankincense and Myrrh," BA, XXIII

12 [Sept. 1960], 70–95.) ■ χρηματισθέντες aor. part. χρηματίζομαι to be informed; in classical Gr. to do business, to manage public affairs, then to advise, to consult on public affairs. In later Gr. to give an authoritative answer as by an oracle or to give a divine command or warning (McNeile). κατ᾽ = κατά manner. ὄναρ dream. ἀνακάμψαι aor. inf. ἀνακάμπτω to bend or to turn back, to return (AS). πρός to. δι᾽= διά through, by. ἄλλος another. ὁδός way. ἀνεχώρησαν aor. ἀναχωρέω to go away, to return, often used in the sense to take refuge from danger (MM). χώρα land, here home country.

13 ■ ἀναχωρησάντων aor. part. gen. abs. "when, after they …" s.v.12. ἰδού behold. κυρίος lord, ruler. φαίνεται s.v.7. κατ᾽ ὄναρ s.v.12. λέγων s.v.2. ἐγερθείς aor. pass. part. ἐγείρω to wake, pass. to wake up, to rise, to get up. παράλαβε aor. imp. παραλαμβάνω to take to oneself. παδίον s.v.8. μήτηρ s.v.11. φεῦγε imp. φεύγω to flee, to seek safety in flight (BAG). ἴσθι

4

imp. εἰμί to be. ἐκεῖ there. ἕως ἄν w. subj. until, until whenever;
the ἕως is temp.; ἄν indicates that the time of fulfillment is
indefinite (IBG, 133). εἴπω aor. subj. λέγω to say. μέλλω to be
about to, used with the inf. to express imminence (BD, 181). γάρ
for (explanatory). ζητεῖν inf. ζητέω to seek. ἀπολέσαι aor. inf.
The gen. of the article w. the inf. to express purpose. ἀπόλλυμι
to ruin, to destroy, to kill (s. TDNT and CBB). ■ παρέλαβεν 14
aor. νύξ night. ἀνεχώρησεν s.v.12. ■ ἦν impf. εἰμί. ἕως w. gen. 15
until, to. τελευτή end, death. ἵνα w. the subj. that, in order that
(to express purpose). πληρωθῇ aor. subj. pass. πληρόω to fulfill. ῥηθέν aor. pass. part. λέγω. ὑπό w. gen. by. διά w. gen.
through. ἐκάλεσα aor. s.v.7. υἱός son.

■ τότε s.v.7. ἰδών aor. part. ὁράω to see. Temporal use of 16
the part. ὅτι that. ἐνεπαίχθη aor. pass. ἐμπαίζω to ridicule, to
make fun of, to mock, to deceive, to trick (BAG). Used in the
LXX Exodus 10:2 for God mocking the Egyptians. ὑπό by (w.
pass.). μάγος s.v.1. ἐθυμώθη aor. pass. θυμόω to anger, pass.
to be angry. λίαν very. ἀποστείλας aor. part. ἀποστέλλω to
send. ἀνεῖλεν aor. ἀναιρέω to take away, to do away with, to
kill. πᾶς s.v.3. παῖς youth, child. ὅριον boundary, pl. region.
ἀπό from. διετής two years old. κατωτέρω adv. under. κατά
w. acc. according to, in accordance with. ὅς s.v.6. ἠκρίβωσεν
s.v.7. παρά s.v.4. ■ ἐπληρώθη aor. pass. s.v.15. ῥηθέν s.v.15. 17
διά through. λέγοντος s.v.2. ■ φωνή voice, call, cry. ἠκούσθη 18
aor. pass. s.v.3. κλαυθμός crying. Nouns expressing actions are
formed with –μος (BD, 58, 59; s. also MH, 350, 351, 355).
ὀδυρμός lamentation, mourning. πολύς much, great, loud.
κλαίουσα part. κλαίω to cry loudly. τέκνον child. ἤθελεν
impf. θέλω to wish, to will. παρακληθῆναι aor. pass. inf.
παρακαλέω pass. to be comforted. ὅτι because. εἰσίν pres. εἰμί
to be.

■ τελευτήσαντος aor. part. τελευτάω to die; gen. abs. 19
when, after. ἰδοὺ ἄγγελος κυρίου φαίνεται κατ᾿ ὄναρ s.v.13.
■ λέγων s.v.2. ἐγερθεὶς παράλαβε τὸ παιδίον καὶ τὴν 20
μητέρα αὐτοῦ s.v.13. πορεύου imp. s.v.8. γῆ s.v.6.
τεθνήκασιν perf. θνήσκω to die, perf. to be dead. γάρ for
(explanatory). ζητοῦντες part. s.v.13, to seek after something.
ψυχή soul, life. ■ παρέλαβεν s.v.14. εἰσῆλθεν aor. 21
εἰσέρχομαι to go in ■ ἀκούσας s.v.3. ὅτι that. βασιλεύω to 22
be king. Verbs ending in –εύω indicate the exercise of a profession (MH, 398–400). ἀντί w. gen. instead of. Clear example of
the preposition indicating substitution. πατήρ father. ἐφοβήθη
aor. φοβέομαι to be afraid. ἐκεῖ there, indicating motion (BD,
56). ἀπελθεῖν aor. inf. ἀπέρχομαι to go away, to depart.

5

χρηματισθείς s.v.12. ἀνεχώρησεν s.v.12. μέρος part. pl. re-
23 gion, area. ■ ἐλθών s.v.8. κατῴκησεν aor. κατοικέω to live,
dwell, settle down. πόλις city. λεγομένην pres. pass. part.
ὅπως w. subj. in order that. πληρωθῇ s.v.15. ῥηθέν s.v.15.
κληθήσεται fut. pass. καλέω s.v.7.

Ch. 3

1   ■ ἡμέρα day. ἐκεῖνος that. Indefinite determination of
time which points back to a date which has preceded it (Meyer).
παραγίνομαι to come, to arrive, to be present. A historic
present (McNeile). βαπτιστής baptizer. Most nouns ending in
–της indicate one who preforms an action (MH, 365ff.).
κηρύσσων part. κηρύσσω to proclaim as a herald. Matthew
uses this word for John, for Jesus, and for the disciples. He
emphasizes the binding and official legalistic character of the
proclamation (CBB; s. also TDNT). ἔρημος desert, wilderness.
Indicates the lower Jordan valley and possibly the eastern slopes
of the valley (s. Robert W. Funk, "The Wilderness," JBL,
2 LXXVII [Sept. 1959], 205–214). ■ μετανοεῖτε imp. μετανοέω
to repent, to change one's thinking, to turn about. The primary
sense in Judaism is always a change in man's attitude toward
God and in the conduct of life (Moore, Judaism, I, 507; s. also
TDNT; CBB). ἤγγικεν perf. ἐγγίζω to draw near. Perfect =
has drawn near but not necessarily arrived. γάρ for (explanatory.). βασιλεία kingdom, rule of a king. The rule of God on earth
3 as promised in the OT. οὐρανός heaven. ■ οὗτος, αὕτη, τοῦτο
this. ἐστίν pres. εἰμί to be. ῥηθείς aor. pass. part. λέγω. διά
through. φωνή voice, call. βοῶντος part. βοάω to shout, to call
out loudly. ἑτοιμάσατε aor. imp. ἑτοιμάζω to prepare. ὁδός
way. κύριος lord, ruler. εὐθείας adj. fem. pl. εὐθύς straight.
ποιεῖτε imp. ποιέω to make. τρίβους. acc. pl. τρίβος a beaten
path, a way that is familiar and well known (BAG). (For the OT
quotation in the DSS, s. 1QS 8:14f.; also, Fitzmyer, Essays, 3–58,
4 esp. 34–36.) ■ εἶχεν impf. ἔχω to have. The customary impf.
denoting that which regularly or ordinarily occurs in the past
time (DM, 188). ἔνδυμα, garment, clothing. τριχῶν gen. pl.
θρίξ hair. κάμηλος camel. ζώνη belt, girdle. δερμάτινος made
out of leather. Adjectives ending in –ινος signify material, origin, or kind (MH, 359). περί w. acc. around. ὀσφῦς hips. τροφή
food, nourishment. ἦν impf. εἰμί. ἀκρίδες nom. pl. ἀκρίς grasshopper, locust. μέλι honey. ἄγριος found in the open field, wild
5 (BAG). ■ τότε then. ἐξεπορεύετο impf. ἐκπορεύομαι to go
out, to come out. The impf. shows the repetition of the act as the
crowds kept going out to him (RWP). πρός w. acc. to. πᾶς each,

whole, pl. all. περίχωρος neighboring subst. region, neighborhood. ■ ἐβαπτίζοντο impf. pass. βαπτίζω to baptize, originally 6
to dip under. Verbs ending in –ιζω often are causative (MH,
409). Baptism symbolizes the putting off of the old life and the
identification with the new life. (For Jewish proselyte baptism s.
SB, I, 102–112; for the washings of the DSS in connection with
repentance, s. 1QS 5:13–25; 2:25–31:13.) ὑπ᾿ = ὑπό.
ἐξομολογούμενοι pres. part. ἐξομολογέομαι to confess, to
acknowledge, to agree to, indicating a public acknowledgment
(RWP). ἁμαρτία sin.

■ ἰδών aor. part. ὁράω to see. πολύς many. ἐρχομένους 7
part. ἔρχομαι to go, to come. ἐπί for, indicating purpose.
βάπτισμα baptism. εἶπεν aor. λέγω. γέννημα that which is
produced or born, child, offspring (BAG). Nouns ending in –μα
generally indicate the result of the action (MH, 355). ἔχιδνα
poison snakes. τίς who? ὑπέδειξεν aor. ὑποδείκνυμι to show
by tracing out, to make known (AS). ὑπό conveys the idea of
thoughts making their way up into the mind (MH, 327). φυγεῖν
aor. inf. φεύγω to escape, to flee. It suggests the fleeing of snakes
from a field when the harvest begins (McNeile). ἀπό w. gen.
from. μελλούσης part. μέλλω to be about to. ὀργή wrath. ■ 8
ποιήσατε aor. imp. οὖν (draws conclusion from the preceding).
καρπός fruit. ἄξιος corresponding to worthy. μετάνοια repentance, a change of mind, s.v.2. ■ δόξητε aor. subj. δοκέω to 9
suppose, to consider, to think. μή w. subj. = a neg. imp. "Do
not suppose that you are to say" (BAG). ἑαυτοῖς dat. refl. pron.
of the 3rd per. πατήρ father. John makes a reference to the
merits of the fathers, particularly to the merits of Abraham.
Abraham was represented sitting at the gate of gehenna to deliver any Israelite who might have been consigned to its terrors
(Edersheim, LT, I, 271). ὅτι that. δύναμαι to be able to. λίθος
stone. Perhaps an illusion to the rabbinical use of rocks referring
to the patriarchs and to their merits (s. Schechter, Some Aspects
of Rabbinic Theology, 173). ἐγεῖραι aor. inf. ἐγείρω to raise up.
τέκνον child. ■ ἤδη already. ἀξίνη axe. ῥίζα root. δένδρον 10
tree. κεῖται perf. pass. τίθημι to lie. ποιοῦν part. καλός good.
ἐκκόπτεται pres. pass. ἐκκόπτω to cut down. A gnomic pres.,
a maxim or generalization, something that is always true (IBG,
8). πῦρ fire. βάλλεται pres. pass. βάλλω to throw. ■ ἐν instru- 11
mental (BD, 104). ὕδωρ, ατος water. εἰς w. acc. with a view to.
Perhaps also, "because of" (DM, 104). ὀπίσω w. gen. after.
ἰσχυρότερος comp. ἰσχυρός strong. μού gen. of comp. than.
οὗ gen. ὅς rel. pron. who. ἱκανός worthy. ὑπόδημα sandal.
βαστάσαι aor. inf. βαστάζω to pick up and to carry. A slave's

7

12 office in Judea, Greece, and Rome (EGT). ■ πτύον winnowing
   shovel, a forklike shovel, with which the threshed grain was
   thrown into the wind (BAG). χείρ hand. διακαθαριεῖ fut.
   διακαθαρίζω to clean. διά is perfective and describes the carrying of action *through* to a definite result (MH, 301). ἅλων
   threshing floor. Used of the threshed grain still lying on the
   threshing floor (BAG). συνάξει fut. συνάγω to lead together,
   to gather together. σῖτος wheat, grain. ἀποθήκη storehouse,
   barn. ἄχυρον chaff. κατακαύσει fut. κατακαίω to burn up,
   completely burned up. κατά is perfective (RWP). ἄσβεστος
   unquenchable.

13 ■ τότε s.v.5. παραγίνεται s.v.1. ἀπό w. gen. from. ἐπί to,
   toward. πρός to. βαπτισθῆναι aor. inf. pass. Infinitive used to
14 express purpose. s.v.6. ὑπ᾿s.v.6. ■ διεκώλυεν impf. διακωλύω
   to prevent. It is the conative impf. to try to prevent (RWP).
   λέγων s.v.2. χρεία need, necessity. ἔχω to have. ἔρχῃ pres.
15 s.v.7. ■ ἀποκριθείς aor. part. ἀποκρίνομαι to answer. εἶπεν
   s.v.7. ἄφες aor. imp. ἀφίημι to allow, to allow to happen. ἄρτι
   now. οὕτως so. γάρ for (explanatory). πρέπον ἐστίν it is fitting, suitable, proper, right. πληρῶσαι aor. inf. πληρόω to
   fulfill. πᾶς s.v.5. δικαιοσύνη righteousness, the righteousness
   of life through obedience in accordance with the divine will.
   Jesus acknowledges the standard of righteousness as valid and
   affirms the fact He must establish it as the will of God in the
16 kingdom (GW, 126–127). ἀφίησιν pres.ἀφίημι.■ βαπτισθείς
   aor. pass. part. temp. use of the part. εὐθύς immediately, at once.
   ἀνέβη aor. ἀναβαίνω to go up. ὕδωρ s.v.11. ἰδού s.2:1.
   ἠνεῴχθησαν aor. pass. ἀνοίγω to open. οὐρανός s.v.2. εἶδεν
   aor. ὁράω to see. πνεῦμα spirit. θεός God. καταβαῖνον part.
   καταβαίνω to go down, to come down. ὡσεί as, like.
17 περιστερά dove. ἐρχόμενον s.v.7. ■ φωνή s.v.3. οὗτος s.v.3.
   ἐστίν s.v.6. υἱός son. ἀγαπητός beloved. (For verbal nouns
   ending in –ητος RG, 1095–1097.) ὅς s.v.11. εὐδόκησα aor.
   εὐδοκέω to be pleased with.

Ch. 4

1   ■ τότε then, at that time. In the NT esp. loved by Matt. He
   uses it 90 times. ἀνήχθη aor. pass. ἀνάγω to lead up. ἔρημος
   desert, wilderness. ὑπό by (w. pass.). πνεῦμα spirit.
   πειρασθῆναι aor. inf. pass. πειράζω to tempt, to try, to put one
   to the test, often with the intent to evil (Trench, *Synonyms*, 280,
2 281). διάβολος slanderer, devil (CBB). ■ νηστεύσας aor. part.
   νηστεύω to fast. ἡμέρα day. νύξ, κτος night. acc. of time, for
   forty days and forty nights. ὕστερον adv. later, afterward.

8

ἐπείνασεν aor. πεινάω to be hungry. ■ προσελθών aor. part. 3 προσέρχομαι to come to (esp. often w. Matt.). πειράζων part. εἰ if. Introduces a conditional sentence which assumes the condition to be a reality and the conclusion follows logically and naturally from that assumption. (For this and other conditional sentences, s. RG, 1004–1022.) υἱός son. εἶ pres. εἰμί to be. θεός God. The devil assumes the deity of the son. εἰπέ aor. imp. λέγω. ἵνα that. Often used with ἵνα when it denotes a command (BD, 200). λίθος stone, rock. οὗτοι masc. pl. this. ἄρτος bread. γένωνται aor. subj. γίνομαι to become. ■ ἀποκριθείς aor. 4 part. ἀποκρίνομαι to answer. γέγραπται, perf. pass. γράφω to write, perf. it stands written. ἐπ᾿= ἐπί w. dat. Of that upon which a state of being, an action, or a result is based; hence, to live on bread (BAG). μόνος alone. ζήσεται fut. ζάω to live. ἄνθρωπος man. ἀλλά but, except. πᾶς each, every. ῥῆμα word, thing. ἐκπορευομένῳ part. ἐκπορεύομαι to go out, to come out. διά w. gen. through (instrumental). στόμα mouth. ■ παραλαμβάνω to take with, to lead. Historical pres. with 5 vivid picturesqueness (RWP). εἰς to. ἅγιος holy. πόλις city. ἔστησεν aor. ἵστημι to place. ἐπί w. acc. on. πτερύγιον dimin. of πτέρου wing. Indicates the tip or extremity of anything, the pinnacle or summit of the temple (BAG). ἱερόν holy place, temple ■ βάλε aor. imp. βάλλω to cast. σεαυτόν acc. refl. pron. 6 2nd per. κάτω adv. down. γάρ then, for (explanatory). ὅτι used as quotation marks to indicate that the words are quoted. (For the recitative use s. RG, 1027, 1028.) ἄγγελος angel, messenger. ἐντελεῖται fut. mid. ἐντέλλω to give an order, to command. περί w. gen. concerning. ἐπί w. gen. upon. χείρ hand. ἀροῦσίν fut. αἴρω to lift up, to take up, to carry. μήποτε w. subj. lest. προσκόψῃς aor. subj. προσκόπτω to strike against something, to stumble against something. πρός on, against. πούς, δός foot. ■ ἔφη impf. φημί to say. πάλιν again, once 7 again. ἐκπειράσεις fut. ἐκπειράζω. The ἐκ is intensive. To put to a decisive test (MH, 309). κύριος lord, ruler. ■ πάλιν again. 8 εἰς to. ὄρος mountain. ὑψηλός high. λίαν very. δείκνυσιν pres. δείκνυμι to show. A vivid historical pres. (RWP). βασιλεία kingdom. κόσμος world, earth. δόξα brightness, splendor, glory. ■ δώσω fut. δίδωμι to give. ἐάν w. subj. It 9 introduces the condition with the prospects of fulfillment (RG, 1016ff.). πεσών aor. part. πίπτω to fall down. Participle expressing manner. προσκυνήσῃς aor. subj. προσκυνέω s. 2:2. ■ ὕπαγε imp. ὑπάγω to go away. σατανᾶς (Heb.) adversary 10 (s. TDNT; CBB). προσκυνήσεις fut. λατρεύσεις fut. λατρεύω to serve, to work for a reward, to work; in the NT used

11 of religious service (CBB). ■ ἀφίησιν pres. ἀφίημι to leave, to
depart. ἰδού behold. προσῆλθον aor. προσέρχομαι.
διηκόνουν impf. διακονέω inceptive impf. "they began to minister." They brought him food (Bengel).

12   ■ ἀκούσας aor. part. ἀκούω to hear. Temporal use of the
part. ὅτι that. παρεδόθη. aor. pass. παραδίδωμι to hand over,
to deliver over. ἀνεχώρησεν aor. ἀναχωρέω to go away, to
13 depart, often to escape danger (MM). εἰς to, into. ■ καταλιπών
aor. part. καταλείπω to leave, to leave behind. ἐλθών aor. part.
ἔρχομαι to go, to come. κατῴκησεν aor. κατοικέω to live.
(For the use of εἰς in this case s. BD, 110f.) παραθαλάσσιος
14 situated on the sea. ὅριον border, pl. region. ■ ἵνα in order that.
The divine determination (Meyer). πληρωθῇ aor. subj. pass.
πληρόω to fulfill. ῥηθέν aor. pass. part. λέγω to say. διά s.v.4.
15 λέγοντος pres. part. ■ γῆ earth, land. ὁδός way, street. Adverbial acc. (MT, 247). θάλασσα sea. Perhaps an obj. gen. "A way
leading to the sea" (MT, 212). πέραν w. gen. on the other side,
16 across. ἔθνος nation, pl. often heathen nations. ■ λαός people.
καθήμενος part. κάθημαι to sit. σκοτία darkness. φῶς light.
εἶδεν aor. ὁράω to see. μέγας great. χώρα land, here area,
region. σκιά shadow. θάνατος death. ἀνέτειλεν aor.
ἀνατέλλω intr. to rise, to dawn.

17   ■ ἀπὸ τότε from then on. ἤρξατο aor. ἄρχομαι to begin.
It either describes the beginning of a continuous action or marks
a fresh start or phase in the narrative (McNeile). κηρύσσω to
proclaim as a herald. λέγω to say. μετανοῖτε imp. μετανοέω
to change one's mind, to repent s. Matthew 3:2. ἤγγικεν perf.
ἐγγίζω to draw near. βασιλεία kingdom (s. TDNT; CBB). The
message of Jesus was the same as that of John the Baptist.

18   ■ περιπατῶν pres. part. περιπατέω to go about, to walk
around. Participle used to express contemporaneous action.
παρά w. acc. along. θάλασσα sea. εἶδεν s.v.16. ἀδελφός
brother. λεγόμενος pres. pass. part. λέγω to say, to name.
βάλλοντος pres. part. s.v.6. ἀμφίβληστρον casting net. A net
which is thrown over the shoulders and spreads out into a circle
as it falls upon the water (Trench, Synonyms, 236). ἦσαν imp.
εἰμί to be. γάρ for (explanatory). ἁλιεύς fisher. (For a discussion of fishing and fishermen s. Wilhelm H. Wuellner, The Mean-
19 ing of "Fishers of Men.") ■ δεῦτε pl. of δεῦρο an adv. of place
with the force of a command. "Come here" (EGT). ὀπίσω w.
gen. after. Used in the sense "be my pupils." The disciples were
in constant attendance on their teacher (Meyer). ποιήσω fut.
20 ποιέω to make, to appoint to an office (McNeile). ■ εὐθέως at
once. ἀφέντες aor. part. ἀφίημι s.v.11. δίκτυον net. (For the

different words for fishing nets s. Trench, *Synonyms*, 235–237.)
ἠκολούθησαν aor. ἀκολουθέω to follow. Often used of the
willing and obedient disciple who follows his teacher as one who
learns and one who serves (CBB). ■ προβάς aor. part. 21
προβαίνω to go, to go ahead. Participle used temp. ἐκεῖθεν
from there. ἄλλος another. πλοῖον boat. μετά w. gen. with
(accompaniment). πατήρ father. καταρτίζοντας pres. part.
καταρτίζω to make fitted, or equipped for a duty or function
(McNeile). ἐκάλεσεν aor. καλέω to call.

■ περιηγεν impf. περιάγω to go about. Jesus was going 23
around (impf.) in all Galilee (RWP). ὅλος all. διδάσκων pres.
part. διδάσκω to teach. συναγωγή synagogue. (For information about the synagogue s. Moore, *Judaism*, I, 281–307.)
κηρύσσων s.v.17. εὐαγγέλιον the good news, specifically the
gospel. βασιλεία s.v.17. θεραπεύων part. θεραπεύω to serve,
to treat medically, to heal, to restore (BAG). The three participles—teaching, proclaiming, healing—summarize the Lord's
work in Galilee (McNeile). πᾶς s.v.4. νόσος sickness, disease,
the chronic or serious disease. μαλακία sickness, the occasional
sickness (RWP). λαός people. ■ ἀπῆλθεν aor. ἀπέρχομαι to 24
go away, to spread. ἀκοή rumor, report. προσήνεγκαν aor.
προσφέρω to bring to. κακῶς adv. κακός bad. ἔχοντας part.
ἔχω to have. ποικίλος various kinds, diversified. βάσανος torture, torment, severe pain. συνεχομένους pres. pass. part.
συνέχω to hold together. "Held together" or "compressed" is
the idea of the part. (RWP). δαιμονιζομένους part.
δαιμονίζομαι to be possessed by a demon. σεληνιαζομένους
part. σεληνιάζομαι to be brought under the influence of the
moon, to be epileptic (MM). παραλυτικός lame, paralyzed.
ἐθεράπευσεν aor. ■ ἠκολούθησαν s.v.20. ὄχλος crowd, 25
crowd of people. πολύς many. ἀπό w. gen. from. πέραν s.v.15.

Ch. 5

■ ἰδών aor. part. ὁράω to see. ὄχλος crowd, crowd of 1
people. ἀνέβη aor. ἀναβαίνω to go up. ὄρος mountain.
καθίσαντος aor. part. καθίζω to sit, to sit down. Participle is
used as gen. abs. afterward, after (BD, 218). προσῆλθαν aor.
προσέρχομαι to come to. μαθητής student, pupil, disciple
(μανθάνω to learn). ■ ἀνοίξας aor. part. ἀνοίγω to open. 2
στόμα mouth. ἐδίδασκεν impf. διδάσκω to teach. The inceptive impf., he began to teach. (For a study of the word teaching
and its historical context s. TDNT.) (For the purpose of the
Sermon on the Mount s. J. Dwight Pentecost, "The Purpose of
the Sermon on the Mount," Bib Sac, 115 [April, July, Oct.

3 1958], 128ff., 212ff., 313ff.) ■ μακάριος blessed, fortunate, happy (BAG). πτωχός poor, poor as a beggar. πνεῦμα spirit. The dat. gives the sphere of the poverty (McNeile). (For the use of the phrase "poor in spirit" in DSS, s. 1QM 14:7; 1QH 14:3; regarding the "poor," s. 1QM 11:9; 1QH 5:22.) ἐστίν pres. εἰμί to be. αὐτῶν ἐστιν "it belongs to them." αὐτῶν poss. gen.
4 οὐρανός heaven. ■ πενθοῦντες pres. part. πενθέω to lament, to mourn for the dead. To grieve with a grief which so takes possession of the whole being that it cannot be hid (Trench, Synonyms; s. also TDNT). παρακληθήσονται fut. pass. παρακαλέω to comfort, pass. to find comfort, to receive comfort.
5 ■ πραΰς meek, gentle. The humble and gentle attitude which expresses itself in a patient submissiveness to offense, free from malice and desire for revenge (P. Leivestad, "The Meekness and Gentleness of Christ, II Cor. X. 1," NTS, 12 [Jan. 1966], 159; s. also NTW 103, 104). κληρονομήσουσιν fut. κληρονομέω to inherit, to receive as a possession. γῆ land,
6 earth. ■ πεινῶντες pres. part. πεινάω to hunger, to hunger for something. διψῶντες pres. part. διψάω to thirst. (For verbs in άω s. MH, 384.) δικαιοσύνη righteousness. χορτασθήσονται
7 fut. pass. χορτάζω to feed, to fill, to satisfy. ■ ἐλεήμων merciful, sympathetic. ἐλεηθήσονται fut. pass. ἐλεέω to have mercy or pity, to be merciful or show mercy, pass. to find or be shown mercy (BAG). It indicates being moved to pity and compassion by the tragedy and includes the fear that this could happen to
8 me (CBB). ■ καθαρός clean. καρδία heart. The heart is the center of the inner life of the person where all the spiritual forces and functions have their origin (TDNT). ὄψονται fut. ὁράω to
9 see. ■ εἰρηνοποιός to make peace. υἱός son. κληθήσονται fut.
10 pass. καλέω to call, to name, pass. to be given a name. ■ δεδιωγμένοι perf. pass. part. διώκω to pursue, to persecute.
11 ἕνεκεν w. gen. because of, on account of. ■ ἐστέ pres. εἰμί. ὅταν w. subj. if, when. ὀνειδίσωσιν aor. subj. ὀνειδίζω to reproach, to revile, to heap insults upon (BAG). διώξωσιν aor. subj. εἴπωσιν aor. subj. λέγω. πᾶς every, each. It may be used to include everything belonging, in kind, to the class designated by the noun: "every kind of, all sorts of " (BAG). πονηρός bad, evil, wicked. καθ᾽ = κατά w. gen. against. Indicates the hostile
12 relation (Schl.). ψευδόμενοι part. ψεύδομαι to lie. ■ χαίρετε imp. χαίρω to rejoice, to be happy. ἀγαλλιᾶσθε imp. ἀγαλλιάομαι to rejoice greatly. μισθός reward. πολύς great. οὕτως so. γάρ for. ἐδίωξαν aor. πρό w. gen. before.
13 ■ ἅλας salt. ἐάν w. subj. if. μωρανθῇ aor. subj. pass. μωραίνω to play the fool, to become foolish, of salt to become

tasteless, insipid (RWP). τίς τί who, what. ἁλισθήσεται fut.
pass. ἁλίζω to salt, to make salty, pass. to be salted. οὐδέν
nothing. ἰσχύω strong, to be able, w. οὐδέν to be good for
nothing (BAG). ἔτι yet. εἰ μή except. βληθέν aor. pass. part.
βάλλω to throw. ἔξω out. καταπατεῖσθαι pres. mid. inf.
καταπατέω to tread down, to trample. ὑπό w. gen. by (w.
pass.). ἄνθρωπος man. (For an explanation of salt losing its
savor and the idea of salt indicating productivity rather than
preservation, s. E.P. Deatrick, "Salt, Soil, Savor," BA, XXV
[May 1962], 41–48.) ■ φῶς light. κόσμος world, mankind. 14
δύναμαι to be able. πόλις city. κρυβῆναι aor. inf. pass.
κρύπτω or κρύβω to hide, pass. to hide or conceal oneself.
ἐπάνω w. gen. upon. ὄρος mountain. κειμένη part. κεῖμαι to
lie. Used of location of a place (BAG). ■ οὐδέ and, neither. καίω 15
to light. λύχνος oil lamp. τιθέασιν pres. τίθημι to set, to place.
ὑπό w. acc. under. μόδιος a grain measuring vessel containing
about a peck (BAG) (s. also HDCG). ἀλλ᾽= ἀλλά but. ἐπί w.
acc. on. λυχνία lampstand. λάμπω to shine. πᾶς s.v.11. οἰκία
house. (For lamps and lampstands, s. Robert H. Smith, "The
Household Lamps of Palestine in New Testament Times," BA,
XXIX [Feb. 1966], 2–27.) ■ οὕτως "so," makes the comparison. 16
λαμψάτω aor. imp. 3rd sing. λάμπω. The disciples of Jesus are
to allow the light which they received from the heavenly Father
through Jesus to shine in the world in order that they may glorify
God (TDNT). ἔμπροσθεν w. gen. before. ὅπως w. subj. in
order that (purpose). ἴδωσιν aor. subj. ὁράω to see. καλός
good, beautiful. ἔργον work, deed. δοξάσωσιν aor. subj.
δοξάζω to praise, to glorify. οὐρανός s.v.3.

■ νομίσητε aor. subj. to consider, to think. ὅτι that. ἦλθον 17
aor. ἔρχομαι. καταλῦσαι aor. inf. καταλύω to tear down, to
destroy, to annul. Infinitive used to express purpose. νόμος law.
πληρῶσαι aor. inf. πληρόω to fulfill. In an absolute way (s.
C.F.D. Moule. "Fulfillment–Words in the New Testament: Use
and Abuse," NTS, 14 [April 1968], 316ff.). ■ ἀμήν (Heb.) "cer- 18
tainly." (For the Heb. word s. TWOT.) In Judaism the word was
a strengthening or confirming answer or agreement with another
person's statement. For example, a prayer or praise or an oath
(SB, I, 242f.). Jesus did not use the word to apply to others but
to introduce His own words. This gives strength and authority
to what He says. (Klaus Berger, "Zur Geschichte der Ein-
leitungsformel Amen, Ich Sage Euch," ZNW, 63 [1972], 45–75.)
γάρ for. λέγω to say. ἕως ἄν w. subj. until. παρέλθῃ aor. subj.
παρέρχομαι to pass by, to come to an end. οὐρανός s.v.3. ἰῶτα
to Gr. letter iota, used to represent the Heb. letter yod, the

smallest letter in the Heb. alphabet. κεραία horn, projection, hook as a part of a letter (BAG). οὐ μή not in any wise. (For the double neg. s. M, 187–192.) πᾶς everything. (For the use of πᾶς s. IBG, 93–95; RG 771–774.) γένηται aor. subj. γίνομαι to
19 become, to come to pass, to happen. ■ ὅς ἐάν = ὅς ἄν whoever. The relative clause has the character of a conditional clause and refers to a general assertion or supposition (BD, 192). οὖν then, therefore. λύσῃ aor. subj. λύω to loose, to repeal, to annul, to abolish (BAG). ἐντολή command, law. οὗτος this. ἐλάχιστος superl. least, from μικρός small. Paronomasia—the reoccurance of the same word in close proximity. The one who breaks the *least* commandment will be the *least* in the kingdom of heaven (BD, 258). διδάξῃ aor. subj. s.v.2. οὕτως s.v.16. ἄνθρωπος man. κληθήσεται s.v.9. βασιλεία s.v.3. ποιήσῃ aor. subj. ποιέω to do. μέγας large, great. The positive used for the superl.
20 probably under Hebraic influence (MT 31). ■ γάρ for. ὅτι used as quotation marks in a direct quotation. ἐάν s.v.13. περισσεύσῃ subj. περισσεύω to exceed, to overflow like a river out of its banks (RWP). δικαιοσύνη s.v.6. πλεῖον more, in a greater measure. Used as a heightened comp. (BD, 129). γραμματεύς scribe. gen. of comp. εἰσέλθητε aor. subj. εἰσέρχομαι to go in, to come in, to enter.
21 ■ ἠκούσατε aor. ἀκούω to hear. ὅτι that. ἐρρέθη aor. pass. λέγω. ἀρχαῖος old, pl. the old ones, men of earlier generations. φονεύσεις fut. φονεύω to murder, to kill. φονεύσῃ aor. subj. ἔνοχος to be caught in, to be liable, to be guilty. ἔσται fut. εἰμί
22 to be. κρίσις judging, judgment. ■ ὀργιζόμενος part. ὀργίζομαι to be angry. εἴπῃ aor. subj. λέγω. ῥακά fool, empty head. συνέδριον Sanhedrin, highest court of the Jews. μωρός foolish, stupid. *Raca* expresses contempt for a man's head, "you stupid." *More* expresses contempt for his heart and character, "you scoundrel" (EGT). γέεννα gehenna, the city dump of Jerusalem, as a picture of the final place of judgment for the
23 wicked. (For a description of the word s. TDNT.) πῦρ fire. ■ προσφέρῃς pres. subj. προσφέρω to bring, to present offerings and gifts. δῶρον gift, present. ἐπί w. acc. upon. θυσιαστήριον altar. (For words ending in – τήριον meaning "place," s. RG, 154; MH, 343.) κἀκεῖ = καὶ ἐκεῖ "and there." μνησθῇς aor. subj. μιμνήσκομαι to remember, to think about. ἔχω to have.
24 τί something. κατά w. gen. against. ■ ἄφες aor. imp. ἀφίημι to leave, to leave behind. ἔμπροσθεν s.v.16. ὕπαγε pres. imp. ὑπάγω to go. πρῶτον first. διαλλάγηθι aor. imp. διαλλάσσομαι to reconcile, pass. to be reconciled. Denotes mutual concession after mutual hostility (Lightfoot, *Notes*). τότε

then. ἐλθών aor. part. ἔρχομαι coming, to come, to go. Participle used as a circumstantial part. πρόσφερε imp. ■ ἴσθι imp. 25
εἰμί. εὐνοῶν pres. part. εὐνοέω to be well disposed, to make
friends. The pres. tense is written to express an imperative (RG,
375). ἀντίδικος opponent in a law case. ταχύ quickly. ἕως ὅτου
w. pres. ind. meanwhile, as. εἶ pres. εἰμί. μετ᾽= μετά w. gen.
with. ὁδός way. μήποτε w. aor. subj. less. παραδῷ aor. subj.
παραδίδωμι to give over, to turn over to. κριτής the one who
makes a decision, judge. ὑπηρέτης helper, one who serves.
φυλακή prison. βληθήσῃ fut. pass βάλλω to throw, to cast.
■ ἐξέλθῃς aor. subj. ἐξέρχομαι to come out, to go out. ἐκεῖθεν 26
from there. ἀποδῷς aor. subj. ἀποδίδωμι to give back, to pay
back. ἔσχατος last. κοδράντης (lat.) quadrans, a Roman coin
or a coin used at the time of our Lord, worth about 1.5 cents
(UBD, 724).

   ■ μοιχεύσεις fut. μοιχεύω to commit adultery. ■ βλέπων 27/28
pres. part. βλέπω to see, to look upon. γυνή, αικός woman.
πρός w. inf. often expresses purpose, but sometimes weakened
to "with reference to." It may express tendency and ultimate
goal rather than purpose (MT, 144; s. also M, 218). ἐπιθυμῆσαι
aor. inf. ἐπιθυμέω to desire, to long for. ἤδη already.
ἐμοίχευσεν aor. An aor. after a fut. condition is, to a certain
extent, futuristic ([BD, 171]; s. also RG, 846f.). καρδία heart.
■ εἰ if. ὀφθαλμός eye. δεξιός right. σκανδαλίζω to cause to 29
fall. The substantive means to stick in the trap that springs and
closes the trap when the animal touches it (RWP). ἔξελε aor.
imp. ἐξαιρέω to take out, to tear out. βάλε aor. imp. βάλλω.
συμφέρει to be advantageous, to be profitable, to be good, to be
useful. Here it is well trans. "it is better . . . than" (BAG). ἵνα
w. subj. "that." This clause is the subject of συμφέρει (RG,992).
ἀπόληται aor. subj. ἀπόλλυμαι to be destroyed, to be ruined,
to be lost. μέλος member. ὅλος whole. σῶμα body. βληθῇ aor.
subj. pass. βάλλω. ■ χείρ hand. ἔκκοψον aor. imp. ἐκκόπτω 30
to cut off. ἵνα s.v.29. ἀπέλθῃ aor. subj. ἀπέρχομαι to go away.
   ■ ἐρρέθη aor. pass. λέγω. ἀπολύσῃ aor. subj. ἀπολύω to 31
release, to divorce. δότω aor. imp. 3rd. δίδωμι to give.
ἀποστάσιον, bill of divorcement. The written notice was a
protection to the wife (RWP). (For the Jewish practice s. M,
Gittin; SB, 1, 303–312.) ■ ἀπολύων part. παρέκτος w. gen. 32
except. λόγος word, matter, reason. πορνεία unchastity, fornication of every kind of unlawful sexual intercourse (BAG). ποιεῖ
pres. ποιέω to make. μοιχευθῆναι aor. inf. pass.
ἀπολελυμένην perf. pass. part. γαμήσῃ aor. subj. γαμέω to
marry, used of the man. μοιχᾶται pass. μοιχάω to cause one

to commit adultery, pass. to be an adulterer, to commit adultery.

33　■ πάλιν again. ἐπιορκήσεις fut. ἐπιορκέω to swear falsely, to break an oath. ἀποδώσεις fut. ἀποδίδωμι to give away, to fulfill one's duty to someone, to keep oaths (BAG). ὅρκος oath, pl. even when one oath is intended (BAG). (For a Jewish view of oaths, s. M, Shebuoth; SB, I, 321–336; s. also 1QS 5:8.)

34　■ μή ... ὅλως = an unconditional neg. (Schl., 182). ὀμόσαι aor. inf. ὄμνυμι to swear. ὅλως adv. at all. μήτε ... μήτε

35　neither ... nor. ὅτι because. θρόνος throne. θεός God. ■

36　ὑποπόδιον footstool. πούς foot. ■ ὀμόσῃς aor. subj. w. μή = neg. imp. δύνασαι s.v.14. θρίξ, τρίχος hair. λευκός bright, shining, white. ποιῆσαι aor. inf. ἤ or. μέλας black. ■ ἔστω imp.

37　3rd. εἰμί. ναί yes.

38/39　　■ ἀντί w. gen. instead of. ὀδούς, ὀδόντος tooth. ■ ἀντιστῆναι aor. inf. ἀνθίστημι to set against, to set oneself against, to oppose, to resist, to withstand. ὅστις who, whoever. ῥαπίζω to hit, to slap. σιαγών cheek. στρέψον aor. imp.

40　στρέφω to turn. ἄλλος other. ■ θέλοντι part. θέλω to will, to wish. κριθῆναι aor. inf. pass. κρίνω to separate, to judge, pass. to dispute, quarrel, debate, to go to law with someone (BAG). χιτών tunic. A sort of shirt or undergarment, and would be demanded at law (RWP). λαβεῖν aor. inf. λαμβάνω to take.

41　ἱμάτιον garment, outer clothing, cloak. ■ ἀγγαρεύσει fut. ἀγγαρεύω to compel, forcibly to impress someone to service, to compel him to serve whether he liked it or not (NTW, 16). μίλιον mile. A Roman mile, a thousand paces, then a fixed

42　measure about 4,854 feet (BAG). ■ αἰτοῦντι pres. part. αἰτέω to ask. δός aor. imp. δίδωμι to give. ἀπό w. gen. from. δανείσασθαι aor. inf. mid. δανίζω to lend money, mid. to borrow money. ἀποστράφῃς aor. subj. ἀποστρέφομαι to turn away.

43　　■ ἀγαπήσεις fut. ἀγαπάω to love. The fut. is used for injunctions in the legal language of the OT (BD, 183). πλησίος near, close–by, neighbor, fellowman. μισήσεις fut. μισέω to hate. ἐχθρός enemy. (For DSS instructions to hate the enemy,

44　s. 1QS 1:10; 2:4–9; 1QM 4:1.) ■ ἀγαπᾶτε imp. προσεύχεσθε imp. προσεύχομαι to pray. ὑπέρ for, on behalf of. διωκόντων

45　part. s.v.10. ■ ὅπως w. subj. aor. in order that. γένησθε aor. subj. γίνομαι. υἱός son. πατήρ father. ὅτι because. ἥλιος sun. ἀνατέλλω to cause to rise, transitive and causative in meaning (BD, 163). ἐπί w. acc. on, upon. ἀγαθός good. βρέχω to cause

46　to rain. δίκαιος righteous. ἄδικος unrighteous. ■ ἀγαπήσητε aor. subj. ἀγαπῶντας pres. part. τίς what. μισθός s.v.12. οὐχί = οὐ. With questions it expects a positive answer. τελώνης tax

16

collector. (For a study of the word s. TDNT.) ποιοῦσιν pres.
■ ἀσπάσησθε aor. subj. ἀσπάζομαι to greet. More significant   47
in the East; symbolic here of friendly relations (EGT). μόνον
only. ποιεῖτε pres. ἐθνικός Gentile, heathen. ■ ὑμεῖς you (pl.)   48
emphatic. τέλειος perfect. ὡς as. οὐράνιος heavenly, belonging
to heaven, living in heaven.

Ch. 6

■ προσέχετε imp. προσέχω to beware, to give heed to, to   1
watch out for. ποιεῖν inf. ποιέω to do. Used with δικαιοσύνη
meaning "to practice piety," and δικαιοσύνη is the general title
for acts of devotion and religious duty which conform to the will
of God (GW, 129). ἔμπροσθεν w. gen. before, in the presence
of. πρός to, indicates purpose. θεαθῆναι aor. inf. pass. θεάομαι
to see, to behold, to look at. αὐτοῖς dat. of agency (MT, 240).
εἰ δὲ μή γε but, if not, otherwise (s. Margaret Thrall, *Greek
Particles in the New Testament*, 9, 10). μισθός reward.
■ ὅταν w. subj. when, whenever. ἐλεημοσύνη kind deed,   2
alms, charitable giving (BAG). Nothing is more marked in rabbinic ethics than the stress laid upon charity in every sense of the
word (Montefiore and Loewe, *A Rabbinic Anthology*, 412; for
rabbinic views on charity s. Montefiore and Loewe, 412-439,
and Moore, *Judaism*, II, 162-179). σαλπίσῃς aor. subj.
σαλπίζω to sound the trumpet, either in a figurative or literal
sense (McNeile). ὥσπερ just as, even as. ὑποκριτής actor,
interpreter, one who impersonates another, hypocrite (RWP).
ῥύμη a narrow street. ὅπως w. subj. in order that. δοξασθῶσιν
aor. subj. pass. δοξάζω to give honor, to praise, to glorify.
ἀπέχω to receive payment in full. Often used in the sense of
receipting an account which has been paid in full (NTW, 17-20).
■ ποιοῦντος pres. part. ποιέω gen. abs. "when you . . . . "   3
γνώτω aor. imp. 3rd sing. γινώσκω to know. ἀριστερός left.
τί what. δεξιός right. ■ ᾗ subj. εἰμί to be. κρυπτός hidden,   4
secret. ἀποδώσει fut. ἀποδίδωμι to give back, to repay, to
reward.
■ ὡς as. ὅτι because. φιλοῦσιν pres. φιλέω to like, to love.   5
γωνία corner. πλατεῖα a wide street. ἑστῶτες perf. part.
ἵστημι to stand. Standing was the usual attitude in prayer
(McNeile). φανῶσιν aor. subj. φαίνομαι to appear, to show
oneself. ■ ταμεῖον storeroom, innermost secret room (BAG).   6
κλείσας aor. part. κλείω to close. πρόσευξαι aor. imp.
προσεύχομαι to pray. ■ βατταλογήσητε aor. subj.   7
βατταλογέω to babble, either in the sense of repeating the
words or babbling or chattering (RWP). Perhaps a reference to

17

the heathen magical formulas, a repetition of meaningless sounds (F.W. Beare, "Speaking with Tongues," JBL, LXXXIII [Sept. 1964], 229). ἐθνικός heathen. δοκοῦσιν pres. δοκέω to suppose, to think so. ὅτι that. πολυλογία much speaking. εἰσακουσθήσονται fut. pass. εἰσακούω to listen to, to hear
8 and answer prayer. ■ ὁμοιωθῆτε aor. subj. pass ὁμοιόω to make like, pass. to be like. οἶδα defective perf. w. the pres. meaning, to know. χρείαν ἔχω w. gen. to have need of. αἰτῆσαι
9 aor. inf. αἰτέω to ask. ■ οὕτως so, in the following manner. ἀγιασθήτω aor. imp. 3rd sing. pass. ἀγιάζω to treat as holy, to reverence (BAG). (For the aor. imp. in prayers, s. W.F. Bak-
10 ker, The Greek Imperative.) ■ ἐλθάτω aor. imp. 3rd. sing. ἔρχομαι to come. The petition is for the future advent of God to establish His sovereignty on earth (McNeile). βασιλεία kingdom, rule of a king. γενηθήτω aor. imp. 3rd sing. γίνομαι
11 to become, to come to pass, to be done, to happen. ■ ἐπιούσιος for the coming day (RWP). "The bread that we need, give us today, day after day." (For this translation and a study of the
12 word s. TDNT; BAG.) δός aor. imp. δίδωμι. ■ ἄφες aor. imp. ἀφίημι to let go, to cancel, to remit, to pardon (BAG). ὀφείλημα debt, what is owed, one's due (BAG). ὡς as, in the sense of "because" (BD, 236). ἀφήκαμεν aor. ἀφίημι.
13 ὀφειλέτης debtor. ■ εἰσενέγκῃς aor. subj. εἰσφέρω to bring in, to lead into. περρασμός test, temptation. ῥῦσαι aor. imp.
14 ῥύομαι to rescue, to deliver. ■ ἐάν w. subj. if. ἀφῆτε aor. subj. ἀφίημι. παράπτωμα transgression. οὐράνιος belonging to heaven, heavenly.
16   ■ νηστεύητε pres. subj. νηστεύω to fast, to sit and fast. (For Jewish fasting, s. Moore, Judaism, II, 257–266.) γίνεσθε pres. imp. γίνομαι. σκυθρωπός sad, gloomy, sullen look. ἀφανίζω to render invisible or unrecognizable, of one's face, to disfigure, that is, with ashes and by leaving the hair and beard unattended or by coloring the face to look pale as though fasting (McNeile). Perhaps there is a play on words with φανῶσιν. They neglect their appearance in order that they may appear.
17 νηστεύοντες pres. part. contemporaneous time. ■ νηστεύων pres. part. belongs to σύ. ἄλειψαι aor. imp. ἀλείφομαι to
18 anoint oneself. νίψαι aor. imp. νίπτομαι to wash oneself. ■ κρυφαῖος hidden.
19   ■ θησαυρίζετε pres. imp. θησαυρίζω to gather treasure. θησαυρός treasure-chest, treasure. ὅπου rel. where. σής moth. βρῶσις eating. ἀφανίζω s.v.16. κλέπτης thief. διορύσσω to
20 dig through, to break in. ■ οὔτε ... οὔτε neither ... nor. οὐδέ s.v.15.

■ λύχνος light, lamp (s. TDNT). σῶμα body. ἐάν s.v.14. 22
οὖν therefore. ᾖ s.v.4. ἁπλοῦς clear, sound, healthy (BAG; s.
also RWP). ὅλος whole, complete. φωτεινός shining brightly,
light. ■ σκοτεινός dark. εἰ if. φῶς light. σκότος darkness. 23
πόσος adj. of number, magnitude, degree, how much, how great,
how many (AS). "What a terrible kind of darkening that is"
(McNeile). The conclusion of the argument from the lesser to
the greater (s. also Rom. 5:9).

■ μισήσει fut. μισέω to hate, in this context to neglect, to 24
disregard, to slight ἀνθέξεται fut. ἀντέχομαι to hold fast to,
to stick by. Used in the sense of sticking by one's rights (MM).
(For the local force of the prep. in composition, s. MH, 297.)
καταφρονήσει fut. καταφρονέω to despise, to look down
upon. The prep. indicates that the action is unfavorable to the
object (MH, 316). μαμωνᾶς possession, earthly goods (TDNT).

■ μεριμνᾶτε imp. μεριμνάω to be concerned for, to be 25
anxious about. ψυχή soul. The life principle embodied in the
body (McNeile). Dative = dat. of advantage (MT, 238). τί
what? φάγητε αοι. subj. ἐσθίω to eat. πίητε αοr. subj. πίνω to
drink. μηδέ = οὐδέ s.v.15. ἐνδύσησθε aor. subj. ἐνδύομαι to
clothe oneself with, to put on. οὐχί in questions, expects a positive answer. πλεῖον imp. πολύς much, much more. τροφή food.
Genitive = gen. of comparison, "than." ἔνδυμα clothing. ■ 26
ἐμβλέψατε aor. imp. ἐμβλέπω to look at, to consider.
πετεινόν bird. σπείρω to sew. θερίζω to harvest. συνάγω to
gather, to gather together. ἀποθήκη barn, storehouse. μᾶλλον
more. Strengthens the comparative force of διαφέρετε (Meyer).
διαφέρω to differ, to be different, to be worth more than, to be
superior to (BAG). ■ μεριμνῶν part. expresses means. 27
προσθεῖναι aor. inf. προστίθημι to add to. ἐπί w. acc. upon,
to. ἡλικία size, age. The passage can refer to the length of life
or to the size or stature of the person (TDNT; MM). πῆχυς
originally forearm, then cubit, as a length of measure, about 18
inches or can refer to a measure of time (BAG). ■ περί w. gen. 28
concerning, about. τί why? μεριμνᾶτε pres. καταμάθετε aor.
imp. καταμανθάνω to learn thoroughly, to observe well, to
consider carefully (AS), to understand, to take in this fact about
(M, 117, 118). κρίνον lily. ἀγρός field. πῶς how. αὐξάνω int.
to grow. κοπιῶσιν pres. κοπιάω to labor with wearisome effort, to toil (T). Not so much the actual exertion as the weariness
which follows on this straining of all his powers to the utmost
(Trench, Synonyms, 378). νήθω to spin. ■ περιεβάλετο aor. 29
mid. περιβάλλω to put around, to put on, περιβάλλομαι mid.
to clothe oneself. ὡς as. ■ χόρτος grass. Mere weeds to be cut 30

19

down and used as fuel (EGT). σήμερον today. ὄντα part. εἰμί.
αὔριον tomorrow. κλίβανος oven, furnace. βαλλόμενον pres.
pass. part. βάλλω to cast. οὕτως so. ἀμφιέννυμι to clothe.
31 ὀλιγόπιστος little faith, a small amount of trust. ■
μεριμνήσητε aor. subj. w. μή as a neg. imp. τί s.v.25.
περιβαλώμεθα aor. subj. mid. The deliberative subj. (DM, 171;
32 MT 98,99). ■ ἔθνος people, pl. heathen. ἐπιζητοῦσιν pres.
ἐπιζητέω to look for, to seek after. The prep. is directive, indicating the concentration of the verb's action upon some object
(MH, 312). Present indicates a a continual seeking after. οἶδα
33 s.v.8. χρήζω to have need of, w. gen. ἅπας = πᾶς. ■
δικαιοσύνη righteousness, conduct in agreement with His
(God's) will (GW, 129). καί "and," "so." To introduce a result
which comes from what precedes (BAG). προστεθήσεται fut.
34 pass. προστίθημι to add to. ■ αὔριον tomorrow, the next day.
μεριμνήσει fut. ἑαυτῆς gen. refl. pron. 3rd per. ἀρκετός
enough, sufficient. κακία trouble, misfortune. Used in the sense
of damage done to a crop by hail (MM). "Each day has enough
trouble of its own" (BAG).

Ch. 7

1 ■ κρίνετε imp. κρίνω to judge, habit of censoriousness,
sharp, unjust criticism (RWP). κριθῆτε aor. pass. subj. may refer
2 to divine judgment or to human judgment (McNeile). ἐν instrumental. κρίμα judgment as from a judge. κριθήσεσθε fut.
pass. μέτρον measure. μετρεῖτε pres. μετρέω to measure.
3 μετρηθήσεται fut. pass. ■ τί why. κάρφος a splinter, a piece
of dry wood or chaff, a very small particle that may irritate
(RWP). σός your. δοκός beam. κατανοεῖς pres. κατανοέω to
4 notice, to take note of, to perceive. ■ ἤ or. πῶς how. ἐρεῖς fut.
λέγω to say. ἄφες aor. imp. ἀφίημι to allow. ἐκβάλω aor. subj.
ἐκβάλλω to cast out, to remove. ἰδού to see, to behold. ἡ δοκός
beam, a log upon which planks in a house rest, a post sticking
out grotesquely (RWP). The article is used as the article of
5 previous reference or renewed mention (IBG,117). ■ ἔκβαλε
aor. imp. τότε then, afterward. διαβλέψεις fut. διαβλέπω to
see clearly, sharply. The prep. is prefective (MH,301). ἐκβαλεῖν
6 aor. inf. ■ δῶτε aor. subj. δίδωμι to give, w. μή = neg. imp.
ἅγιος holy. κύων, κυνός dog. μηδέ = οὐδέ and not, neither.
βάλητε aor. subj. βάλλω to cast. μαργαρίτης pearl.
ἔμπροσθεν w. gen. before. χοῖρος a young pig, swine. μήποτε
w. ind. fut. and aor. subj. lest. καταπατήσουσιν fut.
καταπατέω to trample. πούς foot. στραφέντες aor. part.
στρέφομαι to turn around. ῥήξωσιν aor. subj. ῥήγνυμι to tear

20

in pieces.

■ αἰτεῖτε imp. αἰτέω to ask. δοθήσεται fut. pass. δίδωμι. 7
κρούετε imp. κρούω to knock. ἀνοιγήσεται fut. pass. ἀνοίγω
to open. ■ αἰτῶν part. λαμβάνω to take, to receive. ζητῶν part. 8
■ τίς who. μή uscd when a neg. answer to a question is expected. 9
(For the Semitic structure of this verse see, BD, 246.) ἐπιδώσει
fut. ἐπιδίδωμι to give to. The ἐπί is directive (MH, 312). ■ 10
ἰχθύς fish. ὄφις snake. Stones on the shore, and possible water
snakes, suggested themselves as substitute (McNeile). ■ εἰ if. 11
Introduces a first-class condition, ὄντες part. εἰμί. οἴδατε defective perf. with the pres. meaning, οἶδα to know. διδόναι pres.
inf. πόσω μᾶλλον how much more? δώσει fut. δίδωμι.
αἰτοῦσιν part. ■ ὅσος sums up the sermon to this point 12
(McNeile). ἐάν w. subj. "if." Introduces a third-class conditional
clause. θέλητε subj. θέλω to wish, to want. ποιῶσιν subj.
ποιέω to do, to make.

■ εἰσέλθατε aor. imp. εἰσέρχομαι to come in, to go in. 13
διά w. gen. through. στενός narrow. ὅτι because. πλατύς wide.
εὐρύχωρος wide, roomy, broad. ἀπάγουσα part. ἀπάγω to
lead. ἀπώλεια destruction. εἰσερχόμενοι part. ■ τεθλιμμένη 14
perf. pass. part. θλίβω to press, to be narrow. ὀλίγοι few.
εὑρίσκοντες part. s.v.7.

■ προσέχετε pres. imp. προσέχω to turn one's mind to, 15
to pay attention, to give heed. πρός, used with verbs to be on
guard, to give heed to (BD, 83). ὅστις generical or generalized
rel. pron. whoever, everyone who. ἔνδυμα clothing. Perhaps a
reference to a dress worn by a prophet (EGT). ἔσωθεν inwardly.
λύκυς wolf. ἅρπαξ raging, ravenous. ■ ἐπιγνώσεσθε fut. 16
ἐπιγινώσκω an exact knowledge, to know fully, to recognize.
μήτι, used in questions which expect a neg. answer. συλλέγω
to gather together. ἄκανθα thorn bushes. σταφυλή grapes.
τρίβολος thistles. σῦκον figs. ■ σαπρός decayed, rotten. Used 17
of things unusable, unfit, bad (BAG). ■ ἐνεγκεῖν aor. inf. φέρω 18
to bear. ■ ἐκκόπτεται pres. pass. ἐκκόπτω to cut down. ■ ἄρα 19/20
then, expresses an inference. Used to emphasize the preceding
word.

■ κύριος Lord. Often occurs as a form of polite address, but 21
here it is more than that. It is addressed to Him in His supreme
power in the last day (McNeile). εἰσελεύσεται fut.
εἰσέρχομαι. ■ ἐροῦσιν fut. λέγω. ὄνομα name. The dat. here 22
is instrumental (McNeile). ἐπροφητεύσαμεν aor. προφητεύω
to prophesy. δύναμις power, miracle. ■ ὁμολογήσω fut. 23
ὁμολογέω to make a statement, in the legal sense to bear witness. An act of proclamation in which the relation of man to

21

Jesus is expressed in a binding and valid form (TDNT). ὅτι recitative, used as quotation marks to introduce a direct quote. οὐδέποτε never. ἔγνων aor. γινώσκω to know. The words "I never knew you" were used by the rabbis as a banish formula (SB). ἀποχωρεῖτε pres. impf. ἀποχωρέω to depart, to go away. ἐργαξόμενοι pres. part. ἐργάζομαι to work. ἀνομία lawlessness.

24 ■ ὁμοιωθήσεται fut. pass. ὁμοιόω to compare, to liken. φρόνιμος understanding, practically wise, sensible (AS). 25 ᾠκοδόμησεν aor. οἰδοκομέω to build. ■ κατέβη aor. καταβαίνω to go down, to fall down. βροχή rain (used in the papyri for artifical inundations) (McNeile). ἦλθον aor. ἔρχομαι. ποταμός flood. ἔπνευσαν aor. πνεώ to blow. ἄνεμος wind. προσέπεσαν aor. προσπίπτω to fall upon. ἔπεσεν aor. πίπτω to fall. τεθεμελίωτο plperf. pass. θεμελιόω 26 to found, to lay the foundation. ■ μωρός foolish, unreflecting, foolish deeds, heart thoughts arising from a lack of knowledge or the inability to make correct decisions (s. CBB, s. also 27 TDNT). ἄμμος sand. ■ προσέκοψαν aor. προσκόπτω to strike against, to beat against. πτῶσις fall.

28 ■ ὅτε when. ἐτέλεσεν aor. τελέω to complete, to end. ἐξεπλήσσοντο impf. pass. ἐκπλήσσω to amaze, to astound, pass. to be amazed, to be astounded, to be beside one's self. The impf. represents a past event as still taking place at the time when an event in the aor. suddenly intervenes (MT, 66). ἐπί w. the 29 dat. expressing the reason. ■ γάρ for (explanatory). διδάσκων part. διδάσκω.

Ch. 8

1 ■ καταβάντος aor. part. καταβαίνω to go down (part. used as gen. abs.). ἠκολούθησαν aor. ἀκολουθέω to follow, to 2 be a traveling companion. ■ προσέλθων aor. part. προσέρχομαι to come to. προσεκύνει impf. προσκυνέω to worship by falling at the feet. The inceptive impf. "he began to worship." ἐάν w. the subj. if. It indicates some doubt regarding the condition. The doubt is not about the power but about the will (EGT). θέλῃς pres. subj. θέλω to wish, to will. καθαρίσαι 3 aor. inf. καθαρίζω to cleanse. ■ ἐκτείνας aor. part. ἐκτείνω to stretch out. ἥψατο aor. ἅπτω to touch, to take hold of (used w. the gen.). καθαρίσθητι aor. imp. pass. ἐκαθαρίσθη aor. pass. 4 ■ ὅρα pres. imp. ὁράω to see. εἴπῃς aor. subj. λέγω. ὕπαγε pres. imp. ὑπάγω to go forth. δεῖξον aor. imp. δείκνυμι to show. προσένεγκον aor. imp. προσφέρω to bring to, to carry to, to offer. προσέταξεν aor. προστάσσω to instruct, to com-

mand. μαρτύριον proof, testimony (s. Lev. 14:1–32. For the
Jewish view of leprosy, s. SB, IV, 745–763, M, Negaim). Judaism
expected the removal of this affliction in the time of Messianic
salvation (TDNT).
■ εἰσελθόντες aor. part. εἰσέρχομαι to go in, to come in 5
(part. used as gen. abs.). ἑκατόνταρχος leader of a hundred
men, centurion. παρακαλῶν part. παρακαλέω to call for help.
■ παῖς son (used here w. the meaning servant). A friendly term 6
of address which indicates that the one serving had a personal
relation w. his master (Schl.) βέβληται perf. pass. βάλλω to
throw, pass. to lie on a sick bed. παραλυτικός lame, paralyzed.
δεινῶς adv. δεινός terrible. βασανιζόμενος pass. part.
βασανίζω to torment. ■ ἐλθών aor. part. ἔρχομαι to come, to 7
go. θεραπεύσω fut. θεραπεύω to heal. The fut. indicates a
promise w. certainty (Schl.). ■ ἀποκριθεὶς aor. part. 8
ἀποκρίνομαι to answer. ἔφη impf. φημί to speak. ἱκανός sufficient, worthy. στέγη roof. εἰσέλθῃς aor. subj. εἰπέ aor. imp.
λέγω. ἰαθήσεται fut. pass. ἰάομαι to heal. ■ ἐξουσία author- 9
ity, authority to rule, authority by virtue of office. πορεύθητι
aor. imp. πορεύομαι to go, to march (for comparison w.
ἔρχομαι, s. BD, 172). ἔρχου pres. imp. ποίησον aor. imp.
ποιέω to do, to make. ■ ἀκούσας aor. part. ἀκούω to hear. 10
ἐθαύμασεν aor. θαυμάζω to be amazed. ἀκολουθοῦσιν part.
s.v.1. τοσαύτην fem. acc. τοσοῦτος so great. εὗρον aor.
εὑρίσκω to find. ■ ἀνατολή east. δυσμή west. ἥξουσιν fut. 11
ἥκω to come. ἀνακλιθήσονται fut. ἀνακλίνομαι to recline at
a table. Used of the Messianic banquet (BAG). (For the Jewish
custom of eating while reclining at the table, s. SB, IV, 618f.).
■ ἐκβληθήσονται fut. pass. ἐκβάλλω to cast out. ἐξώτερος 12
outer. Comparative in form only. κλαυθμός crying. βρυγμός
gnashing of teeth. The wailing indicates suffering, the gnashing
of teeth, despair (Meyer). ὀδόντων gen. pl. ὀδούς tooth. ■ 13
ἐπίστευσας aor. act. πιστεύω to believe. γενηθήτω aor. imp.
3rd sing. γίνομαι to be, to become, to happen. ἰάθη aor. pass.
ἰάομαι.
■ ἐλθών aor. part. ἔρχομαι. πενθερά mother of the wife, 14
mother-in-law. βεβλημένην perf. pass. part., s.v.6.
πυρέσσουσαν pres. part. πυρέσσω to have a fever. ■ ἥψατο 15
s.v.3. ἀφῆκεν aor. ἀφίημι to depart. πυρετός fever. ἠγέρθη
aor. pass. ἐγείρω act. to wait, pass. to rise, to get up. διηκόνει
impf. διακονέω to wait on someone at the table, to serve. Inceptive impf. "she began to serve." The previous aor. expresses a
point, the impf. begins a linear action (s. Bakker, 26). ■ ὀψία 16
evening. γενομένης aor. part. γίνομαι gen. abs. (when it was

23

evening). προσήνεγκαν aor. act., s.v.4. προσφέρω.
δαιμονιζομένους pres. part. δαιμονίζω to be possessed by a
demon or an evil spirit. ἐξέβαλεν aor., s.v.12. κακῶς ἔχω to be
17 ill, sick. ἔχοντας part. ἐθεράπευσεν aor., s.v.7. ■ πληρωθῇ
aor. subj. pass. πληρόω to fulfill. ῥηθέν aor. pass. part. λέγω to
say. αὐτός he, himself (emphatic, s. MT, 40, 41). ἔλαβεν aor.
λαμβάνω to take away. ἐβάστασεν aor. βαστάζω to take
away, to bear.

18   ■ ἰδών aor. part. ὁράω to see. ἐκέλευσεν aor. κελεύω to
command (for this verb w. the aor. inf., s. BD, 174). ἀπελθεῖν
aor. inf. ἀπέρχομαι to go away, to leave. πέραν the other side.

19 ■ προσελθών aor. part. προσέρχομαι to come to. εἰς "a"
(used as an indef. art. RWP). διδάσκαλος teacher (for a study
of this word and particularly the rabbi teacher position in Judaism, s. TDNT). ἀκολουθήσω fut. s.v.1. The word speaks of the
rabbi teacher–student relation. ὅπου (ἐ) άν w. a subj. "wher-
20 ever." ἀπέρχῃ subj. ■ ἀλώπηξ fox. φωλεός den, hole for animals. πετεινόν bird. κατασκήνωσις dwelling place, nest. ποῦ
21 where. κλίνῃ pres. subj. κλίνω to incline, to lay. ■ ἕτερος another (for the use of ἕτερος, s. RG, 748–750). ἐπίτρεψον aor.
imp. ἐπιτρέπω to allow, to permit. θάψαι aor. inf. θάπτω to
22 bury. ■ ἀκολούθει pres. imp. a call discipleship. ἄθες aor. imp.
ἀφίημι to leave, to let. νεκρός dead. Perhaps refers to the
spiritual dead (Allen), or may have the meaning dying (AM).
The urgency of following Jesus unreservedly is greater than
burial duties (Hill). (For the background of this passage, s. Luke
9:59f.)

23   ■ ἐμβάντι aor. part. ἐμβαίνω to step in, to embark. The
24 part. is used as a dat. abs. (EGT). ■ σεισμός shaking, used of
a storm or an earthquake. ἐγένετο aor. γίνομαι. ὥστε so that,
used w. the inf. to express results. καλύπτεσθαι pres. pass. inf.
καλύπτω to cover over. κῦμα wave, billow. αὐτός he, in contrast to the others. ἐκάθευδεν impf. καθεύδω to sleep. The
impf. "he kept on sleeping" stands in contrast to the aor.
25 (MT,66). ■ προσελθόντες s.v.2. ἤγειραν aor. s.v.15. σῶσον
aor. imp. σῴζω to save, to rescue. The aor. is used by people in
straitened circumstances (Bakker, 130). ἀπολλύμεθα pres.
ἀπόλλυμι to be destroyed. The pres. graphically describes the
26 dangerous situation. ■ τί why? δειλός cowardly, timid.
ὀλιγόπιστος w. little trust, small in faith. ἐγερθείς aor. pass.
part. ἐπετίμησεν aor. ἐπιτιμάω to rebuke. Suggests that the
elements are treated as evil powers which must be subdued as a
sign of the kingdom over which Christ is king (Hill; s. also Matt.
27 17:18). ἄνεμος wind. γαλήνη calm. ■ ἄνθρωπος men, either

24

the disciples in the boat (Filson) or the people who will subsequently hear (McNeile). ποταπός what sort of, what kind.
ὑπακούω to listen to, to obey.

■ ὑπήντησαν aor. ὑπαντάω to meet. μνημεῖον monu- 28
ment, tomb. χαλεπός hard, difficult, dangerous, violent. λίαν
very. ἰσχύω to be strong, to be able. τις anyone. παρελθεῖν aor.
inf. παρέρχομαι to go by, to pass by. ■ ἔκραξαν aor. κράζω 29
to cry, to scream. ἦλθες aor. ἔρχομαι. τί ἡμῖν καὶ σοί "What
to us and you?" It represents a Heb. idiom suggesting the two
parties have no common concern (Tasker). βασανίσαι aor. inf.,
s.v.6. ■ μακρός long, temporal and spatial. μακράν far, a long 30
way. ἀγέλη heard. χοίρων gen. pl. χοῖρος pig, swine (gen. used
as gen. of apposition or definition RG, 499). It was forbidden for
Jews to raise pigs (M, Baba Kama, 7; SB, I, 492, 493).
βοσκομένη pres. pass. part. βόσκω to feed, to herd, pass. to
graze. ■ παρεκάλουν impf. παρακαλέω to beseech. The impf. 31
indicates they continually asked. εἰ "if." The condition is accepted as true. ἀπόστειλον aor. imp. ἀποστέλλω. ■ 32
ἐξελθόντες aor. part. ἐξέρχομαι. ἀπῆλθον aor. s.v.18.
ὥρμησεν aor. ὁρμάω to set out, to rush. κρημνός steep bank,
precipice. ἀπέθανον aor. ἀποθνήσκω to die. ■ βόσκοντες 33
pres. part. βόσκω. ἔφυγον aor. φεύγω to flee. ἀπήγγειλαν
aor. ἀπαγγέλω to report. ■ ἐξῆλθεν aor. ἐξέρχομαι. 34
ὑπάντησις meeting (for the grammatical use of this, s. M, 14).
ἰδόντες aor. part. ὁράω to see. παρεκάλεσαν aor. μεταβῇ aor.
subj. μεταβαίνω to depart to another place. ὅριον boundary, pl.
area.

Ch. 9

■ ἐμβάς aor. part. ἐμβαίνω to step into, to embark. 1
διεπέρασεν aor. διαπεράω to cross over. ἦλθεν aor. ἔρχομαι
to come. ■ προσέφερον impf. προσφέρω to bring to, to carry. 2
The impf. suggests that they came bringing the man to Jesus as
He arrived in Capernaum (Hill). παραλυτικός lame, paralyzed.
βεβλημένον perf. pass. part. βάλλω to throw. ἰδών aor. part.
ὁράω to see. αὐτῶν "their." Used of him who was born, and of
them who bear him (Bengel). θάρσει imp. θαρσέω to be of
good cheer. ἀφίενται pres. pass. ἀφίημι to depart, pass. to be
forgiven. The pres. means either "are in a state of remission" or
"are at this moment remitted," an aoristic pres. (McNeile).■ 3
βλασφημεῖ pres. βλασφημέω to speak evil of, to defame, to
blaspheme. ■ εἰδώς part. def. perf. w. the pres. meaning οἶδα to 4
know. ἐνθύμησις reflection, thought. ἱνατί (γένηται) "in order that what might happen?", Why, for what reason? (BAG).

ἐνθυμεῖσθε pres. ἐνθυμέομαι to consider, reflect, to think.
5 ■ εὐκοπώτερος comp. εὔκοπος easy. εἰπεῖν aor. inf. λέγω.
ἔγειρε pres. imp. ἐγείρω intr. only in imp. "Arise!" περιπάτει
6 pres. imp. περιπατέω to walk, to go about. ■ εἰδῆτε subj. οἶδα.
ἐξουσία authority. ἀφιέναι pres. inf. ἀφίημι. ἆρον aor. imp.
αἴρω to lift up, to take up. ὕπαγε pres. imp. ὑπάγω to go, to
7 go away. ■ ἐγερθείς aor. pass. part. ἐγείρω pass. to arise.
8 ἀπῆλθεν aor. ἀπέρχομαι to depart. ■ ἐφοβήθησαν aor. pass.
φοβέομαι to be afraid, to fear. ἐδόξασαν aor. δοξάζω to praise,
to glorify. δόντα aor. part. δίδωμι to give. τοιοῦτος such as
this, of such a kind. ἀνθρώποις dat. "On behalf of men" (AM).
9 ■ παράγων part. παράγω intr. to pass by. εἶδεν aor.
ὁράω. καθήμενον pres. part. κάθημαι to sit. τελώνιον tax
office, probably near the beach in order to handle business connected with ships coming to Galilee from the east side of the lake
(Filson). (For tax collectors and their position in Judaism, s.
TDNT; SB, I, 377–380.) λεγόμενος pres. pass. part. λέγω here,
"to be named." ἀκολούθει pres. imp. ἀκολουθέω to follow, "be
My disciple," "attach yourself to My person in order to hear and
follow Me" (Hill). ἀναστάς aor. part. ἀνίσταμι to arise.
10 ἠκολούθησεν aor. ■ ἐγένετο aor. γίνομαι to become, to happen. ἀνακειμένου pres. part. ἀκάκειμαι to recline at the table.
ἁμαρτωλός sinful, sinner. In this context, for those who either
could not because of ignorance or would not observe the intrica-
cies of the Jewish law as elaborated by the traditions of the
scribes (Tasker). συνανέκειντο impf. συνανάκειμαι to lie
11/12 with one at the table. ■ διὰ τί for what reason? Why? ■
ἀκούσας aor. part. ἀκούω to hear. χρεία need. ἰσχύοντες
pres. part. ἰσχύω strong, to be healthy. ἰατρός doctor, physi-
13 cian. κακῶς ἔχω to have it bad, to be sick. ■ πορευθέντες aor.
part. πορεύομαι to go. μάθετε aor. imp. μανθάνω to learn, "go
and learn." A common formula used by the rabbi (SB, I, 499).
ἔλεος mercy. A rendering of the Hebrew word חסד, "covenant
loyalty." καλέσαι aor. inf. καλέω to call. Infinitive used to
express purpose. The same word used of inviting to a feast (AM).
14 ■ προσέρχονται from προσέρχομαι approach.
15 λέγοντες part. λέγω. διὰ τί s.v.11. νηστεύω to fast ■ μή used
in questions which expect a neg. answer. νυμφών wedding hall.
υἱοὶ τοῦ νυμφ. "sons of the bride chamber." A Hebrew idiom
for wedding guests (RWP). πενθεῖν inf. πενθέω to mourn. ἐφ᾿
ὅσον so long as. ἐλεύσονται fut. ἔρχομαι. ὅταν w. a subj.
when. ἀπαρθῇ aor. subj. pass. ἀπαίρω to take away.
16 νηστεύσουσιν fut. ■ ἐπιβάλλει pres. ἐπιβάλλω to throw
over, to lay on, to put on. ἐπίβλημα a patch. ῥάκους gen. sing.

ῥάκος a piece of cloth. ἄγναφος unshrunken, unbleached, new
(BAG). ἱμάτιον garment. παλαιός old. Old in the sense of
worn out (Trench, *Synonyms*). αἴρω to take away, to tear, tear
away.πλήρωμα fullness, that which fills, a patch put on to fill
a gap (McNcile). χείρων comp. κακός bad. σχίσμα tear. ■ 17
νέος new, fresh. ἀσκός a leather bag, wineskin (BAG). εἰ δὲ μή
γε but, if not, otherwise (s. Matt. 6:1). ῥήγνυνται pass.
ῥήγνυμι to tear, burst. ἐκχεῖται pres. pass. ἐκχέω to pour out.
ἀπόλλυμαι pres. to be lost, to be destroyed. ἀμφότεροι both.
συντηροῦνται pres. pass. συντηρέω protect, keep safe. The
prep. is perfective (M, 113).

■ λαλοῦντος pres. part. λαλέω to speak, gen. abs. to ex- 18
press contemporaneous time, "while he was speaking." ἄρχων
leader, ruler. εἰς "a" (used as an indef. article). προσεκύνει
impf. προσκυνέω to fall down and do reverence. ὅτι, used as
quotation marks to introduce a direct quotation. ἄρτι just now.
ἐτελεύτησεν aor. τελευτάω to die. "Just now died" (RWP).
ἐπίθες aor. imp. ἐπιτίθημι to lay upon, to place upon. Aorist
imp. used by one in difficult circumstances (s. Matt. 8:25).
ζήσεται fut. ζάω to live. ■ ἐγερθείς s.v.7. ἠκολούθει impf. 19
inceptive, "he began to follow." ■ αἱμορροοῦσα pres. part. 20
αἱμορροέω to suffer w. a hemorrhage. In modern medical terminology, menorrhagia (Tasker). ἔτη acc. pl. ἔτος year, acc. of
time "for twelve years." προσελθοῦσα aor. part. fem.
προσέρχομαι to come to. ἥψατο aor. ἅπτομαι to touch, take
hold. κράσπεδον hedge, border, hem or tassel which was worn
on the four corners of the outer garment (BAG). ἱμάτιον the
outward garment worn over the shirt (AM). ■ ἐάν w. the subj. 21
if. It views the condition as possible. ἅψωμαι aor. subj.
ἅπτομαι to touch. σωθήσομαι fut. pass. σώζω to save, to
heal. ■ στραφείς aor. pass. part. στρέφομαι to turn, to turn 22
around. σέσωκεν perf. act. The perf. tense indicates "you have
received healing and are now in perfect health" (GI, 33). ἐσώθη
aor. pass. σώζω. ■ αὐλητής flute player. The poorest families 23
were expected to provide two flute players and one wailing
woman (Hill). θορυβούμενον pres. pass. part. θορυβέω throw
into disorder, pass. be troubled, distressed, aroused (BAG). ■ 24
ἀναχωρεῖτε pres. imp. ἀναχωρέω to go away. ἀπέθανεν aor.
ἀποθνήσκω to die. κοράσιον little girl. καθεύδω to sleep.
κατεγέλων impf. καταγελάω to laugh, to scorn. The prep. is
perfective, the impf. indicates repeated laughter of scorn (RWP).
■ ἐξεβλήθη aor. pass. ἐκβάλλω to cast out. εἰσελθών aor. part. 25
εἰσέρχομαι to go in. ἐκράτησεν aor. κρατέω take hold of,
grasp, w. the gen. ἠχέρθη aor. pass. ■ ἐξῆλθεν aor. ἐξέρχομαι 26

to go out. φήμη report, fame.

27 ■ παράγοντι s.v.9. τυφλός blind. κράζοντες pres. part.
κράζω to scream, to cry. ἐλέησον aor. imp. ἐλεέω to have
28 compassion, to show mercy. ■ προσῆλθον aor. πιστεύετε
pres. imp. πιστεύω to believe, to have faith, trust. ποιῆσαι aor.
29 inf. ποιέω to do, to make. ■ γενηθήτω aor. imp. 3rd sing.
30 γίνομαι to become, to happen. ■ ἠνεώχθησαν aor. pass.
ἀνοίγω to open. ἐνεβριμήθη aor. ἐμβριμάομαι to snort. As
an expression of anger, to sternly warn (BAG). ὁρᾶτε pres. imp.
31 ὁράω. γινωσκέτω pres. imp. 3rd sing. γινώσκω to know. ■
ἐξελθόντες aor. part. ἐξέρχομαι. διεφήμισαν aor.
διαφημίζω to spread abroad.

32 ■ ἐξερχομένων pres. part. gen. abs. προσήνεγκαν aor.
προσφέρω s.v.2. κωφός dull, deaf and dumb. δαιμονιζόμενον
part. δαιμονίζομαι to be possessed by a demon, by an evil
33 spirit. ■ ἐκβληθέντος aor. part. pass. ἐκβάλλω gen. abs.
ἐλάλησεν aor. ἐθαύμασαν aor. θαυμάζω to be amazed.
ἐφάνη aor. pass. φαίνομαι to shine, to appear.

35 ■ περιῆγεν impf. περιάγω to go about. διδάσκων pres.
part. διδάσκω to teach. κηρύσσων pres. part. κηρύσσω to
proclaim. θεραπεύων pres. part. θεραπεύω to heal. The three
participles summarize the ministry of Jesus as He went about
36 from place to place. ■ ἐσπλαγχνίσθη aor. pass.
σπλαγχνίζομαι to have pity, to be filled w. compassion, tenderness (MM). (For a study of the word, s. CBB.) ἐσκυλμένοι
perf. pass. part. σκύλλω to flay, to skin. Used in the papyri w.
the meaning to distress, to harass, to worry, to trouble (MM).
The people were harassed, importuned, bewildered by those who
should have taught them (Allen). ἐρριμμένοι perf. pass. part.
ῥίπτω to cast down, to prostrate either from drunkenness or
from a mortal wound (AM). Both participles refer to the people
37 as sheep, mishandled and lying helpless (McNeile). ■ θερισμός
harvesting. The ending indicates activity. It indicates either
"spiritual susceptibility" (EGT) or "judgment" at the end of the
38 age (Hill). ■ δεήθητε aor. imp. δέομαι to ask, to beg (used w.
the gen.). ἐκβάλῃ aor. subj. ἐκβάλλω to cast out, here, to send
out.

Ch. 10

1 ■ προσκαλεσάμενος aor. mid. part. προσκαλέω to call
to one's self. ἔδωκεν aor. δίδωμι to give. ὥστε so that (ex-
2 presses results). ■ ἀπόστολος apostle, one sent out. It indicates
one sent out w. the personal authority and as a representative of
the one sending (s. TDNT, CBB). ἐστίν pres. sing. εἰμί to be.

The verb is sing. because the subject is n. pl. πρῶτος first. "First and foremost" (Tasker). λεγόμενος pres. pass. part. λέγω to say, to name. ■ παραδούς aor. act. part. παραδίδωμι to give 4 over, to betray.

■ ἀπέστειλεν aor. ἀποστέλλω to send forth. 5 παραγγείλας aor. act. part. παραγγέλλω to instruct, to give orders. ἔθνος people, pl. heathen, those who are not Jews. ἀπέλθητε aor. subj. ἀπέρχομαι to go away, to depart (used w. μή for a neg. to express a neg. imp.) εἰσέλθητε aor. subj. εἰσέρχομαι to go in. ■ ἀπολωλότα perf. part. ἀπόλλομι to 6 destroy, to lose, to perish. ■ πορευόμενοι pres. part. ἤγγικεν 7 perf. act. ἐγγίζω to draw near (s. Matt. 3:2). ■ ἀσθενοῦντας 8 pres. part. ἀσθενέω to be without strength, to be sick. θεραπεύετε pres. imp. θεραπεύω to heal. ἐγείρετε pres. imp. ἐγείρω to awaken. καθαρίζετε pres. imp. καθαρίζω to cleanse. ἐκβάλλετε pres. imp. ἐκβάλλω to cast out. δωρεάν adv. as a gift, without payment, freely. ἐλάβετε aor. (ind.) λαμβάνω to take, to receive. δότε aor. imp. δίδωμι to give. ■ κτήσησθε aor. 9 subj. κτάομαι to procure for one's self, to get, gain, to acquire. ἄργυρος silver. χαλκός copper. ζώνη belt, girdle. Used for carrying money (RWP). ■ πήρα traveling bag or bread bag, a 10 beggar's collecting bag (LAE, 109). ῥάβδος staff. ■ ὅς ἄν w. the 11 subj. whoever. ἐξετάσατε aor. imp. ἐξετάζω to examine, to inquire, to question. τίς who. κἀκεῖ = καὶ ἐκεῖ and there. μείνατε aor. imp. μένω to remain. ἕως ἄν w. the subj. as long as, until. ἐξέλθητε aor. subj. ἐξέρχομαι to go out. ■ 12 εἰσερχόμενοι part. ἀσπάσασθε aor. imp. ἀσπάζομαι to greet. ■ ἐάν or if, w. the subj. indicates the condition is probable. 13 ᾖ subj. εἰμί. ἐλθάτω aor. imp. 3rd sing. ἔρχομαι to come. εἰρήνη peace. Equivalent to the Hebrew shalom indicating wholeness, prosperity, well being (AM, s. also CBB, TDNT). ἐπιστραφήτω aor. imp. 3rd sing. ἐπιστρέφομαι to turn about, to return. ■ δέξηται aor. subj. δέχομαι to receive as a guest. 14 ἀκούσῃ aor. subj. ἀκούω to hear. ἐξερχόμενοι pres. part. ἔξω w. the gen. out of. ἐκτινάξατε aor. imp. ἐκτινάσσω to shake off. κονιορτός dust. "To shake off the dust" indicates total abandonment (Hill). (For the Jewish custom, s. SB, I, 571.) ■ 15 ἀμήν truly (s. Matt. 5:18). ἀνεκτότερος comp. ἀνεκτός bearable, endurable. ἔσται fut. εἰμί. κρίσεως gen. sing. κρίσις. Judgment (for the lack of the article, s. BD, 134f.). ἤ than.

■ ἰδού see, behold, ἀποστέλλω s.v.5. μέσος in the middle, 16 midst. λύκος wolf. The figure denotes false prophets or some general menace, or here the Jewish adversaries (Hill). γίνεσθε pres. imp. γίνομαι to become, to be. φρόνιμος understanding,

29

wise. ὄψις snake. A symbol of cunningness (TDNT). ἀκέραιος unmixed, pure. περιστερά dove. Used as a symbol of Israel —
17 patient, submissive, faithful (Hill). ■ προσέχετε pres. imp. προσέχω to beware of. παραδώσουσιν fut. παραδίδωμι s.v.4. συνέδριον the Sanhedrin, council (s. TDNT).
18 μαστιγώσουσιν fut. μαστιγόω to whip, to flog. ■ καί ... δέ "and ... and." The καί introduces that which is similar. The δέ that which is different (EGT). ἀχθήσεσθε fut. pass. ἄγω to
19 lead. ἕνεκεν w. gen. because of, for the sake of. ■ παραδῶσιν aor. subj. παραδίδωμι s.v.4. μεριμνήσητε aor. subj. μεριμνάω to be anxious, to have anxiety, an ingressive aor. "do not become anxious" (RWP). λαλήσητε aor. subj. λαλέω to
20 speak. δοθήσεται fut. pass. δίδωμι. ■ λαλοῦντες pres. part. λαλοῦν pres. part. n. πνεῦμα spirit, the Holy Spirit, not a promise of a universal outpouring, but an endowment of power for a
21 specific kind of situation (GW, 250). ■ ἐπαναστήσονται fut. ἐπανίσταμι to rise up against. The pres. ἐπί is directive w. hostility implied (MH, 312). γονεῖς parents. θανατώσουσιν
22 fut. θανατόω to kill. ■ ἔσεσθε fut. εἰμί. μισούμενοι pres. pass. part. μισέω to hate. The fut. of the verb and the pres. part. used to form a periphrastic fut. pass. It will go on through the ages (RWP). ὑπομείνας aor. part.ὑπομένω to remain under, to en-
23 dure. τέλος the end. σωθήσεται fut. pass. σῴζω to save. ■ διώκωσιν pres. subj. διώκω to persecute. φεύγετε pres. imp. φεύγω to flee. οὐ μή "certainly not," a strong and emphatic neg. (For this construction, s. M, 188–192.) τελέσητε aor. subj. τελέω to complete, to come to the end. ἔλθῃ aor. subj. ἔρχομαι.
25 ■ ἀρκετός enough, sufficient. γένηται aor. subj. γίνομαι. (For the use of ἵνα not expressing purpose, s. M, 206–209.) εἰ "if" (views the condition as true). οἰκοδεσπότης lord or head of the house. ἐπεκάλεσαν aor. ἐπικαλέω to call, to name. πόσῳ μᾶλλον how much more. οἰκιακός members of a household (here in the sense of relatives, BAG).
26 ■ φοβηθῆτε aor. subj. φοβέομαι to be afraid. κεκαλυμμένον perf. pass. part. καλύπτω to hide, to cover over. ἀποκαλυφθήσεται fut. pass. ἀποκαλύπτω to uncover, pass. to be revealed. γνωσθήσεται fut. pass. γινώσκω to
27 know. ■ εἴπατε aor. imp. λέγω. οὓς ear. κηρύξατε aor. imp.
28 κηρύττω. ■ φοβεῖσθε pres. imp. (For the use of this verb w. μή as the translation of a Heb. idiom, s. RG, 577.) ἀποκτεννόντων pres. part. ἀποκτεννω (ἀποκτείνω) to kill. δυναμένων part. δύναμαι to be able to. ἀποκτεῖναι aor. inf. ἀπολέσαι aor. inf. ἀπόλλυμι. γέεννα Gehenna, hell (s. TDNT). οὐχί strong form
29 of οὐ used in questions which expect a positive answer. ■

στρουθίον sparrow (for the significance of this saying in the light of commercial life, s. LAE, 272-275). ἀσσάριον the Roman "as" about one-sixteenth of a denarius, less than one-half cent (AM), gen. of price. πωλεῖται pres. pass. πωλέομαι to sell, pass. to offer for sale, to be sold. εἰς, μία, ἕν one (for the construction ἕν . . . οὐ, "no one, not one," s. BD, 159). πεσεῖται fut. mid. πίπτω to fall. ■ ὑμῶν your (pl.) emphatic position. 30 τρίχες nom. pl. θρίξ, τριχός hair. ἠριθμημέναι perf. pass. part. ἀριθμέω to count. ■ διαφέρω to be different, to be worth 31 more than (w. gen. of comparison).

■ ὅστις general rel. pron. whoever. ὁμολογήσει fut. 32 ὁμολογέω to confess, to acknowledge, to affirm solidarity w. Him in action and even in death (Hill). ἔμπροσθεν w. gen. before. ■ ἀρνήσηται aor. subj. ἀρνέομαι to deny, to declare 33 that one does not know or have dealings w. someone (Hill). ἀρνήσομαι fut.

■ νομίσητε aor. subj. νομίζω to think, to suppose. ἦλθον 34 aor. ἔρχομαι. βαλεῖν aor. inf. βάλλω to cast, to throw, to bring. The aor. inf. indicates a sudden hurling of the sword where peace is expected (RWP). The inf. expresses purpose. ■ διχάσαι aor. 35 inf. διχάζω to divide in two, to set at variance. νύμφη bride, young wife. πενθερά mother-in-law, ■ φιλῶν pres. part. φιλέω 37 to love. The state of mind compelled naturally by sense and emotion (McNeile). ὑπέρ w. acc. beyond, more than. ■ 38 σταυρός cross. The emphasis is on self-renunciation to the point of being a lonely outcast (Hill). ■ εὑρών aor. part. 39 εὑρίσκω to find. ἀπολέσει fut. ἀπόλλυμι. ἀπολέσας aor. part. εὑρήσει fut. εὑρίσκω.

■ δεχόμενος pres. mid. part. δέχομαι to receive, to wel- 40 come. ἀποστείλαντα aor. part. ■ εἰς in (for its use here, s. RG, 41 593). λήμψεται fut. λαμβάνω. μισθός reward. The gen. may be considered subjective gen. meaning "reward offered by a righteous man" (GW, 137f.). ■ ὅς ἐάν whoever. ποτίσῃ aor. 42 subj. ποτίζω to give to drink. ψυχρός cold. ἀπολέσῃ aor. subj. ἀπόλλυμι.

Ch. 11

■ ἐγένετο aor. γίνομαι to become, to happen. ἐτέλεσεν 1 aor. τελέω to end, to complete. διατάσσων pres. part. διατάσσω to order, to direct, to command. μετέβη aor. μεταβαίνω to depart. τοῦ w. inf. to express purpose.

■ ἀκούσας aor. part. ἀκούω to hear. δεσμωτήριον prison, 2 the ending expresses place (MH, 342f.). πέμψας aor. part. πέμπω to send. ■ σύ you (emphatic). εἶ pres. εἰμί to be. 3

ἐρχόμενος part. ἔρχομαι to come, to go, "the Coming One," virtually a title for the Messiah (Tasker). προσδοκῶμεν ind. or
4 subj. προσδοκάω to wait for, to expect. ■ ἀποκριθείς aor. part. ἀποκρίνομαι to answer. πορευθέντες aor. part. πορεύομαι to go. The part. is circumstantial and may be translated as an imp. ἀπαγγείλατε aor. imp. ἀπαγγέλλω to report,
5 to proclaim. ■ ἀναβλέπω to see again, the prep. ἀνά has the force of "again" (MH, 295). περιπατοῦσιν pres. περιπατέω to walk about. καθαρίζονται pres. pass. καθαρίζω to cleanse, pass. to be cleansed. ἐγείρονται pres. pass. ἐγείρω to rise, to be raised. πτωχός poor, abject poverty (NTW, 110). εὐαγγελίζονται pass. εὐαγγελίζω to evangelize, to bring the good news. (For the Jewish expectation of the healing of diseases
6 at the time of the Messiah, s. SB, I, 593f.) ■ ὃς ἐάν w. subj. whoever. The rel. sentence contains the condition for the main clause. σκανδαλισθῇ aor. subj. pass. σκανδλίζω to cause to
7 stumble (s. TDNT, NTW). ■ πορευομένων part. used as gen. abs. ἤρξατο aor. ἄρχομαι to begin. τί what? or why? ἐξήλθατε aor. ἐξέρχομαι to go out, to come out. θεάσασθαι aor. inf. θεάομαι to see, to look at, to gaze at a show or demonstration (AM). The inf. expresses purpose. κάλαμος reed. ἄνεμος wind. σαλευόμενον pres. pass. part. σαλεύω to agitate, to shake.
8 ■ ἀλλά but, rather, or has the force of "if not" (McNeile). ἰδεῖν aor. inf. ὁράω to see. The inf. expresses purpose. μαλακός soft, refers here to soft garments (for the use of adjectives as nouns, s. IBG, 96). ἠμφιεσμένον perf. pass. part. ἀμφιέννυμι to clothe. φοροῦντες pres. part. φορέω to wear constantly,
9 denotes the repeated or habitual action (AS). ■ ναί yes. περισσότερον comp. περισσός exceeding the usual number or size, extraordinary, remarkable, comp. greater (BAG).
10 προφήτου gen. of comparison. ■ γέγραπται perf. pass. γράφω. κατασκευάσει fut. κατασκευάζω to prepare, to
11 make ready. ■ ἐγήγερται perf. pass. ἐγείρω to rise up, to appear on the stage of history (McNeile). γεννητός born. (For adj. w. this ending, s. MH, 370.) μείζων comp. μέγας large, great. μικρότερος comp. μικρός small, little, the least. The comp. is used w. the force of superl. (s. RG, 667ff.). No greater person has arisen than John the Baptist because he stood on the threshold of the kingdom. Yet the least disciple who, through following Jesus, already participates in the reality of the kingdom is greater
12 than John (Hill). ■ βιάζεται mid. or pass. βιάζω. The mid. form means to apply force, to enter forcibly. The pass. form means to be violently treated, to be oppressed, to suffer violence (BAG). (For a discussion of the passage, s. McNeile, RWP.) βιαστής

one who uses violence. ἀρπάζω to snatch, to rob. ■ 13
ἐπροφήτευσαν aor. προφητεύω to prophesy. ■ εἰ if. 14
δέξασθαι aor. inf. δέχομαι to welcome, to receive. (s. 1QS
9:11.) μέλλων part. μέλλω to be about to do something. ■ ἔχων 15
part. ἔχω. ὦτα acc. pl. οὖς, ὦτος ear ἀκουέτω pres. imp. 3rd
sing.
   ■ τίνι dat. sing. to whom. ὁμοιώσω fut. ὁμοιόω to com- 16
pare, to liken to. γενεά generation. ὅμοιος like. παιδίον child.
καθημένοις part. κάθημαι to sit. ἀγορά market place.
προσφωνοῦντα pres. part. προσφωνέω to call to, to call out.
   ■ ηὐλήσαμεν aor. αὐλέω to play the flute. ὠρχήσασθε aor. 17
ὀρχέομαι to dance. ἐθρηνήσαμεν aor. θρηνέω to mourn, to
lament. ἐκόψασθε aor. κόπτομαι to strike one's self on the
breast, a sign of sorrow. ■ ἦλθεν aor. ἔρχομαι. μήτε ... μήτε 18
"neither ... nor." ἐσθίων part. ἐσθίω to eat. πίνων part. πίνω
to drink. ■ φάγος glutton. οἰνοπότης wine drinker, drunkard. 19
ἐδικαιώθη aor. pass. δικαιόω to declare righteous, to recognize
as righteous, proved to be in the right and accepted by God
(GW, 138). ἀπό from, by (for the causal or instrumental use, s.
IBG, 73).
   ■ ἤρξατο s.v.7. ὀνειδίζω to reproach, revile. ἐγένοντο 20
s.v.1. πλεῖστος superl. πολύς much, "very many mighty
works" (RWP). The elative use of the superl. (M, 79f.). ὅτι
because, gives the reason for the accusation. μετενόησαν aor.
μετανοέω to repent, s. Matt. 3:2. ■ εἰ if, introduces a contrary 21
to fact conditional clause "if ... had been done ... ἄν ... would
have repented" (MT, 91f.). γενόμεναι aor. part. γίνομαι.
σάκκος sack, sackcloth. The fabric from which a sack is made
is usually dark in color (BAG). σποδός ashes. ■ ἀνεκτότερος 22
comp. ἀνεκτός bearable, endurable. ἔσται fut. εἰμί. ἤ than,
used w. comp. ■ ἕως w. gen. unto. ὑψωθήσῃ fut. pass. ὑψόω to 23
lift up. ᾅδης hades, the underworld, the kingdom of the dead.
καταβήσῃ fut. (2nd sing.) καταβαίνω to go down.
ἐγενήθησαν aor. γίνομαι. ἔμεινεν aor. μένω to remain. μέχρι
w. gen. until. σήμερον today.
   ■ ἀποκριθείς s.v.4. ἐξομολογοῦμαι to confess, often used 25
in the LXX as the equivalent "to give praise" (AM; s. also
TDNT). ἔκρυψας aor. 2nd sing. κρύπτω to hide. σοφός wise.
συνετός understanding. ἀπεκάλυψας aor. 2nd sing.
ἀποκαλύπτω to unveil, to reveal. νήπιος infant, minor. ■ ὁ 26
πατήρ father (nom. is used for voc., s. BD, 81). οὕτως because,
introducing the reason for this contentment (EGT). εὐδοκία
good pleasure, good will, satisfaction. ἐγένετο s.v.1,
ἔμπροσθεν before. ■ παρεδόθη aor. pass. παραδίδωμι to de- 27

liver over. ἐπιγινώσκω to know, sometimes it means "exact knowledge." The prep. is directive (MH, 312). εἰ μή may, accept. τις anyone (neg. no one). ἐάν = ἄν (BD, 57). βούληται pres. subj. βούλομαι to will. ἀποκαλύψαι aor. inf. (For a dis-

28 cussion of the exegetical problems of this v., s. McNeile.) ∎ δεῦτε come, come on. κοπιῶντες pres. part. κοπιάω to become weary, tired, to work hard. πεφορτισμένοι perf. pass. part. φορτίζω to burden. The perf. expresses a state of weariness (RWP). κἀγώ = καὶ ἐγώ (emphatic). ἀναπαύσω fut.

29 ἀναπαύω to cause to rest, to give rest, to refresh. ∎ ἄρατε aor. imp. αἴρω to lift up, to take up. ζυγός yoke, symbol of obligation and subjection (Moore, *Judaism*, I, 465; SB, I, 608–610). μάθετε aor. imp. μανθάνω to learn. ὅτι either "that" or "because." πραΰς gentle, meek (s. Matt. 5:5). ταπεινός lowly, humble. καρδία heart. καί and, w. fut. introduces a result. εὑρήσετε fut.

30 εὑρίσκω to find. ἀνάπαυσις refreshing, refreshment, rest. ∎ χρηστός useful, comfortable. φορτίον burden. ἐλαφρός light. "To take the yoke of Jesus" is not burdensome, but is characterized by humility and concern for the despised (Hill).

Ch. 12

1   ∎ ἐπορεύθη aor. πορεύομαι to go. σπόριμος sown, grain fields. ἐπείνασαν aor. πεινάω to hunger, inceptive aor. "became hungry" (Tasker). ἤρξαντο aor. ἄρχομαι to begin. τίλλω to pluck, to pluck off. στάχυς head of grain. ἐσθίω to

2 eat. ∎ ἰδόντες aor. part. ὁράω to see. ποιοῦσιν pres. ποιέω to do. ἔξεστιν it is lawful, it is allowed. Jewish tradition prohibited reaping or threshing on the sabbath (M, Shabbath, 7, 2). (For the sabbath, s. M, Shabbath; Moore, *Judaism*, II, 21–39.) ποιεῖν

3 pres. inf. ∎ ἀνέγνωτε aor. ἀναγινώσκω to read. τί what.

4 ἐποίησεν aor. ποιέω. ∎ εἰσῆλθεν aor. εἰσέρχομαι to go in, to come in. πρόθεσις setting forth presentation, "loaves of presentation" (BAG). ἔφαγον aor. ἐσθίω. ἔξον pres. part. ἔξεστι allowed, permitted. ἦν impf. εἰμί. φαγεῖν aor. inf. εἰ μή

5 except. ∎ ἱερόν holy place, temple. βεβηλοῦσιν pres.

6 βεβηλόω to defile, to make common. ἀναίτιος guiltless. ∎ τοῦ ἱεροῦ gen. of comparison. μείζων comp. μέγας large, great.

7 ∎ εἰ "if" w. ἄν used for a contrary to fact conditional clause. ἐγνώκετε plperf. γινώσκω to know, to understand. (For the use of the plperf. in conditional clauses, s. DM, 290.) ἔλεος mercy (s. Matt. 9:13). κατεδικάσατε aor. ind. καταδικάζω to condemn (in the legal sense, MM).

9   ∎ μεταβάς aor. part. μεταβαίνω to depart. ἦλθεν aor.

10 ἔρχομαι to come, to go. ∎ ἔχων pres. part. ἔχω. ξηρός dried,

withered. ἐπηρώτησαν aor. ἐπερωτάω to question. The pres.
is directive (MH, 312). λέγοντες pres. part. λέγω. εἰ used to
introduce a question (for this usage, s. BD, 226). θεραπεῦσαι
aor. inf. θεραπεύω to heal. The rabbis allowed help for the sick
if the sick person's life was in danger (M, Yoma 8, 6; s. also Hill).
κατηγορήσωσιν aor. subj. κατηγορέω to accuse, to bring accusation against (w. gen.). ▪ ἔσται fut. εἰμί. ἕξει fut. ἔχω. ἐάν 11
if. The condition is probable. ἐμπέσῃ aor. subj. ἐμπίπτω to fall
into. βόθυνος ditch. οὐχί w. questions which expect a positive
answer. κρατήσει fut. κρατέω to take hold of. ἐγερεῖ fut.
ἐγείρω to raise up ▪ πόσῳ how much? οὖν therefore. διαφέρω 12
(s. Matt. 10:3l). ὥστε wherefore, therefore (drawing a conclusion). ▪ ἔκτεινον aor. imp. ἐκτείνω to stretch out. ἐξέτεινεν 13
aor. ἀπεκατεστάθη aor. pass. ἀποκαθίστημι to restore, to
restore to the same condition. ▪ ἐξελθόντες aor. part. 14
ἐξέρχομαι to go out. συμβούλιον plan, purpose (consultation
and its result, BAG). ἔλαβον aor. λαμβάνω to take. ὅπως w.
subj. in order that. ἀπολέσωσιν aor. subj. ἀπόλλυμι to destroy.

▪ γνούς aor. part. γινώσκω to know. ἀνεχώρησεν aor. 15
ἀναχωρέω to depart, to go away. ἠκολούθησαν aor.
ἀκολουθέω to follow. ἐθεράπευσεν aor. ▪ ἐπετίμησεν aor. 16
ἐπιτιμάω to rebuke (s. Matt. 8:26). ποιήσωσιν aor. subj. s.v.2.
▪ πληρωθῇ aor. subj. pass. πληρόω to fulfill. ῥηθέν aor. pass. 17
part. λέγω. ▪ παῖς child, servant. ᾑρέτισα aor. αἱρετίζω to 18
choose. ἀγαπητός beloved. εὐδόκησεν aor. εὐδοκέω to be
pleased w., to be well-pleased, to take pleasure in. θήσω fut.
τίθημι to place. κρίσις judgment, justice. ἔθνος people, pl.
nations, heathen. ἀπαγγελεῖ fut. ἀπαγγέλλω to report, to proclaim. In the work of the servant, there is accomplished a work
of righteousness, judgment, of justice for the Gentiles (Hill).
▪ ἐρίσει fut. ἐρίζω to quarrel, to wrangle. κραυγάσει fut. 19
κραυγάζω to cry (excitedly), to scream. ἀκούσει fut. ἀκούω
to hear. τις anyone. πλατεῖα wide street. ▪ κάλαμος reed. 20
συντετριμμένον perf. pass. part. συντρίβω to shatter, to
crush. κατεάξει fut. κατάγνυμι to break (for the form, s. BD,
50). λίνον flax, linen, lamp wick. τυφόμενον pres. pass. part.
τύφω to produce smoke, pass. to smolder, glimmer. σβέσει fut.
σβέννυμι to extinguish. ἕως ἄν w. subj. until. ἐκβάλῃ aor. subj.
ἐκβάλλω to cast out, to bring forth. νῖκος victory. κρίσις justice. ▪ ἐλπιοῦσιν fut. ἐλπίζω to hope, to put one's hope in 21
someone.

▪ προσηνέχθη aor. pass. προσφέρω to bring to, to bring. 22
δαιμονιζόμενος pres. mid. pass. part. δαιμονίζομαι to be pos-

sessed w. a demon, w. an evil spirit. τυφλός blind. κωφός dumb.
ἐθεράπευσεν aor. s.v.10. ὥστε w. inf. it expresses results "so
23 that." λαλεῖν pres. inf. λαλέω to speak. ■ ἐξίσταντο impf.
ἐξίσταμι to be beside one's self, w. astonishment. The impf.
vividly portrays the situation, they were almost beside themselves w. excitement (RWP). ἔλεγον impf. λέγω to speak, to
say, "they were continually saying" or "they began to say" (inceptive impf.). μήτι expects a neg. answer "can this possibly
be?" They can hardly believe what the facts seem to suggest
24 (EGT). οὗτος this one (emphatic) "this man" (McNeile). ■
25 ἀκούσαντες aor. part. s.v.19. ἄρχων ruler, prince. ■ εἰδώς
part. οἶδα to know (defective perf. w. pres. meaning).
ἐνθύμησις thought, reasoning. μερισθεῖσα aor. pass. part.
fem. μερίζω to divide. ἑαυτῆς refl. pron. 3rd fem. sing.
ἐρημοῦται pres. pass. ἐρημόω to destroy, to desolate. ἤ or
σταθήσεται fut. pass. ἵστημι to place, to set, pass. to stand,
26 to stand firm. ■ εἰ if, the condition is assumed by the speaker to
27 be true. ἐφ᾽= ἐπί. ἐμερίσθη aor. pass. ■ βεελξεβούλ "Baal the
28 prince" (AM; s. also TDNT; SB, I, 631–635). ■ ἄρα then, introduces the conclusion based on the condition. ἔφθασεν aor.
29 φθάνω to come before, to precede, to arrive. ■ εἰσελθεῖν aor.
inf. εἰσέρχομαι to come in. ἰσχυρός strong, w. the article it is
used as a noun "the strong one." The article is generic but hints
at the particular strong man that is meant (McNeile). σκεῦος
vessel, pl. property. ἁρπάσαι aor. inf. ἁρπάζω to snatch, to
rob. δήσῃ aor. subj. δέω to bind. διαρπάσει fut. διαρπάζω to
plunder thoroughly. The prep. is prefective and describes the
30 carrying of action through to a definite result (MH, 301). ■
συνάγων pres. part. συνάγω to gather together, to gather.
31 σκορπίζω to scatter. ■ βλασφημία abusive speech (TDNT).
32 ἀφεθήσεται fut. pass. ἀφίημι to release, to forgive. ■ ὃς ἐάν
whoever. εἴπῃ aor. subj. λέγω to speak, to say. οὔτε … οὔτε
neither … nor. μέλλων part. μέλλω to be about to do.
33   ■ ἤ … ἤ either … or. ποιήσατε aor. imp. s.v.2. σαπρός
34 bad, decayed, rotten. γινώσκεται pass. s.v.15. ■ γέννημα that
which is produced, child, offspring. ἔχιδνα viper, snake, "brood
of vipers," a stinging rebuke to pharisaic hypocrisy (Hill).
36 περίσσευμα abundance, overflow. λαλεῖ pres. ■ ῥῆμα word.
ἀργός useless, ineffective (Tasker). λαλήσουσιν fut.
ἀποδώσουσιν fut. ἀποδίδωμι to render, to give back (w.
37 λόγον to give account). ■ δικαιωθήσῃ fut. pass. δικαιόω to
justify, to declare in the right. καταδικασθήσῃ fut. pass.
καταδικάζω to condemn.
38   ■ ἀπεκρίθησαν aor. ἀποκρίνομαι to answer. λέγοντες

s.v.10. σημεῖον sign. ἰδεῖν aor. inf. ὁράω to see. ■ ἀποκριθείς 39
aor. part. γενεά generation. μοιχαλίς an adulteress, apostate,
disobedient and unfaithful to God (Allen). ἐπιζητεῖ pres.
ἐπιζητέω to seek after. The prep. is directive. It indicates not
just "his looking for" but "his demanding as a necessary preliminary to faith" (Tasker). δοθήσεται fut. pass. δίδωμι to give. εἰ
μή except. ■ ὥσπερ just as. κοιλία belly, stomach. κῆτος sea 40
monster, huge fish. ■ ἀναστήσονται fut. ἀνίσταμι to rise up, 41
to come forward, that is to say as witnesses (Meyer).
κατακρινοῦσιν fut. κατακρίνω to condemn. μετενόησαν
aor. μετανοέω to repent. εἰς because of (causal, s. BD, 112;
DM, 104). κήρυγμα proclamation, message delivered by a herald. πλεῖον comp. ■ βασίλισσα queen. νότος south wind, 42
south, kingdom of the south. ἐγερθήσεται fut. pass. ἐγείρω to
rise up. ἦλθεν s.v.9. περάτων gen. pl. πέρας, ατος border, end.
ἀκοῦσαι aor. inf. Infinitive used to express purpose. σοφία
wisdom. Solomon was wise, but here is Wisdom itself (Bengel).

■ ἀκάθαρτος unclean. ἐξέλθῃ aor. subj. s.v.14. διέρχομαι 43
to go through, to pass through. ἄνυδρος dry, waterless. ζητοῦν
pres. part. ζητέω to seek. ■ ἐπιστρέψω fut. ἐπιστρέφω to turn 44
about, to return. ὅθεν from where. ἐξῆλθον aor. ἐλθόν aor. act.
part. σχολάζοντα pres. part. σχολάζω to have leisure time, to
be unoccupied, stand empty. σεσαρωμένον perf. pass. part.
σαρόω to sweep, to sweep clean. κεκοσμημένον perf. pass.
part. κοσμέω to put into order, to decorate. ■ παραλαμβάνω 45
to take w. πονηρότερος comp. worse. ἑαυτοῦ gen. of comparison. εἰσελθόντα aor. part. s.v.4. κατοικεῖ pres. κατοικέω to
dwell, to settle down. The prep. of the verb is perfectivizing
(MH, 316). ἔσχατος last. τὰ ἔσχατα here "the last or latter
condition." χείρων comp. κακός bad comp. worse. τῶν
πρώτων gen. of comparison "the first or former condition."

■ λαλοῦντος pres. part. s.v.22. Participle used as gen. abs. 46
"while he was speaking." εἰστήκεισαν plperf. act. ἵστημι to
stand, w. the sense of the impf. they had been standing while
Jesus was speaking (EGT). ζητοῦντες part. s.v.43. λαλῆσαι
aor. inf. ■ ἑστήκασιν perf. ἐκτείνας aor. part. s.v.13. ■ ὅστις 47/49/50
general rel. pron. whoever. ποιήσῃ aor. subj. s.v.2.

Ch. 13

■ ἐξελθών aor. part. ἐξέρχομαι to go out. ἐκάθητο impf. 1
κάθημαι to sit. ■ συνήχθησαν aor. pass. συνάγω to gather 2
together, pass. to assemble. ἐμβάντα aor. part. ἐμβαίνω to
embark, to get into. καθῆσθαι pres. inf. Infinitive used to express result. αἰγιαλός shore, beach. εἰστήκει plperf. ἵστημι to

stand. Used w. the impf. sense, had taken a stand and so stood
3 (RWP). ■ ἐλάλησεν aor. λαλέω to speak. παραβολή parable.
(For the meaning of the word, s. TDNT; R.C. Trench, *Notes on
the Parables;* Joachim Jeremias, *The Parables of Jesus.*) ἐξῆλθεν
4 aor. ἐξέρχομαι. σπείρων pres. part. σπείρω to sow. ■ ὅ μέν
... ὅ δέ "the one ... the other," "one ... another" (BD, 131).
ἔπεσεν aor. πίπτω to fall. ἐλθόντα aor. part. ἔρχομαι to come.
πετεινόν bird. κατέφαγεν aor. κατεσθίω to eat up. The prep.
5 of the verb is perfective "to eat up completely." ■ πετρώδης
stony. ἐξανέτειλεν aor. ἐξανατέλλω to spring up. βάθος
6 depth. ■ ἀνατείλαντος aor. part. ἀνατέλλω to rise (used of the
sun). ἐκαυματίσθη aor. pass. καυματίζω to burn, to scorch.
ῥίξα root. ἐξηράνθη aor. pass. ξηραίνω to dry, to dry out, to
7 become dry, to wither. ■ ἄκανθα thorns. ἀνέβησαν aor.
ἀναβαίνω to come up. ἀπέπνιξαν aor. ἀποπνίγω to choke,
8 to choke off, an effective aor. (RWP). ■ ἐδίδου impf. δίδωμι to
9 give, yield. ■ ὦτα pl. οὖς ὠτός ear. ἀκουέτω pres. imp. 3rd sing.
ἀκούω to hear.
10   ■ προσελθόντες aor. part. προσέρχομαι to come to.
11 λαλεῖς pres. ■ ἀποκριθείς aor. part. ἀποκρίνομαι to answer.
δέδοται perf. pass. δίδωμι, γνῶναι aor. inf. γινώσκω to know.
12 ■ ὅστις whoever. δοθήσεται fut. pass. δίδωμι.
περισσευθήσεται fut. pass. περισσεύω to be more than
enough, to be extremely rich or abundant. ἀρθήσεται fut. pass.
13 αἴρω to take away. ■ λαλῶ pres. act. ὅτι because. βλέποντες
pres. part. βλέπω to see. ἀκούοντες pres. part. The part. refer
to the Heb. inf. abs. as used in the quotation from Isa. 6:9, 10.
συνιοῦσιν pres. συνίω = συνίημι to gain insight, to com-
14 prehend, to understand (BAG). ■ ἀναπληροῦται pres. pass.
ἀναπληρόω to fulfill, "is being fulfilled" (Allen) or an aoristic
pres. (RWP). λέγουσα fem. part. ἀκοή hearing, that which is
heard, report, rumor. ἀκούσετε fut. συνῆτε aor. subj. συνίημι.
15 βλέψετε fut. ἴδητε aor. subj. ὁράω to see. ■ ἐπαχύνθη aor.
pass. παχύνω to make fat, to make dull, pass. to become dull,
to be insensitive (TDNT). βαρέως adv. βαρύς heavy. ἤκουσαν
aor. ἐκάμμυσαν aor. καμμύω to shut (fr. καταμύω "to shut
down" RWP). μήποτε w. subj. lest expressing neg. purpose.
ἴδωσιν aor. subj. ὁράω. ἀκούσωσιν aor. subj. συνῶσιν aor.
subj. συνίημι. ἐπιστρέψωσιν aor. subj. ἐπιστρέφω to turn
16 about, to return. ἰάσομαι fut. ind. ἰάομαι to heal. ■ ὑμῶν
emphatic, contrasted w. those described in v. 14 (McNeile).
17 μακάριος blessed, happy. ■ ἐπεθύμησαν aor. ἐπιθυμέω to
desire, to long for. ἰδεῖν aor. inf. ὁράω. εἶδαν aor. ὁράω.
ἀκοῦσαι aor. inf.

■ ἀκούσατε aor, imp σπείραντος aor. part. ■ ἀκούοντος 18/19
pres. part. gen. abs. "while everyone is listening" (RWP). (For
the construction of the part. w. which is often considered as a
Hebraic influence, Casus Pendens, s. MH, 423–425.) συνιέντος
part. συνίημι to comprehend, to understand. (For the interpretation of this parable emphasizing the hearing and obeying of
God's word in the light of Deut. 6:4, 5, s. B. Gerhardsson, "The
Parable of the Sower and its Interpretation," NTS, 14 [Jan.
1968], 165–193.) ἁρπάζω to snatch, to rob, to plunder.
ἐσπαρμένον perf. pass. part. σπείρω. οὗτος this refers to the
pers., not the seed (McNeile). σπαρείς aor. pass. part. σπείρω.
■ ἀκούων pres. part. λαμβάνων pres. part. λαμβάνω to re- 20
ceive, to accept. ■ ἑαυτῷ refl. pron. 3rd sing. πρόσκαιρος 21
lasting for a time, temporary. γενομένης aor. part. to become,
to happen, gen. abs. θλῖψις pressure, tribulation (Trench, Synonyms, 202–204). ἤ or. διωγμός persecution. σκανδαλίζεται
pres. pass. σκανδαλίζω to cause to stumble, to cause to fall.
■ μέριμνα care, concern, "worldly concerns and interest" 22
(Hill). ἀπάτη deceitfulness or pleasure (MM). πλοῦτος riches
(subj. gen.) συμπνίγω to choke, lit. "to choke together." (For
the perfectivizing prep. w. the verb, s. MH, 325f.) ἄκαρπος
unfruitful. ■ συνιείς pres. part. δή a strengthening particle, "in 23
reality" (EGT). καρποφορεῖ pres. καρποφορέω to bring forth
fruit, to produce. ποιεῖ pres. ποιέω to do, to make, to produce.
■ παρέθηκεν aor. παρατίθημι to place along side, to put 24
before. ὡμοιώθη aor. pass. ὁμοιόω to compare. σπείραντι aor.
part. s.v.3. ■ ἐν w. dat. and the inf. to express contemporary time 25
"while ... " καθεύδω to sleep. ἦλθεν aor. ἔρχομαι s.v.4.
ἐπέσπειρεν aor. ἐπισπείρω to sow upon, to sow afterward, to
resow (MM). ζιζάνιον a poisonous weed which is related to
wheat and in the early stages of growth it is hard to distinguish
from it (J. Jeremias, The Parables of Jesus, 224). ἀπῆλθεν aor.
ἀπέρχομαι to go away. ■ ἐβλάστησεν aor. βλαστάνω to 26
sprout, to put forth. χόρτος grass. ἐποίησεν aor. s.v.23. ἐφάνη
aor. φαίνομαι to appear. ■ προσελθόντες s.v.10. 27
οἰκοδεσπότης master of the house. οὐχί used in questions
which expect a positive answer. ἔσπειρας aor. 2nd sing. πόθεν
where, from where. ■ ἔφη 3rd sing. of impf. and aor. φημί to 28
say. θέλω to wish, to want. (For this word used to introduce a
question w. the deliberative subj., s. BD, 185.) ἀπελθόντες aor.
part. ἀπέρχομαι a circumstantial part. συλλέξωμεν aor. subj.
συλλέγω to bring together, to collect, to gather up, a deliberative subj. "shall we gather" (RG, 934). ■ φησίν pres. φημί. οὐ 29
used in questions expecting a neg. answer. μήποτε lest.

συλλέγοντες pres. act. part. ἐκριζώσητε aor. subj. ἐκριζόω to uproot, to pull out by the roots. ἅμα together, together with.

30 ■ ἄφετε aor. imp. ἀφίημι to leave, to leave alone. συναυξάνομαι to grow, to grow together. ἀμφότεροι both. θερισμός harvest. ἐρῶ fut. λέγω. θεριστής harvester, the ending indicates the agent (MH, 365). συλλέξατε aor. imp. δήσατε aor. imp. δέω to bind. δέσμη bundle. κατακαῦσαι aor. inf. κατακαίω to burn up. The prep. in the verb is perfective not just "to burn" but "to burn up." The inf. is used to express purpose. συναγάγετε aor. imp. συνάγω to gather together. ἀποθήκη storage room, barn.

31 ■ ὅμοιος like, similar. κόκκος grain, a single grain. σίναπι mustard, popularly viewed as the smallest of all seeds (BAG).

32 λαβών aor. part. s.v.20. ἔσπειρεν aor. ■ ὅ which, refers to grain but neuter by attraction (EGT). μικρότερον comp. μικρός small. σπερμάτων gen. of comp. ὅταν w. subj. when, whenever. αὐξηθῇ aor. subj. αὐξάνομαι to grow. μεῖζον comp. μέγας large, great. λάχανον an edible plant, vegetable (gen. of comp.). γίνομαι s.v.21. ἐλθεῖν aor. inf. ἔρχομαι, used w. ὥστε to express results. κατασκηνοῦν pres. inf. κατασκηνόω to live, to inhabit, inf. expressing result. κλάδος branch.

33 ■ ἐλάλησεν s.v.3. ζύμη leaven. In Jewish imagery leaven refers to what is unclean or evil (Hill). ἐνέκρυψεν aor. ἐγκρύπτω to hide, to conceal in. ἄλευρον wheat flour. σάτον seah. A Heb. measure of grain containing about a peck and a half (BAG; s., also SB, I, 670). ἕως οὗ until. ἐζυμώθη aor. pass. ζυμόω to ferment, to leaven.

34 ■ οὐδέν nothing. ἐλάλει impf. pointing to a regular prac-
35 tice, not merely to a single occasion (EGT). ■ πληρωθῇ aor. subj. pass. πληρόω to fill, to fulfill. ῥηθέν aor. pass. part. λέγω to say. λέγοντος pres. part. ἀνοίξω fut. ἀνοίγω to open. στόμα mouth. ἐρεύξομαι fut. ἐρεύγομαι to spue out, to bellow, to roar, to speak out loud, to utter (AS). κεκρυμμένα perf. pass. part. κρύπτω to hide. καταβολή foundation, beginning.

36 ■ ἀφείς aor. part. ἀφίημι s.v.30. προσῆλθον aor. προσέρχομαι s.v.10. διασάφησον aor. imp. διασαφέω to explain "make thoroughly clear right now" (RWP). ζιζάνιον
38 s.v.25. ■ πονηρός evil, "the sons of the evil one" = "those
39 whose character is evil" (McNeile). ■ σπείρας aor. part. διάβολος slanderer, the devil. θερισμός harvest. συντέλεια
40 completion. ■ συλλέγεται pres. pass. s.v.28. πυρί dat. sing. πῦρ πυρός fire, instrumental dat. κατακαίεται pass. s.v.30.
41 ἔσται fut. εἰμί. ■ ἀποστελεῖ fut. ἀποστέλλω to send. συλλέξουσιν fut. σκάνδαλον the stick in a trap, the trap itself,

the cause or occasion of stumbling. Here used of persons "the devil's children" who work against God and try to cause as many as possible to fall (TDNT). ποιοῦντας part. s.v.23. ἀνομία lawlessness. ▪ βαλοῦσιν fut. βάλλω to throw, to cast. κάμινος 42 furnace. κλανθμός loud crying, weeping. βρυγμός gnashing, grinding. ὀδούς, ὀδ όντος tooth, "the gnashing of teeth" is used as an expression of anger and frustration of the damned (SB, I, 673). ▪ ἐκλάμψουσιν fut. ἐκλάμπω to shine out, to shine forth, 43 suggestive of the sun emerging from behind the cloud (EGT).

▪ θησαυρός treasure, treasure chest. κεκρυμμένῳ perf. 44 pass. part. εὑρών aor. act. part. εὑρίσκω to find. ἔκρυψεν aor, κρύπτω to hide. ἀπό for, cause of (for the causal use, s. BD, 113). αὑτοῦ "his joy" subjective gen. not obj. (McNeile). ὑπάγω to go out. πωλεῖ pres. πωλέω to sell. ὅσος how large? how many? ἀγοράζω to buy. ▪ ἔμπορος merchant. ζητοῦντι 45 pres. part. ζητέω to seek, to look for. μαργαρίτης pearl. ▪ 46 πολύτιμος costly, very valuable. ἀπελθών aor. part. ἀπέρχομαι to go out. πέπρακεν perf. act. πιπράσκω to sell. Perhaps an example of the aoristic perf., though the word has no aorist form (s. M, 142–145; MKG, 265f.). ἠγόρασεν aor. ἀγοράζω. ▪ σαγήνη dragnet, the long-draw net or sweep-net. 47 They are open to include a large extent of the sea, then drawn together and all which they contain is enclosed (Trench, Synonyms, 236). βληθείσῃ aor. pass. part. βάλλω to cast. γένος kind, sort. συναγαγούσῃ aor. part. s.v.2. ▪ ἐπληρώθη aor. 48 pass. s.v.35. ἀναβιβάσαντες aor. part. ἀναβιβάζω to bring up, to pull up (the prep. in the verb is a local, MH, 295). αἰγιαλός shore, beach. καθίσαντες aor. part. καθίζω to sit, to take one's seat. συνέλεξαν aor. s.v.28. ἄγγος vessel, container. σαπρός worthless, unsuitable for eating (Hill). ἔβαλον aor. βάλλω. ▪ 49 συντέλεια s.v.39. ἐξελεύσονται fut. ἐξέρχομαι to go out. ἀφοριοῦσιν fut. ἀφορίζω to separate, to set apart. μέσον middle, midst. ▪ βαλοῦσιν fut. s.v.42.   50

▪ συνήκατε aor. συνίημι s.v.13. ▪ μαθητευθείς aor. 51/52 pass. part. μαθητεύω to make a disciple, to be a disciple (s. McNeile; TDNT). τῇ βασιλείᾳ dat. of reference "w. respect to the kingdom" (Hill; DM, 85). ἐκβάλλω to bring out, lit. to throw out. θησαυρός storehouse. καινός new. παλαιός old.

▪ ἐγένετο aor. γίνομαι s.v.21. ἐτέλεσεν aor. τελέω to 53 end, to complete. μετῆρεν aor. μεταίρω to go away. ▪ ἐλθών 54 aor. part. πατρίς fatherland, country, native place. ἐδίδασκεν impf. διδάσκω to teach. The impf. suggests more than one occasion (Filson). ὥστε so that, expresses result. ἐκπλήσσεσθαι pres. pass. inf. ἐκπλήσσω to amaze, to as-

55 tound, pass. to be amazed, be overwhelmed. ■ *οὗτος* "this one," "this fellow," used contemptuously (Tasker). *τέκτων* carpenter, woodworker, builder (BAG). The article "the" with carpenter indicates possibly that He was the only one in the town, well-
57 known to all (EGT). ■ *ἐσκανδαλίζοντο* impf. pass., the opposite of "to believe in him." They refused to believe in Him
58 (TDNT). *ἄτιμος* without honor. *εἰ μή* except. ■ *ἐποίησεν* aor. s.v.23. *ἀπιστία* unbelief.

Ch. 14

1   ■ *ἤκουσεν* aor. *ἀκούω* to hear. *τετραάρχης*. (For a study of the man Herod Antipas, s. Harold Hoehner, *Herod Antipas*.)
2 *ἀκοή* rumor, report. ■ *παισίν* dat. pl. *παῖς* children, servants, the courtiers (RWP). *αὐτός* he (emphatic) indicating the terror-striken conscious (Meyer). *ἠγέρθη* aor. pass. *ἐγείρω* to awake, pass. to be raised. *ἐνεργοῦσιν* pres. *ἐνεργέω* to be at work in,
3 to be operative in, to energize. ■ *κρατήσας* aor. part. *κρατέω* to seize, to arrest. *ἔδησεν* aor. *δέω* to bind. *ἀπέθετο* aor. mid. *ἀποτίθημι* to put away (the prep. in the verb has local force,
4 MH, 297f.). ■ *ἔλεγεν* impf. implies a repeated rebuke
5 (McNeile). *ἔξεστιν* it is lawful, it is allowed. ■ *θέλων* pres. part. *θέλω* to wish, to will, to want. *ἀποκτεῖναι* aor. inf. *ἀποκτείνω* to kill. *ἐφοβήθη* aor. *φοβέομαι* to fear. *εἶχον* impf. *ἔχω* to
6 have, to consider, to look upon, to view (BAG). ■ *γενέσια* birthday celebration. *γενομένοις* aor. part. *γίνομαι* to become, to happen. *ὠρχήσατο* aor. *ὀρχέομαι* to dance. *ἤρεσεν* aor.
7 *ἀρέσκω* to please. ■ *ὅθεν* from where (causal), because. *ὅρκος* oath. *ὡμολόγησεν* aor. *ὁμολογέω* to confess on oath, to promise. *δοῦναι* aor. inf. *δίδωμι* to give. *ὃ ἐάν* whatever. *αἰτήσηται*
8 aor. subj. mid. *αἰτέω* to ask, to request. ■ *προβιβασθεῖσα* aor. pass. part. *προβιβάζω* to bring forward, to bring to the point, give instructions (McNeile). *δός* aor. imp. 2 sing. *δίδωμι*. *φησίν* pres. *φημί* to say. *πίναξ* a board, plank, anything flat like
9 a table or plate, dish (Hill). ■ *λυπηθείς* aor. pass. part. *λυπέω* to grieve, to pain, pass. become sad, sorrowful, distressed (BAG). *συνανακειμένους* pres. part. *συνανάκειμαι* to recline together at the table. *ἐκέλευσεν* aor. *κελεύω* to command, to
10 order. *δοθῆναι* aor. pass. inf. *δίδωμι*. ■ *πέμψας* aor. part. *πέμπω* to send. *ἀπεκεφάλισεν* aor. *ἀποκεφαλίζω* to behead.
11 ■ *ἠνέχθη* aor. pass. *φέρω* to carry, to bring. *ἐδόθη* aor. pass. *δίδωμι*. *κοράσιον* girl. The dimin. "little girl" (Hill). *ἤνεγκεν*
12 aor. act. *φέρω*. ■ *προσελθόντες* aor. part. *προσέρχομαι* to come to. *ἦραν* aor. *αἴρω* to lift up, to carry away. *πτῶμα* body, corpse. *ἔθαψαν* aor. *θάπτω* to bury. *ἐλθόντες* aor. part.

ἔρχομαι to come, to go. ἀπήγγειλαν aor. ἀπάγγελλω to report, to announce.

■ ἀκούσας aor. part. used temporarily to express antece- 13 dent time "after he heard." ἀνεχώρησεν aor. ἀναχωρέω to go away, to withdraw, to retire. ἐκεῖθεν from there. ἴδιος for one's self, private. ἠκολούθησαν aor. ἀκολουθέω to follow. πεζῇ by land. ■ ἐξελθών aor. part. ἐξέρχομαι to go out; that is "disem- 14 bark" (Tasker). εἶδεν aor. ὁράω to see. ἐσπλαγχνίσθη aor. pass. (deponent) σπλαγχνίζομαι to pity, to have compassion on (see Matt. 9:36). ἐθεράπευσεν aor. θεραπεύω to heal. ἄρρωστος without strength, sick. ■ ὀψία evening. γενομένης 15 aor. part, γίνομαι, part. used as gen. abs. προσῆλθον aor. προσέρχομαι. λέγοντες pres. part. ὥρα hour, the hour for the customary meal (Allen). ἤδη already. παρῆλθεν aor. παρέρχομαι to go by, to pass. ἀπόλυσον aor. imp. ἀπολύω to dismiss, to send away. ἀπελθόντες aor. part. ἀπέρχομαι to go away. κώμη village. ἀγοράσωσιν aor. subj. ἀγοράζω to buy, used w. ἵνα to express purpose. ἑαυτοῖς refl. pron. 3rd per. βρῶμα food. ■ χρείαν ἔχω to have need. ἀπελθεῖν aor. inf. 16 act. ἀπέρχομαι epexegetical, to explain the need (IBG, 127). δότε aor. imp. δίδωμι. ὑμεῖς "you" emphatic, stands in contrast w. their "send away" (RWP). φαγεῖν aor. inf. ἐσθίω to eat. ■ εἰ μή except. ἰχθύς fish. Bread and fish form the basic diet of 17 the poor of Galilee (Hill). ■ φέρετε pres. imp. ■ κελεύσας aor. 18/19 part. κελεύω to command, generally designates verbal orders from a superior (Thayer). ἀνακλιθῆναι aor. inf. pass. ἀνακλίνω to lay down, pass. to sit down, to take one's place (at table) (Hill). χόρτος grass. λαβών aor. part. λαμβάνω to take. ἀναβλέψας aor. part. ἀναβλέπω to look up. εὐλόγησεν aor. εὐλογέω to bless, to express praise and thanks. It was customary to pray at the beginning of the meal and at the end as an expression of dependence on God for all man's needs and of gratitude for His constant goodness (Moore, *Judaism*, II, 216f.; s. also SB, I, 685f.; M, Berakoth, 6-8). κλάσας aor. part. κλάω to break. ἔδωκεν aor. δίδωμι. ■ ἔφαγον aor. ἐσθίω to eat. 20 ἐχορτάσθησαν aor. pass. χορτάζω to satisfy, pass. to be satisfied, to be filled, an effective aor. (RWP). περισσεῦον pres. part. περισσεύω to exceed or remain over, to abound, to be in abundance. κλάσμα broken pieces. The –μα ending indicating a pass. idea "that which was broken." κόφινος basket, probably a large, heavy basket for carrying things (BAG). πλήρης full. ■ ἐσθίοντες pres. part. ἦσαν impf. εἰμί. ὡσεί (w. numbers) 21 about. χωρίς w. gen., without, except. παιδίον child.

■ εὐθέως adv. immediately, at once. ἠνάγκασεν aor. 22

ἀναγκάζω to compel. ἐμβῆναι aor. inf. ἐμβαίνω to embark.
προάγω to go before. πέραν the other side. ἕως οὗ (w. the subj.
23 until). ἀπολύσῃ aor. subj. ■ ἀπολύσας aor part. temp. ἀνέβη
aor. ἀναβαίνω to go up. ὄρος mountain, here "hill country"
(AM). προσεύξασθαι aor. mid. inf. προσεύχομαι to pray, inf.
24 used to express purpose. ἦν s.v.21. ■ στάδιον stade, about 600
feet (Filson). ἀπεῖχεν plperf. ἀπέχω to be distant, to be away.
βασανιζόμενον pres. pass. part. βασανίζω to torture, to torment, to harass (harassed by the waves, BAG). κῦμα wave.
25 ἐναντίος opposed, against, contrary to. ἄνεμος wind. ■
τετάρτη φυλακή the fourth watch, between 3 and 6 A.M. The
Romans divided the night into four watches of three hours each,
beginning at 6 P.M. (Tasker). The dat. is temp. expressing a point
of time (MT, 243). ἦλθεν aor. ἔρχομαι. περιπατῶν pres. part.
περιπατέω to walk. Participle of manner "he came walking."
26 ■ ἰδόντες aor. part. ὁράω. ἐταράχθησαν aor. pass. ταράσσω
to be terrified. ὅτι used to indicate quotation marks in direct
speech, recitative. φάντασμα appearance, apparition, ghost.
27 ἔκραξαν aor. κράζω to cry out, to scream. ■ ἐλάλησεν aor.
λαλέω to speak. θαρσεῖτε pres. imp. θαρσέω to be cheerful,
to have courage. φοβεῖσθε pres. imp. The pres. imp. w. the neg.
indicates that an action in progress should discontinue (s. Bak-
28 ker, 35ff.; MKG, 247). ■ ἀποκριθείς aor. part. ἀποκρίνομαι
to answer. εἶ pres. εἰμί. κέλευσον aor. imp. ἐλθεῖν aor. inf.
29 ἔρχομαι. ■ ἐλθέ aor. imp. ἔρχομαι. καταβάς aor. act. part.
30 καταβαίνω to disembark, to go down. περιεπάτησεν aor. ■
βλέπων pres. part. βλέπω to see. Temporal use of the part.
expressing contemporaneous action. ἐφοβήθη aor. ἀρξάμενος
aor. mid. part. ἄρχομαι to begin. καταποντίζεσθαι pres. pass.
inf. καταποντίζω to throw into the sea, to drown, pass. to be
sunk, to be drowned (BAG). σῶσον aor. imp. σώζω to rescue,
31 to save. ■ ἐκτείνας aor. act. part. ἐκτείνω to stretch out.
ἐπελάβετο aor. mid. ἐπιλαμβάνω to take hold of, to grasp (w.
gen.). ὀλιγόπιστος little faith. εἰς τί why. ἐδίστασας aor. act.
32 διστάζω to doubt. ■ ἀναβάντων aor. part. ἀναβαίνω (gen.
33 abs.). ἐκόπασεν aor. κοπάζω to stop, to cease, to rest. ■
προσεκύνησαν aor. προσκυνέω to fall down and worship.
ἀληθῶς adv. truly.
34   ■ διαπεράσαντες aor. part. διαπεράω to pass over, to
cross over. The prep. in the verb describes the carrying of the
action through to a definite result describing a journey to a goal
35 (MH, 301). ■ ἐπιγνόντες aor. act. part. ἐπιγινώσκω to recognize. ἀπέστειλαν aor. ἀποστέλλω to bring to, to carry to.
36 κακῶς ἔχω to have it bad, to be sick. ἔχοντας pres. part. ■

παρεκάλουν impf. παρακαλέω to ask, to beseech. The impf. indicates the continual asking. ἄψωνται aor. subj. ἅπτομαι to touch (w. gen.). κράσπεδον edge, end. ὅσοι as many as. ἥψαντο aor. ἅπτομαι. διεσώθησαν aor. pass. διασῴζω to save, to heal completely. The prep. w. the verb is perfective indicating a thorough healing (MH, 301f.).

Ch. 15

■ Ἱεροσόλυμα Jerusalem. The rabbis of Jerusalem were 1 held in high esteem and their wisdom was especially praised (SB, I, 691). ■ παραβαίνω to transgress. παράδοσις tradition. The 2 body of commentary added to the law and transmitted orally. The scribes and Pharisees regarded it as of equal importance with the law. It was later written and codified and formed the Mishnah (Hill). (S. further Moore, *Judaism*, I, 251-262; SB, I, 691-695; TDNT, VI, 661f.) πρεσβύτερος older, elder, the learned ones (s. TDNT). νίπτονται pres. mid. νίπτω to wash. (For the custom of hand washing, s. M, Yadaim; SB, I, 695-704; LT, II, 10-15.) ὅταν w. subj. when, whenever. ἐσθίωσιν subj. ἐσθίω to eat. ■ ἀποκριθείς aor. part. ἀποκρίνομαι to answer. 3 καί "also." διά w. acc. "because of your tradition" (RWP). ἐντολή commandment. Jesus counterattacks, the disciples transgress the unwritten tradition, they transgress God's commandment (Hill). ■ τίμα pres. imp. τιμάω to' honor. 4 κακολογῶν pres. part. κακολογέω to speak evil of, to insult. ἤ or. τελευτάτω imp. 3rd sing. τελευτάω to die. ■ ὅς ἄν w. 5 subj., introduces a rel. clause which forms the hypothetical condition of a conditional sentence. εἴπῃ aor. subj. λέγω. δῶρον gift, present, a reference to practice of korban in which a man dedicates his property to God and is not obligated to take care of his parents (Hill; M, Nedarim; SB, I, 711-717). ὠφελήθης aor. pass. ὠφελέω to profit, to benefit. ■ οὐ μή not at all, a 6 strong neg. (s. MT, 96). τιμήσει fut. "need not honor" (BD, 184). ἠκυρώσατε aor. ἀκυρόω to make without authority, null and void, used in the papyri in the legal sense to cancel or make void a will or a death (MM). ■ ὑποκριτής hypocrite, a legalist 7 who manipulates the law w. casuistry and hair-splitting interpretations for his own benefit (AM, CXV-CXXIII). ἐπροφήτευσεν aor. προφητεύω to prophesy. ■ χεῖλος lip. 8 τιμᾷ pres. act. πόρρω far, far away. ἀπέχω to be distant, to be far away. ■ μάτην adv. in vain, to no end. σέβομαι to worship, 9 the honoring of God through acts of obedience to His will (CBB; TDNT). διδάσκοντες pres. part. διδάσκω to teach. ἔνταλμα commandment.

10   ■ προσκαλεσάμενος aor. mid. part. προσκαλέω to summon, to call to. ἀκούετε pres. imp. ἀκούω to hear. συνίετε pres.
11   imp. συνίημι to understand, to comprehend. ■ εἰσερχόμενον pres. mid. part. εἰσέρχομαι to come in, to go in. στόμα mouth. κοινοῖ pres. act. κοινόω to make common, to defile. ἐκπορευόμενον pres. mid. part. ἐκπορεύομαι to go out, to go
12   forth. ■ προσελθόντες aor. part. προσέρχομαι. οἶδα defective perf. w. pres. meaning "to know." ἀκούσαντες aor. part. temp. "when they heard." ἐσκανδαλίσθησαν aor. pass. σκανδαλίζω to cause to stumble, indicating deep religious offense at the preaching of Jesus which causes and includes denial
13   and rejection of Jesus (TDNT). ■ φυτεία plant, a cultivated plant (EGT), a figure common among Judaism and the Dead Sea community (Hill). ἥν rel. pron. fem. sing. acc. ἐφύτευσεν aor. φυτεύω to plant. ἐκριζωθήσεται fut. pass. ἐκριζόω to tear out
14   by the roots. ■ ἄφετε aor. imp. ἀφίημι to leave, to leave alone. τυφλός blind. ὁδηγός guide. ἐάν w. subj. if. ὁδηγῇ pres. subj. ὁδηγέω to lead along the way. ἀμφότεροι both. βόθυνος ditch.
15   πεσοῦνται fut. mid. πίπτω to fall. ■ φράσον aor. imp. φράζω
16   to explain, to interpret. ■ ἀκμήν adverbial acc. still, places emphasis at the beginning of a sentence, "Even at this crucial juncture, are you without understanding?" (Hill). καί also.
17   ἀσύνετος without understanding, not comprehending. ■ νοεῖτε pres. act. νοέω to comprehend, to understand. εἰσπορευόμενον pres. mid. part. εἰσπορεύομαι to go in. κοιλία stomach. χωρεῖ pres. χωρέω to go out. ἀφεδρών drain, latrine (for sanitary conditions, s. Edward Neufeld, "Hygiene Conditions in Ancient Israel," BA, XXXIV [May, 1971], 42–
18   66). ἐκβάλλεται pres. pass. ἐκβάλλω to throw out. ■
19   ἐξέρχομαι to go out. κἀκεῖνα = καὶ ἐκ. ■ διαλογισμός disputing, doubts, reason. φόνος murder. μοιχεία adultery. πορνεία illicit sexual activity (TDNT). κλοπή theft. ψευδομαρτυρία false witness. βλασφημία slander, blaspheming.
20   ■ κοινοῦντα pres. part. ἄνιπτος unwashed. φαγεῖν aor. inf. ἐσθίω. Infinitive used as noun. Subject of the verb (BD, 205).
21   ■ ἐξελθών aor. part. ἐξέρχομαι s.v.18. ἀνεχώρησεν aor.
22   ἀναχωρέω to depart. μέρος part, pl. region. ■ ὅριον boundary, pl. area. ἔκραζεν impf. κράζω to cry out. The impf. indicates she kept on calling out (Filson). ἐλέησον aor. imp. ἐλεέω to have mercy, pity, to show mercy. δαιμονίζομαι to be possessed
23   w. a demon. ■ ἀπεκρίθη aor. s.v.3. ἠρώτων impf. ἐρωτάω to ask, to inquire, to request. ἀπόλυσον aor. imp. ἀπολύω to send away. Send her away w. her request granted (Meyer). ὄπισθεν

w. gen. after. ■ ἀπυκριθείς aor. pass. part. s.v.3. ἀπεστάλην 24
aor. pass. ἀποστέλλω. ἀπολωτότα perf. part. ἀπόλλυμι to
lose, to be lost. ■ ἐλθοῦσα aor. part. fem. ἔρχομαι to come, to 25
go. προσεκύνει impf. προσκυνέω to worship. The continual
action of the impf. indicates her persistence (Filson). βοήθει
pres. imp. βοηθέω to help. The pres. imp. here pictures an
excited request to begin an action which is not going on (Bakker,
83f.; MKG, 272). ■ λαβεῖν aor. inf. λαμβάνω to take. βαλεῖν 26
aor. inf. βάλλω to cast, to throw. κυνάριον dog, little dog. A
house dog or lap dog in contrast to a dog of the street or farm
(BAG). ■ ναί certainly. ψιχίον crumb, little morsel, dimin. 27
form. πιπτόντων pres. part. s.v.14. ■ γενηθήτω aor. imp. 3 28
sing. γίνομαι to become, to happen. ἰάθη aor. pass. ἰάομαι to
heal.

■ μεταβάς aor. part. μεταβαίνω to pass over, to withdraw, 29
to depart. ἦλθεν aor. ἔρχομαι s.v.25. ἀναβάς aor. part.
ἀναβαίνω to go up. ἐκάθητο impf. κάθημαι to sit down, to sit.
■ προσῆλθον aor. προσέρχομαι. ἔχοντες pres. part. ἔχω to 30
have. ἑαυτῶν refl. pron. 3rd person. χωλός lame. κυλλός cripple, crippled, deformed, used of a limb of the body which is in
any way abnormal or incapable of being used (BAG). τυφλός
blind. κωφός dumb, deaf. ἔρριψαν aor. ῥίπτω to cast, to fling,
not carelessly but in haste (RWP). ἐθεράπευσεν aor.
θεραπεύω to heal. The aor. summarizes His acts. ■ θαυμάσαι 31
aor. inf. θαυμάζω to marvel, to wonder at. The inf. used w.
ὥστε to express results. βλέποντας pres. part. βλέπω to see.
λαλοῦντας pres. part. λαλέω to speak, to talk. ὑγιής well.
περιπατοῦντας pres. part. περιπατέω to walk about.
ἐδόξασαν aor. δοξάζω to glorify, to praise.

■ σπλαγχνίζομαι to have compassion. ἡμέρα day, a pa- 32
renthetic nom. (RG, 460; MT, 231). προσμένω to remain w.
φάγωσιν aor. subj. ἐσθίω to eat, indirect question w. the deliberative subj. (RWP). ἀπολῦσαι aor. inf. s.v.23. νῆστις not
eating, hungry. μήποτε w. subj. lest. ἐκλυθῶσιν aor. subj. pass.
ἐκλύω pass. to be without strength, to be weary. ■ πόθεν where. 33
τοσοῦτος so much. χορτάσαι aor. inf. χορτάζω to satisfy, to
fill w. food. The inf. used to express result. ■ πόσος how many. 34
ἰχθύδιον dimin. small fish (for diminutives w. this ending, s.
MH, 344–346). ■ παραγγείλας aor. part. παραγγέλλω to 35
give instruction, to command. ἀναπεσεῖν aor. inf. ἀναπίπτω
to sit down, to recline for eating. It denotes the act rather than
the stage (AS). ■ ἔλαβεν aor. λαμβάνω s.v.26. ἰχθύς fish. 36
εὐχαριστήσας aor. part. εὐχαριστέω to give thanks.
ἔκλασέν aor. κλάω to break. ἐδίδου impf. δίδωμι to give. The

47

37 impf. pictures the repeated giving. ■ ἔφαγον aor.
ἐχορτάσθησαν aor. pass. περισσεῦον pres. part. περισσεύω
to be in abundance, to be in excess. ἦραν aor. αἴρω to lift up.
σπυρίς basket, a flexible mat basket used for carrying fish or
38/39 fruit (Tasker). ■ ἐσθίοντες pres. part. ἐσθίω ■ ἀπολύσας aor.
part. ἐνέβη aor. ἐμβαίνω to embark, to get into. ὅριον s.v.22.

Ch. 16

1   ■ προσελθόντες aor. part. προσέρχομαι to come to.
πειράζοντες pres. part. πειράζω to try, to test, to tempt
(Trench, Synonyms). ἐπηρώτησαν aor. ἐπερωτάω to ask, to
ask for; prep. w. the verb is directive and concentrates the verb's
action upon some object (MH, 312). σημεῖον sign, here used in
the sense of a proof that Jesus had God on His side. ἐπιδεῖξαι
aor. inf. ἐπιδείκνυμι to show (for the prep. w. the verb, s. MH,
2 312). ■ ἀποκριθείς aor. part. ἀποκρίνομαι to answer. ὀψία
evening. γενομένης aor. part. γίνομαι to become, to happen;
part. used as gen. abs. εὐδία fair or calm weather (RWP).
3 πυρράζω to be red like fire. ■ πρωΐ early morning. χειμών
rainy, stormy weather. στυγνάζων pres. part. στυγνάζω to be
or become dark, gloomy. γινώσκω to know, w. inf. to know how
to (BD, 199, 200). διακρίνω to divide, to discern. καιρός time.
4 δύναμαι to be able to. ■ γενεά generation. μοιχαλίς adulter-
ous. ἐπιζητεῖ pres. ἐπιζητέω to seek, to seek after (for the prep.
w. the verb, s. MH, 312). δοθήσεται fut. pass. δίδωμι to give.
εἰ μή except. καταλίπων aor. part. καταλείπω to leave behind. ἀπῆλθεν aor. ἀπέρχομαι to go away.
5   ■ ἐλθόντες aor. part. ἔρχομαι to come, to go. ἐπελάθοντο
aor. mid. ἐπιλανθάνομαι to forget. λαβεῖν aor. inf. λαμβάνω
6 to take. ■ ὁρᾶτε pres. imp. ὁράω to see, to beware. προσέχετε
pres. imp. προσέχω to pay attention to, to give heed to. ζύμη
leaven. (For the symbol of leaven see Matt. 13:33.) Jesus meant
their teaching, the rigid legalism and casuistical sophistry of the
Pharisees and the political opportunism and the worldly materi-
7 alism of the Sadducees (Tasker). ■ διελογίζοντο impf. mid.
διαλογίζομαι to reason, to dispute. ἑαυτοῖς ref. pron. 3rd per.
either each man in his own mind or among themselves (EGT).
λέγοντες part. ὅτι either causal "because" or recitative indicat-
8 ing quotation marks. ἐλάβομεν aor. λαμβάνω ■ γνούς aor. act.
part. γινώσκω. ὀλιγόπιστος little faith, trust, confidence, assurance in the power of Christ to provide food as He had done
9 before (Allen). ■ οὔπω not yet. νοεῖτε pres. νοέω to grasp with
the mind, to understand. μνημονεύω to remember. πόσος how
10/12 many. κόφινος s. Matt. 14:20. ■ σπυρίς s. Matt. 15:37. ■

48

συνῆκαν aor. συνίημι to comprehend, to understand.
■ ἐλθών s.v.5. μέρος part, pl. area. ἠρώτα impf. ἐρωτάω 13
to ask, inceptive impf. "he began to question" (RWP). ■ οἱ μέν 14
some. ἄλλοι others. ἕτερος other(s) distinguishes them not
merely numerically but also generically (EGT). ἤ or. ■ ὑμεῖς 15
you emphatic. ■ ἀποκριθείς s.v.2. εἰ pres. 2nd per. sing. ὁ 16
χριστός the Messiah, the anointed one, used without the article
it has the character of a personal name, with the article it is a title
of the one promised in the Old Testament (SB, I, 6ff., TDNT).
ζῶντος pres. part. ζάω to live. ■ μακάριος blessed, happy. 17
σάρξ and αἷμα is a Jewish way of referring to man in his
entirety, but in his natural weakness (Hill). ἀπεκάλυψεν aor.
ἀποκαλύπτω to unveil, to reveal. ■ κἀγώ = καὶ ἐγώ "I also." 18
πέτρα rock. A small detachment of the massive ledge (πέτρος)
(RWP). οἰκοδομήσω fut. οἰκοδομέω to build; "upon this rock
of revealed truth I will build my church" (Allen). ἐκκλησία
assembly, church (s. TDNT; CBB; NTW). πύλη gate. ᾅδης
hades, the underworld, death (TDNT; SB, IV, 1016–1029).
κατισχύσουσιν fut. κατισχύω to overpower, to have strength
against, to gain mastery over (RWP). ■ δώσω fut. δίδωμι to 19
give. κλείς key. ὅς ἐάν whoever. δήσῃς aor. subj. δέω to bind.
λύσῃς aor. subj. λύω to loose. ἔσται fut. εἰμί with the perf.
pass. part. δεδεμένον. ἔσται fut. εἰμί with the perf. pass. part.
λελυμένον. This construction is the fut. perf. pass. periphrastic
trans. "will have been bound," "will have been loosed." It is the
church on earth carrying out heaven's decisions, not heaven
ratifying the church's decision (AM). ■ διεστείλατο aor. mid. 20
διαστέλλομαι to instruct, to order. Another reading has
ἐπετίμησεν aor. ἐπιτιμάω to reprove, to sternly warn, to seriously warn. μηδενί dat. sing. μηδείς no one. εἴπωσιν aor. subj.
λέγω
■ ἤρξατο aor. ἄρχομαι to begin. The verb is emphatic and 21
indicates that a new stage in the self-revelation of Jesus has now
been reached (Tasker). δεικνύω to show. δεῖ it is necessary (w.
acc. and inf.). ἀπελθεῖν aor. inf. ἀπέρχομαι s.v.4. παθεῖν aor.
inf. πάσχω to suffer. ἀποκτανθῆναι aor. pass. inf. ἀποκτείνω
to kill. ἐγερθῆναι aor. pass. inf. ἐγείρω pass. to be raised. ■ 22
προσλαβόμενος aor. mid. part. προσλαμβάνω to take to
oneself, to take aside. ἐπιτιμᾶν pres. inf. ἐπιτιμάω s.v.20.
ἵλεως gracious, merciful, "may God be gracious to you," that is,
"may God in His mercy spare you this" (BAG). οὐ μή never,
an emphatic neg. ἔσται fut. εἰμί ■ στραφείς aor. part. 23
στρέφομαι to turn, to turn oneself. ὕπαγε pres. imp. ὑπάγω
to depart. The pres. imp. often is used to express an order involv-

ing motion (Bakker, 82). ὀπίσω behind. σκάνδαλον occasion to sin. φρονεῖς pres. φρονέω to set one's mind on, to be intent
24 on. ■ ἐλθεῖν aor. inf. s.v.5. ἀπαρνησάσθω aor. imp. 3rd sing. ἀπαρνέομαι to deny, to deny oneself, an act in wholly unselfish manner, give up his personality (BAG). ἀράτω aor. imp. 3rd sing. αἴρω to take up. ἀκολουθείτω pres. imp. 3rd sing. ἀκολουθέω to follow after, used often in the sense of following
25 like a disciple. ■ ὅς ἐάν whoever. θέλῃ pres. subj. σῶσαι aor. inf. σῴζω to save. ἀπολέσει fut. ἀπόλλυμι to loose. ἀπολέσῃ aor. subj. ἕνεκεν w. gen. because of, for the sake of. εὑρήσει fut.
26 εὑρίσκω to find. ■ ὠφεληθήσεται fut. pass. ὠφελέω to benefit, to help, to aid, pass. to have benefit, to profit. ἐάν introduces a supposed case (RWP). κερδήσῃ aor. subj. κερδαίνω to win, to gain, to make a profit. ζημιωθῇ aor. subj. pass. ζημιόω to suffer loss, to suffer confiscation (Allen). ἤ aor. δώσει fut. δίδωμι to give. ἀντάλλαγμα something given in exchange. The prep. ἀντι in the noun indicates reciprocity and implies the equivalence of the object to that against which it is set (MH, 297). A man must surrender his life and nothing less to God, no
27 exchange is possible (McNeile). ■ μέλλω to be about to, used with the inf. to express the fut. ἀποδώσει fut. ἀποδίδωμι to give back, to repay. πρᾶξιν acc. πρᾶξις deed, conduct, the sum of one's doings including that self-denial, adherence to their faith
28 and confession (Meyer). ■ ἑστώτων perf. act. part. ἵστημι to stand. ὅστις rel. pron. "who." Used either in the sense of ὅς, or in the classical sense with a generic meaning, that is, "which, as others of the same class" (s. IBG, 123, 124; M, 91, 92). γεύσωνται aor. subj. γεύομαι to taste (w. gen.). ἕως ἄν w. subj. until. ἴδωσιν aor. subj. ὁράω to see. ἐρχόμενον pres. part.

Ch. 17

1 ■ μεθ᾿ = μετά w. acc. after. ἕξ six. Means "on the sixth day" (McNeile). παραλαμβάνω to take with. ἀναφέρω to
2 take up. ὑψηλός high. ἴδιος for one's self, privately. ■ μετεμορφώθη aor. pass. μεταμορφόω to transform, to change, to change from an earthly to a supernatural figure (TDNT). ἔμπροσθεν w. gen. before. ἔλαμψεν aor. λάμπω to shine, to gleam. ἱμάτιον outward garment. ἐγένετο aor. γίνομαι to
3 become, to happen. λευκός bright, shining, gleaming. ■ ὤφθη aor. pass. ὁράω to see. pass. to fear. (For a sing. verb with a pl. subject s. BD, 74f.) συλλαλοῦντες pres. part. συλλαλέω to
4 talk with. ■ ἀποκριθείς aor. part. ἀποκρίνομαι to answer. καλός good, nice. ἐστίν pres. εἰμί to be. ἡμᾶς us, emphasized by its position, acc. used w. the inf. εἶναι pres. inf. εἰμί. (For the

inf. explaining the adj. s. DM, 219.) εἰ θέλεις "if you desire."
In Hellenistic use equal to "please" (BD, 190). ποιήσω fut. ind.
ποιέω to do, to make. σκηνή tent, booth, dwelling place. ■ 5
λαλοῦντος pres. part. λαλέω gen. abs. expressing contemporaneous time "while he was speaking." νεφέλη cloud. φωτεινός
shining, bright, radiant. ἐπεσκίασεν aor. ἐπισκιάζω to overshadow them. Here the acc. pictures the motion of the cloud as
it enveloped them (McNeile). λέγουσα pres. act. part. fem. sing.
λέγω to speak. It was the shekina from which the divine Voice
proceeded (McNeile). ἀγαπητός beloved. εὐδόκησα aor.
εὐδοκέω to be pleased with. ἀκούετε pres, imp ἀκούω to hear,
to listen to. ■ ἀκούσαντες aor. act. part. ἔπεσαν aor. πίπτω 6
to fall. ἐφοβήθησαν aor. pass. φοβέομαι to be afraid. σφόδρα
very, exceedingly. ■ προσῆλθεν aor. προσέρχομαι to come 7
to, to go to. ἁψάμενος aor. mid. part. ἅπτομαι to touch (w.
gen.). ἐγέρθητε aor. imp. pass. ἐγείρω to rise up. pass. to get
up. φοβεῖσθε pres. imp. φοβέομαι. The pres. imp. w. the neg.
indicates the action in progress should cease "stop being afraid"
(s. Bakker, 35ff.). ■ ἐπάραντες aor. part. ἐπαίρω to lift up. 8
εἶδον aor. ὁράω. εἰ μή except.
■ καταβαινόντων pres. part. καταβαίνω to go down. 9
Used as gen. abs. expressing contemporaneous time "while they
were going down." ἐνετείλατο aor. ἐντέλλομαι to command.
εἴπητε aor. subj. λέγω. The prohibitive subj. implies that the
action is not yet existent and should not arise (MKG, 273).
ὅραμα that which was seen, vision. ἕως οὗ until. ἐγερθῇ aor.
subj. pass. ■ ἐπηρώτησαν aor. ἐπερωτάω to ask, to inquire. δεῖ 10
it is necessary (w. acc. and inf.). ἐλθεῖν aor. inf. ἔρχομαι to
come. (For the rabbinical teaching on Elijah s. SB, IV, 764–798.)
■ ἀποκαταστήσει fut. ἀποκαθίστημι to restore to the for- 11
mer condition (s. TDNT). ■ ἦλθεν aor. ἔρχομαι. ἐπέγνωσαν 12
aor. ἐπιγινώσκω to know, to recognize, to acknowledge.
ἐποίησαν aor. ἐν "to" ("to do something to someone" BD, 86).
The reference is to His execution (McNeile). ὅσα acc. pl. ὅσος
as great, how great, as much as. ἠθέλησαν aor. θέλω. (For the
aor. form s. BD, 36.) πάσχω to suffer. ■ συνῆκαν aor. συνίημι 13
to understand, to comprehend.
■ ἐλθόντων aor. part. used as gen. abs. s.v.10. γονυπετῶν 14
pres. part. γονυπετέω to fall on the knees and beg (TDNT).
■ ἐλέησον aor. imp. ἐλεέω to have mercy, to show compassion. 15
σεληνιάζομαι to be moonstruck, to have epilepsy. The sickness
often was attributed to demons (SB, I, 758; s. also HDCG).
κακῶς ἔχω (some mss. κακῶς πάσχω to suffer). πίπτει pres.
πίπτω to fall. The customary pres. (s. RG, 880). ■ 16

51

προσήνεγκα aor. προσφέρω to bring to. ἠδυνήθησαν aor.
pass. δύναμαι to be able. θεραπεῦσαι aor. inf. θεραπεύω to
17 heal ■ ἀποκριθείς s.v.4. γενεά generation. ἄπιστος faithless,
unbelieving. διεστραμμένη perf. pass. part. διαστρέφω distorted, twisted in two, corrupt (RWP). The perf. expresses a state
or condition consequent upon an action (s. G.L. McKay, "Syntax and Exegesis," Tyndale Bulletin, 23 [1972], 47f.). ἕως πότε
until when, how long. ἔσομαι fut. εἰμί to be. ἀνέξομαι fut. mid.
ἀνέχω to bear up, to endure. φέρετε pres. imp. φέρω to bring.
18 ■ ἐπετίμησεν aor. ἐπιτιμάω to rebuke. The word of command
that brought the hostile powers under control (H.C. Kee, "The
Terminology of Mark's Exorcism Stories," NTS, 14 [Jan. 1968],
246). ἐξῆλθεν aor. ἐξέρχομαι to come out, to go out.
19 ἐθεραπεύθη aor. pass. παῖς child. ■ προσελθόντες aor. part.
προσέρχομαι. κατ ἰδίαν s.v.1. ἐκβαλεῖν aor. inf. ἐκβάλλω
20 to cast out. ■ ὀλιγοπιστία little faith. ἐάν w. subj. if. ἔχητε
pres. subj. ἔχω. κόκκος grain. σινάπεως gen. sing. σίναπι
mustard, mustard seed. Popularly considered the smallest of all
seeds (BAG). ἐρεῖτε fut. λέγω. μετάβα aor. imp. μεταβαίνω
to transfer, to move to another place. ἔνθεν from there.
μεταβήσεται fut. mid. ἀδυνατήσει fut. ἀδυνατέω to be unable, to be impossible.
22   ■ συστρεφομένων pres. mid. part. συστρέφομαι to gather together, to come together. Participle used as gen. abs. μέλλω
s.v.12. παραδίδοσθαι pres. pass. inf. παραδίδωμι to deliver
23 over. ἀποκτενοῦσιν fut. ἀποκτείνω to kill. ■ ἐγερθήσεται
fut. pass. s.v.7. ἐλυπήθησαν aor. pass. λυπέω to cause pain, to
grieve, pass. to become sad, sorrowful, distressed. (The aor. is
ingressive, "they became distressed.") σφόδρα very.
24   ■ ἐλθόντων s.v.14. προσῆλθον s.v.7. δίδραχμον a double
drachma. A coin worth two drachmas, approximately 36 cents.
The amount required for the annual temple tax (BAG). (For the
temple tax s. SB, I, 760–770.) λαμβάνον pres. part. λαμβάνω
to take. εἶπαν aor. λέγω. τελεῖ pres. τελέω to complete, to pay.
25 ■ προέφθασεν aor. προφθάνω to anticipate, to get before one
in doing a thing (RWP). "Jesus spoke to him first" (for the use
with the part. s. RG, 1120). δοκεῖ μοι the impersonal use of
δοκέω with the dat. It appears or seems to be. "What do you
think?" τέλος tax, tribute. κῆνσος tax. The former taxes on
wares, the latter a tax on persons; that is, indirect and direct
26 taxation (EGT). ἀλλότριος foreign, foreigners. ■ εἰπόντος aor.
part. gen. sing. λέγω part. used as gen. abs. "after he said." ἔφη
impf. φημί to say. ἄρα "then," draws an inference from the
preceding. γέ particle emphasizing the previous word.

ἐλεύθερος free. ■ σκανδαλίσωμεν aor. subj. σκανδαλίζω to 27
cause to stumble, to offend. πορευθείς aor. part. πορεύομαι to
go. βάλε aor. imp. βάλλω to cast. ἄγκιστρον fishhook.
ἀναβάντα aor. active part. acc. sing. ἀναβαίνω to come up.
ἆρον aor. imp. αἴρω to take, to lift up. ἀνοίξας aor. part.
ἀνοίγω to open. εὑρήσεις fut. εὑρίσκω to find. στατήρ a
stater. A silver coin equal to 4 drachma worth about 80 cents
(BAG). λαβών aor. part. λαμβάνω. δός aor. imp. δίδωμι to
give. ἀντί w. gen., for

Ch. 18

■ προσῆλθον aor. προσέρχομαι to come to. λέγοντες 1
part. λέγω to say. τίς who? ἄρα "then" points back to the tax
collection incident (RWP). μείζων comp. μέγας great. ἐστίν
pres. εἰμί to be. ■ προσκαλεσάμενος aor. mid. part. 2
προσκαλέω to call to one's self. παιδίον child. ἔστησεν aor.
ἵστημι to place. μέσον mid. ■ ἐάν w. subj. "if." στραφῆτε aor. 3
pass. subj. στρέφω to turn about, to turn around, "unless ye turn
around so as to go in an opposite direction" (EGT). γένησθε
aor. subj. γίνομαι to become. οὐ μή not at all. εἰσέλθητε aor.
subj. εἰσέρχομαι to go in. ■ ὅστις whoever. ταπεινώσει fut. 4
ταπεινόω to lower, to make low, to humble. ἑαυτόν refl. pron.
3rd per. sing. "himself." "He will be the greatest who.has the
least idea that he is great" (McNeile). ■ ὅς ἐάν whoever. 5
δέξηται aor. subj. δέχομαι to receive, to receive as a guest, to
welcome. τοιοῦτος such as this, of such a kind. ἐπὶ τῷ ὀνόματι
"on the ground of my Name" (McNeile).

■ σκανδαλίσῃ aor. subj. σκανδαλίζω to cause to fall, to 6
offend, to cause to stumble. πιστευόντων pres. part. πιστεύω
to put trust in (εἰς), to believe on. συμφέρει to be advantageous
or profitable. The next clause is the subject of the verb. "That a
millstone be hung around his neck is advantageous for him" (s.
RG, 992). κρεμασθῇ aor. subj. pass. κρεμάννυμι to hang.
μύλος millstone. ὀνικός donkey. The large upper millstone
driven by an ass (EGT). τράχηλος neck. καταποντισθῇ aor.
subj. pass. καταποντίζω to flow into the sea, pass. to be
drowned. πέλαγος the open sea. ■ οὐαί woe. Indicating the 7
causal origin of the woe for humanity (Meyer). ἀπό the cause
of stumbling, the reason of offense (s. TDNT). ἀνάγκη necessary, necessity. ἐλθεῖν aor. inf. ἔρχομαι to come. πλήν nevertheless. δι᾿ = διά w. gen. through. ■ εἰ "if." The condition is 8
viewed as true. πούς foot. ἔκκοψον aor. imp. ἐκκόπτω to cut
off. βάλε aor. imp. βάλλω to cast. εἰσελθεῖν aor. inf. κυλλός
cripple. χωλός lame. ἤ "than," used after comp. ἔχοντα pres.

part. acc. sing. ἔχω to have. βληθῆναι aor. inf. pass. βάλλω.
πῦρ fire. αἰώνιος everlasting. (For the term "everlasting fire"
9 in the DSS, s. 1Qs 2:8.) ■ ἔξελε aor. imp. ἐξαιρέω to take out.
μονόφθαλμος one eyed. γέεννα gehenna. Hell (s. TDNT).
10   ■ ὁρᾶτε pres. imp. ὁράω see, see to it. καταφρονήσητε
aor. subj. καταφρονέω to despise. The subj. with the neg. expresses a prohibition. It indicates that the action should not arise
(MKG). διὰ παντός always. βλέπουσι pres. βλέπω to see.
12 The pres. emphasizes the continuous action. ■ δοκεῖ ὑμῖν
"What do you think?" (s. Matt 17:25). γένηται aor. subj.
γίνομαι w. dat. indicates possession. "If a certain man had."
ἀνθρώπῳ dat. showing possession. πλανηθῇ aor. subj. pass.
πλανάω to lead astray, pass. to go astray. οὐχί in questions
expecting a positive answer. ἀφήσει fut. ἀφίημι to leave.
πορευθείς aor. part. πορεύομαι to go. ζητεῖ pres. ζητέω to
13 seek, to look for. πλανώμενον pres. part. ■ εὑρεῖν aor. inf.
εὑρίσκω to find. The inf. is used with the verb "if he happened
to find" (s. BD, 201). χαίρω to rejoice, to be happy.
14 πεπλανώμενον perf. pass. part. ■ ἔμπροσθεν w. gen. before.
Targum expression used out of reverence to God. With the
meaning "it is not the will of my Father" (Martin McNamara,
Targum and Testament, 95). ἀπόληται aor. subj. ἀπόλλυμι to
perish.
15   ■ ἁμαρτήσῃ aor. subj. ἁρματανω to sin. ὕπαγε pres. imp.
ὑπάγω to go, to go forth. The pres. imp. often is used to express
an order involving motion (Bakker, 82). ἔλεγξον aor. imp.
ἐλέγχω to bring to light, to expose. "Show him his fault while
you are with him alone" (BAG). μεταξύ w. gen., between.
ἀκούσῃ aor. subj. ἀκούω to hear, to listen to. ἐκέρδησας aor.
16 ind. 2nd sing. κερδαίνω to win, to gain. ■ παράλαβε aor. imp.
παραλαμβάνω to take, to take with. ἐάν w. subj. to express
purpose. μετά w. gen. by. στόμα mouth. σταθῇ aor. subj. pass.
17 ἵστημι to place, pass. to stand. ῥῆμα word. ■ παρακούσῃ aor.
subj. παρακούω to ignore, to refuse to hear. The prep. indicates
to hear a "side" (MH, 319). ἐκκλησία assembly, a small body
of the Lord's followers (McNeile). ἔστω pres. imp. 3rd sing.
εἰμί. ὥσπερ as. ἐθνικός heathen.
18   ■ ὅσα ἐάν whatever. δήσητε aor subj. δέω to bind. ἔσται
fut. εἰμί. δεδεμένα perf. pass. part. (For this construction ·s.
Matt. 16:19.) λύσητε aor. subj. λύω to loose. λελυμένα perf.
19 pass. part. ■ ὅτι = to quotation marks (recitative use).
συμφωνήσωσιν aor. subj. συμφωνέω to be in agreement, lit.
"to produce a sound together." (For the prep. s. MH, 324f.)
πρᾶγμα matter. αἰτήσωνται aor. subj. αἰτέω to ask, to re-

quest. οὗ gen. sing. of the rel. pron. Genitive by attraction (MT, 324). γενήσεται fut. γίνομαι ■ οὗ where. συνηγμένοι perf. 20 pass. part. συνάγω to come together, to gather together. The perf. pictures the state of being gathered together.

■ προσελθών aor. part. προσέρχομαι s.v.1. ποσάκις as 21 often as. ἁμαρτήσει fut. s.v.15. εἰς w. acc. against. ἀφήσω fut. ἀφίημι to release, to forgive. ἑπτάκις seven times. Three times was considered the normal number of times to forgive (Allen). ■ οὐ not. Does not belong with the verb but with "seven" (EGT). 22 ἑβδομηκοντάκις ἑπτά seven times seventy, that is, unlimited. ■ ὡμοιώθη aor. pass. ὁμοιόω to compare, to make like, pass. 23 to be made like or to become like. ἠθέλησεν aor. (ἐ) θέλω to will, to wish. συνᾶραι aor. inf. συναίρω w. λόγον "I compare accounts, make a reckoning" (LAE 117). ■ ἀρξαμένου aor. 24 mid. part. ἄρχομαι to begin. Used as gen. abs. προσήχθη aor. pass. προσάγω to lead or bring to. ὀφειλέτης debtor. τάλαντον talent. A measure of weight, then a unit of coinage (BAG). A talent was worth 6,000 denarii, or about 1,000 dollars. The debt here would be about 10 or 12 million dollars (RWP). ■ ἔχοντος pres. part. ἔχω to have. Used as gen. abs. either temp. 25 or causal (BD, 218). ἀποδοῦναι aor. inf. ἀποδίδωμι to give back, to pay back. ἐκέλευσεν aor. κελεύω to order, to command (w. acc. and inf.). πραθῆναι aor. pass. inf. πιπράσκω to sell. ἀποδοθῆναι aor. pass. inf. ἀποδίδωμι The two infs. are used with the verb to command (BD, 201). ■ πεσών aor. part. πίπτω 26 to fall. προσεκύνει impf. προσκυνέω to fall down and worship, to do reverence to. The imp. is inceptive, "he began to." μακροθύμησον aor. imp. μακροθυμέω to have patience. The word indicates one who has the power to avenge himself yet refrains from the exercise of this power (Trench, Synonyms, 195). The aor. imp. used by one in difficult circumstances is not intended to create an understanding but to display complete dependence on the one appealed to (Bakker, 100f.). ἀποδώσω fut. ἀποδίδωμι ■ σπλαγχνισθείς aor. pass. part. 27 σπλαγχνίζομαι to be moved with compassion. The part. could be causal. ἀπέλυσεν aor. ἀπολύω to release. δάνειον loan. ἀφῆκεν aor. ἀφίημι to release, "to cancel the loan" (BAG). ■ ἐξελθών aor. part. ἐξέρχομαι to go out. εὗρεν aor. εὑρίσκω 28 to find. σύνδουλος fellow slave. ὤφειλεν imp. ὀφείλω to owe a debt. δηνάριον denarius. A Roman silver coin worth about 18 cents. It was the workman's average daily wage (BAG). It was a six hundred-thousandth of his own remitted debt (McNeile). κρατήσας aor. part. κρατέω to cease. ἔπνιγεν impf. πνίγω to choke. Inceptive imp. "he began choking." ἀπόδος aor. imp.

55

ἀποδίδωμι. εἰ "if." Assumes the reality of the case. The ex-
29 pression of pitiless logic (Meyer). ■ παρεκάλει imp.
παρακαλέω to beseech, to ask. The imp. indicates persistent
30 requesting. ■ ἤθελεν imp. θέλω. Imperative of persistent refusal
(RWP). ἀπελθών aor. part. ἀπέρχομαι to go out. ἔβαλεν aor.
βάλλω to cast. ἀποδῷ aor. subj. ἀποδίδωμι. ὀφειλόμενον
pres. pass. part. (For imprisonment because of debt s. LAE, 270.)
31 ■ ἰδόντες aor. part. ὁράω to see. γενόμενα aor. part. s.v.3.
ἐλυπήθησαν aor. pass. λυπέω s. Matt. 17:23. σφόδρα very.
ἐλθόντες aor. part. s.v.7. διεσάφησαν aor. διασαφέω to ex-
32 plain, to report. ■ προσκαλεσάμενος s.v.2. ὀφειλή debt.
33 ἀφῆκα aor. s.v.27. παρεκάλεσας aor. ind. 2nd sing. ■ ἔδει
imp. δεῖ it is necessary, one must (w. acc. and inf.). ἐλεῆσαι aor.
34 inf. ἐλεέω to show mercy, to be merciful. ἠλέησα aor. ■
ὀργισθείς aor. part. ὀργίζομαι to be angry, aor. to become
angry. παρέδωκεν aor. παραδίδωμι to deliver over.
35 βασανιστής one who tortures, jailer. ἕως οὗ until. ■ ποιήσει
fut. ποιέω to do. ἀφῆτε aor. subj. ἀφίημι.

Ch. 19

1   ■ ἐγένετο aor. γίνομαι to become, to happen. ἐτέλεσεν
aor. τελέω to end, to complete. μετῆρεν aor. μεταίρω to depart. ἦλθεν aor. ἔρχομαι to come, to go. ὅριον border, pl. area,
2 region. πέραν w. gen. the other side. ἠκολούθησαν aor.
ἀκολουθέω to follow. ἐθεράπευσεν aor. θεραπεύω to heal.
3   ■ προσῆλθον aor. προσέρχομαι to come to.
πειράζοντες pres. part. πειράζω to try, to tempt. λέγοντες
pres. part. λέγω. εἰ if, whether, used in indirect questions.
ἔξεστιν it is lawful, it is allowed. ἀπολῦσαι aor. inf. ἀπολύω
4 to release, to divorce. (For Jewish divorce s. Matt. 5:31.) ■
ἀποκριθείς aor. pass. part. ἀποκρίνομαι to answer. ἀνέγνωτε
aor. ἀναγινώσκω to read. κτίσας aor. part. κτίζω to create.
ἄρσην male. θηλῦς female. ἐποίησεν aor. ποιέω to do, to
5 make. ■ εἶπεν aor. λέγω to speak. ἕνεκα w. gen. because of.
καταλείψει fut. καταλείπω to leave. The prep. with the verb
is perfective (MH, 316). κολληθήσεται fut. pass. κολλάω to
join closely together, to unite, pass. cling. ἔσονται fut. εἰμί to
6 be. ■ ὥστε "therefore," draws a conclusion from the preceding.
εἰσίν pres. εἰμί. συνέζευξεν aor. συνζεύγνυμι to join together, to yoke together. The aor. is timeless (RWP). χωριζέτω
7 pres. imp. 3rd sing. χωρίζω to divide, to separate. ■ ἐνετείλατο
aor. mid. ἐντέλλω to command. δοῦναι aor. inf. δίδωμι to give.
8 βιβλίον book. Here bill of divorcement. ■ ὅτι "because" or the
equivalent of quotation marks. πρός w. acc. "in accordance

with," "in view of" (BD, 124). "With a view to" (McNeile).
σκληροκαρδία hardness of heart. ἐπέτρεψεν aor. ἐπιτρέπω
to allow, to permit. γέγονεν perf. γίνομαι. ■ ὃς ἄν whoever. 9
The rel. clause has the character of the conditional clause in a
conditional sentence. ἀπολύσῃ aor. subj. ἐπί w. dat. "on the
basis of," "because." πορνεία prostitution, unchastity, of every
kind of unlawful sexual intercourse (BAG; s. also TDNT).
γαμήσῃ aor. subj. γαμέω to marry. μοιχᾶται pres. mid.
μοιχάομαι to commit adultery. ■ ἐστίν pres. εἰμί. αἰτία mat- 10
ter, case. συμφέρει it is profitable, it is beneficial. γαμῆσαι aor.
inf. ■ χωροῦσιν pres. χωρέω to make room, to have room for, 11
to contain, to comprehend, understand (BAG). δέδοται perf.
pass. δίδωμι. ■ εὐνοῦχος eunuch, an emasculated man, keeper 12
of the bed chamber in an oriental harem (TDNT; EGT). ὅστις
which ones, indicates those belonging to a class. κοιλία womb.
ἐγεννήθησαν aor. pass. γεννάω to bare, pass. to be born.
εὐνουχίσθησαν aor. pass. εὐνουχίζω to castrate. εὐνούχισαν
aor. ἑαυτούς reflex. pron. 3rd per. διά w. acc. because of.
δυνάμενος pres. part. δύναμαι to be able to. χωρεῖν pres. inf.
χωρείτω pres. imp. 3rd sing.

■ προσηνέχθησαν aor. pass. προσφέρω to bring to. 13
ἐπιθῇ aor. subj. ἐπιτίθημι to place upon. προσεύξηται aor.
subj. προσεύχομαι to pray. The placing of hands was a symbol
of prayer and blessing (EGT). ἐπετίμησαν aor. ἐπιτιμάω to
rebuke. ■ ἄφετε aor. imp. ἀφίημι to allow. κωλύετε pres. imp. 14
κωλύω to hinder. The pres. imp. with the neg. is used to stop
an action in progress. ἐλθεῖν aor. inf. ἔρχομαι s.v.1. τοιούτων
gen. pl. such as this, of such a kind, gen. of possession. Possessors
of the kingdom are to be like children and all others who have
the child-like spirit (McNeile). ■ ἐπιθείς aor. act. part. 15
ἐπιτίθημι s.v.13. ἐπορεύθη aor. πορεύομαι to go, to leave.
ἐκεῖθεν from there.

■ προσελθών aor. part. s.v.3. ποιήσω fut. s.v.4. σχῶ aor. 16
subj. ἔχω ingressive aor. "may get," "may acquire" (RWP).
αἰώνιος eternal. "Eternal life" contains a temporal reference but
stresses the qualitative reference. It refers to the Jewish concept
of "the life of the age to come" (s. GW, 163–201; MTW, 24–32).
■ ἐρωτᾷς pres. ἐρωτάω to ask. εἰ "if" assumes the reality of 17
the condition. εἰσελθεῖν aor. inf. εἰσέρχομαι to come in, to go
in. τήρει pres. imp. (some mss. τήρησον aor. imp.). τηρέω to
keep, to hold, to observe. ■ ποῖος which ones, or possibly "what 18
sort of" (Filson). ἔφη impf. φημί to say. φονεύσεις fut.
φονεύω to kill. μοιχεύσεις fut. μοιχεύω to commit adultery
s.v.9. κλέψεις fut. κλέπτω to steal. ψευδομαρτυρήσεις fut.

ψευδομαρτυρέω to give false witness, to perjure (AM). (For the use of the fut. for the imp. under Semitic influence, s. MH, 458.)
19 ■ τίμα pres. imp. τιμάω to honor. ἀγαπήσεις fut. ἀγαπάω to
20 love. ὁ πλησίον the one near, neighbor. ■ νεανίσκος young man. ἐφύλαξα aor. φυλάσσω to guard, to observe. ὑστερέω
21 to be in need of, to lack, to fail. ■ τέλειος perfect, complete, perhaps "true," that is, "true to God, true to the covenant" (AM). εἶναι inf. εἰμί. ὕπαγε pres. imp. ὑπάγω. πώλησον aor. imp. πωλέω to sell. ὑπάρχοντα pres. part. ὑπάρχω to be present, to be at one's disposal, part. possessions. δός aor. imp. δίδωμι to give. πτωχός poor. ἕξεις fut. ἔχω. θησαυρός treasure. δεῦρο adv. come, come here (used with the imp.). ἀκολούθει pres. imp. ἀκολουθέω to follow (as a disciple). (S.
22 MNTW, 32–37.) ■ ἀκούσας aor. part. ἀκούω to hear. ἀπῆλθεν aor. ἀπέρχομαι to go away. λυπούμενος pres. pass. part. λυπέω to make sorry, pass. to be sorry, to be sad. ἦν impf. εἰμί. ἔχων pres. part. κτήματα acc. pl. κτῆμα probably "landed property," more definite than "possessions" (McNeile).
23   ■ πλούσιος rich. δυσκόλως difficult, with difficulty
24 (RWP). εἰσελεύσεται fut. εἰσέρχομαι. ■ εὐκοπώτερον comp. εὔκοπος easy. κάμηλος camel. τρῆμα opening, eye. ῥαφίς needle. A proverbial way of expressing something unusually difficult, well nigh impossible (Hill). εἰσελθεῖν aor. inf. The two infs. are used as the subj. of the verb (s. IBG, 127) than.
25 ■ ἐξεπλήσσοντο impf. pass. ἐξπλήσσω to be beside oneself, to be astonished. The impf. may point to a continuous mood culminating at that moment (EGT). λέγοντες part. ἄρα then (draws a logical conclusion). δύναμαι s.v.12. σωθῆναι aor. pass. inf. σῴζω to be rescued, to be saved (s. NTW; TDNT).
26 ■ ἐμβλέψας aor. part. ἐμβλέπω to look at. τοῦτο this (refers to the being saved, Meyer). ἀδύνατος impossible. δύνατος pos-
27 sible. ■ ἀποκριθείς s.v.4. ἡμεῖς "we" (emphatic). ἀφήκαμεν aor. ἀφίημι to leave, to forsake. ἠκολούθησαν aor. s.v.2.
28 ἔσται fut. εἰμί ■ ἀκολουθήσαντες aor. part. παλιγγενεσία regeneration, "the new world." Jewish hopes awaited a renewal both of the land and of the entire world (Hill). (S. HJP, II, ii, 177ff.; CBB; SB, III, 840–847.) καθίσῃ aor. subj. καθίζω to sit. καθήσεσθε fut. κάθημαι to sit. κρίνοντες pres. part. κρίνω to
29 judge, to govern (McNeile). φυλή tribe. ■ ἕνεκεν s.v.5. πολλαπλασίων manifold (v. 1 reading ἑκατονταπλασίων a hundredfold). λήμψεται fut. λαμβάνω to take, to receive. κληρονομήσει fut. κληρονομέω to inherit.

Ch. 20

■ οἰκοδεσπότης ruler of a house, householder. ἐξῆλθεν 1
aor. ἐξέρχομαι to go out. πρωΐ early, "at the same time with
early dawn" (RWP). μισθώσασθαι aor. mid. inf. μισθόω to
hire. Infinitive used to express purpose, vineyard. (For this parable in the light of the Jewish teaching s. SB, IV, 484–500.) ■ 2
συμφωνήσας aor. part. συμφωνέω to agree (s. Matt. 18:19).
ἐκ "for" represents the agreement (RWP). δηνάριον denarius,
a Roman coin worth about 18 cents. A normal day's wage for
laborers (BAG). ἡμέρα day, acc. of time "the whole day" (BD,
88). ἀπέστειλεν aor. ἀποστέλλω to send. ■ ἐξελθών aor. 3
part. περί w. acc. "about." εἶδεν aor. ὁράω to see. ἑστῶτας
perf. part. ἵσταμι to stand. ἀγορά market place. ἀργός idle.
■ ὑπάγετε pres. imp. ὑπάγω to go out. ὃς ἐάν whatever. ᾖ pres. 4
subj. εἰμί to be. δίκαιος right, just. δώσω fut. δίδωμι to give.
■ ἀπῆλθον aor. ἀπέρχομαι to go out. ἐποίησεν aor. ποιέω 5
to do, to make. ὡσαύτως in the same way. ■ εὗρεν aor. 6
εὑρίσκω to find. ἑστήκατε perf. ἵσταμι. ■ ὅτι = quotation 7
marks. ἐμισθώσατο aor. mid. ■ ὀψία evening. γενομένης aor. 8
part. γίνομαι to become. part. used as gen. abs. Payment according to Jewish law was at sunset, that is, 6 P.M. s. Lev. 19:13
(Tasker). ἐπίτροπος overseer, administrator. κάλεσον aor.
imp. καλέω to call. ἀπόδος aor. imp. ἀποδίδωμι to give, to
render, to pay. μισθός reward, payment. ἀρξάμενος aor. mid.
part. ἄρχομαι to begin. ἔσχατος last. ■ ἐλθόντες aor. part. 9
ἔρχομαι. ἔλαβον aor. λαμβάνω to take, to receive. ἀνά prep.
used distributively "each, apiece" (BD, 110). ■ ἐνόμισαν aor. 10
νομίζω to think, to suppose. πλεῖον comp. πολύς more.
λήμψονται fut. λαμβάνω. ■ λαβόντες aor. part. temp. use of 11
the part. ἐγόγγυζον imp. γογγύζω to murmur, to complain, the
inceptive impf. "... they began to ...." κατά w. gen. against.
■ λέγοντες part. μίαν acc. sing. εἷς μία, ἕν one, acc. of time. 12
ἐποίησαν aor. ποιέω to do, here to work. βαστάσασι aor.
part. dat. pl. βαστάζω to bear, to carry. βάρος burden.
καύσων heat. ■ ἀποκριθείς aor. part. ἀποκρίνομαι to an- 13
swer. ἑνί dat. sing. ἕν one. ἑταῖρος friend. General address to
someone whose name is not known (BAG). It implies a rebuke
(MA). ἀδικέω to treat unrighteously. οὐχί in questions which
expect a positive answer. συνεφώνησας aor. ■ ἆρον aor. imp. 14
take, take up. σόν acc. sing. "yours." δοῦναι aor. inf. δίδωμι.
■ ἔξεστιν it is allowed. ποιῆσαι aor. inf. ἐν either instrumental 15
"with" or local "on my property" (s. Jeremias, Parables).
ὀφθαλμός eye "evil eye" designates envy, and jealousy (Hill).
■ ἔσονται fut. εἰμί.   16

17 ■ ἀναβαίνων pres. part. ἀναβαίνω to go up (v. 1 reading μέλλων part. μέλλω to be about to). παρέλαβεν aor.
18 παραλαμβάνω to take to the side. κατ' ἰδίαν privately. ■ παραδοθήσεται fut. pass. παραδίδωμι to give over, to hand over. A technical term of release in courts; "hand over into the custody of" (BAG). ἀρχιερεύς high priest. κατακρινοῦσιν fut. κατακρίνω to condemn. The prep. indicates action unfavorable to the object (MH, 316). The verb indicates Jesus' death will
19 follow a trial to establish legal responsibility (Hill). ■ παραδώσουσιν fut. παραδίδωμι. ἔθνος folk, heathen. εἰς τό w. inf. to show purpose. ἐμπαῖξαι aor. inf. ἐμπαίζω to scourge. μαστιγῶσαι aor. inf. μαστιγόω to crucify. The Jews condemn, the Gentiles scourge and crucify (EGT). τρίτῃ third, dat. of time, on the third day. ἐγερθήσεται fut. pass. ἐγείρω to raise up, pass. to rise, to be raised.
20 ■ προσῆλθεν aor. προσέρχομαι to come to. προσκυνοῦσα pres. part. fem. sing. προσκυνέω to worship. αἰτοῦσα pres. part. fem. sing. αἰτέω to request, to ask. τις
21 something. ■ τί "what?" εἰπέ aor. imp. καθίσωσιν aor. subj. καθίζω to cause to sit down, to seat. δεξιός right. εὐώνυμος left. Such locations indicate positions of honor and authority.
22 Compare Josephus, Antiquities, VI. XI. 9 (Hill). ■ ἀποκριθείς s.v.13. οἶδα defective perf. with a pres. meaning, to know. αἰτεῖσθε pres. mid. δύναμαι to be able to. πιεῖν aor. inf. πίνω
23 to drink. ποτήριον cup. A metaphor of sorrow (Allen). ■ πίεσθε fut. mid. καθίσαι aor. inf. δοῦναι s.v.14. ἡτοίμασται
24 perf. pass. ἑτοιμάζω to prepare. ■ ἀκούσαντες aor. part. ἀκούω to hear. ἠγανάκτησαν aor. ἀγανακτέω to be moved with indignation, implies that they expressed their indignation
25 (Tasker). ■ προσκαλεσάμενος aor. mid. part. προσκαλέομαι to call to oneself. ἄρχων pres. part. ἄρχω used as a noun, ruler. κατακυριεύω to lord it over, to be master. κατεξουσιάζω w. gen. to exercise authority over someone, to play the tyrant
26 (RWP). ■ θέλῃ pres. subj. γενέσθαι aor. inf. s.v.8. ἔσται fut.
27 εἰμί. διάκονος servant, attendant, minister. ■ εἶναι inf. εἰμί.
28 δοῦλος slave. ■ ὥσπερ just as. ἦλθεν aor. ἔρχομαι s.v.9. διακονηθῆναι aor. pass. inf. διακονέω to minister, to serve, pass., to be ministered to. διακονῆσαι aor. inf. λύτρον ransom, the price paid for the release of a slave (AM). (For this important theological term s. the following: APC, 9–48; NTW, 76–83; GW, 49–81.) ἀντί for, instead of. There is the notion of exchange and substitution (RWP). πολλοί many. A Semitic way of expressing "all" (Hill).
29 ■ ἐκπορευομένων pres. mid. part. ἐκπορεύομαι to go out,

to go forth, gen. abs. ἠκολούθησεν aor. ἀκολουθέω to follow.
■ τυφλός blind. καθήμενοι pres. part. κάθημαι to sit. 30
ἀκούσαντες s.v.24. παράγω to go by. ἔκραξαν aor. κράζω to
cry out, to scream. λέγοντες s.v.12. ἐλέησον aor. imp. ἐλεέω
to have compassion, to show mercy. ■ ἐπετίμησεν aor. 31
ἐπιτιμάω to rebuke. σιωπήσωσιν aor. subj. σιωπάω to be
quiet. μεῖζον comp. μέγας great, comp. more. ■ στάς aor. part. 32
ἵσταμι to stand. ἐφώνησεν aor' φωνέω to call. ποιήσω aor.
subj. s.v.5. ■ ἀνοιγῶσιν aor. pass. subj. ἀνοίγω to open. ■ 33/34
σπλαγχνισθείς aor. pass. part. σπλαγχνίζομαι to be moved
with compassion (s. MNTW, 156ff.) ἥψατο aor. mid. ἅπτυμαι
ω touch (w. gen.). ὄμμα eye. εὐθέως at once. ἀνέβλεψαν aor.
ἀναβλέπω to see again. The prep. has the force of "again" (MH,
295).

Ch. 21

■ ἤγγισαν aor. ἐγγίζω to draw near. ἦλθον aor. ἔρχομαι 1
to come, to go. ἐλαία olive tree. ἀπέστειλεν aor. ἀποστέλλω
to send. ■ πορεύεσθε pres. imp. πορεύομαι to go. κώμη vil- 2
lage. κατέναντι w. gen. before, opposite (RG, 643f.). εὑρήσετε
fut. εὑρίσκω to find. ὄνος donkey. δεδεμένην perf. pass. part.
δέω to bind. πῶλος a colt. λύσαντες aor. part. λύω to loose.
ἀγάγετε aor. imp. ἄγω to lead. ■ εἴπῃ aor. subj. λέγω. ἐρεῖτε 3
fut. ■ γέγονεν perf. γίνομαι to become, to happen. πληρωθῇ 4
aor. subj. pass. πληρόω to fulfill. ῥηθέν aor. pass. part. λέγω.
■ εἴπατε aor. imp. λέγω. πραΰς meek (s. Matt. 5:5). 5
ἐπιβεβηκώς perf. pass. part. ἐπιβαίνω to get up on, to mount,
perf. mounted, sitting. ὑποζύγιον beast of burden, donkey (lit.
"under the yoke" BAG). ■ πορευθέντες aor. pass. part. 6
ποιήσαντες aor. act. part. ποιέω to do, to make. συνέταξεν
aor. συντάσσω to command, to instruct. ■ ἤγαγον aor. ἄγω. 7
ἐπέθηκαν aor. ἐπιτίθημι to place upon. ἐπεκάθισεν aor.
ἐπικαθίζω to seat oneself. ἐπάνω w. gen. upon, on. αὐτῶν
them, refers to the garments, not to the animals (RWP). ■ 8
πλεῖστος superl. πολύς. ἔστρωσαν aor. στρώννυμι to spread
out. ἔκοπτον impf. κόπτω to cut. κλάδος branch. ἐστρώννυον
impf. The impf. compared with the aor. shows the growing enthusiasm of the crowd (RWP). ■ προάγοντες pres. part. 9
προάγω to proceed, to go before. ἀκολουθοῦντες pres. part.
ἀκολουθέω to follow. ἔκραζον impf. κράζω to shout. The impf.
pictures the repeated shouting. ὡσαννά Hosanna a Heb. expression from Ps. 118:25 originally "Save, we pray." Here used
as a cry of greeting, an homage "glory, or hail, or welcome to
David's son" (Allen). εὐλογημένος perf. pass. part. εὐλογέω to

61

praise, to bless. ἐρχόμενος pres. part. "The one who is coming,"
perhaps a Messianic title (Hill). ὕψιστος superl. ὕψι the highest.
The angels are invoked to shout hosanna to God (McNeile).
Psalm 118 was used liturgically at the Feasts of Tabernacles,
10 Dedication, and Passover (Hill). ■ εἰσελθόντος aor. part.
εἰσέρχομαι to come in, to go in; part. used as gen. abs. ἐσείσθη
aor. pass. σείω to shake, to stir. Shaken as by an earthquake
11 (Filson). ■ ἔλεγον impf.
12   ■ εἰσῆλθεν aor. εἰσέρχομαι s.v.10. ἐξέβαλεν aor.
ἐκβάλλω to throw out (with force). πωλοῦντας pres. part.
πωλέω to sell. ἀγοράζοντας pres. part. ἀγοράζω to buy.
κολλυβιστής moneychanger. (For money changing in the temple s. LT, I, 367–374; M, Shek., 1, 3, 6.) κατέστρεψεν aor.
καταστρέφω to turn over. κάθεδρα chair, seat. περιστερά
13 dove. ■ γέγραπται perf. pass. γράφω to write. προσευχή
worship, prayer. κληθήσεται fut. pass. καλέω to call. ποιεῖτε
pres. s.v.6. σπήλαιον cave, den. λῃστής robber. Jesus' action
is in fulfillment of Mal. 3:1ff. and is to be taken as a Messianic
sign (Hill).
14   ■ προσῆλθον aor. προσέρχομαι to come to. τυφλός
15 blind. χωλός lame. ἐθεράπευσεν aor. θεραπεύω to heal. ■
ἰδόντες aor. part. ὁράω to see. ἀρχιερεύς high priest.
θαυμάσιος wonderful, wonder. ἐποίησεν aor. παῖς child.
κράζοντας pres. part. s.v.9. λέγοντας pres. part.
16 ἠγανάκτησαν aor. ἀγανακτέω to be unwilling. ■ εἶπαν aor.
λέγω. ναί yes. οὐδέποτε never. ἀνέγνωτε aor. ἀναγινώσκω
to read. θηλαζόντων pres. part. θηλάζω to suck, to nurse.
κατηρτίσω aor. mid. 2nd sing. καταρτίζω to furnish, to pre-
17 pare. αἶνος praise. ■ καταλιπών aor. part. καταλείπω to depart, to leave. ἐξῆλθεν aor. ἐξέρχομαι to go out. ἔξω outside.
ηὐλίσθη aor. pass. αὐλίζομαι to spend the night, to find lodging. Not necessarily spending the night in the open (McNeile).
18   ■ πρωΐ early. ἐπαναγαγών aor. part. ἐπανάγω to return.
19 ἐπείνασεν aor. πεινάω to be hungry. ■ ἰδών s.v.15. συκῆ fig
tree. ἦλθεν s.v.1. εὗρεν aor. εὑρίσκω s.v.2. εἰ μή except.
φύλλον leaf. μόνον only. οὐ μηκέτι no longer. γένηται aor.
subj. γίνομαι s.v.4. Subjunctive used in prohibition ἐξηράνθη
aor. pass. ξηραίνω to dry up, pass., to be dried up. παραχρῆμα
20 adv. at once, immediately, on the spot (Thayer). ■ ἐθαύμασαν
aor. θαυμάζω to wonder at, to marvel. λέγοντες pres. part.
21   ■ ἀποκριθείς aor. pass. part. ἀποκρίνομαι to answer. ἔχητε
aor. subj. ἔχω. διακριθῆτε aor. subj. pass. διακρίνω to be divided in mind, to waver, to doubt (RWP). ποιήσετε fut. s.v.6. κἄν
= καὶ ἐάν even if. εἴπητε s.v.3. ἄρθητι aor. imp. pass. αἴρω

to cast, to throw. **γενήσεται** fut. **γίνομαι**. ■ **ὄσος** as great, how 22
great, whatever. **ἄν** used with the preceding "whatever."
αἰτήσητε aor. subj. **αἰτέω** to ask, to request. **πιστεύοντες** pres.
part. **πιστεύω** to believe, to trust. The part. expresses either
condition or manner. **λήμψεσθε** fut. mid. **λαμβάνω** to take, to
receive.
   ■ **ἐλθόντος** aor. part. **ἔρχομαι** s.v.1. Participle used as gen. 23
abs. **προσῆλθον** s.v.14. **διδάσκοντι** pres. part. dat. sing.
ἀρχιερεύς s.v.15. **πρεσβύτερος** elder. **λέγοντες** part. **ποῖος**
what kind of? **ἔδωκεν** aor. **δίδωμι** to give. ■ **ἀποκριθείς** s.v.21. 24
ἐρωτήσω fut. **ἐρωτάω** to question, to ask. **ὃς ἐάν** "which, if."
The relative clause has the character of a condition (BD, 192).
εἴπητε s.v.3. **ἐρῶ** fut. **λέγω**. ■ **πόθεν** where. **διαλογίζοντο** 25
impf. mid. **διαλογίζομαι** to discuss, to reason. The impf. points
to continual action describing their hopeless quandary (RWP).
διὰ τί why? **ἐπιστεύσατε** aor. s.v.22. ■ **φοβούμεθα** pres. mid. 26
φοβέομαι to be afraid, to fear. ■ **οἶδα** defective perf. w. pres. 27
meaning "to know." **ἔφη** impf. **φημί** to say.
   ■ **τί ὑμῖν δοκεῖ** "What does it seem to you?" "What do you 28
think?" (s. Matt. 17:25). **προσελθών** aor. part. **προσέρχομαι**.
ὕπαγε pres. imp. **ὑπάγω** to go forth. **ἐργάζου** pres. imp. mid.
ἐργάζομαι to work. **ἀμπελών** vineyard. ■ **ἀπῆλθεν** aor. 29
ἀπέρχομαι to go forth. ■ **δεύτερος** the second. **ὡσαύτως** like- 30
wise. **ὕστερον** later. **μεταμεληθείς** aor. pass. part.
μεταμέλομαι to be sorry, to be sorry afterward (RWP; s. also
TDNT; Trench, *Synonyms* 255ff.). ■ **ἐκ** "of" (s. BD, 90). 31
ἐποίησεν aor. s.v.6. **τελώνης** tax collector. **πόρνη** prostitute.
προάγω to go before, precede. (For the prep. in the verb s. MH,
322f.) ■ **ἦλθεν** s.v.1. **ἐν ὁδῷ δικαιοσύνης** "with the path of 32
righteousness," that is, with the message of righteousness. The
obligation of obedience to the divine will as both preached and
practiced by John (GW, 124, 125). **ἐπιστεύσατε** aor. s.v.22.
ἰδόντες s.v.15. **μετεμελήθητε** aor. pass. s.v.30. **τοῦ** with the
inf. expresses either purpose or result (s. IBG, 128f.).
   ■ **ἀκούσατε** aor. imp. s.v.16. **οἰκοδεσπότης** master of the 33
house, a householder. **ὅστις** who (s. M, 91f.). **ἐφύτευσεν** aor.
φυτεύω to plant. **φραγμός** fence. Protection against wild beasts
(McNeile). **περιέθηκεν** aor. **περιτίθημι** to place around.
ὤρυξεν aor. **ὀρύσσω** to dig. **ληνός** winepress. The winepress
consists of two parts, where the grapes were crushed and where
the juice fell (McNeile; TDNT). **ᾠκοδόμησεν** aor. **οἰκοδομέω**
to build. **πύργος** tower. For the winedressers and watchmen
(RWP). **ἐξέδοτο** aor. mid. **ἐκδίδωμι** to lease out. **γεωργός**
farmer, tenant farmer. They had to pay a portion of the crops

each year as their rent (Tasker). ἀπεδήμησεν aor. ἀποδημέω
34 to go on a journey. ■ ἤγγισεν s.v.1. ἀπέστειλεν s.v.1. λαβεῖν
35 aor. inf. λαμβάνω s.v.22, the inf. used to express purpose. ■
λαβόντες aor. part. λαμβάνω. ἔδειραν aor. δέρω to flay, to
skin, to beat. ἀπέκτειναν aor. ἀποκτείνω to kill.
36 ἐλιθοβόλησαν aor. λιθοβολέω to stone to death. ■ πλείονας
37 comp. πολύς more. τῶν πρώτων gen. of comp. ■ ὕστερον
finally, at last, superl. emphasizing the end of a series (BD, 34).
ἐντραπήσονται fut. pass. ἐντρέπω to make someone ashamed,
to be put to shame, to have regard or respect for someone
38 (BAG). ■ κληρονόμος heir. δεῦτε come, come on.
ἀποκτείνωμεν aor. subj. hortatory, "let us kill." σχῶμεν aor.
subj. ἔχω hortatory, "let us get his inheritance" (RWP).
39/40 κληρονομία inheritance. ■ ἐξέβαλον s.v.12. ■ ἔλθῃ aor. subj.
41 ἔρχομαι. ποιήσει fut. ■ ἀπολέσει fut. ἀπόλλυμι to destroy.
ἐκδώσεται fut. mid. ἐκδίδωμι to lease out. ἀποδώσουσιν fut.
42 ἀποδίδωμι to pay, to give back, to give over. ■ ἀνέγνωτε aor.
s.v.16. λίθος stone. The acc. is inverse attraction of the antecedent to the case of the relative (MT, 324). ἀπεδοκίμασαν aor.
ἀποδοκιμάζω to reject after scrutiny, to declare useless (BAG).
οἰκοδομοῦντες pres. part. w. the article used as a noun.
ἐγενήθη aor. pass. γίνομαι s.v.4. γωνία corner. ἐγένετο aor.
43 mid. γίνομαι. ■ διὰ τοῦτο because of this, because.
ἀρθήσεται fut. pass. αἴρω s.v.21. δοθήσεται fut. pass. δίδωμι
to give. ἔθνει dat. sing. ἔθνος folk, nation. ποιοῦντι pres. part.
44 ■ πεσών aor. act. part. πίπτω to fall. συνθλασθήσεται fut.
pass. συνθλάω to crush. πέσῃ aor. subj. λικμήσει fut. λικμάω
to break into small pieces or to scatter as dust (Allen).
45 ■ ἀκούσαντες aor. part. ἔγνωσαν aor. act. γινώσκω to
46 know, to understand. ■ ζητοῦντες pres. part. ζητέω to seek,
concessive use of the part. "although . . . ." κρατῆσαι aor. inf.
κρατέω to seize, to arrest. ἐφοβήθησαν aor. pass. ἐπεί since,
because. εἰς "as" used with the pred. acc. or double acc. (s. RG,
481ff.; IBG, 70). εἶχον impf. ἔχω.

Ch. 22

1/2 ■ ἀποκριθείς aor. pass. part. ἀποκρίνομαι. ■ ὡμοιώθη
aor. pass. ὁμοιόω to compare, to make alike, pass. to be like.
ὅστις rel. pron. who, emphasizing the class or kind to which one
belongs. γάμους wedding feast, pl. because the festivities lasted
3 for days (EGT; TDNT). ■ ἐποίησεν aor. ποιέω to send.
καλέσαι aor. inf. καλέω to call, to summon. κεκλημένους
perf. pass. part. καλέω. The words imply the guest had been
invited previously; the announcement now being that the feast

was ready (McNeile). ἤθελον impf. (ἐ) θέλω. The impf. pictures
the repeated rejection. ἐλθεῖν aor. inf. ἔρχομαι to come. ■ 4
εἴπατε aor. imp. λέγω. ἄριστον breakfast, toward midday,
with which the series of meals connected with the marriage was
to begin (Meyer). ἡτοίμακα perf. ἐτοιμάζω to prepare. ταῦρος
steer. σιτιστός fattened ones, verbal from the verb to feed with
wheat or other grain, to fatten (RWP). τεθυμένα perf. pass. part.
θύω to slaughter. ἔτοιμος ready. δεῦτε come! ■ ἀμελήσαντες 5
aor. part. ἀμελέω to neglect, to be unconcerned. ἀπῆλθον aor.
ἀπέρχομαι to go forth. ὅς μέν ... ὅς δέ used indef. "one ...
another" (BD, 131). ἐμπορία trade, business. ■ κρατήσαντες 6
aor. part. κρατέω to seize. ὕβρισαν aor. ὑβρίζω to treat in an
arrogant or spiteful manner, to mistreat, to insult. Treatment
which is calculated publicly to insult and openly to humiliate the
person who suffers from it (MNTW; s. also TDNT).
ἀπέκτειναν aor. ἀποκτείνω to kill. ■ ὠργίσθη aor. pass. 7
ὀργίζω to anger, pass. to be angry, ingressive aor. "he became
angry." πέμψας aor. part. πέμπω to send. στράτευμα army,
bands of soldiers (RWP). ἀπώλεσεν aor. ἀπόλλυμι to destroy.
φονεύς murderer. ἐνέπρησεν aor. ἐμπί(μ)πρημι to set on fire,
to burn. ■ πορεύεσθε pres. imp. mid. πορεύομαι to go. 9
διέξοδος outlet, street crossing, more probably the place where
a street cuts through the city boundary and goes out into the
open country (BAG). εὕρητε aor. subj. εὑρίσκω to find.
καλέσατε aor. imp. ■ ἐξελθόντες aor. part. ἐξέρχομαι to go 10
out. συνήγαγον aor. συνάγω. εὗρον aor. τε ... καί both ...
and. ἐπλήσθη aor. pass. πίμπλημι to fill, to be full.
ἀνακειμένων pres. part. ἀνάκειμαι to recline (at the table).
■ εἰσελθὼν aor. part. εἰσέρχομαι to go in. θεάσασθαι aor. 11
mid. inf. θεάομαι to look at, to view, inf. used to express purpose. εἶδεν aor. ὁράω to see. ἐνδεδυμένον perf. pass. part.
ἐνδύω to put on, to clothe. (For the use of the negative with the
part. s. M, 231f.) ἔνδυμα garment, clothes. Perhaps only clean
clothes were expected (AM). ■ ἑταῖρος friend (s. Matt. 20:13). 12
εἰσῆλθες aor. εἰσέρχομαι. ἔχων pres. part. ἐφιμώθη aor. pass.
φιμόω to put to silence, to muzzle. ■ διάκονος servant, min- 13
ister. δήσαντες aor. part. δέω to bind. ἐκβάλετε aor. imp.
ἐκβάλλω to cast out. ἐξώτερος adjectival comp. of the adv.
used as superl.; fartherest, extreme, "the darkness fartherest out"
(BAG). κλαυθμός loud crying, wailing. βρυγμός gnashing,
grinding. ὀδούς tooth. ■ κλητός called. ἐκλεκτός chosen, elect. 14
■ πορευθέντες aor. pass. part. s.v.9. συμβούλιον counsel. 15
ἔλαβον aor. λαμβάνω to take. ὅπως in order that, introduces
a purpose clause (BD, 186). παγιδεύσωσιν aor. subj.

16 παγιδεύω to ensnare, to catch in a trap. ■ λέγοντας pres. part. οἶδα to know. μέλει σοι "it is a care or concern," "you court

17 no man's favor" (BAG). ■ εἰπόν aor. imp. λέγω. δοκεῖ σοι "what do you think?" ἔξεστιν is lawful, "Is it warranted by anything in the Law or the Scribal tradition?" (McNeile). δοῦναι aor. inf. δίδωμι to give. κῆνσος poll tax, to be paid by all males over 14 and females over 12, up to the age of 65

18 (McNeile). ■ γνούς aor. act. part. γινώσκω to know, to recog-

19 nize. πειράζω to tempt. ■ ἐπιδείξατε aor. imp. ἐπιδείκνυμι to show. νόμισμα coin. προσήνεγκαν aor. προσφέρω to bring to. δηνάριον denarius. A Roman silver coin, a workman's aver-

20 age daily wage (BAG). ■ εἰκών image. ἐπιγραφή inscription. The imperial tax was paid in coins which bore the head of the emperor, and inscriptions which described the religious and cul-

21 tic claims of the Caesar (Hill). ■ ἀπόδοτε aor. imp. ἀποδίδωμι to give back. It has the sense of giving back what is due (AM).

22 ■ ἀκούσαντες aor. part. ἀκούω to hear. ἐθαύμασαν aor. θαυμάζω to be amazed. ἀφέντες aor. part. ἀφίημι to leave. ἀπῆλθαν s.v.5.

23   ■ προσῆλθον aor. προσέρχομαι to come to. ἀνάστασις resurrection. ἐπηρώτησαν aor. ἐπερωτάω to ask about (the

24 prep. in the verb is directive). ■ ἀποθάνῃ aor. subj. ἀποθνήσκω to die. ἐπιγαμβρεύσει fut. ἐπιγαμβρεύω to become related by marriage, to marry as next of kin. ἀναστήσει

25 fut. ἀνίστημι to raise up. ■ γήμας aor. part. γαμέω to marry. ἐτελεύτησεν aor. τελευτάω to die. ἀφῆκεν aor. ἀφίημι s.v.22.

27/28 ■ ὕστερον latter, last. ἀπέθανεν aor. ἀποθνήσκω. ■ εἰμί w.

29 gen. shows possession. ἔσχον aor. ἔχω. ■ πλανᾶσθε pres. pass. πλανάω to lead astray, pass. to go astray, to be mislead. εἰδότες

30 part. οἶδα to know. γραφή Scripture. ■ οὔτε ... οὔτε neither, nor. γαμοῦσιν pres. γαμίζονται pres. pass. γαμίζω to give a

31 woman in marriage, pass., to be given in marriage. ■ ἀνέγνωτε

32 aor. ἀναγινώσκω to read. ῥηθέν aor. pass. part. λέγω. ζώντων pres. part. ζάω to live. The argument stands on the use

33 of the gen. (McNeile). ■ ἀκούσαντες s.v.22. ἐξεπλήσσοντο impf. pass. ἐκπλήσσω to be beside oneself, to be amazed, over-whelmed. διδαχή teaching.

34   ■ ἐφίμωσεν aor. s.v.12. συνήχθησαν aor. pass. συνάγω

35 to gather together, to come together. ■ ἐπηρώτησεν s.v.23. νομικός lawyer, a man learned in the law of Moses, that is, a scribe belonging to the Pharisaic party (Hill). πειράζων pres.

36 part. s.v.18. ■ μέγας positive of the adj. used as superl. "the

37 greatest" (BD, 127). ■ ἔφη impf. φημί to say. ἀγαπήσεις fut.

39 ἀγαπάω to love. διανοίᾳ understanding. ■ πλησίον adv. near,

used as a noun, neighbor. ■ κρέμαται pres. κρεμάννυμι to 40
hang.

■ συνηγμένων perf. pass. part. συνάγω s.v.34. gen. abs. 41
■ τοῦ Δαυίδ gen. of relationship (RG, 501f.). (For the Messiah 42
as the Son of David s. SB, I, 525; Moore, *Judaism*, II, 328f.;
Fitzmyer, *Essays*, 113–126; CEC 109f.; cf. also 4QFlor. 1:11-
13.) ■ κάθου pres. imp. κάθημαι to sit. θῶ aor. subj. τίθημι to 44
set, to place. ἐχθρός enemy. ὑποκάτω under. (For Ps. 110 in
rabbinical literature s. SB, IV, 452–465.) ■ ἐδύνατο impf. 46
δύναμαι. ἀποκριθῆναι aor. pass inf s.v.1. ἐτόλμησεν aor.
τολμάω to dare.

Ch. 23

■ ἐλάλησεν aor. λαλέω to speak. ■ κάθεδρα chair. A soft 1/2
seat with a back (Jastrow, II, 1434). Not simply a metaphor for
there was an actual stone seat in front of the synagogue where
the authoritative teacher sat (Hill). ἐκάθισαν aor. καθίζω to
take a seat, to sit. The aor. is a timeless aor. (RWP). ■ εἴπωσιν 3
aor. subj. λέγω. ποιήσατε aor. imp. ποιέω to do. τηρεῖτε pres.
imp. τηρέω to observe. The aor. imp. indicates "start to do," the
pres. "continue to observe" (s. Bakker, 434). ποιεῖτε pres. imp.
ποιοῦσιν pres. ■ δεσμεύω to bind, to tie on. φορτίον burden. 4
βαρύς heavy. ἐπιτιθέασιν pres. ἐπιτίθημι to place upon.
ὦμος shoulder. δάκτυλος finger, instrumental dat. "with the
finger." κινῆσαι aor. inf. κινέω to move, to remove. ■ πρὸς τό 5
with the inf. used to express purpose (TDNT). θεαθῆναι aor.
pass. inf. θεάομαι to look upon, used in the sense of careful and
deliberate vision which interprets its object (AS). πλατύνω to
make wide. φυλακτήριον means of protection, amulet, protec-
tive charms, phylacteries, small leather cases containing portions
of Scripture. These were strapped to the left hand and to the
forehead (s. SB, IV, 250–276; HBD, III, 869–874; NBD, 995).
μεγαλύνω to make large. κράσπεδον fringes, tassels. These
were worn on the corner of the outer garment in accord with
Num. 15:38f.; Deut. 22:12. But the Pharisees lengthened theirs
in order to call attention to their piety (Hill). ■ φιλοῦσιν pres. 6
φιλέω to love. πρωτοκλισία place of honor at a dinner, beside
the master of the house or host (BAG). δεῖπνον dinner, the
main meal. πρωτοκαθεδρία chief seat. These were on the platform facing the congregation with their backs to the chest in
which the rolls of Scripture were kept. (McNeile). ■ ἀσπασμός 7
greeting. Disciples were never to greet their masters since this
implied a certain equality (AM). καλεῖσθαι pres. pass. inf.
καλέω to call. ῥαββί master, teacher (TDNT). ■ κληθῆτε aor. 8

subj. pass. καλέω used w. the neg. to express a prohibition of an
9/10 action that should not arise. ■ καλέσητε aor. subj. ■
11/12 καθηγητής teacher. ■ μείζων comp. μέγας ■ ὑψώσει fut.
ὑψόω to lift up, to exalt. ταπεινωθήσεται fut. pass. ταπεινόω
to make low, to humble. ταπεινώσει fut. ὑψωθήσεται fut. pass.
13   ■ οὐαί woe. κλείω to shut, to lock. εἰσέρχομαι to go in,
to come in. εἰσερχομένους pres. mid. part. conative use of the
pres. "Those who are in the process of entering—trying to enter"
(McNeile). ἀφίετε pres. ἀφίημι to allow. εἰσελθεῖν aor. inf.
εἰσέρχομαι
15   ■ περιάγω to go about, to travel about. ξηρά dry land.
ποιῆσαι aor. inf. προσήλυτος proselyte (s. TDNT; Moore,
Judaism, I, 323–353). γένηται aor. subj. γίνομαι to become.
γέεννα gehenna, "son of gehenna," one fitted and destined for
gehenna (McNeile). διπλότερον comp. δίπλους double. ὑμῶν
gen. of comp.
16   ■ ὁδηγός guide. τυφλός blind. ὃς ἄν whoever. The relative
clause has the character of a condition. ὀμόσῃ aor. subj. ὄμνυμι
to swear. νάος temple. οὐδέν ἐστιν "it is nothing," the formula
for a non-binding oath (EGT). χρυσός gold. ὀφείλω to be indebted, bound to performance, the formula for a binding oath
17 (EGT). ■ μωρός foolish, fool. ἁγίασας aor. part. ἁγιάζω to
18 sanctify, to make holy. ■ θυσιαστήριον altar. ἐπάνω w. gen.,
19/20 upon. ■ ἁγιάζον pres. act. part. ὀμόσας aor. act. part.
21 ὄμνυμι ■ κατοικοῦντι pres. act. part. dat. sing. κατοικέω to
22 dwell, to reside. ■ καθημένῳ pres. part. κάθημαι to sit.
23   ■ ἀποδεκατοῦτε pres. ἀποδεκατόω to tithe, to give a
tenth. (For the tithe s. M, Maaseroth; M, Maaser Sheni.)
ἡδύοσμον mint. ἄνηθον dill, used for seasoning (Filson).
κύμινον cumin, used as spice and medicine (Filson). ἀφήκατε
aor. ind. ἀφίημι. βαρύτερα comp. βαρύς. κρίσις justice. The
respect for the rights of others which gives a just judgment (Hill).
ἔλεος mercy. ἔδει impf. δεῖ it is necessary. ποιῆσαι aor. inf.
24 ἀφεῖναι aor. inf. ἀφίημι. ■ διϋλίζοντες pres. part. διϋλίζω to
strain out by filtering through (RWP). (Note the prep. "through"
in compound. S. MH, 300f.) κώνωψ gnat. κάμηλος camel.
καταπίνοντες pres. part. καταπίνω to swallow, to drink down.
(Note the prep. "down" in the compound.)
25   ■ καθαρίζω to cleanse. ἔξωθεν outside. ποτήριον cup.
παροψίς dish. (For the cleaning of vessels s. M, Kleim.) ἔσωθεν
inside. γέμω to be full. ἁρπαγή robbery, plunder. Obtained by
violent or dishonest practices (Filson). ἀκρασία lack of self-
control which shows itself in an unrestrained desire for gain
26 (McNeile). ■ καθάρισον aor. imp. ἐντός inside. ἐκτός outside.

■ παρομοιάζω to be like, to compare. τάφος grave. 27
κεκονιαμένοις perf. pass. part. κονιάω to make white, to whit-
en with chalk or lime. Before the Passover it was customary to
whitewash graves that people might not unintentionally touch
them or contract ceremonial defilement (Allen). φαίνομαι to
appear. ὡραῖος beautiful. ὀστέον bone. ■ μεστός full (w. gen.). 28
ὑπόκρισις hypocrite, casuist, one who engages in legal hair-
splitting (AM, CXII–CXXIII). ἀνομία lawlessness. (For the
alpha privative which negates the word, s. A.C. Moorhouse,
Studies in the Greek Negatives, 41–68.)

■ οἰκοδομειτε pres. οἰκοδομέω to build. κοσμεῖτε pres. 29
act. κοσμέω to put into order, to decorate. The erecting of
monuments to mark the graves of Israel's heroes may have been
initiated by Herod the Great's building of a monument at David's tomb. Such monuments may have had an expiatory character (Hill). μνημεῖον monument. ■ ἤμεθα impf. ind. 1st pl. 30
εἰμί. ἄν used to introduce the second part of a contrary to fact
conditional clause. ■ ὥστε therefore. μαρτυρεῖτε pres. act. 31
μαρτυρέω to testify. φονευσάντων aor. act. part. φονεύω to
kill. ■ πληρώσατε aor. imp. πληρόω to fill, to fill up. "Perform 32
then that with the hand that which you cherish in the heart"
(Bengel). μέτρον measure. ■ ὄφις snake. γέννημα that which 33
is born, brood. ἔχιδνα a poisonous snake. (s. Matt. 3:7). φύγητε
aor. subj. φεύγω to flee. The subj. is used in doubtful or deliberate question. "How shall (can) you escape?" (BD, 185; s. also
MKG, 244). ■ διὰ τοῦτο because of this. ἀποστέλλω to send. 34
σοφός wise. ἀποκτενεῖτε fut. ἀποκτείνω to kill. σταυρώσετε
fut. σταυρόω to crucify. μαστιγώσετε fut. μαστιγόω to
scourge. διώξετε fut. διώκω to hunt, to pursue, to persecute.
■ ἔλθῃ aor. subj. ἔρχομαι to come, to go. αἷμα δίκαιον inno- 35
cent blood (Hill). ἐκχυννόμενον pres. pass. part. ἐκχέω to shed,
to pour out. ἐφονεύσατε aor. μεταξύ between. ■ ἥξει fut. ἥκω 36
to come. γενεά generation.
    ■ ἀποκτείνουσα pres. act. part. fem. sing. λιθοβολοῦσα 37
pres. act. part. fem. sing. λιθοβολέω to stone. The part. with the
article are almost substantives, "the killer of . . . the stoner of
. . ." (McNeile; s. M, 127f.). ἀπεσταλμένους perf. pass. part.
ἀποστέλλω. ποσάκις how often. ἠθέλησα aor. θέλω.
ἐπισυναγαγεῖν aor. act. inf. ἐπισυνάγω to gather together.
(For the double prep. w. the verb s. MH, 312.) τρόπος like, in
like manner. ὄρνις bird, hen, the mother bird (McNeile).
νοσσίον a young bird. πτέρυξ wing. ἠθελήσατε aor. θέλω
■ ἴδητε aor. subj. ὁράω to see. εἴπητε aor. subj. λέγω. 39
εὐλογημένος perf. pass. part. εὐλογέω to bless, to praise, pass.,

blessed.

Ch. 24

1   ■ ἐξελθών aor. part. ἐξέρχομαι to go out. ἐπορεύετο impf. πορεύομαι to go, to precede. προσῆλθον aor. προσέρχομαι to come to. ἐπιδεῖξαι aor. act. inf. ἐπιδείκνυμι to show, to
2 point out. οἰκοδομή building. ■ ἀποκριθείς aor. pass. part. ἀποκρίνομαι to answer. ἀφεθῇ aor. subj. pass. ἀφίημι to leave, pass., to be left. καταλυθήσεται fut. pass. καταλύω to throw down, to destroy, to demolish.
3   ■ καθημένου pres. part. κάθημαι to sit. κατ᾿ ἰδίαν privately. εἰπέ aor. imp. πότε when. σημεῖον sign. παρουσία presence, arrival, coming (TDNT; CBB; NTW). συντέλεια end, consumation. (For a prophetical study of Matt. 24; 25 s. John F. Walvoord, "Christ's Olivet Discourse on the End of the Age," Bib Sac, 128, 129 [1971–72].) Matthew supplies no answer re-
4 garding the destruction of the temple (McNeile). ■ βλέπετε pres. imp. to beware. μή "lest." πλανήσῃ aor. subj. πλανάω to
5 lead astray. ■ ἐλεύσονται fut. ἔρχομαι to come, to go.
6 πλανήσουσιν fut. ■ μελλήσετε fut. μέλλω to be about to. (For the use of this word to express the durative fut. s. MKG, 307, "you will continually hear.") πόλεμος war. ἀκοή rumor. ὁρᾶτε pres. imp. ὁράω to see. (For the use of the two imps. s. RG, 949.) θροεῖσθε pres. imp. θροέομαι to cry aloud, to scream, pass., to be terrified by an outcry (RWP). δεῖ it is necessary. γενέσθαι aor. mid. inf. γίνομαι to become, to happen.
7 οὔπω not yet. ■ ἐγερθήσεται fut. pass. ἐγείρω pass., to rise up, to rise up against. ἔθνος folk, nation. λιμός famine. σεισμός earthquake. κατὰ τόπους "in various places." (For the distribu-
8 tive use of the prep. w. the acc. s. RG, 608.) ■ ἀρχή beginning. ὠδίν birth pangs, labor pains, travail. The Jews used the phrase to signify the time of unprecedented trouble which was to precede the Messianic salvation (Allen; s. also HJP, II, ii, 154–156;
9 Moore, *Judaism*, II, 361f.). ■ παραδώσουσιν fut. παραδίδωμι to deliver over. θλῖψις pressure, tribulation. ἀποκτενοῦσιν fut. ἀποκτείνω to kill. μισούμενοι pres. pass. part. μισέω to hate.
10 ■ σκανδαλισθήσονται fut. pass. σκανδαλίζω to cause to
11 stumble (s. TDNT). μισήσουσιν fut. act. ■ ψευδοπροφήτης
12 false prophet. ■ πληθυνθῆναι aor. pass. inf. πληθύνω to increase, to multiply, pass., to be multiplied, to grow. The prep. is used with the inf. to express cause (MT, 142f.). ἀνομία lawlessness (s. Matt 23:28). ψυγήσεται fut. pass. ψύχω to make cold,
13 pass., to become cold. ■ ὑπομείνας aor. act. part. ὑπομένω to
14 endure. σωθήσεται fut. pass. σῴζω to save, to rescue. ■

κηρυχθήσεται fut. pass. κηρύσσω. οἰκουμένη the inhabited earth. μαρτύριον witness. ἥξει fut. ἥκω to come.

■ ὅταν whenever. ἴδητε aor. subj. ὁράω. βδέλυγμα 15 abomination, detestable thing. ἐρήμωσις desolation. "An abominable thing that layeth waste" (McNeile). A reference to the Anti-Christ (the man of sin) 2 Thess. 2:3f. (Hill). ῥηθέν aor. pass. part. λέγω. ἑστός perf. act. part. ἵσταμι to place, perf., to stand. ἀναγινώσκων pres. act. part. ἀναγινώσκω to read. νοείτω pres. imp. νοέω to understand. ■ φευγέτωσαν pres. 16 imp. 3rd pl. φεύγω to flee. ■ δῶμα roof. καταβάτω aor. imp. 17 3rd sing. καταβαίνω to come down. ἆραι aor inf. αἴρω to pick up, to take. Infinitive used to express purpose. ■ ἐπιστρεψάτω 18 aor imp. 3rd sing. ἐπιστρέφω to turn about, to return. ὀπίσω back, behind. ■ οὐαί woe. γαστήρ stomach. ἐχούσαις pres. 19 act. part. fem. dat. pl. ἔχω "to have something in the stomach," that is, "to be pregnant." θηλαζούσαις pres. act. part. fem. θηλάζω to suck, to nurse. ■ προσεύχεσθε pres. mid. imp. 20 προσεύχομαι to pray. γένηται aor. subj. γίνομαι. φυγή flight, escape. χειμών storm, winter. σαββάτῳ dat. of time. ■ γέγονεν perf. γίνομαι ■ εἰ μή "if not," "except," introduces 21/22 a contrary to fact conditional clause. ἐκολοβώθησαν aor. pass. κολοβόω to mutilate, to curtail, to shorten (BAG). ἐσώθη aor. pass. σώζω to save, to rescue. ἐκλεκτός elect, chosen. κολοβωθήσονται fut. pass. ■ εἴπῃ aor. subj. πιστεύσητε aor. 23 subj. πιστεύω to trust, to believe; with neg. it is a prohibition not to start an action. ■ ψευδόχριστος false Christ. δώσουσιν 24 fut. δίδωμι to give. τέρας wonder, that which is startling, imposing, amazement, waking (Trench, Synonyms; TDNT; CBB). πλανῆσαι aor. inf. πλανάω. Infinitive used to express result. ■ προείρηκα perf. προλέγω to say beforehand. ■ εἴπωσιν aor. 25/26 subj. ἔρημος desert. ἐξέλθητε aor. subj. ἐξέρχομαι. ταμιεῖον hidden, secret room. ■ ἀστραπή lightning. ἀνατολαί east. 27 φαίνομαι to shine. δυσμαί west. ■ ὅπου (ἐ)άν w. subj. wher- 28 ever. πτῶμα corpse, a fallen one. συναχθήσονται fut. pass. συνάγω to gather together. ἀετός eagle, vulture.

■ εὐθέως adv. immediately. σκοτισθήσεται fut. 29 σκοτίζομαι to become dark, to be dark. σελήνη moon. δώσει fut. δίδωμι. φέγγος light, radiance. ἀστήρ star. πεσοῦνται fut. mid. πίπτω to fall. σαλευθήσονται fut. pass. σαλεύω to shake, to cause to move to and fro. ■ φανήσεται fut. φαίνομαι. 30 κόψονται fut. mid. κόπτω to strike, to strike the breast as a sign of mourning. φυλή tribe. ὄψονται fut. ὁράω to see. ἐρχόμενον pres. mid. part. νεφέλη cloud. δόξα glory. ■ ἀποστελεῖ fut. 31 ἀποστέλλω to send. σάλπιγξ trumpet. ἐπισυνάξουσιν fut.

ἐπισυνάγω to bring together, to gather together, s. Matt. 23:37.
ἄνεμος wind. ἄκρον end.

32   ■ συκῆ fig tree. μάθετε aor. imp. μανθάνω. κλάδος
branch. ἀπαλός tender. φύλλον leaf. ἐκφύῃ pres. subj. ἐκφύω
33 to put forth. θέρος summer. ■ ἴδητε aor. subj. ὁράω. θύρη door.
The putting forth of the fig tree from its state of winter dryness,
symbolizes the future reviviscence of the Jewish people (Alford).
34 ■ παρέλθῃ aor. subj. παρέρχομαι to pass by, to pass away.
35 γενεά race, generation. ■ παρελεύσεται fut. παρέρχομαι.
παρέλθωσιν aor. subj. παρέρχομαι. The dissolution of heaven
and earth would constitute the end of the present age. "The
world shall pass away and my prediction of it shall not fail"
(McNeile).

36/38   ■ οἶδα defective perf. with a pres. meaning, to know. ■
κατακλυσμός flood. τρώγοντες pres. part. τρώγω to gnaw, to
nibble, to munch, to chew raw fruit or vegetables (McNeile).
πίνοντες pres. part. πίνω to drink. γαμοῦντες pres. part.
γαμέω to marry. γαμίζοντες pres. part. γαμίζω to give in
marriage. The parts. are not periphrastic but are descriptive
predicates (EGT). A description of a mode of life without concern and without any foreboding of an impending catastrophe
(Meyer). ἄχρι w. gen. until. εἰσῆλθεν aor. εἰσέρχομαι to go
39 in. κιβωτός ark. ■ ἔγνωσαν aor. γινώσκω. ἦλθεν aor.
40 ἔρχομαι. ἦρεν aor. αἴρω. ■ παραλαμβάνεται pres. pass.
παραλαμβάνω to take to oneself, to take along with, to take
away. The pres. tense pictures what is fut. as though it were
41 already taking place (Meyer). ἀφίεται pres. pass. ἀφίημι. ■
ἀλήθουσαι pres. act. part. fem. pl. ἀλήθω to grind. The work
usually performed by the lower order of female slaves (Meyer).
42 μύλος mill, mill stone. ■ γρηγορεῖτε pres. imp. γρηγορέω to
watch. The pres. imp. indicates a constant vidual. ποία what
43 kind, that of time. ■ ἐκεῖνο refers to that which follows (s. BD,
151f.). γινώσκετε pres. ind. or imp. εἰ w. the ind. and ἄν to
introduce a contrary to fact conditional clause. ᾔδει plperf.
οἶδα. οἰκοδεσπότης ruler of the house. φυλακή night watch.
ἐγρηγόρησεν aor. γρηγορέω εἴασεν aor. ἐάω to allow.
διορυχθῆναι aor. pass. inf. διορύσσω to dig through, to break
through. Dig through the tile roof or under the floor (RWP).
44 ■ γίνεσθε pres. imp. ἕτοιμος ready. ἦ . . . ὥρα "at which hour,"
dat. of time. δοκεῖτε pres. δοκέω to think, to be of an opinion.
45   ■ φρόνιμος sensible, thoughtful, wise. κατέστησεν aor.
καθίστημι to appoint, to constitute. οἰκετεία household
slaves. δοῦναι aor. inf. δίδωμι. The inf. used to express purpose.
46 ■ μακάριος happy. ἐλθών aor. part. ἔρχομαι. The part. used

to express contemporaneous time, "when he comes." εὑρήσει fut. εὑρίσκω to find. ποιοῦντα pres. act. part. acc. masc. sing. ποιέω to do, to make. So performing as was assigned to him. ■ ὑπάρχω, ὑπάρχοντα possessions. καταστήσει fut. 47 καθίστημι. ■ χρονίζω to delay, to take time. ■ ἄρξηται aor. 48/49 subj. ἄρχομαι to begin. τύπτω to strike, to beat. σύνδουλος fellow servant. ἐσθίῃ pres. subj. ἐσθίω to eat. πίνῃ pres. subj. μεθυόντων pres. part. μεθύω to be drunk, "with those who are drunken." ■ προσδοκᾷ pres. act. προσδοκάω to wait for, to 50 expect. ■ διχοτομήσει fut. διχοτομέω to cut in two. In Exod. 51 29:17 the verb is used of dividing a sacrificial victim into pieces (McNeile). (For the treatment of Heb. slaves, s. SB, IV, 698–744.) μέρος lot, part. θήσει fut. τίθημι to place, to assign. κλαυθμός loud crying.

Ch. 25

■ ὁμοιωθήσεται fut. pass. ὁμοιόω to make alike, to com- 1 pare. The kingdom is not like the virgins, but their story illus- trates an aspect of it (McNeile). παρθένος virgin. λαβοῦσαι aor. act. part. fem. pl. λαμβάνω to take. λαμπάς lamp, prob- ably the so-called "Herodian" lamp (s. Matt 5:15). ἐξῆλθον aor. ἐξέρχομαι to go out. ὑπάντησις meeting. This represents the third state of the matrimonial procedure. First engagement, then bethrothal, then the marriage. The bridegroom accompanied by his friends went to fetch the bride from her father's house and brought her back in procession to his own home where the marriage feast was held (Tasker). νυμφίος bridegroom. ■ 2 μωρός foolish. φρόνιμος wise, sensible, thoughtful. ■ ἔλαβον 3 aor. λαμβάνω. ■ ἀγγεῖον vessel, flask. ■ χρονίζοντος pres. 4/5 act. part. χρονίζω to delay, to take one's time. Participle used as gen. abs. ἐνύσταιξαν aor. νυστάζω to nod, to become drowsy, to doze. "They all became drowsy" (BAG). The ingres- sive aor. ἐκάθευδον impf. καθεύδω to sleep. They dropped off to sleep and then went on sleeping (RWP). ■ κραυγή cry, loud 6 calling. γέγονεν perf. γίνομαι to become, to happen. The perf. probably is used here as a historic pres. (M, 146; s. also K.L. McKay, "The Use of the Ancient Greek Perfect Down to the End of the Second Century A.D.," *Bulletin of the Institute of Classical Studies*, 12 [1965], 1–21). ■ ἠγέρθησαν aor. pass. 7 ἐγείρω to awaken, to arouse from sleep. ἐκόσμησαν aor. κοσμέω to put in order, to trim the lamps, to make presentable (s. R.H. Smith, BA, 29 [Feb. 1966], 5). ■ εἶπαν aor. λέγω. δότε 8 aor. imp. δίδωμι to give. σβέννυνται pres. pass. σβέννυμι to extinguish, pass., to go out. ■ ἀπεκρίθησαν aor. pass. 9

ἀποκρίνομαι to answer. μήποτε probably, perhaps (BAG). ἀρκέσῃ aor. subj. ἀρκέω to be enough, sufficient. πορεύεσθε pres. imp. πορεύομαι to go. πωλοῦντας pres. part. πωλέω to
10 sell. ἀγοράσατε aor. imp. ἀγοραζω to buy. ■ ἀπερχομένων pres. mid. part. ἀπέρχομαι to go away. Participle used as gen. abs. "while they were going away." ἀγοράσαι aor. inf., used to express purpose. ἦλθεν aor. ἔρχομαι to come, to go. ἕτοιμος ready. εἰσῆλθον aor. γάμος pl. wedding festivities. ἐκλείσθη aor. pass. κλείω to shut, to lock; effective aor. "to shut, to stay
11 shut" (RWP). ■ ὕστερον later. ἄνοιξον aor. imp. ἀνοίγω to
12 open. ■ ἀποκριθείς aor. pass. part. οἶδα defective perf. w. pres.
13 meaning, to know. ■ γρηγορεῖτε pres. imp. γρηγορέω to watch, to be ready.
14   ■ ἀποδημῶν pres. part. ἀποδημέω to go on a journey, about to go away from one's people, on the point of going abroad (RWP). ἐκάλεσεν aor. καλέω to call. παρέδωκεν aor. παραδίδωμι to deliver over, to give to. ὑπάρχοντα pres. part.,
15 part. used as a noun, goods, possession. ■ ἔδωκεν aor. δίδωμι. τάλαντον a measure of money worth 6,000 denarii (one denarius was a day's wage, RWP). (S. also Matt. 18:24.) ἀπεδήμησεν
16 aor. ■ εὐθέως adv. immediately. πορευθείς aor. pass. part. πορεύομαι. λαβών aor. part. λαμβάνω. ἠργάσατο aor. mid. ἐργάζομαι to be active, to work. ἐκέρδησεν aor. κερδαίνω to
17/18 profit, to gain. ■ ὡσαύτως likewise. ■ ἀπελθών aor. part. ἀπέρχομαι. ὤρυξεν aor. ὀρύσσω to dig. ἔκρυψεν aor.
19 κρύπτω to hide. ἀργύριον silver money. ■ ἔρχεται historical pres. συναίρω λόγον μετά a commercial term, "to compare
20 accounts, to make a reckoning" (LAE, 117). ■ προσελθών aor. part. προσέρχομαι to come to. προσήνεγκεν aor. προσφέρω
21 to bring to. ἴδε aor. imp. ὁράω. to see. ■ ἔφη impf. φημί to say. εὖ adv. "well done!," "excellent!" (EGT). καταστήσω fut. καθίστημι to appoint. εἴσελθε aor. imp. εἰσέρχομαι. χαρά
24 joy. ■ εἴληφας perf. act. part. λαμβάνω. ἔγνων aor. γινώσκω to know. σκληρός hard, severe. θερίζων pres. part. θερίζω to harvest. ἔσπειρας aor. act. 2nd sing. σπείρω to sow. συνάγων pres. part. διεσκόρπισας aor. διασκορπίζω to scatter, to scat-
25 ter seed or to winnow (BAG). ■ φοβηθείς aor. pass. part.
26 φοβέομαι to be afraid. σός "yours." ■ ὀκνηρός idle, lazy.
27 ᾔδεις plperf. οἶδα. ■ ἔδει impf. δεῖ it is necessary (w. acc. and inf.). βαλεῖν aor. inf. βάλλω. to throw, here to bring. τραπεζίτης moneychanger, banker. ἐλθών aor. part. ἔρχομαι. ἐκομισάμην aor. mid. κομίζω to bring, mid., to get back, recover. τόκος interest. The maximum rate for money loans in the empire was 12 percent (W.W. Buckland, *A Textbook of*

Roman Law, 465). ■ ἄρατε aor. imp. αἴρω to lift up, to take 28
away. ἔχοντι pres. act. part. dat. masc. sing. ■ δοθήσεται fut. 29
pass. δίδωμι. περισσευθήσεται fut. pass. περισσεύω to
abound, to have an abundance, to make to abound. ἔχοντος
pres. part. gen. sing. A Semitic construction of *casus pendes*. The
part. is to be translated in the place of the resumptive pron.
"from the one who does not have" (s. McNeile: MH, 432f.).
ἀρθήσεται fut. pass. αἴρω. ■ ἀχρεῖος useless. ἐκβάλετε aor. 30
imp. ἐκβάλλω to cast out.

■ ἔλθῃ aor. subj. ἔρχομαι. καθίσει fut. καθίζω to sit, to 31
take one's seat. ■ συναχθήσονται fut. pass. συνάγω. 32
ἀφορίσει fut. ἀφορίζω to separate. ποιμήν shepherd. ἔριφος
kid, goat. ■ στήσει fut. ἵστημι to place. δέξιος right. 33
εὐώνυμος left. ■ ἐρεῖ fut. λέγω. δεῦτε "come here!" 34
εὐλογημένοι perf. pass. part. εὐλογέω to bless, to praise.
κληρονομήσατε aor. imp. κληρονομέω to inherit, to receive
an inheritance. ἡτοιμασμένην perf. pass. part. ἑτοιμάζω to
prepare. καταβολή foundation. ■ ἐπείνασα aor. πεινάω to be 35
hungry. ἐδώκατε aor. δίδωμι. φαγεῖν aor. inf. ἐσθίω to eat,
inf. used to express purpose. ἐδίψησα aor. διψάω to be thirsty.
ἐποτίσατε aor. ποτίζω to give to drink. ξένος stranger. ἤμην
impf. 1st sing. εἰμί (s. BD, 49). συνηγάγετε aor. συνάγω.
■ γυμνός naked. περιεβάλετε aor. περιβάλλω to cast about, 36
to clothe. ἠσθένησα aor. ἀσθενέω to be weak, to be sick.
ἐπεσκέψασθε aor. ἐπισκέπτομαι to visit. ἤλθατε aor.
ἔρχομαι. ■ ἀποκριθήσονται fut. pass. εἴδομεν aor. ὁράω. 37
πεινῶντα pres. part. ἐθρέψαμεν aor. τρέφω to nourish, to give
to eat. διψῶντα part. ■ ἐφ᾽ ὅσον "in so far as" (EGT). 40
ἐποιήσατε aor. ποιέω to do. ἐλάχιστος superl. μικρός "the
least."

■ κατηραμένοι perf. pass. part. καταράομαι to curse (s. 41
CBB; TDNT). διάβολος slanderer, devil. ■ ἀσθενής weak, 43
sick. ■ διηκονήσαμεν aor. διακονέω to serve, to minister. 44
■ ἀπελεύσονται fut. ἀπέρχομαι. κόλασις punishment (s. 46
TDNT).

Ch. 26

■ ἐγένετο aor. γίνομαι to become, to happen. ἐτέλεσεν 1
aor. τελέω to end, to bring to completion. ■ οἶδα defective perf. 2
with the pres. meaning, to know. πάσχα passover (s. TDNT;
Moore, *Judaism*,II, 40f.; M, Pesahim). παραδίδοται pres. pass.
παραδίδωμι to deliver over, to betray. Used as a technical term
of release in court, "hand over into the custody of " (BAG). εἰς
τό w. inf. indicates purpose. σταυρωθῆναι aor. pass. inf.

3 σταυρόω to crucify. ■ συνήχθησαν aor. pass. συνάγω pass.,
to gather together. Points to a meeting of the Sanhedrin (EGT).
ἀρχιερεύς high priest. πρεσβύτερος elders. αὐλή courtyard.
4 λεγόμενος pres. pass. part. ■ συνεβουλεύσαντο aor. mid.
συμβουλεύω to give advice, mid., to counsel together. ἵνα w.
subj. after a v. of effort or plan (EGT). δόλος deceit, cunning,
treachery, as they would trap a wild beast (RWP). κρατήσωσιν
aor. subj. κρατέω to seize, to take into custody, to arrest.
5 ἀποκτείνωσιν aor. subj. ἀποκτείνω to kill. ■ ἑορτή feast,
festival. θόρυβος turmoil, uproar. γένηται aor. subj. γίνομαι.
6/7 ■ γενομένου aor. mid. part. γίνομαι gen. abs. ■
προσῆλθεν aor. προσέρχομαι to come to. ἔχουσα pres. act.
part. fem. sing. ἀλάβαστρον alabaster, then alabaster flask for
ointment. A vessel with a long neck which was broken off when
the contents were used (BAG). μύρον ointment, a highly perfumed or aromatic oil, or compound of such substances.
βαρύτιμος lit. "heavy with price." very expensive. The ointment was estimated at over 300 denarii (McNeile). κατέχεεν
aor. καταχέω to pour over, to pour down. ἀνακειμένου pres.
8 part. ἀνάκειμαι to recline at the table. ■ ἰδόντες aor. part.
ὁράω to see. ἠγανάκτησαν aor. ἀγανακτέω to be indignant,
to be angry. εἰς τί "for what reason?," "why?," "but why to no
9 purpose?" (LNT, 269). ἀπώλεια destruction, waste. ■ ἐδύνατο
impf. δύναμαι. πραθῆναι aor. pass. inf. πιπράσκω to sell.
(Used with the gen. of price.) δοθῆναι aor. pass. inf. δίδωμι to
give. Almsgiving was expected from the passover pilgrims as an
10 accompaniment of their worship (McNeile). ■ γνούς aor. act.
part. γινώσκω to know. κόπους παρέχειν w. dat. to cause
someone trouble. ἠργάσατο aor. mid. ἐργάζομαι to work, to
12 do. ■ βαλοῦσα aor. act. part. βάλλω to throw, of liquids, to
pour. πρὸς τό w. inf. used to express purpose. ἐνταφιάσαι aor.
inf. ἐνταφιάζω to prepare for burial, to bury. ἐποίησεν aor.
13 ποιέω to do. ■ κηρυχθῇ aor. pass. subj. κηρύσσω.
λαληθήσεται fut. pass. λαλέω to speak. μνημόσυνον remembrance, memorial.
14/15 ■ πορευθείς aor. pass. part. πορεύομαι to go. ■ δοῦναι
aor. inf. δίδωμι. παραδώσω. fut. παραδίδωμι s.v.2. ἔστησαν
aor. ἵστημι to place, to place in the scales, to weigh (McNeile).
ἀργύριον silver money. Thirty silver shekels, a reference to
Zech. 11:12. If a man's ox gored a servant he had to pay this
amount (Exod. 21:32) (RWP). The total bribe was about a
16 month's wages (Filson). ■ ἐζήτει impf. ζητέω to seek. εὐκαιρία
the right time, opportunity. παραδῶ aor. subj. παραδίδωμι.
17 ■ τὰ ἄζυμα unleavened bread, the feast of unleavened

bread (s. RWP; SB, I, 987, 988). προσῆλθον s.v.7.
ἐτοιμάσωμεν aor. subj. ἐτοιμάζω to prepare. φαγεῖν aor. inf.
ἐσθίω to eat. πάσχα s.v.2. ▪ ὑπάγετε pres. imp. ὑπάγω to go. 18
δεῖνα someone, a certain one. Used of a person or thing one
cannot or does not wish to name (BAG). εἴπατε aor. imp. λέγω.
ποιῶ pres. s.v.12. ▪ ἐποίησαν aor. συνέταξεν aor. 19
συντάσσω to command, to give an order. ἡτοίμασαν aor.
▪ ὀψία evening. γενομένης aor. mid. part. s.v.6. ἀνέκειτο impf. 20
ἀνάκειμαι s.v.7. ▪ ἐσθιόντων pres. part. gen. abs. "while they 21
were eating." παραδώσει fut. παραδίδωμι s.v.2. ▪ 22
λυπούμενοι pres. pass. part. λυπέω to make sorry, pass. to be
sorry, to be sad. ἤρξαντο aor. ἄρχομαι to begin. εἷς ἕκαστος
each (intensified) (s. BD, 160). μήτι used in a question which
expects a neg. answer. ▪ ἀποκριθείς aor. part. ἀποκρίνομαι 23
to answer. ἐμβάψας aor. act. part. ἐμβάπτω to dip into.
τρύβλιον a deep bowl. The food was dipped into a sauce composed of fruits, spices, and vinegar (McNeile). ▪ γέγραπται 24
perf. pass. γράφω to write. παραδίδοται pres. pass. ἐγεννήθη
aor. pass. γεννάω to bear, to be born. Used in a contrary to fact
conditional clause. ▪ παραδιδούς pres. act. part. εἶπας aor. ind. 25
2nd sing. λέγω s.v.64.

▪ λαβών aor. part. λαμβάνω to take. εὐλογήσας aor. 26
part. εὐλογέω to bless, to give thanks (s. TDNT). (For the
blessings used at such meals s. Hill.) ἔκλασεν aor. κλάω to
break. δούς aor. act. part. δίδωμι s.v.9. λάβετε aor. imp.
λαμβάνω. φάγετε aor. imp. ἐσθίω. ▪ ποτήριον cup. 27
εὐχαριστήσας aor. part. εὐχαριστέω to give thanks. ἔδωκεν
aor. δίδωμι. πίετε aor. imp. πίνω to drink. ▪ διαθήκη cove- 28
nant (s. TDNT; CBB; NTW; APC). ἐκχυννόμενον pres. pass.
part. ἐκχύννω to pour out. The shed blood indicates "life given
up in death" (APC). ▪ πίω aor. subj. γένημα that which grows, 29
fruit. ἄμπελος grapevine. ▪ ὑμνήσαντες aor. part. ὑμνέω to 30
sing hymns of praise. The second part of the Hallel (Pss. 113–
118) was sung at the close of the Passover meal (BAG). ἐξῆλθον
aor. ἐξέρχομαι to go out.

▪ σκανδαλισθήσεσθε fut. pass. σκανδαλίζω to cause to 31
stumble (s. TDNT). πατάξω fut. πατάσσω to strike, to hit.
ποιμήν shepherd. διασκορπισθήσονται fut. pass.
διασκορπίζω to scatter. (For the prep. in the compound with
the meaning "to and fro" s. MH, 302.) ποίμνη flock. ▪ 32
ἐγερθῆναι aor. pass. inf. ἐγείρω to raise from the dead, to rise.
The inf. is used with the prep. μετά to express subsequent time,
"after ...." προάξω fut. προάγω to go before. ▪ ἀποκριθείς 33
s.v.23. ἐγώ "I," emphatic in contrast to others.

σκανδαλισθήσονται fut. pass. The volative fut. expresses
34 determination of the will (RG, 874). ■ ἔφη impf. φημί to say.
πρίν w. acc. and inf. "before." ἀλέκτωρ rooster. φωνῆσαι aor.
inf. φωνέω to call, here, to crow. The cock crowing marked the
third Roman watch 12–3 A.M. (McNeile). ἀπαρνήσῃ fut.
ἀπαρνέομαι to deny. The prep. of the compound perfectivizes
35 the verb "to completely deny" (s. MH, 298). ■ δέῃ pres. subj.
δεῖ it is necessary. ἀποθανεῖν aor. inf. ἀποθνῄσκω to die. οὐ
μή emphatic neg. εἶπαν aor.

36　　　　■ καθίσατε aor. imp. καθίζω to sit down. αὐτοῦ adv. of
place "here." ἕως οὗ w. subj. as long as, until, while. ἀπελθών
aor. part. ἀπέρχομαι to go forth. προσεύξωμαι aor. subj.
37 προσεύχομαι to pray. ■ παραλαβών aor. part.
παραλαμβάνω to take with. ἤρξατο s,v.22. λυπεῖσθαι pres.
pass. inf. s.v.22. ἀδημονεῖν pres. inf. ἀδημονέω to be troubled,
to be distressed. It implies a restless, distracted, shrinking from
some trouble or thought of trouble which nevertheless cannot be
38 escaped (McNeile). ■ περίλυπος lit. "surrounded by sorrow,"
overwhelmed with distress (EGT). (For the prep. in this compound s. MH, 321f.) μείνατε aor. imp. μένω to remain.
γρηγορεῖτε pres. imp. γρηγορέω to watch, "keep awake"
39 physically (McNeile). ■ προσελθών aor. part. προσέρχομαι
to go before. μικρόν a little, adv. acc. "a little way," "short
distance." ἔπεσεν aor. πίπτω to fall. προσευχόμενος pres.
mid. part. παρελθάτω aor. imp. 3rd sing. παρέρχομαι to pass
by. The aor. imp. indicates the feeling of dependence which
leaves everything to the Father (s. Bakker, 101). ποτήριον cup.
40 (For the meaning here s. HDCG, I, 37f.) ■ εὑρίσκω to find,
historical pres. καθεύδοντας pres. part. καθεύδω to sleep.
ἰσχύσατε aor. ind. ἰσχύω to have strength, to be able.
41 χρηγορῆσαι aor. act. inf. ■ προσεύχεσθε pres. imp.
εἰσέλθητε aor. subj. εἰσέρχομαι to go in to. πειρασμός temptation. πνεῦμα spirit. πρόθυμος ready, willing. σάρξ flesh. The
distinction is between man's physical weakness (flesh) and the
noble desires of his will (willing spirit) (Hill). ἀσθενής weak.
42 ■ προσηύξατο aor. προσεύχομαι. εἰ "if," introduces a first-
class condition assumed to be true. παρελθεῖν aor. inf.
παρέρχομαι. ἐὰν μή "if not," "except," condition of the third
class undetermined. This delicate distinction between the conditional clauses accurately presents the real attitude of Jesus
toward this subtle temptation (RWP). γενηθήτω aor. imp. 3rd
43 sing. γίνομαι s.v.1. ■ ἐλθών aor. part. ἔρχομαι. εὗρεν aor.
εὑρίσκω. βεβαρημένοι perf. pass. part. βαρέω to make heavy,
to be heavy (with sleep). The perf. emphasizes the present state.

■ ἀφείς aor. part. ἀφίημι to leave. εἰπών aor. part. ■ 44/45
καθεύδετε pres. imp. ἀναπαύεσθε pres. mid. imp.
ἀναπαύομαι to take one's rest. ἤγγικεν perf. ἐγγίζω to draw
near. παραδίδοται s.v.24. ■ ἐγείρεσθε pres. imp. pass. s.v.32. 46
ἄγωμεν subj. ἄγω to go, cohortative subj. "let us go."
παραδιδούς pres. part. "the one who betrays." Judas sold information where Jesus could be found and taken inconspicuously
(s. Josef Blinzler, The Trial of Jesus).

■ λαλοῦντος pres. part. gen. abs. "while he was yet speak- 47
ing." ἦλθεν aor. ἔρχομαι s.v.36. μάχαιρα sword. ξύλον wood,
stick, club (McNeile). ■ ἔδωκεν aor. s.v.27. φιλήσω aor. subj. 48
φιλέω to love, to kiss. κρατήσατε aor. imp. s.v.4. ■ 49
προσέλθών aor. part. s.v.7. χαῖρε pres. imp. χαίρω form of
greeting, "hello." κατεφίλησεν aor. καταφιλέω intensified by
the prep., to kiss fervently (RWP). The disciple was not to greet
the master first. This was a sign of insubordination (AM). ■ 50
ἑταῖρος friend. ἐφ᾽ ὅ "for what?" "why?" (s. GI, 69–71; LAE,
125–131). πάρει pres. πάρειμι to be present, to come.
ἐπέβαλον aor. ἐπιβάλλω to seize, to lay hands upon.
ἐκράτησαν aor. ■ ἐκτείνας aor. part. ἐκτείνω to stretch out. 51
ἀπέσπασεν aor. ἀποσπάω to draw out. πατάξας aor. part.
s.v.31. ἀφεῖλεν aor. ἀφαιρέω to take away, to cut off. ὠτίον
ear. ■ ἀπόστρεψον aor. imp. ἀποστρέφω to turn away, to put 52
away. λαβόντες s.v.26. ἐν by (instrumental use of the prep.).
ἀπολοῦνται fut. ἀπόλλυμι to perish. ■ δοκεῖς pres. δοκέω to 53
suppose, to think. οὐ in the question expects a positive answer.
παρακαλέσαι aor. inf. παρακαλέω to summons, to call to
one's side for help. παραστήσει fut. παρίστημι to stand by.
The prep. in the compound is local (s. MH, 319). Both of these
verbs are used in connection with military matters (EGT).
πλείω comparative, πολύς more than. λεγιών legion. The principle unit of the Roman army containing about 6,000 men (s.
IDB, III, 110; BC, V, 427–431). ■ πληρωθῶσιν aor. subj. pass. 54
πληρόω to fulfill. δεῖ s.v.35. γενέσθαι aor. inf. γίνομαι s.v.1.
■ λῃστής robber. One who uses violence to possess himself of 55
other's property thus differing from a thief (EGT). ἐξήλθατε
s.v.30. συλλαβεῖν aor. inf. συλλαμβάνω to seize, to take. καθ᾽
ἡμέραν daily. ἐκαθεζόμην impf. καθέζομαι to sit. διδάσκων
pres. part. ■ γέγονεν perf. γίνομαι. ἀφέντες aor. part. ἀφίημι 56
s.v.44. ἔφυγον aor. φεύγω to flee.

■ κρατήσαντες aor. act. part. s.v.4. ἀπήγαγον aor. 57
ἀπάγω to lead away. ἀρχιερεύς s.v.3. (For the trial of Jesus,
s. David R. Catchpole, The Trial of Jesus; Josef Blinzler, The
Trial of Jesus; A.N. Sherwin-White, Roman Society and Roman

58 *Law in the New Testament.*) ■ ἠκολούθει impf. ἀκολουθέω.
The impf. pictures His continual following. μακρόθεν from afar,
from a distance. εἰσελθών aor. part. εἰσέρχομαι to go in, to
come in. ἐκάθητο impf. κάθημαι to sit. ὑπηρέτης servant,
minister, helper. ἰδεῖν aor. inf. ὁράω to see. Infinitive to express
59 purpose. ■ συνέδριον Sanhedrin. The Sanhedrin did not possess
the general right of execution except in reference to the violation
of the innermost temple court (AM; Sherwin-White, 38ff.).
ἐζήτουν impf., indicating the continual search.
ψευδομαρτυρία false witness. θανατώσωσιν aor. subj.
60 θανατόω to kill. ■ εὗρον aor. s.v.43. προσελθόντων aor. part.
s.v.7. gen. abs. used to express concession "although." ὕστερον
61 at last. ■ εἶπαν aor. λέγω. ἔφη s.v.34. καταλῦσαι aor. inf.
καταλύω to destroy. διὰ τριῶν ἡ μερῶν lit. "through three
days" (EGT). οἰκοδομῆσαι aor. inf. οἰκοδομέω to erect, to
62 build.   ■   ἀναστάς   aor.   ἀνίστημι   to   stand   up.
καταμαρτυροῦσιν pres. καταματυρέω to give testimony
63 against (w. gen.). ■ ἐσιώπα impf. σιωπάω to be silent. The
impf. indicates He continually remained silent during the various accusations. ἐξορκίζω to cause someone to take an oath, to
charge someone under oath. To put someone under oath using
divine names and titles renders the oath binding (McNeile).
64 ζῶντος pres. part. ζάω to live. εἴπῃς aor. subj. λέγω. ■ σὺ
εἶπας aor. "you (emphatic) said it." The phrase is affirmative in
content, and reluctant in formulation (D.R. Catchpole, "The
Answer of Jesus to Caiaphas [Matthew 26:64]," NTS, 17 [Jan.
1971], 213–226). πλήν "moreover," "indeed," "Yes, I am. Indeed I tell you that you will see Me immediately vindicated"
(M.E. Thrall, *Greek Particles in the New Testament*, 78). ὄψεσθε
65 fut. mid. ὁράω to see. ■ διέρρηξεν aor. διαρρήγνυμι to rip, to
tear. The tearing of the garment may have been a spontaneous
expression of real horror (McNeile). Those judging the trial of
a blasphemer were required to stand and tear their garments
upon hearing the blasphemy (s. M, Sanhedrin, 7, 5).
ἐβλασφήμησεν aor. βλασφημέω to blaspheme (s. TDNT).
66 ἠκούσατε aor. ἀκούω to hear. ■ τί ὑμῖν δοκεῖ used impersonally w. dat. "What is it to you?," that is, "What do you think?"
67 ἀποκριθέντες aor. pass. part. ἔνοχος guilty. ■ ἐνέπτυσαν aor.
ἐμπτύω to spit on. A sign of the strongest rejection and contempt (NBD). ἐκολάφισαν aor. κολαφίζω to strike with the
fist. ἐρράπισαν aor. ῥαπίζω to strike with a club, also to strike
68 with the open hand, esp. in the face (BAG; s. Isa. 50:6). ■
προφήτευσον aor. imp. προφητεύω to prophesy. παίσας aor.
part. παίω to hit, to strike. Jesus is subject to indignities by

which it is thought the hollowness of His claim will be revealed
(Hill).

■ προσῆλθεν aor. s.v.7. ἦσθα impf. 2nd sing. εἰμί (s. 69
BD,49). ■ ἠρνήσατο aor. s.v.34. οἶδα s.v.2. ■ ἐξελθόντα aor. 70/71
act. part. ἐξέρχομαι s.v.30. He retired into the dimmer light of
the vestibule close to the gateway (McNeile). πυλών gate, gateway, entrance. εἶδεν aor. ὁράω. ■ ὅρκος oath. ὅτι = quotation 72
marks. ■ ἑστῶτες perf. act. part. ἵσταμι to stand. λαλιά 73
speech. (For the language and dialect of those of Galilee s.
Harold Hoehner, Herod Antipas, 61–64.) δῆλος clear, evident.
■ ἤρξατο s.v.22. καταθεματίζω to curse, to wish oneself ac- 74
cursed if he lies (TDNT). ὀμνύω to swear. ἐφώνησεν aor.
s.v.34. ■ ἐμνήσθη aor. pass. μιμνήσκομαι to remember. 75
εἰρηκότος perf. act. part. λέγω. ἔκλαυσεν aor. κλαίω to weep.
πικρῶς bitterly.

Ch. 27

■ πρωΐα early morning. γενομένης aor. mid. part. 1
γίνομαι to become, sometimes in the sense "to be," gen. abs.
συμβούλιον consultation. ἔλαβον aor. λαμβάνω to take.
Used with the preceding word, to form a plan, to consult, to plot
(BAG). It is not the interrogation of the accused or the examination of testimony (Catchpole, The Trial of Jesus, 191). ὥστε
"that," used to introduce intended results, that is, purpose (BD,
198). θανατῶσαι aor. inf. θανατόω to kill. ■ δήσαντες aor. 2
act. part. δέω to bind. ἀπήγαγον aor. act. ἀπάγω to lead out.
παρέδωκαν aor. παραδίδωμι to deliver over. ἡγεμών governor, ruler. (For material on Pontius Pilate s. HA, 172–183.)
■ ἰδών aor. part. ὁράω to see. παραδούς aor. act. part. 3
παραδίδωμι to deliver over, to betray. κατεκρίθη aor. pass.
κατακρίνω to pronounce judgment against, to condemn.
μεταμεληθείς aor. pass. part. μεταμέλομαι to regret, to repent, wishing it were undone (EGT; s. also Matt. 21:30).
ἔστρεψεν aor. στρέφω to bring back, to return. ■ ἥμαρτον aor. 4
ἁμαρτάνω to sin. παραδούς aor. act. part., used to express
manner. εἶπαν aor. λέγω. ὄψῃ fut. mid. 2nd sing. ὁράω "see to
it yourself," "you take care of that!," the volitive fut. (s. BD,
183). ■ ῥίψας aor. part. ῥίπτω to throw, to put or lay down. He 5
placed the money in the treasury (McNeile). ἀνεχώρησεν aor.
ἀναχωρέω to depart, to go away. ἀπελθών aor. part.
ἀπέρχομαι to go out. ἀπήγξατο aor. mid. ἀπάγχω direct mid.
to hang oneself (RWP). ■ ἔξεστιν it is lawful. βαλεῖν aor. inf. 6
βάλλω to cast, to put. κορβανᾶς temple treasury. τιμή price.
The price of blood was polution to the treasury (McNeile). ■ 7

81

ἠγόρασαν aor. ἀγοράζω to buy. κεραμεύς potter. ταφή
8 grave. ξένος stranger. ■ ἐκλήθη aor. pass. καλέω to call, to
9 name. ■ ἐπληρώθη aor. pass. πληρόω to fulfill. ῥηθέν aor.
pass. part. λέγω. τετιμημένου perf. pass. part. τιμάω to set a
10 price on, to estimate, to value. ἐτιμήσαντο aor. mid. ■ ἔδωκαν
aor. δίδωμι to give. εἰς here "for." συνέταξεν aor. ind.
συντάσσω to arrange, to order.
11   ■ ἐστάθη aor. pass. ἵστημι to place. The sentence of the
Sanhedrin had to be carried out by the procurator (s. Sherwin-
White, 44ff.). It is also suggested the religious leaders sought to
avoid responsibility by having a third party carry out the sentence (s. LNT, 422f.). ἐπηρώτησεν aor. ἐπερωτάω to question.
σύ "you" emphatic. The term "King of the Jews" indicated "a
leader of the resistance" (Sherwin-White, 24). ἔφη impf. φημί
12 to say. ■ ἐν τῷ w. inf. indicates contemporaneous time "while."
κατηγορεῖσθαι pres. pass. inf. κατηγορέω to bring a charge
13 against. ἀπεκρίνατο aor. ἀποκρίνομαι to answer. ■ πόσος
how much, how great, how many. καταμαρτυροῦσιν pres. act.
14 καταματυρέω to witness against (w. gen.). ■ ἀπεκρίθη aor.
pass. ἀποκρίνομαι. ῥῆμα word. θαυμάζειν pres. inf.
θαυμάζω to be astounded, to wonder, the inf. used to express
results. Those who did not defend themselves were given three
opportunities of changing their mind before sentence was finally
given against them (Sherwin-White, 25).
15   ■ εἰώθει plperf. of the perf. form εἴωθα to be accustomed
(s. BAG). ἀπολύω to release. ἤθελον impf. θέλω. (For the
custom of releasing a prisoner at Passover and comments on M,
16 Pesachim 7, 6 s. Josef Blinzler, *The Trial of Jesus*.) ■ ἐπίσημος
outstanding, notorious. It may refer to the high reputation in
which he was held by the more rebellious Jews (McNeile).
17 λεγόμενος pres. pass. part. ■ συνηγμένων perf. pass. part.
συνάγω to gather together, to assemble, gen. abs. ἀπολύσω
18 fut. ■ ᾔδει plperf. οἶδα to know. φθόνος envy, jealousy (s. IDB,
19 II, 806f.). ■ καθημένου pres. part. κάθημαι to sit, to take one's
seat, gen. abs. βῆμα tribunal, judicial bench. ἀπέστειλεν aor.
ἀποστέλλω to send. δίκαιος righteous, innocent (s. GW,
20 121f.). ἔπαθον aor. πάσχω to suffer. ὄναρ dream. ■ ἔπεισαν
aor. πείθω to persuade. αἰτήσωνται aor. mid. subj. αἰτέω to
ask, to request. ἀπολέσωσιν aor. subj. ἀπόλλυμι to destroy.
21/22 ■ ἀποκριθείς aor. pass. part. ἀποκρίνομαι. ■ ποιήσω fut.
ποιέω to do, to do with. σταυρωθήτω aor. pass. imp. 3rd sing.
23 σταυρόω to crucify. ■ ἐποίησεν aor. ἔκραζον impf. κράζω to
scream; impf. pictures the continual action. The crowd clamored
for crucifixion because it meant "cursed by God" (s. TDNT

under σταυρός). ■ ὠφελεῖ pres. ὠφελέω to be of use, to profit. 24
λαβών aor. part. λαμβάνω. ἀπενίψατο aor. mid. ἀπονίπτω
to wash, to wash off. The practice of washing hands was a symbol
for the removal of guilt (Tasker). κατέναντι w. gen. over,
against, before. ■ ἀπέλυσεν aor. φραγελλώσας aor. part. 26
φραγελλόω to scourge. (For the horrible practice of scourging,
s. J. Blinzler, The Trial of Jesus.) σταυρωθῇ aor. pass. subj.
   ■ παραλαβόντες aor. part. παραλαμβάνω to take with. 27
πραιτώριον the official residence of a governor (s. McNeile).
συνήγαγον aor. συνάγω. σπεῖρα cohort (s. reference in Matt.
26.53). ■ ἐκδύσαντες aor. part. ἐκδύω to undress. χλαμύς a 28
man's outer garment, a cloak used by travelers and soldiers
(BAG). κόκκινος scarlet. This scarlet mantel on Jesus was a
mock imitation of the royal purple (RWP). περιέθηκαν aor.
περιτίθημι to place around. ■ πλέξαντες aor. part. πλέκω to 29
plait. στέφανος wreath, circlet. ἄκανθα thorn. ἐπέθηκαν aor.
ἐπιτίθημι to place upon. The circlet of thorns was meant as a
cheap (and painful) imitation of the radiant circlet depicted on
the coins of Tiberius Caesar (AM). κάλαμος reed, corresponding to the scepter in the emperor's hand as depicted on the coins
(AM). γονυπετήσαντες aor. part. γονυπετέω to fall on the
knees. ἐνέπαιξαν aor. ἐμπαίζω to ridicule, to make fun of, to
mock (s. Matt. 20:19). χαῖρε "hail!" (s. Matt. 26:49). The soldiers used the familiar "Ave Caesar" in their mockery of Jesus
(RWP). ■ ἐμπτύσαντες aor. part. ἐμπτύω to spit on. ἔλαβον 30
s.v.1. ἔτυπτον impf. τύπτω to strike. The impf. indicates "they
repeatedly struck him on the head" (Filson). ■ ἐξέδυσαν aor. 31
ἐκδύω. ἐνέδυσαν aor. ἐνδύω to put on. ἀπήγαγον s.v.2. εἰς τό
w. inf. to express purpose. σταυρῶσαι aor. inf. s.v.22.
   ■ εὗρον aor. εὑρίσκω to find. ἠγγάρευσαν aor. 32
ἀγγαρεύω to compel, to forcibly impress someone into service
(s. NTW, 15–17). ἄρῃ aor. subj. αἴρω to lift up, to carry.
σταυρος cross (s. TDNT; J. Blinzler, The Trial of Jesus). ■ 33
ἐλθόντες aor. part. ἔρχομαι to come, to go. κρανίον skull.
■ ἔδωκαν s.v.10. πιεῖν aor. inf. πίνω to drink. χολή gall. 34
μεμιγμένον perf. pass. part. μείγνυμι to mix. A man about to
be executed could beg a "grain of incense" (a narcotic) in wine
in order to dull his senses and alleviate pain (Hill). γευσάμενος
aor. part. γεύομαι to taste. ἠθέλησεν aor. θέλω. ■ 35
σταυρώσαντες aor. part. διεμερίσαντο aor. mid. διαμερίζω
to distribute, to distribute among themselves. The soldiers who
carried out the sentence had a right to the clothes of the criminal
(AM). ■ ἐτήρουν impf. τηρέω to watch. ■ ἐπέθηκαν aor. 36/37
ἐπιτίθημι to place upon, to place. ἐπάνω w. gen. over. αἰτία

cause, guilt. γεγραμμένην perf. pass. part. γράφω to write. The
inscription was written with black or red letters on a white
38 background (J. Blinzler, *The Trial of Jesus*). ■ σταυροῦνται
39 pres. pass. λῃστής robber (s. Matt. 26:55). ■
παραπορευόμενοι pres. part. παραπορεύομαι to pass alongside of, to pass by. ἐβλασφήμουν impf. βλασφημέω to revile,
to defame. The impf. pictures the continual defaming.
κινοῦντες pres. part. κινέω to move, to shake. To shake the
40 head as a sign of scorn and derision (BAG). ■ καταλύων pres.
part. καταλύω to destroy. οἰκοδομῶν pres. part. οἰκοδομέω to
build. σῶσον aor. imp. σῴζω to save, to rescue. κατάβηθι aor.
41 imp. καταβαίνω to come down. ■ ἐμπαίζοντες pres. part.
42 s.v.29. ■ ἔσωσεν aor. σῴζω. σῶσαι aor. inf. καταβάτω aor.
43 imp. καταβαίνω. ■ πέποιθεν perf. πείθω s.v.20. The perf. has
the pres. meaning of depend on, trust in (BD, 176). ῥυσάσθω
44 aor. imp. ῥύομαι to rescue. ■ τὸ αὐτό the same thing.
συσταυρωθέντες aor. pass. part. συσταυρόω to crucify together. ὠνείδιζον impf. ὀνειδίζω to reproach, to heap insults
upon, the inceptive impf., "they began to reproach him" (RWP).
45   ■ ἐγένετο aor. γίνομαι s.v.1. γῆ land, earth, indicates all
46 Palestine or the whole world (s. Hill). ■ ἀνεβόησεν aor.
ἀναβοάω to cry out. ἠλί (Heb.) "my God." λεμά (Heb.)
"why?" σαβαχθάνι (Aram.) "Why did You forsake Me?" (s.
Allen). θεέ voc. (s. BD, 25). ἐγκατέλιπες aor. ἐγκαταλείπω
to abandon, to leave in the lurch. (For the prep. in compound s.
MH, 305.) ἑστηκότων perf. act. part., ἵστημι to stand.
ἀκούσαντες aor. part. ἀκούω to hear. φωνεῖ pres. φωνέω to
48 call. ■ δραμών aor. act. part. τρέχω to run. λαβών s.v.24.
σπόγγος sponge. πλήσας aor. part. πίμπλημι to fill (w. gen.).
ὄξος sour wine, vinegar. *Posca*, a wine vinegar which was the
favorite drink of soldiers and the lower ranks of society (BAG;
McNeile). περιθείς aor. part. περιτίθημι. ἐπότεζεν impf.
ποτίζω to give to drink. The conative impf. "they tried to give
49 him to drink" (s. IBG, 9; RG, 885). ■ ἄφες aor. imp. ἀφίημι
to leave alone. ἴδωμεν aor. subj. ὁράω to see, cohortative subj.
"let us see." σώσων fut. part. σῴζω to save, to rescue. The fut.
50 part. used to express purpose (s. BD, 178, 215f.). ■ κράξας aor.
part. s.v.23. ἀφῆκεν aor. ἀφίημι to let go, to send away. Not
51 the divine Spirit but "the spirit of life" (Hill). ■ καταπέτασμα
curtain, veil. (For the veils of the temple s. LT, II, 611f.; SB, I,
1043–1046.) ἐσχίσθη aor. pass. σχίζω to split, to divide, to
tear apart. ἄνωθεν from above. ἐσείσθη aor. pass. σείω to
shake (used of an earthquake). (For extra biblical references to
52 this event s. LT, II, 610; Allen.) ■ μνημεῖον tomb.

ἀνεῴχθησαν aor. pass. ἀνοίγω to open. κεκοιμημένων perf. pass. part. κοιμάομαι pass,. to sleep, to fall asleep. ἠγέρθησαν aor. pass. ἐγείρω to raise, pass. to rise. ■ ἐξελθόντες aor. part. 53 ἐξέρχομαι. ἔγερσις resurrection. εἰσῆλθον aor. εἰσέρχομαι to come in, to go in. ἐνεφανίσθησαν aor. pass. ἐμφανίζω to appear. ■ ἑκατόνταρχος leader of a hundred men, centurion. 54 (For Roman army divisions s. Matt. 25:53.) τηροῦντες pres. part. ἰδόντες s.v.3. γινόμενα pres. part. s.v.1. ἐφοβήθησαν aor. φοβέομαι to be afraid. ■ μακρόθεν from afar. θεωροῦσαι 55 pres. part. θεωρέω to look at (as a spectator) (AS). ἠκολούθησαν aor. ἀκολουθέω to follow. διακονοῦσαι pres. act. part. fem. pl. διακονέω to minister.

■ ὄψιος late. γενομένης aor. mid. part. s.v.1. Jesus died 57 shortly before 3 P.M. on Friday. The Sabbath would begin at sundown; before it came and all work ceased, the body should be buried (Filson). (For material regarding the day of the cruci-fixion— Friday—and the year—AD 33, see Harold Hoehner, "Chronological Aspects of the Life of Christ Part IV: The Day of Christ's Crucifixion," Bib Sac 131 [July–Sept. 1974], 241–264; "Part V: The Year of Christ's Crucifixion," Bib Sac 131 [Oct–Dec], 332–348.) ἦλθεν aor. ἔρχομαι s.v.33. τοὔνομα = τὸ ὄν. ἐμαθητεύθη aor. pass. μαθητεύομαι to be a disciple. ■ προσελθών aor. part. προσέρχομαι to come to. ἠτήσατο 58 aor. mid. αἰτέω to ask, mid. to ask for oneself. Bodies of crimi-nals were sometimes given to their friends for burial (McNeile). ἐκέλευσεν aor. κελεύω to command. ἀποδοθῆναι aor. pass. inf. ἀποδίδωμι to give up, to give. ■ λαβών aor. part. 59 λαμβάνω s.v.1. ἐνετύλιξεν aor. ἐντυλίσσω to wrap up. (For the wrapping of the body in linen in preparation for burial, s. J. Blinzler, The Trial of Jesus.) ■ ἔθηκεν aor. τίθημι to place. 60 ἐλατόμησεν aor. λατομέω to hew out of the rock. προσκυλίσας aor. act. part. προσωλίω to roll, to roll up to. ἀπῆλθεν aor. ἀπέρχομαι s.v.5. ■ καθήμεναι prcs. mid. part. 61 fem. pl. s.v.19.

■ ἐπαύριον on the next day, dat. of time. παρασκευή 62 preparation, the day of preparation. Friday, on which day every-thing had to be prepared for the Sabbath (BAG). συνήχθησαν aor. pass. συνάγω s.v.17. ■ ἐμνήσθημεν aor. pass. 63 μιμνήσκομαι to remember, ingressive aor. "we have just re-called" (RWP). πλάνος "deceiving" as substantive, "deceiver." ζῶν pres. part. ζάω to live. Temporal part. to express contempo-raneous time. ■ κέλευσον aor. imp. ἀσφαλισθῆναι aor. pass. 64 inf. ἀσφαλίζω to make safe, to guard. μήποτε lest. ἐλθόντες s.v.33. κλέψωσιν aor. subj. κλέπτω to steal. εἴπωσιν aor. subj.

ἠγέρθη aor. pass. s.v.52. ἔσται fut. Used after μήποτε to express the feeling of apprehension (BD, 188). πλάνη error, deception. χείρων comparative κακός. τῆς πρώτης gen. of
65 comp. "as the first." ■ ἔφη s.v.11. ἔχετε pres. imp. κουστωδία (Lat.) watch, guard. ὑπάγετε pres. imp. ὑπάγω to go forth.
66 ἀσφαλίσασθε aor. mid. imp. οἶδα s.v.18. ■ πορευθέντες aor. part. πορεύομαι to go. ἠσφαλίσαντο aor. mid. σφραγίσαντες aor. act. part. σφραγίζω to seal. Probably by a cord stretched across the stone and sealed at each end (RWP).

Ch. 28

1 ■ ὀψέ w. gen., after, "after the Sabbath" (BAG). ἐπιφωσκούσῃ pres. part. ἐπιφώσκω to shine forth, to dawn. ἦλθεν aor. ἔρχομαι to come, to go. θεωρῆσαι aor. inf. θεωρέω
2 to see, to view. Infinitive used to express purpose. ■ σεισμός earthquake. ἐγένετο aor. γίνομαι to become, to happen. γάρ "for," explains the preceding. καταβάς aor. part. καταβαίνω to go down. προσελθών aor. part. προσέρχομαι to go to, to come to. ἀπεκύλισεν aor. ἀποκυλίω to roll away. ἐκάθητο
3 imp. κάθημαι to sit. ἐπάνω w. gen., upon. ■ εἰδέα appearance.
4 ἀστραπή lightning. χιών snow. ■ φόβος fear. αὐτοῦ "of him" (obj. gen.). ἐσείσθησαν aor. pass. σείω to shake, "paralyzed with fear." The expression indicates faces waxen and immobile with fear (AM). τηροῦντες pres. part. τηρέω to watch, to guard.
5 ἐγενήθησαν aor. pass. γίνομαι ■ ἀποκριθείς aor. pass. part. ἀποκρίνομαι to answer. φοβεῖσθε pres. imp. φοβέομαι to be afraid. Present imp. with the neg. "stop being afraid." οἶδα def. perf. w. pres. meaning, to know. ἐσταυρωμένον perf. pass. part.
6 σταυρόω to crucify. ζητεῖτε pres. ζητέω to seek. ■ ἠγέρθη aor. pass. ἐγείρω to awaken, to raise, pass. to rise. δεῦτε come! come on! adv. used as hortatory particle (BAG). ἴδετε aor. imp.
7 ὁράω to see. ἔκειτο impf. pass. κεῖμαι to lie. ■ ταχύ quickly. πορευθεῖσαι aor. pass. part. fem. pl. πορεύομαι to go. Circumstantial part. to be translated as imp. εἴπατε aor. imp. λέγω.
8 προάγω pres. to go before. ὄψεσθε fut. mid. ὁράω. ■ ἀπελθοῦσαι aor. act. part. fem. pl. ἀπέρχομαι to go away. μνημεῖον tomb. ἔδραμον aor. τρέχω to run. ἀπαγγεῖλαι aor. inf. to report, to bring news from (s. MH, 297). Infinitive used
9 to express purpose. ■ ὑπήντησεν aor. ὑπαντάω to meet. χαίρετε pres. imp. χαίρω. The form of greeting (s. Matt. 26:49). ἐκράτησαν aor. κρατέω to seize. προσεκύνησαν aor.
10 προσκυνέω to worship. ■ ὑπάγετε pres. imp. ὑπάγω to go forth. ἀπαγγείλατε aor. imp. ἀπέλθωσιν aor. subj. ἀπέρχομαι.

■ πορευομένων pres. mid. part. gen. abs. ἐλθόντες aor. 11
part. ἔρχομαι. γενόμενα aor. mid. part. γίνομαι. ■ 12
συναχθέντες aor. pass. part. συνάγω to gather together, to
assemble. συμβούλιον consultation, plan, decision. λαβόντες
aor. part. λαμβάνω to take. Used with the preceding word to
mean "to form a plan," "to deceive," "to plot" (BAG).
ἀργύριον silver. ἱκανός enough, large enough, much. ἔδωκαν
aor. δίδωμι to give. ■ ἔκλεψαν aor. κλέπτω to steal. 13
κοιμωμένων pres. mid. part. κοιμάομαι to sleep. The part.
used temporally to express contemporaneous time "while we
slept." ■ ἀκουσθῇ aor. pass. subj. ἀκούω to hear. If this comes 14
to a hearing, a trial (EGT). πείσομεν fut. πείθω to persuade.
ἀμέριμνος without care, "we will put it right with the Procurator, so that you need not trouble" (MM). ποιήσομεν fut. ποιέω
to do, s. preceding word. ■ ἐποίησαν aor. ἐδιδάχθησαν aor. 15
pass. διδάσκω to teach, to instruct. διεφημίσθη aor. pass.
διαφημίζω to make known by word of mouth, to spread the
news about (BAG).

■ ἐπορεύθησαν aor. pass. πορεύομαι s.v.7. ἐτάξατο aor. 16
mid. τάσσω to assign, to order, mid., to appoint by one's own
authority (AS). ■ ἰδόντες aor. part. s.v.6. ἐδίστασαν aor. 17
διστάζω to doubt. ■ ἐδόθη aor. pass. δίδωμι s.v.12. ■ 18/19
πορευθέντες aor. part. s.v.7. (For the translation of the part. as
imp. as well as the setting of the term "to make disciples," s.
Cleon Rogers, "The Great Commission," Bib Sac, 130 [July
1973], 258–267; s. also SSM, 455–457.) μαθητεύσατε aor. imp.
μαθητεύω to make a disciple. βαπτίζοντες pres. part.
βαπτίζω to baptize, part. of manner. ■ διδάσκοντες pres. part., 20
part. of manner. τηρεῖν pres. inf. τηρέω to guard, to keep, to
observe. ἐνετειλάμην aor. ἐντέλλομαι to command.
συντέλεια completion.

THE GOSPEL OF MARK

Ch. 1

1 ἀρχή beginning, used without the article indicates it was intended as a title (M, 82). It is either the title for the whole gospel of Mark or for verses 1-13 (s. Cranfield). εὐαγγέλιον gospel, good news (s. Cranfield; TDNT; NTW; CBB). The following gen. "Jesus Christ" is obj. gen. "the good news about

2 Jesus Christ" (Taylor). ■ γέγραπται perf. pass. γράφω to write, perf., "it stands written." Refers to the regulative and authoritative character of the document (MM). κατασκευάσει

3 fut. κατασκευάζω to prepare, to make ready, to furnish. ■ βοῶντος pres. part. βοάω to shout, to cry out. ἑτοιμάσατε aor. imp. ἑτοιμάζω to make ready. εὐθύς straight. ποεῖτε pres. imp.

4 ποιέω to do, to make. τρίβος way. ■ ἐγένετο aor. γίνομαι to become, "to appear on the scene." It emphasizes His emergence in accordance with the divine purpose (Taylor). βαπτίζων pres. act. part. βαπτίζων (TDNT; s. Matt. 3:6). κηρύσσων pres. part. κηρύσσων to proclaim as a herald (CBB; Cranfield). μετάνοια change of mind, repentance (s. Matt. 3:2; Cranfield).

5 ἄφεσις release, forgiveness (TDNT; CBB). ■ ἐξεπορεύετο impf. mid. ἐκπορεύομαι to go out. ἐβαπτίζοντο impf. pass., the impf. indicates that they repeatedly came out and were baptized. ποταμός river. ἐξομολογούμενοι pres. mid. part. ἐξομολογέομαι to confess, to confess publicly, to avow openly (Taylor). It is possible that a spoken confession of sin preceded

6 the actual baptism (Cranfield). ■ ἦν impf. εἰμί used with the two parts. "clothed," "eating" to form the periphrastic impf. and denotes habitual action "was clothed (as his custom was)" (Taylor). ἐνδεδυμένος perf. pass. part. ἐνδύομαι to put on (clothing), perf., to be clothed. The following accs. are normal after the pass. of this verb (Cranfield). θρίξ, τρίχος hair. δερμάτινος made of leather. ὀσφύς hip. ἔσθων pres. part. ἔσθω to eat. (For

7 the form s. MH, 238.) ■ ἐκήρυσσεν impf. λέγων pres. part. λέγω to say, to speak. ἔρχομαι pres. mid., to come. The pres. sounds the note of immediacy (Taylor). ἰσχυρότερος comp. ἰσχυρός strong, mighty. μου gen. of comp. ἱκανός fit, sufficient, worthy. Denotes any kind of sufficiency or fitness

(Gould). κύψας aor. part. κύπτω to stoop. λῦσαι aor. inf. λύω to loose. ἱμάς strap. The thong of the sandal which held it together (RWP). ὑπόδημα sandal. αὐτοῦ his. (For the resumptive pronoun used after a relative, s. W.F. Bakker, *Pronomen Alurndans and Prvnomen Coniunctum,* 39.) ■ ἐβάπτισα aor. 8 The aor. represents John's course as already fulfilled in view of the coming of Messiah (Swete). βαπτίσει fut.

■ ἐγένετο s.v.4. ἦλθεν aor. ἔρχομαι s.v.7. ἐβαπτίσθη 9 aor. pass. s.v.4. ■ εὐθύς immediately, at once, so then, a favorite 10 word of Mark occurring 41 times. (For the meaning s. Taylor.) ἀναβαίνων pres. part. ἀναβαίνω to go up. εἶδεν aor. ὁράω to see. σχιζομένους pres. pass. part. σχίζω to split, to divide. The pres. part. indicates action already in progress (Cranfield). The idea is that of a fixed separation of heaven from the earth, only to be broken in special circumstances (Taylor). περιστερά dove. καταβαῖνον pres. part. καταβαίνω to come down. ■ εἰ 11 pres. 2nd per. sing. εἰμί to be. ἀγαπητός beloved. εὐδόκησα aor. εὐδοκέω to be pleased.

■ ἐκβάλλω to cast out, to drive out, the historical pres. 12 ■ ἦν s.v.6. πειραζόμενος pres. pass. part. πειράζω to try, to 13 test, to tempt, used here of an actual solicitation to evil (Gould). The pres. part. could be used to express purpose (comp. Matt. 4:1 where the inf. of purpose is used). διηκόνουν impf. διακονέω to serve, to minister to, the inceptive impf. "they began to ministcr to."

■ παραδοθῆναι aor. pass. inf. παραδίδωμι to deliver 14 over, to deliver up as a prisoner (s. Cranfield). ἦλθεν s.v.9. κηρύσσων s.v.4. ■ λέγων s.v.7. ὅτι recitative equivalent to 15 quotation marks. πεπλήρωται perf. pass. πληρόω. (For this phrase s. Swetc.) ἤγγικεν perf. ἐγγίζω to draw ncar (s. Matt. 3:2). μετανοεῖτε pres. imp. μετανοέω to repent, to change one's mind, s.v.4. πιστεύετε pres. imp. (TDNT). Here with the prep. probably a Semitism (Cranficld).

■ παράγων pres. part. παράγω to pass by, to go along. 16 εἶδεν s.v.10. ἀμφιβάλλοντας pres. part. ἀμφιβάλλω to cast a net. ἦσαν impf. εἰμί. ἁλιεύς fishermen (s. Matt. 4:18). ■ εἶπεν 17 aor. λέγω. δεῦτε adv. come here. ποιήσω fut. s.v.3. With the acc. and the inf. meaning "to cause someone to do something" (Cranfield). γενέσθαι aor. mid. inf. s.v.4. ■ ἀφέντες aor. part. 18 ἀφίημι to leave. δίκτυον net. ἠκολούθησαν aor' ἀκολουθέω to follow, to follow as a disciple. It implies personal adherence and association (Carrington). ■ προβάς aor. part. προβαίνω to 19 go forward. ὀλίγον adv. a little, a little further. καταρτίζοντας pres. part. καταρτίζω to put in order, mending, cleaning, fold-

ing, and making the nets ready for another night's fishing (Cran-
20 field). ■ ἐκάλεσεν aor. καλέω to call. μισθωτός a hired worker. ἀπῆλθον aor. ἀπέρχομαι to go forth.
21   ■ εἰσπορεύομαι to go in, historical pres. εἰσελθών aor.
part. εἰσέρχομαι to go in. συναγωγή synagogue (s. Matt. 4:23;
TDNT). ἐδίδασκεν impf. διδάσκω to teach, inceptive impf.
22 "he began to teach" (Cranfield). ■ ἐξεπλήσσοντο impf. pass.
ἐκπλήσσω to be astonished, to be amazed, to strike a person
out of his senses by some strong feeling such as fear, wonder, or
even joy (Gould). διδάσκων pres. part. used in the periphrastic
construction. ἐξουσία authority. The authority of a rabbi or
God-given authority (Cranfield; s. also TDNT). γραμματεύς
23 scribe (s. Matt. 2:4). ■ ἀνέκραξεν aor. ἀνακράζω to cry aloud,
to shout, indicating strong emotion, either the cries of the suffer-
24 er or of the unclean spirit (Taylor). ■ λέγων s.v.7. τί ἡμῖν καὶ
σοί an idiom meaning "What have we and you in common?,"
"Why do you interfere w. us?," "Mind your own business!"
(Cranfield; Taylor). ἦλθες s.v.9. ἀπολέσαι aor. inf. ἀπόλλυμι
to destroy. Infinitive used to express purpose. οἶδα defective
25 perf. w. pres. meaning to know. ■ ἐπετίμησεν aor. ἐπιτιμάω
to rebuke (s. Matt. 17:18). φιμώθητι aor. pass. imp. φιμόω to
silence, to muzzle, "be muzzled" like an ox (RWP). ἔξελθε aor.
26 imp. ἐξέρχομαι to go out. ■ σπαράξαν aor. act. part.
σπαράσσω to tear, to pull to and fro, to convulse. Medical
writers used the word of the convulsive action of the stomach
(Gould). φωνῆσαν aor. part. φωνέω to make a sound, to call
out, to cry out. These parts. are used temporally expressing
27 antecedent time ("After"). ἐξῆλθεν aor. ■ ἐθαμβήθησαν aor.
pass. θαμβέω to be astounded, to be amazed (s. Taylor). ὥστε
used w. inf. and acc. to introduce a result clause. συζητεῖν pres.
inf. συζητέω to question, to discuss. καινός new, in respect of
quality as distinct from time (Cranfield). ἐπιτάσσει pres. act.
to command. ὑπακούουσιν pres. act. 3rd pl. to obey.
29/30   ■ ἐξελθόντες aor. part. ■ πενθερά mother-in-law.
κατέκειτο impf. mid. κατάκειμαι to lie. πυρέσσουσα pres.
31 part. πυρέσσω to suffer w. a fever. ■ προσελθών aor. part.
προσέρχομαι to come to. ἤγειρεν impf. ἐγείρω to raise, to
awaken. κρατήσας aor. part. κρατέω to take hold of, used w.
partitive gen. and the part. expresses contemporaneous action
(Taylor). ἀφῆκεν aor. ἀφίημι s.v.18. διήκονει impf. inceptive
32 "she began to serve." ■ ὀψία evening. γενομένης aor. mid. part.
γίνομαι s.v.4. ἔδυσεν (ἔδυ) aor. δύω to go down, to set (for the
form, s. BD, 51). ἔφερον impf. φέρω to carry, to bring. The impf.
indicates they brought them in a steady stream (RWP). ἔχοντας

pres. part. ἔχω. In this construction to have it bad, to suffer from a sickness. δαιμονιζομένους pres. part. δαιμονίζομαι to be possessed by demon. ■ ἐπισυνηγμένη perf. pass. part. 33 ἐπισυνάγω to gather together, to assemble. The part. is used in a periphrastic construction. The tense vividly describes the growing crowds (Taylor). θύρα door. The acc. dwells on the thought of the flocking up to the door which preceded, and the surging, moving, mass before it (Swete). ■ ἐθεράπευσεν aor. 34 θεραπεύω to heal. ποικίλος various kinds, diversified, manifold. ἐξέβαλεν aor. ἐκβάλλω s.v.12. ἤφιεν impf. ἀφίημι to allow. λαλεῖν pres. inf. λαλέω to speak. ἤδεισαν plperf. οἶδα to know.

■ πρωΐ adv. early. ἔννυχα adv. at night. ἀναστάς aor. 35 part. ἀνίστημι to arise. ἀπῆλθεν s.v.20. προσηύχετο impf. προσεύχομαι to pray. The impf. denotes what He was doing when He was sought by the others (Gould). ■ κατεδίωξεν aor. 36 καταδιώκω to pursue closely, to follow down, to track down. The prep. in the v. is perfective (Taylor). ■ εὗρον aor. εὑρίσκω 37 to find. ■ ἄγωμεν pres. subj. ἄγω to lead, to go. Hortatory subj. 38 "let us go." ἀλλαχοῦ elsewhere. ἐχόμενος pres. mid. part. ἔχω. The mid. part. has the meaning "near," "neighboring." κωμόπολις a small town having only the status of a village (Cranfield). κηρύξω aor. subj. s.v.4. Subjunctive used to express purpose. ἐξῆλθον aor. either leaving Capernaum or coming from the heavenly Father (s. Alexander). ■ κηρύσσων pres. 39 part. expressing manner.

■ ἔρχεται pres. mid. historical pres. λεπρός leprous, used 40 as a substitutive leper (s. IDB, III, 111-113). παρακαλῶν pres. part. παρακαλέω to call for help. Participle of manner. γονυπετῶν pres. part. γονυπετέω to fall to the knees. ἐάν if. Indicates the condition is uncertain. θέλῃς pres. subj. θέλω to will. καθαρίσαι aor. inf. καθαρίζω to cleanse, to make clean. ■ σπλαγχνισθείς aor. pass. part. σπλαγχνίζομαι to be 41 moved w. compassion. ἐκτείνας aor. part. ἐκτείνω to stretch out. ἤψατο aor. mid. ἅπτομαι to touch (w. gen.) καθαρίσθητι aor. pass. imp. ■ ἀπῆλθεν aor. s.v.20. ἐκαθαρίσθη aor. pass. 42 ■ ἐμβριμησάμενος aor. mid. part. ἐμβριμάομαι (w. dat.) to 43 scold, censure, warn sternly (BAG), "moved by deep feeling toward him" (s. Taylor; Cranfield). ἐξέβαλεν aor. ἐκβάλλω s.v.12. ■ ὅρα pres. imp. ὁράω to see. εἴπῃς aor. subj. λέγω w. 44 neg. used to forbid the starting of an action. ὕπαγε pres. imp. ὑπάγω to go, to go away. δεῖξον aor. imp. δείκνυμι to show. προσένεγκε aor. imp. προσφέρω to carry to, to bring an offering, to offer (s. Matt. 8:4 for regulations regarding lepers).

προσέταξεν aor. προστάσσω to command, to give an order.
45 μαρτύριον witness, proof (s. Cranfield). ■ ἐξελθών aor. part.
ἐξέρχομαι to go out. ἤρξατο aor. ἄρχομαι to begin.
διαφημίζω to make known by word of mouth, to spread the
news about (BAG). ὥστε used w. inf. to express result.
εἰσέλθειν aor. inf. εἰσέρχομαι to go in, s.v.6. ἤρχοντο impf.
"the people kept on coming." πάντοθεν "from everywhere."

Ch. 2

1   ■ εἰσελθών aor. part. εἰσέρχομαι to go in. δἰ ἡμερῶν
"after some days." The prep. w. gen. has the idea of "through"
and is used here temporarily "after" (s. BD, 119). ἠκούσθη aor.
2 pass. ἀκούω to hear. ■ συνήχθησαν aor. pass. συνάγω to
gather together, to assemble. ὥστε w. inf. and the acc. to express
result. χωρεῖν pres. inf. χωρέω to make room, to have space for,
to contain. τὰ πρὸς τὴν θύραν either acc. of reference, "so that
there was no longer room for them even about the door," or to
be taken w. inf., "so that even the space about the door could no
longer contain them" (Cranfield). ἐλάλει impf. λαλέω to speak.
3 ■ ἔρχονται historical pres. φέροντες pres. part. φέρω to carry,
part. of manner. παραλυτικός paralyzed, one lame w. paralysis.
4 αἰρόμενον pres. pass. part. αἴρω to lift up, to carry. ■
δυνάμενοι pres. mid. part. δύναμαι to be able to.
προσενέγκαι aor. inf. προσφέρω to carry, to bring to. διά w.
acc. because of. ἀπεστέγασαν aor. ἀποστεγάζω to unroof, to
remove the roof. ἐξορύξαντες aor. part. ἐξορύσσω to dig out,
to tear out. The roof probably was formed by beams and rafters
across which matting, branches, and twigs, covered by earth
trodden hard, were laid (Taylor). χαλῶσι pres. χαλάω to let
down. κράβατος pallet. It was the poor man's bed (Swete).
5 κατέκειτο impf. κατάκειμαι to lie. ■ ἰδών aor. part. ὁράω to
see. ἀφίενται pres. pass. ἀφίημι to release, to forgive, an aoris-
6 tic pres. indicating punctiliar action (s. RG, 864f.). ■ ἦσαν impf.
εἰμί used w. part. to build the periphrastic impf. καθήμενοι
pres. part. κάθημαι to sit. διαλογιζόμενοι pres. mid. part.
διαλογίζομαι to reason, to debate, to balance accounts (Tay-
7 lor). ■ βλασφημεῖ pres. βλασφημέω to blaspheme (s. TDNT,
8 CBB). ἀφιέναι pres. inf. εἰ μή "except." ■ ἐπιγνούς aor. part.
9 ἐπιγνώσκω to perceive, to recognize, to know. ■
εὐκοπώτερος comp. εὔκοπος w. easy labor, easy. εἰπεῖν aor.
inf. λέγω to say. ἔγειρε pres. imp. ἐγείρω to rise. ἆρον aor. imp.
αἴρω to take up. περιπάτει pres. imp. περιπατέω to walk
about. The pres. imp. often is used to express an order involving
10 motion (Bakker, 82). ■ ἵνα w. subj. used to express purpose.

εἰδῆτε subj. of defective perf. w. pres. meaning οἶδα to know.
■ ὕπαγε pres. imp. s. Mark 1:44. ■ ἠγέρθη aor. pass. ἐγείρω 11/12
to raise, pass. to rise. ἄρας aor. part. αἴρω to take up, to lift up.
ἐξῆλθεν aor. ἐξέρχομαι to go out. ἐξίστασθαι pres. mid. inf.
ἐξίστημι to amaze, to be amazed, to be beside one's self. Infinitive used to express result. δοξάζειν pres. inf. δοξάζω to think,
to praise, to give glory to (s. TDNT, CBB). εἴδομεν aor. ὁράω
to see.

■ ἤρχετο impf. mid. ἔρχομαι. The two impfs. of this v. 13
indicate the coming and going of successive groups of hearers
(Taylor). ■ παράγων pres. part. παράγω to go by. εἶδεν aor. 14
ὁράω. τελώνιον custom office, toll house (s. Matt. 9:9; HA,
73–79). It may have been a tax station on the trade route or a
place for port duties and fishing tolls (HA, 76). ἀκολούθει pres.
imp. ἀκολουθέω to follow, to follow as a disciple (TDNT).
ἀναστας aor. act. part. ἀνίστημι to get up, to rise up.
ἠκολούθησεν aor. ■ κατακεῖσθαι pres. mid. inf. κατάκειμαι 15
to recline (at the table). Generally used of festive meals where
entertainment was provided (Cranfield). τελώνης tax collector,
publican, Not the Roman publicani but native Jews who had
been contracted to collect taxes in a town or small district (HA,
78). συνανέκειντο impf. συνανάκειμαι to recline at the table
together. ἦσαν impf. εἰμί. ἠκολούθουν impf. ■ ἰδόντες aor. 16
part. s.v.5. ἔλεγον impf. ■ ἀκούσας aor. part. ἀκούω to hear. 17
ἰσχύοντες pres. part. ἰσχύω to be strong. ἰατρός doctor, physician. ἔχοντες pres. part. ἔχω w. adv. "to have it badly," "to be
sick." ἦλθον aor. ἔρχομαι s.v.3. καλέσαι aor. inf. καλέω to
call, inf. of purpose.

■ νηστεύοντες pres. part. νηστεύω to fast. ■ εἶπεν aor. 18/19
s.v.9. νυμφών the bride chamber, "sons of the bride chamber,"
refers to either the groomsman or the wedding guest (s. Taylor).
ἐν ᾧ while. ■ ἐλεύσονται fut. mid. ἀπαρθῇ aor. pass. subj. 20
ἀπαίρω to take away. νηστεύσουσιν fut. ■ ἐπίβλημα lit. 21
"that which is place upon," patch. ῥάκος cloth. ἄγναφος new,
that which was not treated by the fuller, "a patch of undressed
cloth" (Taylor). ἐπίραπτει to sew on, the gnomic pres.
πολαιός old. εἰ δὲ μή otherwise. αἴρω s.v.3. Here the meaning
is to tear. πλήρωμα fullness, patch. χεῖρον comp. worse.
σχίσμα division, tear. ■ βάλλει pres. to throw, to put. οἶνος 22
wine. νέος new. fresh. ἀσκός skin, leather bag or bottle, wineskin (s. Taylor). ῥήξει fut. ῥήγνυμι to rip ἀπόλλυται pres.
ἀπόλλυμι to destroy, to ruin, mid. to be ruined.

■ ἐγένετο aor. mid. γίνομαι to become, to happen, to 23
come to pass. Used w. inf. to emphasize the actual occurrence

93

of the action denoted by the verb (BAG). παραπορεύεσθαι
pres. mid. inf. παραπορεύομαι to pass by. διά w. gen. through.
ἤρξαντο aor. mid. ἄρχομαι to begin. ποιεῖν pres. inf. ποιέω
to make. τίλλοντες pres. part. τίλλω to pluck, to pick. στάχυς
head or ear of grain. The word suggests the party was pushing
its way through the corn where there was no path. As they went,
24 they plucked the ears and ate (Swete). ■ ἔλεγον inceptive impf.
"they began to say." ἴδε aor. imp. ὁράω to see. ἔξεστιν it is
25 allowed, it is lawful. ■ ἀνέγνωτε aor. ἀναγινώσκω to read.
ἐποίησεν aor. ἔσχεν aor. ἔχω to have. ἐπείνασεν aor. πεινάω
26 to be hungry. ■ εἰσῆλθεν aor. s.v.1. ἐπί w. gen. "in time of"
or "in the passage about" (RWP). ἄρτος προσθέσεως the
shewbread. The twelve newly baked loaves of bread placed every
Sabbath in two rows on a table before God in the Tabernacle and
later eaten by priests (Lev. 24:5-9) (Taylor). ἔφαγεν aor. ἐσθίω
to eat. φαγεῖν aor. inf. ἔδωκεν aor. δίδωμι to give. οὖσιν pres.
27 part. εἰμί to be. ■ διά w. acc. because of, for.

Ch. 3

1   ■ ἐξηραμμένην perf. pass. part. ξηραίνω to dry out, to
become dry, to wither, to be withered. The perf. points to a
withered state and may show that it was not from birth but was
2 the result of injury by accident or disease (RWP). ■
παρετήρουν impf. act. παρατηρέω to observe from the side,
to observe minutely, going along as it were w. the object for the
purpose of watching its movements (Swete). ποῖς σάββασιν
dat. of time. θεραπεύσει fut. θεραπεύω to heal.
κατηγορήσωσιν aor. subj. κατηγορέω w. gen. to accuse, to
3/4 bring charges against. ■ ἔγειρε pres. imp. "stand up!" ■ ἔξεστιν
it is allowed, it is lawful. ποιῆσαι aor. inf. ποιέω to do.
κακοποιέω to do evil. ἐσιώπων impf. act. σιωπάω to be silent.
5   ■ περιβλεψάμενος aor. mid. part. περιβλέπω to look around.
The prep. compound is local (s. MH, 321f.). συλλυπούμενος
pres. mid. part. συλλυπέομαι to be grieved w., to feel sympathy. The prep. compound may be perfective "utterly distressed"
(MH, 325). πώρωσις hardening. ἔκτεινον aor. imp. ἐκτείνω to
stretch out. ἐξέτεινιν aor. ἀπεκατεστάθη aor. pass.
6 ἀποκαθίστημι to restore again (s. MM). ■ συμβούλιον consolation. ἐδίδουν impf. δίδωμι to give, to give counsel, to plot
(BAG; Taylor). ὅπως w. subj. to express purpose. ἀπολέσωσιν
aor. subj. ἀπόλλυμι to destroy.

7   ■ ἀνεχώρησεν aor. ἀναχωρέω to depart. ἠκολούθησεν
8 aor. act. ἀκολουθέω to follow. ■ ἐποίει impf. "the things he was
9 continually doing." ἦλθον aor. ἔρχομαι to come. ■ πλοιάριον

dimin., a small boat. προσκαρτερῇ pres. subj. προσκαρτερέω
w. dat. to attach one's self to, to wait on. The idea is that the boat
is at the disposal of Jesus as a refuge from the pressure of the
crowd (Taylor). θλίβωσιν pres. subj. θλίβω to pressure, to
squeeze. ■ ἐθεράπευσεν aor. s.v.2. ὥστε w. inf. to express 10
result. ἐπιπίπτειν pres. inf. to fall upon. ἅψωνται aor. subj.
ἅπτομαι w. gen. to touch. μάστιξ whip, scourge, disease,
thought of as divine chastisements (Alexander). ■ ἀκάθαρτος 11
unclean. ἐθεώρουν impf. θεωρέω to see, the iterat. impf., "every
time they saw." προσέπιπτον impf. προυπίπτω to fall before.
ἔκραζον impf. κράζω to cry out, to scream. ■ πολλά adv., 12
much, very. ἐπετίμα impf. ἐπιτιμάω w. dat. to rebuke, to sternly charge (s. Matt. 17:18).

■ προσκαλεῖται pres. mid. προσκαλέω to call to one's 13
self, to summon. ἤθελεν impf. θέλω to will. ἀπῆλθον aor.
ἀπέρχομαι to go forth, to go out. ■ ὦσιν subj. εἰμί. ■ ἐξουσία 14/15
authority (s. TDNT). ■ ἐπέθηκεν aor. ἐπιτίθημι to place upon, 16
to give a name. ■ βροντή thunder. ■ παρέδωκεν aor. 17/19
παραδίδωμι to deliver over, to betray.

■ συνέρχομαι pres. mid., to come together, historical pres. 20
δύνασθαι pres. mid. inf. δύναμαι to be able to, used w. ὥστε
to express result. φαγεῖν aor. inf. ἐσθίω to eat. ■ οἱ παρ᾽ αὐτοῦ 21
"the ones w. him," "his family" (s. Cranfield). ἐξῆλθον aor.
ἐξέρχομαι to go out (from Nazareth to Capernaum). κρατῆσαι
aor. inf. κρατέω to take hold of, to arrest. The family wanted to
get hold of Jesus, to take control of His actions (Taylor). ἐξέστη
aor. ἐξίστημι to be out of one's mind. (For the view that it was
the crowd that was out of control w. enthusiasm and Jesus'
followers sought to calm them, s. Henry Wansbrough, "Mark
3:21—Was Jesus Out of His Mind?" NTS, 18 [January, 1972],
231-235.) ■ καταβάντες aor. part. καταβαίνω to come down. 22
ἄρχοντι pres. part. masc. dat. sing. ἄρχω to be a ruler, prince.
■ προσκαλεσάμενος aor. mid. part. s.v.13. ■ ἐφ᾽ = ἐπί w. acc. 23/24
against. μερισθῇ aor. pass. subj. μερίζω pass., to be divided.
σταθῆναι aor. pass. inf. ἵστημι to stand. ■ δυνήσεται fut. 25
s.v.20. ■ εἰ "if." Introduces a conditional clause which the 26
speaker assumes to be true. "Suppose Satan to have actually
risen up against himself . . . then he is at this moment in an
unstable condition, his end has come" (Swete). ἀνέστη aor.
ἀνίστημι to stand up, to rise up. ἐμερίσθη aor. pass. ■ σκεῦος 27
vessel, pl. goods. διαρπάσαι aor. inf. διαρπάζω to plunder.
The prep. in compound is perfective, "to thoroughly ransack"
(RWP). δήσῃ aor. subj. δέω to bind. ■ ἀμήν (Heb.) "truly." He 28
solemnly guarantees the truth of what He is about to say. It is

the equivalent of "as I live, saith the Lord" in the OT (Cranfield;
s. also Matt. 5:18, TDNT). ἀφεθήσεται fut. pass. ἀφίημι to
29 release, to forgive. ἁμάρτημα sin, the act of sin (Swete). ■ εἰς
against. ἄφεσις release, forgiveness. ἔνοχος w. gen. liable,
30 guilty of. ■ ὅτι because.
31 ■ ἔξω outside. στήκοντες pres. part. στήκω. Late pres.
form from the perf. of ἵστημι, to stand (BAG). καλοῦντες pres.
32 part. καλέω to call. A request for an interview (Taylor). ■
ἐκάθητο impf. κάθημαι to sit. ζητοῦσιν pres. ζητέω to seek.
33/34 ■ ἀποκριθείς aor. pass. part. ἀποκρίνομαι to answer. ■
περιβλεψάμενος aor. mid. part. s.v.5. κύκλος in a circle. ἴδε
aor. imp. ὁράω to see.

Ch. 4

1 ■ συνάγεται pres. pass. συνάγω to gather together, to
assemble, historical pres. πλεῖστος superl. πολύς much, many.
The elative use of the superl. (BD, 33). ὥστε w. inf. to express
result. ἐμβάντα aor. part. ἐμβαίνω to get in, to embark.
καθῆσθαι pres. inf. κάθημαι to sit. Infinitive used to express
2 result. ■ ἐδίδασκεν impf., inceptive impf. "he began to teach."
παραβολή parable. A brief utterance connected with a com-
3 parison or image (Lane; s. Matt. 13:3; Cranfield). ■ ἀκούετε
pres. imp. ἀκούω to hear, to listen. This recalls the Shema of
Deut. 6:4 (Swete; s. also Matt. 13:19). σπείρων pres. part.
σπείρω to sow (seed). σπεῖραι aor. inf. Infinitive used to ex-
4 press purpose. ■ ἔπεσεν aor. πίπτω to fall. πετεινά birds.
5 κατέφαγεν aor. κατεσθίω to eat up. ■ πετρώδης rocklike,
stony, of shallow soil with underlying rock (AS). εἶχεν impf.
ἔχω to have. ἐξανέτειλεν aor. ἐξανατέλλω to spring up. διά
6 w. inf. to express cause. ■ ἐκαυματίσθη aor. pass. καυματίζω
to burn, to scorch, "it felt the burning heat" (Swete). ἐξηράνθη
7 aor. pass. ξηραίνω to dry up. ■ ἄκανθα thorn. ἀνέβησαν aor.
ἀναβαίνω to go up, to grow up. Used in LXX of the springing
up of vegetation (Taylor). συνέπνιξαν aor. συμπνίγω to press
closely, to choke. Used of plants whose food and light is cut off
8 by weeds (BAG). ἔδωκεν aor. δίδωμι to give. ■ ἐδίδου impf.
ἀναβαίνοντα pres. part. s.v.7. αὐξανόμενα pres. pass. part.
9 αὐξάνω pass. to grow. ■ οὖς, ὠτός ear. ἀκουέτω pres. imp. 3rd
sing., s.v.3.
10 ■ κατὰ μόνας alone. ἠρώτων impf. ἐρωτάω to question,
11 to ask. ■ μυστήριον mystery, that which man cannot know
apart from God's revelation (s. TDNT; CBB). δέδοται perf.
12 pass. δίδωμι. ■ ἴδωσιν aor. subj. ὁράω to see. συνιῶσι pres.
subj. συνίημι to comprehend, to understand. μήποτε lest.

96

ἐπιστρέψωσιν aor. subj. ἐπιστρέφω to turn around, to repent. For those who are not disciples the purpose of the parables is to conceal the truth and to prevent repentance and forgiveness (Taylor). ἀφεθῇ aor. pass. subj. ἀφίημι to release, to forgive.
■ οἶδα defective perf. w. pres. meaning to know. γνώσεσθε 13 fut. mid. γινώσκω to know. οἶδα is used in reference to knowledge which comes from intuition or insight, γινώσκω of that which is gained by experience or acquaintance (Swete). ■ 15 σπείρεται pres. pass. ἀκούσωσιν aor. subj. αἴρει pres. to lift up, to take away. ἐσπαρμένον perf. pass. part. σπείρω to sow. ■ πρόσκαιρος temporary, lasting for a time. γενομένης aor. 17 mid. part. gen. abs. "when tribulation or persecution comes." σκανδαλίζονται pres. pass. σκανδαλίζω to cause to stumble. They are trapped at once because their faith is so feeble (Taylor; s. also TDNT). ■ μέριμνα concern, care. ἀπάτη deceit. 19 ἐπιθυμία desire, longing. The prep. in the compound is directive "having one's passion toward" (Taylor). εἰσπορευόμεναι pres. part. εἰσπορεύομαι to come in. ἄκαρπος unfruitful. ■ 20 σπαρέντες aor. pass. part. σπείρω. παραδέχονται pres. mid. to receive, to accept. This denotes a favorable reception (Gould). καρποφοροῦσιν pres. act. καρποφορέω to bear fruit.
     ■ μήτι used w. a question expecting a strong neg. answer 21 (Gould). A rabbinical way of expressing a prohibition (s. LNT, 199f.). ἔρχεται pres. mid. Perhaps an indication that Jesus was thinking of Himself and His mission (Cranfield). λύχνος lamp. (s. Matt. 5:15). The definite article used here could refer to a special lamp. Perhaps the Hanukkah lamp (LNT, 200). ἵνα used to express purpose or intent. μόδιος bushel. A dry measure containing nearly two gallons (Taylor). τεθῇ aor. pass. subj. τίθημι to place. The man who lit the Hanukkah lamp. w. the intention of afterward covering or hiding it, did not do his duty by lighting the lamp (LNT, 207). σύχ used in a question expecting a positive answer. λυχνία lampstand. The possible interpretation of this difficult saying is "just as the little light kindled at Hanukkah is intended to burn itself out in praise of God and His miracles, so people did not scruple to push it under the bed, so it is sinful to disregard Heavenly illumination or in any way to impair its capacity to illuminate" (LNT, 207). ■ κρυπτός hid- 22 den. φανερωθῇ aor. pass. subj. φανερόω to make clear, to manifest. ἀπόκρυφος secret, hidden. ἔλθῃ aor. subj. ■ 23 ἀκουέτω pres. imp. 3rd sing.
     ■ μετρεῖτε pres. act. μετρέω to measure. μετρηθήσεται 24 fut. pass. προστεθήσεται fut. pass. προστίθημι to add to. "Your attention to the teaching will be the measure of the profit

25 you will receive from it" (Swete). ■ δοθήσεται fut. pass. δίδωμι
to give. ἀρθήσεται fut. pass. αἴρω.

26/27   ■ βάλῃ aor. subj. βάλλω to cast. ■ καθεύδῃ pres. subj.
καθεύδω to sleep. ἐγείρηται pres. subj. pass. ἐγείρω pass., to
rise, to awaken. νύξ, -κτός night. The sleeping and rising go on
continually from day to day (RG, 470). βλαστᾷ pres. subj.
βλαστάω to grow. μηκύνηται pres. pass. subj. μηκύνω to
make long, pass. to become long, to grow (BAG). ὡς after verbs
28 of saying, thinking "how" (Taylor). ■ χόρτος grass, the green
shoot. εἶτεν then (s. BD, 19). στάχυς head or ear of grain.
29 σῖτος wheat, grain. ■ παραδοῖ aor. subj., to give over, to allow.
δρέπανον sickle. παρέστηκεν perf. act. παρίστημι to place
beside; perf. of a point of time, to be here, to have come (BAG).
30   ■ ὁμοιώσωμεν pres. subj. ὁμοιόω to make alike, to compare. θῶμεν aor. subj. τίθημι to place. Used of setting forth an
idea in symbolism (AS). The subjs. are deliberative subjs. (IBG,
31 22). ■ κόκκος kernel, seed. σίναπι mustard. μικρότερος
32 comp. μικρός small. ■ μεῖζον comp. μέγας large. λάχανον
plant, vegetable, gen. of comparison. ποιεῖ pres. ποιέω to make,
to produce. κλάδος branch. σκιά shadow. κατασκηνοῦν pres.
inf. κατασκηνόω to put up a tent, to dwell.
33   ■ ἐλάλει impf. λαλέω to speak. ἠδύναντο impf. δύναμαι.
34 ■ χωρίς w. gen. without. ἐπέλυεν impf. ἐπιλύω to untie, to
release, to explain, to expound.
35   ■ ὀψία evening, late afternoon. γενομένης aor. part.
γίνομαι to become, gen. abs. διέλθωμεν aor. subj. διέρχομαι
to go through, to go across. (For the prep. w. compound, s. MH,
36 300f.) Hortatory subj. ■ ἀφέντες aor. part. ἀφίημι to dismiss,
37 to send away. παραλαμβάνω to take w. ■ λαῖλαψ a furious
storm, a hurricane, squall (Taylor). κῦμα wave. ἐπέβαλλεν
impf. ἐπιβάλλω threw upon, intr. to strike upon. "The waves
were beating into the boat" (Gould). ὥστε used w. inf. to express
result. ἤδη already. γεμίζεσθαι pres. pass. inf. γεμίζω to fill,
38 pass. to become full. ■ πρύμνην the stern of a ship. κεφάλαιον
pillow, cushion. Presumably a rower's wooden or leathern seat
used as a headrest (Taylor); or it may have been the pillow that
was customarily kept for those not involved in sailing or fishing
(Lane). καθεύδων pres. part. used in a periphrastic construction. μέλει σοι "Is it no concern to you?" ἀπολλύμεθα "we are
39 perishing." ■ διεγερθείς aor. pass. part. διεγείρω to wake up,
"to arouse completely" (Taylor). ἐπετίμησεν aor. ἐπιτιμάω to
rebuke, to sternly warn (s. Matt. 17:18). εἶπεν aor. λέγω.
σιώπα pres. imp. σιωπάω to be silent. πεφίμωσο perf. pass.
imp. φιμόω to muzzle, to silence. The perf. indicates "put the

muzzle on and keep it on" (RG, 908; s. also M, 176; MKG, 264f.). ἐκόπασεν aor. κοπάζω to grow weary, to cease. Used in the LXX of water in repose after a storm or flood (Swete). γαλήνη calm. ■ δειλός cowardly, timid. ■ ἐφοβήθησαν aor. 40/41 φοβέομαι to be afraid. φόβυς fear. (For the cognate acc., s. RG, 477f.; BD, 84f.) ὑπακούω to listen to, to obey.

Ch. 5

■ ἦλθον aor. ἔρχομαι to come, to go. ■ ἐξελθόντος aor. 1/2 part. ἐξέρχομαι to go out, to come out, gen. abs. ὑπήντησεν aor. ὑπαντάω to meet. ■ κατοίκησις living quarters, dwelling. 3 According to the Talmud there were four signs of madness; walking abroad at night, spending the night on a grave, tearing one's clothes, destroying what one was given (Lane). ἅλυσις chain. ἐδύνατο impf. δύναμαι to be able. δῆσαι aor. inf. δέω to bind. ■ διά because, but here the construction indicates not 4 the reason but the circumstances mentioned by way of explanation (Cranfield). πολλάκις often. πέδη bonds for the feet, shackles. δεδέσθαι perf. pass. inf. δέω. The perf. indicates the condition or state. διεσπάσθαι perf. pass. inf. διασπάω. to tear apart. συντετρῖφθαι perf. pass. inf. συντρίβω to shatter, to smash, to crush. ἴσχυεν impf. ἰσχύω to be strong. δαμάσαι aor. inf. δαμάζω to tame. ■ κράζων pres. part. κράζω to cry 5 out, to scream. This and the following part. used in a periphrastic construction emphasize the repeated action. κατακόπτων pres. part. κατακόπτω to cut to pieces. The prep. compound is perfective. His body in this way may have been gashed and scarred all over (Swete). ■ ἰδών aor. part. ὁράω to see. μακρόθεν adv. 6 from afar. ἔδραμεν aor. act. πρέχω to run. προσεκύνησεν aor. προσκυνέω to worship, to worship by falling on the knees. ■ κράξας aor. part. ὕψιστος superl. most high. ὁρκίζω to ad- 7 jure, to implore. βασανίσῃς aor. subj. 2nd sing. βασανίζω to examine, to torture. ■ ἔλεγεν impf. ἔξελθε aor. impf. ■ 8/9 ἐπηρώτα impf. ἐπερωτάω to consult, to inquire of, to ask (Taylor). λεγιών legion, a unit of the Roman army containing approximately six thousand men (s. Matt. 26:53). ■ παρεκάλει 10 impf. παρακαλέω to call to, to beseech, to plead w. ἀποστείλῃ aor. subj. ἀποστέλλω to send away.

■ πρός w. dat. by, near by. ἀγέλη herd. χοῖρος pig, swine. 11 βοσκομένη pres. part. βόσκομαι to graze, to feed. Participle used in a periphrastic construction. ■ παρεκάλεσαν aor. 12 λέγοντες pres. part. πέμψον aor. imp. πέμπω to send. εἰσέλθωμεν aor. subj. εἰσέρχομαι to go in. ■ ἐπέτρεψεν aor. 13 ἐπιτρέπω to allow. εἰσῆλθον aor. ὥρμησεν aor. ὁρμάω to set

out, to rush. κατά w. gen. down. κρημνός cliff, precipice, steep
bank. ώς (w. numbers) about. έπγίγοντο impf. pass. πνίγω to
14 choke, to drown. ■ βόσκοντες pres. part. βόσκω to feed, to
graze a herd. έφυγον aor. φεύγω to flee. άπήγγειλαν aor.
άπαγγέλλω to bring news, to report, "for those in the city and
for those in the fields." Not an incidence of είς used in the sense
of έν (s. John J. O'Rourke, "A Note Concerning the Use of ΕΙΣ
and ΕΝ in Mark," JBL, 85 [Sept., 1966], 349–351). ίδεῖν aor.
inf. γεγονός perf. part. γίνομαι to become, to happen. The perf.
emphasizes the continuing state or condition of that which had
15 happened. ■ θεωροῦσιν pres. θεωρέω to see. δαιμονιζόμενον
pres. mid. part. δαιμονίζομαι to be possessed by a demon. The
"imperfective" part., "the man who used to be (or, who had until
now been) a demonic." (T.L. McKay, "Syntax in Exegesis," TB,
23 [1972], 48.) καθήμενον pres. part. κάθημαι to sit.
ίματισμένον perf. pass. part. ίματίζω to clothe, to be clothed.
The perf. emphasizing his pres. condition or state.
σωφρονοῦντα pres. act. part. σωφρονέω to be of sound mind,
to be in one's right mind. The man was master of himself again
(Swete; s. also TDNT; CBB). έσχηκότα perf. act. part. έχω to
have. Not an aoristic perf. but expressing an "ex-state"; i.e.,
"having had and now free of" (McKay TB, 23 [1972], 48).
16 έφοβήθησαν aor. φοβέομαι to fear, to be afraid. ■
διηγήσαντο aor. διηγέομαι to relate, to set out in detail (Taylor). (For the prep. compound, s. MH, 301.) έγένετο aor.
17 γίνομαι. ■ ήρξαντο aor. άρχομαι to begin. παρακαλεῖν pres.
18 inf. άπελθεῖν aor. inf. άπέρχομαι to go away. ■ έμβαίνοντος
pres. part. έμβαίνω to get in, to embark. δαιμονισθείς aor.
19 pass. part. ῇ subj. είμί. ■ άφῆκεν aor. άφίημι to release, to
allow. ύπαγε pres. imp. ύπάγω to go, to go forth. άπάγγειλον
aor. imp. πεποίηκεν perf. ποιέω to do. ήλέησεν aor. έλεέω to
show mercy, to be merciful (s. TDNT). The change from perf.
to aor. is deliberate. The man has received blessings which abide
20 and which are a definite boon in his cure (Taylor). ■ άπῆλθεν
aor. κηρύσσειν pres. inf., to proclaim, to proclaim as a herald.
έποίησεν aor. έθαύμαζον impf. θαυμάζω to marvel, to wonder.
21   ■ διαπεράσαντος aor. part. διαπεράω to cross over, gen.
abs. συνήχθη aor. pass. συνάγω to gather together, to assem-
22 ble. ■ έρχεται pres. mid. historical pres. άρχισυνάγωγος leader or president of a synagogue. The official whose duty it was to
take care of the physical arrangements for the worship services
23 (BAG; s. also SB, IV, 115–152; TDNT). ίδων s.v.6. ■
παρακαλεῖ pres. s.v.10. θυγάτριον daughter. The dimin. ap-

pears to be used as a term of affection, "my little daughter"
(Taylor). ἐσχάτως ἔχει "to be at the point of death" (Gould).
ἐλθών aor. part. s.v.1. ἐπιθῇς aor. subj. ἐπιτίθημι to place
upon. Used w. ἵνα in the sense of an imp. (s. IGB, 144f.). σωθῇ
aor. pass. subj. σῴζω to save, to heal. ζήσῃ aor. subj. ζάω to
live. ■ ἀπῆλθεν s.v.20.   24

    ἠκολούθει impf. ἀκολουθέω to follow. συνέθλιβον impf.
συνθλίβω to press together, to press upon. ■ οὖσα pres. part. 25
fem. sing. εἰμί to be. ῥύσις flow, suffering from hemorrhage
(Swete). δώδεκα ἔτη "twelve years," acc. of time. ■ παθοῦσα 26
aor. act. part. fem. sing. πάσχω to suffer. ἰατρός doctor.
δαπανήσασα aor. act. part. fem. sing. δαπανάω to spend, to
spend freely. ὠφεληθεῖσα aor. pass. part. ὠφελέω to profit, to
receive benefit, pass. to receive help. χείρων comp. worse.
ἐλθοῦσα aor. part. ἔρχομαι. ■ ἀκούσασα aor. fem. part. 27
ἀκούω to hear. ἥψατο aor. ἅπτομαι to touch. ■ ἔλεγεν s.v.8. 28
ἅψωμαι aor. subj. σωθήσομαι fut. pass. ■ ἐξηράνθη aor. pass. 29
ξηραίνω to dry, to dry up. πηγή spring, fountain, source. ἔγνω
aor. γινώσκω to know. ἴαται perf. pass. ἰάομαι to heal. According to Jewish teaching her touch should have made Jesus
unclean (M, Zabim 5,1), but Jesus made her clean. μάστιξ
scourge, plague. ■ ἐπιγνούς aor. part. ἐπιγινώσκω to know, to 30
recognize. ἐξελθοῦσαν s.v.2. ἐπιστραφείς aor. pass. part.
ἐπιστρέφω to turn around. ■ συνθλίβοντα pres. part. ■ 31/32
περιεβλέπετο impf. mid. περιβλέπω to look around, to look
about one's self. ἰδεῖν aor. inf. ὁράω to see. ποιήσασαν aor.
act. part. fem. sing. ποιέω to do, to make. ■ φοβηθεῖσα aor. 33
part. s.v.15. τρέμουσα pres. part. τρέμω to shake, to tremble.
εἰδυῖα fem. part. of defective perf. οἶδα w. pres. meaning to
know. γέγονεν perf. s.v.14. ἦλθεν s.v.1. προσέπεσεν aor.
προσπίπτω to fall down before someone. ■ σέσωκεν perf. act. 34
The perf. emphasizes the pres. state as a result of a completed
action. Perhaps Mark had a double meaning, the religious sense
of the word being suggested as well as the sense to heal (Cranfield). ἴσθι imp. εἰμί "continue whole and well" (RWP; s. also
M, 174, 226).

    ■ λαλοῦντος pres. part. λαλέω to speak, gen. abs. 35
ἀπέθανεν aor. ἀποθῄσκω to die. σκύλλω to flay, to skin, to
trouble, to annoy. ■ παρακούσας aor. part. παρακούω to hear 36
beside, to overhear, to refuse to hear (s. Taylor). λαλούμενον
pres. pass. part. φοβοῦ pres. imp. φοβέομαι w. neg. to stop an
action in progress, "stop fearing!" πίστευε pres. imp. πιστεύω
to believe, to trust. ■ ἀφῆκεν aor. ἀφίημι (w. inf.) to allow, to 37
permit. συνακολουθῆσαι aor. act. inf. συνακολουθέω to fol-

38 low along, to follow w. ■ θεωρεῖ pres. θεωρέω to see, to observe,
   historical pres. θόρυβος turmoil, uproar. κλαίοντας pres. part.
   κλαίω to cry, loud weeping. ἀλαλάζοντας pres. part.
   ἀλαλάζω to shout, to wail. The two parts. explain the turmoil
39 (Cranfield). ■ εἰσελθών aor. part. s.v.12. θορυβεῖσθε pres.
   pass. θορυβέω to throw into disorder, pass. to be troubled, dis-
40 tressed, aroused. καθεύδω to sleep. ■ κατεγέλων impf.
   καταγελάω w. gen. to laugh at, to deride, to jeer at. The prep.
   compound is perfective (Taylor). ἐκβαλών aor. part. ἐκβάλλω
   to send out. παραλαμβάνω to take w. εἰσπορεύομαι to go in.
41 ■ κρατήσας aor. part. κρατέω w. gen. to take hold of. ταλιθά
   (Aramaic) fem. form, "youth" (Gould). κοῦμ (Aramaic) arise!
   μεθερμηνευόμενον pres. pass. part. μεθερμηνεύω to translate.
   κοράσιον dimin. form, girl, little girl. ἔγειρε imp. ἐγείρω to
42 arise. ■ ἀνέστη aor. ἀνίστημι to stand up, to arise.
   περιεπάτει impf. περιπατέω to walk about, inceptive impf.,
   "she began to walk about." ἐξέστησαν aor. ἐξίστημι to be
43 astonished, to be bewildered. ■ διεστείλατο aor. mid.
   διαστέλλω to divide or distinguish, mid. to give an explicit
   order, to command (Swete). γνοῖ aor. subj. γινώσκω to know.
   δοθῆναι aor. pass. inf. δίδωμι. Infinitive used after a verb of
   saying (s. Taylor). φαγεῖν aor. inf. ἐσθίω to eat.

Ch. 6

1 ■ ἐξῆλθεν aor. ἐξέρχομαι to go out. ἀκολουθοῦσιν pres.
2 ἀκολουθέω to follow, historical pres. ■ γενομένου aor. part.
   γίνομαι to become, to happen, gen. abs. ἤρξατο aor. ἄρχομαι
   to begin. ἀκούοντες pres. part. ἀκούω to hear. ἐξεπλήσσοντο
   impf. pass. ἐκπλήσσω to amaze, pass. to be amazed, to be
   overwhelmed. λέγοντες pres. part. λέγω. πόθεν where, from
   where. δοθεῖσα aor. pass. part. δίδωμι to give. γινόμεναι pres.
3 mid. part. ■ τέκτων builder, carpenter, woodworker, one who
   works with hard material (Lane). ἐσκανδαλίζοντο impf. pass.
   σκανδαλίζω to cause to stumble, pass. to be offended (s.
4 TDNT). ■ ἄτιμος without honor. (For the Alpha prefix forming
   the neg., s. A.C. Moorhouse, Studies in the Greek Negatives,
5 41–68.) συγγενής relative, kinsman. ■ ἐδύνατο impf. δύναμαι
   to be able. ποιῆσαι aor. inf. ποιέω to do. ἄρρωστος weak, sick.
   ἐπιθείς aor. ἐπιτίθημι to place upon. ἐθεράπευσεν aor.
6 θεραπεύω to heal. ■ ἐθαύμασεν aor. θαυμάζω to wonder, to
   be amazed.
        περιῆγεν impf. περιάγω to go about, to go around.
7 διδάσκων pres. part. διδάσκω to teach. ■ προσκαλεῖται
   pres. mid. προσκαλέομαι to summons, to call. ἤρξατο s.v.2.

ἐδίδου impf. δίδωμι to give. ■ παρήγγειλεν aor. 8
παραγγέλλω to give instruction, to command. αἴρωσιν pres.
subj. αἴρω to lift up, to take. ῥάβδος staff. πήρα leather pouch,
wallet (s. Matt. 10:10). ζώνη belt. Ancient custom was to keep
small change in the girdle (Taylor; s. also Matt. 10:9). ■ 9
ὑπυδεδεμένους perf. mid. part. ὑποδέω to bind under, to put
on shoes. σανδάλιον sandals. ἐνδύσησθε pres. mid. subj.
ἐνδύω mid. clothe, to put on clothes. ■ εἰσέλθητε aor. subj. 10
εἰσέρχομαι to go in, to come in. μένετε pres. imp. μένω to
remain. ἐξέλθητε aor. subj. s.v.1. ■ δέξηται aor. subj. δέχομαι 11
to welcome, to receive. ἀκούσωσιν aor. subj. s.v.2.
ἐκπορευόμενοι pres. mid. part. ἐκπορεύομαι to go out.
ἐκτινάξατε aor. imp. ἐκτινάσσω to shake, to shake off. χοῦς
earth, dust (s. Matt. 10:14). ■ ἐξελθόντες aor. part. s.v.1. 12
ἐκήρυξαν aor. κηρύσσω to proclaim as a herald (s. TDNT).
μετανοῶσιν pres. subj. μετανοέω to change the mind, to repent. ■ ἐξέβαλλον impf. ἐκβάλλω to cast out, to drive out. 13
ἤλειφον impf. ἀλείφω to anoint w. oil. ἐθεράπευον impf. s.v.5.
■ ἤκουσεν aor. s.v.2. ἐγένετο aor. s.v.2. βαπτίζων pres. 14
act. part. βαπτίζω to dip, to baptize (s. Matt. 3:6; TDNT).
ἐγήγερται perf. pass. ἐγείρω to raise, pass. to rise, to be resurrected. The perf. indicates has risen and is therefore alive and
among us again (Swete). ἐνεργοῦσιν pres. act. ἐνεργέω to be
operative, to be at work. ■ ἀκούσας aor. part. ἀπεκεφάλισα 16
aor. ἀποκεφαλίζω to behead. ἠγέρθη aor. pass. (For a detailed
discussion of this passage, s. HA, 184–197.) ■ ἀποστείλας aor. 17
part. s.v.7. ἐκράτησεν aor. κρατέω to seize, to arrest. ἔδησεν
aor. δέω to bind. ἐγάμησεν aor. γαμέω to marry (s. HA, 131–
136). ■ ἔξεστιν it is lawful, it is allowed. (For the unlawfulness 18
of this marriage, s. HA, 137–146.) ■ ἐνεῖχεν impf. ἐνέχω w. dat. 19
to have it in for someone, to hold a grudge (s. Taylor). ἤθελεν
impf. θέλω to will, to want. ἀποκτεῖναι aor. inf. ἀποκτείνω to
kill. ■ ἐφοβεῖτο impf. φοβέομαι to fear. The impf. pictures the 20
continual fearing. εἰδώς defective perf. part. w. pres. meaning
οἶδα to know. συνετήρει impf. συντηρέω to guard, to keep
safe. The prep. compound is perfective (s. Taylor; M, 116).
ἠπόρει impf. ἀπυρέω to be at a loss, in doubt. ἡδέως adv.
gladly. ἤκουεν impf. ■ γενομένης aor. mid. part. gen. abs. 21
εὔκαιρος opportune, suitable. γενέσια birthday. δεῖπνον dinner. ἐποίησεν aor. s.v.5. μεγιστᾶνες the great ones, courtiers.
χιλίαρχος literally the leader of a thousand soldiers, later the
commander of a cohort. Roughly, equivalent to our present-day
major or colonel (HA, 119; BAG). ■ εἰσελθούσης aor. act. part. 22
fem. sing. gen. abs. ὀρχησαμένης aor. mid. part. ὀρχέομαι to

103

dance, not necessarily a sensual dance (HA, 157). ἤρεσεν aor. ἀρέσκω to please. συνανακειμένοις pres. mid. part. συνανάκειμαι to recline at the table w. someone. κοράσιον girl, dimin. little girl, a young girl at or near marriageable age, probably around fourteen years old. (For the meaning of the term and the identity of the girl, s. HA, 151–156.) αἴτησον aor. imp. αἰτέω to ask, to request. θέλῃς pres. subj. θέλω. δώσω fut.

23 δίδωμι to give. ■ ὤμοσεν aor. ὄμνυμι to swear. (For the oath of Herod, s. HA, 165–167.) αἰτήσῃς aor. subj. ἥμισυς half.

24 ■ ἐξελθοῦσα aor. part. fem. sing. s.v.1. αἰτήσωμαι aor. subj. mid. The change from act. to mid. is intentional and indicates the

25 urgency of the request. The subj. is deliberative (Taylor). ■ σπουδή haste, speed. ἠτήσατο aor. mid. λέγουσα pres. act. part. fem. sing. ἐξαυτῆς immediately. δῷς aor. subj. δίδωμι to

26 give. πίναξ a board, plate, dish. ■ περίλυπος sorrowful, very sad. ὅρκος oath. The pl. suggests repeated oaths (Taylor). ἠθέλησεν aor. ἀθετῆσαι aor. inf. ἀθετέω to set aside, "would

27 not break faith w. her," "disappoint her" (Swete). ■ σπεκουλάτωρ used to denote a member of the headquarters staff of a legionary commander in the Roman imperial army or of a provincial governor whose duties included the carrying out of executions, hence, "executioner" (Cranfield). ἐπέταξεν aor. ἐπιτάσσω to instruct, to command. ἐνέγκαι aor. inf. φέρω to

28 carry, to bring. ἀπελθών aor. part. ἀπέρχομαι to go out. ■

29 ἤνεγκεν aor. φέρω. ἔδωκεν aor. δίδωμι. ■ ἀκούσαντες aor. part. s.v.2. ἦλθον aor. ἔρχομαι to go, to come. ἦραν aor. αἴρω to take up, to take away. πτῶμα body, corpse. ἔθηκαν aor. τίθημι to place.

30 ■ συνάγονται pres. pass. συνάγω to gather together, to assemble. ἀπήγγειλαν aor. ἀπαγγέλλω to report. ἐποίησαν

31 aor. s.v.5. ἐδίδαξαν aor. διδάσκω. ■ δεῦτε "come!" ἀναπαύσασθε aor. imp. ἀναπαύομαι to cease, to rest. ὑπάγοντες pres. act. part. ὑπάγω to depart, to go forth. φαγεῖν aor. inf. ἐσθίω to eat. εὐκαίρουν impf. εὐκαιρέω to have time,

32/33 to have opportunity. ■ ἀπῆλθον aor. s.v.27. ■ εἶδον aor. ὁράω to see. ἐπέγνωσαν aor. ἐπιγινώσκω to know, to recognize. πεζῇ by foot. συνέδραμον aor. συντρέχω to run together.

34 προῆλθον aor. προέρχομαι to go before. ■ ἐξελθών aor. part. ἐσπλαγχνίσθη aor. pass. σπλαγχνίζομαι to have pity, to feel sympathy, to be moved w. compassion (s. MNTW, 156–160). ἔχοντα pres. part. ἔχω. ποιμήν shepherd. The figure denotes

35 the lack of spiritual guidance (Gould). ἤρξατο s.v.2. ■ γενομένης s.v.2. προσελθόντες aor. part. προσέρχομαι to

36 come to. ■ ἀπόλυσον aor. imp. ἀπολύω to free, to release, to

dismiss. ἀπελθόντες s.v.27. κύκλῳ in a circle. ἀγοράσωσιν
aor. subj. ἀγοράζω to purchase, to buy (at the market square).
φάγωσιν aor. subj. ■ ἀποκριθείς aor. pass. part. ἀποκρίνομαι 37
to answer. δότε aor. imp. δίδωμι s.v.2. δηνάριον denar, a Roman coin worth about eighteen cents. It was the workman's
average daily wage (BAG). διακόσιοι two hundred. This and
the preceding gen., gen. of price. δώσομεν fut. δίδωμι. ■ 38
ὑπάγετε pres. imp. ἴδετε aor. imp. ὁράω to see. γνόντες aor.
act. part. γινώσκω to know. ■ ἐπέταξεν s.v.27. ἀνακλῖναι 39
aor. act. inf. (or ἀνακλιθῆναι aor pass. inf.) ἀνακλίνω to
cause to recline, to recline. συμπόσιον originally a drinking
party, then a party of guests of any kind, a company. The repetition of the word indicates distribution (RWP). χλωρός green.
χόρτος grass. ■ ἀνέπεσαν aor. ἀναπίπτω to fall back, to 40
recline. πρασιά a garden bed, refers to the arrangement in rows.
It often was customary for the students of the rabbis to sit in rows
which were compared to the rows of vines in the vineyard or to
well-ordered gardens (s. SB, II, 13; Cranfield). ■ λαβών aor. 41
part. λαμβάνω to take. ἀναβλέψας aor. part. ἀναβλέπω to
look up. εὐλόγησεν aor. εὐλογέω to praise, to give thanks, to
bless (s. TDNT). κατέκλασεν aor. κατακλάω to break up, to
break in pieces. ἐδίδου impf. The impf. suggests the successive
distributions of bread (Taylor). παρατιθῶσιν pres. subj.
παρατίθημι to set before, to serve a meal. ἐμέρισεν aor.
μερίζω to divide. ■ ἔφαγον aor. ἐσθίω to eat. ἐχορτάσθησαν 42
aor. pass. χορτάζω to give to eat, to satisfy, to be filled, to be
satisfied (w. food). ■ ἦραν aor. αἴρω s.v.8. κλάσμα piece, that 43
which was broken. κόφινος a wicker-work basket, in which the
Jews carried food (Taylor; s. Matt. 14:20). ■ φαγόντες aor. act. 44
part.

■ ἠνάγκασεν aor. ἀναγκάζω to compel, to force. 45
ἐμβῆναι aor. inf. ἐμβαίνω to get in, to embark. ■ 46
ἀποταξάμενος aor. mid. part. ἀποτάσσομαι to depart, to say
good-by. προσεύξασθαι aor. inf. προσεύχομαι to pray. ■ 47
γενομένης aor. mid. part. gen. abs. μέσον middle. ■ ἰδών aor. 48
part. ὁράω to see. βασανιζομένους pres. pass. part. βασανίζω
to test, to torture, to distress. ἐλαύνω to drive as of ships or
chariots. They drove the boat w. oars (RWP). ἐναντίος against.
τέταρτος fourth. φυλακή watch. Implies the Roman reckoning
of four night watches. It would be about three o'clock in the
morning (Taylor). περιπατῶν pres. part. περιπατέω to walk
about, part. used to express manner. ἤθελεν impf. s.v.22.
παρελθεῖν aor. inf. παρέρχομαι to go by, to pass by. ■ ἔδοξαν 49
aor. δοκέω to suppose. φάντασμα an apparition, ghost. It was

a popular belief that spirits of the night brought disaster (Lane).
ἀνέκραξαν aor. ἀνακράζω to cry out, to scream. The appear-
50 ance drew forth a shriek of terror (Swete). ■ εἶδαν aor. ὁράω.
ἐταράχθησαν aor. pass. ταράσσω to shake, to gather, to stir
up, to unsettle, to throw into confusion. ἐλάλησεν aor. λαλέω
to speak. θαρσεῖτε pres. imp. θαρσέω to be brave, to be of good
cheer. φοβεῖσθε pres. mid. imp. φοβέομαι to be afraid, to fear,
51 pres. imp. w. neg. used to prohibit an action in progress. ■ ἀνέβη
aor. ἀναβαίνω to go up. ἐκόπασεν aor. κοπάζω to become
tried, to cease. ἐκ περισσοῦ adv. beyond measure, exceedingly.
ἐξίσταντο impf. ἐξίστημι to be beside one's self, to be aston-
52 ished, to be amazed. ■ συνῆκαν aor. συνίημι to understand,
to comprehend. πεπωρωμένη perf. pass. part. πωρόω to hard-
en, to form a callus (AS). The perf. pictures the state of condition
of hardness.
53   ■ διαπεράσαντες aor. part. διαπεράω to pass over, to
cross over. ἦλθον aor. προσωρμίσθησαν aor. pass.
προσορμίζω mid. and pass. to land, to cast anchor. They
brought the boat to the moorings, casting anchor, or lashing her
54 to a post on the shore (Swete). ■ ἐξελθόντων aor. part. s.v.1.
55 ἐπίγνοντες aor. part. ■ περιέδραμον aor. περιτρέχω to run
about. ἤρξαντο s.v.2. κράβατος mattress, pallet, the poor
man's bed (BAG). περιφέρειν pres. inf. to carry about. ἤκουον
56 impf. s.v.2. ■ εἰσεπορεύετο impf. εἰσπορεύομαι to go in.
ἀγορά market place. ἐτίθεσαν impf. τίθημι to place.
ἀσθενοῦντας pres. part. ἀσθενέω to be weak, to be sick.
παρεκάλουν impf. παρακαλέω to beseech, to plead w. The
impf. indicates the continual beseeching. κράσπεδον border.
ἅψωνται pres. subj. ἅπτομαι w. gen. to touch. ἥψαντο aor.
mid. ἐσῴζοντο impf. pass. σῴζω to save, to heal.

Ch. 7
1   ■ συνάγονται pres. pass. συνάγω to gather together, to
2 assemble. ἐλθόντες aor. part. ἔρχομαι to go, to come. ■
ἰδόντες aor. part. ὁράω to see. κοινός common, profane, un-
3 clean. ἄνιπτος unwashed. ■ πυγμή fist. The dat. could be modal "w. the fist," w. the fist held out while water is poured over
it. It could be instrumental dat. where the fist is rubbed in the
hand to wash it. Or it could be dat. of measure, "by elbow
length" (Swete). νίψωνται aor. mid. subj. νίπτω to wash, mid.
to wash one's self. κρατοῦντες pres. part. κρατέω to seize, to
4 hold, to hold fast. παράδοσις tradition. ■ παρέλαβον aor.
παραλαμβάνω to receive, denoting the process of receiving a
thing by transmission (Gould). κρατεῖν pres. inf. ποτήριον

cup. ξέστης pitcher, jug. χάλκιον a bronze or copper vessel, kettle. ■ ἐπερωτῶσιν pres. ἐπερωτάω to ask, to ask about 5 something (s. Mark 5:9). περιπατοῦσιν pres. περιπατέω to walk about, in the Hebraic sense of living or conducting one's life (Taylor). ■ ἐπροφήτευσεν aor. προφητεύω to prophesy. 6 ὑποκριτής hypocrite, casuist (s. Matt. 23:28). γέγραπται perf. pass. γράφω "it stands written." χεῖλος lip. τιμᾷ pres. τιμάω to honor. πόρρω adv. far, far away. ἀπέχω to be away. ■ μάτην 7 adv. in vain, to no purpose. σέβομαι to worship, indicates a proper conduct in relation to those worthy of honor (CBB; s. also TDNT). διδάσκοντες pres. part. διδάσκω to teach. διδασκαλία doctrine, a definite course of instruction (Swete). ἔνταλμα commandment. ■ ἀφέντες aor. part. ἀφίημι to re- 8 lease, to leave, commandment, the oral law (commandments of men) w. its burdensome rules about ceremonial washings contravenes the divine intention and even sets it at naught (Taylor). ■ ἔλεγεν impf. καλῶς well. Used here w. irony (BD, 262). 9 ἀθετεῖτε pres. ἀθετέω to set aside, to reject, to cancel (s. MM, 12). ■ τίμα pres. imp. κακολογῶν pres. part. κακολογέω to 10 speak evil of, to insult. τελευτάτω pres. imp. 3rd sing. τελευτάω to die. ■ εἴπῃ aor. subj. λέγω. κορβᾶν offering, gift. 11 A formula pronounced over some object to remove it from profane use (s. Joseph A. Fitzmyer, "The Aramaic Qorban Inscription from Jebel Hallet Et-Turi and Mark 7:11-Matt. 15:5," JBL, 78 [March 1959], 60–65. He states the new inscription provides a perfect contemporary parallel; s. also TDNT). ὅ ἐάν whatever. ὠφελήθης aor. pass. subj. ὠφελέω to help, to benefit, pass. to have benefit from, to profit. ■ οὐκέτι no longer. Once the for- 12 mula was used (perhaps hastily), he evidently was not allowed to change his mind (s. Cranfield). ἀφίετε pres. ἀφίημι w. inf. to allow. ποιῆσαι aor. inf. ποιέω to do. ■ ἀκυροῦντες pres. act. 13 part. ἀκυρόω to cancel, to render null and void, to revoke. Often used of annulling wills and contracts (MM). ᾗ dat. by attraction. παρεδώκατε aor. παραδίδωμι to give further, to pass on, to transmit by teaching. Used of passing on tradition. παρόμοιος almost the same, like. ποιεῖτε present.

■ προσκαλεσάμενος aor. mid. part. προσκαλέομαι to 14 call to one's self. ἀκούσατε aor. imp. ἀκούω w. gen. listen to, to hear. σύνετε aor. imp. συνίημι to understand, to comprehend. ■ ἔξωθεν outside. εἰσπορευόμενον pres. mid. part. 15 εἰσπορεύομαι to go in. κοινῶσαι aor. inf. κοινόω to make common, to defile. ἐκπορευόμενα pres. mid. part. ἐκπορεύομαι to go out. κοινοῦντα pres. part. ■ εἰσῆλθεν aor. 17 εἰσέρχομαι to go out. ἐπηρώτων impf. ἐπερωτάω inceptive

18 impf., "they began to question." ■ ἀσύνετος without understanding, not comprehending. It is the man who lacks discernment (Swete). νοεῖτε pres. νοέω to understand, to apprehend.
19 ■ κοιλία stomach. ἀφεδρών toilet. καθαρίζων pres. part.
20 καθαρίζω to cleanse, to declare clean. βρῶμα food. ■ κοινοῖ
21 pres. s.v.15. ■ ἔσωθεν inside. διαλογισμός consideration,
thought. Not merely evil thoughts but evil devisings which issue
in degraded acts and vices now mentioned (Taylor). πορνεία
immorality, illicit sexual indulgence (s. TDNT). κλοπή theft.
22 φόνος murder. ■ μοιχεία adultery. πλεονεξία greed, the desire
to have more often at the expense of others (s. TDNT; NTW,
97–99). πονηρία bad, evil, wicked (s. Trench, Synonyms).
δόλος deceit. ἀσέλγεια unrestrained, unbridled, shameless living (s. NTW, 26,27). πονηρός evil, wicked, "evil eye." Semitic
expression for envy, jealousy, a jealous grudge (Swete).
βλασφημία blasphemy, slander. ὑπερηφανία pride.
ἀφροσύνη foolish, senseless. Used esp. of religious insensibility
(Cranfield).
24 ■ ἀναστάς aor. act. part. ἀνίστημι to arise. ἀπῆλθεν aor.
ἀπέρχομαι to depart, to go forth. εἰσελθών aor. act. part.
s.v.17. ἤθελεν impf. θέλω to will, to want. γνῶναι aor. act. inf.
γινώσκω to know. ἠδυνάσθη aor. δύναμαι to be able, an Ionic
form for the aor. (Cranfield). λαθεῖν aor. inf. λανθάνω to be
25 hidden, concealed. ■ ἀκούσασα aor. act. part. fem. ἀκούω to
hear. θυγάτριον daughter, dimin. form used to express endear-
ment. ἀκάθαρτος unclean. ἐλθοῦσα aor. part. fem., s.v.1.
26 προσέπεσεν aor. προσπίπτω to fall down. ■ ἠρώτα impf.
ἐρωτάω to ask, to request. ἐκβάλῃ aor. subj. βάλλω to throw
27 out, to cast out. ■ ἔλεγεν impf. ἄφες aor. imp. ἀφίημι to allow.
πρῶτον first. χορτασθῆναι aor. pass. inf. χορτάζω to feed,
pass. to be full, to be satisfied. λαβεῖν aor. inf. λαμβάνω to take.
κυνάριον dog, dimin. little dog (s. Matt. 15:26). The dimin.
suggests that the reference is to the little dogs that were kept as
28 pets (Cranfield). βαλεῖν aor. inf. βάλλω to throw. ■ ἀπεκρίθη
aor. pass. ἀποκρίνομαι to answer. ὑποκάτω under. ψιχίον
29 crumb, dimin. form. ■ ὕπαγε pres. imp. ὑπάγω to go away, to
30 go. ἐξελήλυθεν perf. ἐξέρχομαι to go out. ■ ἀπελθοῦσα aor.
act. part. fem. εὗρεν aor. εὑρίσκω to find. βεβλημένον perf.
pass. part. βάλλω to cast, to lie. ἐξεληλυθός perf. part.
ἔρχομαι.
31   ■ ἐξελθών aor. part. ἐξέρχομαι to go out. ἦλθεν aor. s.v.1.
32 ■ φέρουσιν pres., historical pres. to carry, to bring. κωφός dull,
dumb, deaf. μογιλάλος speaking w. difficulty, having an im-
pediment in speech (Cranfield). The recovery of hearing by the

deaf was a note of the messianic age (Swete). παρακαλοῦσιν
pres. παρακαλέω to beseech, to plead. ἐπιθῇ aor. subj.
ἐπιτίθημι to place upon. ■ ἀπολαβόμενος aor. mid. part. 33
ἀπολαμβάνω to take from, to draw a person aside privately.
ἔβαλεν aor., here in the sense of putting, placing. δάκτυλος
finger. οὖς, ὠτός ear. πτύσας aor. part. πτύω to spit. (For the
Jewish custom, s. SB, II, 15f.) ἥψατο aor. mid. ἅπτομαι w. gen.
to touch. ■ ἀναβλέψας aor. part. ἀναβλέπω to look up. 34
ἐστέναξεν aor. στενάζω to groan, to sigh. ἐφφαθά (Aramaic)
"be opened," "be released." The idea is not of the particular part
of the pers. being opened, but of the whole pers. being opened
or released. It is the command that shatters the fetters by which
Satan has held his victim bound (Cranfield). διανοίχθητι aor.
pass. imp. διανοίγω to open. ■ ἠνοίγησαν aor. pass. ἀνοίγω 35
to open. ἐλύθη aor. pass. λύω to loose. ἐλάλει impf. λαλέω to
speak, inceptive impf. "he began to speak." ὀρθῶς adv. straight,
correctly. ■ διεστείλατο aor. mid. διαστέλλω to command, to 36
charge. λέγωσιν pres. subj. διεστέλλετο impf. mid.
περισσότερον comp. περισσός beyond measure, exceeding.
ἐκήρυσσον impf. κηρύσσω to proclaim, to herald. The impf.
expresses repeated action. ■ ὑπερπερισσῶς adv., beyond all 37
measure, exceedingly. ἐξεπλήσσοντο impf. pass. ἐκπλήσσω
pass. to be astounded (s. Mark 1:22). λέγοντες pres. part.
πεποίηκεν perf. ποιέω to do, to make. ἄλαλος dumb. λαλεῖν
pres. inf.

Ch. 8

■ ὄντος pres. part. εἰμί gen. abs. ἐχόντων pres. part. ἔχω 1
to have, gen. abs. φάγωσιν aor. subj. ἐσθίω to eat, deliberative
subj. προσκαλεσάμενος aor. mid. part. προσκαλέω to summons, to call someone to one's self. ■ σπλαγχνίζομαι ἐπί to 2
have compassion on (s. Mark 6:34). προσμένω to remain w.
■ ἀπολύσω aor. subj. ἀπολύω to release, to send away. νῆστις 3
hungry. ἐκλυθήσονται fut. pass. ἐκλύω to be weary, to become
tired, to faint; "they will be exhausted" (Gould). ■ 4
ἀπεκρίθησαν aor. pass. ἀποκρίνομαι to answer. δυνήσεται
fut. δύναμαι to be able. χορτάσαι aor. act. inf. χορτάζω to
feed, to fill w. food, to satisfy. ■ ἠρώτα imp. ἐρωτάω to ask. 5
εἶπαν aor. λέγω. ■ ἀναπεσεῖν aor. inf. ἀναπίπτω to recline. 6
λαβών aor. part. λαμβάνω to take. εὐχαριστήσας aor. part.
εὐχαριστέω to give thanks. ἔκλασεν aor. κλάω to break.
ἐδίδου impf. δίδωμι to give (s. Mark 6:41). παρατιθῶσιν pres.
subj. παρατίθημι to serve (food). παρέθηκαν aor. ■ εἶχον 7
impf. ἔχω. ἰχθύδιον dimin., small fish. εὐλογήσας aor. part.

εὐλογέω to praise, to bless, to give thanks. παρατιθέναι pres.
8 act. inf. ■ ἔφαγον aor. ἐχορτάσθησαν aor. pass. ἦραν aor.
αἴρω to lift up, to pick up. κλάσμα fragment. It was common
after a banquet to gather up the remaining pieces of bread which
were the size of an olive (SB, IV, 625ff.). σπυρίς a mat basket
for provisions. In Acts 9:25 it is large enough to carry a man
10 (Taylor). ■ ἐμβάς aor. part. ἐμβαίνω to get in, to embark.
ἦλθεν aor. ἔρχομαι to go, to come.
11   ■ ἐξῆλθον aor. ἐξέρχομαι to go out, to come out. ἤρξαντο
aor. ἄρχομαι to begin. συζητεῖν pres. inf. συ(ν)ζητέω to discuss, to debate, to argue. ζητοῦντες pres. part. ζητέω to seek.
σημεῖον sign. πειράζοντες pres. part. πειράζω to try, to test,
12 to tempt. ■ ἀναστενάξας aor. part. ἀναστενάζω to sigh deeply. ζητεῖ pres. εἰ "if," a strong negation, a Heb. oath formula w.
the meaning "if I do such a thing, may I die!" (s. Taylor; MH,
13 468f.). δοθήσεται fut. pass. δίδωμι to give. ■ ἀφείς aor.
ἀφίημι to leave, to depart. ἀπῆλθεν aor. ἀπέρχομαι to go
away.
14   ■ ἐπελάθοντο aor. ἐπιλανθάνομαι to forget. λαβεῖν aor.
15 inf., s.v.6. εἰ μή except. ■ διεστέλλετο impf. mid. διαστέλλω
to charge, to command. λέγων pres. part. ὁρᾶτε pres. imp.
ὁράω to see. βλέπετε pres. imp. βλέπω to see, to take heed.
16 ζύμη leaven (s. Matt. 13:33). ■ διελογίζοντο impf.
17 διαλογίζομαι to reason, to discuss, to debate. ■ γνούς aor. act.
part. γινώσκω to know. οὔπω not yet. νοεῖτε pres. νοέω to
understand, to perceive. συνίετε pres. συνίημι to bring together, to comprehend. πεπωρωμένην perf. pass. part. πωρόω
to harden. The perf. indicates the state of hardness. Hardening
flows on from the heart to the sight, the hearing, and the memory
18/19 (Bengel). ■ μνημονεύω to remember. ■ ἔκλασα s.v.6. κόφινος
basket (s. Mark 6:43). ἤρατε aor., s.v.8.
22   ■ παρακαλοῦσιν pres. παρακαλέω to summon, to plead
23 w. ἄψηται aor. subj. ἅπτομαι w. gen., to grasp, to touch. ■
ἐπιλαβόμενος aor. mid. part. ἐπιλαμβάνω w. gen., to take
hold of, to place hands upon. ἐξήνεγκεν aor. ἐκφέρω to carry
out. πτύσας aor. part. πτύω to spit. ὄμμα eye. ἐπιθείς aor.
part. ἐπιτίθημι to place upon. ἐπηρώτα impf. ἐπερωτάω to
ask. εἰ "if." (For this word introducing direct quotation, s. BD,
24 226.) ■ ἀναβλέψας aor. part. ἀναβλέπω to look up. The man
involuntarily raised his eyes (Swete). ὁρῶ pres., s.v.15.
περιπατοῦντας pres. part. περιπατέω to walk about. A suggested translation is "I can actually see people, for they look to
25 me like trees—only they walk!" (Cranfield). ■ ἐπέθηκεν aor.
διέβλεψεν aor. διαβλέπω to see clearly. The aor. indicates the

definite point at which the man achieved clear sight (Cranfield). ἀπεκατέστη aor. ἀποκαθίστημι to restore. ἐνέβλεπεν impf. ἐμβλέπω to turn and fix the eyes upon, to see. Implies the power to concentrate the attention on a particular object (Swete). The impf. indicates the continuing action. τηλαυγῶς adv., clearly from afar. The meaning is that the man sees everything clearly at a distance (Taylor). ■ ἀπέστειλεν aor. ἀποστέλλω to send 26 away. εἰσέλθῃς aor. subj. εἰσέρχομαι to go in, to come in. Used w. a neg. as a prohibition.

■ ἐξῆλθεν s.v.11. ἐπηρώτα s.v 23. ■ ἀποκριθείς aor. 27/29 pass. part, s.v.4. εἰ pres. εἰμί. ■ ἐπετίμησεν aor. ἐπιτιμάω to 30 rebuke, to warn. λέγωσιν pres. subj.

■ ἤρξατο aor. mid. s.v.11. δεῖ it is necessary, denotes a 31 logical necessity (AS). παθεῖν aor. inf. πάσχω to suffer. ἀποδοκιμασθῆναι aor. pass. inf. ἀποδοκιμάζω to reject after testing. ἀποκτανθῆναι aor. pass. inf. ἀποκτείνω to kill. ἀναστῆναι aor. inf. ἀνίστημι to rise. ■ παρρησία freely 32 speaking, frankness, boldness of speech, used adverbially, "plainly" (s. Taylor). ἐλάλει impf. λαλέω to speak. προσλαβόμενος aor. mid. part. προσλαμβάνω to take to one's self. ἤρξατο s.v.11. ἐπιτιμᾶν pres. inf. ■ ἐπιστραφείς aor. pass. part. 33 ἐπιστρέφω to turn around, to turn to. The Lord turned around sharply as if to face the speaker (Swete). ἰδών aor. part. ὁράω to see. ὕπαγε pres. imp. ὑπάγω to go away. φρονεῖς pres. φρονέω to be minded, to think about. The verb keeps in view the direction which thought takes (Taylor). Here it could mean "to take someone's side" (Cranfield). ■ προσκαλεσάμενος 34 aor. mid. part., s.v.1. ἐλθεῖν aor. inf., s.v.10. ἀπαρνησάσθω aor. imp. ἀπαρνέομαι to deny. The basic idea is to say "no." It is to disown one's self, to turn away from the idolatry of self-centeredness (Cranfield). ἀράτω aor. imp. αἴρω s.v.8. ἀκολουθείτω pres. imp. ἀκολουθέω to follow. ■ θέλῃ pres. 35 subj. ψυχή life, soul. σῶσαι aor. inf. σῴζω to rescue, to save. ἀπολέσει fut. ἀπόλλυμι to loose, to destroy, to ruin. σώσει fut. ■ ὠφελεῖ pres. ὠφελέω to have benefit, to profit. κερδῆσαι 36 aor. act. inf. κερδαίνω to gain, to make a profit. κόσμος world. Here used of the prizes of business and social life (Taylor). ζημιωθῆναι aor. pass. inf. ζημιόω to confiscate, or find, to inflict a penalty of any kind, pass. to suffer loss, to loose (s. Swete). ■ δοῖ aor. subj. δίδωμι to give. ἀντάλλαγμα price. The 37 price received in exchange for an article of commerce (Swete). ■ ἐπαισχυνθῇ aor. subj. ἐπαισχύνομαι w. acc. to be ashamed. 38 ἐπαισχυνθήσεται fut. pass. ἔλθῃ aor. subj. s.v.10.

111

Ch. 9

1 ■ ἔλεγεν impf. λέγω to say. ἑστηκότων perf. act. part. ἵστημί in the perf. to stand. γεύσωνται aor. mid. subj. γεύομαι to taste. ἴδωσιν aor. subj. ὁράω to see. ἐληλυθυῖαν perf. act. part. fem. ἔρχομαι to come. The perf. tense indicates "already established w. power" (GI, 42). The Transfiguration points forward to and is a foretaste of the Resurrection and of the Second Coming (Cranfield).

2 ■ παραλαμβάνει pres. to take w., historical pres. μετεμορφώθη aor. pass. μεταμορφόω to transform (s. TDNT).

3 ἔμπροσθεν before. ■ ἐγένετο aor. mid. γίνομαι to become, to happen. στίλβοντα pres. part. στίλβω to gleam, to glitter. Used of polished or bright surfaces (Taylor). λευκός white. λίαν very. γναφεύς bleacher, fuller, one who cleans woolen cloth by the use of nitrium (Lane). λευκᾶναι aor. inf. λευκαίνω to make

4 white. ■ ὤφθη aor. pass. ὁράω to see, pass. to appear. ἦσαν impf. εἰμί to be. Used w. inf. to form the periphrastic.

5 συλλαλοῦντες pres. part. συλλαλέω to talk together. ■ ἀποκριθείς aor. pass. part. ἀποκρίνω to answer. εἶναι pres. inf. εἰμί "It is a good thing that we are here" (Cranfield). ποιήσωμεν aor. subj. ποιέω to do, to make, a hortatory subj. σκηνή tent, booth. Peter was probably thinking of the booths used to celebrate the Feast of Tabernacles (Swete). (See also

6 Lev. 23:40–43.) ■ ἤδει plperf. of the defective perf. w. pres. meaning οἶδα to know. ἀποκριθῇ aor. pass. subj. ἔκφοβος

7 terrified. ■ ἐπισκιάζουσα pres. part. fem. ἐπισκιάζω to over- shadow. ἀγαπητός beloved. ἀκούετε pres. imp. ἀκούω w. gen.

8 to listen to, to hear. ■ ἐξάπινα adv. suddenly. περιβλεψάμενοι aor. mid. part. περιβλέπω to look around. εἶδον aor. ὁράω.

9 ■ καταβαινόντων pres. part. καταβαίνω to go down, gen. abs. διεστείλατο aor. mid. διαστέλλω to command. διηγήσωνται aor. mid. subj. διηγέομαι to relate, to narrate, to tell. ἀναστῇ

10 aor. subj. ἀνίστημι to rise up, to arise. ■ ἐκράτησαν aor. κρατέω to grasp, to hold fast, to retain in their memory (s. Swete). συζητοῦντες pres. part. συζητέω to seek together, to

11 question, to dispute. ἀναστῆναι aor. inf. ■ ἐπηρώτων impf. ἐπερωτάω to ask, to question. λέγοντες pres. part. δεῖ it is

12 necessary. ἐλθεῖν aor. inf. ἔρχομαι s.v.1. ■ ἔφη impf. φημί to say, to speak. ἐλθών aor. part. ἀποκαθιστάνω to restore. γέγραπται perf. pass. γράφω to write, perf. "it stands written." πάθῃ aor. pass. subj. πάσχω to suffer. ἐξουδενηθῇ aor. pass.

13 subj. ἐξουδενέω to consider as nothing, to despise. ■ καί also. ἐλήλυθεν perf. ἔρχομαι. ἐποίησαν aor. ἤθελον impf. θέλω to wish, to want, to will.

■ ἐλθόντες aor. act. part., s.v.1. εἶδον s.v.8. ■ ἰδόντες aor. 14/15
part. ὁράω. ἐξεθαμβήθησαν aor. pass. ἐκθαμβέομαι to be
amazed, to be extremely amazed. The prep. in the verb is perfective (RWP). προστρέχοντες pres. part. προστρέχω to run to
someone. ἠσπάζοντο impf. mid. ἀσπάζομαι to greet. ■ 16
ἐπηρώτησεν aor., s.v.11. συζητεῖτε pres. ■ ἀπεκρίθη aor., 17
s.v.5. ἤνεγκα aor. θέρω to carry, to bring. ἔχοντα pres. part.
ἔχω to have. ἄλαλος dumb, not able to speak. ■ καταλάβῃ 18
aor. subj. καταλαμβάνω to take hold of, to seize. Nouns related
to this verb were used as medical terms in reference to seizures
and persons subjected to them (Swete). ῥήσσω the meaning of
the verb is either "to tear," "to rend," or "to strike or dash
down" (s. Taylor). ἀφρίζω to foam. τρίζω to grind. Used of any
sharp or grinding sound (Swete). ξηραίνεται pass. ξηραίνω to
dry out, to wither. It pictures complete exhaustion (Taylor).
εἶπα aor. 1st pers. sing. λέγω to say. ἐκβάλωσιν aor. subj.
ἐκβάλλω to throw out, to cast out, to drive out. ἴσχυσαν aor.
ἰσχύω to be strong, to be able. ■ ἀποκριθείς aor. pass. part., 19
s.v.5. ἔσομαι fut. εἰμί. ἀνέξομαι fut. ἀνέχομαι w. gen. to
endure, to put up w. ■ ἰδών aor. part. συνεσπάραξεν aor. 20
συνσπαράσσω to tear to pieces, to pull about, to convulse.
πεσών aor. part. πίπτω to fall. ἐκυλίετο impf. pass. κυλίω to
roll. ἀφρίζων pres. part., s.v.19. ■ γέγονεν perf., s.v.3. The perf. 21
emphasizes the state or conditon. παιδιόθεν from childhood.
(For the use of the adv. w. the strengthening prep., s. MH, 164.)
■ ἔβαλεν aor. βάλλω to throw. ἀπολέσῃ aor. subj. ἀπόλλυμι 22
to destroy. δύνῃ aor. subj. 2nd per. sing. δύναμαι to be able.
βοήθησον aor. imp. βοηθέω to hurry to help, to help.
σπλαγχνισθείς aor. part. σπλαγχνίζομαι to have compassion. ■ τὸ εἰ δύνῃ the article has the effect of making this clause 23
into a noun "as to your 'if you can' !" (Cranfield; s. also Taylor;
RG, 766). πιστεύοντι pres. part. dat. sing. πιστεύω to believe,
to trust. ■ κράξας aor. part. κράζω to scream. ἔλεγεν impf. 24
βοήθει pres. imp. ■ ἐπισυντρέχω to run together. The prep. 25
compound is directive. The word describes a crowd converging
on a single point, perhaps from several directions (Taylor).
ἐπετίμησεν aor. ἐπιτιμάω to command, to rebuke, to charge
(s. Matt. 17:18). ἐπιτάσσω to order, to command. ἔξελθε aor.
imp. ἐξέρχομαι to come out. εἰσέλθῃς aor. subj. εἰσέρχομαι
to go in. Used w. the neg. to form a prohibition "don't ever go
in again!" ■ κράξας aor. act. part., s.v.24. σπαράξας aor. act. 26
part. σπαράσσω to convulse. ἐξῆλθεν aor. ἐγένετο s.v.3.
ὥστε used w. inf. to express results. ἀπέθανεν aor.
ἀποθνῄσκω to die. ■ κρατήσας aor. part., s.v.10, w. gen. to 27

seize, to take hold of. ἤγειρεν aor. ἐγείρω to raise. ἀνέστη aor.
28 ἀνίστημι to stand up. ■ εἰσελθόντος aor. part. gen. abs.
ἐπηρώτων impf., inceptive impf. ἠδυνήθημεν aor. pass.
29 δύναμαι. ἐκβαλεῖν aor. inf. ■ ἐξελθεῖν aor. inf.
30 ■ ἐξελθόντος aor. part., s.v.25. παρεπορεύοντο aor. mid.
inf. παραπορεύομαι to travel. διά w. gen. through. ἤθελεν
31 s.v.13. γνοῖ aor. subj. γινώσκω to know. ■ ἐδίδασκεν impf.
διδάσκω to teach. γάρ "for." It gives the explanation of the
preceding. παραδίδοται pres. pass. παραδίδωμι to deliver
over (s. Cranfield), futuristic pres. It startles and arrests attention. It affirms and gives a sense of certainty (RG, 870).
ἀποκτενοῦσιν fut. ἀποκτείνω to kill. ἀποκτανθείς aor. pass.
32 part. μετά after. ἀναστήσεται fut., s.v.9. ■ ἠγνόουν impf.
ἀγνοέω not to understand, not to know, to be ignorant.
ἐφοβοῦντο impf. mid. φοβέομαι to fear, to be afraid.
ἐπερωτῆσαι aor. inf., s.v.11.
33   ■ ἦλθον aor., s.v.1. γενόμενος aor. mid. part., s.v.3.
ἐπηρώτα s.v.11. διελογίζεσθε impf. διαλογίζομαι to discuss,
34 to dispute. ■ ἐσιώπων impf. σιωπάω to be silent.
διελέχθησαν aor. pass. διαλέγομαι to discuss, to conduct a
discussion. The prep. in the compound recalls the two parties in
a conversation (MH, 302). μείζων comp. μέγας. The comp.
35 used here to express the superl. (s. BD, 32f.). ■ καθίσας aor.
part. καθίζω to take a seat, to sit down. ἐφώνησεν aor. φωνέω
36 to call. εἶναι s.v.5. ἔσται fut. εἰμί. ἔσχατος last. ■ λαβών aor.
part. λαμβάνω to take. ἔστησεν aor. ἵστημι to place.
ἐναγκαλισάμενος aor. mid. part. ἐναγκαλίζομαι to take in
37 one's arms, to embrace. εἶπεν s.v.18. ■ τοιοῦτος of such a
character, character, such a one. δέξηται aor. subj. δέχομαι to
receive, to welcome. ἐπί w. dat. "because of," "on the ground
of" (Taylor). ἀποστείλαντα aor. part. ἀποστέλλω to send.
38   ■ ἔφη s.v.12. εἴδομεν s.v.8. ἐκβάλλοντα pres. part.,
s.v.18. ἀκολουθεῖ pres. ἀκολουθέω to follow, to follow as a
disciple. ἐκωλύομεν impf. κωλύω to prevent, to hinder. The
impf. is conative, "we sought to stop him" (Taylor; s. also M,
39 129). ὅτι because. ἠκολούθει impf. ■ κωλύετε pres. imp. The
pres. imp. used w. neg. to stop an action in progress (s. MKG,
272f.). ποιήσει fut., s.v.5. δυνήσεται fut. δύναμαι.
40 κακολογῆσαι aor. inf. κακολογέω to speak evil of. ■ ὑπέρ w.
41 gen. "for." ■ ποτίσῃ aor. subj. ποτίζω to give to drink.
ἀπολέσῃ aor. subj., s.v.22.
42   ■ σκαναδαλίσῃ aor. subj. σκανδαλίζω to cause to stumble, to cause someone to stumble in his faith (Cranfield).
πιστευόντων pres. part. πιστεύω to believe, to trust.

περίκειμαι to place about, to place around. μύλος ὀνικός the
upper millstone. The millstone turned by an ass, in contrast w.
the handmill served by a woman (Taylor). τράχηλος throat,
neck. βέβληται perf. pass. βάλλω s.v.22. The perf. emphasizes
the state or condition. ■ ἀπόκοψον aor. imp. ἀποκόπτω to cut 43
off. κυλλός crooked, cripple. εἰσελθεῖν aor. inf., s.v.25.
ἀπελθεῖν aor. inf. ἀπέρχομαι to go away. γέεννα hell (s.
TDNT). ἄσβεστος unquenchable. ■ χωλός lame. βληθῆναι 45
aor. pass. inf. βάλλω. ■ ἔκβαλε aor. imp. μονόφθαλμος one- 47
eyed. ■ σκώληξ worm Used to emphasize the unending de- 48
struction and decay of the pers. (TDNT) or pictures the unending gnawing inflicted on man himself by his sins (Gould).
τελευτᾷ pres. τελευτάω to come to an end, to die. σβέννυται
pres. pass. σβέννυμι to extinguish. ■ ἁλισθήσεται fut. pass. 49
ἁλίζω to salt. ■ ἅλας salt, salt grain. ἄναλος not salty. γένηται 50
aor. subj., s.v.3. ἀρτύσετε fut. ἀρτύω to prepare, specifically to
season. εἰρηνεύετε pres. imp. εἰρηνεύω to be peaceable, to keep
peace.

Ch. 10

■ ἀναστάς aor. part. ἀνίστημι to arise, to indicate the 1
beginning of an action (usually motion) expressed by another
verb, to set out, to get ready (BAG). συμπορεύομαι to accompany, to travel w. someone. εἰώθει plperf. of the perf. form
εἴωθα to be accustomed to. The form is used here as an impf.
(RWP). ἐδίδασκεν impf. διδάσκω to teach. There is absolutely
no reason for rejecting that Jesus spoke here in Greek (J.N.
Sevenster, *Do You Know Greek?*, 190). ■ προσελθόντες aor. 2
part. προσέρχομαι to come to. ἐπηρώτων impf. ἐπερωτάω to
ask, to question. ἔξεστιν it is allowed, it is lawful. ἀπολῦσαι
aor. inf. ἀπολύω to release, to divorce. πειράζοντες pres. act.
part. πειράζω to tempt, to try. ■ ἀποκριθείς aor. pass. part. 3
ἀποκρίνομαι to answer. ἐνετείλατο aor. mid. ἐντέλλομαι to
command. ■ ἐπέτρεψεν aor. ἐπιτρέπω to allow. ἀποστάσιον 4
divorcement (s. Matt. 5:31). γράψαι aor. act. inf. γράφω to
write. ■ πρός w. acc. in accordance w., in view of (s. BD, 124). 5
σκληροκαρδία hardness of heart. ἔγραψεν aor. ■ ἄρσην 6
male. θῆλυς female. ἐποίησεν aor. ποιέω to do, to make. ■ 7
ἕνεκεν because of. καταλείψει fut. καταλείπω to leave. ■ 8
ἔσονται fut. 3rd pl. εἰμί to be. ■ συνέζευξεν aor. συζεύγνυμι 9
to join together. χωριζέτω pres. imp. χωρίζω to separate. ■ 11
ἀπολύσῃ aor. subj. γαμήσῃ aor. subj. γαμέω to marry.
μοιχᾶται pres. mid. μοιχάω to commit adultery. ■ 12
ἀπολύσασα aor. act. part. fem. (For Jesus' teaching on mar-

riage and divorce, s. LNT, 363–388.)

13 ■ προσέφερον impf. προσφέρω to bring to, to carry to.
ἅψηται aor. mid. subj. ἅπτομαι w. gen. to touch. Subjunctive
used w. ἵνα to express purpose. The purpose of the touching is
to obtain a blessing (Taylor; s. also SB, I, 807f.). ἐπετίμησαν
14 aor. ἐπιτιμάω to rebuke. ■ ἰδών aor. part. ὁράω to see.
ἠγανάκτησεν aor. ἀγανακτέω to be vexed, to be indignant,
ingressive aor. to become indignant (Gould). ἄφετε aor. imp.
ἀφίημι to allow. κωλύετε pres. imp. κωλύω to hinder.
15 τοιοῦτος of such a kind, of such a character, character. ■
δέξηται aor. subj. δέχομαι to receive, to welcome. εἰσέλθῃ
16 aor. subj. εἰσέρχομαι to come in. ■ ἐναγκαλισάμενος aor.
mid. part. ἐναγκαλίζομαι to embrace, to take in one's arms.
κατευλόγει impf. κατευλογέω to wish one well, to bless. The
force of the prep. in the compound is intensive. He blessed them
fervently, in no perfunctory way, but w. emphasis (Swete). The
impf. pictures the repeated action. τιθείς aor. part. τίθημι to
place.

17 ■ ἐκπορευομένου pres. mid. part. ἐκπορεύομαι to go out.
προσδραμών aor. act. part. προστρέχω to run to.
γονυπετήσας aor. part. γονυπετέω to fall to one's knees.
ἐπηρώτα s.v.2. ποιήσω fut., s.v.6. κληρονομήσω fut.
κληρονομέω to inherit. Inheriting eternal life was a fixed ex-
18 pression in Judaism (Lane). ■ εἶπεν aor. λέγω to say, to speak.
ἀγαθός good. In reference to God perfect (CBB; also TDNT).
19 ■ οἶδα defective perf. w. pres. meaning to know. φονεύσῃς aor.
subj. φονεύω to kill, to murder. μοιχεύσῃς aor. subj., s.v.11.
κλέψῃς aor. subj. κλέπτω to steal. ψευδομαρτυρήσῃς aor.
subj. ψυδομαρτυρέω to give a false witness. ἀποστερήσῃς aor.
subj. ἀποστερέω to rob, to deprive, to defraud of. Used of
keeping back wages from one hired and in classical Gr. of refusing to return goods or money deposited w. another for safe
20 keeping (Taylor). τίμα pres. imp. τιμάω to honor. ■ ἔφη impf.
φημί to say. ἐφυλαξάμην aor. mid. φυλάσσω to guard, to
keep. The aor. is intended to sum up his accomplishments.
21 νεότης youth. ■ ἐμβλέψας aor. part. ἐμβλέπω to look at.
ἠγάπησεν aor. ἀγαπάω to love. ὑστερεῖ pres. ὑστερέω to
come short of, to fail, to be lacking (Taylor; cf. Rom 3:23).
ὕπαγε pres. imp. ὑπάγω to go. πώλησον aor. imp. πωλέω to
sell. δός aor. δίδωμι to give. ἔξεις fut. ἔχω to have. δεῦρο
"Come!" ἀκολούθει imp. ἀκολουθέω to follow, to follow as a
22 disciple. ■ στυγνάσας aor. act. part. στυγνάζω to be sad, to
become sad. Used of the saddening of the face of nature or the
human face. Used of a dark stormy night or the somber, gloomy

man who broods over unwelcome thoughts (Swete). ἀπῆλθεν aor. ἀπέρχομαι to go away. λυπούμενος pres. mid. part. λυπέομαι to be sad, to be sorry. ἦν impf. εἰμί to be. ἐχών pres. part. ἔχω to have. Used in a periphrastic construction. **■** 23 περιβλεψάμενος aor. mid. part. περιβλέπω to look around. δύσκολος w. difficulty. χρῆμα "a thing one used," pl. wealth, riches (Taylor). εἰσελεύσονται fut. mid. εἰσέρχομαι to go in. **■** ἐθαμβοῦντο impf. pass. θαμβέω to scare, to terrify, pass. to 24 be amazed. ἀποκριθείς aor. pass. part., s.v.3. εἰσελθεῖν aor. inf. **■** εὐκοπώτερος comp. εὔκοπος easy, without trouble. 25 τρυμαλιά hole, perforation, opening. ῥαφίς needle. διελθεῖν aor. inf. διέρχομαι to go through. **■** ἐξεπλήσσοντο impf. 26 ἐκπλήσσομαι pass. to be amazed, to be overwhelmed. λέγοντες pres. act. part. σωθῆναι aor. pass. inf. σῴζω to rescue, to save. **■** ἀδύνατος impossible. **■** ἤρξατο aor. mid. 27/28 ἄρχομαι to begin. ἀφήκαμεν aor. ἀφίημι to leave. ἠκολευθήκαμεν perf. The perf. indicates "we have left all and are following you." **■** ἕνεκεν because of, on account of. **■** ἐάν 29/30 "if he shall not," more freely "without" (s. Taylor). λάβῃ aor. subj. λαμβάνω to take, to receive. ἑκατονταπλασίων a hundredfold. διωγμός persecution. ἐρχομένῳ pres. mid. part., s.v.2. **■** ἔσονται fut. εἰμί. 31

■ ἦσαν impf. εἰμί to be. ἀναβαίνοντες pres. part. 32 ἀναβαίνω to go up. ἦν s.v.22. προάγων pres. part. προάγω to go before, to precede, to lead forward. The part. is used in a periphrastic construction. ἀκολουθοῦντες pres. part., s.v.21. ἐφοβοῦντο impf. mid. φοβέομαι to fear, to be afraid. παραλαβών aor. part. παραλαμβάνω to take w., to take along. ἤρξατο s.v.28. μέλλοντα pres. part. μέλλω to be about to. The part. is used w. the pres. inf. to express a fut. w. a durative value, "the things which will be happening" (s. MKG, 307f.). συμβαίνειν pres. inf. Used w. dat. "to happen to." **■** 33 παραδοθήσεται fut. pass. παραδίδωμι to deliver over (s. Mark 9:31). κατακρινοῦσιν fut. κατακρίνω to condemn, to make a decision against someone. **■** ἐμπαίξουσιν fut. ἐμπαίζω 34 to mock, to play his game w. someone (TDNT). ἐμπτύσουσιν fut. to spit on. μαστιγώσουσιν fut. μαστιγόω to beat w. a whip, to scourge. ἀποκτενοῦσιν fut. ἀποκτείνω to kill. ἀναστήσεται fut. mid. ἀνίστημι to rise, to rise up.

■ προσπορεύομαι to come to. αἰτήσωμεν aor. subj. 35 αἰτέω to ask, to request. ποιήσῃς aor. subj., s.v.6. **■** ποιήσω 36 aor. subj., deliberative subj. **■** δός aor. imp. s.v.21. καθίσωμεν 37 aor. subj. καθίζω to sit, to take one's seat. **■** οἶδα s.v.19. 38 αἰτεῖσθε pres. mid. αἰτέω to ask, to request, mid. somewhat

stronger than the act. "to ask for one's self" (s. M, 160; s. also
TDNT). πιεῖν aor. inf. πίνω to drink. ποτήριον cup. The cup
belongs to the royal banquet at which the king sits beside his
most honored guest. It also is associated w. the allotted share of
joy or suffering which is the portion of men and of nations in the
course of their life (Swete). βαπτισθῆναι aor. pass. inf.
39 βαπτίζω to dip, to baptize. ■ πίεσθε fut. mid.
40 βαπτισθήσεσθε fut. pass. ■ καθίσαι aor. act. inf. δοῦναι aor.
inf., s.v.21. ἡτοίμασται perf. pass. ἑτοιμάζω to make ready, to
prepare. The perf. indicates it has been prepared and stands
41 ready. ■ ἀκούσαντες aor. act. part. ἀκούω to hear. ἤρξαντο
42 aor. mid., s.v.28. ἀγανακτεῖν pres. inf., s.v.14. ■
προσκαλεσάμενος aor. part. προσκαλέομαι to call to one's
self, to summons. δοκοῦντες pres. part. δοκέω to appear, to
suppose. Possibly "those who aspire to rule" (but s. Cranfield).
ἄρχω w. gen. to rule over. κατακυριεύω w. gen. to be lord over,
to rule over. The compound prep. in the verb gives the sense of
using lordship over people to their disadvantage and to one's
own advantage (Cranfield). κατεξουσιάζω w. gen. to exercise
43 authority over. ■ θέλῃ pres. subj. γενέσθαι aor. inf. γίνομαι
44/45 to become, to be. ἔσται fut. εἰμί. ■ εἶναι inf. εἰμί. ■ καὶ γὰρ
either emphatic "for the Son of man Himself" (Taylor) or "for
also." The Son of man is not exempt from this rule; His kingship
is also that of service and not of lordship (Gould). ἦλθεν aor.
διακονηθῆναι aor. pass. inf. διακονέω to serve, to minister,
pass. to be ministered to. διακονῆσαι aor. act. inf. The infs. are
used to express purpose. λύτρον ransom, the price paid for
release (s. Matt. 20:38; Cranfield). ἀντί w. gen. instead of, in
place of. It is the prep. of substitution. He took our place (Leon
Morris, The Cross in the New Testament, 54).
46   ■ ἐκπορευομένου s.v.17. προσαίτης beggar. The prep.
compound is directive and indicates to ask to or for one's self (s.
MH, 324). προσαιτῶν the variant reading, pres. part.
προσαιτέω to beg. The part. in this case is one of manner.
ἐκάθητο impf. κάθημαι to sit. The iterat. or customary impf.
47 "he used to sit," "it was his custom to sit" (s. RG, 884). ■
ἀκούσας aor. part., s.v.41. κράζειν pres. inf., to cry out, to
scream. ἐλέησον aor. imp. ἐλεέω to have mercy, to show mercy.
48 ■ ἐπετίμων impf. s.v.13. The impf. indicates "they continually
rebuked him." σιωπήσῃ aor. subj. σιωπάω to keep silent, to
49 be silent. ἔκραζεν impf. "he continually cried out." ■ στάς aor.
part. ἵστημι to stand, to remain. φωνήσατε aor. imp. φωνέω
to call. φωνοῦσιν pres., historical pres. θάρσει pres. imp.
θαρσέω to be cheerful, to have courage. ἔγειρε pres. imp. rise,

arise. ■ ἀποβαλών aor. act. part. ἀποβάλλω to throw off. 50
ἀναπηδήσας aor. act. part. ἀναπηδάω to jump up, to spring
up. ἦλθεν aor. ἔρχομαι. ■ ἀποκριθείς s.v.3. ῥαββουνί master, 51
teacher (s. TDNT). ἀναβλέψω aor. subj. ἀναβλέπω to look up,
to see again. ■ ὕπαγε s.v.21. σέσωκεν perf., s.v.26. The perf. 52
emphasizes the state or condition of being healed. ἀνέβλεψεν
aor. ἠκολούθει impf., s.v.21, inceptive impf. "he began to follow."

Ch. 11

■ ἐγγίζουσιν pres., to be near, to draw near, historical pres. 1
■ ὑπάγετε pres. imp. ὑπάγω to go forth, to go. κατέναντι adv. 2
opposite. εἰσπορευόμενοι pres. mid. part. εἰσπορεύομαι to go
in, to come in. εὑρήσετε fut. εὑρίσκω to find. πῶλος the young
of any animal, generally a horse, but in the LXX and the papyri,
also the colt or foal of a donkey (Taylor). δεδεμένον perf. pass.
part. δέω to bind. ἐκάθισεν aor. καθίζω to sit, to take one's
seat. λύσατε aor. imp. λύω to loosen, to untie. φέρετε prep.
imp. φέρω to bring. ■ εἴπῃ aor. subj. λέγω. ποιεῖτε pres. ind. 3
ποιέω to do, to make. εἴπατε aor. imp. ■ ἀπῆλθον aor. 4
ἀπέρχομαι to go out. εὗρον aor. ἄμφοδος street. ■ 5
ἑστηκότων perf. part. ἵστημι, perf. to stand. ἔλεγον impf.
λύοντες pres. part. ■ ἀφῆκαν perf. ἀφίημι to allow. ■ 6/7
ἐπιβάλλουσιν pres., to place upon, to cast upon, historical
pres. ■ ἔστρωσαν aor. στρώννυμι to spread out. στιβάς kind 8
of bed or mattress made of straw, rushes, reeds, leaves, etc. Here
leaves, leafy branches (BAG). κόψαντες aor. part. κόπτω to
cut. ■ προάγοντες pres. part. προάγω to go before. 9
ἀκολουθοῦντες pres. part. ἀκολουθέω to follow. ἔκραζον
impf. κράζω to cry out, to scream. ὡσαννά (Heb.) hosanna,
save, we pray, save now (s. Matt. 21:9). εὐλογημένος perf. pass.
part. εὐλογέω to bless, to give thanks (s. TDNT). ■ ὕψιστος the 10
highest, pl. heaven. ■ εἰσῆλθεν aor. εἰσέρχομαι to go in, to 11
come in. περιβλεψάμενος aor. mid. part. περιβλέπω to look
about, to look around. ὀψέ late. οὔσης part. εἰμί to be, gen. abs.
either temporal or causal. ἐξῆλθεν aor. ἐξέρχομαι to go out.
■ ἐξελθόντων aor. act. part. gen. abs. ἐπείνασεν aor. 12
πεινάω to be hungry, ingressive aor. to become hungry. ■ ἰδών 13
aor. part. ὁράω to see. συκῆ fig tree. μακρόθεν from afar off.
ἔχουσαν pres. part. ἔχω to have. φύλλον leaf, pl. leaves, foliage. ἦλθεν aor. ἔρχομαι to come, to go. ἄρα "in these circumstances" (Lane). εὑρήσει fut., s.v.2. ἐλθών aor. part. εὗρεν aor.
ἦν impf. εἰμί to be. σῦκον fig. In the Messianic age figs and all
other products of nature will always be in season (s. Richard H.

Hiers, "Not the Season for Figs," JBL, 87 [December 1968],
394–400). This indicates the promised OT kingdom would not
14 at this time be established. ■ ἀποκριθείς aor. pass. part.
ἀποκρίνομαι to answer. εἶπεν aor. λέγω to say. φάγοι aor.
opt. ἐσθίω to eat. The opt. here expresses prohibition (M, 165).
ἤκουον impf. ἀκούω to hear.
15   ■ εἰσελθών aor. part., s.v.11. ἤρξατο aor. mid. ἄρχομαι
to begin. ἐκβάλλειν pres. inf., to cast out, to drive out.
πωλοῦντας pres. part. πωλέω to sell. ἀγοράζοντας pres. act.
part. ἀγοράζω to buy. κολλυβιστής moneychanger (s. Matt.
21:12). καθέδρα seat, chair. περιστερά pigeon. κατέστρεψεν
aor. καταστρέφω to turn down, to overthrow, to turn over.
16 ■ ἤφιεν impf. ἀφίημι to allow. διενέγκῃ aor. subj. διαφέρω to
carry through. No one was allowed to enter the Temple Mount
w. his staff, sandal, or wallet or w. dust on his feet (s. M, Bera-
17 koth, IX, 5; s. also Swete). ■ ἐδίδασκεν impf. διδάσκω to
teach, inceptive impf. "he began to teach." ἔλεγεν impf.
γέγραπται perf. pass. γράφω to write. κληθήσεται fut. pass.
καλέω to call. πεποιήκατε perf., s.v.3. The perf. emphasizes
the past action w. a continuing result or state. σπήλαιον hole,
18 den, cave. λῃστής robber, bandit. ■ ἤκουσαν aor. act. ἐζήτουν
impf. ζητέω to seek. The impf. pictures the repeated action.
ἀπολέσωσιν aor. subj. ἀπόλλυμι to destroy, to ruin.
ἐφοβοῦντο impf. φοβέομαι to be afraid, to fear. ἐξεπλήσσετο
19 impf. mid. ἐκπλήσσομαι to be astounded. ■ ἐγένετο aor.
γίνομαι to become, "when it got late" (Cranfield).
ἐξεπορεύοντο impf. mid. ἐκπορεύομαι to go out.
20   ■ παραπορευόμενοι pres. mid. part. παραπορεύομαι to
pass by. εἶδον aor. ὁράω to see. ἐξηραμμένην perf. pass. part.
ξηραίνω to dry up, to wither. The impf. pictures the abiding
21 results (Taylor). ῥίζα root. ■ ἀναμνησθείς aor. pass. part.
ἀναμιμνήσκομαι to remember, to be reminded. ἴδε aor. imp.
ὁράω to see. κατηράσσω aor. mid. 2nd per. sing. καταράομαι
22/23 to curse. ἐξήρανται perf. pass. ■ ἔχετε pres. imp. ■ εἴπῃ s.v.3.
ἄρθητι aor. pass. imp. αἴρω to lift up, pass. to be lifted up.
βλήθητι aor. pass. imp. βάλλω to throw. διακριθῇ aor. pass.
subj. διακρίνομαι to hesitate, to doubt. πιστεύῃ pres. subj.
πιστεύω to believe, to trust. λαλεῖ pres. λαλέω to speak, to
24 say. ἔσται fut. εἰμί ■ διά w. acc. because of. προσεύχομαι to
pray. αἰτεῖσθε pres. mid. αἰτέω to ask, to ask for one's self (s.
Mark 10:38). πιστεύετε pres. imp. ἐλάβετε aor. λαμβάνω to
25 receive. ■ στήκετε pres. στήκω to stand. προσευχόμενοι
pres. mid. part. ἀφίετε pres. imp. to forgive. ἀφῇ aor. subj.
παράπρωμα a false step, a fall from the right course, an error,

a mistake in judgment, a blunder, transgression (s. Swete; Trench, *Synonyms*; TDNT).

■ περιπατοῦντας pres. part. περιπατέω to walk about, 27 gen. abs. ■ ἔλεγον impf., s.v.5. ἔδωκεν aor. δίδωμι to give. 28 ποιῆς pres. subj. ■ ἐπερωτήσω fut. ἐπερωτάω to ask a ques- 29 tion. ἀποκρίθητε aor. pass. imp., s.v.14. ἐρῶ fut. λέγω. ■ 31 διελογίζοντο impf. mid. διαλογίζομαι to discuss, to dispute. εἴπωμεν aor. subj., s.v.3. ἐπιστεύσατε aor. ind., s.v.23. ■ 32 ἐφοβοῦντο s.v.18. εἶχον impf. ἔχω to have, to hold, to think (s. BD, 204). ἀποκριθέντες aor. pass. part., s.v.14. οἶδα defective perf. w. pres. meaning, to know.

Ch. 12

■ ἤρξατο aor. ἄρχομαι to begin. λαλεῖν pres. inf. λαλέω 1 to speak. ἀμπελών vineyard. (For a study of this parable in the light of Jewish law, s. LNT, 286–308.) ἐφύτευσεν aor. φυτεύω to plant. περιέθηκεν aor. περιτίθημι to place around. φραγμός a fence, wall, hedge. This was necessary to keep the vines from running over another's property (LNT, 292). It also was for protection against wild animals (Taylor). ὤρυξεν aor. ὀρύσσω to dig. ὑπολήνιον the trough for the juice under the press in which the grapes were crushed (Cranfield). ᾠκοδόμησεν aor. οἰκοδομέω to build. πύργος tower. ἐξέδοτο aor. mid. ἐκδίδωμι to give out, to farm out, to lease. γεωργός farmer, tenant farmer. Those who had made a contract w. the landlord to tend the vineyard in return for part of its produce (s. LNT, 293f.). ἀπεδήμησεν aor. ἀποδημέω to travel, to make a trip. ■ ἀπέστειλεν aor. ἀποστέλλω to send. λάβῃ aor. subj. 2 λαμβάνω to take, to receive. Normally the vineyard produced grapes for wine only in the fourth year. The fruit of the vineyard was possibly the vegetables grown between the vines. It was necessary for the owner to receive a token payment of the harvest in order to retain ownership (s. LNT, 295ff.). ■ λαβόντες 3 aor. act. part. ἔδειραν aor. δέρω to beat. κενός empty. ■ 4 ἐκεφαλαίωσαν aor. κεφαλαιόω to strike on the head. ἠτίμασαν aor. ἀτιμάζω to dishonor, to insult. ■ ἀπέκτειναν 5 aor. ἀποκτείνω to kill. δέροντες pres. act. part. ἀποκτέννοντες pres. act. part. ■ ἀγαπητός beloved. 6 ἐντραπήσονται fut. pass. ἐντρέπω pass., to reverence, to re-spect. ■ εἶπαν aor. λέγω. κληρονόμος heir. The one who 7 would take over the property. δεῦτε "Come!" (s. BD, 184). ἀποκτείνωμεν pres. or aor. subj., hortatory subj. Since the own-er of the vineyard had not received pay for three years, the tenants hoped to destroy the evidence by killing the son and thus

8 having a claim to the vineyard (s. LNT, 300–306). ■ ἐξέβαλον
9 aor. ἐκβάλλω to cast out, to throw out. ■ ποιήσει fut. ποιέω
to do, to make. ἐλεύσεται fut. ἔρχομαι to come, to go.
ἀπολέσει fut. ἀπόλλυμι to destroy, to ruin. δώσει fut. δίδωμι
10 to give. ■ ἀνέγνωτε aor. ἀναγινώσκω to read.
ἀπεδοκίμασαν aor. ἀποδοκιμάζω to reject, to reject after
examining. οἰκοδομοῦντες pres. act. part. ἐγενήθη aor. pass.
γίνομαι to become. γωνία corner. (For the grammatical struc-
11 ture of this v., s. MH, 423f.; Taylor.) ■ ἐγένετο aor. mid.
12 θαυμαστός wonderful, incomprehensible. ■ ἐζήτουν impf.
ζητέω to seek, to look for. The impf. emphasizes they repeatedly
sought. κρατῆσαι aor. inf. κρατέω to seize. ἐφοβήθησαν aor.
pass. φοβέομαι to fear, to be afraid of. ἔγνωσαν aor. γινώσκω
to know, to recognize. πρὸς αὐτούς "with reference to them"
(Lane). ἀφέντες aor. part. ἀφίημι to leave. (For the Semitic use
of the redundant part., s. MH, 452–454.) ἀπῆλθον aor.
ἀπέρχομαι to go away.
13   ■ ἀγρεύσωσιν aor. subj. ἀγρεύω to catch or take by hunt-
14 ing or fishing (AS). ■ ἐλθόντες aor. part., s.v.9. οἴδαμεν defective perf. w. pres. meaning οἶδα to know. ἀληθής true, upright
(Taylor). μέλει σοι "you are not concerned about." ἔξεστιν it
is lawful. δοῦναι aor. inf. δίδωμι to give. κῆνσος tribute, poll
15 tax (s. Matt. 22:17). δῶμεν aor. subj., deliberative subj. ■ εἰδώς
part. οἶδα. ὑπόκρισις hypocrisy, an attempt to evade the law
(s. Matt 23:28). πειράζετε to test, to try, to tempt. φέρετε pres.
16 imp. φέρω to carry, to bring. ἴδω aor. subj. ὁράω to see. ■
ἤνεγκαν aor. act. φέρω. εἰκών image. ἐπιγραφή inscription (s.
17 Matt. 22:20). εἶπαν s.v.7. ■ ἀπόδοτε aor. imp. ἀποδίδωμι to
give back, to pay. The compound verb implies that the tribute
is a debt (Swete). ἐξεθαύμαζον impf. θαυμάζω to be astounded, to be amazed.
18   ■ ἐπηρώτων impf. ἐπερωτάω to question. λέγοντες pres.
part. (For the Semitic construction of the part., s. MH, 454.)
19 ■ ἔγραψεν aor. γράφω. ἀποθάνῃ aor. subj. ἀποθνήσκω to
die. καταλίπῃ aor. subj. καταλείπω to leave behind. ἀφῇ aor.
subj. ἀφίημι to leave. λάβῃ aor. subj., s.v.2. ἐξαναστήσῃ aor.
20 subj. ἐξανίστημι to raise up. ■ ἔλαβεν aor. ἀποθνήσκων pres.
21/23 part. ἀφῆκεν aor. ■ ἀπέθανεν aor. καταλιπών aor. part. ■
ἀναστῶσιν aor. subj. ἀνίστημι to rise up, to rise. ἔσχον aor.
24 ἔχω ■ ἔφη impf. φημί to say, to speak. πλανᾶσθε pres. mid.
πλανάομαι to go astray, to be deceived, to be misled. εἰδότες
25 part. οἶδα s.v.14. ■ γαμοῦσιν pres. γαμέω to marry.
26 γαμίζονται pres. pass. γαμίζω to give in marriage. ■
ἐγείρονται pres. pass. ἐγείρω to rise, to be raised. ἀνέγνωτε

aor., s.v.10. ■ ζώντων pres. part. ζάω to live.   27
■ προσελθών aor. part. προσέρχομαι to come to. 28
ἄκουσας aor. part. ἀκούω w. gen. to hear, to listen to.
συζητούντων pres. part. συζητέω to examine together, to dispute. εἰδώς part. οἶδα s.v.14. ἀπεκρίθη aor. pass.
ἀποκρίνομαι to answer. ἐπηρώτησεν aor., s.v.18. ■ ἄκουε 29
pres. imp. ■ ἀγαπήσεις fut. ἀγαπάω to love. The fut. w. the 30
force of the imp. is a translation of the Heb. impf. used as a
jussive (s. MH, 458). ■ πλησίος the next one, neighbor. μείζων 31
comp. μέγας great, τούτων gen. of comparison. ■ ἀγαπᾶν 33
pres. inf. σύνεσις understanding. περισσότερος comp.
περισσός beyond measure, over and above, more exceeding.
πάντων gen. of comparison. ὁλοκαύτωμα burnt offering.
θυσία sacrifice. ■ ἰδών aor. part., s.v.14. νουνεχῶς wisely, 34
thoughtfully. μακράν far. The acc. fem. used as an adv. (Taylor). ἐτόλμα impf. τολμάω to dare. ἐπερωτῆσαι aor. active
inf.

■ ἀποκριθείς aor. pass. part., s.v.28. (For the Semitic use 35
of the part., s. MH, 453.) διδάσκων pres. part., part. of manner.
■ κάθου pres. mid. imp. κάθημαι to sit, to sit down. θῶ aor. 36
subj. τίθημι to place, to set, to establish, to make. ἐχθρός enemy. ὑποκάτω w. gen. under. ■ ἤκουεν impf., s.v.28. ἡδέως adv. 37
gladly.

■ βλέπετε pres. imp. βλέπω to see, to beware of. 38
θελόντων pres. part. to desire, to wish. στολή cloak, not only
the cloak worn by the common people, but esp. the cloak of
honor, the scholars' or officers' distinction (s. Jastrow, I, 537; SB,
II, 31–33). περιπατεῖν pres. inf. περιπατέω to walk about.
ἀσπασμός greetings. ■ πρωτοκαθεδρία the chief seat, the 39
bench in the synagogues in front of the ark where the Scriptures
were contained while facing the congregation. It was reserved
for the officials and persons of high distinction (s. LT, I, 436).
πρωτοκλισία first or chief place at the table. The place of the
most honored guest on the couch around the table (s. Swete).
δεῖπον dinner, the main meal, generally in the evening (s. SB,
IV, 611–639; LT, II, 205–210). ■ κατέσθιοντες pres. act. part. 40
κατεσθίω to devour, to eat up. χήρα widow. πρόφασις alleged motive or cause, esp. a motive or cause that is falsely
alleged; pretext, pretense (Cranfield). προσευχόμενοι pres.
mid. part. προσεύχομαι to pray. λήμψονται fut. mid.
λαμβάνω to take, to receive.

■ καθίσας aor. act. part. καθίζω to sit, to take one's seat. 41
γαζοφυλακεῖον treasury. Probably a reference to the thirteen
trumpet-like chests placed at intervals around the walls of the

123

court of the women in the Herodian temple (s. Swete). ἐθεώρει
impf. θεωρέω to watch to observe. The impf. pictures his repeated watching of the different persons who passed by. χαλκός
copper, brass, bronze money. πλούσιος rich. ἔβαλλον impf.

42 "they were repeatedly casting." ■ ἐλθοῦσα aor. part. ἔρχομαι
s.v.9. πτωχός poor, abject poverty, one who has literally nothing
and is in imminent danger of real starvation (NTW, 110).
ἔβαλεν aor. λεπτόν the smallest Jewish coin. A small copper
coin worth normally about one-eighth of a cent (BAG; s. Lane;
F.W. Madden, *History of Jewish Coinage and of the Money in
the Old and New Testament*, 296–302). κοδράντης a Roman
coin equal to about a fourth of a cent (BAG). Mark gives the
Roman coinage for the benefit of his Roman readers (Taylor).

43 ■ προσκαλεσάμενος aor. mid. part. προσκαλέομαι to summons, to call to one's self. πλεῖον comp. πολύς. πάντων gen.
of comparison. βαλλόντων pres. part. περισσεύοντος pres.
part. περισσεύω to be in abundance. ὑστέρησις deficiency,
want, need. βίος living, livelihood, the means by which life is
sustained (AS).

Ch. 13

1   ■ ἐκπορευομένου pres. mid. part. ἐκπορεύομαι to go out,
gen. abs. ἴδε aor. imp. ὁράω to see. ποταπός what sort of, how
fashioned. οἰκοδομή building. (For a description of the temple,
s. Josephus, *Jewish War*, V, 184–247; *Antiquities*, XV, 380–425.)

2 ■ ἀφεθῇ aor. pass. subj. ἀφίημι to leave. καταλυθῇ aor. pass.
subj. καταλύω to destroy, to completely demolish (RWP).

3   ■ καθημένου pres. part. κάθημαι to sit down, gen. abs.

4 ἐπηρώτα impf. ἐπερωτάω to question, to ask. ■ εἶπον aor.
imp. λέγω. σημεῖον sign. μέλλῃ pres. subj. μέλλω to be about
to. Used w. inf. to express the fut. συντελεῖσθαι pres. pass. inf.
συντελέω to complete, to bring to an end. The prep. in the

5 compound is perfective (Taylor). ■ ἤρξατο aor. mid. ἄρχομαι
to begin. βλέπετε pres. imp. πλανήσῃ aor. subj. πλανάω to

6 lead astray, to cause to wander. ■ ἐλεύσονται fut. mid.

7 ἔρχομαι to go, to come. πλανήσουσιν fut. ■ ἀκούσητε aor.
subj. ἀκούω to hear. πόλεμος war. θροεῖσθε pres. mid. imp.
θροέομαι to raise an outcry, pass. of the alarm occasioned by
a sudden cry or of mental uneasiness in general (Swete). The
pres. imp. w. the neg. has the idea "do not immediately be
alarmed" (s. MKG, 272). δεῖ it is necessary. γενέσθαι aor. mid.

8 inf. γίνομαι to become, to happen. ■ ἐγερθήσεται fut. pass.
ἐγείρω to rise up. σεισμός earthquake. κατὰ τόπους distributive use of the prep. from place to place, everywhere, here and

there. λιμός famine. ἀρχή beginning. ὠδίνων pl. birth pains (s. Matt. 24:8). ■ παραδώσουσιν fut. παραδίδωμι to deliver 9 over. συνέδριον a local Jewish council, court (s. Moore, *Judaism*, 261f.). δαρήσεθε fut. pass. δέρω to beat. ἡγεμών ruler, governor. σταθήσεσθε fut. pass. ἵστημι to place, to set, to stand. μαρτύριον witness. (For the threefold aspect of this witness, s. Cranfield.) ■ κηρυχθῆναι aor. pass. inf. ■ ἄγωσιν pres. 10/11 subj. ἄγω to lead. παραδιδόντες pres. part. προμεριμνᾶτε pres. imp. προμεριμνάω to concern one's self, to be anxious beforehand. λαλήσητε aor. subj. λαλέω to speak. δοθῇ aor. pass. subj. δίδωμι to give. λαλεῖτε pres. imp. λαλοῦντες pres. part. ■ ἐπαναστήσονται fut. ἐπανίστημι to rise up against. 12 γονεύς pl. parents. θανατώσουσιν fut. θανατόω to kill. ■ 13 μισούμενοι pres. pass. part. μισέω to hate. ὑπομείνας aor. act. part. ὑπομένω to endure. σωθήσεται fut. pass. σῴζω to rescue, to save.

■ ἴδητε aor. subj. βδέλυγμα that which is detestable, 14 abomination. ἐρήμωσις making into a desert, desolating, desolation. ἑστηκότα perf. part. masc. ἵστημι perf. to stand. ἀναγινώσκων pres. part. ἀναγινώσκω to read. νοείτω pres. imp. νοέω to understand, to comprehend. φευγέτωσαν pres. imp. 3rd pl. φεύγω to flee. ■ καταβάτω aor. imp. καταβαίνω 15 to come down. εἰσελθάτω aor. imp. εἰσέρχομαι to go in. ἆραι aor. act. inf. αἴρω to take away, to remove. Infinitive used to express purpose. ■ ἐπιστρεψάτω aor. imp. ἐπιστρέφω to turn 16 about. ■ ἐχούσαις pres. part. fem. used in the idiom "to be 17 pregnant." θηλαζούσαις pres. part. fem. θηλάζω to nurse, to suck. ■ προσεύχεσθε pres. mid. imp. προσεύχομαι to pray. 18 γένηται aor. subj. χειμών wintertime. ■ γέγονεν perf. 19 τοιοῦτος of such a kind, of such a character. ἔκτισεν aor. κτίζω to make, to create. ■ ἐκολόβωσεν aor. κολοβόω to shorten. 20 ἐσώθη aor. pass. ἐκλεκτός chosen, elect. ἐξελέξατο aor. mid. ἐκλέγω to choose, mid. to choose out, to pick out for one's self. ■ εἴπῃ aor. subj. λέγω. πιστεύετε pres. imp. πιστεύω to be- 21 lieve, to trust. ■ ψευδόχριστος false christ. ψευδοπροφήτης 22 false prophet. ποιήσουσιν fut. ποιέω to make, to do. ἀποπλανᾶν pres. inf. ἀποπλανάω to lead astray, to cause to wander. The prep. compound is either local or perfective, to lead away (s. MH, 297ff.). Used w. πρός to indicate subjective purpose (Taylor). ■ προείρηκα perf. προλέγω to say beforehand. 23

■ σκοτισθήσεται fut. pass. σκοτίζω to darken, to make 24 dark. σελήνη moon. δώσει fut. φέγγος light, ray, beam. ■ 25 πίπτοντες pres. part. πίπτω to fall. σαλευθήσονται fut. pass. σαλεύω to shake. ■ ὄψονται fut. mid. ὁράω to see. ἐρχόμενον 26

125

27 pres. mid. part. ■ ἀποστελεῖ fut. ἀποστέλλω to send.
ἐπισυνάξει fut. ἐπισυνάγω to assemble, to gather together.
ἄκρος end.

28   ■ συκῆ fig tree. μάθετε aor. imp. μανθάνω to learn.
κλάδος branch. ἀπαλός tender. The fig tree is mentioned because in Palestine, where most trees are evergreens, the rising of
the sap in its branches and the appearance of leaves is a sure sign
that winter is past (Taylor). ἐκφύῃ pres. subj. ἐκφύω to put
forth, to sprout. φύλλον leaf, pl. foliage. γινώσκετε pres. imp.

29 γινώσκω to know, to recognize. θέρος summer. ■ ἴδητε aor.
subj. γινόμενα pres. mid. part. "when you see these things

30 happening." ■ παρέλθῃ aor. subj. παρέρχομαι to pass by, to
pass away. γενεά generation, race (s. Swete). μέχρις οὗ until.

31 γένηται aor. mid. subj. ■ παρελεύσονται fut. mid.

32/33   ■ οἶδα defective perf. w. pres. meaning to know. ■
ἀγρυπνεῖτε pres. imp. ἀγρυπνέω to chase sleep away, to be

34 watchful (s. MH, 290). ■ ἀπόδημος to be away from home, to
be away on a journey. ἀφείς aor. part. ἀφίημι to leave. δούς aor.
part. δίδωμι. θυρωρός doorkeeper, the one who stood guard at
the entrance of a courtyard which served several houses (s. SB,
II, 47f.). ἐνετείλατο aor. mid. ἐντέλλομαι to command.
γρηγορῇ pres. subj. γρηγορέω to watch, to keep awake, to be

35 on the alert (BAG). ■ γρηγορεῖτε pres. imp. μεσονύκτιον
midnight, acc. of time. ἀλεκτοροφωνία the crowing of a rooster. "At cockcrow," the name of the third watch of the night
(12–3 AM) (BAG). πρωΐ early morning. These words denote the

36 four watches of the night, from six to six (Gould). ■ ἐλθών aor.
part. ἐξαίφνης suddenly. εὕρῃ aor. subj. εὑρίσκω to find.
καθεύδοντας pres. act. part. καθεύδω to sleep.

Ch. 14

1   ■ ἦν impf. εἰμί equivalent to, "was about to be." Mark
looks back on the event as past (Swete). πάσχα passover, the
passover lamb, the passover feast, or the passover meal (s. Matt.
26:2; SB, IV, 41–76). ἄζυμος unleavened, the feast of unleavened bread celebrated in connection w. passover. ἐζήτουν impf.
ζητέω to seek. δόλος deceit, guile, trickery. κρατήσαντες aor.
part. κρατέω to seize. ἀποκτείνωσιν pres. subj. ἀποκτείνω to

2 kill. ■ ἑορτή feast. μήποτε lest, used to express neg. purpose.
ἔσται fut. ind. The fut. ind. represents the danger as real and
imminent, and adds force to the depreciation (Swete). θόρυβος
tumult, uproar, riot.

3   ■ ὄντος gen. abs. κατακειμένου pres. mid. part.
κατάκειμαι to recline at the table, gen. abs. ἦλθεν aor.

126

ἔρχομαι to come, to go. ἔχουσα pres. part. ἀλάβαστρον an alabaster vase (s. Matt. 26:7). μύρον sweet-smelling oil, perfume. νάρδος spikenard. A plant native to India (BAG). πιστικός genuine. (For this word, s. Taylor.) πολυτελής very expensive. συντρίψασα aor. part. fem. συντρίβω to crush. The breaking of the flask was perhaps the expression of the wholeheartedness of her devotion (Cranfield). κατέχεεν impf. καταχέω to pour down, to pour over, inceptive impf. "she began to pour." ■ ἀγανακτοῦντες pres. part. ἀγανακτέω to be un- 4 willing, to be angry, ἀπώλεια destruction, ruin, waste. γέγονεν perf. γίνομαι to become, to happen, to be. ■ ἠδύνατο aor. 5 δύναμαι. πραθῆναι aor. pass. inf. πιπράσκω to sell. ἐπάνω over, more than. δοθῆναι aor. pass. inf. δίδωμι to give. ἐνεβριμῶντο perf. mid. ἐμβριμάομαι to snort, an expression of anger and displeasure, to warn sternly (BAG; s. also Mark 1:43). ■ ἄφετε aor. imp. ἀφίημι to leave. παρέχω to cause, in 6 this context to cause trouble. ἠργάσατο aor. mid. ἐργάζομαι to work, to do. ■ θέλητε pres. subj. ἐποίησεν aor. inf. ποιέω 7 to do. ■ ἔσχεν aor. ἔχω to have. προέλαβεν aor. 8 προλαμβάνω to take beforehand, to anticipate. μυρίσαι aor. inf. μυρίζω to anoint. ἐνταφιασμός to lay out, preparation for burial (Taylor). ■ κηρυχθῇ aor. pass. subj. κηρύσσω to preach, 9 to herald. λαληθήσεται fut. pass. λαλέω to speak, to tell. μνημόσυνον memorial.

■ ἀπῆλθεν aor. ἀπέρχομαι to go out. παραδοῖ aor. subj. 10 παραδίδωμι to deliver over. ■ ἀκούσαντες aor. part. ἀκούω 11 to hear. ἐχάρησαν aor. act. χαίρω to rejoice, to be glad. ἐπηγγείλαντο aor. mid. ἐπαγγέλλομαι to promise. δοῦναι aor. inf. δίδωμι to give. ἐζήτει s.v.1. εὐκαίρως a good time, opportunity.

■ ἔθυον impf. θύω to slay, to sacrifice (an animal), custom- 12 ary impf. ἀπελθόντες aor. part., s.v.10. ἑτοιμάσωμεν aor. subj. ἑτοιμάζω to prepare. φάγῃς aor. subj. ἐσθίω to eat. ■ ὑπάγετε 13 pres. imp. ὑπάγω to go forth. ἀπαντήσει fut. ἀπαντάω to meet. κεράμιον a jar or vessel of pottery. βαστάζων pres. part. βαστάζω to carry. ἀκολουθήσατε aor. imp. ἀκολουθέω to follow. ■ εἰσέλθῃ aor. subj. εἰσέρχομαι to go in. εἴπατε aor. 14 imp. λέγω. οἰκοδεσπότης master of the house, landlord. κατάλυμα inn, guest room (Taylor). ■ δείξει fut. δείκνυμι to 15 show. ἀνάγαιον a room upstairs. ἐστρωμένον perf. pass. part. στρώννυμι to spread out, carpeted or perhaps provided w. carpeted divans (Swete; s. also Taylor). ἕτοιμος ready, prepared. ἑτοιμάσατε aor. imp. ■ ἐξῆλθον aor. ἐξέρχομαι to go 16 out. ἦλθον s.v.3. εὗρον aor. εὑρίσκω to find. ἡτοίμασαν aor.

17/18 ■ γενομένης aor. mid. part. gen. abs., s.v.4. ■ ἀνακειμένων
pres. mid. part. ἀνάκειμαι to recline at the table, gen. abs.
ἐσθιόντων pres. part. gen. abs. παραδώσει fut. παραδίδωμι
19 s.v.10. ■ ἤρξαντο aor. mid. ἄρχομαι to begin. λυπεῖσθαι pres.
mid. inf. λυπέομαι to be sad, to be sorrowful. εἰς κατὰ εἷς "one
20 by one." (For this construction, s. Taylor.) ■ ἐμβαπτόμενος
21 pres. mid. part. ἐμβάπτω to dip in. τρύβλιον bowl. ■
γέγραπται perf. pass. γράφω to write. παραδίδοται pres.
pass., s.v.10. ἐγεννήθη aor. pass. γεννάω to bear, pass. to be
born.

22   ■ λαβών aor. act. part. λαμβάνω to take. εὐλογήσας aor.
act. part. εὐλογέω to give thanks, to praise, to bless. ἔκλασεν
aor. κλάω to break. ἔδωκεν aor. δίδωμι to give. λάβετε aor.
23 imp. ■ εὐχαριστήσας aor. part. εὐχαριστέω to thank, to say
24 thanks. ἔπιον aor. πίνω to drink. ■ διαθήκη covenant, testament, will (s. Matt 26:28). ἐκχυννόμενον pres. pass. part.
25 ἐκχύννω to pour out, to shed. ■ γένημα that which is produced,
26 fruit. ■ ὑμνήσαντες aor. part. ὑμνέω to sing a hymn. ἐξῆλθον
s.v.16.

27   ■ σκανδαλισθήσεσθε fut. pass. σκανδαλίζω to cause to
stumble, to offend, pass. to be offended (s. TDNT). γέγραπται
perf. pass., s.v.21. πατάξω fut. πατάσσω to strike, to hit.
ποιμήν shepherd. διασκορπισθήσονται fut. pass.
28 διασκορπίζω to scatter. ■ ἐγερθῆναι aor. pass. inf. ἐγείρω to
rise up, pass. to be raised. προάξω fut. προάγω to go forward,
29/30 to go before. ■ ἔφη impf. φημί to say. ■ ἀλέκτωρ rooster.
φωνῆσαι aor. inf. φωνέω to call, to make a sound, to crow.
31 ἀπαρνήσῃ aor. subj. ἀπαρνέομαι to deny. ■ ἐκπερισσῶς
beyond measure, exceedingly. ἐλάλει impf., s.v.9. δέῃ pres.
subj. δεῖ it is necessary. συναποθανεῖν aor. inf.
συναποθνήσκω to die together. ἀπαρνήσομαι fut. (s. BD,
184).

32   ■ καθίσατε aor. imp. καθίζω to sit, take one's seat.
33 προσεύξωμαι aor. mid. subj. προσεύχομαι to pray. ■ ἤρξατο
aor. mid., s.v.19. ἐκθαμβεῖσθαι pres. mid. inf. ἐκθαμβέομαι
to be amazed, to be distressed. Here denotes a being in the grip
of a shuddering horror in the face of the dreadful prospect before
him (Cranfield). ἀδημονεῖν pres. inf. ἀδημονέω to be sorely
34 troubled, to be in anguish (Taylor). ■ περίλυπος very sorrowful,
surrounded w. sorrow. μείνατε aor. imp. μένω to remain.
γρηγορεῖτε press. imp. γρηγορέω to be awake, to be watchful,
35 to watch. ■ προελθών aor. part. προέρχομαι to go forward, to
go further. μικρόν adv. a little. ἐπίπτεν impf. πίπτω to fall.
προσηύχετο impf. mid. to pray. παρέλθη aor. subj.

παρέρχομαι to go by, to pass by. The substance of the prayer is given in indirect speech (Taylor). ■ παρένεγκε aor. imp. 36 παραφέρω to take away, to remove. ■ καθεύδοντας pres. part. 37 καθεύδω to sleep. ἴσχυσας aor. ἰσχύω to be strong, to be able. γρηγορῆσαι aor. act. inf. ■ προσεύχεσθε pres. mid. imp. 38 ἔλθητε aor. subj. πρόθυμος willing, eager. ἀσθενής weak, without strength. ■ ἀπελθών s.v.12. προσηύξατο aor. mid. 39 εἰπών aor. part. λέγω. ■ ἐλθών aor. part. εὗρεν aor., s.v.16. 40 καταβαρυνόμενοι pres. pass. part. καταβαρύνω to be weighed down, to be heavy. ᾔδεισαν plperf. of the defective perf. οἶδα to know. ἀποκριθῶσιν aor. pass. subj. ἀποκρίνομαι to answer. ■ καθεύδετε pres. imp. ἀναπαύεσθε 41 pres. mid. imp. ἀναπαύομαι to cease, to rest. ἀπέχει it is sufficient, "enough of this!" (For this and other possible meanings of the word, s. Cranfield.) ἦλθεν aor., s.v.3. παραδίδοται pass., s.v.10. ■ ἐγείρεσθε impf. pass., s.v.28. ἄγωμεν pres. subj. 42 ἄγω hortative subj. "let us go." παραδιδούς pres. part. ἤγγικεν perf. ἐγγίζω to draw near.

■ λαλοῦντος pres. part. gen. abs., s.v.9. παραγίνομαι to 43 come to. μάχαιρα a short sword, a knife. ξύλον wood, a stout stick or perhaps a club (Swete). ■ δεδώκει plperf. δίδωμι to 44 give. (For the plperf. without the augment, s. BD, 36.) παραδιδούς pres. part. σύσσημον a sign, signal. φιλήσω fut. φιλέω to kiss. κρατήσατε aor. imp., s.v.1. ἀπάγετε pres. imp. ἀπάγω to lead forth, to lead away. ἀσφαλῶς adv., safely. ■ 45 ἐλθών aor. part. προσελθών aor. part. προσέρχομαι to come to. κατεφίλησεν aor. καταφιλέω to kiss fervently (s. Matt. 26:49). The compound indicates a prolonged kissing designed to give the crowd a chance to see the one to be seized (Cranfield). ■ ἐπέβαλαν aor. ἐπιβάλλω to place, to lay hands upon (in a 46 hostile sense; s. Swete). ἐκράτησαν aor. ■ παρεστηκότων 47 perf. act. part. παρίστημι to stand by. σπασάμενος aor. mid. part. σπάομαι to draw out, to draw. ἔπαισεν aor. παίω to strike, to hit. ἀφεῖλεν aor. ἀφαιρέω to cut off. ὠτάριον ear (dimin. form). ■ ἀποκριθείς aor. pass. part. (For the redundant 48 use of the part., s. MH, 453.) λῃστής robber. ἐξήλθατε aor., s.v.16. συλλαβεῖν aor. inf. συλλαμβάνω to arrest, to take as prisoner. ■ ἤμην impf. εἰμί. διδάσκων pres. part. ἐκρατήσατε 49 aor. πληρωθῶσιν aor. pass. subj. πληρόω to fill, to fulfill. ■ 50 ἀφέντες aor. part. ἀφίημι to leave, to forsake. ἔφυγον aor. φεύγω to flee.

■ νεανίσκος youth, young man. συνηκολούθει impf. 51 συνακολουθέω to follow w. περιβεβλημένος perf. pass. part. περιβάλλω to put around, to put on, to be clothed. σινδών fine linen cloth or a garment made out of it (Cranfield). Either a light summer "square" hastily caught up or a night dress (Swete). γυμνός naked, possibly in the sense of light clad (s. Taylor).

52 κρατοῦσιν pres. ■ καταλιπών aor. part. καταλείπω to leave behind.

53 ■ ἀπήγαγον aor., s.v.44. συνέρχομαι to accompany, to
54 go w. ■ μακρόθεν from a distance, from afar. ἠκολούθησεν aor. ἀκολουθέω to follow. αὐλή courtyard. The open court around which the chambers of the Temple were built (Swete). συγκαθήμενος pres. mid. part. συγκάθημαι to sit together. θερμαινόμενος pres. mid. part. θερμαίνομαι to warm one's self. The two parts. are used in a periphrastic construction. φῶς
55 light, fire. ■ συνέδριον the Sanhedrin (s. TDNT; also Matt. 25:59). ἐζήτουν impf., s.v.1. θανατῶσαι aor. inf. θανατόω to
56 kill. ηὕρισκον impf., s.v.16. ■ ἐψευδομαρτύρουν impf.
57 ψευδομαρτυρέω to give a false witness. ■ ἀναστάντες aor.
58 part. ἀνίσταμι to stand up, to rise up. ■ ἠκούσαμεν aor. ἀκούω to hear. καταλύσω fut. καταλύω to destroy. χειροποίητος made w. human hands. ἀχειροποίητος not made. w. human hands. (For the significance of the endings, s.
60 M, 221f.) οἰκοδομήσω fut. οἰκοδομέω to build. ■ ἐπηρώτησεν aor. ἐπερωτάω to question. καταμαρτυροῦσιν
61 pres. καταμαρτυρέω w. the gen. to witness against. ■ ἐσιώπα impf. σιωπάω to be silent. ἀπεκρίνατο aor. mid. ἐπηρώτα
62 impf., inceptive impf. ■ εἰμί "I am" (s. Matt. 26:64). ὄψεσθε fut. mid. ὁράω to see. καθήμενον pres. part. κάθημαι to sit.
63 ἐρχόμενον pres. mid. part., s.v.3. ■ διαρήξας aor. part.
64 διαρρήγνυμι to tear into, to rip (s. Matt. 26:65). ■ βλασφημία slander, blasphemy. (For blasphemy in connection w. v. 62, s. Catchpole, The Trial of Jesus, 135–141.) φαίνομαι to appear. κατέκριναν aor. κατακρίνω to decide against, to condemn.
65 ἔνοχος guilty (s. BD, 98). ■ ἤρξαντο aor. mid., s.v.19. ἐμπτύω to spit on. περικαλύπτω to cover all around, to blindfold. κολαφίζω to strike w. the fist, derived from the word meaning "knuckles" (MH, 407). προφήτευσον aor. imp. προφητεύω to prophesy. ῥάπισμα a slap on the cheek w. the open hand (Taylor). ἔλαβον aor. λαμβάνω s.v.22, "they caught him w. blows" (Swete).

66 ■ ὄντος part. εἰμί gen. abs. παιδίσκη a female slave, maid.
67 ■ ἰδοῦσα aor. part. fem. ὁράω to see. ἐμβλέψασα aor. part. fem. ἐμβλέπω to look at. Indicates that she looked straight at
68 him (Cranfield). ■ ἠρνήσατο aor. mid. ἀρνέομαι to say no, to deny. οἶδα defective perf. w. pres. meaning to know. ἐπίσταμαι to understand. ἐξῆλθεν aor., s.v.16. προαύλιον the

vestibule leading to the courtyard. ■ παρεστῶσιν perf. part. 69
παρίσταμαι perf. to stand by, to be a bystander. ■ ἠρνεῖτο 70
impf. mid. The impf. suggests repeated denials (Cranfield). ■ 71
ἀναθεματίζω to curse. Peter invokes an anathema on himself
if his denials are false (Swete). ὁμνύναι pres. inf. ὄμνυμι to
swear. ■ ἐφώνησεν aor., s.v.30. ἀνεμνήσθη aor. pass. 72
ἀναμιμνήσκω pass. to remember. ἐπιβαλών aor. part.
ἐπιβάλλω to throw upon, "to put his mind on" (RWP), "to set
about to, to begin" (BD, 162, s. also M, 131). ἔκλαιεν impf.
κλαίω to weep, to cry, inceptive impf.

Ch. 15

■ πρωΐ early, at daybreak from five to six A.M. (Swete). It 1
was common for the Roman officials to be at work very early (s.
Sherwin-White, 45f.). συμβούλιον council, according to the
variant reading here either to reach a decision or to hold consultation (BAG; Taylor). δήσαντες aor. act. part. δέω to bind.
ἀπήνεγκαν aor. ἀποφέρω to carry away, to take away. Used
in the papyri of one who is transferred from a village prison to
the prison of the metropolis (M, 39). παρέδωκαν aor.
παραδίδωμι to turn over, to deliver over to. ■ ἐπηρώτησεν 2
aor. ἐπερωτάω to question. ἀποκριθείς aor. pass. part.
ἀποκρίνομαι to answer. (For the Semitic construction, s. MH,
453.) ■ κατηγόρουν impf. κατηγορέω to accuse. The impf. 3
pictures the repeated accusation. ■ ἐπηρώτα impf. ἴδε aor. 4
impf. ὁράω to see. πόσος how large, pl. how many.
κατηγοροῦσιν pres. ■ ἀπεκρίθη aor. pass. θαυμάζειν pres. 5
inf. to be astounded, to wonder, to be amazed. Infinitive used to
express result.

■ ἀπέλυεν impf. ἀπολύω to release. The impf. is a custom- 6
ary impf. "it was customary to release," "he was in the habit of
releasing" (Gould). παρῃτοῦντο impf. mid. παραιτέομαι to
ask from another, to beg. ■ λεγόμενος pres. pass. part. 7
στασιαστής insurrectionist. δεδεμένος perf. pass. part.
στάσις insurrection. φόνος murder. πεποιήκεισαν plperf.
ποιέω to do, to make, to commit. (For the lack of the augment,
s. BD, 36.) ■ ἀναβάς aor. part. ἀναβαίνω to go up. ἤρξατο 8
aor. mid. ἄρχομαι to begin. αἰτεῖσθαι pres. mid. inf. αἰτέομαι
to ask, to request. ἐποίει impf. ■ ἀπολύσω fut. ■ ἐγίνωσκεν 9/10
impf. γινώσκω to know. φθόνος jealousy. παραδεδώκεισαν
plperf. ■ ἀνέσεισαν aor. ἀνασείω to stir up. ἀπολύσῃ aor. 11
subj. ■ ποιήσω fut. ■ ἔκραξαν aor. κράζω to cry out, to 12/13
scream. σταύρωσον aor. imp. σταυρόω to crucify. ■ 14
ἐποίησεν aor. ■ βουλόμενος pres. mid. part. βούλομαι to will, 15

to wish, to want. **ἱκανός** sufficient. Used in the idiom to satisfy (s. Taylor; RG, 1385). **ποιῆσαι** aor. inf. **φραγελλώσας** aor. part. **φραγελλόω** to flog (s. Matt. 27:26). **σταυρωθῇ** aor. pass. subj.

16　　■ **ἀπήγαγον** aor. **ἀπάγω** to lead out, to lead away. **αὐλή** courtyard, palace. **πραιτώριον** the official residence of a governor. Here it is either Herod's palace or the Tower of Antonia

17 (Taylor). **συγκαλοῦσιν** pres. **συγκαλέω** to call together. ■ **ἐνδιδύσκω** to put on. **πορφύρα** purple. The cloak of one of the soldiers, possibly a castoff and faded rag, but w. color enough left in it to suggest the royal purple (Swete). **περιτιθέασιν** pres. **περιτίθημι** to place about. **πλέξαντες** aor. part. **πλέκω** to plant. **ἀκάνθινος** out of thorns, from thorns. (For the ending

18 signifying material, s. MH, 359.) ■ **ἀσπάζεσθαι** pres. mid. inf.

19 **ἀσπάζομαι** to greet. ■ **ἔτυπτον** impf. **τύπτω** to strike, to hit. **κάλαμος** reed. **ἐνέπτυον** impf. **ἐμπτύω** to spit on. **τιθέντες** pres. part. **τίθημι** to place. Used w. the word "knee" to kneel. **προσεκύνουν** impf. **προσκυνέω** to worship, to pay homage, a mockery in terms of Caesar worship or oriental ideas of kingship

20 (Taylor). ■ **ἐνέπαιξαν** aor. **ἐμπαίζω** to mock (s. TDNT). **ἐξέδυσαν** aor. **ἐκδύω** to take off, to remove (clothing) **ἐνέδυσαν** aor. **ἐνδύω** to put on. **σταυρώσωσιν** aor. subj., s.v.13.

21　　■ **ἀγγαρεύω** to compel, forcibly to impress someone into service, to compel him to serve whether he likes it or not (s. NTW, 16f.). **παράγοντα** pres. part. **παράγω** to pass by. **ἐρχόμενον** pres. mid. part. **ἔρχομαι** to go, to come. **ἄρῃ** aor.

22 subj. **αἴρω** to lift up, to take up. ■ **μεθερμηνευόμενος** pres.

23 pass. part. **μεθερμηνεύω** to translate. **κρανίον** skull. ■ **ἐδίδουν** impf. **δίδωμι** to give, the conative impf. "they tried to give" (Swete). **ἐσμυρνισμένον** perf. pass. part. **σμυρνίζω** to drug w. myrrh. In accordance w. Jewish customs based on Proverbs 31:6, wine drugged w. myrrh was given in order to dull the senses

24 (Cranfield). **ἔλαβεν** aor. **λαμβάνω** to take, to receive. ■ **διαμερίζονται** pres. mid. **διαμερίζω** to distribute, mid. to divide among themselves. **βάλλοντες** pres. part. **βάλλω** to throw.

25 **κλῆρος** lot; that is, pebble or small stick (BAG). ■ **τρίτος** third

26 (about 9 o'clock). **ἐσταύρωσαν** aor. ■ **ἐπιγραφή** inscription. **ἐπιγεγραμμένη** perf. pass. part. **ἐπιγράφω** to inscribe, to write

29 upon (s. Matt. 27:37). ■ **παραπορευόμενοι** pres. mid. part. **παραπορεύομαι** to go by, to pass by. **ἐβλασφήμουν** impf. **βλασφημέω** to slander, to blaspheme (s. Mark 14:64). **κινοῦντες** pres. part. **κινέω** to move, to shake. **οὐά** "ah!" or "ha!" indicating wonder, real or assumed (Taylor). **καταλύων**

132

pres. part. καταλύω to destroy, to demolish. οἰκοδομῶν pres. part. οἰκοδομέω to build. ■ σῶσον aor. imp. σῴζω to save, to 30 rescue. The jest was the harder to endure since it appealed to the consciousness of power held back only by the self-restraint of a sacrificed will (Swete). καταβάς aor. act. part. καταβαίνω to come down, to go down. ■ ἐμπαίζοντες pres. part. ἔσωσεν aor. 31 σῶσαι aor. act. inf. ■ καταβάτω aor. imp. ἴδωμεν aor. subj., 32 s.v.4. πιστεύσωμεν aor. subj. πιστεύω to believe, to trust. συνεσταυρωμένοι perf. pass. part. συσταυρόω to co-crucify, to crucify together, to crucify w someone. The perf. emphasizes the state or condition. ὠνείδιζον impf. ὀνειδίζω to reproach, to insult.

   ■ γενομένης aor. mid. part. γίνομαι to become, to happen, 33 gen. abs. ἐγένετο aor. mid. ■ ἐβόησεν aor. βοάω to cry out, to 34 shout, to cry aloud. ἐλωΐ "My God." λαμά "why?" σαβαχθάνι "why have you forsaken me?" (s. Matt. 27:46). ἐγκατέλιπες aor. 2nd per. sing. ἐγκαταλείπω to forsake, to leave. ■ παρεστηκότων perf. act. part. παρίστημι perf. to be 35 a bystander, to stand aside. ἀκούσαντες aor. act. part. ἀκούω to hear. ἴδε s.v.4. φωνεῖ pres. φωνέω to call. ■ δραμών aor. act. 36 part. τρέχω to run. γεμίσας aor. part. γεμίζω to fill, σπόγγος sponge. ὄξος sour wine (s. Matt. 27:48). περιθείς aor. part. ἐπότιζεν impf. ποτίζω to give to drink. ἄφετε aor. imp. ἀφίημι to leave, to leave alone. ἴδωμεν aor. subj., s.v.4. hortative subj. "let us see." καθελεῖν aor. inf. καθαιρέω to take down. ■ ἀφείς 37 aor. part. In this context "having uttered" (Cranfield). ἐξέπνευσεν aor. ἐκπνέω to breathe out, to expire, to die. ■ 38 καταπέτασμα curtain, veil (s. Matt. 27:51). ἐσχίσθη aor. pass. σχίζω to split, pass. to be torn. ■ ἰδών aor. part. 39 κεντυρίων centurion. ἐξ ἐναντίας opposite. υἱὸς θεοῦ Son of God. The anarthrous predicate and its position emphasize nature and character (s. John 1:1). ■ μακρόθεν from afar. θεωροῦσαι 40 pres. act. part. fem. pl. θεωρέω to see, to view. ■ ἠκολούθουν 41 impf. ἀκολουθέω to follow. διακονέω to serve, to minister to. συναβᾶσαι aor. part. συναναβαίνω to go up together, to go up w.

   ■ ἤδη already. γενομένης aor. mid. part., s.v.33. 42 παρασκευή preparation. Here used technically of the day of preparation for a Sabbath or the Passover (Taylor). προσάββατον the day before the Sabbath; that is, Friday (BAG). ■ ἐλθών aor. act. part., s.v.21. εὐσχήμων prominent, 43 noble, influential, wealthy (s. Taylor). βουλευτής counselor, a member of the Sanhedrin (Swete). προσδεχόμενος pres. mid. part. προσδέχομαι to await, to expect. τολμήσας aor. act.

part. τολμάω to dare, to have courage, to be brave enough, "he summoned up courage" (BAG). εἰσῆλθεν aor. εἰσέρχομαι to
44 go in. ᾐτήσατο aor. mid., s.v.8. ■ ἐθαύμασεν aor., s.v.5. τέθνηκεν perf. act. ἀποθνῄσκω to die, perf. to be dead. προσκαλεσάμενος aor. mid. part. προσκαλέομαι to summons, to call to one's self. ἐπηρώτησεν s.v.2. ἀπέθανεν aor. The distinction in tenses is noticeable. The perf. implies an existing condition, the aor. describes an observed event (Taylor).
45 ■ γνούς aor. act. part. γινώσκω to know. ἐδωρήσατο aor. mid. δωρέομαι to give, to present, to bestow. The verb suggests a
46 gracious act (Taylor). πτῶμα one that is fallen, corpse. ■ ἀγοράσας aor. part. ἀγοράζω to buy. σινδών fine linen. καθωλών aor. part., s.v.36. ἐνείλησεν aor. ἐνειλέω to wrap, to roll, to wrap in (s. Matt. 27:59). κατέθηκεν aor. κατατίθημι to lay down, to place a body in a tomb (BAG). λελατομημένον perf. pass. part. λατομέω to hew, to cut out of stone. προσεκύλισεν aor. προσκυλίω to roll to, to roll up. Rock tombs were common in the neighborhood of Jerusalem, sometimes containing chambers and sometimes a single room provided w. a bench or shelf on which the body was placed, the entrance being closed by a large flat stone rolled or pushed into
47 position (Taylor). ■ ἐθεώρουν impf., s.v.40. τέθειται perf. pass. τίθημι to place, to lay.

Ch. 16

1 ■ διαγενομένου aor. mid. part. διαγίνομαι to pass, to elapse, gen. abs. "when the Sabbath was over," after sunset on the day following the crucifixion (Swete). ἠγόρασαν aor. ἀγοράζω to buy. ἄρωμα spice, probably perfumed oils rather than aromatic herbs (Taylor). ἐλθοῦσαι aor. part. fem.
2 ἀλείψωσιν aor. subj. ἀλείφω to anoint. ■ ἀνατείλαντος aor. part. gen. sing. ἀνατέλλω to rise. Used of the sun rising, gen.
3/4 abs. ■ ἀποκυλίσει fut. ἀποκυλίω to roll away. ■ ἀναβλέψασαι aor. part. fem. pl. ἀναβλέπω to look up. θεωροῦσιν pres. θεωρέω to see, historical pres. ἀνκεκύλισται perf. pass. ἀνακυλίω to roll back. The perf. indicates the state
5 or condition after a completed action. σφόδρα very. ■ εἰσελθοῦσαι aor. part. fem. pl. εἰσέρχομαι to go in. εἶδον aor. ὁράω to see. καθήμενον pres. part. κάθημαι to sit. περιβεβλημένος perf. pass. part. περιβάλλω to place around, perf. pass. to be clothed w. στολή robe, esp. a long-flowing robe (BAG). ἐξεθαμβήθησαν aor. ἐκθαμβέομαι to be amazed. The
6 women were startled and awe-stricken (Swete). ■ ἐκθαμβεῖσθε pres. mid. imp. The pres. imp. w. the neg. indicates the stopping

134

of an action in progress. ζητεῖτε pres. ζητέω to seek, to look for. ἐσταυρωμένον perf. pass. part. σταυρόω to crucify. ἠγέρθη aor. pass. ἐγείρω to raise, pass. to rise. ἴδε aor. imp. ὁράω. ἔθηκαν aor. τίθημι to place, to lay. ■ ὑπάγετε pres. imp. 7 ὑπάγω to go forth, to go. εἴπατε aor. imp. λέγω. ὄψεσθε fut. ὁράω. ■ ἐξελθοῦσαι aor. part. fem. ἐξέρχομαι to go out. 8 ἔφυγον aor. φεύγω to flee. τρόμος trembling, fear. ἔκστασις bewilderment. ἐφοβοῦντο impf. mid. φοβέομαι to fear, to be afraid.

■ (For the textual problem concerning Mark 16:9–20, s. 9 Bruce M. Metzger, *A Textual Commentary on the Greek New Testament*, 122–126; John W. Burgon, *The Last Twelve Verses of the Gospel According to Mark;* William R. Farmer, *The Last Twelve Verses of Mark*). ἀναστάς aor. part. ἀνίστημι to rise. ἐφάνη aor. φαίνομαι to appear. ἐκβεβλήκει plperf. ἐκβάλλω to cast out, to drive out. ■ πορευθεῖσα aor. pass. part. 10 πορεύομαι to go. ἀπήγγειλεν aor. ἀπαγγέλλω to report, to announce. aor. mid. part. γενομένοις to become, to happen, to be. πενθοῦσι pres. part. dat. pl. πενθέω to mourn. κλαίουσιν pres. part. κλαίω to cry, to weep. ■ κἀκεῖνοι = καὶ ἐκεῖνοι. 11 ἀκούσαντες aor. part. ἀκούω to hear. ζῇ pres. ζάω to live. ἐθεάθη aor. pass. θεάομαι to see, to behold, to look at. ἠπίστησαν aor. ἀπιστέω to disbelieve, to refuse to believe.

■ περιπατοῦσιν pres. part. περιπατέω to walk about, to 12 go about. ἐφανερώθη aor. pass. φανερόω to make clear, to make visible, pass. to become visible, to be revealed, to appear. μορφή form. πορευομένοις pres. mid. part. dat. pl. ■ 13 ἀπελθόντες aor. part. ἀπέρχομαι to go away, to depart. (For the Semitic use of the part., s. MH, 452.) ἐπίστευσαν aor. πιστεύω to believe.

■ ἀνακειμένοις pres. mid. part. ἀνάκειμαι to recline at 14 the table. ὠνείδισεν aor. ὀνειδίζω to rebuke, to insult. σκληροκαρδία hard-heartedness. θεασαμένοις aor. mid. part. ἐγηγερμένον perf. pass. part., s.v.6. The perf. indicates the state or condition after the completed act. ■ κηρύξατε aor. imp. 15 κηρύσσω to preach, to proclaim. ■ πιστεύσας aor. act. part. 16 βαπτισθείς aor. pass. part. βαπτίζω to baptize. σωθήσεται fut. pass. σῴζω to rescue, to save. ■ ἀπιστήσας aor. act. part., 17 s.v.11. κατακριθήσεται fut. pass. κατακρίνω to decide against, to condemn. παρακολουθήσει fut. παρακολουθέω to follow, to accompany, to follow along the side. λαλήσουσιν fut. λαλέω to speak. ■ ὄφις snake. ἀροῦσιν fut. αἴρω to lift up, to 18 pick up. θανάσιμος deadly. πίωσιν aor. subj. πίνω to drink. βλάψῃ aor. subj. βλάπτω to harm, to injure. ἄρρωστος weak,

sick. ἐπιθήσουσιν fut. ἐπιτίθημι to place upon. ἕξουσιν fut.
ἔχω. Used w. καλῶς to be well, to be healthy.

19   ■ λαλῆσαι aor. inf. ἀνελήμφθη aor. pass. ἀναλαμβάνω
to take up. ἐκάθισεν aor. καθίζω to sit down, to take one's seat.

20 ■ ἐξελθόντες aor. part., s.v.8. ἐκήρυξαν aor., s.v.15.
συνεργοῦντος pres. part. συνεργέω to work along w., to cooperate w., gen. abs. βεβαιοῦντος pres. part. βεβαιόω to confirm.
ἐπακολουθούντων pres. part. ἐπακολουθέω to follow, to accompany. παρηγγελμένα perf. pass. part. παραγγέλλω to
command. συντόμως briefly. ἐξήγγειλαν aor. ἐξαγγέλλω to
report, to proclaim. ἐξαπέστειλεν aor. ἐξαποστέλλω to send
out. ἄφθαρτος indestructible, immortal.

THE GOSPEL OF LUKE

ἐπειδήπερ inasmuch as, since. A triple compound particle 1
("since," "truly," "indeed") expressing cause w. reference to a
fact already well known (s. Arndt; Godet; BD, 238).
ἐπεχείρησαν aor. ἐπιχειρέω to put the hand to, to undertake,
to attempt. No thought of censure, the other writers are mentioned as precedents rather than failures (BC, II, 493).
ἀνατάξασθαι aor. mid. inf. ἀνατάσσω to arrange in a row, to
draw up again, in order; that is, to arrange afresh so as to show
the sequence of events (Plummer). διήγησις narrative. It indicates a narration of a verified and well-witnessed report (I.I. Du
Plessis, "Once More: The Purpose of Luke's Prologue," Nov T,
16 [Oct. 1974], 263). πεπληροφυρημένων perf. pass. part.
πληροφορέω to fill completely, to fulfill, either in the sense of
to be fully persuaded or to be accomplished (s. Arndt; BAG;
LAE, 86f.). ■ παρέδοσαν aor. παραδίδωμι to deliver, to trans- 2
mit in both oral and written form (Ellis). αὐτόπτης eyewitness.
This reflects the conviction that the Christian faith is rooted not
in speculative creation but in historical reality (Ellis). The eyewitnesses are Luke's guarantee for a true report (Du Plessis,
265). ὑπηρέτης minister. They not only had personal knowledge of the facts but also practical experience of the facts (Plummer). γενόκενοι aor. mid. part. γίνομαι to become, to be. ■ 3
ἔδοξε aor. δοκέω to appear, to seem. μοι used impersonally w.
dat. of advantage "it appears good to me." κἀμοί = καὶ ἐμοί.
παρηκολουθηκότι perf. act. part. παρακολουθέω to follow
along. The mid. tracing, investigating, whereby one arrives at a
knowledge of the matter (Meyer). (For a good criticism of Cadbury's treatment of this word, s. Stonehouse, 121ff.) The perf.
emphasizes the state reached after investigation. ἄνωθεν from
the beginning, from the first. ἀκριβῶς accurately. Points to the
painstaking character of researches (Arndt). καθεξῆς in order,
one after the other, successively (s. BC, II, 504f.). It could refer
to topical order or chronological order. γράψαι aor. acc. inf.
γράφω to write. κράτιστος most noble, most excellent, honorary form of address used to persons who hold a higher official

4 or social position than the speaker (BAG). ■ ἐπιγνῶς aor. subj.
ἐπιγινώσκω to know. The prep. compound emphasizes a directive knowledge (MH, 312). κατηχήθης aor. pass. κατηχέω to
instruct, "to sound down into the ears, teach orally" (Plummer).
ἀσφάλεια certainty, safety, security, "the truth" about some
matters reported or discussed (BC, II, 509; s. also RWP). The
position of the word gives its solemn emphasis. Theophilus shall
know that the faith he has embraced has an impregnable historical foundation (Plummer).
5   ■ ἐγένετο aor. mid., s.v.2. (see also Luke 2:1). ἐφημερία
daily service. Then a course of priests who were on duty for a
week. The whole body of priests was divided into twenty-four
families or courses of service (s. RWP; HJP, Div. II, I 216–229;
6 SB, II, 55–68). ■ ἀμφότερος both. ἐνάντιον before.
πορευόμενοι pres. part. πορεύομαι to go. Hebraic expression
indicating the conduct of life. ἐντολή commandment.
δικαίωμα ordinance, things declared right (s. TDNT).
ἄμεμπτος blameless, unblamed (s. Trench, Synonyms, 380).
7 ■ στεῖρα barren, sterile. προβεβηκότες perf. part. προβαίνω
8 to go forward, to advance. ■ ἐγένετο aor. mid., s.v.2. (For the
construction and use, s. Arndt.) ἱερατεύω to be a priest, to
function as a priest. (For verbs w. this ending indicating the
exercise of a profession, s. MH, 398f.) τάξις row, order (s.v.5).
9 ■ ἔθος custom. ἔλαχεν aor. λαγχάνω to receive, to obtain
something by lot, to be appointed or chosen by lot. The casting
of lots took place twice a day at the morning and at the evening
offering of incense (Plummer). θυμιᾶσαι aor. inf. θυμιάω to
burn incense, to offer incense as a sacrifice (s. SB, II, 71–75; M,
Yoma 5, 1; M, Tamid 5, 4; 6, 2, 3; LT, I, 137ff.). εἰσελθών aor.
10 act part. εἰσέρχομαι to go in. ■ προσευχόμενον pres. part.
προσεύχομαι to pray. θυμίαμα incense, offering of incense.
11 ■ ὤφθη aor. pass. ὁράω to see, pass. to appear. ἑστώς perf. act.
part. ἵστημι perf. to stand. θυσιαστήριον altar of incense. The
right side was the south side, and the angel would be between
12 the altar and the golden candlestick (Plummer). ■ ἐταράχθη
aor. pass. ταράσσω to trouble, to disturb. ἰδών aor. part. ὁράω
13 to see. ἐπέπεσεν aor. ἐπιπίπτω to fall upon. ■ φοβοῦ pres.
imp. φοβέομαι to fear, to be afraid. The pres. imp. w. neg. is
used to prohibit an action in progress. εἰσηκούσθη aor. pass.
εἰσακούω to hear, to attend to. (For the effect of the prep.
compound, s. MH, 304.) δέησις request prayer. Implies personal need (Plummer). γεννήσει fut. γεννάω to bear, to give
birth. καλέσεις fut. καλέω to call, to name. The fut. used w. the
14 force of an imp. ■ ἀγαλλίασις rejoicing, refers to a demonstra-

tive rejoicing (Arndt). χαρήσονται fut. χαίρω to be glad, to
rejoice. ■ σίκερα strong drink. Denotes any intoxicating bever- 15
age prepared from either grain or fruit (IDB, IV, 448). (For
regulations regarding a Nazarite, s. M, Nazir; SB, II, 80–88.) πίῃ
fut. πίνω to drink. πλησθήσεται fut. pass. πίμπλημι to fill.
κοιλία body cavity, womb, uterus. The expression means either
"from birth" (BAG) or "before birth" (Godet). ■ ἐπιστρέψει 16
fut. ἐπιστρέφω to turn about, to cause to return. ■ 17
προσελεύσεται fut. προσέρχομαι to go before. ἐπιστρέψαι
aor. inf., inf. to express purpose. ἑτοιμάσαι aor. inf. ἑτοιμάζω
to prepare, to make ready. κατεσκευασμένον perf. pass. part.
κατασκευάζω to furnish, to equip, to prepare. The perf. emphasizes the state of preparedness. ■ γνώσομαι fut. γινώσκω to 18
know, to recognize. ■ ἀποκριθείς aor. pass. part. ἀποκρίνομαι 19
to answer. (For the Hebraic construction of the part., s. MH,
453.) παρεστηκώς perf. act. part. παρίστημι to stand, to
stand beside, implies ministering (Plummer). ἀπεστάλην aor.
pass. ἀποστέλλω to send, to send w. authority, to accomplish
a mission (s. TDNT; CBB). εὐαγγελίσασθαι aor. mid. inf.
εὐαγγελίζομαι to bring good news. Infinitive used to express
purpose. ■ σιωπῶν pres. part. σιωπάω to be silent. Participle 20
used in a periphrastic construction. δυνάμενος pres. mid. part.
δύναμαι to be able. γένηται aor. subj., s.v.2. πληρωθήσονται
fut. pass. πληρόω to fulfill, to fill.

■ προσδοκῶν pres. part. προσδοκάω to expect, to wait 21
for. Participle used in a periphrastic construction. ἐθαύμαζον
impf. θαυμάζω to marvel, to wonder, to wonder at. The impf.
pictures the continual action. χρονίζειν pres. inf., to delay. The
inf. used w. the prep. expressing contemporaneous time "while
he delayed." (For the Semitic construction, s. MH, 450.) ■ 22
ἐξελθών aor. part. ἐξέρχομαι to go out. ἐδύνατο impf.
ἐπέγνωσαν aor. ἐπιγινώσκω to know, to recognize. ὀπτασία
vision. ἑώρακεν perf. ὁράω to see. διανεύων pres. part.
διανεύω to nod. The part. used in a periphrastic construction
indicating continuous action (s. IBG, 16ff.). διέμενεν impf.
διαμένω to remain. The prep. in the compound is perfective.
Both the compound and the tense emphasize the fact that it was
not mere temporary seizure (Plummer). ■ ἐπλήσθησαν aor. 23
pass. λειτουργία ministry, literally "service rendered to the
people." Used in the religious sense denoting the service a priest
renders to God (Arndt). ἀπῆλθεν aor. ἀπέρχομαι to go away.
■ συνέλαβεν aor. συλλαμβάνω to conceive, to become preg- 24
nant. περιέκρυβεν aor. περικρύβω to conceal, to hide. The
compound verb implies all round, complete concealment (Plum-

25 mer). ■ πεποίηκεν perf. ποιέω to do. The perf. implies the state
or condition as a result of the completed action. ἐπεῖδεν aor.
ἐφοράω to look upon, to concern one's self w., to look w. favor
on someone (BAG). ἀφελεῖν aor. inf. ἀφαιρέω to take away.
The inf. used as object of the verb. ὄνειδος reproach.

26/27   ■ ἀπεστάλη aor. pass., s.v.19. ■ παρθένος virgin.
ἐμνηστευμένην perf. pass. part. μνηστεύω pass. to be engaged
28 (s. Matt. 1:19). ■ εἰσελθών aor. part., s.v.9. κεχαριτωμένη
perf. pass. part. χαριτόω to bestow grace, to show favor to
someone. Here it is the divine favor for a special vocation (Mof-
29 fat, Grace, 100; Robinson, Ephesians, 226ff.; TDNT). ■
διεταράχθη aor. pass. διαταράσσω to confuse, to perplex.
The prep. compound intensifies the verb "she was thoroughly
confused." διελογίζετο impf. mid. διαλογίζομαι to reason, to
debate, to consider, to reckon up different reasons (RWP).
30 ποταπός what sort of, what kind of. ■ φοβοῦ pres. imp., s.v.13.
31 εὗρες aor. εὑρίσκω to find. ■ συλλήμψῃ fut. συλλαμβάνω
32 s.v.24. τέξῃ fut. τίκτω to bear, to give birth. ■ ὕψιστος superl.
the highest, the most high. κληθήσεται fut. pass. καλέω to call.
33/35 ■ βασιλεύσει fut. βασιλεύω to be king, to reign. ■
ἐπελεύσεται fut. ἐπέρχομαι to come upon. ἐπισκιάσει fut.
ἐπισκιάζω to overshadow. γεννώμενον pres. pass. part.
36 γεννάω s.v.13. ■ συγγενίς relative, kinswoman. συνείληφα
perf. συλλαμβάνω. γῆρας old age. καλουμένη pres. pass.
37 part. καλέω. ■ ἀδυνατήσει fut. ἀδυνατέω to be impossible.
38 ■ γένοιτο aor. opt. γίνομαι to become, to happen. The opt.
generally is used to express a wish (s. BD, 194). Here it is an
expression of submission (Plummer). ἀπῆλθεν s.v.23.
39   ■ ἀναστᾶσα aor. part. fem. ἀνίστημι to arise. (For the
40 Semitic use the redundant part., s. MH, 453.) ■ εἰσῆλθεν aor.,
41 s.v.9. ἠσπάσατο aor. mid. ἀσπάζομαι to greet. ■ ἤκουσεν
aor. ἀκούω to hear. ἐσκίρτησεν aor. σκιρτάω to leap, to jump.
42 βρέφος unborn child, baby. ἐπλήσθη aor. pass. s.v.15. ■
ἀνεφώνησεν aor. ἀναφωνέω to call out. εὐλογημένη perf.
pass. part. εὐλογέω to bless. ἐν among. Hebraic way of express-
43/45 ing a superl. ■ ἔλθῃ aor. subj. ἔρχομαι to come, to go. ■
μακάριος happy (s. Matt. 5:3). πιστεύσασα aor. part. fem.
πιστεύω to believe, to trust. λελαλημένοις perf. pass. part.
λαλέω to speak.
47/48   ■ ἠγαλλίασεν aor. ἀγαλλιάω to rejoice. ■ ἐπέβλεψεν
aor. ἐπιβλέπω to look upon. μακαριοῦσιν fut. μακαρίζω to
49 call or consider blessed, happy, fortunate. ■ ἐποίησεν aor.,
50 s.v.25. ■ φοβουμένοις pres. mid. part., s.v.13. Fearing God is
51 the OT description of piety (Plummer). ■ βραχίων arm.

διεσκόρπισεν aor. διασκορπίζω to scatter. ὑπερήφανος
haughty, arrogant. ■ καθεῖλεν aor. καθαιρέω to bring down. 52
ὕψωσεν aor. ὑψόω to lift up ■ πεινῶντας pres. part. πεινάω 53
to hunger, to be hungry. ἐνέπλησεν aor. ἐμπίμπλημι to fill, to
satisfy. πλουτοῦντας pres. part. πλουτέω to be rich.
ἐξαπέστειλεν aor. ἐξαποστέλλω to send out. ■ ἀντελάβετο 54
aor. mid. ἀντιλαμβάνω mid., to lay hold of in order to support
or to succour (Plummer). μνησθῆναι aor. pass. part.
μυμνήσκομαι to remember. The inf. is used to express result
(s. BD, 198). ■ ἔμεινεν aor. μένω to remain. ὑπέστρεψεν aor. 56
ὑποστρέφω to return. ■ ἐπλήσθη aor. pass., s.v.15. τεκεῖν 57
aor. inf. s.v.31. ■ συνέχαιρον impf. συγχαίρω to rejoice to- 58
gether. ■ περιτεμεῖν aor. inf. περιτέμνω to cut around, to 59
circumcise. ἐκάλουν impf. Conative impf. "they were attempting to name him" (s. Arndt). ■ ἀποκριθεῖσα aor. pass. part. 60
fem. s.v.19. κληθήσεται fut. pass., s.v.13. ■ ἐνένευον impf. 62
ἐννεύω to nod, to signal by nodding. The article used here
introduces an indirect question (RG, 766). θέλοι pres. opt. θέλω
to will, to want. The opt. is used in indirect discourse (s. BD,
195). καλεῖσθαι pres. pass. inf. ■ αἰτήσας aor. part. αἰτέω to 63
ask fur, to request. πινακίδιον a small tablet, small wooden
boards, covered w. a film of wax, were used (Ellis; s. also SB, II,
108ff.). ἔγραψεν aor. γράφω to write. ■ ἀνεῴχθη aor. pass. 64
ἀνοίγνυμι to open. ἐλάλει impf. λαλέω to speak. Inceptive
impf. "he began to speak." ■ περιοικοῦντας pres. part. 65
περιοικέω to live around, to live by, neighboring. ὀρεινή hill
country. διελαλεῖτο impf. pass. διαλαλέω to discuss, to talk w.
The prep. compound and the impf. indicate it was continuous
talk back and forth between the people (RWP). ■ ἔθεντο aor. 66
mid. τίθημι to place, to lay.
    ■ ἐπροφήτευσεν aor. προφητεύω to prophesy. ■ 67/68
ἐπεσκέψατο aor. mid. ἐπισκέπτομαι to look upon, to visit.
λύτρωσις redemption, release. The reference here is no doubt
to political redemption but is accompanied by and based upon
moral and spiritual reformation (Plummer). ■ ἤγειρεν aor. 69
ἐγείρω to wake, to raise up. κέρας horn. Used as a symbol of
strength. ■ ἐλάλησεν aor. ■ μισούντων pres. part. μισέω to 70/71
hate. ■ ποιῆσαι aor. inf. Infinitive used to express the purpose 72
of "the raising up." μνησθῆναι aor. pass. inf., s.v.54. ■ ὤμοσεν 73
aor. ὄμνυμι to swear. δοῦναι aor. inf. δίδωμι to give. The inf.
gives the contents and purpose of the oath (Plummer). ■ 74
ἄφοβος without fear, fearless. ῥυσθέντας aor. pass. part.
ῥύομαι to rescue, to deliver. λατρέυειν pres. inf. to serve. Compare Heb. 12:28. ■ ὁσιότης piety, devoutness, personal piety or 75

devoutness which arises out of respect for the eternal laws (s.
76 TDNT). ■ κληθήσῃ fut. pass. προπορεύσῃ fut. mid.
προπορεύομαι to go before, to go forth. ἑτοιμάσαι aor. inf.,
78 s.v.17. ■ σπλάγχνον compassion, "the heart of mercy" (Arndt;
79 s. also TDNT). ἐπισκέψεται fut. mid. ■ ἐπιφᾶναι aor. inf.
ἐπιφαίνω to appear, to show one's self. σκιά shadow.
καθημένοις pres. mid. part. κάθημαι to sit. κατευθῦναι aor.
inf. κατευθύνω to make straight, to guide. Infinitive used to
express purpose.
80   ■ ηὔξανεν impf. αὐξάνω to grow. ἐκραταιοῦτο impf.
pass. κραταιόω to grow strong. Imperfect indicates He continued to grow strong. ἀνάδειξις commissioning, installation,
showing.

Ch. 2

1   ■ ἐγένετο aor. mid. γίνομαι to become, to happen. (For
the use of this verb in Luke, s. Plummer, 45.) ἐξῆλθεν aor.
ἐξέρχομαι to go out. ἀπογράφεσθαι pres. mid. inf.
ἀπογράφω to register, to record, mid. to register one's self. The
inf. expresses either the content or the purpose of the edict.
2 οἰκουμένη world, the inhabited earth. ■ ἀπογραφή enroll-
ment, tax registration. ἡγεμονεύοντος pres. part. ἡγεμονεύω
to govern, to be governor. (For the system of taxation and the
problem of the governorship of Quirinius, s. Arndt; William
Ramsey, The Bearing of Recent Discovery on the Trustworthi-
ness of the New Testament, 238–300; Harold Hoehner, "Chronological Aspects of the Life of Christ: The Date of Christ's Birth,"
Bib Sac 130 [Oct. 1974], 340–348; and other bibliographical
references by HA, 299.) It has been suggested that Quirinius had
3 authority over Syria at two different times. ■ ἐπορεύοντο impf.
4 πορεύομαι to go, to travel. ■ ἀνέβη aor. ἀναβαίνω to go up.
5 καλεῖται pres. pass. καλέω to call, to name. ■ ἀπογράψασθαι
aor. mid. inf. ἐμνηστευμένη perf. pass. part. μνηστεύω pass.
6 to be engaged (s. Matt. 1:19). ἔγκυος pregnant. ■ ἐπλήσθησαν
aor. pass. πίμπλημι to fill, to fulfill. τεκεῖν aor. inf. τίκτω to
7 give birth. ■ ἔτεκεν aor. πρωτότοκος first-born.
ἐσπαργάνωσεν aor. σπαργανόω to wrap in strips of cloth
intended to strengthen the back and bones and provide proper
growth (HDCG, II, 685). ἀνέκλινεν aor. ἀνακλίνω to lay
down, to place in a reclining position. φάτνη a trough or box for
feeding cattle (s. IDB, III, 257). κατάλυμα lodging, inn, guest
room. (For a description of a possibly similar building, s. RWP.)
8   ■ ποιμήν shepherd. Shepherds had a low reputation and
were looked upon w. great suspicion (s. TDNT; SB, II, 113f.).

ἀγραυλοῦντες pres. part. ἀγραυλέω literally, "to make the
field the courtyard," to spend their life in the open air (Plummer). φυλάσσοντες pres. part. φυλάσσω to guard. ■ ἐπέστη 9
aor. ἐφίστημι to come upon suddenly and unexpected.
περιέλαμψεν aor. περιλάμπω to shine around. ἐφοβήθησαν
aor. pass. φοβέομαι to be afraid. ■ φοβεῖσθε pres. mid. imp. 10
Present imp. w. neg. indicating the prohibition of an action in
progress. ■ ἐτέχθη aor. pass. τίκτω to give birth. ■ εὑρήσετε 11/12
fut. εὑρίσκω to find. ἐσπαργανωμένον perf. pass. part., s.v.7.
κείμενον pres. part. κεῖμαι to lie. ■ ἐξαίφνης suddenly. 13
στρατιά army, a band of soldiers; however, this army an-
nounces peace (Bengel). αἰνούντων pres. part. αἰνέω to praise,
gen. pl. The construction is according to sense (RWP). ■ 14
εὐδοκία good pleasure. It refers to God's good pleasure (Arndt;
s. also Fitzmyer, Essays 101–104; for the phrase in DSS, s. 1QH
4:32, 33; 11:9; 1QS 8:6).

■ ἀπῆλθον aor. ἀπέρχομαι to go away. ἐλάλουν impf. 15
λαλέω to speak. The impf. pictures the repeated action.
διέλθωμεν aor. subj. διέρχομαι to pass through, to go through.
The compound verb refers to the intervening country (Plummer). The subj. is cohortatory "let us go." δή indeed. It has the
force of urgency (Arndt). ἴδωμεν aor. subj. ὁράω to see, cohortatory subj. γεγονός perf. part. γίνομαι. ἐγνώρισεν aor.
γνωρίζω to make known. ■ ἦλθαν aor. ἔρχομαι to go. 16
σπεύσαντες aor. part. σπεύδω to hurry, part. of manner.
ἀνεῦραν aor. ἀνευρίσκω to find. The compound implies a
search in order to find (Plummer). ■ ἰδόντες aor. part. ὁράω to 17
see. λαληθέντος aor. pass. part. ■ ἀκούσαντες aor. part. 18
ἀκούω. ἐθαύμασαν aor. θαυμάζω to wonder, to be amazed.
■ συνετήρει impf. συντηρέω to keep in mind, to hold or treas- 19
ure up (in one's memory) (BAG). συμβάλλουσα pres. part.
συμβάλλω to reflect upon, "placing together for comparison"
(RWP). ■ ὑπέστρεψαν aor. ὑποστρέφω to return. ἤκουσαν 20
aor. ἀκούω. εἶδον aor. ὁράω. ■ ἐπλήσθησαν aor. pass., s.v.6. 21
περιτεμεῖν aor. inf. περιτέμνω to circumcise. (For the rite of
circumcision among the Jews, s. SB, IV, 23–40; TDNT.) ἐκλήθη
aor. pass. καλέω s.v.4. κληθέν aor. pass. part. συλλημφθῆναι
aor. pass. inf. συλλαμβάνω to conceive, to become pregnant.
(For the use of the inf. w. prep. w. a temporal meaning "before,"
s. RG, 107f.) ■ καθαρισμός cleansing (s. Lev. 12:1–8). 22
ἀνήγαγον aor. ἀνάγω to lead up. παραστῆσαι aor. inf.
παρίστημι to present. (For the redemption of the first-born, s.
Exod. 13:2–12; SB, II, 120ff.) ■ γέγραπται perf. pass. γράφω 23
to write. διανοῖγον pres. part. διανοίγω to open. κληθήσεται

24 fut. pass. καλέω s.v.4. ■ δοῦναι aor. inf. δίδωμι to give.
εἰρημένον perf. pass. part. λέγω. ζεῦγος yoke, to pair. τρυγών
turtledove, the offering of the poor (Plummer). νοσσός young,
offspring, particularly used of birds. περιστερά pigeon, tamed
pigeon.

25   ■ εὐλαβής cautious, esp. conscientious, here conscientious
in matters of religion (Plummer). παράκλησις consolation. A
comprehensive term for the fulfillment of the messianic hope
26 (SB, II, 124). ■ κεχρηματισμένον perf. pass. part. χρηματίζω
to impart a revelation, to instruct, to warn. The word was used
in the papyri in the sense of to transact business as well as a
revelation from a deity (s. MM). The part. is used in a periphrastic construction. ἰδεῖν aor. inf., s.v.15. πρὶν ἤ ἄν w. subj.
27 "before." ἴδῃ aor. subj. ■ ἦλθεν s.v.16. εἰσαγαγεῖν aor. inf.
εἰσάγω to bring in. Infinitive used w. prep. in a temporal sense
(s. RG, 1072f.). ποιῆσαι aor. inf. ποιέω to do. εἰθισμένον
28 perf. pass. part. ἐθίζω to accustom, perf. the custom. ■ ἐδέξατο
aor. mid. δέχομαι to receive. ἀγκάλη arm, bent as to receive
something (BAG). εὐλόγησεν aor. εὐλογέω to bless. It was the
custom in Jerusalem to bring a small child to a rabbi that he
30 might bless the child and pray for it (SB, II, 138). ■ εἶδον aor.,
31/33 s.v.20. ■   ἡτοίμασας aor. ἐτοιμάζω to prepare. ■
θαυμάζοντες pres. part., s.v.18. Participle used in a periphrastic
34 construction. ■ κεῖται pres. ind. of an old defective verb, here
used as the pass. of τίθημι to place, to appoint (s. RWP).
ἀντιλεγόμενον pres. pass. part. ἀντιλέγω to speak against, to
contradict, to oppose. The Son experiences contradiction from
the world which reaches its culmination in the crucifixion (Mey-
35 er). ■ διελεύσεται fut. διέρχομαι to pass through. ῥομφαία
a large wide sword. Such a weapon signifies extreme anguish
(Plummer). ἀποκαλυφθῶσιν aor. pass. subj. ἀποκαλύπτω to
unveil, to reveal. Used w. ὅπως to express a purpose of the
"appointing" in v. 34 (Arndt). διαλογισμός consideration,
thought, scheme, an undertone of hostility is suggested
(Leaney).

36   ■ προβεβηκυῖα perf. act. part. fem. προβαίνω to advance. ζήσασα aor. part. fem. ζάω to live. παρθενία virginity.
37 ■ ἀφίστατο impf. mid. ἀφίστημι to depart. λατρεύουσα
38 pres. part. fem. λατρεύω to minister (s. Luke 1:74). ■
ἐπιστᾶσα aor. part. ἐφίστημι to approach, to come up, to
stand by. ἀνθωμολογεῖτο impf. mid. ἀνθομολογέομαι to give
thanks. The compound prep. in the verb indicates thanksgiving
in return for benefits (MH, 297). The inceptive impf. ἐλάλει
impf.

■ ἐτέλεσαν aor. τελέω to complete. ἐπέστρεψαν aor. 39
ἐπιστρέφω to return. ■ ηὔξανεν impf. αὐξάνω to grow. 40
ἐκραταιοῦτο impf. pass. κραταιόω to make strong, pass. to be
strengthened, to grow strong. πληρούμενον pres. pass. part.
πληρόω to fill.

■ ἐπορεύοντο impf. mid. to go, to travel, to make a journey, 41
customary impf. ■ ἐγένετο aor. mid. s.v.1. ἀναβαινόντων pres. 42
part., s.v.4, gen. abs. ■ τελειωσάντων aor. act. part. τελειόω 43
to end, to complete. ὑπέμεινεν aor. ὑπομένω to remain behind.
ἔγνωσαν aor. γινώσκω to know. ■ νομίσαντες aor. part. 44
νομίζω to suppose, to believe. ἀνεζήτουν impf. ἀναζητέω to
look for, to seek. The prep. denotes thoroughness and the impf.
gives the repeated action "they searched up and down, back and
forth, a thorough search and prolonged" (RWP). ■ εὑρόντες 45
aor. part., s.v.12. ὑπέστρεψαν aor. ἀναζητοῦντες pres. part.
■ εὗρον aor. καθεζόμενον pres. mid. part. καθέζομαι to sit. 46
ἐπερωτῶντα pres. part. ἐπερωτάω to ask a question, to inquire.
The prep. compound is directive (MH, 312). (For questions and
answers in the rabbinical method of teaching. s. SB, II, 150.)
■ ἐξίσταντο impf. ἐξίστημι to be amazed, to be astonished. 47
■ ἰδόντες aor. part., s.v.15. ἐξεπλάγησαν aor. pass. 48
ἐκπλήσσω to strike out, to drive out by blow, pass, to be
overwhelmed, to be astonished. ἐποίησας aor. 2nd per. sing.,
s.v.27. ὀδυνώμενοι pres. mid. part. ὀδυνάομαι to suffer pain.
■ ἐζητεῖτε impf. ᾔδειτε plperf. of the defective perf. w. a pres. 49
meaning οἶδα to know. δεῖ it is necessary. ■ συνῆκαν aor. 50
συνίημι to bring together, to understand, to comprehend.
ἐλάλησεν aor., s.v.15. ■ κατέβη aor. καταβαίνω to go down. 51
ὑποτασσόμενος pres. pass. part. ὑποτάσσω pass. submit
one's self, to subordinate one's self, to obey. διετήρει impf.
διατηρέω to keep, to guard safely. The prep. compound is perfective and describes the carrying of action through to a definite
result (MH, 301). προέκοπτεν impf. προκόπτω to advance.
ἡλικία height, stature (Godet).

Ch. 3

■   ἡγεμονία   leadership,   government,   reign. 1
ἡγεμονεύοντος pres. part. ἡγεμονεύω to be governor.
τετρααρχοῦντος pres. part. τετρααρχέω to be tetrarch; that is,
a governor of a fourth, that is, one of four provinces, later a
governor of any division (Plummer). (For the life and times of
Herod Antipas, s. HA. See also Harold Hoehner, "Chronological
Aspects of the Life of Christ: The Commencement of Christ's
Ministry," Bib Sac 131 [Jan–March], 147–162.) ■ ἐγένετο aor. 2

3   mid. γίνομαι to become, to happen (s. Luke 2:1). ■ ἦλθεν aor.
ἔρχομαι to come, to go. κηρύσσων pres. part. (For John's
4   preaching of baptism and repentence, s. Matt. 3:1,2.) ■
γέγραπται perf. pass. γράφω to write. The perf. indicates "it
stands written" (s. MM). βοῶντος pres. part. βοάω to shout, to
call aloud. ἑτοιμάσατε aor. imp. ἑτοιμάζω to prepare. ποιεῖτε
5   pres. imp. ποιέω to do, to make. τρίβος way, path. ■ φάραγξ
a valley shut in by precipices, a ravine (Plummer).
πληρωθήσεται fut. pass. πληρόω to fill. βουνός hill.
ταπεινωθήσεται fut. pass. ταπεινόω to make low. σκολιός
crooked, curved. τραχύς uneven, rough. λεῖος smooth, even.
6   ■ ὄψεται fut. mid. ὁράω to see.
7   ■ βαπτισθῆναι aor. pass. inf. βαπτίζω to baptize. Infinitive used to express purpose. ἔχιδνα snake (for a similar expression, "adder or snake eggs" in DSS, s. CD 5:14). ὑπέδειξεν
aor. ὑποδείκνυμι to show, to show under, to point out, to give
a tip or private hint (RWP). φυγεῖν aor. inf. φεύγω to flee.
8   μελλούσης pres. part. fem. sing. μέλλω to be about to. ■
ποιήσατε aor. imp., s.v.4. ἄρξησθε aor. mid. subj. ἄρχομαι to
begin. Used as a Semitic construction "do not say" (Arndt; s.
also MH, 455). ἐγεῖραι aor. inf. ἐγείρω to awake, to raise up.
9   ■ ἀξίνη axe. κεῖται perf. pass. τίθημι perf. pass. to lie (s. Luke
10 2:34). ■ ἐπηρώτων impf. ἐπερωτάω to question, to inquire,
inceptive impf. ποιήσωμεν aor. subj., deliberative subj. "what
11 shall we do?" ■ ἀποκριθείς aor. pass. part. ἀποκρίνομαι to
answer. (For the Semitic construction, s. MH, 453.) μεταδότω
aor. imp. 3rd sing. μεταδίδωμι to give, to share. βρῶμα food.
13 ποιείτω pres. imp. 3rd sing. ■ διατεταγμένον perf. pass. part.
διατάσσω to command, to prescribe. πράσσετε pres. imp.
14 πράσσω to do, to extort, to exact tribute (s. Plummer). ■
στρατευόμενοι pres. mid. part. στρατεύομαι to be a soldier.
διασείσητε aor. subj. διασείω to extort money by violence,
literally to shake violently; that is, to shake down (BAG). Used
in the papyri in the sense "to intimidate" (MM).
συκοφαντήσητε aor. subj. συκοφαντέω to accuse falsely, to
extort by blackmail (for this word, s. Arndt). ἀρκεῖσθε pres.
imp. pass. ἀρκέω pass. to be enough, to be sufficient. ὀψώνιον
food, ration, pay. The average soldier received two hundred and
twenty-five denarii a year (a denarius, worth about 18 cents, was
the normal day's wages) from which deductions were made for
food, clothing and arms (OCD, 1014). (For the meaning "provi-
sions/shoppings," see C.C. Caragounis, " ΟΨΩΝΙΟΝ: A Reconsideration of Its Meaning," Nov T, 16 [Jan., 1974], 49–51.)
15 ■ προσδοκῶντος pres. part. προσδοκάω to await w. ex-

pectation, gen. abs. διαλογιζομένων pres. mid. part. διαλογίζομαι to discuss, to reason, to debate. ■ ἀπεκρίνατο 16 aor. mid. ἰσχυρότερος comp. ἰσχυρός strong, mighty. ἱκανός sufficient, worthy. λῦσαι aor. inf. λύω. ἱμάς, άντος leather straps. ■ πτύον winnowing shovel. διακαθᾶραι aor. inf. 17 διακαθαίρω to thoroughly clean. ἅλων threshing floor. συναγαγεῖν aor. inf. συνάγω to gather together. ἀποθήκη storehouse, barn. ἄχυρον chaff. κατακαύσει fut. κατακαίω to burn, to burn up. ἄσβεστος unquenchable. ■ παρακαλῶν pres. 18 part. παρακαλέω to urge, to exhort, part. of manner. εὐηγγελίζετο impf. mid. εὐαγγελίζομαι to proclaim the good news (s. TDNT). ■ ἐλεγχόμενος pres. pass. part. ἐλέγχω to 19 bring to light, to expose, to convict or convince someone of something, to reprove (BAG). ἐποίησεν aor. ■ προσέθηκεν 20 aor. προστίθημι to add to, "he added this also on top of all—he shut up John in prison" (Plummer). κατέκλεισεν aor. κατακλείω to shut up, literally, to shut down.

■ βαπτισθῆναι aor. pass. inf., inf. used w. prep. to express 21 time. βαπτισθέντος aor. pass. part., gen. abs. προσευχομένου pres. mid. part. προσεύχομαι to pray. ἀνεῳχθῆναι aor. pass. inf. ἀνοίγω to open. ■ καταβῆναι aor. inf. καταβαίνω to 22 come down. σωματικός bodily. γενέσθαι aor. mid. inf. (s. Luke 2:1). εὐδόκησα aor. εὐδοκέω to have pleasure, to be pleased.

■ ἀρχόμενος pres. mid. part., s.v.8. It refers to Jesus begin- 23 ning His ministry (Plummer). ὡσεί about, around. A person's age frequently was given in multiples of five. Luke's chronology is only very general (Ellis; s. also v. 1). ἐνομίζετο impf. pass. νομίζω to suppose.

Ch. 4

■ ὑπέστρεψεν aor. ὑποστρέφω to return. ἤγετο impf. 1 pass. ἄγω to lead. ■ πειραζόμενος pres. pass. part. πειράζω to 2 try, to tempt. The pres. part. used here may be used to express purpose. Compare Matt. 4:1 (s. also RG, 891). ἔφαγεν aor. ἐσθίω to eat. συντελεσθεισῶν aor. pass. part. συντελέω to finish, to complete. The prep. compound is perfective. Participle used is gen. abs. ἐπείνασεν aor. πεινάω to be hungry. ■ εἰπέ 3 aor. imp. γένηται aor. mid. subj. γίνομαι to become. ■ 4 ἀπεκρίθη aor. ἀποκρίνομαι to answer. γέγραπται perf. pass. γράφω to write. ζήσεται fut. mid. ζάω to live. ■ ἀναγαγών 5 aor. act. part. ἀνάγω to lead up. ἔδειξεν aor. δείκνυμι to show. στιγμὴ χρόνου "in a point of time." It intimates the kingdoms were represented, not in a series of pageants, but simultaneously

147

6 (Plummer). ■ δώσω fut. δίδωμι to give. παραδέδοται perf.
7 pass. παραδίδωμι to deliver over. ■ προσκυνήσῃς aor. subj.
προσκυνέω to worship, to worship by falling on the knees.
8 ■ ἀποκριθείς aor. pass. part. (s. Luke 3:11). προσκυνήσεις
9 fut. λατρεύσεις fut. λατρεύω to minister, to serve. ■ ἤγαγεν
aor. ἄγω to lead. ἔστησεν aor. ἵστημι to place, to stand. βάλε
10 aor. imp. βάλλω to throw. ■ ἐντελεῖται fut. ἐντέλλομαι to
command, to give instructions. διαφυλάξαι aor. inf.
διαφυλάσσω to guard, to watch over. Used esp. for divine
11 guardianship (MM). ■ ἀροῦσιν fut. αἴρω to lift up. μήποτε w.
subj. "lest." Used to express neg. purpose. προσκόψῃς aor. subj.
12 προσκόπτω to strike against, to stumble on. ■ εἴρηται perf.
pass. λέγω. ἐκπειράσεις fut. ἐκπειράζω to tempt, to test, to
try, to test out. The prep. compound might suggest the daring of
13 the act or the effort to put to a decisive test (MH, 309). ■
συντελέσας aor. part. ἀπέστη aor. ἀφίστημι to depart.
14   ■ ὑπέστρεψεν s.v.1. ἐξῆλθεν aor. ἐξέρχομαι to go out.
15 ■ ἐδίδασκεν impf. διδάσκω to teach. The impf. emphasizes the
continuing action. δοξαζόμενος pres. pass. part. δοξάζω to
glorify, to praise, to hold in high esteem.
16   ■ ἦλθεν aor. ἔρχομαι to come, to go. τεθραμμένος perf.
pass. part. τρέφω to nourish, to bring up, to rear. εἰσῆλθεν aor.
εἰσέρχομαι to go in. εἰωθός perf. part. of an old form ἔθω to
be accustomed. Synagogue attendance was expected of every
devout Jew (Ellis). ἀνέστη aor. ἀνίστημι to stand up.
ἀναγνῶναι aor. inf. ἀναγινώσκω to read. (For the reading of
17 the Scripture in the synagogue service, s. TT, 42–50.) ■ ἐπεδόθη
aor. pass. ἐπιδίδωμι to give to. ἀνοίξας aor. part. ἀνοίγω to
open. εὗρεν aor. εὑρίσκω to find. γεγραμμένον perf. pass.
18 part., s.v.4. ■ εἵνεκεν because of. ἔχρισεν aor. χρίω to anoint.
εὐαγγελίσασθαι aor. mid. inf. εὐαγγελίζομαι to proclaim
good news. Infinitive used to express purpose. ἀπέσταλκεν aor.
ἀποστέλλω to send, to send as an authoritative representative
(s. TDNT). κηρύξαι aor. inf. κηρύσσω. αἰχμάλωτος prisoner
captured in war, captive. ἀνάβλεψις restoration of sight.
ἀποστεῖλαι aor. inf. τεθραυσμένους perf. pass. part. θραύω
19 to break in pieces, to shatter. ■ ἐνιαυτός year. δεκτός acceptable. That in which He is pleased to show mankind extraordinary
20 favors (Godet). ■ πτύξας aor. part. πτύσσω to fold, to roll
together. ἀποδούς aor. part. ἀποδίδωμι to give back.
ἐκάθισεν aor. καθίζω to sit down, to take one's seat. The one
teaching generally sat to teach. ἀτενίζοντες pres. part. ἀτενίζω
to look or gaze intently. The prefix of the word is not alpha
privative but copulative or intensive (RWP). The part. is used in

148

a periphrastic construction. ■ ἤρξατο aor. ἄρχομαι to begin. 21
πεπλήρωται perf. pass. πληρόω to fill, to fulfill. ■ 22
ἐμαρτύρουν impf. καρτυρέω to be a witness, to testify.
ἐθαύμαζον impf. θαυμάζω to wonder, to be amazed, to admire.
■ πάντως adv. (in answers to questions) "certainly." ἐρεῖτε fut. 23
λέγω. θεράπευσον aor. imp. θεραπεύω to heal. ἠκούσαμεν
aor. ἀκούω to hear. γενόμενα aor. mid. part., s.v.3. ποίησον
aor. imp. ποιέω ■ ἐκλείσθη aor. pass. κλείω to shut, to close. 25
ἐπί about. ἐγένετο aor. s.v.3. ■ ἐπέμφθη aor. pass. πέμπω to 26
send. ■ ἐπί w. gen. at the time of. ἐκαθαρίσθη aor. pass. 27
καθαρίζω to cleanse. ■ ἐπλήσθησαν aor. pass. πίμπλημι to 28
fill. θυμός anger, partitive gen. used w. the verb "filled w." The
construction indicates the control and domination of the total
person. ■ ἀναστάντες aor. part. ἀνίστηνι. ἐξέβαλον aor. 29
ἐκβάλλω to throw out, to drive out. ἤγαγον aor., s.v.1. ὀφρύς
brow, ridge. ᾠκοδόμητο plperf. pass. οἰκοδομέω to build.
κατακρημνίσαι aor. inf. κατακρημνίζω to throw someone
over a cliff. The inf. is used w. a particle to express intended
result (RWP). ■ διελθών aor. part. διέρχομαι to pass through, 30
to go through.

■ κατῆλθεν aor. κατέρχομαι to go down. διδάσκων pres. 31
part. used in periphrastic construction expressing continual or
repeated action. ■ ἐξεπλήσσοντο impf. pass. ἐκπλήσσω to be 32
astounded. ■ ἀνέκραξεν aor. ἀνακράζω to cry out, to scream 33
out. ■ ἔα interjection of anger or dismay "ah." ἦλθες aor. 2nd 34
per. sing., s.v.16. ἀπολέσαι aor. inf. ἀπόλλυμι to destroy, to
ruin. Infinitive used to express purpose. οἶδα defective perf. w.
pres. meaning to know. ■ ἐπετίμησεν aor. ἐπιτιμάω to charge, 35
to sternly command (s. Matt. 17:18; cf. 1QM 14:10.) φιμώθητι
aor. pass. imp. φιμόω to muzzle, pass. to be silent. ἔξελθε aor.
imp., s.v.14. ῥῖψαν aor. part. ῥίπτω to throw, to fling. The verb
expresses violence (s. RWP). βλάψαν aor. part. βλάπτω to
damage, to injure. ■ ἐγένετο aor. mid., s.v.3. συνελάλουν impf. 36
συλλαλέω to talk together, to discuss. ■ ἐξεπορεύετο impf. 37
ἐκπορεύομαι to go out. ἦχος echo, report.

■ ἀναστάς aor. part., s.v.16. εἰσῆλθεν aor. εἰσέρχομαι 38
to go in. συνεχομένη pres. pass. part. συνέχω pass. to be held
by something, to suffer. The part. is used in a periphrastic construction. πυρετός fever. The ancient physicians distinguished
fevers by the terms "great" and "small." (For this and the previous word. s. MLL 3,4.) ἠρώτησαν aor. ἐρωτάω to ask, to
request. ■ ἐπιστάς aor. part. ἐφίστημι to stand by or near, to 39
approach. ἐπάνω over. Jesus stepped up to the bed or rug on
which the patient lay and bent over her (Arndt). ἀφῆκεν aor.

ἄφιημι to leave. ἀναστᾶσα aor. part. διηκόνει impf.
40 διακονέω to serve, to minister, inceptive impf. ■ δύνοντος pres.
part. δύνω to go down (of the sun), to set. Participle used in gen.
abs. ἀσθενοῦντας pres. part. ἀσθενέω to be weak, to be sick.
ἤγαγον aor., s.v.1. ἐπιτιθείς aor. part. ἐπιτίθημι to place
41 upon. ἐθεράπευεν impf., s.v.23. ■ ἐξήρχετο impf. mid.
κραυγάζοντα pres. part. κραυγάζω to scream, to cry out.
ἐπιτιμῶν pres. part. εἴα impf. ἐάω to allow. ᾔδεισαν plperf.
οἶδα. εἶναι pres. inf. Infinitive used in indirect discourse.
42 ■ γενομένης aor. mid. part. gen. abs. ἐπεζήτουν impf.
ἐπιζητέω to seek after, to look for. The prep. marks the direction of the search (Plummer). The impf. describes the continual
action. κατεῖχον impf. κατέχω to hold back, to restrain. The
43 conative impf. "they tried to restrain him." ■ εὐαγγελίσασθαι
aor. mid. inf., s.v.18. δεῖ (w. acc. and inf.) "it is necessary."
ἀπεστάλην aor. pass. ἀποστέλλω to send, to send as an official representative (s. TDNT).

Ch. 5

1   ■ ἐγένετο aor. mid. γίνομαι to become, to happen (s. Luke
2:1). ἐπικεῖσθαι pres. mid. inf. ἐπίκειμαι to lie upon, to press
around, to press upon. ἑστώς perf. part. ἵστημι perf. to stand.
2 ■ εἶδεν aor. ὁράω to see. πλοιάριον small boat, an open craft
some twenty to thirty feet in length (Ellis). ἁλεεύς seaman,
fisherman. ἀποβάντες aor. part. ἀποβαίνω to go forth, to go
3 away. ἔπλυνον impf. πλύνω to wash, to clean. ■ ἐμβάς aor.
part. ἐμβαίνω to get in, to embark. ἠρώτησεν aor. ἐρωτάω to
ask, to request. ἐπαναγαγεῖν aor. inf. ἐπανάγω to put out to
sea. ὀλίγον adv. a little. καθίσας aor. part. καθίζω to sit down.
4 ἐδίδασκεν impf. διδάσκω to teach, inceptive impf. ■
ἐπαύσατο aor. mid. παύομαι to cease, to stop. λαλῶν pres.
part. λαλέω to speak. ἐπανάγαγε aor. imp. βάθος deep.
χαλάσατε aor. imp. χαλάω to let down. A nautical term for
5 lowering cargo or boats (RWP). ἄγρα catch. ■ ἀποκριθείς aor.
pass. part. ἀποκρίνομαι to answer (s. MH, 453). ἐπιστάτης
overseer, director, master, implying authority and used here of
one who has the right to give orders (Plummer). κοπιάσαντες
aor. part. κοπιάω to work, to work w. effort. The part. could be
concessive "although we have worked." ἐλάβομεν aor.
λαμβάνω to take, to receive. ἐπί w. dat. "in reliance on Your
6 Word" (Arndt). χαλάσω fut. ■ ποιήσαντες aor. part. ποιέω.
συνέκλεισαν aor. συγκλείω to close together. διερρήσσετο
impf. pass. διαρρήγνυμι to rip apart, pass. to burst, inceptive
7 impf. ■ κατένευσαν aor. κατανεύω to motion to. μέτοχος

partner. ἐλθόντας aor. part. ἔρχομαι to come. συλλαβέσθαι aor. mid. inf. συλλαμβάνω to take hold together, to help. ἦλθαν aor. ἔρχομαι. ἔπλησαν aor. πίμπλημι to fill. βυθίζεσθαι pres. pass. inf. βυθίζω to cause to sink, pass. to sink. The inf. used w. the particle to express result. The pres. tense is inceptive (Arndt). ■ ἰδών aor. part. ὁράω to see. 8 προσέπεσεν aor. προσπίπτω to fall down before (w. dat.). ἐξελθε aor. imp. ἐξέρχομαι to depart, to go away. ἁμαρτωλός sinful. ■ θάμβος amazement. περιέσχεν aor. περιέχω to en- 9 compass, to seize. ■ κοινωνός partner, associate, one who 10 shares, stronger than the term used in v. 7. It denotes an association and a common undertaking (Godet; s. also TDNT; CBB; MNTW). φοβοῦ pres. imp. φοβέομαι to fear, w. the neg. indicating a prohibition of existing action. ζωγρῶν pres. part. ζωγρέω to capture alive, to catch alive. Participle used in a periphrastic fut. construction emphasizing linear or durative action (s. MT, 89; MKG, 307f.). ■ καταγαγόντες aor. part. 11 κατάγω to lead down, nautical term to bring boats to land. ἄφεντες aor. part. ἀφίημι to leave. ἠκολούθησαν aor. ἀκολουθέω to follow, to follow as a disciple.

■ ἐγένετο aor. mid., s.v.1. πλήρης full. (For the medical 12 use of this term, s. MLL, 5f.) λέπρα leprosy (s. Matt. 8:4). πεσών aor. part. πίπτω to fall. ἐδεήθη aor. pass. δέομαι to want for one's self, to beg, to request. θέλῃς pres. subj. to want. καθαρίσαι aor. inf. καθαρίζω to cleanse. ■ ἐκτείνας aor. part. 13 ἐκτείνω to stretch out. ἥψατο aor. mid. ἅπτομαι to touch (w. the gen.). καθαρίσθητι aor. pass. imp. ἀπῆλθεν aor. ἀπέρχομαι to go away. ■ παρήγγειλεν aor. παραγγέλλω to 14 command, to charge. εἰπεῖν aor. inf. λέγω. δεῖξον aor. imp. δείκνυμι to show. προσένεγκε aor. imp. προσφέρω to carry to, to offer a sacrifice. προσέταξεν aor. προστάσσω to instruct, to command. μαρτύριον witness, proof. ■ διήρχετο 15 impf. διέρχομαι to go through, to spread abroad. The impf. indicates the fame of Jesus kept going (RWP). συνήρχοντο impf. mid. συνέρχομαι to accompany, to travel w. someone. ἀκούειν pres. inf., s.v.1. Infinitive used for purpose. θεραπεύεσθαι pres. pass. inf. θεραπεύω to heal. Infinitive to express purpose. ■ ὑποχωρῶν pres. part. ὑποχωρέω to with- 16 draw, to slip away secretly (RWP). Participle used in a periphrastic construction. προσευχόμενος pres. mid. part. προσεύχομαι to pray. Participle in periphrastic construction.

■ ἐγένετο aor. mid., s.v.1. διδάσκων pres. part. periphras- 17 tic construction. καθήμενοι pres. part. κάθημαι to sit. νομοδιδάσκαλος teachers of the law. Used in the rabbinical

writings of those who give "halacha," i.e., authoritative interpretations of Scripture (Ellis). ἐληλυθότες perf. part. ἔρχομαι to
come, to go. ἰᾶσθαι pres. mid. ἰάομαι to heal. Infinitive used
18 w. prep. to express purpose (s. MT, 143). ■ φέροντες pres. part.
φέρω to carry. παραλελυμένος perf. pass. part. παραλύω to
weaken, to disable. The perf. emphasizes the state or condition
paralyzed. Luke is in strict agreement w. the medical writers in
using the verb instead of the more popular adj. (MLL, 6).
ἐζήτουν impf. ζητέω to seek. εἰσενεγκεῖν aor. inf. εἰσφέρω to
19 carry in. θεῖναι aor. inf. τίθημι to lay, to place. ■ εὑρόντες aor.
part. εὑρίσκω to find. ποίας gen. sing. fem. "what sort of," gen.
of place "by what sort of (way)" (s. BD, 99f.). εἰσενέγκωσιν
aor. subj., deliberative subj. of indirect question retained in the
direct (RWP). ἀναβάντες aor. part. ἀναβαίνω to go up.
κέραμος tile. Because of the Gentile influence in Palestine at
the time it would not be unusual for Jewish homes to have had
tile roofs (Geldenhuys). καθῆκαν aor. καθίημι to let down.
κλινίδιον (dimin. of κλίνη) pallet, stretcher. (For examples
where the word is used of a light couch for carrying the sick, s.
20 MLL, 116.) ■ ἰδών aor. part., s.v.8. ἀφέωνται perf. pass.
21 ἀφίημι to release, to forgive. ■ ἤρξαντο aor. mid. ἄρχομαι to
begin. διαλογίζεσθαι pres. mid. inf. διαλογίζομαι to reason
w., to debate w., to consider. ἀφεῖναι aor. inf. ἀφίημι. εἰ μή
22 except. ■ ἐπιγνούς aor. part. ἐπιγινώσκω. The verb implies a
thorough and accurate knowledge (Plummer). ἀποκριθείς aor.
23 pass. part., s.v.5. ■ εὐκοπώτερος comp. εὔκοπος easy. ἔγειρε
pres. imp. arise, περιπάτει pres. imp. περιπατέω to walk
24 about. ■ εἰδῆτε perf. subj. οἶδα to know. ἀφιέναι pres. inf.
ἄρας aor. part. αἴρω to lift up, to take up. πορεύου pres. mid.
25 imp. πορεύομαι to go. ■ ἀναστάς aor. part. ἀνίστημι to stand
up. κατέκειτο impf. mid. κατάκειμαι to lie, customary impf.
"upon which he used to lie." ἀπῆλθεν aor., s.v.13. δοξάζων
26 pres. part. δοξάζω to glorify, to praise. ■ ἔλαβεν aor., s.v.5.
ἐδόξαζον impf. ἐπλήσθησαν aor. pass. πίμπλημι s.v.7.
εἴδομεν aor., s.v.2. παράδοξος incredible, literally "things
which are contrary to opinion or belief" (Arndt).
27   ■ ἐξῆλθεν aor., s.v.8. ἐθεάσατο aor. θεάομαι to see, to
observe, to look at. τελώνιον tax station, custom house (s. Mark
28 2:14). ἀκολούθει pres. imp., s.v.11. ■ καταλιπών aor. part.
καταλείπω to leave, to forsake. ἀναστάς s.v.25. ἠκολούθει
29 impf. ■ ἐποίησεν aor., s.v.6. δοχή banquet. (For a description
of a Jewish banquet, s. SB, IV, 611–639.) κατακείμενοι pres.
30 mid. part., s.v.25. Here to recline at the table. ■ ἐγόγγυζον impf.
31 γογγύζω to murmur, to complain. ■ ἀποκριθείς aor. pass.

part., s.v.5. ■ ἐλήλνθα perf. ἔρχομαι s.v.7. καλέσαι aor. inf. 32
καλέω to call. Infinitive used to express purpose.

■ νηστεύω to fast (s. Geldenhuys). πυκνός often. 33
ποιοῦνται pres. mid., s.v.6. ■ νυμφών marriage hall, wedding 34
room. The Hebraic expression designating the attendance of the
bridegroom (Arndt). ἐν ᾧ while, so long as. ποιῆσαι aor. inf.
νηστεῦσαι aor. inf. ■ ἐλεύσονται fut. mid. ἔρχομαι. ἀπαρθῇ 35
aor. pass. subj. ἀπαίρω to take away, implying rejection and
violent death (Ellis). ■ ἐπίβλημα patch. σχίσας fut. aor. part. 36
σχίζω to tear, to rip. εἰ δὲ μή γε "but if otherwise" (s. Plummer). συμφωνήσει fut. συμφωνέω to fit, to harmonize, to
agree. ■ ῥήξει fut. ῥήγνυμι to tear, to burst. ἐκχυθήσεται fut. 37
pass. ἐκχέω to pour out. ἀπολοῦνται fut. mid. ἀπόλλυμι to
ruin, to lose. ■ βλητέον verbal adj. from βάλλω "one must put" 38
(s. M, 221f.). ■ πιών aor. part. πίνω to drink. χρηστός good, 39
useful, pleasant.

Ch. 6

■ ἐγένετο aor. mid. γίνομαι to become, to happen (s. Luke 1
2:1). ἔτιλλον impf. τίλλω to pluck, to pick. ἤσθιον impf.
ἐσθίω to eat. στάχυς ear of grain. ψώχοντες pres. part. ψώχω
to rub. ■ εἶπαν aor. λέγω. ■ ἀποκριθείς aor. pass. part. 2/3
ἀποκρίνομαι to answer. ἀνέγνωτε aor. ἀναγινώσκω to read.
ἐποίησεν aor. ἐπείνασεν aor. πεινάω to be hungry. ■ 4
εἰσῆλθεν aor. εἰσέρχομαι to go in. λαβών aor. part.
λαμβάνω to take. ἔφαγεν aor. ἐσθίω to eat. ἔδωκεν aor.
δίδωμι to give. φαγεῖν aor. inf.

■ εἰσελθεῖν aor. inf. δεξιός right. There is a mark of par- 6
ticularity here such as a physician would observe (MLL, 7).
ξηρός dried, withered. ■ παρετηροῦντο impf. mid. 7
παρατηρέω to observe, to watch closely, esp. w. sinister intent
perhaps from looking sideways out of the corner of one's eyes
(Plummer). θεραπεύω to treat medically, to heal. εὕρωσιν aor.
subj. εὑρίσκω to find. κατηγορεῖν pres. inf. κατηγορέω w.
gen. to accuse. ■ ᾔδει plperf. of the defective perf. οἶδα to know. 8
ἔγειρε pres. imp. arise. στῆθι aor. imp. ἵστημι to stand.
ἀναστάς aor. part. ἀνίστημι to stand up. ἔστη aor. ἵστημι
to stand. ■ ἐπερωτάω to ask, to direct a question to someone. 9
ἀγαθοποιῆσαι aor. inf. ἀγαθοποιέω to do good. σῶσαι aor.
inf. σῴζω to save, to rescue, to heal. ἀπολέσαι aor. inf.
ἀπόλλυμι to destroy, to ruin. ■ περιβλεψάμενος aor. mid. 10
part. περιβλέπω to look about. The mid. voice gives a personal
touch (RWP). ἔκτεινον aor. imp. ἐκτείνω to stretch out.
ἀπεκατεστάθη aor. pass. ἀποκαθίστημι to completely re-

153

11 store. Used as a technical medical term to cure (BAG). ■
ἐπλήσθησαν aor. pass. πίμπλημι to fill (w. gen.). ἀνοία madness, mad fury, a loss of reason which is caused by extreme
excitement (Plummer). διελάλουν impf. διελαλέω to discuss,
to speak back and forth. (For the force of the prep. in compound,
s. MH, 302.) ποιήσαιεν aor. opt. The potential opt. expressing
hesitancy, a weighing of possibilities (Arndt).
12   ■ ἐγένετο aor. mid., s.v.1. ἐξελθεῖν aor. inf. ἐξέρχομαι to
go out. προσεύξασθαι aor. mid. inf. προσεύχομαι to pray.
Infinitive used to express purpose. διανυκτερεύων pres. part.
διανυκτερεύω to watch through the night. Medical writers used
it of whole night vigils (RWP). The part. used in a periphrastic
13 construction. ■ προσεφώνησεν aor. προσφωνέω to summons, to call to. ἐκλεξάμενος aor. mid. part. ἐκλέγω to chose,
to select. The word implies the telling over in preference to
others for one's own advantage (Plummer). ὠνόμασεν aor.
14 ὀνομάζω to name, to give a name to. ■ καλούμενον pres. pass.
15 part. καλέω to call, to name. ■ ζηλωτής zealous, referring to the
personal character (BC, I, 425f.) or zealot, referring to a political
party which radically opposed the Roman rule (s. IDB, IV,
936ff.; H.P. Kingdon, "The Origins of the Zealots," NTS 19
16 [Oct., 1972], 74–81). ■ προδότης betrayer.
17   ■ καταβάς aor. part. καταβαίνω to go down. ἔστη s.v.8.
18 πεδινός flat, level. παράλιος along the sea. ■ ἦλθον aor.
ἔρχομαι to come. ἀκοῦσαι aor. inf. ἀκούω to hear. Infinitive
of purpose. ἰαθῆναι aor. pass. inf. ἰάομαι to heal. Infinitive of
purpose. ἐνοχλούμενοι pres. pass. ἐνοχλέω to trouble. (For
medical examples of the word, s. MLL, 8.) ἐθεραπεύοντο impf.
19 pass., s.v.7. ■ ἐζήτουν impf. ζητέω to seek. ἅπτεσθαι pres.
mid. inf. ἅπτομαι to touch (w. gen.). ἐξήρχετο impf. ἰᾶτο impf.
mid.
20/21   ■ ἐπάρας aor. part. ἐπαίρω to lift up. ■ πεινῶντες pres.
part., s.v.3. χορτασθήσεσθε fut. pass. χορτάζω to feed, to fill,
to satisfy, pass. to be satisfied. κλαίοντες pres. part. κλαίω to
22 cry, to weep. γελάσετε fut. γελάω to laugh. ■ μισήσωσιν aor.
subj. μισέω to hate. ἀφορίσωσιν aor. subj. ἀφορίζω to mark
off from by boundary, to separate, excommunication from the
congregation as well as from social intercourse (Plummer).
ὀνειδίσωσιν aor. subj. ὀνειδίζω to reproach, to heap insults on.
23 ἐκβάλωσιν aor. subj. ἐκβάλλω to cast out, to throw out. ■
χάρητε aor. imp. χαίρω to rejoice. σκιρτήσατε aor. imp.
σκιρτάω to skip, to jump, to leap. ἐποίουν impf., s.v.2, custom-
24 ary impf. ■ ἀπέχετε pres. ind. act. to receive. The word was
used in a commercial sense to acknowledge the receipt of full

payment (s. MM; LAE, 110f.). Beyond the present possession of riches these people have nothing to hope for (Arndt). ■ 25 ἐμπεπλησμένοι perf. pass. part. ἐμπίμπλημι to fill up, to satisfy. πεινάσετε fut., s.v.3. γελῶντες pres. part., s.v.21. πενθήσετε fut. πενθέω to mourn. κλαύσετε fut. κλαίω s.v.21. ■ εἴπωσιν aor. subj. λέγω. 26

■ ἀγαπᾶτε pres. imp. ἀγαπάω to love. ποιεῖτε pres. imp. 27 ■ εὐλογεῖτε pres. imp. εὐλογέω to bless. The granting or ac- 28 knowledgment of power leading to success. Here general kindness shown to enemies (CBB; TDNT). καταρωμένους pres. mid. part. καταράομαι to curse, the attempt to bring evil upon someone (CBB; TDNT). προσεύχεσθε pres. mid. imp., s.v.12. ἐπηρεαζόντων pres. part. ἐπηρεάζω to abuse, to mistreat, to display a despiteful spirit (Arndt). ■ τύπτοντι pres. part. τύπτω 29 to hit, a violent blow w. the fist rather than a|contemptuous slap (Plummer). σιαγών cheek, jawbone. πάρεχε pres. imp. παρέχω to offer. αἴροντος pres. part. αἴρω to take, to take away. ἱμάτιον coat, outward garment. χιτών undergarment (s. Matt. 5:40). κωλύσῃς aor. subj. κωλύω to hinder, to prevent. The subj. used w. a neg. to express a prohibition. ■ αἰτοῦντι 30 pres. part. αἰτέω to ask, to request. δίδου pres. imp. δίδωμι to give. ἀπαίτει pres. imp. ἀπαιτέω to ask for something back. ■ ποιῶσιν pres. subj. ■ ἀγαπῶντας pres. act. part. χάρις 31/32 thanks, favor. ■ ἀγαθοποιῆτε pres. subj. ἀγαθοποιέω to do 33 good. Subjunctive used in a conditional clause w. the condition being probable. ■ δανείσητε aor. subj. δανείζω to lend money. 34 λαβεῖν aor. inf. λαμβάνω to take, to receive. ἀπολάβωσιν aor. subj. ἀπολαμβάνω to receive again. ■ ἀπελπίζοντες pres. 35 part. ἀπελπίζω to hope to have something in return (Arndt) or to give up in despair (Plummer). Used in medical language to denote a disease one despairs of curing (MLL, 118f.). ■ γίνεσθε 36 pres. mid. imp., s.v.1. οἰκτίρμων merciful, compassionate (TDNT).

■ κρίνετε pres. imp. κρίνω to judge. κριθῆτε aor. pass. 37 imp. καταδικάζετε pres. imp. καταδικάζω to condemn, to pass sentence against. ἀπολύετε pres. imp. ἀπολύω to release, to forgive. ἀπολυθήσεσθε fut. pass. ■ δοθήσεται fut. pass., 38 s.v.30. πεπιεσμένον perf. pass. part. πιέζω to press down. σεσαλευμένον perf. pass. part. σαλεύω to shake. ὑπερεκχυννόμενον pres. mid. part. ὑπερεκχύννομαι to over-flow. The picture is of grain poured into a container, pressed down and then shaken so that every little corner is filled and the grain is poured in until it runs over (Arndt). δώσουσιν fut. 3rd per. pl. used impersonally. Sometimes used when the subject is

God (s. BD, 72). κόλπος the fold formed by a loose garment
overhanging a girdle (Plummer). μετρεῖτε pres. μετρέω to measure. ἀντιμετρηθήσεται fut. pass. ἀντιμετρέω to measure
back again. The prep. in compound expresses reciprocal action
39 (MH, 297). ■ ὁδηγεῖν pres. inf. ὁδηγέω to lead, to show the
40 way. ἐμπεσοῦνται fut. mid. ἐμπίπτω to fall in. ■
κατηρτισμένος perf. pass. part. καταρτίζω to complete, to
finish, to equip. When the disciple has received complete preparation from his teacher, he will be equal to his teacher but not
41 surpassing (Meyer). ■ κάρφος splinter, anything small and dry.
δοκός beam. The main beam receiving the other beams in a roof
or floor (Plummer). κατανοεῖς pres. κατανοέω to notice, to
42 observe carefully, to consider, to look at w. reflection. ■ ἄφες
aor. imp. ἀφίημι to leave, to leave alone. ἔκβαλε aor. imp.
διαβλέψεις fut. διαβλέπω to see clearly, to see accurately.
ἐκβαλεῖν aor. inf.
44 ■ ἄκανθα thorn bush. σῦκον figs. βάτος a bramble bush.
σταφυλή grapes. τρυγῶσιν pres. τρυγάω to pick grapes, to
45 gather fruit. ■ λαλεῖ pres. λαλέω to speak.
46/47 ■ καλεῖτε pres., s.v.15. ■ ἀκούων pres. part. ἀκούω to
hear, to listen to, to hear and obey. ποιῶν pres. part. The participles of continued action are significant (Arndt). ὑποδείξω fut.
48 ὑποδείκνυμι to show. ■ οἰκοδομοῦντι pres. part. οἰκοδομέω
to build. ἔσκαψεν aor. σκάπτω to dig. ἐβάθυνεν aor. βαθύνω
to make deep, to deepen. ἔθηκεν aor. τίθημι to lay. θεμέλιον
foundation. πλήμμυρα a flood. γενομένης aor. mid. part., gen.
abs. προσέρρηξεν aor. προσρήγνυμι to break against.
ἴσχυσεν aor. ἰσχύω to be strong, to be able. σαλεῦσαι aor. inf.
49 οἰκοδομῆσθαι perf. pass. inf. ■ ἀκούσας aor. part. ποιήσας
aor. part. οἰκοδομήσαντι aor. part. συνέπεσεν aor.
συμπίπτω to fall together. ῥῆγμα breaking, ruin, collapse.
Used of a "breach" in a dam (MM). As a medical term "lacera-
tion," "rupture" (MLL, 56).

Ch. 7

1   ■ ἐπειδή after. Normally the word is causal but here temporal (RWP). ἐπλήρωσεν aor. πληρόω to fulfill, to end, to con-
2 clude. εἰσῆλθεν aor. εἰσέρχομαι to go in. ■ ἑκατόνταρχος
leader of a hundred men, centurion (s. IDB, I, 547f.). ἤμελλεν
impf. μέλλω to be about to. Used w. inf. to express fut. The impf.
w. inf. expresses futurity or intention reckoned from a moment
in the past, "he was going to die," "he was at the point of death"
(MKG, 307). τελευτᾶν pres. inf. τελευτάω to die. ἔντιμος
3 costly, valuable, honored. ■ ἀκούσας aor. part. ἀκούω to hear.

ἀπέστειλεν aor ἀποστέλλω to send, to send an official in an
authoritative position. ἐρωτῶν pres. part. ἐρωτάω to ask, to
request. ἐλθών aor. part. ἔρχομαι to come. διασώσῃ aor. subj.
διασώζω to save, to rescue, to heal. Medical writers used the
term w. the meaning to escape from a severe illness or an epi-
demic, to get through the attack (MLL, 10). ■ παραγενόμενοι 4
aor. mid. part. παραγίνομαι to come to. παρακάλουν impf.
παρακαλέω to call for help, to appeal to, to urge. The impf.
emphasizes the continual urging. σπουδαῖος eagerly, earnestly.
παρέξῃ fut. mid. 2nd per. sing. παρέχομαι to grant something
to someone. ■ ἀγαπᾷ pres. ἀγαπάω to love. ᾠκοδόμησεν aor. 5
οἰκοδομέω to build. ■ ἐπορεύετο impf. mid. πορεύομαι to go. 6
μακράν far. ἀπέχοντος pres. part. ἀπέχω to be away, gen. abs.
ἔπεμψεν aor. πέμπω to send. σκύλλου pres. pass. imp.
σκύλλω to trouble, mid., to fatigue, to cause trouble (Arndt).
ἱκανός sufficient, worthy. στέγη roof. εἰσέλθῃς aor. subj. ■ 7
ἠξίωσα aor. ἀξιόω to judge worthy. ἐλθεῖν aor. inf. εἰπέ aor.
imp. λέγω. ἰαθήτω aor. pass. imp. ἰάομαι to heal. ■ 8
τασσόμενος pres. pass. part. τάσσω to place or station, to
appoint, to put someone over, to put in charge. The pres. part.
is adjectival, "for I am a man who is habitually placed under
authority" (Plummer). πορεύθητι aor. pass. imp. ἔρχου pres.
imp. ποίησον aor. imp. ποιέω. ■ ἐθαύμασεν aor. θαυμάζω to 9
wonder, to be amazed. στραφείς aor. pass. part. στρέφω to
turn, pass. to turn around. ἀκολουθοῦντι pres. part.
ἀκολουθέω to follow. τοσοῦτος so great, so large. εὗρον aor.
εὑρίσκω to find. ■ ὑποστρέψαντες aor. part. ὑποστρέφω to 10
return. πεμφθέντες aor. pass. part. ὑγιαίνοντα pres. part.
ὑγιαίνω to be healthy. The servant was not only cured but was
also in good health (MLL, 11).

■ ἐγένετο aor. mid. γίνομαι to become, to happen (s. Luke 11
2:1). ἑξῆς next, in a series, of time on the next day, afterward
(BAG). ἐπορεύθη aor. pass. συνεπορεύοντο impf. mid.
συμπορεύομαι to travel together. ■ ἤγγισεν aor. ἐγγίζω to 12
draw near, to approach. ἐξεκομίζετο impf. pass. ἐκκομίζω to
carry out, esp. to bury. τεθνηκώς perf. part. ἀποθνήσκω to die,
perf. to be dead. μονογενής only, only child. χήρα widow.
Jesus' compassion on the weeping widow who for the second
time was robbed of her provider and protector is probably to be
understood as a Messianic act (TDNT). ἱκανός here, "much,
many, numerous." ■ ἰδών aor. part. ὁράω to see. 13
ἐσπλαγχνίσθη aor. pass. σπλαγχνίζομαι to be moved w.
compassion, to have compassion upon (s. TDNT). κλαῖε pres.
imp. κλαίω to cry, to weep loudly. The pres. imp. w. neg. indi-

14 cates the discontinuing of an action in progress. ■ προσελθών aor. part. προσέρχομαι to come to. ἥψατο aor. mid. ἅπτομαι to touch (w. gen.). σορός an open coffin, a portable frame on which the body was laid (Arndt). βαστάζοντες pres. part. βαστάζω to carry. ἔστησαν aor. ἵστημι to stand. ἐγέρθητι
15 aor. pass. imp. ἐγείρω to raise, pass. to rise up. ■ ἀνεκάθισεν aor. ἀνακαθίζω to sit up. Used by medical writers to describe patients sitting up in bed (MLL, 11). ἤρξατο aor. mid. ἄρχομαι to begin. λαλεῖν pres. inf. λαλέω to speak, to utter a sound
16 (Arndt). ἔδωκεν aor. δίδωμι to give. ■ ἔλαβεν aor. λαμβάνω to take, to seize. ἐδόξαζον impf. δοξάζω to glorify, to hold in high esteem, inceptive impf. ἠγέρθη aor. pass. ἐγείρω. ἐπεσκέψατο aor. mid. ἐπισκέπτομαι to look at, to go to see, to visit. Used of God's gracious visitation in bringing salvation
17 (BAG). ■ ἐξῆλθεν aor. ἐξέρχομαι to go out.
18 ■ ἀπήγγειλαν aor. ἀπαγγέλλω to report. προσκαλεσάμενος aor. mid. part. προσκαλέω to call to, to
19 summons. ■ ἔπεμψεν aor., s.v.6. προσδοκῶμεν pres. ind. or pres. subj. (deliberative subj.) προσδοκάω to wait for, to ex-
20 pect. ■ παραγενόμενοι pres. mid. part., s.v.4. ἀπέστειλεν aor.
21 act., s.v.3. ■ ἐθεράπευσεν aor. θεραπεύω to treat medically, to heal. μάστιξ whip, scourge, plague, suffering. ἐχαρίσατο aor.
22 mid. χαρίζομαι to be gracious to, to graciously grant. ■ ἀποκριθείς aor. pass. part. ἀποκρίνομαι to answer. (For the Semitic use, s. MH, 453.) θέντες aor. part., s.v.6. ἀπαγγείλατε aor. imp. εἴδετε aor. ὁράω. ἠκούσατε aor., s.v.3. ἀναβλέπουσιν pres. to see again. περιπατοῦσιν pres.
23 περιπατέω to walk about. ■ σκανδαλισθῇ aor. pass. subj. σκανδαλίζω to cause to stumble, to take offense (s. TDNT).
24 ■ ἀπελθόντων aor. part. ἀπέρχομαι to go away, gen. abs. ἤρξατο aor. mid. s.v.15. ἐξήλθατε s.v.17. θεάσασθαι aor. mid. inf. θεάομαι to see, to watch. σαλευόμενον pres. pass.
25 part. σαλεύω to shake. ■ ἰδεῖν aor. inf. ὁράω. Infinitive of purpose. μαλακός soft. ἠμφιεσμένον perf. pass. part. ἀμφιέννυμι to clothe, to dress. (For the acc. used w. the pass., s. BD, 87.) ἔνδοξος distinguished, splendid. τρυφή indulgent, luxurious. ὑπάρχοντες pres. part. ὑπάρχω to be, to exist.
26 βασίλειον palace. ■ ναί yes, certainly. A strong emphatic particle, confirmatory of a preceding statement (DM, 262). περισσότερος comp. περισσός over and above, excessively, comp. more exceedingly, to a greater degree. προφήτου gen. of
27 comparison. ■ γέγραπται perf. pass. γράφω to write. κατασκευάσει fut. κατασκευάζω to prepare, to build, to con-
28 struct. ■ μείζων comp. μέγας. Ἰωάννου gen. of comparison.

μικρότερος comp. μικρός. ■ αὐτοῦ gen. of comparison. 29
ἐδικαίωσαν aor. δικαιόω to declare righteous, to justify. Here
"to recognize and acknowledge the righteousness of God" (GW,
138). βαπτισθέντες aor. pass. part. βαπτίζω to baptize. ■ 30
ἠθέτησαν aor. ἀθετέω to set aside, to annul. Used of grain
rejected by the inspector as unfit for food (MM).
    ■ ὁμοιώσω fut. ὁμοιόω to compare. ■ καθημένοις pres. 31/32
mid. part. κάθημαι to sit. προσφωνοῦσιν pres. part.
προσφωνέω to call to. ηὐλήσαμεν aor. αὐλέω to play the
flute. ὠρχήσασθε aor. mid. ὀρχέομαι to dance. ἐθρηνήσαμεν
aor. θρηνέω to mourn, to lament. ἐκλαύσατε aor. κλαίω to
weep. ■ ἐλήλυθεν perf. ἔρχομαι. ■ φάγος glutton. οἰνοπότης 33/34
wine drinker, drunkard.
    ■ ἠρώτα s.v.33. φάγῃ aor. subj. ἐσθίω to eat. εἰσελθών 36
aor. part., s.v.1. κατεκλίθη aor. pass. κατακλίνω to cause to lie
down, pass. to recline at the table. ■ ἁμαρτωλός sinful, devoted 37
to sin (RWP). ἐπιγνοῦσα aor. part. fem. ἐπιγινώσκω to know,
"having learned definitely" (Arndt). κομίσασα aor. part. fem.
κομίζω to bring. ἀλαβάστρον alabaster, a very soft stone from
which flasks or vases were made for the keeping of perfume
(Arndt) μύρον ointment, perfume. ■ στᾶσα aor. part. ἵστημι 38
to stand. κλαίουσα pres. part., s.v.13. The outward act of weeping is the result and expression of the inward state of grief
(Geldenhuys). ακρουν tear. βρέχειν pres. inf. to wet (s. BD,
164). θρίξ hair. ἐξέμασσεν impf. ἐκμάσσω to wipe off, to dry.
κατεφίλει impf. καταφιλέω to kiss, to kiss affectionately. Kissing the feet was a common mark of deep reverence, esp. to
leading rabbis (Plummer; s. also SB, I, 995f.; TDNT). ἤλειφεν
impf. ἀλείφω to anoint. Not the religious word for anoint, but
the general word (Trench, Synonyms, 136f.). ■ ἰδών aor. part., 39
s.v.13. καλέσας aor. part. καλέω to call, to invite. ἐγίνωσκεν
impf. γινώσκω to know. Used w. in a contrary to fact conditional sentence. ποταπός "what sort of?" literally, "from what
country?" (AS). ■ ἀποκριθείς aor. pass. part., s.v.22. εἰπεῖν 40
aor. inf. εἰπέ aor. imp., s.v.7. ■ χρεοφειλέτης debtor, one who 41
owes an obligation or debt (RWP). δανειστής moneylender, a
professional moneylender (Arndt). ὤφειλεν impf. ὀφείλω to
owe. δηνάριον denarius. A Roman silver coin worth normally
about 18 cents. It was a workman's average daily wage (BAG).
    ■ ἐχόντων pres. part., gen. abs. causal. ἀποδοῦναι aor. inf. 42
ἀποδίδωμι to pay back, to give back. ἐχαρίσατο aor. mid.,
s.v.21. He made them a present of what they owed (Plummer).
πλεῖον comp. πολύς. ■ ὑπολαμβάνω to take up, to assume, 43
to suppose w. an air of supercilious indifference (Plummer).

ὀρθῶς adv. right, correctly. ἔκρινας aor. 2nd sing. κρίνω to
44 judge. ■ στραφείς aor. pass. part., s.v.9. εἰσῆλθον aor. ἔδωκας
aor. 2nd sing., s.v.15. ἔβρεξεν aor., s.v.38. ἐξέμαξεν aor., s.v.38.
45 ■ φίλημα kiss. διέλειπεν impf. διαλείπω to stop, to cease.
46 καταφιλοῦσα pres. act. part. fem., s.v.38. ■ ἔλαιον olive oil.
ἤλειψας aor. (For the anointing and washing of the body, s. SB,
47 I, 426–429.) ■ οὗ χάριν because of which, on account of.
ἀφέωνται perf. pass. ἀφίημι to release, to forgive. ἠγάπησεν
49 aor. ἀφίεται pres. pass. ■ συνανακείμενοι pres. mid. part.
συνανάκειμαι to sit at the table together, to recline at the table
50 together. ἀφίησιν pres. ■ σέσωκεν perf. σῴζω to rescue, to
save, to deliver. It was her faith, not her love, that saved her
(Caird). πορεύου pres. imp., s.v.6.

Ch. 8

1 ■ ἐγένετο aor. mid. γίνομαι to become, to happen (s. Luke
2:1). The formula often is used to introduce a temporal element
(s. Klaus Beyer, *Semitiche Syntax im Neuen Testament*, 29–62).
καθεξῆς one after the other, successively, afterward. διώδευεν
impf. διοδεύω to pass through, to travel through. κατὰ πόλιν
from city to city. (For the distributive use of the prep., s. RG,
2 608.) ■ τεθεραπευμέναι perf. pass. part. θεραπεύω to treat
medically, to heal. The perf. emphasizes the pres. state or condition. καλουμένη pres. pass. part. καλέω to call, to name.
3 ἐξεληλύθει plperf. ἐξέρχομαι to come out. ■ ἐπίτροπος overseer, finance minister, one who is concerned w. the finances and
personal property of an owner (HA, 303f.). διηκόνουν impf.
διακονέω to minister, w. rel. pron. "who are of such a character
as to minister to them." They were persons of substance (Plummer). The impf. pictures the continual ministering.
4 ■ συνιόντος pres. part. σύνειμι to come together, gen.
abs. ἐπιπορευομένων pres. mid. part. ἐπιπορεύομαι to go on
5 a journey to, to go to, gen. abs. ■ ἐξῆλθεν aor. ἐξέρχομαι to
go out. σπείρων pres. part. σπείρω to sow. σπεῖραι aor. inf.
ἔπεσεν aor. πίπτω to fall. κατεπατήθη aor. pass. καταπατέω
to trample on, to trample down. κατέφαγεν aor. κατεσθίω to
6 eat up. ■ κατέπεσεν aor. καταπίπτω to fall down. φυέν aor.
part. neuter φύομαι to spring up, to sprout, to grow. ἐξηράνθη
7 aor. pass. ξηραίνω to dry up. ἰκμάς moisture. ■ ἄκανθα
thorns, thornbush. συμφυεῖσαι aor. part. fem. pl. συμφύομαι
to grow together. ἀπέπνιξαν aor. ἀποπνίγω to choke, to
8 choke off so as to exterminate it (Plummer). ■ ἐποίησεν aor.
ποιέω. ἐφώνει impf. φωνέω to call. The impf. is best interpreted as denoting repeated action (Arndt). ἀκουέτω imp. 3rd sing.

■ ἐπηρώτων impf. ἐπερωτάω to ask, to direct questions to. 9
εἴη opt. εἰμί, opt. of indirect discourse, a mark of elegant speech
(Arndt). ■ δέδοται perf. pass. δίδωμι to give. γνῶναι aor. inf. 10
γινώσκω to know. οἱ λοιποί the rest. Those outside the circle
of Christ's disciples (Plummer). βλέποντες pres. part. βλέπω
to see. συνιῶσιν pres. subj. συνίημι to understand, to comprehend.

■ τοῦ θεοῦ subjective gen. A word which comes from God 11
(RWP). ■ ἀκούσαντες aor. act. part. πιστεύσαντες aor. act. 12
part. πιστεύω to believe, to trust. σωθῶσιν aor. pass. subj.
σώζω to save, to rescue. ■ ἀκούσωσιν aor. subj. ἀφίστανται 13
pres. ἀφίστημι to go away, to withdraw, to fall away. ■ πεσόν 14
aor. part. πίπτω to fall. ἡδονή pleasure. πορευόμενος pres.
mid. part. πορεύομαι to go, "as they go on their way" (Arndt).
συμπνίγονται pres. pass. συμπνίγω to choke, to choke until
dead. The prep. in compound is perfective (MH, 325).
τελεσφοροῦσιν pres. τελεσφορέω to bear fruit to maturity, to
bring to maturity. ■ κατέχω to hold down, to hold fast. 15
καρποφοροῦσιν pres. καρποφορέω to bear fruit.

■ λύχνος lamp (s. Matt. 5:15). ἅψας aor. part. ἅπτω to 16
light. καλύπτω to hid. τίθησιν pres. τίθημι to set, to place.
λυχνία lampstand. εἰσπορευόμενοι pres. mid. part.
εἰσπορεύομαι to go in (on this v., s. Mark 4:21f.). ■ κρυπτός 17
hidden. γενήσεται fut. mid., s.v.1. ἀπόκρυφος hidden, hidden
away, from the public eye (Plummer). γνωσθῇ aor. pass. subj.
γινώσκω to know. ἔλθῃ aor. subj. ἔρχομαι. ■ δοθήσεται fut. 18
pass. δίδωμι to give. ἀρθήσεται fut. pass. αἴρω to take away.

■ ἠδύναντο aor. mid. δύναμαι. συντυχεῖν aor. inf. 19
συντυγχάνω (w. dat.) to eat w., to come together w. ■ 20
ἀπηγγέλη aor. pass. ἀπαγγέλλω to report. ἑστήκασιν perf.
ἵστημι to stand ἰδεῖν aor. inf. ὁράω to see. ■ ἀποκριθείς aor. 21
pass. part. ἀποκρίνομαι to answer (s. MH, 453).

■ ἐγένετο aor. mid., s.v.1. ἐνέβη aor. ἐμβαίνω to go in, to 22
get in, to embark. διέλθωμεν aor. subj. διέρχομαι to go
through. The prep. in compound emphasizes the passing through
a point and the arrival at the destination (s. MH, 300ff.). Hortatory subj. ἀνήχθησαν aor. pass. ἀνάγω to lead up, to put out
to sea. ■ πλεόντων pres. part. πλέω to sail gen. abs. 23
ἀφύπνωσεν aor. ἀφυπνόω to fall asleep. κατέβη aor.
καταβαίνω to come down, to go down. λαῖλαψ a violent
storm, a whirlwind or tornado (Arndt). συνεπληροῦντο impf.
pass. συμπληρόω to fill completely. The prep. in compound is
perfective (MH, 325). The impf. pictures the process of completely filling. ἐκινδύνευον impf. κινδυνεύω to be in danger.

24 ■ προσέλθοντες aor. part. προσέρχομαι to come to.
διήγειραν aor. διεγείρω to wake up. ἐπιστάτης master, overseer (s. Luke 5:5). διεγερθείς aor. pass. part. ἐπετίμησεν aor.
ἐπιτιμάω to rebuke (s. Matt. 17:18). κλύδων wave, a boisterous
surge, a violent agitation (RWP). ἐπαύσαντο aor. mid.
25 παύομαι to cease, to stop. γαλήνη calm, stillness. ■
φοβηθέντες aor. pass. part. φοβέομαι to be afraid.
ἐθαύμασαν aor. θαυμάζω to wonder, to be amazed.
26   ■ κατέπλευσαν aor. καταπλέω to sail down; i.e. from the
27 high seas toward the coast, to sail toward the coast. ■ ἐξελθόντι
aor. part., s.v.5, dat. used w. the verb. ἐνεδύσατο aor. mid.
ἐνδύω to put on, to clothe one's self. ἱμάτιον the outer garment,
clothes, here any kind of garment (Arndt). ἔμενεν impf. μένω
28 to remain, customary impf. ■ ἰδών aor. part., s.v.20.
ἀνακράξας aor. part. ἀνακράζω to cry out. προσέπεσεν aor.
προσπίπτω to fall forward, to fall down before. βασανίσῃς
aor. subj. βασανίζω to rub on a touch stone, to test the genuineness, to examine, to torture. The NT gives it merely the general
sense of inflicting bodily or mental pain (Arndt; s. also TDNT).
29 ■ παράγγελλεν impf. παραγγέλλω to command, to charge.
The impf. emphasizes repeated action. ἐξελθεῖν aor. inf.
συνηρπάκει plperf. συναρπάζω to seize by violence, to drag
away. The prep. in compound is perfective and denotes the
establishment of a permanent hold (M,113), "seize and keep a
firm hold of" (MM). ἐδεσμεύετο impf. pass. δεσμεύω to bind.
ἅλυσις chain. πέδη fetter, bond for the feet. It could be made
of hair or of material that was used in the manufacture of ropes
(Arndt). φυλασσόμενος pres. pass. part. φυλάσσω to guard,
to watch. διαρήσσων aor. part. διαρρήγνυμι to tear into. The
prep. intensifies the meaning of the verb (RWP). ἠλαύνετο
30 impf. pass. ἐλαύνω to drive. ■ ἐπηρώτησεν aor. s.v.9. λεγιών
legion (s. Matt. 26:53). εἰσῆλθεν aor. εἰσέρχομαι to go into.
31 ■ παρεκάλουν impf. παρακαλέω to ask, to beseech. ἐπιτάξῃ
aor. subj., s.v.25. ἄβυσσος abyss, depth, underworld. The prison of disobedient spirits (s. TDNT; Ellis; Cremer). ἀπελθεῖν
aor. inf. ἀπέρχομαι to go away.
32   ■ βοσκομένη pres. pass. part. βόσκω to feed, pass. to
graze. ἐπιτρέψῃ aor. subj. ἐπιτρέπω to allow. εἰσελθεῖν aor.
33 inf. εἰσέρχομαι. ■ ὥρμησεν aor. ὁρμάω to rush. κρημνός a
steep and rocky slope (Plummer). ἀπεπνίγη aor. pass., s.v.7.
34 ■ γεγονός perf. part. ἔφυγον aor. φεύγω to flee. ἀπήγγειλαν
35 aor., s.v.20. ■ ἐξῆλθον aor. εὗρον aor. εὑρίσκω to find.
καθήμενον pres. mid. part. κάθημαι to sit. ἱματισμένον perf.
pass. part. ἱματίζω to clothe. The perf. part. emphasizes the

state or condition. σωφρονοῦντα pres. part. σωφρονέω to be
of sound mind, to be in one's right mind. Used of mental health
in contrast to madness (BAG). ἐφοβήθησαν aor. pass. ▪ ἐσώθη 36
aor. pass. σῴζω to rescue, to save, to heal. δαιμονισθείς aor.
pass. part. δαιμονίζομαι to be possessed by an evil spirit. ▪ 37
ἠρώτησεν aor. ἐρωτάω to ask, to request. συνείχοντο impf.
pass. συνέχω to hold together, pass. to be seized. ἐμβάς aor.
part. ὑπέστρεψεν aor. ὑποστρέφω to return. ▪ ἐδεῖτο impf. 38
δέομαι to ask, to request, to beg. The impf. pictures the continual asking. ἐξεληλύθει plperf. ἐξέρχομαι. ἀπέλυσεν aor.
ἀπολύω to release, to send away, to dismiss. ▪ ὑπόστρεφε pres. 39
imp. διηγοῦ pres. imp. διηγέομαι to tell, to debate, to describe.
ἀπῆλθεν aor.

▪ ἀπεδέξατο aor. mid. ἀποδέχομαι to receive, to wel- 40
come, implies a cordial reception (EGT). προσδοκῶντες pres.
part. προσδοκάω to await, to expect. Participle used in a periphrastic construction. A vivid picture of the attitude of the
people toward Jesus (RWP). ▪ ἦλθεν aor., s.v.12. ὑπῆρχεν 41
impf. ὑπάρχω to be. πεσών aor. part., s.v.5. εἰσελθεῖν aor. inf.,
s.v.30. ▪ μονογενής only child (s. Luke 7:12). ἀπέθνησκεν 42
impf. ἀποθνήσκω to die. Imperfect "she is dying." This is from
the viewpoint of the father (Plummer).

ὑπάγειν pres. inf. to go away, to depart. Infinitive used w.
prep. to express contemporaneous time. συνέπνιγον impf.,
s.v.14. The prep. expresses the pressing together all around him
(Plummer). ▪ ῥύσις flow. ἴσχυσεν aor. ἰσχύω to be able. 43
θεραπευθῆναι aor. pass. inf., s.v.2. ▪ ἥψατο aor. mid. 44
ἅπτομαι w. gen. to touch. κράσπεδον border, perhaps the
tassel, one on each corner of the overgarment (Arndt). ἔστη aor.
ἵστημι to stand. In medical writers to denote the stoppage of
bodily discharges (MLL, 15). ▪ ἁψάμενος aor. mid. part. 45
ἅπτομαι. ἀρνουμένων pres. mid. part. ἀρνέομαι to say no, to
deny, gen. abs. ἀποθλίβω to press upon, to crowd. Used of
pressing out grapes (RWP). ▪ ἔγνων aor., s.v.10. ἐξεληλυθυῖαν 46
perf. part. fem. sing. ἐξέρχομαι to go out. ▪ ἰδοῦσα aor. part. 47
fem. s.v.20. ἔλαθεν aor. λανθάνω to be hidden. τρέμουσα
pres. part. τρέμω to tremble. προσπεσοῦσα aor. part. fem.,
s.v.28. ἀπήγγειλεν aor., s.v.20. ἰάθη aor. pass. ἰάομαι to heal.
▪ σέσωκεν perf., s.v.36. πορεύου pres. imp. πορεύομαι to go. 48

▪ λαλοῦντος pres. part. λαλέω to speak, gen. abs. 49
τέθνηκεν perf. ἀποθνήσκω perf. to be dead. σκύλλε pres.
imp. σκύλλω to trouble, to cause inconvenience to. Present
imp. w. neg. used to discontinue an action in progress. ▪ 50
ἀκούσας aor. part., s.v.8. ἀπεκρίθη aor. pass., s.v.21. φοβοῦ

pres. imp., s.v.25. πίστευσον aor. imp., s.v.12. Note the change of tense, "cease to fear; only make an act of faith" (Plummer).

51 σωθήσεται fut. pass. ■ ἐλθών aor. part. ἀφῆκεν aor. ἀφίημι
52 to allow. ■ ἔκλαιον impf. κλαίω to weep loudly. ἐκόπτοντο impf. mid. κόπτομαι to beat the breast or head in mourning. κλαίετε pres. imp. used w. a neg. as a command to stop the
53 action which is in progress. ἀπέθανεν aor. ἀποθνήσκω. ■ κατεγέλων impf. καταγελάω to deride, to laugh scornfully at (used w. gen.). εἰδότες perf. part. of the defective perf. οἶδα to
54 know. ■ κρατήσας aor. part. κρατέω w. gen. to grasp, to take hold of. ἐφώνησεν aor. φωνέω to call aloud. ἔγειρε pres. imp.
55 ■ ἐπέστρεψεν aor. ἐπιστρέφω to return. ἀνέστη aor. ἀνίστημι to arise. διέταξεν aor. διατάσσω to instruct, to command. δοθῆναι aor. pass. inf. δίδωμι to give. φαγεῖν aor.
56 inf. ἐσθίω to eat. ■ ἐξέστησαν aor. ἐξίστημι to be beside one's self, to be astounded. παρήγγειλεν aor., s.v.29. εἰπεῖν aor. inf. γεγονός perf. part., s.v.1.

Ch. 9

1 ■ συγκαλεσάμενος aor. mid. part. συγκαλέω to call together, to summons. ἔδωκεν aor. δίδωμι to give. ἐξουσία authority (TDNT; CBB). θεραπεύειν pres. inf., to treat medically,
2 to heal, inf. explaining the authority and power. ■ ἀπέστειλεν aor. ἀποστέλλω to send out, to send out as an official or authoritative representative (TDNT). ἰᾶσθαι pres. mid. inf.
3 ἰάομαι to heal. ■ αἴρετε pres. imp. αἴρω to take. ἔχειν pres. inf. The inf. is used to express a command (s. RG, 1092; BD,
4 196). ■ εἰσέλθητε aor. subj. εἰσέρχομαι to come into, to go into. μένετε pres. imp. μένω to remain. ἐξέρχεσθε pres. mid.
5 imp. ἐξέρχομαι to go out. ■ δέχωνται pres. subj. δέχομαι to receive. κονιορτός dust. ἀποτινάσσετε pres. imp. to shake off
6 (s. Matt. 10:14). ■ διήρχοντο impf. mid. διέρχομαι to go through.

7 ■ ἤκουσεν aor. ἀκούω to hear. τετραάρχης tetrarch. Luke calls him by his correct title (HA, 149). διηπόρει impf. διαπορέω to be thoroughly at a loss, unable to find a way out (RWP). λέγεσθαι pres. pass. inf. used w. prep. to express cause. ἠγέρθη aor. pass. ἐγείρω to raise, pass. to rise. (For discussion of the popular opinion regarding the supposed resurrection of
8 John, s. HA, 187–189.) ■ ἐφάνη aor. φαίνομαι to appear.
9 ἀνέστη aor. ἀνίστημι to raise up, to rise. ■ ἀπεκεφάλισα aor. ἀποκεφαλίζω to behead. ἐζήτει impf. ζητέω to seek. The impf. pictures the continual seeking. ἰδεῖν aor. inf. ὁράω to see. The statement could be taken as a form of sarcasm or irony (HA,

190f.).

■ ὑποστρέψαντες aor. part. ὑποστρέφω to return. 10
διηγήσαντο aor. mid. διηγέομαι to report, to narrate, to tell.
ἐποίησαν aor. ποιέω to do, to make. παραλαβών aor. part.
παραλαμβάνω to take to one's self. ὑπεχώρησεν aor.
ὑποχωρέω to withdraw. καλουμένην pres. pass. part. καλέω
to call, to name. ■ γνόντες aor. part. γινώσκω to know. 11
ἠκολούθησαν aor. ἀκολουθέω to follow. ἀποδεξάμενος aor.
mid. part. ἀποδέχομαι to receive, to welcome (s. Luke 8:40).
ἐλάλει impf λαλέω to speak. ἰᾶτο impf. mid. ■ ἤρξατο aor. 12
mid. ἄρχομαι to begin. κλίνειν pres. inf. to bend, to bow down,
intr. to decline. Used of the day coming to an end, probably
between 3:00 and 6:00 P.M. (Arndt). προσελθόντες aor. part.
προσέρχομαι to come to. ἀπόλυσον aor. imp. ἀπολύω to
release, to dismiss. πορευθέντες aor. pass. part. πορεύομαι to
go, to journey. καταλύσωσιν aor. subj. καταλύω halt, literally,
"to unharness the pack animals," to rest, to find lodging (BAG).
εὕρωσιν aor. subj. εὑρίσκω to find. ἐπισιτισμός provision,
esp. provisions for a journey (RWP). ■ δότε aor. imp. δίδωμι 13
to give. φαγεῖν aor. inf. ἐσθίω to eat. ἀγοράσωμεν aor. subj.
ἀγοράζω to buy, to buy in the market place. The subj. is used
in 3rd class conditional clause w. εἰ instead of ἐάν (RWP). ■ 14
κατακλίνατε aor. imp. κατακλίνω to recline. κλισία a group
of people eating together, a company reclining. ■ εὐλόγησεν 16
aor. εὐλογέω to bless, to give thanks. κατέκλασεν aor.
κατακλάω to break. ἐδίδου impf. The impf. pictures the repeated act of giving. παραθεῖναι aor. inf. παρατίθημι to place
before, to serve food. Jesus' act would remind a Jew of the
miracle of the manna (Ellis). ■ ἔφαγον aor., s.v.13. 17
ἐχορτάσθησαν aor. pass. χορτάζω to feed, to satisfy. ἤρθη
aor. pass. αἴρω to take up. περισσεύσαν aor. part. περισσεύω
to be in abundance, to be left over. κόφινος basket (s. Matt.
14:20; Mark 6:43).

■ ἐγένετο aor. mid. γίνομαι to become, to happen (s. Luke 18
2:1; 8:1). προσευχόμενον pres. mid. part. προσεύχομαι to
pray. συνῆσαν impf. σύνειμι w. dat. to be together.
ἐπηρώτησεν aor. ἐπερωτάω to question, to direct a question
to. ■ ἀποκριθέντες aor. pass. part. ἀποκρίνομαι to answer. 19
(For the Semitic use, s. MH, 453.) ἀνέστη aor., s.v.8. ■ 20
χριστόν the anointed, the Christ (s. TDNT). The acc. is used
w. the unexpressed inf. (RWP).

■ ἐπιτιμήσας aor. ἐπιτιμάω to rebuke, to sternly charge. 21
παρήγγειλεν aor. παραγγέλλω to command, to order. Used
esp. of transmitted orders of a military commander (AS). ■ 22

εἰπών aor. part. δεῖ it is necessary. παθεῖν aor. inf. πάσχω to suffer. ἀποδοκιμασθῆναι aor. pass. inf. ἀποδοκιμάζω to reject after investigation (Plummer; TDNT). ἀποκτανθῆναι aor. pass. inf. ἀποκτείνω to kill. ἐγερθῆναι aor. pass. inf., s.v.7. The
23 infs. here are dependent on the verb "it is necessary." ▪ ἀρνησάσθω aor. mid. imp. ἀρνέομαι to say no, to deny. ἀράτω aor. imp. αἴρω s.v.3. ἀκολουθείτω pres. imp., s.v.11.
24 Here the word indicates to follow as a disciple (s. TDNT). ▪ θέλῃ pres. subj. σῶσαι aor. inf. σῴζω to save, to rescue. ἀπολέσει fut. ἀπόλλυμι to lose, to destroy. ἀπολέσῃ aor.
25 subj. σώσει fut. ▪ ὠφελεῖται press. pass. ὠφελέω to help, to benefit, to be of use. κερδήσας aor. part. κερδαίνω to gain, to win (s. Mark 8:36). ἀπολέσας aor. part. ζημιωθείς aor. pass.
26 part. ζημιόω to suffer loss (s. Mark 8:36). ▪ ἐπαισχυνθῇ aor. pass. subj. ἐπαισχύνομαι to be ashamed. Shame in the eyes of men. The subj. is used in an indefinite rel. clause (RWP).
27 ἐπαισχυνθήσεται fut. pass. ἔλθῃ aor. subj. ἔρχομαι. ▪ ἑστηκότων perf. part. ἵστημι to stand. γεύσωνται aor. mid. subj. γεύομαι to taste. ἴδωσιν aor. subj. ὁράω to see.
28 ▪ ἐγένετο aor. mid. (s. Luke 2:1; 8:1). παραλαβών aor. part. παραλαμβάνω to take w. ἀνέβη aor. ἀναβαίνω to go up. προσεύξασθαι aor. mid. inf., s.v.18. Infinitive used w. prep. to
29 express time, "while" (s. BD, 208). ▪ εἶδος appearance. λευκός white. ἐξαστράπτων pres. part. ἐξαστράπτω to flash forth as
30 lightning, to gleam. ▪ συνελάλουν impf. συλλαλέω to speak together, to converse. The impf. pictures the continued conver-
31 sation. ▪ ὀφθέντες aor. pass. part. ὁράω to see, pass. to appear. ἔξοδος departure, going out. The word contains the ideas both of death and ascension (Godet). ἤμελλεν impf. μέλλω to be about to. Used w. inf. to express the fut. In the impf. it expresses fut. or intention reckoned from a moment in the past (MKG, 307). The concept of divine appointment or determination is
32 evident (Arndt). ▪ βεβαρημένοι perf. pass. part. βαρέω to make heavy, to burden, pass. to be heavy. The perf. pictures the state or condition. διαγρηγορήσαντες aor. part. διαγρηγορέω to remain awake. The force of the prep. is either to remain awake in spite of desire to sleep or to become thoroughly awake (RWP; s. also MH, 301). εἶδαν aor. ὁράω.
33 συνεστῶτας perf. part. συνίστημι to stand together. ▪ διαχωρίζεσθαι pres. mid. inf. διαχωρίζω to divide, mid. to depart. Infinitive used w. prep. to express time. ποιήσωμεν aor. subj., s.v.10. εἰδώς part. of the defective perf. οἶδα w. the pres.
34 meaning to know. ▪ ἐπεσκίαζεν impf. ἐπισκιάζω to overshadow. ἐφοβήθησαν aor. φοβέομαι to be afraid. εἰσελθεῖν aor.

inf., s.v.4. ■ ἐκλελεγμένος perf. pass. part. ἐκλέγω to choose. 35
The perf. pictures the state or condition. ἀκούετε pres. imp.
ἀκούω w. the gen. here, listen to. ■ γένεσθαι aor. mid. inf. 36
Infinitive used w. prep. to express time, "after." εὑρέθη aor.
pass. εὑρίσκω to find. ἐσίγησαν aor. σιγάω to be silent,
progressive aor., to become silent. ἀπήγγειλαν aor.
ἀπαγγέλλω to report. ἑώρακαν plperf. ὁράω to see.

■ ἐγένετο aor. mid. (s. Luke 2:1; 8:1). ἐξῆς afterward. 37
κατελθόντων aor. part. κατέρχομαι to come down, to go
down, gen. abs. συνήντησεν aor. συναντάω to meet. ■ 38
ἐβόησεν aor. βοάω to call out, to cry out for help. ἐπιβλέψαι
aor. inf. ἐπιβλέπω to look upon, to regard w. compassion
(Arndt). μονογενής only child (compare Luke 7:12; 8:42). ■ 39
ἐξαίφνης suddenly. The word was used in medical language for
sudden attacks of speechlessness, spasms, etc. (MLL, 19).
σπαράσσω to tear. ἀφρός foam. Used by medical writers to
describe the symptoms of epilepsy. Probably the disease through
which the demons exerted their power over this child (MLL,
17). μόλις hardly, w. difficulty. ἀποχωρεῖ pres. ἀποχωρέω to
leave, to depart. συντρῖβον pres. part. n. συντρίβω to crush,
to mishandle. ■ ἠδυνήθησαν aor. pass. δύναμαι to be able. 40
■ ἀποκριθείς aor. pass. part., s.v.19. διεστραμμένη perf. pass. 41
part. διαστρέφω twisted, turned, distorted. ἀνέξομαι fut. mid.
ἀνέχομαι w. gen. to bear w., to endure. προσάγαγε aor. imp.
προσάγω to bring to, to lead to. ■ προσερχομένου pres. mid. 42
part. προσέρχομαι to come to. ἔρρηξεν aor. ῥήγνυμι to throw
down. The word is used of boxers knocking down, and of wres-
tlers throwing, an opponent (Plummer). συνεσπάραξεν aor.
συσπαράσσω to tear, to pull about, to convulse. ἐπετίμησεν
aor. (s. Matt. 17:18). ἰάσατο aor. mid., s.v.2. ἀπέδωκεν aor.
ἀποδίδωμι to give back. ■ ἐξεπλήσσοντο aor. 43
ἐκπλήσσομαι to be beside one's self, to be astonished.
μεγαλειότης majesty.

θαυμαζόντων pres. part. θαυμάζω to wonder, to be
amazed, gen. abs. ἐποίει impf., s.v.10. ■ θέσθε aor. mid. imp. 44
τίθημι to place, to lay. The meaning of the expression is "store
them in your memory" (Arndt). μέλλει s.v.31. παραδίδοσθαι
pres. pass. inf. παραδίδωμι to deliver over, to betray. ■ 45
ἠγνόουν impf. ἀγνοέω to be ignorant, not to know.
παρακεκαλυμμένον perf. pass. part. παρακαλύπτω to conceal. αἴσθωνται aor. subj. αἰσθάνομαι to perceive.
ἐφοβοῦντο impf. mid., s.v.34. ἐρωτῆσαι aor. inf. ἐρωτάω to
ask, to question.

■ εἰσῆλθεν aor., s.v.4. τό the definite article used before 46

167

indirect speech (s. BD, 140). εἴη opt. εἰμί opt. used in indirect
question in a context of doubt and perplexity (RG, 940; MKG,
47 240ff.). μείζων comp. μέγας. ■ εἰδώς s.v.33. ἐπιλαβόμενος
aor. mid. part. ἐπιλαμβάνομαι to take, to take hold of.
48 ἔστησεν aor. ἵστημι to place, to stand. ■ δέξηται aor. mid.
subj., s.v.5. ἀποστείλαντα aor. part., s.v.2. μικρότερος comp.
μικρός. The comp. is used here as the superl. (s. BD, 32f.).
ὑπάρχων pres. part. ὑπάρχω to be.
49   ■ ἀποκριθείς aor. pass. part., s.v.19. εἴδομεν aor. ὁράω.
50 ἐκωλύομεν impf. κωλύω to hinder, to prevent. ■ κωλύετε pres.
imp. The pres. imp. used w. a neg. here indicates "do not continue" or "do not always" (s. MKG, 272f.).
51   ■ ἐγένετο aor. mid., s.v.18. συμπληροῦσθαι pres. pass.
inf. συμπληρόω to fill, to fulfill. Infinitive used w. prep. to
express time, "when the days were being fulfilled." ἀνάλημψις
taking up, lifting up. It could refer to His death but better to His
ascension (Arndt). ἐστήρισεν aor. στηρίζω to fix firmly; "to
set the face" is a Hebraism implying fixedness of purpose, esp.
52 in the prospect of difficulty or danger (Plummer). ■ ἀπέστειλεν
aor., s.v.2. πορευθέντες aor. pass. part. εἰσῆλθον aor., s.v.4.
53 ἑτοιμάσαι aor. inf. ἑτοιμάζω to prepare. ■ ἐδέξαντο aor. mid.,
54 s.v.5. ■ ἰδόντες aor. part., s.v.9. εἴπωμεν aor. subj., deliberative
subj. preceded by a verb of desire (s. BD, 185). καταβῆναι aor.
pass. inf. καταβαίνω to go down, to come down. ἀναλῶσαι
55 aor. inf. ἀναλίσκω to consume, to destroy. ■ στραφείς aor.
56 pass. part. στρέφω to turn. ■ ἐπορεύθησαν aor. pass.
57   ■ ἀκολουθήσω fut., s.v.11. ἀπέρχῃ pres. subj.
58 ἀπέρχομαι to go away. ■ ἀλώπηξ fox. φωλεός den, hole for
animals. κατασκήνωσις encampments, roost (s. Plummer).
59 κλίνῃ subj. κλίνω to lay. ■ ἀκολούθει pres. imp. The word
indicates to follow as a disciple (s. TDNT). ἐπίτρεψον aor. imp.
ἐπιτρέπω to allow. ἀπελθόντι aor. part. dat. sing. θάψαι aor.
inf. θάπτω to bury. According to Jewish tradition, the obligation to bury a relative took precedence over religious duties and
was considered to be an obligatory act of love (s. Ellis; SB, IV,
578ff.; M, Berakoth, 3, 1f.; Roy A. Harrisville, "Jesus and the
60 Family," Interp. 23 [Oct., 1969], 432ff.). ■ ἄφες aor. imp.
ἀφίημι to allow. ἀπελθών aor. part. διάγγελλε pres. imp.
διαγγέλλω to publish everywhere, to proclaim far and wide
61 (Arndt). ■ ἀποτάξασθαι aor. mid. inf. ἀποτάσσομαι to de-
tach, to separate, "to set myself apart from, bid farewell to, them
62 that are at my house" (Plummer). ■ ἐπιβαλών aor. part.
ἐπιβάλλω to place upon, to place the hand upon. ἄροτρον
plow. βλέπων pres. part. βλέπω. εὔθετος well-placed, fit, suit-

able, useable.

Ch. 10

■ ἀνέδειξεν aor. ἀναδείκνυμι to show forth, to display, to 1
make public, esp. a person's appointment to an office (Plummer).
ἀπέστειλεν aor. ἀποστέλλω to send out, to send out as an
official authoritative representative (s. TDNT). ἀνά distributive,
"by twos." ἤμελλεν impf. μέλλω to be about to. (For the construction, s. Luke 7:2.) ■ δεήθητε aor. pass. imp. δέομαι w. gen. 2
to pray, to ask someone for something. ἐκβάλῃ aor. subj.
ἐκβάλλω to drive out, to cast out. ■ ὑπάγετε pres. imp. ὑπάγω 3
to go, to go forth. ἄρνας acc. pl. ἀρήν lamb. ■ βαστάζετε pres. 4
imp. βαστάζω to carry. Here the pres. imp. w. neg. indicates
"do not always carry" (MKG, 272). βαλλάντιον purse, an old
word for moneybag (RWP). ἀσπάσησθε aor. subj. ἀσπάζω to
greet. ■ εἰσέλθητε aor. subj. εἰσέρχομαι to go in. λέγετε pres. 5
imp. ■ ἐπαναπαήσεται fut. pass. ἀπαναπαύομαι to rest 6
upon. ἀνακάμψει fut. ἀνακάμπτω to return. ■ μένετε pres. 7
imp. μένω to remain. ἔσθοντες pres. part. ἔσθω an old poetic
verb for ἐσθίω (RWP). μεταβαίνετε pres. imp. μεταβαίνω to
change a place, to leave, to depart. The force of the prep. involves the idea of change (MH, 318). ■ εἰσέρχησθε pres. mid. 8
subj. δέχωνται pres. mid. subj. δέχομαι to receive, to welcome.
παρατιθέμενα pres. pass. part. παρατίθημι to set (food) before someone. ■ θεραπεύετε pres. imp. θεραπεύω to treat 9
medically, to heal. ἤγγικεν perf. ἐγγίζω to draw near, perf. to
be at hand (s. Matt. 3:2). ■ ἐξέλθόντες aor. part. ἐξέρχομαι to 10
go out. εἴπατε aor. imp. λέγω. ■ καί "even." The ascensive use. 11
The thing that is added is out of the ordinary and rises to a
climax like the crescendo in music (RG, 1181). κονιορτός dust.
κολληθέντα aor. pass. part. κολλάω to cling to. (For the medical examples of the word, s. MLL, 128f.) ἀπομάσσομαι to
wipe off, to rub off w. the hands (RWP). ■ ἀνεκτότερος comp. 12
ἀνεκτός bearable, endurable.

■ ἐγενήθησαν aor. pass. γίνομαι to become, to happen. 13
γενόμεναι aor. mid. part. ἄν + ind. used in a contrary to fact
conditional sentence. καθήμενοι pres. mid. part. κάθημαι to
sit. μετενόησαν aor. μετανοέω to change the mind, to repent.
■ μή used in questions which expect the answer "no." ὑψωθήσῃ 15
fut. pass. ὑψόω to lift up, to exalt. ᾅδης like the OT sheol. It
means death or the realm of death (Ellis). καταβήσῃ fut.
καταβαίνω to go down. ■ ἀκούων pres. part. ἀκούω w. gen. 16
to hear, to listen to. ἀθετῶν pres. part. ἀθετέω to set aside, to
reject. ἀποστείλαντα aor. part., s.v.1.

169

17   ■ ὑπέστρεψαν aor. ὑποστρέφω to turn about, to return.
18   ■ ἐθεώρουν impf. θεωρέω to see, to be a spectator. The impf.
      points to what was constantly repeated. Every expulsion of de-
      mons meant a fall of Satan (Arndt). ἀστραπή lightning.
19   πεσόντα aor. part. πίπτω to fall. ■ δέδωκα perf. δίδωμι to
      give. The perf. means, "I have given to you, so that you now
      possess it" (Geldenhuys). πατεῖν pres. inf. πατέω to walk. ὄφις
      snake. ἀδικήσει fut. ἀδικέω to commit an injustice, to harm;
20   to do wrong. ■ χαίρετε impf. χαίρω to rejoice. ἐγγέγραπται
      perf. pass. ἐγγράφω to write in, to record. (For the Jewish
      concept of various heavenly books, s. SB, II, 169–176.)
21   ■ ἠγαλλιάσατο aor. mid. ἀγαλλιάω to rejoice.
      ἐξομολογέομαι to confess publicly, to praise, to thank.
      ἀπέκρυψας aor. ἀποκρύπτω to hide. ἀπεκάλυψας aor.
      ἀποκαλύπτω to unveil, to reveal. ἐγένετο aor. mid. γίνομαι.
22   ■ παρεδόθη aor. pass. παραδίδωμι to give over, to transfer.
23   ἀποκαλύψαι aor. act. inf. ■ στραφείς aor. pass. part. στρέφω
24   to turn. ■ ἠθέλησαν aor. θέλω to wish, to desire, to want. ἰδεῖν
      aor. inf. ὁράω. εἶδαν aor. ἀκοῦσαι aor. inf. ἤκουσαν aor.
25   ■ νομικός jurist, lawyer. One conversant w. the law, its
      interpretation and application (s. TDNT). ἀνέστη aor.
      ἀνίστημι to stand up, to rise for a question or participation in
      an argument (Arndt). ἐκπειράζων pres. part. ἐκπειράζω to try,
      to test, to tempt. ποιήσας aor. part. ποιέω. κληρονομήσω fut.
      κληρονομέω to receive as inheritance, to receive a share alloted
26   to you (Arndt). ■ γέγραπται perf. pass. γράφω to write.
      ἀναγινώσκω to read, "how do you read?" i.e., "may I hear your
27   authorities w. exposition?" (LNT, 224). ■ ἀποκριθείς aor. pass.
      part. ἀποκρίνομαι to answer. ἀγαπήσεις fut. ἀγαπάω to
28   love. πλησίον neighbor. ■ ὀρθῶς straight, correctly.
      ἀπεκρίθης aor. pass. ποίει pres. imp. ζήσῃ fut. ζάω to live.
      Future following an imp. forms the 2nd part of a conditional type
29   sentence. (For this Semitic construction, s. MH, 421.) ■ θέλων
      pres. part. θέλω. The part. could be causal. δικαιῶσαι aor. act.
      inf. δικαιόω to declare righteous, to justify, to clear one's self
      of a charge. The lawyer wishes to vindicate himself w. a question
      implying he did not know precisely what his duty was (GW,
30   133). ■ ὑπολαβών aor. part. ὑπολαμβάνω to take up, to take
      up the discussion. κατέβαινεν impf. καταβαίνω to go down.
      λῃστής robber. περιέπεσεν aor. περιπίπτω to fall among, to
      be encompassed by, to be surrounded by robbers. A common
      experience on the road to Jericho (RWP). ἐκδύσαντες aor. part.
      ἐκδύω to remove the clothing, to strip. ἐπιθέντες aor. part.
      ἐπιτίθημι to place upon; here, to inflict blows upon someone.

ἀπῆλθον aor. ἀπέρχομαι to go away. ἀφέντες aor. part.
ἀφίημι to leave. ἡμιθανής half dead. ■ συγκυρία coincidence. 31
This had not been prearranged or planned (Arndt). ἰδών aor.
part. ὁράω. ἀντιπαρῆλθεν aor. ἀντιπαρέρχομαι to pass by
along on the other side. He came alongside, then stepped over
to the opposite side of the road to avoid ceremonial contamination w. a stranger (RWP). The priest and the Levi were obligated
according to the law to help a neighbor in need. They also were
obligated not to defile themselves by touching a dead body.
Since defilement prevented their service in the temple and eating
of the tithe, they chose to pass by on the opposite side rather
than to take a chance on defilement (s. LNT, 211–217). ■ ἐλθών 32
aor. part. ἔρχομαι. ■ ὁδεύων pres. part. ὁδεύω to travel, to be 33
on a journey. ἦλθεν aor. ἔρχομαι. ἐσπλαγχνίσθη aor. pass.
σπλαγχνίζομαι to be deeply moved w. compassion, to have
compassion (TDNT). The irony is that a foreigner, not included
in the Jewish definition of a neighbor, is the one who showed
himself neighbor to the unfortunate Jew (Ellis). ■ προσελθών 34
aor. part. προσέρχομαι to come to. Contrast v. 31. The Samaritan was moved by compassion, and this obviated fears about his
own contamination (LNT, 217). κατέδησεν aor. καταδέω to
bind up. Used in medical language of binding up wounds, ulcers,
etc. (MLL, 27). τραῦμα wound. ἐπιχέων pres. part. ἐπιχέω to
pour upon. (For the medical use of this term as well as the
medicinal use of oil and wine, s. MLL, 28f.) ἐπιβιβάσας aor.
part. ἐπιβιβάζω to set upon. ἤγαγεν aor. ἄγω to lead.
πανδοχεῖον inn. A large structure w. shelter for man and beast
(Arndt). ἐπεμελήθη aor. ἐπιμελέομαι to care for. Used in
medical language of care taken of the sick or some injured part
of the body (MLL, 29). ■ ἐκβαλών aor. part. ἐκβάλλω to throw 35
out, to take out. δηνάριον denarius. A Roman coin worth about
18 cents. It was the workman's average daily wage (BAG).
ἔδωκεν aor. δίδωμι to give. πανδοχεύς innkeeper.
ἐπιμελήθητι aor. pass. imp. προσδαπανήσῃς aor. subj.
προσδαπανάω to spend besides, to spend in addition.
ἐπανέρχεσθαι pres. mid. inf. ἐπανέρχομαι to come back
again. Infinitive used w. prep. to express time. ἀποδώσω fut.
ἀποδίδωμι to give back, to pay back. (For the Samaritan's utter
trust in making the innkeeper his agent esp. in light of his lack
of legal recourse, s. LNT, 218.) ■ δοκεῖ to appear, to seem. 36
γεγονέναι perf. inf. γίνομαι. ἐμπεσόντος aor. part. ἐμπίπτω
to fall in, to fall among. ■ ἔλεος mercy. (For the Heb. content 37
of this word, s. TDNT; CBB.) πορεύου pres. imp. πορεύομαι
to go. ποίει pres. imp. "do constantly," in the sense of lifelong

action (Geldenhuys).

38   ■ εἰσῆλθεν aor., s.v.5. ὑπεδέξατο aor. mid. ὑποδέχομαι
39 to receive, to welcome as a guest. ■ τῇδε dat. sing. fem. ὅδε, this
one here (s. RG, 696). καλουμένη pres. pass. part. καλέω.
παρακαθεσθεῖσα aor. pass. part. fem. παρακαθέζομαι to sit
beside. ἤκουεν impf., s.v.16. The impf. pictures the continual
40 listening. ■ περιεσπᾶτο impf. mid. περισπάομαι to be pulled
or dragged away, to become or be distracted. She was drawn
about in different directions (Plummer). ἐπιστᾶσα aor. part.
ἐφίστημι to place upon, to come to. μέλει σοι "to be of concern to you." κατέλειπεν impf. καταλείπω to leave, to forsake.
The impf. expresses the continuance of the neglect (Plummer).
διακονεῖν pres. inf. διακονέω to minister, esp. to serve at the
table. εἰπὲ aor. imp. συναντιλάβηται aor. subj.
συναντιλαμβάνομαι to help. The mid. voice in the prep. in
compound means to take hold of one's self at the end of his task
41 together w. one (RWP). ■ ἀποκριθείς aor. pass. part., s.v.27.
μεριμνάω to be concerned, to have care. It refers to agitated
state of mind (Geldenhuys). θορυβάζῃ pres. pass. θορυβάζω to
42 cause trouble, pass. to be troubled or distracted. ■ ἐξελέξατο
aor. mid. ἐκλέγομαι to choose, to choose for one's self.
ἀφαιρεθήσεται fut. pass. ἀφαιρέω to take away.

Ch. 11

1   ■ ἐγένετο aor. mid. γίνομαι to become, to happen (s. Luke
8:1). προσευχόμενον pres. mid. part. προσεύχομαι to pray.
ἐπαύσατο aor. mid. παύομαι to stop, to cease. δίδαξον aor.
2 imp. διδάσκω. ἐδίδαξεν aor. ■ προσεύχησθε pres. subj.
λέγετε pres. imp. ἁγιασθήτω aor. pass. imp. ἁγιάζω to declare
holy, to treat as holy (Arndt). ἐλθάτω aor. imp. 3rd sing.
3 ἔρχομαι. ■ ἐπιούσιος daily, for the coming day (s. Matt. 6:11).
4 δίδου pres. imp. δίδωμι to give. ■ ἄφες aor. imp. ἀφίημι to
release, to forgive. ὀφείλοντι pres. part. dat. sing. ὀφείλω to
owe, to owe a debt. (For sins viewed as a debt to God, s. TDNT.)
εἰσενέγκῃς aor. subj. εἰσφέρω to lead into, to bring into, "do
not permit the foes of our soul to catch us in their net" (Arndt).
5   ■ ἕξει fut. ἔχω to have. μεσονύκτιον midnight. εἴπῃ aor.
subj. χρῆσον aor. imp. χράω, κίχρημι to lend. Distinct from
"to lend on interest" as a matter of business. It means "to allow
6 the use of" as a friendly act (Plummer). ■ παρεγένετο aor.
παραγίνομαι to arrive, to come to. παραθήσω fut.
7 παρατίθημι to set before. ■ ἔσωθεν from within. ἀποκριθείς
aor. pass. part. ἀποκρίνομαι to answer. κόπος tiring work,
trouble. πάρεχε pres. imp. παρέχω to cause, to make. The pres.

imp. w. the neg. indicates the stopping of an action in progress.
κέκλεισται perf. pass. κλείω to lock. The perf. indicates the
state after the completed action. εἰς w. force of ἐν (BG, 33).
ἀναστάς aor. part. ἀνίστημι to arise, to get up. δοῦναι aor.
inf. δίδωμι. ■ ἀναίδεια lack of feeling of shame, persistent 8
(Arndt). ἐγερθείς aor. pass. part. ἐγείρω to arise, to get up.
χρήζω w. gen. to need, to have need of. ■ αἰτεῖτε pres. imp. 9
αἰτέω to ask, to request. δοθήσεται fut. pass. δίδωμι to give.
ζητεῖτε pres. imp. ζητέω to seek. εὑρήσετε fut. εὑρίσκω to
find. κρούετε pres. imp. κρούω to hit, to knock. ἀνοιγήσεται
fut. pass. ἀνοίγνυμι to open. (For the construction of the imp.
followed by the fut. as a type of conditional sentence, s. Luke
10:28.) ■ αἰτήσει fut. μή used in questions which expect the 11
answer no. ὄφις snake. ἐπιδώσει fut. ἐπιδίδωμι to give over,
to hand to. ■ ᾠόν egg. ■ ὑπάρχοντες pres. part. ὑπάρχω to be, 12/13
to exist. οἴδατε defective perf. w. pres. meaning οἶδα to know.
διδόναι pres. inf. δίδωμι.

■ ἐκβάλλων pres. part. ἐκβάλλω to throw out, to cast out. 14
Participle used in a periphrastic construction. κωφός dumb.
ἐγένετο aor. mid., s.v.1. ἐξελθόντος aor. part. ἐξέρχομαι to go
out, gen. abs. ἐλάλησεν aor. λαλέω. ἐθαύμασαν aor.
θαυμάζω to wonder, to marvel. ■ ἄρχων leader, prince. ■ 15/16
πειράζοντες pres. part. πειράζω to test, to try, to tempt.
ἐζήτουν impf., s.v.9. ■ εἰδώς perf. part. of defective perf. οἶδα 17
s.v.13. διανόημα thought. The word indicates to think through
or distinguish, intent, purpose (RWP). διαμερισθεῖσα aor.
pass. part. fem. διαμερίζω to divide into. ἐρημοῦται pass.
ἐρημόω to make empty, to destroy, to make desolate. ■ 18
διεμερίσθη aor. pass. σταθήσεται fut. pass. ἵστημι to stand.
■ υἱός son. Here equivalent to "your own people" (Arndt). 19
ἔσονται fut. εἰμί. ■ δάκτυλος finger. ἔφθασεν aor. φθάνω to 20
come, to arrive at. ■ ἰσχυρός strong. καθωπλισμένος perf. 21
pass. part. καθοπλίζω to arm fully, to equip. The prep. in compound is perfective. φυλάσσῃ pres. subj. φυλάσσω to guard.
αὐλή courtyard, palace. ■ ἰσχυρότερος comp. ἰσχυρός. 22
αὐτοῦ gen. of comparison. ἐπελθών aor. part. ἐπέρχομαι to
come upon. νικήσῃ aor. subj. νικάω to conquer. πανοπλία
complete armor, a word indicating the soldier's outfit such as
shield, sword, lance, helmet, etc. (RWP). αἴρω to take away.
ἐπεποίθει plperf. of the perf. πείθω to trust. σκῦλον booty,
spoils. The armor and weapons taken from the body of a slain
enemy (BAG). διαδίδωσιν pres. διαδίδωμι to distribute. ■ ὤν 23
pres. part. εἰμί. συνάγων pres. part. συνάγω to lead together,
to gather together. σκορπίζω to scatter, to scatter out.

24 ■ ἐξέλθῃ aor. subj. ἐξέρχομαι to go out. διέρχομαι to pass through, to go through. ἄννδρος waterless. ζητοῦν pres. part. εὑρίσκον pres. part., s.v.9. ὑποστρέψω fut. ὑποστρέφω to
25 turn back, to return. ἐξῆλθον aor. ■ ἐλθόν aor. part., s.v.2. σεσαρωμένον perf. pass. part. σαρόω to sweep out, to clean. κεκοσμημένον perf. pass. part. κοσμέω to arrange in order.
26 ■ πονηρότερος comp. ἑαυτοῦ gen. of comparison. εἰσελθόντα aor. part. εἰσέρχομαι to go in. κατοικεῖ pres. κοτοικέω to dwell, to take up residence. The prep. in compound indicates "taking up a permanent abode" (Plummer). χείρων comp. κακός. τῶν πρώτων gen. of comparison.
27 ■ ἐπάρασα aor. part. ἐπαίρω to lift up. κοιλία womb. βαστάσασα aor. part. fem. βαστάζω to carry. μαστός breast.
28 ἐθήλασας aor. 2nd per. sing. θηλάζω to suck, to nurse. ■ μενοῦν rather. The word is used correctively, "what you have said is true as far as it goes, but the blessedness of Mary consists in the fact that she shares in the blessedness of those who hear the Word of God and keep it" (Thrall). ἀκούοντες pres. part. ἀκούω. φυλάσσοντες pres. part.
29 ■ ἐπαθροιζομένων pres. part. ἐπαθροίζομαι to throng together, to crowd upon. The prep. in compound is directive indicating the concentration of the verb's action upon some object (MH, 312), gen. abs. ἤρξατο aor. mid. ἄρχομαι to begin.
30/31 δοθήσεται fut. pass. δίδωμι. ■ ἐγένετο aor. mid., s.v.1. ■ νότος south. ἐγερθήσεται fut. pass., s.v.8. κατακρινεῖ fut. κατακρίνω to condemn. ἦλθεν aor. ἔρχομαι. ἀκοῦσαι aor. inf., s.v.28. Infinitive used to express purpose. Σολομῶνος gen.
32 of comparison. ■ ἀναστήσονται fut. ἀνίστημι s.v.7. μετενόησαν aor. μετανοέω to change one's mind, to repent.
33 ■ λύχνος lamp, oil lamp (s. Matt. 5:15). ἅψας aor. part. ἅπτω to light. κρύπτη a dark and hidden place, a cellar. μόδιος a bushel, a peck measure, a grain measure (s. Mark 4:21ff.). λυχνία lampstand. εἰσπορευόμενοι pres. mid. part.
34 εἰσπορεύομαι to go in. φέγγος light, ray, beam. ■ ἁπλοῦς single as opposed to double or faulty and distorted vision (Arndt). ᾖ subj. εἰμί. φωτεινός shining, brilliant. ἐπάν when-
35 ever, after. σκοτεινός dark. ■ σκόπει pres. imp. σκοπέω to see, to look upon, to watch. μή "whether." Here used like an
36 indirect question (s. RG, 1045.) ■ ἔχον pres. part. ἀστραπή flash, lightning. φωτίζῃ pres. subj. φωτίζω to illuminate, to enlighten.
37 ■ λαλῆσαι aor. inf., s.v.14. Infinitive used w. prep. to express time. ἐρωτᾷ pres. ἐρωτάω to ask, to question. ἀριστήσῃ aor. subj. ἀριστάω to eat, to eat breakfast. It is the

174

morning meal after the return from morning prayers (RWP; s.
also SB, II, 204ff.). ἀνέπεσεν aor. ἀναπίπτω to recline, to fall
back on the sofa or lounge (RWP). ■ ἰδών aor. part. ὁράω to 38
see. ἐθαύμασεν aor., s.v.14. ἐβαπτίσθη aor. pass. βαπτίζω to
dip, to wash, pass. to wash one's self. (For the washing of hands,
s. Matt. 15:2.) ■ νῦν now (logical). ἔξωθεν outside. πίναξ plat- 39
ter, dish. ἔσωθεν inside. ἁρπαγή robbery, robbing. It points to
covetousness and greed (Arndt). ■ ἄφρων foolish, ignorant. 40
ποιήσας aor. part. ποιέω to make. ■ πλήν however, neverthe- 41
less. In this case, possibly introducing an inference (s. Thrall,
23f.; s. also Luke 22:21). ἐνόντα pres. part. ἔνειμι to be in,
"those things which are within"; i.e. the heart, "give your heart
as alms, let your heart go out to the poor." (For this and other
suggestive meanings, s. Arndt.) δότε aor. imp., s.v.3.
ἐλεημοσύνη mercy, compassion, alms. ■ οὐαί woe, alas. 42
Denotes a grieving giving up to judgment (Ellis).
ἀποδεκατοῦτε pres. ἀποδεκατόω to pay a tenth, to tithe.
ἡδύοσμον mint. πήγανον rue. A strong-smelling herb w. gray-
green leaves and lemon yellow clusters of flowers (IDB, IV, 129).
λάχανον vegetable, plant. Whatever is used for food and is kept
watch over and grows from the soil is liable to tithes (M, Maaseroth; s. also SB, IV, 640–697). παρέρχομαι to go by, to pass by,
to neglect, to disobey. ἔδει impf. δεῖ it is necessary. ποιῆσαι
aor. inf. παρεῖναι aor. inf. παρίημι to leave undone, to neglect,
to let pass. ■ ἀγαπᾶτε pres. ἀγαπάω to love. πρωτοκαθεδρία 43
chief seat, place of honor, the best seat. This was a semi-circular
bench around the ark and faced the congregation (Plummer).
■ μνημεῖον tomb. ἄδηλος unseen, inconspicuous (s. Matt. 23: 44
27). περιπατοῦντες pres. part. περιπατέω to walk about.
οἴδασιν s.v.13.
    ■ ἀποκριθείς aor. pass. part., s.v.7. ὑβρίζω to insult, to 45
mistreat, to treat shamefully (s. MNTW; TDNT). ■ φορτίζω to 46
burden, to burden down. δυσβάστακτος difficult, heavy to
bear. δάκτυλος finger. προσψαύω w. dat. to touch. A term
used by medical writers to describe the feeling, very gently, of
a sore or tender part of the body, or the pulse (MLL, 62). ■ 47
οἰκοδομεῖτε pres. οἰκοδομέω to build. ἀπέκτειναν aor.
ἀποκτείνω to kill. ■ συνευδοκεῖτε pres. συνευδοκέω to ap- 48
prove of, to entirely approve of. ■ ἀποστελῶ fut. ἀποστέλλω 49
to send, to send as an authoritative official representative.
ἀποκτενοῦσιν fut. διώξουσιν fut. διώκω to persecute. ■ 50
ἐκζητηθῇ aor. pass. subj. ἐκζητέω to require, to demand back,
to require as a debt (Plummer). ἐκκεχυμένον perf. pass. part.
ἐκχέω to pour out, to shed. καταβολή foundation. ■ 51

ἀπολομένου aor. part. ἀπόλλυμι to destroy, to loose, mid. to
52 perish. μεταξύ between. ἐκζητηθήσεται fut. pass., s.v.50. ■
ἤρατε aor. αἴρω to take away. κλείς, κλειδός key. "The key
of knowledge" is the key that opens the treasures of knowledge,
it is the right interpretation of Scripture (Arndt). εἰσήλθατε
53 aor., s.v.26. ἐκωλύσατε aor. κωλύω to hinder. ■ ἐξελθόντος
s.v.14. δεινῶς adv. terribly. ἐνέχω to have it in for someone, to
have a grudge against someone. ἀποστοματίζω to pry w. questions, to entice to answers. Originally to dictate what is to be
54 learned by heart and recited (Plummer). ■ ἐνεδρεύοντες pres.
part. ἐνεδρεύω to prepare an ambush, to lie in wait. θηρεῦσαι
aor. inf. θηρεύω to ensnare, to catch in hunting, to hunt (RWP).

Ch. 12

1   ■ ἐν οἷς "in which things or circumstances," in the mean-
time (RWP). ἐπισυναχθεισῶν aor. pass. part. ἐπισυνάγω to
gather together, gen. abs. καταπατεῖν pres. inf. καταπατέω to
trample on, to walk on. Infinitive used w. ὥστε to express result.
ἤρξατο aor. mid. ἄρχομαι to begin. προσέχετε pres. imp.
2 προσέχω to beware, to take heed. ■ συγκεκαλυμμένον perf.
pass. part. συγκαλύπτω to hide, to conceal completely, to cover up. ἀποκαλυφθήσεται fut. pass. ἀποκαλύπτω to uncover,
3 reveal. γνωσθήσεται fut. pass. γινώσκω to know. ■ ἀνθ᾿ =
ἀντί on account of, because. εἴπατε aor. λέγω. ἀκουσθήσεται
fut. pass. ἀκούω. ἐλαλήσατε aor. λαλέω to speak. ταμιεῖον
store chamber, secret room. κηρυχθήσεται fut. pass.
κηρύσσω to proclaim.

4   ■ φοβηθῆτε aor. pass. subj. φοβέομαι to be afraid, to fear.
The subj. w. the neg. is used to prohibit the starting of an action.
ἀποκτεννόντων pres. part. ἀποκτέννω to kill. περισσότερος
comp. περισσός over and above, excessive, more. ποιῆσαι
5 aor. inf. ποιέω to do. ■ ὑποδείξω fut. ὑποδείκνυμι to show.
φοβήθητε aor. pass. imp. ἀποκτεῖναι aor. inf. ἀποκτείνω to
kill. ἐμβαλεῖν aor. inf. ἐμβάλλω to throw into. γέεννα the
6 valley Gehenna, hell (s. TDNT). ναί yes, certainly. ■ οὐχί
strengthened form of οὐ, not. Used in a question expecting the
answer yes. στρουθίον dimin. sparrow. πωλοῦνται pres. pass.
πωλέω to sell, pass. to offer for sale. ἀσσάριον the sixteenth
part of a denarius worth approximately one cent (Arndt).
ἐπιλελησμένον perf. pass. part. ἐπιλανθάνομαι to forget, to
7 be forgotten. ■ θρίξ, τριχός hair. ἠρίθμηνται perf. pass.
ἀριθμέω to count. φοβεῖσθε pres. mid. imp. w. the neg. "stop
being afraid" or "do not always be afraid." διαφέρω w. gen. to
differ, to be superior to (Plummer; s. also Matt 10:30f.).

■ ὅς ἄν "whoever." ὁμολογήσῃ aor. subj. ὁμολογέω to 8 agree, to confess. The expression w. prep. is Semitic and means "to state about a person what one knows to be true" (Arndt). ■ ἀρνησάμενος aor. mid. part. ἀρνέομαι to say no, to deny. 9 ἀπαρνηθήσεται fut. pass. ἀπαρνέομαι to deny. The prep. in compound is perfective (s. MH, 298). ■ ἐρεῖ fut. λέγω. εἰς 10 against. ἀφεθήσεται fut. pass. ἀφίημι to release, to forgive. βλασφημήσαντι aor. part. dat. sing. βλασφημέω to blaspheme (s. TDNT; CBB). ■ εἰσφέρωσιν subj. εἰσφέρω to bring 11 into, to lead in. μεριμνήσητε aor. subj. μεριμνάω to be concerned, to be anxious. ἀπολογήσησθε aor. pass. subj. ἀπολογέομαι to defend one's self. εἴπητε aor. subj. ■ διδάξει 12 fut. διδάσκω. δεῖ it is necessary. εἰπεῖν aor. inf.

■ εἰπέ aor. imp. λέγω. μερίσασθαι aor. mid. inf. μερίζω 13 to divide, to divide something w. another. ■ κατέστησεν 14 aor. καθίστημι to appoint, to constitute. μεριστής divider, one who divides. ■ ὁρᾶτε pres. imp. ὁράω. φυλάσσεσθε pres. 15 mid. imp. φυλάσσομαι to guard one's self. πλεονεξία covetousness, greediness. The greedy desire to have more (Plummer; s. also MNTW; TDNT). περισσεύειν pres. inf. to be in abundance. The inf. is used w. prep. as a substantive or epexegetical (MT, 146; s. also RWP). ■ εὐφόρησεν aor. εὐφορέω to produce 16 well, to be fruitful. ■ διελογίζετο impf. διαλογίζομαι to con- 17 sider, to think over, to reason. ποιήσω fut. ■ καθελῶ fut. 18 καθαιρέω to tear down. ἀποθήκη storehouse, granary, barn. μείζων comp. μέγας great. ■ ἐρῶ fut. λέγω. κείμενα pres. mid. 19 part. κεῖμαι to lie. Here used of goods "be stored up." ἀναπαύου pres. imp. ἀναπαύομαι to rest, to take one's rest. πίε aor. imp. πίνω to drink. εὐφραίνου pres. mid. imp. εὐφραίνομαι to be happy. ■ ἄφρων without reason, senseless, 20 foolish, expressing a reckless and inconsiderate habit of mind (AS). ἀπαιτοῦσιν pres. ἀπαιτέω to ask from someone, to require. The rabbis used the 3rd pl. to avoid saying "God" (RWP). ἡτοίμασας aor. 2nd sing. ἑτοιμάζω to prepare. ■ θησαυρίζων 21 pres. part. θησαυρίζω to treasure up. πλουτῶν pres. part. πλουτέω to be rich.

■ μεριμνᾶτε pres. imp. φάγητε aor. subj. ἐνδύσησθε aor. 22 subj. ἐνδύομαι to put on, to clothe one's self. ■ πλείων comp. 23 πολύς. τροφή nourishment, food, sustenance, gen. of comparison. ἔνδυμα clothing, gen. of comparison. ■ κατανοήσατε aor. 24 imp. κατανοέω to understand, to take knowledge of, to perceive. κόραξ raven. The name covers the whole of the crow tribe (Plummer). θερίζω to harvest. τρέφω to nourish, to sustain. πόσῳ how much more? ■ μεριμνῶν pres. part. ἡλικία stature, 25

a measure of space used here for a small unit of time "age" (Arndt). προσθεῖναι aor. inf. προστίθημι to add to. πῆχυς
26 cubit, a measure of length about 18 inches (BAG). ■ ἐλάχιστος superl. ὀλίγος small, slight, superl. least, smallest. μεριμνᾶτε
27 pres. ■ κρίνον lily. νήθω to spin. ὑφαίνω to weave. περιεβάλετο aor. mid. περιβάλλομαι to put around one's self,
28 to clothe. ■ χόρτος grass. ὄντα part. εἰμί. αὔριον tomorrow. κλίβανος oven, furnace. ἀμφιάζω to clothe. ὀλιγόπιστος
29 small faith, little faith. ■ ζητεῖτε pres. imp. ζητέω to seek. πίητε aor. subj. μετεωρίζεσθε pres. pass. imp. μετεωρίζω to be raised from the ground, suspended in mid-air, to be anxious, to be
30 worried (Arndt; s. also BAG). ■ ἐπιζητοῦσιν pres. ἐπιζητέω to seek, to look for. οἶδα defective perf. w. pres. meaning to
31 know. χρῄζω to need. ■ πλήν however, adversative use (Thrall, 21; s. Luke 22:21). προστεθήσεται fut. pass. προστίθημι to add to. (For the imp. followed by the fut. as a type of conditional
32 sentence, s. Luke 10:28.) ■ φοβοῦ pres. mid. imp. εὐδόκησεν aor. εὐδοκέω to have pleasure, to be pleased. δοῦναι aor. inf.
33 δίδωμι to give. ■ πωλήσατε aor. imp. δότε aor. imp. ἐλεημοσύνη compassion, alms, contribution. ποιήσατε aor. imp. βαλλάντιον moneybag, purse. παλαιούμενα pres. pass. part. παλαιόω to make whole, pass. to become whole. ἀνέκλειπτος unfailing, inexhaustible. σής moth. διαφθείρω to corrupt.
35 ■ ἔστωσαν imp. 3rd pl. εἰμί. ὀσφῦς hips, waist. περιεζωσμέναι perf. pass. part. περιζώννυμι to fasten up the garments w. a belt. Participle used in a perf. pass. periphrastic imp. construction. The perf. has the meaning "be the kind of person who never needs to be told to gird them up, because he will always live in this condition" (GI, 41). καιόμενοι pres. pass. part. καίω to light, to burn, periphrastic pres. mid. imp.,
36 already burning and continuously burning (RWP). ■ προσδεχομένοις pres. mid. part. προσδέχομαι to await, to expect. ἀναλύσῃ aor. subj. ἀναλύω to break up, to loose, to untie, to depart, to return. The picture is the breaking up of a feast or a camp (Plummer). ἐλθόντος aor. part. ἔρχομαι to go, gen. abs. κρούσαντος aor. part. κρούω to knock on.
37 ἀνοίξωσιν aor. subj. ἀνοίγνυμι to open. ■ ἐλθών aor. part. εὑρήσει fut. εὑρίσκω to find. γρηγοροῦντας pres. part. γρηγορέω to remain awake, to watch. περιζώσεται fut. mid., s.v.35. ἀνακλινεῖ fut. ἀνακλίνω to cause to recline, esp. at a table. παρελθών aor. part. παρέρχομαι to go along, to come to, to come. διακονήσει fut. διακονέω to serve, esp. at
38/39 table. ■ ἔλθῃ aor. subj. εὕρῃ aor. subj. ■ γινώσκετε pres. imp.

γινώσκω to know. ᾔδει plperf. of οἶδα. ἀφῆκεν aor. ἀφίημι
to allow, to permit. διορυχθῆναι aor. pass. inf. διορύσσω to
dig through, to break in. ■ γίνεσθε pres. mid. imp. γίνομαι to 40
become, to be. ἕτοιμος ready, prepared. δοκεῖτε pres. δοκέω to
suppose, to think.

■ ἄρα then, therefore. οἰκονόμος steward, a trusted slave 42
commissioned w. the responsibility of the oversight of the
household (s. TDNT). καταστήσει fut. καθίστημι to appoint,
to commission. θεραπεία ministry, household, a body of
domestic servants (s. RWP). διδόναι pres. inf. δίδωμι to give.
σιτομέτριον a measured portion of food, ration (Plummer).
■ ποιοῦντα pres. part. ■ χρονίζω to take time, to delay. 43/45
ἄρξηται aor. subj. ἄρχομαι to begin. τύπτω to beat.
μεθύσκεσθαι pres. mid. inf. μεθύσκομαι to be drunk, to
become drunk, to get drunk. ■ ἥξει fut. ἥκω to come. 46
προσδοκᾷ pres. προσδοκάω to expect. διχοτομήσει fut.
διχοτομέω to cut in two pieces. θήσει fut. τίθημι to place, to
give. ■ γνούς aor. part. γινώσκω to know. ἑτοιμάσας aor. 47
part. ποιήσας aor. part. δαρήσεται fut. pass. δέρω to skin, to
flay, to flog. (For customs regarding old Jewish slavery, s. SB, IV,
698–744.) ■ ἐδόθη aor. pass. δίδωμι. ζητηθήσεται fut. pass. 48
ζητέω to seek, to require. παρέθεντο aor. mid. παρατίθημι to
give over, to commit, to entrust. αἰτήσουσιν fut. αἰτέω w. acc.
to ask from someone, to require, great endowments or a great
responsibility (Arndt).

■ ἦλθον aor. βαλεῖν aor. inf. εἰ "how I wish that" (RWP). 49
ἀνήφθη aor. pass. ἀνάπτω to kindle, to set on fire. ■ 50
βαπτισθῆναι aor. pass. inf. βαπτίζω to baptize. συνέχομαι
to be afflicted, to suffer. τελεσθῇ aor. pass. subj. τελέω to
complete, to finish, to end. ■ παρεγενόμην aor. παραγίνομαι 51
to arrive, to come. δοῦναι aor. inf. δίδωμι to give. Infinitive
used to express purpose. διαμερισμός division. ■ 52
διαμεμερισμένοι perf. pass. part. διαμερίζω to divide, to divide into.

■ ἴδητε aor. subj. ὁράω. ἀνατέλλουσαν part. ἀνατέλλω 54
to rise. δυσμαί west. ὄμβρος rain. ■ νότος south wind. 55
πνέοντα pres. part. πνέω to blow. καύσων hot, burning. ■ 56
δοκιμάζω to examine, to prove, to come to a conclusion after
an examination.

■ ἀντίδικος opponent, adversary in a law case. δός aor. 57
imp. δίδωμι to give. ἀπηλλάχθαι perf. pass. inf. ἀπαλλάσσω
to free, mid. to be released from, to be rid of. Used here in a legal
sense and the perf. emphasizes a state of completion, "to be rid
of him for good" (RWP). κατασύρῃ subj. κατασύρω to drag

away. παραδώσει fut. παραδίδωμι to deliver over, to turn
over. πράκτωρ officer, the subordinate officer carrying out the
judgment of the court (Arndt). βαλεῖ fut. βάλλω to throw, to
59 cast. ■ ἐξέλθῃς aor. subj. ἐξέρχομαι to come out. λεπτόν a
small copper coin worth about one-eighth of a cent (BAG; s. also
Mark 12:42). ἀποδῷς aor. subj. ἀποδίδωμι to give back, to pay
back.

Ch. 13

1   ■ παρῆσαν impf. πάρειμι to be present, to come.
ἀπαγγέλλοντες pres. part. ἀπαγγέλλω to report. ἔμιξεν aor.
μείγνυμι to mix. It has been suggested that this incident occurred at a passover, perhaps the year before Jesus' death (s.
2 Ellis; HA, 175ff.). ■ ἀποκριθείς aor. pass. part. ἀποκρίνομαι
to answer. (For the Semitic construction, s. MH, 453.) δοκεῖτε
pres. δοκέω to suppose. παρά "more than." ἐγένοντο aor. mid.
γίνομαι to become, to be. πεπόνθασιν perf. πάσχω to suffer.
3 ■ μετανοῆτε pres. subj. μετανοέω to change the mind, to re-
4 pent. ἀπολεῖσθε fut. ἀπόλλυμαι to perish. ■ ἔπεσεν aor.
πίπτω to fall. πύργος tower. ἀπέκτεινεν aor. ἀποκτείνω to
kill. ὀφειλέτης debtor, sinner. (For the idea of sin as a debt to
God, s. TDNT.) κατοικοῦντας pres. part. κατοικέω to dwell,
5 to live. ■ μετανοήσητε aor. subj. ὡσαύτως in the same manner
(Plummer).
6   ■ πεφυτευμένην perf. pass. part. φυτεύω to plant.
ἀμπελών vineyard. ἦλθεν aor. ἔρχομαι. ζητῶν pres. part.
7 ζητέω to seek, to look for. εὗρεν aor. εὑρίσκω to find. ■
ἀμπελουργός vineyard keeper. ἔτος year, parenthetical nom.
used to express time (BD, 79f.). It was four years from the time
of planting that mature fruit was expected (s. LNT, 295; M,
Orlah). Here the three years are counted from the time when the
fig tree would normally be expected to bear, not from the time
of planting (RWP). ἔκκοψον aor. imp. ἐκκόπτω to cut off.
ἱνατί why? καί also, in addition (Plummer). καταργεῖ pres.
8 καταργέω to make idle, to make ineffective, to use up. ■ ἄφες
aor. imp. ἀφίημι to allow. σκάψω aor. subj. σκάπτω to dig.
βάλω aor. subj. βάλλω to throw. κόπριον manure, fertilizer.
9 ■ ποιήσῃ aor. subj. μέλλον next year, for the future. (For the
construction of this sentence in the suppression or breaking off
under the influence of strong emotion, s. Arndt; RG, 1203.)
ἐκκόψεις fut. The parable has its application to Israel as a nation
which required repentance (Arndt).
10   ■ διδάσκων pres. part. διδάσκω to teach. Participle used
11 in a periphrastic construction. ■ ἀσθένεια weakness, sickness.

συγκύπτουσα pres. part. συγκύπτω to bend together. Medical word for curvature of the spine (RWP). ἀνακῦψαι aor. inf.
ἀνακύπτω to bend up, to raise one's self up, to stand erect.
παντελής complete perf. at all. ■ ἰδών aor. part. ὁράω to see. 12
προσεφώνησεν aor. προσφωνέω to call to. ἀπολέλυσαι
perf. pass. 2nd sing. ἀπολύω to release. The perf. indicates, "you
have been freed and are in the state of freedom" (Arndt). The
word is used in medical writers for the releasing from disease; i.e.
relaxing tendons, membranes, etc. (MLL, 21). ■ ἐπέθηκεν aor. 13
ἐπιτίθημι to lay upon, to place upon. παραχρῆμα at once,
immediately. ἀνωρθώθη aor. pass. ἀνορθόω to straighten up
again. A medical term meaning, "to straighten, to put into natural position, abnormal or dislocated parts of the body" (MLL,
22). ἐδόξαζεν impf. δοξάζω to glorify, inceptive impf. "she
began to glorify." ■ ἀποκριθείς aor. pass. part., s.v.2. 14
ἀγανακτῶν pres. part. ἀγανακτέω to be aroused, to be indignant, to be angry. ἐθεράπευσεν aor. θεραπεύω to treat medically, to heal. δεῖ it is necessary. θεραπεύεσθε pres. pass. imp.
■ ἀπεκρίθη aor. pass. ὑποκριτής hypocrite, casuist (s. Matt. 15
23:27). βοῦς ox. ὄνος donkey. φάτνη stable, stall. ἀπαγαγών
aor. part. ἀπάγω to lead out. ποτίζω to give to drink. ■ υἷσαν 16
pres. part. εἰμί. ἔδησεν aor. δέω to bind. ἔδει impf. λυθῆναι
aor. pass. inf. ■ λέγοντος pres. part. gen. abs. κατῃσχύνοντο 17
impf. mid. καταισχύνομαι to be ashamed, "were put to
shame" (Plummer). ἀντικείμενοι pres. part. ἀντίκειμαι to be
opposed, to resist. ἔχαιρεν impf. χαίρω to rejoice. ἔνδοξος
glorious. γινομένοις pres. mid. part., s.v.2.
    ■ ὁμοιώσω fut. ὁμοιόω to compare, to make alike. ■ 18/19
κόκκος grain. σίναπι mustard. λαβών aor. part. λαμβάνω.
ἔβαλεν aor., s.v.8. κῆπος garden ηὔξησεν aor. αὐξάνω to
grow. ἐγένετο aor. mid. κατεσκήνωσεν aor. κατασκηνόω to
dwell, to make a nest. ■ ζύμη leaven. λαβοῦσα aor. part. 21
ἔκρυψεν aor. κρύπτω to hide. ἄλευρον flour. σάτον seah. A
Jewish measure for grain about a peck and a half (BAG).
ἐζυμώθη aor. pass. ζυμόω to leaven, to ferment. (For this parable, s. Matt. 13:33.)
    ■ διεπορεύετο impf. mid. διαπορεύομαι to journey 22
through, to pass through. κατά w. acc. through, distributive use,
"from village to village." διδάσκων pres. part., s.v.10. πορεία
journey. ποιούμενος pres. mid. part., s.v.9, "making his way to
Jerusalem" (RWP). ■ εἰ. Used to introduce a direct question and 23
is either a Hebraism or an ellipsis (RG, 1176, 1024). σῳζόμενοι
pres. pass. part. σῴζω to rescue, to save. ■ ἀγωνίζεσθε pres. 24
mid. imp. ἀγωνίζομαι to engage in an athletic contest, to fight,

to struggle, to strive. **εἰσελθεῖν** aor. inf. **εἰσέρχομαι** to go in.
στενός narrow. **ζητήσουσιν** fut., s.v.6. **ἰσχύσουσιν** fut.
25 **ἰσχύω** to be strong, to be able. ■ **ἐγερθῇ** aor. pass. subj. **ἐγείρω**
to rise, pass. to raise, to get up. **ἀποκλείσῃ** aor. subj. **ἀποκλείω**
to lock up. **ἄρξησθε** aor. mid. subj. **ἄρχομαι** to begin. **ἑστάναι**
perf. inf. **ἵστημι** to stand. **ἄνοιξον** aor. **ἀνοίγω** to open.
ἀποκριθείς aor. pass. part., s.v.2. **ἐρεῖ** fut. **λέγω**. **οἶδα** defective
26 perf. w. pres. meaning to know. ■ **ἄρξεσθε** fut. mid. **ἐφάγομεν**
aor. **ἐσθίω** to eat. **ἐπίομεν** aor. **πίνω** to drink. **πλατεῖα** wide,
27 wide street. **ἐδίδαξας** aor. ■ **ἀπόστητε** aor. imp. **ἀφίστημι** to
28 depart, to go away. **ἐργάτης** worker. ■ **κλαυθμός** loud crying
wailing. **βρυγμός** grinding, gnashing of teeth. **ὄψησθε** aor. mid.
subj. **ὁράω** to see. **ἐκβαλλομένους** pres. pass. part. **ἐκβάλλω**
29 to cast out, to drive out. ■ **ἥξουσιν** fut. **ἥκω** to come. **ἀνατολή**
east. **δυσμή** west. **βορρᾶς** north. **νότος** south.
ἀνακλιθήσονται fut. pass. **ἀνακλίνω** to recline (at the table).
31 ■ **προσῆλθαν** aor. **προσέρχομαι** to come to. **ἔξελθε** aor.
imp. **ἐξέρχομαι** to go out. **πορεύου** pres. mid. imp. **πορεύομαι**
to go. **ἐντεῦθεν** from here. This incident probably took place just
before Jesus left Galilee (HA, 218). **ἀποκτεῖναι** aor. inf., s.v.4.
Evidently a threat by Herod to get out of Antipas' domain (HA,
32 219f.). ■ **πορευθέντες** aor. pass. part. **εἴπατε** aor. imp. **ἀλώπηξ**
fox. The person described as a fox is looked down upon as weak
and wily, and as lacking real power and dignity (HA, 220, 343–
347). **ἴασις** healing. **ἀποτελέω** to complete. **αὔριον** tomorrow.
The expression "today and tomorrow" means "day by day."
Along w. the reference to the third day it is a Semitic idiom for
a short and definite period (HA, 221). **τελειοῦμαι** pres. pass.
τελειόω to complete, to finish. Here it is passive and means "I
33 am brought to completion" (HA, 222). ■ **δεῖ** it is necessary.
ἐχομένῃ pres. mid. part. **ἔχω**. Here "the next day" (s. Plummer). **ἐνδέχεται** pres. mid. "it is fitting." Here "it will not do."
The idea of necessity enters in (Arndt). **ἀπολέσθαι** aor. inf.,
34 s.v.3. ■ **ἀποκτείνουσα** pres. part. to kill. **λιθοβολοῦσα** pres.
part. **λιθοβολέω** to stone. **ἀπεσταλμένους** perf. pass. part.
ἀποστέλλω to send, to send out as an authoritative representative. **ἠθέλησα** aor. **θέλω** to wish, to desire. **ἐπισυνάξαι** aor.
inf. **ἐπισυνάγω** to gather together. **ὄρνις** hen (s. Matt. 23:39).
35 **νοσσιά** nest, brood. **πτέρυξ** wing. ■ **ἀφίεται** pres. pass.
ἀφίημι to leave, to forsake. It means "you have it entirely to
yourselves to possess and protect; for God no longer dwells in
it and protects it" (Plummer). **ἴδητε** aor. subj. **ὁράω**. **ἥξει** fut.,
s.v.29. **εἴπητε** aor. subj. **εὐλογημένος** perf. pass. part. **εὐλογέω**
to bless, to praise.

■ ἐγένετο aor. mid. γίνομαι to become, to happen (s. Luke 1
2:1; 8:1). ἐλθεῖν aor. inf. ἔρχομαι to come, to go. Infinitive used
w. prep. to express time (s. MT, 145f.). φαγεῖν aor. inf. ἐσθίω
to eat. ἦσαν impf. εἰμί. παρατηρούμενοι pres. mid. part.
παρατηρέω to stand by the side and watch (s. Luke 6:7). Participle used in a periphrastic construction. ■ ἰδού behold, look. 2
ὑδρωπικός dropsy. A medical term denoting a pers. suffering
from dropsy (MLL, 24). ■ ἀποκριθείς aor. pass. part. 3
ἀποκρίνομαι to answer (s. Luke 13:2). ἔξεστιν it is lawful, it
is allowed. θεραπεῦσαι aor. inf. θεραπεύω to handle medically, to heal. ■ ἡσύχασαν aor. ἡσυχάζω to be silent, ingres- 4
sive aor. "they became silent" (RWP). ἐπιλαβόμενος aor. mid.
part. ἐπιλαμβάνομαι to take hold of. ἰάσατο aor. mid. ἰάομαι
to heal. ἀπέλυσεν aor. ἀπολύω to release (s. Luke 13:12). ■ 5
βοῦς ox. φρέαρ well. πεσεῖται fut. mid. πίπτω to fall.
ἀνασπάσει fut. ἀνασπάω to pull up, to pull out. In the DSS
it was forbidden to give help to an animal on the Sabbath; either
to aid in delivering the young or to pull it out of a ditch (s. CD,
11:13–15). ■ ἴσχυσαν aor. ἰσχύω to be strong, to be able. 6
ἀνταποκριθῆναι aor. pass. inf. ἀνταποκρίνομαι to answer
back, to reply. (For the force of the prep. compound, s. MH,
297.)

■ κεκλημένους perf. pass. part. καλέω to call, to invite. 7
ἐπέχων pres. part. ἐπέχω (the word "mind" is to be supplied as
the object), to hold the mind on something, to notice. He directed his attention to this (Plummer). πρωτοκλισία chief seat, the
first place. In a group of three cushions or couches used for
reclining, the one in the center was the place of honor (s. SB, IV,
611–635). ἐξελέγοντο impf. mid. ἐκλέγω to choose, mid. to
choose for one's self. ■ κληθῇς aor. pass. subj. καλέω. 8
κατακλιθῇς aor. pass. subj. κατακλίνομαι to sit down, to
recline (esp. when eating). Used w. neg. to express prohibition,
implying the action is not yet existent and should not arise (s.
MKG, 273). ἐντιμότερος comp. ἔντιμος honored. σοῦ gen. of
comparison. ᾖ pres. subj. εἰμί. ■ ἐλθών aor. part. καλέσας aor. 9
part. ἐρεῖ fut. λέγω to say, to speak. δός aor. imp. δίδωμι to
give. ἄρξῃ fut. mid. ἄρχομαι to begin. The verb marks the
contrast between the brief, self-assumed promotion and the permanent merited humiliation (Plummer). αἰσχύνη shame.
κατέχειν pres. inf. to take, to hold down. ■ πορευθείς aor. pass. 10
part. πορεύομαι to go. ἀνάπεσε aor. imp. ἀναπίπτω to fall
back, to lie back, to recline at the table. ἔλθῃ aor. subj.
κεκληκώς perf. part. καλέω to call, to invite. ἐρεῖ fut. λέγω to

say. Used w. ἵνα, here perhaps to express results rather than
purpose (Plummer; s. also RG, 984f.). προσανάβηθι aor. imp.
προσαναβαίνω to come up to. It pictures the host as beckon-
ing to the guest to come up to him (Arndt). συνανακειμένων
pres. mid. part. συνανάκειμαι to recline at the table together

11 (w. dat.). ■ ὑψῶν pres. part. ὑψόω to lift up, to exalt.
ταπεινωθήσεται fut. pass. ταπεινόω to make low, to humble.

12 ὑψωθήσεται fut. pass. ■ κεκληκότι perf. act. part. dat. sing.
καλέω to call, to invite. ποιῇς pres. subj. ποιέω. ἄριστον
breakfast, the early morning meal (s. Luke 11:37). δεῖπνον dinner, the main meal (s. SB, IV, 611–639). φώνει pres. imp.
φωνέω to call, to invite. The pres. imp. indicates "do not habitually invite." It is the exclusive invitation of rich neighbors that
is forbidden (Plummer). συγγενής relative. γείτων neighbor.
ἀντικαλέσωσιν aor. subj. ἀντικαλέω to invite in return. (For
the reciprocal action expressed in the prep., s. MH, 297.)

13 γένηται aor. mid. subj. ἀνταπόδομα repayment. ■ δοχή
reception, banquet. It could be a reference to the messianic
victory banquet after the destruction of His enemies (LNT, 126–
155). κάλει pres. imp. ἀνάπηρος crippled, maimed. The prep.

14 is intensive, "very maimed" (Plummer). χωλός lame. ■ ἔσῃ fut.
εἰμί. ἀνταποδοῦναι aor. inf. ἀνταποδίδωμι to pay back again,
to pay back in return. ἀνταποδοθήσεται fut. pass. ἀνάστασις
resurrection.

15   ■ ἀκούσας aor. part. ἀκούω to hear. φάγεται fut. mid.
16/17 ἐσθίω to eat. ■ ἐποίει impf. ἐκάλεσεν aor. ■ ἀπέστειλεν aor.
ἀποστέλλω to send, to send out as an official and authoritative
representative. εἰπεῖν aor. inf., inf. of purpose. ἔρχεσθε pres.

18 mid. imp. ■ ἤρξαντο aor. mid. ἀπὸ μιᾶς "unanimously, w. one
accord" (BD, 126). παραιτεῖσθαι pres. mid. inf. παραιτέομαι
to ask someone for something, to make an excuse, to beg off (s.
RWP). ἠγόρασα aor. ἀγοράζω to buy. ἀνάγκη necessity, con-
straint. ἐξελθών aor. part. ἐξέρχομαι to go out. ἰδεῖν aor. inf.
ὁράω to see. ἐρωτάω to ask, to request. ἔχε pres. imp.

19 παρῃτημένον perf. part. (For the construction, s. RWP.) ■
ζεῦγος yoke. δοκιμάσαι aor. inf. δοκιμάζω to try out, to prove

20/21 by testing, inf. of purpose. ■ ἔγημα aor. γαμέω to marry. ■
παραγενόμενος aor. mid. part. παραγίνομαι to come.
ἀπήγγειλεν aor. ἀπαγγέλλω to report. ὀργισθείς aor. pass.
part. ὀργίζομαι to become angry, ingressive aor.
οἰκοδεσπότης ruler of a house. ἔξελθε aor. imp. πλατεῖα
wide, wide street. ῥύμη street, lane. χωλός lame, cripple. The
physically blemished were barred from full participation in
Jewish worship. This was also stressed in the Qumran commun-

ity (Ellis). **εἰσάγαγε** aor. imp. **εἰσάγω** to lead in, to bring in.
■ **γέγονεν** perf. **γίνομαι. ἐπέταξας** aor. **ἐπιτάσσω** to com- 22
mand, to give an order. ■ **φραγμός** hedges, fences. Poor travel- 23
ers were accustomed to camping in the shelter of the hedges and
fences (Arndt). **ἀνάγκασον** aor. imp. **ἀναγκάζω** to compel.
The compelling was by persuasion (Plummer). **εἰσελθεῖν** aor.
inf. **γεμισθῇ** aor. pass. subj. **γεμίζω** to fill, pass. to become full.
■ **γεύσεται** fut. mid. **γεύομαι** to taste, to eat. There shall be no 24
food sent to them as a token of recognition (LNT, 141).

   ■ **συνεπορεύοντο** impf. mid. **συμπορεύομαι** to go to- 25
gether, to accompany. **στραφείς** aor. pass. part. **στρέφομαι** to
turn one's self, to turn. ■ **μισεῖ** pres. **μισέω** to hate. It signifies 26
"loving less" (Arndt). (For the rabbinical teaching regarding
preferential treatment of the teacher over the Father, s. M, Baba
Netzia 2, 11.) ■ **σταυρός** cross (s. Matt. 10:38). (For the con- 27
cept of discipleship s. Matt. 28:19.) ■ **θελών** pres. part. **θέλω.** 28
πύργος tower. **οἰκοδομῆσαι** aor. inf. **οἰκοδομέω** to build.
καθίσας aor. act. part. **καθίζω** to sit down. This represents long
and serious consideration (Plummer). **ψηφίζω** to count, to calculate. **δαπάνη** cost. **ἀπαρτισμός** completion, to finish off, to
finish up. (For the force of the prep., s. MH, 299.) ■ **θέντος** aor. 29
part. **τίθημι** to place, to lay, gen. abs. **θεμέλιον** foundation.
ἰσχύοντος pres. part., s.v.6. **ἐκτελέσαι** aor. inf. **ἐκτελέω** to
bring to completion, to complete. **θεωροῦντες** pres. part.
θεωρέω to see, to watch. **ἄρξωνται** aor. mid. subj., s.v.9.
ἐμπαίζειν pres. inf. to mock. ■ **λέγοντες** pres. part. **ἤρξατο** 30
aor. mid. **οἰκοδομεῖν** pres. inf. **ἴσχυσεν** aor. ■ **πορευόμενος** 31
pres. mid. part., s.v.10. **συμβαλεῖν** aor. inf. **συμβάλλω** w. dat.
to throw together, to fight. **πόλεμος** war. **βουλεύσεται** fut.
mid. **βουλεύομαι** to confer, to take counsel, to deliberate w.
one's self. **ἐν** "by," "with." Instrumental use of the prep. (RWP).
ὑπαντῆσαι aor. inf. **ὑπαντάω** to meet. **ἐρχομένῳ** pres. mid.
part. ■ **πόρρω** far. **ὄντος** pres. part. gen. abs. **πρεσβεία** 32
embassy, delegation. **ἀποστείλας** aor. part., s.v.17. **ἐρωτᾷ**
s.v.18. ■ **ἀποτάσσομαι** to say good-by to, to renounce, to 33
forsake (w. dat.). **τὰ ὑπάρχοντα** possessions.

   ■ **οὖν** "to be sure" (DM, 255). **ἅλας** salt. **μωρανθῇ** aor. 34
pass. subj. **μωραίνω** to make foolish, to make useless (s. Matt.
5:13). **ἀρτυθήσεται** fut. pass. **ἀρτύω** to season. ■ **κοπρία** ma- 35
nure heap, rubbish heap. **εὔθετος** fit, suitable. **ἀκουέτω** pres.
imp. 3rd sing.

Ch. 15

1   ■ ἦσαν impf. εἰμί to be. ἐγγίζοντες pres. part. ἐγγίζω to
2 come near. Participle used in a periphrastic construction. ■
διεγόγγυζον impf. διαγογγύζω to murmur, to murmur among
themselves, throughout their whole company (Plummer). The
impf. pictures the continual action. προσδέχεται pres. mid. to
receive, to welcome. συνεσθίει pres. act. to eat together, to eat
3/4 w. someone. ■ εἶπεν aor. λέγω to say, to speak. ■ ἀπολέσας
aor. part. ἀπόλλυμι to lose. ἀπολωλός perf. part. εὕρη aor.
5 subj. εὑρίσκω to find. ■ εὑρών aor. part. ἐπιτίθημι to place
upon. ὦμος shoulder. χαίρων pres. part. χαίρω to rejoice. Par-
6 ticiple of manner. ■ ἐλθών aor. part. ἔρχομαι. συγκαλεῖ pres.
συγκαλέω to call together. γείτων neighbor. συγχάρητε aor.
7 imp. συγχαίρω to rejoice together. εὗρον aor. ■ μετανοοῦντι
pres. part. μετανοέω to change the mind, to repent (s. Matt.
3:2). ἤ "then." χρεία need, necessity.
8   ■ δραχμή drachma. A Greek silver coin worth normally
about 18 or 19 cents. It was the price of a sheep or one-fifth the
price of an ox (BAG). ἀπολέσῃ aor. subj. ἀπόλλυμι to lose.
ἅπτω to light. σαροῖ pres. σαρόω to sweep, to clean. ζητεῖ
pres. ζητέω to search. ἐπιμελῶς carefully, diligently. The prep.
compound is directive. It is directed concern (s. MH, 312ff.).
9 ■ φίλη female friend, girl friend. ἀπώλεσα aor. ἀπόλλυμι to
10 lose. ■ ἐνώπιον in the presence of.
12   ■ νεώτερος comp. νεός new, young. δός aor. imp. δίδωμι
to give. ἐπίβαλλον pres. part. ἐπιβάλλω to fall to, to be appropriate. It is the share which hypothetically is bound to come to
him (LNT, 106). μέρος part. οὐσία possession, property. The
younger son's part was probably about two-ninths (LNT, 109).
διεῖλεν aor. διαιρέω to divide. The father made a formal and
legal division of his goods. Though there was no further legal
claims to an inheritance, responsibility to the family was not
13 relieved (LNT, 108ff.). ■ συναγαγών aor. part. συνάγω to
gather together. Perhaps in the sense, "to turn everything into
cash" (BAG). The buyer of the property was not to possess it
before the death of the father (s. M, Baba Bathra 8, 7).
ἀπεδήμησεν aor. ἀποδημέω to be out of the land, to be away
from home, to go on a journey to a distant country.
διεσκόρπισεν aor. διασκορπίζω to scatter, to scatter in various directions, to squander (Arndt). ζῶν pres. part. ζάω to live.
Participle of means or manner. ἀσώτως adv. without saving,
14 dissolutely. Used of debauched and profligate living. ■
δαπανήσαντος aor. act. part. δαπανάω to spend, gen. abs.
ἐγένετο aor. mid. γίνομαι. ἤρξατο aor. mid. ἄρχομαι to be-

gin. ὑστερεῖσθαι pres. mid. inf. ὑστερέομαι to come late, to be behind, to fall short, to be in want, to suffer need. ■ 15 πορευθείς aor. pass. part. ἐκολλήθη aor. pass. κολλάω to glue together, to join. It denotes that he forced himself on a citizen of the country (Arndt). ἔπεμψεν aor. πέμπω to send. βόσκειν to feed, to graze. χοῖρος pig. He was occupied in the most degraded occupation known to the Jews (LNT, 112). ■ 16 ἐπεθύμει impf. ἐπιθυμέω to desire, to long for. κεράτιον the pods of the carob tree whose sweet-tasting pods were shaped like little horns (RWP). The rabbis considered this the equivalent of being in the direst need (Leaney). ἤσθιον impf. ἐδίδου impf. ■ ἔφη impf. φημί to say. μίσθιος hired worker. ■ ἀναστάς 17/18 aor. part. ἀνίστημι to stand up, to get up. ἐρῶ fut. λέγω. ἥμαρτον aor. ἁμαρτάνω to sin. He sinned against God and his father in disobeying the fifth commandment. Having squandered his goods, he was not able to fulfill his moral obligation to his father (LNT, 111f.). ■ κληθῆναι aor. pass. inf. καλέω to call, 19 to name, ποίησον aor. imp. ποιέω to do, to make. ■ ἦλθεν aor. 20 ἔρχομαι. ἀπέχοντος pres. part. ἀπέχω to be far off. εἶδεν aor. ὁράω to see. ἐσπλαγχνίσθη aor. pass. σπλαγχνίζομαι to be moved w. compassion (s. MNTW; TDNT). δραμών aor. part. τρέχω to run. ἐπέπεσεν aor. ἐπιπίπτω to fall upon. τράχηλος neck. κατεφίλησεν aor. καταφιλέω to kiss, to kiss fervently, the sign of forgiveness (J. Jeremias, The Parables of Jesus). ■ 22 ἐξενέγκατε aor. imp. ἐκφέρω to bring out. στολή robe, a stately robe. Instead of giving medals of honor, robes were given. He is treated as the guest of honor (Jeremias). δότε aor. imp. δίδωμι to give. δακτύλιος ring, signet ring. He is to consider himself as his father's deputy (LNT, 113). ὑπόδημα sandal, shoe. A sign that the servants accepted him as master (LNT, 114). ■ φέρετε 23 pres. imp. φέρω to bring, to carry. μόσχος a young animal, calf. θύσατε aor. imp. θύω to kill, to slaughter. The killing of the fatted calf is the height of hospitality (LNT, 114). φαγόντες aor. part. ἐσθίω to eat. εὐφρανθῶμεν aor. subj. εὐφραίνομαι to make merry, to rejoice, to be happy, hortatory subj. ■ ἀνέζησεν 24 aor. ἀναζάω to live again, to begin to live (GI, 150f.). εὑρέθη aor. pass.

■ πρεσβύτερος comp. πρέσβυς old. συμφωνία music. It 25 means a band of players or singers (Plummer). χορός choral dance, dancing. ■ προσκαλεσάμενος aor. mid. part. 26 προσκαλέω to summons, to call to one's self. ἐπυνθάνετο impf. πυνθάνομαι to inquire, to question. εἴη opt. εἰμί. Optative used in indirect discourse corresponding to the potential opt. of the direct question (BD, 195). ■ ἔθυσεν aor. ὑγιαίνοντα 27

pres. part. ὑγιαίνω to be healthy. ἀπέλαβεν aor.
28 ἀπολαμβάνω to receive back. ■ ὠργίσθη aor. pass.
ὀργίζομαι to be angry, to become angry, ingressive aor. ἤθελεν
impf. θέλω to wish, to desire. εἰσελθεῖν aor. inf. εἰσέρχομαι
to go in. ἐξελθών aor. part. ἐξέρχομαι to go out. παρεκάλει
impf. The impf. indicates "he kept on beseeching him" (RWP).
29 ■ ἀποκριθείς aor. pass. part. ἀποκρίνομαι to answer.
παρῆλθον aor. παρέρχομαι to pass by, to neglect, to transgress. The aor. indicates not even once in contrast w. so many
years of service (RWP). ἔδωκας aor. δίδωμι to give. ἔριφος kid.
Worth at the highest about 20 cents (Arndt). εὐφρανθῶ aor.
30 subj. pass ■ οὗτος "this one." Used contemptuously.
καταφαγών aor. part. κατεσθίω to eat up, to devour. ἡ
32 prep. is perfective. ■ εὐφρανθῆναι aor. pass. inf. χαρῆναι aor.
inf. ἔδει impf. δεῖ it is necessary, one must. The parable was told
to entreat the respectable Jews to rejoice w. God over the restoration of sinners (Caird).

Ch. 16

1   ■ καί "also," connects this parable w. what has just been
related (Arndt). οἰκονόμος steward, manager of an estate. One
who has been given the authority and the responsibility to handle the affairs of the estate for the owner (s. LNT, 52ff.; TDNT).
διεβλήθη aor. pass. διαβάλλω to bring charges w. hostile intent, either falsely and slanderously or justly (BAG). ὡς "because." Used w. part. for giving the alleged ground of a charge
against one (RWP). διασκορπίζων to scatter, to squander (s.
Luke 15:13). It refers to the steward's wastefulness, carelessness,
2 neglect of duty (Geldenhuys). ■ φωνήσας aor. act. part. φωνέω
to call. ἀπόδος aor. imp. ἀποδίδωμι to give back, to render.
λόγος account. οἰκονομία stewardship, trusted responsibility.
δύνῃ pres. 2nd sing. δύναμαι. (For the form, s. BD, 46f.)
οἰκονομεῖν pres. inf. οἰκονομέω to be a steward, to exercise the
3 responsibility of managing an estate. ■ ποιήσω aor. subj. ποιέω
deliberative subj. ἀφαιρεῖται pres. mid. ἀφαιρέω to take away
from. σκάπτειν pres. inf. to dig. Digging is the hardest kind of
work (BAG). ἐπαιτεῖν pres. inf. to ask for something, to beg.
4 αἰσχύνομαι to be ashamed. ■ ἔγνων aor. γινώσκω to know,
"I've got it." It is a burst of daylight to the puzzled, darkened
man (RWP). μετασταθῶ aor. pass. subj. μεθίστημι to remove,
to transfer. δέξωνται aor. mid. subj. δέχομαι to receive, to
5 welcome. ■ προσκαλεσάμενος aor. mid. part. προσκαλέω to
summons, to call someone to one's self. χρεοφειλέτης debtor.
6 ὀφείλω to owe, to owe a debt. ■ βάτος bath. A Heb. liquid

measure between eight and nine gallons (BAG). ἔλαιον olive
oil. δέξαι aor. imp. δέχομαι. γράμμα writing, reference to a
written contract. καθίσας aor. part. καθίζω to sit down.
γράψον aor. imp. γράφω to write. It has been suggested that the
steward was releasing the debtors from unlawful interest (usury)
which was condemned by biblical law (s. LNT, 56–74). ▪ κόρος 7
cor. A measure for grain, flour, etc., between ten and twelve
bushels (BAG). ▪ ἐπήνεσεν aor. ἐπαινέω to praise, to approve, 8
to sanction, to ratify (LNT, 64). His master agrees w. him in
following the laws of God and honesty. The steward gains approval by doing what the law of God required of him (LNT, 72).
ἀδικία unrighteous, refers to his previous condition. φρονίμως
adv. wisely. ἐποίησεν aor. φρονιμώτερος comp. Worldly
people both by training and instinct act in some crisis upon the
assumption that God's standards are the right standards (LNT,
76). ▪ ποιήσατε aor. imp. ἐκ "of," "by," "apart from." The 9
translation "and not" has been suggested (s. Pasquale Colella,
"Zu Lk 16:7," ZNW, 64 [1973], 125f.). μαμωνᾶς mammon,
livelihood, possession. (For a comprehensive listing of the examples of this word, s. H.P. Rüger, "Μαμωνᾶς," ZNW, 64 [1973],
127–131.) ἐκλίπῃ aor. subj. ἐκλείπω fail, where the unrighteous mammon ceases to be of service (Arndt). αἰώνιος eternal.
σκηνή tent. ▪ ἐλάχιστος superl. ὀλίγος elative superl. "very 10
little" (RWP). ▪ ἐγένεσθε aor. mid. γίνομαι to become, to be, 11
to prove to be (Plummer). πιστεύσει fut. πιστεύω to have faith
in, to entrust. ▪ ἀλλότριος another's, that which belongs to 12
another. δώσει fut. δίδωμι to give. ▪ οἰκέτης slave, a 13
household servant. δουλεύω to be a slave, to be enslaved, to
serve as a slave. μισήσει fut. μισέω to hate. ἀγαπήσει fut.
ἀγαπάω to love. ἀνθέξεται fut. mid. ἀντέχομαι to cling to, to
hold fast to someone, to be devoted to. καταφρονήσει fut.
καταφρονέω to despise (w. gen.).

▪ ἤκουον impf. "they were listening." φιλάργυρος lover 14
of money. ὑπάρχοντες pres. part. ὑπάρχω to exist, to be.
ἐξεμυκτήριζον impf. ἐκμυκτηρίζω to turn up the nose, to
show disrespect or contempt (Arndt). ▪ δικαιοῦντες pres. part. 15
δικαιόω to justify, to declare righteous. ὑψηλός high, exalted.
βδέλυγμα abomination, that which is detestable. It orginally
meant something that offends on account of its stench (Arndt).
▪ εὐαγγελίζεται pres. pass. εὐαγγελίζομαι to proclaim good 16
news. βιάζεται pres. mid. βιάζομαι to use force, to force one's
way, best taken as conative pres. "everybody tries to press into
it" (Arndt). (For the mid. force, s. BS, 258.) ▪ εὐκοπώτερος 17
comp. εὔκοπος easy. παρελθεῖν aor. inf. παρέρχομαι to go

by, to pass away. κεραία horn, one of the little horns or minute projections which distinguish Heb. letters (Plummer). πεσεῖν

18 aor. inf. πίπτω to fall. ■ ἀπολύων pres. part. ἀπολύω to release, to divorce. γαμῶν pres. part. γαμέω to marry. μοιχεύω to commit adultery. ἀπολελυμένην perf. pass. part. fem. sing. Christ has spoken of the continual obligation of the law; He now gives an isolated example (Meyer).

19   ■ δέ and, now. (For the connection of thoughts in this chapter, see LNT, 78–99.) ἐνεδιδύσκετο impf. mid. ἐνδιδύσκομαι to clothe one's self, customary impf. "he customarily clothed himself." πορφύρα purple. βύσσος fine linen. The outer garment was dyed purple, the inner garment was of fine linen made of flax (Arndt). εὐφραινόμενος pres. mid. part. εὐφραίνομαι to be glad, to enjoy one's self. λαμπρῶς splendid-

20 ly, sumptuously. ■ πτωχός poor, poor as a beggar (s. TDNT; MNW). ἐβέβλητο plperf. pass. βάλλω to throw, to place. He had been placed there and was still there. πυλών gate. εἱλκωμένος perf. part. ἑλκόωμαι to be full of sores. A medical

21 term meaning to be ulcerated (MLL, 31). ■ ἐπιθυμῶν pres. part. ἐπιθυμέω to desire, to long for. Luke uses this word w. the inf. to express the unfulfilled desire or longing (Jeremias, *The Parables of Jesus*). χορτασθῆναι aor. pass. inf. χορτάζω to satisfy, to feed until one is full. ἀλλὰ καί "further," "what is more." The two particles are combined in a progressive sense (Thrall, 14). κύων, κυνός dog. ἐπέλειχον impf. ἐπιλείχω to lick. The prep. in compound could be local, "to lick over" (RWP). ἕλκος

22 wound, ulcer (s. MLL, 32). ■ ἐγένετο aor. mid. γίνομαι (s. Luke 2:1; 8:1). ἀποθανεῖν aor. inf. ἀποθνήσκω to die. ἀπενεχθῆναι aor. pass. inf. ἀποφέρω to carry away. κόλπος bosom. It indicates the place of honor at a banquet (s. John 13:23; Jeremias, *Parables*). ἀπέθανεν aor. ἐτάφη aor. pass.

23 θάπτω to bury. ■ ᾅδης hades, the underworld, the place of the dead (s. TDNT). ἐπάρας aor. part. ἐπαίρω to lift up. βάσανος torment, torture. Originally the touchstone by which metals were tested, then the rack for torturing people (RWP; s. SB, IV,

24 1016–1165). ὁρᾷ pres. ὁράω historical pres. ■ ἐλέησον aor. imp. ἐλεέω to have mercy on, to show mercy. πέμψον aor. imp. πέμπω to send. The aor. imp. is used in the state of emergency, a cry for help (s. Bakker, 100f.). βάψῃ aor. subj. βάπτω to dip. ἄκρον tip. δάκτυλος finger. καταψύξῃ aor. subj. καταψυχω to cool off, to make cool. ὀδυνάομαι to be in anguish, to be in severe pain. (For medical examples of the word, s. MLL, 32f.)

25 ■ μνήσθητι aor. imp. μιμνήσκομαι to remember. ἀπέλαβες aor. ἀπολαμβάνω to take from, to receive. παρακαλεῖται

pres. pass. παρακαλέω to encourage, to comfort. ὀδυνᾶσαι
pres. (For the form, s. BD, 45.) ■ μεταξύ w. gen. between. 26
χάσμα division, chasm. ἐστήρικται perf. pass. στηρίζω to set
up, to firmly establish, perf. that which stands, fixed. θέλοντες
pres. part. θέλω to wish, to want. διαβῆναι aor. inf. διαβαίνω
to pass through. δύνωνται pres. mid. subj. δύναμαι.
διαπερῶσιν pres. subj. διαπεράω to cross over. ■ πέμψῃς aor. 27
subj. The rich man showed love for his brothers, but had no love
for Lazarus (LNT, 90). ■ διαμαρτύρηται pres. mid. subj. 28
διαμαρτύρομαι to witness to, to warn. The prep. compound
may mean "bear witness successfully" or "bear witness
thoroughly, earnestly" (Plummer). ἔλθωσιν aor. subj. ἔρχομαι
to come, to go. ■ ἀκουσάτωσαν aor. imp. 3rd pl. ■ πορευθῇ 29/30
aor. subj. πορεύομαι to go, to make a journey. μετανοήσουσιν
fut. μετανοέω to repent, to change one's mind. ■ ἀναστῇ aor. 31
subj. ἀνίστημι to rise, to rise up. πεισθήσονται fut. pass.
πείθω to persuade. The story teaches the necessity of giving
earnest heed to the warnings of God's Word.

Ch. 17

■ ἀνένδεκτος impossible from the verb meaning to admit 1
to one's self, hence, "inadmissible," "unallowable" (RWP).
ἐλθεῖν aor. inf. ἔρχομαι. The inf. is used either as the subj.
(IBG, 129) or to express design (Plummer). ■ λυσιτελεῖ pres. 2
act. λυσιτελέω literally, "it pays the taxes, repays the outlay,"
it is well, it is advantageous, it is worth its while (Plummer).
μυλικός that which belongs to the mill (millstone). περίκειμαι
to place around, to be placed around. τράχηλος neck. ἔρριπται
perf. pass. ῥίπτω to throw, to hurl. σκανδαλίσθῃ aor. subj.
σκανδαλίζω to cause to stumble (s. TDNT). ■ προσέχετε 3
pres. imp. προσέχω to give attention, to take heed. ἁμάρτῃ
aor. subj. ἁμαρτάνω to sin. ἐπιτίμησον aor. imp. ἐπιτιμάω to
rebuke, to warn sternly. μετανοήσῃ aor. subj. μετανοέω to
change one's mind, to repent. ἄφες aor. imp. ἀφίημι to release,
to forgive. ■ ἑπτάκις seven times. Symbolizes any large number 4
(Arndt). ἁμαρτήσῃ aor. subj. εἰς against. ἐπιστρέψῃ aor. subj.
ἐπιστρέφω to turn to. ἀφήσεις fut. 2nd sing.

■ πρόσθες aor. imp. προστίθημι to add to, to give in 5
addition, to increase. It involves increasing the substance rather
than adding a new substance (GI, 51). ■ κόκκος grain. σίναπι 6
mustard. ἐλέγετε impf. used in a contrary to fact conditional
clause. The verb in the condition is pres. rather than the normal
impf. This implies the disciples had some faith (GI, 51f.).
συκάμινος mulberry tree. ἐκριζώθητι aor. pass. imp. ἐκριζόω

to rip out by the roots, to uproot. φυτεύθητι aor. pass. imp. φυτεύω to plant. ὑπήκουσεν aor. ὑπακούω to listen to, to obey. Used in a contrary to fact conditional clause.

7   ■ ἀροτριῶντα pres. part. ἀροτριάω to plow. ποιμαίνοντα pres. part. ποιμαίνω to be a shepherd. εἰσελθόντι aor. part. dat. sing. εἰσέρχομαι to come in. ἐρεῖ fut. λέγω. εὐθέως immediately. παρελθών aor. part. παρέρχομαι to come to. ἀνάπεσε aor. imp. ἀναπίπτω to fall
8 back, to recline at the table. ■ οὐχί strengthened form of οὐ used in the question expecting the answer yes. ἑτοίμασον aor. imp. ἑτοιμάζω to prepare. δειπνήσω fut. δειπνέω to eat, to dine. περιζωσάμενος aor. mid. part. περιζώννυμι to gird yourself about, to tie up your tunic so that it will not interfere w. your movements (s. Arndt). διακόνει impf. διακονέω to minister, to serve (at the table). φάγω aor. subj. ἐσθίω to eat. πίω aor. subj. πίνω to drink. μετά w. acc. after. φάγεσαι fut. mid. ἐσθίω. πίεσαι fut. mid. πίνω. This reflects the current custom (Gel-
9 denhuys). ■ μή used in questions expecting the answer no. χάριν ἔχω thanks. Here, "to have gratitude toward one" (RWP). ἐποίησεν aor. ποιέω to do. διαταχθέντα aor. pass.
10 part. διατάσσω to order, to command. ■ ποιήσητε aor. subj. λέγετε pres. imp. ὅτι equivalent to quotation marks. ἀχρεῖος unprofitable, useless. (For the alpha privative, s. A.C. Moor- house, *Studies in the Greek Negatives*, 41–68.) ὠφείλομεν impf. ὀφείλω to be obligated, to owe a debt. ποιῆσαι aor. inf. πεποιήκαμεν perf.

11   ■ ἐγένετο aor. γίνομαι (s. Luke 2:1; 8:1). διήρχετο impf.
12 διέρχομαι to go through. ■ εἰσερχομένου pres. mid. part. gen. abs., s.v.7. ἀπήντησαν aor. ἀπαντάω to meet. ἔστησαν aor.
13 ἵστημι to stand. πόρρωθεν far away, at a distance (concerning leprosy, s. Matt. 8:4). ■ ἦραν aor. αἴρω to lift up. ἐλέησον aor.
14 imp. ἐλεέω to have mercy on, to have compassion on. ■ ἰδών aor. part. ὁράω to see. πορευθέντες aor. pass. part. ἐπιδείξατε aor. imp. ἐπιδείκνυμι to show. ἐκαθαρίσθησαν aor. pass.
15 καθαρίζω to cleanse. ■ ἰάθη aor. pass. ἰάομαι to heal. ὑπέστρεψεν aor. ὑποστρέφω to turn around, to return. δοξάζων pres. part. δοξάζω to esteem, to glorify, to praise.
16 ■ ἔπεσεν aor. πίπτω to fall. εὐχαριστῶν pres. part. εὐχαριστέω to be thankful, to give thanks. Participle of man-
17 ner. ■ ἀποκριθείς aor. pass. part. ἀποκρίνομαι to answer.
18 (For the Hebraic use of the part., s. MT, 155ff.) ■ εὑρέθησαν aor. pass. εὑρίσκω to find. ὑποστρέψαντες aor. act. part. δοῦναι aor. inf. δίδωμι to give. εἰ μή except. ἀλλογενής one
19 of another race, foreigner. ■ ἀναστάς aor. part. ἀνίστημι to

192

rise up. (For the construction of the part., s. Matt. 28:19.)
πορεύου pres. mid. imp. σέσωκεν perf. σῴζω to rescue, to
save, to heal. The perf. indicates the state or condition.

■ ἐπερωτηθείς aor. pass. part. ἐπερωτάω to ask a ques- 20
tion, to direct a question to. ἀπεκρίθη aor. pass., s.v.17.
παρατήρησις observation, a watching closely. Used by medical
writers to denote medical observation of disease (MLL, 153).
■ ἐροῦσιν fut. λέγω. ἐντός w. gen. within, in the midst of, 21
among (s. Arndt; BAG). ■ ἐλεύσονται fut. mid. ἔρχομαι. 22
ἐπιθυμήσετε fut. ἐπιθυμέω to desire, to long for. ἰδεῖν aor. inf.
ὁράω to see. ὄψεσθε fut. mid. ὁράω. ■ ἀπέλθητε aor. subj. 23
ἀπέρχομαι to go away, to depart. The subj. w. the neg. is used
as a prohibition, the aor. indicating do not start the action.
διώξητε aor. subj. διώκω to pursue. ■ ἀστραπή lightning. 24
ἀστράπτουσα pres. part. ἀστράπτω to flash, to lightning. ἐκ
τῆς. The word χώρας (region) is to be supplied. λάμπω to
shine. ■ δεῖ it is necessary. παθεῖν aor. inf. πάσχω to suffer. 25
ἀποδοκιμασθῆναι aor. pass. inf. ἀποδοκιμάζω to reject after
examination (s. TDNT). ■ ἐγένετο aor. mid., s.v.11. ■ ἤσθιον 26/27
impf. ἐσθίω to eat. ἔπινον impf., s.v.8. ἐγάμουν impf. γαμέω
to marry. ἐγαμίζοντο impf. pass. γαμίζω to give in marriage.
The impfs. vividly portray the continual action of the past time.
They were not merely living their ordinary lives, but they were
wholly given up to external things (Plummer). εἰσῆλθεν aor.,
s.v.7. κιβωτός ark. ἦλθεν aor. ἔρχομαι. κατακλυσμός flood,
from the verb meaning "to dash against," and signifies an overwhelming inundation (Arndt). ἀπώλεσεν aor. ἀπόλλυμι to
ruin, to destroy. The last three verbs in the aor. stand in contrast
to the previous impfs. (RWP). ■ ἠγόραζον impf. ἀγοράζω to 28
buy, to purchase at the marketplace. ἐπώλουν impf. πωλέω to
sell. ἐφύτευον impf. φυτεύω to plant. ᾠκοδόμουν impf.
οἰκοδομέω to build. ■ ἐξῆλθεν aor. ἐξέρχομαι to go out. 29
ἔβρεξεν aor. βρέχω to rain. Rather than used impersonally, the
subject of the verb is probably the Lord (BD, 72). θεῖον sulphur.
■ ἀποκαλύπτεται pres. pass. ἀποκαλύπτω to unveil, to re- 30
veal. The futuristic use of the pres. gives a confident assertion
intended to arrest attention w. a vivid and realistic tone (MT,
63). ■ καταβάτω aor. imp. 3rd sing. καταβαίνω to come 31
down. ἆραι aor. inf. αἴρω to lift up, to take. Infinitive of purpose. ἐπιστρεψάτω aor. imp. 3rd sing., s.v.4. ■ μνημονεύετε 32
pres. imp. μνημονεύω to remember. ■ ζητήσῃ aor. subj. ζητέω 33
to seek, to look for. περιποιήσασθαι aor. mid. inf.
περιποιέομαι to preserve for one's self, to preserve one's life.
ἀπολέσει fut. ἀπόλλυμι s.v.27. ζωογονήσει fut. ζωογονέω to

34 give life to, to make alive, to preserve a life. ■
   παραλημφθήσεται fut. pass. παραλαμβάνω to accept, to re-
35 ceive, to take. ἀφεθήσεται fut. pass. ἀφίημι to leave. ■
37 ἀλήθουσαι pres. act. part. fem. ἀλήθω to grind. ■ ἀετός vulture. ἐπισυναχθήσονται fut. pass. ἐπισυνάγω to gather together.

Ch. 18

1 ■ πρός used w. inf. indicates purpose, but is sometimes
   weakened to "w. reference to" (MT, 144). δεῖν pres. inf. δεῖ "it
   is necessary." ἐγκακεῖν pres. inf. ἐγκακέω to give in to evil, to
   become weary, to lose heart, to turn coward (RWP). Real courage requires that we leave the problem w. God (J.M. Derrett,
   "Law in the New Testament: The Unjust Judge," NTS, 18 [Jan.,
2 1972] 191). ■ φοβούμενος pres. mid. part. φοβέομαι to fear,
   to be afraid. ἐντρεπόμενος pres. mid. part. ἐντρέπομαι to turn
3 to confusion, to put to shame, mid. to reverence. ■ χήρα widow.
   A widow would go to court without an advocate only in a desper-
   ate situation (Derrett, NTS, 188). ἤρχετο impf. mid. ἔρχομαι
   iterat. impf., she came over and again. ἐκδίκησον aor. imp.
   ἐκδικέω to avenge someone, to procure justice for someone.
   Here "take up my case" (Derrett, NTS, 187). ἀντίδικος adver-
4 sary, opponent (in court). ■ ἤθελεν impf. θέλω to wish, to want.
   The impf. pictures his continual rejection. εἰ "if, also." With this
   construction the condition is treated as a matter of indifference.
5 The matter is belittled (RG, 1026f.). ■ γέ a particle of emphasis,
   "yet because she troubles me" (Plummer). παρέχω "to cause
   trouble." The inf. is used w. the prep. to express cause.
   ἐρχομένη pres. mid. part. The pres. indicates the continual coming, the part. could be conditional or manner. ὑπωπιάζῃ pres.
   subj. ὑπωπιάζω to strike in the eye, to give a black eye to, here
   in the sense of "to annoy" (Plummer) or "to disgrace" in the
6 sense of losing prestige (Derrett, NTS, 190ff.). ■ ἀκούσατε aor.
7 act. imp. ἀκούω. ■ ποιήσῃ aor. subj. ποιέω. ἐκδίκησις vengeance. A technical term for administrative justice (Derrett,
   NTS, 186). βοώντων pres. part. βοάω to cry aloud, to call for
   help. μακροθυμεῖ pres. μακροθυμέω to be patient, to delay.
8 God will not delay (Derrett, NTS, 189; s. also Arndt). ■
   ποιήσει fut. ἐλθών aor. part. ἔρχομαι.
9 ■ πεποιθότας perf. part. πείθω to persuade, perf. be persuaded, to trust in. ἐξουθενοῦντας pres. part. ἐξουθενέω to
10 regard as nothing, to despise. ■ ἀνέβησαν aor. ἀναβαίνω to go
11 up. προσεύξασθαι aor. inf. προσεύχομαι to pray. ■ σταθείς
   aor. pass. part. ἵστημι to stand. προσηύχετο impf. mid.

εὐχαριστέω to be thankful, to give thanks. It was customary to began a prayer w. a note of thanksgiving. In this case it turned out to be an expression of self-admiration (Arndt). ἅρπαξ swindler, extortioner (s. LAE, 316f.). μοιχός adulterer. οὗτος this one. Used in a contemptuous sense. ■ νηστεύω to fast (s. 12 TDNT; SB, II, 241ff., IV, 77–114; M, Taanith). δίς twice, on Mondays and Thursdays (Plummer). ἀποδεκατεύω to tithe, to pay a tenth. κτάομαι to own, to possess. ■ μακρόθεν from afar, 13 far off. ἑστώς perf. part. ἵστημι to stand. ἤθελεν s.v.4. ἐπᾶραι aor. inf. ἐπαίρω to lift up. ἔτυπτεν impf. τύπτω to strike, to hit. στῆθος breast. ἱλάσθητι aor. pass. imp. ἱλάσκομαι to propitiate, pass. to be propitiated, to be merciful or gracious (s. APC, 125–185; TDNT). ■ κατέβη aor. καταβαίνω to go down. 14 δεδικαιωμένος perf. pass. part. δικαιόω to justify, to declare righteous. The perf. looks at the completed state; that is, the state of having been declared to be in the right (s. TDNT; APC, 224–274). ὑψῶν pres. part. ὑψόω to lift up, to exalt. ταπεινωθήσεται fut. pass. ταπεινόω to make low, to humble. ταπεινῶν pres. part. ὑψωθήσεται fut. pass.

■ προσέφερον impf. προσφέρω to bring to. βρέφος baby, 15 infant. ἅπτηται pres. mid. subj. ἅπτομαι to touch (w. gen.). The iterat. pres. He touched one after the other (RWP). ἰδόντες aor. part. ὁράω to see. ἐπετίμων impf. ἐπιτιμάω to rebuke, inceptive impf. "they began to rebuke." ■ προσεκαλέσατο aor. 16 mid. προσκαλέω to summons, to call to one's self. ἄφετε aor. imp. ἀφίημι to allow. ■ κωλύετε pres. imp. κωλύω to hinder, 17 to forbid. δέξηται aor. subj. δέχομαι to receive, to welcome. εἰσέλθῃ aor. subj. εἰσέρχομαι to go into.

■ ἐπηρώτησεν aor. ἐπερωτάω to question, to ask a ques- 18 tion. ποιήσας aor. part., s.v.7. κληρονομήσω fut. κληρονομέω to receive as an inheritance, to inherit. ■ οἶδα 20 defective perf. w. a pres. meaning to know. μοιχεύσῃς aor. subj. μοιχεύω to commit adultery. Used w. a neg. as a prohibition forbidding that the action should arise (s. MKG, 273). φονεύσῃς aor. subj. φονεύω to murder, to commit murder. κλέψῃς aor. subj. κλέπτω to steal. ψευδομαρτυρήσῃς aor. subj. ψευδομαρτυρέω to be a false witness, to give false witness. τίμα pres. imp. τιμάω to honor. ■ ἐφύλαξα aor. φυλάσσω to 21 guard, to keep, to observe. ■ ἀκούσας aor. part., s.v.6. λείπω 22 to be lacking. πώλησον aor. imp. πωλέω to sell. διάδος aor. imp. διαδίδωμι to distribute. The prep. compound implies the giving to various ones (s. MH, 302). ἕξεις fut. ἔχω to have. (For the construction of an imp. followed by the fut. indicating a type of a conditional sentence, s. Beyer, *Semitische Syntax*, 238–255.)

195

δεῦρο "come!" ἀκολούθει pres. imp. ἀκολουθέω to follow, to
23 follow as a disciple (s. TDNT). ■ περίλυπος surrounded by
sorrow, extremely sorrowful. ἐγενήθη aor. pass. γίνομαι to
24/25 become. ■ δυσκόλως adv. difficult. ■ εὐκοπώτερος comp.
εὔκοπος easy, without difficulty. τρῆμα hole, eye of a needle.
βελόνη needle. Used in medical writers of a surgical needle used
26 in operations (MLL, 60f.). εἰσελθεῖν aor. inf., s.v.17. ■
28 σωθῆναι aor. pass. inf. σῴζω to save, to rescue. ■ ἀφέντες aor.
part., s.v.16. Here to forsake, to leave. ἠκολουθήσαμεν aor.
29/30 ■ ἀφῆκεν aor. ἀφίημι. ἕνεκεν because of, on account of. ■
λάβῃ aor. subj. λαμβάνω to receive. πολλαπλασίων manifold, much more.
31   ■ παραλαβών aor. part. παραλαμβάνω to take along, the
notion of taking aside is involved but not prominent (Plummer).
τελεσθήσεται fut. pass. τελέω to bring to completion, to com-
32 plete. γεγραμμένα perf. pass. part. γράφω to write. ■
παραδοθήσεται fut. pass. παραδίδωμι to deliver over to.
ἔθνος Gentile. ἐμπαιχθήσεται fut. pass. ἐμπαίζω to mock (s.
Mark 10:34). ὑβρισθήσεται fut. pass. ὑβρίζω to treat outra-
geously, to treat someone seditiously (s. MNTW; TDNT).
33 ἐμπτυσθήσεται fut. pass. ἐμπτύω to spit on. ■
μαστιγώσαντες aor. part. μαστιγόω to scourge (s. Matt. 27:
26; TDNT). ἀποκτενοῦσιν fut. ἀποκτείνω to kill.
34 ἀναστήσεται fut. ἀνίσταμι to rise. ■ συνῆκαν aor. συνίημι
to comprehend, to understand. κεκρυμμένον perf. pass. part.
κρύπτω to conceal, to hide. ἐγίνωσκον impf. γινώσκω to
know.
35   ■ ἐγένετο aor. mid. (s. Luke 2:1; 8:1). ἐκάθητο impf.
κάθημαι to sit. ἐπαιτῶν pres. part. ἐπαιτέω to ask for, to beg.
36 ■ ἀκούσας aor. part., s.v.6. διαπορευομένου pres. mid. part.
διαπορεύομαι to travel through, to pass through. ἐπυνθάνετο
37 impf. πυνθάνομαι to inquire. εἴη opt. εἰμί. ■ ἀπήγγειλαν aor.
38 ἀπαγγέλλω to report. ■ ἐβόησεν aor., s.v.7. ἐλέησον aor. imp.
39 ἐλεέω to have mercy on. ■ προάγοντες pres. part. προάγω to
go before. ἐπετίμων impf., s.v.15. σιγήσῃ aor. subj. σιγάω to
be silent, to be quiet. ἔκραζεν impf. κράζω to shout, to scream.
40 The impf. pictures the repeated action. ■ σταθείς aor. pass.
part., s.v.14. ἐκέλευσεν aor. κελεύω to order, to command.
41 ἀχθῆναι aor. pass. inf. ἄγω to lead. ■ ποιήσω fut., s.v.7.
ἀναβλέψω aor. subj. ἀναβλέπω to look up, to see again, to
42 regain sight (s. MH, 295). ■ ἀνάβλεψον aor. imp. σέσωκεν
43 perf., s.v.26. ■ ἀνέβλεψεν aor. ἠκολούθει impf., s.v.22. ἰδών
s.v.15. ἔδωκεν aor. δίδωμι to give. αἶνος praise.

Ch. 19

■ εἰσελθών aor. part. εἰσέρχομαι to go in. διήρχετο 1
impf. mid. διέρχομαι to go through, to pass through. ■ 2
καλούμενος pres. pass. part. καλέω to call. ἀρχιτελώνης chief
tax collector, superintendent of tax collectors. He was in the
service of the government or foreign bankers who had bought
the privilege of collecting taxes (Arndt). (For tax collectors and
the Jewish view of them as those who used force and fraud to
gain riches, s. LNT, 280ff.; TDNT.) ■ ἐζήτει impf. ζητέω to 3
seek. The impf. pictures his continual effort. ἰδεῖν aor. inf. ὁράω
to see. ἠδύνατο impf. mid. δύναμαι to be able. ἀπό (w. gen.)
from, here in a causal sense. The multitude was the source of the
hindrance (Plummer). ἡλικία stature, size. ■ προδραμών aor. 4
part. προτρέχω to run before. ἀνέβη aor. ἀναβαίνω to go up,
to climb up. συκομορέα fig-mulberry tree. It has leaves like
those of the mulberry tree, while its fruit is like that of a fig tree
(Arndt). ἴδῃ aor. subj. ὁράω. ἐκείνης gen. w. the word "way"
to be understood. The gen. case is used in connection w. the
prep. in the compound verb or is adverbial in use (RWP).
ἤμελλεν impf. μέλλω to be about to. ■ ἦλθεν aor. ἔρχομαι. 5
ἀναβλέψας aor. part. ἀναβλέπω to look up. σπεύσας aor.
part. σπεύδω to hurry. (For the part. used in connection w. the
imp., s. Matt. 28:19.) κατάβηθι aor. pass. imp. καταβαίνω to
come down. δεῖ it is necessary. μεῖναι aor. inf. μένω to remain,
to stay. Jesus was putting pressure on him to clean up his life so
that He could visit w. him (LNT, 283). ■ κατέβη aor. 6
ὑπεδέξατο aor. mid. ὑποδέχομαι to welcome, to receive as a
guest. χαίρων pres. part. χαίρω to rejoice, to be glad. ■ ἰδόντες 7
aor. part. ὁράω. διεγόγγυζον impf. διαγογγύζω to murmur, to
complain, to grumble w. one another. εἰσῆλθεν aor.
καταλῦσαι aor. inf. καταλύω to take up one's quarters, to
lodge, to rest, inf. of purpose. It was thought to be wicked to eat
the fruit of a person whose earnings were tainted (LNT, 28l).
■ σταθείς aor. pass. part. ἵστημι to stand. ἥμισυς half. τὰ 8
ὑπάρχοντα pres. part., that which one has, possessions. εἰ introduces a first-class conditional clause in which the subject
views the condition as real. ἐσυκοφάντησα aor. συκοφαντέω
to obtain through extortion or blackmail. ἀποδίδωμι to pay
back, to give back. τετραπλοῦν four times, fourfold. His intention to make restoration indicates his repentence and makes it
possible for Jesus to eat w. him without contamination (s. LNT,
283ff.). ■ ἐγένετο aor. mid. γίνομαι. ■ ζητῆσαι aor. inf. Infini- 9/10
tive of purpose. σῶσαι aor. inf σῴζω to save, to rescue. Infinitive of purpose. ἀπολωλός perf. part. ἀπόλλυμι to ruin, to

destroy, to be lost. The perf. pictures the state or condition.

11 ■ ἀκουόντων pres. part. ἀκούω to hear, gen. abs.
προσθείς aor. part. προστίθημι to add. Here used in the Hebraic sense of an adv., "again," "further." (For the Hebraic adverbial use of an auxiliary verb, s. MH, 445f.) διά used w. acc.
of inf. to express cause, "because He was near Jerusalem" (s.
MT, 142f.). δοκεῖν pres. inf. δοκέω to seem, to appear, to suppose. παραχρῆμα immediately. ἀναφαίνεσθαι pres. pass. inf.

12 ἀναφαίνομαι pass., to appear, to manifest itself. ■ εὐγενής of
noble birth. A significant term since to be a member of the
aristocracy was highly prized (Arndt). ἐπορεύθη aor. pass.
πορεύομαι to go, to travel. λαβεῖν aor. inf. λαμβάνω to receive, inf. of purpose. ὑποστρέψαι aor. inf. ὑποστρέφω to

13 return. ■ καλέσας aor. part., s.v.2. ἔδωκεν aor. δίδωμι to give.
μνᾶ mina. A Gr. monetary unit worth in normal times about
eighteen to twenty dollars (BAG). πραγματεύσασθε aor. mid.
imp. πραγματεύομαι to carry on business, esp. as a banker or

14 trader (Plummer). ἐν ᾧ while, until (s. BD, 193). ■ πολίτης
citizen. ἐμίσουν impf. μισέω to hate. ἀπέστειλαν aor.
ἀποστέλλω to send, to send as an official authoritative repre-

15 sentative. βασιλεῦσαι aor. inf. βασιλεύω to be king. ■
ἐγένετο s.v.9. ἐπανελθεῖν aor. inf. ἐπανέρχομαι to return
again. The aor. inf. used w. prep. to express time, "after he
returned" (s. MT, 145f.). λαβόντα aor. part. φωνηθῆναι aor.
pass. inf. φωνέω to call, inf. in indirect discourse (s. RG, 1036f.).
δεδώκει plperf. δίδωμι. γνοῖ aor. subj. γινώσκω.
διεπραγματεύσατο aor. mid. διαπραγματεύομαι to gain by
trading, to earn. The compound points to the result of the activ-

16 ity enjoined (Arndt). ■ παρεγένετο aor. mid. παραγίνομαι to
come on the scene, to come, to present one's self.
προσηργάσατο aor. mid. προσεργάζομαι to produce in addition, to gain. The prep. compound indicates "in addition,"

17 "besides," "more" (RWP). ■ ἐλάχιστος superl. μικρός little,

18 small. ἐγένου aor. mid. ἴσθι pres. imp. εἰμί. ■ ἦλθεν aor., s.v.5.

19/20 ἐποίησεν aor. ποιέω. ■ γίνου pres. mid. imp. ■ ἀποκειμένην
perf. pass. part. ἀποτίθημι to lay aside, to put away.
σουδάριον (from Latin) a face cloth for wiping perspiration,

21 corresponding to our handkerchief (BAG). ■ αὐστηρός harsh,
severe, originally that which is harsh and stringent in taste. It
signifies a person who would not permit any trifling (Arndt; s.
also Trench, Synonyms, 47f.). ἔθηκας aor. τίθημι to place, to
lay, to set, to put down. ἔσπειρας aor. 2nd sing. σπείρω to sow.

22 ■ κρινῶ fut. κρίνω to judge. ᾔδεις plperf. of the defective perf.

23 οἶδα to know. ■ τράπεζα table, banker's table. ἐλθών aor. part.

ἔρχομαι to come, to go, forms a conditional clause of a contrary to fact conditional sentence (s. BD, 182). ἔπραξα aor. πράσσω to do, to collect. Used of collecting taxes, duties, and interest (BAG). ■ παρεστῶσιν perf. part. παρίσταμαι to stand by. 24 ἄρατε aor. imp. αἴρω to take, to take away. δότε aor. imp. δίδωμι. ■ δοθήσεται fut. pass. δίδωμι. ἀρθήσεται fut. pass. 26 αἴρω. ■ πλήν moreover, here the meaning is progressive, "and, 27 what is more" (Thrall, 23; s. Luke 22:21). θελήσαντας aor. part. ἀγάγετε aor. imp. ἄγω to lead. κατασφάξατε aor. imp. κατασφάζω to slaughter, to cut down. ἔμπροσθεν w. gen. before.

■ εἰπών aor. part. ἐπορεύετο impf. mid., s.v.12. 28 ἀναβαίνων pres. part., s.v.4. ■ ἐγένετο aor. mid., s.v.9. 29 ἤγγισεν aor. ἐγγίζω to be near, to come near. ἀπέστειλεν aor., s.v.14. ■ ὑπάγετε pres. imp. ὑπάγω to go, to go forth. 30 εἰσπορευόμενοι pres. mid. part. εἰσπορεύομαι to go in. εὑρήσετε fut. εὑρίσκω to find. πῶλος a young animal, a young donkey, colt. δεδεμένον perf. pass. part. δέω to bind, to tie. ἐκάθισεν aor. καθίζω to sit. λύσαντες aor. part. λύω to loose. ■ ἐρωτᾷ pres. subj. ἐρωτάω to question, to ask. ἐρεῖτε fut. 31 λέγω to say. ■ ἀπελθόντες aor. part. ἀπέρχομαι to go away. 32 ἀπεσταλμένοι perf. pass. part. εὗρον aor. ■ λυόντων pres. 33 part. gen. abs. ■ ἤγαγον aor. ἄγω to lead. ἐπιρίψαντες aor. 35 part. ἐπιρρίπτω to throw upon. ἐπεβίβασαν aor. ἐπιβιβάζω to place upon. ■ πορευομένου pres. mid. part. gen. abs. 36 ὑπεστρώννυον impf. ὑποστρώννυμι to spread out under. The impf. pictures the continual and repeated action.

■ ἐγγίζοντος pres. part. gen. abs. κατάβασις going down, 37 descent. ἤρξαντο aor. mid. ἄρχομαι to begin. αἰνεῖν pres. inf. αἰνέω to praise. εἶδον aor. ὁράω to see. ■ εὐλογημένος perf. 38 pass. part. εὐλογέω to bless, to praise. ■ ἐπιτίμησον aor. imp. 39 ἐπιτιμάω to rebuke, to warn, to threaten. ■ ἀποκριθείς aor. 40 pass. part. ἀποκρίνομαι to answer. (For the Semitic use, s. MH, 453.) ἐάν used w. ind. in a first-class conditional clause where the condition is assumed as real (RWP; s. also BD, 189f.). σιωπήσουσιν fut. σιωπάω to be quiet, to be silent. κράξουσιν fut. κράζω to cry out, to scream.

■ ἰδών aor. part. ὁράω. ἔκλαυσεν aor. κλαίω to cry, to 41 weep. The word means to lament w. sobs (Arndt). ■ εἰ "if," 42 introduces a contrary to fact conditional clause w. the conclusion broken off and not expressed (s. RWP). ἔγνως aor., s.v.15. ἐκρύβη aor. pass. κρύπτω to conceal, to hide. ■ ὅτι because. 43 ἤξουσιν fut. ἥκω to come. παρεμβαλοῦσιν fut. παρεμβάλλω to throw or raise up beside. χάραξ, κος stake.

Here the sing. is collective designating the palisades, a wall made of stakes erected by Roman soldiers during the siege of the city (Arndt; s. also Josephus, *Wars* V, 6, 2; V, 9, 4). περικυκλώσουσιν fut. περικυκλόω to encircle. συνέξουσιν fut. συνέχω to hold together, to press hard, to crowd someone.

44 πάντοθεν from all sides. ■ ἐδαφιοῦσιν fut. ἐδαφίζω to level to the ground, to shatter against the ground (Geldenhuys). ἀφήσουσιν fut. ἀφίημι to leave. ἐπισκοπή visitation.

45 ■ εἰσελθών aor. part., s.v.1. πωλοῦντας pres. part. πωλέω
46 to sell. ■ γέγραπται perf. pass. γράφω to write. ἐποιήσατε aor., s.v.18. σπήλαιον cave, den. λῃστής robber. (For this incident, s. Matt. 21:12.)

47 ■ διδάσκων pres. part. διδάσκω part. used in a periphrastic construction. ἐζήτουν impf., s.v.3. ἀπολέσαι aor. inf.
48 ἀπόλλυμι to destroy. ■ εὕρισκον impf. The impf. indicates they were not to find, in spite of thier searching and meditating (Arndt). ποιήσωσιν aor. subj., s.v.18, deliberative subj. ἐξεκρέματο impf. mid. ἐκκρεμάννυμαι to hang upon.

Ch. 20

1 ■ ἐγέντο aor. mid. γίνομαι to become, to happen (s. Luke 2:1; 8:1). διδάσκοντος pres. part. διδάσκω to teach, gen. abs. εὐαγγελιζομένου pres. mid. part. εὐαγγελίζομαι to proclaim good news, gen. abs. ἐπέστησαν aor. ἐφίστημι to stand by, to
2 approach. ■ εἰπόν aor. imp. ποῖος what kind. δούς aor. part.
3 δίδωμι to give. ■ ἀποκριθείς aor. pass. part. ἀποκρίνομαι to answer (s. MH, 453). ἐρωτήσω fut. ἐρωτάω to question, to ask.
5 εἴπατε aor. imp. ■ συνελογίσαντο aor. mid. συλλογίζομαι to bring together accounts, to reason, to reason together. εἴπωμεν aor. subj. ἐρεῖ fut. λέγω. ἐπιστεύσατε aor. πιστεύω
6 to believe. ■ καταλιθάσει fut. καταλιθάζω to stone, to throw stones down upon. πεπεισμένος perf. pass. part. πείθω to persuade. The perf. indicates a settled state of persuasion (RWP).
7 εἶναι perf. inf. εἰμί. Infinitive used in indirect discourse. ■ εἰδέναι inf. of the defective perf. οἶδα w. pres. meaning to know.

9 ■ ἤρξατο aor. mid. ἄρχομαι to begin. ἐφύτευσεν aor. φυτεύω to plant. ἐξέδοτο aor. mid. ἐκδίδωμι to lease, to give out. ἀπεδήμησεν aor. ἀποδημέω to leave the country, to go
10 on a journey. (For this parable, s. Mark 12:1–12.) ■ ἀπέστειλεν aor. ἀποστέλλω to send, to send as an authoritative representative (s. TDNT). δώσουσιν fut. δίδωμι to give. ἐξαπέστειλαν aor. ἐξαποστέλλω to send out, to send away. δείραντες aor.
11 part. δέρω to flay, to beat. ■ προσέθετο aor. mid. προστίθεμι.

Used in the Hebraic sense "again" (s. Luke 19:11). πέμψαι aor.
inf. πέμπω to send. ἀτιμάσαντες aor. part. ἀτιμάω to dishon-
or. ■ τραυματίσαντες aor. part. τραυματίζω to wound. 12
ἐξέβαλον aor. ἐκβάλλω to throw out. ■ ποιήσω fut. πέμψω 13
fut. ἴσως perhaps, probably, presumably (s. MM).
ἐντραπήσονται fut. pass. ἐντρέπομαι to show respect to. ■ 14
ἰδόντες aor. part. ὁράω to see. διελογίζοντο impf.
διαλογίζομαι to reason. ἀποκτείνωμεν pres. or aor. subj.
ἀποκτείνω to kill, hortatory subj. γένηται aor. mid. subj. ■ 15
ἐκβαλόντες aor. part. ἀπέκτειναν aor. ■ ἐλεύσεται fut. mid. 16
ἔρχομαι to come, to go. ἀπολέσει fut. ἀπόλλυμι to destroy.
ἀκούσαντες aor. part. ἀκούω to hear. γένοιτο aor. mid. opt.
The only use of this phrase outside of Paul's epistles. The meaning is "may the whole story never happen!" (Arndt). ■ 17
ἐμβλέψας aor. part. ἐμβλέπω to look at, to fix one's gaze upon.
γεγραμμένον perf. pass. part. γράφω to write, perf. "it stands
written." (For the legal and authoritative implications of this
word, s. BS, 112ff.) ἀπεδοκίμασαν aor. ἀποδοκιμάζω to reject after examination. οἰκοδομοῦντες pres. part. οἰκοδομέω
to build. ἐγενήθη aor. pass. γίνομαι. γωνία corner. ■ πεσών 18
aor. part. πίπτω to fall. συνθλασθήσεται fut. pass. συνθλάω
to shatter. πέσῃ aor. subj. λικμήσει fut. λικμάω to winnow
chaff from grain, to blow away like chaff, to sweep out of sight
or out of existence (Plummer). (For the meaning "to grind to
powder," s. BS, 225f.) ■ ἐζήτησαν aor. ζητέω to seek, to try. 19
ἐπιβαλεῖν aor. inf. ἐπιβάλλω to place upon, to lay hands upon
someone. ἐφοβήθησαν aor. pass. φοβέομαι to be afraid, to
fear. ἔγνωσαν aor. γινώσκω to know. πρός in reference to, w.
respect to.
        ■ παρατηρήσαντες aor. part. παρατηρέω to watch in- 20
tently (s. Luke 6:7). ἐγκάθετος spy, agent, one who is hired to
trap one by crafty words (RWP). ὑποκρινομένους pres. mid.
part. ὑποκρίνομαι to pretend (s. TDNT). ἐπιλάβωνται aor.
subj. ἐπιλαμβάνομαι to lay hold upon, to seize. ὥστε w. inf.
Used to express intended result (BD, 198). The sense would be,
"such words as it would enable them to hand him over" (IBG,
143). παραδοῦναι aor. inf. παραδίδωμι to deliver over. ■ 21
ἐπηρώτησαν aor. ἐπερωτάω to ask. λαμβάνω to receive.
Used in the expression "to accept the face" which is a Hebraism
meaning "to regard w. favor," "to show partiality" (s. Geldenhuys). ■ ἔξεστιν it is allowed, it is lawful. The question is framed 22
as a question in Jewish law because there was no specific command in the law. The authority and ability of Jesus as a teacher
was being tested (LNT, 315–323). φόρος tribute. δοῦναι aor.

23 inf. δίδωμι to give. ■ κατανοήσας aor. part. κατανοέω to take
note of, to perceive, to consider carefully. πανουργία lit.
"readiness to do anything," skill, in the neg. sense craftiness,
24 trickery (BAG). ■ δείξατε aor. imp. δείκνυμι to show.
δηνάριον denarius. A Roman silver coin with a picture of Caesar (s. Matt. 22:20). εἰκών image. ἐπιγραφή inscription. Some
25 feel Jesus was alluding to Ecclesiastes 7:2 (LNT, 324–328). ■
τοίνυν therefore, draws an inference and a consequence from
the preceding (s. BD, 235). ἀπόδοτε aor. imp. ἀποδίδωμι to
render, to give what is proper and due. Jesus' answer is that
human governments are to be obeyed as long as they do not
conflict w. God's law and God is to be obeyed (LNT, 333–337).
26 ■ ἴσχυσαν aor. ἰσχύω to be able. ἐπιλαβέσθαι aor. mid. inf.
θαυμάσαντες aor. part. θαυμάζω to marvel, to wonder.
ἐσίγησαν aor. σιγάω to be silent, to become silent.
27   ■ προσελθόντες aor. part. προσέρχομαι to come to, to
approach. ἀντιλέγοντες pres. part. ἀντιλέγω to speak in opposition to, to oppose, to contradict, to deny. εἶναι inf.
28 ἐπηρώτησαν s.v.21. ■ ἔγραψεν aor., s.v.17. ἀποθάνῃ aor.
subj. ἀποθνῄσκω to die. ἄτεκνος childless. ᾖ subj. εἰμί. λάβῃ
aor. subj., s.v.21. ἐξαναστήσῃ aor. subj. ἐξανίστημι to raise
29/31 up out of, to raise up. ■ λαβών aor. part. ἀπέθανεν aor. ■
33 ἔλαβεν aor. κατέλιπον aor. καταλείπω to leave behind. ■
34 ἔσχον aor. ἔχω to have. ■ γαμοῦσιν pres. γαμέω to marry.
35 γαμίσκονται pres. pass. γαμίσκω to give in marriage. ■
καταξιωθέντες aor. pass. part. καταξιόω to consider worthy.
τυχεῖν aor. inf. τυγχάνω (w. gen.) to attain, to meet, to experi-
36 ence. ■ ἀποθανεῖν aor. inf. ἰσάγγελος angel like, equal to
37 angels. ὄντες part. εἰμί. ■ ἐγείρονται pres. pass. ἐγείρω to rise,
pass. to raise, to be raised. καί even, also. ἐμήνυσεν aor. μηνύω
disclose, intimate, reveal. Used esp. of making known what was
38 secret (Plummer). ■ ζώντων pres. part. ζάω to live. ζῶσιν pres.
39/40 ■ ἀποκριθέντες aor. pass. part. s.v.3. ■ ἐτόλμων impf.
τολμάω to dare. ἐπερωτᾶν pres. inf., s.v.21.
42/43   ■ κάθου imp. κάθημαι to sit. ■ θῶ aor. subj. τίθημι to
place, to make. ὑποπόδιον footstool, acc. used predicatively. It
predicates something of a noun already in the acc., "as . . . " (s.
44 IBG, 35). ■ καλεῖ pres. καλέω to call.
45/46   ■ ἀκούοντος pres. part. gen. abs., s.v.16. ■ προσέχετε
pres. imp. προσέχω to give heed to, to be aware of. θελόντων
pres. part. θέλω to wish, to want. περιπατεῖν pres. inf.
περιπατέω to walk about. στολή robe, a stately robe generally
reaching to the feet or train-like sweeping the ground (Trench,
Synonyms, 186). φιλούντων pres. part. φιλέω to love, to be

fond of. πρωτοκαθεδρία, κλισία seat of honor. (For the seat
of honor at the synagogue and at banquets, s. Luke 11:43; Mark
12:39.) ■ κατεσθίω to eat up. πρόφασις pretext. μακρός long. 47
λήμψονται fut., s.v.21. περισσότερος comp. περισσός
excessive, abundant.

Ch. 21

   ■ ἀγαβλέψας aor. part. ἀναβλέπω to look up. εἶδεν aor. 1
ὁράω to see. βάλλοντας pres. part. βάλλω to throw.
γαζοφυλακεῖον contribution box (s. Mark 12:41). ■ πενιχρός 2
needy, poor. It describes the man for whom life and living is a
struggle (NTW). λεπτόν the smallest bronze coin (s. Mark 12:
42). ■ πτωχός poor, poor to the point of being a beggar (Arndt; 3
TDNT). πλεῖον comp. πολύς much, comp. more. πάντων gen.
of comparison. ἔβαλεν aor. ■ περισσεύοντος pres. part. 4
περισσεύω to be in abundance, to be in excess. ὑστέρημα
lack, poverty. It is more than poverty; it signifies destitution
(Arndt). βίος living, livelihood (s. Mark 12:44).
   ■ λεγόντων pres. part. ἀνάθημα a gift dedicated to God. 5
Used of costly offerings presented to the gods and suspended or
exposed to view in the temple. It expresses that which is dedicated to God for its own honor as well as for God's glory (s. Trench,
Synonyms, 16ff.). κεκόσμηται perf. pass. κοσμέω to adorn.
■ ταῦτα "these things" acc. of general reference (RWP). Also 6
explained as an independent nominative (s. M, 69; DM, 70).
ἐλεύσονται fut. mid. ἔρχομαι to come. ἀφεθήσεται fut. pass.
ἀφίημι to leave. καταλυθήσεται fut. pass. καταλύω to destroy.
   ■ ἐπηρώτησαν aor. ἐπερωτάω to direct a question to, to 7
ask. μέλλη subj. μέλλω to be about to. Used w. inf. to express
fut. (s. MKG, 307). ■ πλανηθῆτε aor. pass. subj. πλανάω to 8
deceive, to lead astray, pass. to be led astray. ἤγγικεν perf.
ἐγγίζω to draw near, to be near. πορευθῆτε aor. pass. subj.
πορεύομαι to go. Subjunctive used w. neg. to express a command not to start an action. ■ ἀκούσητε aor. subj. ἀκούω to 9
hear. ἀκαταστασία disturbance, upheaval, revolution.
πτοηθῆτε aor. pass. subj. πτοέομαι to terrify, to frighten, pass.
to be alarmed, to be startled. δεῖ it is necessary. γενέσθαι aor.
mid. inf. γίνομαι to become, to happen. ■ ἐγερθήσεται fut. 10
pass. ἐγείρω to raise, pass. to rise. ■ σεισμός earthquake. κατὰ 11
τόπους everywhere, various places, distributive use of prep.
φόβητρον terrible sight or event, horror. ■ πρό before. The 12
prep. is used of time (Plummer). ἐπιβαλοῦσιν fut. ἐπιβάλλω
to throw upon, to lay (hands) upon. διώξουσιν fut. διώκω to

persecute. παραδιδόντες pres. part. παραδίδωμι to deliver
over. ἀπαγομένους pres. pass. part. ἀπάγω to lead away. A
13 technical term in Athenian legal language (EGT). ■
ἀποβήσεται fut. ἀποβαίνω to turn out, to turn out for you
14 (dat. of advantage) (RWP). ■ θέτε aor. imp. τίθημι to place, to
determine. προμελετᾶν pres. inf. προμελετάω to practice
beforehand, to prepare. The proper term for preparing a speech
(Geldenhuys). ἀπολογηθῆναι aor. pass. inf. ἀπολογέομαι to
15 defend one's self. ■ δώσω fut. δίδωμι to give. στόμα mouth,
here the power of speech. σοφία wisdom, the choice of matter
and form (Plummer). δυνήσονται fut. δύναμαι to be able.
ἀντιστῆναι aor. inf. ἀνθίσταμι to stand against, to withstand.
ἀντειπεῖν aor. inf. ἀντιλέγω to speak against. ἀντικείμενοι
pres. mid. part. ἀντίκειμας to lie over against, to be opposed.
16 (For the prep. in compound, s. MH, 297.) ■ παραδοθήσεσθε
fut. pass. παραδίδωμι to deliver over. θανατώσουσιν fut.
θανατόω to kill. ἐξ out of, "some of you." The partitive gen. w.
17 the prep. is used as the object (s. BD, 91). ■ μισούμενοι pres.
18 pass. part. μισέω to hate. ■ ἀπόλητας aor. subj. ἀπόλλυμαι
19 to destroy, to perish. ■ ὑπομονή patience, endurance, lit. "remaining under" indicates an active endurance which opposes the
evil while patiently waiting on the Lord (s. TDNT; CBB).
κτήσεσθε fut. κτάομαι to possess, to acquire.
20   ■ ἴδητε aor. subj., s.v.1. κυκλουμένην pres. pass. part.
κυκλόω to encircle. στρατόπεδον army camp. γνῶτε aor. imp.
21 γινώσκω. ■ φευγέτωσαν pres. imp. 3rd per. pl. φεύγω to flee.
ἐκχωρείτωσαν pres. imp. 3rd. pl. ἐκχωρέω to go out.
εἰσερχέσθωσαν pres. mid. imp. 3rd. pl. εἰσέρχομαι to go into.
22 ■ ἐκδίκησις punishment, vengeance. πλησθῆναι aor. pass. inf.
πίμπλημι to fill, to fulfill. γεγραμμένα perf. pass. part.
γράφω. (For the OT character of this prophecy, s. C.H. Dodd,
23 More New Testament Studies, 74–80.) ■ θηλαζούσαις pres.
part. fem. dat. pl. θηλάζω to nurse, to breast feed, to give suck.
24 ἀνάγκη distress, calamity (s. Matt. 24:8). ■ πεσοῦνται fut.
mid. πίπτω to fall. αἰχμαλωτισθήσονται fut. pass.
αἰχμαλωτίζω to take captive. πατουμένη pres. pass. part.
πατέω to walk on, to tread on. ἄχρι οὗ w. subj. until.
πληρωθῶσιν aor. pass. subj. πληρόω to fill, to fulfill. It is
possible that Luke understands the final signs (25–33) to follow
the Gentile "times" and if so a fut. repossession by the Jews is
anticipated (Ellis).
25   ■ συνοχή distress, dismay. ἀπορία perplexity. ἦχος roaring, gen. of possession, shading over into an expression of cause,
"perplexity caused by the roaring of the sea" (Arndt). σάλος

rolling or tossing motion esp. of the waves in a rough sea (BAG).
■ ἀποψυχόντων pres. part. ἀποψύχω to breathe out, to faint, 26
to expire, gen. abs. προσδοκία expectation. ἐπερχομένων
pres. mid. part. ἐπέρχομαι to come upon. οἰκωμένη inhabited
earth, the land that is built upon. σαλευθήσονται fut. pass.
σαλεύω to shake. ■ ὄψονται fut. mid. ὁράω to see. ■ 27/28
ἀρχομένων pres. mid. part. ἄρχομαι to begin. ἀνακύψατε aor.
imp. ἀνακύπτω to stand erect, to be elated. Used of being elated
after sorrow (Plummer). ἐπάρατε aor. imp. ἐπαίρω to lift up.
ἀπολύτρωσις redemption, release for the payment of a price,
deliverance (s. APC, 37–48; TDNT; GW, 71ff.).

■ ἴδετε aor. imp. ■ προβάλωσιν aor. subj. προβάλλω to 29/30
put forth, to sprout. βλέποντες pres. part. θέρος summer. ■ 31
γινόμενα pres. mid. part. γινώσκετε pres. imp. ■ παρέλθῃ 32
aor. subj. παρέρχομαι to go by, to pass away. (For the term
"last generation" in DSS, s. 1QpHab 2:7; 7:2; CD 1:12.)
γένηται aor. mid. subj. ■ παρελεύσονται fut. mid. 33
παρέρχομαι.

■ προσέχετε pres. imp. προσέχω to give attention, to give 34
heed. βαρηθῶσιν aor. pass. subj. βαρέω to weigh down, to
depress. κραιπάλη drunken nausea. Signifies the distressing
after effects of intoxication (Arndt; for medical examples of the
word, s. MLL, 167). μέθη drunkenness. βιωτικός belonging to
daily life, worldly, secular, everyday (s. MH, 379). ἐπιστῇ aor.
subj. ἐφίσταμι to come upon (suddenly and unexpectedly).
αἰφνίδιος suddenly, unexpectedly. ■ παγίς snare, trap. 35
ἐπεισελεύσεται fut. mid. ἐπεισέρχομαι to come over.
καθημένους pres. mid. part. κάθημαι to sit, to dwell. ■ 36
ἀγρυπνεῖτε pres. imp. ἀγρυπνέω to be awake. δεόμενοι pres.
mid. part. δέομαι to request, to pray. κατισχύσητε aor. subj.
κατισχύω to be able to. ἐκφυγεῖν aor. inf. ἐκφεύγω to flee.
μέλλοντα pres. part. σταθῆναι aor. pass. inf. ἵστημι to stand.

■ διδάσκων pres. part. used in a periphrastic construction. 37
ηὐλίζετο impf. mid. αὐλίζομαι to spend the night, to find lodging. ■ ὤρθριζεν impf. ὀρθρίζω to rise early in the morning, to 38
come early in the morning. ἀκούειν pres. inf., inf. of purpose.

Ch. 22

■ ἤγγιζεν impf. ἐγγίζω to be near, to draw near. 1
λεγομένη pres. pass. part. ■ ἐξήτουν impf. ζητέω to seek. The 2
impf. indicates continual action but not a special meeting of the
Sanhedrin (Arndt). ἐφοβοῦντο impf. mid. φοβέομαι to be
afraid, to fear. ■ εἰσῆλθεν aor. εἰσέρχομαι to go in, to come 3
in. ὄντα pres. part. εἰμί. ■ ἀπελθών aor. part. ἀπέρχομαι to 4

depart, to go away. συνελάλησεν aor. συλλαλέω to talk together, to confer. παραδῷ aor. subj. παραδίδωμι to hand over,
5 to deliver over. ■ ἐχάρησαν aor. χαίρω to rejoice, to be glad.
συνέθεντο aor. mid. συντίθεμι to make an agreement to-
6 gether. δοῦναι aor. inf. δίδωμι. ■ ἐξωμολόγησεν aor.
ἐξομολογέω to consent, to promise. εὐκαιρία opportunity,
convenient time. ἄτερ w. gen. without, apart from.
7   ■ ἦλθεν aor. ἔρχομαι. ἔδει impf. δεῖ it is necessary.
8 θύεσθαι pres. mid. inf. θύω to offer, to slay. ■ ἀπέστειλεν aor.
ἀποστέλλω to send. εἰπών aor. part. λέγω to say.
πορευθέντες aor. pass. part. πορεύομαι to go. ἑτοιμάσατε
aor. imp. ἑτοιμάζω to prepare, to make ready. φάγωμεν aor.
9 subj. ἐσθίω to eat. ■ ἑτοιμάσωμεν aor. subj., deliberative subj.
10 ■ εἰσελθόντων aor. part., s.v.3. gen. abs. συναντήσει fut.
συναντάω to meet. βαστάζων pres. part. βαστάζω to carry.
11 ἀκολουθήσατε aor. imp. ἀκολουθέω to follow. ■ ἐρεῖτε fut.
12 λέγω. ■ δείξει fut. δείκνυμι to show. ἀνάγαιον an upstairs
room. ἐστρωμένον perf. pass. part. στρώννυμι to spread out.
Here the term could indicate the floor consisting of tiles but
more likely it describes the room as furnished, supplied w. rugs
13 and couches (Arndt). ■ εὗρον aor. εὑρίσκω to find. εἰρήκει
plperf. λέγω to say. ἡτοίμασαν aor.
14   ἐγένετο aor. mid. γίνομαι to become, to be. ἀνέπεσεν
15 aor. ἀναπίπτω to recline (at the table), lit. to fall back. ■
ἐπιθυμία desire. ἐπεθύμησα aor. ἐπιθυμέω to desire, to long
for. (For the Hebraic construction w. the dat. of the verbal
substitutive w. the cognate verb as a translation of the Heb. inf.
abs., s. BD, 106.) φαγεῖν aor. inf. παθεῖν aor. inf. πάσχω to
16 suffer. ■ πληρωθῇ aor. pass. subj. πληρόω to fill, to fulfill.
17 ■ δεξάμενος aor. mid. part. δέχομαι to receive. The cup was
handed to Him (Plummer). εὐχαριστήσας aor. part.
εὐχαριστέω to bless, to give thanks. λάβετε aor. imp.
λαμβάνω to take. διαμερίσατε aor. imp. διαμερίζω to distrib-
18/19 ute. ■ πίω aor. subj. πίνω to drink. ἔλθῃ aor. subj. ■ λαβών aor.
part. ἔκλασεν aor. κλάω to break. ἔδωκεν aor. δίδωμι to give.
διδόμενον pres. pass. part. ποιεῖτε pres. imp. ποιέω to do.
20 ἀνάμνησις remembrance, memorial. ■ δειπνῆσαι aor. inf.
δειπνέω to dine, to eat a meal. Infinitive used w. prep. to express
time, "after" (s. MT, 143f.). διαθήκη covenant, will (s. Matt.
26:28). ἐκχυννόμενον pres. pass. part. ἐκχύννω to pull out, to
21 shed. ■ πλήν however. Here it seems to indicate a breakoff in
the thought and a transition to a different point (Thrall, 22; s.
also the detailed study of this word in Jerker Blomquist, *Greek*
22 *Particles in Hellenistic Prose*, 75–100). ■ ὡρισμένον perf. pass.

part. ὁρίζω to mark off the boundary, to determine. The perf.
indicates a state arising from a completed action in the past.
■ ἤρξαντο aor. mid. ἄρχομαι to begin. συζητεῖν pres. inf. 23
συζητέω to discuss w. εἴη pres. opt. εἰμί opt. of indirect speech,
a mark of culture (Arndt). μέλλων pres. part. μέλλω to be about
to. Used w. inf. to express fut. (s. MKG, 307).

■ φιλονεικία contentiousness, lit. love of strife, contention 24
(Arndt). μείζων comp. μέγας great. ■ ἐξουσιάζοντες pres. 25
part. ἐξουσιάζω to have authority over (w. gen.). καλοῦνται
pres. pass. ■ γινέσθω pres. mid. imp. 3rd sing. νεώτερος comp. 26
νέος young, the lowest in rank (Plummer). ἡγούμενος pres.
mid. part. ἡγέομαι to lead, to be the leader. διακονῶν pres.
part. διακονέω to serve, to minister. ■ ἀνακείμενος pres. mid. 27
part. ἀνάκειμαι to recline at the table. ■ διαμεμενηκότες perf. 28
part. διαμένω to remain throughout. The idea of persistent loyalty is enforced by the compound verb, the perf. tense, and the
prep. "who have perseveringly remained w. me and continue to
do so" (Plummer). ■ διατίθεμαι to decree, to ordain, to assign. 29
διέθετο aor. mid. ■ ἔσθητε pres. subj. ἐσθίω. πίνητε pres. subj. 30
καθήσεσθε fut. mid. κάθημαι to sit. κρίνοντες pres. part.
κρίνω to judge. The Passover celebrated two events, the deliverance from Egypt and the anticipated coming Messianic deliverance (Ellis).

■ ἐξητήσατο aor. mid. ἐξαιτέομαι to ask for, to demand. 31
The mid. voice indicates the personal interest of Satan (Arndt).
■ ἐδεήθην aor. pass. δέομαι to ask for, to pray, to voice a 32
petition based on a real need (Arndt). ἐκλίπῃ aor. subj.
ἐκλείπω to leave off, to fail utterly. The prep. compound is
perfective (MH, 309). ἐπιστρέψας aor. part. ἐπιστρέφω to
turn, to return. στήρισον aor. imp. στηρίζω to establish, to
support, to strengthen. ■ φωνήσει fut. φωνέω to make a sound, 34
to call. Here to crow. ἀπαρνήσῃ aor. subj. ἀπαρνέομαι to
deny. εἰδέναι inf. of the defective perf. w. a pres. meaning οἶδα
to know.

■ βαλλάντιον moneybag, purse. πήρα knapsack, wallet. 35
ὑστερήσατε aor. ὑστερέω to lack. ■ ἀράτω aor. imp. 3rd sing. 36
αἴρω to take up. πωλησάτω aor. imp. 3rd sing. πωλέω to sell.
ἀγορασάτω aor. imp. 3rd sing. ἀγοράζω to buy. ■ 37
γεγραμμένον perf. pass. part. γράφω to write. τελεσθῆναι
aor. pass. inf. τελέω to complete. The bringing to completion of
what one wills or what another wills (TDNT). ἐλογίσθη aor.
pass. λογίζομαι to count, to reckon, to consider, to class.

■ ἐξελθών aor. part. ἐξέρχομαι to go out. ἠκολούθησαν 39
aor. pass., s.v.10. ■ γενόμενος aor. mid. part., s.v.14. 40

προσεύχεσθε pres. mid. imp. προσεύχομαι to pray.
41 εἰσελθεῖν aor. inf., s.v.3. ■ ἀπεσπάσθη aor. pass. ἀποσπάω
to tear away, to withdraw. προσηύχετο impf. mid. The impf.
42 pictures repeated action. ■ εἰ "if." Introduces a conditional
clause which is considered to be true. παρένεγκε aor. imp.
παραφέρω to carry by, to remove. πλήν either a balancing
adversative particle, "nevertheless," or it introduces a condition,
"on the condition that" (Thrall, 69ff.; s. Luke 22:21). γινέσθω
43 pres. mid. imp. 3rd sing. ■ ὤφθη aor. pass. ὁράω to see, pass.
44 to appear. ἐνισχύων pres. part. ἐνισχύω to strengthen. ■
ἀγωνία conflict (an athletic conflict), struggle. ἐκτενέστερον
comp. ἐκτενής stretched fervently, earnestly. ἐγένετο aor. mid.
ἱδρώς sweat. θρόμβος thick clots. Used in medical language for
a clot of coagulated blood (MLL, 82f.). καταβαίνοντες pres.
45 part. καταβαίνω to go down, to fall down. ■ ἀναστάς aor.
part. ἀνίστημι to stand up. εὗρεν aor., s.v.13. κοιμωμένους
pres. mid. part. κοιμάομαι to sleep. λύπη sorrow, grief, anxie-
46 ty. ■ εἰσέλθητε aor. subj.
47   ■ λαλοῦντος pres. part. λαλέω to speak, gen. abs.
προήρχετο impf. mid. προέρχομαι to go before. φιλῆσαι aor.
48/49 inf. φιλέω to kiss. ■ παραδίδως pres. 2nd sing., s.v.4. ■ ἰδόντες
aor. part. ὁράω to see. ἐσόμενον fut. part. εἰμί "what was about
to happen." εἰ, normally used when indirect question here is due
to an ellipsis, "tell us whether we shall strike" (Arndt).
50 πατάξομεν fut. πατάσσω to strike (w. a sword). ■ ἐπάταξεν
aor. ἀφεῖλεν aor. ἀφαιρέω to take away, to cut off. οὖς ear.
51 ■ ἀποκριθείς aor. pass. part. ἀποχρίνομαι to answer. ἐᾶτε
impf. ἐάω to allow. ἀψάμενος aor. mid. part. ἅπτομαι to
52 touch. ὠτίον ear. ἰάσατο aor. mid. ἰάομαι to heal. ■
παραγενομένους aor. mid. part. παραγίνομαι to be present.
53 λῃστής robber. ἐξήλθατε aor. ξύλον wood, club. ■ ὄντος pres.
part. εἰμί gen. abs. ἐξετείνατε aor. ἐκτείνω to stretch out.
54   ■ συλλαβόντες aor. part. συλλαμβάνω to seize, to arrest.
ἤγαγον aor. ἄγω to lead. εἰσήγαγον aor. εἰσαγω to lead into.
ἠκολούθει impf., s.v.10. (For the references to the trial and
crucifixion of Christ, s. the parallel accounts in Matt. and Mark.)
55 ■ περιαψάντων aor. part. περιάπτω to kindle around, to make
a good fire that blazes all over (RWP). συγκαθισάντων aor.
part. συγκαθίζω to sit together, gen. abs. ἐκάθητο impf.,
56 s.v.30. ■ ἰδοῦσα aor. part. fem. sing., s.v.49. ἀτενίσασα aor.
57 part. fem. sing. ἀτενίζω to gaze at, to look steadily at. ■
ἠρνήσατο aor. ἀρνέομαι to say no, to deny. Two meanings are
implicit, to refuse to recognize and to abandon and deny solidarity w. someone (Ellis). οἶδα defective perf. w. a pres. meaning to

208

know. ■ βραχύς a little (after a little while). ἔφη impf. φημί to 58
say. ■ διαστάσης aor. part. διΐστημι. ὡσεί of time, to pass. 59
διϊσχυρίζετο impf. mid. διϊσχυρίζομαι to make one's self
strong, to make an emphatic declaration, to insist (s. RWP).
■ παραχρῆμα immediately. ἐφώνησεν aor., s.v.34. ἀλέκτωρ 60
rooster. ■ στραφείς aor. pass. part. στρέφομαι to turn, to turn 61
one's self. ἐνέβλεψεν aor. ἐμβλέπω to look at (w. dat.).
ὑπεμνήσθη aor. pass. ὑπομιμνήσκομαι to remember. πρίν
used w. inf. "before." φωνῆσαι aor. inf. ■ ἐξελθών aor. part. 62
ἔκλαυσεν aor. κλαίω to weep. πικρῶς adv. bitterly. (For a
comparison of this section w. Mark's account, s. Catchpole, *The
Trial of Jesus,* 160–174.)

■ συνέχοντες pres. part. συνέχω to hold together, to hold 63
in custody (BAG). ἐνέπαιζον impf. ἐμπαίζω to play a game w.,
to mock. δέροντες pres. part. δέρω to flay, to beat. ■ 64
περικαλύψαντες aor. part. περικαλύπτω to put a veil around,
to blindfold. ἐπηρώτων impf. ἐπερωτάω to question.
προφήτευσον aor. impf. προφητεύω to prophecy. παίσας
aor. part. παίω to strike. ■ βλασφημοῦντες pres. part. 65
βλασφημέω to slander, to blaspheme.

■ ἐγένετο aor. mid., s.v.14. συνήχθη aor. pass. συνάγω 66
to come together, to assemble. ἀπήγαγον aor. ἀπάγω to lead
away. ■ εἰπόν aor. imp. λέγω. εἴπω aor. subj. πιστεύσητε aor. 67
subj. πιστεύω to believe. ■ ἐρωτήσω aor. subj. ἐρωτάω to 68
question. ἀποκριθῆτε aor. pass. subj., s.v.51. ■ ἔσται fut. εἰμί. 69
καθήμενος pres. mid. part., s.v.56. ■ ἔφη impf., s.v.58. ■ 70/71
ἠκούσαμεν aor. ἀκούω to hear.

Ch. 23

■ ἀναστάν aor. part. ἀνίστημι to arise. ἤγαγον aor. ἄγω 1
to lead. ■ ἤρξαντο aor. mid. ἄρχομαι to begin. κατηγορεῖν 2
pres. inf. κατηγορέω to speak against someone, to accuse.
οὗτος "this one," used contemptuously. εὕρομεν aor. εὑρίσκω
to find. Indicates either "to catch in the act" or "to discover by
investigation" (Plummer). διαστρέφοντα aor. part.
διαστρέφω to turn this way and that, to distort, to pervert,
implying sedition (RWP). κωλύοντα pres. part. κωλύω to forbid. διδόναι pres. inf. δίδωμι to give, to pay. The accusation
brought against Jesus is presented by Luke as being purely political in content (Blinzler). ■ ἠρώτησεν aor. ἐρωτάω to question. 3
ἀποκριθείς aor. pass. part. ἀποκρίνομαι to answer (s. MH,
453). ἔφη, impf. φημί to say. ■ αἴτιος guilty. ■ ἐπίσχυον impf. 4/5
ἐπισχύω to grow strong, to insist. The prep. in compound indicates "to add up in strength" and the impf. indicates they kept

insisting (RWP). ἀνασείω to stir up, to incite. διδάσκων pres.
part. ἀρξάμενος aor. mid. part.

6 ■ ἀκούσας aor. part. ἀκούω. ἐπηρώτησεν aor.
7 ἐπερωτάω to question, to ask. ■ ἐπιγνούς aor. part.
ἐπιγινώσκω to know, to recognize. The prep. compound is
directive. It directs the verb's action upon some object (MH,
312). ἀνέπεμψεν aor. ἀναπέμπω to send, to send up. In this
case for judicial examination (Arndt). Pilate evidently sent Jesus
to Herod Antipas as a diplomatic move to try to please Herod.
He also felt that Herod would reach the same conclusion of
8 innocence in this awkward case (HA, 233–239). ■ ἰδών aor.
part. ὁράω to see. ἐχάρη aor. χαίρω to rejoice. λίαν very.
ἱκανός enough (long). θέλων pres. part. Participle used in a
periphrastic construction. ἰδεῖν aor. inf. ὁράω. ἤλπιζεν impf.
ἐλπίζω to hope. The periphrastic construction and the impf.
indicate the continuance of the wishing and hoping (Plummer).
9 ■ ἐπηρώτα impf. Pictures the repeated questioning.
10 ἀπεκρίνατο aor. mid. ■ εἱστήκεισαν plperf. ἵστημι to place,
perf. to stand. εὐτόνως adv. at full pitch, vigorously (HA, 240).
11 κατηγοροῦντες pres. part., s.v.2. ■ ἐξουθενήσας aor. part.
ἐξουθενέω to count as nothing, to treat w. contempt, to despise.
στράτευμα army. Here the pl. may indicate only a modest
detachment of soldiers, his bodyguard (HA, 241). ἐμπαίξας
aor. act. part. ἐμπαίζω to play a game w., to mock. περιβαλών
aor. part. περιβάλλω to throw about, to put on. ἐσθής robe.
λαμπρός bright. Such a robe was used of the candidate for an
office. Jesus was ridiculed and mocked as the candidate for the
kingship of the Jews (HA, 243). ἀνέπεμψεν aor., s.v.7. Here to
12 send back. ■ ἐγένοντο aor. mid. γίνομαι to become.
προϋπῆρχον impf. προϋπάρχω to be before, to exist previously (s. BD, 213). ἔχθρα enmity, hostility.
13 ■ σωψκαλεσάμενος aor. mid. part. συγκαλέω to call
together, to summons, "he called them together about himself"
14 (s. HA, 243). ■ προσηνέγκατε aor. προσφέρω to bring to.
ἀποστρέφοντα aor. part. ἀποστρέφω to turn someone away
from, to pervert, "to seduce the people from their allegiance"
(Plummer). ἀνακρίνας aor. part. ἀνακρίνω to examine, to ex-
15 amine judicially. εὗρον aor. κατηγορεῖτε pres. ■
πεπραγμένον perf. pass. part. πράσσω to do, to practice. The
16 perf. looks at the abiding results of an act which was done. ■
παιδεύσας aor. part. παιδεύω to teach, to admonish, "to give
him a lesson," either by beating or warning (Sherwin-White,
18 27f.). ἀπολύσω fut. ἀπολύω release. ■ ἀνέκραγον aor.
ἀνακράζω to cry out. παμπληθεί all together. αἶρε pres. imp.

αἴρω to take away. The pres. imp. is the emotional and impatient
command to become involved in the action of "taking away" (s.
Bakker, 82f.). ἀπόλυσον aor. imp., effective aor. draws attention to the terminating point, "release him quickly and decisive-
ly." ■ στάσις uprising, insurrection. γενομένην aor. mid. part. 19
φόνος murder. βληθείς aor. pass. part. βάλλω to throw. ■ 20
προσεψώνησεν aor. προσφωνέω to call to, to call out, to
address someone. ἀπολῦσαι aor. inf. ■ ἐπεφώνουν impf. 21
ἐπιφωνέω to call forth, to shout, to yell. The impf. pictures the
continuous action. σταύρου pres. imp. σταρόω to crucify. The
pres. imp. is full of emotion for the people are irritated even more
by the evasive answers of Pontius Pilate (Bakker, 83). ■ 22
ἐποίησεν aor. ποιέω. ■ ἐπέκειντο impf. mid. ἐπίκειμαι lit., 23
to lie upon, to press upon, to be urgent. The verb was used for
the rush and swirl of a tempest (RWP). αἰτούμενοι pres. mid.
part. αἰτέομαι to ask. σταυρωθῆναι aor. pass. inf. κατίσχυον
impf. κατισχύω to gain power over, to prevail. The prep. in
compound indicates an unfavorable action (MH, 316). ■ 24
ἐπέκρινεν aor. ἐπικρίνω to give a sentence, to pronounce a
legal decision, the final decision (Arndt). γενέσθαι aor. mid. inf.
■ ἀπέλυσεν aor. βεβλημένον perf. pass. part. βάλλω. 25
ἠτοῦντο impf. mid. παρέδωκεν aor. παραδίδωμι to deliver
over.
    ■ ἀπήγαγον aor. ἀπάγω to lead away. ἐπιλαβόμενοι 26
aor. mid. part. ἐπιλαμβάνομαι to seize, to lay hold upon (s.
Mark 15:21). ἐπέθηκαν aor. ἐπιτίθημι to place upon. ■ 27
ἠκολούθει impf. ἀκολουθέω to follow. ἐκόπτοντο impf. mid.
κόπτομαι to hit one's self on the chest as a sign of mourning.
ἐθρήνουν impf. θρηνέω to lament, to wail. ■ στραφείς aor. 28
pass. part. στρέφομαι to turn one's self, to turn. κλαίετε pres.
imp. κλαίω to weep, to cry. The pres. imp. w. the neg. indicates
the stopping of an action in progress. πλήν but. Used in an
adversative function (Thrall, 21, 68; s. Luke 22:21). ■ ἐροῦσιν 29
fut. λέγω. στεῖρα sterile. κοιλία stomach, womb. ἐγέννησαν
aor. γεννάω to bare, to give birth. μαστός breast. ἔθρεψαν aor.
τρέφω to nourish, to give nourishment. ■ ἄρξονται fut. mid., 30
s.v.2. πέσατε aor. imp. πίπτω to fall. βουνός hill. καλύψατε
aor. imp. καλύπτω to hide, to conceal. ■ ὑγρός moist. ξύλον 31
wood. ξηρός dry. The proverb perhaps from the carpentry
profession. The meaning is if an innocent person has to suffer so
severely, what will happen to those who are guilty? (Arndt).
γένηται aor. mid. subj., s.v.8.
    ■ ἤγοντο impf. pass., s.v.1. ἀναιρεθῆναι aor. pass. inf. 32
ἀναιρέω to take up, to take away, to put to death. ■ ἦλθον aor. 33

211

ἔρχομαι. καλούμενον pres. pass. part. καλέω to call, to name.
34 ἐσταύρωσαν aor., s.v.21. ■ ἄφες aor. imp. ἀφίημι to release,
to forgive. οἶδα defective perf. w. pres. meaning to know.
διαμεριζόμενοι pres. mid. part. διαμερίζομαι to divide up
35 into parts for one's self, to distribute. ἔβαλον aor., s.v.19. ■
εἱστήκει plperf., s.v.10. θεωρῶν pres. part. θεωρέω to watch.
ἐξεμυκτήριζον impf. ἐκμυκτηρίζω to turn up the nose at, to
mock (s. Luke 16:14). λέγοντες pres. part. ἔσωσεν aor. σῴζω
36 to rescue, to save. σωσάτω aor. imp. 3rd sing. ■ ἐνέπαιξαν
aor., s.v.11. προσερχόμενοι pres. mid. part. προσέρχομαι to
come to. ὄξος vinegar, a sour wine drink (s. Matt. 27:48).
37 προσφέροντες pres. part. προσφέρω to bring to. ■ σῶσον
38 aor. imp. ■ ἐπιγραφή inscription (s. Matt. 27:37).
39 　　　■ κρεμασθέντων aor. pass. part. κρέμαμαι to hang, mid.
to be hanging. ἐβλασφήμει impf. βλασφημέω to blaspheme,
to slander. οὐχί used in questions expecting the answer, yes. A
40 more bitter taunt than "if thou art" (Plummer). ■ ἐπιτιμῶν
pres. part. ἐπιτιμάω to rebuke. ἔφη s.v.3. φοβῇ pres. mid.
41 φοβέομαι to be afraid, to fear. ■ δικαίως adv. justly.
ἐπράξαμεν aor., s.v.15. ἄτοπος out of place, out of line, wrong.
42 ■ μνήσθητι aor. imp. μιμνήσκομαι to remember. A prayer
petition found on gravestones that one be remembered at the
resurrection (s. E.E. Ellis, "Present and Future Eschatology in
43 Luke," NTS, 12 [October, 1965], 36). ἔλθῃς aor. subj. ■
παράδεισος paradise, a Persian word meaning a park or enclosed garden, then used in Judaism as the abode of the redeemed between death and the resurrection (s. TDNT, SB, II,
264–269).
45 　　　■ ἐκλιπόντος aor. part. ἐκλείπω to fail, to leave out, to fail
utterly, gen. abs. ἐσχίσθη aor. pass. σχίζω to rip, to tear.
46 καταπέτασμα curtain, veil (s. Ellis; also Matt. 27:51). ■
φωνήσας aor. part. φωνέω to call, to cry out. παρατίθεμαι to
deposit w. another, to give him charge, to commit. ἐξέπνευσεν
47 aor. ἐκπνέω to breathe out, to expire, to die. ■ ἰδών aor. part.,
s.v.8. γενόμενον aor. mid. part. ἐδόξαζεν impf. δοξάζω to
48 glorify. ὄντως adv. truly, certainly. ■ συμπαραγενόμενοι aor.
mid. part. συμπαραγίνομαι to come together, to arrive along
w. θεωρία show, spectacle. θεωρήσαντες aor. part. τύπτοντες
pres. part. τύπτω to strike. στῆθος breast, chest. ὑπέστρεφον
49 impf. ὑποστρέφω to return. ■ συνακολουθοῦσαι pres. act.
part. fem. pl. συνακολουθέω to follow along w., to accompany.
ὁρῶσαι pres. act. part. fem. pl. ὁράω to see.
50 　　　■ βουλευτής council member. This marks Joseph as a
51 member of the Sanhedrin (Arndt). ■ προσεδέχετο impf. mid.

212

προσδέχομαι to wait for, to expect. ■ προσελθών aor. part. 52
προσέρχομαι s.v.36. ᾐτήσατο aor. mid. αἰτέομαι to ask, to
request. ■ καθελών aor. part. καθαιρέω to take down. 53
ἐνετύλιξεν aor. ἐντυλίσσω to wrap, to wrap in, to wrap up.
ἔθηκεν aor. τίθημι to place. λαξευτός to cut in the rock.
κείμενος perf. pres. pass. part. used as pass. of τίθημι to be laid,
to lie. ■ παρασκευή preparation. ἐπέφωσκεν impf. 54
ἐπιφώσκω to dawn, to give light. In a figurative way, to approach (Arndt), inceptive impf. "began to approach." ■ 55
κατακολουθήσασαι aor. act. part. fem. pl. κατακολουθέω to
follow after. The prep. compound describes following right over
an intervening space until the goal is reached (s. MH, 316).
συνεληλυθυῖαι perf. pass. part. fem. pl. συνέρχομαι to come
w., to accompany. Used in a periphrastic construction.
ἐθεάσαντο aor. mid. θεάομαι to see, to observe, to watch.
ἐτέθη aor. pass. τίθημι to place. ■ ὑποστρέψασαι aor. part. 56
fem. pl., s.v.48. ἡτοίμασαν aor. ἐτοιμάζω to prepare. ἄρωμα
spice, sweet-smelling herbs (Arndt). μύρον ointment (s. Luke
7:37).

ἡσύχασαν aor. ἡσυχάζω to rest.

Ch. 24

■ ὄρθρου βαθέως early, lit. at deep dawn, gen. of time 1
(RWP). ἦλθον aor. ἔρχομαι to come. φέρουσαι pres. part.
fem. pl. φέρω to bring, to carry. ἡτοίμασαν aor. ἐτοιμάζω to
prepare. ■ εὗρον aor. εὑρίσκω to find. ἀποκεκυλισμένον 2
perf. pass. part. ἀποκυλίω to roll away. ■ εἰσελθοῦσαι aor. 3
part. fem. pl. εἰσέρχομαι to go into. ■ ἐγένετο aor. mid. 4
γίνομαι (s. Luke 2:1; 8:1). ἀπορεῖσθαι pres. mid. inf. ἀπορέω
to be at a loss, to be perplexed. ἐπέστησαν aor. ἐφίστημι to
come upon suddenly or unexpected and stand by, to step up as
suddenly, to burst upon one (RWP). ἀστραπτούσῃ pres. part.
fem. dat. sing. ἀστράπτω to flash, lightening. ■ ἔμφοβος 5
afraid, frightened. γενομένων aor. mid. part. γίνομαι to
become, to be, gen. abs. κλινουσῶν pres. part. fem. gen. pl.
κλίνω to bend, to bow. ζητεῖτε pres. ζητέω to seek. ζῶντα pres.
part. ζάω to live, "the living one." ■ ἠγέρθη aor. pass. ἐγείρω 6
to raise, pass. to rise. μνήσθητε aor. pass. imp. μιμνήσκομαι
to remember. ἐλάλησεν aor. λαλέω to say, to speak. ■ δεῖ it 7
is necessary. παραδοθῆναι aor. pass. inf. παραδίδωμι to deliver over. σταυρωθῆναι aor. pass. inf. σταυρόω to crucify.
ἀναστῆναι aor. pass. inf. ἀνίστημι to stand up, to rise. ■ 8
ἐμνήσθησαν aor. pass. ■ ὑποστρέψασαι aor. act. part. fem. 9
pl. ὑποστρέφω to return. ἀπήγγειλαν aor. ἀπαγγέλλω to

11 report. ■ *ἐφάνησαν* aor. *φαίνομαι* to appear, to show one's
self. *λῆρος* idle talk, nonsense. Used in medical language of the
wild talk of the sick during delirium (MLL, 178). *ἠπίστουν*
impf. *ἀπιστέω* to disbelieve. The impf. pictures the continual
disbelief.

13 ■ *πορευόμενοι* pres. mid. part. *πορεύομαι* to go.
ἀπέχουσαν pres. part. fem. sing. *ἀπέχω* to be at a distance.
στάδιον stade. A measure of distance about 107 feet, 60 stade,
14 about seven miles (RWP). ■ *ὡμίλουν* impf. *ὁμιλέω* to talk w.,
to converse. *συμβεβηκότων* perf. part. *συμβαίνω* to happen,
15 to occur. ■ *συζητεῖν* pres. inf. *συζητέω* to investigate together,
to discuss. *αὐτός* himself, emphatic use (s. IBG, 121). *ἐγγίσας*
aor. part. *ἐγγίζω* to be near, to come near. *συνεπορεύετο* impf.
mid. *συμπορεύομαι* to go w., to travel w. The impf. pictures the
16 continual action. ■ *ἐκρατοῦντο* impf. pass. *κρατέω* to lay hold
of, to take possession, to hold, to restrain. They were blocked or
restrained by supernatural power (Ellis). *ἐπιγνῶναι* aor. inf.
17 *ἐπιγινώσκω* to know, to recognize. ■ *ἀντιβάλλω* pres. to
place or put against, to exchange words. (For the reciprocal
action indicated by the prep. compound. s. MH, 297.)
περιπατοῦντες pres. part. *περιπατέω* to walk. *ἐστάθησαν*
aor. pass. *ἵστημι* to stand. *σκυθρωπός* w. a sad, gloomy, or
18 sullen look. ■ *ἀποκριθείς* aor. pass. part. *ἀποκρίνομαι* to
answer. *παροικεῖς* pres. *παροικέω* to live as a stranger, to
inhabit or live in, "have you been living alone (all by yourself)?"
19 (s. RWP). *ἔγνως* aor. *γινώσκω* to know. ■ *ποῖος* what kind of?
20 what? *ἐγένετο* aor. mid. ■ *παρέδωκαν* aor., s.v.7.
21 *ἐσταύρωσαν* aor., s.v.7. ■ *ἠλπίζομεν* impf. *ἐλπίζω* to hope.
Imperfect used w. a verb of wishing. It indicates failure to realize
the desire or the perception that it cannot be realized (SMT, 15).
μέλλων pres. part. *μέλλω* to be about to. Used w. pres. inf. to
express durative fut. (MKG, 307). *λυτροῦσθαι* pres. mid. inf.
λυτρόω to redeem, to release by payment of a price, to fulfill the
obligation of the OT family protector (kinsman redeemer, goel;
s. TDNT; CBB; APC, 9–59). *ἀλλά γε καί* "moreover." The
second and third of these particles form a combination expressing a progressive idea reinforced by the one in the mid. for the
sake of emphasis (s. Thrall, 12–15). *ἄγει* used impersonal, "one
is keeping the third day" or personal, "he (that is, Jesus) now
22 passes the third day since" (s. Arndt). ■ *ἐξέστησαν* aor.
23 *ἐξίστημι* to amaze, to startle. *ὀρθρινός* early. ■ *εὑροῦσαι* aor.
act. part. fem. pl., s.v.2. *ἦλθον* aor., s.v.1. *ὀπτασία* appearance,
vision. *ἑωρακέναι* perf. act. inf. *ὁράω* to see. Infinitive used in
24 indirect discourse. *ζῆν* pres. inf., s.v.5. ■ *ἀπῆλθον* aor.

ἀπέρχομαι to go away. εἶδον aor. ὁράω. ■ ἀνόητος not under- 25
standing, unintelligent, foolish. βραδύς slow. πιστεύειν pres.
inf. used w. a prep. πιστεύω to believe on, to repose one's trust
upon, suggesting more of a state (ἐπί dat.; M, 68). ἐλάλησεν
aor., s.v.6. ■ ἔδει impf., s.v.7. παθεῖν aor. inf. πάσχω to suffer 26
(s. TDNT; for the suffering Messiah, s. SB, II, 273–299).
εἰσελθεῖν aor. inf., s.v.3. ■ ἀρξάμενος aor. mid. part. ἄρχομαι 27
to begin. διηρμήνευσεν aor. διερμηνεύω to interpret, to explain. The verb is used of interpreting a foreign language (Plummer).

■ ἤγγισαν aor. ἐπορεύοντο impf. mid. προσεποιήσατο 28
aor. mid. προσποιέω to act as though, to pretend. He would
have departed if they had not begged Him to remain (Plummer).
πορρώτερον comp. πόρρω forward, farther. ■ παρεβιάσαντο 29
aor. mid. παραβιάζομαι to use force to accomplish something,
to urge strongly, to prevail upon, effective aor., they successfully
constrained Him (Arndt). μεῖνον aor. imp. μένω to remain.
κέκλικεν perf. κλίνω to decline (used of the day), to approach
its end. εἰσῆλθεν aor. μεῖναι aor. inf., inf. of purpose. ■ 30
κατακλιθῆναι aor. pass. inf. κατακλίνομαι to sit down, to lie
down, to recline (by eating). Infinitive used w. prep. to express
time, "while" (s. MT, 145f.). λαβών aor. part. λαμβάνω to
take, to receive. εὐλόγησεν aor. εὐλογέω to bless, to give
thanks. κλάσας aor. part. κλάω to break. ἐπεδίδου impf.
ἐπιδίδωμι to give to, to distribute, inceptive impf. ■ 31
διηνοίχθησαν aor. pass. διανοίγω to open. ἐπέγνωσαν aor.
ἄφαντος invisible. ■ καιομένη pres. mid. part. καίομαι to 32
burn. Periphrastic construction emphasizing continuance of the
emotion (Plummer). ἐλάλει impf. διήνοιγεν impf. ■ 33
ἀναστάντες aor. part., s.v.7. ὑπέστρεψαν aor., s.v.9.
ἠθροισμένους perf. pass. part. ἀθροίζω to gather together, to
assemble. ■ ὄντως adv., truly, certainly. ἠγέρθη aor. pass., s.v.6. 34
ὤφθη aor. pass. ὁράω to see, pass., to appear. ■ ἐξηγοῦντο 35
impf. mid. ἐξηγέομαι to lead out, to rehearse, to explain.
ἐγνώσθη aor. pass. γινώσκω to know. κλάσις breaking.

■ λαλούντων pres. part. gen. abs. ἔστη aor. ἵστημι. ■ 36/37
πτοηθέντες aor. pass. part. πτοέω to terrify, pass. to be terrified, to be alarmed, to be frightened. ἐδόκουν impf. δοκέω to
suppose, to believe, to seem. θεωρεῖν pres. inf. θεωρέω to see,
to watch. ■ τεταραγμένοι perf. pass. part. ταράσσω to agi- 38
tate, to stir up, to shake up, to trouble, periphrastic construction.
διαλογισμός consideration, esp. doubt. ■ ἴδετε aor. imp. 39
ὁράω. ψηλαφήσατε aor. imp. ψηλαφάω to touch, to feel.
ὀστέον bone. ἔχοντα pres. part. ■ ἀπιστούντων pres. part., 41

gen. abs. θαυμαζόντων pres. part. θαυμάζω to wonder, to be
42 amazed. βρώσιμος eatable. ἐνθάδε here. ■ ἐπέδωκαν aor.
43 ἐπιδίδωμι. ὀπτός roasted, baked, broil. ■ ἔφαγεν aor. ἐσθίω
to eat.
44   ■ πληρωθῆνω aor. pass. inf. πληρόω to fill, to fulfill.
γεγραμμένα perf. pass. part. γράφω to write. ψαλμός psalm.
45 ■ διήνοιξεν aor. συνιέναι pres. inf. συνίημι to understand, to
46/47 comprehend. ■ γέγραπται perf. pass. ■ κηρυχθῆναι aor. pass.
49 inf. κηρύσσω to proclaim, to preach. ■ ἐξαποστέλλω to send
out, to send out as a personal authoritative representative
(TDNT; CBB). καθίσατε aor. imp. καθίζω to sit, to spend
some time in a place (Plummer). ἐνδύσησθε aor. pass. subj.
ἐνδύω to clothe, pass. to be clothed.
50   ■ ἐξήγαγεν aor. ἐξάγω to lead out. ἐπάρας aor. part.
51 ἐπαίρω to lift up. ■ ἐγένετο aor. mid., s.v.4. εὐλογεῖν pres. inf.
Infinitive used w. prep. to express contemporaneous time (s.
MT, 145). διέστη aor. διίστημι to set apart, to separate, to
52/53 part, to depart. ■ ὑπέστρεψαν aor., s.v.33. ■ εὐλογοῦντες pres.
part. (For the reason of the disciples' joy, s. Plummer.)

THE GOSPEL OF JOHN

(For a discussion of the authorship of this Gospel, s. Westcott IX–LXVII; Morris, *Studies* 139–292; Adolf Schlatter, "Die Sprache und Heimat des Vierten Evangelisten," *Johannes und Sein Evangelium*, K.H. Rengstorf [ed.] 28–201.)

ἀρχή beginning. Refers to the period before creation and 1 is more qualitative than temporal (Brown). ἦν impf. εἰμί. The impf. expresses continuous timeless existence (Bernard), and is contrasted w. ἐγένετο of v.3 (Barrett). πρός w. acc. "w. God," that is, accompaniment or "toward God," that is, relationship (Brown). θεός God. The word is without the article and is the predicate emphasizing quality, "the word had the same nature as God" (s. Phillip B. Harner, "Qualitative Anarthrous Predicate Nouns," JBL, 92 [March, 1973], 75–78). λόγος word. A description of Jesus basically from the OT Scriptures designating Him as the divine Revealer of God's wisdom and power (s. Brown; Morris; Hoskyns. S. further Bernard; Dodd; TDNT; CBB; Ladd, 237–242). ■ οὗτος this. It implies and emphasizes 2 the whole previous definition (Westcott). ■ ἐγένετο aor. mid. 3 γίνομαι to become. The creative activity is viewed as one event in contrast to the continuous existence in vv. 1 and 2 (RWP). χωρίς without, apart. It implies causality and presence (Brown). γέγονεν perf. (For the possible grammatical constructions, s. Brown; s. also 1QH 1:20; 1QS 3:15.) ■ ζωή life. The right and 4 power to bestow activity, to make alive. Here it points to one particular part of creation, to mankind (Lightfoot). φῶς light, that which enables men to recognize the operation of God in the world (Hoskyns). ■ σκοτία darkness. φαίνω pres. ind. act. to 5 shine, "the light keeps on giving light" (RWP). κατέλαβεν aor. καταλαμβάνω to seize, to grasp, to overcome, to grasp w. the mind, to understand. Perhaps John combined the two meanings, the darkness neither understood nor quenched the light (Barrett; for the importance of light and darkness in the DDS, s. 1QS; Morris, *Studies*, 324f.; Ladd, 234–236; J.H. Charlesworth, "A Critical Comparison of the Dualism in 1QS iii, 13–iv, 26 and the 'Dualism' contained in the Fourth Gospel," NTS 15 [July,

1969], 389–418).

6 ■ ἀπεσταλμένος perf. pass. part. ἀποστέλλω to send, to
commission, to send as an authoritative personal representative
(s. TDNT; CBB). The perf. indicates the permanent character of
his mission (Morris). παρά w. gen. from, from the side of. It
does not indicate the same close relation as in v. 1 (Morris).

7 ■ ἦλθεν aor. ἔρχομαι to come. μαρτυρήσῃ aor. subj.
μαρτυρέω to witness, to be a witness. Used to explain the previous, that is, the epexegetic use (Barrett). πιστεύσωσιν aor.

9 subj. to believe. ■ ἀληθινός real, genuine, authentic. The opposite is not necessarily false but impf., shadowy. Christ is the perf.
light in whose radiance all other lights seem dim (Bernard; s. also
Morris). φωτίζω pres. ind. to shed light upon, to bring light, to
instruct. Only He can make clear to every individual the meaning and purpose of his or her life (Lightfoot). The pres. indicates
the revelation is only in Him (Bultmann). ἐρχόμενον pres. mid.
part. refers either to each person born or to Christ as the light

10 who came into the world (s. Brown). ■ ἔγνω aor. γινώσκω to
know, to recognize, more than intellectual knowledge, rather "to

11 be in right relation" (Morris). ■ ἴδιος one's own, belonging to
one, personal. It describes the land and people of Israel as being
the home and family of God (Westcott). παρέλαβον aor.
παραλαμβάνω to receive, to take to one's side, common verb

12 to welcome (RWP). ■ ὅσος "as many as" introduces a casus
pendus (a dangling construction) which is resumed by the pronoun (s. Bernard; MH, 423ff.). ἔλαβον aor. λαμβάνω to receive. ἔδωκεν aor. δίδωμι to give. γενέσθαι aor. mid. inf.
γίνομαι to become. Men are not by nature the children of God,
only by receiving Christ do they gain the right to become the
children of God (Barrett). πιστεύουσιν pres. part. used w. the
following prep. εἰς; it indicates an active commitment to a person. It is the acceptance of Jesus and of what He claims to be
and a dedication of one's life to Him (Brown; s. also M, 67f.).

13 ■ αἵματα pl. "bloods." Perhaps the blood of father and mother.
This and the following phrases emphasize that no human agency
is or can be responsible for such a birth (Barrett). σάρξ flesh.
Here it is not the wicked principle opposed to God, rather the
severe of the natural, the powerless, and the superficial (Brown).
ἐγεννήθησαν aor. pass. γεννάω to give birth, to bear, pass. to
be born.

14 ■ σάρξ flesh. Here it stands for the whole man (Brown).
ἐγένετο aor. mid. The word came on the human scene—as flesh,
man (Barrett). ἐσκήνωσεν aor. σκηνόω to live in a tent, to
settle, ingressive aor. to take up one's temporary dwelling place

(Bernard). The flesh of Jesus Christ is the new localization of
God's presence on earth; Jesus is the replacement of the ancient
tabernacle (Brown). ἐθεασάμεθα aor. mid. θεάομαι to watch
as in a theater, to view, to see, to contemplate (s. Brown, 502).
To attribute to the word "behold" in such a context a purely
spiritual sense, is to set at nought the evidence (Godet). δόξα
glory, that which brings honor and praise to someone. Here the
manifestation of God's presence and power (Dodd, 207; s. also
TDNT). μονογενής only, unique (Morris; s. also John 3:16).
πλήρης full. χάρις grace. ἀλήθεια truth. These terms are based
on the OT concepts of grace and truth related to God's loyalty
and faithfulness to His covenant and covenant people (Barrett).
(For the OT background, s. Lester J. Kuyper, "Grace and Truth:
An Old Testament Description of God, and Its Use in the Johannine Gospel," Interpretation, 18 [January, 1964], 3–19; TDNT.)
■ μαρτυρεῖ pres., historical pres. κέκραγεν perf. ind. act. 15
κράζω to cry, to cry out. A technical rabbinic term for the loud
voice of prophet who intends to be heard (Hoskyns). The perf.
pictures the sounding effects of his voice (Bernard; but s. M,
147). ■ πλήρωμα fullness, that which is filled (in the pass. 16
sense) or that which fills (act. sense; s. Morris; TDNT). ἀντί
instead of, either the idea of replacement—the old covenant is
replaced by the new covenant (Brown)—or the idea of accumulation—the total life is of grace as it perceives one grace is
exchanged only for another (Barrett). ■ ἐδόθη aor. pass. δίδωμι. 17
■ ἑώρακεν perf. ὁράω to see. πώποτε ever, yet at any time. ὤν 18
pres. part. εἰμί to be. κόλπος bosom. A Heb. idiom expressing
the intimate relationship of child and parent, of friend and friend
(Tasker). ἐξηγήσατο aor. mid. ἐξηγέομαι to lead out, to explain, to rehearse facts, to recount a narrative. Often used for the
publishing or explaining of divine secrets (Barrett).

■ ἀπέστειλαν aor. ἀποστέλλω s.v.6. ἐρωτήσωσιν aor. 19
subj. ἐρωτάω to ask, to question. ■ ὡμολόγησεν aor. 20
ὁμολογέω to agree, to confess. ἠρνήσατο aor. mid. ἀρνέομαι
to deny. The first term marks the ready self-devotion of the
testimony, the second the completeness of it (Westcott). The
terms taken together indicate "he declared without any qualification, avowing" (Brown). ■ ἠρώτησαν aor. ἐρωτάω. 21
ἀπεκρίθη aor. pass. ἀποκρίνομαι to answer. ὁ προφήτης "the
prophet." The article refers to the known or promised prophet
intended by Deut. 18:15 (Meyer; s. also the study of background
material in Meeks; 1QS 9:11.) ■ δῶμεν aor. subj. used w. ἵνα to 22
express purpose. πέμψασιν aor. part. dat. pl. πέμπω to send.
■ ἔφη impf. φημί to say, to speak. βοῶντος pres. part. gen. sing. 23

βοάω to shout, to cry out. It describes the cry which answers to
strong feeling (Westcott). εὐθύνατε aor. imp. εὐθύνω straight-
24 en, to make straight. ■ ἀπεσταλμένοι perf. pass. part., s.v.6.
26 ■ ἀπεκρίθη aor. pass., s.v.21. στήκω to stand. οἴδατε perf. ind.
act. from the defective perf. οἶδα w. a pres. meaning to know.
(For a discussion of the meaning and its contrast to its synonym,
27 s. Brown, Appendix 1.) ■ ἵνα. Used here w. the adj. "worthy"
and the subj. where normally the inf. is used (s. RWP). αὐτοῦ
repeated after the rel. pron. and is best regarded as a Semitism
(Barrett). ἱμάς leather strap. ὑπόδημα sandal, shoe. The loosing and carrying of sandals was the duty of a slave, and a disciple
was exempt from this because of its menial character (s. Ber-
28 nard). ■ ἐγένετο aor. mid., s.v.3.
29 ■ ἐπαύριον adv., tomorrow, that is, on the following day.
The word "day" in the dat. (dat. of time) is understood (RWP).
ἴδε aor. imp. ὁράω to see, "behold." This favorite word of John
is no longer a real imp. but an exclamation (Morris). ἀμνός
lamb. Evidently a reference to the various uses of the lamb as a
sacrifice in the OT. All that these sacrifices foreshadowed was
perfectly fulfilled in the sacrifice of Christ (Morris). (For the
possible specific references of what was intended, s. Morris;
Brown.) αἴρων pres. part. αἴρω to lift up, to take away, to carry
off, to bear (s. TDNT). The pres. is the futuristic (Brown) or
timeless (Bultmann) or historical (Godet). ἁμαρτία sin. The
sing. refers to the mass of sin (Godet) and the guilt incurred (s.
30 Hoskyns). ■ γέγονεν perf., s.v.3. πρῶτος first, as a comp. it has
31 a temporal significance "before" (Brown). ■ ἤδειν plperf. οἶδα.
φανερωθῇ aor. pass. subj. φανερόω to manifest, to make clear,
32 to reveal. ἦλθον aor., s.v.7. ■ ἐμαρτύρησεν aor., s.v.7.
τεθέαμαι perf., s.v.14. The perf. emphasizes the continuing effects of the past action. καταβαῖνον pres. part. καταβαίνω to
come down. ὡς as. περιστερά dove. ἔμεινεν aor. μένω to
33 remain. ■ ἴδῃς aor. subj. ὁράω to see. μένον pres. part. neuter
sing. (For the idea of ritual cleansing with water and the cleans-
34 ing of the spirit, s. 1QS 3:7, 8; 4:21.) ■ ἑώρακα perf., s.v.18.
μεμαρτύρηκα perf. The perf. emphasizes that his testimony
was continuous up to the time of speaking (Bernard).
35/36 ■ εἱστήκει plperf. ἵστημι to stand. ■ ἐμβλέψας aor. part.
ἐμβλέπω to look at, signifies an intent, earnest gazing (Bernard). περιπατοῦντι pres. act. part. περιπατέω to walk. ἴδε
37 aor. imp. ὁράω s.v.29. ■ ἤκουσαν aor. ἀκούω to hear.
λαλοῦντος pres. part. (For John's use of this verb, s. Morris.)
ἠκολούθησαν aor. ἀκολουθέω to follow, to follow as a disciple
38 (s. TDNT). ■ στραφείς aor. pass. part. στρέφομαι to turn, to

turn around. θεασάμενος aor. mid. part., s.v.14. ραββί (Heb.)
rabbi, lit. "my great one," teacher (s. TDNT).
μεθερμηνευόμενον pres. pass. part. μεθερμηνεύω to translate,
to interpret. ■ ἔρχεσθε pres. mid. imp., s.v.7. ὄψεσθε fut. mid. 39
ὁράω to see. (For the imp. followed by καί and the fut. as a
Semitic type of conditional sentence, s. K. Beyer, Semitische
Syntax im Neuen Testament, 238–258.) ἦλθαν aor., s.v.7. εἶδαν
aor. ὁράω. ■ ἀκουσάντων aor. act. part. ἀκολουθησάντων 40
aor. act. part. ■ πρῶτον first, taken either as an adj. that is, he 41
found his own brother first and later found someone else, or as
an adv. the first thing he did was to find his brother (Tasker).
εὑρήκαμεν perf. ind. act. εὑρίσκω to find. χριστός the anointed, Messiah, Christ (s. CBB; TDNT). ■ ἤγαγεν aor. ἄγω to 42
lead. κληθήσῃ fut. pass. καλέω, to call. ἑρμηνεύεται pres.
pass., to translate, to interpret.

      ■ ἠθέλησεν aor. θέλω to will, to want. The aor. indicates 43
"he resolved" and the subject is probably Jesus (Morris).
ἐξελθεῖν aor. inf. ἐξέρχομαι to go out. ἀκολούθει pres. imp.,
s.v.37. ■ ἔγραψεν aor. γράφω to write. The prominent position 45
of the verb may indicate that Philip and Nathanael had previously discussed the fulfillment of these Scriptures (Morris). ■ τι 46
ἀγαθόν "anything good." A scornful question (Barrett). ἔρχου
pres. imp. ■ ἀληθῶς truly. δόλος deceit, cunning, treachery. It 47
indicates his religious and moral integrity (Lindars). ■ πόθεν 48
where. ἀπεκρίθη aor. pass., s.v.21. φωνῆσαι aor. inf. φωνέω
to call. Infinitive used w. a prep. to express time, "before" (s.
MT, 144). ὄντα pres. part. εἰμί to be. συκῇ fig tree. The rabbis
often sat under a fig tree for study or for teaching (Bultmann).
■ ὑποκάτω w. gen. under. μείζω neuter comp. μέγας great. 50
τούτων gen. of comparison. ὄψῃ fut. ὁράω to see. ■ ἀνεῳγότα 51
perf. act. part. ἀνοίγω to open. The perf. indicates the completed state "to be opened." A reference to Jacob's vision in
Gen. 28:10ff. (s. Bernard). ἀναβαίνοντας pres. part.
ἀναβαίνω to go up. καταβαίνοντας s.v.32. The thought is that
the Son of man is the means of bridging the gap between earth
and heaven (Morris).

                                                                        Ch. 2

      ■ γάμος wedding. (For the Jewish custom regarding wed- 1
dings, s. SB, II, 372–399; IDB, III, 285f.; LNT, 228–246.)
ἐγένετο aor. mid. γίνομαι to become, to be. ■ ἐκλήθη aor. 2
pass. καλέω to call, to invite. (For the moral obligation of the
guests to bring gifts and the duty of reciprocation, s. LNT, 229–
234.) ■ ὑστερήσαντος aor. act. part. ὑστερέω to fall short, to 3

4 run short, to fail, gen. abs. ■ τί ἐμοὶ καὶ σοί "what is it to Me and to you?" "You have no right to blame Me. The problem is taken care of." It is an answer of remonstrance putting off an impatient urging (s. LNT, 238–243). γύναι woman, vocative not disrespectful but a certain disassociation is pres. (Schnackenburg). ὥρα hour, "I shall choose the appropriate moment," referring to His intention to provide the needed wine (s. LNT,
5 242). ■ ὅ τι ἄν "whatever." λέγῃ pres. subj. ποιήσατε aor. imp.
6 ■ λίθινος stone. Adjectives w. this ending generally signify material, origin, or kind (MH, 359). Stone was used because it did not itself contract uncleanness (Barrett). ὑδρία waterpot. κείμεναι pres. mid. part. κεῖμαι to lie, of vessels to stand. χωροῦσαι pres. act. part. χωρέω to have room for, to contain. ἀνά each, prep. used in a distributive sense. μετρητής measure,
7 a liquid measure about nine gallons (BAG). ■ γεμίσατε aor. imp. γεμίζω to fill, to fill w. (w. gen.). ἄνω "up to the brim." There was no room left for adding anything to the water in the
8 jars (Bernard). ■ ἀντλήσατε aor. imp. ἀντλέω to draw, to draw out. Often used of drawing water from a well but here from a water jar (Brown). φέρετε pres. imp. φέρω to carry. ἀρχιτρίκλινος superintendent of a banquet whose duty it was
9 to arrange the tables and food (AS). ἤνεγκαν aor. φέρω. ■ ἐγεύσατο aor. mid. γεύομαι to taste. γεγενημένον perf. mid. part. γίνομαι to become. The perf. emphasizes the state or condition arising from a past completed action. ᾔδει plperf. οἶδα to know. πόθεν where, from where. ἠντληκότες perf. act. part.
10 ἀντλέω. φωνέω to call, to call out. νυμφίος groom. ■ μεθυσθῶσιν aor. pass. subj. μεθύσκω pass. to become drunk, to be drunk. His words do not imply that the guests were already drunk (Sanders). ἐλάσσω comp. masc. μικρός lesser, inferior. τετήρηκας perf. τηρέω to guard, to keep back, to preserve.
11 ■ ἐποίησεν aor. ποιέω to do. ἀρχή beginning. σημεῖον sign, an act or miracle w. a meaning designed to lead to belief in Jesus as the Messiah, the Son of God (s. Schnackenburg; Brown; TDNT). ἐφανέρωσεν aor. φανερόω to manifest, to make visible, to make clear. His Messianic glory was manifested in the abundance of wine which was the OT figure for joy of the final days (Brown). ἐπίστευσαν aor. πιστεύω to believe in, to trust
12 in. ■ κατέβη aor. καταβαίνω to go down. ἔμειψαν aor. μένω to remain.
13/14   ■ πάσχα passover. ἀνέβη aor. ἀναβαίνω to go up. ■ εὗρεν aor. εὑρίσκω to find. πωλοῦντας pres. part. πωλέω to sell. βοῦς ox. πρόβατον sheep. περιστερά pigeon. κερματιστής moneychanger, properly one who exchanges

222

large money into small (Morris). καθημένους pres. mid. part.
κάθημαι to sit. ■ ποιήσας aor. act. part. φραγέλλιον whip. 15
No sticks or weapons were allowed in the temple precinct
(Brown). σχοινίον cord, probably of twisted rushes (Westcott).
ἐξέβαλεν aor. ἐκβαλλω to cast out, to drive out. κολλυβιστής
moneychanger. ἐξέχεεν aor. act. ind. ἐκχέω to pour out. (For
the form, s. MH, 215, 265.) κέρμα small coin. τράπεζα table.
ἀνέτρεψεν aor. ἀνατρέπω to turn over. ■ ἄρατε aor. imp. 16
αἴρω to lift up, to take away. ποιεῖτε pres. imp. used w. a neg.
to prohibit an action in progress. ἐμπόριον a place of trade, a
house of merchandise, gen. of apposition (s. Barrett). ■ 17
ἐμνήσθησαν aor. pass. μιμνήσκομαι to remember.
γεγραμμένον perf. pass. part. γράφω to write. ζῆλος zeal followed by the obj. gen. "zeal for thine house" (Tasker).
καταφάγεται fut. mid. κατεσθίω to eat up, to consume. ■ 18
ἀπεκρίθησαν aor. pass. ἀποκρίνομαι to answer. οὖν "in response." (For the responsive use of the particle, s. DM, 254.)
σημεῖον sign, s.v.11 (s. also Morris, 684–691; Peter Riga, "Signs
of Glory: The Use of 'Semeion' in St. John's Gospel," Interpretation 17 [October, 1963], 402–424). ποιεῖς pres. ind. act. ■ 19
λύσατε aor. imp. λύω to loose, to destroy. It is a permissive imp.
not a command (RWP). ἐγερῶ fut. ἐγείρω to raise up. (For the
imp. followed by the fut., s. John 1:39.) ■ οἰκοδομήθη aor. pass. 20
οἰκοδομέω to build, to erect, complexive aor. summing up the
whole process of building which is not yet completed (it was
completed in A.D. 63) (Brown; s. also H.W. Hoehner,"Chronological Aspects of the Life of Christ," Bib Sac 131 [Jan., 1974],
49–52; for DSS instructions concerning temple building, s. Yiga-
el Yadin, "The Temple Scroll," BA 30 [Dec., 1967], 137–139).
■ ἠγέρθη aor. pass. ἐγείρω.   22
    ■ θεωροῦντες pres. part. θεωρέω to see. ἐποίει impf. 23
ποιέω. ■ ἐπίστευεν impf. to trust, to entrust one's self. ■ 24/25
μαρτυρήσῃ aor. subj. μαρτυρέω to witness, to give witness.
ἐγίνωσκεν impf.

Ch. 3

    ■ ἄνθρωπος man, "a man of the Pharisees." An unusual 1
expression probably linking this to the closing of the previous
chapter so to bring out Jesus' knowledge of man (Morris).
ἄρχων leader. ■ ἦλθεν aor. ἔρχομαι to come. οἶδα defective 2
perf. w. a pres. meaning to know. ἐλήλυθας perf. ἔρχομαι.
σημεῖον sign (s. John 2:11, 18). ᾖ pres. subj. εἰμί. ■ ἀπεκρίθη 3
aor. pass. ἀποκρίνομαι to answer. γεννηθῇ aor. pass. subj.
γεννάω. The pass. can either mean "to be born" or "to be

begotten" (s. Brown). ἄνωθεν "from above," the heavenly world
from whose power a man must be renewed (Schnackenburg),
"again," "anew." The translation "reborn from above" includes
both meanings of the word (Morris). ἰδεῖν aor. inf. ὁράω to see.
4 Here "to experience, encounter, participate in" (Brown). ■
γέρων old. ὤν pres. part. εἰμί. κοιλία stomach, womb.
δεύτερον second, a second time. εἰσελθεῖν aor. inf.
6 εἰσέρχομαι to go into. ■ γεγεννημένον perf. pass. part.
γεννάω. The perf. tense conveys that which has been born and
7 at pres. comes before us in this light (Westcott). ■ θαυμάσῃς
aor. subj. θαυμάζω to wonder, to marvel. δεῖ it is necessary (w.
8 inf.). ■ πνεῦμα wind. πνεῖ pres. act. πνέω to blow. The gnomic
use of the pres. (s. IBG, 8). πόθεν where, from what place. ποῦ
9/10 where, to what place. ■ γενέσθαι aor. mid. inf. γίνομαι. ■ ὁ
διδάσκαλος the teacher. The article emphasizes the status of
11 Nicodemus as a great teacher (Barrett). ■ ἐπίγειος earthly.
12 ■ εἴπω aor. subj. ἐπουράνιος heavenly. (For the terms earthly
13 and heavenly, s. Schnackenburg.) ■ ἀναβέβηκεν perf.
ἀναβαίνω to go up, to ascend. The perf. indicates "no man has
gained the heights of heaven" (Morris). εἰ μή except. καταβάς
14 aor. act. part. καταβαίνω to descend, to come down. ■ ὕψωσεν
aor. ὑψόω to lift up, to make high. ὄφις snake. ὑψωθῆναι aor.
15 pass. inf. ■ πιστεύων pres. act. part. ἔχῃ pres. subj. Subjunctive
used w. ἵνα to express purpose. αἰώνιος eternal. Eternal life is
the life of the age to come which is gained by faith, cannot be
destroyed, and is a pres. possession of the one who believes (s.
GW, 192–201; Brown, 505–508; Dodd, 144–150).
16   ■ ἠγάπησεν aor. ἀγαπάω to love (s. TDNT; James Moffatt, Love in the New Testament; Brown, 497ff.). μονογενής
unique, only one of its kind (s. TDNT). ἔδωκεν aor. ind. δίδωμι
to give. ἀπόληται aor. mid. subj. ἀπόλλυμαι to destroy, to
17 perish (s. TDNT). ■ ἀπέστειλεν aor. ἀποστέλλω to send, to
send as an authoritative representative. κρίνῃ aor. subj. κρίνω
to decide, to judge, to condemn as the contrast w. "to be saved"
18 (Morris). σωθῇ aor. pass. subj. σῴζω to rescue, to save. ■
κρίνεται pres. pass. κέκριται perf. pass. The perf. indicates he
has entered into a continuing state of condemnation because he
has refused to enter a continuing state of belief (Morris).
19 πεπίστευκεν perf. πιστεύω to believe. ■ κρίσις judgment.
Here the process of judging, not the sentence of condemnation
(Morris). Men are judged by the work and person of Jesus (Barrett). φῶς light. The revelation brings to light what man truly is
20 (TDNT). ■ φαῦλος bad, foul, worthless. πράσσων pres. part.
πράσσω to do. ἐλεγχθῇ aor. pass. subj. ἐλέγχω properly sift-

ed, tried, tested, and then, if need be, convicted, to show how
faulty they are and to reprove (Westcott). ■ ποιῶν pres. part. 21
(For the construction "doing the truth" in DSS, s. 1QS 1:5; 5:3;
8:2.) φανερωθῇ aor. pass. subj. φανερόω to manifest, to bring
to light. εἰργασμένα perf. pass. part. ἐργάζομαι to work, to
produce by work. The perf. may point to the permanence of such
works (Morris).

■ ἦλθεν aor., s.v.2. διέτριβεν impf. διατρίβω to remain, 22
to spend some time. ἐβάπτιζεν impf. βαπτίζω to baptize. The
impf. points to the repeated action. ■ βαπτίζων pres. part. 23
παρεγίνοντο impf. mid. παραγίνομαι to come on the scene,
to appear, to come. Imperfect indicates "they kept on coming."
ἐβαπτίζοντο impf. pass. ■ βεβλημένος perf. pass. part. βάλλω 24
to throw, to cast. Participle used in a periphrastic construction.
■ ἐγένετο aor. mid. γίνομαι to become, to arise. οὖν "now" (s. 25
DM, 254). ζήτησις questioning, controversy. ἐκ from. The dispute arose from, originated w., the disciples of John (Barrett).
καθαρισμός cleansing, purification. ■ μεμαρτύρηκας perf. 26
s.v.11. ἴδε aor. imp. ὁράω to see. ■ ἀπεκρίθη aor. pass., s.v.3. 27
ᾖ subj. εἰμί. δεδομένον perf. pass. part. δίδωμι to give. Participle used in a periphrastic construction to express the perf. subj.
■ ἀπεσταλμένος perf. pass. part., s.v.17. ἔμπροσθεν before. 28
■ ἔχων pres. part. νύμφη bride. νυμφίος bridegroom. φίλος 29
τοῦ νυμφίου "the friend of the groom." The groom's closest
friend who takes care of arranging the wedding (Brown; Jastrow
II, 1543). ἑστηκώς perf. part. ἵστημι, perf. to stand.
πεπλήρωται perf. pass. πληρόω to fill, to fulfill. ■ αὐξάνω to 30
grow, to increase. ἐλαττοῦσθαι pres. pass. inf. ἐλαττόω to
make less, inferior, to decrease. ■ ἄνωθεν s.v.3. ἐπάνω w. gen. 31
above. ὤν s.v.4. ■ ἑώρακεν perf., s.v.11. ἤκουσεν aor. ἀκούω 32
to hear. ■ λαβών aor. part. λαμβάνω to take, to receive. 33
ἐσφράγισεν aor. σφραγίζω to seal, to certify, to acknowledge
as a seal does on a document (BAG; CMM). ■ ἀπέστειλεν aor., 34
s.v.17. ῥῆμα word, that which is spoken. μέτρον measure. The
Father gives the Spirit to the Son without measure (Morris).
■ δέδωκεν perf. δίδωμι to give. ■ πιστεύων pres. part. 35/36
ἀπειθῶν pres. part. ἀπειθέω to be disobedient. Disbelief is
regarded in its activity (Westcott). ὄψεται fut. mid. ὁράω to see.
It means to participate in God's kingdom (Lindars).

Ch. 4

■ οὖν when, now, indicates a succession of either time or 1
events (DM, 253). ἔγνω aor. γινώσκω. ἤκουσαν aor. ἀκούω
to hear. πλείονας comp. πολύς "more." ■ καίτοι γε although 2

(s. BD, 234; Thrall, 37; Jerker Blomquist, *Greek Particles in Hellenistic Prose*, 35–45). ἐβάπτιζεν impf. emphasizing the re-
3 peated act. ■ ἀφῆκεν aor. ἀφίημι to leave. ἀπῆλθεν aor.
4 ἀπέρχομαι to go out, to leave. ■ ἔδει impf. δεῖ it is necessary, to have to, not geographical necessity but means that God's will
5 or plan is involved (Brown). διέρχομαι to pass through. ■ λεγομένην pres. pass. part. πλησίον w. gen. near to, near.
6 χωρίον piece of land, parcel. ἔδωκεν aor. δίδωμι to give. ■ πηγή well, spring. κεκοπιακώς perf. part. κοπιάω to labor, to grow weary from work. The perf. emphasizes the state of weariness. ὁδοιπορία walking, journey. ἐκαθέζετο impf. mid. καθέζομαι to sit, to be sitting. οὕτως thus, so, either modifying the verb "he sat right down" or the part. "tired as he was" (Brown). ἐπί w. dat. upon, "upon the curbstone of the well" (RWP). ὡς w. numbers "about," that is about noon, the natural time to rest while the sun was at its height (Bernard).
7   ■ ἀντλῆσαι aor. inf. ἀντλέω to draw. Infinitive used to express purpose. δός aor. imp. δίδωμι. πεῖν aor. inf. πίνω to
8 drink. ■ ἀπεληλύθεισαν plperf. ἀπέρχομαι. ἀγοράσωσιν
9 aor. subj. ἀγοράζω to buy, to buy at the marketplace. ■ ὤν pres. part. εἰμί. οὔσης fem. part. εἰμί. συγχράομαι to have dealings w., to use together w.; that is, Jews do not use vessels w. the Samaritans for fear of becoming unclean (s. Barrett; Morris; M,
10 Niddah IV, 1). ■ ἀπεκρίθη aor. pass. ἀποκρίνομαι to answer. ἤδεις plperf. of the defective perf. οἶδα to know. δωρεά gift. ἤτησας aor. αἰτέω to ask. ζῶν pres. part. ζάω to live, "living water"; that is, fresh, flowing water; but also water creating and maintaining life (Barrett; for the expression in DSS, s. CD 19:34.
11 There it means the law which is a "well of living water.") ■ ἄντλημα bucket for drawing water. φρέαρ well. βαθύς deep.
12 ■ μείζων comp. μέγας great, greater. πατρός gen. of compari-
13 son. ἔπιεν aor. πίνω. θρέμμα cattle. ■ πίνων pres. part.
14 διψήσει fut. διψάω to thirst, to be thirsty. ■ πίῃ aor. subj. δώσω fut. δίδωμι to give. γενήσεται fut. mid. γίνομαι. ἁλλομένου pres. mid. part. ἅλλομαι spring up, leap. Used of
15 quick movement by living beings like jumping (Brown). ■ διψῶ pres. subj. διέρχωμαι pres. mid. subj.
16   ■ ὕπαγε pres. imp. go. The pres. imp. often is used to express an order involving motion (Bakker, 82). φώνησον aor.
18 imp. φωνέω to call. ἐλθέ aor. imp. ἔρχομαι. ■ ἔσχες aor. ἔχω to have. According to rabbinical teaching, a woman was to be married only twice or at the most three times (SB, II, 437). ἀληθής truly, "this is a true thing" (RWP). εἴρηκας perf. λέγω.
20 ■ προσεκύνησαν aor. προσκυνέω to worship. δεῖ it is neces-

226

sary. ■ πίστευε pres. imp. προσκυνήσετε fut. ■ σωτηρία 21/22
deliverance, salvation (s. TDNT). ■ ἀληθινός true, genuine. 23
προσκυνητής worshiper. τοιοῦτος such, of such a kind.
προσκυνοῦντας pres. act. part. ■ πνεῦμα spirit. The predicate 24
without the article emphasizes the character and nature (s. John
1:1). ■ ἔλθῃ aor. subj. ἔρχομαι. ἀναγγελεῖ fut. ἀναγγέλλω 25
to announce. The word is used of the fresh and authoritative
message of the advocate, 16:13ff. (Westcott). The Messiah is the
supernatural person who will declare divine truth to men (Barrett). ■ λαλῶν pres. part.   26

■ ἐθαύμαζον impf. θαυμάζω to be astonished, to marvel. 27
It denotes incredulous surprise (MM). The surprise arises because He was talking to a woman. This was held to be improper
esp. for a rabbi (s. M, Aboth 1, 5; Moore, *Judaism*, II, 269f.).
ἐλάλει impf. λαλέω. μέντοι really, actually. ■ δεῦτε adv. serv- 29
ing as hortatory particle "come! come on!" (BAG). ἴδετε aor.
imp. ὁράω to see. ἐποίησα aor. ποιέω. μήτι not necessarily
expecting a neg. answer but rather a cautious opinion (s.
Schnackenburg). ■ ἐξῆλθον aor. ἐξέρχομαι to go out. ἤρχοντο 30
impf. mid. The impf. pictures the long procession as they ap-
proached Jesus (RWP).

■ ἐν τῷ μεταξύ "in the meanwhile"; that is, before the 31
Samaritan villagers arrived (Bernard). ἠρώτων impf. ἐρωτάω to
question, to ask. φάγε aor. imp. ἐσθίω to eat. ■ βρῶσις food, 32
properly the process of eating but here synonymous w. food
(Barrett). φαγεῖν aor. inf. ■ μή used in questions expecting an 33
answer no. ἤνεγκεν aor. φέρω to carry, to bring. ■ βρῶμα food. 34
ἵνα does not express purpose but rather introduces a noun clause
used as subject or predicate nominative (s. M, 208). πέμψαντος
aor. act. part. πέμπω to send. τελειώσω aor. subj. to accomplish, to finish, to bring to consummation, to complete, to bring
to completion that work which was begun by the Father
(Schnackenburg). ■ τετράμηνος the fourth month. θερισμός 35
harvest. Between the end of sowing and the beginning of harvest
four months intervened (Barrett; s. also "The Gezer Calendar,"
ANET, 320). ἐπάρατε aor. imp. ἐπαίρω to lift up. θεάσασθε
aor. mid. imp. θεάομαι to look at, to contemplate (s. John 1:14).
χώρα field. λευκός white. Perhaps referring to the people in
their white clothes (s. Morris). ■ θερίζων pres. part. θερίζω to 36
harvest. μισθός reward, recompense. σπείρων pres. part.
σπείρω to sow. ὁμοῦ together. χαίρῃ pres. subj. ■ ἐν τούτῳ 37
"in this." It may refer to the previous (v.36) but more probably
to the following (v.38) (Barrett). ■ ἀπέστειλα aor. 38
ἀποστέλλω to send, to send as an official and authoritative

representative. κεκοπιάκατε perf. ind. act., s.v.6. κόπος work,
labor. εἰσεληλύθατε perf. εἰσέρχομαι to go into, to enter into.
39 ■ ἐπίστευσαν aor. μαρτυρούσης pres. act. part. fem. gen.
40 sing. μαρτυρέω to give witness, to testify. ■ ἠρώτων impf., to
ask, to request. μεῖναι aor. inf. μένω to remain. ἔμεινεν aor.
42 ■ λαλιά speech. Not in the sense of gossip but as human and
outward speech about something (Schnackenburg). ἀκηκόαμεν
perf. act. ἀκούω. ἀληθῶς truly. σωτήρ savior. The term "savior
of the world" often was used of the Roman emperor (s. LAE,
364f.; TDNT).
43/44/45   ■ ἐξῆλθεν aor., s.v.30. ■ ἐμαρτύρησεν aor., s.v.39. ■ οὖν
"then," "therefore" (s. DM, 253f.). ἦλθεν aor. ἔρχομαι to go,
to come. ἐδέξαντο aor. mid. δέχομαι to receive, to welcome.
ἑωρακότες perf. act. part. ὁράω. ἐποίησεν aor.
46   ■ βασιλικός belonging to the king, royal officer. Either a
person of royal blood or a servant of the king (Brown). ἠσθένει
47 impf. ἀσθενέω to be sick. ■ ἀκούσας aor. act. part. ἀπῆλθεν
aor., s.v.3. ἠρώτα s.v.31. καταβῇ aor. subj. καταβαίνω to go
down, to descend. ἰάσηται aor. mid. subj. ἰάομαι to heal.
ἤμελλεν impf. μέλλω to be about to, "was going to die," "was
at the point of death." (For the use of the inf. to express futurity
48 reckoned from a moment in the past, MKG, 307.) ■ σημεῖον
sign (s. John 2:11). τέρας wonder. Directs attention to the
miraculous but in the NT not used alone (Morris). ἴδητε aor.
subj. ὁράω to see. His faith required the support of sight (Westcott). πιστεύσητε aor. subj. The pl. indicates the individual was
49 representative of a whole class (Bernard). ■ κατάβηθι aor. imp.
καταβαίνω. πρίν used w. inf. in a temporary sense "before."
50 ἀποθανεῖν aor. act. inf. ἀποθνήσκω. ■ πορεύου pres. imp.
2nd sing. πορεύομαι to travel, to go. ζῇ pres. ind. ζάω to live,
Semitic, covering both recovery from illness and return to life
from death (Brown). ἐπίστευσεν aor. ἐπορεύετο impf. mid.
51 ■ καταβαίνοντος pres. act. part. gen. abs. ὑπήντησαν aor.
52 ὑπαντάω to meet. ■ ἐπύθετο aor. mid. πυνθάνομαι to inquire.
κομψότερον adv. comp. of κομψός nicely. ἔσχεν aor. ἔχω to
have. Used w. the preceding adv. meaning "to be well," w. the
ingressive aor. "to get better" (Barrett). ἐχθές yesterday. (For
53 the reckoning of time, s. Morris.) ἀφῆκεν aor., s.v.3. ■ ἔγνω
54 aor., s.v.1. ■ παλιν δεύτερον "again, the second sign." The
term "again" is pleonastic (Brown).

Ch. 5
1/2   ■ ἀνέβη aor. ἀναβαίνω to go up. ■ ἔστιν pres., historical
pres. (Schnackenburg). προβατική having to do w. sheep.

Either sheep gate or sheep pool (s. Morris; Barrett).
κολυμβήθρα diving pool, swimming pool, pool. (For the identification as the pool of St. Anne, s. Morris; Schnackenburg.)
ἐπιλεγομένη pres. pass. part. ἐπιλέγω to name, to be named.
■ κατέκειτο impf. κατάκειμαι to lie, customary impf. "a multi- 3
tude used to lie." ἀσθενούντων pres. part. ἀσθενέω to be
weak, to be sick. χωλός lame. ξηρός dry, withered, disabled w.
atrophied limbs (Brown). ■ ἀσθένεια weakness, sickness. ■ 5/6
ἰδών aor. part. ὁράω to see. κατακείμενον pres. mid. part.
γνούς aor. part. γινώσκω to know. ὑγιής whole, well.
γενέσθαι aor. mid. inf. γίνομαι to become. ■ ἀπεκρίθη aor. 7
pass. ἀποκρίνομαι to answer. ἀσθενῶν pres. part. ταραχθῇ
aor. pass. subj. ταράσσω to stir up, to trouble. βάλῃ aor. subj.
βάλλω to throw, to bring. It may express the necessary haste of
movement (Westcott). ■ ἔγειρε pres. imp. ἐγείρω to rise. ἆρον 8
aor. imp. αἴρω to pick up, to lift up. κράβατος mat, pallet,
mattress used by the poor as bedding (Brown). περιεπάτει pres.
imp. περιπατέω to walk about. ■ ἐγένετο aor. mid. γίνομαι. 9
ἦρεν aor. αἴρω. περιεπάτει impf., inceptive impf. "he began to
walk about."
     ■ τεθεραπευμένῳ perf. pass. part. θεραπεύω to treat 10
medically, to heal. The perf. pictures his state or condition and
puts some stress on the permanence of the cure (Morris).
ἔξεστιν it is lawful, it is allowed. ἆραι aor. inf. αἴρω to lift up,
to take. (For Sabbath requirements, s. Matt. 12:2.) ■ ποιήσας 11
aor. act. part. ■ ἠρώτησαν aor. ἐρωτάω to ask. εἰπών aor. part. 12
λέγω to say, to speak. ■ ἰαθείς aor. pass. part. ἰάομαι to heal. 13
ᾔδει plperf. of the defective perf. w. a pres. meaning οἶδα to
know. ἐξένευσεν aor. ἐκνεύω to turn the head aside, to dodge
(Barrett). ὄντος pres. part. εἰμί gen. abs. ■ ἴδε aor. imp. ὁράω 14
to see. γέγονας perf. γίνομαι. ἁμάρτανε pres. imp.
ἁμαρτάνω to sin. The pres. imp. w. the neg. indicates "do not
continue to sin any longer." χεῖρον comp. κακός. γένηται aor.
mid. subj. γίνομαι. ■ ἀπῆλθεν aor. ἀπέρχομαι to go away. 15
■ ἐδίωκον impf. διώκω to persecute. ἐποίει impf. The impf. 16
could be inceptive (Morris) or customary, "he was in the habit
of doing" (Westcott). ■ ἀπεκρίνατο aor. mid. ἀποκρίνομαι to 17
answer. The mid. indicates a legal force, to make answer to the
charge, to make a defense (s. Morris; MM). ■ ἐζήτουν impf. 18
ζητέω to seek. ἀποκτεῖναι aor. inf. ἀποκτείνω to kill. ἔλυεν
impf. λύω to loose, to break. ἴσος equal. ποιῶν pres. part. In
rabbinic teaching a rebellious son is said "to make himself equal
w. his father" (Lightfoot).
     ■ ποιεῖν pres. inf. βλέπῃ pres. subj. βλέπω. ποιοῦντα 19

20 pres. part. ποιῇ pres. subj. ■ φιλέω from the original meaning "treat someone as one of their own" develop the meaning "the natural inclination to a relative, love for a relative," to love (TDNT; s. also Brown). μείζονα comp. μέγας. τούτων gen. of comparison. δείξει fut. δείκνυμι to show. θαυμάζητε pres. subj. θαυμάζω to be astonished, to wonder. Used w. the particle
21 to express purpose. ■ ἐγείρω to raise. ζωοποιέω to make alive.
22/23 ■ δέδωκεν perf. δίδωμι to give. ■ τιμῶσι pres. subj. τιμάω to honor. τιμῶν pres. part. πέμψαντα aor. part. πέμπω to send.
24 ■ ἀκούων pres. part. πιστεύων pres. part. αἰώνιος eternal (s. John 3:15). κρίσις judgment. Includes fut. judgment and also the judgment that was in process throughout the ministry of Jesus (Barrett). μεταβέβηκεν perf. μεταβαίνω to go or pass from one place to another, to transfer, to move one's living quarters (Schnackenburg). The perf. indicates the completed state, the believer has passed into eternal life which begins here
25 (Bernard). ■ ἀκούσουσιν fut. ἀκούω to hear, to hear and do, to be obedient as commonly used in the OT (Barrett). ἀκούσαντες aor. part. ζήσουσιν fut. ζάω to live. Refers to the
26 spiritually dead being made alive (s. Tasker). ■ ἔδωκεν aor.
27 δίδωμι to give. ■ ὅτι because. υἱὸς ἀνθρώπου "Son of man." Without the article emphasizing humanity or equal to the ex-
28 pression w. the article (Morris). ■ θαυμάζετε pres. imp. w. the
29 neg. prohibits an action in progress. ■ ἐκπορεύσονται fut. mid. πορεύομαι to go out. ἀνάστασις resurrection. φαῦλος bad, worthless. πράξαντες aor. part. πράσσω to do.
30/31   ■ πέμψαντός aor. act. part., s.v.23. ■ ἀληθής true, genuine. The legal principle here is from Deut. 19:15 where a man cannot be convicted of a crime on the testimony of one witness
32 (Brown; s. also M, Kethuboth, 2,9). ■ ἄλλος another. Not the Baptist but the Father (Barrett). μαρτυρῶν pres. act. part. οἶδα
33 defective perf. w. the pres. meaning "to know." ■ ἀπεστάλκατε perf. ἀποστέλλω to send, to send as an authoritative representative. μεμαρτύρηκεν perf. The tense indicates the testimony still has value (Brown). Those of Qumran considered themselves as "witnesses of the truth" and "sons of
34 the truth" (1QS 8:6; 4:5; 1QM 17:8; 1QH 6:29.) ■ σωθῆτε aor. pass. subj. σώζω to save, to rescue. Used w. the particle to
35 express purpose. ■ λύχνος lamp (s. Matt 5:15). καιόμενος pres. pass. part. καίω to light, pass. to burn. φαίνων pres. part. φαίνω to shine. ἠθελήσατε aor. θέλω to wish, to want to. ἀγαλλιαθῆναι aor. pass. inf. ἀγαλλιάομαι to be glad, to be
36 overjoyed. ■ μείζω comp., s.v.20, predicate acc. τελειώσω aor.
37 subj. τελειόω to complete. ■ ἀκηκόατε perf. ἀκούω. εἶδος

appearance, form. ἑωράκατε perf. ὁράω. ■ μένοντα pres. part. 38
μένω to remain. ἀπέστειλεν aor. ■ ἐρευνᾶτε pres. ind. 39
ἐρευνάω to search, to investigate. Corresponding to the Heb.
technical term used by the rabbis and in the Qumran literature
for the study of the Scripture (Schnackenburg). ὅτι because.
μαρτυροῦσαι pres. act. part. fem. pl. ■ ἐλθεῖν aor. inf. 40
ἔρχομαι to come. ἵνα pres. subj. Used w. the particle to express
purpose.

■ ἔγνωκα perf. γινώσκω. ■ ἐλήλυθα perf. ἔρχομαι. 42/43
ἔλθῃ aor. subj. ἔρχομαι. λήμψεσθε fut. mid. λαμβάνω to
receive. ■ πιστεῦσαι aor. inf. λαμβάνοντες pres. part. ■ 44/45
δοκεῖτε pres. imp. κατηγορήσω fut. κατηγορέω (w. gen.) to
accuse. A legal technical term to bring charges in court (BAG).
κατηγορῶν pres. part. The pres. part. perhaps having the force
of the fut. (s. BD, 175). ἠλπίκατε perf. ἐλπίζω to hope. The
perf. indicates that the hope continues in the pres. and is not
merely an emotion of the past (Bernard). ■ ἐπιστεύετε impf. 46
Used in a contrary to fact conditional clause. ἔγραψεν aor.
γράφω. ■ πιστεύσετε fut. Used as the conclusion of a condi- 47
tional sentence which views the condition as true.

Ch. 6

■ ἀπῆλθεν aor. ἀπέρχομαι to go away, to depart. πέραν 1
the other side. ■ ἠκολούθει impf. ἀκολουθέω to follow. The 2
impf. denotes the continuous action "they kept following" (Morris). ἑώρων impf. ἀσθενούντων pres. part. ἀσθενέω to be
weak, to be sick. ■ ἀνῆλθεν aor. ἀνέρχομαι to go up, to come 3
up. ἐκάθητο impf. mid. κάθημαι to sit down, to sit. ■ ἐπάρας 5
aor. part. ἐπαίρω to lift up. θεασάμενος aor. mid. part.
θεάομαι to see, to view. ἀγοράσωμεν aor. subj. ἀγοράζω to
buy at the marketplace, deliberative subj. φάγωσιν aor. subj.
ἐσθίω to eat. ■ πειράζων pres. part. πειράζω to test. Used here 6
in the neutral sense of testing (Morris). ᾔδει plperf. of the defective perf. w. the pres. meaning οἶδα to know. ἔμελλεν impf.
μέλλω to be about to. Used w. the inf. to express the fut. (MKG,
307). ■ δηνάριον denarius. A Roman silver coin worth normal- 7
ly about 18 cents (BAG). βράχυς short, small. λάβῃ aor. subj.
λαμβάνω to receive. ■ παιδάριον lad, small boy, a double 9
dimin. (Brown). κρίθινος made of barley. (For adj. w. this suffix
signifying material, origin or kind, s. MH, 359.) ὀψάριον cooked
food w. a special meaning of pickled fish (Barrett; MM). ■ 10
ποιήσατε aor. imp. ἀναπεσεῖν aor. inf. ἀναπίπτω to recline,
to sit down. χόρτος grass. ἀνέπεσαν aor. ὡς w. numbers
"about." ■ ἔλαβεν aor. λαμβάνω to receive, to take. 11

εὐχαριστήσας aor. act. part. εὐχαριστέω to give thanks, not a sacramental reference (Bernard). διέδωκεν aor. διαδίδωμι to distribute. ἀνακειμένοις pres. mid. part. ἀνάκειμαι to recline
12 (at the table). ἤθελον impf. θέλω to wish, to desire. ■ ἐνεπλήσθησαν aor. pass. ἐμπίμπλημι to fill up, to fill, pass. to be satisfied (w. enough to eat). συναγάγετε aor. imp. συνάγω to gather together. περισσεύσαντα aor. act. part. περισσεύω to be in abundance, to be left over. ἀπόληται aor. subj. ἀπόλλυμαι to perish, to be lost. Used w. the particle to
13 express purpose. ■ συνήγαγον aor. ἐγέμισαν aor. γεμίζω to fill. κόφινος basket, probably of wicker (s. Morris).
14 βεβρωκόσιν perf. part. βιβρώσκω to eat. ■ ἰδόντες aor. part. ὁράω to see. ἐποίησεν aor. ὁ προφήτης "the prophet" (s. John
15 1:21; Meeks, 87–91; 1QS 9:11). ■ γνούς aor. part. γινώσκω to know. ἁρπάζω to rob, to seize. A violent word w. connotations of force (Brown). ποιήσωσιν aor. subj. ἀνεχώρησεν aor. ἀναχωρέω to depart, to go away.
16 ■ ἐγένετο aor. mid. γίνομαι to become. κατέβησαν aor.
17 καταβαίνω to go down. ■ ἐμβάντες aor. part. ἐμβαίνω to embark, to get into (a boat). ἤρχοντο impf. mid. The impf. may be conative, "they were trying to cross," or emphasize continuing action, "they were in process of crossing" (Morris). ἐγεγόνει
18 plperf. γίνομαι. ἐληλύθει plperf. ἔρχομαι. ■ πνέοντος pres. part. πνέω to blow, gen. abs. causal. διηγείρετο impf. pass. διεγείρω to wake up, to arouse, pass. "was becoming aroused"
19 (BAG). ■ ἐληλακότες perf. act. part. ἐλαύνω to row. στάδιον stade, about 607 feet (BAG). The lake is about 13 miles long and at its greatest width 8 miles wide (s. IDB, II, 348; ZPEB, II, 643–648). περιπατοῦντα pres. part. περιπατέω to walk about.
20 ἐφοβήθησαν aor. pass. φοβέομαι to be afraid. ■ φοβεῖσθε pres. mid. imp. Used w. a neg. to prohibit an action in progress.
21 ■ λαβεῖν aor. inf. λαμβάνω. ὑπῆγον impf. ὑπάγω. progressive impf. "to which land they had been going" (RWP).
22 ■ ἑστηκώς perf. part. ἵσταμι perf. to stand. εἶδον aor. ὁράω. πλοιάριον small ship, boat. εἰ μή except. συνεισῆλθεν
23 aor. συνεισέρχομαι to go into together. ■ ἦλθεν aor. ἔρχομαι. ἔφαγον aor. ἐσθίω to eat. εὐχαριστήσαντος aor.
24 part., s.v.11 (gen. abs.). ■ ἐνέβησαν aor. ἐμβαίνω s.v.17.
25 ζητοῦντες pres. part. ζητέω to seek. ■ εὑρόντες aor. part. εὑρίσκω to find. γέγονας perf. act. 2nd sing. γίνομαι to become, to be. The perf. brings two ideas together, "When did you come?" and "How long have you been here?" (Morris).
26 ■ ἀπεκρίθη aor. pass., s.v.7. σημεῖον sign, s. John 2:18. ἐχορτάσθητε aor. pass. χορτάζω to feed, to feed until full, to

be satisfied (w. food). ■ ἐργάζεσθε pres. mid. imp. ἐργάζομαι 27 to work, to earn by working (Barrett). The pres. imp. w. the neg. in this case may be conative, "stop trying to earn." βρῶσις food. ἀπολλυμένην pres. mid. part. ἀπόλλυμι s.v.12. μένουσαν pres. act. part. fem. μένω to remain. This food remains forever and also has the effect of producing a life that lasts forever (Morris). δώσει fut. δίδωμι to give. ἐσφάγισεν aor. σφραγίζω to seal, to certify (s. John 3:33). The sacrificial animals were examined and sealed if perfect. Perhaps the thought of Christ as an accepted sacrifice is indicated (Westcott). ■ 28 ποιῶμεν pres. subj., deliberative subj. "What shall we do?" ἐργαζώμεθα pres. mid. subj. The meaning here is "to perform a work" (Barrett). ἔργα τοῦ θεοῦ the works that God desires of men (Brown). ■ πιστεύητε pres. subj. Used w. the particle as 29 explanatory of the preceding (Barrett). ἀπέστειλεν aor. ἀποστέλλω to send, to send as an authoritative representative (s. TDNT). ■ ἴδωμεν aor. subj. ὁράω to see. ■ μάννα manna. 30/31 The miraculous provision of the manna in the desert provided the rabbis w. suitable language to describe the rich gifts of God in the Messianic age (Hoskyns; s. SB, II, 481). γεγραμμένον perf. pass. part. γράφω to write. ἔδωκεν aor. δίδωμι. φαγεῖν aor. inf. ἐσθίω to eat. ■ δέδωκεν perf. δίδωμι. δίδωσιν pres. 32 ■ καταβαίνων pres. act. part. καταβαίνω to come down, to 33 descend. διδούς pres. part. δίδωμι.

■ δός aor. imp. δίδωμι. ■ ὁ ἄρτος τῆς ζωῆς the bread that 34/35 gives life, that is, everlasting life (Morris). ἐρχόμενος pres. mid. part. πεινάσῃ aor. subj. πεινάω to be hungry. πιστεύων pres. part. διψήσει fut. διψάω to thirst, to be thirsty ever. ■ εἶπον 36 aor. May refer to v.26 or to words like them spoken at some earlier time (Westcott). ἑωράκατε perf. ὁράω. ■ δίδωσιν pres. 37 The pres. is used here where the Son awaits, in v.39 the perf. expresses the gift as completed in the will of the Father (Morris). ἥξει fut. ἥκω to come. ■ καταβέβηκα perf. καταβαίνω to go 38 down, to come down. πέμψαντος aor. part. πέμπω to send. ■ ἀπολέσω aor. subj. ἀπόλλυμι to destroy, to lose, "that I 39 should not lose one of the whole company" (Barrett). ἀναστήσω aor. subj. ἀνίστημι to raise up. ■ θεωρῶν pres. 40 part., s.v.19. ἔχῃ pres. subj. Not as fut., but as pres. already as a divine power before resurrection (Westcott). ἀναστήσω aor. subj. or fut. ind. The volitive fut., a promise (RWP).

■ ἐγόγγυζον impf. γογγύζω to murmur, to complain, in- 41 ceptive impf., "they began to complain." καταβάς aor. part. καταβαίνω. ■ οὗτος "this one." An element of discouragement 42 (Brown). οἴδαμεν defective perf. w. a pres. meaning, οἶδα to

233

43 know. ∎ γογγύζετε pres. imp. used w. a neg. to stop an action
44 in progress. ∎ ἐλθεῖν aor. inf. ἔρχομαι. to come. ἑλκύσῃ aor.
subj. ἑλκύω to draw. (For the possible implications of this word,
"the idea of resistance," "to take possession of," "to bring near,"
referring to the conversion of proselytes, s. Morris; Barrett.)
45 ἀναστήσω fut. ind., s.v.40. ∎ ἔσονται fut. εἰμί. διδακτός
taught, the substantivized verbal adj., as a pass., as the gen. to
designate the agent (MT, 234). ἀκούσας aor. part. μαθών aor.
46 part. μανθάνω to learn. ∎ ἑώρακεν perf. ὤν pres. part. εἰμί.
49/50 ∎ ἀπέθανον aor. ἀποθνήσκω to die. ∎ ἀποθάνῃ aor. subj.
51 ∎ ζῶν pres. part. ζάω to live. καταβάς aor. part., s.v.38. φάγῃ
aor. subj., s.v.31. It refers to the act of appropriating Christ
(Morris). ζήσει fut. ζάω. δέ an unusual position but introduces
a fresh thought (Barrett).
52   ∎ ἐμάχοντο impf. mid. μάχομαι to fight, to rage a war of
words (RWP), inceptive imp. δοῦναι aor. inf. δίδωμι to give.
53/54 ∎ πίητε aor. subj. πίνω to drink. ∎ τρώγων pres. part. τρώγω
to nibble, to munch, to eat audibly, to crunch. The pres. tense
points to a continuing appropriation (Morris). πίνων pres. part.
55/57/58 ∎ πόσις drink. ∎ διά w. acc. "because of." καί "also." ∎
59 ἔφαγον aor., s.v.31. ∎ συναγωγή the absence of the definite
article marks the character of the assembly rather than the place
itself (Westcott). διδάσκων pres. part.
60   ∎ σκληρός dried, rough, harsh. ἀκούειν pres. inf. "to hear
61/62 w. appreciation" (Morris). ∎ εἰδώς perf. part. οἶδα s.v.42. ∎
θεωρῆτε pres. subj. θεωρέω to see. (For the possible constructions of this elliptical sentence, s. Brown; Barrett.)
ἀναβαίνοντα pres. part. ἀναβαίνω to go up, to ascend.
63 πρότερον formerly. ∎ ζωοποιοῦν pres. act. part. ζωοποιέω to
64 make alive. ὠφελεῖ pres. ὠφελέω to profit, to be useful. ∎ ᾔδει
plperf. οἶδα. παραδώσων fut. part. παραδίδωμι to deliver
65 over, to betray. ∎ εἴρηκα perf. λέγω. ᾖ pres. subj. εἰμί.
δεδομένον perf. pass. part. δίδωμι to give. Used to form the
periphrastic perf. pass. subj.
66   ∎ ἐκ τούτου either "for this reason" or "from this time"
67 (Barrett). ἀπῆλθον aor., s.v.1. περιεπάτουν impf., s.v.19. ∎ μή
68 used in a question expecting the answer no. καί also. ∎
ἀπεκρίθη aor. pass., s.v.7. ἀπελευσόμεθα fut. mid.
69 ἀπέρχομαι to go away. ∎ πεπιστεύκαμεν perf. ind. act. The
perf. implies "we have come to a place of faith and continue
there" (Morris). ἐγνώκαμεν perf. ind. act. γινώσκω to know.
The perf. implies "we have recognized the truth and hold it"
(Barrett). ὁ ἅγιος "dedicated" by God to convey the words of
70 eternal life to mankind (Tasker). ∎ ἐξελεξάμην aor. mid.

ἐκλέγω to select, to choose out for one's self. διάβολος slanderer, devil. Satan has made Judas his ally, a subordinate devil (Barrett). ■ ἔμελλεν impf., s.v.6. παραδιδόναι pres. inf., 71 s.v.64.

Ch. 7

■ περιεπάτει impf. περιπατέω to walk, to conduct one's 1 life, to pass one's time. The impf. of customary action (Barrett). ἐζήτουν impf. ζητέω to seek. The impf. pictures the progressive attitude (RWP). ἀποκτεῖναι aor. inf. ἀποκτείνω to kill. ■ 2 ἑορτή feast, festival. σκηνοπηγία the setting up of tents or dwellings. (For the popular great and holy Feast of Tabernacles, s. SB, II, 774-812; Edersheim, Temple, 268-287; M, Sukkah.) ■ μετάβηθι aor. pass. imp. μεταβαίνω to leave, to depart. 3 ἐντεῦθεν from here. ὕπαγε pres. imp. ὑπάγω to go. ἵνα used w. the fut. ind. which may put a slight emphasis on the actuality of the beholding (Morris). θεωρήσουσιν fut. θεωρέω to see. The brothers want Jesus to show off His miraculous power in Jerusalem (Brown). ■ κρυπτός hidden, secret. παρρησία open, 4 public. "Public" was considered to be the presence of ten Israelites (SB, II, 486). φανέρωσον aor. imp. φανερόω to manifest, to make clear. ■ ἐπίστευον impf. The impf. pictures the con- 5 tinual attitude. They believed that Jesus might be able to dazzle Jerusalem w. miracles but had not begun to perceive the meaning of what they had already beheld (Barrett). ■ καιρός time, the 6 suitable time, the right time, the favorable opportunity (s. Morris). ■ ἀνάβητε aor. imp. ἀναβαίνω to go up, to ascend. 8 πεπλήρωται perf. pass. πληρόω to fill, to fulfill. Perhaps Jesus uses a play on words w. the term "ascend" (Brown), or He simply is refusing to go w. the disciples at that time (s. Morris). ■ εἰπών aor. act. part. λέγω. ἔμεινεν aor. ind. μένω to remain. 9 ■ ἀνέβησαν aor. ἀναβαίνω. φανερῶς adv. openly. ■ 10/12 γογγυσμός murmuring. Perhaps here muttering, as of men who did not dare to speak plainly and loudly what they felt (Westcott). ■ μέντοι particle mostly adversative, though, to be sure, 13 indeed, however (s. BAG). παρρησίᾳ openly, boldly, w. confidence. The basic idea in the word is freedom of speech, when the words flow freely (Morris). ἐλάλει impf.

■ μεσούσης pres. act. part. fem. μεσόω to be in the mid- 14 dle, gen. abs. ἀνέβη aor., s.v.10. ἐδίδασκεν impf., inceptive impf. "he began to teach." ■ ἐθαύμαζον impf. θαυμάζω to 15 wonder, to marvel at. γράμματα letters, education. Refers particularly to rabbinical learning under another rabbi (s. Brown). οἶδεν defective perf. w. a pres. meaning οἶδα to know.

μεμαθηκώς perf. act. part. μανθάνω to learn, to study, not
16 having passed through the school of the masters (Godet). ■
ἀπεκρίθη aor. pass. ἀποκρίνομαι to answer. πέμψαντος aor.
17 act. part. πέμπω to send. ■ θέλῃ pres. subj., that is, "if it be any
man's will to do His will" (Westcott). γνώσεται fut. mid.
γινώσκω. πότερον interrogative used in a disjunctive question
18/19 "whether" (BAG). ■ λαλῶν pres. part. ζητῶν pres. part. ■
21 ἔδωκεν aor. δίδωμι. ἀποκτεῖναι aor. inf., s.v.1. ■ ἐν ἔργον
"one work," a reference to the healing in 5:1–15 (Brown).
22 ἐποίησα aor. ■ δέδωκεν perf. δίδωμι. περιτομή circumcision.
23 ■ λυθῇ aor. pass. subj. λύω to loose, to break laws, to annul, to
24 cancel (AS). χολάω to be angry. ὑγιής well, healthy. ■ κρίνετε
pres. imp. κρίνω to judge. The pres. imp. w. the neg. indicates
the stopping of an action which is in progress. ὄψις appearance.
26 ■ ἴδε aor. imp. ὁράω. μήποτε whether, perhaps, "can it be
27 possible that . . . ?" (Barrett). ἔγνωσαν aor. γινώσκω. ■ πόθεν
where, from where. ἔρχηται pres. mid. subj. ἔρχομαι to come.
28 ■ ἔκραξεν aor. κράζω to cry out. Used by John to introduce
solemn pronouncements (Barrett). διδάσκων pres. part.
ἐλήλυθα perf. ἔρχομαι. ἀληθινός true, denotes genuineness.
29 God is the ultimate reality (Tasker). ■ ἀπέστειλεν aor.
ἀποστέλλω to send, to send as an authoritative representative.
30 ■ οὖν therefore. Because of His claim to be sent from God
(Westcott). πιάσαι aor. inf. πιάζω to seize, to arrest.
ἐπέβαλεν aor. ἐπιβάλλω to cast upon, to lay hands upon.
31 ἐληλύθει plperf. ἔρχομαι. ■ ἐπίστευσαν aor. ἔλθῃ aor. subj.
ἔρχομαι. πλείων comp. πολύς. ποιήσει fut. ὧν gen. of comparison. ἐποίησεν aor.
32 ■ ἤκουσαν aor. ἀκούω to hear. γογγύζοντος pres. part.
γογγύζω to murmur, s.v.12. ὑπηρέτης attendant. Here temple
34 police (s. Brown). πιάσωσιν aor. subj. ■ ζητήσετε fut.
35 εὑρήσετε fut. εὑρίσκω to find. ἐλθεῖν aor. inf. ἔρχομαι. ■
μέλλω. (For its use w. the inf. to form the perf., s. John 6:6.)
διασπορά dispersion, diaspora. Jews living outside Palestine (s.
TDNT). The following gen. describes the area of the dispersion
(Schnackenburg).
37 ■ ἔσχατος last. (For a description of the ceremony of pouring water and wine over the altar, see Edersheim, *The Temple*,
281f; Morris.) εἱστήκει plperf. ἵστημι perf. to stand. ἔκραξεν
aor., s.v.28. διψάω to thirst. ἐρχέσθω pres. mid. imp. 3rd sing.
38 πινέτω impf. 3rd sing. πίνω to drink. ■ πιστεύων pres. part.
καθώς just as. (For the use and construction, s. Morris; Brown.)
ποταμός river. κοιλία stomach. Denotes the hidden, innermost recesses of the human body (BAG). ρεύσουσιν fut. ρέω

to flow. ζῶντος pres. part. ζάω to live. ■ ἔμελλον impf., s. John 39
6:6. οὐδέπω not yet. ἐδοξάσθη aor. pass. δοξάζω to glorify.
■ ἀκούσαντες aor. part. ■ σπέρμα seed, ancestry. ■ 40/42/43
σχίσμα division, split. ἐγένετο aor. mid. γίνομαι. ■ ἤθελον 44
impf., s.v.1.
    ■ ἠγάγετε aor. ἄγω to lead, here to bring. ■ 45/46
ἀπεκρίθησαν aor. pass., s.v.16. οὐδέποτε never, not at any
time. ἐλάλησεν aor. ■ πεπλάνησθε perf. pass. πλανάω to 47
lead astray, to deceive. ■ ἐπίστευσεν aor. ■ γινώσκων pres. 48/49
part. ἐπάρατος accursed. (For examples of how the learned
rabbis despised those who were not concerned w. the law, s. SB,
II, 494–519; Barrett.) ■ ἐλθών aor. part. ἔρχομαι. ὤν pres. part. 50
εἰμί. ■ ἀκούσῃ aor. subj. γνῷ aor. subj. γινώσκω. ■ 51/52
ἐρεύνησον aor. imp. ἐρευνάω to search, to examine, to investigate. ἴδε s.v.26. ■ ἐπορεύθησαν aor. pass. πορεύομαι to go. 53

Ch. 8

    ■ ἐπορεύθη aor. pass. πορεύομαι to go. ■ ὄρθρος day- 1/2
break, "early in the morning," gen. of time. παρεγένετο aor.
mid. παραγίνομαι to come to. ἤρχετο impf. mid. ἔρχομαι.
καθίσας aor. part. καθίζω to sit down. ἐδίδασκεν impf., inceptive impf. "he began to teach." ■ μοιχεία adultery. 3
κατειλημμένην perf. pass. part. καταλαμβάνω to seize, to
take. The perf. indicates "taken w. shame upon her." It points
to her continuing character as an adulteress (Morris). It has been
suggested that the husband set a deliberate trap in order to
divorce her or have her stoned (s. LNT, 160–164; Morris).
στήσαντες aor. part. ἵστημι to place, to stand. ■ 4
κατείληπται perf. pass. ἐπ᾽ αὐτοφώρῳ (caught) in the act.
Used of catching a thief or one in adultery (BAG). μοιχευομένη
pres. mid. part. μοιχεύομαι to commit adultery. ■ ἐνετείλατο 5
aor. mid. ἐντέλλομαι to command. τοιοῦτος such a one.
λιθάζω to stone. Only under the condition of persistence after
previous warning and after the actual witness of the act by two
competent witnesses was one to be stoned for adultery (s. LNT,
160ff.). ■ πειράζοντες pres. part. πειράζω to test, to tempt. 6
ἔχωσιν pres. subj. κατηγορέω w. the gen. to accuse. They
wanted to know if she could lawfully in the circumstances be
stoned (LNT, 174). κύψας aor. part. κύπτω to stoop. δάκτυλος
finger. Writing w. the finger was symbolic of divine legislation
(LNT, 177). κατέγραφεν impf. καταγράφω to write down, to
register (s. MM). It has been suggested that Jesus wrote down
Exodus 23:1b indicating it was wrong to join w. the wicked, here
indicating the conspiracy against the woman (s. LNT, 175–182).

7 ■ ἐπέμενον impf. ἐπιμένω to remain. ἐρωτῶντες pres. part.
ἐρωτάω to ask. ἀνέκυψεν aor. ἀνακύπτω to raise one's self up,
to stand erect, to look up. ἀναμάρτητος without sin. Used
generally of innocence (s. Hoskyns). βαλέτω aor. imp. 3rd sing.
βάλλω to throw. Jesus insists upon the innocence and therefore
8 the competence of the accuser and witness (LNT, 182). ■
κατακύψας aor. part. κατακύπτω to stoop down. ἔγραφεν
impf. It is suggested that He wrote Exodus 23:7a indicating they
should keep away from a false matter and leave judgment and
9 retribution to God (LNT, 183f.). ■ ἀκούσαντες aor. part.
ἀκούω. ἐξήρχοντο impf. mid. ἐξέρχομαι to go out. The inceptive or interat. impf. "they began to go out and continued one
by one." ἀρξάμενοι aor. mid. part. ἄρχομαι to begin.
κατελείφθη aor. pass. καταλείπω to leave alone. οὖσα pres.
10 part. fem. εἰμί. ■ ἀνακύψας aor. part. κατέκρινεν aor.
11 κατακρίνω to condemn. ■ πορεύου pres. mid. imp. μηκέτι no
longer. ἁμάρτανε pres. imp. ἁμαρτάνω to sin.
12   ■ αὐτοῖς. It can refer to the Pharisees and the crowds in the
temple (RWP). ἐλάλησεν aor. λαλέω to speak. φῶς light. (For
the meaning of this and the description of the Jewish ceremony
of lighting the huge golden candlesticks at the Feast of the
Tabernacles, s. M, Sukkah 5. 2–4; Barrett; Morris; s. 1QS 3:20;
4:8; 1QM 17:6; CD 5:18.) ἀκολουθῶν pres. part. ἀκολουθέω
to follow, to follow as a disciple (s. TDNT). περιπατήσῃ aor.
14 subj. περιπατέω to walk, to walk about. ἕξει fut. ἔχω. ■
ἀπεκρίθη aor. pass. ἀποκρίνομαι to answer. οἶδα defective
perf. w. a pres. meaning to know. πόθεν where, from where.
15 ἦλθον aor. ἔρχομαι. ποῦ where, where to. ■ κατά w. the acc.
according to. It gives the norm of judgment, "after the flesh" and
draws attention to the imperfection of their judgment (Morris).
16 ■ ἀληθινός true, verified (s. Brown). πέμψας aor. part. πέμπω
17 to send. ■ γέγραπται perf. pass. γράφω to write. The perf.
indicates "it stands written" and indicates the legal authority (s.
18/19 MM). ■ μαρτυρῶν pres. part. ■ ᾔδειτε plperf. οἶδα. Used in
20 a contrary to fact conditional clause. ■ ῥῆμα speech. ἐν by,
denoting nearness (Brown). γαζοφυλάκειον treasury. Probably
situated in the Court of the Women (Barrett). διδάσκων pres.
part. ἐπίασεν aor. πιάζω to seize, to arrest. ἐλήλυθει plperf.
ἔρχομαι.
21   ■ ζητήσετε fut. ζητέω to seek. ἀποθανεῖσθε fut. mid.
22 ἀποθήσκω to die. ἐλθεῖν aor. inf. ἔρχομαι. ■ μήτι. Introduces
a hesitant question, "You don't suppose . . . do you?" (s. M, 170).
23 ἀποκτενεῖ fut. ἀποκτείνω to kill. ■ κάτω below, beneath. ἄνω
above. Jewish technical terms for "heavenly" and "earthly" (s.

238

Schnackenburg). ■ πιστεύσητε aor. subj. The aor. means 24
"make an act of faith," "come to believe" (Morris). ■ τὴν 25
ἀρχήν adv. acc. "from the beginning," "at all." (For this difficult
construction, s. Brown; Schnackenburg.)■ πέμψας aor. part., 26
s.v.16. ἥκουσα aor. ἀκούω. ■ ἔγνωσαν aor. γινώσκω. ἔλεγεν 27
impf. Here "to talk about." ■ ὑψώσητε aor. subj. ὑψόω to lift 28
up. A reference both to the cross and to the exaltation (Barrett).
γνώσεσθε fut. mid. γινώσκω. ἐδίδαξεν aor. ■ ἀφῆκεν aor. 29
ἀφίημι to leave. ἀρεστός verbal adj. of ἀρέσκω to please, "the
things pleasing." The service is positive act. energetic (Westcott). ■ λαλοῦντος pres. part. gen. abs. ἐπίστευσαν aor.   30
■ πεπιστευκότας perf. act. part. Perhaps referring to those 31
who have made an outward profession (Morris; but s. also
Schnackenburg). μείνητε aor. subj. μένω to remain. ἀληθῶς
adv. truly. ■ γνώσεσθε fut. mid. s.v.28. ἐλευθερώσει fut. 32
ἐλευθερόω to free, liberation from sin, a synonym for salvation
(Barrett). ■ ἀπεκρίθησαν aor. pass., s.v.14. δεδουλεύκαμεν 33
perf. δουλεύω to be enslaved, to serve as a slave. γενήσεσθε
fut. mid. γίνομαι. ■ ποιῶν pres. part. ■ ἐλευθερώσῃ aor. subj. 34/36
ὄντως really, actually. ἔσεσθε fut. εἰμί. ■ οἶδα defective perf. 37
w. a pres. meaning, s.v.14. ἀποκτεῖναι aor. inf., s.v.22. χωρέω
to make room for, to contain. They have never really made room
for His word at all (Tasker). ■ ἑώρακα perf. ὁράω to see. The 38
tense would seem to imply that Jesus had a preexistent vision
which continues into the pres. (Brown). ἠκούσατε aor., s.v.26.
ποιεῖτε pres. ind. or imp. (s. Westcott).
    ■ λελάληκα perf. λαλέω. ■ πορνεία fornication, unlawful 40/41
sexual relation. ἐγεννήθημεν aor. pass. γεννάω to bear, pass.
to be born. ■ ἠγαπᾶτε impf. ἀγαπάω to love. Used in a con- 42
trary to fact conditional clause. ἐξῆλθον aor. ἐξέρχομαι to go
out. ἥκω to come, to be pres. ἐλήλυθα perf. ἔρχομαι.
ἀπέστειλεν aor. ἀποστέλλω to send, to send as an authoritative representative (s. TDNT). ■ λαλιά speech. Denotes the 43
form of expression, the outward shape of the discourse (Morris).
λόγος word. Signifies the content (Morris). ■ διάβολος slan- 44
derer, devil. (For the construction here, s. BD, 140.)
ἀνθρωποκτόνος murderer. Because he robbed Adam of immortality (Barrett). ἔστηκεν impf. στήκω to stand, to stand
fast. λαλῇ pres. subj. ψεῦδος lie. ψεύστης liar. ■ ἐγώ. Placed 45
first for emphasis (Bernard). ■ ἐλέγχω to convict, to prove, to 46
convince w. proofs. ■ ὤν pres. part. εἰμί.   47
    ■ καλῶς adv. well. The meaning here is "Are we not right 48
in saying?" (Barrett). ■ ἀτιμάζω to dishonor. ■ ζητῶν pres. 49/50
part. κρίνων pres. part. ■ τηρήσῃ aor. subj. τηρέω to guard, to 51

52 keep, to observe. **θεωρήσῃ** aor. subj. to see. ■ **ἐγνώκαμεν** perf. **γινώσκω**. **ἀπέθανεν** aor. **ἀποθνήσκω** to die. **γεύσηται** aor.
53/54 mid. subj. **γεύομαι** to taste. ■ **πατρός** gen. of comparison. ■
55 **δοξάσω** aor. subj. **δοξάζω** to glorify. **δοξάζων** pres. part. ■
56 **εἴπω** aor. subj. **λέγω**. ■ **ἠγαλλιάσατο** aor. mid. **ἀγαλλιάομαι**
to rejoice, to be overjoyed (Morris). **ἴδῃ** aor. subj. **ὁράω**. Used
w. **ἵνα** to express content (s. IBG, 145f.). **εἶδεν** aor. **ὁράω**
58 **ἐχάρη** aor. pass. **χαίρω** to be glad, to rejoice. ■ **γενέσθαι** aor.
mid. inf. **γίνομαι** to become, aor. "to come into existence"
(Morris). Infinitive used w. the prep. to express time "before" (s.
59 MT, 144). ■ **ἦραν** aor. **αἴρω** to lift up, to pick up. **βάλωσιν** aor.
subj. **βάλλω** to throw. **ἐκρύβη** aor. pass. **κρύπτω** to hide, to
conceal.

Ch. 9

1 ■ **παράγων** pres. part. **παράγω** to go by, to pass by. **εἶδεν**
2 aor. **ὁράω** to see. **τυφλός** blind. **γενετή** birth. ■ **ἠρώτησαν** aor.
ἐρωτάω to question, to ask. **ἥμαρτεν** aor. **ἁμαρτάνω** to sin.
γονεῖς parents. **ἵνα** "so that." Expresses result (s. RG, 997f.).
3 **γεννηθῇ** aor. pass. subj. **γεννάω** to bear, pass. to be born. ■
ἀπεκρίθη aor. pass. **ἀποκρίνομαι** to answer. **φανερωθῇ** aor.
4 pass. subj. **φανερόω** to make clear, to manifest. ■ **δεῖ** it is necessary (used w. the inf.). **ἐργάζεσθαι** pres. mid. inf. to work.
5/6 **πέμψαντος** aor. part. **πέμπω** to send. ■ **ὦ** pres. subj. **εἰμί**.
ἔπτυσεν aor. **πτύω** to spit. The curative value of saliva was
highly esteemed in antiquity (s. Morris; Barrett). **χαμαί** on the
ground. An old adv. either in the dat. or locative (RWP).
ἐποίησεν aor. **πηλός** mud, clay. (For the forbidding of knead-
ing on the Sabbath, s. M, Shabbath 7, 2.) **πτύσμα** saliva, spittle.
7 **ἐπέθηκεν** aor. **ἐπιτίθημι** to place upon. ■ **ὕπαγε** pres. imp.
ὑπάγω to go. **νίψαι** aor. imp. **νίπτομαι** to wash. **κολυμβήθρα**
pool. **ἑρμηνεύεται** pres. pass. **ἑρμηνεύω** to translate.
ἀπεσταλμένος perf. pass. part. **ἀποστέλλω** to send. It was
from Siloam that the water used in the libations at the Feast of
Tabernacles was drawn (Barrett). **ἀπῆλθεν** aor. **ἀπέρχομαι**
to go away. **ἐνίψατο** aor. mid. **ἦλθεν** aor. **ἔρχομαι**. **βλέπων**
8 pres. part. ■ **γείτων** neighbor. **θεωροῦντες** pres. part. **θεωρέω**
to see. **προσαίτης** beggar. **καθήμενος** pres. mid. part.
κάθημαι to sit. **προσαιτῶν** pres. part. **προσαιτέω** to ask from
someone, to beg (s. MH, 324). The pres. indicates he had his
10 regular place and was a familiar figure (RWP). ■ **ἠνεῴχθησαν**
11 aor. pass. **ἀνοίγω** to open. ■ **λεγόμενος** pres. pass. part.
ἐπέχρισεν aor. **χρίω** to anoint. **ἀπελθών** aor. part.
ἀπέρχομαι. **νιψάμενος** aor. mid. part. **ἀνέβλεψα** aor.

ἀναβλέπω to see again. ■ οἶδα defective perf. w. a pres. mean- 12
ing to know.

■ ἦν impf. εἰμί. ἀνέῳξεν aor. ἀνοίγω to open. ■ ἠρώτων 14/15
impf. ἐρωτάω. Emphasizes the repeated questioning. ■ 16
ἁμαρτωλός sinful. τοιοῦτος such a thing, such as this. σχίσμα
division. ■ ἠνέῳξεν aor. ἀνοίγω to open. 17
■ ἐπίστευσαν aor. ἐφώνησαν aor. φωνέω to call. ■ 18/19
ἐγεννήθη aor. pass. ■ ἤνοιξεν aor. ἀνοίγω. ἐρωτήσατε aor. 21
imp. ἡλικία age, full age, to come to maturity, one who is 13
years and one day old (SB, II, 534). λαλήσει fut. ■ ἐφοβοῦντο 22
impf. mid. φοβέομαι to fear. συνετέθειντο plperf. mid.
συντίθημι to agree. ὁμολογήσῃ aor. subj. ὁμολογέω to confess. ἀποσυνάγωγος to excommunicate, to be separated from
the synagogue (s. Brown; SB, IV, 293–333). γένηται aor. mid.
subj. γίνομαι. ■ δός aor. imp. δίδωμι to give. ■ ὤν pres. part. 24/25
εἰμί. ■ ἠκούσατε aor. ἀκούω to hear. μή. An unusual way of 27
adjuring the man to speak the truth (Lindars). Used in questions
expecting the answer "no." γενέσθαι aor. mid. inf. γίνομαι.
■ ἐλοιδόρησαν aor. λοιδορέω to abuse, to revile (s. TDNT). 28
■ λελάληκεν perf. λαλέω. ■ θαυμαστός wonderful, remarka- 29/30
ble. ■ θεοσεβής devout, God-fearing. ᾖ subj. εἰμί. ποιῇ pres. 31
subj. ■ ἠκούσθη aor. pass. ἀκούω to hear. γεγεννημένου perf. 32
pass. part. γεννάω. ■ ἠδύνατο aor. mid. δύναμαι to be able. 33
Used in a contrary to fact conditional clause (s. RG, 922f.,
1014ff.). ■ ὅλος totally, predicate nom. (RWP). ἐξέβαλον aor. 34
ἐκβάλλω to throw out.
■ εὑρών aor. part. εὑρίσκω to find. ■ καί. Used to in- 35/36
troduce the apodosis which is here a question and has the force
"who then" (under the circumstances set forth in the protasis)
(BD, 227). πιστεύσω aor. subj. ■ ἑώρακας perf. ὁράω. ■ ἔφη 37/38
impf. φημί to say, to speak. προσεκύνησεν aor. προσκυνέω
to worship. The action of bowing down to worship is used in
John 4:20–24 to describe the worship due to God (Brown). ■ 39
βλέπωσιν pres. subj. γένωνται aor. mid. subj. γίνομαι.
■ ἤκουσαν aor. ἀκούω. ὄντες pres. part. εἰμί. ■ ἦτε subj. 40/41
εἰμί. εἴχετε impf. ἔχω. Used in a contrary to fact conditional
clause. The addition of ἄν produces the effect of italicizing the
word "if" (M, 200).

Ch. 10

■ εἰσερχόμενος pres. mid. part. εἰσέρχομαι go in. αὐλή 1
a courtyard, sheepfold. Here it seems to be a yard in front of the
house, surrounded by a stone wall which was probably topped
w. briers (Brown). ἀναβαίνων pres. part. ἀναβαίνω to go up,

to climb over. ἀλλαχόθεν from another place. κλέπτης thief, one who steals. λῃστής robber, bandit. The combination may denote a readiness to engage in violence as well as dishonesty 2/3 (Morris). ■ ποιμήν shepherd (s. TDNT; CBB). ■ θυρωρός doorkeeper. Perhaps an undershepherd or possibly one fold served more than one flock and had an independent porter (Barrett). ἴδιος one's own. φωνέω pres. ind. Eastern shepherds commonly give names to their sheep descriptive of some trait or 4 characteristic of the animal (Bernard). ■ ἐκβάλῃ aor. subj. ἐκβάλλω to drive out. The word has an air of force (Morris). ἔμπροσθεν w. the gen. before, in front of. οἶδα defective perf. 5 w. a pres. meaning to know. ■ ἀλλότριος stranger. 6 ἀκολουθήσουσιν fut. φεύξονται fut. mid. φεύγω to flee. ■ παροιμία proverb, parable (s. Barrett). ἔγνωσαν aor. γινώσκω. ἐλάλει impf.

7   ■ θύρα door, gate. Jesus is the door through which the sheep pass and the door through which alone men can rightly 8 approach the sheep (Hoskyns). ■ ἦλθον aor. ἔρχομαι. 9 ἤκουσαν aor. ἀκούω to hear. ■ εἰσέλθῃ aor. subj. εἰσέρχομαι. σωθήσεται fut. pass. σῴζω to save, to rescue. ἐξελεύσεται fut. mid. ἐξέρχομαι. νομή pasture. εὑρήσει fut. 10 εὑρίσκω to find. ■ εἰ μή except. κλέψῃ aor. subj. κλέπτω to steal. θύσῃ aor. subj. θύω to slaughter, to kill for food (Morris). ἀπολέσῃ aor. subj. ἀπόλλυμι to destroy. ἔχωσιν pres. subj. περισσόν abundance, superfluous, more than is really necessary (Sanders), "have it to the full," "to have a surplus" (Ber- 11 nard). ■ καλός good, beautiful, in the sense of an ideal or model 12 of perfection (s. Brown; Barrett). ■ μισθωτός a hired man, one paid to do his work (s. Morris). ὤν pres. part. εἰμί. λύκος wolf. ἀφίημι to forsake, to leave. ἁρπάζω to snatch, to seize, to take suddenly and vehemently, to drag away. σκορπίζω to scatter. 13/16 ■ μέλει μοι to be of concern to someone. ■ δεῖ it is necessary, one must (used w. the inf.). ἀγαγεῖν aor. inf. ἄγω to lead. ἀκούσουσιν fut. γενήσεται fut. mid. γίνομαι. ποίμνη flock. 17 ■ λάβω aor. subj. λαμβάνω. It may be used w. a particle to 18 express purpose (s. Barrett). ■ ἦρεν aor. αἴρω to take away. ἐξουσία authority, right, legal authority (s. Schnackenburg). θεῖναι aor. inf. τίθημι to lay down. λαβεῖν aor. inf. λαμβάνω. ἔλαβον aor.
19/20   ■ σχίσμα division, split. ἐγένετο aor. mid. γίνομαι. ■ 21 μαίνομαι to rage, to rave, to be mad. ■ δαιμονιζομένου pres. mid. part. δαιμονίζομαι to be possessed w. an evil spirit. (For the Jewish view of demons, s. SB, IV, 501–535.) One who has a demon was not to be listened to (TDNT). μή. Used in hesitant

questions expecting the answer no. ἀνοῖξαι aor. inf.
■ ἐγένετο aor. mid. γίνομαι. ἐγκαίνια renewal, rededica- 22
tion, dedication. Used here for the Feast of Dedication (s. 1
Macc. 4:36–59; 2 Macc. 10:1–8; Edersheim, *Temple*, 333–336).
χειμών winter. The eight-day feast began on the 25th of the
month of Kislev; that is December. ■ περιεπάτει impf. 23
περιπατέω to walk about. στοά porch w. columns (s. Edersheim, *Temple*, 43f.). ■ ἐκύκλωσαν aor. κυκλόω to encircle. 24
ἕως πότε "how long?" αἴρω s.v.18. Here lit. "to take away our
life"; that is, "to hold in suspense" (Brown). εἰπόν aor. imp.
λέγω. παρρησίᾳ adv. openly, plainly. ■ ἀπεκρίθη aor. pass. 25
ἀποκρίνομαι to answer. ■ ἀπόλωνται aor. subj. ἀπόλλυμι to 28
be lost. ἁρπάσει fut., s.v.12. ■ δέδωκεν perf. δίδωμι. πάντων 29
gen. of comparison. μείζων comp. μέγας. ■ ἕν n. "one thing." 30
Identity is not asserted, but essential unity is (Morris).
■ ἐβάστασαν aor. βαστάζω to take up. λιθάσωσιν aor. 31
subj. λιθάζω to stone. ■ ἔδειξα aor. δείκνυμι to show. ποῖος 32
which kind of. ■ ὤν part., s.v.12. ■ γεγραμμένον perf. pass. 33/34
part. γράφω to write. εἶπα aor. λέγω. ■ λυθῆναι aor. pass. inf. 35
λύω to break, to set aside, to nullify (s. Brown). γραφή Scripture. It means any particular passage of Scripture (Lindars). ■ 36
ἡγίασεν aor. ἁγιάζω to set apart, to sanctify, to consecrate.
Used in the rel. clause which is an acc. of reference (Barrett).
ἀπέστειλεν aor. ἀποστέλλω to send. ■ πιστεύητε pres. subj. 38
πιστεύετε pres. imp. γνῶτε aor. subj. γινώσκω to know. The
aor. indicates "that we may come to know" (Morris).
γινώσκητε pres. subj. "and keep on knowing" (Morris). ■ 39
ἐζήτουν impf. ζητέω to seek. πιάσαι aor. inf. πιάζω to seize.
ἐξῆλθεν aor. ἐξέρχομαι to go out.
■ ἀπῆλθεν aor. ἀπέρχομαι to go away. πέραν w. the gen. 40
"the other side." βαπτίζων pres. part. βαπτίζω to baptize.
■ ἦλθον aor., s.v.8. ἐποίησεν aor. ἀληθής true. ■ ἐπίστευσαν 41/42
aor.

Ch. 11

■ ἀσθενῶν pres. part. ἀσθενέω to be weak, to be sick. 1
Participle used in a periphrastic construction. ■ ἀλείψασα aor. 2
part. ἀλείφω to anoint. μύρον ointment, perfume. ἐκμάξασα
aor. part. fem. ἐκμάσσω to wipe. θρίξ hair. ἠσθένει impf.
ἀσθενέω. ■ ἀπέστειλαν aor. ἀποστέλλω to send. ἴδε aor. 3
imp. ὁράω to see. ■ ἀκούσας aor. part. ἀσθένεια "w. a view 4
to death." This construction is more reassuring indicating the
sickness is not "dangerous" (Bernard). δοξασθῇ aor. pass. subj.
δοξάζω to glorify. ■ ἠγάπα impf. ἀγαπάω to love. ■ ἤκουσεν 5/6

7 aor. ἀκούω. ἔμεινεν aor. μένω to remain. ■ ἔπειτα then.
8 ἄγωμεν pres. subj. ἄγω to go, hortatory subj. ■ ἐζήτουν impf.
9 ζητέω to seek. λιθάσαι aor. inf. λιθάζω to stone. ■ ἀπεκρίθη
aor. pass. ἀποκρίνομαι to answer. περιπατῇ pres. subj.
11 περιπατέω to walk, to walk about. ■ κεκοίμηται perf. pass.
κοιμάω to sleep, to fall asleep. The perf. emphasizes the pres.
state. The word is used here as a euphemism for death (Brown).
ἐξυπνίσω aor. subj. ἐξυπνίζω to awake someone out of sleep.
12 ■ εἶπαν aor. λέγω. σωθήσεται fut. pass. σῴζω to rescue, to
13 recover from illness (Barrett). ■ εἰρήκει plperf. λέγω. ἔδοξαν
aor. δοκέω to suppose. κοίμησις sleep. ὕπνου gen. of descrip-
14 tion or possibly obj. gen. (RWP). ■ παρρησίᾳ openly.
15 ἀπέθανεν aor. ἀποθνήσκω to die. ■ πιστεύσητε aor. subj.
The aor. points to a single act "to come to have faith" (Brown).
16 ἤμην impf. εἰμί. ■ λεγόμενος pres. pass. part. συμμαθητής
fellow-disciple, dat. of agent. ἀποθάνωμεν aor. subj.
ἀποθνήσκω hortatory subj.
17 ■ ἐλθών aor. part. ἔρχομαι. εὗρεν aor. εὑρίσκω to find.
19 ■ ἐληλύθεισαν plperf. ἔρχομαι. παραμυθήσωνται aor. pass.
subj. παραμυθέομαι to comfort, to console. (For the Jewish
20 custom, s. SB, IV, 592–607; LT, II 316–320.) ■ ὑπήντησεν aor.
ὑπαντάω to meet. ἐκαθέζετο impf. mid. καθέζομαι to sit, to
21 be sitting down. ■ ἦς impf. Used in a contrary to fact conditional
22 clause. ■ οἶδα defective perf. w. a pres. meaning, "to know."
23 αἰτήσῃ aor. subj. αἰτέω to ask. δώσει fut. δίδωμι. ■
ἀναστήσεται fut. mid. ἀνίσταμι to rise. (For Jewish refer-
25 ences to the resurrection, s. Barrett.) ■ πιστεύων pres. part.
26/27 ζήσεται fut. mid. ζάω to live. ■ ζῶν pres. part. ■ πεπίστευκα
perf. The perf. indicates a faith once given and permanently
remaining (Morris).
28 ■ ἀπῆλθεν aor. ἀπέρχομαι to go away. ἐφώνησεν aor.
29 φωνέω to call. λάθρα secretly. πάρειμι to be present. ■
ἐγείρεται pres. pass. ἐγείρω to raise, pass. to rise. ταχύ quick-
30/31 ly. ἤρχετο impf. mid. ἔρχομαι. ■ ἐληλύθει plperf., s.v.19. ■
ὄντες pres. part. εἰμί. παραμυθούμενοι pres. mid. part.
ἰδόντες aor. act. part. ὁράω. ἀνέστη aor. ἀνίστημι. ἐξῆλθεν
aor. ἐξέρχομαι to go out. ἠκολούθησαν aor. ἀκολουθέω to
follow. δόξαντες aor. part. δοκέω. κλαύσῃ aor. subj. κλαίω to
32 weep, to cry. ■ ἦλθεν aor. ἔρχομαι. ἔπεσεν aor. πίπτω to fall.
33 ■ εἶδεν aor. ὁράω. κλαίουσαν pres. part. συνελθόντας aor.
part. συνέρχομαι to go together, to go w. someone.
ἐνεβριμήσατο aor. mid. ἐμβριμάομαι to snort as an expression of anger, to be moved w. the deepest emotions. Perhaps
the anger was at the illness and handicaps which were looked on

as a manifestation of Satan's kingdom of evil (Brown). ἐτάραξεν
aor. ταράσσω to shake, to trouble, to be disturbed, to shudder
(Brown). He now voluntarily and deliberately accepts and makes
His own the emotion and the experience from which it is His
purpose to deliver men (Lightfoot). ■ τεθείκατε perf. τίθημι to 34
place, to lay. ἔρχου pres. mid. imp. ■ ἐδάκρυσεν aor. δακρύω 35
to shed tears. The aor. signifies "He burst into tears" (Morris).
■ ἐφίλει impf. ■ ἐδύνατο aor. mid. ἀνοίξας aor. part. ἀνοίγω 36/37
to open. ποιῆσαι aor. inf.

■ ἐμβριμώμενος pres. mid. part. σπήλαιον cave, prob- 38
ably w. a horizontal shaft which was used as a grave (s. Barrett).
ἐπέκειτο plperf. pass. τίθημι pass. to lie. ■ ἄρατε aor. imp. 39
αἴρω to take away. The stone would be extremely heavy in order
to keep beasts of prey out of the tomb (Lightfoot).
τετελευτηκότος perf. act. part. τελευτάω to die. ὄζω to smell,
to give off an odor, pleasant or unpleasant. "By this time the
smell must be offensive" (BAG). ■ ὄψῃ fut. ὁράω. ■ ἦραν aor. 40/41
αἴρω. ■ ᾔδειν plperf. οἶδα. περιεστῶτα perf. part. 42
περιΐσταμι, perf. to stand about, to stand around. ■ 43
ἐκραύγασεν aor. κραυγάζω to shout. δεῦρο adv. of place used
as an imp. "here!" Jesus' command is wonderfully succinct;
"Here! outside!" (Morris). ■ τεθνηκώς perf. part. ἀποθνήσκω 44
to die, perf. to be dead. δεδεμένος perf. pass. part. δέω to bind.
κειρία bandage, grave clothes. ὄψις face. σουδάριον (Latin)
napkin, a cloth used for wiping off perspiration. There is some
reason to think that only the faces of the poor were covered in
this way (Barrett). περιεδέδετο plperf. pass. περιδέω to bind
about, to bind around. λύσατε aor. imp. λύω to loose. ἄφετε
aor. imp. ἀφίημι to release, to let go.

■ ἐλθόντες aor. part., s.v.17. θεασάμενοι aor. mid. part. 45
θεάομαι to see, to behold, to view. ἐποίησεν aor. ἐπίστευσαν
aor. ■ ἀπῆλθον aor., s.v.28. ■ συνήγαγον aor. συνάγω to 46/47
summons together, to call together. συνέδριον Sanhedrin (s.
TDNT). ποιοῦμεν pres. ind. "What are we now doing?" It
implies the answer "nothing" (Barrett). ■ ἀφῶμεν aor. subj. 48
ἀφίημι s.v.44. πιστεύσουσιν fut. ἐλεύσονται fut. mid.
ἔρχομαι. ἀροῦσιν aor. αἴρω s.v.39. ■ ὤν pres. part., s.v.31. 49
ἐνιαυτός year, "that fateful year" (s. Morris), gen. of time (MT,
235). ■ συμφέρει it is profitable, it is to one's advantage. 50
ἀποθάνῃ aor. subj., s.v.16. ἀπόληται aor. mid. subj. ἀπόλλυμι
to perish. ■ ἐπροφήτευσεν aor. προφητεύω to prophesy. (For 51
unintentional prophecy among the rabbis, s. Hoskyns; SB, II,
546.) ἔμελλεν impf., s. John 6:6. μέλλω. ■ διεσκορπισμένα 52
perf. pass. part. διασκορπίζω to scatter. Sin scatters men, but

salvation in Christ brings them together (Morris). συναγάγῃ
53 aor. subj. συνάγω. ■ οὖν then, now (s. DM, 253).
ἐβουλεύσαντο aor. mid. βουλεύομαι to will, to take counsel.
That which had been a desire before now becomes a settled plan
(Westcott). ἀποκτείνωσιν aor. act. subj. ἀποκτείνω to kill.
54 ■ οὖν therefore. Denotes a much stricter sequence of
thought than often in this Gospel (Morris). περιεπάτει impf.
περιπατέω s.v.9. λεγομένην pres. pass. part., s.v.16.
55 ■ ἀνέβησαν aor. ἀναβαίνω to go up. ἁγνίσωσιν aor.
56 subj. ἁγνίζω to sanctify, to purify (s. Brown). ■ ἐζήτουν impf.,
s.v.8. ἑστηκότες perf. part. ἵστημι to stand. ἔλθῃ aor. subj.
57 ἔρχομαι. ■ δεδώκεισαν plperf. δίδωμι. The plperf. may indicate the permanent nature of the order (Morris). γνῷ aor. subj.
γινώσκω. μηνύσῃ aor. subj. μηνύω to make known, to report,
to give information to the authorities (s. MM). ὅπως w. the subj.
to express purpose (s. BD, 186f.). πιάσωσιν aor. subj. πιάζω
to seize, to arrest.

Ch. 12

1   ■ πρό before. (For the use of the prep. here, s. M,
2 100f.) ἦλθεν aor. ἔρχομαι. ἤγειρεν aor. ἐγείρω to raise. ■
ἐποίησαν aor. δεῖπνον banquet (s. SB, IV, 611–639). διηκόνει
impf. διακονέω to minister, to serve tables. ἀνακειμένων pres.
3 mid. part. ἀνάκειμαι to recline at the table. ■ λαβοῦσα aor.
part. fem. λαμβάνω. λίτρα a (Roman) pound (12 ounces)
(BAG). μύρον nard, ointment of nard. νάρδος spikenard, a
fragrant oil derived from the root and spike (hair stem) of the
nard plant which grows in the mountains of northern India
(Brown). πιστικός fit to be trusted, genuine (MH, 379f.).
πολύτιμος of great worth, expensive. ἤλειψεν aor. ἀλείφω to
anoint. ἐξέμαξεν aor. ἐκμάσσω to wipe off, to dry off.
4 ἐπληρώθη aor. pass. πληρόω to fill. ὀσμή odor. ■ μέλλων
5 pres. part. μέλλω s. John 6:6. ■ ἐπράθη aor. pass. πιπράσκω
to sell. δηνάριον denarius. A Roman silver coin worth normally
about 18 cents. A workman's average daily wage (BAG). ἐδόθη
6 aor. pass. δίδωμι. ■ ἔμελεν impf. μέλει (w. dat.) to have concern for. γλωσσόκομον a small box or case, originally one for
the mouthpiece of a flute (Morris; s. also MM). βαλλόμενα
pres. pass. part. βάλλω to throw, to put. ἐβάσταζεν impf.
7 βαστάζω to carry, to take away, to steal (s. BS, 257). ■ ἄφες
aor. imp. ἀφίημι to leave alone. ἐνταφιασμός preparation for
burial. τηρήσῃ aor. subj. τηρέω to keep. Used here to express
purpose, "the purpose was that she might keep" (Brown).
9/10   ■ ἔγνω aor. γινώσκω. ἴδωσιν aor. subj. ὁράω. ■

ἐβουλεύσαντο aor. mid. βουλεύομαι to take counsel.
ἀποκτείνωσιν aor. subj. ἀποκτείνω to kill. ■ ὑπῆγον impf. 11
ὑπάγω to go. Here it means that many of the Jews left their
former Jewish allegiance and way of life to become disciples
(Barrett). ἐπίστευον impf. The impf. pictures the repeated action.

■ ἐλθών aor. part. ἔρχομαι. ἀκούσαντες aor. part. ■ 12/13
ἔλαβον aor. λαμβάνω. βαΐον palm branch. φοῖνιξ palm tree,
"the palm branches of the palm trees" (RWP). To carry palms
was a mark of triumphant homage to a victor or a king (Bernard).
ἐξῆλθον aor. ἐξέρχομαι to go out. ὑπάντησις meeting. The
special idea of the word was the official welcome of a newly
arrived dignitary (M, 14). ἐκραύγαζον impf. κραυγάζω to
shout. ὡσαννά hosanna (s. Matt. 21:9). εὐλογημένος perf.
pass. part. εὐλογέω to bless, to attribute power to (s. CBB;
TDNT). ■ εὑρών aor. part. εὑρίσκω to find. It could mean "to 14
find after search," "to find by the agency of others" (Barrett).
ὀνάριον dimin. donkey. ἐκάθισεν aor. καθίζω to sit down.
■ πῶλος colt, young animal, young donkey. ὄνος donkey. ■ 15/16
ἔγνωσαν aor., s.v.9. ἐδοξάσθη aor. pass. δοξάζω to glorify.
ἐμνήσθησαν aor. pass. μιμνήσχομαι to remember.
ἐποίησαν aor. ■ ἐμαρτύρει impf. μαρτυρέω to give testimony 17
to, to bear witness. The impf. pictures the continual action and
they proclaimed what had been done as testimony to the power
of Jesus (Barrett). οὖν then, now, indicating a succession of
events (s. DM, 253). ὤν pres. part. εἰμί. Here the pres. part.
denotes a continued action antecedent to that of the principal
verb (SMT, 58). ἐφώνησεν aor. φωνέω to call. ἤγειρεν aor.,
s.v.1. ■ ὑπήντησεν aor. ὑπαντάω to meet. ἤκουσαν aor. 18
ἀκούω to hear. πεποιηκέναι perf. act. inf. ποιέω. ■ εἶπαν aor. 19
λέγω. ἴδε aor. imp. ὁράω. ἀπῆλθεν aor. ἀπέρχομαι to go out.

■ Ἕλληνες Greeks by birth (Schnackenburg), those of non- 20
Jewish birth (Barrett). ἀναβαινόντων pres. act. part.
ἀναβαίνω to go up. προσκυνήσωσιν aor. subj. προσκυνέω
to worship. (For the worship of half proselytes, s. SB, II, 548–
551.) ■ προσῆλθον aor. προσέρχομαι to come to, to go to. 21
ἠρώτων impf. ἐρωτάω to ask, to make a request. ἰδεῖν aor. inf.
ὁράω to see. ■ ἐλήλυθεν perf. ἔρχομαι. δοξασθῇ aor. pass. 23
subj., s.v.16. ■ κόκκος seed, grain. πεσών aor. part. πίπτω to 24
fall. ἀποθάνῃ aor. subj. ἀποθνήσκω to die. ■ φιλῶν pres. act. 25
part. φιλέω to love. μισῶν pres. act. part. μισέω to hate.
φυλάξει fut. φυλάσσω to guard, to preserve. The use of this
verb indicates that the life is a pres. possession which will extend
into eternity (Schnackenburg). ■ διακονῇ pres. subj. 26

ἀκολουθείτω pres. imp. 3rd sing. ἀκολουθέω to follow, to follow as a disciple (s. TDNT). The sense is that a man must follow Jesus if he would serve Him (Tasker). εἰμὶ pres., pres. of anticipation; He refers to the state of the celestial glory of Jesus, as the promise (Godet). ἔσται fut. εἰμί. τιμήσει fut. τιμάω to honor.

27   ■ τετάρακται perf. pass. ταράσσω to trouble (s. John 11:33). The perf. emphasizes the state or condition. εἴπω aor. subj. λέγω, deliberative subj. The words represent a rhetorical question and reveal the human shrinking from death (Morris).

28/29 ἦλθον aor., s.v.1. ■ δόξασον aor. imp. ■ ἐστώς perf. part. ἵστημι perf. to stand. βροντή thunder. γεγονέναι perf. inf.

30 γίνομαι. λελάληκεν perf. λαλέω. ■ ἀπεκρίθη aor. pass.

31 ἀποκρίνομαι. γέγονεν perf. γίνομαι. ■ ἐκβληθήσεται fut.

32 pass. ἐκβάλλω to cast out, to throw out. ■ ὑψωθῶ aor. pass.

33 subj. ὑψόω to lift up. ἑλκύσω fut. ἑλκύω to drag, to draw. ■ σημαίνων pres. part. σημαίνω to signify, to indicate. Not to be considered a technical term for the prophecy of an oracle (s. TDNT). ἤμελλεν impf. μέλλω. (For the construction, s. John

34 6:6.) ■ ἠκούσαμεν aor., s.v.18. δεῖ it is necessary. ὑψωθῆναι

35 aor. pass. inf. ■ περιπατεῖτε pres. imp. περιπατέω to walk, to walk about. καταλάβῃ aor. subj. καταλαμβάνω to overcome, to overtake (s. John 1:5). περιπατῶν pres. act. part. οἶδα defec-

36 tive perf. w. a pres. meaning to know. ■ πιστεύετε pres. imp. υἱοὶ φωτός "sons of light." This is a common designation in the DSS (s. 1QS 1:9, 2:16; 1QM 1:1, 3, etc.) γένησθε aor. subj. γίνομαι. ἐλάλησεν aor.

    ἀπελθών aor. part. ἀπέρχομαι s.v.19. ἐκρύβη aor. pass.

37 κρύπτω to conceal, to hide, pass. to hide one's self. ■ τοσοῦτος so many. In this case not "so great" (Westcott). πεποιηκότος perf. part. ποιέω gen. abs. The perf. points to the permanent character (Morris). ἔμπροσθεν w. the gen. before, in the presence of. ἐπίστευον impf. The impf. emphasizes the repeated unbelief or the continual stubbornness of the unbelief (Schnack-

38 enburg). ■ πληρωθῇ aor. pass. subj., s.v.3. ἐπίστευσεν aor. ἀκοή report. βραχίων arm. ἀπεκαλύφθη aor. pass.

39/40 ἀποκαλύπτω to reveal. ■ ἠδύνατο impf. mid. δύναμαι. ■ τετύφλωκεν perf. τυφλόω to blind. The perf. emphasizes the continuing state. ἐπώρωσεν aor. πωρόω to harden. It describes the formation of a "callus" in a part of the body (Westcott). ἴδωσιν aor. subj., s.v.9. νοήσωσιν aor. subj. νοέω to understand, to comprehend. The aor. may be ingressive, "to realize" (M, 117). στραφῶσιν aor. pass. subj. στρέφω pass. to be converted. It has the sense of a middle voice, "to turn themselves"

(Brown). ■ **εἶδεν** aor. ὁράω. ■ **ὅμως** "nevertheless even," "but 41/42 yet even" (s. RWP). **ὡμολόγουν** impf. ὁμολογέω to confess. The tense marks the continued shrinking from the act of faith (Westcott). **ἀποσυνάγωγος** excommunicated, expelled from the synagogue. **γένωνται** aor. subj., s.v.36. ■ **ἠγάπησαν** aor. 43 ἀγαπάω to love. (For the term "glory of men" in DSS, s. 1Q 4:23.)

■ **ἔκραξεν** aor. κράζω to shout, to cry out. **πιστεύων** pres. 44 part. **πέμψαντα** aor. part. πέμπω to send. ■ **θεωρῶν** pres. part. 45 ■ **ἐλήλυθα** perf., s.v.23. **μείνῃ** aor. subj. μένω to remain. ■ 46/47 **φυλάξῃ** aor. subj., s.v.25. ■ **ἀθετῶν** pres. part. ἀθετέω to set 48 aside, to reject. **λαμβάνων** pres. part. **κρίνοντα** pres. part. **κρινεῖ** fut. ■ **δέδωκεν** perf. δίδωμι. **εἴπω** aor. subj. **λαλήσω** 49 aor. subj. ■ **εἴρηκεν** perf. λέγω.   50

Ch. 13

■ **εἰδώς** perf. part. of the defective perf. οἶδα w. a pres. 1 meaning to know. **ἦλθεν** aor. ἔρχομαι. The aor. expresses what has just happened (M, 135). **μεταβῇ** aor. subj. μεταβαίνω to depart, to transfer. Well chosen to express transference from one world to another (Barrett). **ἀγαπήσας** aor. part. ἀγαπάω to love. Love becomes an important concept in this section of Christ's dealing w. His disciples (s. Dodd, 398ff.). **εἰς τέλος** "to the end" or "to the utmost." Perhaps both meanings are intended (Morris). **ἠγάπησεν** aor. ἀγαπάω. ■ **γινομένου** aor. mid. 2 part. gen. abs. **βεβληκότος** perf. part. βάλλω to throw, to place or put something into the heart (BAG). **παραδοῖ** aor. subj. παραδίδωμι to betray, to deliver over. ■ **ἔδωκεν** aor. δίδωμι. 3 **ἐξῆλθεν** aor. ἐξέρχομαι to go out. ■ **ἐγείρεται** pres. pass. 4 ἐγείρω to arise, historical pres. **λαβών** aor. act. part. λαμβάνω. **ἱμάτιον** linen, towel (s. SB, II, 556f.). **διέζωσεν** aor. διαζώννυμι to tie around one's self. ■ **νιπτήρ** basin or jug. 5 Washing was done by pouring water over the feet from one vessel into another (Morris). **ἤρξατο** aor. mid. ἄρχομαι to begin. **νίπτω** to wash. **ἐκμάσσω** to wipe off. **διεζωσμένος** perf. pass. part. It was the duty of the non-Jewish servant to wash the feet of his master. A Jewish slave was not required to do this (s. SB, II, 557). ■ **σύ** and **μου**, both pronouns are emphatic and 6 special stress is on the second (Bernard). ■ **ἀπεκρίθη** aor. pass. 7 ἀποκρίνομαι to answer. **γνώσῃ** fut. γινώσκω. ■ **οὐ μή** "not 8 in anywise." **νίψῃς** aor. subj. μέρος part. Jesus' answer points us to a washing free from sin which only Christ can give (Morris). ■ **λελουμένος** perf. pass. part. λούω to wash, to bathe. The 10 former verb tends to be used for washing a part of the body; here

for the whole body (Brown). The perf. emphasizes the state and character of one who has been bathed. νίψασθαι aor. mid. inf. καθαρός clean. Jesus symbolically declares the complete purification through the humiliation of the death of the Messiah (Hoskyns).
11 kyns). ■ ᾔδει plperf. οἶδα. παραδιδόντα pres. part.
12 ■ ἔνιψεν aor. ἔλαβεν aor. λαμβάνω. ἀνέπεσεν aor. ἀναπίπτω to recline, to recline at the table. πεποίηκα perf.
13 ■ φωνεῖτε pres. φωνέω to call, to address. Used for addressing one w. his title (RWP). διδάσκαλος nom. the articular nom.
14 used in address (M, 70; BD, 81). ■ ὀφείλω to owe a debt, to be obligated. Used to express human and ethical obligations (CBB;
15 TDNT). ■ ὑπόδειγμα example, pattern, illustration (Barrett;
16 MM). ἐποίησα aor. ποιῆτε pres. subj. ■ μείζων comp. μέγας Used w. the gen. of comparison. πέμψαντος aor. part. πέμπω
17 to send. ■ εἰ used w. the ind. introducing a condition and carries the implication that in fact they did know them (Morris). ἐάν introduces a conditional clause which has less certainty (Mor-
18 ris). ■ ἐξελεξάμην aor. mid. ἐκλέγω to choose, to select for one's self. πληρωθῇ aor. pass. subj. πληρόω to fill, to fulfill (s. Matt. 5:17). τρώγων pres. part. τρώγω to chew, to eat. ἐπῆρεν
19 aor. ἐπαίρω to lift up. πτέρνα heel. ■ γενέσθαι aor. mid. inf.
20 γίνομαι. πιστεύητε aor. mid. subj. ■ πέμψω fut.
21   ■ εἰπών aor. part. λέγω. ἐταράχθη aor. pass. ταράσσω to trouble, to be disturbed (s. John 11:33). ἐμαρτύρησεν aor. μαρτυρέω to bear witness. Used here in the sense of making an important and solemn declaration (Barrett). παραδώσει fut.
22 παραδίδωμι to betray, to deliver over. ■ ἔβλεπον impf. ἀπορούμενοι pres. mid. part. ἀπορέω to be at a loss, to be
23 disturbed. ■ ἀνακείμενος pres. part. ἀνάκειμαι to lie at the
24 table, to recline. ἠγάπα impf. ἀγαπάω. ■ νεύω to nod, to signal
25 by nodding the head. εἰπέ aor. imp. λέγω. ■ ἀναπεσών aor. part. ἀναπίπτω. στῆθος chest. (For the seating arrangement
26 and other customs of a meal, s. SB, IV, 611–639.) ■ βάψω fut. βάπτω to dip. ψωμίον this small piece of bread. δώσω fut.
27 δίδωμι. βάψας aor. part. ■ εἰσῆλθεν aor. εἰσέρχομαι to go in. ποίησον aor. imp. τάχιον comp. "more quickly" (s. Morris).
28/29 ■ ἔγνω aor. γινώσκω. ■ ἐδόκουν impf. δοκέω to suppose. ἐπεί since, because. γλωσσόκομον bag, purse (s. John 12:6). ἀγόρασον aor. imp. ἀγοράζω to buy. δῷ aor. subj. δίδωμι.
30 ■ ἐξῆλθεν aor., s.v.3.
31   ■ ἐδοξάσθη aor. pass. δοξάζω to glorify. Used intransitively "to display one's importance, greatness, or glory." It indicates that God has made a full display of His glory in the person of the Son of man (G.B. Caird, "The Glory of God in the Fourth

Gospel: An Exercise in Biblical Semantics," NTS 15 [April, 1969], 265–277). ■ δοξάσει fut. ■ τεκνίον little child. A dimin. 32/33 expressing affection (Morris). ζητήσετε fut. ζητέω to seek. ἐλθεῖν aor. inf. ἔρχομαι. ■ ἀγαπᾶτε pres. subj. ἠγάπησα aor. 34 ἀγαπάω. Used to express purpose (Bultmann). This is the new commandment of the new covenant (Brown). ■ γνώσονται fut. 35 mid., s.v.7. ἔχητε pres. subj.

■ ἀπεκρίθη aor. pass., s.v.7. ἀκολουθῆσαι aor. pass. inf. 36 ἀκολουθέω to follow, to follow as a disciple. ὕστερον later. ■ θήσω fut. τίθημι to place, to lay down. ■ φωνήσῃ aor. subj. 37/38 φωνέω to call, to crow. ἀρνήσῃ aor. subj. ἀρνέομαι to deny.

Ch. 14

■ ταρασσέσθω pres. pass. imp. 3rd sing. ταράσσω to 1 trouble (s. John 11:33). The pres. subj. w. the neg. indicates the stopping of an action in progress (MKG, 272). πιστεύετε pres. imp. Jesus is urging His followers to continue to believe and in this way not to let their hearts be troubled (Morris). ■ μονή 2 dwelling place. John may be referring to places where the disciples can dwell in peace by remaining w. the Father (Brown). ἑτοιμάσαι aor. inf. ἑτοιμάζω to prepare. Infinitive used to express purpose. ■ ἐάν here, "when" (Brown). πορευθῶ aor. 3 pass. subj. ἑτοιμάσω aor. subj. παραλήψομαι fut. mid. παραλαμβάνω to take w. someone. ἦτε pres. subj. εἰμί. ■ οἶδα 4 defective perf. w. a pres. meaning to know. ■ καί "that is to say," 6 epexegetical use of the particle (s. BD, 228). The repetition of the definite article refers to Christ as the real truth, life, etc., and all other, His transitory (MT, 178). ■ ἐγνώκειτε plperf. 7 γινώσκω. (For the type of conditional clause here, s. Brown.) ᾔδειτε plperf. οἶδα. ἀπ' ἄρτι "from now on." ἑωράκατε perf. ὁράω to see. The perf. indicates the lasting results. ■ δεῖξον aor. 8 imp. δείκνυμι to show. ἀρκέω to be strong, to be enough, to be sufficient. ■ τοσοῦτος so great, "so long a time." ἔγνωκας perf. 9 γινώσκω. ἑωρακώς perf. ■ πιστεύων pres. part. ποιήσει fut. 12 μείζων comp. μέγας. Used w. the gen. of comparison. ■ ἄν 13 generalizes and includes anything at all (Morris). αἰτήσητε aor. subj. αἰτέω to ask. δοξασθῇ aor. pass. subj. δοξάζω to glorify.

■ ἀγαπᾶτε pres. subj. ἀγαπάω to love. τηρήσετε fut. 15 τηρέω to guard, to keep. ■ ἐρωτήσω fut. ἐρωτάω to ask. Gen- 16 erally used of the prayers of Jesus Himself (Bernard). παράκλητος advocate, comforter. (For the meaning of this term, s. Brown II, 1135–1144; MNTW; CBB; TDNT.) δώσει fut. δίδωμι. ᾖ pres. subj. εἰμί. ■ λαβεῖν aor. inf. λαμβάνω. 17 ■ ἀφήσω fut. ἀφίημι to leave, to forsake. ὀρφανός orphan, 18

used of children left without a father and also used of disciples
19/20 left without a master (Barrett). ∎ ζήσετε fut. ζάω to live. ∎
21 γνώσεσθε fut. mid. γινώσκω. ∎ ἔχων pres. part. τηρῶν pres.
part., used as subject of sentence in a casus pendens construction, followed by a resumptive pron. (s. MH, 423). ἀγαπῶν
pres. part. The article is used here w. the predicate signifying that
the predicate is identical w. the subject and the only one of its
kind (s. Harner, 75; s. John 1:1). ἀγαπηθήσεται fut. pass.
ἀγαπήσω fut. ἐμφανίσω fut. ἐμφανίζω to reveal, to manifest,
to make visible. The presentation in a clear, conspicuous form
22/23 (Westcott). ∎ γέγονεν perf. γίνομαι. μέλλω s. John 6:6. ∎
ἀπεκρίθη aor. pass. ἀποκρίνομαι to answer. ἐλεύσόμεθα fut.
24 mid. ἔρχομαι. ποιησόμεθα fut. mid. ∎ πέμψαντός aor. part.
πέμπω to send.
25/26   ∎ λελάληκα perf. λαλέω to speak. ∎ πέμψει fut. διδάξει
fut. ὑπομνήσει fut. ὑπομιμνήσκω to cause to remember, to
27 bring to remembrance. ∎ δειλιάτω imp. 3rd sing. δειλιάω to be
28 afraid, to be cowardly, to be timid. ∎ ἠκούσατε aor. ἠγαπᾶτε
29 impf. ἀγαπάω. ἐχάρητε aor. χαίρω. ∎ εἴρηκα perf. λέγω.
πρίν used w. the inf. to express time, "before." γενέσθαι aor.
mid. inf. γίνομαι. γένηται aor. mid. subj. πιστεύσητε aor.
30 subj. The aor. may mean "come to trust" (Morris). ∎ λαλήσω
31 fut. ∎ γνῶ aor. subj. γινώσκω. ἐνετείλατο aor. mid. ἐντέλλω.
ἐγείρεσθε pres. pass. imp. ἐγείρω to arise. ἄγωμεν pres. subj.
ἄγω to go, hortatory subj.

Ch. 15

1   ∎ ἄμπελος vine. (For the Jewish symbol of the vine, s.
Barrett; Hoskyns.) ἀληθινός true, genuine. γεωργός farmer,
one who tills the soil. Refers in a specialized way to a vinedresser
2 (Brown). ∎ κλῆμα cane, shoot of a vine (Morris). φέρον pres.
part. φέρω to carry, to bear. αἴρω to lift up, to take away.
καθαίρω to cleanse, here in the sense of "cleanse by pruning"
(Bernard). πλείων comp. πολός. φέρῃ pres. subj. Used to ex-
3 press purpose. ∎ δία w. the acc. the cause of. λελάληκα perf.
The perf. may indicate that the word may remain w. them (Mor-
4 ris). ∎ μείνατε aor. imp. μένω to remain. (S. Jürgen Heise,
Bleiben: Menein in den Johanneischen Schriften.) μένῃ pres.
5 subj. ∎ μένων pres. part. χωρίς w. the gen. without, apart from.
6 ∎ ἐβλήθη aor. pass. βάλλω to throw. ἔξω out, here "out of the
vineyard" (Morris). ἐξηράνθη aor. pass. ξηραίνω to dry out,
pass. to become dry, to wither. συνάγουσιν the subject "they"
may refer to the unnamed servants (Bernard) or it is the Semitic
custom of using the 3rd per. pl. as the pass. (Brown). καίεται

pres. pass. καίω to burn. ■ μείνητε aor. subj. μένω. θέλητε 7
pres. subj. αἰτήσασθε aor. mid. imp. αἰτέω to ask. γενήσεται
fut. mid. γίνομαι. ■ ἐν τούτῳ the pron. looks back, and at the 8
same time the thought already indicated is developed in the
words which follow (Westcott). ἐδοξάσθη aor. pass. δοξάζω to
glorify. The aor. views the glorification as complete (Morris).
φέρητε aor. subj. φέρω. γενήσθε aor.; a variant reading
γενήσεσθε fut. mid. If the fut. is adopted, it has a kind of
independence "and then you will become" (BD, 186). ■ 9
ἠγάπησεν aor. ἀγαπάω to love. ■ τηρήσητε aor. subj. τηρέω 10
to guard, to observe. μενεῖτε fut. τετήρηκα perf.

■ ᾖ subj. εἰμί. πληρωθῇ aor. pass. subj. πληρόω to fulfill. 11
■ ἀγαπᾶτε pres. subj. ■ μείζων comp. μέγας used w. a gen. of 12/13
comparison. The ἵνα sentence w. the subj. is explanatory (Barrett). θῇ aor. subj. τίθημι to lay, to lay down. ■ ποιῆτε pres. 14
subj. ■ εἴρηκα perf. λέγω. ἤκουσα aor. ἀκούω. ἐγνώρισα aor. 15
γνωρίζω to make known. The aor. contemplates the completed
work of Christ (Barrett). ■ ἐξελέξασθε aor. mid. ἐκλέγω to 16
choose, to choose for one's self. ἔθηκα aor. τίθημι. ὑπάγητε
aor. ὑπάγω to go, to go forth. αἰτήσητε aor. subj. δῷ aor. subj.
δίδωμι. ■ ταῦτα "these." It indicates all that Jesus has com- 17
manded them is designed to teach them the lesson of mutual love
(SM).

■ γινώσκετε pres. imp. μεμίσηκεν perf. μισέω to hate. 18
The perf. points to a permanent attitude (Morris). ■ ἦτε impf. 19
εἰμί. ἄν. Used in a contrary to fact conditional clause. ἐφίλει
impf. φιλέω to love. ■ μνημονεύετε pres. imp. μνημονεύω to 20
remember, followed by the gen. ἐδίωξαν aor. διώκω to persecute. διώξουσιν fut. ἐτήρησαν aor. τηρήσουσιν fut. ■ 21
ποιήσουσιν fut. πέμψαντα aor. part. πέμπω to send. ■ ἦλθον 22
aor. ἔρχομαι. ἐλάλησα aor. εἴχοσαν impf. ἔχω. The impf. w.
this ending is common in the LXX and occurs in the papyri and
inscriptions (RWP; s. also MH, 194f.). πρόφασις excuse. It is
what is put forth to justify it, whether this is the real reason or
a mere excuse (Morris). ■ ἑωράκασιν perf. ὁράω to see. ■ 24/25
γεγραμμένος perf. pass. part. ἐμίσησεν aor. δωρεάν without
cause.

■ ἔλθῃ aor. subj. ἔρχομαι. παράκλητος (s. John 14:16). 26
μαρτυρήσει fut. ματυρέω to bear witness. ■ μαρτυρεῖτε pres. 27
imp. It could be understood also as ind. (Brown).

Ch. 16

■ λελάληκα perf. σκανδαλισθῆτε aor. pass. subj. 1
σκανδαλίζω to cause to stumble (s. TDNT). ■ 2

ἀποσυνάγωγος expelled from the synagogue. ποιήσουσιν fut.
ἀποκτείνας aor. part. ἀποκτείνω to kill. δόξῃ aor. subj. δοκέω
to suppose. λατρεία service. Denotes worship as well as the
3 more general idea of the service of God (Morris). ■ ἔγνωσαν
4 aor. γινώσκω. ■ ἔλθῃ aor. subj. ἔρχομαι.
5   ἤμην impf. εἰμί. ■ πέμψαντα aor. part. πέμπω to send.
6/7 ■ πεπλήρωκεν perf. πληρόω to fulfill. ■ συμφέρει it is expedient, it is of an advantage, it is profitable. παράκλητος (s. John
14:16). πορευθῶ aor. pass. subj. πορεύομαι to go, to go away.
8 πέμψω fut. ■ ἐλθών aor. part. ἔρχομαι. ἐλέγξει fut. ἐλέγχω
to expose, to convict, to cross-examine for the purpose of con-
vincing or refuting an opponent, esp. used of legal proceedings
(s. Morris). δικαιοσύνη righteousness. Christ's own righteousness as the standard and source (MRP, 143). κρίσις judgment.
9 ■ ὅτι "because" or "that." (For the possible construction, s.
10/11 Barrett.) ■ οὐκέτι no longer. ■ κέκριται perf. pass. κρίνω to
judge.
12   ■ βαστάζω to bear. The basic idea is that they cannot
13 understand now (Brown). ■ ὁδηγήσει fut. ὁδηγέω to show the
way, the figure of a guide who introduces the traveler into an
unknown country (Godet). λαλήσει fut. ἐρχόμενα pres. mid.
14 part. ἀναγγελεῖ fut. ἀναγέλλω to proclaim. ■ δοξάσει fut.
δοξάζω to glorify. λήμψεται fut. mid. λαμβάνω. ἀναγγελεῖ
fut. Repetition of this word puts emphasis on this aspect of the
Spirit's work (Morris).
16/17   ■ ὄψεσθε fut. mid. ὁράω. ■ οἶδα defective perf. w. a pres.
18/20 meaning to know. ■ ἤθελον impf. θέλω. ■ κλαύσετε fut.
κλαίω to cry, to weep. θρηνήσετε fut. θρηνέω to mourn. The
reference is to the loud wailing and lamentation that is the customary reaction to death in the Near East (Brown). χαρήσεται
fut. χαίρω to rejoice. λυπηθήσεσθε fut. pass. λυπέω pass. to
21 be sad. γενήσεται fut. mid. γίνομαι. ■ τίκτῃ pres. subj. τίκτω
to give birth. ἦλθεν aor. ἔρχομαι. γεννήσῃ aor. subj. γεννάω
to give birth. The previous pres. depicts the woman as in the act
of childbirth, the aor. here sees the process as complete (Morris).
23 ἐγεννήθη aor. pass. ■ ἐρωτήσετε fut. αἰτήσητε aor. subj.
24 αἰτέω to ask. δώσει fut. δίδωμι. ■ ᾐτήσατε aor. αἰτέω.
αἰτεῖτε pres. imp. ᾖ pres. subj. εἰμί. πεπληρωμένη perf. pass.
part. Used to form the periphrastic perf. pass. subj. Used to
express purpose (RWP).
26/27   ■ αἰτήσεσθε fut. mid. ■ πεφιλήκατε perf.
πεπιστεύκατε perf. The perf. tense of these verbs implies a
continuous attitude of life (Brown). ἐξῆλθον aor. ἐξέρχομαι to
28/29/31 go out. ■ ἐλήλυθα perf. ἔρχομαι. ■ ἴδε aor. imp. ὁράω. ■

ἀπεκρίθη aor. pass. ἀποκρίνομαι to answer. ■ σκορπισθῆτε 32
aor. pass. subj. σκορπίζω to scatter. ἀφῆτε aor. subj. ἀφίημι
to forsake. ■ ἔχητε pres. subj. θαρσεῖτε pres. imp. θαρσέω to 33
have courage, to be courageous. νενίκηκα perf. νικάω to conquer. The perf. tense denotes an abiding victory (Morris).

Ch. 17

■ ἐλάλησεν aor. ἐπάρας aor. part. ἐπαίρω to lift up. 1
ἐλήλυθεν perf. ἔρχομαι. δόξασον aor. imp. δοξάζω to glorify.
δοξάσῃ aor. subj. ■ ἔδωκας aor. δίδωμι. δέδωκας perf. The 2
perf. denotes the permanence of the gift (Morris). δώσῃ aor.
subj. δίδωμι "grace" in the Pauline epistles, "giving" in the
fourth gospel (s. Morris). ■ ἵνα "that," explanatory use. 3
ἀπέστειλας aor. ἀποστέλλω to send, to send as a personal
authoritative representative (s. TDNT). ■ ἐδόξασα aor. 4
τελειώσας aor. part. τελειόω to bring to completion, to reach
the goal, to finish. It looks back upon the completed life of Jesus,
and probably upon His death too (Barrett). ἵνα expresses either
purpose or it is explanatory (s. Brown). ποιήσω aor. subj. ■ 5
εἶναι inf. εἰμί.

■ ἐφανέρωσα aor. φανερόω to make clear, to reveal. The 6
aor. sums up the work of the ministry and is parallel to v.4
(Barrett). τετήρηκαν perf. τηρέω to keep. (For the form, s. BD,
44.) ■ ἔγνωκαν perf. γινώσκω. ■ ἔλαβον aor. λαμβάνω. 7/8
ἔγνωσαν aor. γινώσκω. ἐξῆλθον aor. ἐξέρχομαι to go out.
ἐπίστευσαν aor. ■ δέδωκας perf. ■ δεδόξασμαι perf. pass. 9/10
The perf. indicates the state of glorification and may be proleptic
pointing forward to the glory that was yet to come, but which
was certain (Morris). ■ τήρησον aor. imp. ἐν the "in" is both 11
local and instrumental. They are to be both marked w. and
protected by the divine name (Brown). ὦσιν subj. εἰμί. ■ ἤμην 12
impf. εἰμί ἐτήρουν impf. ἐφύλαξα aor. φυλάσσω to guard.
The aor. sums up the process represented by the impf. (Barrett).
ἀπώλετο aor. mid. ἀπόλλυμι to destroy, to be lost, to perish.
ἀπώλεια destruction, perdition, damnation (s. Brown).
πληρωθῇ aor. pass. subj. πληρόω to fulfill. ■ πεπληρωμένην 13
perf. pass. part. ■ ἐμίσησεν aor. μισέω to hate. ■ ἄρῃς aor. 14/15
subj. αἴρω to lift up, to take away. τηρήσῃς aor. subj. ■ 17
ἁγίασον aor. imp. ἁγιάζω to sanctify, to set apart and dedicate
a person or thing for the service of God and to dedicate as a
sacrifice (Hoskyns). ἀλήθεια truth. (For the construction without the article, s. John 1:1.) ■ ἀπέστειλα aor. The aor. is used 18
proleptically referring to the commission after the resurrection
(Morris). ■ ἡγιασμένοι perf. pass. part. ἁγιάζω. 19

20/21   ■ πιστευόντων pres. part. ■ ἵνα. The first two clauses
express the content of prayer and the third expresses purpose
23 (Brown). πιστεύῃ pres. subj. ■ τετελειωμένοι perf. pass. part.
used in a periphrastic construction to form the perf. pass. subj.
used to express purpose. The perf. indicates a permanent state
as the goal and final result (RWP). γινώσκῃ pres. subj.
24 ἠγάπησας aor. ἀγαπάω to love. ■ θεωροῦσιν pres. subj.
25 θεωρέω to see. ■ καί "both," that is, "both the world and these"
26 (s. Morris). ■ ἐγνώρισα aor. γνωρίζω to make known. ᾖ subj.
εἰμί.

Ch. 18
1   ■ εἰπών aor. part. λέγω participle to express antecedent
time, "after." ἐξῆλθεν aor. ἐξέρχομαι to go out. χείμαρρος
brook. One containing water perhaps only in the winter (Barrett). κῆπος garden. Refers to a plot of land where vegetables
or flowers are planted and sometimes trees as well (Brown). Such
gardens were forbidden in Jerusalem (s. SB, I, 992f.). εἰσῆλθεν
2 aor. εἰσέρχομαι to go in. ■ ᾔδει plperf. of the defective perf.
οἶδα to know. παραδιδούς pres. part. παραδίδωμι to betray,
3 to deliver over. συνήχθη aor. pass. συνάγω. ■ λαβών aor.
part. λαμβάνω. σπεῖρα cohort (s. Morris). ὑπηρέτης minister,
the temple police (s. Brown). φανός torch. λαμπάς lantern,
4/5 lamp. ὅπλον weapon. ■ εἰδώς pres. part. οἶδα. ■ ἀπεκρίθησαν
aor. pass. ἀποκρίνομαι to answer. εἰστήκει plperf. ἵστημι
6 perf. to stand. ■ ἀπῆλθαν aor. ἀπέρχομαι to go away. ἔπεσαν
7 aor. πίπτω to fall. χαμαί to the ground. ■ ἐπηρώτησεν aor.
8 ἐπερωτάω to question, to ask. ■ ἄφετε aor. imp. ἀφίημι to
9 allow. ■ πληρωθῇ aor. pass. subj. πληρόω to fulfill. δέδωκας
perf. δίδωμι. ἀπώλεσα aor. ἀπόλλυμι to perish, to be lost.
10 ■ εἵλκυσεν aor. ἑλκύω to draw. ἔπαισεν aor. παίω to strike.
ἀπέκοψεν aor. ἀποκόπτω to cut off. ὠτάριον dimin. ear, the
11 external part of the ear (s. Brown). δεξιός right. ■ βάλε aor.
imp. βάλλω to throw, to place. θήκη scabbard, here the recepta-
cle into which a thing is put (Barrett). πίω aor. subj. πίνω to
drink.

12   ■ συνέλαβον aor. συλλαμβάνω to seize, to take into
14 custody. ■ συμφέρει it is useful, it is advantageous (s. John
16:7). ἀποθανεῖν aor. inf. ἀποθνήσκω to die.

15   ■ ἠκολούθει impf. ἀκολουθέω to follow. γνωστός
known. συνεισῆλθεν aor. συνεισέρχομαι to go in together.
16 αὐλή courtyard. ■ εἰστήκει s.v.5. θυρωρός doorkeeper.
εἰσήγαγεν aor. εἰσάγω to lead into. The subject is uncertain;
the meaning might be "he brought Peter in" or "she admitted

Peter" (Morris). ■ παιδίσκη maidservant. ■ ἀνθρακιά char- 17/18
coal fire. πεποιηκότες perf. part. ψῦχος cold. ἐθερμαίνοντο
impf. mid. θερμαίνομαι to warm one's self. ἑστώς perf. part.
ἵστημι. θερμαινόμενος pres. mid. part.

■ οὖν then, now. Here it indicates a succession of events (s. 19
DM, 253f.). ἠρώτησεν aor. ἐρωτάω to question. ■ ἀπεκρίθη 20
aor. pass., s.v.5. λελάληκα perf. ἐδίδαξα aor. ἐλάλησα aor.
■ ἐρώτησον aor. imp. ἀκηκοότας perf. act. part. ἀκούω. ἴδε 21
aor. imp. ὁράω. ■ εἰπόντος aor. part. gen. abs. παρεστηκώς 22
perf. part. παρίσταμι to stand along side of. ἔδωκεν aor.
δίδωμι. ῥάπισμα slap, a blow on the face w. the flat of the hand
(Barrett). ■ μαρτύρησον aor. imp. μαρτυρέω to testify, "pro- 23
duce some evidence of it" (Brown). ■ ἀπέστειλεν aor. 24
ἀποστέλλω to send. δεδεμένον perf. pass. part.

■ εἶπον aor. The subject is presumably the servants and 25
police mentioned in v.18 (Brown). ἠρνήσατο aor. mid.
ἀρνέομαι to deny. ■ συγγενής relative. ὤν part. εἰμί.
ἀπέκοψεν aor., s.v.10. ὠτίον ear. εἶδον aor. ὁράω. ■ ἀλέκτωρ 27
rooster. ἐφώνησεν aor. φωνέω to call, here to crow.

■ μιανθῶσιν aor. pass. subj. μιαίνω to defile. φάγωσιν 28
aor. subj. ἐσθίω to eat. πάσχα passover, not necessarily referring to the main passover meal but the remaining meals that will
be taken in the passover season (Tasker). ■ ἐξῆλθεν aor., s.v.1. 29
κατηγορία accusation. ■ ἀπεκρίθησαν aor. pass., s.v.5. 30
ποιῶν pres. part. παρεδώκαμεν aor. παραδίδωμι s.v.2. ■ 31
λάβετε aor. imp. λαμβάνω. κρίνατε aor. imp. κρίνω to judge.
ἔξεστιν it is lawful, it is allowed. ἀποκτεῖναι aor. inf.
ἀποκτείνω to kill (s. Morris, 786ff.; Sherwin-White, 36–43).
■ πληρωθῇ aor. pass. subj. σημαίνων pres. part. σημαίνω to 32
signify, to indicate. ἤμελλεν impf. μέλλω to be about to. (For
the construction w. the inf. to express the fut., s. John 6:6.) ■ 33
ἐφώνησεν s.v.27. ■ ἠγωνίζοντο impf. mid. ἀγωνίζομαι to 36
fight. The impf. indicates "they would be fighting," that is, fighting now (Morris). παραδοθῶ aor. pass. subj. παραδίδωμι. νῦν
non-temporal use following a sentence expressing an unfulfilled
condition "but as it is," "but as the case now stands" (Thrall, 31).
■ οὐκοῦν an augmentative particle seeking a definite answer 37
"very well; so you are a king?" (Barrett). γεγέννημαι perf. pass.
γεννάω to bear, pass. to be born. ἐλήλυθα perf. ἔρχομαι.
μαρτυρήσω aor. subj.

■ εἰπών aor. part. ■ συνήθεια custom (s. Blinzler, The 38/39
Trial of Jesus). ■ ἐκραύγασαν aor. κραυγάζω to scream. 40

Ch. 19

1 ■ ἔλαβεν aor. λαμβάνω. ἐμαστίγωσεν aor. μαστιγόω
2 to scourge (s. Matt. 27:26). ■ πλέξαντες aor. part. πλέκω to
plait. ἄκανθα thorn (s. Brown). ἐπέθηκαν aor. ἐπιτίθημι to
place upon. πορφυροῦς purple (s. Morris). περιέβαλον aor.
3 περιβάλλω to cast about, to put around. ■ ἤρχοντο impf. mid.
ἔρχομαι. χαῖρε imp. "Hail," followed by the nom. of address
w. the article "Hail, you king!" (Barrett). ἐδίδοσαν impf.
δίδωμι. The impf. speaks of repeated action. ῥάπισμα slap (s.
4 John 18:22). ■ ἐξῆλθεν aor. ἐξέρχομαι to go out. ἴδε aor. imp.
5 ὁράω. γνῶτε aor. subj. γινώσκω. ■ φορῶν pres. part. φορέω
to wear, to carry. ἀκάνθινος thorny, made of thorns. (For the
6 suffix indicating material, s. MH, 359.) ■ εἶδον aor. ὁράω.
ἐκραύγασαν aor. κραυγάζω to scream. σταύρωσον aor. imp.
7 σταυρόω to crucify. λάβετε aor. imp. λαμβάνω. ■
ἀπεκρίθησαν aor. pass. ἀποκρίνομαι to answer. ἀποθανεῖν
aor. inf. ἀποθνήσκω to die. ἐποίησεν aor.
8 ■ ἤκουσεν aor. ἀκούω. μᾶλλον more. ἐφοβήθη aor. pass.
9 φοβέομαι to fear, to be afraid. ■ εἰσῆλθεν aor. εἰσέρχομαι to
10 go into. ἔδωκεν aor. δίδωμι. ■ ἀπολῦσαι aor. inf. ἀπολύω to
11 release. σταυρῶσαι aor. inf. ■ δεδομένον perf. pass. part.
δίδωμι. ἄνωθεν from above (s. John 3:3). παραδούς aor. part.
παραδίδωμι to deliver over, to betray. μείζων comp. μέγας.
12 ■ ἐζήτει impf. ζητέω to seek. The conative impf. implies a series
of attempts which were shouted down (Brown). ἀπολύσῃς aor.
subj.
13 ■ ἀκούσας aor. part. w. the gen. ἤγαγεν aor. ἄγω.
ἐκάθισεν aor. καθίζω to sit down, to take one's seat. βῆμα
15 judgment seat (s. Blinzler). λεγόμενον pres. pass. part. ■ ἆρον
16 aor. imp. αἴρω to take away. σταυρώσω fut. ■ παρέδωκεν aor.
παραδίδωμι. σταυρωθῇ aor. pass. subj.
    παρέλαβον aor. παραλαμβάνω to take, to take custody
17 of. The subject is probably the soldiers (Morris). ■ βαστάζων
18/19 pres. part. βαστάζω to carry. ■ ἐσταύρωσαν aor., s.v.6. ■
ἔγραψεν aor. ἔθηκεν aor. τίθημι to place. γεγραμμένον perf.
20 pass. part. ■ ἀνέγνωσαν aor. ἀναγινώσκω to read.
21/22 ἐσταυρώθη aor. pass. ■ γράφε pres. imp. γέγραφα perf. The
perf. tense marks the permanence and abiding character of his
act. It was the expression of a legal decision (Bernard).
23 ■ ἔλαβον aor., s.v.1. ἐποίησαν aor. ἄρραφος without a
24 seam. ὑφαντός woven. ■ σχίσωμεν aor. subj. σχίζω to divide,
to split, hortatory subj. λάχωμεν aor. subj. λαγχάνω to obtain
by casting lots, to cast lots. πληρωθῇ aor. pass. subj. πληρόω
to fulfill. (For the ancient Jewish understanding of Ps. 22, s. SB,

II, 574–580.) διεμερίσαντο aor. mid. διαμερίζω to divide, to
distribute, mid. to divide among themselves. ἔβαλον aor.
βάλλω to throw, to cast. οὖν "so then," resumptive (MT, 337).
■ εἱστήκεισαν plperf. ἵστημι perf. to stand. ■ ἰδών aor. part. 25/26
ὁράω. παρεστῶτα perf. part. παρίστημι to stand alongside.
ἠγάπα impf. ἀγαπάω to love.
    ■ εἰδώς part. οἶδα. τετέλεσται perf. pass. τελέω to bring 28
to an end. It has the connotation of completion (Brown).
τελειωθῇ aor. pass. subj. τελειόω to accomplish. Used here in
the sense of the fulfillment of Scripture (Morris). ■ σκεῦος 29
vessel. ἔκειτο impf. κεῖμαι to set. ὄξος vinegar, a diluted vine-
gary wine drunk by soldiers and laborers (Brown). σπόγγος
sponge. ὕσσωπος hyssop. περιθέντες aor. part. περιτίθημι to
put around. προσήνεγκαν aor. προσφέρω to bring to someone. ■ κλίνας aor. part. κλίνω to bow. παρέδωκεν aor., s.v.16. 30
The verb indicates "to give up voluntarily" (Bernard).
    ■ μείνῃ aor. subj. μένω to remain. ἠρώτησαν aor. 31
ἐρωτάω to ask. κατεαγῶσιν aor. pass. subj. κατάγνυμι to
break. σκέλος leg. ■ ἦλθον aor. ἔρχομαι. κατέαξαν aor. 32
συσταυρωθέντος aor. pass. part. συσταυρόω to co-crucify, to
crucify together. ■ ἐλθόντες aor. part. ἔρχομαι. εἶδον aor., 33
s.v.6. τεθνηκότα perf. part. ἀποθνήσκω s.v.7. ■ λόγχη spear- 34
head, lance, a shaft tipped w. an iron point (Morris). πλευρά
side. ἔνυξεν aor. νύσσω to stab, to pierce. ἐξῆλθεν aor. A
possible translation is "and there came out immediately blood,
even fluid (water)," and it may be an allusion to the passover (s.
J.M. Ford, "Mingled Blood From the Side of Christ" [John
19:34], NTS, 15 [April, 1969], 337, 338). ■ ἑωρακώς perf. part. 35
ὁράω. μεμαρτύρηκεν perf. μαρτυρέω to bear witness. The
perf. signifies "he has said it on a permanent record" (Morris).
πιστεύητε pres. subj. The purpose clause probably modifies the
whole idea in the verse (Brown). ■ ἐγένετο aor. mid. γίνομαι. 36
ὀστοῦν bone. συντριβήσεται fut. pass. συντρίβω to shatter,
to crush. ■ ὄψονται fut. mid. ὁράω. ἐξεκέντησαν aor. 37
ἐκκεντέω to pierce.
    ■ ὤν pres. part. εἰμί. κεκρυμμένος perf. pass. part. 38
κρύπτω to hide, to conceal. The part. is used adverbially (Barrett). ἄρῃ aor. subj. αἴρω. ἐπέτρεψεν aor. ἐπιτρέπω to allow,
to permit. ἦρεν aor. αἴρω. ■ μίγμα mixture. σμύρνα myrrh. 39
ἀλόη aloes. A powdered aromatic sandalwood used for perfum-
ing bedding or clothes. Its purpose probably was to counteract
unpleasant odor and slow down corruption (Brown). λίτρα a
Roman pound (12 ounces) (BAG). ■ ἔλαβον aor., s.v.1. 40
ἔδησαν aor. δέω to bind. ὀθόνιον linen bandage. The body is

wrapped in the bandages, the spices being sprinkled between the
folds (Barrett; s. also Blinzler). ἄρωμα spices, aromatic oil (s.
41 Brown). ἐνταφιάζω to bury. ■ ἐσταυρώθη aor. pass., s.v.20.
42 τεθειμένος perf. pass. part. τίθημι s.v.19. ■ ἔθηκαν aor. (For
the form, s. BD, 47f.)

Ch. 20

1 ■ οὔσης pres. part. fem. εἰμί gen. abs. ἠρμένον perf. pass.
part. αἴρω to take away. This seems to imply that the stone was
lifted out of the groove in which it ran. The perf. may give an
2 air of finality (Morris). ■ ἐφίλει impf. φιλέω to love. ἦραν aor.
αἴρω. οἶδα defective perf. w. a pres. meaning to know. ἔθηκαν
3 aor. τίθημι s. John 19:42. ■ ἐξῆλθεν aor. ἐξέρχομαι to go out.
4 ἤρχοντο impf. ἔρχομαι. ■ ἔτρεχον impf. ὁμοῦ together.
προέδραμεν aor. προτρέχω to run before, to outrun (s.
Brown). τάχιον comp. adv. ταχύς fast. ἦλθεν aor. ἔρχομαι.
5 ■ παρακύψας aor. part. παρακύπτω to bend over. The verb
conveys the idea of bending over; that is to see something better,
"to peer into," "to peep into" (Morris). εἰσῆλθεν aor.
6 εἰσέρχομαι to go into. ■ ἀκολουθῶν pres. part. ἀκολουθέω
7 to follow. ■ σουδάριον handkerchief, a cloth used to wipe off
perspiration, probably the size of a small towel or large napkin
(Brown). ἐντετυλιγμένον perf. pass. part. ἐντυλίσσω to wrap.
8/9 ■ ἐλθών aor. part. ἔρχομαι. εἶδεν aor. ὁράω. ■ ᾔδεισαν plperf.
10 οἶδα. ἀναστῆναι aor. inf. ἀνίστημι to rise. ■ ἀπῆλθον aor.
ἀπέρχομαι to go out.
11   ■ εἱστήκει plperf. ἵσταμι perf. to stand. κλαίουσα pres.
12 part. fem. κλαίω to cry, to weep. παρέκυψεν aor. ■
καθεζομένους pres. mid. part. καθέζομαι to sit down. ἔκειτο
13 impf. κεῖμαι. ■ ἔθηκαν aor. τίθημι. ἦραν aor., s.v.2. ἐστράφη
aor. pass. στρέφομαι to turn around. ἑστῶτα perf. part.
15 ἵσταμι. ■ δοκοῦσα pres. part. fem. δοκέω to suppose.
κηπουρός gardener. ἐβάστασας aor. βαστάζω to carry, to
16 carry away. εἰπέ aor. imp. λέγω. ἀρῶ fut. αἴρω. ■ στραφεῖσα
17 aor. part. fem. στρέφομαι. ■ ἅπτου pres. imp. ἅπτομαι w. the
gen. to touch, to grasp, to cling. Jesus is asking her not to hold
onto Him (s. Brown). ἀναβέβηκα perf. ἀναβαίνω to ascend,
18 to go up. πορεύου pres. imp. πορεύομαι to go. ■ ἀγγέλλουσα
pres. part. fem. ἀγγέλλω to report. ἑώρακα perf. ὁράω.
19   ■ κεκλεισμένων perf. pass. part. κλείω to shut. ἔστη aor.
20 ἵστημι to stand. ■ εἰπών aor. part. λέγω. ἔδειξεν aor.
δείκνυμι to show. ἐχάρησαν aor. pass. χαίρω to be glad, to
21 rejoice. ἰδόντες aor. part., s.v.8. ■ ἀπέσταλκεν perf.
22 ἀποστέλλω to send. ■ ἐνεφύσησεν aor. ἐμφυσάω to breathe

upon. This is a preparatory event different from Pentecost (Hoskyns; s. also Morris). λάβετε aor. imp. λαμβάνω. ■ ἀφῆτε aor. 23 subj. ἀφίημι to release, to forgive. ἀφέωνται perf. pass. ἀφίημι. κρατῆτε pres. subj. κρατέω to hold, to retain. The church, not just the apostles, is now given authority to declare that certain sins are forgiven and certain sins are retained (Morris). κεκράτηνται perf. pass.

■ ἦλθεν aor., s.v.4. ■ ἑωράκαμεν perf., s.v.18. ἴδω aor. 24/25 subj. ὁράω. ἦλος nail. δάκτυλος finger. πιστεύσω aor. subj. ■ κεκλεισμένων perf. pass. part., s.v.19. ■ φέρε pres. imp. 26/27 φέρω to bring, to take. ἴδε aor. imp. ὁράω. βάλε aor. imp. βάλλω. γίνου pres. mid. imp. γίνομαι. ■ ἀπεκρίθη aor. pass. 28 ἀποκρίνομαι to answer. ■ πεπίστευκας perf. ἰδόντες aor. 29 part. πιστεύσαντες aor. ἐνώπιον w. gen. in the presence of, before.

■ γεγραμμένα perf. pass. part. ■ γέγραπται perf. pass. 30/31 The tense indicates that what he has written stands (Morris). πιστεύητε pres. subj. ἔχητε pres. subj.

Ch. 21

■ ἐφανέρωσεν aor. φανερόω to manifest, to make visible. 1 ■ ἁλιεύειν pres. inf., inf. of purpose, to fish. ἐξῆλθον aor. 3 ἐξέρχομαι to go out. ἐνέβησαν aor. ἐμβαίνω to get in, to embark. ἐπίασαν aor. πιάζω to catch. ■ γινομένης pres. mid. 4 part. fem. gen. abs. ἔστη aor. ἵστημι to stand. αἰγιαλός shore, beach. ᾔδεισαν plperf. οἶδα to know. ■ προσφάγιον relish. 5 Here best understood of some staple article of food of the genus fish. A part of an ordinary meal (MM). ἀπεκρίθησαν aor. pass. ἀποκρίνομαι to answer. ■ βάλετε aor. imp. βάλλω to throw. 6 δίκτυον net, casting net. εὑρήσετε fut. εὑρίσκω to find. ἔβαλον aor. βάλλω. ἑλκύσαι aor. inf. ἑλκύω to draw. ἴσχυον impf. ἰσχύω to be strong, to be able. Obedience to Christ, not luck, is the important thing (Morris). ■ ἠγάπα impf. ἀγαπάω 7 to love. ἀκούσας aor. part. ἐπενδύτης outer garment. Peter was working in a loin cloth, but for sake of modesty and reverence he put on his outer garment (Brown). διεζώσατο aor. mid. διαζώννομι to gird one's self by pulling up the tunic and allowing a fold to fall over the belt. ■ ἦλθον aor. ἔρχομαι. ὡς w. 8 numbers "about," "approximately." πῆχυς cubit, about 18 inches. Here "about a hundred yards away" (BAG). σύροντες pres. part. σύρω to draw, to drag. ■ ἀπέβησαν aor. ἀποβαίνω 9 to get out, to disembark. ἀνθρακιά charcoal fire. κειμένην pres. mid. part. κεῖμαι to lie. ὀψάριον fish. Normally refers to dried or preserved fish but here used to describe freshly caught

fish (Brown). ἐπικείμενον pres. mid. part. ἐπίκειμαι to lay
10/11 upon. ■ ἐνέγκατε aor. imp. φέρω to bring, to carry. ■ ἀνέβη
aor. ἀναβαίνω to go up. Here used of embarking on a ship
(Morris). εἵλκυσεν aor. ἑλκύω. ὄντων part. εἰμί gen. abs.
concessive "although." ἐσχίσθη aor. pass. σχίζω to tear, to rip,
12 to break. ■ ἀριστήσατε aor. imp. ἀριστέω to take breakfast
which was the first meal of the day (Barrett). ἐτόλμα impf.
τολμάω to dare. ἐξετάσαι aor. inf. ἐξετάζω to inquire, to ask.
14 εἰδότες part. οἶδα. ■ ἐφανερώθη aor. pass. ἐγερθείς aor. pass.
ἐγείρω to rise.
15   ■ ἠρίστησαν aor., s.v.12. πλέον comp. πολύς "more
than," gen. of comparison (s. Brown). φιλέω to love. (For a
discussion of this word and its synonym in the contest, s. Morris.) βόσκε pres. imp. βόσκω to feed as a herdsman, to tend.
16 ἀρνίον lamb. ■ ποίμαινε pres. imp. ποιμαίνω to shepherd, to
17 tend to sheep. προβάτιον sheep. ■ ἐλυπήθη aor. pass. λυπέω
18 pass. to be sad. ■ νεώτερος comp. νέος young. ἐζώννυες impf.
ζώννυμι to gird one's self, s.v.7. περιεπάτεις impf. περιπατέω
to go about. ἤθελες impf. θέλω. γηράσῃς aor. subj. γηράσκω
to become old. ἐκτενεῖς fut. ἐκτείνω to stretch out. ζώσει fut.
19 ζώννυμι. οἴσει fut. φέρω s.v.10. ■ σημαίνων pres. part.
σημαίνω to signify. δοξάσει fut. δοξάζω to glorify. εἰπών aor.
part. λέγω. ἀκολούθει pres. imp. ἀκολουθέω to follow.
20   ■ ἐπιστραφείς aor. pass. part. ἐπιστρέφομαι to turn
about. ἠγάπα impf., s.v.7. ἀκολουθοῦντα pres. part.
ἀνέπεσεν aor. ἀναπίπτω to recline at the table. παραδιδούς
21 pres. part. παραδίδωμι to betray, to deliver over. ■ ἰδών aor.
23 part. ὁράω. θέλω pres. subj. ■ ἐξῆλθεν aor., s.v.3. ἀποθνήσκω
pres. The pres. tense indicates "that disciple dies not" (Morris).
24   ■ μαρτυρῶν pres. part. μαρτυρέω to testify, to give witness. γράψας aor. part.
25   ■ ἐποίησεν aor. γράφηται pres. pass. subj. (For a defense
of the integrity and importance of this chapter, s. S.S. Smalley,
"The Sign in John 21," NTS, 20 [April, 1974], 275–288).

ACTS

πρῶτον "first," used for πρότερον "former." The first of two, not implying a third (GR, 662f.). λόγος book, treaty. This was a customary name for a division of the work which covered more than one roll of papyrus (LC). ἐποιησάμην aor. mid. ποιέω to make. The mid. is the usual construction for mental acts (RWP). ὧν gen. by attraction. ἤρξατο aor. mid. ἄρχομαι to begin. The verb is emphatic and is not a Semitic auxiliary. As the Gospel tells us what Jesus began to do and teach, so Acts tells what He continued to do and teach by His Holy Spirit (Bruce). ■ ἐντειλάμενος aor. mid. part. ἐντέλλομαι to in- 2 struct, to command. ἐξελέξατο aor. mid. ἐκλέγω to select, to choose. ἀνελήμφθη aor. pass. ἀναλαμβάνω to take up. Used of the ascension of Christ (Haenchen). ■ παρέστησεν aor. 3 παρίστημι to present. ζῶντα pres. part. ζάω to live. παθεῖν aor. inf. πάσχω to suffer. Used w. the inf. to express time, "after" (s. MT, 143). τεκμήριον sign, proof. In logic "demonstrative proof" (LC). In medical language "demonstrative evidence" (MLL, 184). ὀπτανόμενος pres. mid. part. ὀπτάνομαι to let one's self be seen, to appear to someone. It is not used in the sense of a vision (Haenchen; s. also MM). ■ συναλιζόμενος 4 pres. mid. part. συναλίζω lit., "to eat salt w.," "to eat w.," or possibly "to dwell w." (Bruce—ET). παρήγγειλεν aor. παραγγέλω to command. ἠκούσατε aor. ἀκούω to hear. ■ 5 βαπτισθήσεσθε fut. pass.

■ συνελθόντες aor. part. συνέρχομαι to come together. 6 ἠρώτων impf. ἐρωτάω to question, to ask. ἀποκαθιστάνω to restore, to restore to its former state. An eschatological technical term for the restoration of the right order through God in the end time (Haenchen; for the Jewish expectations, s. Moore, *Judaism* II, 323–376; SB, IV, 799–976). ■ γνῶναι aor. inf. γινώτκω. 7 Jesus refuses to answer the question not in respect of the matter itself but in respect of the time inquired after (Meyer). ἔθετο aor. mid. τίθημι to place, to set. ■ λήμψεσθε fut. λαμβάνω. 8 ἐπελθόντος aor. part. ἐπέρχομαι to come upon. ἔσεσθε fut. εἰμί. ἔσχατον last, end. ■ βλεπόντων pres. part. gen. abs. 9

263

ἐπήρθη aor. pass. ἐπαίρω to lift up. ὑπέλαβεν aor.
10 ὑπολαμβάνω to take up. ■ ἀτενίζοντες pres. part. ἀτενίζω to
gaze. Used by medical writers to denote a peculiar fixed look
(MLL, 76). παρειστήκεισαν plperf. παρίσταμι perf. to
11 stand. ἐσθής clothing. ■ ἐστήκατε perf. ἵστημι perf. to stand.
12   ■ ὑπέστρεψαν aor. ὑποστρέφω to return. ἐλαιών, ῶνος
olive yard, olivet. Nouns w. this suffix denote a place where
13 persons or things are found (Bruce). ■ ὑπερῷον an upstairs
room. Traditionally the study and the room for prayer of a rabbi
(LC). ἀνέβησαν aor. ἀναβαίνω to go up. καταμένοντες pres.
14 part. καταμένω to remain. ■ προσκαρτεροῦντες pres. part.
προσκαρτερέω to be strong, to be steadfast, like the English
"carry on" (RWP). The part. used in a periphrastic construction.
15 ὁμοθυμαδόν together w. one mind or purpose. ■ ἀναστάς aor.
part. ἀνίστημι to arise. ἐπὶ τὸ αὐτό all together. The phrase
seems to be a semi-technical term like "in church fellowship"
16 (Bruce). ■ ἔδει impf. δεῖ it is necessary. πληρωθῆναι aor. pass.
inf. πληρόω to fulfill. προεῖπεν aor. προλέγω to say beforehand. ὁδηγός guide. συλλαβοῦσιν aor. part. συλλαμβάνω to
17 seize, to arrest. ■ κατηριθμημένος perf. pass. part.
καταριθμέω to number. ἔλαχεν aor. λαγχάνω to obtain by lot.
Here "to obtain the rank" (LC; for the council of 12 men and
18 3 priests in DSS, s. 1QM 8:1f.). ■ ἐκτήσατο aor. mid. κτάομαι
to acquire, to get for one's self. ἀδικία unrighteousness. The
gen. is either objective, "the reward he received for his unrighteousness," or a Semitic adjectival gen., "his unrighteous reward"
(Bruce). πρηνής head first, flat on the face (EGT). ἐλάκησεν
aor. λακέω to crack, to burst. An accompanying noise is implied
19 (Bruce). ἐξεχύθη aor. pass. ἐκχέω to pour out. ■ κληθῆναι aor.
20 pass. inf. καλέω. ■ γέγραπται perf. pass. γράφω. γενηθήτω
aor. imp. 3rd sing. γίνομαι. ἔπαυλις homestead, a country
house, cottage, cabin (RWP). ἔστω pres. imp. εἰμί. λαβέτω aor.
22 imp. λαμβάνω. ■ ἀρξάμενος aor. mid. part., s.v.1.
23 ἀνελήμφθη aor. pass., s.v.2. ■ ἔστησαν aor. ἵστημι to set up,
here to nominate (s. Alex). ἐπεκλήθη aor. pass. ἐπικαλέω to
24 call, to name, to give a surname. ■ προσευξάμενοι aor. mid.
part. προσεύχομαι to pray. καρδιογνώστης knower of the
heart. A favorite expression of postapostolic Christianity (Haenchen). ἀνάδειξον aor. imp. ἀναδείκνυμι to show. ἐξελέξω
25 aor. mid. subj. 2nd per. ἐκλέγω s.v.2. ■ λαβεῖν aor. inf.
λαμβάνω. παρέβη aor. παραβαίνω to go aside, to turn aside.
26 πορευθῆναι aor. pass. inf. ■ ἔδωκαν aor. δίδωμι. ἔπεσεν aor.
πίπτω to fall. συγκατεψηφίσθη aor. pass. συγκαταψηφίζω
mid. "to join in a vote of condemnation," pass. to be chosen (by

a vote), together w.; then, to be added (BAG). The method employed by the Jews was to put the names written on stones into a vessel and shake it until one fell out (LC).

Ch. 2

■ συμπληροῦσθαι pres. pass. inf. συμπληρόω pass. to 1 fill completely of time, to approach, to come. The inf. used w. the prep. to express time "after" (s. MT, 145). πεντεκοστή Pentecost. (For the Jewish celebration of Pentecost, s. TDNT; SB, II, 597–602; Edersheim, *Temple*, 206, 207.) ■ ἐγένετο aor. 2 γίνομαι. ἄφνω suddenly. ἦχος sound, noise. Used in Luke 21:25 for the roar of the sea. It was "an echoing sound as of a mighty wind borne vibrantly" (RWP). φερομένης pres. pass. part. φέρω to carry, pass. to be driven. ἐπλήρωσεν aor. πληρόω to fill. καθήμενοι pres. mid. part. κάθημαι to sit. Periphrastic construction w. the part. ■ ὤφθησαν aor. pass. 3 ὁράω. διαμεριζόμεναι pres. pass. part. διαμερίζω to distribute, mid. parting themselves asunder or distributing themselves (RWP). γλῶσσα tongue, tongue shaped (s. SB, II, 602f.). ὡσεί as. ἐκάθισεν aor. καθίζω to take one's seat, to sit. ἕκαστος each. Each one present received the Spirit without conditions (s. Bruner, 163). ■ ἐπλήσθησαν aor. pass. πίμπλημι to fill. 4 ἤρξαντο aor. mid. ἄρχομαι to begin. καθώς just as. ἐδίδου impf. δίδωμι. ἀποφθέγγομαι to utter, to speak. Used of weighty or oracular utterance (Bruce) but not for ecstatic speech (Haenchen). The filling w. the Spirit was an experience to be repeated on several occasions; but the Spirit-baptism took place once for all (Bruce—ET).

■ κατοικοῦντες pres. part. κατοικέω to dwell, to reside in 5 a place (RWP). εὐλαβής pious, devout. ■ γενομένης aor. mid. 6 part. γίνομαι gen. abs. συνεχύθη aor. pass. συγχέω to pour together, to confound, to be perplexed. It describes the surprising effect of the miracle (Haenchen). ἤκουον impf. ἀκούω. διάλεκτος dialect, manner of speech (Bruce). Luke's choice of this word indicates that the speaking in tongues was the use of other languages (s. Bruner, 164). ■ ἐξίσταντο aor. impf. mid. 7 ἐξίστημι to be beside one's self, to be astonished. ἐθαύμαζον impf. θαυμάζω to wonder, to marvel. ■ ἐγεννήθημεν aor. pass. 8 γεννάω to bear, pass. to be born. ■ ἐπιδημοῦντες pres. part. 10 ἐπιδημέω to be away from home, to be on a journey. ■ 11 προσήλυτος proselyte. In the LXX used of a sojourner in the land of Israel, later used to denote those Gentiles who undertook the complete observance of the Jewish law and had to be circumcised, baptized and offer sacrifices (Bruce; s. also TDNT; SB, II,

12 715–723). μεγαλεῖος pl. mighty deeds. ■ διηποροῦντο perf.
13 mid. διαπορέω to be at a loss, to be perplexed. ■
διαχλευάζοντες pres. part. διαχλευάζω to mock, to ridicule.
The prep. compound indicates the flinging of ridicule at another
party (MH, 302). γλεῦκος sweet wine, probably the fresh made
wine which has not yet been kept long enough and is still fer-
menting (LC). μεμεστωμένοι perf. pass. part. μεστόω to fill.
The perf. emphasizes the state or condition.
14 ■ σταθείς aor. pass. part. ἵστημι to stand up, to rise.
ἐπῆρεν aor. ἐπαίρω to lift up. ἀπεφθέγξατο aor. mid.
ἀποφθέγγομαι s.v.4. ἔστω pres. imp. εἰμί. ἐνωτίσασθε aor.
16 imp. ἐνωτίζομαι to give ear to. ■ εἰρημένον perf. pass. part.
17 λέγω. ■ ἐκχεῶ fut. ἐκχέω to pour out. προφητεύσουσιν fut.
mid. προφητεύω. ἐνυπνιασθήσονται fut. pass.
19 ἐνυπνιάζομαι to dream. ■ δώσω fut. δίδωμι. ἀτμίς vapor.
20 καπνός smoke. ■ μεταστραφήσεται fut. pass. μεταστρέφω
to change, to turn into. The prep. compound has the idea of
21 change (s. MH, 318). ■ ἐπικαλέσηται aor. mid. subj.
ἐπικαλέω to call upon. σωθήσεται fut. pass. σῴζω to save, to
rescue.
22 ■ ἀκούσατε aor. imp. ἀποδεδειγμένον perf. pass. part.
ἀποδείκνυμι to appoint, to designate (s. LC), to authenticate
23 (Haenchen). ἐποίησεν aor. ■ ὡρισμένη perf. pass. part. ὁρίζω
to mark off by boundaries, to determine. The perf. emphasizes
a state of completion. God had willed the death of Jesus (RWP).
βουλή counsel. πρόγνωσις foreknowledge. ἔκδοτος given up,
delivered up. (For verbal adj. w. this ending, s. M, 221f.)
προσπήξαντες aor. part. προσπήγνυμι to nail to. ἀνείλατε
aor. ἀναιρέω to kill. Here human freedom and divine necessity
24 join hands (Haenchen). ■ ἀνέστησεν aor. ἀνίστημι to raise
up. ὠδίν pain, pl. birth pains. κρατεῖσθαι pres. pass. inf.
25 κρατέω to hold fast. ■ προορώμην impf. mid. προοράω to see
beforehand or without the temporal idea, "to have before one's
eyes" (s. Haenchen). σαλευθῶ aor. pass. subj. σαλεύω to
26 shake, pass. to be moved. ■ ηὐφράνθη aor. pass. εὐφραίνομαι
to rejoice. ἠγαλλιάσατο aor. mid. ἀγαλλιάομαι to be glad.
κατασκηνώσει fut. κατασκηνόω to dwell, to live in a tent (s.
27 John 1:14). ■ ἐγκαταλείψεις fut. ἐγκαταλείπω to abandon, to
28 leave. ἰδεῖν aor. inf. ὁράω. διαφθορά corruption. ■ ἐγνώρισας
aor. γνωρίζω to make known. πληρώσεις fut. πληρόω to
fulfill.
29 ■ ἐξόν part. ἔξεστιν it is lawful, it is allowed. εἰπεῖν aor.
inf. λέγω. ἐτελεύτησεν aor. τελευτάω to die. ἐτάφη aor. pass.
30 θάπτω to bury. ■ εἰδώς part. οἶδα. ὤμοσεν aor. ὀμνύω to

266

swear. ὀσφύς loins, "fruit of his loins"; that is, one of his descendants (Bruce). καθίσαι aor. inf. καθίζω to sit. ■ προϊδὼν 31 aor. part. προοράω to see beforehand. ἐλάλησεν aor. ἐγκατελείφθη aor. pass. ■ ὑψωθείς aor. pass. part. ὑψόω to lift 33 up, to exalt. λαβών aor. part. λαμβάνω. ἐξέχεεν aor. ἐκχέω to pour out. ■ ἀνέβη aor. ἀναβαίνω to ascend. κάθου pres. mid. 34 imp., s.v.2. ■ θῶ aor. subj. τίθημι to place, to set, to make. (For 35 this use of the subj. for the fut., s. RWP.) ■ ἀσφαλῶς assuredly. 36 Used to emphasize the conclusion which he is about to draw from his three texts (EGT). γινωσκέτω pres. imp. ἐσταυρώσατε aor. σταυρόω to crucify.

■ ἀκούσαντες aor. part. κατενύγησαν aor. pass. 37 κατανύσσω to pierce, to sting sharply. Used of painful emotion, which penetrates the heart as if stinging (Meyer). ποιήσωμεν aor. subj., deliberative subj. ■ μετανοήσατε aor. 38 imp. μετανοέω to change one's mind, to repent (s. Matt. 3:2). βαπτισθήτω aor. pass. imp. 3rd sing. βαπτίζω to baptize. Baptism was the outward sign of repentence (Bruce). εἰς "for" or "because of" (DM, 104). The phrase could be connected with the command "Repent." λήμψεσθε fut. mid. λαμβάνω. ■ 39 προσκαλέσηται aor. mid. subj. προσκαλέομαι to call to. ■ πλείων comp. πολύς. διεμαρτύρατο aor. mid. 40 διαμαρτύρομαι to make a solemn attestation or call to witness. The perfective use of the prep. compound (RWP). παρεκάλει impf. παρακαλέω to exhort, to encourage (s. TDNT). The impf. pictures the repeated action. σώθητε aor. pass. imp. σῴζω. σκολιός crooked. ■ ἀποδεξάμενοι aor. mid. part. 41 ἀποδέχομαι to receive, to welcome. ἐβαπτίσθησαν aor. pass. προσετέθησαν aor. pass. προστίθημι to add to. Luke does not say anything about the newly baptized ones speaking in tongues, although according to v.38 they received the Holy Spirit (Haenchen). ■ προσκαρτεροῦντες pres. part. 42 προσκαρτερέω s. Acts 1:41. κλάσις breaking. The breaking of bread refers either to an ordinary meal or to the celebration of the Lord's Supper (s. LC).

■ ἐγίνετο impf. mid. γίνομαι. ■ πιστεύσαντες aor. part. 43/44 ■ κτῆμα possession, personal property. ἐπίπρασκον impf. 45 πιπράσκω to sell, customary impf. "they sold from time to time" (RWP). διεμέριζον impf., s.v.3. ■ κλῶντες pres. part. 46 κλάω to break. μετελάμβανον impf. μεταλαμβάνω to partake of, to share in. ἀφελότης singleness, generosity (Bruce). ■ αἰνοῦντες pres. part. αἰνέω to praise. προσετίθει impf. 47 προστίθημι pres. pass. part.

267

Ch. 3

1   ■ *ἀνέβαινον* impf. *ἀναβαίνω* to go up, descriptive impf.
they were ascending the terraces to the temple court (RWP).
2   ■ *ἐβαστάζετο* impf. pass. *βαστάζω* to carry. The impf.
denotes the action was simultaneous to the going up (Meyer).
ἐτίθουν impf. *τίθημι* to place, customary impf. *ὡραῖος* beautiful (s. Haenchen). *αἰτεῖν* pres. inf., inf. of purpose. *ἐλεημοσύνη*
alms   (s.   Matt.   6:2).   *εἰσπορευομένων*   pres.   part.
3 *εἰσπορεύομαι.* ■ *μέλλοντας* pres. part. to be about to.
εἰσιέναι pres. inf. *εἴσειμι* to go in. *ἠρώτα* impf. *ἐρωτάω* to
4 ask, to request. *λαβεῖν* aor. inf. *λαμβάνω.* ■ *ἀτενίσας* aor.
5 part. *ἀτενίζω* to gaze. *βλέψον* aor. imp. ■ *ἐπεῖχεν* impf. *ἐπέχω*
to hold fast w. the dat. to aim at, to fix one's attention upon.
6 *προσδοκῶν* pres. part. *προσδοκάω* to expect. ■ *περιπάτει*
7 pres. imp. *περιπατέω* to walk, to walk about. ■ *πιάσας* aor.
part. *πίαζω* to seize. *ἤγειρεν* aor. *ἐγείρω* to raise. *παραχρῆμα*
immediately. *ἐστερεώθησαν* aor. pass. *στερεόω* to make firm,
solid, ingressive aor. to become strong. In medical language
applied to the bones in particular (MLL, 35). *βάσις* foot.
8 *σφυδρόν* ankle, ankle bone (s. LC). ■ *ἐξαλλόμενος* pres. mid.
part. *ἐξάλλομαι* to leap out, to leap up. *περιεπάτει* impf.
περιπατέω. εἰσῆλθεν aor. *εἰσέρχομαι* to go in. *περιπατῶν*
10 pres. part. *περιπατέω* to walk about. ■ *ἐπεγίνωσκον* impf.
ἐπιγινώσκω to recognize, to know, inchoative impf. "they began to perceive" (RWP). *ἐπλήσθησαν* aor. pass. *πίμπλημι* to
fill. *συμβεβηκότι* perf. act. part. *συμβαίνω* to happen. The
perf. pictures the continuing results.
11   ■ *κρατοῦντος* pres. part. *κρατέω* to hold, gen. abs.
12 *συνέδραμεν* aor. *συντρέχω* to run together. ■ *ἀπεκρίνατο*
aor. mid. *ἀποκρίνομαι* to answer. *ἐπὶ τούτῳ* either masc. (the
healed man) or n. (the act of healing; s. Haenchen).
13 *πεποιηκόσιν* perf. act. part. ■ *ἐδόξασεν* aor. *δοξάζω* to glorify. *παῖς* child, servant (s. TDNT). *παρεδώκατε* aor.
παραδίδωμι to deliver over. *ἠρνήσασθε* aor. mid. *ἀρνέομαι*
14 to deny. *κρίναντος* aor. part. *κρίνω* to judge, gen. abs. ■
ἠτήσασθε aor. mid. *αἰτέω. χαρισθῆναι* aor. pass. inf.
χαρίζομαι to do a favor, to give over to. In the legal context,
15 to release (s. TDNT; Bruce). ■ *ἀρχηγός* originator, author,
leader (s. Haenchen; TDNT). *ἀπεκτείνατε* aor. *ἀποκτείνω* to
16 kill. ■ *ἐστερέωσιν* aor., s.v.7. *ἔδωκεν* aor. *δίδωμι. ὁλοκληρία*
17 wholeness, completeness, soundness in all parts. ■ *ἐπράξατε*
18 aor.   *πράσσω*   to   do.   ■   *προκατήγγειλεν*   aor.
προκαταγγέλλω to report beforehand, to announce fully
beforehand (RWP). *παθεῖν* aor. inf. *πάσχω* to suffer.

ἐπλήρωσεν aor. πληρόω to fulfill. ■ μετανοήσατε aor. imp. 19
μετανοέω to change one's mind, to repent (s. Matt. 3:2).
ἐπιστρέψατε aor. imp. ἐπιστρέφω to turn to. The prep. compound is directive (s. MH, 312). ἐξαλειφθῆναι aor. pass. inf.
ἐξαλείφω to wash over, to wipe out, to obliterate, to cancel a
debt (s. NTW). ■ ἀνάψυξις to cool again, to refresh. 20
ἀποστείλῃ   aor.   subj.   ἀποστέλλω   to   send.
προκεχειρισμένον perf. pass. part. προχειρίζομαι to choose
for one's self, to select, to appoint. It has been inferred that if the
Jewish nation had accepted the gospel then, the kingdom of God
would speedily have been established on earth. The nation as a
whole declined this offer and Acts records the progressive acceptance of the gospel by the Gentiles (Bruce). ■ δέξασθαι aor. 21
mid. inf. δέχομαι to receive. ἀποκατάστασις restoration. The
establishment of all that had been promised in the OT (Williams;
s. also Acts 1:6). ἐλάλησεν aor. ■ ἀναστήσει fut. ἀνίστημι 22
to raise up. ἀκούσεσθε fut. ἀκούω. λαλήσῃ aor. subj. ■ 23
ἐξολεθρευθήσεται fut. pass. ἐξολεθρεύω to destroy, to utterly
destroy, perfective use of the prep. compound. ■ καθεξῆς in 24
order, in succession. κατήγγειλαν aor. καταγγέλλω to proclaim. ■ διέθετο aor. mid. διατίθημι to make a covenant. 25
ἐνευλογηθήσονται fut. pass. εὐλογέω to bless. ■ ἀναστήσας 26
aor. part. ἀνίστημι. ἀπέστειλεν aor. ἀποστέλλω.

Ch. 4

■ ἐπέστησαν aor. ἐφίστημι to come upon. ■ 1/2
διαπονούμενοι pres. mid. part. διαπονέομαι to be annoyed, to
be worked up, to be indignant, perfective use of the prep. compound (RWP). ■ ἐπέβαλον aor. ἐπιβάλλω to lay hands upon. 3
ἔθεντο aor. mid. τίθημι to place. τήρησις prison, place of
custody, probably in one of the chambers of the temple (RWP).
■ ἀκουσάντων aor. part. ἐπίστευσαν aor. ἐγενήθη aor. pass. 4
■ συναχθῆναι aor. pass. inf. συνάγω to come together, to 5
convene. ■ στήσαντες aor. part. ἵστημι to place, to stand. 7
ἐπυνθάνοντο impf. mid. πυνθάνομαι to inquire. ἐποιήσατε
aor. ■ πλησθεις aor. pass. part. τίμπλημι to fill. ■ 8/9
ἀνακρινόμεθα pres. pass. ἀνακρίνω to examine. In Attic Gr.
it refers to a preliminary hearing but later to any legal inquiry
(LC). εὐεργεσία good deed. σέσωσται perf. pass. σῴζω to
save, to heal. The perf. indicates the continuing state. ■ ἔστω 10
pres. imp. εἰμί. ἐσταυρώσατε aor. σταυρόω to crucify.
ἤγειρεν aor. ἐγείρω to raise. παρέστηκεν perf. παρίσταμι to
stand, to stand before someone. ■ ἐξουθενηθεις aor. pass. part. 11
ἐξουθενέω to despise. γενόμενος aor. mid. part. γίνομαι.

γωνία corner, either the highest cornerstone right under the roof or the cornerstone under the building (RWP).

12 ■ δεδομένον perf. pass. part. δίδωμι. σωθῆναι aor. pass.
13 inf. σῴζω. ■ θεωροῦντες pres. part. θεωρέω to see. παρρησία boldness, freedom of speech. Here of the confidence and forthrightness w. which the apostles spoke under the prompting of the Holy Spirit (Bruce). καταλαβόμενοι aor. mid. part. καταλαμβάνω to grasp, to perceive, mid. indicates the grasping w. the mind (Bruce). ἀγράμματος uneducated, unable to write. Here it denotes the lack of rabbinic training (Meyer). ἰδιώτης layman, one who is not an expert, unskilled, commoner (Bruce). ἐθαύμαζον impf. θαυμάζω to recognize, to realize, inceptive
14 impf. ■ ἑστῶτα perf. part. ἵστημι to stand. τεθεραπευμένον perf. pass. part. θεραπεύω to treat medically, to heal. ἀντειπεῖν aor. inf. ἀντιλέγω to say something against, to speak against.
15 ■ κελεύσαντες aor. part. κελεύω to command. συνέβαλλον
16 impf. συμβάλλω to confer. ■ ποιήσωμεν aor. subj., delibera-
17 tive subj. γέγονεν perf. γίνομαι. ■ πλείων comp. πολύς. διανεμηθῇ aor. pass. subj. διανέμω to distribute, to divide into portions, to spread abroad (EGT). ἀπειλησώμεθα aor. mid. subj. ἀπειλέω to threaten, hortatory subj. "let us threaten."
18 ■ καλέσαντες aor. part. παρήγγειλαν aor. παραγγέλλω to
19 command. καθόλου at all. ■ ἀποκριθέντες aor. pass. part. ἀποκρίνομαι to answer. (For the Semitic use of the redundant part., s. MH, 453.) κρίνατε aor. imp. κρίνω to judge, to decide.
20/21 ■ εἴδαμεν aor. ὁράω. ■ προσαπειλησάμενοι aor. mid. part. προσαπειλέω to threaten further. The prep. compound indicates "in addition" (Bruce). εὑρίσκοντες pres. part. causal (M, 230). κολάσωνται aor. mid. subj. κολάζομαι to punish.
22 γεγονότι perf. part. γίνομαι. ■ γεγόνει plperf.
23 ■ ἀπολυθέντες aor. pass. part. ἀπήγγειλαν aor.
24 ἀπαγγέλλω to report. ■ ἦραν aor. αἴρω to lift up. δεσπότης lord, sovereign lord. A word used in connection w. servants
25 (Bruce). ποιήσας aor. part. ■ ἐφρύαξεν aor. φρυάσσω to snort, to be arrogant, haughty, insolent (BAG). ἐμελέτησαν
26 aor. μελετάω to devise, to plan. ■ παρέστησαν aor. παρίσταμι to stand, to stand by someone. συνήχθησαν aor.
27/28 pass. συνάγω. ■ ἔχρισας aor. χρίω to anoint (s. TDNT). ■ ποιῆσαι aor. inf. προώρισεν aor. προορίζω to determine beforehand, to mark out with a boundary before. γενέσθαι aor.
29 mid. inf. γίνομαι. ■ ἔπιδε aor. imp. ἐφοράω to look upon.
31 ἀπειλή threat. δός aor. imp. δίδωμι to give. ■ δεηθέντων aor. pass. part. δέομαι to pray, to make a request. ἐσαλεύθη aor. pass. σαλεύω to shake, "shook as w. an earthquake"; a sign of

divine assent (Bruce). συνηγμένοι perf. pass. part. συνάγω to gather together, to assemble. ἐπλήσθησαν aor. pass. πίμπλημι. ἐλάλουν impf.

■ ὑπαρχόντων pres. part. ὑπάρχω to exist, to be, pl. part. 32 possessions. ■ ἀπεδίδουν impf. ἀποδίδωμι to give, to give 33 back. ■ ἐνδεής in need, needy. κτήτωρ owner. Frequent in 34 papyri for owners of real estate (Bruce). πωλοῦντες pres. part. πωλέω to sell. ἔφερον impf. φέρω to bring. πιπρασκομένων pres. pass. part. πιπράσκω to sell. ■ ἐτίθουν impf. τίθημι 35 s.v.3. διεδίδοτο impf. pass. διαδίδωμι to distribute. καθότι in proportion as, according as. ■ ἐπικληθείς aor. pass. part. 36 ἐπικαλέω to name, to call by the surname. μεθερμηνευόμενον pres. pass. part. μεθερμηνεύω to translate. ■ πωλήσας aor. 37 part. ἤνεγκεν aor. φέρω. ἔθηκεν aor. τίθημι. (For the common ownership of goods in DDS, s. 1QS 1:12f.)

Ch. 5

■ ἐπώλησεν aor. πωλέω to sell. κτῆμα possession, landed 1 property (Bruce). ■ ἐνοσφίσατε aor. mid. νοσφίζομαι to 2 embezzle, to secretly take a part of a larger quantity which had been given to one as a trust (s. LC). συνειδυίης perf. part. fem. sing. σύνοιδα to share knowledge w., to be implicated. ἐνέγκας aor. part. φέρω to carry, to bring. ἔθηκεν aor. τίθημι to place. ■ ἐπλήρωσεν aor. πληρόω to fill. ψεύσασθαι aor. mid. inf. 3 ψεύδομαι to lie, to lie to someone, inf. of purpose. νοσφίσασθαι aor. mid. inf. ■ μένον pres. part. n. μένω to 4 remain. πραθέν aor. pass. part. πιπράσκω to sell. τί ὅτι "Why (is it) that . . . ?" elliptical construction (Bruce). ἔθου aor. mid. τίθημι. ■ πέσων aor. part. πίπτω to fall. ἐξέψυξεν aor. 5 ἐκψύχω to breathe out, to expire. A term used by medical writers (MLL, 37). ■ ἀναστάντες aor. part. ἀνίστημι to arise. 6 (For the Semitic construction, s. BG, 126f.) συνέστειλαν aor. συστέλλω to gather together, to wrap up. Used by medical writers in the sense "to bandage" (s. MLL, 38; but s. also LC). ἐξενέγκαντες aor. part. ἐκφέρω to carry out. Used in the technical sense to carry out for burial (Bruce). ἔθαψαν aor. θάπτω to bury.

■ εἰδυῖα part. fem. οἶδα. γεγονός perf. part. γίνομαι. ■ 7/8 ἀπεκρίθη aor. pass. ἀποκρίνομαι to answer. εἰπέ aor. imp. λέγω. τοσοῦτος so large, so much, gen. of price. ἀπέδοσθε aor. mid. ἀποδίδωμι to sell. ■ συνεφωνήθη aor. pass. συμφωνέω 9 to agree together, impersonal use w. the dat. It was agreed together by you, or for you (RWP). πειράσαι aor. inf. πειράζω to tempt. θαψάντων aor. part. θάπτω. ■ ἔπεσεν aor. πίπτω. 10

εἰσέλθόντες aor. part. εἰσέρχομαι. εὗρον aor. εὑρίσκω.
12   ■ ἐγίνετο impf. mid. γίνομαι. The impf. pictures the repeated occurence. ὁμοθυμαδόν w. one accord. In Hellenistic
13 Gr. "together" (s. LC). ■ ἐτόλμα impf. τολμάω to dare.
κολλᾶσθαι pres. mid. inf., to join. Perhaps w. the idea of attach-
ing one's self without a regular introduction (s. Bruce).
14 ἐμεγάλυννεν impf. μεγαλύνω to make large, to magnify. ■
προσετίθεντο impf. pass. προστίθημι to add to. The impf.
15 pictures the repeated action. πιστεύοντες pres. part. ■
πλατεῖα street. τιθέναι pres. inf. τίθημι s.v.2. κλινάριον bed,
little bed. κράβατος pallet, camp bed (s. RWP; EGT).
16 ἐπισκιάσῃ aor. subj. ἐπισκιάζω to overshadow. ■ συνήρχετο
impf. mid. συνέρχομαι to come together. πέριξ adv. surrounding. ὀχλουμένους pres. pass. part. ὀχλέω to trouble, to torment.
ἐθεραπεύοντο impf. pass. θεραπεύω to heal.
17   ■ ἀναστάς aor., s.v.6. οὖσα pres. part. εἰμί. Used here in
the sense of introducing some technical phrase and has the
meaning of "local," "existing" (Bruce). ἐπλήσθησαν aor. pass.
18 πίμπλημι to fill. ■ ἐπέβαλον aor. ἐπιβάλλω to place upon (s.
Acts 4:3). ἔθεντο aor. mid. τίθημι to place. δημόσιος public,
19 publicly. ■ διά. Here used w. the gen. "at night" (BD, 119).
ἤνοιξε aor. ἀνοίγω to open. ἐξαγαγών aor. part. ἐξάγω to lead
20 out. ■ πορεύεσθε pres. mid. imp. πορεύομαι to go. σταθέντες
aor. pass. part. ἵστημι to stand, pass. to take a stand (RWP).
21 λαλεῖτε pres. imp. ■ ὄρθρος dawn, early morning, daybreak.
ἐδίδασκον impf., inceptive impf. παραγενόμενος aor. mid.
part. παραγίνομαι to come on the scene, to appear.
συνεκάλεσαν aor. συγκαλέω to summons. καί "that is,"
epexegetical use (s. BG, 154). ἀπέστειλαν aor. ἀποστέλλω to
send. δεσμωτήριον prison. ἀχθῆναι aor. pass. inf. ἄγω to lead.
22   ■ ἀναστρέψαντες aor. part. ἀναστρέφω to turn again, to be
23 turned. ἀπήγγειλαν aor. ἀπαγγέλλω to report. ■
κεκλεισμένον perf. pass. part. κλείω to close, to shut. The perf.
emphasizes the state, "shut tight" (RWP). ἀσφάλεια safety.
ἑστῶτας perf. part. ἵστημι to stand. ἀνοίξαντες aor. part.
24   ■ ἤκουσαν aor. ἀκούω to hear. διηπόρουν impf. διαπορέω to
be perplexed. γένοιτο aor. mid. opt. γίνομαι "as to what this
would become." The conclusion of a conditional clause w. the
condition "if the thing should be allowed to go on" not expressed
25/26 (RWP). ■ διδάσκοντες pres. part. ■ ἀπελθών aor. part.
ἀπέρχομαι to go away. ἦγεν impf. ἄγω. ἐφοβοῦντο impf. mid.
φοβέομαι to be afraid, to fear. λιθασθῶσιν aor. pass. subj.
λιθάζω to stone.
27   ■ ἀγαγόντες aor. part. ἄγω. ἔστησαν aor. ἵστημι to

place, to stand. ἐπηρώτησεν aor. ἐπερωτάω to question. ■ 28
παρηγγείλαμεν aor. παραγγέλλω to command, to charge.
Often used as a legal term indicating a summons to court or the
complaint against the defendent (LC). (For the Semitic construction w. the verb and the dat. of the noun translating the inf.
abs., s. MH, 443f.) πεπληρώκατε perf. πληρόω to fill. The
perf. emphasizes the continuing result. ἐπαγαγεῖν aor. inf.
ἐπάγω to bring. ■ ἀποκριθείς aor. pass. part., s.v.8. 29
πειθαρχέω to obey, to obey one in authority (EGT). ■ ἤγειρεν 30
aor. ἐγείρω to raise. διεχειρίσασθε aor. mid. διαχειρίζομαι
to take in hand, to do away w. A euphemism for "kill" (MH,
302). κρεμάσαντες aor. part. κρεμάννυμι to hang. ■ ἀρχηγός 31
s. Acts 3:15. ὕψωσεν aor. ὑψόω to lift up, to exalt. δοῦναι aor.
inf. δίδωμι. ■ ἔδωκεν aor. δίδωμι. πειθαρχοῦσιν pres. part. 32
■ διεπρίοντο impf. pass. διαπρίομαι to saw through, to 33
cut to the quick, to infuriate (BAG). ἀνελεῖ aor. inf. ἀναιρέω
to kill. ■ ἐκέλευσεν aor. κελεύω to command. ποιῆσαι aor. inf. 34
■ προσέχετε pres. imp. προσέχω to give heed, to pay atten- 35
tion, "hold your mind (noun, unexpressed) for or on yourselves"
(RWP). ■ ἀνέστη aor. ἀνίστημι. προσεκλίθη aor. pass. 36
προσκλίνομαι to attach one's self, to follow. ἀνῃρέθη aor.
pass. ἀναιρέω. ἐπείθοντο impf. mid. πείθομαι to obey.
διελύθησαν aor. pass. διαλύω to scatter, to destroy. ■ 37
ἀπέστησεν aor. ἀφίστημι to cause to revolt, to mislead.
ἀπώλετο aor. mid. ἀπόλλυμι to destroy, to perish.
διεσκορπίσθησαν aor. pass. διασκορπίζω to scatter. ■ 38
ἀπόστητε aor. imp. ἀφίστημι to keep away from. ἄφετε aor.
imp. ἀφίημι to leave, to leave alone. ᾖ pres. subj. εἰμί.
καταλυθήσεται fut. pass. καταλύω to destroy, to loosen down
like a falling house (RWP). ■ δυνήσεσθε fut. mid. δύναμαι. 39
καταλῦσαι aor. inf. θεομάχος fighting against God. εὑρεθῆτε
aor. pass. subj. ἐπείσθησαν aor. πείθομαι. ■ 40
προσκαλεσάμενοι aor. part. προσκαλέω to flog, to beat. The
punishment was for minor offenses (EGT). ἀπέλυσαν aor.
ἀπολύω to release. ■ ἐπορεύοντο impf. mid. χαίροντες pres. 41
part. κατηξιώθησαν aor. pass. καταξιόω to consider worthy.
ἀτιμασθῆναι aor. pass. inf. ἀτιμάζω to dishonor. ■ ἐπαύοντο 42
impf. mid. παύομαι to cease.

Ch. 6

■ πληθυνόντων pres. part. πληθύνω to fill, here intr. to 1
increase. Genitive abs. expressing contemporaneous time.
παρεθεωροῦντο impf. pass. παραθεωρέω to look beyond, to
overlook, to neglect. διακονία ministry. It suggests a daily dis-

pensation of alms or of food to the widows (LC; TDNT).
2 καθημερινός daily. χήρα widow. ■ προσκαλεσάμενοι aor.
mid. part. προσκαλέω to summons. ἀρεστός fit, pleasing.
καταλείψαντας aor. part. καταλείπω to leave behind, to
3 abandon. ■ ἐπισκέψασθε aor. mid. imp. ἐπισκέπτομαι to
oversee, to supervise. μαρτυρουμένους pres. pass. part.
μαρτυρέω to give testimony, to bear witness, to be well reported
of (s. BS, 265; LAE, 88). καταστήσομεν fut. καθίστημι to
appoint. The twelve were to give their approval to the congrega-
4 tion's selection of the seven (Bruce). ■ προσκαρτερήσομεν
5 fut. προσκαρτερέω to hold fast to, to continue in. ■ ἤρεσεν
aor. ἀρέσκω to please. ἐξελέξαντο aor. mid. ἐκλέγω to select,
6 to choose. ■ ἔστησαν aor. ἵστημι to place, to stand.
προσευξάμενοι aor. mid. part. προσεύχομαι to pray.
7 ἐπέθηκαν aor. ἐπιτίθημι to place upon. ■ ηὔξανεν impf.
αὐξάνω to grow. The impf. pictures the continual growth.
ἐπληθύνετο impf. pass. πληθύνω to increase. σφόδρα very.
ὑπήκουον impf. ὑπακούω to listen to, to obey.
8/9   ■ ἐποίει impf. ■ ἀνέστησαν aor. ἀνίστημι to arise.
λεγομένης pres. part., here "so called." συζητοῦντες pres.
10 part. συζητέω to dispute, to question together. ■ ἴσχυον impf.
ἰσχύω to be strong, to be able. ἀναστῆναι aor. inf. ἀνθίστημι
11 to stand against, to successfully withstand. ἐλάλει impf. ■
ὑπέβαλον aor. ὑποβάλλω to put up, to prompt. It applies to the
secret instigation of persons who are supplied w. suggestions of
what they are to say, much as in the modern "frame-up" (LC).
12 ἀκηκόαμεν perf. ἀκούω. ■ συνεκίνησαν aor. συγκινέω to
throw into a commotion, to stir violently. ἐπιστάντες aor. part.
ἐφίστημι to come upon, ingressive aor. "they rushed at him"
(RWP). συνήρπασαν aor. συναρπάζω to seize. ἤγαγον aor.
14 ἄγω to lead. ■ καταλύσει fut. καταλύω to destroy. ἀλλάξει
fut. ἀλλάσσω to change. παρέδωκεν aor. παραδίδωμι to give
over, to transmit. Stephen saw clearly the inevitability of a break
w. Judaism. He may have spoken of the transitory character of
15 the Mosaic ceremonial (Bruce). ■ ἀτενίσαντες aor. part.
ἀτενίζω to gaze. καθεζόμενοι pres. mid. part. καθέζομαι to
sit.

Ch. 7

1   ■ εἰ introduces a direct question. The accused is asked to
2 defend himself against the charge (Haenchen). ■ ἀκούσατε aor.
imp. ὤφθη aor. pass. ὁράω, pass. to appear. ὄντι part. dat. sing.
εἰμί. κατοικῆσαι aor. inf. κατοικέω to live, to be at home, inf.
used w. πρὶν ἤ to express antecedent time "before" (s. MT, 140).

274

■ ἔξελθε aor. imp. ἐξέρχομαι to go out. συγγένεια kinship, 3
relatives. δεῦρο adv. here. Here used as imp. come, come here.
δείξω aor. subj. δείκνυμι to show. ■ κατῴκησεν aor. 4
κατοικέω. ἀποθανεῖν aor. inf. ἀποθνήσκω to die.
μετῴκισεν aor. μετοικίζω to cause to dwell, to settle. (For the
idea of transfer or change indicated by the prep. compound, s.
MH, 318.) ■ ἔδωκεν aor. δίδωμι. βῆμα step, "stepping of a 5
foot" (s. RWP). ἐπηγγείλατο aor. mid. ἐπαγγέλλω to promise. δοῦναι aor. inf. δίδωμι. κατάσχεσις possession. ὄντος
pres. part. gen. abs. ■ ἐλάλησεν aor. ἔσται fut. εἰμί. πάροικος 6
foreign, alien, sojourner. ἀλλότριος foreign. δουλώσουσιν fut.
δουλόω to serve as a slave, to be enslaved. κακώσουσιν fut.
κακόω to treat badly, to harm, to mistreat. ■ ἐξελεύσονται fut. 7
mid. ἐξέρχομαι. λατρεύσουσιν fut. λατρεύω to serve. ■ 8
διαθήκη treaty, covenant (s. TDNT; IDB I, 714–723). οὕτως
so, thus. Possibly emphatic while there was still no holy place
(LC). ἐγέννησεν aor. γεννάω to beget. περιέτεμεν aor.
περιτέμνω to circumcise.

■ ζηλώσαντες aor. part. ζηλόω to boil w. zeal then w. 9
envy, to be jealous (RWP). ἀπέδοντο impf. mid. ἀποδίδωμι to
sell. ■ ἐξείλατο aor. mid. ἐξαιρέω to take out, to tear out, to 10
deliver. κατέστησεν aor. καθίστημι to appoint. ἡγούμενον
pres. mid. part. ἡγέομαι to rule, to govern. ■ ηὕρισκον impf. 11
εὑρίσκω. χόρτασμα food. Originally of animals, foodstuffs.
Later in the sense of men's food as well (Bruce). ■ ἀκούσας aor. 12
part. ἐξαπέστειλεν aor. ἐξαποστέλλω to send out. ■ 13
ἐγνωρίσθη aor. pass. γνωρίζω to make known. (For the construction w. the dat., s. BD, 102.) ἐγένετο aor. mid. γίνομαι.
■ ἀποστείλας aor. part. ἀποστέλλω to send. μετεκαλέσατο 14
aor. mid. μετακαλέομαι to summon to one's self, to send forth.
■ κατέβη aor. καταβαίνω to go down. ἐτελεύτησεν aor. 15
τελευτάω to die. ■ μετετέθησαν aor. pass. μετατίθημι to 16
transfer, to move from one place to another. (For the significance of the prep. compound, s. MH, 318.) ὠνήσατο aor. mid.
ὠνέομαι to sell.

■ ἤγγιζεν impf. ἐγγίζω to draw near, to be near. 17
ὡμολόγησεν aor. ὁμολογέω to agree, to promise. ηὔξησεν
aor. αὐξάνω to grow. ἐπληθύνθη aor. pass. πληθύνω pass. to
multiply, to increase. ■ ἀνέστη aor. ἀνίστημι to arise. ᾔδει 18
plperf. (= impf.) οἶδα. ■ κατασοφισάμενος aor. mid. part. 19
κατασοφίζομαι to exploit, to deal wisely. It implies crafty or
deceitful ill treatment (LC). ἐκάκωσεν aor., s.v.6. ποιεῖν pres.
inf. Infinitive used as an explanatory phrase involving some idea
of purpose (Bruce; s. also BD, 206). βρέφος infant. ἔκθετος

exposed, cast out. ζωογονεῖσθαι pres. pass. inf. ζωογονέω to
20 produce life. Here to preserve life (Haenchen). ■ ἐγεννήθη aor.
pass. γεννάω. ἀστεῖος belonging to the city, w.
city manners
and polish, elegant, fine (s. RWP). τῷ θεῷ ethical dat. "fair to
God" (RWP). ἀνετράφη aor. pass. ἀνατρέφω to bring up, to
21 nourish. ■ ἐκτεθέντος aor. pass. part. ἐκτίθημι to set out, to
expose, gen. abs. ἀνείλατο aor. mid. ἀναιρέομαι to lift up.
Used of acknowledging or adopting as one's child (Bruce).
ἀνεθρέψατο aor. mid. ἀνατρέφω. εἰς υἱόν acc. w. prep. used
for the predicate acc., is probably due to Semitic influence (s.
22 BD, 86). ■ ἐπαιδεύθη aor. pass. παιδεύω to train a child, to
instruct.
23   ■ ἐπληροῦτο impf. pass. πληρόω to fulfill, to complete.
ἀνέβη aor. ἀναβαίνω to go up, to come up. Used of things
coming up into one's mind (AS). ἐπισκέψασθαι aor. mid. inf.
ἐπισκέπτομαι to visit, to go to see for one's self, w. one's own
24 eyes, to help if possible (RWP). ■ ἀδικούμενον pres. pass. part.
ἀδικέω to wrong, to act unjustly toward, pass. to suffer injustice.
ἠμύνατο aor. mid. ἀμύνω mid. to avenge one's self.
καταπονουμένῳ pres. pass. part. καταπονέω to subdue, to
torment, to oppress. πατάξας aor. part. πατάσσω to strike, to
25 hit. ■ ἐνόμιζεν impf. νομίζω to suppose. συνιέναι pres. inf.
συνίημι to comprehend, to understand. συνῆκαν aor.
26 συνίημι. ■ ὤφθη aor. pass. ὁράω. μαχομένοις pres. mid. part.
μάχομαι to fight. συνήλλασεν impf. συναλλάσσω to reconcile, conative impf. "tried to reconcile." εἰπών aor. part. λέγω.
27 ■ ἀπώσατο aor. mid. ἀπωθέομαι to push away. δικαστής
28 judge. ■ ἀνελεῖν aor. inf. ἀναιρέω to kill. ἀνεῖλες aor.
29 ἀναιρέω. ■ ἔφυγεν aor. φεύγω to flee.
30/31   ■ πληρωθέντων aor. pass. part. πῦρ flame. ■ ἐθαύμαζεν
impf. θαυμάζω to wonder, to be amazed. ὅραμα appearance.
κατανοῆσαι aor. inf. κατανοέω to take knowledge of, to take
notice of, "to master the mystery." (For the force of the prep.
32 compound, s. M, 117.) ■ γενόμενος aor. mid. part. γίνομαι.
33 ἐτόλμα impf. τολμάω to dare. ■ λῦσον aor. imp. λύω to loose.
34 ἔστηκας perf. ἵστημι to stand. ■ κάκωσις ill treatment.
στεναγμός sighing, groaning. ἤκουσα aor. ἀκούω. ἐξελέσθαι
aor. mid. ἐξαιρέω to deliver. ἀποστείλω aor. subj.
35 ἀποστέλλω hortatory subj. "let me send." ■ ἠρνήσατο aor.
mid. ἀρνέομαι to deny. λυτρωτής one who ransoms, redeemer.
ἀπέσταλκεν perf. ἀποστέλλω. ὀφθέντος aor. pass. part.
36 ὁράω. ■ ἐξήγαγεν aor. ἐξάγω to lead out. ποιήσας aor. part.
37 ἐρυθρός red. ■ εἴπας aor. part. λέγω. ἀναστήσει fut.
38 ἀνίστημι to raise up, to awaken. λαλοῦντος pres. part.

ἐδέξατο aor. mid. δέχομαι to receive, to welcome. ζῶντα pres. part. ζάω to live. ■ ἠθέλησαν aor. θέλω. ὑπήκοος obedient. 39 γενέσθαι aor. mid. inf. γίνομαι. ἐστράφησαν aor. pass. στρέφω to turn. ■ ποίησον aor. imp. προπορεύσονται fut. 40 mid. προπορεύομαι to go before, to precede, as Jehovah had gone before them in the pillar of cloud and as images were carried by the heathen in their marches (Alex). ■ 41 ἐμοσχοποίησαν aor. μοσχοποιέω to make a calf. ἀνήγαγον aor. ἀνάγω to lead up, to bring a sacrifice (s. MM). εὐφραίνοντο impf. mid. εὐφραίνομαι to rejoice, impf. pictures the continuing action. ■ ἔστρεψεν aor. στρέφω. παρέδωκεν 42 aor. παραδίδωμι to deliver over. γέγραπται perf. pass. The perf. indicates the permanency of the authoritative record. βίβλος book (s. Matt 1:1). μή expects a neg. answer. σφάγιον animal sacrifice. προσηνέγκατε aor. προσφέρω to bring to, to sacrifice. ■ ἀνελάβετε aor. ἀναλαμβάνω to take up, to take. 43 ἄστρον star, constellation. Perhaps a reference to the Assyrian and Egyptian worship of the god of the planet Saturn (Bruce— ET). μετοικιῶ fut. μετοικίζω to remove to a new abode, to cause to migrate (s.v.4.). ἐπέκεινα w. gen. beyond. (For the OT quote in DSS, s. CD 6:14f.)

■ διετάξατο aor. mid. διατάσσομαι to command. 44 ποιῆσαι aor. inf. ἑωράκει plperf. ὁράω. ■ εἰσήγαγον aor. 45 εἰσάγω to bring in. διαδεξάμενοι aor. mid. part. διαδέχομαι to receive through another, to receive in succession (RWP). κατάσχεσις possession. ἐξῶσεν aor. ἐξωθέω to drive out. ■ 46 εὗρεν aor. εὑρίσκω. ἠτήσατο aor. mid. αἰτέω to ask, mid. to ask a favor for one's self. εὑρεῖν aor. inf. σκήνωμα tent, dwelling place. Used by David in the humility of his request (Meyer). ■ οἰκοδόμησεν aor. οἰκοδομέω to build. ■ χειροποίητος 47/48 made w. human hands. ■ ὑποπόδιον footstool. κατάπαυσις 49 rest.

■ σκληροτράχηλος stiff-necked. Used in the LXX to de- 51 scribe the rebellious tendency of Israel (LC). ἀπερίτμητος un-circumcised. ἀντιπίπτω to fall against, to resist. ■ ἐδίωξαν aor. 52 διώκω to persecute, pursue. ἀπέκτειναν aor. ἀποκτείνω to kill. προκαταγγείλαντας aor. part. προκαταγγέλλω to an-nounce beforehand. ἔλευσις coming. A messianic term denot-ing Messiah's advent (Bruce). προδότης traitor, betrayer. φονεύς murderer. ■ ἐλάβετε aor. λαμβάνω. ἐφυλάξατε aor. 53 φυλάσσω to observe, to keep.

■ διεπρίοντο impf. mid. διαπρίομαι to cut to the quick 54 (s. Acts 5:33). ἔβρυχον impf. βρύχω to bite w. loud noise, to grind or gnash the teeth, inceptive impf. "they began" (RWP).

277

55 ■ ἀτενίσας aor. part. ἀτενίζω to gaze. ἑστῶτα perf. part.
56 ἵστημι to stand. ■ διηνοιγμένους perf. pass. part. διανοίγω
57 to open. ■ κράξαντες aor. part. κράζω to scream. συνέσχον
aor. συνέχω to hold, to hold together. ὥρμησαν aor. ὁρμάω
58 to rush. ■ ἐκβαλόντες aor. part. ἐκβάλλω to throw out.
ἐλιθοβόλουν impf. λιθοβολέω to stone, inceptive impf. "they
began." ἀπέθεντο aor. mid. ἀποτίθημι to put away, to put
59 down. καλουμένου pres. pass. part. ■ ἐπικαλούμενον pres.
mid. part. ἐπικαλέομαι to call upon, to call to. δέξαι aor. imp.
60 δέχομαι to receive, to welcome. ■ θείς aor. part. τίθημι to
place, here to kneel down. γόνυ knee. ἔκραξεν aor. στήσῃς
aor. subj. ἵστημι to lay, to establish. The neg. is equivalent to
"forgive" (LC). ἐκοιμήθη aor. pass. κοιμάομαι to go to sleep,
an unexpectedly beautiful word for so brutal a death (Bruce).

Ch. 8

1 ■ συνευδοκῶν pres. part. συνευδοκέω to agree w., to
approve of, to have pleasure w. The periphrastic construction
describes a condition, not a momentary excitement (Haenchen).
ἀναίρεσις killing, murder.
ἐγένετο aor. mid. γίνομαι. διωγμός persecution.
2 διεσπάρησαν aor. pass. διασπείρω to scatter. ■
συνεκόμισαν aor. συγκομίζω to gather up for burial (LC).
3 κοπετός mourning, lamentation. ■ ἐλυμαίνετο impf.
λυμαίνομαι to devastate, to ruin. Used of physical injury, particularly of the mangling by wild beast (LC). The impf. pictures
the continual action. κατά used in the distributive sense, "from
house to house." εἰσπορευόμενος pres. mid. part.
εἰσπορεύομαι to go into. σύρων pres. part. σύρω to drag.
παρεδίδου impf. παραδίδωμι to deliver over.
4 ■ διασπαρέντες aor. pass. part. διασπείρω s.v.1.
5 διῆλθον aor. διέρχομαι to go through. ■ κατελθών aor. part.
6 κατέρχομαι to go down. ἐκήρυσσεν impf. ■ προσεῖχον impf.
προσέχω to give heed to. Used in the sense of paying attention
7 and giving a favorable response (Bruce). ἐποίει impf. ■ βοῶντα
pres. part. βοάω to call aloud. ἐξήρχοντο impf. mid. ἐξέρχομαι
to come out. παραλελυμένοι perf. mid. part. παραλύομαι to
be weakened, to be disabled. Luke's use of the verb instead of
the adj. is in strict agreement w. that of the medical writers
(MLL, 6). ἐθεραπεύθησαν aor. pass. θεραπεύω to heal.
9 ■ προϋπῆρχεν impf. προϋπάρχω to be before, to exist
previously. μαγεύων pres. part. μαγεύω to practice magic.
Used w. the previous verb to form a periphrastic construction
"he was existing previously practicing magic" (RWP).

278

ἐξιστάντων pres. part. ἐξίστημι to astonish, to amaze, to
cause one to be beside himself. ■ ἐξεστακέναι perf. act. inf. 11
ἐξίστημι. ■ ἐπίστευσαν aor. ἐβαπτίζοντο impf. pass. 12
βαπτίζω to baptize. They received baptism but had nevertheless not yet received the Holy Spirit (Bruner, 173f.). ■ 13
βαπτισθείς aor. pass. part. προσκαρτερῶν pres. part.
προσκαρτερέω to attend constantly, to adhere to. θεωρῶν
pres. part. θεωρέω to see, to watch. γινομένας pres. mid. part.
ἐξίστατο impf. pass.

   ■ ἀκούσαντες aor. part. δέδεκται perf. mid. δέχομαι to 14
receive, to welcome. ἀπέστειλαν aor. ἀποστέλλω to send, to
send as an official authoritative representative (s. TDNT). ■ 15
καταβάντες aor. part. καταβαίνω to descend, to go down.
προσηύξαντο aor. mid. προσεύχομαι to pray. λάβωσιν aor.
subj. λαμβάνω. Used w. the particle to express purpose. ■ 16
ἐπιπεπτωκός perf. act. part. ἐπιπίπτω to fall upon.
βεβαπτισμένοι perf. pass. part. ὑπῆρχον impf. ὑπάρχω to be
present, to be. ■ ἐπετίθεσαν impf. ἐπιτίθημι to lay upon. The 17
iterat. impf. emphasizing the repetition (s. MT, 67). ἐλάμβανον
impf. ■ δίδοται pres. pass. δίδωμι. προσήνεγκεν aor. 18
προσφέρω to bring to. χρῆμα pl. money. ■ δότε aor. imp. 19
δίδωμι. ἐπιθῶ aor. subj. ἐπιτίθημι. λαμβάνῃ pres. subj. ■ εἴη 20
opt. εἰμί. Optative used to express a wish that can be fulfilled
(s. RG, 939f.; MKG, 241f.). ἀπώλεια destruction. δωρέα gift,
free gift. ἐνόμισας aor. νομίζω to suppose. ■ μερίς part. 21
κλῆρος lot, inheritance. ἔναντι before. ■ μετανόησον aor. 22
imp. μετανοέω to change one's mind, to repent. δεήθητι aor.
pass. imp. δέω to ask, to pray. ἀφεθήσεται fut. pass. ἀφίημι
to forgive. (For the construction w. the particles, "in the hope
that perhaps," s. IBG, 158.) ἐπίνοια thought, intent, plot. Used
in the bad sense of evil or hostile schemes or stratagems (LC).
■ χολή gall. πικρία bitterness. ■ ἀποκριθείς aor. pass. part. 23/24
ἀποκρίνομαι to answer. ἐπέλθῃ aor. subj. ἐπέρχομαι to come
upon. εἰρήκατε perf. λέγω.

   ■ διαμαρτυράμενοι aor. mid. part. διαμαρτύρομαι to 25
testify, to bear witness, to solemnly declare (s. MH, 302).
λαλήσαντες aor. part. ὑπέστρεφον impf. ὑποστρέφω to return. εὐηγγελίζοντο impf. mid. (For the importance of the
conversion of the Samaritans, s. C.H.H. Scobie, "The Origins
and Development of Samaritan Christianity," NTS, 19 [July,
1973] 390–414; BHS, 55–72.)

   ■ ἐλάλησεν aor. ἀνάστηθι aor. imp. ἀνίστημι to arise. 26
πορεύου pres. imp. πορεύομαι to go. μεσημβρία midday,
noon. ■ ἀναστάς aor. part. ἀνίστημι. ἐπορεύθη aor. pass. 27

εὐνοῦχος eunuch. δυνάστης treasurer. ἐληλύθει plperf.
ἔρχομαι. προσκυνήσων fut. part. προσκυνέω to worship.
28 Participle used to express purpose. ■ ὑποστρέφων pres. part.,
s.v.25. ἅρμα wagon, probably an ox wagon (Bruce).
ἀνεγίνωσκεν impf. ἀναγινώσκω to read, impf. picturing the
29 continual action. ■ πρόσελθε aor. imp. προσέρχομαι to go to.
30 κολλήθητι aor. pass. imp. κολλάομαι to join. ■ προσδραμών
aor. part. προστρέχω to run to. ἤκουσεν aor. ἀκούω. ἆρα
interrogative particle intensified used to indicate doubt on Phil-
31 ip's part (RWP). ■ δυναίμην pres. opt. δύναμαι. ὁδηγήσει
fut. ὁδηγέω to show the way, to lead. ἀναβάντα aor. part.
ἀναβαίνω to get up. καθίσαι aor. inf. καθίζω to sit down.
32 ■ σφαγή slaughter. ἤχθη aor. pass. ἄγω to lead. κείροντος
33 pres. part. κείρω to shear. ■ ἤρθη aor. pass. αἴρω to lift up, to
take away. διηγήσεται fut. mid. διηγέομαι to relate, to narrate.
34/35   ■ ἀποκριθείς aor. part. ■ ἀρξάμενος aor. mid. part.
36/38 ἄρχομαι to begin. ■ βαπτισθῆναι aor. pass. inf. ■ ἐκέλευσεν
aor. κελεύω to command. στῆναι aor. inf. ἵστημι to stand.
39 ■ κατέβησαν aor. καταβαίνω to ascend, to go up. ἥρπασεν
40 aor. ἁρπάζω to snatch, to carry off. ■ εὑρέθη aor. pass.
εὑρίσκω to find, idiomatic for "he came" (GI, 158).

Ch. 9

1   ■ ἐμπνέων pres. part. ἐμπνέω to breathe in, to inhale,
followed by the gen. indicating what was breathed. Threatening
and murder were the atmosphere which he breathed and by
which and in he lived (EGT; s. BD, 95f.). προσελθών aor. part.
2 προσέρχομαι to come to. ■ ᾐτήσατο aor. mid. αἰτέω to request, to ask for one's self. ὅπως w. subj. that, in order that. εὕρῃ
aor. subj. εὑρίσκω. ὁδός way (s. TDNT). ὄντας pres. part. εἰμί.
δεδεμένους perf. pass. part. δέω to bind. The perf. emphasizes
3 the condition. ἀγάγῃ aor. subj. ἄγω to lead. ■ ἐγένετο aor. mid.
γίνομαι. ἐξαίφνης suddenly. περιήστραψεν aor.
4 περιαστράπτω to flash around. ■ πεσών aor. part. πίπτω to
6 fall. ἤκουσεν aor. ἀκούω. ■ ἀλλά but. Introduces the imp.
which adds something new to the context (Haenchen).
ἀνάστηθι aor. pass. imp. ἀνίστημι to arise. εἴσελθε aor. imp.
7 εἰσέρχομαι to go into. λαληθήσεται fut. pass. ■
συνοδεύοντες pres. part. συνοδεύω w. dat. to accompany, to
travel w. someone. εἱστήκεισαν plperf. ἵστημι to stand. ἐνεός
8 speechless. θεωροῦντες pres. part. θεωρέω to see. ■ ἠγέρθη
aor. pass. ἐγείρω to raise, pass. to rise. ἀνεῳγμένων perf. pass.
part. ἀνοίγω to open. (For the form, s. BD, 53.) Participle used

as gen. abs. ἔβλεπεν impf. χειραγωγοῦντες pres. part. χειραγωγέω to lead by the hand. εἰσήγαγον aor. εἰσάγω to lead into. ■ ἔφαγεν aor. ἐσθίω to eat. ἔπιεν aor. πίνω to drink. 9
■ ὅραμα vision. Not necessarily a night vision, but de- 10 scribes a condition in which the person's consciousness is opened for a heavenly message (Haenchen). ■ πορεύθητι aor. 11 pass. imp. ῥύμη street. εὐθύς straight. ζήτησον aor. imp. ζητέω to seek. ■ εἰσελθόντα aor. part. εἰσέρχομαι s.v.6. ἐπιθέντα 12 aor. part. ἐπιτίθημι to place upon. ἀναβλέψῃ aor. subj. ἀναβλέπω to see again, to regain sight (s. LC). ■ ἀπεκρίθη aor. 13 pass. ἀποκρίνομαι to answer. ἤκουσα aor. ■ δῆσαι aor. inf. 14 δέω s.v.2. ἐπικαλουμένους pres. mid. part. ἐπικαλέομαι to call upon. ■ πορεύου pres. mid. imp. σκεῦος vessel, instrument. 15 The word means implements in general (LC). ἐκλογή choice, gen. of quality used in the Hebraic sense, "intrument of choice" that is, "chosen vessel" (Bruce). βαστάσαι aor. inf. βαστάζω to bear, to carry. ■ ὑποδείξω fut. ὑποδείκνυμι to show. παθεῖν 16 aor. inf. πάσχω to suffer. ■ ἀπῆλθεν aor. ἀπέρχομαι to go 17 away. ἀπέσταλκεν perf. ἀποστέλλω to send, to send as an authoritative representative (TDNT). ὀφθείς aor. pass. part. ὁράω. ἤρχου impf. mid. ἔρχομαι. πλησθῇς aor. pass. subj. πίμπλημι to fill. ■ ἀπέπεσαν aor. ἀποπίπτω to fall off. λεπίς 18 scaly substance, flakes (s. LC). (For the medical use of the term, s. MLL, 39f.) ἀναστάς aor. part. ἐβαπτίσθη aor. pass. βαπτίζω to baptize. ■ ἐνίσχυσεν aor. ἐνισχύω to receive 19 strength.
■ ἐκήρυσσεν impf., inceptive impf. "he began to preach." 20 ■ ἐξίσταντο aor. mid. ἐξίστημι to be beside one's self, to be 21 amazed. πορθήσας aor. part. πορθέω to destroy, to ravage, to destroy or sack a city, to destroy any human fellowship (s. Haenchen; LC). ἐληλύθει plperf. ἔρχομαι. δεδεμένους perf. pass. part., s.v.2. ■ ἐνεδυναμοῦτο impf. pass. ἐνδύναμαι to receive 22 power, to fill w. power. It is used of religious and spiritual strength (EGT). The impf. pictures the continual increase of strength. συνέχυννεν impf. συγχύννω to pour together, to confuse, to confound, to throw into consternation (BAG). κατοικοῦντας pres. part. κατοικέω to prove, putting together. Used here of putting the prophetic Scriptures alongside their fulfillment (Bruce).
■ ἐπληροῦντο impf. pass. πληρόω to fulfill. 23 συνεβουλεύσαντο aor. mid. συμβουλεύομαι to counsel together, to plot. ἀνελεῖν aor. inf. ἀναιρέω to kill. ■ ἐγνώσθη 24 aor. pass. γινώσκω. ἐπιβουλή plot. παρετηροῦντο impf. mid. παρατηρέω to watch, to observe (s. Luke 6:7). ἀνέλωσιν aor.

25 subj. ἀναιρέω. ■ τεῖχος wall. καθῆκαν aor. καθίημι to let
down. χαλάσαντες aor. part. χαλάω to lower. σπυρίς basket,
a large woven basket suitable for hay and straw or for bales of
wool (LC).

26   ■ παραγενόμενος aor. mid. part. παραγίνομαι to arrive.
ἐπείραζεν impf. πειράζω to try, to attempt. The impf. pictures
the repeated attempts. ἐφοβοῦντο impf. mid. φοβέομαι to be
27 afraid,   to   fear.   ■   ἐπιλαβόμενος   aor.   mid.   part.
ἐπιλαμβάνομαι to take hold of, to be concerned w., to take an
interest in. ἤγαγεν aor. ἄγω. διηγήσατο aor. mid. διηγέομαι
to relate, to describe. The subject could be either Paul or Barnabas. ἐλάλησεν   aor.   ἐπαρρησιάσατο   aor.   mid.
28 παρρησιάζομαι to speak freely, openly, boldly. ■
εἰσπορευόμενος pres. mid. part. εἰσπορεύομαι to go in. Par-
29 ticiple used in a periphrastic construction. ■ ἐλάλει impf.
συνεζήτει impf. συζητέω to dispute, to argue. The impf. indicates Paul argued often (Haenchen). ἐπεχείρουν impf.
30 ἐπιχειρέω to put the hand to, to try. ■ ἐπιγνόντες aor. part.
ἐπιγινώσκω to realize, to know. The verb without any object
is perhaps idiomatic (LC). κατήγαγον aor. κατάγω to lead
down. ἐξαπέστειλαν aor. ἐξαποστέλλω to send away.

31   ■ οἰκοδομουμένη pres. pass. part. οἰκοδομέω to build, to
edify, to build up (s. TDNT). παράκλησις comfort, encouragement, followed by subjective gen. ἐπληθύνετο impf. pass.
πληθύνω to increase, to multiply.

32   ■ ἐγένετο aor. mid., s.v.3. (For the Hebraic construction,
s. M, 16f.; Beyer 29–62.) διερχόμενον pres. mid. part.
διέρχομαι to pass through. διὰ πάντων that is, through all the
areas mentioned in v.31 (Haenchen). κατελθεῖν aor. inf.
κατέρχομαι to go down; that is, to come down from Jerusalem
33 (s. LC). ■ εὗρεν aor. εὑρίσκω. κατακείμενον pres. mid. part.
κατάκειμαι to be lying down. κράβατος mattress, mat (s.
Mark 2:4). παραλελυμένος perf. pass. part. παραλύω pass. to
34 be paralyzed. ■ ἰάομαι pres. mid. to heal, aoristic pres. (s.
RWP). ἀνάστηθι aor. pass. imp., s.v.6. στρῶσον aor. imp.
στρώννυμι to make one's bed or to get ready to eat (s. Bruce).
35 ἀνέστη aor. ἀνίστημι. ■ οἵτινες = οἵ (s. MKG, 174; BG, 68).
ἐπεστρεψαν aor. ἐπιστρέφω to turn to.

36   ■ διερμηνευομένη pres. pass. part. διερμηνεύω to trans-
37 late. ἐποίει impf. ■ ἐγένετο aor. mid. s.v.32. ἀσθενήσασαν
aor. part. fem. ἀσθενέω to be weak, to be sick. ἀποθανεῖν aor.
inf. ἀποθνήσκω to die. λούσαντες aor. part. λούω to wash.
38 ἔθηκαν aor. τίθημι to place, to put. ■ οὔσης pres. part. fem.
εἰμί gen. abs. ἀκούσαντες aor. part. ἀπέστειλαν aor.

ἀποστέλλω s.v.17. παρακαλοῦντες pres. part. παρακαλέω to ask, to beseech, to urge. ὀκνήσῃς aor. subj. ὀκνέω to delay. διελθεῖν aor. inf. διέρχομαι. ■ ἀναστάς aor. part., s.v.11. 39 συνῆλθεν aor. συνέρχομαι to lead up. παρέστησαν aor. παρίστημι to come to and stand by. χήρα widow. κλαίουσαι pres. part. κλαίω to weep, to cry loudly. ἐπιδεικνύμεναι pres. mid. part. ἐπιδείχνυμι to show, to display. Perhaps the mid. indicates the exhibitors owned and were wearing Tabitha's gift (LC). ■ ἐκβαλών aor. part. ἐκβάλλω to put out. θείς aor. part. 40 τίθημι. γόνυ knee. προσηύξατο aor. mid. προσεύχομαι to pray. ἐπιστρέψας aor. part., s.v.35. ἀνάστηθι aor. pass. imp., s.v.6. ἤνοιξεν aor. ἀνοίγω to open, s.v.8. ἀνεκάθισεν aor. ἀνακαθίζω to sit up. ■ δούς aor. part. δίδωμι. ἀνέστησεν aor. 41 ἀνίστημι to raise up. ζῶσαν pres. part. fem. ζάω to live. ■ 42 γνωστός known. ἐπίστευσαν aor. ■ μεῖναι aor. inf. μένω to 43 remain. βυρσεύς tanner. The work of a tanner was "defiling" according to Jewish law (LC).

Ch. 10

■ ἑκατοντάρχης centurion (s. BC, V, 427–445). ■ 1/2 εὐσεβής pious. φοβούμενος pres. mid. part. φοβέομαι to fear. These two terms denote Gentiles who, though not full proselytes, attached themselves to the Jewish religion, practicing its monotheistic and imageless worship (Bruce; s. also TDNT; BC, V, 74–96). ποιῶν pres. part. ἐλεημοσύνη alms (s. Matt. 6:2). δεόμενος pres. mid. part. δέομαι to ask, to pray. διὰ παντός always. ■ φανερῶς adv. clearly. ■ ἀτενίσας aor. part. ἀτενίζω 3/4 to gaze. ἀνέβησαν aor. ἀναβαίνω to ascend, to go up. μνημόσυνον remembrance. ■ πέμψον aor. imp. πέμπω to 5 send. μετάπεμψαι aor. mid. imp. μεταπέμπομαι to send for. The mid. indicates the sending of another for one's own sake (RWP). ■ ξενίζεται prcs. pass. ξενίζω to receive as a guest, to 6 entertain as a stranger. ■ ἀπῆλθεν aor. ἀπέρχομαι to go away. 7 φωνήσας aor. part. φωνέω to call. οἰκέτης household servant. προσκαρτερούντων pres. part. προσκαρτερέω to be true. ■ ἐξηγησάμενος aor. mid. part. ἐξηγέομαι to relate. 8 ἀπέστειλεν aor. ἀποστέλλω to send.

■ ἐπαύριον on the following day. ὁδοιπορούντων pres. 9 part. ὁδοιπορέω to journey, gen. abs. προσεύξασθαι aor. mid. inf. προσεύχομαι to pray, inf. of purpose. ■ ἐγένετο aor. mid. 10 γίνομαι. πρόσπεινος very hungry. ἤθελεν impf. θέλω. γεύσασθαι aor. mid. inf. γεύομαι to eat. παρασκευαζόντων pres. part. παρασκευάζω to prepare, gen. abs. ἔκστασις ecstasy, trance, a state in which a man stands outside himself (Bruce).

11 ■ ἀνεῳγμένον perf. pass. part. ἀνοίγω to open. καταβαῖνον
pres. part. καταβαίνω to descend. ὀθόνη linen cloth. ἀρχή
corner. These two words were a technical medical phrase "the
ends of a bandage" used for the ends of a sheet (MLL, 218).
12 καθιέμενον pres. pass. part. καθίημι to let down. ■ ὑπῆρχεν
impf. ὑπάρχω to exist, to be. τετράπους four-footed (animals).
13 ἑρπετόν reptile. πετεινά (pl.) birds. ■ ἀναστάς aor. part.
ἀνίστημι to arise. θῦσον aor. imp. θύω to kill. Here not used
in its original sense of "to sacrifice" (Bruce). φάγε aor. imp.
14 ἐσθίω to eat. ■ μηδαμῶς "not at all," "by no means." ἔφαγον
15 aor. ἐσθίω. ■ ἐκαθάρισεν aor. καθαρίζω to cleanse, to purify.
κοίνου pres. imp. κοινόω to consider common, to count as
profane (s. LC). The pres. imp. w. the neg. implies that he is not
16 to go on doing what he is already doing (Bruce). ■ ἀνελήμφθη
aor. pass. ἀναλαμβάνω to take up.
17   ■ διηπόρει impf. διαπορέω to be perplexed. The original
meaning intensified by the prep. compound is "to be completely
at a loss what road to take" (RWP). εἴη opt. εἰμί.
ἀπεσταλμένοι perf. pass. part. ἀποστέλλω. διερωτήσαντες
aor. part. διερωτάω to ask. The prep. compound intensifies and
gives the meaning "to ask constantly or continually" (EGT).
ἐπέστησαν aor. ἐφίστημι to approach, to stand before.
18 πυλῶν house door. ■ ἐπυνθάνοντο impf. mid. πυνθάνομαι to
inquire. εἰ if, whether. Introduces either a direct or indirect
19 quotation (s. LC). ἐνθάδε here. ■ διενθυμουμένου pres. mid.
part. διενθυμέομαι to think about, to think through and
through, in and out (RWP), gen. abs. ζητοῦντες pres. part.
20 ζητέω to seek. ■ κατάβηθι aor. imp. καταβαίνω to go down.
πορεύου pres. mid. imp. πορεύομαι to go. διακρινόμενος
pres. mid. part. διακρίνομαι to question, to doubt. ἀπέσταλκα
21/22 perf. ἀποστέλλω. ■ καταβάς aor. part. καταβαίνω. ■
μαρτυρούμενος pres. pass. part. μαρτυρέω to give witness.
(For the pass., s. Acts 6:3.) ἐχρηματίσθη aor. pass.
χρηματίζομαι to instruct, to give a divine warning (Bruce; s.
23 also MM). μεταπέμψασθαι aor. mid. inf. ■ ἀκοῦσαι aor. inf.
εἰσκαλεσάμενος aor. mid. part. εἰσκαλέω to call in. ἐξένισεν
aor., s.v.6.
24   συνῆλθον aor. συνέρχομαι to accompany, to go w. ■
προσδοκῶν pres. part. προσδοκέω to expect, to await, to direct the mind toward anything (RWP). Participle used in a periphrastic construction. συγκαλεσάμενος aor. mid. part.
συγκαλέω to call together, to summon. συγγενής relative.
25 ἀναγκαῖος intimate, familiar. ■ εἰσελθεῖν aor. inf.
εἰσέρχομαι. The construction of the inf. w. the gen. of the

284

article is probably a Semitic influence and supposes some
"futurity," "when Peter was about to go in" (s. BG, 133; RG,
1067f.). συναντήσας aor. part. συναντάω to meet. πεσών
aor. part. πίπτω to fall. προσεκύνησεν aor. προσκυνέω to
worship. ■ ἀνάστηθι aor. pass. imp. ἀνίστημι to stand up, rise. 26
■ συνομιλῶν pres. part. συνομιλέω to talk w. 27
συνεληλυθότας perf. part. συνέρχομαι. ■ ἀθέμιτος unlaw- 28
ful, contrary to the divinely constituted order of things, breaking
a taboo. It denotes profanity (LC). ἀλλόφυλος "of another
tribe," one that is not a Jew. Not all intercourse w. Gentiles was
absolutely prohibited, but that which rendered a Jew ceremonially unclean, such as entering a Gentile house or handling articles belonging to Gentiles (Bruce; s. also SB, IV, 353–414).
κάμοί = καὶ ἐμοί. (For the adverbial use of the conjunctive,
s. BG, 153.) ἔδειξεν aor. δείκνυμι to show. ■ ἀναντιρρήτως 29
adv. not speaking back, without raising any objection.
μεταπεμφθείς aor. pass. part. μεταπέμπασθε aor. mid. ■ 30
ἤμην impf. εἰμί. τὴν ἐνάτην the ninth (hour), acc. of time.
ἔστη aor. ἵστημι to stand. ἐσθής clothing. λαμπρός shining,
bright. ■ εἰσηκούσθη aor. pass. εἰσακούω to hear, to attend 31
to (s. MH, 304). ἐμνήσθησαν aor. pass. μιμνήσκω to remember. ■ μετακάλεσαι aor. imp. μετακαλέω to summons. ■ 32/33
ἐξαυτῆς at once. ἔπεμψα aor. ἐποίησας aor. Used w. the aor.
part. as a means of expressing a polite request, "please do so and
so" (Bruce). προστεταγμένα perf. pass. part. προστάσσω to
command. Cornelius is a military man and he employs a military
term (RWP).

■ ἀνοίξας aor. part. καταλαμβάνομαι to grasp w. the 34
mind, to perceive. προσωπολήμπτης literally, "acceptor of
faces, or persons," to have favorites (LC). ■ ἐργαζόμενος pres. 35
mid. part. ἐργάζομαι to work, to do. To work righteousness is
used in its widest sense but may denote almsgiving (Bruce). It
is not that righteousness is itself acceptable, but in the Jewish
tradition it is that which leads to acceptability (MRP, 132).
δεκτός acceptable. ■ εὐαγγελιζόμενος pres. mid. part. to pro- 36
claim good news (s. TDNT). ■ ἀρξάμενος aor. mid. part. 37
ἄρχομαι to begin. ἐκήρυξεν aor. ■ ἔχρισεν aor. χρίω to anoint 38
(s. TDNT; CBB). διῆλθεν aor. διέρχομαι to pass through, to
go about from place to place. εὐεργετῶν pres. part. εὐεργετέω
to do well, to do good. Possibly w. reference to the royal title of
Hellenistic kings (LC; DC, I, 34). ἰώμενος pres. mid. part.
ἰάομαι to heal. καταδυναστευομένους pres. pass. part.
καταδυναστεύω to oppress, to exploit, to dominate someone
(s. BAG). ■ ἀνεῖλαν aor. ἀναιρέω to kill. κρεμάσαντες aor. 39

part. κρεμάννυμι to hang. ξύλον wood (s. J.M. Baumgarten, "Does TLH in the Temple Scroll Refer to Crucifixion?" JBL, 91
40 [Dec., 1972], 472–481). ■ ἔδωκεν aor. δίδωμι to give, here to make. In this sense it seems to be a Semitism (LC). ἐμφανής
41 visible. γενέσθαι aor. mid. inf. γίνομαι. ■ προκεχειροτονημένοις perf. pass. part. προχειροτονέω to choose or designate by hand, to choose beforehand (s. RWP). συνεφάγομεν aor. συνεσθίω to eat w. someone. συνεπίομεν aor. συμπίνω to drink w. someone. ἀναστῆναι aor. inf.
42 ἀνίστημι. ■ παρήγγειλεν aor. παραγγέλλω to command, to charge. κηρύξαι aor. inf. διαμαρτύρασθαι aor. mid. inf. διαμαρτύρομαι to witness (s. Acts 2:40). ὥρισμένος perf. pass. part. ὁρίζω to mark out the boundary, to ordain. ζώντων
43 pres. part. ζάω to live. ■ λαβεῖν aor. inf. λαμβάνω.
44   ■ λαλοῦντος pres. part. gen. abs. "as he was speaking." This happened before he had finished what he meant to say
45 (Alex). ἐπέπεσεν aor. ἐπιπίπτω to fall upon. ■ ἐξέστησαν aor. ἐξίστημι to be beside one's self, to be amazed. ἐκκέχυται
46 perf. pass. ἐκχέω to pour out. ■ ἤκουον impf. ἀκούω. μεγαλυννόντων pres. part. μεγαλύνω to magnify, to praise.
47 ἀπεκρίθη aor. pass. ἀποκρίνομαι to answer. ■ κωλῦσαι aor. inf. κωλύω to hinder, to forbid. βαπτισθῆναι aor. pass. inf.
48 βαπτίζω to baptize. ἔλαβον aor. λαμβάνω. ■ προσέταξεν aor. προστάσσω. ἠρώτησαν aor. ἐρωτάω to ask, to request. ἐπιμεῖναι aor. inf. ἐπιμένω to remain.

Ch. 11

1   ■ ἤκουσαν aor. ἀκούω. ἐδέξαντο aor. mid. δέχομαι to
2 receive, to welcome. ■ ἀνέβη aor. ἀναβαίνω to go up. διεκρίνοντο impf. mid. διακρίνομαι to take issue, to dispute w. someone. (For the force of the prep. compound indicating a to and fro, s. MH, 302.) The inceptive impf. περιτομή circumci-
3 sion. ■ εἰσῆλθες aor. εἰσέρχομαι to go into. ἔχοντας pres.
4 part. συνέφαγες aor. συνεσθίω to eat w. someone. ■ ἀρξάμενος aor. mid. part. ἄρχομαι to begin. ἐξετίθετο impf. mid. ἐκτίθημι to set forth, to explain, a deliberate and detailed
5 narrative (RWP). καθεξῆς in order, in succession. ■ ἤμην impf. εἰμί. προσευχόμενος pres. mid. part. προσεύχομαι to pray. ἔκστασις trance (s. Acts 10:6). καταβαῖνον pres. part. καταβαίνω to go down, to come down. ὀθόνη a sheet made of fine linen. ἀρχή corner, end (s. Acts 10:11). καθιεμένην pres.
6 pass. part. καθίημι to let down. ■ ἀτενίσας aor. part. ἀτενίζω to gaze. κατενόουν impf. κατανοέω to put the mind down, to understand, to take notice of. εἶδον aor. τετράπους four-footed.

286

θηρίον wild animal. ■ ἀναστάς aor. part. ἀνίστημι to rise up. 7
θῦσον aor. imp. θύω to slay (s. Acts 10:13). φάγε aor. imp.
ἐσθίω to eat. ■ μηδαμῶς not at all. ■ ἀπεκρίθη aor. pass. 8/9
ἀποκρίνομαι to answer. ἐκαθάρισεν aor. καθαρίζω to
cleanse. κοίνου pres. mid. imp. κοινόω to make common, mid.
to consider common (s. Acts 10:15). ■ ἐγένετο aor. mid. 10
γίνομαι. ἀνεσπάσθη aor. pass. ἀνασπάω to pull up. ■ 11
ἐπέστησαν aor. ἐφίστημι to come upon and stand by.
ἀπεσταλμένοι perf. pass. part. ἀποστέλλω to send. ■ 12
συνελθεῖν aor. inf. συνέρχομαι to go w., to accompany.
διακρίναντα aor. part. διακρίνω to make a distinction or possibly w. the meaning "without hesitation" (s. LC). ■ 13
ἀπήγγειλαν aor. ἀπαγγέλλω to announce, to report.
σταθέντα aor. pass. part. ἵστημι pass. to stand. εἰπόντα aor.
part. λέγω. ἀπόστειλον aor. imp. μετάπεμψαι aor. mid. imp.
μεταπέμπω to send for. ἐπικαλούμενον pres. pass. part.
ἐπικαλέω to call by the first name. ■ λαλήσει fut. σωθήσῃ fut. 14
pass. σώζω to rescue, to save (s. TDNT; CBB). ■ ἄρξασθαι 15
aor. mid. inf. ἄρχομαι. ἐπέπεσεν aor. ἐπιπίπτω to fall upon.
■ ἐμνήσθην aor. μιμνήσκομαι to remember. ἐβάπτισεν aor. 16
βαπτίζω to baptize. βαπτισθήσεθε fut. pass. ■ ἴσος same. 17
ἔδωκεν aor. δίδωμι. πιστεύσασιν aor. part. dat. pl. κωλῦσαι
aor. inf. κωλύω to forbid. ■ ἡσύχασαν aor. ἡσυχάζω to be 18
silent, ingressive aor. "they became silent." ἐδόξασαν aor.
δοξάζω to glorify. Their opposition ceased and their praise began (Bruce).

■ διασπαρέντες aor. pass. part. διασπείρω to scatter. 19
γενομένης aor. mid. part. γίνομαι. διῆλθον aor. διέρχομαι to
pass through, to go about. ■ ἐλθόντες aor. part. ἔρχομαι. 20
ἐλάλουν impf. εὐαγγελιζόμενοι pres. mid. part.
εὐαγγελίζομαι to tell the good news (s. TDNT). ■ 21
ἐπέστρεψεν aor. ἐπιστρέφω to turn to. ■ ἠκούσθη aor. pass. 22
ἀκούω. οὔσης part. fem. εἰμί. ἐξαπέστειλαν aor.
ἐξαποστέλλω to send out, to send out as an authoritative representative (s. TDNT). ■ παραγενόμενος aor. mid. part. 23
παραγίνομαι to arrive. ἐχάρη aor. χαίρω. παρεκάλει impf.
παρακαλέω to exhort. πρόθεσις purpose, "w. purpose of
heart," that is "w. determination" (Bruce). ■ προσετέθη aor. 24
pass. προστίθημι to add to. ■ ἐξῆλθεν aor. ἐξέρχομαι to go 25
out. ἀναζητῆσαι aor. inf. ἀναζητέω to search for. The prep.
compound indicates to seek up and down, back and forth; to
make a thorough search till success comes (RWP). ■ εὑρών aor. 26
part. εὑρίσκω. ἤγαγεν aor. ἄγω to lead. συναχθῆναι aor.
pass. inf. συνάγω to gather together, to be taken in as a guest

(LC). διδάξαι aor. inf. χρηματίσαι aor. inf. χρηματίζω to give instruction.

27/28 ■ κατῆλθον aor. κατέρχομαι to come down. ■ ἀναστάς aor. part., s.v.7. ἐσήμαινεν impf. σημαίνω to signify, to make known. λιμός famine. μέλλω to be about to. Used w. inf. to

29 express the fut. ἔσεσθαι fut. inf. εἰμί (s. MKG, 308). ■ εὐπορεῖτο impf. mid. εὐπορέω to be well off, to have plenty, here "according to his financial ability" (BAG). ὥρισαν aor. ὁρίζω to fix a boundary, to determine, to appoint, "they arranged." Perhaps each one set aside a fixed sum out of his property or income as a contribution to the fund (Bruce).

30 πέμψαι aor. inf. πέμπω to send. ■ ἐποίησαν aor. ἀποστείλαντες aor. part., s.v.11.

Ch. 12

1 ■ ἐπέβαλεν aor. ἐπιβάλλω to cast upon, to lay hands on, to seize. κακῶσαι aor. inf. κακόω to afflict, to do harm to. (For verbs w. this ending having a factitive or an instrumental mean-

2 ing, s. MH, 394f.) Infinitive of purpose. ■ ἀνεῖλεν aor. ἀναιρέω to kill. μάχαιρα sword, instrumental dat. (For execution w. the

3 sword at that time, s. Haenchen; SB, II, 706.) ■ ἀρεστός pleasing, verbal adj. followed by the dat. (RWP). προσέθετο aor. mid. προστίθημι to add to, to proceed. A Semitic construction common in OT (Bruce; s. also MH, 445). συλλαβεῖν aor. inf. συλλαμβάνω to arrest. τὰ ἄζυμα "days of unleavened bread." (For the Feast of Unleavened Bread, s. IDB, III, 663f.; TDNT;

4 M, Pesahim.) ■ πιάσας aor. part. πιάζω to seize. ἔθετο aor. mid. τίθημι to place. παραδούς aor. part. παραδίδωμι to deliver over. τετράδιον quaternion, a company of four soldiers for each watch of three hours (LC). ἀναγαγεῖν aor. inf. ἀνάγω to lead up. Peter was in the inner prison or lower ward and so would

5 be led up (RWP). ■ ἐτηρεῖτο impf. pass. τηρέω to guard. ἐκτενῶς adv. earnestly (LC).

6 ■ ἤμελλεν impf. μέλλω to be about to. (For the use of the impf. w. the inf. to express intention reckoned from a moment in the past, s. MKG, 307.) προαγαγεῖν aor. inf. προάγω to lead out. In the language of the law court "to bring before" (BAG). κοιμώμενος pres. mid. part. κοιμάομαι to sleep. μεταξύ between. δεδεμένος perf. pass. part. δέω to bind. The perf. indi-

7 cates the state or condition. ἅλυσις chain. ἐτήρουν impf. ἐπέστη aor. ἐφίστημι to stand by. ἔλαμψεν aor. λάμπω to shine. οἴκημα room, euphemism for prison (LC). πατάξας aor. part. πατάσσω to strike, to hit. πλευρά side. ἤγειρεν aor. ἐγείρω to wake up. ἀνάστα aor. imp. ἀνίστημι to rise up, to

get up. τάχος hurry, quickness. Used w. prep. adverbially "quickly" (s. IBG, 78). ἐξέπεσαν aor. ἐκπίπτω to fall off. ■ 8 ζῶσαι aor. mid. imp. ζώννυμι to gird one's self, to bind the tunic w. a wide belt. During the night the long-flowing undergarment was loosened, but fastened up by day, so as not to impede movements (EGT). ὑπόδησαι aor. mid. imp. ὑποδέω to bind under, to tie on sandals. περιβαλοῦ aor. mid. imp. περιβάλλω to throw about (one's self), to put on. ἀκολούθει pres. imp. ἀκολουθέω to follow. ■ ἐξελθών aor. part. ἐξέρχομαι to go 9 out. ἠκολούθει impf. ἀκολουθέω. ᾔδει plperf. οἶδα. Used here as the impf. ἐδόκει impf. δοκέω to suppose, to think. ὅραμα vision. ■ διελθόντες aor. part. διέρχομαι to go through. 10 σιδηροῦς iron. φέρουσαν pres. part. fem. φέρω to carry, to lead. αὐτόματος automatically, of its own accord (s. LC). ἠνοίγη aor. pass. ἀνοίγω to open. προῆλθον aor. προέρχομαι to go forward, to proceed, here "to go one block farther" (BAG). ῥύμη street or alley. They went along the main street until its intersection (LC). The acc. is acc. of extent, of space (s. BD, 88). ἀπέστη aor. ἀφίστημι to go away, to depart. ■ γενόμενος aor. 11 mid. part. γίνομαι "coming to himself." ἐξαπέστειλεν aor. ἐξαποστέλλω to send out. ἐξείλατο aor. mid. ἐξαιρέω to remove above, to rescue. προσδοκία expectation. ■ συνιδών 12 aor. part. συνοράω to see together, to see clearly, to be aware of, "having realized the position" (Bruce). (For the perfective force of the prep. compound, s. MH, 325.) ἐπικαλουμένου pres. pass. part. ἐπικαλέω to name. ἱκανός considerable, many. συνηθροισμένοι perf. pass. part. συναθροίζω to bring together, pass. to be gathered, to meet. προσευχόμενοι pres. mid. part. προσεύχομαι to pray. Participle used to form the periphrastic impf. The praying apparently had been going on all night (RWP). ■ κρούσαντος aor. act. part. κρούω to knock, 13 gen. abs. πυλών gateway, entrance. The gate entrance was separated from the living quarters by a courtyard (s. Haenchen). προσῆλθεν aor. προσέρχομαι to come to. ὑπακοῦσαι aor. inf. ὑπακούω to answer the door. Used technically of the doorkeeper, whose duty it is to listen for the signals of those who wish to enter, and to admit them if they are entitled to do so (BAG). Infinitive used to express purpose. ■ ἐπιγνοῦσα aor. act. part. 14 fem. sing. ἐπιγινώσκω to recognize. ἤνοιξεν aor. ἀνοίγω. εἰσδραμοῦσα aor. part. εἰστρέχω to run in. ἀπήγγειλεν aor. ἀπαγγέλλω to report. ἑστάναι perf. inf. ἵστημι to stand. Infinitive used in indirect discourse (s. IBG, 153). ■ μαίνῃ pres. 15 mid. 2nd per. sing. μαίνομαι to be mad, to be crazy. διϊσχυρίζετο impf. mid. διϊσχυρίζομαι to insist. An old word

of vigorous and confident assertion, originally "to lean upon"
(RWP). ἔχειν pres. inf., here "it is," "the situation is so" (BAG).
16 Infinitive used in indirect discourse. ■ ἐπέμενεν impf. ἐπιμένω
to remain, to continue. (For the use of this word w. the part., s.
BD, 213.) κρούων pres. part. ἀνοίξαντες aor. part. ἐξέστησαν
17 aor. ἐξίστημι to be amazed, to be beside one's self. ■
κατασείσας aor. part. κατασείω to signal or motion to w. the
hand. σιγᾶν pres. inf. σιγάω to be silent. διηγήσατο aor. mid.
διηγέομαι to relate, to narrate. ἐξήγαγεν aor. ἐξάγω to lead
out. ἀπαγγείλατε aor. imp. ἐπορεύθη aor. pass. πορεύομαι to
go.
18   ■ γενομένης aor. mid. part., gen. abs. τάραχος commotion. ἄρα therefore, then, inferential particle. ἐγένετο aor. mid.
19 γίνομαι. ■ ἐπιζητήσας aor. part. ἐπιζητέω to look for. εὑρών
aor. part. εὑρίσκω. ἀνακρίνας aor. part. ἀνακρίνω to examine, to question thoroughly. ἐκέλευσεν aor. κελεύω to command. ἀπαχθῆναι aor. pass. inf. ἀπάγω to lead away to execution. Perhaps used in the sense of "to arrest," "to lead off to
prison." According to Justinian's Code a guard who allowed a
prisoner to escape became liable to the same penalty as had
awaited the prisoner (Bruce). κατελθών aor. part. κατέρχομαι
to go down. διέτριβεν impf. διατρίβω to remain.
20   ■ θυμομαχῶν pres. part. θυμομαχέω to fight desperately,
here "to be furious," "to be exasperated" (Bruce). ὁμοθυμαδόν
together, w. one accord. παρῆσαν impf. πάρειμι to be present.
πείσαντες aor. act. part. πείθω to persuade. κοιτών bedroom,
lit. "the one over the bedroom of the king." Used as a title for
the one in charge of the king's bedroom (s. LC). ἠτοῦντο impf.
mid. αἰτέω to ask. Imperfect pictures the continual asking.
τρεφέσθαι pres. pass. inf. τρέφω to feed, to support, to provide
w. food. The Phoenician cities depended largely on the grain
fields of Galilee for their food and Herod had cut off their supply
(Rackham). βασιλικός royal, belonging to a king. (For adj.
21 ending w. this suffix, s. MH, 378.) ■ τακτός set, appointed, dat.
of time. According to Josephus, it was a festival in honor of the
emperor, possibly on the first of August, the anniversary of his
birthday (Bruce). ἐνδυσάμενος aor. mid. part. ἐνδύω to put on,
to dress. ἐσθής clothing, raiment. According to Josephus, it was
a robe made of silver which glittered in the sun (s. Bruce, ET).
καθίσας aor. part. καθίζω to sit down, ingressive aor. to take
one's seat. ἐδημηγόρει impf. δημηγορέω to make a speech,
22 inceptive impf. "he began to make a speech." ■ ἐπεφώνει impf.
23 ἐπιφωνέω to cry out loudly, to cheer (LC). ■ ἐπάταξεν aor.
ἀνθ' ὧν because. ἔδωκεν aor. δίδωμι. σκωληκόβρωτος eaten

by worms. The word is used of diseased grain (s. MM). ἐξέψυξεν aor. ἐκψύχω to die, to breathe out. A term used by medical writers (s. MLL, 37). (For the life and death of Herod Agrippa I, s. Josephus, Ant. XVIII, 6; XVIX, 5–9; Schürer HJP [NEE] I, 442–454.)

■ ηὔξανεν impf. αὐξάνω to grow. ἐπληθύνετο impf. pass. 24 πληθύνω to increase. ■ ὑπέστρεψαν aor. ὑποστρέφω to re- 25 turn. πληρώσαντες aor. part. πληρόω to fill, to fulfill. συμπαραλαβόντες aor. act. part. συμπαραλαμβάνω to take someone along w. ἐπικληθέντα aor. pass. part. ἐπικαλέω s.v.12.

Ch. 13

■ οὖσαν pres. part. fem. sing. εἰμί. Used w. prep. which in 1 this case is distributive (s. RWP). καλούμενος pres. pass. part. σύντροφος a companion in education, playmate, intimate friend (s. Deissmann, BS, 311f.; MM). ■ λειτουργούντων pres. 2 part. λειτουργέω to serve. Used in classical Gr. to describe the service voluntarily rendered to the state. Later it indicated the performing of services which the state required. Still later it was used to describe any kind of service. In NT times it was the word for the service that a priest or servant rendered in a temple (NTW, 74f.). Perhaps the service rendered here was that of prayer (TDNT). νηστευόντων pres. part. νηστεύω to fast. ἀφορίσατε aor. imp. ἀφορίζω to mark off w. a boundary, to separate. δή a particle used here to emphasize the imp. (Bruce). προσκέκλημαι perf. mid. προσκαλέω to call, to call to one's service (Bruce). The perf. emphasizes that the divine decision was already made before it was revealed (Haenchen) ■ 3 νηστεύσαντες aor. part. προσευξάμενοι aor. mid. part. προσεύχομαι to pray. ἐπίθεντες aor. act. part. ἐπιτίθημι to place upon. The laying on of hands here expressed the fellowship w. the two and the recognition of the divine call (Bruce). ἀπέλυσαν aor. ἀπολύω to release, to let go, to send off.

■ αὐτοί "they." The pron. is used here unemphatic (Haen- 4 chen; s. also IBG,121). ἐκπεμφθέντες aor. pass. part. ἐκπέμπω to send out. κατῆλθον aor. κατέρχομαι to go down. ἀπέπλευσαν aor. ἀποπλέω to sail away. ■ γενόμενοι aor. 5 mid. part. γίνομαι. Used in the sense "to arrive." κατήγγελλον impf. καταγγέλλω to report, to proclaim, incep- tive impf. "they began to proclaim." ὑπηρέτης assistant, atten- dant, a helper who willingly submits himself to the carrying out of the will of the one over him (s. TDNT). ■ διελθόντος aor. 6 act. part. διέρχομαι to pass through. εὗρον aor. act. εὑρίσκω

291

to find. μάγος magician (s. BC, V, 164–188). ψευδοπροφήτης
7 false prophet. ■ ἀνθύπατος proconsul, one who is head of the
government in a senatorial province (BAG). (For a discussion of
Sergius Paulus, s. BRD, 150–172; for a more neg. view, s. BC,
V, 455f.) συνετός intelligent. ἐπεζήτησεν aor. ἐπιζητέω to
8 seek, to look for. ἀκοῦσαι aor. act. inf. ■ ἀνθίστατο impf. mid.
ἀνθίστημι to stand against, to withstand. The impf. pictures
the continual action and may be understood as conative "he
tried to oppose." μεθερμηνεύεται pres. pass. μεθερμηνεύω to
translate. ζητῶν pres. part. ζητέω to seek. διαστρέψαι aor. inf.
διαστρέφω to pervert, to distort. (For the force of the prep.
9 compound, s. MH, 302.) ■ ὁ καί "who is also." (For this phrase,
s. Deissmann, BS, 313–317; Haenchen.) πλησθείς aor. pass.
part. πίμπλημι to fill. ἀτενίσας aor. act. part. ἀτενίζω to gaze
at someone or something. This is not to be considered the evil
eye used by the rabbis to inflict punishment (Haenchen; s. SB,
10 II, 713f.). ■ δόλος deceit, treachery. Properly bait for fish, then
any cunning contrivance for deceiving or catching (LS).
ῥαδιουργία ease in doing, recklessness, wickedness. Used in
the papyri in the general sense of "false pretenses" (MM).
παύσῃ fut. παύω to cease, volitive fut. slightly imp. w. an
implied reproach (Bruce; RG, 874). διαστρέφων pres. part.
11 ■ ἔσῃ fut. εἰμί. ἔπεσεν aor. πίπτω to fall. ἀχλύς cloud. Used
by medical writers of an inflammation which brings a cloudy
appearance into the eye (LC; MLL, 44). ἐζήτει impf.
12 χειραγωγός one who leads another by the hand. ■ γεγονός
perf. act. part. γίνομαι. ἐκπλησσόμενος pres. mid. part.
ἐκπλήσσομαι to be astonished.
13   ■ ἀναχθέντες aor. pass. part. ἀνάγω to set sail.
ἀποχωρήσας aor. pass. part. ἀποχωρέω to depart, to leave, to
14 desert. ὑπέστρεψεν aor. ὑποστρέφω to return. ■ διελθόντες
aor. part., s.v.6. παρεγένοντο aor. mid. παραγίνομαι to arrive.
15 ἐκάθισαν aor. καθίζω to take one's seat. ■ ἀνάγνωσις reading. (For the synagogue and its service, s. Moore, Judaism I,
281–307; TDNT; SB, IV, 153–188.) The service consisted of the
Shema, prayer by the leader, reading of the law, and a sermon
by a member of the congregation (Bruce). ἀπέστειλαν aor.
ἀποστέλλω to send. ἀρχισυνάγωγος head of the synagogue.
One of his duties was to select the readers and the speakers for
16 the service (RWP). λέγετε pres. imp. ■ ἀναστάς aor. act. part.
ἀνίστημι to stand up. κατασείσας aor. act. part. κατασείω
to shake down, to shake or wave as a signal (AS).
        φοβούμενοι pres. mid. part. φοβέομαι to fear (s. Acts
10:2). ἀκούσατε aor. imp. (For an analysis of Paul's sermon

according to the method of rabbinical preaching, s. J.W. Bowker, "Speeches in Acts: A Study in Proem and Yellammedenu Form," NTS, 14 [Oct. 1967], 96–111.) ■ ἐξελέξατο aor. mid. 17 ἐκλέγω to choose, to elect. The mid. indicates a selection for one's self. ὕψωσεν aor. ὑψόω to exalt. παροικία sojourn, living in a place as a stranger or foreigner (s. TDNT; TDOT). βραχίων arm. ἐξήγαγεν aor. act. ἐξάγω to lead out. ■ ὡς w. numbers 18 "approximately."   τεσσερακονταέτης   forty   years. ἐτροποφόρησεν aor. act. τροποφορέω to bear or put up w. someone, to endure (s. LC). ■ καθελών aor. part. καθαιρέω to 19 destroy. κατεκληρονόμησεν aor. κατακληρονομέω to divide according to lots, to distribute an inheritance, to take for a possession, to give for a possession (s. Bruce). ■ ἔδωκεν aor. 20 δίδωμι. ■ ᾐτήσαντο aor. mid. αἰτέω to ask, mid. to ask for 21 one's self, to avail one's self of one's right to ask (BG, 76). ■ 22 μεταστήσας aor. act. part. μεθίστημι to remove, to depose. ἤγειρεν aor. ἐγείρω to raise up. (For the use of the prep. w. the acc. to replace the predicate after this verb, s. M, 71.) μαρτυρήσας aor. part. μαρτυρέω to bear witness, to testify. εὗρον aor., s.v.6. ποιήσει fut. ■ ἤγαγεν aor. ἄγω to lead. ■ 23/24 προκηρύξαντος aor. act. part. προκηρύσσω to proclaim beforehand, gen. abs. εἴσοδος entrance, coming. ■ ἐπλήρου 25 impf. πληρόω to fulfill, to complete. The impf. indicates that John had not finished his course at the time referred to (LC). ὑπονοέω to suppose, to suspect. The prep. compound conveys the idea of thoughts making their way up into the mind (MH, 327). ὑπόδημα sandal. λῦσαι aor. inf. λύω to loose.

■ ἐξαπεστάλη aor. pass. ἐξαποστέλλω to send out. ■ 26/27 κατοικοῦντες pres. part. κατοικέω to live, to dwell. ἀγνοήσαντες aor. part. ἀγνοέω to be ignorant, not to recognize. ἀναγινωσκομένας pres. pass. part. ἀναγινώσκω to read. κρίναντες aor. act. part. κρίνω to judge, to condemn. ἐπλήρωσαν aor. ■ αἰτία charge, followed by the gen. "the 28 reason for a capital punishment" (BAG). εὑρόντες aor. act. part. εὑρίσκω. ἀναιρεθῆναι aor. pass. inf. ἀναιρέω to put to death. ■ ἐτέλεσαν aor. τελέω to complete. γεγραμμένα perf. pass. 29 part. καθελόντες aor. part. καθαιρέω to take down. The technical term for removal after crucifixion (AS). ἔθηκαν aor. τίθημι to place. ■ ὤφθη aor. pass. ὁράω to see. πλείων comp. 31 πολύς. Used here w. no sense of comparison (LC). συναναβᾶσιν aor. act. part. dat. pl. συναναβαίνω to accompany, to go up w. someone. ■ γενόμενην aor. mid. part., s.v.5. 32 ■ ἐκπεπλήρωκεν perf. act. ἐκπληρόω to fulfill. The perf. em- 33 phasizes the completed action w. continuing results.

ἀναστήσας aor. act. part. ἀνίστημι to raise up. γέγραπται perf. pass. γεγέννηκα perf. act. γεννάω to beget. The day of the king's anointing was ideally the day in which he was born into
34 a new relation of sonship toward Jehovah (Bruce). ■ μέλλοντα pres. act. part. μέλλω to be about to. Used w. inf. to express the fut. (s. MKG, 307). εἴρηκεν perf. λέγω. ὅτι recitative, equivalent to quotation marks. δώσω fut. δίδωμι. ὅσιος pious, divine decrees in contrast to human statutes (BAG). The word is used to translate the Heb. *hesed* which means conduct in accordance w. the covenant and refers here to "the inviolable covenant w.
35 David" (Nelson Glueck, *Hesed in the Bible*, 78). ■ ἰδεῖν aor. inf. ὁράω. Jesus was raised from the dead so that He as the Son of
36 David can in the future rule over Israel. ■ ὑπηρετήσας aor. act. part. ὑπηρετέω to serve (s. TDNT). ἐκοιμήθη aor. pass. κοιμάω to fall asleep. προσετέθη aor. pass. προστίθημι to add. An expression arising from the practice of burying families
38 together (Alford). ■ ἔστω pres. imp. εἰμί. καταγγέλλεται pres. pass. καταγγέλλω to proclaim, to announce. ἠδυνήθητε aor. pass. δύναμαι. δικαιωθῆναι aor. pass. inf. δικαιόω to justify, to declare righteous. The law could never justify anyone from anything. Complete justification is afforded by Christ to
39 every believer (Bruce). ■ πιστεύων pres. act. part. δικαιοῦται
40 pres. pass. ■ μή "lest." (For this particle used to express neg. purpose, s. RG, 987f.) ἐπέλθῃ aor. subj. ἐπέρχομαι to come
41 upon. εἰρημένον perf. pass. part. λέγω. ■ ἴδετε aor. imp. ὁράω. καταφρονητής one who despises, despiser, one who "thinks down" on another. θαυμάσατε aor. imp. θαυμάζω to wonder, to be amazed. ἀφανίσθητε aor. pass. imp. ἀφανίζω to vanish away, pass. to be made to vanish, to destroy utterly so as to be invisible (LC). πιστεύσητε aor. subj. ἐκδιηγῆται pres. mid. subj. ἐκδιηγέομαι to declare, to relate in detail. The double prep. in compound indicates to declare right through to the end (MH, 311).

42   ■ ἐξιόντων pres. part. gen. pl. ἔξειμι to go out, gen. abs. παρεκάλουν impf. παρακαλέω to ask, to beseech, inceptive impf. "they began to beseech." μεταξύ between, commonly
43 used to mean "next" (Bruce). λαληθῆναι aor. pass. inf. ■ λυθείσης aor. pass. part. fem. gen. sing., gen. abs. ἠκολούθησαν aor. pass. ἀκολουθέω to follow. σεβομένων pres. mid. part. σέβομαι to be devout. προσήλυτος proselyte (s. TDNT; SB, II, 715ff.; BC, V, 74–96). ἐπείθον impf. πείθω to persuade, conative impf. "they were trying to persuade" (RWP), "urged" (Bruce).

44   ■ σχεδόν almost. συνήχθη aor. pass. συνάγω. ἀκοῦσαι

aor. act. inf. Infinitive of purpose. ■ ἐπλήσθησαν aor. pass. 45
πίμπλημι s.v.9. ἀντέλεγον impf. ἀντιλέγω to speak against,
to contradict. λαλουμένοις pres. pass. part. βλασφημοῦντες
pres. act. part. βλασφεμέω to blaspheme, to slander, to defame.
■ παρρησιασάμενοι aor. mid. part. παρρησιάζομαι to be 46
bold, suggests also abnormal eloquence and emotion (LC).
ἀναγκαῖος necessary. ἀπωθεῖσθε pres. mid. to push away
from one's self. ■ ἐντέταλται perf. mid. ἐντέλλομαι to com- 47
mand. τέθεικα perf. τίθημι. ■ ἀκούοντα pres. part. ἔχαιρον 48
impf. ἐδόζαζον impf. δυξάζω to glorlfy. ἐπίστευσαν aor.
τεταγμένοι perf. pass. part. τάσσω to appoint, perhaps here in
the sense "enrolled," "inscribed" (Bruce). ■ διεφέρετο impf. 49
pass. διαφέρω to carry through. ■ παρώτρυναν aor. 50
παροτρύνω to incite, to stir up. εὐσχήμων prominent, of high
standing, perhaps here "rich" (LC; s. also TDNT). ἐπήγειραν
aor. ἐπεγείρω to rouse up, to excite, to stir up. ἐξέβαλον aor.
ἐκβάλλω to cast out. ■ ἐκτιναξάμενοι aor. mid. part. 51
ἐκτινάσσομαι to shake off. κονιορτός dust. The shaking off
of dust might mean that the missionaries cleared themselves of
all further responsibilities (s. BC, V, 271ff.). ■ ἐπληροῦντο 52
impf. pass. πληρόω to fill.

Ch. 14

■ ἐγένετο aor. mid. γίνομαι. (For the construction of this 1
verb w. the inf., s. Luke 8:1.) κατὰ τὸ αὐτό "together" or
perhaps w. the meaning "in the same way" or "at one time" (s.
LC). εἰσελθεῖν aor. act. inf. εἰσέρχομαι to go in. λαλῆσαι
aor. inf. πιστεῦσαι aor. inf. The inf. is used here to express
actual result (s. RG, 1000). ■ ἀπειθήσαντες aor. part. ἀπειθέω 2
to disobey, used here as the opposite of believe. Unbelief and
disobedience are both involved in the rejection of the gospel
(Bruce). ἐπήγειραν aor. ἐπεγείρω to excite, to stir up.
ἐκάκωσαν aor. κακόω to make evil, to injure, to irritate (LC).
■ διέτριψαν aor. διατρίβω to stay, to remain. 3
παρρησιαζόμενοι pres. mid. part. παρρησιάζομαι to speak
freely, to be bold. ἐπί w. dat., upon the basis of, in reliance upon
(IBG, 50). μαρτυροῦντι pres. act. part. dat. sing. μαρτυρέω to
testify, to bear witness. διδόντι pres. part. The part. indicates
how witness was carried out (s. Haenchen). ■ ἐσχίσθη aor. 4
pass. σχίζω to split, to divide. ■ ὁρμή impulse, inclination, 5
attempt (s. TDNT). ὑβρίσαι aor. inf. ὑβρίζω to mistreat, to
treat shamefully. It expresses insulting and outrageous treatment
which is calculated publicly to insult and openly to humiliate the
person who suffers from it (MNTW, 83; s. also TDNT).

6 λιθοβολῆσαι aor. inf. λιθοβολέω to stone. ■ συνιδόντες aor.
part. συνοράω to see together, to become conscious of, to perceive, "to get wind of it" (Bruce). κατέφυγον aor. καταφεύγω
to flee, to take refuge. Used in the koine as a kind of technical
expression for suppliants "fleeing" or "resorting" to anyone for
7 help (MM). ■ εὐαγγελιζόμενοι pres. mid. part.
εὐαγγελίζομαι to proclaim good news. The part. used in periphrastic construction emphasizes the continual action.

8   ■ ἀδύνατος without strength, weak, impotent. (For the
medical use of this term, s. MLL, 46.) ἐκάθητο impf. κάθημαι
to sit, perhaps the customary use of the impf. "he used to sit"
(s. DM, 188). κοιλία womb. περιεπάτησεν aor. περιπατέω
9 to walk, to walk about. ■ ἤκουεν impf. ἀκούω. The impf. pictures the continual action of listening. λαλοῦντος pres. act. part.
gen. sing. ἀτενίσας aor. part. ἀτενίζω to gaze. σωθῆναι aor.
pass. inf. σῴζω to save, to rescue, to heal. The inf. combines
10 here both purpose and result (RWP). ■ ἀνάστηθι aor. pass.
imp. ἀνίστημι to stand up. ἥλατο aor. ἅλλομαι to leap, to
jump up. περιεπάτει impf. act. περιπατέω inceptive impf. "he
began to walk." Note the use of the previous aor. w. the impf.
11 here. ■ ἐποίησεν aor. ἐπῆραν aor. ἐπαίρω to lift up.
ὁμοιωθέντες aor. pass. part. ὁμοιόω to make like, to become
12 like. κατέβησαν aor. καταβαίνω to come down. ■ ἐκάλουν
impf. ἐπειδή since, because. ἡγούμενος pres. mid. part.
ἡγέομαι to lead. The part. is used as a noun "the leader of the
13 talk." ■ ὄντος part. εἰμί. ταῦρος bull, ox. στέμμα garland,
wreath, either made of flowers or wool used to adorn the victim
(BAG; Williams). πυλών gate. The great gateway which led into
the temple area (Rackham). ἐνέγκας aor. act. part. φέρω to
bring. ἤθελεν impf. θέλω, the desiderative impf. used in ex-
14 pressing a wish (IBG, 9). ■ ἀκούσαντες aor. part.
διαρρήξαντες aor. act. part. διαρρήγνυμι to rip in two.
ἐξεπήδησαν aor. ἐκπηδάω to leap out, to rush out. The prep.
compound retains its local force (s. Haenchen). κράζοντες pres.
15 part. κράζω to scream. ■ ὁμοιοπαθής w. the same nature. Used
of similar feelings, circumstances, and experiences (BAG).
μάταιος vain, empty. It emphasizes the aimlessness, the leading
to no object or end (Trench, Synonyms, 180f.; TDNT). ζῶντα
16 pres. act. part. ζάω to live. ■ παρῳχημέναις perf. mid. part.
παροίχομαι to go by. εἴασεν aor. ἐάω to permit, to allow.
17 ■ καίτοι "and yet." ἀμάρτυρος without a witness. (For the
prefix used to negate the meaning of the word, s. Moorhouse,
61ff.) ἀφῆκεν aor. ἀφίημι to leave. ἀγαθουργῶν pres. act.
part. ἀγαθουργέω to do good. The participles in this v. are

either causal (RWP) or explanatory (EGT). οὐρανόθεν from
heaven. (For the ending of the adv. w. the ablative quality of
indicating source, s. MH, 164.) ὑετός rain. ἐμπιπλῶν pres. act.
part. ἐμπίμπλημι to fill. εὐφροσύνη gladness, cheerfulness.
■ μόλις scarcely, barely, w. effort. κατέπαυσαν aor. 18
καταπαύω to restrain, to cause to cease. The prep. compound
is perfective. The articular inf. in the gen. case used w. a neg.
following this verb is a common Gr. idiom (RG, 1171). ■ 19
ἐπῆλθαν aor. ἐπέρχομαι to come upon, to come to.
πείσαντες aor. act. part. πείθω to persuade. λιθάσαντες aor.
act. part. λιθάζω to stone. ἔσυρον impf. σύρω to drag.
νομίζοντες pres. part. νομίζω to suppose. τεθνηκέναι perf.
act. inf. ἀποθνῃσκω to die, perf. to be dead. The perf. emphasizes the state or condition. ■ κυκλωσάντων aor. act. part. 20
κυκλόω to encircle, gen. abs. ἀναστάς aor. act. part.
ἀνίστημι. εἰσῆλθεν aor. εἰσέρχομαι. ἐπαύριον the following (day).

■ μαθητεύσαντες aor. act. part. μαθητεύω to make a 21
disciple (s. Matt. 28:19). ὑπέστρεψαν aor. ὑποστρέφω to return. ■ ἐπιστηρίζοντες pres. part. ἐπιστηρίζω to strengthen. 22
παρακαλοῦντες pres. part. παρακαλέω to exhort, to encourage. The word is used of exhorting troops who are about to go
into battle (MNTW, 134; TDNT). δεῖ it is necessary. Used w.
the acc. and the inf. ■ χειροτονήσαντες aor. act. part. 23
χειροτονέω to elect by show of hands, to appoint. Here the
selection was made by Paul and Barnabas (Haenchen). κατά.
The prep. is used here distributively, "from church to church."
προσευξάμενοι aor. mid. part. προσεύχομαι to pray.
νηστεία fasting. παρέθεντο aor. mid. παρατίθημι to place
before, mid. to deposit w. another, to commend a person to the
care of another (MM). πεπιστεύκεισαν plperf. ■ διελθόντες 24
aor. part. διέρχομαι to pass through. ■ λαλήσαντες aor. act. 25
part. ■ ἀπέπλευσαν aor. ἀποπλέω to sail, to sail from. 26
παραδεδομένοι perf. pass. part. παραδίδωμι to deliver over
to, to commit. The part. is used in a perf. pass. periphrastic
construction. ἐπλήρωσαν aor. πληρόω to fulfill, to complete.
■ παραγενόμενοι aor. mid. part. παραγίνομαι to arrive. 27
συναγαγόντες aor. act. part. συνάγω to gather together.
ἀνήγγελλον impf. ἀναγγέλλω to report, to carry back good
tidings (EGT). ἤνοιξεν aor. act. ἀνοίγω to open. ■ διέτριβον 28
impf. διατρίβω to stay, to remain.

Ch. 15

1 ■ κατελθόντες aor. act. part. κατέρχομαι to come down. ἐδίδασκον impf., inceptive impf. "They began to teach and kept it up" (RWP). περιτμηθῆτε aor. pass. subj. περιτέμνω to circumcise. ἔθος custom. σωθῆναι aor. pass. inf. σῴζω to rescue,

2 to save. ■ γενομένης aor. mid. part. γίνομαι, gen. abs. στάσις uprising, faction, discord. ζήτησις questioning, dispute, discussion. ἔταξαν aor. τάσσω to arrange. The subject of the verb implies that the brethren at Antioch appointed Paul and Bar-

3 nabas as their delegates (LC). ζήτημα question. ■ προπεμφθέντες aor. pass. part. προπέμπω to accompany, to help on one's journey w. food, money by arranging for companions means of travel, etc., to send on one's way (BAG). διήρχοντο impf. διέρχομαι to pass through. ἐκδιηγούμενοι pres. mid. part. ἐκδιηγέομαι to narrate, to tell in detail (s. Acts 13:41). ἐπιστροφή turning to, conversion. ἐποίουν impf. Used in the sense "to cause," "to bring about" w. the dat. of advantage

4 (BAG). ■ παραγενόμενοι aor. mid. part. παραγίνομαι to arrive. παρεδέχθησαν aor. pass. παραδέχομαι to receive, to welcome. ἀνήγγειλαν aor. ἀναγγέλλω to report. ἐποίησεν

5 aor. ■ ἐξανέστησαν aor. ἐξανίστημι to arise. The prep. compound is perfective (s. MH, 308f.). αἵρεσις group, party. It does not refer to a heresy or sect (LC). πεπιστευκότες perf. act. part. δεῖ "it is necessary." αὐτούς "they" acc. used w. inf. It refers to Gentile believers or perhaps those like Titus in particular among Paul's companions who were not circumcised (Williams). παραγγέλλειν pres. act. inf. to command, to charge. Used esp. of the transmitted orders of a military commander (AS).

6 ■ συνήχθησαν aor. pass. συνάγω to gather together, to

7 assemble. ἰδεῖν aor. inf. ὁράω. ■ ἀναστάς aor. act. part. ἀνίστημι to arise. ἐπίστασθε pres. mid. ἐπίσταμαι to understand, to be acquainted w. ἐξελέξατο aor. mid. ἐκλέγω to select, to make a choice. ἀκοῦσαι aor. inf. used either to define

8 the choice or to express result. πιστεῦσαι aor. inf. ■ καρδιογνώστης one who knows the heart (s. Acts 1:24). ἐμαρτύρησεν aor. μαρτυρέω to bear witness. Used in the sense of confirmation or approval (s. TDNT). δούς aor. act. part. δίδωμι. The part. expresses how the approval was expressed (s.

9 Haenchen). ■ διέκρινεν impf. διακρίνω to make a difference, distinction. μεταξύ between. καθαρίσας aor. act. part. καθαρίζω to cleanse. The part. is either causal or explanatory.

10 ■ ἐπιθεῖναι aor. act. inf. ἐπιτίθημι to place upon, an epexegetic inf. explaining wherein their tempting God lay (Bruce). ζυγός yoke. Used in Jewish writers in the sense of "obligation," but

here the figure suggests a burden rather than a religious duty
(LC). ἰσχύσαμεν aor. ἰσχύω to be able. βαστάσαι aor. inf.
βαστάζω to carry, to bear. ■ σωθῆναι aor. pass. inf.   11
■ ἐσίγησεν aor. σιγάω to be quiet, ingressive aor. "to   12
become silent." ἤκουον impf. ἐξηγουμένων pres. mid. part.
ἐξηγέομαι to explain, to go through or lead out a narrative of
events (RWP). ἐποίησεν aor. ■ σιγῆσαι aor. inf. ἀπεκρίθη   13
aor. pass. ἀποκρίνομαι to answer. ἀκούσατε aor. imp. ■   14
ἐξηγήσατο aor. mid. ἐπεσκέψατο aor. mid. ἐπισκέπτομαι to
look upon, to visit, to make provision for. Here it means that
God made provision for the call of the Gentiles (LC). λαβεῖν
aor. inf. λαμβάνω. ■ γέγραπται perf. pass. ■ ἀναστρέψω fut. 15/16
ἀναστρέφω to turn again. ἀνοικοδομήσω fut. ἀνοικοδομέω
to build again. πεπτωκυῖαν perf. act. part. fem. πίπτω to fall.
κατεστραμμένα perf. pass. part. καταστρέφω to turn down,
to ruin. The perf. part. emphasizes the condition "the ruined
portions of it" (RWP). ἀνορθώσω fut. ἀνορθόω to erect again,
to rebuild, to restore. ■ ὅπως that, in order that. Used w. the 17
subj. to express purpose (s. MT, 105). ἐκζητήσωσιν aor. subj.
ἐκζητέω to seek out. κατάλοιπος rest, remaining.
ἐπικέκληται perf. pass. to call upon. ἐπ᾽ αὐτούς. The use of a
pron. repeating the relat. is due to Semitic influence (s. BD, 65;
W.F. Bakker, Pronomen Abundens and Pronomen Coniunctum,
33–42; for the use of the OT quote in DSS, s. CD 7:15). ■   18
γνωστός known. ■ κρίνω to judge, to decree. It is the definite 19
sentence of a judge, and implies that he is acting by an authority
which is personal (s. LC). παρενοχλεῖν pres. inf. to trouble, to
annoy. The pres. tense indicates "stop annoying" (LC).
ἐπιστρέφουσιν pres. act. part. ἐπιστρέφω to turn to. The
pres. part. is an acknowledgment of a work actually in progress
(EGT). ■ ἐπιστεῖλαι aor. act. inf. ἐπιστέλλω to send, to send 20
to, to instruct. In the papyri the general use is in connection w.
sending a letter or other written communications, but used in
official documents it had the meaning "instruct," "enjoin"
(MM). ἀλίσγημα pollution, contamination. It implies ritual
rather than moral pollution (LC). πορνεία illicit sexual relation.
Perhaps used here to refer to the breaking of the Jewish marriage
law prohibiting those of close kin to marry (Bruce; TDNT; SB,
II, 729f.). πνικτός strangled, choked to death. Used of animals
killed without having the blood drained from them (BAG; SB,
II, 730f.). ■ κηρύσσοντας pres. part. ἀναγινωσκόμενος pres. 21
pass. part. ἀναγινώσκω to read.
■ ἔδοξε aor. δοκεῖ "it seems good." It is the technical term 22
in Gr. of all periods for "voting" or "passing" a measure in the

299

assembly (LC). ἐκλεξαμένους aor. mid. part. πέμψαι aor. act.
inf. πέμπω to send. καλούμενον pres. pass. part. ἡγουμένους
23 pres. mid. part. ἡγέομαι to lead. Here "leaders." ■ γράψαντες
24 aor. act. part. nom. abs. (s. RG, 459). ■ ἐπειδή since, seeing that.
ἠκούσαμεν aor. ἀκούω. ἐτάραξαν aor. ταράσσω to disturb,
to throw into confusion (Haenchen). ἀνασκευάζοντες pres.
part. ἀνασκευάζω to destroy, to pervert. It means reversing
what has been done, tearing down what has been built, or cancelling what has been agreed upon (LC). Also, a military metaphor, of plundering a town (Bruce). διεστειλάμεθα aor. mid.
27 διαστέλλομαι to order, to give strict commands. ■
ἀπαγγέλλοντας pres. part. ἀπαγγέλλω to report. The part.
28 may be used to express purpose (LC). ■ πλέων comp. πολύς.
ἐπιτίθεσθαι pres. mid. inf. ἐπάναγκες adv. by compulsion,
29 necessarily, here "the necessary things" (BAG). ■ εἰδωλόθυτον
that which is offered to an idol. διατηροῦντες pres. part.
διατηρέω to keep carefully. πράξετε fut. πράσσω. ἔρρωσθε
perf. pass. imp. ῥώννυμι to make strong, to be made strong, to
keep well, farewell, common at the close of letters (RWP).
30 ■ ἀπολυθέντες aor. pass. part. ἀπολύω to release, to dismiss. κατῆλθον aor. κατέρχομαι to go down. συναγαγόντες
aor. part. συνάγω. ἐπέδωκαν aor. ἐπιδίδωμι to give over, to
deliver. In later Gr. a technical term for sending in a report or
31 handing over a letter (Bruce). ■ ἀναγνόντες aor. act. part.
ἀναγινώσκω to read. ἐχάρησαν aor. pass. χαίρω to rejoice,
32 ingressive aor. "they burst into exultant joy" (RWP). ■ ὄντες
pres. part. εἰμί. παρεκάλεσαν aor. παρακαλέω to exhort, to
encourage, to comfort (MNTW, 134). ἐπεστήριξαν aor.
33 ἐπιστηρίζω to strengthen. ■ ποιήσαντες aor. act. part.
35 ἀποστείλαντας aor. act. part. ἀποστέλλω. ■ διέτριβον impf.
διατρίβω to remain. διδάσκοντες pres. act. part.
εὐαγγελιζόμενοι pres. mid. part. εὐαγγελίζομαι to proclaim
the good news, to evangelize.
36 ■ ἐπιστρέψαντες aor. act. part. ἐπιστρέφω s.v.19.
ἐπισκεψώμεθα aor. mid. subj., s.v.14, hortatory subj. "let us
visit." κατηγγείλαμεν aor. καταγγέλλω to proclaim. This
verb w. compound prep. often emphasizes the solemn style of
the proclamation (CBB). ἔχουσιν "how they have it," "how
their state is," their internal and external Christian condition
37 (Meyer). ■ ἐβούλετο impf. mid. βούλομαι to will, to want, to
wish. The impf. indicates Barnabas stuck to his decision (RWP).
συμπαραλαβεῖν aor. act. inf. συμπαραλαμβάνω to take
along together w., to take someone along as a helper (MM). The
pres. inf. in v.38 compared to the aor. inf. here indicates to have

someone w. them day by day (s. M, 130). ■ ἠξίου impf. act. 38
ἀξιόω to consider worthy, to consider suitable. He did not think
Mark fit or worthy to be taken w. them (Alex.). (For a milder
view of the situation w. the idea that the impf. shows that Paul
merely "requested," and not even pressingly, s. GI, 95.)
ἀποστάντα aor. act. part. ἀφίστημι to depart, to desert, to
give up. συνελθόντα aor. act. part. συνέρχομαι to accompany.
■ ἐγένετο aor. mid. γίνομαι. παροξυσμός irritation, provoca- 39
tion, quarrel (s. TDNT). ἀποχωρισθῆναι aor. pass. inf.
ἀποχωρίζω to separate, to depart. Infinitive used to express
result. (For the construction, s. RG, 999f.) παραλαβόντα aor.
act. part. παραλαμβάνω to take w. ἐκπλεῦσαι aor. act. inf.
ἐκπλέω to sail away. Infinitive used to express result. The quarrel had at least one good result, that two missionary expeditions
set out instead of one (Bruce). ■ ἐπιλεξάμενος aor. mid. part. 40
ἐπιλέγω to choose, to select. ἐξῆλθεν aor. ἐξέρχομαι to go
out. παραδοθείς aor. pass. part. παραδίδωμι to deliver over,
to commend. ■ διήρχετο impf. mid., s.v.3. ἐπιστηρίζων pres. 41
act. part., s.v.32.

■ κατήντησεν aor. καταντάω to come down to, to arrive 1
at. ■ ἐμαρτυρεῖτο impf. pass. μαρτυρέω pass. to be well spoken 2
of, to be approved. ■ ἠθέλησεν aor. θέλω. ἐξελθεῖν aor. inf. 3
ἐξέρχομαι to go out. λαβών aor. act. part. λαμβάνω.
περιέτεμεν aor. act. περιτέμνω to circumcise. ὄντας pres.
part. εἰμί. ᾔδεισαν plperf. οἶδα w. defective perf. the plperf. is
equivalent to the impf. (s. MH, 221). ὑπῆρχεν impf. ὑπάρχω
to be, to exist. The impf. probably indicates that his father was
dead (Bruce). ■ διεπορεύοντο impf. mid. διαπορεύομαι to 4
travel through. παρεδίδοσαν impf. παραδίδωμι to deliver.
The impf. indicates they kept on delivering them in city after city
(RWP). φυλάσσειν pres. inf. to observe. Infinitive used to express purpose (s. IBG, 139). δόγμα decree, decision. The noun
is derived from the verb which is used in Acts 15:22, 28.
κεκριμένα perf. pass. part. κρίνω to decide. The perf. emphasizes the permanence of the conclusion (RWP). ■ ἐστερεοῦντο 5
impf. pass. στερεόω to make firm, to strengthen (s. Acts 3:7).
ἐπερίσσευον impf. περισσεύω to increase. The impf. indicates the continual increase.

■ διῆλθον aor. διέρχομαι to go through. κωλυθέντες aor. 6
pass. part. κωλύω to hinder. The part. could be causal and the
action is simultaneous or antecedent w. the main verb that is not
subsequent (RWP). (For a discussion of the aor. part. possibly

expressing subsequent action, s. BG, 87f.; G.M. Lee, "The Past
Participle of Subsequent Action," Nov T, 17 [July, 1975], 199.)
7 λαλῆσαι aor. inf. ■ ἐπείραζον impf. πειράζω to try, to attempt. πορευθῆναι aor. pass. inf. πορεύομαι to travel, to go.
8 εἴασεν aor. ἐάω to allow. ■ παρελθόντες aor. act. part.
παρέρχομαι to pass by. κατέβησαν aor. καταβαίνω to go
9 down. ■ ὅραμα vision. ὤφθη aor. pass. ὁράω pass. to appear.
ἑστώς perf. act. part. ἵστημι perf. to stand. παρακαλῶν pres.
act. part. παρακαλέω to encourage, to beseech, to entreat (s.
Acts 15:32). διαβάς aor. part. διαβαίνω to pass through, to
come over. (For the circumstantial part. expressing a command,
s. Matt. 28:19; BG, 129f.) βοήθησον aor. imp. βοηθέω to help.
(For the view that the man of Macedonia was Luke, s. PTR,
10 202f.) ■ ἐζητήσαμεν aor. ζητέω to seek. The 1st per. pl. subject
is the beginning of the first long "we passage," continuing to the
arrest of Paul and Silas in Philippi (LC). συμβιβάζοντες pres.
part. συμβιβάζω to put together, to conclude, to infer.
προσκέκληται perf. mid. προσκαλέω to call.
εὐαγγελίσασθαι aor. mid. inf. εὐαγγελίζομαι to proclaim the
good news. Infinitive of purpose.
11 ■ ἀναχθέντες aor. pass. part. ἀνάγω to lead up, pass. to
set sail. εὐθυδρομήσαμεν aor. εὐθυδρομέω to run a straight
course; that is, they found a favorable wind, probably from the
northeast, enabling them to make Samothrace (LC). τῇ
ἐπιούσῃ "on the following (day)," dat. of time w. the word
12 "day" to be supplied. ■ κολωνία colony. A Roman colony was
like a piece of Rome or Italy transplanted abroad (Bruce; for
information regarding Roman colonies, s. LC; IDB, I, 657; CC,
175f.). διατρίβοντες pres. part. διατρίβω to remain. Participle
13 used in a periphrastic construction. ■ ἐξήλθομεν aor.
ἐξέρχομαι s.v.3. ποταμός river. The river would be the Gan-
gites (Angites) which flows into the Strymon (Williams). The
omission of the article is one of the touches of familiarity which
show the hand of one who knew Philippi well (PTR, 213; s. RG,
792). ἐνομίζομεν impf. νομίζω to suppose, to be the custom.
(For the textual problem here, s. Bruce M. Metzger, *A Textual
Commentary on the Greek New Testament*, 447.) προσευχή
prayer, a place of prayer (s. Deissmann, BS, 222). καθίσαντες
aor. part. καθίζω to take one's seat, to sit down. ἐλαλοῦμεν
impf., inceptive impf. "we began to speak." συνελθούσαις aor.
14 part. συνέρχομαι to come together, to gather. ■
πορφυρόπωλις one who sells purple. Thyatira was famous for
its dyeing (PTR, 214). There was a great demand for this fabric
as it was used for the official toga at Rome and in Roman colo-

nies (RWP). (For the cloth industry under the Roman Empire, s.A.H.M. Jones, *The Roman Economy*, 350–364.) σεβομένη pres. mid. part. σέβομαι to worship, to fear (s. TDNT). ἤκουεν impf. ἀκούω. The impf. pictures the attentive listening. διήνοιξεν aor. διανοίγω to open. προσέχειν pres. inf. to hold to, to give attention to, to give heed to. λαλουμένοις perf. pass. part. ■ ἐβαπτίσθη aor. pass. βαπτίζω to baptize. ὁ οἶκος 15 αὐτῆς "her house." Her household probably included servants and other dependents, perhaps some of the women of v.13 (Bruce). κεκρίκατε perf. κρίνω to judge, to decide. εἰσελθόντες aor. part. εἰσέρχομαι to go in. μένετε pres. imp. μένω to remain. παρεβιάσατο aor. mid. παραβιάζομαι to urge strongly, to insist.

■ ἐγένετο aor. mid. γίνομαι. πορευομένων pres. mid. 16 part., s.v.7, gen. abs. παιδίσκη slave girl. ἔχουσαν pres. part. πύθων python, divination, prophecy. The word was used for the serpent that guarded the Delphic oracle and later was slain by Apollo. The word came to designate spirit of divination, then also a ventriloquist, who was believed to have such a spirit dwelling in his belly (BAG; LC). The word is in opposition to "spirit." ὑπαντῆσαι aor. inf. ὑπαντάω to meet. παρεῖχεν impf. παρέχω to bring in, to provide, to supply. The impf. pictures a steady source of income (RWP). μαντευομένη pres. mid. part. μαντεύομαι to soothsay, to give an oracle. It refers to the tumult of the mind, the fury, the temporary madness, under which those were, who were supposed to be possessed by the god during the time they delivered their oracles (Trench, *Synonyms*, 22). In the LXX it always is employed of lying prophets (EGT). This is the instrumental use of the part. ■ κατακολουθοῦσα 17 pres. part. κατακολουθέω to follow. The prep. compound indicates the following after someone over an intervening space (s. MH, 316). ἔκραζεν impf. κράζω to scream. Imperfect, because she did it many days (Bruce). ■ ἐποίει impf. "she kept on doing 18 it." διαπονηθείς aor. pass. part. διαπονέω to be worked up, to be indignant (s. Acts 4:2). ἐπιστρέψας aor. part. ἐπιστρέφω to turn to. παραγγέλλω to command. The word is esp. used of the transmitted orders of a military commander (AS). ■ 19 ἐπιλαβόμενοι aor. mid. part. ἐπιλαμβάνω to seize. εἵλκυσαν aor. ἑλκύω to drag. ἀγορά marketplace. Here it indicates "the courthouse" (LC). ἄρχοντας acc. pl. rulers, magistrates. A general Gr. name for the magistrates of a city. (For their function in a Roman colony, s. LC; Sherwin-White, 74f.) ■ 20 προσαγαγόντες aor. part. προσάγω to lead to. στρατηγοί leader of an army, general, city official. The author uses the most common Hellenistic title to render the untranslatable term *duoviri* (Sherwin-White, 93). After the pattern of the consuls at Rome, the chief magistrates of a Roman colony were two in number and their official title was *duoviri*, that is, "the two men" (Rackham). ἐκταράσσουσιν pres. to trouble, to agitate, to throw into confusion. The prep. compound is perfective (s. MH,

21 309). ὑπάρχοντες pres. part., s.v.3. ■ ἔθος custom. ἔξεστιν lawful, it is allowed. παραδέχεσθαι pres. mid. inf. to receive, to adopt. The two charges were the causing of riots and the introduction of an alien religion. (For a discussion of these

22 charges, s. Sherwin-White, 79ff.) ■ συνεπέστη aor. συνεφίστημι to rise up together, to join in an attack (BAG). περιρήξαντες aor. part. περιρήγνυμι to strip off all around. The magistrates had the clothes of the apostles torn off (Bruce). ἐκέλευον impf. κελεύω to command. The official order generally given was "go, lictors; strip off their garments; let them be scourged" (CH, 234). ῥαβδίζειν pres. inf. to beat w. rods. The beating w. rods was done by the lictors (s.v.35) as a means of police coercion (TDNT). The Lex Porciae de Tergo Civium prohibited the scourging of Roman citizens without appeal

23 (OCD, 604). ■ ἐπιθέντες aor. part. ἐπιτίθημι to lay on. ἔβαλον aor. βάλλω to throw. παραγγείλαντες aor. part.

24 δεσμοφύλαξ jailer. ἀσφαλῶς safely. ■ λαβών aor. part. λαμβάνω. ἐσώτερος inner. The comp. has perhaps superl. force "inmost" (Bruce). ἠσφαλίσατο aor. mid. ἀσφαλίζω to make safe, to secure. ξύλον wood, stock. A Roman instrument of torture w. more than two holes for the legs so that they could be forced widely apart unto a position which soon became intolerably painful (LC).

25 ■ μεσονύκτιον midnight. προσευχόμενοι pres. mid. part. προσεύχομαι to pray. ὕμνουν impf. ὑμνέω to sing a hymn of praise addressed directly to God (Trench, *Synonyms*, 297f.; TDNT). The impf. pictures continual singing. ἐπηκροῶντο impf. ἐπακροάομαι to listen to. Employed in medical language for the placing of the ear to the human body, in order to detect the nature of internal disease by the sound (MLL, 234). The

26 prep. compound is directive. ■ ἄφνω suddenly. σαλευθῆναι aor. pass. inf. σαλεύω to shake. Infinitive used w. ὥστε to express result. δεσμωτήριον prison. ἠνεῴχθησαν aor. pass. ἀνοίγω to open. παραχρῆμα immediately. ἀνέθη aor. pass.

27 ἀνίημι to loosen, to release. ■ ἔξυπνος out of sleep, awake, aroused. γενόμενος aor. mid. part. γίνομαι. ἀνεῳγμένας perf. pass. part. ἀνοίγω. σπασάμενος aor. mid. part. σπάω to draw. μάχαιρα sword. ἤμελλεν impf. μέλλω to be about to.

(For the construction w. the inf. expressing futurity or intention
reckoned from a moment in the past, s. MKG, 307.) ἀναιρεῖν
pres. inf. to kill. νομίζων pres. part. ἐκπεφευγέναι perf. inf.
ἐκφεύγω to flee, to escape. The prep. is perfective (s. MH, 310).
■ ἐφώνησεν aor. φωνέω to call. πράξῃς aor. subj. πράσσω to 28
do. The aor. subj. w. the neg. is used to prohibit the beginning
of an action (s. MKG, 273). ■ αἰτήσας aor. part. αἰτέω to ask. 29
εἰσεπήδησεν aor. εἰσπηδάω to leap in, to rush in, to burst in
(s. MM). προσέπεσεν aor. προσπίπτω to fall down before
someone. ■ προαγαγών aor. part. προάγω to lead forth, to 30
bring out. δεῖ it is necessary. σωθῶ aor. pass. subj. σῴζω to
rescue, to save. ■ πίστευσον aor. imp. σωθήσῃ fut. pass. (For 31
the use of the imp. followed by the fut. to form a type of Hebraic
conditional sentence, s. John 1:38.) ■ ἐλάλησαν aor. ■ 32/33
παραλαβών aor. part. παραλαμβάνω to take w. ἔλουσεν aor.
λούω to wash. (For the use of this word w. the prep., s. Deissmann; BS, 227.) ■ ἀναγαγών aor. part. ἀνάγω. παρέθηκεν 34
aor. παρατίθημι to set before. An individual table was placed
beside each guest (Bruce). ἠγαλλιάσατο aor. mid.
ἀγαλλίαομαι to rejoice, to be full of joy. πανοικεῖ w. one's
whole household. An expression common in the closing greetings of private letters (MM). πεπιστευκώς perf. act. part.

■ ἀπέστειλαν aor. ἀποστέλλω to send. ῥαβδοῦχος lic- 35
tor, rod-bearers. They were attendants serving the magistrate
who prepared the way for the magistrate, carried out punish-
ments and summons (s. OCD, 609). ἀπόλυσον aor. imp.
ἀπολύω to release. ■ ἀπήγγειλεν aor. ἀπαγγέλλω to report. 36
ἀπέσταλκαν perf. ἀποστέλλω. ἀπολυθῆτε aor. pass. subj.
ἐξελθόντες aor. act. part. ἐξέρχομαι. πορεύεσθε pres. mid.
imp. ■ δείραντες aor. act. part. δέρω to flay, to skin, to strike. 37
δημοσίᾳ publicly. ἀκατάκριτος uncondemned, or possibly
"untried," "without a trial" (LC). λάθρα secretly. ἐλθόντες
aor. part., s.v.7. ἐξαγαγέτωσαν aor. imp. ἐξάγω to lead out, to
conduct. ■ ἠρώτων impf. ἐρωτάω to ask. ἀπελθεῖν aor. inf. 39
ἀπέρχομαι to go forth, to go out. ■ παρεκάλεσαν aor. act. 40
παρακαλέω to encourage, to comfort.

Ch. 17

■ διοδεύσαντες aor. part. διοδεύω to take the road 1
through. The road was the Via Egnatia. This verb probably was
chosen to emphasize the way (Bruce). ■ εἰωθός custom, habit. 2
εἰσῆλθεν aor. εἰσέρχομαι to go into. διελέξατο aor. mid.
διαλέγομαι to reason, to revolve in the mind, to teach w. the
method of question and answer, to give a discourse, but always

3 w. the idea of intellectual stimulus (RWP). ■ διανοίγων pres. part. διανοίγω to open. παρατιθέμενος pres. mid. part. παρατίθημι to place alongside, to allege, to present evidence. Here it is the bringing forward in proof passages of Scripture (EGT). The pres. part. emphasizes the continuing action and describes the means or methods of Paul's reasoning and argumentation. ἔδει impf. δεῖ it is necessary. παθεῖν aor. act. inf. πάσχω to suffer. ἀναστῆναι aor. act. inf. ἀνίστημι to rise. καταγγέλλω proclaim. The word often emphasizes the elevat-

4 ed and solemn style of the proclamation (CBB). ■ ἐπείσθησαν aor. pass. πείθω to persuade, pass. "were persuaded." προσεκληρώθησαν aor. pass. προσκληρόω to join w. σεβομένων pres. mid. part. σέβομαι to be devout, pious, to be

5 God-fearing (s. Acts 10:2). ■ ζηλώσαντες aor. part. ζηλόω to be jealous. προσλαβόμενοι aor. mid. part. προσλαμβάνω to take to one's self, to accept in the circle of acquaintances, to take along w. one's self as companion or helper (BAG). ἀγοραῖος one who hangs out at the marketplace, loafer, gangster (Bruce). ὀχλοποιήσαντες aor. act. part. ὀχλοποιέω to gather a crowd, to collect a mob. ἐθορύβουν impf. θορυβέω to cause an uproar, to trouble, to throw into confusion. ἐπιστάντες aor. act. part. ἐφίστημι to stand before, to approach, to appear. ἐζήτουν impf. ζητέω to seek, to try. προαγαγεῖν aor. act. inf. προάγω

6 to lead before, to bring out before. ■ εὑρόντες aor. part. εὑρίσκω. ἔσυρον impf. σύρω to drag. πολιτάρχης ruler of the city. Used mainly of the Macedonian title for the non-Roman magistrates of a city (LC). The title is found in some nineteen inscriptions. The majority of these is used for magistrates in Macedonian cities (Bruce). βοῶντες pres. part. βοάω to shout. ἀναστατώσαντες aor. part. ἀναστατόω to stir up sedition, to upset. Used of a letter of a bad little boy whose mother said, "he

7 drives me mad" (s. LAE, 202). ■ ὑποδέδεκται perf. mid.

8 ὑποδέχομαι to receive, to entertain. ἀπέναντι against. ■ ἐτάραξαν aor. ταράσσω to stir up, to confuse, to trouble.

9 ἀκούοντας pres. part. ■ λαβόντες aor. part. λαμβάνω. ἱκανόν security. It is the equivalent of the Latin satis accipere which is used in connection w. the offering and giving of security in civil and criminal procedures (Sherwin-White, 95). ἀπέλυσαν aor. ἀπολύω to release. (For the relation of these events to things mentioned in 1 and 2 Thess., s. Bruce.)

10 ■ διὰ νυκτός "in the night"; "during" or "in the course of the night" (s. IBG). ἐξέπεμψαν aor. ἐκπέμπω to send out, to send away. παραγενόμενοι aor. mid. part. παραγίνομαι to arrive. ἀπῄεσαν impf. ἄπειμι to go away, "they went their

way" (LC). ■ εὐγενέστερος comp. εὐγενής of noble birth, 11
well-born, noble-minded (BAG). ἐδέξαντο aor. mid. δέχομαι
to receive. προθυμία willingness, eagerness. καθ' ἡμέραν
daily. ἀνακρίνοντες pres. part. ἀνακρίνω to examine, to sift up
and down, to make careful and exact research as in legal processes (RWP). ἔχοι pres. opt., "if these things have it so." (For
the opt. in indirect questions, s. MT, 130f.; RG, 1043f.) ■ 12
ἐπίστευσαν aor. εὐσχήμων of rank, of position, perhaps
"rich" or refers to character rather than position (LC). ■ 13
ἔγνωσαν aor. γινώσκω. κατηγγέλη aor. pass. καταγγέλλω
s.v.3. σαλεύοντες pres. act. part. σαλεύω to shake, to cause to
waiver, to agitate. ταράσσοντες pres. act. part. ■ 14
ἐξαπέστειλαν aor. ἀποστέλλω to send out. ὑπέμειναν aor.
ὑπομένω to remain, to remain behind. (For the prep. compound, s. MH, 327.) ■ καθιστάνοντες pres. act. part. 15
καθίστημι to bring down to a place. ἤγαγον aor. ἄγω. ἐντολή
instruction. ὡς τάχιστα as quickly as possible. ἔλθωσιν aor.
subj. ἔρχομαι, subj. used in an indirect command (s. RG, 1046).
ἐξῄεσαν impf. ἔξειμι to go out.

■ ἐκδεχομένου pres. mid. part. ἐκδέχομαι to expect, gen. 16
abs. παρωξύνετο impf. pass. παροξύνω pass. to be angry (s.
Acts 15:39). θεωροῦντος pres. act. part. θεωρέω to see, to
observe. Paul probably could distinguish the statues of the gods
from those of ordinary men, because the former had no inscriptions (DCNT, 125). κατείδωλος full of images. (For the prep.
compound and the coining of this word, s. MH, 317.) The prep.
may mean "thick with," "luxuriant with" as used of vegetation
(R.E. Wycherly, "St. Paul at Athens," JTS, NTS, 19 [1968],
619,620). οὖσαν pres. part. εἰμί. ■ διελέγετο impf. mid. 17
διαλέγομαι s.v.2. παρατυγχάνοντας pres. act. part.
παρατυγχάνω to happen to be near or present. The idea of
"chance" is not necessarily implied (MM). ■ συνέβαλλον impf. 18
συμβάλλω to throw together, to discuss, to meet w., to quarrel.
θέλοι pres. opt., potential opt. used in an incomplete conditional
clause w. the protasis implied, "What would he wish to say, if
he could say anything?" "What might he be trying to say?" (s.
DM, 174; IBG, 151). σπερμολόγος seed picker. First used of
birds that pick up grain, then of men who pick up odds and ends
in the market, and then transferred to men who were zealous
seekers of the second rate at second hand, and finally to generally worthless persons (LC). καταγγελεύς announcer.
εὐηγγελίζετο impf. mid. εὐαγγελίζομαι to proclaim good
news. ■ ἐπιλαβόμενοι aor. mid. part. ἐπιλαμβάνω to take 19
hold of. ἄρειος πάγος the Areopagus or Hill of Ares (Mars'

307

Hill). The word is to be understood either as the geographical place or it refers to a governmental council in the city of Athens. Among the many functions of this council was that of supervising education, particularly of controlling the many visiting lecturers (BAG; PTR, 245f.; LC). (For the suggestion that the whole incident took place near the northwest angle of the Agora in or near the Stoa Basileios, see C.J. Hemer, "Paul at Athens: A Topographical Note," NTS, 20 [April, 1974], 341-350.) ἤγαγον aor., s.v.15. γνῶναι aor. act. inf. γινώσκω.

20 λαλουμένη pres. pass. part. ■ ξενίζοντα pres. act. part. ξενίζω
21 to surprise or astonish w. something new or strange. ■ ἐπιδημοῦντες pres. act. part. ἐπιδημέω to reside as a foreigner. ηὐκαίρουν impf. εὐκαιρέω to have time, to have leisure or opportunity. Followed by the prep. it means "to devote one's leisure to" (AS). καινότερος comp. καινός new. The comparison can often have the force of a superl. (s. BD, 127). The true comparison would mean "something newer than what they had heard" (RG, 665).

22   ■ σταθείς aor. pass. part. ἵστημι to stand. δεισιδαιμονέστερος comp. δεισιδαίμων God-fearing, religious, religiosity. It expresses respect for or fear of the supernatural (Williams; s. also LC). The comp. here means "more
23 religious than usual" (RWP). ■ διερχόμενος pres. mid. part. διέρχομαι to pass through. ἀναθεωρῶν pres. part. ἀναθεωρέω to look at, to observe. The prep. compound is perfective (MH, 296). σέβασμα object of worship. εὗρον aor. εὑρίσκω. βωμός altar. ἐπεγέγραπτο plperf. pass. ἐπιγράφω to inscribe. ἄγνωστος unknown. (For examples and evidences of altars to unknown gods in and around Athens, s. BC, V, 240-246; Haen-
24 chen.) ■ ποιήσας aor. act. part. χειροποίητος made w. human
25 hands. ■ ἀνθρώπινος human. (For the formation of adj. w. this ending signifying material, origin, or kind, s. MH, 359.) θεραπεύεται pres. pass. θεραπεύω to care for, to attend, to serve. προσδεόμενος pres. mid. part. προσδέομαι to want, to
26 need in addition. διδούς pres. part. ■ ἐποίησεν aor. ὁρίσας aor. act. part. ὁρίζω to mark out boundaries, to determine.The aor. part. is not "later" in time than the main verb. The determination of man's home preceded his creation in the divine plan (M, 133). προστεταγμένους perf. pass. part. προστάσσω to
27 appoint, to assign, to prescribe, to fix. ὁροθεσία boundary. ■ ψηλαφήσειαν aor. opt. ψηλαφάω to touch, to feel. The opt. is used here in a type of incomplete conditional sentence expressing aim or purpose (s. MT, 127; RG, 1021). The verb gives the idea of groping after God in the darkness, when the light of His

full revelation is not available (Bruce). εὕροιεν aor. opt.
εὑρίσκω. καί γε "and yet," "although," a concessive expression (Bruce; s. also Thrall, 37f.). ■ κινέομαι to move. The 28
verb might mean simultaneously: "we are moved by Him" and
"we move in Him" (DCNT, 127). ποιητής poet. εἰρήκασιν
perf. λέγω. (For the quotations from the Gr. poet Aratus and
also possibly from Epimenides, s. BC, V, 246–251.) ■ ἄργυρος 29
silver. χάραγμα an engraved work, an inscription engraved.
τέχνη art. ἐνθύμησις design. θεῖος divine. Dio Chrysostom
considered sculpture to be one source of man's conception of the
divine (DCNT, 128; DC XII, 44, 80). ■ ἀγνοία ignorance. 30
ὑπεριδών aor. act. part. ὑπεροράω to overlook. A verb frequent in the LXX and is applied to a thing which is not attended
to, and is left without favorable help or without severe punishment (Bengel). πανταχοῦ everywhere. ■ ἔστησεν aor. ἵστημι 31
to set, to appoint. μέλλει pres. to be about to. Used w. the inf.
to express the fut. ἐν ἀνδρί "by a man." (For the use of the prep.
expressing agency, s. the examples quoted by Haenchen.)
ὥρισεν aor. ὁρίζω. παρασχών aor. part. παρέχω to furnish,
to bring forward evidence (RWP). ἀναστήσας aor. act. part.
ἀνίστημι to raise.

■ ἀκούσαντες aor. act. part. ἐχλεύαζον impf. χλευάζω to 32
mock, to sneer, to scoff, inceptive impf. "they began to scoff."
ἀκουσόμεθα fut. mid. ■ ἐξῆλθεν aor. ἐξέρχομαι to go out. 33
■ κολληθέντες aor. pass. part. κολλάομαι to join. 34
ἐπίστευσαν aor.

Ch. 18

■ χωρισθείς aor. pass. part. χωρίζομαι to depart. ■ εὑρών 1/2
aor. act. part. προσφάτως recently. ἐληλυθότα perf. part.
ἔρχομαι. διατεταχέναι perf. inf. διατάσσω to decree, to order. (For the decree of Claudius to expel the Jews from Rome,
s. BC, V, 295f.; 459f.; JPF, I, 180–183.) προσῆλθεν aor.
προσέρχομαι to come to. ■ ὁμότεχνος the same trade. ἔμενεν 3
impf. μένω to remain. ἠργάζοντο impf. mid. ἐργάζομαι to
work. σκηνοποιός leather worker, tentmaker (s. LC). The rabbis emphasize the necessity of learning a trade. Excellent is the
study of the law together w. worldly occupation, for toil in them
both puts sin out of mind (M, Aboth 2, 2). At Tarsus there was
a large group of "linen-workers" (DC XXXIV, 21). ■ διελέγετο 4
impf. mid. διαλέγομαι to discuss, to dispute, to argue (s. Acts
17:2). ἔπειθεν impf. πείθω to persuade.

■ κατῆλθον aor. κατέρχομαι to go down. συνείχετο 5
impf. mid. συνέχω mid. to be occupied w. or absorbed in some-

thing, "Paul was wholly absorbed in preaching" (BAG), inceptive impf. When Silas and Timothy came down to Corinth Saul
was able to give all his time to preaching (LC).
διαμαρτυρόμενος pres. mid. part. διαμαρτύρομαι to testify,
to solemnly declare. The prep. compound is intensive (IBG, 88).

6　■ ἀντιτασσομένων pres. mid. part. ἀντιτάσσομαι to oppose,
to resist. βλασφημούντων pres. act. part. βλασφημέω to slander, to blaspheme. ἐκτιναξάμενος aor. mid. part. ἐκτινάσσω

7 to shake off (s. BC, V, 274f.). ■ μεταβάς aor. part. μεταβαίνω
to go away. σεβομένου pres. mid. part. σέβομαι to fear, to
reverence, to worship (s. Acts 10:2). συνομοροῦσα pres. part.

8 συνομορέω to be right next to, to adjoin. ■ ἀρχισυνάγωγος
leader in the synagogue (s. Acts 13:15). ἐπίστευσεν aor.
ἀκούοντες pres. part. ἐπίστευον impf. The impf. pictures the

9 repeated action. ἐβαπτίζοντο impf. pass. βαπτίζω. ■ φοβοῦ
pres. mid. imp. φοβέομαι to be afraid. The pres. imp. w. the neg.
indicates the discontinuing of an action in progress (s. MKG,
272). λάλει pres. imp. σιωπήσῃς aor. subj. σιωπάω to be
silent. The aor. subj. used w. a neg. to prevent the beginning of

10 an action which is not in progress (s. MKG, 273). ■ ἐπιθήσεται
fut. mid. ἐπιτίθημι to attack. κακῶσαι aor. act. inf. κακόω to
do harm, to injure. The inf. expresses either purpose or result.

11 ■ ἐκάθισεν aor. καθίζω to sit, to remain. ἐνιαυτός year.
διδάσκων pres. part.

12 　　　■ ἀνθύπατος proconsul. Gallio, brother of Seneca, the
philosopher and tutor of Nero was, according to an inscription
at Delphi, proconsul in Corinth between A.D. 51 and 53 (s. BC,
V, 460–464; IDB, II, 351). ὄντος pres. part. εἰμί gen. abs.
κατεπέστησαν aor. κατεφίστημι to rise up against someone.
ὁμοθυμαδόν w. one mind, together. ἤγαγον aor. ἄγω to lead.

13 βῆμα bench, judges. ■ ἀναπείθω to persuade, in a neg. sense
to seduce, to mislead (s. MM). The prep. compound is perfective

14 and suggests success (MH, 296). ■ μέλλοντος pres. part. μέλλω
to be about to. ῥαδιούργημα to prank, crime, particularly implies fraud and deception (LC; MM). ἀνεσχόμην aor.
ἀνέχομαι to bear w., to tolerate. Used of listening patiently

15 while others are allowed to speak (Bruce). ■ ὄψεσθε fut. mid.

16 ὁράω ■ ἀπήλασεν aor. ἀπελαύνω to drive away.

17 term than just "to send away" (Haenchen). ■ ἐπιλαβόμενοι
aor. mid. part. ἐπιλαμβάνω to take, to lay hold of. ἔτυπτον
impf. τύπτω to beat, inceptive impf., they began to beat. ἔμελεν
impf. μέλει to be concerned about something. (For Paul's
experience before Gallio in the light of Roman law and for a
defense of its integrity, s. Sherwin-White, 99–107.)

■ προσμείνας aor. part. προσμένω to remain. 18 ἀποταξάμενος aor. mid. part. ἀποτάσσομαι to say farewell. ἐξέπλει impf. ἐκπλέω to sail, inceptive impf. "they began to sail." κειράμενος aor. mid. part. κείρομαι to shear, mid., to have one's hair cut. εὐχή vow. A temporary Nazarite vow of thirty days during which abstinence from wine was practiced and the hair was not cut. The cutting of the hair marked the termination of the vow (s. Bruce; LC; M, Nazir). ■ κατήντησαν 19 aor. καταντάω to arrive. κατέλιπεν aor. καταλείπω to leave behind. αὐτού here. εἰσελθών aor. part. εἰσέρχομαι to go in. διελέξατο aor. mid. διαλέγομαι (s. Acts 17:2). ■ ἐρωτώντων 20 pres. act. part. ἐρωτάω to ask, to request, gen. abs. πλείων comp. πολύς. μεῖναι aor. inf. μένω. ἐπένευσεν aor. ἐπινεύω to approve by a nod, to consent. ■ ἀνακάμψω fut. ἀνακάμπτω 21 to turn back, to return again. θέλοντος pres. part., gen. abs. ἀνήχθη aor. pass. ἀνάγω to set sail. ■ κατελθών aor. part. 22 κατέρχομαι. ἀναβάς aor. part. ἀναβαίνω to disembark. ἀσπασάμενος aor. mid. part. ἀσπάζομαι to greet. κατέβη aor. καταβαίνω to go down. ■ ποιήσας aor. part. ἐξῆλθεν aor. 23 ἐξέρχομαι to go out. καθεξῆς in order, successively. στηρίζων pres. part. στηρίζω to strengthen.

■ λόγιος learned, "a man of culture" (s. MM). 24 κατήντησεν s.v.19. ὤν pres. part. εἰμί. ■ κατηχημένος perf. 25 pass. part. κατηχέω to instruct, to teach by repeating, dinning into the ears, to teach orally by word of mouth (RWP). Participle used in a periphrastic construction. ζέων pres. part. ζέω to boil, literally "boiling over in his spirit," that is, full of enthusiasm (Brucc). ἐλάλει impf. ἀκριβῶς accurately. ἐπιστάμενος pres. mid. part. ἐπίσταμαι to know, to understand. ■ ἤρξατο aor. 26 mid. ἄρχομαι to begin. ἀκούσαντες aor. act. part. προσελάβοντο aor. mid. προσλαμβάνομαι to take to one's self (s. Acts 17:19). ἀκριβέστερον adv. comp. more accurately. ἐξέθεντο aor. mid. ἐκτίθημι to set forth, to explain. ■ 27 βουλομένου pres. mid. part., gen. abs. διελθεῖν aor. inf. διέρχομαι to pass through. προτρεψάμενοι aor. mid. part. προτρέπομαι to urge forward, to push on, to encourage. ἔγραψαν aor. ἀποδέξασθαι aor. mid. inf. ἀποδέχομαι to welcome, to receive, to accept gladly. παραγενόμενος aor. mid. part. παραγίνομαι to arrive. συνεβάλετο aor. mid. συμβάλλω to throw together, to help, to be helpful. πεπιστευκόσιν perf. act. part. The perf. emphasizes the state of belief. ■ εὐτόνως vigorously. διακατηλέγχετο impf. mid. 28 διακατελέγχομαι to refute, to confute w. rivalry in a contest (RWP). δημοσίᾳ publicly. ἐπιδεικνύς to set forth, to point out,

311

to prove.

Ch. 19

1   ■ ἐγένετο aor. mid. γίνομαι. (For this Hebraic construction, s. Luke 8:1.) διελθόντα aor. act. part. διέρχομαι to pass
through. ἀνωτερικός higher, upper. It may refer to the "upper
country" meaning the region above and behind Ephesus (Williams). It may, however, refer to the higher lying and more direct
route from Antioch to Ephesus (PTR, 265; s. also W.M. Ramsay,
The Historical Geography of Asia Minor, 164f.). ἐλθεῖν aor. inf.

2   ἔρχομαι. εὑρεῖν aor. inf. ■ ἐλάβετε aor. λαμβάνω.
πιστεύσαντες aor. part. The part. expresses contemporaneous
action "on believing," that is, "when you became Christians"
(LC). The coincident aor. part. is doctrinally important (M,

3   131). ἠκούσαμεν aor. ἀκούω. ■ εἰς "into." Used w. the baptismal formula "into the name of." (For a discussion of the meaning
and the suggestion that it characterized the rite in a fundamental
way; that is, a "Jesus baptism" or a "John baptism," s. Lars
Hartman, "Into the Name of Jesus," NTS, 20 [July, 1974], 432–

4   440.) ἐβαπτίσθητε aor. pass. βαπτίζω to baptize. ■
ἐβάπτισεν aor. μετάνοια change of mind, repentance (s. Matt.
3:2). ἐρχόμενον pres. mid. part. The part. w. the prep. is placed
first in the clause to give it prominence, thus stressing the
preparatory nature of John's ministry (Bruce). πιστεύσωσιν
aor. subj. The subj. gives both a content and the purpose (s.

5/6 Alford). ■ ἀκούσαντες aor. part. ■ ἐπιθέντος aor. part.
ἐπιτίθημι to place upon. ἐλάλουν impf. ἐπροφήτευσον impf.
προφητεύω to prophesy. (For an explanation of this event in
the light of the transitional period, s. Roy L. Aldrich, "The
Transition Problem in Acts," Bib Sac 114 [July, 1957], 235–242;
s. also BHS, 83–89.)

8   ■ εἰσελθών aor. part. εἰσέρχομαι to go in.
ἐπαρρησιάζετο impf. mid. παρρησιάζομαι to speak freely, to
speak boldly. The impf. pictures the repeated action. μήν month.
διαλεγόμενος pres. mid. part. διαλέγομαι to discuss, to dispute, to argue (s. Acts 17:2). πείθων pres. part. πείθω to per-

9   suade. ■ ἐσκληρύνοντο impf. pass. σκληρύνω to harden, pass.
to be or become hardened, to be obstinate (Bruce). ἠπείθουν
impf. act. ἀπειθέω to be disobedient, to refuse to believe.
κακολογοῦντες pres. part. κακολογέω to speak evil about.
ἀποστάς aor. act. part. ἀφίστημι to depart, to withdraw.
ἀφώρισεν aor. ἀφορίζω to separate. καθ᾽ ἡμέραν daily.
σχολή lecture hall. The day's work activity generally ended at
11:00 A.M. Paul worked manually from daybreak until 11:00

A.M., then devoted the next five hours to the still more exhausting business of Christian dialectic (Bruce; LC). ■ κατοικοῦντας 10 pres. part. κατοικέω to live, to dwell. ἀκοῦσαι aor. inf. Infinitive used w. ὥστε to express actual result (s. RG, 999f.).

■ τυχούσας aor. act. part. τυγχάνω to hit upon, to happen. 11 The part. is used to mean "not common," "extraordinary" (AS). Here it indicates that which is unusual or extraordinary (Bruce). ἐποίει impf. ■ ἀσθενοῦντας pres. part. ἀσθενέω to be weak, 12 to be sick. ἀποφέρεσθαι pres. pass. inf. ἀποφέρω to carry away. χρώς skin. σουδάριον sweat rag, cloths worn around the head and used to wipe the sweat off (LC). σιμικίνθιον apron. These were worn by the working men (Rackham). ἀπαλλάσσεσθαι pres. pass. inf., pass. to be released, to be cured, to leave, to depart. (For the frequent occurrence of this word of the medical writers, s. MLL, 47.) ■ ἐπεχείρησαν aor. 13 ἐπιχειρέω to attempt, to undertake. περιερχομένων pres. mid. part. περιέρχομαι to go about. ἐξορκιστής exorcist. (For Jewish views of demonism and exorcism, s. SB, IV, 501–535; Josephus, Antiquities VIII, 45–49.) ὁρκίζω to cause to swear, to adjure, to charge. ■ ποιοῦντες pres. part. ■ ἀποκριθέν aor. 14/15 pass. part. ἀποκρίνομαι to answer. ■ ἐφαλόμενος aor. mid. 16 part. ἐφάλλομαι to leap, to jump, to spring upon like a panther (RWP). κατακυριεύσας aor. act. part. κατακυριεύω to become master of, to subdue. The prep. compound is perfective and indicates an action unfavorable to its object (MH, 316). ἀμφότεροι both, all (s. Haenchen; MM). ἴσχυσεν aor. ἰσχύω to be strong, to overcome. γυμνός naked. τετραυματισμένους perf. pass. part. τραυματίζω to wound. The perf. emphasizes the state or condition. ἐκφυγεῖν aor. inf. ἐκφεύγω to flee, to escape. The inf. is used to express actual result (s.v.10). ■ 17 γνωστός known. ἐπέπεσεν aor. ἐπιπίπτω to fall upon. ἐμεγαλύνετο impf. pass. μεγαλύνω to make large, to magnify. ■ πεπιστευκότων perf. act. part. ἤρχοντο impf. mid. ἔρχομαι. 18 ἐξομολογούμενοι pres. mid. part. ἐξομολογέομαι to confess, public confession. ἀναγγέλλοντες pres. act. part. ἀναγγέλλω to make known. πρᾶξις deed, spell. A technical term for a specific magical spell (s. Deissmann; BS, 323). ■ περίεργα 19 things belonging to magic. A technical term for magic (s. Deissmann; BS, 323). πραξάντων aor. act. part. πράσσω to do, to practice. συνενέγκαντες aor. act. part. συμφέρω to bring together. κατέκαιον impf. κατακαίω to burn up. συνεψήφισαν aor. συμψηφίζω to reckon together. εὗρον aor. ἀργύριον silver, silver pieces worth about one thousand dollars (RWP). ■ 20 ηὔξανεν impf. αὐξάνω to grow. The impf. pictures the continual growth. ἴσχυεν impf.

21 ■ ἐπληρώθη aor. pass. πληρόω to fulfill, to complete. ἔθετο aor. mid. τίθημι to place, to purpose. διελθών aor. part., s.v.1. εἰπών aor. part. λέγω. γενέσθαι aor. mid. inf. γίνομαι. The inf. is used w. prep. to express time, "after" (s. MT, 143).

22 δεῖ it is necessary. ἰδεῖν aor. inf. ὁράω. ■ ἀποστείλας aor. act. part. ἀποστέλλω to send. διακονούντων pres. part. ἐπέσχεν

23 aor. ἐπέχω to stay, to wait. ■ ἐγένετο aor. mid. (s. Luke 8:1).

24 ■ ἀργυροκόπος silversmith. ποιῶν pres. part. ναός temple, shrine. Although shrines of terra cotta and marble have been found during excavations, no silver shrines have come to light thus far. However, theft, war, and plunder would decrease the number of shrines or images that survived, and any object of precious metal might be destroyed or melted down for other uses (s. Floyd V. Filson, "Ephesus and the New Testament," BA, 8 [Sept. 1945], 73–80). These probably were small shrines representing the goddess Artemis sitting in a niche w. her lions beside her (PTR, 278). παρείχετο impf. mid. παρέχω to furnish, to

25 supply. τεχνίτης craftsman, artisan. ■ συναθροίσας aor. act. part. συναθροίζω to assemble, to gather together. He was organizing the whole trade in a protest (Bruce). εὐπορία wealth,

26 affluence. ■ σχεδόν almost. οὗτος "this." Used here to express contempt (s. RG, 697; MT, 44). πείσας aor. act. part., s.v.8. μετέστησεν aor. μεθίστημι to change, to pervert. The prep.

27 compound has the idea of change (s. MH, 318). ■ ἀπελεγμός exposure, rejection after examination, disrepute (RWP). ἐλθεῖν aor. part., s.v.1. θεά goddess. (For the worship and greatness of Artemis of Ephesus, s. BC, V, 251–256.) λογισθῆναι aor. pass. inf. λογίζομαι to reckon, to judge, to consider. καθαιρεῖσθαι pres. pass. inf. καθαιρέω to tear down, to destroy. μεγαλειότης greatness, majesty. (For a description of the famous temple which was considered one of the seven wonders of the world, s. BC, V, 252f.; Strabo XIV. 1. 22, 23.)

28 ■ ἀκούσαντες aor. part. γενόμενοι aor. mid. part.

29 γίνομαι. ἔκραζον impf. act. κράζω to scream. ■ ἐπλήσθη aor. pass. πίμπλημι to fill. σύγχυσις confusion. ὥρμησαν aor. act. ὁρμάω to rush. ὁμοθυμαδόν together, w. one mind, w. one accord. θέατρον theater. The great temple of Ephesus was the regular meeting place of the assembly (Sherwin-White, 87). The large theater was approximately 495 ft. in diameter and would accomodate approximately 24,500 persons (s. Merrill M. Parvis,"Ephesus in the Early Christian Era," BA, 8 [Sept. 1945], 61–73). συναρπάσαντες aor. act. part. συναρπάζω to seize. The prep. compound is perfective (s. MH, 325). συνέκδημος

traveling companion. ■ βουλομένου pres. mid. part. βούλομαι 30
to will. εἰσελθεῖν aor. inf. εἰσέρχομαι s.v.8. εἴων impf. act.
ἐάω to allow. ■ ὄντες pres. part. εἰμί. πέμψαντες aor. act. part. 31
πέμπω to send. παρεκάλουν impf. παρακαλέω to ask, to
beseech, to plead. δοῦναι aor. act. inf. δίδωμι. (For a discussion
of the Asiarchs, s. BC, V, 256–262.) ■ συγκεχυμένη perf. pass. 32
part. συγχέω to pour together, to confuse. The perf. emphasizes
the state or condition. πλείων comp. πολύς. ᾔδεισαν plperf.
οἶδα. συνεληλύθεισαν plperf. συνέρχομαι to come together.
■ συνεβίβασαν aor. συμβιβάζω to bring together, to prove, 33
to instruct (Haenchen). προβαλόντων aor. act. part.
προβάλλω to put forward. κατασείσας aor. part. κατασείω
to motion w. the hand, to shake down. Here it indicates the rapid
waving of the hand up and down to get a hearing (RWP). ἤθελεν
impf. θέλω. ἀπολόγεισθαι pres. mid. inf. to defend one's self.
■ ἐπιγνόντες aor. act. part. ἐπιγινώσκω to know, to recog- 34
nize. κράζοντες pres. part. ■ καταστείλας aor. part. 35
καταστέλλω to calm down, to quiet down. γραμματεύς town
clerk. (For the importance of this position in the city government of that day, s. Sherwin-White, 86f.) νεωκόρος temple
guardian, temple warden (s. Sherwin-White, 88f.). διοπετής
fallen from heaven, an image fallen from heaven. ■ 36
ἀναντίρρητος incontestable. (For the neg. force of the prefix,
s. Moorhouse, 47–68.) δέον ἐστίν it is necessary.
κατεσταλμένους perf. pass. part. καταστέλλω. προπετής
rash, reckless, thoughtless. ■ ἠγάγετε aor. ἄγω to lead. 37
ἱερόσυλος temple robber, one who commits sacrilege.
βλασφημοῦντας pres. act. part. βλασφημέω to blaspheme.
τὴν θέον goddess. The fem. article w. the masc. noun was the
regular term for the great goddess of the city. The town clerk
uses the technical term (Bruce). ■ λόγος matter, case. 38
ἀγοραῖος market days, court days. ἀνθύπατος proconsul.
ἐγκαλείτωσαν pres. act. imp. 3rd per. pl. ἐγκαλέω to accuse,
to call one in, to bring a charge against (RWP). ■ ἔννομος 39
lawful. The technical term for the regularly appointed meeting
of the people. (For the accuracy of this terminology and of
Luke's description of the entire event, s. Sherwin-White, 84–92.)
ἐπιλυθήσεται fut. pass. ἐπιλύω to explain, to decide, to settle.
■ ἐγκαλεῖσθαι pres. pass. inf. ὑπάρχοντος pres. act. part. gen. 40
abs. δυνησόμεθα fut. mid. ἀποδοῦναι aor. act. inf. ἀποδίδωμι
λόγον to give account. συστροφή disorderly gathering, commotion. ἀπέλυσεν aor. ἀπολύω to dismiss.

Ch. 20

1 ■ **παύσασθαι** aor. mid. inf. **παύω** to cease. (For the inf. w. prep. to express time, s. Acts 19:21.) **μεταπεμψάμενος** aor. mid. part. **μεταπέμπω** to send after, to summons. **παρακαλέσας** aor. act. part. **παρακαλέω** to encourage, to exhort. **ἀσπασάμενος** aor. mid. part. **ἀσπάζομαι** to greet, to draw to one's self in embrace either in greeting or farewell. Here
2 it is in farewell (RWP). **ἐξῆλθεν** aor. **ἐξέρχομαι** to go out. ■
3 **διελθών** aor. act. part. **διέρχομαι** to go through. ■ **ποιήσας** aor. part. **μήν** month. The acc. is used to express the extent of time answering the question, "How long?" (BD, 88; RG, 469f.). **γενομένης** aor. mid. part. **γίνομαι.** **ἐπιβουλή** plot. Perhaps the plot was to kill Paul as he took a pilgrim ship carrying Jews to the Passover (PTR, 287; Haenchen). **μέλλοντι** pres. part. **μέλλω** to be about to. **ἀνάγεσθαι** pres. mid. part. to set sail. **ἐγένετο** aor. mid. **γίνομαι.** **γνώμη** opinion, decision, "he decided." **ὑποστρέφειν** pres. act. inf. to return, epexegetic inf.
4 used to explain the decision (s. IBG, 127). ■ **συνείπετο** impf.
5 mid. **συνέπομαι** to accompany. ■ **προελθόντες** aor. act. part. **προέρχομαι** to go before, to go ahead. **ἔμενον** impf. **μένω** to
6 remain, to wait for. ■ **ἐξεπλεύσαμεν** aor. **ἐκπλέω** to set sail, to sail away. **διετρίψαμεν** aor. **διατρίβω** to spend, to stay.

7 ■ **συνηγμένων** perf. pass. part. **συνάγω** to gather together, pass. to assemble. **κλάσαι** aor. act. inf. **κλάω** to break, inf. used to express purpose. **διελέγετο** impf. mid. **διαλέγομαι** to instruct, to teach (s. Acts 17:2). **ἐξιέναι** pres. inf. **ἔξειμι** to go out. **παρέτεινεν** impf. **παρατείνω** to stretch beside, to pro-
8 long. **μεσονύκτιον** midnight. ■ **λαμπάς** lamp. **ὑπερῷον** up-
9 stairs. **οὗ** where. ■ **καθεζόμενος** pres. mid. part. **καθέζομαι** to sit. **θυρίς** window. **καταφερόμενος** pres. pass. part. **καταφέρω** to bear down, "to drop off to sleep." The pres. tense describes the progressive action. The hot, oily atmosphere caused by the crowd and the torches made it difficult for one who had probably put in a hard day's work to keep awake (Bruce). **ὕπνος** sleep. **βαθύς** deep. **διαλεγομένου** pres. mid. part. **πλεῖων** comp. **πολύς.** **κατενεχθείς** aor. pass. part. **καταφέρω.** The aor. in contrast to the pres. part. indicates that sleep finally overtook him and he fell fast asleep (s. Alford). **ἔπεσεν** aor. **πίπτω** to fall. **τρίστεγος** third story. **κάτω** down. **ἤρθη** aor. pass. **αἴρω** to lift
10 up, to pick up. ■ **καταβάς** aor. act. part. **καταβαίνω** to go down. **ἐπέπεσεν** aor. **ἐπιπίπτω** to fall upon. **συμπεριλαβών** aor. part. **συμπεριλαμβάνω** to embrace, to take hold, to gather around. **θορυβεῖσθε** pres. mid. imp. **θορυβέομαι** to throw into disorder, to be troubled, to be distressed. The pres. imp. w. the

neg. indicates the stopping of an action in progress (s. MKG,
272). ■ ἀναβάς aor. part. ἀναβαίνω to go up. κλάσας aor. 11
part. γευσάμενος aor. mid. part. γεύομαι to taste, to eat.
ὁμιλήσας aor. part. ὁμιλέω to be in company w., to converse
w. αὐγή daylight. ■ ἤγαγον aor. ἄγω to lead. ζῶντα pres. act. 12
part. ζάω to live. παρεκλήθησαν aor. pass. παρακαλέω to
comfort, to encourage. μετρίως adv. moderately. Used w. neg.
"exceedingly."

■ ἀνήχθημεν aor. pass. ἀνάγω. The 1st per. pl. begins 13
again in this section. ἀναλαμβάνειν pres. act. inf. to take up,
to take along as a traveling companion, to take on board (BAG).
διατεταγμένος perf. mid. part. διατάσσομαι to give orders,
to give instruction, periphrastic use of the part. πεζεύειν pres.
act. inf. to go by foot, to travel by land (s. LC). ■ συνέβαλλεν 14
impf. συμβάλλω to bring together, to meet. The impf. may
imply that Paul was seen and taken in by boat as he was nearing
Assos (Bruce). Some manuscripts have the aor. instead of the
impf. (s. BC, III, 194). ἀναλαβόντες aor. act. part.
ἀναλαμβάνω. ■ ἀποπλεύσαντες aor. act. part. ἀποπλέω to 15
sail away. ἐπιούσῃ the word "day" is to be supplied, "on the
following day." κατηντήσαμεν aor. καταντάω to arrive, to
reach a destination. ἄντικρυς face to face w., opposite (RWP).
παρεβάλομεν aor. παραβάλλω to throw alongside, to approach, to come near. As a technical term in seamen's speech to
come near by ship, to cross over (BAG). ἐχομένῃ "on the following (day)." ■ κεκρίκει plperf. κρίνω to decide. 16
παραπλεῦσαι aor. act. inf. παραπλέω to sail by. γένηται aor.
mid. subj. γίνομαι. Used w. particle to express purpose.
χρονοτριβῆσαι aor. act. inf. χρονοτριβέω to spend time.
ἔσπευδεν impf. σπεύδω to hurry. εἴη opt. εἰμί. γενέσθαι aor.
mid. inf. γίνομαι.

■ πέμψας aor. part. πέμπω to send. μετεκαλέσατο aor. 17
mid. μετακαλέω to call, to summons. The prep. compound has
the idea of change; that is, to call from one place to another (s.
MH, 318; RWP). ■ παρεγένοντο aor. mid. παραγίνομαι to 18
arrive. ἐπίστασθε pres. mid. ἐπίσταμι to know, to understand, primarily expresses the knowledge obtained by proximity
to the thing known; then knowledge viewed as a result of a
prolonged practice (T). ἐπέβην aor. ἐπιβαίνω to step on, to set
foot on. ἐγενόμην aor. mid., s.v.3. ■ δουλεύων to serve as a 19
slave (TDNT; CBB). ταπεινοφροσύνη humility. The recognition of one's own weakness as well as the recognition of God's
power (s. Trench, *Synonyms*, 148–153; TDNT). δάκρυον tear.
συμβάντων aor. act. part. συμβαίνω to come together, to

20 happen to. ■ ὑπεστειλάμην aor. mid. ὑποστέλλω to draw
back in fear, to shrink from. The opposite of to speak boldly.
συμφερόντων pres. act. part. συμφέρω to be profitable, to be
of an advantage. ἀναγγεῖλαι aor. act. inf. ἀναγγέλλω to an-
21 nounce, to proclaim. διδάξαι aor. inf. δημοσιᾳ publicly. ■
διαμαρτυρόμενος pres. mid. part. διαμαρτύρομαι to testify
22 (s. Acts 2:40). ■ δεδεμένος perf. pass. part. δέω to bind. The
perf. emphasizes the state or condition. συναντήσοντα fut. act.
part. συναντάω to meet w., to happen to. εἰδώς perf. part.
23 οἶδα. ■ πλήν "except that," "only," conjunction w. a limitive
24 force (Thrall, 20; L). ■ οὐδενὸς λόγου ποιέομαι "I reckon my
life of no account" (Bruce). ὡς used to express purpose, "in
order that" (RG, 987). τελειώσω fut. or aor. subj. τελειόω to
complete, to finish. δρόμος run, course. ἔλαβον aor. λαμβάνω.
διαμαρτύρασθαι aor. mid. inf.
25   ■ ὄψεσθε fut. mid. ὁράω. διῆλθον aor. διέρχομαι s.v.2.
26 ■ αἷμα blood. In this connection Paul means "I am free of blame
in reference to each one, if he (on account of unbelief) falls a prey
28 to death" (Meyer). ■ προσέχετε pres. imp. προσέχω to take
heed, to pay attention to. ἔθετο aor. mid. τίθημι to place, to
appoint. ἐπίσκοπος overseer, bishop. ποιμαίνειν pres. act. inf.
to shepherd, to tend or feed the flock, inf. of purpose.
περιεποιήσατο aor. mid. περιποιέω to secure, to acquire.
29 ἴδιος own. ■ εἰσελεύσονται fut. mid. εἰσέρχομαι to go into.
ἄφιξις departure. φειδόμενοι pres. mid. part. φείδομαι to
30 spare (w. the gen.). ■ ἀναστήσονται fut. mid. ἀνίστημι to
arise, to rise up. λαλοῦντες pres. act. part. διεστραμμένα perf.
pass. part. διαστρέφω to turn aside, to twist, to pervert, to
31 distort. ■ γρηγορεῖτε pres. imp. γρηγορέω to stay awake, to
watch. The pres. imp. would indicate a continual watchfulness.
μνημονεύοντες pres. part. μνημονεύω to remember.
νουθετῶν pres. part. νουθετέω to instruct, to warn, to admonish. To instruct one who has gone astray by warning him of the
32 danger, admonishing him to return (s. TDNT; CBB). ■
παρατίθεμαι to commit to. δυναμένῳ pres. mid. part.
οἰκοδομῆσαι aor. act. inf. οἰκοδομέω to build, to build up.
δοῦναι aor. act. inf. δίδωμι. ἡγιασμένοις perf. pass. part.
33 ἁγιάζω to sanctify. ■ ἀργύριον silver. ἐπεθύμησα aor.
34 ἐπιθυμέω to desire, to covet (w. the gen.). ■ οὖσιν part. εἰμί.
ὑπηρέτησαν aor. ὑπηρετέω to serve, to minister (s. TDNT).
35 ■ ὑπέδειξα aor. ὑποδείκνυμι to show under one's eyes, to give
an object lesson, to show (RWP). κοπιῶντας pres. part.
κοπιάω to work, to toil. The verb emphasizes the hardness of
the work and the weariness it brings (LC). ἀντιλαμβάνεσθαι

pres. mid. inf. to help, to take another's part, to succour (w. the gen.) (EGT). ἀσθενούντων pres. part. ἀσθενέω to be sick, to be weak.

■ εἰπών aor. part. λέγω. θείς aor. part. τίθημι. γόνυ knee, 36 "to place the knee," "to kneel." προσηύξατο aor. mid. προσεύχομαι to pray. ■ κλαυθμός crying, weeping. 37 ἐπιπέσοντες aor. part. ἐπιπίπτω to fall upon. τράχηλος neck. κατεφίλουν impf. καταφιλέω to kiss (s. Mark 14:45). ■ 38 ὀδυνώμενοι pres. mid. part. ὀδυνάομαι to be distressed, to be moved by pain, to sorrow. μάλιστα especially. εἰρήκει plperf. λέγω. προέπεμπον impf. προπέμπω to send forward, to accompany, to escort.

■ ἐγένετο aor. mid. γίνομαι. (For the construction, s. Luke 1 8:1.) ἀναχθῆναι aor. pass. inf. ἀνάγω mid. or pass. to put out to sea, to set sail. ἀποσπασθέντας aor. pass. part. ἀποσπάω to tear away, to part. εὐθυδρομήσαντες aor. act. part. εὐθυδρομέω to run a straight course. The prevailing wind was northeast (Bruce). τῇ ἑξῆς w. the word "day" supplied "on the next day." ■ εὑρόντες aor. part. διαπερῶν pres. part. 2 διαπεράω to cross over. ἐπιβάντες aor. act. part. ἐπιβαίνω to embark, to go aboard. ἀνήχθημεν aor. pass. ἀνάγω. ■ 3 ἀναφάναντες aor. part. ἀναφαίνω to cause to appear, probably a nautical technical term to sight (BAG). The word lit. means "we made it visible to ourselves"; that is, by drawing near (BD, 163). καταλίποντες aor. part. καταλείπω to leave behind. εὐώνυμος left. ἐπλέομεν impf. πλέω to sail. κατήλθομεν aor. κατέρχομαι to come down. ἐκεῖσε there. ἀποφορτιζόμενον pres. mid. part. ἀποφορτίζομαι to make light, to unload. An impf. periphrastic construction used as the customary impf., "the ship had the characteristic of " (BD, 175). γόμος freight, cargo. ■ ἀνεύροντες aor. part. ἀνευρίσκω to seek out, to find by 4 searching. The prep. compound is perfective (MH, 296). ἐπεμείναμεν aor. ἐπιμένω to remain. ■ ἐξαρτίσαι aor. act. 5 inf. ἐξαρτίζω to fulfill, to complete. Here in the sense of accomplishing the days; that is, finishing the time, the seven days during which we had to remain for the cargo to be unloaded or for other business (EGT). προπεμπόντων pres. part. προπέμπω to accompany, to escort, gen. abs. θέντες aor. pass. part. τίθημι to place, to kneel down. αἰγιαλός beach. προσευξάμενοι aor. mid. part. προσεύχομαι to pray. ■ 6 ἀπησπασάμεθα aor. mid. ἀπασπάζομαι to give parting greetings, to say farewell. ἐνέβημεν aor. ἐμβαίνω to embark, to get on board. ὑπέστρεψαν aor. ὑποστρέφω to return.

7 ■ διανύσαντες aor. part. διανύω to accomplish, to complete. The prep. has the idea of carrying an action through to a definite result (MH, 301). κατηντήσαμεν aor. καταντάω to arrive. ἀσπασάμενοι aor. mid. part. ἀσπάζομαι to give greet-

8 ings, to greet. ἐμείναμεν aor. μένω to remain. ■ εἰσελθόντες aor. act. part. εἰσέρχομαι to go into. εὐαγγελιστής evangelist, one who brings the good news. A possible secular use of the word describes one as the proclaimer of the oracle announcements (MM). Words ending w. this suffix indicate the agent who per-

9 forms the action (MH, 360f.). ■ προφητεύουσαι pres. act. part.

10 προφητεύω to prophesy. ■ ἐπιμενόντων pres. act. part. gen.

11 abs. πλείων comp. πολύς. ■ ἐλθών aor. part. ἔρχομαι. ἄρας aor. act. part. αἴρω to lift up, to take. ζώνη belt. δήσας aor. act. part. δέω to bind, to tie. παραδώσουσιν fut. act. παραδίδωμι

12 to deliver over to. ■ ἠκούσαμεν aor. ἀκούω. παρεκαλοῦμεν impf. παρακαλέω to urge, to exhort, conative impf. "we tried to persuade him from going up" (RWP). ἐντόπιος one belonging to the place, resident. ἀναβαίνειν pres. inf. Infinitive used to express purpose. The pres. inf. indicates "to stop going up"

13 (Bruce). ■ ἀπεκρίθη aor. pass. ἀποκρίνομαι to answer. κλαίοντες pres. part. κλαίω to weep, to cry. συνθρύπτοντες pres. part. συνθρύπτω to crush together, to break up, to pound to bits (s. LC). δεθῆναι aor. pass. inf. δέω. ἀποθανεῖν aor. act. inf. ἀποθνήσκω to die. ἑτοίμως ready. ἔχω to have, here "to

14 be" (s. BAG). ■ πειθομένου pres. pass. part. πείθω to persuade. ἡσυχάσαμεν aor. ἡσυχάζω to be still, to be quiet, ingressive aor. "we became silent." εἰπόντες aor. act. part. λέγω. τοῦ κυρίου placed first for emphasis. γινέσθω pres. mid. imp.

15 ■ ἐπισκευασάμενοι aor. mid. part. ἐπισκευάζω to prepare, to pack up (LC). ἀνεβαίνομεν impf. ἀναβαίνω to go up.

16 ■ συνῆλθον aor. συνέρχομαι to go w. someone, to accompany. ἄγοντες pres. part. ἄγω to lead, to bring, "bringing us to Mnason." ξενισθῶμεν aor. pass. subj. ξενίζω to entertain guests, to show hospitality. The subj. used here in the rel. clause expresses purpose (BD, 191). ἀρχαῖος old, early, it may mean that he was an early disciple or even from the beginning, the great Pentecost (EGT).

17 ■ γενομένων aor. mid. part. γίνομαι gen. abs. ἀσμένως w. joy, gladly. ἀπεδέξαντο aor. mid. ἀποδέχομαι to welcome,

18 to receive. ■ ἐπιούσῃ "on the next (day)." εἰσῄει impf. εἴσειμι to go into. παρεγένοντο aor. mid. παραγίνομαι to arrive.

19 ■ ἐξηγεῖτο impf. mid. ἐξηγέομαι to narrate, to explain in detail. (For the prep. compound, s. MH, 310.) ὧν gen. pl., gen. by

attraction to the antecedent instead of the normal acc. (s. RWP).
ἐποίησεν aor. ■ ἀκούσαντες aor. act. part. ἐδόξαζον impf. 20
δοξάζω to glorify. μυριάς "tens of thousands." A Gr. idiom for
a great number (LC). πεπιστευκότων perf. act. part. ζηλωτής
zealous. The word here does not indicate the political party of
the Zealots (Bruce). (For a description of the political party, s.
H.P. Kingdon, "Who Were the Zealots and Their Leaders in
A.D. 66?" NTS, 17 [Oct., 1970], 68–72.) ■ κατηχήθησαν aor. 21
pass. κατηχέω to instruct, to inform. (For Jewish attacks against
Paul as found in extrabiblical Jewish writings, s. SB, II, 753–
755.) ἀποστασία apostasy, falling away. ■ πάντως certainly, 22
of course, originally it is a word of assurance, "by all means," but
has been weakened and could be uncertain in force, "probably"
(LC; s. also G.M. Lee, "Πάντως 'Perhaps'?" ZNW, 64 [1973],
152). ἀκούσονται fut. mid. ἐλήλυθας perf. act. ἔρχομαι. ■ 23
ποίησον aor. imp. εὐχή vow (s. Acts 18:18). ■ παραλαβών 24
aor. part. παραλαμβάνω to take, to take w. someone.
ἁγνίσθητι aor. pass. inf. ἁγνίζω to sanctify, to purify. The
pass. is used here as a refl. pass., "purify yourself " (s. RG, 819).
δαπάνησον aor. imp. δαπανάω to spend money on someone,
to pay the expenses. ξυρήσονται fut. mid. ξυράομαι to shave,
mid. to shave one's self, to let one's self be shaved. (For the fut.
ind. used w. ἵνα to express purpose, s. MT, 100. For the Jewish
custom, s. SB, II, 755.) γνώσονται fut. mid. γινώσκω.
κατήχηνται perf. pass. φυλάσσων pres. part. φυλάσσω to
guard, to observe. ■ ἐπεστείλαμεν aor. ἐπιστέλλω to send to, 25
to send a message by letter, to write. From the usage of the word
in official documents, the meaning readily passed over into "instruct," "enjoin" (MM). κρίναντες aor. act. part. κρίνω to
decide, to determine, to judge. φυλάσσεσθαι pres. mid. inf.
εἰδωλόθυτον meat offered to an idol. It refers to sacrificial
meat, part of which was burned on the altar, part of which was
eaten at a solemn meal in the temple, and part of which was sold
in the market for home use (BAG). πνικτός strangled. ■ 26
ἐχομένη ἡμέρα the following day. ἁγνισθείς aor. pass. part.
διαγγέλλων pres. part. διαγγέλλω to announce, to declare.
προσηνέχθη aor. pass. προσφέρω to bring an offering, to offer. The aor. ind. contemplates the final result (RWP).
προσφορά offering.

■ ἔμελλον impf. μέλλω to be about to. Used w. the inf. to 27
express futurity or intention reckoned from a moment in the
past, "the days were going to be completed" (s. MKG, 307).
συντελεῖσθαι pres. pass. inf. συντελέω to complete.
θεασάμενοι aor. mid. part. θεάομαι to see, to observe.

συνέχεον impf. συγχέω to pour together, to cause confusion, to stir up. The impf. pictures the continual action. ἐπέβαλαν aor. ἐπιβάλλω to place upon, to place hands upon, to seize.

28 ■ κράζοντες pres. act. part. κράζω to scream. βοηθεῖτε pres. imp. βοηθέω to help. πανταχῆ everywhere. διδάσκων pres. part. εἰσήγαγεν aor. εἰσάγω to lead into. κεκοίνωκεν perf. κοινόω to make common, to defile. The perf. pictures the abiding condition. It was a capital offense for a Gentile to be found within the barrier which divided the court of the Gentiles from

29 the court of Israel (s. LC; LAE, 80f.; M, Kelim I, 8). ■ προεωρακότες perf. act. part. προοράω to see previously, to

30 see before. ἐνόμιζον impf. νομίζω to suppose. ■ ἐκινήθη aor. pass. κινέω to move. ἐγένετο aor. mid., s.v.1. συνδρομή running together. ἐπιλαβόμενοι aor. mid. part. ἐπιλαμβάνω to seize. εἷλκον impf. ἕλκω to drag. ἐκλείσθησαν aor. pass. κλείω to shut. αἱ θύραι doors. The Levitical temple police closed the doors separating the temple from the court of the

31 Gentiles (Haenchen). ■ ζητούντων pres. part. ζητέω to seek, to try. ἀποκτεῖναι aor. act. inf. ἀποκτείνω to kill. ἀνέβη aor. ἀναβαίνω to go up. φάσις report. χιλίαρχος the leader of a thousand soldiers, the military tribune, the commander of a cohort, about six hundred men (BAG). These usually were young men doing military service at the beginning of their offi-

32 cial career (BC, V, 428). συγχύννεται pres. pass., s.v.27. ■ ἐξαυτῆς immediately. παραλαβών aor. act. part., s.v.24. ἑκατοντάρχης leader of a hundred men, centurion. κατέδραμεν aor. act. κατατρέχω to run down. ἐπαύσαντο aor. mid. παύω to stop, to cease. τύπτοντες pres. part. τύπτω

33 to beat. ■ ἐγγίσας aor. part. ἐγγίζω to draw near, to be near. ἐπελάβετο aor. mid. ἐπιλαμβάνω. ἐκέλευσεν aor. κελεύω to command. δεθῆναι aor. pass. inf., s.v.13. ἅλυσις chain. ἐπυνθάνετο impf. mid. πυνθάνομαι to investigate, to inquire. εἴη opt. εἰμί. Optative used in indirect discourse (s. RG, 1044).

34 πεποιηκώς perf. act. part. ■ ἐπεφώνουν impf. ἐπιφωνέω to call to. δυναμένου pres. mid. part., gen. abs. γνῶναι aor. act. inf. γινώσκω. ἀσφαλής certainty. ἄγεσθαι pres. pass. inf., s.v.16. παρεμβολή barracks. These were the barracks of the Roman garrison called Antonia located northwest of the temple connected to the temple by two flights of stairs (s. BC, V, 478f.;

35 Josephus, Wars V, 5, 8). ■ ἀναβαθμός step. συνέβη aor. συμβαίνει to happen. βαστάζεσθαι pres. pass. inf. βαστάζω

36 to carry. βία force, violence. ■ ἠκολούθει impf. ἀκολουθέω to follow. αἶρε pres. imp., s.v.11.

37   ■ μέλλων pres. part. εἰσάγεσθαι pres. pass. inf. ἔξεστιν

it is allowed, it is lawful. εἰπεῖν aor. inf. λέγω. ■ ἀναστατώσας 38
aor. act. part. ἀναστατόω to cause a revolt. ἐξαγαγών aor. act.
part. ἐξάγω to lead out. σικάριος assassin. Assassins, armed w.
short daggers (sicai) under their cloaks, mingled w. the crowd,
struck down their opponents, then pretended to call for help
(Josephus, *Wars* II, 13, 3). The Egyptian mentioned was a Jew
who proclaimed himself as a prophet. He gathered a large following intending to lead them to the Mount of Olives promising that
at his command the walls of Jerusalem would collapse. His force
was attacked by Felix but the Egyptian himself escaped (Josephus, *Wars* II, 13, 5; Ant. XX, 8, 6; HJP [NEE], I, 464). ■ 39
ἄσημος insignificant. πολίτης citizen. (For the city of Tarsus,
s. Strabo, VI, 311, 341–353; DC XXXIII–XXXIV.) ἐπίτρεψον
aor. imp. ἐπιτρέπω to permit, to allow. λαλῆσαι aor. act. inf.
■ ἐπιτρέψαντος aor. part. gen. abs. ἑστώς perf. act. part. 40
ἵστημι to stand. κατέσεισεν aor. κατασείω to wave w. the
hand (s. Acts 19:33). γενομένης aor. mid. part., gen. abs.
προσεφώνησεν aor. προσφωνέω to speak to, to deliver a
speech.

Ch. 22

■ ἀκούσατε aor. imp. ἀπολογία defense. The personal 1
pron. is to be taken w. the noun, "hear my defense" (Bruce).
■ ἀκούσαντες aor. act. part. προσεφώνει impf. προσφωνέω 2
to speak to. παρέσχον aor. παρέχω to offer, to provide, to give.
ἡσυχία quietness. ■ γεγεννημένος perf. pass. part. γεννάω to 3
bear, pass. to be born. ἀνατεθραμμένος perf. pass. part.
ἀνατρέφω to nourish, to nurse up, to bring up. πεπαιδευμένος
perf. pass. part. παιδεύω to instruct, to train. (For Jewish education, s. CC, 154f.) ἀκρίβεια strictness, exactness. ζηλωτής zealot, zealous. ὑπάρχων pres. part. ὑπάρχω to exist, to be. ■ 4
ἐδίωξα aor. διώκω to pursue, to hunt an animal, to persecute.
δεσμεύων pres. part. δεσμεύω to bind, to put in chains.
παραδιδούς pres. part. παραδίδωμι to deliver over. ■ 5
πρεσβυτέριον the elderhood, the Sanhedrin (s. JPF, I, 379–
400). δεξάμενος aor. mid. part. δέχομαι to receive.
ἐπορευόμην impf. mid. πορεύομαι to travel, to go. ἄξων fut.
act. part. ἄγω to lead. The fut. part. used to express purpose (s.
BD, 178f.). ἐκεῖσε there, to that place. If the original force "to
that place" be pressed, it refers to those Christians who had gone
to Damascus to escape the persecution in Jerusalem (Bruce).
ὄντας pres. part. εἰμί. δεδεμένους perf. pass. part. δέω to bind.
τιμωρηθῶσιν aor. subj. pass. τιμωρέω to punish, subj. used to
express purpose.

6 ■ ἐγένετο aor. mid. γίνομαι. (For the construction, s. Luke 8:1.) ἐγγίζοντι pres. act. part. ἐγγίζω to draw near, to come near. μεσημβρία midday, noon. ἐξαίφνης suddenly. περιαστράψαι aor. act. inf. περιαστράπτω to shine all
7 around (s. Acts 9:3). ■ ἔπεσα aor. πίπτω to fall. ἔδαφος
8 ground. ἤκουσα aor. ἀκούω. ■ ἀπεκρίθην aor. pass.
9 ἀποκρίνομαι to answer. ■ ἐθεάσαντο aor. mid. θεάομαι to
10 see, to view. λαλοῦντος pres. part. ■ ποιήσω aor. subj. ἀναστάς aor. part. ἀνίστημι to stand up, to arise. πορεύου pres. mid. imp. λαληθήσεται fut. pass. τέτακται perf. pass.
11 τάσσω to command. ποιῆσαι aor. inf. ■ ἐνέβλεπον impf. ἐμβλέπω to look at, to see. χειραγωγούμενος pres. pass. part. χειραγωγέω to lead by the hand. συνόντων pres. part. σύνειμι to be present, to accompany, to be with someone.
12 ■ εὐλαβής pious, godly. μαρτυρούμενος pres. pass. part.
13 κατοικούντων pres. act. part. κατοικέω to live, to dwell. ■ ἐλθών aor. part. ἔρχομαι. ἐπιστάς aor. act. part. ἐφίστημι to come to. ἀνάβλεψον aor. imp. ἀναβλέπω to see again. ἀνέβλεψα aor. ind. to look up. The verb has the double mean-
14 ing, "to see again" and "to look up" (s. MH, 295f.). ■ προεχειρίσατο aor. mid. προχειρίζομαι to take into one's hands beforehand, to plan, to purpose, to determine (RWP). γνῶναι aor. act. inf. γινώσκω. ἰδεῖν aor. inf. ὁράω. ἀκοῦσαι
15 aor. inf. ■ ἔσῃ fut. εἰμί. ἑώρακας perf. ὁράω. The perf. denotes a continuing effect on the subject that Paul had seen the Lord and this is what establishes him permanently as an apostle (BD,
16 176). ■ βάπτισαι aor. mid. imp. βαπτίζω to baptize, causative mid. "get yourself baptised" (RG, 808). ἀπόλουσαι aor. mid. imp. ἀπολούω to wash away. ἐπικαλεσάμενος aor. mid. part. ἐπικαλέω to call upon. The calling upon the Lord effects the washing away of sin.
17 ■ ὑποστρέψαντι aor. act. part. ὑποστρέφω to return. προσευχομένου pres. mid. part. προσεύχομαι to pray.
18 γενέσθαι aor. mid. inf. γίνομαι. ἔκστασις trance. ■ σπεῦσον aor. act. imp. σπεύδω to hurry. ἔξελθε aor. imp. ἐξέρχομαι to go out. ἐν τάχει quickly. παραδέξονται fut. mid.
19 παραδέχομαι to receive, to welcome. ■ ἤμην impf. εἰμί. φυλακίζων pres. part. φυλακίζω to put into prison. δέρων pres. act. part. δέρω to flay, to skin, to beat. πιστεύοντας pres. act.
20 part. ■ ἐξεχύννετο impf. pass. ἐκχύννω to pour out, to shed. The impf. pictures the continual act. ἐφεστώς perf. act. part. ἐφίστημι to stand by. συνευδοκῶν pres. part. συνευδοκέω to consent, to be pleased w. φυλάσσων pres. part. φυλάσσω to
21 guard, to watch. ἀναιρούντων pres. part. ἀναιρέω to kill. ■

ἐξαποστελῶ fut. ἐξαποστέλλω to send out, to send as an official representative w. the authority of the one sending (s. TDNT; CBB).

■ ἤκουον impf. ἀκούω. ἐπῆραν aor. ἐπαίρω to lift up. 22 αἴρε pres. imp. αἴρω to take away. καθῆκεν impf. καθήκω usually impersonal, "it comes to someone," "it is proper," "it is fitting." Verbs expressing obligation or necessity are used in the impf. when the obligation is not lived up to, or has not been met (RG, 886). ζῆν pres. inf. ζάω to live. ■ κραυγαζόντων pres. act. 23 part. κραυγάζω to scream, to cry out, gen. abs. ῥιπτούντων pres. act. part. ῥιπτέω to throw off. Perhaps here the meaning "to shake," "to wave" (LC). βαλλόντων pres. act. part. βάλλω to throw. ἀήρ air. ■ ἐκέλευσεν aor. κελεύω to command. 24 χιλίαρχος leader of a thousand men (s. Acts 21:31), tribune. He appears as the commander-in-chief in Jerusalem. Probably commander of a Cohors Italica whose officers were tribunes (HJP [NEE] I, 366; Sherwin-White, 155). εἰσάγεσθαι pres. pass. inf. εἰσάγω to lead in, to bring in. εἴπας aor. part. λέγω. (For the form of the aor., s. BD, 43.) ἀνετάζεσθαι aor. pass. inf. ἀνετάζω to examine. The word was used of government clerks whose business it was to examine documents and glue them into books (MM). Scourging was not a punishment but was considered to be the simplest method of finding out the truth or obtaining a confession. It was the legal method of examining a slave or alien (LC). ἐπιγνῷ aor. subj. ἐπιγινώσκω to recognize, to know. The prep. compound is directive (s. MH, 312). ἐπεφώνουν impf. ἐπιφωνέω to call to. ■ προέτειναν aor. 25 προτείνω to stretch forward, probably the technical term of tying up a person for a whipping (Bruce). ἱμάς strap, thong. The dat. could be either instrumental, "ticd w. straps," or purpose, "for the whip" (BAG; LC). ἑστῶτα perf. act. part. ἵστημι perf. to stand. ἀκατάκριτος uncondemned. ἔξεστιν it is lawful. μαστίζειν pres. act. inf. to whip, to scourge. ■ προσελθών aor. 26 act. part. προσέρχομαι to come to, to go to. ἀπήγγειλεν aor. ἀπαγγέλλω to report. ■ λέγε pres. imp. σύ "you," emphatic 27 position, a question of surprise (Meyer). ■ κεφάλαιον capital, 28 sum, gen. of price (BD, 97). πολιτεία citizenship. (For a discussion of Roman citizenship and Acts, s. Sherwin-White, 144–185; CC, 176.) ἐκτησάμην aor. mid. κτάομαι to obtain. γεγέννημαι perf. pass. γεννάω to bear, pass. to be born. Not to be taken in the sense of "to become" but indicates Paul's father was a Roman citizen and Paul was born w. this right (Sherwin-White, 151). Citizenship may have been proven by certificates on small wooden blocks or metal certificates as car-

29 ried by the soldiers (Sherwin-White, 148f.). ■ ἀπέστησαν aor.
    ἀφίστημι to stand away, to depart. μέλλοντες pres. act. part.
    ἐφοβήθη aor. pass. φοβέομαι to be afraid. ἐπιγνούς aor. act.
    part. ἐπιγινώσκω to recognize, to know. δεδεκώς perf. act.
    part. δέω to bind. Participle used in a periphrastic construction.
30 ■ βουλόμενος pres. mid. part. βούλομαι to will, to wish.
    γνῶναι aor. act. inf., s.v.14. τὸ τί κατηγορεῖται "of what he
    was accused." This is an explanation of the preceding word
    "certainty" (RWP). The article is used w. the indirect interrogra-
    tive making the clause substantival but does not change the
    meaning (MT, 182). ἔλυσεν aor. λύω to loose, to release.
    ἐκέλευσεν aor., s.v.24. συνελθεῖν aor. inf. συνέρχομαι to
    come together, to convene. καταγαγών aor. part. κατάγω to
    lead down. ἔστησεν aor. ἵστημι to place, to stand.

Ch. 23

1   ■ ἀτενίσας aor. act. part. ἀτενίζω to gaze, to look at
    intently. συνείδησις conscience (s. Rom. 2:15). πεπολίτευμαι
    perf. mid. πολιτεύομαι to live as a citizen, to live in the reli-
2   gious sense (Haenchen). ■ ἐπέταξεν aor. ἐπιτάσσω to com-
    mand, to charge. παρεστῶσιν perf. part. παρίστημι to stand
3   near or by someone. τύπτειν pres. inf. to strike, to hit. ■ εἶπεν
    aor. λέγω to say, to speak. μέλλω to be about to. Used w. the
    inf. to express the fut. A type of "predictive curse" (LC). τοῖχος
    wall. κεκονιαμένε perf. pass. part. voc. κονιάω to whitewash.
    The "whitewashed wall" contrasted the decent exterior w. the
    unclean contents (Bruce). κάθη pres. mid. 2nd sing. κάθημαι
    to sit. (For the form, s. BD, 50.) κρίνων pres. part. κρίνω to
    judge. παρανομῶν pres. part. παρανομέω to act contrary to
4   the law. τύπτεσθαι pres. pass. inf. ■ λοιδορεῖς pres. act. 2nd
5   sing. to abuse, to reproach, to heap abuse upon (TDNT). ■ ᾔδειν
    plperf. οἶδα. Perhaps Paul did not recognize the high priest
    because of weak eyesight or he spoke w. irony (Bruce).
    γέγραπται perf. pass. ἐρεῖς fut. λέγω. κακῶς adv. evil.
6   ■ γνούς aor. act. part. γινώσκω. ἔκραζεν impf. κράζω to
    scream. κρίνομαι pres. pass. (For the various legal terms used
    in Paul's trials, s. A.A. Trites, "The Importance of Legal Scenes
    and Language in the Book of Acts," Nov T [Oct. 1974], 278–
7   284.) ■ λαλοῦντος pres. act. part. gen. abs. ἐγένετο aor. mid.
    γίνομαι. στάσις sedition, revolution, riot. ἐσχίσθη aor. pass.
8   σχίζω to split, to divide. ■ εἶναι pres. inf. εἰμί. Infinitive used
9   in indirect assertion (RWP). ■ κραυγή scream. ἀναστάντες
    aor. act. part. ἀνίστημι to rise up. διεμάχοντο impf. mid.
    διαμάχομαι to fight, to fight it out. The prep. compound indi-

cates a fighting between, back and forth, fearlessly (RWP).
ἐλάλησεν aor. act. ■ γινομένης pres. mid. part. gen. abs. 10
φοβηθείς aor. pass. part. φοβέομαι to be afraid, to fear.
διασπασθῇ aor. pass. subj. διασπάω to tear into. (For the
force of the prep., s. MH, 302.) ἐκέλευσεν aor. καταβάν aor.
part. καταβαίνω to go down. ἁρπάσαι aor. act. inf. ἁρπάζω
to seize, to snatch, to take by force.

■ ἐπιοῦσα νύξ the following night. ἐπιστάς aor. part. 11
ἐφίστημι to come upon, to stand by. θάρσει pres. imp.
θαρσέω to be brave, to be courageous. διεμαρτύρω aor. mid.
διαμαρτύρομαι to testify, to give witness, to solemnly declare
(MH 302). δεῖ it is necessary. μαρτυρῆσαι aor. act. inf.
μαρτυρέω to be a witness.

■ γενομένης aor. mid. part. γίνομαι. ποιήσαντες aor. 12
part. συστροφή conspiracy, plot (s. LC). ἀνεθεμάτισαν aor.
ἀναθεματίζω. Used w. refl. pron. to place one's self under a
curse, to take a vow. (For the Jewish teaching on vows, s. M,
Nedarim.) φαγεῖν aor. inf. ἐσθίω to eat. πεῖν aor. inf. πίνω to
drink. ἀποκτείνωσιν aor. subj. ἀποκτείνω to kill. ■ πλείων 13
comp. πολύς. συνωμοσία conspiracy. ποιησάμενοι aor. mid.
part. ■ προσελθόντες aor. part. προσέρχομαι to come to. 14
ἀνάθεμα curse, that which is set aside for destruction (s.
TDNT). γεύσασθαι aor. mid. inf. γεύομαι to taste, to eat.
■ ἐμφανίσατε aor. imp. ἐμφανίζω to give information, to lay 15
information before. Here used in a semi-technical sense (LC).
ὅπως w. subj. to express purpose, in order that. καταγάγῃ aor.
subj. κατάγω to lead down. μέλλοντας pres. part. used w. ὡς
to give the alleged reason (RWP). διαγινώσκειν pres. act. inf.
to decide, to determine. A legal technical term here "to determine his case by thorough investigation" (BAG).
ἀκριβέστερον adv. comp. ἀκριβής exact, accurate. ἐγγίσαι
aor. act. inf. ἐγγίζω to be near, to draw near. ἀνελεῖν aor. inf.
ἀναιρέω to kill. ■ ἀκούσας aor. part. ἐνέδρα ambush. 16
παραγενόμενος aor. mid. part. παραγίνομαι to come, to arrive. Here either in the sense "having been present" or "having
arrived (at the barracks)" (Bruce). εἰσελθών aor. part.
εἰσέρχομαι to go in. ἀπήγγειλεν aor. ἀπαγγέλλω to report.
■ προσκαλεσάμενος aor. mid. part. προσκαλέω to sum- 17
mons. ἑκατοντάρχης centurion. ἄπαγε pres. imp. ἀπάγω to
lead out, to lead away. ἀπαγγεῖλαι aor. act. inf. ■ παραλαβών 18
aor. part. παραλαμβάνω to take along. ἤγαγειν aor. ἄγω to
lead, to bring. ἠρώτησεν aor. ἐρωτάω to question. ἀγαγεῖν
aor. inf. ἄγω. λαλῆσαι aor. inf. ■ ἐπιλαβόμενος aor. mid. 19
part. ἐπιλαμβάνω to take, to take hold of (w. gen.) so as to give

confidence to the youth (Bengel). ἀναχωρήσας aor. part.
ἀναχωρέω to go back, to withdraw. (For the prep. compound,
s. MH, 295.) ἐπυνθάνετο impf. mid. πυνθάνομαι to inquire,
20 inceptive impf. "he began to inquire." ■ συνέθεντο aor. mid.
συντίθημι to place together, to arrange, to agree. ἐρωτῆσαι
21 aor. inf. αὔριον tomorrow. ■ πεισθῇς aor. pass. subj. πείθω to
persuade, pass. to be persuaded, to consent, to obey. The aor.
subj. w. neg. indicates the forbidding or starting of an action not
in progress. ἐνεδρεύουσιν pres. act. to lie in ambush, to lie in
wait for. ἀνέλωσιν aor. subj. ἀναιρέω to kill. προσδεχόμενοι
pres. mid. part. προσδέχομαι to wait for. ἐπαγγελία consent.
The word often means promise but its original sense is "a favora-
22 ble message" (LC). ■ ἀπέλυσε aor. ἀπολύω to release.
παραγγείλας aor. act. part. παραγγέλλω to command, to
charge. ἐκλαλῆσαι aor. act. inf. ἐκλαλέω to speak out, to di-
vulge. Infinitive used in an indirect command. (For this construction and also the change to direct quotation, s. RG, 1046f.)
ἐνεφάνισας aor. ἐμφανίζω to report, to inform.
23   ■ ἑτοιμάσατε aor. imp. ἑτοιμάω to make ready.
πορευθῶσιν aor. pass. subj. πορεύομαι to go, to travel.
δεξιολάβος "taking (a spear) in the right hand." In military
phraseology the spear was always connected w. the right, as the
shield w. the left (MH, 273). The spearman, bowman, slinger, or
24 perhaps bodyguard (BAG). ■ κτῆνος animal, horses, or mules
(LC). παραστῆσαι aor. act. inf. παρίστημι to stand by, to
provide. ἐπιβιβάσαντες aor. part. ἐπιβιβάζω to cause to sit
upon, to mount. διασώσωσι aor. subj. διασῴζω to rescue, to
bring through safely. The prep. compound describes the carrying
of action through to a definite result (MH, 301). ἡγεμών gover-
25/26 nor. ■ γράψας aor. part. ■ κράτιστος most excellent, excellency, a term of address. χαίρειν pres. inf. to greet, "greetings."
27   ■ συλλημφθέντα aor. pass. part. συλλαμβάνω to arrest, to
seize. ἀναιρεῖσθαι pres. pass. inf. ἐξειλάμην aor. mid.
ἐξαιρέω to rescue, to take out. μαθών aor. act. part. μανθάνω
28 to learn. ■ βουλόμενος pres. mid. part. βούλομαι to will, to
wish. ἐπιγνῶναι aor. inf. ἐπιγινώσκω to recognize, to know.
ἐνεκάλουν impf. ἐγκαλέω w. dat. to accuse, "to call in" in a bad
sense; that is, calling a man in to accuse him (MH, 305).
29 κατήγαγον aor. κατάγω. ■ εὗρον aor. ἐγκαλούμενον pres.
30 pass. part. ζήτημα question. ἔγκλημα accusation. ■
μηνυθείσης aor. pass. part. μηνύω to disclose, to inform, to
report, gen. abs. ἔσεσθαι fut. inf. εἰμί. Infinitive used in indirect
discourse (s. RG, 877). ἐξαυτῆς at once. ἔπεμψα aor. πέμπω
to send, epistolary aor. (Bruce). κατήγορος accuser.

■ διατεταγμένον perf. pass. part. διατάσσω to com- 31
mand. ἀναλαβόντες aor. act. part. ἀναλαμβάνω to take up, to
conduct. ἤγαγον aor. ἄγω. ■ ἐπαύριον "on the following 32
(day)." ἐάσαντες aor. act. part. ἐάω to allow. ὑπέστρεψαν aor.
ὑποστρέφω to return. ■ ἀναδόντες aor. part. ἀναδίδωμι to 33
give up, to hand over. παρέστησαν aor. παρίστημι. ■ 34
ἀναγνούς aor. act. part. ἀναγινώσκω to read. ἐπερωτήσας
aor. part. ἐπερωτάω to question, to ask. ποῖος what kind of ?
ἐπαρχεία province. πυθόμενος aor. mid. part. πυνθάνομαι to
inquire, to learn by inquiring. ■ διακούσομαι fut. διακούω to 35
listen through, a legal term for "hold a hearing" (LC).
παραγένωνται aor. mid. subj. παραγίνομαι to arrive, to be
present. κελεύσας aor. part. πραιτώριον praetorium, originally the headquarters of the praetor or military commander
then the official residence of the Roman governor of the province. The word is used here of a palace in Caesarea, built by
Herod the Great, which served as a residence for the procurator
(Bruce). φυλάσσεσθαι pres. pass. inf. φυλάσσω to guard.

Ch. 24

■ κατέβη aor. καταβαίνω to go down. ῥήτωρ public 1
speaker, orator, a speaker in court, attorney, a lawyer acquainted
w. Roman and Jewish law (Haenchen). ἐνεφάνισαν aor.
ἐμφανίζω to inform, to bring an accusation, to indict. ἡγεμών
governor. (For the legal aspects and accuracy of this section, s.
Sherwin-White, 48–70; s. also BC, V, 306–338.) ■ κληθέντος 2
aor. pass. part. καλέω to call, to summons, gen. abs. ἤρξατο aor.
mid. ἄρχομαι to begin. κατηγορεῖν pres. act. inf. to accuse, to
bring a legal accusation. τυγχάνοντες pres. act. part. τυγχάνω
(w. gen.) to happen to, to happen, to come about. διόρθωμα
reform. γινομένων pres. mid. part., gen. abs. πρόνοια forethought, foresight. ■ πάντῃ adv. in every way, in every place, 3
everywhere. The two words used together are rhetorical allitera-
tion (Bruce). κράτιστος most excellent. ■ πλείων comp. 4
πολύς "any more," "any longer." ἐγκόπτω to hinder or perhaps here to make weary, to delay (LC; TDNT). ἀκοῦσαι aor.
act. inf. συντόμως briefly. ἐπιείκεια mildness, moderation,
clemency (TDNT; NTW, 38). ■ εὑρόντες aor. part. λοιμός 5
pest, plague, pestilence. The point is to create the right atmosphere—Paul was a political, not a theological offender (LC; s.
also Sherwin-White, 50f.). κινοῦντα pres. part. κινέω to incite.
οἰκουμένη world, the inhabited earth. πρωτοστάτης ringlead-
er, used of a man in the front rank (Bruce). αἵρεσις party, sect.
■ ἐπείρασεν aor. πειράζω to attempt, to try. βεβηλῶσαι aor. 6

inf. βεβηλόω to profane, to desecrate. ἐκρατήσαμεν aor. κρατέω to seize, to arrest. A slight euphemism for mob lynch-
8 ing! (Williams). ■ δυνήσῃ fut. mid. 2nd sing. ἀνακρίνας aor. act. part. ἀνακρίνω to examine. The word often is used of the interrogation of a prisoner (LC). ἐπιγνῶναι aor. act. inf. ἐπιγινώσκω to recognize, to know, "to get at the facts"
9 (Bruce). ■ συνεπέθεντο aor. mid. συνεπιτίθημι to join in the attack, to attack together. φάσκοντες pres. act. part. φάσκω to say, to speak, to insist. The verb seems often to mean an asser-tion against a challenge (LC). ἔχειν pres. act. inf. to have, here, "to be."
10   ■ ἀπεκρίθη aor. pass. ἀποκρίνομαι to answer. νεύσαντος aor. part. νεύω to wave, to motion w. the hand, gen. abs. ὄντα part. εἰμί. ἐπιστάμενος pres. mid. part. ἐπίσταμαι
11 to know. εὐθύμως w. good courage, cheerfully. ■ δυναμένου pres. mid. part. πλείους comp. nom. pl. (for the form, s. BD, 16), more, here "more than." (For the construction here, s. RG, 666.) ἀνέβην aor. ἀναβαίνω to go up. προσκυνήσων fut. part. προσκυνέω to worship. Future part. used to express purpose.
12 ■ εὗρον aor. διαλεγόμενον pres. mid. part. διαλέγομαι to discuss, to teach, to dispute (s. Acts 17:2). ποιοῦντα pres. act.
13 part. ■ παραστῆσαι aor. act. inf. παρίστημι to place along-side, to prove, to provide proof, to substantiate, "to put evidence
14 alongside of argument" (LC). ■ ὁμολογέω to confess, to admit. πατρῷος ancestral. Paul insisted that he had not forsaken the faith of his fathers (Bruce). πιστεύων pres. act. part. γεγραμμένοις perf. pass. part. The perf. emphasizes the perma-
15 nent state of authority of that which was written. ■ μέλλειν pres. act. inf. to be about to. Infinitive used in an indirect asser-tion. ἔσεσθαι fut. inf. εἰμί. (For the construction w. the fut. inf.
16 as being closer to classical Gr., s. MT, 79; MKG, 308.) ■ ἐν τούτῳ "therefore," the causal or instrumental use of the prep. (s. BG, 40). ἀσκέω to exercise, to take pains, to drill. The word has a note of moral strictness about it, without the later sense of asceticism (Bruce). ἀπρόσκοπος without offense, unharmed, uninjured. In the papyri it is used to refer to the maintenance of an unspoiled record in one's own self-judgment (LC). διὰ
17 παντός "always." ■ ποιήσων fut. part. The fut. part. is used to express purpose. παρεγενόμην aor. mid. παραγίνομαι to
18 come. προσφορά offering. ■ ἐν αἷς "in which," referring to the offerings of v.17. ἡγνισμένον perf. pass. part. ἁγνίζω to sancti-
19 fy, to dedicate, to purify. ■ τινὲς δὲ ἀπὸ τῆς Ἀσίας "but some of the Jews from Asia." No verb appears for these words. Paul stops to explain that they are not here, a Pauline anacoluthon

330

(RWP). The Roman law was very strong against accusers who abandoned their charges (Sherwin-White, 52). ἔδει impf. δεῖ it is necessary. ἔχοιεν pres. opt. The opt. is used to express the condition of a fourth-class conditional clause indicating the remoteness of the hypothesis (RG, 1020f.). The conditional clause is mixed w. the apodosis of the second class; that is, contrary to fact (RG, 1022). ■ αὐτοί οὗτοι "these themselves." 20 εἰπάτωσαν aor. imp. λέγω. στάντος aor. act. part. ἵστημι to stand, gen. abs. ■ ἤ "than," "what else than," "except" (RWP). 21 ἐκέκραξα aor. ἐκκράζω to scream out. ἐστώς perf. act. part. ἵστημι. κρίνομαι pres. pass.

■ ἀνεβάλετο aor. ἀναβάλλομαι to postpone. A legal 22 technical term to adjourn a trial (BAG). ἀκριβέστερον adv. comp. The comp. is used in the sense of elative superl. "knowing for certain" (BG, 49). εἰδώς perf. part. οἶδα. εἴπας aor. act. part. λέγω. καταβῇ aor. sub. καταβαίνω to go down, to come down. διαγνώσομαι fut. mid. διαγινώσκω to examine, to determine, to decide. ■ διαταξάμενος aor. mid. part. 23 διατάσσω to command. τηρεῖσθαι pres. pass. inf. τηρέω to guard. ἄνεσις relaxing, indulgence, privilege, "free custody." He was still bound but the indulgence involved food and the visits of friends and the remission from the severe form of custody (EGT). ὑπηρετεῖν pres. inf. to minister to.

■ παραγενόμενος aor. mid. part. παραγίνομαι. 24 μετεπέμψατο aor. mid. μεταπέμπομαι to send for, to summons. ἤκουσεν aor. ἀκούω. ■ δικαιοσύνη righteousness, jus- 25 tice in the widest sense, the rendering to everyone his due. (Alex.). ἐγκράτεια self-control, the control of the passions and desires, often used regarding the controlling of sexual desires (TDNT). κρίμα judgment. μέλλοντος pres. part. ἔμφοβος terrified, "being struck w. fear, trembling." Truth makes Felix fear even a prisoner in bonds (Bengel). γενόμενος aor. mid. part. γίνομαι. τὸ νῦν ἔχον (pres. part.) "as for the present or holding the now," acc. of time (RWP). πορεύου pres. mid. imp. πορεύομαι to go. μεταλαβών aor. act. part. μεταλαμβάνω to receive, to have. An idiom meaning "to have spare time." The prep. compound implies a different or subsequent occasion (LC). μετακαλέσομαι fut. mid. μετακαλέω to send for. ■ ἅμα at 26 the same time. ἐλπίζων pres. act. part. χρῆμα pl. money. δοθήσεται fut. pass. δίδωμι. πυκνότερον adv. comp. either in the comp. sense "the more often" (because of his financial expectations) or used as an elative superl. "very often" (Bruce). μεταπεμπόμενος pres. mid. part. ὡμίλει impf. ὁμιλέω to converse w., to talk to. The impf. pictures the repeated action.

27   ■ διετία two years. πληρωθείσης aor. pass. part. πληρόω
to fulfill, to complete. ἔλαβεν aor. λαμβάνω. διάδοχος succes-
sor. (For a summary of the events during the rule of Felix and
Festus and the events leading to the appointment of Festus, s.
JPF, I, 365–370; BC, V, 464–467.) θέλων pres. part. χάριτα
acc. sing. favor. (For the form of the acc., s. BD, 27.)
καταθέσθαι aor. mid. inf. κατατίθημι to lay down, to grant
or do someone a favor. κατέλιπε aor. καταλείπω to leave
behind, to leave. δεδεμένον perf. pass. part. δέω to bind.

Ch. 25

1   ■ ἐπιβάς aor. part. ἐπιβαίνω to enter, to come into, to set
foot upon. ἐπαρχεία province, the district governed by a prefect
2   (LC). ἀνέβη aor. ἀναβαίνω to go up. ■ ἐνεφάνισαν aor.
ἐμφανίζω to make known, to bring charges against (s. Acts
3   24:1). παρεκάλουν impf. παρακαλέω to urge. ■ αἰτούμενοι
pres. mid. part. αἰτέω to ask. μεταπέμψηται aor. mid. subj.
μεταπέμπομαι to summons, subj. used w. particle to express
purpose. ἐνέδρα ambush, plot (s. Acts 23:16). ποιοῦντες pres.
4   act. part. ἀνελεῖν aor. act. inf. ἀναιρέω to kill. ■ ἀπεκρίθη aor.
pass. ἀποκρίνομαι to answer. τηρεῖσθαι pres. pass. inf. τηρέω
to guard, to watch over. Infinitive used in indirect discourse. εἰς
"in," "at." (For the use of the prep. in a local sense without
expressing motion, s. BD, 110f.; BG, 33f.) μέλλειν pres. inf. to
be about to. Infinitive used in indirect discourse. ἐκπορεύεσθαι
5   pres. mid. inf. ■ οἱ ἐν ὑμῖν δυνατοί "the men of power or
influence among you." A phrase used frequently for the Jewish
notables. The word may include the ability to speak as well as
the prestige of position (LC). συγκαταβάντες aor. act. part.
συγκαταβαίνω to come down together, to go down together.
ἄτοπος not in place, improper. κατηγορείτωσαν pres. imp.
κατηγορέω to accuse, to bring a charge against.
6   ■ διατρίψας aor. act. part. διατρίβω to spend, to stay.
πλείων comp. πολύς. καταβάς aor. part. καταβαίνω to go
down. καθίσας aor. part. καθίζω to sit down, to take one's seat.
βῆμα judge's bench, judgment seat. This was a necessary for-
mality in order that his decision might have legal effect (Bruce).
ἐκέλευσεν aor. κελεύω to command. ἀχθῆναι aor. pass. inf.
7   ἄγω to lead. ■ περιέστησαν aor. περιΐστημι to stand around.
καταβεβηκότες perf. act. part. καταβαίνω. βαρύς heavy,
weighty, serious. αἰτίωμα charges. Used in the papyri in the
sense of "blame" (MM). καταφέροντες pres. act. part.
καταφέρω to bring against, to bring down upon. ἴσχυον impf.
ἰσχύω to be strong, to be able. ἀποδεῖξαι aor. act. inf.

ἀποδείκνυμι to prove, to demonstrate. ■ ἀπολογουμένου 8
pres. mid. part. ἀπολογέομαι to defend one's self, gen. abs.
ἥμαρτον aor. ἁμαρτάνω to sin, to offend. ■ θέλων pres. part. 9
καταθέσθαι aor. mid. inf. κατατίθημι (s. Acts 24:27).
ἀποκριθείς aor. pass. part. ἀναβάς aor. act. part. ἀναβαίνω.
κριθῆναι aor. pass. inf. κρίνω to judge. ■ ἑστώς perf. part. 10
ἵστημι to stand. δεῖ it is necessary. κρίνεσθαι pres. pass. inf.
ἠδίκηκα perf. ἀδικέω to do that which is not right, to commit
a crime. κάλλιον adv. comp. καλός. Comparative used as an
clative superl. "very well." ■ ἀδικῶ pres. ind. act. "I am guilty," 11
an Attic use (Bruce). The perf. (in v.10) is used for individual
trespasses, the pres. only for the general result (BD, 168).
πέπραχα perf. act. πράσσω to do, to commit. παραιτέομαι
"I beg myself off," an idiomatic use of Hellenistic Gr. (LC),
conative pres. "I am not trying to beg myself off " (s. SMT, 8).
ἀποθανεῖν aor. act. inf. ἀποθνήσκω to die. (For the inf. used
w. the article as the object of the verb, s. MT, 140; IBG, 127.)
χαρίσασθαι aor. mid. inf. χαρίζομαι to give freely or graciously as a favor, to pardon. ἐπικαλέομαι to call upon, to
appeal. According to the Roman right of provocatio a Roman
citizen had the right to be tried before Caesar. (For a discussion
of this right and its relation to Acts and Luke's historical accuracy, s. Sherwin-White, 57–70.)

■ διαγενομένων aor. mid. part. διαγίνομαι to pass by, to 13
intervene, gen. abs. κατήντησαν aor. καταντάω to come
down, to arrive. ἀσπασάμενοι aor. mid. part. ἀσπάζομαι to
greet. The greeting and the arrival were at the same time (Haenchen). ■ πλείους comp. s.v.6. διέτριβον impf. διατρίβω s.v.6. 14
ἀνέθετο aor. mid. ἀνατίθημι to lay before, to communicate w.
a view to consultation (MM). καταλελειμμένος perf. pass.
part. καταλείπω to leave behind. ■ γενομένου aor. mid. part. 15
γίνομαι gen. abs. ἐνεφάνισαν aor., s.v.2. καταδίκη sentence,
condemnation. ■ ἀπεκρίθην aor. pass., s.v.4. 16
κατηγορούμενος pres. pass. part., s.v.5. ἔχοι pres. opt. The opt.
is used in a temporal clause but is due to indirect discourse (RG,
970). τόπος place, opportunity. λάβοι aor. opt. λαμβάνω. ■ 17
συνελθόντων aor. part. συνέρχομαι to come together. ἐνθάδε
here. ἀναβολή delay, postponement. ποιησάμενος aor. mid.
part. ἑξῆς "on the next (day)." καθίσας aor. part. ἐκέλευσα
aor. s.v.6. ἀχθῆναι aor. pass. inf., s.v.6. ■ σταθέντες aor. part. 18
ἵστημι to stand. ἔφερον impf. φέρω to bring. ὧν rel. pron. gen.
pl. (For the construction here, s. RG, 719.) ὑπενόουν impf.
ὑπονοέω to suppose. ■ δεισιδαιμονία superstitition. 19
τεθνηκότος perf. act. part. ἀποθνήσκω to die, perf. to be dead.

ἔφασκεν impf. φάσκω to say, to affirm, to insist (s. Acts 24:9).
20 ζῆν pres. inf. to live. ■ ἀπορούμενος pres. mid. part.
ἀπορέομαι to be perplexed, to be in doubt which way to turn
(RWP). βούλοιτο pres. mid. opt. βούλομαι to wish, to will, opt.
21 in indirect discourse. κρίνεσθαι pres. pass. inf., s.v.10. ■
ἐπικαλεσαμένου aor. mid. part., s.v.11, gen. abs. τηρηθῆναι
aor. pass. inf., s.v.4. τηρεῖσθαι pres. pass. inf., s.v.4. ἀναπέμψω
fut. or aor. subj. ἀναπέμπω to send up, to send to a superior.
It indicates the sending of a prisoner to a superior tribunal (LC).
22 ■ ἐβουλόμην impf. mid. "I should like" (Bruce). ἀκοῦσαι aor.
act. inf. ἀκούσῃ fut.
23   ■ ἐλθόντος aor. part. gen. abs. φαντασία pomp, pagean-
try. εἰσελθόντων aor. part. εἰσέρχομαι to go into.
ἀκροατήριον audience chamber, doubtless in Herod's praetorium (Bruce). κατ' ἐξοχήν prominence "par excellence." ■
24 κελεύσαντος aor. act. part. ἤχθη aor. pass. ἄγω. ■
συμπαρόντες pres. part. συμπάρειμι to be present together.
θεωρεῖτε pres. imp. θεωρέω to see, to view. ἐνέτυχον aor.
ἐντυγχάνω to meet, to approach, to appeal, to petition.
25 βοῶντες pres. act. part. βοάω to scream, to yell. ■
κατελαβόμην aor. mid. καταλαμβάνω to seize, mid. to grasp,
26 to understand. πεπραχέναι perf. inf., s.v.11. ἔκρινα aor. ■
ἀσφαλής certain. γράψαι aor. act. inf. προήγαγον aor.
προάγω to lead before. μάλιστα especially. σχῶ aor. subj.
27 ἔχω. γράψω aor. subj. ■ ἄλογος unreasonable, without reason.
πέμποντα pres. part. σημᾶναι aor. inf. σημαίνω to signify, to
indicate.

Ch. 26

1   ■ ἐπιτρέπεται pres. pass. ἐπιτρέπω to allow, "it is allowed for you." (For the impersonal pass., s. BD, 164.) The
aoristic pres. used of an action coincident in time w. the act of
speaking, and conceived of as a simple event (SMT, 9). ἐκτείνας
aor. act. part. ἐκτείνω to stretch out. ἀπελογεῖτο impf. mid.
ἀπολογέομαι to defend one's self, inceptive impf. "he began to
2 make his defense." ■ ἥγημαι perf. mid. ἡγέομαι to consider,
to regard. The perf. here carries the sense of the pres. "I consider" (BD, 176). μακάριος happy (s. TDNT). μέλλων pres. part.
3 μέλλω to be about to. Used w. the inf. to express fut. ■ μάλιστα
especially. This may go w. the whole following phrase, as giving
a special reason for Paul's pleasure or only w. the following word
"because you are specially expert" (Bruce). γνώστης one who
knows, expert. (For material regarding Agrippa II, s. HJP [NEE]
I, 471–483; JPF, I, 300–304.) ὄντα pres. part. εἰμί.

μακροθύμως adv. patiently. ἀκοῦσαι aor. inf. ■ μὲν οὖν "well, 4
then" (Bruce). βίωσις manner of life. νεότης youth. ἀρχή beginning, explanatory of preceding—the commencement of his
training, which was not only amongst his own nation, but also
especially at Jerusalem (EGT). γενομένην aor. mid. part.
γίνομαι. ἴσασι perf. act. 3rd per. pl. οἶδα. (For the use of the
old form instead of the vernacular Hellenistic, s. MH, 221.) ■ 5
προγινώσκοντες pres. act. part. προγινώσκω to know before,
to know previously. ἄνωθεν from the beginning, for a long time.
The word deals w. a condition now existent and of long standing
(LC). θέλωσι pres. act. subj. ἀκριβέστατος superl. ἀκριβής
accurate, strict. The true superl. force "strictest" (Bruce).
θρησκεία rite, worship. It indicates the practical side of religion, its customs (LC). ἔζησα aor. ζάω to live. ■ ἔστηκα perf. 6
ἵστημι perf. to stand. κρινόμενος pres. pass. part. κρίνω to
judge. ■ δωδεκάφυλον twelve tribes. ἐκτένεια earnestly. Used 7
in the papyri w. the meaning "effort" (MM). λατρεῦον pres.
part. λατρεύω to worship, to serve. καταντῆσαι aor. act. inf.
καταντάω to go down, to arrive. ■ ἄπιστος unbelievable, in- 8
credible. κρίνεται pres. pass. εἰ "that." ■ ἔδοξα aor. δοκέω to 9
seem, to think. ἐμαυτῷ "myself." The use of the refl. pron.
strengthens the subject of the sentence (Haenchen). δεῖ it is
necessary. ἐναντίος in opposition to. πρᾶξαι aor. act. inf.
πράσσω to do. ■ ἐποίησα aor. κατέκλεισα aor. κατακλείω 10
to shut up, to shut down like a trap door (RWP). λαβών aor.
part. λαμβάνω. ἀναιρουμένων pres. pass. part. ἀναιρέω to
kill, gen. abs. κατήνεγκα aor. καταφέρω to bring down, to cast
down. Used w. the following word "to cast down my pebble" (a
black one). The ancient Greeks used white pebbles for acquittal,
black ones for condemnation (RWP). ψῆφος pebble. ■ τιμωρῶν 11
pres. part. τιμωρέω to punish. The synagogue punishment of
scourging is probably intended (Haenchen). ἠνάγκαζον impf.
ἀναγκάζω to force, to compel, the conative impf. "I tried to
compel them." He does not say that he succeeded in making
them blaspheme (Bruce). περισσῶς exceeding, extreme.
ἐμμαινόμενος pres. mid. part. ἐμμαίνομαι to be enraged, here
"being furiously enraged at them" (BAG). ἐδίωκον impf. διώκω
to hunt, to pursue, to persecute.
   ■ ἐν οἷς "under these circumstances" (Bruce). 12
πορευόμενος pres. mid. part. πορεύομαι to go, to travel.
ἐπιτροπή permission, w. the order, commission. Paul was a
commissary (Bengel). ■ βασιλεῦ vocative, "O king!" 13
οὐρανόθεν from heaven. περιλάμψαν aor. act. part.
περιλάμπω to shine around. ■ καταπεσόντων aor. act. part. 14

335

καταπίπτω to fall down. *σκληρός* difficult. *κέντρον* goad. A sharp-pointed stick used to prod an ox at the plow (LC).

15/16 *λακτίζειν* pres. act. inf. to kick. ■ *εἶπα* aor. *λέγω*. ■ *ἀνάστηθι* aor. act. imp. *ἀνίστημι* to rise up, to arise. *στῆθι* aor. act. imp. *ἵστημι* to stand. *ὤφθην* aor. pass. *ὁράω* to see, pass. to appear to. *προχειρίσασθαι* aor. mid. inf. *προχειρίζω* to determine,

17 to appoint (s. Acts 22:14). *ὀφθήσομαι* fut. pass. *ὁράω*. ■ *ἐξαιρούμενος* pres. mid. part. *ἐξαιρέω* to rescue, to take out, to choose. *ἀποστέλλω* to send as an authoritative representa-

18 tive (s. TDNT). ■ *ἀνοῖξαι* aor. act. inf. *ἀνοίγω* to open, inf. of purpose. *ἐπιστρέψαι* aor. act. inf. *ἐπιστρέφω* to turn, inf. of purpose but subordinate and explanatory of the previous inf. (s. EGT). *λαβεῖν* aor. act. inf. *λαμβάνω* to take, to receive. Again, subordinate to the previous inf. expressing the final result aimed at (EGT). *κλῆρος* share, part, portion, inheritance. *ἡγιασμένοις* perf. pass. part. *ἁγιάζω* to sanctify. The perf. emphasizes the state or condition.

19 ■ *ὅθεν* therefore. This rel. adv. gathers up all that Paul had said (RWP). *ἐγενόμην* aor. mid. *γίνομαι*. *ἀπειθής* disobedi-

20 ent. *ὀπτασία* vision. ■ *ἀπήγγελλον* impf. *ἀπαγγέλλω* to pro-

21 claim. *πράσσοντας* pres. act. part. ■ *συλλαβόμενοι* aor. mid. part. *συλλαμβάνω* to seize. *ἐπειρῶντο* impf. mid. *πειράομαι* to try, to attempt, conative impf. emphasizing the unsuccessful attempt. *διαχειρίσασθαι* aor. mid. inf. *διαχειρίζομαι* to take

22 in hand, to lay hands on, to kill. ■ *ἐπικουρία* aid, help. *τυχών* aor. act. part. *τυγχάνω* (w. gen.) to obtain. *ἔστηκα* perf. act. *ἵστημι* to stand. It emphasizes Paul's stability and fidelity (RWP). *μαρτυρόμενος* pres. mid. part. *μαρτύρομαι* to wit-

23 ness, to testify. *ἐλάλησαν* aor. ■ *παθητός* suffer, subject to suffering, capable of suffering (s. BD, 36; RG, 157).

24 ■ *ἀπολογουμένου* pres. mid. part. gen. abs. *μαίνῃ* pres. ind. mid. 2nd per. sing. *μαίνομαι* to be mad, to be out of one's

25 mind. *περιτρέπει* pres. ind. act. to turn, to turn around. ■ *σωφροσύνη* sobriety, soundness of mind, rational. It indicates the condition of an entire command over the passions and de- sires (s. Trench, *Synonyms*, 69f.). Paul says he is speaking words which are understandable and capable of being proven, those

26 which do not have to do w. ecstasy (TDNT). ■ *παρρησιαζόμενος* pres. mid. part. *παρρησιάζομαι* to speak openly, to speak boldly, to speak freely. *λανθάνειν* pres. inf. to be hidden, to escape notice. The pres. indicates that Paul regards the whole course of events as still unfinished, and believes that Agrippa is watching it (LC). Infinitive used in indirect discourse after the verb "I am persuaded." *γωνία* corner. *πεπραγμένον*

perf. pass. part. πράσσω. The perf. indicates the abiding result.
■ ἐν ὀλίγῳ "in a short time," "rapidly" (s. LC). πείθεις pres. 28
ind. act. 2nd sing. to persuade. ποιῆσαι aor. act. inf. to make,
to do, "in short, you are trying to persuade me to act the Christian" (Bruce). ■ εὐξαίμην aor. opt. mid. εὔχομαι to wish, to 29
pray, potential opt. used in the conclusion of an unexpressed
fourth-class conditional clause expressing what would happen on
the fulfillment of some supposed condition (s. MT, 121f.; RG,
1021). καί ... καί "both ... and." The phrase here may mean
"w. few or many words" (Williams) or "concerning both small
and great" (BG, 41). ἀκούοντας pres. act. part. γενέσθαι aor.
mid. inf. γίνομαι. παρεκτός except.

■ ἀνέστη aor. ἀνίστημι to stand up. συγκαθήμενοι pres. 30
mid. part. συγκάθημαι to sit together, to sit w. ■ 31
ἀναχωρήσαντες aor. act. part. ἀναχωρέω to retire, to depart.
ἐλάλουν impf. The impf. describes the eager conversation of the
dignitaries about Paul's wonderful speech (RWP). ■ 32
ἀπολελύσθαι perf. pass. inf. ἀπολύω to release, to free.
ἐδύνατο impf. mid. ἐπεκέκλητο plperf. ind. mid. ἐπικαλέω to
appeal, to call upon. Expresses more than the aor. would have
done; Paul's appeal to Caesar was not a mere act in the past, but
had put him in a definite position in the eyes of the law (Bruce).

Ch. 27

■ ἐκρίθη aor. pass. κρίνω to judge, to decide, to determine. 1
ἀποπλεῖν pres. act. inf. to sail. (For the use of the inf. w. the
article in the gen., s. RG, 1067f.) παρεδίδουν impf.
παραδίδωμι to deliver over. δεσμώτης prisoner. σπεῖρα cohort. Σεβαστός worthy of reverence, Augusta, emperor. An
honorary title frequently given to auxiliary troops (BAG; BC, V,
443f.; HJP [NEE], I, 364). ■ ἐπιβάντες aor. act. part. 2
ἐπιβαίνω to embark, to go aboard. μέλλοντι pres. part. μέλλω
to be about to. Used w. inf. to express the fut. ὄντος pres. part.
εἰμί gen. abs. ■ κατήχθημεν aor. pass. to come down, to land. 3
κατάγω adv. humanely, kindly. χρησάμενος aor. mid. part.
χράομαι (w. dat.) to use, to deal w., to show to. ἐπέτρεψεν aor.
ἐπιτρέπω to allow. πορευθέντι aor. pass. part. πορεύομαι to
go. ἐπιμέλεια attention, care. τυχεῖν aor. act. inf. τυγχάνω (w.
gen.) to obtain, to receive. Infinitive expressing purpose. ■ 4
κακεῖθεν "and from there." ἀναχθέντες aor. pass. part.
ἀνάγω. ὑπεπλεύσαμεν aor. ὑποπλέω to sail under, to sail by
the side of an island in such a way that the island protects the
ship from the wind (BAG). ἄνεμος wind. The prevailing wind
through the summer months was west or northwest so the ship

sailed east and north of the island (Bruce; for the various winds,
5 s. BC, V, 338–344). ἐναντίος contrary, against. ■ πέλαγος
open sea. διαπλεύσαντες aor. act. part. διαπλέω to sail across.
6 κατήλθαμεν aor. κατέρχομαι to come down. ■ εὑρών aor.
act. part. πλέον pres. act. part. n. sing. ἐνεβίβασεν aor.
ἐμβιβάζω to cause to enter, to put on board. The ship they got
on seems to have been a corn ship. Egypt was the chief granary
of Rome and the corn trade between Rome and Egypt was of the
7 greatest importance (Bruce). ■ ἱκανός many. βραδυπλοοῦντες
pres. act. part. βραδυπλοέω to sail slowly. μόλις w. difficulty.
γενόμενοι aor. mid. part. γίνομαι. προσεῶντος pres. act. part.
8 προσεάω to permit to go farther. ■ παραλεγόμενοι pres. mid.
part. παραλέγω to coast along, doubtless by hugging the shore,
and using every breath of land breeze they managed to creep
slowly along (LC). καλούμενον pres. pass. part. λιμήν harbor,
port, here "Fair Havens," a small bay protected by islands, but
was not a very good winter harbor (Bruce).
9   ■ διαγενομένου aor. mid. part. διαγίνομαι to come in
between, to intervene, to pass. ἐπισφαλής dangerous. πλοῦς
voyage, navigation. A voyage after the middle of September was
thought risky and after December 11th dangerous (Williams).
νηστεία Fast. The Fast was the Day of Atonement. In A.D. 59
the Fast was on October 5th and Luke indicates it was more
dangerous than ever (Bruce; s. also LC). παρεληλυθέναι perf.
act. inf. παρέρχομαι to pass by. παρῄνει impf. παραινέω to
warn, to offer advice. The impf. pictures the continual action.
10 ■ ὕβρις injury. The word is used of a loss at sea (Williams).
ζημία loss. φορτίον freight. ἔσεσθαι fut. inf. εἰμί. (For the use
11 of the fut. inf. in this construction, s. MKG, 308.) ■ κυβερνήτης
pilot, the officer responsible for its safe navigation and for the
discipline of the crew (LC). ναύκληρος captain. He was a merchant shipowner, who usually acted as captain of his own ship
(Bruce; PTR, 324f.). ἐπείθετο impf. mid. πείθω to yield, to
persuade, mid. to be persuaded, to obey. λεγομένοις pres. pass.
12 part. ■ ἀνεύθετος unsuitable. ὑπάρχοντος pres. act. part.
ὑπάρχω to exist, to be, gen. abs. παραχειμασία wintering.
πλείονες comp. πολλοί. ἔθεντο aor. mid. τίθημι to place, to
put, here "to take counsel," "to give counsel." ἀναχθῆναι aor.
pass. inf. ἀνάγω. δύναιντο pres. opt. mid. used in a condition
of the fourth class w. the idea of purpose implied and indirect
discourse (RWP). καταντήσαντες aor. act. part. καταντάω to
come, to arrive. παραχειμάσαι aor. act. inf. παραχειμάζω to
spend the winter. βλέποντα pres. act. part. λίψ southwest wind.
χῶρος northwest wind (s. BC, V, 338–344).

■ ὑποπνεύσαντος aor. act. part. ὑποπνέω to blow under, 13
to blow softly, gently. νότος south wind. δόξαντες aor. act. part.
δοκέω to suppose, to seem, to appear to. κεκρατηκέναι perf.
act. inf. κρατέω to seize, to obtain. ἄραντες aor. part. αἴρω to
lift up, to take up, "to weigh anchor." ἆσσον comp. nearer.
παρελέγοντο impf. mid. παραλέγω (s.v.8). ■ ἔβαλεν aor. 14
βάλλω to throw, to dash, to rush. Here in this context "their
rush down from it," that is, from Crete (Bruce; for the use of the
prep. w. gen. meaning "down from," s. RG, 606). τυφωνικός
tempestuous. The word refers to the whirling motion of the
clouds and sea caused by the meeting of opposite currents of air
like a typhoon (Bruce). (For adjectives w. this suffix meaning
"pertaining to," "w. the characteristic of," s. MH, 378.)
εὐρακύλων northeast wind, Euraquilo (s. BC, V, 344). ■ 15
συναρπασθέντος aor. pass. part. συναρπάζω to seize violently. It was as if the ship was seized by a great monster (RWP).
δυναμένου pres. mid. part. ἀντοφθαλμεῖν pres. act. inf., lit.
"facing the eye," to face into. Perhaps the origin of the phrase
lay in the custom of putting an eye on each side of the bow of
the ship (Williams). ἐπιδόντες aor. act. part. ἐπιδίδωμι to give
way to. ἐφερόμεθα impf. pass. φέρω to carry, here "we were
being carried," "we were being driven." ■ νησίον little island. 16
(For the possibility that some nouns w. this ending do not have
a dimin. meaning, s. MH, 340ff.) ὑποδραμόντες aor. act. part.
ὑποτρέχω to run under; that is, for protection against the wind.
(For the purpose of this maneuver, s. PTR, 328f.) ἰσχύσαμεν
aor. ἰσχύω to be able. περικρατής having power, bringing in
command. Used here w. the inf. "to get the boat under control"
(BAG). γενέσθαι aor. mid. inf. γίνομαι. σκάφη dinghy, a
small boat which was sometimes towed, sometimes kept on
deck, used for landing or for pulling the ship's head around.
(LC). ■ βοήθεια help, pl. helps, tackle. It means either ropes or 17
sails or perhaps the maneuvers dictated by the professional skill
of the sailors (LC). ἐχρῶντο impf. mid. χράομαι to use.
ὑποζωννύντες pres. act. part. ὑποζώννυμι to undergird, to
brace. A nautical technical term used of securing the ship. (For
the various methods which were possibly used in securing the
ship, s. BC, V, 345–354.) φοβούμενοι pres. mid. part.
φοβέομαι to be afraid, to fear. μή "lest" (used after a verb of
fear). ἐκπέσωσιν aor. act. subj. ἐκπίπτω nautical technical
term to drift off course, to run aground (BAG). χαλάσαντες
aor. part. χαλάω to lower, to let down. σκεῦος gear. The phrase
"lowering the gear" could mean either lowering the sail or drop-
ping the sea anchor or lowering such gear such as sails, rigging,

18 anchors, cables, etc. (s. Bruce). ■ σφοδρῶς adv. very, exceedingly. χειμαζομένων pres. pass. part. χειμάζω to expose to bad
weather, to toss in a storm. ἑξῆς "on the following (day)."
ἐκβολή throwing out, jettisoning. ἐποιοῦντο impf. mid. inceptive impf. "they began to make an ejection." A technical term
19 for throwing the cargo overboard (LC). ■ αὐτόχειρ "with their
own hands." This emphatic word marks a climax of precaution-
ary operations (Bruce). σκευή gear, presumably spare sails and
20 tackle (LC). ἔρριψαν aor. ρίπτω to throw, to hurl. ■ ἄστρον
star. ἐπιφαινόντων pres. act. part. ἐπιφαίνω to appear.
χειμών storm. ἐπικειμένου pres. mid. part. ἐπίκειμαι to lie
upon. Used to describe the pressure of a violent tempest (T).
περιῃρεῖτο impf. pass. περιαιρέω to take away, to remove. The
force of the prep. compound could be local but is perhaps better
as intensive (MH, 321). The impf. implies that the situation was
continually getting worse (Bruce). σῴζεσθαι pres. pass. inf.
σῴζω to save, to rescue.

21   ■ ἀσιτία without food. They had no appetite. (For the
medical use of this word, s. MLL, 276.) σταθείς aor. pass. part.
ἵστημι to put, aor. pass. to stand, to step up or to stand to say
something or make a speech (BAG). ἔδει impf. δεῖ it is necessary. πειθαρχήσαντας aor. act. part. πειθαρχέω to listen to,
to obey. ἀνάγεσθαι pres. pass. inf. κερδῆσαι aor. act. inf.
κερδαίνω to gain. The word may have the sense of "gain by
avoiding what would be detrimental" or "to incur," "to obtain"
22 (LC). ■ παραινῶ pres. ind. act. to advise, to recommend.
εὐθυμεῖν pres. act. inf. to be cheerful, to cheer up. ἔσται fut.
23 εἰμί. πλήν except (s. Luke 22:21). ■ παρέστη aor. παρίστημι
24 to stand beside. ■ φοβοῦ pres. mid. imp. used w. a neg. to stop
an action in progress. παραστῆναι aor. inf. κεχάρισται perf.
mid. χαρίζομαι to give, to grant, "has given as a present"
25 (Bruce). πλέοντας pres. part. ■ εὐθυμεῖτε pres. imp.
λελάληται perf. pass. The perf. emphasizes the abiding result
26 of what was spoken. ■ ἐκπεσεῖν aor. inf. ἐκπίπτω s.v.17.

27   ■ ἐγένετο aor. mid. γίνομαι. διαφερομένων pres. pass.
part. διαφέρω to carry through, to drive about. The idea here
is "drifting across" (LC). ὑπενόουν impf. ὑπονοέω to think, to
suspect, inceptive impf. "they began to think." The prep. compound conveys the idea of thoughts making their way up into the
mind (MH, 327). προσάγειν pres. act. inf. to come near, to
approach, "they began to suspect that land was near (approach-
28 ing) them" (BAG). ■ βολίσαντες aor. act. part. βολίζω to
throw down the lead into the sea, to take soundings (RWP).
εὗρον aor. ὀργυιά fathom, about six feet, as a nautical technical

340

term used to measure the depth of water (BAG). βραχύς little, short. διαστήσαντες aor. part. διΐστημι to go away, to pass, here either "after a short interval" (Bruce) or "after they had sailed a short distance farther" (BAG). ■ τραχύς rough, rocky. 29 πρύμνη stern. ῥίψαντες aor. act. part. ῥίπτω to throw, to hurl. ἄγκυρα anchor. The anchors were to act as a brake casting them from the stern and were intended to keep the prow of the ship pointing to the shore (Bruce). ηὔχοντο impf. mid. εὔχομαι to pray, to wish for. The impf. pictures the continual action. ■ 30 ζητούντων pres. part. ζητέω to seek, to attempt, gen. abs. φυγεῖν aor. act. inf. φεύγω to flee. πρόφασις pretext, pretense. πρῷρα bow, prow. ἐκτείνειν pres. act. inf. to stretch out, to let out. ■ μείνωσιν aor. subj. μένω to remain. Subjunctive used in 31 a third-class conditional clause. σωθῆναι aor. pass. inf. σῴζω. ■ ἀπέκοψαν aor. ἀποκόπτω to cut off. σχοινίον rope. 32 εἴασαν aor. ἐάω to let, to allow. ■ ἄρχι οὗ "until," here w. the 33 impf. until it was about to become day; that is, before daybreak (Haenchen; s. also BD, 193). ἤμελλεν impf. μέλλω. παρεκάλει impf. παρακαλέω to encourage, to exhort. The impf. pictures the repeated action. Verbs of asking and commanding have the idea of an incomplete action in the past since they await a fulfillment in a further action by another agent (MT, 164f.). μεταλαβεῖν aor. inf. μεταλαμβάνω to take, to partake of food. προσδοκῶντες pres. act. part. προσδοκάω to wait. διατελεῖτε pres. ind. act. to accomplish, to continue. προσλαβόμενοι aor. mid. part. προσλαμβάνω to take, mid. to take to one's self. Probably Paul means that they had taken no regular meals, only bits of food now and then (RWP). ■ πρός 34 w. gen. "in the interest of" (BD, 125). ἀπολεῖται fut. mid. ἀπόλλυμι to perish, to be lost. The expression is proverbial in the OT meaning the saving of life (LC). ■ εἴπας aor. act. part. 35 λέγω. λαβών aor. act. part. λαμβάνω. εὐχαρίστησεν aor. εὐχαριστέω to thank, to give thanks, giving thanks for one's food was a normal Jewish custom (Bruce). ἤρξατο aor. mid. ἄρχομαι to begin. ■ εὔθυμος cheerful. προσελάβοντο aor. 36 mid. προσλαμβάνω to take, to take to one's self. Used w. the partitive gen. (RWP). ■ ἤμεθα impf. εἰμί. (For this Hellenistic 37 form, s. BD, 49.) ■ κορεσθέντες aor. pass. part. κορέννυμι to 38 satisfy. ἐκούφιζον impf. κουφίζω to lighten, inceptive impf. "they began to make the ship lighter." ἐκβαλλόμενοι pres. mid. part. ἐκβάλλω to throw out.

■ ἐπεγίνωσκον impf. ἐπιγινώσκω to know, to recognize. 39 κόλπος bay. κατενόουν impf. κατανοέω to perceive. The impf. may indicate that one after another of them noticed

341

(Bruce). ἔχοντα pres. act. part. αἰγιαλός beach. ἐβουλεύοντο impf. mid. βουλεύομαι to take counsel, to decide, to plan. The impf. mid. shows the process of deliberation and doubt (RWP). ἐξῶσαι aor. act. inf. ἐξωθέω to drive out, as a seaman's techni-
40 cal term "to beach," "to run ashore" (BAG). ■ περιελόντες aor. part. περιαιρέω to take away, to cast off. The prep. compound is intensive (MH, 321). εἴων impf. ἐάω to allow. ἀνέντες aor. part. ἀνίημι to loosen, to release. ζευκτηρία bands, lashings, straps. The word is used in the papyri in connection w. the mechanism of a water wheel (MM). πηδάλιον rudder. ἐπάραντες aor. part. ἐπαίρω to set, to hoist. ἀρτέμων foresail, the forward mast or the sail on it (LC). πνεούσῃ pres. part. "to the blowing (wind)." κατεῖχον impf. κατέχω to hold down, inceptive impf. "they began to hold the ship steadily for the
41 beach" (RWP). ■ περιπεσόντες aor. part. περιπίπτω to fall around, to encounter, to fall into, here "to strike a reef" (BAG). διθάλασσος w. the sea on both sides. Perhaps a sand bank or reef (BAG). ἐπέκειλαν aor. ἐπικέλλω to run ashore. ἐρείσασα aor. part. fem. ἐρείδω to jam fast, to become firmly fixed. ἔμεινεν aor. μένω. ἀσάλευτος unmoveable, unshakable. ἐλύετο impf. pass. λύω to loosen, to break up, inceptive impf.
42 "the stern began to break up." ■ βουλή plan. ἀποκτείνωσιν aor. act. subj. ἀποκτείνω to kill. ἐκκολυμβήσας aor. part. ἐκκολυμβάω to swim away. διαφύγῃ aor. subj. διαφεύγω to
43 escape. ■ βουλόμενος pres. mid. part. βούλομαι to wish, to want to. διασῶσαι aor. act. inf. διασῴζω to save, to rescue. The prep. compound describes the carrying of action through to a definite result, "to bring safely through" (MH, 301). ἐκώλυσεν aor. κωλύω to hinder. ἐκέλευσεν aor. κελεύω to command. κολυμβᾶν pres. act. inf. to swim. ἀπορίψαντος aor. act. part. ἀπορίπτω to leap off. ἐξιέναι pres. inf. ἔξειμι to go
44 to land. ■ σανίς plank. διασωθῆναι aor. pass. inf. διασῴζω.

Ch. 28

1 ■ διασωθέντες aor. pass. part. διασῴζω to rescue completely (s. Acts 27:43). ἐπέγνωμεν aor. ἐπιγινώσκω to know,
2 to recognize. καλεῖται pres. pass. ■ βάρβαρος one who does not speak Gr., foreigner. The Maltese were Phoenicians speaking some dialect of Punic or Phoenician (LC). παρεῖχον impf. παρέχω to offer, to provide, to show. τυχοῦσαν aor. act. part. τυγχάνω to hit, to meet w. The part. used w. the neg. means "not common," "ordinary." φιλανθρωπία love for mankind, kindness, hospitality. ἅψαντες aor. act. part. ἅπτω to light (a fire). πυρά fire, bonfire, a fire of brush wood in the open (LC).

προσελάβοντο aor. mid. προσλαμβάνω to receive, to take to, "they brought us all to it" (Bruce). ὑετός rain. ἐφεστῶτα perf. act. part. ἐφίστημι to set upon, to come upon, to be present, "the rain that stood upon them"; that is, the pouring rain (RWP). ψῦχος cold. ■ συστρέψαντος aor. act. part. gen. abs. 3 συστρέφω to twist together, to roll together in a bundle. φρύγανον brush, dry wood, brush wood. ἐπιθέντος aor. part. ἐπιτίθημι to place upon, gen. abs. ἔχιδνα snake. θέρμη heat. ἐξελθοῦσα aor. part. ἐξέρχομαι to come out. καθῆψεν aor. καθάπτω to fasten on, to bite (LC). (For the medical use of the term indicating the introduction of poison matter into the body, s. MLL, 288.) ■ κρεμάμενον pres. mid. part. κρεμάννυμι to 4 hang. θηρίον animal, beast. Term used by medical writers of venomous serpents (MLL, 51). πάντως adv. perhaps (s. Acts 21:22). φονεύς murderer. δίκη justice, perhaps a reference to justice as a goddess, Dike (Rackham; TDNT). εἴασεν aor. ἐάω to allow, to let. ■ ἀποτινάξας aor. part. ἀποτινάσσω to shake 5 off. ἔπαθεν aor. act. πάσχω to suffer. ■ προσεδόκων impf. 6 προσδοκάω to await, to expect. The impf. pictures the continuing action, they stood watching him for some time (Bruce). πίμπρασθαι pres. pass. inf. πίμπρημι to swell. It was the usual medical word for inflammation (MLL, 50). πίπτειν pres. inf. to fall down. (For the medical use of the term, s. MLL, 50f.) ἄφνω suddenly. ἐπὶ πολύ "for a long (time)." προσδοκώντων pres. part. gen. abs. θεωρούντων pres. part. θεωρέω to see, gen. abs. ἄτοπος out of place, harm. The word was used in medical language to denote anything unusual in the symptoms of a disease or something that was out of the way; that is, deadly or fatal (MLL, 289). γινόμενον pres. mid. part. ἔλεγον impf., inceptive impf. "they began to say." ■ ὑπῆρχεν impf. ὑπάρχω to exist, 7 to be. χωρία land, property. ἀναδεξάμενος aor. mid. part. ἀναδέχομαι to receive. φιλοφρόνως friendly, courteously, hospitably. ἐξένισεν aor. ξενίζω to entertain. ■ ἐγένετο aor. 8 mid. γίνομαι. πυρετός fever. δυσεντέριον dysentery. (For the medical use of the term in this v., s. MLL, 52f.) συνεχόμενον pres. pass. part. συνέχω to be sick, "to be afflicted w. attacks" (LC). εἰσελθών aor. part. εἰσέρχομαι to come into. προσευξάμενος aor. mid. part. προσεύχομαι to pray. ἰάσατο aor. mid. ἰάομαι to heal. ■ γενομένου aor. mid. part. γίνομαι 9 gen. abs. προσήρχοντο impf. mid. προσέρχομαι to come to. ἐθεραπεύοντο impf. pass. θεραπεύω to treat medically, to heal. ■ ἐτίμησαν aor. τιμάω to honor. The context is opposed to the 10 possible rendering "paid us large fees" (LC). ἀναγομένοις pres. mid. part. ἀνάγω to sail. ἐπέθεντο aor. mid. ἐπιτίθημι to place upon, to put onboard.

11   ■ ἀνήχθημεν aor. pass. ἀνάγω to sail. παρακεχειμακότι perf. act. part. παραχειμάζω to spend the winter. παράσημον
12 figurehead, sign. ■ καταχθέντες aor. pass. part. κατάγω to go down, to land. ἐπεμείναμεν aor. ἐπιμένω to remain, to remain
13 there. The prep. compound is directive (s. MH, 312). ■ περιελθόντες aor. part. περιέρχομαι to go around. Alternate reading περιελόντες aor. part. περιαιρέω to weigh anchor, to cast loose. κατηντήσαμεν aor. καταντάω to arrive. ἐπιγενομένου aor. mid. part. ἐπιγίνομαι to arise, to come on,
14 gen. abs. νότος south wind. δευτεραῖος "on the 2nd day." ■ οὗ where. εὑρόντες aor. act. part. παρεκλήθημεν aor. pass. παρακαλέω to ask, to urge, "we were invited" (LC). ἐπιμεῖναι aor. act. inf. ἐπιμένω. Ῥώμην Rome. The article would denote
15 Rome as the goal of the entire journey (BD, 137). ■ κακεῖθεν "and from there." ἀκούσαντες aor. act. part. ἀπάντησις meeting. φόρον forum. ταβέρνα tavern, "Tres Tabernae," a roadside house thirty-three miles from Rome on the Appian Way (LC). εὐχαριστήσας aor. part. εὐχαριστέω to give thanks. ἔλαβε
16 aor. λαμβάνω. θάρσος courage. ■ εἰσήλθομεν aor. εἰσέρχομαι to go in. ἐπετράπη aor. pass. ἐπιτρέπω to allow, to permit. φυλάσσοντι pres. part. φυλάσσω to guard. Paul was not in prison but in charge of a soldier detailed to guard him (LC). He was still bound to a soldier by a light chain so that he could not go in and out as he pleased (EGT).

17   ■ ἐγένετο aor. ind. mid., s.v.8. συγκαλέσασθαι pres. mid. inf. συγκαλέω to call together, to summons. ὄντας pres. part. εἰμί. συνελθόντων aor. act. part. συνέρχομαι to come together, to assemble, gen. abs. ἐναντίος contrary, hostile. ποιήσας aor. part. παρεδόθην aor. pass. παραδίδωμι to deliv-
18 er over. ■ οἵτινες "who." Used for the normal rel. pron. esp. after part. where the rel. pron. could be confused w. the article (BD, 153). ἀνακρίναντες aor. act. part. ἀνακρίνω to examine. ἐβούλοντο impf. mid. βούλομαι to will, to want to. ἀπολῦσαι
19 aor. act. inf. ἀπολύω to release. ■ ἀντιλεγόντων pres. part. ἀντιλέγω to speak against, to object, gen. abs. ἠναγκάσθην aor. pass. ἀναγκάζω to compel, to force. ἐπικαλέσασθαι aor. mid. inf. ἐπικαλέω to appeal to (s. Acts 25:11, 12). ἔχων pres. part. κατηγορεῖν pres. act. inf. to accuse, to bring an accusation
20 against someone. ■ παρεκάλεσα aor. παρακαλέω s.v.14. ἰδεῖν aor. inf. ὁράω. Infinitive used to express purpose. προσλαλῆσαι aor. act. inf. προσλαλέω to talk to. εἵνεκεν because of. ἅλυσις chain. περίκειμαι to lie around, to wear. Paul does not lie around the chain, but the chain lies around him

(RWP). ■ ἐδεξάμεθα aor. mid. δέχομαι to receive. 21
παραγενόμενος aor. mid. part. παραγίνομαι to come.
ἀπήγγειλεν aor. ἀπαγγέλλω to report. ἐλάλησεν aor. ■ 22
ἀξιοῦμεν pres. act. to consider worthy, to think right or proper.
ἀκοῦσαι aor. act. inf. γνωστός known. πανταχοῦ everywhere.
ἀντιλέγεται pres. pass.
    ■ ταξάμενοι aor. mid. part. τάσσω to arrange, to appoint. 23
ξενία lodging. The living quarters that Paul had rented (Haenchen). πλείων comp. πολύς. ἐξετίθετο impf. mid. ἐκτίθημι to
lay out, to set forth. Perhaps the mid. indicates that the apostle
vindicates his own conduct (EGT). διαμαρτυρόμενος pres.
mid. part. διαμαρτύρομαι to testify, to bear witness. πείθων
pres. part. πείθω to persuade. πρωΐ early. ἑσπέρα evening.
■ ἐπείθοντο impf. pass. The impf. either pictures the repeated 24
action or is inceptive, "some began to be persuaded" (RWP).
λεγομένοις pres. pass. part. ἠπίστουν impf. ἀπιστέω to disbelieve. (For the alpha as a neg. prefix, s. Moorhouse 41-68.)
■ ἀσύμφωνος out of harmony, without agreement. ἀπελύοντο 25
impf. mid. ἀπολύω to dismiss, mid. "to loose one's self," "to
depart." εἰπόντος aor. act. part. λέγω gen. abs. ■ πορεύθητι 26
aor. pass. imp. πορεύομαι to go. εἰπόν aor. imp. λέγω.
ἀκούσετε fut. συνῆτε aor. subj. συνίημι to comprehend, to
understand. βλέποντες pres. part. βλέψετε fut. ἴδητε aor. subj.
ὁράω. ■ ἐπαχύνθη aor. pass. παχύνω to make fat, to become 27
fat, to make dull, pass. to become dull (TDNT). βαρέως adv.
heavy, heavily. ἤκουσαν aor. ἀκούω. ἐκάμμυσαν aor.
καμμύω to shut, to close the eyes. ἀκούσωσιν aor. subj.
ἐπιστρέψωσιν aor. subj. ἐπιστρέφω to turn, to turn back.
ἰάσομαι fut. mid., s.v.8. ■ ἔστω pres. imp. εἰμί. ἀπεστάλη 28
aor. pass. ἀποστέλλω to send, to send as an authoritative representative (TDNT).
    ■ ἐνέμεινεν aor. ἐμμένω to remain. διετία two years. 30
Perhaps the two years indicate that the time period for Paul's
accusers to appear had elapsed (s. BC, V, 330). ἀπεδέχετο impf.
mid. ἀποδέχομαι to receive, to welcome. ■ κηρύσσων pres. 31
part. διδάσκων pres. part. ἀκωλύτως adv. without hindrance.
The adv. is of constant occurrence in legal documents in the
papyri (MM).

ROMANS

δοῦλος slave, bondservant. The term emphasizes the bond- 1
age and the belonging to another (CBB; TDNT). (For the concept of slavery in the ancient world, s. Philemon 21f.) The following genitives show possession. κλητός called. The verbal adj.
w. this ending usually has a pass. sense (BG, 47; s. also M, 221).
ἀφωρισμένος perf. pass. part. ἀφορίζω to mark off, to separate
by a boundary. The absence of the article w. the words in v.1
indicate the nature or quality (BG, 55). ■ προεπηγγείλατο aor. 2
mid. προεπαγγέλλω to promise before, to promise previously
or in advance. γραφή writing, Scripture. The absence of the
article throws the stress on "holy" (SH). ■ περὶ τοῦ υἱοῦ αὐτοῦ 3
to be connected closely w. the word "gospel" (Lightfoot, Notes).
γενομένου aor. mid. part. γίνομαι. ■ ὁρισθέντος aor. pass. 4
part. ὁρίζω to mark out the boundary, to decree, to appoint (s.
S. Lewis Johnson, Jr., "The Jesus that Paul Preached," Bib Sac,
128 [April, 1971], 129f.; L.C. Allen, "The Old Testament Background of [προ] ὁρίζειν in the New Testament," NTS, 17 [Oc-
tober, 1970], 104–108; TDNT). ἁγιωσύνη holiness. Here it
indicates a spirit or disposition of holiness which characterized
Christ spiritually (Johnson, 132). ■ ἐλάβομεν aor. λαμβάνω. 5
The pl. refers only to Paul and his stylistic method avoiding the
emphasis on "I" (Kuss). ἀποστολή apostleship, the office of an
apostle. ὑπακοή obedience. ■ οὖσιν pres. part. εἰμί. ἀγαπητός 7
beloved. (For verbal adjectives w. this ending, s.v.1.)
■ καταγγέλλεται pres. pass. καταγγέλλω to proclaim, to 8
report, to publicly report (Barrett). ■ λατρεύω to serve, to serve 9
for pay then to do service for a deity (TDNT). ἐν τῷ πνεύματί
μου "with (in) my spirit." It is by using his spirit that Paul
renders God service (Barrett). ἐν τῷ εὐαγγελίῳ "in the gospel."
The prep. here denotes the external sphere (Lightfoot, Notes).
ἀδιαλείπτως adv. without ceasing, constantly. μνεία remembrance, mention. ■ δεόμενος pres. mid. part. δέομαι to pray, to 10
make a request. εἴ πως "if perhaps." By omitting the apodosis
of the conditional sentence, the first clause may be taken as a
wish (MT, 91). εὐοδωθήσομαι fut. pass. εὐοδόω to cause one

347

to journey prosperously, to make one succeed (Godet). ἐλθεῖν
11 aor. act. inf. ἔρχομαι. ■ ἐπιποθέω to long for. The prep. compound marks the direction of the desire (SH). ἰδεῖν aor. inf.
ὁράω. μεταδῶ aor. subj. μεταδίδωμι to share w. someone.
χάρισμα a gift (freely and graciously given), a favor bestowed
(BAG). πνευματικός spiritually, pertaining to the spirit. The
suffix indicates a dynamic relation to the idea involved in the
root (MH, 378). στηριχθῆναι aor. pass. inf. στηρίζω to
strengthen. The pass. indicates it is God who will strengthen
(Godet). The inf. is used w. prep. to express purpose (s. MT,
12 143). ■ συμπαρακληθῆναι aor. pass. inf. συμπαρακαλέω to
encourage together, to encourage mutually. Here it signifies "I
w. you, Christians of Rome" (Godet). Infinitive used to express
13 purpose. ■ προεθέμην aor. mid προτίθημι to place before, to
purpose, to intend. ἐκωλύθην aor. pass. κωλύω to hinder.
δεῦρο adv. here, until now. σχῶ aor. subj. ἔχω to have, to get.
14 The idea expressed is that of gathering fruit (Murray). ■
βάρβαρος one who does not speak Gr. properly; one who
speaks an unintelligible language then applied to people who did
not familiarly use Gr., and so were regarded as uncultured
(Dodd). σοφός wise. ἀνόητος ignorant, not understanding.
ὀφειλέτης one who owes a debt. (For the binding obligation
15 placed upon debtors in the ancient world, s. SEH I, 382f.) ■ τὸ
κατ' ἐμέ either to be taken as the subject w. the next word as
the predicate, "for my part, I am all readiness" (EGT) or the
prep. is to be taken as a circumlocution for the poss. gen., "my
readiness" (BD, 120). πρόθυμος ready, willing eager.
εὐαγγελίσασθαι aor. mid. inf. εὐαγγελίζομαι to evangelize,
to proclaim the good news.
16   ■ ἐπαισχύνομαι to be ashamed. πιστεύοντι pres. act.
part. Ἕλλην Gr. Here it refers to anyone who is not a Jew
17 (Gifford). ■ δικαιοσύνη the phrase could mean "the righteous
standing which God gives" or "the righteous character which
God is" or "the righteous activity which comes from God." (For
a review of these meanings, s. MRP, 9–14; Cranfield). ἐν αὐτῷ
"in it," that is, in the gospel. ἀποκαλύπτεται pres. pass.
ἀποκαλύπτω to reveal. ἐκ "out of." The prep. here may indicate the source of the righteousness. (For the various interpretations of this phrase, s. S. Lewis Johnson, Jr., "The Gospel that
Paul Preached," Bib Sac, 128 [October, 1971], 336f.)
γέγραπται perf. pass. The perf. emphasizes the permanent and
authoritative character of that which was written (s. MM).
ζήσεται fut. mid. ζάω to live.
18   ■ ἀποκαλύπτεται pres. pass. The word need not be totally

eschatological but has the sense of God's displeasure at sin, the sense that God will not overlook sin (Lightfoot, *Notes*). ὀργή wrath. The word indicates the deep-seated anger of God against sin. This anger arises from His holiness and righteousness (s. TDNT; CBB; Trench, *Synonyms*, 130–134; Cranfield). ἀσέβεια ungodliness. ἀδικία unrighteousness. The first represents impiety toward God and the second injustice toward men (Hodge). ἀλήθεια truth. The knowledge of God as communicated to the human conscience (Godet). κατεχόντων pres. part. κατέχω to hold down, to suppress, to hold fast or firmly. ■ διότι because. 19 It gives the reason of that which precedes (Godet). γνωστός known or knowable. ἐφανέρωσεν aor. φανερόω to make clear, to manifest. ■ ἀόρατος unseen, invisible. (For the use of the 20 prefix as a neg., s. Moorhouse, 41–66.) κτίσις creation. ποίημα that which is made. It refers to the source from which our perception of the invisible things is derived (Murray). νοούμενα pres. pass. part. νοέω to perceive, to gain an insight into (s. TDNT). καθορᾶται pres. pass. καθοράω to see, to see clearly or plainly, distinctly (LS). The force of the prep. compound is intensive or it may relate to the direction of sight, "contemplated" (SH). τε " and," "both." It joins words closely which have between themselves a close or logical affinity (MT, 339). ἀΐδιος eternal. θειότης divinity, divine nature, a summary term for the attributes which constitute deity (SH). (For this term and its contrast with the word "deity" as used in Colossians 2:9, s. TDNT; Cranfield; Trench, *Synonyms*, 7–10.) εἶναι pres. inf. used w. prep. to express purpose or result (MT, 143). ἀναπολόγητος without excuse, without legal defense (Lightfoot, *Notes*). ■ γνόντες aor. act. part. γινώσκω. (For the Jewish 21 teaching regarding the Gentiles knowing God's demands, s. SB III, 36–46.) ἐδόξασαν aor. δοξάζω to form an opinion about, to glorify. ηὐχαρίστησαν aor. εὐχαριστέω to give thanks, to be thankful. ἐματαιώθησαν aor. pass. ματαιόω to render futile, worthless, pass. to be given over to worthlessness, think about worthless things, to be foolish (BAG). διαλογισμός reason, here "inward questionings" (Lightfoot, *Notes*). ἐσκοτίσθη aor. pass. σκοτίζω to darken, ingressive aor. to become darkened. ἀσύνετος unintelligible, without insight. ■ φάσκοντες 22 pres. act. part. φάσκω to affirm, to assert. ἐμωράνθησαν aor. pass. μωραίνω to make foolish, pass. to become foolish. ■ 23 ἤλλαξαν aor. ἀλλάσσω to exchange. They exchanged one thing for another (Hodge). ἄφθαρτος incorruptible. ὁμοίωμα likeness, implies a resemblance which may be accidental. εἰκών image, presupposes an archetype of which it is a copy. The gen.

is gen. of apposition or explanation. (For this word and the preceding, s. Lightfoot, *Notes*.) φθαρτός corruptible. πετεινά (pl.) birds. τετράπους four-footed. ἑρπετά (pl.) creeping things, snakes.

24   ■ διό "therefore." παρέδωκεν aor. παραδίδωμι to deliver over, to hand over. (For the judicial aspect, s. Gifford; SB III, 62f.) ἐπιθυμία lust, desire. ἀκαθαρσία uncleanness. It refers to sexual aberration (Murray). ἀτιμάζεσθαι pres. pass. inf.
25 ἀτιμάζω to dishonor. The inf. is epexegetic (Barrett). ■ μετήλλαξαν aor. μεταλλάσσω to change w., to exchange. ἐσεβάσθησαν aor. pass. σεβάζομαι to worship, to show reverence to. ἐλάτρευσαν aor., s.v.9. παρά w. acc. "more than." Used to express the comp. and here means virtually "instead of" (BD, 123f.). κτίσαντα aor. part. κτίζω to create. εὐλογητός
26 blessed. ■ πάθος passion or a passionate desire. It represents the pass., ungoverned aspect of evil desire (AS). ἀτιμία dishonor, disgrace. (For the prefix as a neg., s.v.20.) θῆλυς female. φυσικός natural, that which pertains to nature. (For the meaning of the suffix, s. MH, 378.) χρῆσις use, function, esp. of
27 sexual intercourse (BAG). ■ ὁμοίως likewise. ἄρσην male. ἀφέντες aor. act. part. ἀφίημι to leave, to forsake. ἐξεκαύθησαν aor. pass. ἐκκαίω to set on fire, pass. to be consumed, to be inflamed. ὄρεξις desire. It is always the reaching out after and toward an object, w. the purpose of drawing that after which it reaches to itself, and making it its own (Trench, *Synonyms*, 326). ἀσχημοσύνη shameless, disgraceful, obscenity (Barrett). κατεργαζόμενοι pres. mid. part. κατεργάζομαι to work, to accomplish. (For the perfectivizing force of the prep. compound, s. M, 112f.) ἀντιμισθία reward, penalty. The prep. compound emphasizes the reciprocal nature of the transaction (BAG). ἔδει impf. δεῖ it is necessary. πλάνη error. (For the Jewish view on sexual perversion of the heathen, s. SB III, 64–74.) ἀπολαμβάνοντες pres. act. part. ἀπολαμβάνω to re-
28 ceive, to receive back, to receive one's due (SH). ■ ἐδοκίμασαν aor. δοκιμάζω to test, to put to the test, to make a decision after a trial. They tested God at first and turned aside from Him (RWP). ἐπίγνωσις cognizance, knowledge. ἀδόκιμος rejected, rejected after a trial, failing the test, disqualified, useless (Cranfield). νοῦς mind, the reasoning faculty, esp. as concerned w. moral action, the intellectual part of conscience (SH). καθήκοντα pres. act. part., that which is proper, or fitting, moral. The word w. a technical term of Stoic philosophy (s.
29 TDNT; Barrett). ■ πεπληρωμένους perf. pass. part. πληρόω to fill. πλεονεξία greediness, the insatiable desire to have more

even at the expense of harming others (s. Lightfoot, *Notes;* NTW, 97ff.; TDNT). μεστός full. φθόνος envy. φόνος murder. ἔρις strife, wrangling. δόλος deceit, cunning, treachery. κακοήθεια malice, the tendency to put the worst construction upon everything (SH; Trench, *Synonyms,* 38–40). ψιθυριστής whisperer, the man who pours his poison against his neighbor by whispering in the ear (Godet). ■ κατάλαλος speaking evil 30 against others, slanderous, slanderer. The prep. compound indicates the action of the word is unfavorable to its object (MH, 316). θεοστυγής "hated of God" (pass.) or "haters of God" (active) (s. Gifford; Kuss). ὑβριστής a man of arrogant insolence. The word contains a mixture of cruelty and pride. The proud insolence and contempt for others displays itself in cruelty for the mere enjoyment of seeing others suffer (s. Trench, *Synonyms,* 202–205; Cranfield; MNTW, 77–85; TDNT). ὑπερήφανος proud, arrogant, one who shows himself above others. It is the proud, insolent, self-sufficient person who in his heart sets himself upon a pedestal above all others, even above God (s. Trench, *Synonyms,* 101f.; MNTW, 85–89; TDNT). ἀλάζων boastful, bragger, one who makes empty boasts and false promises often for the purpose of gain (s. Trench, *Synonyms,* 98–101; MNTW, 38–42; TDNT). ἐφευρετής inventor. γονεύς parents. ἀπειθής disobedient. ■ ἀσύνθετος covenant- 31 breaker, faithless to an agreement. ἄστοργος unloving, without tenderness. It refers to the lack of the feelings of natural tenderness, as seen in a mother who exposes or kills her child, a father who abandons his family, or children who neglect their aged parents (Godet). ἀνελεήμων unmerciful, without pity. ■ 32 δικαίωμα that which is declared right, judgment, ordinance (TDNT; MRP, 209). ἐπιγνόντες aor. part. ἐπιγινώσκω to know. συνευδοκέω to heartily approve (SH).

Ch. 2

■ διό therefore. It refers either to the preceding section 1 (1:18–32) or only to v. 32, or to that which follows in Ch. 2 (Murray). ἀναπολόγητος without excuse, without defense. κρίνων pres. part. κρίνω to judge. κατακρίνω pres. ind. to judge against, to condemn. ■ κρίμα judgment, decision, either 2 good or bad (RWP). τοιοῦτος such as this, of such a kind. πράσσοντας pres. act. part. ■ λογίζομαι pres. ind. mid. 2nd 3 per. sing. to reckon, to consider, to suppose. ■ χρηστότης kind- 4 ness, kindness in general, as expressed in giving favors (Hodge; TDNT). ἀνοχή patience. It is that forbearance or suspense of wrath, that truce w. the sinner, which by no means implies that

the wrath will not be executed at the last (Trench, *Synonyms*, 200). μακροθυμία longsuffering, a long holding out of the mind before it gives room to action or passion (Trench, *Synonyms*, 196; TDNT). καταφρονέω pres. ind. act. to think down on, to despise. ἀγνοῶν pres. part. ἀγνοέω to be ignorant, to ignore (Barrett). ἄγειν pres. act. inf. conative pres. "to try to lead"
5 (Käsemann) ■ σκληρότης hardness. ἀμετανόητος unrepentant. θησαυρίζω to store up, to treasure up. The idea is gradual accumulation (Lightfoot, *Notes*). δικαιοκρισία just judgment, judgment according to that which is right. It denotes God's
6 justice in the narrow, even distributive sense (MRP, 189). ■ ἀποδώσει fut. ἀποδίδωμι to give back, to recompense. Used in the papyri for the paying of a debt or restoring of a due of any
7 kind (MM). ■ ὑπομονή patience, endurance, bearing up under. ἀφθαρσία incorruptible, immortality. ζητοῦσιν pres. part.
8 ζητέω to seek. ■ ἐριθεία selfish ambition (BAG; s. also Barrett; Phil. 2:3). ἀπειθοῦσι pres. act. part. ἀπειθέω to be disobedient. πειθομένοις pres. mid. part. πείθομαι to obey, to be obedient. ἀδικία unrighteousness. θυμός anger, rage. (For this and the
9 following word, s. Trench, *Synonyms*, 130–134; TDNT.) ■ θλῖψις pressure, tribulation. στενοχωρία anguish, torturing confinement (SH). κατεργαζομένου pres. mid. part.
10 κατεργάζομαι to do, to accomplish (s. Rom. 1:27). ■
11 ἐργαζομένῳ pres. mid. part. ■ προσωπολημψία partial, the accepting of the appearance of a pers. A Hebraic term for partiality. The Oriental custom of greeting was to bow one's face to the ground. If the one greeted accepted the pers., he was allowed to
12 lift his head again (TDNT; s. also, SB III, 79–83). ■ ὅσοι as many as, "all alike, whether under the law or not under the law" (Lightfoot, *Notes*). ἀνόμως adv. without law, lawless. ἥμαρτον aor. ἁμαρτάνω to send. A timeless aor. (RWP). ἀπολοῦνται fut. ind. mid. ἀπόλλυμι to perish. κριθήσονται fut. ind. pass.
13 ■ ἀκροατής one who hears. ποιητής one who does. (For the ending of these two nouns indicating the agent who performs the action, s. MH, 364f.) δικαιωθήσονται fut. ind. pass. δικαιόω to justify, to declare righteous, to declare in the right. (For this important term, s. TDNT; APC, 224–280; GW, 82–162; MRP.)
14 ■ ὅταν w. subj. "whenever." ἔχοντα pres. part. φύσις nature,
15 instrumental dat. ποιῶσιν pres. subj. ■ ἐνδείκνυνται pres. ind. mid. to demonstrate, to show. The word implies an appeal to facts (SH). γραπτός written. συμμαρτυρούσης pres. act. part. f. sing. συμμαρτυρέω to testify w., to confirm, to testify in support of someone or something (BAG). συνείδησις conscience. Paul regarded conscience as performing in the gentile

world roughly the same function as was performed by the law
among the Jews (s. Margaret E. Thrall, "The Pauline Use of
Συνείδησις," NTS, 14 [Oct. 1967], 124). μεταξύ between.
κατηγορούντων pres. act. part. κατηγορέω to speak against,
to accuse, to bring a legal accusation against someone, gen. abs.
ἀπολογουμένων pres. mid. part. ἀπολογέομαι to excuse, to
defend, to offer a legal defense, gen. abs. ▪ κρυπτός hidden. 16

▪ ἐπονομάζῃ pres. ind. pass. 2nd per. sing. ἐπονομάζω to 17
put a name upon, pass. to have a name imposed, to bear the name
(SH). ἐπαναπαύῃ pres. ind. mid. 2nd per. sing. to rest upon, to
rely upon, to lean upon (Michel). καυχᾶσαι pres. ind. mid. 2nd
per. sing. to boast, to pride one's self in. ▪ δοκιμάζω pres. ind. 18
act. to test, to examine, to approve after testing. διαφέροντα
pres. part. διαφέρω. The part. could mean either "the things
which excel" or "the things which differ." Here it refers to the
most delicate shades of the moral life alluding to the legal casuistry in which the Jewish schools excelled (Godet).
κατηχούμενος pres. pass. part. κατηχέω to instruct. ▪ 19
πέποιθα perf. ind. act. πείθω to persuade, to be persuaded, to
put one's trust in. ὁδηγός guide, one who leads the way (RWP).
▪ παιδευτής educator, teacher, schoolmaster. The word has the 20
idea of discipline, correction, as well as teaching (SH). ἄφρων
unthinking, foolish, ignorant, obj. gen. νήπιος infant.
μόρφωσις form, the rough sketch, penciling of the form, the
outline or framework without the substance (Lightfoot, Notes).
▪ διδάσκων pres. act. part. κηρύσσων pres. act. part. ▪ 21/22
βδελυσσόμενος pres. mid. part. βδελύσσομαι to abhor, to
detest. εἴδωλον idol. ἱεροσυλέω to rob a temple. Perhaps a
reference to the robbing of heathen temples (Kuss; SB III, 113).
(For the Jewish opposition against heathen idolatry, s. Moore,
Judaism I, 362f.; SB III, 111f.) ▪ βλασφημεῖται pres. pass. 24
βλασφημέω to blaspheme. γέγραπται perf. pass. ▪ ὠφελεῖ 25
pres. ind. act. gnomic pres. Used to express customary action
and general truths (SMT, 8). πράσσῃς pres. subj. The pres.
would emphasize the continual doing of the law. παραβάτης
trangressor, one who steps across a line (RWP). ἦς pres. subj.
εἰμί. ἀκροβυστία uncircumcision. (For the importance of circumcision in Judaism, s. Moore, Judaism II, 16–21; TDNT; SB
IV, 23–40; Gal. 2:3.) γέγονεν perf. ind. act. γίνομαι. The perf.
emphasizes the continuing state or results. ▪ δικαίωμα ordi- 26
nance, righteous to man (s. Rom. 1:32). φυλάσσῃ pres. subj.
φυλάσσω to guard, to observe. λογισθήσεται fut. pass. ▪ 27
κρινεῖ fut. τελοῦσα pres. part. τελέω to bring to an end, to
complete, to fulfill. διά w. gen. "with." Used to describe the

353

attendant circumstances; that is, w. all your advantages of cir-
28 cumcision and the possession of a written law (SH). ■ φανερός
29 visible, open to sight, manifest. ■ οὗ rel. pron. gen. sing., the
antecedent is Ἰουδαῖος. ἔπαινος praise.

Ch. 3

1   ■ περισσός advantage, that which encircles a thing, that
which is in excess, over and above (SH). ὠφέλεια benefit, usefulness. (For the use of the rhetorical question to express clarity,
s. BD, 262.) περιτομή circumcision. The article and the pl. verb
in v.2 shows that it refers to the nation. Paul is thinking of the
promises of the Abrahamic Covenant as the superiority that
Israel had (s. Lewis Johnson, Jr., "Studies in Romans: The Jews
2 and the Oracles of God," Bib Sac, 130 [July, 1973], 239). ■
πρῶτον first, in the first place. ἐπιστεύθησαν aor. pass.
πιστεύομαι to entrust, pass. to be entrusted w. λόγιον saying,
oracle. Here it is a reference to the O.T. promises. The acc. is
used after a pass. verb (s. Johnson, "The Jews and the Oracles
3 of God," 240–246). ■ ἠπίστησαν aor. ἀπιστέω to disbelieve,
to refuse to believe or w. the meaning to be unfaithful (s. SH).
(For the prefix as a neg., s. Rom. 1:20.) ἀπιστία unbelief, unfaithfulness. καταργήσει fut. καταργέω to render inactive, to
4 render invalid (SH). ■ γένοιτο aor. opt. mid. γίνομαι in this
phrase "let it not be." It expresses the abhorrence of an inference
which may be falsely drawn from the argument (SMT, 79).
γινέσθω pres. mid. imp. Here "be found"; that is, become,
relatively to our apprehension (Lightfoot, Notes). δέ "but." The
contrast really means "though every man be found a liar"
(RWP). ἀληθής true. καθάπερ just as. γέγραπται perf. pass.
The perf. emphasizing the completed state and the continual
authority of that which is written. δικαιωθῇς aor. pass. subj.
δικαιόω to declare right, to justify, pass. to be declared to be in
the right (s. Rom. 2:13). νικήσεις fut. νικάω to be victorious,
to conquer. κρίνεσθαι pres. inf. mid. or pass. κρίνω to judge.
(For the use of the inf. w. the prep. to express contemporary
5 action, s. MT, 144f.) ■ ἀδικία unrighteousness. συνίστησιν
pres. ind. act. συνίστημι to bring together, to commend, to
demonstrate, to bring out something (BAG). Used in a first-class
conditional clause where the condition is assumed for the sake
of argument to be true (s. BG, 103). ἐροῦμεν fut. λέγω.
ἐπιφέρων pres. part. ἐπιφέρω to inflict. The sentence expects
6 the answer no (Barrett). ■ γένοιτο aor. opt. mid., s.v.4. ἐπεί
since, if that were so; that is, "if the inflicting of punishment
7 necessarily implied injustice" (SH). κρινεῖ fut. ■ ἐν "by,"

"through." (For the instrumental use of the prep., s. MT, 252f.)
ψεῦσμα lie. ἐπερίσσευσεν aor. περισσεύω to be in abundance, to increase. κἀγώ = καὶ ἐγώ. The word καί "then" is
used to introduce the main clause of a conditional sentence and
connotes a previously expressed circumstance (BG, 155).
ἁμαρτωλός sinful, sinner. κρίνομαι pres. ind. pass. ■ μή used 8
in a question expecting the answer no. (For the construction of
this v., s. RWP.) βλασφημούμεθα pres. pass. βλασφημέω to
slander. ὅτι recitative; that is, equivalent to quotation marks (s.
RG, 951f.). ποιήσωμεν aor. subj., deliberative subj. "let us do."
ἔλθῃ aor. subj. ἔρχομαι. ὧν rel. pron. gen. pl. "whose." It refers
to all who draw these antinomian inferences (Lightfoot, Notes).
κρίμα judgment. ἔνδικος just. (For this passage, s. S. Lewis
Johnson, Jr., "Studies in Romans: Divine Faithfulness, Divine
Judgment, and the Problem of Antinomianism," Bib Sac, 130
[Oct. 1973], 329–337.)

■ προεχόμεθα pres. mid. or pass. προέχω to excel, to be 9
first, or mid. to have an advantage or to hold something before
one's self for protection, or pass. to be excelled, to be in a worse
position (BAG; s. also SH; Käsemann). οὐ πάντως "not all
together," "only in a limited sense" (s. Barrett; S. Lewis Johnson, Jr., "Studies in Romans: The Universality of Sin," Bib Sac,
131 [April, 1974], 166). προῃτιασάμεθα aor. mid
προαιτιάομαι to make a previous accusation, to accuse previously, to incriminate previously. It belongs to the language of the
bar (Godet). ■ γέγραπται perf. pass. The perf. indicates the 10
permanent and authoritative character of that which was written
(s. MM). (For the composite character of the following quotation, s. Fitzmyer, Essays, 66f.) ■ συνίων pres. part. συνίω to 11
understand. ἐκζητῶν pres. part. ἐκζητέω to seek out. ■ 12
ἐξέκλιναν aor. ἐκκλίνω to turn away from, to turn aside from.
ἅμα together. ἠχρεώθησαν aor. pass. ἀχρέομαι to be worthless, to be useless, ingressive aor. "to become worthless." The
idea of the Heb. word is "to go bad or sour" like milk (Lightfoot,
Notes). χρηστότης goodness, the widest sense, w. the idea of
utility (SH). ■ τάφος grave. ἀνεῳγμένος perf. pass. part. 13
ἀνοίγω to open. λάρυγξ throat. ἐδολιοῦσαν impf. act. δολιόω
to deceive, to practice or use deceit. (For the impf. of contract
verbs w. the aor. ending, s. MH, 195.) ἰός poison. ἀσπίς asps,
the Egyptian cobra (RWP). χεῖλος lip. ■ ἀρά curse (s. TDNT). 14
πικρία bitterness. ■ ὀξύς swift, fast. ἐκχέαι aor. act. inf. ἐκχέω 15
to pour out, to shed. ■ σύντριμμα destruction, ruin, fracture (s. 16
MM). ταλαιπωρία misery. ■ ἔγνωσαν aor. γινώσκω. ■ 17/18
ἀπέναντι before, in the presence of. ■ ὅσος "whatever things." 19

λέγει pres. ind. act. λαλεῖ pres. ind. act. The first verb calls attention to the substance of what is spoken, the second to the outward utterance (SH). ἵνα used to express purpose or result (s. BD, 198). φραγῇ aor. subj. pass. φράσσω to shut, to stop, to close or stop the mouth, so that the man must remain silent (BAG). ὑπόδικος liable to judgment or to punishment, a legal term meaning "to answer to," "to bring under the cognizance of." Used in the papyri of officials who are held answerable
20 (MM). γένηται aor. subj. mid. γίνομαι. ■ διότι because. δικαιωθήσεται fut. pass. The fut. may indicate that this will never be the case. The whole context has reference to a judicial trial and verdict (SH; s. also Rom. 2:13). ἐπίγνωσις recognition, knowledge. The prep. w. the gen. indicates "through," "by means of" (IBG).

21   ■ πεφανέρωται perf. pass. φανερόω to make manifest, to make clear. The perf. emphasizes the state or condition. (For a study of the perf., s. K.L. McKay, "The Use of the Ancient Greek Perfect Down to the Second Century A.D.," *Bulletin of the Institute of Classical Studies of the University of London*, 12 [1965], 1–21.) μαρτυρουμένη pres. pass. μαρτυρέω to testify,
22 to bear witness. ■ εἰς πάντας "unto all," "for all." πιστεύοντας pres. act. part. διαστολή difference, distinction.
23 ■ ἥμαρτον aor. ἁμαρτάνω to sin, to miss the mark (s. CBB). ὑστεροῦνται pres. mid. ὑστερέω to come too late, to miss, to fail to reach, to be lacking, to come short of, followed by the gen. (BAG; TDNT). δόξα glory. The following gen. could be obj.; that is, failing to give God glory, or subj., failing to receive the glory God gives, or poss.; that is, failing to conform to His image
24 (s. Murray). ■ δικαιούμενοι pres. pass. part. The pres. tense is iterat. and emphasizes the repeated action in each case (RWP). (For the grammatical connection and use of the part., s. SH; Murray; Cranfield.) δωρεάν freely, as a gift without payment. (For the adverbial use of the acc. in the papyri, s. MM.) ἀπολύτρωσις redemption, release, or deliverance of the pay-
25 ment of a price (s. APC, 37–48; GW, 71f.; TDNT). ■ προέθετο aor. mid. προτίθημι to place before, mid. to purpose, to design or to set forth publicly (SH). ἱλαστήριον that which expiates or propitiates, the means of expiation or the place of propitiation (for example mercy seat) (s. APC, 167–174; GW, 38–47; TDNT). ἔνδειξις demonstration, sign, proof. διά w. acc. because of. πάρεσις passing over; Christ died and thereby manifested God's righteousness because in the past God had merely overlooked man's sins (Barrett; s. also MRT, 210). προγεγονότων perf. act. part. προγίνομαι to happen before,

to happen previously. The prep. compound is temporal. ■ ἀνοχή 26
patience, forbearing (s. Rom. 2:4). δικαιοῦντα pres. act. part.
■ καύχησις boasting. ἐξεκλείσθη aor. pass. ἐκκλείω to 27
shut out, to exclude. ποῖος what sort of? ■ δικαιοῦσθαι pres. 28
pass. inf. ■ εἴπερ if, if on the whole. Used of a thing which is 30
assumed to be (T). δικαιώσει fut. ἀκροβυστία uncircumcision. ■ καταργοῦμεν pres. ind. act., s.v.3. γένοιτο aor. opt. 31
mid., s.v.4. ἱστάνω to establish.

Ch. 4

■ ἐροῦμεν fut. λέγω. εὑρηκέναι perf. act. inf. Infinitive 1
used in indirect discourse (s. BD, 203,204). προπάτωρ forefather, ancestor. ■ ἐδικαιώθη aor. pass. δικαιόω to justify, to 2
declare righteous (s. Rom. 2:13). καύχημα boasting, ground of
boasting (SH). (For the righteousness of Abraham in Jewish
thinking, s. SB III, 186–201.) ■ γάρ for. To be taken as an 3
argumentative particle showing why Abraham has no ground of
boasting (Barrett). ἐλογίσθη aor. pass. λογίζομαι to reckon to
one's account. In the language of an accountant the word means
"to enter in the account book" (s. Ramsey; LP, 286f.). ■ 4
ἐργαζομένῳ pres. mid. part. ἐργάζομαι to work. μισθός pay,
wage, salary (s. MM). λογίζεται pres. pass. ὀφείλημα debt,
that which is owed (s. Rom. 1:14). ■ πιστεύοντι pres. part dat. 5
sing. δικαιοῦντα pres. part. ἀσεβής ungodly. A very strong
word used to place the gratuity of the gift in the strongest light
(Lightfoot, *Notes*). ■ καθάπερ even as. (For Paul's use of the 6
rabbinical exegetical principle of comparing the same word used
in two passages, s. Barrett.) μακαρισμός declaration of blessedness (T). The ending of the word indicates a state or condition
(MH, 355). ■ μακάριος blessed, happy. ἀφέθησαν aor. pass. 7
ἀφίημι to forgive. ἀνομία lawlessness. ἐπεκαλύφθησαν aor.
pass. ἐπικαλύπτω to cover over. ■ οὐ μή "not ever." (For this 8
emphatic neg. use, s. M, 188f.; BG, 149f.) λογίσηται aor. mid.
subj. ■ περιτομή circumcision. ἀκροβυστία uncircumcision. 9
The prep. used here w. acc. primarily designates movement
toward. In this sense "for" (s. IBG, 49). ■ ὄντι pres. part. εἰμί. 10
■ σημεῖον sign. ἔλαβεν aor. λαμβάνω. σφραγίς seal. That 11
which confirms a test or authenticates. Used w. gen. The sign of
circumcision simply confirms righteousness through faith that
was already pres. (BAG; s. also TDNT). λογισθῆναι aor. pass.
inf. Infinitive used to show purpose (contemplated result) or
actual result (RWP). ■ στοιχοῦσιν pres. act. part στοιχέω to 12
walk. A well-known military term meaning strictly "to march in
file" (SH). ἴχνος footstep, track.

357

13   ■ *νόμου* "in the context of law." The prep. w. gen. indicates attendant circumstances (Barrett). The word law without the article refers to law as commandment demanding obedience and applies to all law which falls into this category (Murray). *ἐπαγγελία* promise. *κληρονόμος* heir. (For the Jewish view of Abraham as heir of the world and that this was achieved through

14   his law righteousness, s. SB III, 204–209.) ■ *κεκένωται* perf. pass. *κενόω* to empty. The perf. emphasizes a state or condition brought about by a previous result (s. Rom 3:21). *κατήργεται* perf. pass. *καταργέω* to render inoperative (s. Rom. 3:3). The conditional sentence of this v. could be classified as a second-class conditional sentence where the condition is not true (s.

15   IBG, 148f.). ■ *ὀργή* wrath (s. Rom. 1:18). *παράβασις* trans-
16   gression, stepping over the mark. ■ *βέβαιος* ratified (Lightfoot,
17   Notes). *σπέρμα* seed. ■ *γέγραπται* perf. pass. *ὅτι* recitative, equal to quotation marks. *τέθεικα* perf. act. *τίθημι* to place, to appoint. *κατέναντι* opposite to, in the presence of. (For this prep., s. MH, 129.) *ζωοποιοῦντος* pres. act. part. *ζωοποιέω* to make alive. Refers to God's ability to give a child to Abraham

18   and Sarah in their old age (Godet). *καλοῦντος* pres. part. ■ *ἐλπίς* hope. Here lit. "against (or, beyond) hope, in hope," that is, "hoping against hope" (Barrett). *γενέσθαι* aor. mid. inf. used w. prep. to express purpose. *εἰρημένον* perf. pass. part. *λέγω*.

19   *ἔσται* fut. *εἰμί*. ■ *ἀσθενήσας* aor. act. part. *ἀσθενέω* to be weak, ingressive aor. w. neg., "without showing weakness," "without becoming weak" (SH). *κατενόησεν* aor. *κατανοέω* to see clearly, to discern. (For the prep. compound, s. M, 117.) *νενεκρωμένον* perf. pass. part. *νεκρόω* to kill, pass. to die. The perf. emphasizes the completed state or condition (s. Rom. 3:-21). *ἑκατονταέτης* a hundred years. *που* about. *ὑπάρχων* pres. part. *ὑπάρχω* to exist, to be. *νέκρωσις* death, deadness. (For

20   nouns w. this suffix, s. MH, 373f.) ■ *διεκρίθη* aor. pass. *διακρίνω* to separate, to divide into, to be divided in one's own mind, to waiver (RWP). *ἐνεδυναμώθη* aor. pass. *ἐνδυναμόω* to strengthen, pass. to be strengthened, to be empowered. *δούς* aor.

21   act. part. *δίδωμι*. ■ *πληροφορηθείς* aor. pass. part. *πληροφορέω* to fill completely, to convince fully, pass. to be fully convinced, assured (BAG; TDNT). *ἐπήγγελται* perf. pass.

23   *ἐπαγγέλλω* to promise. *ποιῆσαι* aor. inf. ■ *ἐγράφη* aor. pass.
24   ■ *μέλλει* pres. ind. act. to be about to. Used w. inf. to express fut. (s. MKG, 307). *ἐγείραντα* aor. act. part. *ἐγείρω* to raise.
25   ■ *παρεδόθη* aor. pass. *παραδίδωμι* to deliver up. Perhaps a reference to Isaiah 53:12 (Lightfoot, Notes). *διά* w. acc. because of. The first prep. here could be causal and the second final

(MRP, 196) or both prep. could have a prospective reference (Murray). παράπτωμα transgression, a falling along side, a false step, transgression (TDNT; Cremer, 498f.). ἠγέρθη aor. pass. ἐγείρω. δικαίωσις justification, the judicial vindication and justification (TDNT; MRP, 196).

Ch. 5

■ δικαιωθέντες aor. pass. part. δικαιόω to justify, to de- 1 clare to be in the right (s. Rom. 2:13). The aor. part. expresses time before the main verb and could be here either temporal or causal. πρός w. ■ καί "also" (Godet). προσαγωγή access, 2 introduction (SH). ἐσχήκαμεν perf. ind. act. ἔχομεν. The perf. emphasizes the state "to have received and still possess" (M, 238). ἐστήκαμεν perf. ἵστημι, perf. to stand. καυχώμεθα pres. ind. or subj. It means a triumphant, rejoicing confidence in God (Barrett). ■ καί also. ἐν ταῖς θλίψεσιν "in the tribula- 3 tion." The word refers to pressures, hardships, and sufferings (SH; TDNT; Trench, Synonyms, 202f.). εἰδότες perf. part. of the defective verb οἶδα. ὑπομονή patient endurance, patiently waiting in hope (TDNT; CBB). κατεργάζεται pres. ind. mid. to produce. The prep. compound is perfective carrying the action of the main verb to its conclusion (s. M, 112f.). ■ δοκιμή ap- 4 proved character, the quality of being approved as a result of test and trials (BAG; SH). ■ καταισχύνει pres. ind. act. to put to 5 shame. ἐκκέχυται perf. pass. ἐκχέω to pour out. The word denotes both abundance and diffusion (Lightfoot, Notes). The idea of spiritual refreshment and encouragement is conveyed through the metaphor of watering (SH). The perf. emphasizes the completed state (s. Rom. 3:21). δοθέντος aor. pass. part. δίδωμι. ■ εἴ γε "if indeed." The combination is used to in- 6 troduce a fact of which one was absolutely certain (Thrall, 89f.). ὄντων pres. part. εἰμί gen. abs. ἀσθενής weak. ἀσεβής ungod- ly. ἀπέθανεν aor. ἀποθνήσκω to die. ■ μόλις w. difficulty, 7 scarcely, hardly. ὑπὲρ δικαίου "for a righteous (man)." (For a discussion of the structure of this v., s. Frederik Wisse, "The Righteous Man and the Good Man in Romans 5:7," NTS, 19 [October, 1972], 91–93.) ἀποθανεῖται fut. mid. ἀποθνήσκω. τάχα perhaps, possibly, probably. τολμᾷ pres. ind. act. to dare. ἀποθανεῖν aor. act. inf. ἀποθνήσκω. ■ συνίστησιν pres. ind. 8 act. to bring together, to demonstrate. ὄντων pres. part. gen. pl., gen. abs. expressing contemporaneous time. ■ μᾶλλον more, 9 here "much more," argument from the greater to the less (RWP). (For examples of this method of argument among the rabbis, s. SB III, 223–226.) σωθησόμεθα fut. pass. σῴζω to

save, to rescue, to deliver. Here it means the consummation of
that work of which justification is the commencement. It is a
preservation from all causes of destruction (Hodge; TDNT;
10 CBB). ■ ἐχθροί enemies. κατηλλάγημεν aor. pass.
καταλλάσσω to exchange, to make other a state of enmity, to
exchange enmity for friendship (APC, 187f.; s. also TDNT;
MNTW, 102–106). The prep. compound is perfective and means
"to effect a thorough change back, reconciled" (MH, 298).
11 καταλλαγέντες aor. pass. part. ■ καυχώμενοι pres. mid. part.
καταλλαγή reconciliation. ἐλάβομεν aor. λαμβάνω.
12   ■ εἰσῆλθεν aor. εἰσέρχομαι to come into. διῆλθεν aor.
διέρχομαι to pass through. It contains the force of distribution
"made its way to each individual member of the race" (SH). ἐφ'
ᾧ perhaps best understood as causal, "because" (s. F.W. Danker,
"Romans 5:12: Sin Under Law," NTS, 14 [April, 1968], 424–
439; but s. also GI, 116f.). ἥμαρτον aor. ἁμαρτάνω to sin.
13 ■ ἐλλογεῖται pres. pass. ἐλλογέω to charge to one's account
14 (s. MM). ὄντος pres. act. part. gen. sing. ■ ἐβασίλευσεν aor.
βασιλεύω to be king, to rule as king. ἁμαρτήσαντας aor. act.
part. ὁμοίωμα likeness. It denotes a resemblance which may
however be purely accidental (AS). παράβασις transgression.
τύπος type. The word means a visible mark left by some object.
Then the mark left in history or nature by the antitype (Barrett;
TDNT). μέλλοντος pres. act. part. μέλλω to be about to, here
"the one who is coming."
15   ■ παράπτωμα transgression (s. Rom. 4:25; Trench, Synonyms, 239f.). χάρισμα grace gift, an act of grace (Godet; s.
TDNT; CBB). ἀπέθανον aor., s.v.6. πολλῷ μᾶλλον "how
much more" (s.v.9.). δωρεά gift, the act of giving (Godet).
ὑπερίσσευσεν aor. περισσεύω to be more than enough, to
16 abound. ■ δώρημα gift. It denotes the concrete gift, the blessing
bestowed (Godet). κρίμα judgment, decision. κατάκριμα condemnation, judgment against someone. (For the force of the
prep. compound, s. MH, 316.) δικαίωμα justification, acquittal
17 (s. MRP, 198f.). ■ περισσεία more than enough, abundance.
λαμβάνοντες pres. act. part. It is the gift which man receives,
it is imputed, not infused (SH). βασιλεύσουσιν fut. to be king,
18 to rule as king. ■ ἄρα therefore. It gives a summation of the
doctrine set forth in the whole passage from v.12 onward (Mur-
19 ray). δικαίωσις justification. ■ παρακοή disobedience.
κατεστάθησαν aor. pass. καθίστημι to set down, to consti-
20 tute, to establish. ■ παρεισῆλθεν aor. παρεισέρχομαι to
come in along side, to come into the side of a state of things
already existing (SH). πλεονάσῃ aor. subj. πλεονάζω to be, or

to become more, to be pres. in abundance. Here it is probably intr. (Lightfoot, *Notes*). The subj. is used to express purpose. ἐπλεόνασεν aor. ὑπερεπερίσσευσεν aor. ὑπερπερισσεύω to abound more exceedingly. The prep. compound magnifies (MH, 326). ■ βασιλεύσῃ aor. subj. Subjunctive used to express 21 purpose. αἰώνιος eternal. Eternal life is not only related to the fut., but is organically related to the actual life lived and is a pres. possession of the believer (GW, 189f.).

Ch. 6

■ ἐροῦμεν fut. λέγω. ἐπιμένωμεν pres. subj. ἐπιμένω to 1 stay, to remain, to reside in. The pres. tense indicates the practice of sin as a habit. The subj. is deliberative (RWP). πλεονάσῃ aor. subj. πλεονάζω to be in abundance, to abound, to cause to increase. Subjunctive used to express purpose. ■ γένοιτο aor. 2 opt. mid. γίνομαι (s. Rom. 3:4). ἀπεθάνομεν aor. ἀποθνήσκω to die. τῇ ἁμαρτίᾳ "w. respect to sin," dat. of reference or respect (s. BD, 105f.). ζήσομεν fut. ζάω to live; that is, at any fut. time whatever after the occurrence of our dying (Meyer). ■ ἀγνοεῖτε pres. ind. act. not to know, to be 3 ignorant. ὅσοι as many as, "all of us who" (BAG). ἐβαπτίσθημεν aor. pass. βαπτίζω to baptize. ■ συνετάφημεν 4 aor. pass. συνθάπτω to bury together. εἰς θάνατον "into the death." The prep. conveys the notation of incorporation into (Lightfoot, *Notes*). ὥσπερ just as, even so. ἠγέρθη aor. pass. ἐγείρω pass. to be raised, to rise. καινότης freshness, newness, "in a new state, which is life." The idea of the word is "strangeness," and therefore a change (Lightfoot, *Notes*). περιπατήσωμεν aor. subj. περιπατέω to walk, to walk about, to conduct one's life (s. TDNT). The subj. is used to express purpose. ■ σύμφυτος grown together w. The process of grafting 5 may be in mind (Barrett). γεγόναμεν perf. γίνομαι. ὁμοίωμα likeness (s. Rom. 5:14). ἐσόμεθα fut. εἰμί. ■ γινώσκοντες 6 pres. part. παλαιός old. συνεσταυρώθη aor. pass. συσταυρόω to crucify together. καταργηθῇ aor. pass. subj. καταργέω to render inoperative, to make inactive (s. Rom. 3:13). μηκέτι no longer. ■ ἀποθανών aor. act. part. 7 δεδικαίωται perf. pass. δικαιόω to justify, to declare to be in the right. Here the word means either to be declared to be free from sin or to be acquitted from sin (s. MRP, 200f.). ■ 8 συζήσομεν fut. συζάω to live together. ■ εἰδότες perf. part. of 9 defective verb οἶδα to know. ἐγερθείς aor. pass. part. κυριεύω w. gen. to be lord over, to rule over, the idea of master and slave is pres. (SH). ■ ἐφάπαξ once for all. ■ λογίζεσθε pres. mid. 10/11 imp. λογίζομαι to consider, to reckon. The pres. imp. could mean "do this continually," or "continue doing this" (MKG, 272). ζῶντας pres. part. ζάω. The dat. w. part. could be dat. of respect or dat. of personal interest or advantage (s. DM, 84f.).

12 ■ βασιλευέτω pres. imp. βασιλεύω to be king, to rule as king. The pres. imp. w. neg. means either "do not always," or "do not continue" (MKG, 272). θνητός mortal, subject to death. ὑπακόυειν pres. act. inf. to listen to, to obey. The inf. used w. prep. expresses either purpose or result (MT, 143). ἐπιθυμία. The prep. compound is directive. The basic meaning "drive,"

13 "passion," is directed to an object (s. TDNT; Godet). ■ παριστάνετε pres. imp. παρίστημι to place beside, to put at one's disposal, to present. The word could be used in a military sense (Käsemann). (For the meaning of the pres. imp. w. neg., s.v.12.) μέλη acc. pl. members. ὅπλον tool, weapon. Sin is regarded as a sovereign (v. 12), who demands the military service of its subjects, levys their quota of arms (v. 13), and gives them their soldier's-pay of death (v. 23) (Lightfoot, Notes). ἀδικία unrighteousness. παραστήσατε aor. imp. παρίστημι. The previous pres. imp. calls for the discontinuation of an action. The aor. imp. calls for an immediate decisive new action as a break from the past (Johnson; Bakker, 65). ζῶντας pres. act. part. "alive, after being dead," a common classical expression

14 (Lightfoot, Notes). ■ κυριεύσει fut.

15 ■ ἁμαρτήσωμεν aor. subj. ἁμαρτάνω to sin, deliberative

16 subj. ■ ἤτοι "either." It has the notion of restriction (RG, 1154).

17 ■ ἦτε impf. εἰμί. ὑπηκούσατε aor. ὑπακούω. παρεδόθητε aor. pass. παραδίδωμι to deliver over to. τύπος a type. Incorporation of the antecedant into the rel. clause, "to which form

18 of doctrine ye were delivered" (RWP). ■ ἐλευθερωθέντες aor. pass. part. ἐλευθερόω to free, to make free. The part. could be

19 temporal "after" or causal. ἐδουλώθητε aor. pass. ■ ἀνθρώπινος human, here "to speak in human terms" (BAG). ἀσθένεια weakness; that is, "because of the difficulties of apprehension" (SH). παρεστήσατε aor. παρίστημι. δούλα acc. pl. predicative acc. in a double acc. construction "as servants" (s. MT, 246; RG, 480f.). ἀκαθαρσία uncleanness. ἀνομία lawlessness. ἁγιασμός sanctification, holiness, consecration. It refers to the process or state (Murray) of being set apart for God's service and the development and display of His characteristics

20/22 (s. Cremer; TDNT). ■ ἐλεύθερος free. ■ δουλωθέντες aor.

23 pass. part. ■ ὀψώνιον provisions, wages of a soldier (s. C.C. Caragounis, "Ὀψώνιον: A Reconsideration of its Meaning," Nov T 16 [January, 1974], 35–57; TDNT). (For a description of

soldier's pay, s. Lightfoot, *Notes*; CC, 206–209; BC V, 428.) χάρισμα free gift, grace gift (s. Rom. 5:14).

Ch. 7

■ γινώσκουσιν pres. act. part. dat. pl. He speaks to those 1 who have a knowledge of a general principle of all law (SH). κυριεύω pres. ind. act. to be lord over, to rule (w. gen.). ζῆ pres. ind. act. to live, to be alive. ■ ὕπανδρος under (subjected to) a 2 husband, married. The word may itself include the idea of subordination (Barrett). ζῶντι pres. act. part. dat. sing. ζάω. The part. used as an adj. "living husband" (s. Lightfoot, *Notes*). δέδεται perf. pass. δέω to bind. The perf. emphasizes the state or condition. (For the perf., s. Rom. 3:21.) ἀποθάνῃ aor. subj. ἀποθνήσκω to die. Subjunctive used in a third-class conditional sentence where the condition is probable. κατήργηται perf. pass. καταργέω to render inoperative, to nullify, to annul. The perf. emphasizes she is completely absolved or discharged (SH). ■ ἄρα then. μοιχαλίς adulteress. χρηματίσει fut. 3 χρηματίζω. The basic meaning is to do business, to negotiate. Then to be called, to bear the name or title of. Then in a special sense of giving answers or communications as an oracle (SH). The fut. is gnomic used to state what will customarily happen when occasion offers (SMT, 36). γένηται aor. mid. subj. γίνομαι. γενομένην aor. mid. part. ■ ὥστε therefore, conse- 4 quently. It draws an inference from the preceding and introduces the actual relation w. respect to Christians who are in a position corresponding w. that of the wife (Meyer). ἐθανατώθητε aor. pass. θανατόω to put to death. τῷ νόμῳ dat. of respect or reference (BD, 105). γενέσθαι aor. mid. inf. γίνομαι. Infinitive used w. prep. to express purpose. ἐγερθέντι aor. pass. part. ἐγείρω to rise, pass. to be raised. καρποφορήσωμεν aor. subj. καρποφορέω to bear fruit. Subjunctive used to express purpose. ■ σάρξ flesh, human nature as controlled and directed by sin 5 (Murray; s. TDNT; CBB; Kuss). πάθημα passion. ἁμαρτία pl. sins. ἐνηργεῖτο impf. mid. ἐνεργέω to work within. The pricks and stings of passion were active in our members (SH). The impf. pictures the continual action. καρποφορῆσαι aor. act. inf. Infinitive used to express purpose. ■ κατηργήθημεν aor. pass. 6 καταργέω s.v.2. ἀποθανόντες aor. act. part. ἀποθνήσκω. κατειχόμεθα impf. pass. κατέχω to hold down, to suppress, to hold fast, to confine. καινότης newness. παλαιότης obsoleteness, oldness. The genitives following these two words are genitives of apposition denoting that in which the newness or oldness consists (SH).

7 ■ ἐροῦμεν fut. λέγω. γένοιτο aor. mid. opt. γίνομαι (s. Rom. 3:4). ἔγνων aor. γινώσκω. εἰ μή used to introduce a contrary to fact conditional clause. τε γάρ "and in fact" denotes a second fact of the same kind as the preceding (τέ, also); and the second fact serves as a proof or explanation to the first (γάρ, for) (Godet). ἐπιθυμία desire, lust. ᾔδειν plperf. οἶδα. ἐπιθυμήσεις fut. ἐπιθυμέω to desire, to long for, to covet. It

8 includes every kind of illicit desire (SH). ■ ἀφορμή occasion, pretext, opportunity for something, lit., the starting point or base of operations for an expedition, then generally the resources needed to carry through an undertaking (BAG). λαβοῦσα aor. act. part. λαμβάνω. ἐντολή commandment. κατειργάσατο aor. mid. κατεργάζομαι to achieve, to work out, to bring about

9 (s. Rom. 5:3). ■ ἔζων impf., s.v.1. He had no dread of punishment, no painful conscientiousness of sin (Hodge). ἐλθούσης aor. part. ἔρχομαι gen. abs. ἀνέζησεν aor. ἀναζάω to revive,

10 to live again, to regain life. ■ ἀπέθανον aor. ἀποθνήσκω to

11 die. εὑρέθη aor. pass. ■ ἐξηπάτησεν aor. ἐξαπατάω to deceive completely, to make someone lose the way (RWP). The prep. compound may be intensive ("completely") or perfective ("successfully") (s. MH, 309f.). ἀπέκτεινεν aor. ἀποκτείνω to kill.

12 ■ μέν "undoubtedly." This is intended to guard beforehand the unassailable character of the law (Godet).

13 ■ ἐγένετο aor. mid. γίνομαι. φανῇ aor. pass. subj. φαίνομαι to appear. Used to express purpose. κατεργαζομένη pres. mid. part. γένηται aor. mid. subj. ὑπερβολήν beyond

14 measure, exceedingly. ἁμαρτωλός sinful. ■ σάρκινος fleshly. It denotes the material of which human nature is composed (SH). (For adj. w. this suffix indicating the material of which something is made, s. MH, 359, 378.) πεπραμένος perf. pass. part. πιπράσκω to sell. The perf. emphasizes the state or condi-

15 tion "sold" and therefore its bondslave (Lightfoot, Notes). ■

16 πράσσω to do, to practice. ■ σύμφημι to speak w., to agree, to consent. οὐκέτι no longer. ἐνοικοῦσα pres. part. ἐνοικέω to

18 indwell. ■ παράκειμαι pres. ind. mid. to lie along side, to lie

20/21 at hand, to be within reach (SH). ■ οἰκοῦσα pres. part. ■

22 θέλοντι pres. act. part. dat. sing. ■ συνήδομαι pres. ind. mid.

23 to rejoice w. someone, to joyfully agree. ἔσω inner. ■ ἀντιστρατευόμενον pres. mid. part. ἀντιστρατεύομαι to make a military expedition or take the field against anyone, to oppose, to war against (T). νοῦς mind, the reflective intelligence (RWP). αἰχμαλωτίζοντα pres. act. part. αἰχμαλωτίζω lit. to capture w. a spear, to take a prisoner of war, to subdue (s. LS).

24 ὄντι pres. part. εἰμί. ■ ταλαίπωρος miserable, wretched, dis-

tressed. ῥύσεται fut. mid. ῥύομαι to rescue. The word is used
to denote the act of the soldier who runs at his comrade's cry to
rescue him from the hands of the enemy (Godet). ■ αὐτὸς ἐγώ 25
I, myself. τῷ νοΐ, τῇ σαρκί dat. of reference (s. BD, 105).

Ch. 8

■ ἄρα so, therefore, consequently, an inference drawn from 1
that which precedes (s. Murray). κατάκριμα condemnation, a
judgment against someone. ■ ζωή life. The gen. expresses the 2
effect wrought. The Spirit is the author and giver of life (Gifford). ἠλευθέρωσεν aor. ἐλευθερόω to liberate, to make free.
■ ἀδύνατος impossible. ἐν "in which," "wherein" defining the 3
point in which the impossibility of the law consisted (SH).
ἠσθένει impf. ἀσθενέω to be weak. διὰ τῆς σαρκός "through
the flesh," through the reacting influence of the flesh (Meyer).
πέμψας aor. act. part. πέμπω to send. ὁμοίωμα likeness (s.
Rom. 5:14). κατέκρινεν aor. ind. act. κατακρίνω to condemn.
It refers both to the pronouncement of judgment and the carrying out of the sentence (TDNT). ■ δικαίωμα righteous demand, 4
ordinance (s. Rom. 1:32). πληρωθῇ aor. pass. subj. πληρόω to
fill, to fulfill. περιπατοῦσιν pres. act. part. περιπατέω to walk
about, to conduct one's life (s. TDNT). ■ ὄντες pres. part. εἰμί. 5
φρονοῦσιν pres. ind. act. to think, to set one's mind or heart
upon something. It denotes the whole action of the affections
and will as well as of the reason (SH). ■ διότι because. ἔχθρα 7
hatred, hostility, enmity. ὑποτάσσεται pres. ind. pass.
ὑποτάσσω pass. to be in subjection, to place one's self under.
■ ἀρέσαι aor. act inf. ἀρέσκω to please. ■ ἐν πνεύματι "to be 8/9
under the domination of the Spirit" (SH). εἴπερ "if indeed" (s.
Rom 3:3). οἰκεῖ pres. ind. to dwell. ■ σῶμα body, the physical 10
body (Meyer). ■ ἐγείραντος aor. part. ἐγείρω to raise, to resur- 11
rect. ζωοποιήσει fut. ζωοποιέω to make alive. θνητός mortal,
subject to death. ἐνοικοῦντος pres. part. ἐνοικέω to dwell in.
■ ὀφειλέτης one who owes a moral debt, debtor (s. Rom. 12
1:14). ζῆν pres. act. inf. to live. Infinitive used to explain the
debt. ■ ἀποθνῄσκειν pres. act. inf. πρᾶξις deed, act. 13
θανατοῦτε pres. ind. act. to put to death ζήσεσθε fut. mid.
ζάω. ■ ὅσοι as many as. ἄγονται pres. ind. pass. ἄγω to lead. 14
■ ἐλάβετε aor. λαμβάνω. δουλεία servitude, slavery. υἱοθεσία 15
adoption. The word indicates a new family relation with all the
rights, privileges, and responsibilities. (For the custom of adoption, s. TDNT; OCD, 8f.; Francis Lyall, "Roman Law in the
Writings of Paul—Adoption," JBL, 88 [December, 1969], 458–
466.) ἀββά abba (Aramaic) father. An Aramaic expression used

16 in prayer and in the family circle (BAG; CBB). ■ αὐτό "himself." (For this use of the pron., s. MT, 40f.) συμμαρτνεῖ pres.
act. to bear witness w. someone, to confirm, to testify in support
of someone. Used in the papyri where the signature of each
attesting witness is accompanied by the words "I bear witness w.
and I seal w" (MM). τέκνον child. It expresses the relation of
17 nature and indicates community of life (Godet). ■ κληρονόμος
heir. Paul is still concerned to demonstrate the certainty of fut.
salvation, and argues that if we are heirs of God our inheritance
is secure (Barrett). συγκληρονόμος fellow heir, co-heir. εἴπερ
"if indeed" (s. Rom. 3:30). συνδοξασθῶμεν aor. pass. subj.
συνδοξάζω to glorify together.

18   ■ λογίζομαι to consider, to reckon. ἄξιος that which balances the scales, comparable, worthy (TDNT). πάθημα suffering. πρός. The basic meaning is "near" w. acc. "toward,"
"against." Here "in comparison w." (RG, 622f.; DB, 124f.).
μέλλουσαν pres. part. "coming," "about to be."
19 ἀποκαλυφθῆναι aor. pass. inf. ἀποκαλύπτω to reveal. ■
ἀποκαραδοκία watching eagerly w. outstretched head, eager
waiting. The sense is strengthened by the prep. in compound
which denotes diversion from all other things and concentration
on a single object (SH). κτίσις creation. ἀποκάλυψις uncover-
ing, unveiling, revelation. ἀπεκδέχεται pres. mid. to await expectantly but patiently. The prep. in compound are perfective w.
the idea of readiness and preparedness and the pres. tense indi-
20 cates the going on of the act until he comes (MH, 310). ■
ματαιότης vanity, aimlessness, the inability to reach a goal or
achieve results (Trench, Synonyms, 180–184; TDNT). ὑπετάγη
aor. ind. pass. ὑποτάσσω s.v.7. ἑκών willing, unconstrained,
gladly. It usually stands opposed to violence or compulsion
21 (Cremer, 246). ὑποτάξαντα aor. part. ■ ἐλευθερωθήσεται fut.
22 pass., s.v.2. φθορά corruption, deterioration. ■ συστενάζω
pres. ind. to groan together. συνωδίνω to suffer birth pains
together. The prep. in these two words indicates in all the parts
of which creation is made up (SH). The pres. tense indicates the
23 continual action. ■ ἀπαρχή firstfruits. The first portion of the
harvest, regarded both as a first installment and as a pledge of
the final delivery of the whole (Barrett). The following gen. is
gen. of apposition. The Holy Spirit is regarded as an anticipation
of final salvation, and a pledge that we who have the Spirit shall
in the end be saved (Barrett). ἔχοντες pres. part. υἱοθεσίαν
adoption (s.v.15). ἀπεκδεχόμενοι pres. mid. part. (s.v.19).
ἀπολύτρωσις redemption, release, a deliverance from the "ills
24 that the flesh is heir to" (SH). ■ τῇ ἐλπίδι "in hope." The dat.

is not instrumental but is modal referring to the fact that salvation bestowed in the past is characterized by hope (Murray). ἐσώθημεν aor. pass. σῴζω to save, to rescue. βλεπομένη pres. pass. part. ■ ὑπομονή patience, patient endurance. 25

■ συναντιλαμβάνεται pres. ind. mid. to lend a hand to- 26 gether w., at the same time w. one (RWP), to help, to come to the aid of someone (BAG). ἀσθένεια weakness. προσευξώμεθα aor. mid. subj. προσεύχομαι to pray. δεῖ it is necessary. αὐτὸ τὸ πνεῦμα "the Spirit Himself" (s.v.16). ὑπερεντυγχάνω pres. ind. act. to plead or intercede on behalf of someone. It is a picturesque word of rescue by one who "happens on" one who is in trouble and "in his behalf" pleads w. "unuttered groanings" or w. "sighs that baffle words" (RWP). ἀλάλητος unable to be spoken. ■ ἐρευνῶν pres. part. ἐρευνάω 27 to search, to examine. κατὰ θεόν "according to God." The prep. denotes the standard (Godet). ■ οἴδαμεν perf. of the defective 28 verb w. pres. meaning to know. ἀγαπῶσιν pres. act. part. gen. pl. ἀγαπάω to love. συνεργεῖ pres. ind. to cooperate, to work together, to work w. one another (Gifford). πρόθεσις "according to His purpose." Setting before, purpose (s. TDNT). κλητός dat. pl. called, dat. of advantage. Used to designate the person whose interest is affected (BD, 101). οὖσιν pres. part. εἰμί. ■ ὅτι because. προέγνω aor. ind. act. 3rd per. sing. 29 προγινώσκω to know before, to take note of, to fix the regard upon (SH). προώρισεν aor. προορίζω to mark out w. a boundary beforehand, to predestine. σύμμορφος conformed, having the same form w. It denotes an inward and not merely superficial conformity (RWP; s. TDNT). εἰκών image (s. TDNT; CBB). πρωτότοκος firstborn. The term reflects on the priority and the supremacy of Christ (Murray, s. Col. 1:15). ■ ἐκάλεσεν aor. 30 ἐδικαίωσεν aor. δικαιόω to declare to be in the right, to justify. ἐδόξασεν aor. δοξάζω to glorify. The aor. speaks of God who sees the end from the beginning and in whose decree and purpose all fut. events are comprehended and fixed (Hodge).

■ ἐροῦμεν fut. λέγω. ■ γε an intensive particle here magni- 31/32 fying the deed (RWP). ἐφείσατο aor. mid. φείδομαι to spare. παρέδωκεν aor. παραδίδωμι to deliver over. χαρίσεται fut. mid. χαρίζομαι to give graciously, to give out of grace (s. Rom. 5:15). ■ ἐγκαλέσει fut. ἐγκαλέω to call in, to bring a legal 33 charge against someone. δικαιῶν pres. part. ■ κατακρινῶν 34 pres. part., s.v.3. ἀποθανών aor. part. ἀποθνήσκω. ἐγερθείς aor. pass. part. ἐντυγχάνει pres. s.v.27. ■ χωρίσει fut. χωρίζω 35 to separate. θλῖψις pressure, tribulation. στενοχωρία narrowness, distress. (For these two words, s. Rom. 2:9.) διωγμός

persecution. λιμός hunger. γυμνότης nakedness. κίνδυνος
36 danger. μάχαιρα sword. ■ γέγραπται perf. pass.
θανατούμεθα pres. pass. ἐλογίσθημεν aor. pass. σφαγή
37 slaughter. ■ ὑπερνικῶμεν pres. act. to conquer, to win a victory. The prep. compound intensifies the verb, "we are winning
a most glorious victory" (BAG). ἀγαπήσαντος aor. act. part.
38 ■ πέπεισμαι perf. pass. πείθω to persuade, pass. to be persuaded. ἐνεστῶτα perf. pass. part. ἐνίστημι to place in, perf. to be
at hand, to be pres. It signifies present events and circumstances
39 (Cranfield). δυνάμεις potentate. ■ ὕψωμα height, exaltation.
βάθος depth. δυνήσεται fut. mid. χωρίσαι aor. act. inf.

Ch. 9

1   ■ συμμαρτυρούσης pres. part. συμμαρτυρέω to witness
together (s. Rom. 8:16) gen. abs. συνείδησις conscience (s.
2 Rom. 2:15). ■ λύπη sorrow, grief as a state of mind (SH).
ἀδιάλειπτος continually, unceasing. ὀδύνη pain. It implies the
anguish or smart of the heart which is the result of sorrow (SH).
3 ■ ηὐχόμην impf. mid. εὔχομαι to pray, to wish, idiomatic impf.
"I was on the point of wishing" (RWP; for the desiderative impf.,
s. IBG, 9). ἀνάθεμα a thing or per. devoted to destruction,
4 accursed (Barrett; TDNT). συγγενής relative, kinsman. ■
υἱοθεσία adoption (s. Rom. 8:15). διαθήκη agreement, covenant, treaty (s. TDNT). νομοθεσία giving of the law. λατρεία
religious service. The sum total of the Levitical services institut-
5 ed by the law (Godet). ἐπαγγελία promise. ■ πατέρες fathers.
ὧν pres. part. εἰμί. εὐλογητός blessed.
6   ■ οὐχ οἷον rel. pron. qualitative what sort or manner of,
such as. Used here as an idiom "but it is not as though" (AS).
ἐκπέπτωκεν perf. ἐκπίπτω to fall out, to fall from its place;
7 that is, perished and become of no effect (SH). ■ κληθήσεται
8 fut. pass. καλέω. ■ λογίζομαι pres. ind. pass. to be counted as.
9/10 ■ ἐλεύσομαι fut. mid. ἔρχομαι. ἔσται fut. εἰμί. ■ ῾Ρεβέκκα
perhaps best to be taken as a nom. abs. providing the introduction to what is stated in verses 11 and 12 (Murray). κοίτη bed,
sexual intercourse. Used w. pres. part. ἔχουσα "having" as an
11 idiom meaning "to conceive" (BAG). ■ μήπω not yet.
γεννηθέντων aor. pass. part. γεννάω to bear, pass. to be born.
πραξάντων aor. act. part. πράσσω to do. φαῦλος bad, foul.
Worthlessness is the central notion (Trench, Synonyms, 317f.).
ἐκλογή election, choice. πρόθεσις purpose. μένη pres. subj.
μένω to remain. The pres. tense emphasizes the continual re-
12 maining. ■ καλοῦντος pres. part. ἐρρέθη aor. pass. part. λέγω.
μείζων comp. μέγας. δουλεύσει fut. δουλεύω to serve as a

slave. ἐλάσσων comp. ὀλίγος. ■ γέγραπται perf. pass. The 13
perf. emphasizes the lasting and binding authority of that which
was written (s. M). ἠγάπησα aor. ἀγαπάω to love. ἐμίσησα
aor. μισέω to hate. The Heb. idiom means, "I prefer Jacob to
Esau"; but Paul may again have taken the word literally (Barrett). ■ ἐροῦμεν fut. λέγω. μή used in questions expecting the 14
answer no. γένοιτο aor. mid. opt. γίνομαι (s. Rom. 3:4). ■ 15
ἐλεήσω fut. ἐλεέω to show mercy. οἰκτιρήσω fut. οἰκτίρω to
show compassion. The first of these words expresses the compassion of the heart, the second the manifestion of that feeling
(Godet). ■ θέλοντος pres. part. τρέχοντος pres. part. τρέχω to 16
run. The two words indicate human striving and may reflect the
symbol of an athletic contest (Michel). ἐλεῶντος pres. part.
■ ἐξήγειρα aor. ἐξεγείρω to raise out, to raise up. It is used of 17
God calling up the actors on the stage of history (SH).
ἐνδείξωμαι aor. mid. subj. ἐνδείκνυμι to show, to demonstrate.
διαγγελῇ aor. pass. subj. διαγγέλλω to proclaim. ■ σκληρύνω 18
to harden.
   ■ μέμφεται pres. mid. to blame, to find fault. ἀνθέστηκεν 19
perf. ἀνθίστημι to stand up against, to resist. ■ μενοῦν γε on 20
the contrary. (For the use of this particle, s. Thrall, 34f.)
ἀνταποκρινόμενος pres. mid. part. ἀνταποκρίνομαι to answer back, to talk back, to reply. Reciprocal action is expressed
by the prep. compound (MH, 297). πλάσμα that which is mold-
ed or formed (AS). πλάσαντι aor. part. πλάσσω to form, to
mold. ἐποίησας aor. ind. act. ■ κεραμεύς potter. πηλός clay. 21
The gen. is used w. the word "authority," that is, "authority over
the clay." φύραμα lump of clay. ποιῆσαι aor. inf. Infinitive
used epexegetically to explain the authority. σκεῦος vessel.
ἀτιμία dishonor. That is one vessel designed for noble, one for
ignoble use (Barrett). ■ θέλων pres. part. ἐνδείξασθαι aor. mid. 22
inf. γνωρίσαι aor. inf. γνωρίζω to make known. ἤνεγκεν aor.
φέρω to carry, to bear. μακροθυμία longsuffering (s. Rom.
2:4). κατηρτισμένα perf. pass. part. καταρτίζω to make
ready, to prepare. The perf. emphasizes the state or condition (s.
Rom. 3:21). ἀπώλεια ruin, destruction. ■ γνωρίσῃ aor. subj. 23
Subjunctive used to express purpose. δόξα honor, glory. ἔλεος
mercy. προητοίμασεν aor. προετοιμάζω to prepare before.
The prep. compound is temporal. ■ οὕς whom (pl.) "even us 24
whom He has called." The rel. pron. is attracted to the gender
of the personal pron. (SH). ἐκάλεσεν aor. ■ καλέσω fut. 25
ἠγαπημένην perf. pass. part., s.v.13. ■ ἔσται fut. εἰμί. ἐρρέθη 26
aor. pass. part., s.v.12. κληθήσονται fut. pass., s.v.7. ζῶντος
pres. part. ζάω to live. ■ ἀριθμός number. ἄμμος sand. 27

ὑπόλειμμα rest, remnant. σωθήσεται fut. pass. σῴζω to res-
28 cue, to save. ■ συντελῶν pres. part. συντελέω to bring to an
end, to complete, to finish, to consummate. The prep. compound
29 is perfective (s. MH, 325). ποιήσει fut. ■ προείρηκεν perf.
προλέγω to say before. ἐγκατέλιπεν aor. ἐγκαταλείπω to
leave behind. Used in a second-class conditional clause which is
contrary to fact. ἐγενήθημεν aor. pass. γίνομαι. ὡμοιώθημεν
aor. pass. ὁμοιόω to be like.
30   ■ ἐροῦμεν s.v.14. διώκοντα pres. part. διώκω to hunt, to
pursue, to persecute. κατέλαβεν aor. καταλαμβάνω to lay
31/32 hold on, to obtain. ■ ἔφθασεν aor. φθάνω to arrive at. ■
προσέκοψαν aor. προσκόπτω to cut against, to stumble on or
33 at. πρόσκομμα stumbling, offense. ■ γέγραπται perf. pass.
σκάνδαλον a stumbling block, that which gives offense. (For
this word, s. TDNT; NTW, 111–114.) πιστεύων pres. part.
καταισχυνθήσεται fut. pass. καταισχύνομαι to be ashamed.

Ch. 10

1   ■ εὐδοκία good will, good pleasure, wish or desire inasmuch as a desire is usually directed toward something that
2 causes satisfaction or favor (BAG; s. also TDNT). ■ ζῆλος zeal,
followed by the obj. gen. "zeal for God." ἐπίγνωσις knowledge,
accurate knowledge. The prep. compound is directive (MH,
3 314). ■ ἀγνοοῦντες pres. part. ἀγνοέω to be ignorant, not to
know. (For the suffix as a neg., s. Rom. 1:20.) ζητοῦντες pres.
part. ζητέω to seek. The pres. part. emphasizes the continuing
search. στῆσαι aor. inf. ἵστημι to cause to stand, to establish.
It means to cause to stand erect as a monument raised, not to
the glory of God, but to their own (Godet). ὑπετάγησαν aor.
pass. ὑποτάσσω to put one's self under orders, to obey, pass.
4 to be in subjection (RWP). ■ τέλος end, goal, completion.
πιστεύοντι pres. act. part.
5/6   ■ ποιήσας aor. part. ζήσεται fut. mid. ζάω to live. ■
εἴπῃς aor. subj. λέγω. The aor. subj. w. neg. as a prohibition
forbids the beginning of an action (s. Rom. 6:12). ἀναβήσεται
fut. mid. ἀναβαίνω to go up, to ascend. καταγαγεῖν aor. inf.
κατάγω to lead down. Infinitive used to express purpose. The
thought here is to precipitate the Incarnation. The Messiah has
appeared, and it is therefore impossible to hasten His coming by
perf. obedience to the law and penitence for its transgression
7 (Barrett). ■ καταβήσεται fut. mid. καταβαίνω to go down.
ἄβυσσος abyss, depth, underworld (s. SH; TDNT). ἀναγαγεῖν
aor. inf. ἀνάγω to lead up. Infinitive used to express purpose.
This also is sheer impossibility, since the Resurrection has al-

ready happened (Barrett). ■ ἐγγύς near (used w. dat.) τῆς 8
πίστεως obj. gen. gospel message concerning faith (RWP). ■ 9
ὁμολογήσῃς aor. subj. ὁμολογέω to agree, to confess, to proclaim. As a judicial term, the word indicates the binding and
public declaration which settles a relationship w. legal force
(Käsemann; TDNT). πιστεύσῃς aor. subj. ἤγειρεν aor. ἐγείρω
to raise. σωθήσῃ fut. pass. σῴζω to rescue, to save. ■ 10
πιστεύεται pres. pass. ὁμολογεῖται pres. pass. Both pass. are
the impersonal pass. "it is believed"; that is, "one believes" (s.
RG, 820). ■ καταισχυνθήσεται fut. pass. καταισχύνω to put 11
to shame. ■ διαστολή division, difference. πλουτῶν pres. part. 12
πλουτέω to be rich. ἐπικαλουμένους pres. mid. part.
ἐπικαλέω to call upon. ■ ἐπικαλέσηται aor. mid. subj. 13
■ ἐπίστευσαν aor. πιστεύσωσιν aor. subj., deliberative 14
subj. used in a rhetorical deliberative question (SMT, 77).
ἤκουσαν aor. ἀκούω. ἀκούσωσιν aor. subj., deliberative subj.
κηρύσσοντος pres. part. ■ κηρύξωσιν aor. subj. deliberative 15
subj. ἀποσταλῶσιν aor. pass. subj. ἀποστέλλω to send, deliberative subj. γέγραπται perf. pass. ὡραῖος originally, seasona-
ble, ripe, beautiful, fair, lovely, pleasant (BAG).
εὐαγγελιζομένων pres. mid. part. εὐαγγελίζομαι to proclaim
good news (TDNT; CBB). ■ ὑπήκουσαν aor. ὑπακούω to 16
listen to, to obey, in the sense of give credence to. The word
implies the idea of voluntary submission (SH). ἀκοή hearing,
that which is heard; that is, message report (s. SH). ■ ἄρα then, 17
it follows. ■ μή Used in questions expecting the answer no. 18
μενοῦν γε s. Rom. 9:20. ἐξῆλθεν aor. ἐξέρχομαι to go out
φθόγγος sound, vibration of a musical string (RWP). πέρας
boundary, limit. οἰκουμένη earth, the inhabited earth. ■ ἔγνω 19
aor. act. 3rd per. sing. γινώσκω. παραζηλώσω fut.
παραζηλόω to provoke to jealousy, to make jealous. ἀσύνετος
senseless, not understanding. παροργιῶ fut. παροργίζω to
provoke to anger. ■ ἀποτολμᾷ pres. ind. act. to be bold of one's 20
self; that is, to assume boldness, to make bold (T). The prep.
compound is perfective; that is, "carry daring to its limit" (MH,
298). εὑρέθην aor. pass. ἐμφανής visible, manifest. ἐγενόμην
aor. mid. γίνομαι. ἐπερωτῶσιν pres. part. dat. pl. ἐπερωτάω
to ask for, to inquire. ■ ἐξεπέτασα aor. ἐκπετάννυμι to spread 21
out, to stretch out. ἀπειθοῦντα pres. part. ἀπειθέω to contradict, to speak against.

Ch. 11

■ μή Used in questions expecting the answer no. ἀπώσατο 1
aor. mid. ἀπωθέω to push away, to repel, mid. to push away

from one's self, to reject, to repudiate. γένοιτο aor. mid. opt.
2 γίνομαι (s. Rom. 3:4). φυλή tribe. ■ προέγνω aor. ind. act. 3rd
per. sing. προγινώσκω to foreknow, to know beforehand (s.
Murray at Rom. 8:29). ἐν Ἠλίᾳ "in Elijah," a rabbinic method
of quotation denoting "in the passage of Scripture which contains the history of Elijah" (Godet). ἐντυγχάνει pres. ind. act.
to intercede, to plead w. (w. dat.). The verb means to meet w.,
then to meet w. for the purposes of conversation, to have an
3 interview w., to plead w. or to accuse (SH). ■ ἀπέκτειναν aor.
ἀποκτείνω to kill. θυσιαστήριον altar, place of sacrifice.
κατέσκαψαν aor. κατασκάπτω to dig under or down, to tear
4 down. ὑπελείφθην aor. pass. ὑπολείπω to leave behind. ■
χρηματισμός oracle. The word is used here to emphasize the
localization; the awesomeness is probably the indirectness of the
divine communication (Anthony Hanson, "The Oracle in Romans 11:4," NTS, 19 [April, 1973], 301). κατέλιπον aor.
καταλείπω to leave behind, to reserve. ἐμαυτῷ "for myself,"
refl. pron. It emphasizes the thought that the remnant is preserved by God Himself for His own gracious purpose (Gifford).
5 ἔκαμψαν aor. κάμπτω to bend, to bow. γόνυ knee. ■ οὕτως
so. It refers to the internal resemblance of the two facts, for the
same principle is realized in both (Godet). οὖν then, also. The
words refer to the moral necessity which the one follows the
other and indicates the addition of a new example to the former
(Godet). λεῖμμα rest, remnant. ἐκλογή selection, election.
6 γέγονεν perf. γίνομαι. ■ οὐκέτι no longer. γίνεται pres. ind.
mid. Grace ceases to show itself as that which according to its
nature it is. It becomes what according to its essence it is not;
7 it gives up its specific character (Meyer). ■ ἐπιζητέω pres. ind.
act. to seek for. ἐπέτυχεν aor. ἐπιτυγχάνω to obtain, to reach,
to hit upon. ἐπωρώθησαν aor. pass. πωρόω to harden, to cover
w. a thick skin, to harden by covering w. a callous (T; s. also SH).
8 ■ γέγραπται perf. pass. ἔδωκεν aor. δίδωμι. κατάνυξις
stupefacation. Derived from the verb meaning to strike or prick
9 violently, to stun (SH). ■ γενηθήτω aor. imp. pass. γίνομαι.
παγίς trap, snare. θήρα a net used in hunting as a trap.
ἀνταπόδομα a recompense, a paying back, that which is paid
10 back. ■ σκοτισθήτωσαν aor. pass. imp. σκοτίζω to darken.
νῶτος back. διὰ παντός continually, constantly (BAG).
σύγκαμψον aor. imp. συγκάμπτω to bend together, to bow
down, as of captives whose backs were bent under burdens
(RWP).
11   ■ μή s.v.1. ἔπταισαν aor. πταίω to stumble. πέσωσιν
aor. subj. πίπτω to fall. A man who stumbles may recover

himself, or he may fall completely. Hence, the word is used here
of a complete irrevocable fall (SH). γένοιτο aor. opt. mid. (s.
Rom. 3:4). παράπτωμα transgression, false step (s. TDNT).
παραζηλῶσαι aor. act. inf. παραζηλόω to make jealous, to
provoke to jealousy. Infinitive used w. prep. to express purpose.
■ ἥττημα defeat. πόσῳ μᾶλλον by how much more. (For this   12
type of argument, s. Rom. 5:9.) πλήρωμα fullness.
    ■ ἐφ᾿ ὅσον "inasmuch as," "insofar as" (RWP). δοξάζω to   13
glorify. ■ εἰ "if by any means." The use of the particle w. purpose   14
or aim is a kind of indirect discourse (RWP). παραζηλώσω aor.
subj. or fut. σώσω aor. subj. or fut. σῴζω to rescue, to save.
■ ἀποβολή casting away. καταλλαγή reconciling (s. APC,   15
186–223; TDNT). πρόσλημψις receiving. ■ ἀπαρχή firstfruit   16
(s. Rom. 8:23). φύραμα dough, lump. (For the rabbinical practice based on Num. 15:18, s. SB IV, 665f.) ῥίζα root. κλάδος
branch.
    ■ ἐξεκλάσθησαν aor. pass. ἐκκλάω to break off.   17
ἀγριέλαιος wild olive tree. ὤν pres. part. εἰμί. ἐνεκεντρίσθης
aor. pass. ἐγκεντρίζω to graft in. συγκοινωνός participant,
partner, one who shares something w. someone (BAG; s.
TDNT). πιότης fatness. ἐλαία olive tree. ἐγένου aor. mid. 2nd
per. sing. γίνομαι. ■ κατακαυχῶ pres. mid. imp. 2nd per. sing.   18
κατακαυχάομαι to boast against, to brag. The prep. compound
indicates an action unfavorable to its object (MH, 316). The
pres. imp. w. neg. indicates either to stop an action in progress
or do not make the action a habit (MKG, 272). ■ ἐρεῖς fut.   19
λέγω. κλάδοι branches. Without the article, the character is
emphasized, "beings who had the character of branches" (Godet). ἐγκεντρισθῶ aor. pass. subj. (For the process of grafting
and its relation to the figure of the olive tree, s. Munck, 128–
130.) ■ καλῶς adv. well, "true enough" (Barrett). ἕστηκας   20
perf. ἵστημι to stand. ὑψηλός high. φρόνει pres. imp. φρονέω
to think, to set one's mind upon. φοβοῦ pres. mid. imp.
φοβέομαι to be afraid, to fear. ■ φύσις nature. ἐφείσατο aor.   21
mid. φείδομαι (w. gen.) to spare. The verb is used in a first-class
conditional clause which accepts the condition as a reality.
φείσεται fut. mid. ■ ἴδε aor. imp. ὁράω. χρηστότης goodness,   22
kindness (s. Rom. 2:4). ἀποτομία severity. The word comes
from a verb meaning "to cut right off, to cut short" and emphasizes a rigor which does not bend (Godet). πεσόντας aor. part.
πίπτω to fall, s.v.11. ἐπιμένῃς pres. subj. ἐπιμένω to remain,
to continue. ἐπεί since, otherwise. ἐκκοπήσῃ fut. pass.
ἐκκόπτω to cut out. ■ ἐγκεντρισθήσονται fut. pass.   23
ἐγκεντρίσαι aor. inf. ■ ἐξεκόπης aor. pass. ἐκκόπτω.   24

καλλιέλαιος a cultivated olive tree as opposed to a wild olive tree (BAG). πόσῳ μᾶλλον "by how much more" (s. Rom. 5:9).
25 ■ ἀγνοεῖν pres. act. inf. to be ignorant, not to know. μυστήριον mystery, the plan and purpose of God which was hidden in the past and impossible for human beings to discover but which is now made known by God (s. TDNT; CBB; Cremer, 424f.). ἦτε pres. subj. εἰμί. φρόνιμος wise. πώρωσις the covering w. a callous, dulled perception, hardness (T; s. also v.7). μέρος a part. γέγονεν perf., s.v.5. ἄχρι οὗ w. aor. subj. "until," "until that" (s. Godet). εἰσέλθῃ aor. subj. εἰσέρχομαι to come
26 into, to come in. ■ οὕτως so, accordingly. It continues the thought of what precedes or draws out its implications (Murray). πᾶς Ἰσραήλ "all Israel." It refers to the forgiveness of the whole Jewish people or nation, the whole ethnic group in contrast to the saved remnant of Jews in Paul's day and ours (Johnson). σωθήσεται fut. pass. σῴζω. γέγραπται perf. pass. ἥξει fut. ἥκω to come. ῥυόμενος pres. mid. part. ῥύομαι to rescue, to deliver, Jesus as the Messiah (SH). ἀποστρέψει fut.
27 ἀποστρέφω to turn. ἀσέβεια ungodliness (s. Rom. 1:18). ■ διαθήκη treaty, covenant. ἀφέλωμαι aor. mid. subj.
28 ἀφαιρέομαι to take away, to remove. ■ κατὰ τὸ εὐαγγέλιον "according to the gospel." The relation is thereby designated according to which they are enemies (Meyer). ἐχθροί enemies. It points to the rejection of Israel w. which Paul is dealing throughout this chapter (Murray). δι᾽ ὑμᾶς "because of you," "for your advantage" (Barrett). The prep w. acc. is extended to
29 the final cause (BG, 37). ἀγαπητός beloved. ■ ἀμεταμέλητος not to be sorry afterward, not to be regretted, without regret, irrevocable of something one does not take back (BAG). χάρισμα a gift of grace. God does not go back on His acts of
30 grace (Barrett, s. Rom. 5:15). ■ ἠπειθήσατε aor. ἀπειθέω to be disobedient. ἠλεήθητε aor. pass. ἐλεέω to have mercy or
31 pity, pass. to obtain mercy or pity. ἀπείθεια disobedience. ■
32 ἐλεηθῶσιν aor. pass. subj. ■ συνέκλεισεν aor. συγκλείω to shut together, to shut together like a net (RWP). ἐλεήσῃ aor.
33 subj. ■ βάθος depth. ἀνεξιχνίαστοι unsearchable. (For the prefix used w. the neg., s. Rom. 1:20; for the use of verbal adjectives w. this ending, s. M, 221f.; MH, 188, 370f.) κρίμα literally, not to be tracked out, incomprehensible, inscrutable
34 (BAG). ■ ἔγνω aor. γινώσκω. σύμβουλος fellow counselor,
35 advisor. ἐγένετο aor. mid., s.v.17. ■ προέδωκεν aor. προδίδωμι to give before, to give beforehand, to give in advance. If man could really be the first to do something for God, he would make God his debtor (Godet). ἀνταποδοθήσετει fut.

pass. ἀνταποδίδωμι to recompense, to give back, to repay.
■ ἐξ from, out of. It refers to God as Creator (Godet). διά 36
through. It refers to the government of mankind. Everything is
executed only through Him (Godet). εἰς for. It refers to a final
goal (Godet).

Ch. 12

■ παρακαλέω to admonish, to encourage, to exhort. The 1
word was used in classical Gr. of exhorting troops who were
about to go into battle. Here it is a request based on the apostolic
authority of Paul (MNTW, 134; Michel; s. also TDNT). οὖν
therefore. It refers to the result of the whole previous argument
(SH). οἰκτιρμός mercy, compassion, compassion and pity arising from the miserable state of one in need (s. TDNT; Cremer).
The prep. w. gen. ("by") gives the reader to understand that the
divine mercies are the power by means of which this exhortation
should take possession of his will (Godet). παραστῆσαι aor.
inf. παρίστημι to present, a technical term for presenting a
sacrifice, literally meaning "to place beside" for any purpose
(SH). θυσία offering, sacrifice. ζῶσαν pres. part. ζάω to live.
εὐάρεστος well-pleasing. λογικός pertaining to reason, rational, spiritual. The use of our bodies is characterized by conscience, intelligent, consecrated devotion to the service of God
(Murray). (For adjectives w. this suffix having the idea of
"belonging to," "pertaining to," "w. the characteristics of," s.
MH, 378.) λατρεία service, worship, acc. in apposition to the
object (SH). ■ συσχηματίζεσθε pres. pass. imp. 2
συσχηματίζομαι to form or mold after something. The verb
indicates the adoption or imitation of a pose or received mode
of conduct (Godet). The pres. imp. w. neg. indicates the discon-
tinuance of an action in progress or means that the action is not
to be continually done (MKG, 272f.). μεταμορφοῦσθε pres.
imp. pass. μεταμορφόω to transform, "but be ye transformed in
your inmost nature" (SH). The prep. compound indicates
change; that is, change in form (MH, 318). ἀνακαίνωσις
renewing. νοῦς mind, the thinking power, reason in its moral
quality and activity (Meyer). δοκιμάζειν pres. inf. to prove by
testing, to accept as approved after testing. The inf. w. prep.
expresses the purpose or result (MT, 143).

■ δοθείσης aor. pass. part. δίδωμι. ὄντι pres. part. εἰμί. 3
ὑπερφρονεῖν pres. act. inf. to think over, above or beyond, to
think highly of one's self, to be haughty. Infinitive used in indirect discourse, here indirect neg. command (RWP). δεῖ it is
necessary. φρονεῖν to think, to set the mind or attention on

something (CBB). σωφρονεῖν pres. act. inf. to be of sound mind, to be reasonable, sensible, to keep the proper measure, not going beyond the set boundaries, "to turn the energy of the mind to recognize its limits and respect them" (Godet; TDNT).

4 ἐμέρισεν aor. μερίζω to measure. μέτρον measure. ■ καθάπερ just as. μέλος member. πρᾶξις practice, function.

5 ■ καθ᾽ εἷς "as to each one." A late idiom w. prep. is treated
6 adverbially (RWP). ἀλλήλων one another. ■ διάφορος differing. ἀναλογία proportion, proportionate allowance. (For the
7 use in the papyri, s. MM.) ■ διακονία ministry. The word indicates a personal ministry done in service of another (s. TDNT). Here it probably refers to the administration of alms and attendance to bodily wants (SH). It may also refer to the
8 ministry of the Word (Murray). διδάσκων pres. part. ■ παρακαλῶν pres. part., s.v.1. μεταδιδούς pres. part. μεταδίδωμι to give, to share w. someone. ἁπλότης sincerity, generously, liberally. It refers to open-handed and open-hearted giving out of compassion and a singleness of purpose, not from ambition (SH). προϊστάμενος pres. part. προΐστημι to stand on the first place, to preside. σπουδή zeal. ἐλεῶν pres. part. ἐλεέω to show mercy. ἱλαρότης cheerfulness, gladness, graciousness.

9   ■ ἀνυπόκριτος without hypocrisy. (For the prefix used as a neg., s. Rom. 1:20.) ἀποστυγοῦντες pres. part. ἀποστυγέω to despise, to hate bitterly. It expresses a strong feeling of horror and the prep. compound emphasizes the idea of separation (SH). κολλώμενοι pres. mid. part. κολλάομαι to glue or cement together, to join firmly, to join one's self to (AS). Our attachment to the good is to be that of the devotion illustrated by the bond
10 of marriage (Murray). ■ φιλόστοργος full of tenderness. It denotes the delicate affections mutually rendered by those who cherish one another w. natural affection, as parents and children, brothers and sisters (Godet). τῇ τιμῇ "in or w. honor." The result of true affection is that no one seeks his own honor or position, and everyone is willing to give honor to others (SH). προηγούμενοι pres. mid. part. προηγέομαι to go before and show the way, to consider, to esteem. It either means to try to outdo one another in showing respect or to consider better, to
11 esteem more highly (BAG). ■ ὀκνηρός idle, lazy, irksome, troublesome, not irked by the demands of (Murray). ζέοντες pres. part. ζέω to boil, to be fervent. δουλεύοντες pres. part. δουλεύω
12 to serve as a slave. ■ τῇ ἐλπίδι in hope. The dat. is voc. in the point of hope (EGT). χαίροντες pres. part. θλῖψις pressure, tribulation (s. Rom. 2:9). ὑπομένοντες pres. part. ὑπομένω to

remain under, to endure w. patience. προσκαρτεροῦντες pres. part. προσκαρτερέω to hold fast to, to persevere, to give attention to, to be faithful in (s. TDNT). ■ χρεία need. 13 κοινωνοῦντες pres. part. κοινωνέω to share in, to have fellowship w. (TDNT). φιλοξενία hospitality, fond of strangers. διώκοντες pres. part. διώκω to hunt, to pursue. ■ εὐλογεῖτε 14 pres. imp. εὐλογέω to bless, to invoke God's blessings upon them (Murray). The pres. imp. could be iterat. and calls for habitual action (s. Rom. 6:11). καταρᾶσθε pres. mid. imp. καταράομαι to curse, to invoke a curse. The pres. imp. w. neg. forbids the habitual action. ■ κλαίειν pres. act. inf. to weep. The 15 inf. expresses the force of an imp. (s. RG, 1092f.; IBG, 126). κλαιόντων pres. act. part. ■ φρονοῦντες pres. act. part. 16 ὑψηλός high, exalted. ταπεινός low, humble. συναπαγόμενοι pres. mid. part. συναπάγομαι to lead along w. one, pass. to be carried along w., as by a flood which sweeps everything along w. it and then to give one's self up to (SH). γίνεσθε pres. mid. imp. φρόνιμος wise. ■ ἀποδιδόντες pres. act. part. ἀποδίδωμι to 17 render, to give back, to pay back. προνοούμενοι pres. mid. part. προνοέω to think before, to have regard for, to be preoccupied w. (Godet). ■ εἰρηνεύοντες pres. part. εἰρηνεύω to practice 18 peace, to live in peace. (For verbs ending w. this suffix which expresses the notion of "being or behaving, or acting as," s. MH, 400.) ■ ἐκδικοῦντες pres. part. ἐκδικέω to secure someone's 19 right, to avenge, to revenge. (For the use of the part. in vv. 9–19 w. an imp. sense in a series of exhortations, s. BG, 129f.) δότε aor. imp. δίδωμι. γέγραπται perf. pass. ἐκδίκησις revenge. ἀνταποδώσω fut. ἀνταποδίδωμι to pay back, to recompense. The prep. compound expresses a reciprocal idea (MH, 297). ■ πεινᾷ pres. subj. πεινάω to be hungry. ψώμιζε pres. imp. 20 ψωμίζω to feed w. morsels, then generally to feed (AS). διψᾷ pres. subj. διψάω to be thirsty. πότιζε pres. imp. ποτίζω to give to drink. ποιῶν pres. part. ἄνθραξ coal. σωρεύσεις fut. σωρεύω to pile up, to heap. ■ νικῶ pres. pass. imp. νικάω to 21 conquer, to overcome. νίκα pres. act. imp.

Ch. 13

■ ἐξουσία authority. Here a reference to governmental 1 authorities rather than invisible angelic powers (s. Murray, Appendix C). ὑπερεχούσαις pres. part. f. pl. ὑπερέχω to have or hold over, to be above or supreme. ὑποτασσέσθω pres. pass. imp. ὑποτάσσω to place or rank under, to subject, to obey. οὖσαι pres. part. εἰμί. τεταγμέναι perf. pass. part. τάσσω to draw up an order, to arrange in place, to assign, to appoint (AS).

The part. is used in a periphrastic construction and the perf.
emphasizes the state or condition, "stand ordained by God"
2 (RWP). ■ ὥστε therefore. It presents the logical result (SH).
ἀντιτασσόμενος pres. mid. part. ἀντιτάσσω to arrange one's
self opposite or against, to resist. διαταγή ordinance.
ἀνθέστηκεν perf. ἀνθίστημι to take one's stand against, to
withstand. ἀνθεστηκότες perf. act. part. λήμψονται fut. mid.
3 λαμβάνω. ■ φόβος fear, terror. φοβεῖσθαι pres. mid. inf. to be
4 afraid, to fear. ποίει pres. imp. ἕξεις fut. ἔχω. ■ σοί dat. sing.
"for you," "to you," the ethical dat. (RWP). ποιῇς pres. subj.
φοβοῦ pres. mid. imp. εἰκή without a cause, purposeless, in vain.
μάχαιρα sword. The sword is the symbol of the executive and
criminal jurisdiction of a magistrate and is therefore used of the
power of punishing inherent in the government (SH). φορεῖ
pres. act. to bear, to carry. ἔκδικος avenging. The adj. is used
as a substitutive the avenger, the one who punishes (BAG).
5 πράσσοντι pres. part. πράσσω to do, to practice. ■ ἀνάγκη
necessity, imposed either by the external condition of things, or
by the law of duty, regard to one's advantage, custom, argument
(T). ὑποτάσσεσθαι pres. pass. inf. συνείδησις conscience (s.
6 Rom. 2:15). ■ φόρος tax. τελεῖτε pres. ind. act. to fulfill, to pay.
(For taxation in the Roman Empire, s. CC, 183f.; A.H.M. Jones,
The Roman Economy, 151–158.) προσκαρτεροῦντες pres.
part. προσκαρτερέω to attend constantly, to adhere to (s. Rom.
7 12:12). ■ ἀπόδοτε aor. imp. ἀποδίδωμι to pay back. ὀφειλή
obligation, debt. Here it is the obligations we owe to those in
authority in the state (Murray). τέλος duty, toll, custom.
8   ■ ὀφείλετε pres. imp. ὀφείλω to owe, to be indebted to
someone. ἀγαπᾶν pres. inf. to love. ἀγαπῶν pres. part.
9 πεπλήρωκεν perf. ind. πληρόω to fill, to fulfill. ■ μοιχεύσεις
fut. μοιχεύω to commit adultery. φονεύσεις fut. φονεύω to
murder. κλέψεις fut. κλέπτω to steal. ἐπιθυμήσεις fut.
ἐπιθυμέω to desire, to covet. (For the use of the fut. under
Semitic influence to express a categorical imp., s. BG, 94f.)
ἀνακεφαλαιοῦται pres. pass. ἀνακεφαλαιόω to summarize,
to sum up. A rhetorical term used of the summing up of a speech
or argument and hence of including a large number of separate
10 details under one head (SH). ἀγαπήσεις fut. ■ πλήρωμα fulfillment, a complete fulfillment (Barrett).
11   ■ εἰδότες perf. part. οἶδα. ὕπνος sleep. ἐγερθῆναι aor.
pass. inf. ἐγείρω to raise, pass. to rise. ἐγγύτερον comp. ἐγγύς
12 near, close. ἐπιστεύσαμεν aor. ■ προέκοψεν aor. προκόπτω
to put forward, to advance. ἤγγικεν perf. ἐγγίζω to draw near,
to come close. ἀποθώμεθα aor. mid. subj. ἀποτίθημι to put

378

off, hortatory subj. ἐνδυσώμεθα aor. mid. subj. ἐνδύω to put on, to clothe one's self, hortatory subj. ὅπλον weapon. ■ 13 εὐσχημόνως adv. decently, becomingly. περιπατήσωμεν aor. subj. περιπατέω to walk about, to conduct one's life. κῶμος carousing, reveling. It was used of a nocturnal, riotous procession of half-drunken and frolicsome fellows who paraded through the streets w. torches and music in honor of Bacchus or some other deity. Then it was used generally of feasts and drinking parties that were protracted till late at night and indulged in revelry (T). μέθη drunkenness (s. TDNT; Philo, De Ebrietate). κοίτη bed, sexual intercourse, here unlawful intercourse (SH). ἀσέλγεια debauchery. The word contains the idea of shameless greed, animal lust, sheer self-indulgence which is such a slave to its so-called pleasures that it is lost to shame. It is one who acknowledges no restraints, who dares whatsoever his caprice and wanton petulance may suggest (NTW, 26f.; Trench, Synonyms, 56). ἔρις strife. ζῆλος envy. ■ ἐνδύσασθε aor. mid. imp. 14 πρόνοια forethought, thought in advance, provision. ποιεῖσθε pres. mid. inf. ἐπιθυμία desire, lust (s. Rom. 7:7).

Ch. 14

■ ἀσθενοῦντα pres. part. ἀσθενέω to be weak. The part. 1 denotes one whose faith falters (becomes weak) at a given moment and in a special case (Godet). προσλαμβάνεσθε pres. mid. imp. προσλαμβάνω to take to one's self, to receive. The word is used of God receiving or helping man and of men receiving others into fellowship or companionship (SH). διάκρισις distinguishing, quarrel, "welcome, but not for the purpose of getting into quarrels about opinions" (BAG). διαλογισμός thought, reasoning, questioning. ■ πιστεύει to believe, to have 2 faith; that is, he is completely uninhibited by relics of a pagan or a Jewish past, expressing itself in religious scruples (Barrett). φαγεῖν aor. inf. ἐσθίω to eat. λάχανον vegetable. ■ ἐσθίων 3 pres. part. ἐξουθενείτω pres. imp. 3rd per. sing. ἐξουθενέω to consider as nothing, to treat w. contempt. κρινέτω pres. imp. 3rd per. sing. κρίνω to judge. προσελάβετο aor. mid. προσλαμβάνω. ■ κρίνων pres. part. ἀλλότριος belonging to 4 another, not one's own. οἰκέτης servant, household slave. ἴδιος "to his own master," dat. of reference. It is to his own master that he is responsible (SH). σταθήσεται fut. pass. ἵστημι pass. to stand. (For the pass. deponent, s. RG, 817.) δυνατεῖ pres. act. to be able. στῆσαι aor. inf. ἵστημι to cause to stand. ■ παρά 5 more than. πληροφορείσθω pres. pass. imp. πληροφορέω to fill completely, to convince fully, pass. to be fully convinced,

6 assured, certain (BAG). ■ φρονῶν pres. part. φρονέω to think
7/8 of, to esteem, to regard. ■ ζῇ pres. ind. act. to live. ■ ζῶμεν and
9 ἀποθνήσκωμεν pres. subj. ■ ἀπέθανεν aor. ἀποθνήσκω to
die. ἔζησεν aor. ζώντων pres. part. κυριεύσῃ aor. subj.
10 κυριεύω to be lord, to rule. ■ παραστησόμεθα fut. mid.
11 παρίστημι to stand, to stand beside, to stand before. ■
γέγραπται perf. pass. κάμψει fut. κάμπτω to bend.
ἐξομολογήσεται fut. mid. ἐξομολογέομαι to confess, to ac-
12 knowledge, to give praise. ■ δώσει fut. λόγον δίδωμι to give
an account.

13   ■ κρίνωμεν pres. subj. to judge, hortatory subj. κρίνατε
aor. imp. τιθέναι pres. act. inf. to place. πρόσκομμα stumbling, the opportunity to take offense or to make a misstep
(BAG). σκάνδαλον snare, the stick which caused the trap to
fall, cause of offense, it is that which trips us up or that which
14 lures us into sin (NTW, 111–114; s. also TDNT). ■ πέπεισμαι
perf. pass. πείθω to persuade, pass. to be persuaded, to have
confidence. κοινός common, unclean, defiled. It is a technical
term to express those customs and habits which, although "common" to the world, were forbidden to the pious Jew (SH). εἰ μή
except. λογιζομένῳ pres. mid. part. λογίζομαι to consider, to
15 suppose. ■ βρῶμα food. λυπεῖται pres. pass. λυπέω to cause
sorrow, to hurt. It expresses the painful and bitter feeling produced in the heart of the weak (Godet). ἀπόλλυε pres. imp.
16 ἀπόλλυμι to ruin, to destroy. ἀπέθανεν aor., s.v.9. ■
βλασφημείσθω pres. imp. pass. βλασφημέω to slander, to
17/18 speak evil of. ■ βρῶσις eating. πόσις drinking. ■ ἐν τούτῳ "in
this," that is, by recognizing that food and drink are secondary
matters (Barrett). δουλεύων pres. part. δουλεύω to serve as a
slave. εὐάρεστος pleasing. δόκιμος approved, approved after
19 examination. ■ διώκωμεν pres. subj. διώκω to pursue, hortatory subj. "let us pursue." οἰκοδομή building as a process, figura-
20 tive of spiritual strengthening, edifying, building up (BAG). ■
κατάλυε pres. imp. καταλύω to tear down, to overthrow. It is
the opposite of the building up involved in the word of v. 19
(Murray). The pres. imp. w. the neg. indicates the discontinuing
of an action in progress or that the action should not be a habit
21 (s. Rom. 6:12). ἐσθίοντι pres. part. dat. sing., s.v.3. ■ φαγεῖν
aor. inf., s.v.2. κρέας meat. πιεῖν aor. inf. πίνω to drink.
προσκόπτω pres. act. to strike against, to stumble. Used of
those who strike against a stone or other obstacle in the path.
22 Here it indicates to be induced to sin (T). ■ ἔχε pres. imp.
κρίνων pres. part. δοκιμάζει pres. ind. to approve of after test-
23 ing and examining (SH). ■ διακρινόμενος pres. mid. part.

διακρίνω to judge between, to hesitate, to waiver.

Ch. 15

■ ὀφείλομεν pres. ind. act. to owe someone, to be a debtor 1 (s. Rom. 1:14). ἀσθένημα weak. ἀδύνατος powerless, without strength. βαστάζειν pres. act. inf. to bear. ἀρέσκειν pres. act. inf. to please. ■ πλησίον neighbor, dat. used w. verb. ἀρεσκέτω 2 pres. imp. 3rd per. sing. τὸ ἀγαθόν "for the good," "for his benefit" (Meyer). The end or purpose of pleasing must be the promotion of what is absolutely to their good, further defined by "their edification" (SH). ■ ἤρεσεν aor. ἀρέσκω. γέγραπται 3 perf. pass. ὀνειδισμός reproach, reviling, insult. ὀνειδιζόντων pres. part. ὀνειδίζω to reproach, to heap insults upon. ἐπέπεσαν aor. ἐπιπίπτω to fall upon. ■ ὅσος as great, how 4 great, whatever. προεγράφη aor. pass. προγράφω to write beforehand. The prep. "before" is in contrast w. "today" (SH). παράκλησις consolation, encouragement (s. TDNT). ἔχωμεν pres. subj. Subjunctive used w. particle to express purpose. ■ 5 δῴη aor. act. opt. δίδωμι. The opt. is used to express a wish (s. MT, 120f.; s. also J. Gonda, *The Character of the Indo-European Moods* [Wiesbaden; Otto Harrassowitz, 1956]). φρονεῖν pres. act. inf. to have in mind, to think of, to set one's mind upon. κατὰ Χρ. "according to Christ's example" (Murray). ■ 6 ὁμοθυμαδόν of one accord, w. unity of mind (SH). δοξάζητε pres. subj. δοξάζω to glorify, to cause a good opinion about someone.

■ προσλαμβάνεσθε pres. mid. imp. προσλαμβάνω to 7 receive, to welcome (s. Rom 14:1). προσελάβετο aor. mid. προσλαμβάνω. ■ γεγενῆσθαι perf. pass. inf. γίνομαι. Infini- 8 tive used in indirect discourse after a verb of "saying" (s. BD, 203f.). βεβαιῶσαι aor. inf. βεβαιόω to confirm, to make firm, to establish, to establish a promise is to confirm by fulfilling it (Godet). ■ δοξάσαι aor. inf. The inf. is used to express purpose 9 and is to be related to the εἰς τό of v.8 (Michel). γέγραπται perf. pass. ἐξομολογήσομαι fut. mid. ἐξομολογέω to confess, to praise. ψαλῶ fut. ψάλλω to play a stringed instrument w. the fingers, to sing to a harp, to sing a hymn, to sing praise (AS). ■ εὐφρανθητε aor. pass. imp. εὐφραίνομαι to rejoice. ■ 10/11 αἰνεῖτε pres. imp. αἰνέω to praise. ἐπαινεσάτωσαν aor. imp. 3rd per. pl. ἐπαινέω to approve, to praise. The prep. compound is directive (MH, 312). ■ ἔσται fut. εἰμί. ῥίζα root. 12 ἀνιστάμενος pres. part. ἀνίσταμαι to arise, to rise up in the sense appear, come (BAG). ἄρχειν pres. inf. to rule. ἐλπιοῦσιν fut. ἐλπίζω. (For the use of composite quotations by Paul, s.

13 Rom. 3:10.) ∎ πληρῶσαι aor. opt. πληρόω to fill, to fulfill. (For
   the opt. expressing a wish, s.v.5.) περισσεύειν pres. inf. to
   abound. Infinitive used to express purpose.

14   ∎ πέπεισμαι perf. pass. πείθω to persuade, pass. to be
   persuaded, perf. to have confidence. μεστός full. ἀγαθωσύνη
   goodness. πεπληρωμένοι perf. pass. part., s.v.13. δυνάμενοι
   pres. mid. part. νουθετεῖν pres. act. inf. to admonish, to warn.
   It is an appeal to the mind where opposition is present. The
   person is lead away from a false way through warning, instruction, reminding, teaching, and encouraging and his conduct is to

15 be corrected (CBB; s. also TDNT). ∎ τολμηροτέρως adv.
   comp. τολμηρός bold, daring. ἔγραψα aor. μέρος part, measure, "in some measure," "in part of the epistle" (SH).
   ἐπαναμιμνήσκων pres. part. ἐπαναμιμνήσκω to call back to
   mind again, to remind again (RWP). δοθεῖσαν aor. pass. part.

16 δίδωμι. ∎ λειτουργός minister, one who performs a public
   service, particularly a religious service (s. BAG; TDNT; NTW,
   74–76). ἱερουργοῦντα pres. part. ἱερουργέω to serve as a
   priest, to perform a sacred function, especially to sacrifice (SH).
   γένηται aor. mid. subj. γίνομαι. προσφορὰ offering.
   εὐπρόσδεκτος pleasing, acceptable. ἡγιασμένη perf. pass.

17 part. ἁγιάζω to sanctify, to set apart for divine purposes. ∎

18 καύχησις boasting, glorying. ∎ τολμήσω fut. τολμάω to be
   bold, to dare. κατειργάσατο aor. mid. κατεργάζομαι to ac-

19 complish, to produce. ὑπακοή obedience. ∎ τέρας wonder.
   κύκλῳ in a circle, round about. The idea in the word is that of
   a complete circle and Paul describes the territory already evan-
   gelized in Palestine, Syria, Asia Minor and Greece as lying within a circle; that is, within the circle of the nations around the
   Mediterranean Sea (John Knox, "Romans 15:14–33 and Paul's
   Conception of His Apostolic Mission," JBL, 83 [March, 1964],
   11). πεπληρωκέναι perf. inf. to fulfill, to fill up. To fill up the
   space lacking in preaching the gospel where others have not

20 (Knox, 10). ∎ φιλοτιμούμενον pres. mid. part. φιλοτιμέομαι
   to be fond of honor, to have as one's ambition, to aspire (BAG).
   εὐαγγελίζεσθαι pres. mid. inf. to proclaim the good news, to
   preach the gospel. ὠνομάσθη aor. pass. ὀνομάζω to name, here
   "so named as to be worshipped" (SH). οἰκοδομῶ pres. subj. to

21 build. ∎ γέγραπται perf. pass. ὄψονται fut. mid. ὁράω.
   ἀνηγγέλη aor. pass. ἀναγγέλλω to proclaim. ἀκηκόασιν perf.
   ἀκούω. συνήσουσιν fut. συνίημι to comprehend, to understand.

22   ∎ ἐνεκοπτόμην impf. pass. ἐγκόπτω to cut in, to hinder.
   The impf. pictures the repeated action. ἐλθεῖν aor. inf. ἔρχομαι.

■ ἔχων pres. part. κλῖμα territory, region, district. ἐπιποθία 23
longing. ■ πορεύωμαι pres. mid. subj. πορεύομαι to travel. 24
διαπορευόμενος pres. mid. part. διαπορεύομαι to travel
through. θεάσασθαι aor. mid. inf. θεάομαι to see.
προπεμφθῆναι aor. pass. inf. προπέμπω to send forth, to help
on one's journey w. food, money by arranging for companions,
means of travel, etc., to send on one's way (BAG). Infinitive
used to express purpose. ἐμπλησθῶ aor. pass. subj.
ἐμπίμπλημι to fill. ■ διακονῶν pres. part. ■ ηὐδόκησαν aor. 25/26
εὐδοκέω to be well pleased, to think it good. κοινωνία fellowship, sharing, contribution (s. TDNT). ποιήσασθαι aor. mid.
inf. ■ ὀφειλέτης debtor (s. Rom. 1:14). πνευματικός spiritual. 27
ἐκοινώνησαν aor. κοινωνέω to have a share in. σαρκικός
fleshly, carnal. Here it has no evil associations. It is used with
reference to tangible, material possessions (Murray).
λειτουργῆσαι aor. inf. λειτουργέω to minister, to do a service
(s. v.16). ■ ἐπιτελέσας aor. part. ἐπιτελέω to complete, to 28
bring to completion. σφραγισάμενος aor. mid. part.
σφραγίζω to seal, to seal w. a sign of ownership and a guarantee
of the correctness of the contents (Deissmann; BS, 238f.;
TDNT). ἀπελεύσομαι fut. mid. ἀπέρχομαι to go away, to
depart. ■ ἐρχόμενος pres. mid. part. ἐλεύσομαι fut. mid. 29
ἔρχομαι. ■ παρακαλῶ pres. ind. to urge, to exhort, to encour- 30
age (s. Rom. 12:1). συναγωνίσασθαι aor. mid. inf.
συναγωνίζομαι to fight or contend along w. someone, to strive
together. It is the picture of wrestling in prayer (Michel). ■ 31
ῥυσθῶ aor. pass. subj. ῥύομαι to rescue, to deliver.
ἀπειθούντων pres. part. ἀπειθέω to be disobedient, to be unbelieving. ■ ἐλθών aor. part. ἔρχομαι. συναναπαύσωμαι aor. 32
mid. subj. συναναπαύομαι to rest together w., to refresh together, "I may rest and refresh my spirit w. you" (SH).

Ch. 16

■ συνίστημι to commend, to introduce, commendatory 1
letters were well known in the ancient world (Barrett). οὖσαν
pres. part. εἰμί. ■ προσδέξησθε aor. mid. subj. προσδέχομαι 2
to receive, to welcome. ἀξίως worthily. παραστῆτε aor. subj.
παρίσταμι to stand beside, to help, to assist, to stand beside in
order to hold up (Godet). χρῄζῃ pres. subj. χρῄζω to need, to
have a need. προστάτις helper. The masc. form of the word was
used by the Romans for the legal representative of a foreigner.
In Jewish communities it meant the legal representative or
wealthy patron. Here it indicates the personal help given to Paul
(SH; Michel). ἐγενήθη aor. pass. γίνομαι. ■ ἀσπάσασθε aor. 3

mid. imp. ἀσπάζομαι to greet. (For a study of greetings sent
in letters, s. T.Y. Mullins, "Greeting as a New Testament Form,"
JBL, 87 [December, 1968], 418–426.) συνεργός fellow worker.
4 ■ οἵτινες qualitive pron. signifying "as people who," "who, as
such" (Godet; BG, 69). τράχηλος neck. ὑπέθηκαν aor.
ὑποτίθημι to place under (the axe of the executioner), to risk
5 one's life for another (s. RWP). ■ ἀπαρχή first fruit (s. Rom.
8:23). εἰς "for." The prep. makes Christ the person to whom the
6 first fruits are offered (Godet). ■ ἐκοπίασεν aor. κοπιάω to
7 grow weary, to work w. effort. ■ συγγενής kinsman. Probably
a reference to fellow Jews (Barrett). συναιχμάλωτος fellow
prisoner, fellow captive (s. Rom. 7:23). ἐπίσημος splendid, out-
10 standing. γέγοναν perf. γίνομαι. ■ δόκιμος approved, ap-
12/13 proved after trial. ■ κοπιώσας aor. part. ■ ἐκλεκτός elect.
16 ■ φίλημα kiss. (For this custom, s. TDNT.)
17   ■ σκοπεῖν pres. inf. to observe, to mark, to scrutinize (T);
"to mark and avoid" (SH). διχοστασία division. σκάνδαλον
offense, cause of stumbling (s. Rom. 14:13). ἐμάθετε aor.
μανθάνω to teach. ποιοῦντας pres. part. "causing." ἐκκλίνετε
pres. imp. ἐκκλίνω to come away from someone, to shun, to
18 avoid. ■ τοιοῦτος such a one. χρηστολογία smooth, plausible
speech, fair and insinuating speech (MM). εὐλογία praise, fine
speaking, well-chosen (but untrue) words, false eloquence, or
flattery (BAG). ἐξαπατῶσιν pres. ind. act. to deceive (s. Rom.
19 7:11). ἄκακος without evil, innocent. ■ ἀφίκετο aor. mid.
ἀφικνέομαι to reach, to come from, then to arrive at (RWP).
20 ἀκέραιος unmixed, simple, unsophisticated, innocent. ■
συντρίψει fut. συντρίβω to rub together, to crush, "will throw
him under your feet, that you may trample upon him" (SH).
21/22 τάχος quickly. ■ ἀσπάζομαι pres. mid. s.v.3. ■ γράψας aor.
23 part. ■ ξένος host, one who extends hospitality. οἰκονόμος
steward, manager, city treasurer (s. TDNT).
25   ■ δυναμένῳ pres. mid. part. στηρίξαι aor. inf. στηρίζω
to make firm, to make stable, to establish. ἀποκάλυψις unveiling, revelation. σεσιγημένου perf. pass. part. σιγάω to be silent. The perf. part. emphasizes the state or condition, "a state
26 of silence" (RWP). ■ φανερωθέντος aor. pass. part. φανερόω
to make clear, to manifest, to reveal. προφητικός prophetical.
ἐπιταγή command, commandment. γνωρισθέντος aor. pass.
part. γνωρίζω to make known.

1 CORINTHIANS

κλητός called. Verbal adj. here w. a pass. meaning (s. BG, 1
47f.). ἀπόστολος apostle, one who is called by the Lord, commissioned by Him, carrying His authority (s. TDNT; J. Andrew
Kirk, "Apostleship Since Rengstorf: Towards a Synthesis,"
NTS, 21 [January, 1975], 249–264). Σωσθένης "Sosthenes, the
brother." Probably the Sosthenes of Acts 18:17. The term brother is here probably more than the common bond of brotherhood
true of all believers and refers to a colleague in the Christian
mission; that is, one who makes the ministry his primary occupation (s. E. Earle Ellis, "Paul and His Co-Workers," NTS 17
[July, 1971], 445–452). ■ τῇ ἐκκλησίᾳ "to the church." Here 2
the Christian community in Corinth (Hering; s. also TDNT).
The gen. is poss. and is at once a protest against party spirit; "the
church of God" not of any one individual (RP). οὔσῃ pres. part.
εἰμί. ἡγιασμένοις perf. pass. part. ἁγιάζω to sanctify, to
consecrate, to separate from the secular for sacred use and purposes (s. TDNT; CBB). The perf. emphasizes the state or condition resulting from a previous action (s. Rom 3:21). κλητοί
called, s.v.1. ἐπικαλουμένοις pres. mid. part. ἐπικαλέω to call
upon, to invoke. The pres. tense emphasizes the habitual act
which characterizes their life (s. Hodge). αὐτῶν καὶ ἡμῶν
"theirs and ours." The words could refer to "place" but better
"Lord." Christians share in a common holiness because they
share a common Lord (Barrett). ■ χάρις grace (s. Rom. 5:15). 3
εἰρήνη peace. The Heb. word as used in greetings emphasizes
holiness and prosperity of life and personality (s. TDNT; CBB).

■ πάντοτε always. περὶ w. gen. for, concerning. The mean- 4
ing often overlaps w. ὑπέρ (BD, 121). ἐπὶ "because of." It
indicates the reason (Hering). δοθείσῃ aor. pass. part. δίδωμι.
■ παντί "in everything," "in every respect" (Barrett). 5
ἐπλουτίσθητε aor. pass. πλουτίζω to make rich. λόγῳ speech,
utterance. γνῶσις knowledge. The first is the outward expression and the second the inward conviction (Lightfoot,
Notes). ■ καθὼς just as, inasmuch as. Produces not a mere 6
parallel but rather an explanation of what precedes (RP). τὸ

μαρτύπιον τοῦ Χρ. "the witness of Christ." The gen. could be either objective or subj. ἐβεβαιώθη aor. pass. βεβαιόω to make firm, to make stable, to confirm. It was used in the papyri in the sense of a legally guaranteed security (BS, 104–109). The mystery of Christ was given legal force through the apostle (TDNT).

7 ■ ὑστερεῖσθαι pres. mid. inf. ὑστερέω to come short, to lack. Infinitive used to express contemplated result. It was what was to be looked for in the Corinthians (RP). χάρισμα gift, that which was given out of grace, empowerments given to the church from God or from the risen Lord (E.E. Ellis, " 'Spiritual' Gifts in the Pauline Community," NTS, 20 [January, 1974], 128–144; TDNT). ἀπεκδεχομένους pres. mid. part. ἀπεκδέχομαι to wait eagerly but patiently for something. The double prep. in compound implies a degree of earnestness and intensity of expectation (Lightfoot; s. also MH, 298, 310). The pres. tense emphasizes the continuous action and the part. expresses an attendant circumstance (Grosheide). ἀποκάλυψις unveiling, revelation. It is here followed by the objective gen.

8 ■ βεβαιώσει future βεβαιόω to establish, to confirm (s.v.6). ἕως unto, until. τέλος end, goal. The phrase moves easily from a temporal meaning to the meaning "completely" (Barrett). ἀνέγκλητος without accusation, blameless (s. MM; for the pref.

9 expressing a neg. idea, s. Moorhouse, 42–68). ■ δι'οὗ "through whom." The prep. is used of the principal cause and expresses the indirect calling of God through the gospel and not by a voice from heaven (Grosheide). ἐκλήθητε aor. pass. καλέω to call. κοινωνία fellowship, communion, participation. It expresses the blending of two wills into one common cause (s. TDNT; CBB; RAC). Ἰησοῦ Χριστοῦ. The name reoccurs in every phrase of this preface (Godet).

10 ■ παρακαλέω to entreat, to encourage. Used in the sense of a polite command (Conzelmann; s. Rom. 12:1). διά w. gen. "through," the instrument of the appeal (RWP). τὸ αὐτὸ λέγειν "that you speak the same thing," pres. subj., subj. used after a verb of command. ᾖ pres. subj. εἰμί. σχίσμα split, division. The word pictures the destruction of the unity through force (Weiss). ἦτε pres. subj. εἰμί. κατηρτισμένοι perf. pass. part. καταρτίζω to put in order, to restore, to restore to its former condition, to put into proper condition. The word is used by Herodotus (V, 28) for composing civil disorder (Barrett), periphrastic perf. pass. subj. (RWP). The perf. emphasizes the completed state or condition. νοῦς mind, the intellect in its judging faculty (Grosheide). γνώμη opinion, judgment. It indicates the expressed opinion, the conviction (Grosheide). The former

denotes the general principles, the latter the special application
of those principles (Lightfoot). ■ ἐδηλώθη aor. pass. δηλόω to 11
make clear, to make known. περί w. gen. concerning. ὑπό w.
gen. by. τῶν Χλόης This probably means "by slaves belonging
to Chloe's household" (RP). ἔρις here pl. "strifes," "conten-
tions." The word points to quarrels (Morris). ■ δὲ and, now, 12
"now this is what I mean." ἕκαστος each. ■ μεμέρισται perf. 13
pass. μερίζω to divide, to separate, to divide up and distribute
(Barrett). The perf. pictures the completed action or state. The
tense means "he has already been divided up and distributed"
(s. Lenski). This sentence could be a question or a statement. μή
introduces a question expecting the answer "no." ἐσταυρώθη
aor. pass. σταυρόω to crucify. ἐβαπτίσθητε aor. pass.
βαπτίζω to baptize. ■ ἐβάπτισα aor. εἰ μὴ except, only (s. BD, 14
221). ■ ἵνα w. subj. in order that, expresses purpose. εἴπῃ aor. 15
subj. λέγω to say. ἐμὸν "my," placed before the noun for the
sake of emphasis. ■ καὶ "also." λοιπὸς otherwise, besides that, 16
acc. of general reference "as for anything else" (RWP). οἶδα
defective perf. w. pres. meaning to know. εἰ "if." Used in an
indir. question. ■ ἀπέστειλέν aor. ἀποστέλλω to send, to 17
commission, to commission someone to a special task and to
empower him w. the authority of the one sending (s. TDNT;
CBB; s.v.1). βαπτίζειν pres. inf. The inf. expresses either purpose or explains the idea of sending. εὐαγγελίζεσθαι pres. mid.
inf. εὐαγγελίζομαι to bring good news, to preach the gospel.
(For this word, s. TDNT; RAC VI, 1107–1160.) σοφία wisdom.
What is prohibited is the transformation of words into wisdom.
Paul does not use worldly wisdom (Grosheide). ἵνα that. It
introduces a neg. purpose "lest." κενωθῇ aor. pass. subj. κενόω
to make enmity, "dwindle to nothing, vanish under the weight
of rhetorical ornament and dialectic subtlety" (Lightfoot).
σταυρὸς cross (s. CNT 180–269; Martin Hengel, Crucifixion
[London: SMC, 1977]).

■ λόγος τοῦ σταυροῦ "the word of that cross." The re- 18
peated article is almost demonstrative (RWP). The cross occu-
pies a central place in proclaiming the gospel. It is both the
crowning point of a life of self-renunciation and also the ordained instrument of salvation (Lightfoot). ἀπολλυμένοις pres.
mid. part. ἀπόλλυμι to ruin, to be lost. The prep. in compound
is perfective and the pres. tense indicates that the goal is ideally
reached. A complete transformation of its subjects is required to
bring them out of the ruin implicit in their state (M, 114f.).
μωρία foolishness, nonsense. σῳζομένοις pres. pass. part.
σῴζω to save. The dat. of the first part. is a simple subj. ap-

preciation. The dat. of this part. includes an effective relation and the idea of an effect produced (Godet; s. also Conzelmann).

19 ■ γέγραπται perf. pass. The form expresses the authoritative character of the document, "it stands written" (s. MM). ἀπολῶ fut. ἀπόλλυμι to ruin, to be lost. σύνεσις understanding, a bringing together. The faculty of putting two and two together (MNTW, 148f.; TDNT). (For the DSS, s. I QS III, 15; IV, 22; I QH I, 8.) ἀθετήσω fut. ἀθετέω to do away w. that which has been laid down, to set aside, to disregard, to make void (AS).

20 ■ ποῦ where? συζητητὴς debater. οὐχί a strengthened form of οὐ used in a question which expects the answer yes. ἐμώρανεν

21 aor. μωραίνω to regard as foolish, to make foolish. ■ ἐπειδὴ since, since then, because. σοφίᾳ τοῦ θεοῦ the wisdom of God. ἔγνω aor. γινώσκω. διὰ τῆς σοφίας "through wisdom." εὐδόκησεν aor. εὐδοκέω to please, to have pleasure in. κήρυγμα proclamation, preaching. σῶσαι aor. inf. σῴζω to save, to rescue. The inf. explains what is pleasing to God.

22 πιστεύοντας pres. part. ■ ἐπειδὴ since, because. The conj. is causal but only loosely subordinating (BD, 238). σημεῖον sign. To ask for a sign implies a refusal to take God on trust (Barrett). (For the Jews demanding a sign, s. SB I, 640, 726f.; for signs in the DSS, s. 1 QS 10:4; 1 QH 12:8; 15:20.) αἰτοῦσιν; ζητοῦσιν pres. act. The pres. tense shows the habitual action and describes what is always done. (For the Greeks seeking after knowledge,

23 s. DC XII, 39; XXXVII, 26.) ■ ἡμεῖς δὲ "but we," for emphasis and contrast. ἐσταυρωμένον perf. pass. part. σταυρόω to crucify. The perf. emphasizes the state or condition (s. Rom. 3:21). It refers primarily to the exalted Lord who, in His exaltation, remains the crucified One (E.E. Ellis, " 'Christ Crucified'," RH, 70). σκάνδαλον the stick which an animal stumbled over causing the trap to shut, stumbling block, cause of stumbling, something that trips men up (Barrett; s. also TDNT; NTW, 111–114). μωρία foolishness, nonsense, that which displays a senseless act or thinking or speaking (CBB). The two acc. are in

24 apposition to the object. ■ αὐτοῖς "to them," or "to the called

25 themselves" (Weiss). τε καὶ "both . . . and." ■ μωρός foolish, "the foolish thing of God," is that work of God which the world considers foolishness (Grosheide). σοφώτερος comp. of σοφός followed by the gen. of comparison, wiser than men w. all their strength (Godet). ἀσθενής weak, without strength. ἰσχυρότερος comp. ἰσχυρός strong.

26   ■ βλέπετε pres. indic. act. γάρ for. It is explanatory "you can see what I mean" (Barrett). κλῆσις calling. κατὰ according, according to the standard of. It speaks of wisdom gained

388

according to the flesh; that is, according to natural and human abilities (Weiss). δυνατός powerful. εὐγενής noble, well-born. The social structure of the church at Corinth included those from all levels of society. There were those from the lower levels of society as well as some from the upper levels (s. Gerd Theissen, "Soziale Schichtung in der korinthischen Gemeinde. Ein Beitrag zur Soziologie des hellenistischen Urchristentums," ZNW, 65 [1974], 232–272). ■ ἐξελέξατο aor. mid. ἐκλέγομαι 27 to pick out, to select, to choose for one's self. καταισχύνῃ pres. subj. καταισχύνω to put to shame. The prep. in compound is perfective (RWP). ■ ἀγενής not of noble birth, low, insignifi- 28 cant. (For the neg. force of the pref., s. Rom. 1:20.) ἐξουθενημένα perf. pass. part. ἐξουθενέω to despise, to consider as nothing. (For the force of the prep. in compound and the development of this word, s. MH, 310.) The perf. denotes not only quality but also indicates that that which was once despised will continue to be despised (Grosheide). τὰ μὴ ὄντα pres. part. εἰμί "the things which are not," "things which do not exist." A more contemptible expression in Greek thinking was not possible. Being was everything (Weiss). καταργήσῃ aor. subj. καταργέω to put out of action, to make inactive. The prep. in compound indicates an action unfavorable to its object (MH, 316). ■ ὅπως w. subj. used to express intended results (BD, 196). 29 Here it expresses neg. results. καυχήσηται aor. mid. subj. καυχάομαι to boast, to glory. μὴ πᾶσα σὰρξ no flesh; that is, "no one" an OT expression (Barrett). ■ ἐξ αὐτοῦ "from him" 30 that is, you are born of him in Christ Jesus (Lightfoot). ἐστέ pres. ind. εἰμί. ἐγενήθη aor. pass. γίνομαι. σοφία wisdom, Christ is the true wisdom and union w. Him makes the believer truly wise (Hodge; for Christ as the wisdom of God, s. PW; PRJ, 147–176). ἡμῖν "for us" dat. of advantage. δικαιοσύνη righteousness, the status of being in the right before God (GW, 147; for the view that it means God's loving, gracious, loyal action which believers share in, s. MRP, 155). ἁγιασμὸς holiness, sanctification. ἀπολύτρωσις redemption, release through the payment of a ransom price. Perhaps here pointing to the last great day, the consummation of redemption (Morris). The last three terms are an explanation of the word "wisdom" (Lightfoot). ■ ἵνα w. subj. Used here in an elliptical expression "in 31 order that it might come to pass, work out just as" (BD, 255). γέγραπται perf. pass. s.v.19. καυχώμενος pres. mid. part. s.v.29. The conditional part. used as the subject of the clause is due to Semitic influence (Barrett). καυχάσθω pres. mid. imp. 3rd per. sing.

Ch. 2

1   ■ κἀγώ "and I, accordingly." It emphasizes the apostle's consistency w. the principles laid down in the preceding verses (RP). ἐλθών aor. act. part. ἔρχομαι to come, temporal use of the part. καθ᾽= κατά w. acc. according to. It can indicate the nature or characteristic of a thing or manner (BAG). ὑπεροχή prominence, superiority, excellency. λόγος word, speech. σοφία wisdom. The two nouns are close together in meaning, "eloquence" is rational talk and "wisdom" is wordy cleverness (Barrett). (For the emphasis on oratory in education and the importance of a skilled speaker in the ancient world, s. CC, 151ff.; KP IV, 1396–1414.) καταγγέλλων pres. part. καταγγέλλω to proclaim, to make a solemn proclamation (CBB). The pres. tense emphasizes the continual action and the part. is a part. of manner. In his proclamation Paul placed no reliance upon eloquence or wisdom but it does not mean that he did not employ any kind of speech or wisdom. It is just that these were not prominent in his evangelism (Barrett). μυστήριον τοῦ θεοῦ "the mystery of God," the counsel of God, unknown to man except by revelation, especially concerning His saving work and ultimate purposes in history (ZPEB IV, 327). The gen. is subj. gen. (Lightfoot, *Notes.*) (For the variant reading

2   μαρτύριον "testimony," s. TC, 545.) ■ ἔκρινά aor. κρίνω to judge, to decide. It emphasizes a deliberate act of the will (Lietzmann). The aor. states a fact which had come to its conclusion when Paul arrived at Corinth. He had to go on preaching Christ (Grosheide). εἰδέναι perf. inf. οἶδα to know, "to exhibit the knowledge of, recognize" (Lightfoot). ἐν ὑμῖν "in your midst." εἰ μή except. καί "and this one" specifies the point on which stress was laid, the effect being that of a climax (RP). ἐσταυρωμένον perf. pass. part. σταυρόω to crucify (s. 1 Cor.

3   1:23). ■ κἀγώ s.v.1. Here it points again to Paul's arrival at Corinth (Weiss). ἀσθένεια weakness. τρόμος trembling. The words point to the anxiety or solicitude of mind arising out of a sense of his insufficiency, and of the infinite importance of his work (Hodge). ἐγενόμην aor. mid. γίνομαι to become. Used w.

4   πρός to come to someone, to be w. someone. ■ πειθός persuasive. (For the formation of this word, s. RG, 157.) Paul may be referring to the halakic and haggadic discussions current in Jewish Corinth rather than sophistic rhetoric in Hellenistic Corinth (Wilhelm Wuellner, "Haggadic Homily Genre in I Corinthians 1–3," JBL, 89 [June, 1970], 203). ἀπόδειξις demonstration, proof. The word indicates a compelling decision demanded by the presupposition (s. Fascher). The following genitives are both

obj. (spirit and power are manifested) and subj. (the spirit and power bring proof and conviction) (Barrett). ■ ᾖ pres. subj. εἰμί 5 to be. Used to express purpose. ἐν "in." The prep. marks the medium or sphere in which faith has its root (RP).

■ δέ "but." Paul contrasted the wisdom which he speaks w. 6 that of his opponents (Pearson). αἰών age, the course and current of this world's affairs (Trench; *Synonyms*, 217). ἄρχων pres. part. ἄρχω to rule. The part. "ruler" refers to the human rulers of this world, the great men of authority (s. A.W. Carr, "The Rulers of this Age—I Cor. ii. 6–8," NTS, 23 [October, 1976], 20–35; Gene Miller, "ΑΡΧΟΝΤΩΝ ΤΟΥ ΑΙΩΝΟΣ ΤΟΥΤΟΥ—A New Look at I Corinthians 2:6–8," JBL, 91 [December, 1972], 522–528). καταργουμένων pres. pass. part. καταργέω to make idle, to put out of commission, to remove from power (s. 1 Cor. 1:28). ■ ἀλλά "but." It introduces the 7 positive side again and at the same time gives a strong neg. emphasis (Grosheide). θεοῦ the gen. is placed before the noun for strong emphasis. The wisdom of God is the work of Christ in His crucifixion, as God's secret plan of redemption and the exalted Christ who presently mediates God's hidden wisdom to His people (E.E. Ellis, " 'Wisdom' and 'Knowledge' in I Corinthians," TB, 25 [1974], 95). ἐν μυστηρίῳ "in a mystery" (s.v.1.). ἀποκεκρυμμένην perf. pass. part. ἀποκρύπτω to veil, to hide. προώρισεν aor. προορίζω to mark off w. boundaries beforehand, to predetermine, to predestinate. πρὸ δόξαν ἡμῶν "for our glory." The word indicates our complete salvation (RP).

■ ἔγνωκεν perf. γινώσκω to know, to recognize, to discern. εἰ 8 Used in the ind. w. a contrary to fact conditional clause (s. BD, 182). ἔγνωσαν aor. γινώσκω. ἐσταύρωσαν aor. s.v.2. ■ 9 καθὼς just as, in accordance w. γέγραπται perf. pass. γράφω. The source of Paul's quotation is not known. It may be from a Jewish liturgy, or be based on Isaiah 64:4, or be from an "Apocalypse of Elijah" (Pearson, 35). εἶδεν aor. ὁράω. οὓς ear. ἤκουσεν aor. ἀκούω to hear. καρδία heart. The whole man is viewed from his intentionality; it is the source of the will, emotion, thoughts, and affections (PAT, 448). ἀνέβη aor. ἀναβαίνω to go up, to arise, here "to enter into." ἡτοίμασεν aor. ἑτοιμάζω to prepare. ἀγαπῶσιν pres. part. ἀγαπάω to love. ■ ἀπεκάλυψεν aor. ἀποκαλύπτω to unveil, to reveal. διὰ 10 w. gen. "through." πνεῦμα spirit. Paul denies the views of Philo that the human spirit can know the divine and asserts that only the divine spirit can make known the things of God (PW, 122). ἐραυνᾷ pres. ind. act. to search, to penetrate, to examine, to investigate. The pres. tense indicates that which is always true,

the gnomic pres. (s. IBG, 8). βάθος depth. The deep things of
God designates God's essence, then His attributes, volitions, and
11 plans (Godet). ■ οἶδεν defective perf. w. pres. meaning οἶδα to
know. τοῦ ἀνθρώπου "the things belonging to man," the personal memories, reflections, motives of any human being; all the
thoughts of which he is conscience (RP). τά τοῦ θεοῦ "the
things belonging to God." Used as parallel to the preceding.
ἔγνωκεν perf. ind. act. γινώσκω to know, to recognize, to
12 discern. The perf. emphasizes the continuing knowledge. ■ τὸ
πνεῦμα τοῦ κόσμου "the spirit of the world," the spirit which
animates the world. The gen. is qualitative gen. (Lenski).
ἐλάβομεν aor. λαμβάνω to receive. εἰδῶμεν perf. subj. of the
defective perf. οἶδα. χαρισθέντα aor. pass. part. χαρίζομαι to
give as a gift of grace, to give graciously as a favor (BAG). The
aor. tense indicates that Paul is not speaking only of the future
13 but also of the pres. life of Christians (Barrett). ■ διδακτός
taught. A substantivized verbal adj. w. a pass. meaning followed
by the gen. designating the agent (MT, 234). "Not in words
taught by human wisdom, but in words taught by the Spirit"
(IBG, 40). ἀνθρώπινος human. (For adj. w. this ending signifying material, origin, or kind, s. MH, 359.) πνευματικοῖς spiritual, pertaining to the Spirit. (For adj. w. this ending, s. MH,
378.) The word can be n. "spiritual things" or masc. "spiritual
persons" (s. RP; Barrett). συγκρίνοντες pres. part. συγκρίνω.
The verb has various meanings which are possible in this passage: to bring together, to combine or to compare or to explain,
14 to interpret (BAG; RP). ■ ψυχικός pertaining to the soul or life,
soulish. It describes the natural man who does not possess the
Holy Spirit (s. TDNT; PAT, 334–346; for strong arguments
rejecting the gnostic influence on Paul's use of this term, s.
Pearson, 7–14). δέχεται pres. mid. to receive. The pres. tense
indicates the habitual action. μωρία foolishness, nonsense.
γνῶναι aor. act. inf. γινώσκω. πνευματικῶς adv. spiritually.
Paul rejects Philo's view that man has within him—breathed into
him by God—the capacity for knowing God and the higher
truths of the universe. The wisdom of God comes only through
the Holy Spirit (Pearson, 39). ἀνακρίνεται pres. pass.
ἀνακρίνω to examine, used of judicial hearings, to conduct an
examination, to examine and judge, to call to account, to discern
15 (BAG). The pres. tense indicates that which is always true. ■
πάντα "all things." The spiritual man is able to consider and
appraise all things because he is not only inspired to understand
what he sees; he is also furnished w. a moral standard by which
16 all things may be measured (Barrett). ■ ἔγνω aor. ind. act. s.v.8.

νοῦς mind, thought, plan. A comprehensive name for the thoughts existing in the conscientious (Schlatter). *ὅς* rel. pron. used to express purpose and followed by the fut. (s. BG, 118). *συμβιβάσει* fut. *συμβιβάζω* to put together so as to draw an inference from, to conclude, here to instruct (Lightfoot). *νοῦς Χριστοῦ* "the mind of Christ," the thoughts, counsels, plans and knowledge of Christ known through the agency of the Holy Spirit (s. RP).

Ch. 3

■ *κἀγώ* "and I," emphatic w. a slight contrast to the preced- 1 ing (Grosheide). *ἠδυνήθην* aor. pass. *δύναμαι* to be able. *λαλῆσαι* aor. act. inf. *λαλέω* to speak. *σάρκινος* fleshly, made of flesh. (For nouns w. this ending denoting the material relation, s. RP.) *νήπιος* infant, baby. ■ *γάλα* milk. *ἐπότισα* aor. ind. act. 2 *ποτίζω* to give to drink. *βρῶμα* food, solid food. (For similar terminology appearing in Philo, s. Pearson, 29f.) *οὔπω* not yet. *γὰρ* "and indeed." The word has an intensifying effect (Barrett). *ἔτι νῦν* "even now." ■ *σαρκικός* fleshly, pertaining to the flesh, 3 controlled by the flesh. Words w. this ending denote an ethical or dynamic relation (RP). Flesh is the outlook orientated toward the self, that which pursues its own ends in self-sufficient independence of God (CBB; s. also TDNT; PRJ, 17–35; PAT, 49–95). *ὅπου* where, insofar as. (For the causal use, s. BD, 238.) *ζῆλος* envy. *ἔρις* strife. It is the outward result of envious feeling (RP). *οὐχὶ* A strengthened form of *οὐ* used to introduce a question which expects the answer yes. *κατὰ* according to, "w. merely human motives or feelings." Your walk in life conforms to a merely human standard. The prep. denotes the measure or standard (Lightfoot, *Notes*). *περιπατεῖτε* pres. ind. act. to walk, to conduct one's life. The pres. tense points to an action which was taking place. ■ *ὅταν* "whenever." *οὐκ* used in questions 4 expecting the answer yes. *ἄνθρωποι* human beings. ■ *δι = διά* 5 w. gen. through. *ἐπιστεύσατε* aor. ind. act. *πιστεύω* to believe, ingressive aor. to become a believer, to come to belief. *ἑκάστῳ* dat. of attraction for the abbreviated form "each as the Lord gave to him" (Grosheide). ■ *ἐφύτευσα* aor. *φυτεύω* to 6 plant. *ἐπότισεν* aor. to give to drink, to water. *ηὔξανεν* impf. *αὐξάνω* to cause to grow. The impf. indicates the continuous blessing of God on the work of both Paul and Apollos (RWP). ■ *ὥστε* "therefore." Used w. ind. to draw an inference from the 7 previous sentence (RG, 999; IBG, 144). *οὔτε . . . οὔτε* neither . . . nor. *φυτεύων* pres. part. *ποτίζων* pres. part. *αὐξάνων* pres. part. emphasized by its position in the sentence. ■ *ἕν* one, n. 8

"one thing." The aim, result, and motivating power of their work
are identical (Barrett). μισθός reward, wage, salary. (For the
idea of receiving rewards for work, s. SB IV, 484–500; TDNT.)
9 λήμψεται fut. mid. λαμβάνω to receive. ■ συνεργός fellow
worker. The word w. gen. could mean "fellow workers w. God"
or "fellow workers in God's service." The context indicates that
Paul is speaking of the equal relation of God's workers w. one
another (s. Victor Paul Furnish, " 'Fellow Workers, in God's
Service'," JBL, 80 [December, 1961], 364–370). γεώργιον
working field, cultivated land, field. (For the agricultural picture,
s. ZPEB I, 71–78; IDB I, 56–59; OCD, 29–30.) οἰκοδομή building. Perhaps Paul could be referring to the many buildings and
temples in Corinth. (For architecture and buildings, s. TDNT;
ZPEB I, 287–297; RAC I, 1265–1278.)
10 ■ δοθεῖσαν aor. pass. part. δίδωμι to give. ἀρχιτέκτων
architect, master worker, skilled craftsman (s. Philo, On Dreams
II, 8). θεμέλιος foundation. ἔθηκα aor. τίθημι to lay.
ἐποικοδομεῖ pres. ind. act. to build upon. The pres. tense pictures the continual action and is to be contrasted w. the previous
11 aor. ■ θεῖναι aor. act. inf. τίθημι. παρὰ w. acc. beside, along,
beyond. In comparisons the sense is "than," "more than," "rather than" (DM, 108; IBG, 51). κείμενον pres. mid. part. κεῖμαι
12 to lie, of a foundation "be laid" (BAG). ■ ἀργύριον silver.
τίμιος precious, expensive. Here it means valuable stones for
building such as granite and marble (Hodge). (For the use of
precious metals and stone in building, s. RAC VI, 451–457; SB
III, 333f.) ξύλον wood. χόρτος grass, hay. καλάμη stalk, straw,
13 used as a building material for thatching roofs (BAG). ■
γενήσεται fut. mid. γίνομαι. ἡ ἡμέρα "the day." The article
refers to a day which is well-known (Schlatter). δηλώσει fut.
δηλόω to make visible, to make plain, to make clear. ὅτι because. ἐν dat. πῦρ fire. ἀποκαλύπτεται pres. pass. to unveil,
to reveal. The word "day" is the subject of the verb. The pres.
tense is used to express the fut. It is a confident assertion regarding the fut. (BD, 168). ὁποῖος what kind of, what sort of.
δοκιμάσει fut. δοκιμάζω to approve after testing, used particu-
14 larly of metals which are tried by fire (s. Weiss; TDNT). ■ εἰ
"if," a first-class conditional sentence where the condition is
assumed to be true. μενεῖ fut. μένω to remain. λήμψεται fut.
15 mid. λαμβάνω. ■ κατακαήσεται fut. pass. κατακαίω to burn
up completely. The prep. in compound is perfective (s. MH,
316). ζημιωθήσεται fut. pass. ζημιόω pass. to suffer loss; that
is, he will lose his reward (Hodge). σωθήσεται fut. pass. σώζω
to rescue, to save. ὡς διὰ πυρός "as through fire." The prep. is

to be taken in a local sense; that is, "as one who dashes through
the flames safe, but w. the smell of fire upon him" (Barrett).
■ οἴδατε perf. act. w. pres. meaning to know. The neg. introduc- 16
ing the question expects the answer yes. ναός temple, dwelling
place of a deity, the inward shrine or sanctuary. The reference
is to the one temple of Jerusalem and there may be an allusion
to the dissensions which are corrupting God's temple (Lightfoot,
Notes). οἰκεῖ pres. ind. act. to dwell. ■ φθείρει pres. ind. act. to 17
corrupt, to ruin, to spoil. φθερεῖ fut. ind. act. οἴτινές who,
whoever, ones of such a nature (BG, 68).

■ ἐξαπατάτω pres. imp. ἐξαπατάω to deceive, to cheat. 18
The prep. in compound is perfective "to successfully deceive"
(MH, 311). (For the pres. imp. in the neg., s. Rom. 6:12.) εἰ "if."
It introduces a first-class conditional clause in which the condition is assumed to be true. γενέσθω pres. mid. imp. γίνομαι.
γένηται aor. mid. subj. ■ παρὰ w. dat. "beside," "with," "in the 19
presence of" (DM, 108). γέγραπται perf. pass. γράφω.
δρασσόμενος pres. mid. part. δράσσομαι to catch, to seize.
πανουρχίᾳ cunning, craftiness, trickery, literally, "readiness to
do anything" (BAG). ■ διαλογισμός thought, reasoning. 20
μάταιος empty, vain, useless. It expresses the aimlessness, the
leading to no object or end (s. Trench; Synonyms, 180–184).
(For God destroying the wisdom of the wise as seen in the DSS,
s. 1 QS 5:19f.) ■ ὥστε therefore. It draws a conclusion or infer- 21
ence from the preceding (s.v.7.). καυχάσθω pres. mid. imp.
καυχάομαι to boast, to glory in something or someone. πάντα
"all things." He puts no limit to their possessions in Christ
(Morris). ■ ἐνεστῶτα perf. act. part. ἐνίστημι to be pres. 22
μέλλοντα pres. part. μέλλω to be about to, here "things that are
coming." πάντα ὑμῶν "all things are yours," "all things belong
to you," pred. gen. (RWP).

Ch. 4

■ λογιζέσθω pres. mid. imp. λογίζομαι to reckon, to 1
count, to consider. ἄνθρωπος man, used in the indef. sense
"one" or "a man," "a person" (Meyer; MM). ὑπηρέτης minister, helper, one who is in the service of another (s. TDNT; Acts
13:5). οἰκονόμος steward, manager of a household, often a
trusted slave was put in charge of the whole household. The
word emphasizes that one is entrusted w. great responsibility
and accountability (s. TDNT; CBB). μυστηρίων θεοῦ (s. 1 Cor.
2:1). The gen. expresses that which the steward was entrusted w.
and what he is to administer. ■ ὧδε "in that case," "on that 2
showing," used here to draw an inference "therefore." λοιπός

used here either to strengthen the inference or to introduce a
fresh point "now" and would be the progressive use (s. Thrall,
26f.; Blomqvist, 100–103). ζητεῖται pres. ind. pass. to seek, to
look for. The pres. tense indicates that which is always true. ἵνα
"that." It introduces the clause which is the object of the verb.
πιστός faithful, dependable. εὑρεθῇ aor. pass. subj. εὑρίσκω to
3 find. ■ ἐλάχιστος "it amounts to very little," "it counts for a
very small matter" (RP). The adj. is the superl. of μικρός and
is elative (RWP). (For the use of the prep. after the verb "to be,"
s. RG, 595f.) ἵνα "that," s.v.2. ὑφ᾿= ὑπό w. gen. "by" used w.
a pass. verb to show the agent. ἀνακριθῶ aor. pass. subj.
ἀνακρίνω question, to examine, to interrogate, used of a judicial
examination before the final verdict is given (Weiss; 1 Cor. 2:14).
4 ■ σύνοιδα defective perf. w. a pres. meaning to share knowledge, here "to know about one's self," what is unknown to others
(RP). δεδικαίωμαι perf. ind. pass. δικαιόω to justify, to declare
to be in the right. The form could also be perf. mid. "I have not
5 justified myself." ■ ὥστε "therefore." It draws an inference
from the preceding (s. 1 Cor. 3:7). ἕως ἄν w. subj. "until." ἔλθῃ
aor. act. subj. ἔρχομαι. φωτίσει fut. φωτίζω to illumine, to
bring to light. φανερώσει fut. φανερόω to make visible, to
reveal. γενήσεται fut. mid. γίνομαι. ἕκαστος dat. of advantage "for each one."
6   ■ ταῦτα "these things," n. pl. and refers to the figures of
gardeners, builders, and stewards. (For a discussion of this verse,
s. M.D. Hooker, " 'Beyond the Things Which Are Written': An
Examination of I Cor. 4:6," NTS, 10 [October, 1963], 127–132.)
μετεσχημάτισα aor. μετασχηματίζω to change the form of,
to transform. Here the meaning seems to be "I have applied
these figures of speech to myself and Apollos" (Hooker, 131).
μάθητε aoς. subj. μανθάνω to teach, to instruct. ὑπέρ beyond.
γέγραπται perf. pass. γράφω to write. It was used to refer to
the authoritative character of that which stands written (s. MM).
Paul may be referring to the Scripture passages which he has
quoted or to his own teaching (s. Hooker, 128ff.). εἷς ὑπὲρ τοῦ
ἑνός . . . κατὰ τοῦ ἑτέρου "each on behalf of one and against
another" (Barrett). φυσιοῦσθε either pres. ind. pass. or pres.
subj. pass. by irregular contraction (RWP). φυσιόω to puff up,
7 to inflate, to blow up. ■ διακρίνει pres. ind. to judge between
two, to make a distinction, to make different (s. Weiss; MH,
302). This is probably best taken as a rhetorical question (s.
Barrett). ἔλαβες aor. ind. act. λαμβάνω to receive. καὶ. It
throws emphasis on the verb and w. the conditional particle
8 represents the insistence on what is fact (RP). ■ κεκορεσμένοι

perf. pass. part. κορέννυμι to satisfy w. food, to fill, pass. to be satisfied w. food, to have enough of. Used ironically "you think you already have all the spiritual food you need" (BAG). The perf. emphasizes the completed state or condition. ἐπλουτήσατε aor. πλουτέω to be rich, ingressive aor. to become rich. χωρὶς without. ὄφελον pres. part. n. ὀφείλω to owe. The part. is used in a construction to express an impossible wish; that is, the speaker himself considers the fulfillment of the wish impossible (s. MKG, 252; RG, 1003f.). συμβασιλεύσωμεν aor. subj. συμβασιλεύω to rule together, to be a co-ruler. ■ ἔσχατος last. ἀπέδειξεν aor. ind. 9 ἀποδείκνυμι to show, to expose to view, to exhibit. A technical word of bringing a pers. into the arena. The apostles were brought out to make the grand finale (Lightfoot, *Notes*). ἐπιθανάτιος condemned to die, used of criminals sentenced to death in the arena (PAM, 189). θέατρον theater, play, spectacle (Lightfoot). ἐγενήθημεν aor. pass. γίνομαι to become, to be made. Paul uses the picture to illustrate the humility and indignity to which the apostles are subjected. God is the one who set up this spectacle and He uses the weakness of His servants in order to demonstrate His power and strength (PAM, 189). ■ 10 μωρός foolish, ridiculous. διά w. acc. because, on account of. φρόνιμος sensible, smart. ἔνδοξος honored, distinguished, eminent. ■ πεινῶμεν pres. ind. act. πεινάω to be hungry. διψῶμεν 11 pres. ind. act. διψάω to be thirsty. γυμνιτεύομεν prcs. ind. act. γυμνιτεύω to be naked, to be scantily clothed, to be poorly clothed. κολαφιζόμεθα pres. pass. ind. κολαφίζω to hit w. the fist, to beat w. the fist, not simply struck, but in an insulting manner (like slaves or a condemned man) (Barrett). ἀστατοῦμεν pres. ind. act. ἀστατέω to be homeless, to be without a roof over one's head. ■ κοπιῶμεν pres. ind. κοπιάω 12 to toil, to labor, to do hard work, to work to weariness or exhaustion. ἐργαζόμενοι pres. mid. part. ἐργάζομαι to work. Greeks despised manual labor; St. Paul glories in it (RP). λοιδορούμενοι pres. pass. part. λοιδορέω to abuse w. words. It was a common practice of speakers and politicians to insult and abuse the opponents (TDNT). διωκόμενοι pres. pass. part. διώκω to pursue, to hunt, to persecute. ἀνεχόμεθα pres. mid. ἀνέχομαι to endure, to forbear. ■ δυσφημούμενοι pres. mid. 13 part. δυσφημέω to defame, to slander. περικάθαρμα that which is cleansed all around, that which is removed as a result of a thorough cleansing; that is, dirt, filth. The word was also used of condemned criminals of the lowest class who were sacrificed as offerings for the cleansing of a city (s. TDNT; Lightfoot;

EGT). ἐγενήθημεν aor. pass. s.v.9. περίψημα that which is
removed by the process of cleaning dirt off, scouring, scum. The
previous word indicates a "rinsing," this word indicates a "scrap-
ing" of a dirty vessel. It was used in the papyri in a letter greeting
conveying the idea "your humble and devoted servant" (MM).

14 ■ ἐντρέπων pres. act. part. ἐντρέπω to shame, to make
ashamed. The pres. part. expresses purpose (MT, 157). The pres.
tense may also be viewed as conative "I am not trying to shame
you" (Barrett). νουθετῶν pres. act. part. νουθετέω to admonish, to correct through admonition (s. TDNT). The pres. part.

15 expresses purpose. ■ ἐάν w. subj. introduces a third-class conditional sentence in which the assumption is left undetermined,
but there is some expectation of realization (Funk II, 683).
μύριοι ten thousand. παιδαγωγός child trainer, instructor (s.
Gal. 3:24). ἔχητε pres. subj. ἔχω to have. ἐγέννησα aor.
γεννάω to bear, to produce. Paul describes himself as their
father. The instructor acts as representative of the father but can

16 never take his place (Schlatter). ■ μιμητής imitator, one who
copies or mimics another. γίνεσθε pres. mid. imp. γίνομαι.

17 ■ ἔπεμψα aor. πέμπω. Not the epistolary aor. because Timothy
had not yet reached Corinth and was not the one who delivered
this letter (s. 1 Cor. 16:10) (Lietzmann). ἀναμνήσει fut.
ἀναμιμνήσκω to bring to memory, to remind. The fut. is used
in a rel. clause which expresses purpose (s. RG, 960). ὁδούς
masc. acc. pl. "ways." Here it probably refers to Paul's teachings

18 (s. Weiss). πανταχοῦ everywhere. ■ ἐρχομένου pres. mid. part.
ἔρχομαι to come, gen. abs. expressing a neg. condition "as if I
were not coming." ἐφυσιώθησαν aor. pass. φυσιόω s.v.6.

19 τινές "certain ones." ■ ἐλεύσομαι fut. mid. ἔρχομαι. ταχέως
adv. quickly, soon. θελήσῃ aor. subj. θέλω to wish, to desire.
γνώσομαι fut. mid. γινώσκω. πεφυσιωμένων perf. pass. part.
φυσιόω s.v.6. The perf. emphasizes the completed state or con-

20 dition (s. Rom. 3:21). ■ βασιλεία τοῦ θεοῦ "the kingdom of
God"; that is, God's rule. The verb to be supplied is either "is"

21 or "does not operate" (Barrett). ■ ἐν "with," instrumental use
of the prep. similar to the Hebraic use (s. BD, 117f.; Lietzmann;
Hering). ῥάβδος rod, staff, stick. The figure indicates severity
and is intended as a warning (Lenski). ἔλθω aor. subj. ἔρχομαι,
deliberative subj. "should I come?" πραΰτης meekness, gentleness, restrained patience (s. Matt. 5:5).

Ch. 5

1   ■ ὅλως actually (Barrett), universally, everywhere (Hering). ἀκούεται pres. pass. "is reported"; that is, commonly

known to exist (Lightfoot, *Notes*). πορνεία fornication. It refers to general sexual acts outside of legal marriage (TDNT). καί "even." τοιαύτη of such a kind, such as this. ἥτις which, in the consecutive sense "such as" (s. BG, 68f.). ἔθνεσιν Gentile, those who were not Jews. ὥστε used w. acc. of the inf. to express results "so that." χυναῖκα fem. acc. sing. "his father's wife," the woman was probably the stepmother of the offender and the father had probably died (Barrett). The separation of the gen. from its noun emphasizes both parts of speech (BD, 249). ἔχειν pres. act. inf. The pres. tense emphasizes the continual possession. They were living as man and wife without being married. Both the OT (Lev. 18:7, 8; 20:11) and the rabbis (M Sanhedrin VII, 4) as well as Roman law prohibited such marriages (s. Lietzmann; RAC IV, 685f.; Buckland, 115f.). ■ πεφυσιωμένοι perf. 2 pass. part. φυσιόω to blow up, to puff up, a term used to express pride. The perf. emphasizes the state or condition. οὐχί strengthened form of οὐ. Used in a question expecting the answer yes. μᾶλλον rather. ἐπενθήσατε aor. πενθέω to mourn, to express deep sorrow as one mourning for the dead. ἵνα "that." Used to express desired result (RWP) or a consequence resulting from some quality, "such that" (BD, 192). ἀρθῇ aor. pass. subj. αἴρω to lift up, to take away, to remove. πράξας aor. act. part. πράσσω to do, to practice (variant reading ποιήσας aor. part. ποιέω to do). ■ τῷ σώματι dat. of reference. The word "body" 3 refers to Paul's physical presence or absence (PAT, 268; for a study showing the emphasis on the material aspect of the word, s. SBT). κέκρικα perf. ind. act. κρίνω to judge, to pass judgment. The perf. emphasizes the continuing results of the decision reached. τὸν οὕτως "the one who has so acted," "under circumstances such as these" (Lightfoot, *Notes*). κατεργασάμενον aor. mid. part. κατεργάζομαι to do, to accomplish, to bring an action to fruition. ■ συναχθέντων aor. pass. part. συνάγω to 4 gather together, pass. to be assembled. ■ παραδοῦναι aor. act. 5 inf. παραδίδωμι to deliver over, to turn over, used in a judicial sense. This appears to be a curse of execration w. special reference to satanic affliction of the body (SBT, 143). τὸν τοιοῦτον "such a one." εἰς ὄλεθρον "for destruction." The word refers to destruction and death, often in connection w. God's judgment against sin (s. TDNT; s. also SB III, 358). σωθῇ aor. pass. subj. σῴζω to rescue, to save. ■ καύχημα boasting, boasting uttered 6 (RP). οἴδατε defective perf. w. a pres. meaning οἶδα to know. ζύμη leaven, yeast (s. Matt. 13:33; TDNT). φύραμα that which is mixed or kneaded, a lump or batch of dough (BAG). ζυμοῖ pres. ind. act. to leaven. (For the use of the proverbial saying, s.

399

7 Barrett.) ■ ἐκκαθάρατε aor. imp. ἐκκαθαίρω to clean out, to purge thoroughly. (For the Jewish regulations regarding the removal of all leaven from the house before celebrating the Passover, s. SB III, 359f.) The prep. in compound is perfective (MH, 309f.). παλαιός old; that is, the leaven used in the period before Passover (Barrett). ἦτε pres. subj. εἰμί. νέον new, fresh. ἄζυμοι unleaven. καὶ γάρ "for also." The "also" introduces the obj. relation of things corresponding to the exhortation (Meyer). πάσχα Passover, Passover lamb (s. ZPEB IV, 605–611; M Pesahim). ἐτύθη aor. pass. θύω to kill, to slay, to kill a sacrifice, to
8 slaughter. χριστός in apposition w. the subject. ■ ὥστε therefore, it draws a conclusion from the preceding. ἑορτάζωμεν pres. subj. ἑορτάζω to celebrate the feast, hortatory subj. "let us celebrate." κακίας malice. This is the vicious disposition and the next word is the act. exercise of it (Lightfoot, Notes). ἀζύμοις unleavened loaf. The pl. may be a reference to the unleavened cakes eaten at the Passover or is indefinite "unleavened elements" (RP). εἰλικρίνειας sincerity, purity of motive. Perhaps the literal meaning is "checked by sunlight" (s. TDNT; NTW, 32f.).
9 ■ ἔγραψα aor. not an epistolary aor. but refers to another letter (RP). ἐν τῇ ἐπιστολῇ "in the letter." The article points to a well-known specific letter written by Paul. συναναμίγνυσθαι pres. mid. inf. to mix together, to mix up w., to associate w., inf. used to express purpose. The pres. tense points to a regular association (Grosheide). πόρνος one who engages in illicit sexual activities, a sexually immoral pers. Corinth was well-known to the ancient world for this type of activ-
10 ity. ■ πάντως at all, in general. The meaning here is "not in the abs. sense" (Barrett; s. also BD, 224). πλεονέκτης a covetous pers., one who seeks to fulfill his unsatisfiable desires at all cost and at the expense of others (s. Rom. 1:29). ἅρπαξ robber, extortioner, joined to the previous word w. one article indicating that both words form a single class of those who are absolutely selfish, who covet and sometimes see more than their just share of things (RP). εἰδωλολάτρης idol worshiper, idolator. ἐπεί since, used to introduce the conclusion of a suppressed conditional clause which is contrary to fact (s. RG, 965; BD, 181). ὠφείλετε impf. ὀφείλω to be under obligation to pay a debt, should, must, ought. ἄρα "in that case" (RWP). ἐξελθεῖν aor.
11 act. inf. ἐξέρχομαι to go out from, to depart. ■ ὀνομαζόμενος pres. pass. part. ὀνομάζω to name, to bear the name of. His behavior shows that in truth he is not a Christian (Barrett). ᾖ pres. subj. εἰμί. λοίδορος an abusive pers., one who attacks

another w. abusive language (s. TDNT). μέθυσος drunkard. τοιούτῳ such a one. συνεσθίειν pres. inf. to eat together. The prohibition evidently includes the church's common meal as well as private entertainment (Barrett). ■ τί γάρ μοι "for what 12 is it to me," "for what business of mine is it." ἔξω outside, "those who are outside." An expression used by the rabbis to indicate those who belong to another religion (SB III, 362). ■ κρινεῖ fut. 13 κρίνω to judge. ἐξάρατε aor. imp. ἐξαίρω to exclude, to remove, to drive away. The prep. in compound makes the verb effective, "to put out completely." τὸν πονηρόν the evil one or the article is used in a generic sense referring to the wicked in general (s. BD, 138). ἐξ ὑμῶν αὐτῶν "from yourselves." Perhaps here not reflex (MT, 194; s. BD, 150).

Ch. 6

■ τολμᾷ pres. ind. τολμάω to dare. The pres. tense indi- 1 cates that the action was in process. πρᾶγμα matter, lawsuit. κρίνεσθαι pres. mid. or pass. inf., the permissive mid. or pass. "allow yourselves to be judged" (s. BD, 165, 166). The pres. tense indicates that the trial was being held and no decision had yet been reached. ἐπί w. gen. before, in the presence of (s. RWP). τῶν ἀδίκων the unrighteous ones. These were either pagan judges or, perhaps better, Paul is referring to Jewish judges who tried cases in the synagogue (s. Albert Stein, "Wo trugen die korinthischen Christen ihre Rechtshändel aus?," ZNW, 59 [1968], 86–90; SB III, 364). ■ οὐκ οἴδατε defective perf. w. pres. 2 meaning to know. κρινοῦσιν fut. κρίνω to judge (s. Dan 7:22; SB III, 363). ἀνάξιος unworthy, not equal to the task. (For the neg. pref., s. Rom. 1:20.) κριτήριον law court, tribunal, lawsuit, cause, law preceding (s. Weiss). (For the suf. and its meaning, s. MH, 343.) Genitive used w. the adj. "unworthy" which express value (s. BD, 98). ἐλάχιστος superl. μικρός small, insignificant. ■ κρινοῦμεν fut. μήτιγε "not to speak of" (BD, 220). 3 βιωτικός that which pertains to daily living. It means questions related to our life on earth or to the resources of life such as food, clothing, property, etc. (RP). ■ μὲν οὖν "no but" or "no rather" 4 (RP). ἐξουθενημένους perf. pass. part. ἐξουθενέω to consider as nothing, to despise, to reject w. contempt. It refers either to those in the church who are a little esteemed (Grosheide) or to those outside of the church. καθίζετε pres. ind. or imp. καθίζω to cause to sit, to appoint. ■ ἐντροπήν shame. οὕτως "so," "has 5 it come to this that," "is it to such a degree true that?" (Lightfoot, Notes). ἔνι shortened form for ἔνεστιν to be, to exist, to be found (s. BD, 49). οὐδείς no one, not even one. δυνήσεται

fut. mid. δύναμαι. The fut. is used to designate a sort of consequence resulting from some quality, "such that" (BD, 192).
διακρῖναι aor. act. inf. διακρίνω to judge between two, to
decide. (For the force of the prep. in compound, s. MH, 302f.)
ἀνὰ μέσον between. τοῦ ἀδελφοῦ αὐτοῦ an abridged sentence
conveying a reproach "must his brothers go before strangers?"
6 (Lightfoot, Notes) ■ ἀλλά but in reality. κρίνεται pres. mid. or
pass., s.v.1 καὶ τοῦτο "and that," climactic force of the particle
used w. acc. of general reference (RWP). ἄπιστος unbeliever.
7 (For the neg. force of the pref., s. Rom. 1:20.) ■ ὅλως adv.
altogether, assuredly, actually. ἥττημα defeat. The word was
used of a judicial defeat in court (Schlatter), here used of the
moral and spiritual defeat (Weiss). κρίμα law suit. μεθ'ἑαυτῶν
"w. yourselves." The reflex. pron. emphasizes the idea of corporate unity (Lightfoot, Notes). μᾶλλον adv. rather. ἀδικεῖσθε
pres. ind. mid. or pass. ἀδικέω to wrong someone, to treat
someone unjustly. ἀποστερεῖσθε pres. ind. mid. or pass.
ἀποστερέω to defraud, to steal, to deprive. The two forms here
8 are permissive mid. or pass. (s. MT, 56f.; BD, 165). ■ ὑμεῖς you
9 (emphatic). καὶ τοῦτο "and that," s.v.6. ■ θεοῦ emphatic by its
position. κληρονομήσουσιν fut. κληρονομέω to inherit, to
enter into full possession of (Morris). πλανᾶσθε pres. imp. mid.
or pass. πλανάω to lead astray, to mislead, to deceive, permissive mid. or pass. (s.v.7). The pres. imp. w. the neg. is used to
stop an action in progress "do not continue" (MKG, 272).
εἰδωλολάτρης one who serves idols, idolator. μοιχός adulterer. μαλακός soft, effeminate, a technical term for the pass.
partner in homosexual relations (Barrett; Conzelmann; s. also
RAC IV, 620–650; LAE, 164). ἀρσενοκοίτης a male who has
sexual relations w. a male, homosexual. The Jewish punishment
10 for the sin of homosexuality was stoning (s. SB III, 70f.). ■
πλεονέκτης one desirous of having more and seeks to fulfill his
desires through all means (s. 1 Cor. 5:10). μέθυσος drunkard.
λοίδορος one who uses abusive language (s. 1 Cor. 5:11).
ἅρπαξ robber, one who uses force and violence in stealing. (For
similar lists which were used in the ancient world in a popular
11 game, s. LAE, 316.) ■ καί "and," "and it is true" (Godet).
ταῦτα "these things." The n. is contemptous "such abominations!" (EGT). τινες some. Paul narrows the picture to some,
not all (RWP). ἦτε impf. εἰμί. ἀλλά but, emphasizes strongly
the contrast between their pres. state and their past and the
consequent demand which their changed moral condition makes
upon them (RP). ἀπελούσασθε aor. mid. ἀπολούω to wash,
to wash thoroughly. The prep. in compound points to the com-

plete washing away and the aor. refers to a decisive action (Morris), permissive mid. ἡγιάσθητε aor. pass. ἁγιάζω to sanctify, to make holy. It does not refer to the process of ethical development but means "you were claimed by God as His own and made a member of His holy people" (Barrett). ἐδικαιώθητε aor. pass. δικαιόω to justify, to declare righteous, to declare to be in the right (s. Rom. 2:13).

■ ἔξεστιν it is allowed, it is permitted. Paul is evidently 12 quoting a common saying in Corinth (s. Weiss; Barrett). συμφέρει pres. ind. act. to bring together, to confer a benefit, to be advantageous or profitable or useful (BAG). ἐξουσιασθήσομαι fut. pass. ἐξουσιάζω to bring under the power of someone, to put under the authority of someone. ■ 13 βρῶμα food. κοιλίᾳ stomach, dat. of advantage. καταργήσει fut. καταργέω to make ineffective, to do away w. The organs of digestion will be changed at the resurrection and the physical constitution of the resurrected body will be different from that of the mortal body (SBT, 54). σῶμα body, the physical body, not a reference to the whole pers. w. his personality but rather the physical body (s. SBT, 51–80). ■ ἤγειρεν aor. ἐγείρω to 14 raise up. ἐξεγερεῖ fut. ἐξεγείρω to raise up out of. ■ μέλος 15 member, used in an ecclesiastical and figurative meaning but the figure rests on a strictly physical definition (SBT, 61). ἄρας aor. act. part. αἴρω to take away, to take. ποιήσω aor. subj., deliberative subj. The form could also be fut. ind. act. (s. RWP). πόρνη prostitute. μὴ γένοιτο aor. opt. mid. γίνομαι "let it not be" (s. Rom 3:4). ■ κολλώμενος pres. mid. part. κολλάω to join 16 together, to unite. ἔσονται fut. mid. εἰμί. φησίν pres. ind. φημί to say. εἰς σάρκα μίαν "one flesh." The prep. in place of the pred. nom. is due to Semitic influence (s. MH, 462). The becoming "one flesh" refers to physical union through sexual intercourse (SBT, 62). ■ ἓν πνεῦμα "one spirit." Illicit union w. a 17 harlot effects a oneness of physical relationship which contradicts the Lord's claim over the body and creates a disparity between the body and the spirit (still united to the Lord) (SBT, 69). ■ φεύγετε pres. imp. φεύγω to flee. The pres. imp. indicates 18 it is to be a continual and habitual fleeing. ἁμάρτημα sin, sin as the act or result of the principle of sin. (For the suf. indicating the result of an action, s. MH, 355.) ἐάν used after a rel. pron. giving a generalization "whatever." ποιήσῃ aor. subj. ποιέω. ἐκτός w. gen. outside, without. εἰς w. acc. against. Immorality arises within the body and has as its sole purpose the gratification of the body (Grosheide). ■ ναός temple, the dwelling place 19 of God, the inner sanctuary itself (Lenski). An illusion either to

the temple in Jerusalem or to the temple of Aphrodite near Corinth (s. SBT, 78). οὗ rel. pron. gen. sing. gen. by attraction. ἐστέ pres. ind. εἰμί used w. gen. in the sense of "belonging to"
20 (s. MT, 231). ■ ἠγοράσθητε aor. pass. ἀγοράζω to buy, to buy at the market place. (For the purchasing of slaves in the ancient world, s. FCS, 37ff.). τιμῆς "w. a price," gen. of price. δοξάσατε aor. imp. δοξάζω to cause one to have a good opinion of someone, to glorify. δή then, certainly. Used as an intensive particle and commands an exhortation and indicates that the point at last is clear and may be assumed as true (RG, 1149; BD, 285). ἐν "with." The physical body is man's means of concrete service for God (SBT, 244).

Ch. 7

1   ■ περί w. gen. concerning. (For the elliptical expression w. the gen. of the personal pron., gen. by attraction, s. RP.) ἐγράψατε aor. γράφω to write. Paul now gives his opinion to questions the Corinthians had asked him (Grosheide). καλόν good, that which is useful or pleasing, that which is suitable or appropriate for a situation (T; CBB; TDNT). (For an analysis of the formula "better . . . than," s. G.F. Snyder, "The Tobspruch in the New Testament," NTS, 23 [October, 1976], 117–120.) ἅπτεσθαι pres. mid. inf. ἅπτομαι to touch, followed by the
2 gen. ■ πορνεία fornication, illicit sex. ἐχέτω pres. imp. ἔχω to have. The imp. is hortatory, not merely permissive (RP). (For a study showing that consecrated virginity was not a customary way of life in the most primitive communities, s. J. Massingberd Ford, "St. Paul, The Philogamist (I Corinthians VII in Early
3 Patristic Exegesis)," NTS, 11 [July, 1965], 326–348.) ■ ὀφειλή obligation, debt, due. The specific obligation involved in the marital union (Lenski). ἀποδιδότω pres. imp. ἀποδίδωμι to pay back, to pay one's dues, to render. The pres. imp. indicates habitual duty (Morris). The rabbis required that the marriage partners have regular relations w. one another (s. SB III, 368–
4 371). ■ ἐξουσιάζει pres. ind. act. to exercise authority over, used w. gen. The pres. tense emphasizes a general statement
5 which is always true. ■ ἀποστερεῖτε pres. act. imp. ἀποστερέω to rob, to deprive. εἰ μήτι except, unless in a given case, unless perhaps (s. M 169; BS, 204). σύμφωνος agreement, consent. πρὸς καιρὸν "for a time," "for a period" (no longer) (BD, 124). The rabbis taught that abstinence from intercourse was allowable for generally one to two weeks but disciples of the law may continue abstinence for thirty days against the will of their wives while they occupy themselves in the study of the law

(M Ketuboth V, 6). ἵνα w. subj. that. Either used to express purpose or could be viewed as an imperatival use (s. MT, 94f.). σχολάσητε aor. subj. σχολάζω to have leisure time for, to devote one's self to something (Lightfoot, *Notes*). πάλιν again. τὸ αὐτό "for the same thing," "be together." It refers to being sexually together as before (Lenski). ἦτε pres. subj. εἰμί. πειράζῃ pres. subj. πειράζω to tempt, to try to bring someone to a fall. The subj. is used to express purpose and the pres. tense indicates that Satan may not keep on tempting you (RWP). ἀκρασία lack of self-control, incontinence. Here in the sense of irrepressible desire for sexual relations (Barrett). ■ συγγνώμη 6 concession, allowance, "I do not give this as a binding rule. I state it as what is allowable" (Lightfoot, *Notes*). ■ θέλω to wish, 7 to desire followed by the inf. His desire is not only that they be unmarried, but that they also be able to control themselves (Weiss). At this time Paul may have been unmarried or a widower or his wife may have left him and returned to her family because of his conversion to Christianity (Bruce). χάρισμα gift, gracious gift, a gift given out of grace. ἐκ "from." It gives the source of the gift.

■ ἄγαμος unmarried. (For the neg. pref., s. Rom. 1:21.) 8 χήρα widow. The article may suggest that Paul has in mind the members of the Corinthian church who are widows, but it may also be a generalization (Barrett). καλόν good, s.v.1. μείνωσιν aor. subj. μένω to remain. ■ εἰ w. ind. introduces a condition 9 which is assumed to be true. ἐγκρατεύονται pres. ind. mid. to exercise self-control, to have power over one's self. γαμησάτωσαν aor. imp. γαμέω to marry. Perhaps ingressive aor. "let them seek marriage" (Grosheide). κρεῖττον comp. ἀγαθός better. πυροῦσθαι pres. pass. inf. πυρόω to set afire, pass. to be inflamed. It may mean "to burn w. passion," but may possibly mean "to burn in Gehenna," because of falling into fornication (Bruce). ■ γεγαμηκόσιν perf. act. part. γαμέω to 10 marry. The perf. emphasizes a state or condition (s. Rom. 3:21). παραγγέλλω to give orders, to command, to instruct. Both Paul and the church at Corinth knew the words of Jesus and Paul gives an additional command and expects obedience because he receives revelations from the Lord which he can communicate to the churches (Grosheide). χωρισθῆναι aor. pass. inf. χωρίζω to separate, to divide. The wife is separated, the husband puts away. Then in the converse point of view the believing wife is said to put away and the unbelieving husband is to be separated (Bengel). Infinitive used in indirect discourse. ■ καί 11 even, actually, "if a separation *does* take place" (Barrett).

χωρισθῇ aor. subj. pass. χωρίζω ingressive aor. "she gets separated" (RWP). μενέτω pres. imp. 3rd sing. μένω. τῷ ἀνδρί "to the husband." The definite article is used to denote previous reference; that is, "to her husband" (s. DM, 141; Funk, 556). καταλλαγήτω aor. imp. pass. καταλλάσσω to reconcile, pass. to be reconciled. The prep. in compound is perfective "to effect a thorough change back, to reconcile" (APC, 187ff.). In Judaism it was possible for the wife to return to the husband before the bill of divorcement had been received (SB III, 374).

12 ἀφιέναι pres. inf. ἀφίημι to send away, to divorce. ■ λοιπός rest. Paul refers here to those who have unbelieving partners (Barrett). ἐγώ "I." Paul means that he is not now repeating the teaching of Christ, who is not likely to have said anything on the subj. He is, however, w. inspiration speaking w. apostolic authority (RP). εἰ w. an ind. "if," introduces a condition which is assumed true. ἄπιστος unbelieving. συνευδοκεῖ pres. ind. act. to be pleased together w., to agree together, to approve, to consent. οἰκεῖν pres. act. inf. to live. Used in the sense of being

13 married. μὴ ἀφιέτω pres. imp. ἀφίημι s.v.11. ■ γυνὴ woman, wife. The context indicates that it is "a Christian woman" (Bar-

14 rett). ■ ἡγίασται perf. pass. ἁγιάζω to separate, to sanctify, to set apart for God's service, to consecrate. He was set apart to the service of God, as the guardian of one of His chosen ones (Hodge). The perf. tense refers to the lasting condition (Grosheide). ἐν "in the wife"; that is, through the close tie w. her (Grosheide). ἐπεὶ ἄρα "since otherwise," "since on the contrary supposition it follows . . ." (Lightfoot, Notes). ἀκάθαρτος

15 not clean. (For the neg. pref., s. Rom. 1:20.) ■ εἰ δέ "but if." The particle introduces a condition which is assumed to be true. ἄπιστος unbelieving. χωρίζεται pres. ind. pass. to separate, to separate one's self, to divorce. In the papyri the word was used as a technical expression for divorce (BS, 247). χωριζέσθω pres. imp. pass. δεδούλωται perf. ind. pass. δουλόω to enslave, to be a slave, to be under bondage. ἐν τοῖς τοιούτοις "in such cases." ἐν εἰρήνῃ the prep. may be used in a double sense "God has called you into a peace in which He wishes you to live" (IBG, 79). κέκληκεν perf. ind. act. καλέω to call. The perf. empha-

16 sizes the continuing results or condition (s. Rom. 3:21). ■ σώσεις fut. σῴζω to save, to rescue.

17 　　■ εἰ μή except, only. This looks back to v.15, which contemplates the possibility in certain circumstances of separation (Barrett). (S. also BD, 191.) ἑκάστῳ each one. The word is the subject of the main clause but appears in the dat. through inverse attraction to the subordinate clause (s. RG, 717; BD, 151).

ἐμέρισεν perf. ind. act. μερίζω to divide, to distribute. The perf. looks at the completed action in the past and the continuing results in the present "has assigned his lot in life once for all." The word here refers entirely to the external conditions of life (Lightfoot, *Notes*). περιπατείτω pres. act. imp. περιπατέω to walk about, to conduct one's life. The pres. tense emphasizes the continual or habitual action. διατάσσομαι pres. ind. mid. to command, to ordain, to order. The word was a military term (RWP), a technical term used in connection w. wills, as well as a general word for commanding (MM). ■ περιτετμημένος 18 perf. pass. part. περιτέμνω to circumcise. ἐκλήθη aor. pass. καλέω. ἐπισπάσθω pres. mid. imp. ἐπισπάω a medical technical term "to pull over the foreskin." A method used to conceal circumcision (BAG; SB IV, 33f.; Lietzmann; 1 Macc. 115). ἀκροβυστία uncircumcision. κέκληται perf. pass. καλέω. The perf. emphasizes the continuing result. περιτεμνέσθω pres. pass. imp. περιτέμνω to circumcise. ■ τήρησις keeping, watch- 19 ing, guarding. (For nouns ending w. this suf. which expresses action, s. MH, 373f.) ἐντολῶν gen. pl. obj. gen. ■ κλήσει call- 20 ing. ᾗ rel. pron. dat. sing. fem. locative referring to the state in which he is when he is called by God to become a Christian (Barrett). ἐκλήθη aor. pass. μενέτω pres. imp. μένω to remain. ■ ἐκλήθης aor. pass., s.v.18. μελέτω pres. imp. μέλει imperson- 21 al verb used w. dat. to be a concern to someone "don't let it be a concern to you," "don't worry about it," "stop being concerned about it" (FCS, 175; for the force of the imp., s. Rom 6:11, 12; MKG, 272). ἀλλ'"but." The word here has its full adversative force (FCS, 177). εἰ καί "if, indeed" (FCS, 178; Thrall, 81). ἐλεύθερος free. γενέσθαι aor. mid. inf. γίνομαι. (For an extensive discussion of slavery in the ancient world w. the discussion of why and how a slave was set free, s. FCS, 29–125.) μᾶλλον comp. adv. πολύ "rather," "by all means." χρῆσαι aor. mid. imp. χράομαι to use, to live according to. The object to be supplied would be God's calling "by all means, live according to (your calling in Christ)." The believer's existence is no longer determined by his legal status but if he is to be freed he is to make better use of his vocation (s. FCS, 175–179f.; Grosheide). ■ γάρ "for." This introduces an explanation and 22 further reason why they are not to worry about being in slavery (FCS, 177). ἀπελεύθερος freedman. The following gen. describes who had freed him and to whom he now belongs. (For the social standing and the rights of a freedman as well as his obligations to the one who has freed him, s. FCS, 72–82.) ■ 23 τιμῆς price, gen. sing. gen. of price. ἠγοράσθητε aor. pass.

ἀγοράζω to buy at the market place, to purchase (s. APC,
53–59; TDNT; CBB). The pass. indicates another did the pur-
24 chasing and the aor. looks at the completed transaction. ■ ἐν ᾧ
"in which." It refers to the state or condition. ἐκλήθη aor. pass.,
s.v.18. μενέτω pres. imp. s.v.20. παρὰ w. dat. along side of, in
the presence of. All secular conditions whether of family life, or
caste, or service, are capable of being made the expression of a
Christian character (RP).

25　　　■ παρθένος virgin. It has been suggested that the word
here refers to young widows or widowers who have only been
married once and the question had been raised whether a second
marriage was wrong (s. J.M. Ford, "Levirate Marriage in St. Paul
(I Cor. VII)," NTS, 10 [April, 1964], 361–365). Another suggestion is that it refers to engaged couples w. the meaning "fiance"
and the entire section (verses 25–38) concerns engagement (J.K.
Elliott, "Paul's Teaching on Marriage in I Cor.: Some Problems
Considered," 19 [January, 1973], 219–225). ἐπιταγή commandment (s.v.17); that is, an expressed command, whether a
directly recorded saying of our Lord (as in v. 10) or a direct
intimation to the apostle by revelation (Lightfoot, Notes).
δίδωμι pres. ind. act. to give. Though Paul is giving his own
opinion, it does not mean that this section is not inspired by the
Holy Spirit. ἠλεημένος perf. pass. part. ἐλεέω to show mercy,
pass. to receive mercy. The word indicates to see someone in
need and to have pity and compassion on them and to kindly
help him out of his need (s. TDNT; CBB; Trench, Synonyms,
166–171). The perf. looks at the completed state or condition
and the part. could be used in a causal sense (Barrett). πιστὸς
26 true, faithful, trustworthy. ■ νομίζω to consider, to think, to be
of the opinion. ὑπάρχειν pres. act. inf. to be, to exist. Infinitive
used in indirect discourse. διὰ w. acc. because of. ἐνεστῶσαν
perf. act. part. ἐνίστημι to stand on, to be present. ἀνάγκη
necessity, compulsion of any kind, distress, calamity. It refers to
the whole state of things between the first and second coming
of Christ (Godet). ὅτι used after the main verb in a recitative
sense equivalent to quotation marks (RWP). τὸ οὕτως εἶναι
27 pres. inf. "the being so" (s. BD, 205f.). ■ δέδεσαι perf. ind. pass.
2nd per. sing. δέω to bind, Used w. dat. to indicate the pers. w.
whom one is bound. The perf. indicates the continuing state
resulting from a previous action. (For the lively style of this
section, s. BD, 242.) ζήτει pres. imp. ζητέω to seek. The pres.
imp. w. the neg. could mean "do not immediately . . . ," or "do
not always . . . ," or "do not continue . . ." (MKG, 272). λύσις
loosing, releasing. λέλυσαι perf. ind. pass. 2nd per. sing. λύω

to loose, to release. ■ ἐὰν καί "and if." It introduces a third-class 28
condition indicating the condition is possible. (For the meaning
"although," s. BD, 190.) γαμήσῃς aor. subj. γαμέω to marry,
ingressive aor. to get married. ἥμαρτες aor. ind. act. ἁμαρτάνω
to sin, gnomic aor. indicating that which is always true (Lietzmann; s. BD, 171; Funk, 621). γήμῃ aor. subj. γαμέω. θλῖψις
tribulation, pressure, affliction. τῇ σαρκί dat. of reference, possibly instrumental dat. or dat. of disadvantage. ἕξουσιν fut. ἔχω.
τοιοῦτοι such ones. φείδομαι pres. mid. to spare, conative pres.
"I am trying to spare" (Barrett). ■ φημί to say. καιρός time, 29
time period. συνεσταλμένος perf. pass. part. συστέλλω to
draw together, to limit, to shorten. The time has been drawn
together so as to be small in amount (RP). λοιπός finally, henceforth. The word can be inferential or progressive (s. Blomqvist,
100–103; Thrall, 25–30). ἔχοντες pres. part. ἔχω. The part. is
used w. the particle for an assumed condition (RWP). ὦσιν pres.
subj. εἰμί. ■ κλαίοντες pres. part. to weep, to cry. κατέχοντες 30
pres. act. part. to hold down, to hold firm, to possess, "as not
entering upon full ownership." Earthly goods are a trust, not a
possession (RP). ■ χρώμενοι pres. mid. part. χράομαι to use, 31
to make use of. (For the use of the acc. w. this verb, s. RG, 476.)
καταχρώμενοι pres. mid. part. καταχράομαι to make full use
of, to use to the utmost, "using it down to the ground," "using
it completely up" (RP). (For the use of this word in the papyri,
s. MM.) παράγει to pass by, to pass alongside of, to pass away.
The pres. tense emphasizes the continual action. σχῆμα bearing, manner, outward appearance, form, shape (BAG; TDNT).
κόσμος world. It refers to the world's resources and its opportunities (Bruce). ■ ἀμερίμνους without care, free from care, with- 32
out worry or concern. (For the neg. pref., s. Rom. 1:20.)
μεριμνᾷ pres. ind. act. to have care or concern, to worry about
something, gnomic pres. indicating a general truth (s. SMT, 8;
Funk, 615). ἀρέσῃ aor. subj. ἀρέσκω to please. ■ γαμήσας 33
aor. part. γαμέω. τὰ τοῦ κόσμου "things belonging to the
world," gen. of relationship (s. BD, 89). ■ μεμέρισται perf. ind. 34
pass. μερίζω to divide. The perf. tense emphasizes the state or
condition. ᾖ pres. subj. εἰμί. ἁγία holy, dedicated, consecrated.
τῷ σώματι dat. of reference. The passage indicates that the
human spirit is distinct from the body (s. SBT, 140). γαμήσασα
aor. act. part. fem., s.v.33. ■ αὐτῶν own, refl. use of the pron. 35
or possibly the intensive use (s. RG, 687). σύμφορον that which
is carried together, beneficial, advantageous, profitable, here
used as a noun, benefit, advantage. βρόχος noose, a noose or
slipknot used for lassoing animals (RWP). ἐπιβάλω aor. subj.

ἐπιβάλλω to cast upon, to put upon w. the purpose of catching, "to cast a noose upon one" is a figurative expression, originally borrowed from the chase, for the idea of depriving of freedom (bringing under, binding and limiting relations) (Meyer). εὔσχημον well-shaped, proper, good order, decorum, decency. The word denotes perf. fitness (Godet). εὐπάρεδρον constant, lit. well sitting beside, "for the good position beside the Lord" (RWP). The verb is used in 1 Cor. 9:13 for "waiting upon the altar" (Barrett). ἀπερισπάστως adv. unhindered, lit. without anything drawn around (RWP), without distraction.

36   ■ ἀσχημονεῖν pres. act. inf. to act without decorum, to behave in a dishonorable way (for the noun, s.v.35). ἐπί w. acc. toward. παρθένον αὐτοῦ "his virgin." This refers either to a father and his daughter or to a man and woman who have entered upon a spiritual marriage and now live together without physical relations or a case of levirate marriage and the word means "young widow" or it refers to a man and woman who are an engaged couple (s. Barrett; s. also v. 25). ᾖ pres. subj., s.v.34. ὑπέρακμος past the bloom of youth, beyond marriageable age. The prep. in compound may be understood to express intensification rather than the temporal sense; that is, w. strong passion, oversexed (BAG; s. also Barrett). ὀφείλει pres. ind. act. one is obligated, it is necessary. The word expresses a moral obligation. ποιείτω pres. imp. 3rd per. sing. ποιεώ. γαμείτωσαν pres. imp. 3rd per. pl. γαμέω to marry. Present tense of the imp.

37 points to a general truth. ■ ἕστηκεν perf. ἵστημι to stand. ἐν τῇ καρδίᾳ "in his heart." Here the heart is the center of man from which decisions come (PAT, 328). ἑδραῖος firm, steadfast. ἀνάγκην necessity, s.v.26. ἐξουσία authority. κέκρικεν perf. κρίνω to judge, to come to a decision, to decide. τηρεῖν pres. act. inf. to keep. The meaning is probably "to keep his virgin as she is" (Barrett). The inf. is used in indirect discourse giving the content of the decision. καλῶς adv. well. (For the adj., s.v.1.)

38 ■ γαμίζων pres. act. part. to marry. Verbs w. this ending are generally causative, "to give in marriage," but the word may also mean "to marry," "to enter into marriage" (s. MM; Weiss; Lietzmann). ἑαυτοῦ his. The reflex. here appears to have lost refl.

39 force (IBG, 120). κρεῖσσον comp. ἀγαθός "better." ■ δέδεται perf. ind. pass. δέω to bind. The perf. emphasizes the state or condition resulting from the act of marriage. ὅσον rel. pron. as much as, as long as. ζῇ pres. ind. act. ζάω to live. κοιμηθῇ aor. pass. subj. κοιμάομαι to go to sleep. The term for Christian death (EGT). ᾧ rel. pron. masc. dat. sing. "to whom." The dat. is used w. the verb "to be married to." γαμηθῆναι aor. pass. inf.

γαμέω pass. to be married to, epexegetic inf. used to explain the freedom of the widow (s. Funk, 663f.). ■ μακαριωτέρα comp. 40 μακάριος happy (s. TDNT). ἐάν w. subj. introduces a condition which is probable. μείνῃ aor. subj. μένω to remain.

Ch. 8

■ περί w. gen. "concerning," "about." Paul begins to treat 1 a second point concerning which the Corinthians had questioned him (Grosheide). εἰδωλόθυτον that which was offered as a sacrifice to an idol. The word is of Jewish origin (s. TDNT). Various types of choice animals without blemish were offered to the gods. Part of the meat was burned on the altar and part of it was used for a sacred banquet w. the deity as the honored guest and that which was left was sold at the marketplace (s. OCD, 944; Bruce). The Jews called this meat from sacrifices for the dead; that is, "idols," and the use of such meat was strictly forbidden (s. SB III, 377). οἴδαμεν defective perf. w. pres. meaning. Paul uses the 1st per. pl. to include himself w. the readers (Lietzmann). γνῶσις knowledge. Paul's use of knowledge is not something purely intellectual. It is knowledge which has results and leads to action, especially religious action (Grosheide). Here it is not a reference to gnosticism which developed later (s. PCG, 39f.). φυσιοῖ pres. ind. act. to puff up, to blow up like a billows. The pres. is gnomic emphasizing a general truth. ■ ἐγνωκέναι 2 perf. act. inf. γινώσκω. The perf. emphasizes a knowledge which is acquired and is one's possession. The inf. is used in indirect discourse. ἔγνω aor. ind. act. γινώσκω ingressive aor. "come to know" (RWP). ■ ἔγνωσται perf. ind. pass. he has 3 come to be known and is still known by God (Lenski). ■ βρῶσις 4 eating. (For nouns ending w. this suf. indicating action, s. MII, 373.) εἴδωλον idol. Paul calls that which the statute represents an idol (Schlatter). οὐδείς no one, nobody, used as an adj. "no." εἰ μή except. ■ εἴπερ if indeed, if after all. Here used in a 5 concessive sense (s. BD, 237). λεγόμενοι pres. pass. part. λέγω to say, pass. to be called, "those who continually are called gods" or "so called gods" (Grosheide). εἴτε ... εἴτε "just as indeed." θεοὶ πολλοί many gods (s. Acts 17:16). ■ εἷς one god followed 6 by the word in apposition "the father." κύριος lord, a title used to indicate deity of Jesus Christ. (For a collection of the evidence proving that the Jews at the time of Christ used this term for God, s. Joseph A. Fitzmyer, "Der semitische Hintergrund des neutestamentlichen Kyriostitels," *Jesus Christus in Historie und Theologie*, 267–298). ἐκ and εἰς indicate the origin and goal of God's creation. ἡμεῖς δι᾽ αὐτοῦ "we through Him." Like all men we are created by Christ but we are also redeemed by Him (Grosheide).

7 ■ ἡ γνῶσις "the knowledge." The article points to the specific knowledge he is discussing in this context. συνηθείᾳ familiarity, custom, instrumental dat. συνείδησις conscience (s. Rom. 2:15; TDNT; PAT, 402–446; CBB). μολύνεται pres. pass.

8 μολύνω to stain, to pollute, to contaminate, to defile. ■ παραστήσει fut. ind. act. παρίστημι to present, to present for approbation or condemnation (RP). ἐὰν w. subj. introduces a condition which is possible. φάγωμεν aor. subj. ἐσθίω to eat. ὑστερούμεθα pres. ind. mid. ὑστερέω to fall short, to lack (s. Rom. 3:23). περισσεύομεν pres. ind. act. to have an abun-

9 dance. ■ μή lest. Used w. aor. subj. to express a neg. imp. (s. BD, 184). πρόσκομμα stumbling, hindrance. γένηται aor. mid.

10 subj. γίνομαι. ἀσθενής weak. ■ ἴδῃ aor. subj. ὁράω to see. εἰδώλειον idol temple, idol shrine. κατακείμενον pres. mid. part. κατάκειμαι to lie down, to recline at the table. It would not be uncommon to be invited to a meal in the temple as is evident from some "invitation cards" found among the papyri (s. Bruce). οὐχὶ used to introduce a question which expects the answer yes. ἀσθενοῦς ὄντος weak, used w. part. in apposition to the personal pron. αὐτοῦ. ὄντος pres. part. gen. sing. εἰμί. Perhaps the causal use of the part. οἰκοδομηθήσεται fut. ind.

11 pass. οἰκοδομέω to build up, to strengthen. ■ ἀπόλλυται pres. ind. pass. ἀπόλλυμι to ruin; that is, "to come to sin." It means not to show one's self as a Christian (Grosheide). ἀσθενῶν pres. part. ἀσθενέω to be weak. ἀπέθανεν aor. ind. act.

12 ἀποθνήσκω to die. ■ ἁμαρτάνοντες pres. act. part. ἁμαρτάνω to sin. τύπτοντες pres. part. τύπτω to wound, to strike w. the fist, staff, whip (RWP). The part. could be conditional or indicating the means or manner. ἀσθενοῦσαν pres.

13 part., s.v.11. ■ διόπερ therefore, for this very reason. εἰ w. ind. Used to introduce a condition which is assumed to be true. σκανδαλίζει to cause one to stumble, to offend (s. TDNT; NTW, 111–114). οὐ μή not in anywise. (For the use of this strong neg., s. M 188f.) φάγω aor. subj., s.v.8. σκανδαλίσω aor. subj.

Ch. 9

1 ■ ἐλεύθερος free, the freedom of a Christian (Morris). οὐχὶ used in questions expecting the answer yes. ἑώρακα perf. ind. act. ὁράω to see. The perf. pictures the lasting results of having seen. Having seen the Lord was one of the prerequisites for

2 apostleship (s. Acts 1:22; s. also 1 Cor. 1:1; TDNT). ■ εἰ w. ind.

used to introduce a condition which is assumed to be true.
ἄλλοις "to others," dat. of respect or relation "in the estimation
of others" (s. Funk, 721f.; MT, 238; Barrett). ἀλλά "but at
least." A contrast used w. the emphatic article (BD, 226).
σφραγίς seal, a confirming and guaranteeing sign as well as a
sign of authority (s. TDNT; CBB).

■ ἐμή "my," emphatic by position. ἀπολογία defense. 3
Used elsewhere of defense in a law court (Barrett).
ἀνακρίνουσιν pres. part. ἀνακρίνω to examine, perhaps in the
sense cross-examine, conative pres. those who would like to
examine (Barrett). ■ μὴ οὐκ The first neg. is used in the question 4
expecting the answer no and the second neg. negates the verb
"you would not say that we do not have the authority, would
you?" (s. BD, 220f.; RG, 1173). φαγεῖν aor. act. inf. ἐσθίω to
eat. πεῖν aor. act. inf. πίνω to drink. The inf. is used to explain
the content of the authority. ■ ἀδελφήν sister; that is, a Chris- 5
tian, one who belongs to the same religious belief (s. CBB;
TDNT). περιάγειν pres. act. inf. to lead around. The word does
not emphasize the traveling together on a journey but rather it
means "to have constantly w. one's self"; that is, being married
(Conzelmann). ■ ἤ or. The word continues the question. 6
ἐργάζεσθαι pres. mid. inf. to work; that is, to do manual labor.
■ στρατεύεται pres. mid. ind. to be a soldier, to do military 7
service, to serve in the army. The pres. tense is gnomic emphasizing a timeless truth (s. SMT, 8). ὀψωνίοις provisions, soldiers' wages (s. Rom. 6:28). The dat. could be instrumental. The
soldiers' pay was probably a denarius a day, out of which they
had to equip themselves, secure any simple luxuries, or bribe the
centurions for remissions of duties (BC V, 428). ποτέ at any
time, ever. ἀμπελῶνα vineyard. (For the exact rules governing
the workers eating of the harvest, s. SB III, 379f.) ποιμαίνει
pres. ind. act. to tend a flock. ποίμνη flock. γάλακτος milk.
■ οὐ not. The word negates the verb rather than determining the 8
question (s.v.4.). ■ γέγραπται perf. pass. γράφω. The perf. 9
emphasizes the standing legal authority of that which was written (s. MM). κημώσεις fut. κημόω to muzzle. The fut. is used
under Semitic influence of the legal language of the OT and
expresses a categorical imp. (BG, 94). The Jewish concern for
animals distinguished them from other nations (SB III, 382).
βοῦς ox. ἀλοῶντα pres. act. part. acc. sing. masc. ἀλοάω to
thrash, to tread or trample out. Sledges were drawn by teams of
oxen . . . , and encircled the pile of grain heaped in the center of
the thrashing floor (ZPEB V, 739; IDB IV, 637). μὴ Used to
introduce questions expecting the answer no. μέλει pres. ind.

413

act. to have concern. Used impersonally followed by the dat. of interest and the gen. of thing, "aren't the things of oxen a con-
10 cern to God?" ■ δι᾿ ἡμᾶς "because of us, for our sakes." Either a reference to men in general or specifically to teachers. πάντως assuredly, entirely; that is, in every case (Grosheide). γάρ for. In replies it affirms what was asked, giving the reason for a tacit "yes," "to be sure, just so" (BD, 236). ἐγράφη aor. pass. γράφω. ὀφείλει pres. ind. act. to be obligated to, ought, should. It generally shows a moral obligation. ἀροτριῶν pres. act. part. ἀροτριάω to plow. ἀροτριᾶν pres. act. inf. Used to complete the main verb showing what the obligation is. μετέχειν pres. act.
11 inf. to share in, to partake of. ■ εἰ w. ind. introducing a condition which is assumed to be true. ἐσπείραμεν aor. ind. act. σπείρω to sow, to sow seeds. μέγα great. σαρκικά fleshly, pertaining to the flesh. (For the meaning of this suf., s. MH, 378.) The word here is not identical w. "sinful." The contrast is one between heavenly and earthly, or between spiritual and the material (Grosheide). θερίσομεν fut. ind. act. θερίζω to harvest, to reap. (For the use of the fut. w. εἰ w. the meaning "if subsequently,
12 as actually happened, we . . . ," s. BD, 189.) ■ ὑμῶν "over you" (RG, 500). ἐξουσίας authority, gen. after a verb of sharing. μετέχουσιν pres. ind. act. μετέχω to partake in, to share.

ἐχρησάμεθα aor. mid. χράομαι to use, to make use of. στέγομεν pres. ind. act. to cover, to protect or keep by covering, to bear up against, to endure (T). ἐγκοπή a cutting in, hindrance. Used in the papyri in the literal sense of cutting down (a tree) (MM). δῶμεν aor. act. subj. δίδωμι to give. The subj. is used to
13 express purpose. ■ ἐργαζόμενοι pres. mid. part. ἐργάζομαι to work, here to officiate in religious matters. τὰ ἐκ τοῦ ἱεροῦ the things from the temple or holy place; that is, the altar or the sacrifice. Thus the last clause defines the first (Grosheide). θυσιαστήριον altar, place of sacrifice (for this suf. indicating the place where an action takes place, s. MH, 342–343) "at the altar." The dat. is pure locative (RG, 521). παρεδρεύοντες pres. act. part. to sit constantly beside, to attend constantly (AS). (For the religious connotation of the word in the papyri, s. MM.) συμμερίζονται pres. ind. mid. to share a portion together. The customs Paul refers to were widespread in antiquity. Those who held sacred offices on behalf of others might reasonably expect
14 to be provided for. This Jesus Himself recognized (Barrett). ■ διέταξεν aor. ind. act. διατάσσω to give an order, to command. The tense of the verb indicates that Paul was consciously alluding to a "past" origin in the teaching of Jesus (JNP, 96). καταγγέλλουσιν pres. act. part. masc. dat. pl. καταγγέλλω to

proclaim, to make a solemn proclamation (s. CBB). The dat. is
dat. of favor or advantage (Godet). ἐκ from. The prep. gives the
source of income. ζῆν pres. act. inf. ζάω to live. The inf. is used
in indirect speech (s. BD, 200; IBG, 153). ■ ἐγὼ δὲ but I (em- 15
phatic). He now applies the principle to himself and the apostle
gives a further reason for the renunciation of his undoubted
rights (Hering). κέχρημαι perf. ind. mid. χράομαι to use followed by the object in the dat. The change of tenses from the aor.
to the perf. brings it down to the pres. moment "I have not
availed myself" (RP). γένηται aor. mid. subj. γίνομαι. Subjunctive used in expressing purpose. ἐν in, in my case (Barrett).
ἀποθανεῖν aor. act. inf. ἀποθνῄσκω to die, an epexegetical
inf. explaining what is better. ἤ or. Paul breaks the construction
abruptly (s. MT, 343). καύχημα boasting, reason or ground for
boasting. κενώσει fut. κενόω to make empty, to make void.
■ εὐαγγελίζωμαι pres. mid. subj. εὐαγγελίζομαι to proclaim 16
good news, to evangelize (s. TDNT; CBB; MTW, 41f.). ἀνάγκη
compulsion, necessity. The word in the NT does not have the
meaning "fate" (s. TDNT; Gustav Stählin, "Das Schicksal Im
Neuen Testament und bei Josephus," Josephus-Studien, 321f.).
ἐπίκειται perf. ind. pass. ἐπιτίθημι to place upon, perf. lies
upon. The perf. emphasizes the pres. condition and the meaning
is "presses upon me" (RP). οὐαί woe, alas! An interjection
denoting pain or displeasure (BAG), followed by the dat. of
disadvantage. εὐαγγελίσωμαι aor. mid. subj. ■ ἑκὼν willingly, 17
gladly, of one's own freewill. πράσσω to do, to practice. The
pres. tense emphasizes habitual action and the word is used in
a first-class conditional clause which assumes the reality of the
condition. μισθός payment, reward. Paul's purpose is to intimate that he does not seek his reward in the receiving of financial compensation (Grosheide). ἄκων unwilling, not of one's
own freewill (for the neg. pref., s. Rom. 1:20). οἰκονομία stewardship, responsibility. The word indicates the task given to
responsible and faithful servants who were appointed over the
economy or particular area of responsibility in the household.
The word stresses obligation, responsibility, and faithfulness of
the servant to his master in carrying out the entrusted task (s.
TDNT). (For the use of the word in patristic writers, s. PGL.)
πεπίστευμαι perf. ind. pass. πιστεύω to believe, to entrust.
The perf. emphasizes the completed state or condition reaching
to the pres. time. ■ μού "my," emphatic by position. ἵνα here 18
does not express purpose but gives the content of the reward (s.
BD, 202). εὐαγγελιζόμενος pres. mid. part., s.v.16. ἀδάπανος
without expense, free of charge. θήσω fut. ind. act. τίθημι to

place, to present. εἰς τό w. inf. used to express purpose. καταχρήσασθαι aor. mid. inf. καταχράομαι to make full use of, to use completely, to use to the uttermost. The prep. in compound is perfective (RWP; s. 1 Cor. 7:31).

19 ■ ὤν pres. act. part. εἰμί to be. The part. here is concessive "although I am free." ἐδούλωσα aor. ind. act. δουλόω to enslave, to make a slave of someone. πλείονας comp. πολύς more, the majority or it has the meaning "others, even more" (BD, 127). κερδήσω fut. ind. act. κερδαίνω to win. ■ ἐγενόμην

20 aor. mid. γίνομαι. τοῖς Ἰουδαίοις the individual use of the article "the Jews w. whom I had to deal on each occasion" (BD, 137). ὑπό w. acc. "under." The "law" here is the Torah, as written in the Pentateuch and expounded by orthodox Jewish

21 rabbis (MS, 135). ■ ἄνομος lawless, without the law, however, not in the sense of leading an unregulated and irresponsible life (MS, 135). The addition of the gen. ἄνομος θεοῦ indicates that "the law of God" is something wider and more inclusive than the "law, in the sense of Torah" (MS, 137). ἔννομος legal, subject to law, obedient to the law, "under legal obligation to Christ" (Barrett). (For the relation of this to the spiritual life and walk according to the precepts of Christ, s. MS, 137–148.) κερδάνω

22 aor. act. subj. κερδαίνω s.v.19. ■ γέγονα perf. ind. act. γίνομαι to become. The change from aor. to perf. is significant; this is the permanent result of his past action (RP). πάντως by all means. σώσω fut. σώζω to rescue, to save. (For the use of the fut. in

23 purpose clauses, s. MT, 100.). ■ συγκοινωνός one who shares together, fellow partaker, fellow participant. γένωμαι aor. mid. subj. γίνομαι. Subjunctive used in a purpose clause.

24 ■ οἴδατε defective perf. w. a pres. meaning to know. στάδιον stadium, a running track which was a long parallelogram about 200 yards long and 30 yards wide (s. OCD, 1010f.; Oscar Bronner, "The Apostle Paul and the Isthmian Games," BA, 25 [February, 1962], 1–31; A.H. Harris, Sport in Greece and Rome, 27–33; DGRA, 1055f.). τρέχοντες pres. act. part. τρέχω to run. εἷς one. βραβεῖον prize. The prize given to the winner of an athletic contest. The prize was generally a wreath but the winner was also rewarded w. fame and popularity. καταλάβητε aor. act. subj. καταλαμβάνω to attain, to grasp and hold, effective aor. w. the perfective use of the prep. in compound (RWP). The example of the runners in the arena sets the stage for the

25 theme of self-control which follows (PAM, 87). ■ ἀγωνιζόμενος pres. mid. part. ἀγωνίζομαι to engage in an athletic contest, to strive. (For the attitude of Greeks, Romans, and Jews toward the athletic contest, s. PAM, 16–75; for the

particular neg. attitude of the Jews, s. SB IV, 401–405.) πάντα acc. of general reference "in regards to all things." ἐγκρατεύεται pres. ind. mid. to exercise self-control. The pres. is gnomic and emphasizes that which is always true. All the endeavors of the athlete are in vain if he has not trained his body and abstained from all that might in any harm his physical condition (PAM, 87). φθαρτός perishable. ἄφθαρτος inperishable. λάβωσιν aor. act. subj. λαμβάνω to receive. Paul is not speaking of agonizing for the prize of eternal life but rather for the goal of faithfully proclaiming the gospel (PAM, 87f.). ■ τοίνυν ac- 26 cordingly, therefore. It is used to draw an inference. ἀδήλως uncertainly, "I do not run as one who has no fixed and certain goal" (PAM, 90; s. also Weiss). πυκτεύω to fight w. the fist, to box (s. A.H. Harris, *Sport in Greece and Rome*, 22–25; DGRA, 974). Paul turns to the picture of the boxer in order to reintroduce the principle of self-restriction and self-negation (PAM, 90). ἀήρ, - έρος air. δέρων pres. act. part. to beat. The word could signify the failure of the pugilist to make his blows tell or his actions in carrying on mock contest of a shadow boxer (PAM, 90). ■ ὑπωπιάζω to strike under the eye, to beat black 27 and blue. δουλαγωγῶ to lead into slavery, to make a slave or to treat one as a slave. The two verbs give the picture of the athlete who does all to discipline himself and to keep his body under rigorous control, in order that it might serve and not hinder his progress to the goal (PAM, 91). πως "lest by any means." κηρύξας aor. act. part. κηρύσσω to preach, to proclaim as a herald (s. TDNT). The part. is temporal expressing antecedent time, "after I have preached." ἀδόκιμος rejected as unusable. Used of metals and coins which were rejected for not standing the test (RWP). γένωμαι aor. mid. subj. s.v.23. Paul's fear is that he will be unfaithful in carrying out his commission of preaching the gospel as expected of him (PAM, 96).

Ch. 10

■ ἀγνοεῖν pres. act. inf. ἀγνοέω not to know, to be igno- 1 rant. Used w. acc. and is supplementary to the verb θέλω. (For the neg. force of the pref., s. Rom. 1:21.) πάντες all. The main emphasis in vv. 1–4 rests on the word "all." Paul had received the same privileges (s. Bruce; Grosheide). διῆλθον aor. διέρχομαι to go through, to pass completely through. The prep. in compound is perfective and local (s. MH, 301f.). ■ εἰς into. 2 ἐβαπτίσαντο aor. mid. βαπτίζω to baptize. It means to immerse in Moses; that is, to bring in close relationship w. Moses (Grosheide). The mid. is permissive mid. Some accept the pass.

as the true reading here (s. BD, 166), and the pass. is explained as a permissive pass. "to allow one's self to be . . ." (MT, 57).

3 ■ τὸ αὐτό "the same." πνευματικός spiritual, that which pertains to the spirit. The word is either spiritual in contrast to material or spiritual in its relation to the Holy Spirit. βρῶμα

4 food. ἔφαγον aor. act. ἐσθίω to eat. ■ ἔπιον aor. ind. act. πίνω to drink. πόμα that which one drinks, drink. ἔπινον impf. The impf. pictures the manner of action and shows the continual access to the supernatural source of supply (RWP; BD, 169). ἀκολουθούσης pres. act. part. fem. ἀκολουθέω to follow. (For the Jewish tradition that the well which followed the Israelites in the wilderness, s. SB IV, 406f.; Targum Onkelos and Rashi at Numbers 21:16–19; for the DSS, s. CD 6:3–9.) πέτρα rock (s. Matt. 16:18). ἦν impf. εἰμί. It was not that Christ was the literal rock but He was the spiritual rock that followed and from which Israel drank. The benefits enjoyed by the people are spiritual because they came from Christ who is the source of all blessings

5 (Grosheide; s. also TDNT). ■ εὐδόκησεν aor. εὐδοκέω to be pleased w. Its use w. the prep. ἐν denotes a Semitic influence (s. BD, 111). κατεστρώθησαν aor. ind. pass. καταστρώννυμι to stretch or spread down as of a couch, to lay low, as if by a

6 hurricane (RWP). ■ τύπος type, example. The word is used here in the sense of "an awful, warning example" (Barrett; s. also CBB; TDNT). ἐγενήθησαν aor. pass. γίνομαι. Instead of the usual sing. of the verb after a neuter pl. subject the verb here is pl. through the attraction of the pred. (EGT). εἰς τό w. inf. used here to express purpose; that is, neg. purpose "that we should not be." ἐπιθυμητάς one who lusts, one who has a strong desire. The noun is followed by the obj. gen. indicating the object of the strong desire. (For nouns w. this ending indicating the agent performing an action, s. MH, 365f.) ἐπεθύμησαν aor. ind. act. ἐπιθυμέω to have strong desire, to lust after, to lust. Lust is strong desire of any sort, but in the NT it is more commonly used

7 of evil passions than good desires (Morris). ■ γίνεσθε pres. mid. imp. The pres. imp. w. the neg. is often used to stop an action in progress, "do not continue" (s. MKG, 272f.). γέγραπται perf. ind. pass. γράφω, "it stands written." The term was used of authoritative documents (s. MM). ἐκάθισεν aor. καθίζω to take one's seat, to sit. φαγεῖν aor. act. inf. ἐσθίω to eat. πεῖν aor. act. inf. πίνω to drink. The inf. is used to express purpose. ἀνέστησαν aor. ἀνίστημι to rise up, to get up. παίζειν to play, to amuse one's self, to dance. This word as well as the eating and drinking were considered by the rabbis to mean the

8 committing of idolatry (s. SB III, 410). ■ πορνεύωμεν pres.

subj. πορνεύω to engage in unlawful sexual acts, to commit fornication. The subj. is hortatory "let us not." ἐπόρνευσαν aor. ind. act. ἔπεσαν aor. πίπτω to fall. εἴκοσι τρεῖς twenty-three χιλιάς thousand. ■ ἐκπειράζωμεν pres. subj. ἐκπειράζω to 9 try, to put to the test (s. Matt. 4:1). The prep. in compound is perfective and might suggest the daring of the act or an effort to put to a decisive test (MH, 309), hortatory subj. ὄφις snake. ἀπώλλυντο impf. mid. ἀπόλλυμι to be destroyed, to perish. The impf. pictures the continual action, they continue to perish day by day (RWP). ■ γογγύζετε pres. act. imp. γογγύζω to 10 murmur, to complain, to give audible expression to unwarranted dissatisfaction (Lenski). It contains the idea of a judgment and a condemnation of God by man who instead of giving God thanks and showing obedience sets himself up as a judge over God (s. TDNT; CBB). καθάπερ just as. ἐγόγγυσαν aor. ind. act. γογγύζω and, w. the result that (Barrett). ἀπώλοντο aor. ind. mid. ἀπόλλυμι. ὀλοθρευτής one who destroys, the destroyer. Perhaps a reference to the angel of destruction whom the rabbis called Mashhith (s. SB III, 421f.; Jastrow II, 851; s. Exod. 12:23; TDNT). ■ τυπικῶς adv. typically (s.v.6) 11 συνέβαινεν impf. συμβαίνω to happen. Used w. dat. which indicates to whom the events happened. The impf. pictures the enumerated events as in process of happening; the sing. sums them up as one series (RP). ἐγράφη aor. pass. γράφω. νουθεσία admonition, warning (s. TDNT). τέλη τῶν αἰώνων the ends of the ages. In Jewish writing the term means the beginning of redemption or the time of the appearing of the Messiah or the general meaning "the end" (s. SB III, 416). (For the apparently general use of the term in the DSS, s. 1 QS 4:16f.) Paul believes he and his correspondents are living in the last days of world history before the breaking in of the Messianic Age (Barrett). κατήντηκεν perf. ind. act. καταντάω to come down to a meeting, to arrive at a goal, to come to. The word appears in the papyri as a technical term for the inheritance that comes to an heir (s. TDNT; BAG; MM). It may be that this refers not to "us" but to those of Israel (MT IV, 85). ■ ὥστε therefore, thus 12 then. It indicates that this exhortation to watchfulness is the inference to be drawn from the foregoing examples (Godet). δοκῶν pres. act. part. δοκέω to seem, to be of the opinion, to think. ἑστάναι perf. inf. ἵστημι to stand. βλεπέτω pres. imp. beware. The pres. tense indicates the necessity of continual watchfulness. μή w. subj. lest. It introduces a neg. purpose clause. πέσῃ aor. subj. πίπτω to fall, perhaps here to fall into sin (Weiss). ■ πειρασμός testing, trying, temptation. The verb 13 came to signify the trying intentionally, and w. the purpose of discovering what of good and evil, or power or weakness, was in a person or thing (Trench, *Synonyms*, 280). εἴληφεν perf. ind. act. λαμβάνω to take. The words imply that there was a certain temptation which had captured the Corinthians and which subdued them (Grosheide). εἰ μή except. ἀνθρώπινος human, that which is according to human strength, bearable (Weiss; BAG). The suf. signifies material or kind (MH, 359). ἐάσει fut. ἐάω to allow. The verb is followed by the inf. w. the subject of the inf. in the acc. πειρασθῆναι aor. pass. inf. πειράζω. The pass. indicates that the temptation is from without. ὑπέρ w. acc. above, beyond. ὅ rel. pron. which includes the unexpressed demonstrative pron. "beyond that which" (s. BD, 154). ποιήσει fut. ποιέω. σύν w., in connection w.; that is, "w. the temptation." ἔκβασις a way out, escape. In the papyri it has the meaning "end," "completion" (MM). δύνασθαι pres. mid. inf. to be able. The inf. either explains the way of escape or gives purpose or result of God's making a way of escape (s. BD, 206). ὑπενεγκεῖν aor. act. inf. ὑποφέρω to carry under, to bear, to endure.

14   ■ διόπερ wherefore, for which very reason, "the conclusion of this" (Barrett; DM, 245; Blomqvist, 136f.). εἰδωλολατρία
15 idolatry, the service and worship of idols. ■ φρόνιμος wise, understanding, sensible, the ability to make a decision (s. TDNT). κρίνατε aor. imp. κρίνω to judge. ὑμεῖς you yourself.
16 ■ ποτήριον cup, the cup of blessing was a technical Jewish term used for the cup of wine drunk at the end of a meal. The most honored guest at the table took the cup, lifted it up and said the benediction (Barrett; SB IV, 627ff.). εὐλογοῦμεν pres. ind. act. to bless, to give thanks. The pres. tense views the general Christian practice without going into details (RP). οὐχί introduces a question expecting the answer yes. κοινωνία fellowship, common participation (Barrett; s. also CBB; TDNT). αἵματος τοῦ Χριστοῦ gen. sing. obj. gen. "a participation in the blood of Christ" (RWP). τὸν ἄρτον acc. by inverse attraction to the rel. pron. (s. BD, 154; RG, 717f.). κλῶμεν pres. ind. act. κλάω to break. σώματος τοῦ Χρ. "the body of Christ." A reference to the church as the body of Christ and the fellowship among
17 believers (Kümmel in Lietzmann). ■ ὅτι because. οἱ πάντες the all, "we the whole, the whole number." These words are in apposition w. the subject (RWP). μετέχομεν pres. ind. act. to
18 share w., to be partners in. ■ κατὰ σάρκα "according to the flesh," a reference to historical Israel (Conzelmann). ἐσθίοντες pres. act. part. ἐσθίω. θυσία sacrifice. θυσιαστήριον altar,

place of sacrifice. ■ οὖν then. εἰδωλόθυτον that which is sacri- 19
ficed to an idol (s. 1 Cor. 8:1). ■ ἃ rel. pron. including the 20
demonstrative pron. which is not expressed (s.v.13). δαιμονίοις
"to demons" dat. of advantage. Heathen sacrifices were sacrifices to demons (s. CBB; TDNT; SB III, 51f.; RAC IX, 546–797).
■ οὐ δύνασθε pres. ind. mid. "you are not able." The pres. tense 21
emphasizes that which is always true. ποτήριον cup, the common meal and the common drinking of the heathen created a
close and meaningful relationship between the human partners
and between the god to whom they ate and drank. This was
expecially true when they drank from a common cup (RAC II,
41). πίνειν pres. act. inf. τράπεζα table indicating a common
meal, gen. after a verb of sharing. ■ ἤ or. παραζηλοῦμεν pres. 22
ind. act. to provoke to jealousy, to cause one to be jealous. (For
the prep. compound, s. MH 320.) μὴ introduces a question
which expects the answer no. ἰσχυρότεροι αὐτοῦ "strong as he
(is)," gen. of comparison.

■ ἔξεστιν "it is lawful," "it is allowed." συμφέρει pres. 23
ind. act. to bring together, to help, to confer a benefit, to be
advantageous or profitable or useful (BAG). The pres. tense
indicates that which is always true. οἰκοδομεῖ pres. ind. act. to
build up, to edify. It means to cause to advance spiritually
(Grosheide). ■ μηδεὶς no one. τὸ ἑαυτοῦ "the thing of himself," 24
"that which is his own," "his own ends" (Barrett). ζητείτω pres.
act. imp. ζητέω to seek. The pres. tense points to a habitual
action. ■ μάκελλον stall or shop on the marketplace where 25
meat and other foods were sold. Because of the nearness to the
temple, it was possible that some of the meat in the marketplace
had been sacrificial offerings (s. Lietzmann; TDNT; H.J. Cadbury, "The Macellum of Corinth," JBL 53 [1934], 134–141;
Barrett NTS, 11 [January, 1965], 144). πωλούμενον pres. pass.
part. πωλέω to sell. A middle to lower class household in Corinth buying its supplies in the Macellum would often make pur-
chases that had no connection w. idolatry (Barrett NTS, 11
[January, 1965], 146). ἐσθίετε pres. act. imp. to eat, the imp. of
permission "you may eat" (s. RG, 948). (For a discussion of
Plutarch's arguments against eating meat, s. PTW, 301–316.)
ἀνακρίνοντες pres. act. part. ἀνακρίνω to examine, to make
inquiry. The word was used in a judicial sense of conducting a
hearing or investigation (BAG). Jews were only allowed to buy
meat from the Gentiles if it could be established that it was not
meat offered to idols (s. SB III, 420f.). συνείδησις conscience
(s. Rom. 2:15; PAT, 416–420). ■ τοῦ κυρίου "belongs to the 26
Lord." πλήρωμα fullness, the total content. ■ εἰ "if." It views 27

the possibility as a reality. καλεῖ pres. ind. act. to call, to invite. Christians were evidently frequently invited to dinners by the unbelievers and some of these dinners may have been connected w. heathen gods. (For a study of such invitations w. examples, s. Chan-Hie Kim, "The Papyrus Invitation," JBL, 94 [September, 1975], 391–402.) πορεύεσθαι pres. mid. inf. πορεύομαι to go. παρατιθέμενον pres. pass. part. παρατίθημι to place be-
28 fore. ■ ἐάν used w. subj. to introduce a condition which is possible. εἴπῃ aor. subj. λέγω. ἱερόθυτον that which is sacrificed in a temple. It is different from a word in chapter 8:1; 10:19 and is more appropriate on pagan lips or, in pagan company (Bruce). μηνύσαντα aor. act. part. μηνύω to make known, to
29 give information, to reveal. ■ τὴν ἑαυτοῦ his own. ἱνατί why. κρίνεται pres. ind. pass. κρίνω to judge, pass. to be judged, to
30 be exposed to judgment (Barrett). ■ χάριτι "w. thanks," "w. thanksgiving," dat. of manner (BD, 106). The word "grace" not only meant the gift which was given but the thanks which was expressed for the gift (s. TDNT). βλασφημοῦμαι pres. ind. pass. βλασφημέω to slander, to defame, to injure the reputation of someone (BAG). οὗ "that which," rel. pron. used including
31 the idea of the demonstrative pron. ■ ποιεῖτε pres. act. imp. to
32 do. The pres. tense points to a habitual action. ■ ἀπρόσκοπος without offense, without causing others to stumble (RP). Used in the papyri in the sense of "free from hurt or harm" (MM) and in the sense of "not causing injury" (Preisigke). Ἰουδαίοις Jews (s. Malcolm Love, "Who Were the IOUDAIOI?," Nov T, 18 [April, 1976], 101–130). γίνεσθε pres. mid. imp. ἐκκλησίᾳ
33 church, dat. of disadvantage. ■ πάντα acc. of general reference. σωθῶσιν aor. pass. subj. σῴζω to rescue, to save. Used in a purpose clause.

Ch. 11

1   ■ μιμητής imitator, one who mimics another, from the verb μιμέομαι to imitate, to mimic. The ending of the noun indicates the agent who performs an action (s. MH, 365). γίνεσθε pres. mid. imp. γίνομαι. Χριστοῦ Paul's appeal to the character of Jesus of Nazareth shows Paul's interest in the earthly life of Christ (JNP, 109).
2   ■ ἐπαινῶ pres. ind. act. to praise. πάντα acc. of reference. μέμνησθε perf. ind. mid. μιμνήσκομαι to remember. The perf. indicates that the Corinthians remembered continually (Grosheide). παρέδωκα aor. ind. act. παραδίδωμι to deliver over, to pass on. Often used in the sense of a teacher passing on material which he has learned (s. TDNT; CBB). παράδοσις

tradition, that which is passed on. κατέχετε pres. ind. act. to hold down, to hold fast, to possess (s. MM). ■ εἰδέναι perf. inf. 3 οἶδα. Defective perf. w. pres. meaning to know. κεφαλή head, in its metaphorical sense it may apply to the outstanding and determining part of a whole, but also to origin. Paul does not say that the man is the lord of the woman; he says that he is the origin of her being (Barrett; s. also TDNT). ■ προσευχόμενος 4 pres. mid. part. προσεύχομαι to pray. κατὰ κεφαλῆς down from the head; that is, the veil hanging down from the head (RG, 606f.; s. also MT, 268). καταισχύνει pres. ind. act. to put to shame, to shame, to disgrace. Since the Christian man reflects the glory of Christ if he were to wear a veil concealing his head, he would rob his own head of its chief function of reflecting the glory of Christ (Barrett). ■ ἀκατακαλύπτῳ dat. sing. uncov- 5 ered. For a Jewish woman to appear outside of the house w. an uncovered head was shameful and her husband could divorce her (SB III, 427). The Jewish sense of a woman's head covering indicated the special hairstyle she was to wear which consisted of plaited hair held together w. bands and coverings (s. SB III, 428f.). The women of Tarsus were to have their face covered when they appeared on the street. This was an old custom which was retained in Tarsus (DC 33:48). τὸ αὐτό "one and the same thing w. . . ." (RWP). ἐξυρημένη perf. pass. part. ξυράω to shave. For the Jews a woman w. a shaved head was particularly ugly (SB III, 434). In Cyprus a woman guilty of adultery was to have her hair cut off and was considered a harlot (DC 64:3). A woman w. a shaved head was also the sign of mourning (DC 64:16; s. also De Dea Syria, 6; s. also Barrett). ■ 6 κατακαλύπτεται pres. ind. mid. to cover one's self, to cover one's self w. a veil. The pres. tense is used to express a general principle. κειράσθω aor. imp. mid. κείρω to shear, to cut w. scissors (Lietzmann). αἰσχρός shame, disgrace, followed by the dat. of disadvantage. κείρασθαι aor. mid. inf. The inf. w. the article is used as the subject of the clause (s. Funk, 657). ξυρᾶσθαι pres. mid. inf. ξυράω to shave, to cut w. a razor (s. Lietzmann; s. also v. 5). κατακαλυπτέσθω pres. mid. imp. ■ ὀφείλει one ought to, one is obligated to. The word indicates 7 moral obligation. κατακαλύπτεσθαι pres. mid. inf., s.v.5. εἰκὼν image. δόξα glory. ὑπάρχων pres. act. part. to exist, to be; causal use of the part. ■ καὶ γὰρ "for even," "yes, even" 9 (BD, 236). ἐκτίσθη aor. ind. pass. κτίζω to create. ἀνήρ man, male. ■ ἐξουσία authority, the right to perform an act. The 10 covered head is the woman's authority to pray and worship since it shows her belonging to and obedience to her husband (Schlatter, s. also M.D. Hooker, "Authority on Her Head: An Examination of First Corinthians 11:10," NTS, 10 [April, 1964], 410–416). ἐπὶ τῆς κεφαλῆς "upon her head." διὰ τοὺς ἀγγέλους "because of the angels." Angels were considered to be the guardians of the order of creation (Hooker, 412f.), and were considered to be present at a worship service (Schlatter). (For Qumran parallels to angels being present at worship services, and the interpretation that the lack of covering for a woman signified a physical defect which excluded one from worship, s. Fitzmyer,

11 Essays, 187–204). ■ πλήν however, nevertheless, in any case. It is used in an adversative and modifying sense to conclude a discussion and emphasize what is essential (BD, 234; Blomqvist, 82f.). χωρίς without, separated from. ἐν κυρίῳ in the Lord or perhaps "in the Lord's intention"; that is, in the original creation and its restoration (Barrett). ■ διά w. gen. "through." ἐκ τοῦ

12 θεοῦ "from, out of God." The man is the woman's initial cause, she is his instrumental cause, but both owe their origin to God

13 (s. RP). ■ κρίνατε aor. imp. act. κρίνω to judge, to decide. πρέπον pres. act. part. n. sing. that which is fitting to the circumstances, that which is proper. Followed by the acc. w. the inf.

14 προσεύχεσθαι pres. mid. inf. προσεύχομαι to pray. ■ φύσις "nature herself." κομᾷ pres. subj. act. κομάω to have long hair, to let one's hair grow long. ἀτιμία dishonor. Jewish men wore middle length hair which was usually well-groomed (SB III, 440–442). Sometimes long hair was associated w. homosexuality (Weiss; Philo, The Special Laws, III, 37), but long hair was not uncommon for philosophers, farmers, barbarians, etc. (DC 35:

15 11). ■ κομή long hair, the hairdo which was neatly held in place by means of ribbon or lace. What is required by these verses is an orderly hairdress which distinguishes a woman from a man (Grosheide). ἀντί w. gen. instead of. περιβολαίου that which is thrown about, a wrap, a covering. δέδοται perf. ind. pass.

16 δίδωμι to give. ■ δοκεῖ pres. ind. act. to seem to be, to seem, to intend to be. φιλόνεικος strife-loving, contentious, quarrelsome. συνήθεια custom, habit, usage. He means we have no such custom such as women praying or prophesying w. head uncovered (Morris).

17   ■ παραγγέλλων pres. act. part. παραγγέλλω to transmit a message along from one to another, to declare, to order, to charge. Used especially of the order of the military commander which is passed along the line by his subordinates (T 343). The part. indicates contemporaneous time, "in giving this charge." κρείσσον comp. of ἀγαθός more prominent, preferable, more advantageous, better. ἥσσων comp. of κακός inferior, weaker,

lesser, for the worse. (For both of these words, s. BAG.)
συνέρχεσθε pres. ind. mid. to come together. ■ πρῶτον μέν 18
"first of all," "in the first place." It is not formally caught up by
such a companion phrase as "in the next place," unless we so
regard v. 34b (Bruce). συνερχομένων pres. mid. part.
συνέρχομαι to come together, gen. abs. "when you come together." σχίσμα division. ὑπάρχειν pres. act. inf. used in direct discourse. μέρος τι partly, acc. of extent "to some part"
(RWP). ■ δεῖ followed by the inf. it is necessary to. The word 19
generally expresses logical necessity. αἵρεσις division, different
opinion (s. MM). δόκιμος that which is approved after examination, genuine (s. BS, 259–262; TDNT). φανερός open to sight,
visible, w. reference to outward appearance, manifest as opposed
to conceal (AS, 104). γέγωνται aor. subj. mid. γίνομαι. ■ 20
συνερχομένων pres. mid. part. to come together, to assemble.
οὖν then, now. The word indicates the continuation of the subject from one thought to another or the introduction of a new
phase of thought (DM, 253). τὸ αὐτό the same, here "assemble
together" or "assemble together at the same place." κυριακός
belonging to the Lord. The word was used in the papyri in the
sense of belonging to the Caesar or Imperial (s. Deissmann; BS,
217–219; LAE, 362f.; TDNT) (s. also Rev. 1:10). δεῖπνον dinner, the main meal, supper. ■ ἕκαστος each, each one for him- 21
self. It was not the Lord who was determining the celebration but
the individual (Conzelmann). προλαμβάνει pres. ind. act. to
take before. The prep. here is temporal, "each one takes it before
others have theirs" (Barrett). (For the examples in the papyri
and the suggested "weakening" of the prep. in compound, s.
MM.) φαγεῖν aor. act. inf. ἐσθίω to eat. The prep. used w. inf.
to indicate the area in which some were going ahead of others.
They took what they had brought along and did not permit
others, the poor, to eat from their portion (Grosheide). ὃς μεν
... ὃς δέ "the one, the other." πεινᾷ pres. ind. act. to be hungry.
μεθύει pres. ind. act. to be drunk. The pres. tense vividly points
out the action that was in progress. It could also point to a
habitual action. (For a description of the common meal associated w. the Lord's Supper, s. IDB II, 53–54; for the common meal
of the Greeks and the Romans other than the agape, s. Bengel,
Lietzmann.) ■ μὴ οὐκ used in a question expecting the answer 22
no; "it is certainly not that you do not have houses, is it?"
ἐσθίειν pres. act. inf. to eat. Used w. prep. to express purpose
"for eating and drinking." καταφρονεῖτε pres. ind. act. followed by the gen. to think down upon, to despise.
καταισχύνετε pres. ind. act. to put to shame. The pres. tense

could be conative "are you trying to put to shame?" (s. Barrett). ἔχοντας pres. act. part. ἔχω to have. Adjectival part. used as a noun "those who do not have." εἴπω aor. act. subj. λέγω to say. Deliberative subj. "what shall I say?," "what should I say?" ἐπαινέσω fut. ind. act. or aor. subj. ἐπαινέω to praise. (For an excellent article regarding the struggle between the rich and poor and the social problems at the Lord's Supper in Corinth, s. G. Theissen, "Soziale Integration und sakramentales Handeln," Nov T, 16 [July, 1974], 179–206.)

23　　■ ἐγώ "I." Strongly emphasized and stands in contrast to those at Corinth. παρέλαβον aor. ind. παραλαμβάνω to receive. The word corresponds to the technical term in the rabbinical literature, quibbel, meaning to receive tradition which has been passed on (s. PRJ, 248; SB III, 444). ἀπό from. The prep. can indicate that Paul did not receive his information directly by revelation (Grosheide). It may be, however, that he received the interpretation of the information from the Lord (Barrett). παρέδωκα aor. ind. act. παραδίδωμ to pass on, to hand down. The word corresponds to the rabbinical technical term masar indicating the passing down of tradition. The words mean the chain of historical tradition that Paul received goes back unbroken to the words of Jesus Himself (Ladd, 389). (For the use of masar in the DSS, s. CD 3:3.) ὅτι introduces the content of that which was received. παρέδιδοτο impf. pass. παραδίδωμι to deliver over, to betray. The impf. implies that this betrayal was

24 still going on (Grosheide). ἔλαβεν aor. λαμβάνω. ■ εὐχαριστήσας aor. act. part. εὐχαριστέω to give thanks, temporal use of the part. "after he had given thanks." ἔκλασεν aor. ind. act. κλάω to break. μου "my." Strongly emphasized by its position. τὸ ὑπὲρ ὑμῶν "which was (given) on behalf of you." The word to be supplied here is "given" (s. Luke 22:19). ποιεῖτε pres. imp. ποιέω, The pres. tense emphasizes the repeated action. ἀνάμνησις memorial, remembrance. The word indicates to call back again into memory a vivid experience (s. TDNT). The object of recalling to memory is expressed by the obj. use

25 of the poss. adj. (s. BD, 149). ■ ὡσαύτως in the same manner. ποτήριον cup. (For the cup of blessing which the honored guest lifted up and said the benediction, s. SB IV, 630f.; TDNT.) μετὰ w. acc. after. δειπνῆσαι aor. act. inf. δειπνέω to dine, to eat the main meal. διαθήκη covenant, treaty (s. Matt. 26:28). ἐν τῷ ἐμῷ αἵματι "in my blood." Blood indicated a life given up in death which was the penalty for breaking the covenant (s. Cleon Rogers, "The Covenant with Moses and its Historical Setting," JETS, 14 [1971], 152). ὁσάκις as often as, used w. ἐάν w. the

meaning "every time." The usual construction for a general temporal clause of repetition (RWP). πίνητε pres. subj. πίνω to drink. ▪ γάρ "for." Introduces the apostle's explanation of the 26 Lord's command (RP). ἐσθίητε pres. subj. ἐσθίω. καταγγέλλετε pres. ind. act. καταγγέλλω to proclaim. It is used in the sense of making a solemn announcement by word of mouth (Barrett; CBB). ἄρχι until. οὗ when. ἔλθῃ aor. act. subj. ἔρχομαι. Subjunctive may have an affinity w. a final clause (BD, 193) w. the idea "until the goal is reached, that is till he comes" (Ottfried Hofius, " 'Bis dass er kommt': I Kor. XI. 26," NTS, 14 [April, 1968], 439–441).

▪ ὥστε wherefore, it follows. The word is used to draw a 27 conclusion. ὅς ἄν whoever. ἐσθίῃ pres. subj. ἀναξίως adv. unworthily, not in accordance w. their value (Grosheide). ἔνοχος guilty of, guilty of violating (Hering). When the dat. is used it indicates a crime of which one is guilty; when the gen. is used it indicates against which or against whom the crime is committed (Weiss). ▪ δοκιμαζέτω pres. imp. 3rd per. sing. to examine, 28 to approve after examination (s. TDNT). δοκιμάζω. Used in an indefinite and at the same time general sense "one" (BAG). ▪ κρίμα judgment. The suf. indicates the result of an action; that 29 is, the result of making a decision (s. MH, 355). ἑαυτῷ reflex. pron. dat. of disadvantage. διακρίνων pres. act. part. to judge between, to determine, to distinguish. The part. could be conditional (RWP) or causal. ▪ ἀσθενής weak, sickly. ἄρρωστος 30 powerless, feeble, ill. κοιμῶνται pres. ind. pass. κοιμάω to fall asleep, to die. The pres. tense indicates either an action in progress or a repeated action. ἱκανός a sufficient number, a large amount, many. ▪ εἰ w. ind. used to introduce a contrary to fact 31 conditional clause. διεκρίνομεν impf. διακρίνω s.v.29. ἐκρινόμεθα impf. pass. to judge, pass. to be judged. ▪ 32 κρινόμενοι pres. pass. part. conditional use of the part. "if we are being judged," "when we are being judged." παιδευόμεθα pres. ind. pass. to discipline, to train a child through discipline. (For this figure of speech and the training of children in the ancient world, s. TDNT; RAC VI, 502–559.) κατακριθῶμεν aor. pass. subj. κατακρίνω condemn, to reach a verdict or decision against someone. Subjunctive used in a neg. purpose clause. ▪ ὥστε wherefore, so. The word draws a conclusion from the 33 previous discussion, pres. mid part. to come together, s.v.18. ἐκδέχεσθε pres. mid. imp. ἐκδέχομαι to wait upon, to wait in turn (RWP). It is implied that a proper distribution of food should first be made, and that all then should eat together (Barrett). ▪ πεινᾷ pres. ind. act. to be hungry, s.v.21. ἐν οἴκῳ at 34 home. συνέρχησθε pres. mid. subj. συνέρχομαι. ὡς ἄν whenever. ἔχθω aor. subj. ἔρχομαι. διατάξομαι pres. fut. mid. διατάσσω to put in order.

Ch. 12

1 ■ πνευματικός spiritual. The suf. indicates "that which pertains to the spirit" (s. MH, 378f.). The word can be either masc. (spiritual people) or n. spirit (spiritual things, gifts) (s. Pearson, 47f.; Grosheide). ἀγνοεῖν pres. act. inf. ἀγνοέω to be

2 ignorant (s. 1 Cor. 10:1). ■ ἦτε impf. εἰμί. ἄφωνος without speech, dumb. ὡς ἄν used w. impf. for the notion of repetition (RG, 974). ἤγεσθε impf. pass. ἄγω to lead. ἀπαγόμενοι pres. pass. part. ἀπάγω to lead away, to carry away. It suggests moments of ecstasy experienced in heathen religion, when a human

3 being is possessed by a supernatural (Barrett). ■ ἐν in, through, in control of. λαλῶν pres. act. part. λαλέω to speak. ἀνάθεμα that which is set apart for a deity, that which is abandoned by the gods, a curse, cursed (Grosheide; TDNT). The reference is to demonic powers and the control of these powers over the lives of the Corinthians before they became Christians. It was possible that the demons used the gift of ecstatic speech to curse Jesus (s. Pearson, 49–50f.). εἰπεῖν aor. act. inf. λέγω. κύριος Ἰησοῦς "Jesus is Lord" (s. 1 Cor. 8:6). εἰ μή except. (For the view that Paul is primarily referring to a ruler of the synagogue who is reported to have tutored a Jewish Christian to say these words in order to save membership in the community, s. J.D.M. Derrett, "Cursing Jesus [1 Cor. 13:3]: The Jews as Religious 'Persecutors'," NTS, 21 [July, 1975], 544–554).

4 ■ διαίρεσις distribution (RP) difference, variety (Conzel-
6 mann). ■ ἐνέργημα performance, that which was accomplished through energy. These are the results or effects of the working given by God (RP). ἐνεργῶν pres. act. part. ἐνεργέω to perform, to be at work, to be effective, to produce. τὰ πάντα ἐν πᾶσιν "all things in all." The second "all" could be n. or masc. but the emphasis in the passage is on the working of God within

7 men (Morris). ■ δίδοται pres. pass. δίδωμι to give. The pres. tense points to the habitual and repeated action. φανέρωσις manifestation, a making clear. συμφέρον pres. act. part. n. sing. συμφέρω to bring together, to confer a benefit, to be advantageous, profitable or useful (BAG). Used here w. prep. meaning

8 "w. a view to advantage" that is, "the profit of all" (RP). ■ κατὰ τὸ αὐτὸ πνεῦμα "according to the same spirit." The prep. gives

9 the norm or standard. ■ πίστις faith. Faith here is to be connected w. the miracles referred to in the next few lines (Barrett).

ἰαμάτων healing. The plural relates to the different classes of
sicknesses to be healed (Godet). ■ *διάκρισις* a judging between   10
things, distinguish, discerning. *ἑρμηνεία* interpretation. ■   11
ἐνεργεῖ pres. ind. act. to work in, to energize. The word is often
used of the working of the power of God in a miraculous way
(s. MNTW, 46–54). *διαιροῦν* pres. act. part. *διαιρέω* to distribute. *ἰδίᾳ* individually, by one's self, privately. *καθώς* just as,
accordingly. *βούλεται* pres. ind. mid. *βούλομαι* to will, to determine. The pres. tense emphasizes the habitual or repeated
action. He gives not according to the merit or wishes of men, but
according to his own will (Hodge).

■ *καθάπερ* just as. *σῶμα* body. (For this comparison, s.   12
SBT, 235f.) *μέλος* member. *ὄντα* pres. part. *εἰμί*. The part.
could be concessive, "although they are many." *οὕτως καὶ ὁ*
Χριστός "so also is Christ." Paul draws a comparison and uses
the corporate rather than the solely individual Christ (SBT,
235). ■ *καὶ γάρ* "for even," "yes, even" (BD, 236). *εἰς ἓν σῶμα*   13
"into one body." The prep. describes the result of the process
(Barrett; Weiss). *ἐβαπτίσθημεν* aor. ind. pass. *βαπτίζω*. Paul
is not referring to water baptism but to the spiritual transformation which puts the believer "in Christ," and which is the effect
of receiving the gift of the Spirit which takes place at conversion
(s. BHS, 130f.). *ἐποτίσθημεν* aor. ind. pass. *ποτίζω* to cause
to drink, to give to drink, to water, to irrigate (s. MM; BHS, 131).
■ *ἔστιν* is, consists of. The article w. the subject, "the body" is   14
generic, "a body" (Barrett). ■ *ἐάν* w. subj. "if," "in case." *εἴπῃ*   15
aor. subj. *λέγω*. *ὅτι* because. *οὐ ... οὐκ*. The double negatives
cancel each other and are equivalent to a positive statement
(BD, 223; but s. also RWP). *παρά* "because of this" "along side
of this," "on that score," "for that reason" (IBG, 51). The prep.
w. acc. is causal (RG, 616). ■ *οὖς* ear. ■ *ἀκοή* hearing.   16/17
ὄσφρησις smelling. If the whole body were only one member
the condition would be sad (Grosheide). ■ *νῦν δὲ* "but now,"   18
"but, as it is" (RP). *ἔθετο* aor. ind. mid. *τίθημι* to place, to put.
ἓν ἕκαστον each one. *ἠθέλησεν* aor. ind. act. *θέλω* to wish, to
will. God made unity, but not uniformity. The aor. refers to the
act of creation (RP). ■ *εἰπεῖν* aor. act. inf. *λέγω*. *χρείαν ἔχω*   21
Used w. object in the gen. ■ *ἀλλά* adversative use "on the   22
contrary" (RWP). *μᾶλλον* much rather, to a greater degree.
δοκοῦντα pres. part. *δοκέω* to seem to be, to consider to be,
generally followed by the inf. *ἀσθενέστερος* comp. *ἀσθενής*
weaker. The delicate organs, such as the eye; invisible organs,
such as the heart (Barrett). *ὑπάρχειν* pres. act. inf. to be, to
exist. The inf. is used in connection w. part. even though the two

23 are separated (s. BD, 250). ἀναγκαῖος necessary. ■
ἀτιμότερος comp. ἄτιμος without honor, comp. less honorable. περισσότερος comp. περισσός greater, more.
περιτίθεμεν pres. ind. act. περιτίθημι to place around, to
clothe. The pres. tense is gnomic pointing to that which is always
true. ἀσχήμων unpresentable, indecent, the unpresentable,
that is, private parts (BAG). (For the ancient world's ideas concerning the genitals, s. RAC X, 1–52.) εὐσχημοσύνη decency,
propriety, presentability. Here it is used in the sense, "or treated
24 w. greater modesty" (BAG). ■ εὐσχήμων n. pl. presentable,
decent. συνεκέρασεν aor. συγκεράννυμι to mix together, to
blend together. God mixed the members of the body (Grosheide) in order that it might function harmoniously.
ὑστερουμένῳ pres. mid. or pass. part. to come short, ὑστερέω
to fail, to be inferior, to lack. δούς aor. act. part. δίδωμι to give.
The part. expresses manner telling how the mixing was done.
25 ■ ᾖ pres. subj. εἰμί. The subj. is used here to express purpose;
in this case neg. purpose. σχίσμα division, that which results
from a splitting (s. 1 Cor. 1:10). μεριμνῶσιν pres. subj.
26 μεριμνάω to exercise care for, to exercise concern for. ■
πάσχει pres. ind. to suffer. συμπάσχει pres. ind. to suffer
together. δοξάζεται pres. ind. pass. δοξάζω to honor, pass. to
be honored, to be thought well of. συγχαίρει pres. ind. to rejoice together. The pres. tenses are gnomic indicating that which
is generally true.
27 ■ ἐκ μέρους "from a part." The idiom here means "in-
28 dividually" (Barrett). ■ ἔθετο aor. mid. τίθημι s.v. 18. δεύτερον
acc. sing. secondly. τρίτον acc. sing. thirdly. The acc. is used
adverbially. The notion of subordination is to be found in these
words (Godet). ἰαμάτων gen. pl. healings. ἀντιλήμψις nom.
pl. helpful deeds, assistance. The basic meaning of the word is
an undertaking on behalf of another and is used both in the
papyri and the LXX in the sense of help either from God or from
men (s. BS, 92; MM). κυβέρνησις administration, lit. it refers
to the steering of a ship. The pl. indicates proofs of ability to hold
a leading position in the church (BAG; TDNT). The verb is
applied to the management of a household in an inscription
29 (MM). ■ μή. Used to introduce questions in which the answer
30 "no" is expected, "all are not apostles are they?" ■
31 διερμηνεύουσιν pres. ind. act. to translate, to interpret. ■
ζηλοῦτε pres. imp. ζηλόω to covet, to be zealous for, to earnestly desire. Believers may desire a gift, the Spirit gives them as He
wills (s. Bengel). μείζων comp. μέγας large, great.
    καθ᾿ ὑπερβολήν lit. "according to the excess." It is best

taken to describe the "way" and indicates "a way beyond all comparison" (RWP).

Ch. 13

■ ἐάν w. subj. The word introduces a condition which may 1 be possible, "supposing that." γλῶσσα tongue, language. The dat. form is here instrumental. ἀγάπη love. (For a study of this important word, s. TDNT; CBB; MNTW; James Moffatt, *Love in the New Testament*, especially 178–187; Trench, *Synonyms*, 41–44; s. also 1 John 2:5.) γέγονα perf. act. γίνομαι to become. The perf. would indicate what a per. has become and continues to be (s. McKay). χαλκός copper, brass, bronze. Used w. the following word to indicate a "gong" (BAG; Conzelmann). ἠχῶν pres. act. part. ἠχέω to sound, to ring, to echo, to roar. In connection w. the previous word it indicated a gong which produced a hollow echoing groaning noise (Weiss). κύμβαλον cymbal. Cymbals played a part in the Jewish worship service but even a greater role in the heathen worship of the goddess Cybele and Bacchus (s. TDNT; DGRA, 381f.). ἀλαλάζον pres. act. part. ἀλαλάζω loud sounding, clashing. lit. used in the sense of "raise a war cry, shouting w. triumphant or joy" (AS). ■ ἔχω 2 pres. subj. after ἐάν. εἰδῶ subj. οἶδα. πᾶσαν τὴν γνῶσιν all knowledge. Used w. article it means "all that there is in its entirety" (BD, 144). πᾶσαν τὴν πίστιν "all the faith." μεθιστάναι pres. act. inf. μεθίστημι to remove, to transfer from one place to another. A proverbial expression meaning "to make what seems impossible possible" (Barrett; s. also Matt. 17:20). The inf. is used to express results. οὐθέν nothing, an absolute zero (RWP). ■ ψωμίσω aor. subj. ψωμίζω. The word 3 means either "to spend everything on food," or "to break into crumbs" (Grosheide). The word lit. means "I feed w. small morsels," as a child, or invalid. The meaning here is "if, for the purpose of alms giving, I divide all my property in fragments" (Barrett). ὑπάρχοντα pres. act. part. acc. pl. ὑπάρχω to exist. The part. in pl. means goods, possessions, property. Although giving to charity was held in high esteem by the rabbis and thought to have gained great merit, there were requirements prohibiting one from giving all of his goods; for example, in a year he was not to give more than 20% of his entire possessions (s. SB III, 451; IV, 536–558). παραδῶ aor. subj. παραδίδωμι to give, to hand over. καυχήσωμαι aor. mid. subj. καυχάομαι to boast, to glory. (For a discussion of the variant reading καυθήσομαι fut. subj. pass. καίω to set fire, to burn, s. TC, 563f.; Barrett; Weiss.) ὠφελοῦμαι pres. ind. pass. ὠφελέω to

431

profit, to be of value. The gifts are not valueless, but he is (RP).

4   ■ μακροθυμεῖ pres. ind. act. to be longsuffering, to be patient. It is a long holding out of the mind before it gives room to action or passion—generally to passion (Trench; *Synonyms*, 196). It is the steadfast spirit which will never give in (NTW, 83; s. also TDNT). The idea of the word is that it takes a long time before fuming and breaking into flames. The pres. tense emphasizes the continual and habitual state or action. χρηστεύεται pres. mid. to be useful, to be kind and gracious, to show kindness, one who renders gracious, well-disposed service to others (EGT; TDNT; Trench; *Synonyms*, 323f.). (For verbs w. this ending conveying the idea of "being or behaving, or acting as," s. MH, 400.) ζηλοῖ pres. ind. act. to be fervent, to boil w. envy, to be jealous (s. TDNT). περπερεύεται pres. mid. to brag, to boast, one who talks a lot and acts presumptuously; ostentation is the chief idea and ostentatious boasting leads easily to the next point (RP; s. TDNT). φυσιοῦται pres. mid. φυσιόω to puff up, to

5 puff one's self out like a pair of bellows (RWP). ■ ἀσχημονεῖ to behave indecently or in a shameful manner. Love is tactful and does nothing that would raise a blush (RP). παροξύνεται pres. pass. παροξύνω to irritate, to promote to anger, pass. to be irritated, to be touchy. Selfishness generates the irritability (EGT). λογίζεται pres. mid. to credit someone's account, "doth not register the evil." Love stores up no resentment and bears

6 no malice (RP; s. also TDNT). ■ συγχαίρει pres. ind. act. to rejoice together, to join in rejoicing. Here the rejoicing is at the

7 truth rather than w. the truth (Barrett). ■ στέγει pres. ind. act. to cover (as a roof). The meaning is either to cover in the sense of to protect as a roof or to bear up as to support as a roof (Barrett) or to endure, forbear (s. RP). ὑπομένει to endure, to bear up patiently (s. TDNT; Trench; *Synonyms*, 195f.).

8   ■ οὐδέποτε never. πίπτει pres. act. to fall, to fail. καταργηθήσονται fut. ind. pass. καταργέω to render inoperative, to make ineffective or powerless. παύσονται fut. ind. mid. παύω to cause to rest, to cause to cease, mid. "they shall make themselves cease or automatically cease of themselves" (RWP). (For the dying out and the little use of the gift of tongues in the post-apostolic church, s. Cleon L. Rogers, Jr., "The Gift of Tongues in the Post-Apostolic Church," Bib Sac, 122 [April, 1965], 134–143; S.D. Currie, "'Speaking in Tongues': Early Evidence Outside the New Testament Bearing on *GLOSSAIS*

9 *LALEIN*," Interp., 19 [July, 1965], 277–294.) ■ ἐκ μέρους in

10 part, partially, Both usages in this v. are emphatic (RWP). ■ ὅταν w. subj. when, whenever. ἔλθῃ aor. subj. ἔρχομαι.

καταργηθήσεται fut. ind. pass. s.v.8. ■ ἤμην impf. εἰμί. 11 νήπιος infant, child, minor. ἐλάλουν impf. ind. act. λαλέω to speak, customary impf. "I used to speak." ἐφρόνουν impf. ind. act. φρονέω to think. It points to the thoughts, the interest, and the striving of a child (Lenski), customary impf. γέγονα perf. ind. act. γίνομαι not to be viewed as an aoristic perf. (s. BD, 177) but as a normal perf. emphasizing the resultant condition or state of the subject (s. M 143f.; RG, 900). κατήργηκα perf. ind. act. s.v.8. Here it has the meaning "to put aside." ■ ἄρτι 12 now. A contrast between this dispensation and the fut. (Grosheide). ἔσοπτρον mirror. In Gr. literature a mirror symbolized clarity and self-recognition (Conzelmann). Mirrors of the ancient world were generally made from polished metal and the Corinthian mirrors were famous (RP; Conzelmann; DGRA, 1052f.). (For the legend of letting a mirror down in a spring before the temple of Demeter and looking in the mirror to see if the sick person was to get well or die, s. Pausanias, *Description of Greece* VII, XXI, XII; VIII, XXXVII, VII.) αἴνιγμα riddle, an indistinct image (BAG). πρός before, facing, here "face to face." ἐπιγνώσομαι fut. ind. mid. ἐπιγινώσκω to know, to have specific knowledge. The prep. in compound is directive (s. MH, 312). ἐπεγνώσθην aor. ind. pass. The words bring out the inadequacy of man's present knowledge of God in contrast w. God's knowledge of man now and the knowledge of God that man will have in the future (Barrett). ■ νυνί now, logical not 13 temporal. μένει pres. ind. act. to remain. μείζων comp. μέγας large. The comp. is used here to express the superl. "greatest." (For the contrast of Paul's treatment of love w. the ancient view of virtue, s. Günther Bornkamm, "Der köstlichere Weg: I Kor. 13," *Gesammelte Aufsätze* I, 93–112.)

Ch. 14

■ διώκετε pres. imp. to hunt, to pursue. The pres. imp. calls 1 for a habitual action. ζηλοῦτε pres. imp. to be zealous, to earnestly desire, s. 1 Cor. 12:31. μᾶλλον adv. The comp. may retain its comp. meaning or it may be used to express the superl. (s. Barrett). προφητεύητε pres. subj. to prophesy. The subj. is used to express the aim of the pursuit and desire (s. EGT). ■ 2 γλῶσσα tongue, language (s. TDNT). οὐδεὶς ἀκούει "no one hears" that is, "no one can understand" (Barrett). However, it is possible that the verb retains its normal meaning. πνεύματι dat. sing. If it refers to the Holy Spirit it is instrumental (Bruce). If it is locative it refers to the human spirit (Grosheide). ■ 3 οἰκοδομή edification, building up. παράκλησις exhortation, encouragement, consolation (s. MNTW, 128–135; TDNT; CBB). παραμυθία encouragement, consolation. A synonym w. the previous word. This word, however, is not used in the NT to describe God's consolation (Conzelmann; s. also TDNT).

4 ■ ἑαυτόν himself. Chrysostom says "What a difference between one person and the church " (RP). ἐκκλησία church, assembly. Without the article it refers to the local assembly, the assembly of which he is one member (Barrett). οἰκοδομεῖ pres. ind. act. to edify, to build up. The pres. tense emphasizes the continual action that which is habitual or always true. ■ θέλω to wish, to
5 desire, to want. It is normally followed by the inf. expressing the object of the desire. In this v. it is also followed by ἐκτὸς εἰ μή w. the subj. (s. M 208). διερμηνεύῃ pres. subj. διερμηνεύω to translate. The prep. in compound may indicate either "being a go-between" or "thoroughness." One who interprets his own words intervenes between unintelligible utterance and the hearers (RP). λάβῃ aor. subj. λαμβάνω. The subj. is used to express purpose. The aor. is ingressive "may get edification" (RWP).

6 ■ νῦν δέ "and now." The particle is logical not temporal (s. Weiss). ἐάν w. subj. introduces a condition which is supposable (RWP) "in case." ἔλθω aor. subj. ἔρχομαι. ὠφελήσω fut. ὠφελέω to profit, to benefit. Here followed by the acc. λαλήσω fut. λαλέω. ἐν through, the instrumental use of the prep. ἀποκάλυψις unveiling, revelation. γνῶσις knowledge. προφητεία prophecy. The proclamation of a prophet. The revelation and knowledge are the internal gifts of which prophecy
7 and teaching are the external manifestation (RP). ■ ὅμως. The word could be viewed as displaced and have the meaning "nevertheless," "all the same," or it could be viewed as from the adv. and have the meaning "likewise" (s. BD, 234; MT, 337; BAG). ἄψυχος lifeless. (For the neg. force of the perf., s. Moorhouse, 47ff.) αὐλός flute. The word could refer to various types of wind instruments and was popular in social, religious, and military life (s. DGRA, 1131; RP). κιθάρα lyre, a stringed musical instrument resembling our guitar. It was used in education, lyric poetry, religion, and entertainment (s. OCD, 709; Conzelmann; KP III, 1580). There was a large music hall (odeion) located in Corinth which would seat around 18,000 (s. E.G. Wright, Biblical Archaeology, 262). διαστολή difference, distinction. φθόγγος sound, musical sound, note. It could refer to the notes on a lyre or stops of a flute (s. OCD, 705–713). δῷ aor. subj. δίδωμι to give. γνωσθήσεται fut. ind. pass. γινώσκω. αὐλούμενον pres. pass. part. αὐλέω to play the flute. Here "that which is being played on the flute." κιθαριζόμενον pres. pass.

part. κιθαρίζω to play on the harp or lyre. The pres. part. emphasizes the continuous contemporaneous action, "that which is being played on the lyre." ■ ἄδηλος not clear, uncer- 8 tain, indistinct. παρασκευάσεται fut. mid. παρασκευάζω to prepare, mid. to prepare one's self, to make one's self ready, to make preparations. πόλεμος war, battle (s. Trench; Synonyms, 322). ■ εὔσημος intelligible, that which is well-marked. The 9 adv. was used in the papyri in the sense of "legible," "clearly" (s. MM). δῶτε aor. subj. δίδωμι. γνωσθήσεται fut. ind. pass. s.v.7. λαλούμενον pres. pass. part. λαλέω. ἔσεσθε fut. εἰμί. Used in a periphrastic construction which emphasizes the linear or continuous action (s. IBG, 18). ■ τοσοῦτος so great. Here it 10 indicates a number indefinite but very great (Meyer). τύχοι aor. opt. τυγχάνω to happen, to occur. Used in the construction εἰ τύχοι as a fourth-class conditional clause "if it should happen" (RWP). Used idiomatically w. the meaning "perhaps." ἄφωνος without sound, voiceless; that is, "meaningless sound" (RP). ■ εἰδῶ subj. οἶδα. βάρβαρος barbarian. It denotes a man whose 11 language sounds like "bar bar," that is, whose language makes no sense (Morris). ἐν ἐμοί "in my case," "in my judgment" (M, 103). ■ οὕτως because, since, in the NT it is regularly causal 12 (BD, 238). ζηλωτής zealot, one who is zealous for something, enthusiast. πνευμάτων gen. pl., obj. gen. indicating the object of the strong desire. The pl. refers to the various manifestations of the Spirit (Lenski). ζητεῖτε pres. imp. ζητέω to seek, to seek after. The pres. tense indicates the continuing of an action in progress or the continual action which is to be habitual (s. MKG, 272). περισσεύητε pres. subj. περισσεύω to increase, to abound. The increase could be numerically or spiritually. ■ 13 προσευχέσθω pres. imp. 3rd per. sing. προσεύχομαι to pray. διερμηνεύῃ pres. subj., s.v.5. The one who spoke in tongues evidently knew when he was going to use the gift for he is to pray that he may interpret so that the whole church may be edified. ■ προσεύχωμαι pres. subj. πνεῦμά μου "my spirit." It could 14 refer to the human spirit of Paul (Barrett) or the Holy Spirit or the spiritual gift given by the Holy Spirit (s. Weiss; PAT, 190f.). ἄκαρπος unfruitful. ■ προσεύξομαι fut. mid. The fut. is asser- 15 tive or volitive expressing the determined decision of Paul's will (s. SMT, 34; M, 150; RG, 874). πνεύματι instrumental dat. ψαλῶ fut. ψάλλω to sing a hymn, to sing praises. ■ εὐλογῇς 16 pres. subj. 2nd per. sing. εὐλογέω to speak well of, to praise, to bless, to give thanks. ἀναπληρῶν pres. act. part. ἀναπληρόω to fill, here to fill up the place; that is, "he who fills the role of" (Barrett). ἰδιώτης unskilled, unlearned, a layman in contrast to an expert (s. BAG; TDNT). (For the use of this word and those related to it in the papyri, s. MM; Preisigke I, 689f.) ἐρεῖ fut. λέγω. τὸ ἀμήν amen. It was the Jewish and Christian custom to express agreement and concurrence w. the prayer by responding amen (s. SB III, 456; Barrett). (For the use of the term in the DSS, s. 1 QS 1:20; 2:10, 18.) ἐπί w. dat. to; that is, in response

17 to. ἐπειδή since, because. ■ καλῶς adv. well. εὐχαριστεῖς
18 pres. ind. act. to give thanks. οἰκοδομεῖται pres. pass. ■ μᾶλλον adv. comp. μάλα followed by the gen. of comparison

19 w. the meaning "more than." ■ θέλω I wish, I prefer (RP; LAE, 187, 190). πέντε five, a round number, as used in Judaism (Barrett; SB III, 461). λαλῆσαι aor. act. inf. κατηχήσω aor. act. subj. κατηχέω to instruct, to teach, Paul only uses the word in the sense of theological instruction (Conzelmann). μίριοι ten thousand.

20   ■ παιδία little children. γίνεσθε pres. imp. The pres. imp. w. the neg. is a command to stop an action which is in progress, "do not continue" (s. MKG, 72). φρέσιν dat. pl. φρήν Only used here and in the pl. w. the meaning thinking, understanding (BAG). Dative of respect or reference, "in reference to understanding." κακία wickedness, maliciousness, and ill-will (RP),

21 dat of reference. τέλειος mature. ■ γέγραπται perf. ind. pass. γράφω to write. The perf. points to the continuing authority of that which stands written (s. MM). ἑτερόγλωσσος other tongues, strange languages. χεῖλος lip. εἰσακούσονται fut. mid. εἰσακούω to hear into, to attend to. (For the prep. in

22 compound, s. MH, 304.) ■ ὥστε therefore. The word draws a conclusion from the previous. εἰς after the verb to be it may have a Semitic meaning "to serve as" (s. BD, 80; but also s. Barrett). σημεῖον sign. (For a study of this v., s. J.P.M. Sweet, "A Sign for Unbelievers: Paul's Attitude to Glossolalia." NTS, 13 [April,

23 1967], 240–257.) ■ συνέλθῃ aor. act. subj. συνέρχομαι to come together, to assemble. ἐπὶ τὸ αὐτό "to the same place," "together." λαλῶσιν pres. subj. εἰσέλθωσιν aor. act. subj. εἰσέρχομαι. The subjunctives are used in a third-class conditional clause in which the condition is possible. ἰδιώτης s.v.16. ἐροῦσιν fut. ind. act. λέγω. ὅτι. It introduces either indirect discourse "that" or introduces a direct quotation and is used as quotation marks. μαίνεσθε pres. ind. mid. to be mad, to be crazy. The question introduced by the neg. expects the answer

24 yes. ■ προφητεύωσιν pres. subj. The pres. tense emphasizes the continual action. ἐλέγχεται pres. ind. pass. to convict, to so present the evidence that one is driven to the conclusion that the argument is correct (s. TDNT; T). ἀνακρίνεται pres. ind. pass.

ἀνακρίνω to examine, to cross-examine, to put through a course of questioning as when one is questioned and examined by a judge in a court (Lenski). ■ πέσων aor. part. πίπτω to fall. 25 προσκυνήσει fut. προσκυνέω to worship, to fall down and worship. Used to designate the custom of prostrating one's self before a person and kissing his feet, the hem of his garment, the ground, etc. (BAG; s. also TDNT; CBB). The verb is followed by the dat. ἀπαγγέλλων pres. act. part. to solemnly declare, part. of manner.

■ τί οὖν ἐστιν "what then is the result of this discussion?" 26 (RP) s.v.15. ὅταν w. pres. subj. "whenever," "as often as." συνέρχησθε pres. mid. subj. συνέρχομαι to come together, to assemble. The pres. is iterat. and points to a reoccurring action. ψαλμός song, hymn. The word signifies the singing of praises to God (EGT). Those present may have composed a song or have sung a Christian hymn (Grosheide). ἔχει pres. ind. to have, each one had these gifts because they were given by the Spirit (s. Grosheide). ἑρμηνεία translation, interpretation. πρός w. acc. for, leading to (s. IBG, 53). οἰκοδομή edification, holding up. γινέσθω pres. imp. γίνομαι. The pres. imp. is a command for habitual action. ■ εἴτε if, whether. The construction 27 "whether . . . or" is begun but left unfinished (RP). κατά w. acc. used in a distributive sense "by twos" (s. MT, 268). πλεῖστον adv. superl. πολύς. Used as adverbial acc. "at the most" (RWP). ἀνὰ μέρος "in turn" (s. IBG, 67; MT, 265). In the Jewish synagogue service there were at least seven readers of Scripture who read at least three verses in turn (s. SB III, 465f.; IV, 154–171; HJP II, ii, 79–83; JPF II, 927–933). εἷς one, someone. διερμηνευέτω pres. imp. s.v.5. ■ διερμηνευτής translator, in- 28 terpreter. σιγάτω pres. imp. σιγάω to be silent. The pres. tense indicates that he is not even to speak in a tongue once (RWP). The command indicates that the per. could control the use of the gift. λαλείτω pres. imp. ■ λαλείτωσαν pres. imp. 3rd per. pl. 29 διακρινέτωσαν pres. imp. 3rd per. pl. διακρίνω to separate, to make a distinction, to pass judgment on (BAG). ■ ἀποκαλυφθῇ 30 aor. pass. subj. ἀποκαλύπτω to reveal. καθημένῳ pres. mid. part. κάθημαι to sit, dat. as indirect object. It was the prophet who stood while the congregation sat (Lietzmann; s. also Luke 4:16). ■ καθ᾽ ἕνα "one by one," distributive use of prep. (s. MT, 31 268). μανθάνωσιν pres. subj. μανθάνω to learn. The conjunctive is used to express purpose. παρακαλῶνται pres. pass. subj. παρακαλέω to exhort, to encourage, to comfort (s. MNTW, 128–135). ■ καί also. πνεύματα pl. s.v.12. It is the manifesta- 32 tion of the Spirit or the divine influence under which the proph-

ets spoke (Hodge). ὑποτάσσεται pres. ind. mid. to be in subjection, to be obedient. The prophet exercised self-control and control over the gift. A preacher without self-control is no true
33 prophet (RP). ■ ἀκαταστασία disorder, disturbance, confusion. The disorder could refer to disorder or confusion in the assembly (Barrett) or it could refer to the disorder if the Spirit was not in harmony w. Himself (Conzelmann).

ὡς "as." These words should not be taken w. the preceding
34 but w. the words which follow (Grosheide). ■ ἐκκλησίαι churches, assemblies. Here it refers to the local gathering. ἐπιτρέπω to allow, to permit followed by the inf. In the Jewish synagogue women were not allowed to speak in public and took no active part in the conduct of divine service (JPF II, 920f.; SB
35 III, 467f.). ■ μαθεῖν aor. act. inf. μανθάνω. θέλω to wish, to desire, to will. ἐν οἴκῳ "at home." ἴδιος own. ἐπερωτάτωσαν pres. imp. ἐπερωτάω to ask, to ask about something. The prep. in compound is directive (s. MH, 314). αἰσχρός shameful, disgraceful. Plutarch wrote that not only the arm but the voice of a modest woman ought to be kept from the public, and she should feel shame at being heard, as at being stripped (Barrett). (For a discussion on this passage in the light of other Scriptures
36 dealing w. women in church life, s. PWC, 70–80.) ■ ἐξῆλθεν aor. ind. ἐξέρχομαι to go out. κατήντησεν aor. ind. καταντάω to reach, to arrive. The question is "were you the starting point of the gospel? or were you its only destination?" Paul is attacking the abuses of the Corinthians by pointing out they were not the source of the gospel (s. RP).
37 ■ δοκεῖ pres. ind. act. to suppose. The ind. is used in a first-class conditional clause which assumes that the condition is true. ἐπιγινωσκέτω pres. imp. ἐπιγινώσκω to recognize, to acknowledge completely. ἐντολή commandment. The following
38 gen. "lord" could be poss. gen. or gen. of source. ■ ἀγνοεῖ pres. ind. act. to be ignorant, to disregard. ἀγνοεῖται pres. ind. pass.
39 to be ignored, to be disregarded (s. BAG). ■ ὥστε therefore. The word sums up and draws a conclusion of the previous discussion. ζηλοῦτε pres. act. imp. s.v.1. κωλύετε pres. imp. to hinder, to restrain, to forbid. The pres. imp. w. neg. means either to stop an action in progress or it forbids an habitual action (s. MKG,
40 272f.). ■ εὐχημόνως adv. decently. τάξις "according to order," orderly. Josephus uses the neg. of this word to say that the Roman army did not erect its camp in disorderly parties (Josephus, *Wars* III, 77). Josephus also uses the word indicating that the Essenes only spoke "in turn" (Josephus, *Wars* II, 132). Paul

uses the word to suggest the idea of members of the church doing things at one time, not all at once (Barrett).

Ch. 15

■ γνωρίζω to make known, "I draw your attention" (Barrett). The word was used to introduce a solemn statement (Conzelmann). εὐηγγελισάμην aor. ind. mid. εὐαγγελίζομαι to proclaim good news. The aor. views the total ministry of Paul emphasizing the one gospel which he preached. παρελάβετε aor. ind. act. παραλαμβάνω to receive, to receive as authoritative teaching which was passed on (s. 1 Cor. 11:23). ἐστήκατε perf. ind. act. ἵστημι to stand. ■ σῴζεσθε pres. pass. σῴζω to rescue, to save. The pres. pass. indicates a continuous action which was being performed on the believers. τίνι λόγῳ "by, in which word." The interrogative pron. is used here as a normal rel. pron. (s. RG, 737f.). εἰ "if." The condition is assumed as a reality. κατέχω to hold down, to hold fast. ἐκτὸς εἰ μή except. (For the construction, s. BD, 191.) εἰκῇ adv. without cause, in vain, to no purpose, without due consideration (BAG). ἐπιστεύσατε aor. ind. to believe. Not that Paul really entertains this as a serious possibility, but if the denial of the Resurrection is carried to its logical conclusion, then it would be shown that their belief was fruitless, perhaps because it was exercised superficially or "at random" (Bruce). ■ παρέδωκα aor. παραδίδωμι to deliver over, to pass on, to pass on authoritative teaching (s. 1 Cor. 11:23; for a detailed study of this passage, s. RH, 76–89). ἐν πρώτοις "first of all." The words may indicate priority either in time or importance (Barrett). παρέλαβον aor. ind. act. s. 1 Cor. 11:23. ἀπέθανεν aor. ind. act. ἀποθνῄσκω to die. κατὰ τὰς γραφάς "according to the scriptures." The phrase can be taken to mean "even as the whole tone of the O.T. so foretold concerning Him" (s. Kenneth O. Gangel, "According to the Scriptures," Bib Sac, 125 [April, 1968], 123–128). ■ ἐτάφη aor. ind. pass. θάπτω to bury. ἐγήγερται perf. ind. pass. ἐγείρω to raise. The perf. emphasizes that Christ is risen and indicates a continuing condition which has given rise to a new state of affairs. Christ continues in the risen state (McKay, 12; s. also Gl, 113). τῇ ἡμέρᾳ τῇ τρίτῃ on the day the third, dat. of time. ■ ὤφθη aor. pass. ὁράω to see, pass. to be seen, to appear. He could be seen by human eyes, the appearances were not just visions (Grosheide). εἶτα then, next, adv. denoting sequence (AS). ■ ἔπειτα there upon, thereafter, then. ἐπάνω above, over. (For the use of the adv. w. numbers, s. BD, 99.) πεντακόσιοι 500. ἐφάπαξ (from ἐπί and ἅπαξ), at once, at one time. πλείων comp. πολύς pl. "the majority." μένω pres. act. to

439

remain. ἄρτι now. Paul was writing 20 years or so later (Barrett).
7 ἐκοιμήθησαν aor. pass. κοιμάομαι pass. to fall asleep. ■
πᾶσιν place after the substitutive in order to emphasize the
8 substitutive (BD, 144). ■ ἔσχατον last. Used either in the sense
that Paul is the last of those to be granted such an appearance
or the last of the apostles or he refers to himself as the least of
the apostles (s. PAA, 105). ὡσπερεί like, as though, as it were.
ἔκτρωμα untimely birth, miscarriage. The term points to the
results of the birth and was used to indicate that which is incapable of sustaining life of its own volition and requires divine
intervention if it is to continue. It emphasizes Paul's weakness
and his dependence on God's grace (s. PAA, 104–105; Schlat-
9 ter). ■ ἐλάχιστος superl. of μικρός. The smallest, the least. The
true superl. followed by the gen. of comparison. ἱκανός worthy,
competent, fit. διότι. A strengthened form of ὅτι "because."
10 ἐδιώξα aor. διώκω to hunt, to pursue, to persecute. ■ ἡ εἰς ἐμέ.
The article is used as a rel. pron. "which was extended to me"
(RP). κενός empty,in vain, without success. ἐγενήθη aor. pass.
γίνομαι. περισσότερος comp. περισσός more than sufficient, abundantly. Followed by the comp. gen. ἐκοπίασα aor.
ind. κοπιάω to labor, to work to the point of exhaustion, to work
hard (s. TDNT). It points to the weariness which follows on this
straining of all his powers to the utmost (Trench; Synonyms,
11 378). ■ κηρύσσομεν pres. ind. act. The pres. denotes a constant
fact (Godet). ἐπιστεύσατε aor. ind. act. The aor. points to the
fact of belief.
12   ■ εἰ w. the ind. is used to introduce a condition which is
accepted as true. κηρύσσεται pres. ind. pass. The pres. points
to the continual proclamation. ἐγήγερται perf. ind. pass., s.v.4.
The perf. means "he lives at the present as the risen Savior"
(Grosheide). ἀνάστασις resurrection. It is possible that the
opponents of Paul who deny a resurrection of the dead were
those who were influenced by a Hellenistic, dualistic concept of
after-life current among the sacramentally oriented popular cults
(J.H. Wilson, "The Corinthians Who Say There Is No Resurrection of the Dead," ZNW, 59 [1968], 103; for the views of resur-
14 rection in the ancient world, s. RAC I, 919–938; TDNT). ■
κένος empty, s.v.10. Take out the resurrection, and there is
nothing left (Barrett). ἄρα "then." The word implies the inevi-
15 table nature of the conclusion (Grosheide). ■ εὑρισκόμεθα
pres. ind. pass. εὑρίσκω to find, pass. to be found. The word is
often used of moral judgments respecting character, and conveys
the idea of discovering or detecting (RP). ψευδομάρτυς false
witness. The following gen. is either obj. "a false witness about

God," or subj. gen. "a false witness claiming to be from God." Such a false witness would make his message a myth, a human composition which arises from human wishes, and at the same time he would be claiming that his message was the word of God (Schlatter). ἐμαρτυρήσαμεν aor. ind. act. μαρτυρέω to serve as a witness, to give witness. κατά w. the gen. "again." ἤγειρεν aor. ἐγείρω to rise. ἄρα therefore. ■ εἰ γάρ if indeed. A 16 strengthened form of the particle introducing a condition which is assumed as true "if, as they say, it is true that ..." (BD, 237). ■ μάταιος vain, empty. The word emphasizes the aimlessness 17 and the leading to no object or end (s. Trench; Synonyms, 180f.; s. also CBB). ■ κοιμηθέντες aor. pass. part. κοιμάομαι to fall 18 asleep. ἀπώλοντο aor. ind. mid. ἀπόλλυμι to ruin, to destroy, to perish. ■ εἰ w. the ind. Assumes the condition is true. 19 ἠλπικότες perf. act. part. ἐλπίζω to hope. The part. could be used as a periphrastic perf. emphasizing the continual condition or state of hoping (RWP), or the part. could be considered to be substitutive "we are hopers" (Barrett). ἐλεεινότερος comp. ἐλεεινός pitiable, one who is to be pitied. The comp. is used w. a superl. followed by the gen. of comparison "more deserving of compassion" (RP; s. also BD, 33f.).

■ νυνί "now," not temporal but logical and returns to real- 20 ity (Schlatter). ἀπαρχή firstfruit. The word means the first installment of the crop which foreshadows and pledges the ultimate offering of the whole (Barrett). The word was used in various ways in the papyri: a birth certificate, a certificate of authorization, a yearly offering for a god, inheritance tax (s. Preisigke; MM). κεκοιμημένων perf. pass. part., s.v.6. ■ 21 ἐπειδή since, because. δι'w. gen. "through." ■ ὥσπερ as, just 22 as. ἀποθνησκουσιν pres. ind. act. to die. The pres. tense is frequentative and describes action which reoccurs from time to time w. different individuals (M, 114). ζωοποιηθήσονται fut. ind. pass. ζωοποιέω to make alive. ■ ἕκαστος each. τάγμα 23 rank, order, often used in the military sense denoting a body of troops which can be disposed according to the decision of the commanding officer or it could be applied to any sort of group and could also mean place or position (Barrett; s. also 1 Cor. 14:40). ἔπειτα then, after, thereafter. παρουσία presence, arrival, coming. The word was used as a technical expression for the arrival or visit of the king or emperor (LAE, 368). It was also used for the appearance of a god (Conzelmann; s. TDNT). ■ 24 εἶτα then, after this. The word may indicate that there is also to be an interval between his coming and the end (s. RP; Weiss). τὸ τέλος completion, end. The word was used as a technical

phrase denoting the final consummation (PRJ, 295). ὅταν when, whenever. παραδιδοῖ pres. act. subj. παραδίδωμι to give over, to turn over to someone. The pres. tense pictures a fut. proceeding (RWP). τῷ θεῷ καὶ πατρί. The definite article has here the force of demonstrative w. the meaning of a rel. pron. that is, "to the one who is God and Father" (Weiss). καταργήσῃ aor. subj. καταργέω to make ineffective, to abolish, to bring to an end (s. TDNT). ἀρχή rule, ruler. The nouns here represent the evil
25 powers under whose control the world has come (Barrett). ■ δεῖ impersonal verb, it is needful, it is necessary, the necessity arises out of the sovereign plan of God (s. TDNT). οὗ until. θῇ aor.
26 subj. τίθημι to place, to put. ■ ἔσχατος ἐχθρός. Used as a pred. "as the last enemy." καταργεῖται pres. ind. pass. s.v.24.
27 ■ πάντα γάρ. The first word is emphatic (RP) and the particle gives a causal explanation. ὑπέταξεν aor. ὑποτάσσω to subject. εἴπῃ aor. subj. λέγω. Used to introduce a scriptural quotation "now when it says" (Barrett). ὑποτέτακται perf. ind. pass. ὑποτάσσω. δῆλος clear, plain. ἐκτός outside, except.
28 ὑποτάξαντος aor. act. part. ■ ὑποταγῇ aor. subj. pass. ὑποταγήσεται fut. ind. pass. αὐτός himself. The word is used as an intensifying pronominal adj. (Funk, 562f.). ᾖ pres. subj. εἰμί. The subj. is used in a purpose clause. πάντα ἐν πᾶσιν. Paul refers neither to pantheism nor universalism, but speaks of the new heaven and new earth in which all things are in harmony w. God (s. Barrett; Godet).
29 ■ ἐπεί since, otherwise. τί what. ποιήσουσιν fut. ind. act. to do. Here it means either "what will they have recourse to?" or "what will they gain?" (RP). βαπτιζόμενοι pres. pass. part. βαπτίζω to baptize. The substantival use of the part. w. the article suggests a particular group, not all Christians (Barrett). ὑπέρ w. gen. for, on behalf of. (For literature regarding "baptism for the dead," s. Conzelmann; ZPEB I, 469f.; TDNT; CBB.) ὅλως at all, never. τί καί β. . . . "why then," "why at all, still?"
30 (BD, 228). ■ κινδυνεύομεν pres. ind. act. to be in danger. The pres. tense emphasizes the constant or continual state of danger. πᾶσαν ὥραν every hour, acc. of time, "hourly." The acc. of
31 time means all through every hour (RWP). ■ καθ᾿ ἡμέραν distributive use of the prep. "day after day," "daily." ἀποθνῄσκω pres. ind. act. to die, here "to be in danger of death," or it may mean that Paul abandons life daily and, knowing that he may die, he continually prepares himself for death (Grosheide). νή. A particle used in solemn oaths and means "truly," "yes" (RG, 1150) and is followed by the acc. of the person or thing by which one swears or affirms "yes, truly by my pride in you" (BAG).

■ εἰ Used w. ind. to introduce a condition accepted as true. κατά 32
in accordance w. human standards, "on partly human terms"
(Barrett). ἐθηριομάχησα aor. ind. θηριομαχέω to fight w.
wild animals. It is uncertain if Paul is speaking literally or figuratively. If figuratively the "beasts" may have been the legalists or
Judaizers (Robert E. Osborne, "Paul and the Wild Beasts," JBL,
85 [June, 1966], 230). It may have been evil men whose association corrupts. If there were no resurrection of the body, his
struggles at Ephesus had been in vain (Abraham J. Malherbe,
"The Beasts at Ephesus," JBL, 87 [March, 1968], 80). ὄφελος
profit, benefit, good. φάγωμεν aor. subj. ἐσθίω to eat. πίωμεν
aor. subj. πίνω to drink. The two subjs. are cohortative "let us."
αὔριον tomorrow. ἀποθνῄσκομεν pres. ind. act. s.v.3. The
pres. is used here to express fut. time. (For the quotation from
Isa. 23:13, s. Barrett; for other parallels, s. LAE, 296; Conzelmann.) ■ πλανᾶσθε pres. imp. pass. πλανάω to lead astray, to 33
deceive. The pres. imp. w. the neg. is a command to stop an
action in process. The pass. is permissive pass. "don't allow
yourself to be deceived" (s. BD, 165). φθείρω pres. ind. act. to
corrupt, to ruin, gnomic pres. indicating that which is always
true. ἦθος custom, way, moral. χρηστός useful, good. ὁμιλία
association, company. A possible quotation from Menander,
Thais (for further possible parallels from Menander, s. F.W.
Danker, "Menander and the New Testament," NTS, 10 [April,
1964], 365–368). ■ ἐκνήψατε aor. act. imp. ἐκνήφω become 34
sober, come to one's senses, to wake up. The prep. in compound
points to sobriety attained out of drunkenness (MH, 309). The
aor. imp. calls for immediate action (s. MKG, 272). δικαίως
adv. righteously, truly, really, indeed (s. Lietzmann-Kümmel,
194). ἁμαρτάνετε pres. imp. to sin. The pres. imp. w. the neg.
is a command not to continue an action in progress or a command not to always do an action (s. MKG, 272f.). ἀγνωσία
ignorance followed by the obj. gen. shame.

■ ἐρεῖ fut. λέγω. ποῖος what sort of, what kind of. σώματι 35
dat. sing. instrumental dat. ■ ἄφρων fool, one who is ignorant, 36
one who does not have or use understanding (s. TDNT).
σπείρεις pres. ind. act. to sow. ζωοποιεῖται pres. pass. to make
alive, s.v.22. ἀποθάνῃ aor. subj. to die, s.v.3. ■ γενησόμενον 37
fut. mid. part. γίνομαι "the body that it will become." Perhaps
Paul chose the analogy of the seed precisely because it implies
continuity as well as discontinuity (Ronald J. Sider, "The Pauline Conception of the Resurrection Body in I Corinthians 15:35–
54," NTS, 21 [April, 1975], 432). γυμνός naked, bare. κόκκος
grain. εἰ τύχοι aor. opt. τυγχάνω to happen. The opt. is used

in the idiom meaning "perhaps" (s. BAG). σῖτος wheat. λοιπός remaining. (For rabbinic parallels which use the analogy of bare grains arising w. many coverings to describe the Resurrection, s.
38 PRJ, 305; SB III, 475.) ■ ἠθέλησεν aor. ind. act. θέλω to wish, to will; that is, God gives the seed a body in accordance w. His
39 past decision at creation (Sider, 432). σπέρμα seed. ■ κτῆνος animal, a domesticated animal. πτηνός adj. feathered. Used as a substitutive "bird." ἰχθύς fish. The distinction made between different kinds of flesh was common to rabbinical thought but not as familiar to Hellenistic thinking (SB III, 475f.; PRJ, 305f.).
40 ■ ἐπουράνιος heavenly, celestial; that is, upon heaven or existing in heaven (RWP), not the heavenly body of human beings or angels (Grosheide). ἐπίγειος earthly, terrestrial; that is, the bodies of everything that lives on earth (Grosheide). δόξα good opinion, reputation, brightness, splendor, glory (s. AS; TDNT;
41 CBB). ■ σελήνη moon. ἀστήρ star. The lack of the article points to a characteristic of the class or of the single thing (BD, 132). γάρ "yes, and . . ." (Barrett). διαφέρω to differ. The stars differed in brilliance or brightness (s. Conzelmann; Barrett).
42   ■ οὕτως so, thus. Paul now applies the preceding remarks (Grosheide). σπείρεται pres. ind. pass. s.v.36. φθορά corruption, that which is subject to decay. Corruption is also viewed as an evil power which affects all of creation as a result of Adam's sin (Sider, 433). ἀφθαρσία incorruption, that which is not sub-
43 ject to decay and control by sin. ■ ἀτιμία dishonor. The word was sometimes used of loss of the rights of citizenship. A corpse
44 has no rights (Morris). ἀσθένεια weakness. ■ ψυχικός natural, that which pertains to the soul, a physical body which is suited to earthly life (SBT, 156) and is subject to sin (Sider, 433ff.) πνευματικός spiritual, that which pertains to the spirit. It refers to a physical body renovated by the Spirit of God and therefore suited to heavenly immortality (SBT, 166; Sider, 435). (For the suf. which denotes an ethnical or dynamic relation, s.
45 MH, 378.) ■ γέγραπται perf. pass. γράφω "it stands written." The perf. denotes the abiding authoritative character of that which was written (s. MM). ἐγένετο aor. ind. mid. γίνομαι. Followed by the prep. w. acc. in the place of a pred. nom. "the first Adam became a living soul" (s. MH, 462; BD, 86). ζῶσαν aor. act. part. ζάω to live. ζωοποιοῦν pres. act. part. ζωοποιέω to make alive, life giving. It was in His saving work for men that
46 Christ became a life-giving Spirit (Morris). ■ πρῶτον used as the pred. πνευματικόν "spiritual (body)." ἔπειτα then, s.v.23.
47 ■ ἐκ γῆς "out of the ground," "earthly." The absence of the article stresses that the essential thing is the earth's specific

quality (BD, 132). χοϊκός dusty. The word stresses mortality
due to earthly origin (SBT, 166). ■ οἷος correlative pron. ex- 48
pressing quality, of what sort, such as (s. RG, 291, 731).
ἐπουράνιοι heavenly, celestial. ■ ἐφορέσαμεν aor. φορέω to 49
wear. Used in the papyri in the sense of wearing clothes, a
breastplate or a badge (MM; Preisigke). εἰκών image (s. TDNT;
CBB). φορέσομεν fut. ind. act. The reading of the fut. is accepted instead of the aor. subj. since the context is didactic and
gives a promise instead of hortatory (s. Weiss; TC, 569)
■ φημί to say. σάρξ καὶ αἷμα "flesh and blood." The 50
phrase means our present mortal nature and refers to those who
are still living (RP; s. also Barrett). κληρονομῆσαι aor. inf.
κληρονομέω to inherit, to receive as an inheritance. ■ πάντες 51
οὐ here = οὐ πάντες "not all of us." (For the position of the
neg., s. BD, 224; MT, 287.) κοιμηθησόμεθα fut. ind. act.
κοιμάομαι s.v.6. ἀλλαγησόμεθα fut. ind. pass. ἀλλάσσω to
change, to alter. ■ ἄτομος indivisible, because of smallness, "in 52
a moment" (BAG). ῥιπή throwing, rapid movement, for example, the "casting" of a glance takes an extremely short time.
Here, "in the twinkling of an eye" (BAG). ἐσχάτῃ σάλπιγξ
the last trumpet, the last in a series of trumpets. According to
the Jewish view the Resurrection occurred w. the sound of the
trumpet and there were seven trumpets sounded for the various
stages of resurrection. At the seventh trumpet all were made
alive and stood up on their feet (s. TDNT; SB III, 481).
σαλπίσει fut. ind. pass. σαλπίζω to sound a trumpet. Here
used impersonally, "the trumpet will sound," "the trumpet shall
trumpet" (RG, 392). ἐγερθήσονται fut. ind. pass., s.v.4.
ἄφθαρτος incorruptible, s.v.42. ■ φθαρτός corruptible, that 53
which is subject to decay, s.v.32. ἐνδύσασθαι aor. mid. inf.
ἐνδύω to put on, to put on as clothing. θνητός mortal, that
which is subject to death (s. M, 222). ἀθανασία immortality,
that which is not subject to death. ■ γενήσεται fut. γίνομαι. 54
γεγραμμένος perf. pass. part. γράφω s.v.45. κατεπόθη aor.
ind. pass. καταπίνω to drink down, to swallow down. The prep.
in compound is perfective, "to swallow up." εἰς νίκην "into
victory." The translation of the Semitic phrase meaning "forever," "permanently," "successfully" (s. SL, 153–156; s. also SB
III, 481f.). ■ κέντρον sting. The word represents death as a 55
venomous creature, a scorpion, or a hornet which is rendered
harmless (RP). ■ διδόντι pres. act. part. dat. sing. δίδωμι to 57
give. The pres. tense is used to emphasize the certainty of the
victory (Barrett). ■ ἑδραῖος firm, steadfast. ἀμετακίνητος un- 58
moveable, not capable of being moved from its place.

περισσεύοντες pres. act. part. περισσεύω to abound, to be in abundance. εἰδότες perf. part. οἶδα to know. κόπος effort, labor, s.v.10. κενός empty, vain, s.v.14.

Ch. 16

1 ■ λογεία collection, contribution. The word appears in the papyri in the sense of collection, particularly in the sense of religious collections for a god or temple (s. LAE, 105f.; BS, 142f., 219f.; MM; TDNT). (For the other words Paul uses in speaking of this collection, s. RP.) ὥσπερ just as. διέταξα aor. ind. διατάσσω to arrange, to order, to command, to give express 2 commands (s. MH, 302). ποιήσατε aor. imp. ποιέω to do. ■ κατά w. acc. the distributive use of the prep., "on every first day of the week" (RP). μία σαββάτου a Hebraic expression for "the first day of the week"; that is, Sunday (s. Hering; Conzelmann). τιθέτω pres. imp. 3rd sing. τίθημι to set, to lay, used w. the prepositional phrase "by himself"; that is, in his home (RWP). θησαυρίζων pres. act. part. θησαυρίζω to store up, to save up, part. of means or manner explaining how each one is to lay aside. ὅτι ἐάν the generalized rel. pron. "whatever." εὐοδῶται pres. pass. subj. εὐοδοῦμαι. The form could possibly be perf. ind. pass. or more unlikely perf. subj. pass. (s. M, 54), lit. to send well on one's way, to be lead along a good road. It then has the meaning to get along well, to prosper, to succeed, and was used of having success in business (BAG; Lietzmann). ὅταν when, whenever. ἔλθω aor. subj. ἔρχομαι. γίνωνται pres. 3 mid. subj. γίνομαι subj. used in a purpose clause. ■ παραγένωμαι aor. mid. subj. παραγίνομαι to arrive. The subj. is used w. the indefinite temporal conj. "whenever I arrive" (RWP). δοκιμάσητε aor. subj. δοκιμάζω to approve after examination, to accept as proven, to approve. In an inscription the verb is almost a technical term for passing as fit for a public office (MM). It was also used to indicate a government approved doctor (Preisigke). δι᾽ἐπιστολῶν "through letters," "w. letters." Commendatory letters were well known in antiquity (Barrett; Conzelmann; s. also 2 Cor. 3:1). πέμψω fut. πέμπω to send. ἀπενεγκεῖν aor. act. inf. ἀποφέρω to carry away, to take home, to bring to its destination. It was not the removal of the money from Corinth, but its being conveyed to Jerusalem, that was the important point (RP), inf. used to express purpose. χάρις grace, 4 generosity, favor (s. TDNT; Trench, Synonyms, 167). ■ ἄξιος that which is equal in weight, worthy, right. Paul would make the journey if circumstances were such that the work demanded him going (s. Grosheide). ᾖ subj. εἰμι. πορεύεσθαι pres. mid. inf. to

travel, to make a journey. The inf. is used w. the adj.
πορεύσονται fut. mid. πορεύομαι.

■ διέλθω aor. subj. διέρχομαι to pass through. The follow- 5
ing verb is pres. tense used to express the fut. (s. BD, 168). ■ 6
πρὸς ὑμᾶς "w. you." (For the prep. w. acc. denoting position,
s. IBG, 52f.) τυχόν aor. act. part. n. sing. τυγχάνω to happen,
to occur. The aor. part. is used here as an adv. meaning "possibly," "perhaps" (s. RWP). παραμενῶ fut. παραμένω to remain, to stay, to remain w. someone. The contrast is w. "passing
through" Macedonia. παραχειμάσω fut. παραχειμάζω to
spend the winter. Once winter is passed ships can sail again. The
winter season would thus compel Paul to sojourn at Corinth
(Grosheide). προπέμψητε aor. subj. προπέμπω to send forth,
to help on one's journey w. food, money by arranging for companions, means of travel, etc. (BAG). πορεύωμαι pres. mid.
subj., s.v.4. ■ πάροδος a passing visit, here "in passing" (s. RP). 7
ἰδεῖν aor. inf. ὁράω to see. ἐπιμεῖναι aor. inf. ἐπιμένω to
remain, to stay for a time. ἐπιτρέψῃ aor. subj. ἐπιτρέπω to
allow, to permit. ■ πεντηκοστή Pentecost. Paul was using the 8
Jewish calendar. (For the Jewish celebration of Pentecost, s.
Acts 2:1.) ■ μοί "to me," "for me," dat. of advantage. ἀνέῳγεν 9
perf. ind. pass. ἀνοίγω to open, perf. "to stand open." The verb
is intransitive and means "stands wide open" (RWP). The term
"door" is a metaphor for "opportunity" (Bruce). ἐνεργής effective, active, powerful. The opening of the door promises a rich
field of labor (BAG). (For the usages of the word in the papyri,
such as a mill "in working order" or things or persons which
were "active," s. MM; Preisigke.) ἀντικείμενοι pres. mid. part.
ἀντίκειμαι to lie against someone, to oppose, to be in opposition, to resist.

■ ἔλθῃ aor. subj. ἔρχομαι. ἀφόβως without fear. Paul is 10
not thinking about the outward dangers but about the opposition
that he himself faced (Schlatter). γένηται aor. mid. subj.
γίνομαι to become, to be. ἐργάζεται pres. ind. act. to carry out,
to accomplish, to work at. The pres. tense indicates the pres.
continual and habitual action. ■ ἐξουθενήσῃ aor. act. subj. 11
ἐξουθενέω to consider as nothing, to despise. The prep. in compound not only has a perfective force but it also makes the trans.
idea clear (MH, 310). προπέμψατε aor. imp., s.v.6. ἐκδέχομαι
to expect, to wait for. The idea of the prep. in compound is "to
be ready for" (s. MH, 310).

■ περί concerning. This may mean that the Corinthians in 12
their letter had inquired about Apollos (Barrett). πόλλα n. pl.
used here as an adverb, earnestly, often. παρεκάλεσα aor. ind.

447

act. παρακαλέω to exhort, to encourage, to ask. πάντως adv. at all, "simply" (Barrett). θέλημα wish, will. It refers to either God's will or the will or wish of Apollos (RP). ἐλεύσεται fut. ind. mid., s.v.5. εὐκαιρήσῃ aor. act. subj. εὐκαιρέω to find a good time, to have opportunity.

13 ■ γρηγορεῖτε pres. imp. γρηγορέω to watch, to stay awake, to be alert. The pres. imp. is a command for habitual action. στήκετε pres. imp. στήκω from the verb ἕστηκα perf. from ἵστημι to stand, to stand fast. ἀνδρίζεσθε pres. mid. imp. ἀνδρίζομαι to conduct one's self in a manly or courageous way (BAG). The word is common in the LXX in exhortations (s. Josh. 1:6, 7, 9) (RP). Aristotle uses the word indicating the display of courage which he describes as the mean between fear and confidence (Nichomachean Ethics III, VI, 1, 12). The word was also used in the papyri in the exhortation "therefore do not

14 be fainthearted but be courageous as a man" (s. MM). ■ γίνέσθω pres. mid. imp. γίνομαι.

15 ■ οἴδατε defective perf. w. a pres. meaning to know. ἀπαρχή firstfruit (s. 1 Cor. 15:20). ἔταξαν aor. τάσσω to appoint. They had appointed themselves to the service of their

16 fellow Christians. It was a self-imposed duty (RP). ■ ὑποτάσσησθε pres. mid. subj. ὑποτάσσω to subject one's self, to be in subjection. συνεργοῦντι pres. act. part. συνεργέω to work w., to work together, to cooperate. κοπιῶντι pres. act. part. κοπιάω to labor, to work to the point of exhaustion (s. 1

17 Cor. 15:10). ■ ἐπί w. the dat. over, on the occasion of. παρουσία coming, arrival. ὑστέρημα lack, want, that which comes short. Paul could mean that he had missed his Christian friends, and this trio had renewed his acquaintance w. the city (Morris). ἀνεπλήρωσαν aor. ind. act. ἀναπληρόω to fill up

18 again, to supply. ■ ἀνέπαυσαν aor. ind. ἀναπαύω to give intermission from labor, to refresh (AS). ἐπιγινώσκετε pres. act. imp. to recognize, to acknowledge. τοιοῦτος such a one, one belonging to this class or having this quality.

19 ■ ἀσπάζονται pres. ind. mid. to greet. πολλά n. pl. used
20 as an adv. heartily, s.v.12. ■ ἀσπάσασθε aor. mid. imp. φίλημα kiss. In the ancient world it was customary to give a kiss as a greeting both at the meeting and at the departure. The kiss as symbol of love, fellowship, and thankfulness may have been at this time a liturgical act indicating the forgiveness which had been received and the willingness to partake of the Lord's Supper (s. TDNT; Conzelmann).

21/22 ■ ἀσπασμός greeting. ■ φιλεῖ pres. ind. act. to love (s. TDNT). ἤτω pres. imp. εἰμί. ἀνάθεμα anathema, dedicated for destruction, cursed. μαράναθά or to be divided as μαρὰν ἀθά, an Aramaic expression. The first possible division would be a pres. imp. "our Lord, come!" and understood as a prayer either in a Eucharistic or eschatological context. The second possible division "our Lord comes!" is fut. ind. or as perf. ind. "our Lord is here!" and is understood as a confession. (For a discussion of this phrase, s. EJC, 121–124; TDNT.)

2 CORINTHIANS

Ch. 1

1   οὔσῃ pres. part. εἰμί. ὅλος whole, entire, complete. τῇ Ἀχαΐα Achaia. It refers to the Roman province which included the whole of Greece (s. ZPEB I, 35f.; KP I, 32–38; Strabo XVII. 3. 25), and included Corinth as the capital, Cenchraea (s. Rom. 16:1) and Athens (s. Windisch).

3   ■ εὐλογητός blessed, a Jewish ascription of praise to God acknowledging Him as the source of all blessing (s. TDNT; TDOT; CBB). οἰκτιρμῶν gen. pl. compassion, lament, or sorrow which arises from the pitiful state of the object; then the feeling of compassion and understanding (s. TDNT). The gen. may be Semitic and indicates the character or attribute (s. BG, 14f.). παράκλησις encouragement, consolation, comfort. It is the standing beside a person to encourage him when he is undergoing severe testing (Hughes; s. also MNTW). ■ παρακαλῶν

4 pres. act. part. "the one who encourages or stands beside to comfort." ἐπί w. dat. "on," "on the occasion of." θλῖψις pressure, affliction, crushing (Plummer; Trench, *Synonyms*, 202f.). εἰς τό followed by the acc. w. the inf. used to express purpose. δύνασθαι pres. mid. inf. δύναμαι. θλίψει here without the article "in any kind of affliction." Used previously w. the article it means "all tribulation actually encountered." Here "in any which may be encountered" (BD, 114; MT, 200). ἧς rel. pron. fem. sing. The gen. instead of the acc. is by attraction to the case of its antecedent (s. BD, 154). παρακαλούμεθα pres. ind. pass. παρακαλέω. The pres. tense points to the continual action or its iterat. and points to the comfort received every time trouble

5 and afflictions arise. ■ περισσεύει to abound, to overflow. πάθημα suffering. χριστοῦ to follow Christ is to follow Him into suffering. In this also the disciple must expect to be identi-

6 fied w. the master (Hughes; s. also John 15:20). ■ θλιβόμεθα pres. ind. pass. θλίβω pass. to be afflicted, to suffer pressure (s.v.4). ὑπέρ w. the gen. "w. a view to" (IBG, 65). It points to that which one wants to attain (BD, 121). τῆς ὑμῶν παρακλήσεως "your comfort" obj. gen. ἐνεργουμένης pres. mid. or pass. part. ἐνεργέω to be effective, pass. "is made to

work" by him who bestows it. The mid. appears better "which makes itself felt," "takes effect" (Plummer; Barrett). ὑπομονή remaining under, patience, endurance. It was used of the endurance of that which has come upon man against his will. In classical Gr. it is used also of the ability of a plant to live under hard and unfavorable circumstances. It was later used of that quality which enabled men to die for their god (NTW, 59f.; TDNT; RAC IX, 243–294). ὧν rel. pron. gen. pl. The gen. instead of the acc. is because of attraction to the antecedent "the same sufferings." καί also. πάσχομεν pres. ind. act. The pres. points to the continual suffering or to the repeated suffering. ■ βέβαιος firm, certain (s. 1 Cor. 1:6). εἰδόντες perf. part. from 7 defective verb οἶδα to know. κοινωνός partner, one who has a common share w. another, common participant. Used in the papyri for a partner in business or a participant in a sacrifice (s. MM). Followed by the gen. indicating the thing which is shared. παράκλησις comfort, encouragement. s.v.3.

■ ἀγνοεῖν pres. act. inf. not to know, to be ignorant. ὑπέρ 8 w. gen. "concerning" (s. IBG, 65). γενόμενος aor. mid. part. γίνομαι to become, to happen. Ἀσία Asia; that is, the Roman province, whose capital was Ephesus (Barrett). (For Paul's affliction in Asia, s. Hughes.) καθ᾿ ὑπερβολή lit. "a throwing beyond" then "beyond measure," "exceedingly." ὑπέρ w. acc. above, beyond (s. IBG, 64), "beyond the normal power of endurance" (Hughes). ἐβαρήθημεν aor. ind. pass. βαρέω to weigh down, pass. to be burdened down. Used in the papyri of misfortune or injustice (BAG; MM). ἐξαπορηθῆναι aor. pass. inf. ἐξαπορέομαι to be without a way out, to be in utter despair. The prep. in compound is perfective (MH, 310). The inf. is used to express result, "so that we were utterly without way of escape" (Plummer). ζῆν pres. act. inf. ζάω to live, to remain alive, to continue to live. The gen. of the inf. is used w. the verb explaining the despair, "even to live" (s. M, 217f.). ■ ἀλλά "yes 9 indeed," "certainly." The word is confirmatory or emphatic (s. DM, 240). ἑαυτοῖς "within ourselves." (For the strengthening of the reflex. which was frequent in Attic, s. BD, 148.) ἀπόκριμα response, verdict. A technical term used for an official decision in answer to the petition of an embassy (s. J. Hemer, "A Note on II Cor. 1:9," TB, 23 [1972], 104f.; MM; BS, 257). ἐσχήκαμεν perf. ind. act. ἔχω. The perf. tense means "having gotten, I continue to have" and indicates that though the sentence was not immediately carried out, it remained in force (K.L. McKay, "Syntax in Exegesis," TB, 23 [1972], 48; Barrett). The action completed in the past is conceived in terms of pres. time

for the sake of vividness. This vivid perf. indicates the experience
was a dreadful memory to Paul (RG, 896–897). ἵνα used here
to express purpose, not result, and expresses God's purpose
(Windisch). πεποιθότες perf. act. part. πείθω to persuade, perf.
to have been persuaded, to trust in. ὦμεν pres. subj. εἰμί. Used
in a periphrastic construction. The neg. suggests the discontinu-
ance of an existing condition (Barrett). ἐγείροντι pres. act. part.
ἐγείρω to raise. Perhaps an allusion or quotation from the second prayer of the "Eighteen Petition Prayer" which was quoted
three times a day by every Israelite (s. HJP 2 II, 85–89; s. also
JPF II, 801; M Berakoth 4, 1–7, s. especially 5, 2; SB IV, 208–
10 249). ■ τηλικοῦτος so great, terrible. ἐρρύσατο aor. ind. mid.
ῥύομαι to rescue. The prep. seems to imply peril rather than
death personified but the use of this prep. w. the verb is a common expression (s. Job 33:30; 2 Tim. 4:17, 18) (Plummer).
ῥύσεται fut. ind. mid. ἠλπίκαμεν perf. ind. act. ἐλπίζω to
hope. The perf. means "towards whom we have set our hope, and
11 continue to do so" (EGT). ■ συνυπουργούντων pres. act. part.
συνυπουργέω to work together, to cooperate. The word could
mean cooperation w. Paul or cooperation w. one another or
cooperation w. God (s. Barrett). The part. is used in a gen. abs.
which is either temporal "while" or manner "in that." δέησις
prayer, request. προσώπος face, here it may have the meaning
"person," "from many persons" (Plummer) or it may retain the
lit. meaning "face" and be a picture of "many upturned faces"
(RWP; s. also Hughes). εἰς "for," "to," here in the sense of "the
gracious gift for us." διὰ πολλῶν "through many." The word
may be viewed as n. w. the meaning "through many prayers"
(Schlatter) but as masc. it may be taken w. the verb "may be
thanked for by many" or w. the word "gift" w. the meaning "the
gift which reached us by the agency of many" (s. IBG, 108).
εὐχαριστηθῇ aor. pass. subj. εὐχαριστέω to give thanks. The
subject of the pass. verb is "the gracious gift" that is, Paul's
deliverance (Bultmann) and the pass. is to be understood as "that
you might give thanks for the gift" (s. Lietzmann-Kümmel, 197).
12 ■ καύχησις boasting, glorying. The ending of the noun
means "the act of glorying" but in v. 14 the word is "the thing
boasted of" (RWP). μαρτύριον witness, testimony, evidence (s.
Plummer). The word is an explanation of the previous pron.
"this." συνείδησις conscience (s. Rom. 2:15). ἁπλότητι simplicity, frankness. (For a defense of the variant reading
ἁγιότητι "holiness," s. Hughes; for the adopted reading, s. TC,
575.) εἰλικρινείᾳ sincerity, purity (s. 1 Cor. 5:8; for a discussion
of the etymology "judged by the sun," "determined by sunlight,"

s. GEW I, 450; s. also Hughes). θεοῦ. Probably subj. gen. "God-given simplicity and sincerity" (Plummer). σαρκικός fleshly. Fleshly wisdom is the merely human wisdom which is not the work of the Holy Spirit but of the human nature itself enlightened and unimproved guided by the sinful lust of the flesh (Meyer; s. Rom. 7:14). ἀνεστράφημεν aor. ind. pass. ἀναστρέφω pass. to turn back and forth, to conduct one's self, to live in the sense of the practice of certain principles. It is always used w. the kind of behavior more exactly described (BAG; s. also MM). περισσοτέρως adv. comp. of περισσός abundantly, comp. more abundantly, even more. Here in an elative sense "especially" (BAG). ■ ἄλλα "other things." γράφομεν pres. ind. act. 13 The pres. tense refers to all the letters that Paul writes (Hering). ἀλλ᾽ ή except (s. BD, 233). ἀναγινώσκετε pres. ind. act. to read. ἐπιγινώσκω to acknowledge, to know w. certainty. He is referring to the certainty of the Corinthians' knowledge of his character through first-hand experience (Hughes). τέλος completion, end. ἕως τέλους "to the end," perhaps w. the meaning "completely" (Barrett). ἐπιγνώσεσθε fut. ind. mid. ■ 14 ἐπέγνωτε aor. ind. act. ἐπιγινώσκω s.v.13. ἀπὸ μέρους partially. The phrase determines the degree of recognition (Windisch). ὅτι "that." Here it is not causal (s. Plummer). καύχημα boasting, ground of boasting, s.v.12. The apostle shares the experience of the community because both share something which originates beyond them. For this reason Paul can write "I hope . . . that you can be proud of us as we can be of you, on the day of the Lord Jesus" (PAA, 234). (For this word and the boasting of the apostle, s. PAA, 233–238; CBB; TDNT.)

■ πεποίθησις trust, confidence, s.v.9. ἐβουλόμην impf. 15 mid. βούλομαι to will, to decide. The word implies an act of will, a decision (Barrett). The impf. pictures his former state of mind (RWP). πρότερον adv. formerly, earlier, at first. ἐλθεῖν aor. act. inf. ἔρχομαι. δεύτερος second. χάρις grace, benefit, favor. They would have had two opportunities of receiving spiritual communication from him in person (Hughes). σχῆτε aor. act. subj. ἔχω to have, aor. to get, to receive (M, 110, 247). Subjunctive used in a purpose clause. ■ δι᾽ ὑμῶν w. gen. 16 "through you" (s. Plummer). διελθεῖν aor. act. inf. διέρχομαι to pass through. προπεμφθῆναι aor. pass. inf. προπέμπω to send forth, to outfit for a trip (s. 1 Cor. 16:6). The infinitives are to be taken w. the main verb of v. 15. ■ βουλόμενος pres. mid. 17 part. βούλομαι s.v.15. μήτι ἄρα. Used to introduce a question in which an indignant neg. answer is called for (RWP), "do you think then?" (Barrett). ἐλαφρία lightness, fickleness, vacilla-

tion. ἐχρησάμην aor. ind. mid. χράομαι to use. βουλεύομαι
to make plans, to consider, to decide (s. Windisch). ἵνα w. subj.
Normally introduces a purpose clause but in this case the idea
of result is possible, "w. the result that" (s. Hughes; BD, 198).
ᾖ pres. subj. εἰμί. καί yes. The duplication of the words "yes"
and "no" strengthens the picture of the untrustworthy man who
18 affirms just as fervently as he afterwards denies (Meyer). ▪
19 πιστός faithful, trustworthy. ▪ γάρ "for." The position of the
word emphasizes the gen. τοῦ θεοῦ "God's" (BD, 251) "for it
is this faithful God's Son" (Plummer). κηρυχθείς aor. pass. part.
κηρύσσω to proclaim, to preach, to herald (s. TDNT). ἐγένετο
aor. mid. γίνομαι here, "to be." γέγονεν perf. ind. act. The perf.
emphasizes the continuing state or condition "in Him, yes was
20 and continues to be a reality" (Hughes). ▪ ὅσος rel. pron. indicating quantity "how many." ἐπαγγελία promise. τὸ ἀμήν
amen. A Heb. word meaning "true," "trustworthy" and was used
as a strengthening and confirming statement (s. Barrett; CBB;
TDNT). The use of the article w. the word means "the custom-
21 ary amen" (Plummer). ▪ βεβαιῶν pres. act. part. βεβαιόω to
make firm, to confirm. The word was used in the papyri for
making a legal guarantee and appears often in the guarantee
clause of a bill of sale (Preisigke; MM; BS, 104–109). χρίσας
aor. act. part. χρίω to anoint. The anointing here refers to the
anointing of the Holy Spirit at conversion which every believer
22 receives (s. BHS, 131–134). ▪ σφραγισάμενος aor. mid. part.
σφραγίζω to seal. Goods were sealed as a guarantee indicating
not only ownership but also guaranteed the correctness of the
contents (BS, 239; MM; and especially TDNT). δούς aor. act.
part. δίδωμι to give. ἀρραβών pledge, earnest, down payment.
The term means a deposit which is in itself a guarantee that the
full amount will be paid (Hughes; s. also SB III, 495). τοῦ
πνεύματος gen. of apposition "the guarantee consisting of the
Spirit" (MT, 214).

23   ▪ ἐπικαλοῦμαι pres. ind. mid. to call upon someone, to
invoke, to call upon someone as a witness. The article used w.
the object "God" may be the article of previous reference meaning "I call this God, the God whom I have just described"
(Plummer). ἐπί w. acc. "against." Used w. the verb meaning "he
should punish me if I lie" (Lietzmann). φειδόμενος pres. mid.
part. φείδομαι to spare, to hold back. Followed by the gen. the
part. can be causal or express purpose (s. RWP). ἦλθον aor. ind.
24 act. ἔρχομαι. ▪ κυριεύω to be lord, to exercise authority.
συνεργός fellow-worker. χαρά joy. τῇ πίστει instrumental
dat. (Barrett) or locative indicating the sphere (Plummer).

ἑστήκατε perf. ind. act. ἵστημι perf. to stand. It emphasizes the steadfastness.

■ ἔκρινα ἐμαυτῷ aor. κρίνω to judge, to decide, to make 1 up one's mind. Used w. the dat. of advantage "I decided this for my own sake" (EGT; RG, 539). λύπη sorrow. ἐλθεῖν aor. act. inf. ἔρχομαι. The inf. explains Paul's decision. ■ λυπῶ pres. 2 ind. act. to cause sorrow, to make sorry. καί then. This word accepts the previous statement, and the question shows what a paradox it involves (Plummer). εὐφραίνων pres. act. part. to make happy, to make joyful, to cause one to have good thinking (s. RWP). ἐξ out of. The prep. may suggest "sorrow that arises from me, on my account, sorrow that is occasioned rather than caused by my presence" (Barrett). ■ ἔγραψα aor. ind. act. "I 3 wrote." The reference may be to a lost letter that Paul wrote between 1 and 2 Cor. or it may refer to 1 Cor., particularly to 1 Cor. 16:5ff. (s. Hughes for a discussion of the identity of the epistle). αὐτό pron. 3rd per. sing. n. The words here may be taken in three ways. One an adverbial acc. "precisely this reason," two the direct object of the verb, three a summary of the content of the letter "I wrote to just this effect" (Barrett). ἐλθών aor. act. part. ἔρχομαι. Temporal use of the part. "when I come." σχῶ aor. subj. ἔχω to have, to receive (s. 2 Cor. 1:15). ἔδει impf. δεῖ should, must, it is necessary. Imperfect used for an unrealized pres. obligation (RWP). πεποιθώς perf. act. part. πείθω persuade, perf. to have confidence in, to be confident, to be persuaded. ■ θλῖψις pressure, trouble, affliction (s. 2 Cor. 4 1:4). συνοχῆς holding together, distress, anguish. The lit. meaning is compression and in the papyri it refers to "imprisonment" (MM). (For other usages of the word, s. TDNT.) ἔγραψα aor. ind. act. διά w. the gen. "through," "with." It expresses attendant circumstances (IBG, 57). δάκρυον tear. These words are expressive of deep emotion and intense distress (Plummer). λυπηθῆτε aor. subj. pass. s.v.2. Subjunctive used in a neg. purpose clause. γνῶτε aor. subj. γινώσκω to know. περισσοτέρως adv. comp. πολύς here: "especially" (s. 2 Cor. 1:12).

■ εἰ. Introduces a condition assumed to be true. λελύπηκεν 5 perf. ind. act. λυπέω s.v.2. The perf. indicates that the pain continues to be felt (Windisch). ἀπὸ μέρους in part, to some extent. The phrase may indicate either that not quite all the Corinthians had been distressed (Plummer) or it limits the extent of the effect (Barrett). ἐπιβαρῶ pres. subj. ἐπιβαρέω to weigh

down, to burden. Perhaps w. the meaning "in order not to heap
up too great a burden of words," to exaggerate (s. BAG;
6 Hughes). ■ ἱκανός sufficient, enough. The use of n. instead of
the fem. may be explained as a latinism w. the meaning *satis*, i.e.
"sufficient" (s. Hughes). τοιοῦτος such, such a pers. ἐπιτιμία
punishment, rebuke. The word does not have here the classical
meaning of "possession of political rights," but in the legal sense
of "penalty" (s. Plummer; MM). ὑπὸ τῶν πλειόνων "by the
7 majority," "by the main body of the church" (Barrett). ■
τοὐναντίον on the contrary. μᾶλλον rather. This word may
indicate that there were still some who felt that the punishment
was insufficient (Plummer). χαρίσασθαι aor. mid. inf.
χαρίζομαι to be friendly to someone, to be gracious to someone. It occurs in the LXX w. the meaning "to give a gift." Here
it has the meaning "to forgive" (s. TDNT; Windisch).
παρακαλέσαι aor. act. inf. παρακαλέω to encourage, to exhort, to urge on. It is the word used of the speeches of leaders
and of soldiers who urge each other on. It is the word used to
send hesitant soldiers and sailors courageously into battle
(MNTW, 134). The inf. here are used to express results.
περισσότερος comp. περίσσος exceeding the usual number
or size. Comparative used in the sense of superl. greater, even
more, here, "excessive sorrow" (BAG). The dat. is instrumental.
καταποθῇ aor. pass. subj. καταπίνω to swallow. The prep. is
intensive "to swallow down," "to swallow up completely" or "to
8 engulf" (s. Hughes). ■ κυρῶσαι aor. act. inf. κυρόω to legally
confirm, to ratify. In the papyri the word was used before the
confirming of a sale or the ratification of an appointment (s.
MM). The call for the confirmation of love may have been a
request for a formal act by the congregation to reinstate the
offender in the communion of the church and to assure him of
9 their love (Hodge). ■ ἔγραψα aor. ind. act. s.v.4. γνῶ aor. subj.
γινώσκω. The subj. is used in expressing purpose. The aor. is
ingressive "to come to know" (RWP). δοκιμή approval, proof.
The word indicates the results of a test. εἰς πάντα "in every
respect," "in all things." ὑπήκοος obedience. Paul wanted to
know the church's obedience to his apostolic authority (Bruce).
10 ■ χαρίζομαι s.v.7. κεχάρισμαι perf. ind. mid. The perf.
denotes the continuing state or condition of forgiveness. εἴ τι
κεχάρισμαι "if I have had anything to forgive." He is not
suggesting a doubt as to whether he has granted forgiveness, but
he puts the fact of there being something for him to forgive as
a mere hypothesis (Plummer). δι᾿ὑμᾶς prep. w. the acc. "because of you," "on account of you." ἐν προσώπῳ Χριστοῦ lit.

"before the face of Christ." It is a Semitic construction w. the meaning "in the presence of" (Hughes). ■ πλεονεκτηθῶμεν 11 aor. pass. subj. πλεονεκτέω to take advantage of. The arrogant, grccdy, dcfrauding of somcone often through trickery and treacherous means (NTW; TDNT). νόημα thought, purpose, design, in the sinister sense "devices," 'wiles," "plots," i.e., "evil schemings." The word signifies the function of the intellective faculty (Hughes). ἀγνοοῦμεν pres. ind. act. ἀγνοέω to be ignorant, to be unknowing. (For the neg. pref., s. Moorhouse, 41–66.)

■ ἐλθών aor. part. ἔρχομαι, temporal use of the part. εἰς 12 τὴν Τρῳάδα. The article indicates "to the Troas where we had agreed to meet" (BD, 137). (For an excellent article dealing w. the history and geography of Troas as well as the NT references to this important city, s. C.J. Hemer, "Alexandria Troas," TB, 26 [1975], 79–112.) θύρα door. Used as a symbol of missionary opportunity. ἀνεῳγμένης perf. pass. part. ἀνοίγνυμι to open, perf. pass. "to be standing open." Here was a Roman and cosmopolitan population, reinforced by temporary sojourners suffering in forced delays far from their homes in many parts of the Roman world (Hemer, 103). ἐν κυρίῳ "in the Lord." The Lord Christ is both the content of the apostle's message and also the sphere of his opportunity (Hughes). ■ ἔσχηκα perf. ind. act. 13 ἔχω. The perf. may have the idea of an aor. (BD, 177) but Paul may have wished to accent the strain of his anxiety up to the time of the arrival of Titus (RG, 901). ἄνεσις relief. τῷ πνεύματι "in my spirit," locative use of the dat. Paul writes of his inward distress through anxiousness to hear Titus's report concerning the Corinthians (SBT, 144). τῷ μὴ εὑρεῖν aor. act. inf. εὑρίσκω to find, instrumental use of the inf. "by the not finding Titus as to me" (RWP; MT, 142). ἀποταξάμενος aor. mid. part. ἀποτάσσω mid. to say good-by, to bid farewell to friends (Plummer). ἐξῆλθον aor. ind. act. ἐξέρχομαι to depart.

■ χάρις thanks, preceded by the dat. indicating to whom 14 thanks is given. πάντοτε always. θριαμβεύοντι pres. act. part. θριαμβεύω to lead in a triumph. The picture is the triumphal entry of a military hero into the city of Rome (Lamar Williamson, Jr., "Led in Triumph: Paul's Use of Thriambeuo," Interpretation, 22 [July, 1968], 322). The victorious Roman general marched into the city in a long procession preceded by the city magistrates. They were followed by trumpeters, then the spoils taken from the enemy followed by white oxen intended for sacrifice, then the captives headed by the king of the conquered country, then officials of the victorious army and musicians dancing and playing, and at last the general himself in whose

honor the whole wonderful pagent was taking place (s. ELR, 115–118; DGRA, 1163–1167; KP V, 973–975; H.S. Versnel, *Triumphus* [Leiden, 1970]); Rory B. Egan, "Lexical Evidence on Two Pauline Passages," Nov Test, 19 [January, 1977], 22–62). Paul represents himself as one of the victorious general's soldiers sharing in the glory of his triumph (Barrett). ὀσμή fragrance, sweet smell. It was customary for the triumphal processions to be accompanied by the release of sweet odors from the burning of spices in the streets (Hughes). φανεροῦντι pres. act. part. φανερόω to manifest. The manifestation here is not in
15 the eschatological sense but in the missionary sense. ■ εὐωδία aroma, fragrance. σωζομένοις pres. pass. part. σώζω to save, to rescue. ἀπολλυμένοις pres. pass. part. ἀπόλλυμι to destroy,
16 pass. to perish, to be perishing. ■ ἐκ θανάτου εἰς θάνατον "from death unto death." The rabbis used similar words concerning the law. For some it was a medicine unto healing and to others a medicine unto death (s. SB III, 498; Barrett). ἱκανός sufficient, adequate, "who is sufficient for these responsibilities?" What kind of a minister ought he to be who preaches a gospel which may prove fatal to those who come in contact w.
17 it? (Plummer). ■ οἱ πολλοί the majority. καπηλεύω to peddle, to pawn off a product for gain. The word is used in the LXX in Isa. 1:22 for those who mix wine w. water in order to cheat the buyers (Plummer). It is used by Plato to condemn the pseudo-philosophers (Windisch). It was used in the papyri for a wine dealer and for the running of a junk store (s. MM; Preisigke). The word refers to those who would peddle or merchandise the Word of God for profit. ἀλλά. The repetition of this word gives emphasis in an ascending scale (Plummer). κατέναντι before, in the presence of. ἐν Χριστῷ in union or fellowship w. Christ.

Ch. 3

1   ■ ἀρχόμεθα pres. ind. mid. 1st per. pl. ἄρχομαι to begin. This is sort of an echo of the supposed criticism (Plummer). συνιστάνειν pres. act. inf. συνιστάνω (συνίστημι) to place together, to introduce, to commend. (For the form, s. BD, 46.) χρήζω to need. συστατικός recommendation. ἐπιστολή letter. Letters of recommendation were generally requests for help and hospitality for aid in seeking employment or instruction based on the virtues of the one introduced and the opportunity of the recipient to express his loyalty to the writer (William Baird, "Letters of Recommendation: A Study of II Corinthians 3:1–3," JBL, 80 [June, 1961], 168f.; for examples, s. LAE, 158;
2 1 Cor. 16:3). ■ ἐγγεγραμμένη perf. pass. part. ἐγγράφω to

write in, to inscribe. καρδίαις ἡμῶν. A reference to Paul's own
heart (Baird) or it refers to both Paul and Timothy.
ἀναγινωσκομένη pres. pass. part. ἀναγινώσκω to read. The
pres. tense indicates continual reading, in an iterat. sense. ὑπὸ
πάντων ἀνθρώπων "by all men." Paul is not referring to the
receiving of the letter but the carrying of it. Like a papyrus roll,
it is sealed within him to be revealed to all men when w. open
heart he declares to them the Christian's faith (Baird, 170). ■ 3
φανερούμενοι pres. pass. part. φανερόω to make clear, to manifest. διακονηθεία aor. pass. part. fem. διακονέω to serve, to
minister to. The verb is often used in the sense of "to deliver a
message" (BAG). μελας black. The n. of the adj. has the meaning "ink." Ink could be blotted out or washed off (Plummer),
instrumental dat. (For the making of ink and the use of ink by
the rabbis, s. SB III, 499f.) ζῶντος pres. act. part. to live, "the
spirit of the living God" was the agent of the Corinthians' conversion (Barrett). πλάξ flat stone, tablet. Used in reference to
the tablets of the law (BAG). καρδίαις σαρκίναις "fleshly
hearts." Used in apposition to "tablets." The ending of the adj.
"fleshly" denotes the material out of which something is made
(s. MH 378).

■ πεποίθησις confidence. The substantive is derived from 4
the perf. of πείθω. The word is emphatic by its position (Meyer).
■ ἱκανός sufficient, qualified, capable. λογίσασθαι aor. mid. 5
inf. λογίζομαι to consider, to reckon. Used here in its widest
sense of carrying on any of the ordinary processes of reasoning
(EGT). The inf. expresses either results or is a further explanation of "sufficient." ἱκανότης sufficiency, capability. The adj.
was sometimes used in the LXX to translate Shaddai as the name
of God (s. TDNT) and the thought may be "our sufficiency
comes from the Sufficient One" (Plummer). ■ ἱκάνωσεν aor. 6
ind. act. ἱκανόω to make sufficient. Verbs w. this ending are
usually causal. The verb is followed by the double acc. "as ministers" (s. MT, 246f.). The aor. points to the time when Paul was
called to be an apostle (Plummer). διαθήκη covenant, agreement (s. Jer. 31:31–34; Matt. 26:28). γράμμα that which was
written, letter of the alphabet, letter. ἀποκτεννει pres. ind. act.
to kill. (For the form, s. BAG.) The law demands perf. obedience
and pronounces the sentence of death on the disobedient
(Hodge; s. also Windisch). ζωοποιεῖ pres. ind. act. to make alive.
The indwelling Christ has replaced the old Torah written on
tablets of stone and has become a Torah written within (PRJ,
226).

■ εἰ ... πῶς οὐχὶ μᾶλλον (v.8). Paul uses here argument 7

459

from the greater to the lesser (s. Rom. 5:9). διακονία τοῦ θανάτου obj. gen. "a ministry leading to death." ἐντετυπωμένη perf. pass. part. ἐντυπόω to imprint, to engrave. (For the rabbinical view of the tables engraved in stone, s. SB III, 502–513.) ἐγενήθη aor. ind. pass. γίνομαι to become, to come into existence, to be. ἀτενίσαι aor. act. inf. ἀτενίζω to gaze, to look intently. The rabbis felt that the shining of Moses' face was either from the glory of the Lord or from the writing of the law or from the tablets of the law or from Moses' position as mediator or even from Moses' humility (s. SB III, 513–516). καταργουμένην pres. pass. part. καταργέω to render inoperative, to make of no effect, to do away w., to abolish. The pres. part. indicates the continual action which was taking place at that time. The glory was very splendid but it was very transit

8 (Plummer). ■ μᾶλλον comp. of the adv. μάλα "rather," "even more." It introduces the conclusion of the argument started in v.7. ἔσται fut. εἰμί. This is a logical, not a chronological fut.

9 (Barrett). ■ κατάκρισις condemnation, a judgment against someone. περισσεύω to abound, followed by the dat. which

10 indicates the area in which the abundance is found. ■ καὶ γάρ "for even." A more precise grounding of the previous statement (Meyer). δεδόξασται perf. ind. pass. δοξάζω to think well of, to glorify, pass. to be made glorious. δεδοξασμένον perf. pass. part. μέρος part. ἐν τούτῳ τῷ μέρει 'in this part," "in respect to." ἕνεκεν = ἕνεκα w. the gen. "because of," "on account of." ὑπερβαλλούσης pres. act. part. fem. ὑπερβάλλω to go above and beyond, to surpass, pres. part. surpassing, extraordinary,

11 outstanding (BAG). ■ εἰ γάρ "for if," a continuation of the explanation and support of his argument. μένον pres. act. part. n. sing. μένω "that which remains." The pres. tense emphasizes the continual existence in contrast to that which is passing away.

12 ■ ἔχοντες pres. act. part. ἔχω. παρρησία lit. "speaking all" then "speaking openly" and then the further developed meaning "boldness," "courage," "great freedom" (s. Barrett; TDNT; Windisch). χρώμεθα pres. mid. subj. χράομαι to make use of, to use, followed by the dat. hortatory subj. "let us make

13 use of." ■ καὶ οὐ. Introduces an abbreviated main clause "we do not do as" (s. BD, 255). ἐτίθει impf. ind. act. τίθημι to place, customary impf. "used to place" (RWP). κάλυμμα that which covers, veil. πρός followed by the inf. indicates purpose "w. a view to" (s. MT, 144). ἀτενίσαι aor. act. inf. s.v.7. εἰς τὸ τέλος "unto the end." They should not see the disappearing of the glory on Moses' face and recognize that his service was coming

14 to an end (Schlatter). ■ ἐπωρώθη aor. ind. pass. πωρόω to

harden, to make insensitive, to cover w. thick skin, to petrify
(RWP). νόημα mind. Here the word means "the thinking faculty" (Plummer). ἀνάγνωσις reading. A reference to the public
reading of the law. (For the reading of the Scriptures in the
synagogue, s. JPF II, 927–933; SB IV, 154–165.) παλαιός old.
ἀνακαλυπτόμενον pres. pass. part. ἀνακαλύπτω to unveil, to
reveal. The part. refers to the veil which is not lifted. The whole
sentence illustrates the deep tragedy of Judaism. They hold the
law high and read it in their worship services and they do not
see that it is the document which only pronounces their condemnation (Windisch). ὅτι because. καταργεῖται pres. pass.
καταργέω to render inoperative, to do away w. (s.v.6, 7). ■ 15
ἡνίκα when followed by ἄν w. the subj. introducing an indefinite temporal clause "whenever" (RWP; BD, 237).
ἀναγινώσκηται pres. pass. subj. ἀναγινώσκω to read, to read
aloud. ἐπὶ τὴν καρδίαν "upon their heart." The heart is viewed
as the center of man's being, the spring of will and activity, the
seat of the affections and the understanding (Hughes). κεῖται
pres. ind. mid. to lie. ■ ἐπιστρέψῃ aor. pass. subj. ἐπιστρέφω 16
to turn, mid. and pass. to turn one's self. The prep. in compound
is directive "to turn to." The word gives a graphic parallel to the
account in Exod. 34 where Moses turned from the people and
went in before the Lord, thereupon removing the veil from his
face. The word also involves a deeper significance, for it is used
for the act of turning to the Lord and here involves the experience of evangelical conversion (Hughes). περιαιρεῖται pres.
pass. περιαιρέω to take away, to take away from around. The
compound verb expresses the removing of something which envelops (Plummer), but the prep. may be intensive, i.e. "to
remove completely" (MH, 321; s. also Hughes). ■ οὗ rel. pron. 17
"where." ἐλευθερία freedom, liberty, the end of the dominance
of the written law means liberty (Barrett; s. also CBB; TDNT).
■ πάντες "all." This stands in contrast to Moses and the old 18
covenant. ἀνακεκαλυμμένῳ perf. pass. part., s.v.14. The perf.
indicates the continual state resulting from a previous action.
The veil, once lifted, remains lifted (Hughes).
κατοπτριζόμενοι pres. mid. part. κατοπτρίζω act. "to produce a reflection," mid. "to look at one's self in a mirror." Here
"to look at something as in a mirror, to contemplate something"
(BAG). The pres. part. shows that the beholding is continuous
and free from interruption (Hughes). μεταμορφούμεθα pres.
ind. pass. μεταμορφόω to transform, to change the inward reality to something else (Trench, Synonyms, 264; TDNT; Plummer). ἀπὸ δόξης εἰς δόξαν "from glory unto glory." Christians

seeing in Jesus the image of God, are not deified but are transformed into the same image; the glory they share w. Him ever
increasing from one stage of glory to a higher stage (Barrett).
κυρίου πνεύματος "from the Lord of the Spirit," i.e., from the
Lord who sends the Spirit or it may be taken to mean "of the
Lord who is Spirit." (For the varying interpretations of this
phrase, s. Hughes.)

Ch. 4

1   ■ διὰ τοῦτο "because of this." This is either reference to
the preceding, i.e., because the gospel is good news of the glory
of God or it looks forward, i.e., because of what is said in the next
clause (Barrett). ἔχοντες pres. act. part. ἔχω to have, to possess.
καθώς just as, in accordance w. ἠλεήθημεν aor. ind. pass.
ἐλεέω to show mercy, pass. to be shown mercy, to obtain mercy.
Mercy indicates the compassionate removal of misery (s.
Trench, Synonyms, 169; TDNT; CBB). ἐγκακοῦμεν pres. ind.
act. 1st per. pl. to give into evil, to lose courage. It is the fainthearted coward (RWP). The word is also used in the papyri in
2   the sense of treating someone badly (Preisigke). ■ ἀπειπάμεθα
aor. ind. mid. ἀπειπάμην (ἀπολέγομαι) to speak forth, to
speak off or away from, to renounce (RWP). The aor. is timeless
and does not mean that he had previously practiced what he says
that he has renounced (Plummer). κρυπτός hidden. αἰσχύνη
shame. Τὰ κρυπτὰ τῆς αἰσχύνης "the hidden things of
shame," i.e., the things one hides because one is ashamed of
them (Lietzmann; for a discussion of the various views of this
phrase, s. Bultmann). περιπατοῦντες pres. act. part. to walk, to
conduct one's life. πανουργία (πᾶν ἔργον) readiness to do
anything. In an unfavorable sense, it has the meaning "cunning,
craftiness, trickery." The man who practices this is ready to do
anything, up to every trick (Hughes; TDNT). δολοῦντες pres.
act. part. δολόω to use deceit, to use bait, to ensnare, to corrupt
w. error, to falsify, to corrupt (RWP; T; Trench, Synonyms,
228–231). φανέρωσις openness, clearness, manifestation. The
word is selected in opposition to "the hidden things of shame"
(Plummer). συνιστάνοντες pres. act. part. (s. 2 Cor. 3:1).
3   συνείδησις conscience (s. Rom. 2:15). ■ εἰ w. the ind. assumes
the reality of the condition. καί even, i.e., "even if." With this
construction there is sometimes a tone of contempt and the
matter is belittled (RG, 1026). κεκαλυμμένον perf. pass. part.
καλύπτω to veil, to hide. The perf. looks at the state or circumstance and is used w. an adj. (IBG, 18). ἀπολλυμένοις pres.
pass. part. ἀπόλλυμι to ruin, pass. to perish, to be lost. The

durative verb is perfective and indicates the inevitable doom and the fact that the goal is ideally reached. A complete transformation of its subjects is required to bring them out of the ruin implicit in their state (M, 114f.). ■ αἰών age. It refers to all that 4 floating mass of thoughts, opinions, maxims, speculations, hopes, impulses, aims, aspirations at any time current in the world (Trench; *Synonyms*, 217f.; s. also TDNT). ἐτύφλωσεν aor. ind. act. τυφλόω to blind. νόημα thought, thinking, the ability to reason (s. 2 Cor. 2:11; 3:14). ἄπιστος unbelieving. The fault that leads to their destruction is their own (Barrett). εἰς τό w. the inf. can express either purpose or results (s. IBG, 143). αὐγάσαι aor. act. inf. αὐγάζω. The verb has two meanings (1) to see distinctly or to gaze upon (2) to illumine or beam upon and is used in Lev. 13 and 14 w. the meaning "to appear bright" (Hughes). φωτισμός illumination followed by the gen. of origin "light from the gospel" (MT, 218). εἰκών image, the resemblence of something to a prototype from which it is derived and in whose essence it shares. Christ shares in God's real being and is a perfect manifestation of that being (Hughes; s. also TDNT; CBB). ■ κύριον double acc., i.e., "Christ Jesus as Lord." ■ ὅτι 5/6 "because." This explains why they must preach Christ and not themselves (Plummer). ὁ θεός the Creator of the old creation is also the Creator of the new creation. λάμψει fut. ind. act. λάμπω to shine, to shine forth (s. TDNT). The fut. used to express a command is a translation of the Heb. jussive (s. BD, 183; BG, 94). φωτισμός illumination, enlightenment followed by the gen. of origin or subj. gen., i.e., "the illumining which the knowledge of the glory produces" (Plummer). πρόσωπον face, countenance, per. (BG, 184).

■ θησαυρός treasure, that which is valuable and expensive. 7 ὀστράκινος made of clay, earthenware, pottery. Corinthian pottery was well-known in the ancient world (Strabo, *Geography* VIII, 6.23) and Paul may have been referring to the small pottery lamps which were cheap and fragile or he may have referred to earthenware vases or urns. The point seems to be that the valuable treasure is contained in weak, fragile, and valueless containers (s. Hughes; SB III, 516). The ending of the word signifies material out of which something was made (MH, 359). σκεῦος vessel. ὑπερβολή excess, abundance, extraordinary quality of character (BAG). ᾖ pres. subj. εἰμί. The particle w. the subj. generally indicates purpose but here it may have a causal idea (BG, 140–141). ■ θλιβόμενοι pres. pass. part. θλίβω to subject 8 to pressure, to afflict, that which presses upon or burdens the spirit (Trench; *Synonyms*, 202; TDNT). στενοχωρούμενοι pres. pass. part. στενοχωρέω to pressure into a narrow place. It speaks of the narrowness of room, confined space, and then painfulness of which this is the occasion (Trench; *Synonyms*, 203; TDNT). ἀπορούμενοι pres. mid. part. ἀπορέω to be at a loss, to be in doubt, to be perplexed, to be despondent. In the papyri it was used of one who was ruined by creditors and was at his wits end (MM). ἐξαπορούμενοι pres. mid. part. ἐξαπορέομαι to be completely baffled (Barrett). The prep. in compound is perfective and shows the despondency in its final

9 result of despair (M, 237). ■ διωκόμενοι pres. pass. part. διώκω to hunt, to hunt down like an animal, to persecute. ἐγκαταλειπόμενοι pres. pass. part. ἐγκαταλείπω to desert, to abandon one in difficulty. The word occurs in the LXX in God's promises not to forsake His own (Deut. 31:6–8; Joshua 1:5; 1 Chron. 28:20; Ps. 36:25; 28; s. also Plummer, Bultmann). καταβαλλόμενοι pres. pass. part. καταβάλλω to throw down, to knock down, to strike down w. force. The word was used of throwing an opponent down in wrestling (Windisch) or of striking someone down w. a sword or another weapon (Plummer). ἀπολλύμενοι pres. mid. or pass. part. ἀπόλλυμι to destroy, to perish. The parts. used in this passage are either to be connected w. the verb "we have" in v.7 or they are to be considered exam-

10 ples of abs. part. standing here for the ind. (s. Hughes). ■ πάντοτε always. νέκρωσις dying, the process of dying (Hughes), slaying, putting to death. It refers to Paul's constant exposure to death (Hodge). περιφέροντες pres. act. part. to carry about, to bear about. The pres. tense emphasizes the continual action. The missionaries were perpetually being delivered to death for Christ's sake. They were never free from peril (Plummer). φανερωθῇ aor. pass. subj. φανερόω to make clear, to manifest. The subj. is used w. the particle to express purpose.

11 ■ ἀεί always. γάρ for. The particle gives an explanation of the preceding. ζῶντες pres. act. part. ζάω to live, "the living," "we are ever a living prey" (Plummer). παραδιδόμεθα pres. ind. pass. παραδίδωμι to deliver over, to hand over. The pres. tense emphasizes the continual danger that is faced. διά w. acc. "because." θνητός mortal, subject to death. It emphasizes the

12 material, weakness, and transitoriness of the body (Meyer). ■ ὥστε therefore. It is used here as an inferential particle meaning "and so, accordingly" (IBG, 144). ἐνεργεῖται pres. ind. mid.

13 ἐνεργέω to work, to be at work. ■ τὸ αὐτὸ πνεῦμα τῆς πίστεως "the same spirit" followed by the obj. gen. i.e., the spirit who engenders faith (Barrett). γεγραμμένον perf. pass. part. γράφω to write, perf. "that which stands written." It refers

to an authoritative document (s. MM; BS, 250). ἐπίστευσα aor. ind. act. πιστεύω to believe. Paul quotes Ps. 116:10 as rendered in the LXX (s. Hughes). ἐλάλησα aor. ind. act. λαλέω to speak. ■ εἰδότες perf. part. οἶδα defective perf. w. pres. meaning "to 14 know." The verb expresses knowledge grasped directly or intuitively by the mind (s. Donald W. Burdick, "οἶδα and γινώσκω in the Pauline Epistles," ND, 344-356). ἐγείρας aor. act. part. ἐγείρω to raise up. ἐγερεῖ fut. ind. act. ἐγείρω. παραστήσει fut. ind. act. παρίστημι to present, to cause to stand in the presence of someone (Hughes), to present as a bride is presented to the bridegroom (Plummer). ■ πλεονάσασα aor. act. part. 15 fem. sing. πλεονάζω to make more through the more, to expand, to become more, to increase. Perhaps the idea is "the increasing numbers" (IBG, 108). πλείων comp. πολύς, οἱ πλ the majority, the many. εὐχαριστία thanksgiving. The acc. is the object of the verb περισσεύσῃ. περισσεύσῃ aor. act. subj. περισσεύω to increase, to cause to abound, to make extremely rich (BAG).

■ διό wherefore. ἐγκακοῦμεν pres. ind. act. to lose courage 16 (s.v.1). ἀλλ᾽εἰ w. ind. introduces a condition assumed to be true. ἔξω outward w. the article "the external." ἡμῶν poss. gen. (For the position of the pron., s. BD, 148.) διαφθείρεται pres. ind. pass. to decay. The pres. tense pictures the process of continual decay. ἔσω inward w. the article "the inward." ἀνακαινοῦνται pres. ind. pass. ἀνακαινόω to renew again. The pres. tense emphasizes the continual renewal. ■ παραυτίκα momentary. It 17 indicates a short amount of pres. time including the idea temporary i.e., till life ends or the Lord comes (Plummer; Windisch). ἐλαφρός light, not heavy (s. Matt. 11:30). Affliction for Jesus' sake however crushing it may seem, is in fact light, a weightless trifle (Hughes). θλῖψις pressure, tribulation, affliction. ὑπερβολή excess (s.v.7.) εἰς ὑπερβολήν for or to excess. The two phrases form a double expression which cannot lit. be translated. The meaning is "out of all proportion" (Barrett). βάρος weight. Paul's choice of the expression "the weight of glory" may be influenced from the fact that in Heb. "weight" and "glory" come from the same root (Bruce). κατεργάζεται pres. ind. mid. to produce, to accomplish and it implies a prolonged process, a working out (Plummer). ■ σκοπούντων pres. act. 18 part. σκοπέω to fix one's gaze upon, to concentrate one's attention upon. The part. is used as a gen. abs. (Hughes). βλεπόμενα pres. pass. part. The part. is used as an adj. "the things being seen," i.e., "visible things." πρόσκαιρος for a time, temporary.

Ch. 5

1 ■ οἶδα defective perf. w. a pres. meaning to know (s. 2 Cor. 4:14). ἐπίγειος upon the earth, earthly. Death involves the loss, not only of physical corporeality but also of earthly corporateness (M.J. Harris, ND, 319). σκῆνος tent, gen. of apposition "our earthly tent-dwelling," "the tent which forms our earthly house" (Harris, ND, 318). The figure of a tent picturing the human body suggests impermanence and insecurity and is a common picture of earthly life and its setting in the body (Barrett). From a Jewish point of view the tent could be a reference to the Feast of Tabernacles picturing that the Christian would have to live in a booth before reaching the promised land (PRJ, 313). (For other references to the figure of the tent, s. Windisch; Harris, ND, 318.) καταλυθῇ aor. pass. subj. καταλύω to destroy. In reference to the tent metaphor it describes the act of dismantling a tent (Hughes). οἰκοδομή house, building. ἐκ θεοῦ "from God." The phrase indicates the source of the building as contrasted w. the earthly tent. ἔχω to have, to possess. (For the pres. tense w. the meaning "to possess," s. M 110.) ἀχειροποίητος verbal adj. (χείρ, hand, ποιέω, to make), not made w. hands, not handmade, i.e., not of this creation (Hughes), supernatural, spiritual (Plummer). αἰώνιος eternal, everlasting, not in the sense of pre-existent but it indicates in-

2 definite durability (Plummer). ■ καὶ γάρ "for even," "yes, even" (s. BD, 326). στενάζομεν pres. ind. act. to sigh, to groan because of an undesirable circumstance (BAG). The pres. tense emphasizes the continual groaning in this life. οἰκητήριον a place of living. It denotes a permanent abode or home (s. Jude 6) (Plummer). ἐπενδύσασθαι aor. mid. inf. ἐπενδύομαι to put

3 on over, to put on upon one's self (RWP). ■ εἴ γε "of course if" "if, indeed" (Hughes; IBG, 165). ἐνδυσάμενοι aor. mid. part. ἐνδύομαι to put on, to be clothed. (For the variant reading "to be unclothed," s. TC, 579f.) γυμνός naked, unclothed. εὑρεθησόμεθα fut. ind. pass. εὑρίσκω to find, pass. to be found, to be discovered. Paul's desire not to be found naked reveals not only a characteristically Jewish horror of nakedness, but also that he does not use it in its normal Hellenistic sense

4 (Barrett). ■ καὶ γάρ s.v.2. ὄντες pres. part. εἰμί. The part. w. the article indicates the group to which the subject belongs—"we who are in the tent," i.e., the earthly body (Barrett). βαρούμενοι pres. pass. part. βαρέω to make heavy, to burden, to weigh down. The part. is used adverbially "we groan as weighted down," since we are under a constant depressing burden (Lenski). ἐφ᾽ ᾧ = ἐπὶ τούτῳ ὅτι "in view of the fact that"

(M, 107) "because" (MT, 272). ἐκδύσασθαι aor. mid. inf. ἐκδύομαι to take off, to be unclothed. καταποθῇ aor. pass. subj. καταπίνω to drink down, to swallow down, pass. to be swallowed up. θνητός that which is mortal. It refers to our entire mortal existence (Lenski). The ending of the verbal adj. indicates "libel to death" (RG, 1097; s. also BD, 36). ■ κατεργασάμενος 5 aor. mid. part. κατεργάζομαι to produce, to prepare, to produce a condition or atmosphere, to prepare one for a circumstance (Windisch). εἰς αὐτὸ τοῦτο "for this very purpose." θεός God. The word here is in a position of emphasis (Hughes). δούς aor. act. part. δίδωμι to give. ἀρραβών earnest, down payment (s. 2 Cor. 1:22; s. also MM).

■ θαρροῦντες pres. act. part. θαρρέω to be of good cheer, 6 to be of good courage, to be confident. The part. is in anacolouthon, a break in the sentence structure, and the sentence begins again in v.8 (Barrett). πάντοτε always esp. in view of death. εἰδότες perf. act. part. οἶδα (s. 2 Cor. 4:14). ἐνδημοῦντες pres. act. part. ἐνδημέω to be at home, to be one among his own people, to live in a place (s. RWP). ἐκδημοῦμεν ἀπὸ pres. ind. act. to be gone, to be away from home, to be abroad, to immigrate (Hughes). (For the use of the words "be at home" and "to be abroad," "to be away from home," s. MM; Preisigke.) ■ 7 περιπατοῦμεν pres. ind. act. to walk, to conduct one's life. εἶδος appearance. The word refers to the thing seen, the form or an appearance of an object (Hughes), "we conduct our lives on the basis of faith, not the appearance of things" (Barrett). ■ εὐδοκοῦμεν pres. ind. act. to be well-pleased, to consent, here 8 "we wish rather," "we prefer" (BAG). ἐκδημῆσαι aor. act. inf. (s.v.6). ■ φιλοτιμούμεθα pres. ind. mid. to love, honor, then to 9 be ambitious, to devote one's self zealously to a cause, to be ambitious (s. Hughes). εὐάρεστος pleasing. The word is used in Titus 2:9 of slaves who give satisfaction to their masters (BAG). ■ πάντας all. Used w. the article it means here "the sum total 10 of us" (MT, 201; s. also BG, 61). φανερωθῆναι aor. pass. inf. φανερόω to make clear, to manifest, pass. to be made manifest. They not only have to appear, but have to have their whole character made manifest (Plummer). δεῖ it is necessary. ἔμπροσθεν w. the gen. "before." βῆμα step, platform, tribunal. This was a tribunal where official decisions were given (RAC II, 129–130; for a good description of the "judgment seat" found at the city of Corinth, s. IB I, 683–684). The word was also used in the papyri in the official sense "tribunal, judgment seat" (MM). κομίσηται aor. mid. subj. κομίζω to bring, mid. to carry off, to get for one's self, to receive, to receive as recompense

(BAG). In the NT the mid. has the meaning "to receive back" or "to receive what is one's own" (Hughes; s. also MM). τὰ διὰ τοῦ σώματος "the things (done) through the body." The phrase expresses personal agency in which the body acts as the subject of the doing (SBT, 187). This gives the body its positive meaning for eternity (Schlatter). ἔπραξεν aor. ind. act. πράσσω to do. The aor. pictures the whole life of the individual Christian as seen as a unity. With the prep. the phrase means "w. reference to what he did" (Hughes). φαῦλος worthless, bad, of no account, good-for-nothingness. The word indicates the impossibility of any true gain ever coming forth from it, and the notion of worthlessness is the central notion (Trench, *Synonyms*, 317).

11   ■ εἰδότες perf. act. part. οἶδα defective perf. w. pres. meaning to know (s. 2 Cor. 4:14). φόβος τοῦ κυρίου "fear of the Lord." The fear excited by the thought of standing before the judgment seat of Christ and having one's whole life exposed and estimated (Plummer). The gen. is obj. gen. πείθομεν pres. ind. act. to persuade. The pres. tense may be conative, "we try to persuade" (Barrett; SMT, 8). συνείδησις conscience (s. Rom. 2:15). πεφανερῶσθαι perf. pass. inf. (s.v.10). The perf. indicates Paul's true and integral self has been and continues to be

12   manifested in the conscience of the Corinthians (Hughes). ■ συνιστάνομεν pres. ind. act. to commend (s. 2 Cor. 3:1). ἀφορμή occasion, basis of operation, a place to start from (Plummer). In the papyri the word was used w. the meanings "incitement" or "prompting," "occasion" or "opportunity" (s. MM). διδόντες pres. act. part. δίδωμι. A circumstantial part. to be translated as a main verb. Paul is fond of continuing a construction begun w. a finite verb by means of coordinated part. (BD, 245; IBG, 179; MT, Style 89). καύχημα a boast, the ground or matter of glorying (AS). ἔχητε pres. act. subj. ἔχω. The meaning is "in order that you may have a refutation of those who glory in appearance and not in heart" (Hughes). The subj.

13   is used to express purpose. ■ ἐξέστημεν aor. ind. act. ἐξίστημι to stand out of one's self, to be beside one's self. The word indicates mental imbalance (s. Windisch). θεῷ dat. of advantage. σωφρονοῦμεν pres. ind. act. to be sane, to be sensible, to be in control of one's facilities (s. TDNT; Trench, *Synonyms*, 69-72). (For an example of a heathen prophetess who did not utter her prophecies in wild ecstasy but in self-control and moderation, s.

14   DC I, 56.) ■ ἀγάπη τοῦ Χριστοῦ either obj. gen., i.e. "Paul's love for Christ" or subj. gen. "Christ's love for Paul." It is perhaps best taken as subj. gen. indicating the love which originates or ends w. God in Christ, i.e. Christ's love for him which is prior

to and the explanation of his love for Christ (Hughes; s. also Barrett; RG, 499). συνέχει pres. ind. act. to hold together, to press together, to constrain. The verb implies the pressure which confines and restricts as well as controls (Plummer; Barrett). The pres. tense indicates the continual habit of life. κρίναντας aor. act. part. κρίνω to judge, to decide. The aor. may be perfective aor. indicating the judgment or decision which Paul had come to. The word points to a judgment formed in the past perhaps at or soon after his conversion (Hughes). ἀπέθανεν, ἀπέθανον aor. ind. act. ἀποθνήσκω to die. ἄρα therefore, "that means that" (Barrett; s. also BD, 235). οἱ πάντες all w. the article the word denotes the class named is taken as a whole, i.e. "the sum total of all" (s. BG, 61; MT, 201). ■ ζῶντες pres. act. part. ζάω 15 to live. μηκέτι = οὐκέτι no longer. ἑαυτοῖς reflex. pron. 3rd-per. pl. dat. of advantage "to live for the advantage of one's self." ζῶσιν pres. act. subj. Subjunctive used to express purpose. ἀποθανόντι aor. act. part. dat. of advantage or personal inter-est. ἐγερθέντι aor. pass. part. ἐγείρω to raise, pass. to be raised.

■ ὥστε wherefore. The word is used to draw a conclusion. 16 κατά w. acc. "according to," "according to the standard of." Both prep. phrases "according to the flesh" in this v. are to be taken w. the verbs and not w. the nouns. It is fleshly knowledge that Paul repudiates (Barrett). εἰ καί "even if." The words in-troduce a condition assumed to be true. It indicates that Paul and others really did have a fleshly knowledge of Christ (s. John W. Fraser, "Paul's Knowledge of Jesus: II Cor. 5:16 Once More," NTS, 17 [April, 1971], 300). ἐγνώκαμεν perf. ind. act. γινώσκω to know. Personal acquaintance of "others" is not what is meant here. Paul has a way of looking at, regarding, understanding Christ; now he has a new way of understanding others, including Christ (Fraser, 299). (For arguments showing that Paul was not denying knowledge of the historical Jesus, s. Barrett; JNP, 89ff.; Hughes.) νῦν οὐκέτι "now no longer." This does not mean that Paul had no interest in the historical Jesus, His example, teaching and the traditions about Him. He knew about Jesus. The basic meaning is that Paul had a new, fuller understanding of the "whole Christ" by the Spirit and by faith; and he sees others in a new way according to their standing w. Him, in the "new creation" (Fraser, 312). ■ ὥστε wherefore. 17 Paul draws a second conclusion. κτίσις creation. The one who is in Christ and has experienced the new birth is a part of the new creation. The rabbis used the term "new creature" to describe those whose sins had been forgiven (s. SB II, 415; III, 519; for further parallels w. rabbinic teaching regarding the new creation,

s. PRJ, 119ff.). ἀρχαῖος old, that which comes from an earlier
time. παρῆλθεν aor. ind. act. παρέρχομαι to go by, to pass
away. The aor. is perfective and points to the finality. γέγονεν
perf. ind. act. γίνομαι. The perf. indicates the continuing state
or condition (s. McKay). (For a discussion of the new life in
18 Christ, s. Ladd, 479f.) ■ καταλλάξαντος aor. act. part.
καταλλάσσω to effect a change, to exchange, to reconcile. The
prep. in compound is perfective "to effect a thorough change
back" (s. MH, 298). Reconciliation indicates that Christ's death
removed God's enmity against man (s. APC, 186–223; TDNT;
CBB). δόντος aor. act. part. δίδωμι to give. καταλλαγή reconciliation, gen. of description. It refers to the office and duty of
19 announcing this reconciliation (Hodge). ■ ὡς ὅτι "namely, that
. . ." "how that . . . ." The force of the words is declarative of
what has immediately preceded (Hughes; Alford; s. also RG,
1033). κόσμος world, world of human beings. The acc. is the
direct object of the part. It is the world God reconciles.
καταλλάσσων pres. act. part. The part. may be taken as part
of a periphrastic impf. (Barrett; MT, 88). λογιζόμενος pres.
mid. part. λογίζομαι to place to one's account, to reckon. A
formula used in rabbinic writing (s. SB III, 121f.) and a common
formula in the papyri in the commercial sense of putting down
to one's account (s. MM; Preisigke). αὐτοῖς "against them" dat.
of disadvantage. The pl. pron. takes up the phrase "the world"
(Barrett). παράπτωμα transgression, a false step, blunders (s.
Trench; Synonyms, 245f.; TDNT). θέμενος aor. mid. part.
20 τίθημι to place, to put. ■ ὑπέρ on behalf of, representing. Perhaps the prep. also has the idea of "in place of" (Hughes).
πρεσβεύω to be an ambassador, to carry out the office of an
ambassador. (For verbs w. this ending marking the exercise of
a profession, s. MH, 398.) This was the regular word in the Gr.
east for the emperor's legate (s. MM; TDNT; LAE, 378; Windisch). ὡς. Followed by the gen. abs. it always gives a subj. view
of that which is stated by the gen. abs. The statement is correct.
It may be translated "seeing that" (Plummer). παρακαλοῦντος
pres. act. part. παρακαλέω to urge, to ask, to entreat. δεόμεθα
pres. ind. mid. to ask, to request, to ask for a specific thing. The
pres. tense indicates the continual or habitual action.
καταλλάγητε aor. pass. imp. ingressive aor. "become recon-
21 ciled to God" (Plummer). ■ γνόντα aor. act. part. γινώσκω to
know. It expresses knowledge gained by experience (s. D.W.
Burdick, ND, 344ff.). The part. could be used in a concessive
sense "although he knew no sin." ἁμαρτίαν . . . ἐποίησεν "he
made to be sin." The reference may be an allusion to the scape-

goat at the Day of Atonement (Windisch) or it may refer to the
suffering servant of Isa. 53 w. the idea of sacrifice prominent (s.
Bruce). God placed our sins on the sinless Jesus and as our
substitute in our place God punished Him w. death (Lietzmann).
γενώμεθα aor. mid. subj. γίνομαι to become. δικαιοσύνη "the
righteousness of God." This is the righteousness both that God
requires and that He provides in justification. Paul relates being
"in Christ" to justification (s. GW, 141f.).

Ch. 6

■ συνεργοῦντες pres. act. part. συνεργέω to work w. 1
someone, to cooperate, to work together. The complement to be
supplied after "working w." can only be God (Barrett). The part.
can be taken as causal. παρακαλοῦμεν pres. ind. act. to encourage, to exhort, followed by the acc. w. the inf. κενός empty,
without results, in vain. δέξασθαι aor. mid. inf. δέχομαι to
receive. The aor. may point to the time of conversion and Paul
exhorts them not to have accepted the grace of God in vain, i.e.
not to show by their behavior now that they accepted it then to
no profit (Plummer). The fear is not that they would lose their
salvation but that they would not effectively carry out the ministry of reconciliation which had been committed to them (compare 2 Cor. 5:18). ■ λέγει pres. ind. act. It is used without a 2
stated subject and it may mean either "He (God) says," or "it
(Scripture) says" (Hughes). δεκτός (verbal adj. δέχομαι) acceptable, welcome, favorable (BAG). ἐπήκουσα aor. ind. act.
ἐπακούω to listen to, to hear. It is a technical term for hearing
prayer (Barrett). ἐβοήθησα aor. ind. act. βοηθέω to help.
εὐπρόσδεκτος easily acceptable, pleasant, welcome. Used of a
time which is favorable for bringing God's grace to fruition
(BAG). σωτηρία salvation. The gen. in the phrase "day of
salvation" could be gen. of direction or purpose (BD, 92), i.e. "a
day for salvation," "a day for the proclamation of salvation." It
would then refer again to the fulfilling of the ministry of reconciliation (s. 2 Cor. 5:18). ■ μηδεμίαν fem. acc. sing. μηδείς, 3
μία, ἕν no. A strengthened form used w. another neg. w. the
meaning "no (offense) at all" (BAG). διδόντες pres. act. part.
δίδωμι to give. The pres. tense points to the habitual, continual
action. προσκοπή a striking against, an occasion of stumbling,
to do something which causes others to stumble (T). It indicates
the causing of the foot to strike and the person to stumble (Lenski). μωμηθῇ aor. pass. subj. μωμάομαι to find a defect, to find
fault w., to blame someone (s. Windisch). The word often implies
ridicule as well as blame, w. disgrace as a result (Plummer). The

471

4 subj. is used to express purpose. ■ ἐν παντί "in everything," "in every way." συνιστάνοντες pres. act. part. συνιστάνω (συνίστημι) to bring together, to recommend, to commend (s. 2 Cor. 3:1). θεοῦ διάκονοι "as ministers of God." The nom. means "as God's servants we commend ourselves" (s. RG, 454). The word emphasizes the personal service rendered to another (s. TDNT; CBB). θλίψις pressure, affliction (s. 2 Cor. 1:4). ἀνάγκη necessity, anguish. Here it is used in the sense of suffering, quite possibly it means "tortures" (Barrett). στενοχωρία narrow space, "tight places" (RWP), distress (s. 2 Cor. 4:8).

5 ■ πληγή stripe, wound. ἀκαταστασία instability, often from politics (RWP), disorders. These things consist of troubles inflicted by men (Plummer). κόπος work, labor. The word implies toil unto fatigue, the weariness which follows on the straining of all his powers to the utmost (s. Trench; Synonyms, 379). ἀγρυπνία without sleep, sleeplessness. It refers to the times when Paul voluntarily went without sleep or shortened his hours of rest in order to devote more time to his evangelical work, to his care of all the churches, and to prayer (Hughes). νηστεία fasting, the voluntary foregoing of food in order to get more work done (Plummer). This triplet consists of those troubles which Paul took upon himself in the prosecution of his mission

6 (Plummer). ■ ἀγνότης purity. The word probably refers to purity of life and motive in the comprehensive sense (Hughes), perhaps in the sense of "innocence" (Barrett). γνῶσις knowledge. μακροθυμία longsuffering, patience. It describes the steadfast spirit which will never give in, which can endure delay and bear suffering and is used of God's patience toward sinful men and of the attitude which Christians are to display (NTW, 83–85; TDNT). It refers to a long holding out of the mind before it gives room to action or passion—generally to passion (Trench; Synonyms, 196). χρηστότης usefulness, kindness. ἀνυπόκριτος without hypocrisy, love that is not entirely geniune, i.e. admixed w. insincerity or self-seeking (Hughes). (For the prefix used to

7 negate the word, s. Moorhouse, 47ff.) ■ διά w. gen. "through," "w." ὅπλα used only in the pl. "weapons." Followed by the gen. δικαιοσύνης which refers either to the weapons provided by righteousness, i.e. subj. gen. or to the weapons used in the defense of righteousness (s. Windisch; s. also MRP, 161). δεξιός right, "for the right hand." ἀριστερός left, "for the left hand," i.e. "right hand and left hand weapons," offensive and defensive

8 armor, the shield being carried on the left arm (Plummer). ■ ἀτιμία dishonor, disgrace. δυσφημία slander, evil report.

9 εὐφημία praise, good report. πλάνος deceiver. ■ ἀγνοούμενοι

pres. pass. part. ἀγνοέω to be ignorant, pass. to be unknown. It refers to "being non-entities, not worth knowing," without proper credentials (Plummer). They did not receive recognition in the world of their day because the world, the literature, politics, and scholarship took no notice of them and they were not the source of daily conversation and were not sought out as great orators (Windisch). ἐπιγινωσκόμενοι pres. pass. part. ἐπιγινώσκω to recognize, to acknowledge, pass. to be recognized. They received their recognition from God and hopefully by the Corinthians themselves (Barrett). ἀποθνήσκοντες pres. act. part. ἀποθνήσκω to die. ἰδού "see!" "behold," suddenly and contrary to hope (Bengel). ζῶμεν pres. ind. act. ζάω to live, to be alive. As an apostle, Paul was like a man under sentence of death (Barrett). παιδευόμενοι pres. pass. part. παιδεύω to punish, to discipline. God disciplines His servants for His servants' good (Barrett). θανατούμενοι pres. pass. part. θανατόω to kill, to put to death. See Ps. 118:18, "the Lord hath chastened me sore; but he hath not delivered me over to death." Let believers regard their afflictions not as indications of God's disapprobation, but rejoice in them as opportunities graciously afforded them to glorify His name (Hodge). ■ λυπούμενοι pres. pass. 10 part. λυπέω to cause pain or grief, pass. to be sorry, to be grieved. πτωχός poor, extremely poor, destitute poverty. It describes the abject poverty which has lit. nothing and which is in imminent danger of real starvation (NTW; TDNT). πλουτίζοντες pres. act. part. πλουτίζω to make rich, to make wealthy. ἔχοντες pres. act. part. ἔχω to hold down, to hold as a possession. (For parallel statements in the ancient world, s. Lietzmann; David L. Mealand, " 'As Having Nothing, and Yet Possessing Everything' II Cor. 6:10c," ZNW, 67 [1976], 277–279.)

■ στόμα mouth ἀνέῳγεν perf. ind. act. ἀνοίγω to open, 11 perf. to be opened, to stand open. The phrase means "I am speaking to you frankly, w. an open heart, hiding nothing of my life from you" (Hering). πεπλάτυνται perf. ind. pass. πλατύνω to make wide, to open wide, pass. to be wide open, to have the heart wide open means "there are no secrets in it." Paul tells them "there is room for you in it, and I long to have you there" (Barrett). ■ στενοχωρεῖσθε pres. ind. pass. στενοχωρέω to 12 make narrow, to crowd, to restrict, pass. to be restricted. σπλάγχνα pl. inward parts. It properly refers to the contents of the breast, i.e. the heart, lungs, liver and is used to describe the seat of the deepest emotions and is the strongest word in Gr. for the feeling of compassion (Hughes; MNTW, 156; TDNT).

13   ■ ἀντιμισθία recompense, paying back. The use of the acc. may be an adverbial acc. (IBG, 160), or it may be acc. in apposition to the sentence (s. IBG, 35; MT, 245). ὡς τέκνοις λέγω "I speak as to children." It is in the nature of things that paternal love should meet w. the response of filial love (Hughes).

14   ■ γίνεσθε pres. mid. imp. γίνομαι. The pres. imp. w. the neg. is used either to stop an action in progress or to prohibit a habitual action (s. MKG, 272f.). ἑτεροζυγοῦντες pres. act. part. ἑτεροζυγέω to yoke w. a different yoke, to draft animals that need different kinds of yokes, because they are of different species (BAG), to use a double harnass (Barrett). Paul is probably referring to the prohibitions found in Deut. 22:10 and Lev. 19:19. (For the rabbinical development of this prohibition, s. M. Kilaim VIII, 2f.) The concept of the yoke was used in relation to marriage and in relation to teachers who agreed in their doctrine. A mixed marriage or cooperation w. one who had a different doctrine was considered to be "unequally yoked" Schlatter). The use of the part. w. this verb is sometimes used to denote the beginning of a state or condition "do not lend yourselves to . . ." (BD, 180). ἄπιστος unbelieving, unbeliever. The dat. is used in connection w. the verb "yoked together" (Windisch). μετοχή having a part in, partaking, partnership. κοινωνία fellowship, to have things common or together (s. TDNT; RAC IX, 1100–1145; CBB). πρὸς σκότος w. darkness. (For the term "darkness" particularly in the DSS, s. John 1:5.)

15   ■ συμφώνησις harmony, agreement. The verb related to this noun was used in the papyri w. the meaning "agree w.," "agree together" (s. MM). βελιάρ a Heb. word meaning "worthless" and was used in Jewish writings and the DSS to describe Satan, the prince of lawlessness and darkness (s. Hughes; Bruce; Barrett; TDNT).

16   ■ συγκατάθεσις approval, accent, agreement, union. Used in the papyri of a decision arrived at by a group, an agreement (BAG). ναός temple. The term was properly used of the innermost sanctuary of a temple where the divine presence was supposed to be located (Hughes). ζῶντος pres. act. part. ζάω to live. ὅτι. Used to introduce direct speech and is the equivalent of quotation marks (s. BD, 205; 246f.). ἐνοικήσω fut. ind. act. ἐνοικέω to live in, to dwell in. ἐμπεριπατήσω fut. ind. act. ἐμπεριπατέω to walk about in, to walk about among. ἔσομαι fut. ind. εἰμί. (For Paul's use of the OT in the Pharisaic practice of putting together various Scriptures to prove a point, s. BE,

17   115ff.)   ■ ἐξέλθατε aor. act. imp. ἐξέρχομαι to go out. ἀφορίσθητε aor. pass. imp. ἀφορίζω to separate, pass. to be separated. ἀκάθαρτος unclean. ἅπτεσθε pres. mid. imp.

ἅπτομαι to touch, followed by the gen. εἰσδέξομαι fut. ind. mid. εἰσδέχομαι to receive, to receive w. favor (Plummer). ■ ἔσομαι, ἔσεσθε fut. s.v.16. εἰς. The prep. is used in a Hebraic 18 way to introduce the pred. nom. (s. BG, 10f.). παντοκράτωρ almighty, all powerful, omnipotent.

Ch. 7

■ ἔχοντες pres. act. part. ἔχω. The pres. tense points to the 1 continuous possession. ἐπαγγελία promise. καθαρίσωμεν aor. act. subj. καθαρίζω to cleanse, to purify. (For examples of this verb used w. the prep., s. BS, 216f.) The hortatory use of the subj. "let us . . . ." The aor. tense indicates that a complete break should be made (Hughes). μολυσμός that which stains, defilement, pollution. σαρκὸς καὶ πνεύματος "flesh and spirit." The terms refer to the outward and inward man both of which would be contaminated by contact w. heathen forces (s. Schlatter). ἐπιτελοῦντες pres. act. part. ἐπιτελέω to complete, to perfect, to bring to the goal. The word can also refer to the discharging of religious duties (s. Barrett). The prep. in compound is directive indicating the concentration of the verb's action upon some object (MH, 312). The pres. tense points to a continual advance in holiness (Hughes). ἁγιωσύνη holiness. φόβος θεοῦ "the fear of God." The gen. is objective gen.

■ χωρήσατε aor. act. imp. χωρέω to make room for, to 2 provide a place for, "make room for us in your hearts" (RWP). ἠδικήσαμεν aor. ind. act. ἀδικέω to wrong someone, to treat someone unjustly, to injure (s. BAG). ἐφθείραμεν aor. ind. act. φθείρω to corrupt, to ruin. It may refer to money, or morals, or doctrine (Plummer). ἐπλεονεκτήσαμεν aor. ind. act. πλεονεκτέω to take advantage of someone in order to gain something, to defraud for the purpose of gain. It refers to the selfish attitude of one who is willing to go to all lengths to satisfy his selfishness (s. TDNT; NTW). The three aor. tenses point back to a definite occasion (Hughes). ■ κατάκρισις condemna- 3 tion, the rendering of a decision against someone. προείρηκα perf. ind. act. προλέγω to say before. The prep. in compound is temporal. εἰς τό w. the inf. used to express purpose (s. MT, 143). συναποθανεῖν aor. act. inf. συναποθνήσκω to die w. someone, to die together. συζῆν pres. act. inf. συζάω to live together. ■ παρρησία freedom in speaking, openness, boldness 4 (s. 2 Cor. 3:12). καύχησις boasting. πεπλήρωμαι perf. ind. pass. πληρόω to fill, pass. to be filled. The perf. indicates "I was filled then and am still" (Plummer). The dat. occurs here as instrumental instead of the classical gen. (s. BD, 104).

ὑπερπερισσεύομαι pres. ind. pass. to cause someone to overflow, pass. to overflow, to be overflowing (s. BAG). ἐπί w. the
dat. "amid all my afflictions" (Plummer). •

5   ■ καὶ γάρ "for even." ἐλθόντων aor. act. part. ἔρχομαι
gen. abs. "when we had come." ἔσχηκεν perf. ind. act. ἔχω.
(For the use of the perf. here, s. 2 Cor. 2:13.) ἄνεσις relief.
θλιβόμενοι pres. act. part. θλίβω to exercise pressure on someone, to afflict. The part. is used independently in the sentence
and in this case has the character of the ind. (s. M, 182; RG,
1135). μάχη battle, fight. The fights without were presumably
against adversaries, whether Christian or non-Christian—Paul
had many (Barrett). φόβος fear. The fears within were perhaps
for the safety of Titus, who might have been carrying a large sum
of money, and was seriously overdue, and for the success of the
6 work in Corinth (Barrett; s. also Windisch). ■ παρακαλῶν pres.
act. part. The pres. tense refers to the habitual character of the
comforting God (s. 2 Cor. 1:4). παρεκάλεσεν aor. ind. act.
παρακαλέω to comfort, to encourage. ταπεινός humble, used
here in the psychological sense "downcast," "depressed"
7 (Hughes). παρουσία arrival. ■ παράκλησις comforting, consolation, comfort, encouragement. παρεκλήθη aor. ind. pass.
s.v.6. ἐφ᾽ ὑμῖν "over you," "upon you" (RWP). ἀναγγέλλων
pres. act. part. to report, to announce. The part. is used as a nom.
abs. (Lietzmann). ἐπιπόθησις longing, yearning. The prep. in
compound is directive indicating a "longing towards" (RWP).
ὀδυρμός lamentation, mourning. Evidently the expression of
regret for having saddened Paul by the disorders tolerated in the
church (s. Meyer). ζῆλος zeal, intense interest. ὥστε w. the inf.
and the so-called subject of the inf. is used to express result.
μᾶλλον comp. "rather." It is used either in the sense "I rejoiced
rather than mourning," or "I rejoiced the more" (s. Barrett;
8 Windisch). ■ ὅτι because. εἰ καί "if even," "although." (For this
construction, s. 2 Cor. 4:3.) ἐλύπησα aor. ind. act. λυπέω to
cause pain, to make sorry. μεταμέλομαι pres. ind. mid. to be
sorry, to regret. The verb indicates to change one's feelings about
something (s. TDNT; Trench; Synonyms, 255–261; CBB).
μετεμελόμην impf. ind. mid. The impf. is used in the concessive
clause w. the meaning "although I was in a regretful mood at
9 first" (RWP). πρὸς ὥραν "for a moment," "for an hour." ■
ἐλυπήθητε aor. ind. pass. s.v.8. μετάνοια repentence. It indicates the changing of one's thinking regarding a matter (s.
TDNT; Windisch; CBB). κατὰ θεόν "according to God," "in
the way of God's will" (Barrett). ζημιωθῆτε aor. pass. subj.
ζημιόω to inflict injury or punishment, pass. to suffer damage

or loss, to sustain injury. The pass. is the permissive pass. "to permit one's self to sustain loss" (BAG). ἐκ from. Used here in the causal sense "because of us" (MT, 260). ■ λύπη pain, sor- 10 row. ἀμεταμέλητος verbal adj. "not to be regretted." It refers to either "repentence" or to "salvation" or to both; i.e. "repentence-unto-salvation" (s. Hughes; Barrett). (For the prefix as a neg., s. Moorhouse, 47ff.) ἐργάζεται pres. ind. mid. to work, to produce. κατεργάζεται pres. ind. mid. to work out, to produce its fulfillment in. The compound is intensive and designed to emphasize the inevitability of the outworking of death in the sorrow of the world (Hughes). ■ λυπηθῆναι aor. pass. inf. 11 λυπέω. The inf. is used as a noun (s. BD, 205f.). πόσος "how large?" κατειργάσατο aor. ind. mid. s.v.10. σπούδη eagerness, earnestness, diligence. (For the use of the word in the papyri and examples, s. MM.) ἀλλά "but," "yea." The word is used to introduce an additional point in an emphatic way (BD, 233). ἀπολογία defense; i.e. a defense against an accusation (Barrett). ἀγανάκτησις indignation. Here it indicates the indignation at the shame brought upon the church (Plummer). ἐπιπόθησις longing, yearning, s.v.7. ζῆλος zeal, s.v.7. ἐκδίκησις vengeance, punishment. Perhaps it has the idea of "requital" i.e. seeing that justice is done by bringing the guilty person to ecclesiastical discipline (Hughes). συνεστήσατε aor. ind. act. συνίστημι to commend. ἁγνός pure, immaculate, without guilt. εἶναι pres. inf. The inf. is used here w. the verb "you have demonstrated yourselves to be pure." (For the construction, s. BD, 209.) πρᾶγμα matter, affair. ■ ἄρα then, so, 12 therefore, consequently (s. BD, 235). ἔγραψα aor. ind. act. γράφω to write. ἕνεκεν w. the gen. "because of," "on account of," "for the sake of." ἀδικήσαντος aor. act. part. ἀδικέω to wrong someone, s.v.2. ἀδικηθέντος aor. pass. part. ἀδικέω pass. to be wrong, here "the one who was wronged." The word has a strong legal flavor w. the active indicating the person who was guilty and had committed wrong and the pass. indicating the party against whom the crime was committed (s. Windisch), followed by the gen. of the inf. "for the sake of," "on account of." It is used w. the inf. to express purpose (s. IBG, 83; MT, 144). φανερωθῆναι aor. pass. inf. φανερόω to make clear, to manifest. ἐνώπιον in the presence of, before. ■ 13 παρακεκλήμεθα perf. ind. pass. παρακαλέω s.v.6. The perf. tense means "we have been comforted and continue to be so" (Hughes).

παράκλησις comforting, consolation, s.v.7. περισσοτέρως comp. of adv. strengthened by μᾶλλον = "the

more exceedingly." (For examples of this construction, s. Hughes; BD, 129; MT, 29.) ἐχάρημεν aor. ind. pass. χαίρω to rejoice, to be glad. ἀναπέπαυται perf. ind. pass. ἀναπαύω to refresh, to give rest. The compound verb expresses a temporary relief, e.g. a truce as distinct from a peace (Plummer; s. also MM). The perf. indicates that at the time of writing Titus was
14 still in a state of refreshment (Hughes). ■ ὅτι because. εἰ w. the ind. introduces a condition which is assumed to be true. τι acc. "anything." κεκαύχημαι perf. ind. mid. καυχάομαι to glory, to boast. The perf. brings out the fact that Paul kept up this boasting about the Corinthians when he was speaking to Titus (Lenski). κατῃσχύνθην aor. ind. pass. καταισχύνω to put to shame. ἐγενήθη aor. ind. pass. γίνομαι to become. The perfective use of the aor. "our boasting before Titus proved to be the
15 truth" (Barrett). ■ σπλάγχνα the inward parts, the affections (s. 2 Cor. 6:12). περισσοτέρως abundantly, s.v.13. ἀναμιμνῃσκομένου pres. pass. part. ἀναμιμνῄσκω to remind someone of something, pass. to remember, to recall. The part. is used as a gen. abs. expressing contemporaneous time. τρόμος trembling. The phrase "w. fear and trembling" indicates "a nervous anxiety to do one's duty" (Plummer). ἐδέξασθε aor. ind.
16 mid. δέχομαι to receive. ■ ἐν παντί "in everything." θαρρῶ pres. ind. act. θαρρέω to be confident, to be courageous. The basic meaning of the word is "to dare," "to be bold or daring" (TDNT) but was used also in the papyri in the sense of "to have confidence in" (s. MM).

Ch. 8

1   ■ γνωρίζω to make known, to cause to know, here "we draw your attention to" (Barrett). χάρις grace. The word here means the generous giving on the part of Christians which is considered as a gift of thanksgiving (s. GNT, 174f.; TDNT; CBB). δεδομένην perf. pass. part. δίδωμι to give. The grace of generosity was given to the churches by God (Lietzmann). The perf. emphasizes the state or condition. The prep. ἐν has almost the meaning of the dat.; i.e. "in the case of the churches" (s. BD, 118). Although the area of Macedonia which included Philippi, Thessalonica, and Beroea had at one time been rich, the Romans had taken possession of the gold and silver mines and the coun-
2 try was like a lacerated and disjointed animal (Plummer). ■ δοκιμή proof, test as of metal (RWP). θλῖψις pressure, affliction. περισσεία abundance, superfluity, surplus (s. LAE, 84). κατὰ βάθους "down to depth," "rock bottom." Their poverty had already reached the lowest stage (Plummer; s. also Barrett).

πτωχεία poverty. The word describes abject poverty, which has lit. nothing and which is in imminent danger of real starvation (NTW, 110; s. also TDNT). In many parts of the Roman Empire the bulk of the urban population seems to have been very poor; probably because of high taxes, high rent, and high prices for food (s. Jones, 38; A.M.H. Jones, *The Greek City*, 269; RAC I, 698–705). ἐπερίσσευσεν aor. ind. act. περισσεύω to abound, to overflow. ἁπλότης generosity, liberality. The basic meaning of the word is "simplicity," "single-mindedness" and indicates the true open-heartedness and generosity toward others in which there is no duplicity of motive (Hughes). ■ παρά w. acc. 3 "beyond." αὐθαίρετος (αὐτός, αἱρέω to choose) voluntarily, of one's own accord; i.e. "spontaneously and voluntarily, out of one's own initiative, without request and without coercion" (Windisch; s. also Plummer). ■ παράκλησις beseeching, urg- 4 ing. δεόμενοι pres. mid. part. to ask, to beg. κοινωνία fellowship, sharing (s. TDNT; for the rabbinical practice of sharing through a collection, s. SB III, 316). ἅγιοι holy ones, saints. A term of honor used for the church in Jerusalem. ■ ἠλπίσαμεν 5 aor. ind. act. ἐλπίζω to hope, to expect. ἔδωκαν aor. ind. act. δίδωμι to give. Not only have they given grace and a proof of fellowship, but they have altogether given their own selves (Bengel). θέλημα θεοῦ. Everywhere in Paul's writings the impulse to faithful service is traced up to God's grace (EGT). ■ εἰς τό 6 w. the inf., used here to introduce results "in such a manner that we have urged" (BD, 207; s. also RG, 1003; IBG, 141). παρακαλέσαι aor. act. inf. παρακαλέω to urge, to beseech, to ask. ἵνα "that." It introduces the content of the request (Barrett). προενήρξατο aor. ind. mid. προενάρχομαι to begin previously. ἐπιτελέσῃ aor. subj. ἐπιτελέω to complete, to bring to the goal. The prep. in compound is perfective (RWP). ■ 7 περισσεύετε pres. ind. act. to abound, to overflow, followed by dat. of reference "to abound in reference to." ἵνα used w. subj. to introduce an imp. (s. BD, 195f.; MT, 94f.; BG, 141f.).

■ ἐπιταγή command. διά w. gen. "through." This gives the 8 motive which justifies the request. γνήσιος genuine, sincere. The primary sense "born in wedlock" is overshadowed by derived application (MM). δοκιμάζων pres. act. part. δοκιμάζω to approve by testing, to accept as proven, to approve (s. BAG). ■ διά w. acc. "because of." ἐπτώχευσεν aor. ind. act. 9 πτωχεύω to be poor, ingressive aor. to become poor, to be reduced to abject poverty. The aor. tense makes it evident that the whole event of the Incarnation is referred to, and is viewed as one act (s. Fred. B. Craddock, "The Poverty of Christ; An

Investigation of II Cor. 8:9," Interp. 22 [April, 1968], 165ff.). πτωχεία poverty, s.v.2. πλουτήσητε aor. subj. πλουτέω to be rich, ingressive aor. to become rich; i.e. w. the heavenly riches of union w. God in Christ and the assurance of eternal life

10 (Plummer). ■ γνώμη opinion, advice. συμφέρει to bring together, to be advantageous, profitable or useable (BAG). οἵτινες "who," "those who." It is used to emphasize persons belonging to a certain class and emphasizes the characteristic quality (s. IBG, 124; BAG). τὸ ποιῆσαι aor. act. inf. The inf. w. the article is used as a noun (s. BD, 205). προενήρξασθε aor. ind. mid., s.v.6. ἀπὸ πέρυσι "last year," "from last year" (RWP). If Paul was writing these words in the autumn of A.D. 57, the Corinthian collection would have been initiated not less than some nine months and up to as much as twenty-one months previously

11 (Hughes). ■ ἐπιτελέσατε aor. imp. act., s.v.6. προθυμία readiness, forwardness, eargerness (s. RWP). τοῦ θέλειν pres. act. inf. The inf. is used as a noun. ἐπιτελέσαι aor. act. inf., s.v.6. ἐκ τοῦ ἔχειν pres. act. inf. used w. prep. "out of the having"; i.e. "according to one's resources," "according to your means" (MT, 144). The construction is probably meant to accent the ability

12 growing "out of" the possession of property (RG, 1074). ■ πρόκειται pres. ind. mid. to be present, to lie before one. καθὸ ἐάν "according to whatever he may have." The amount that a man may have is indefinite, therefore the subj. is used, but his not having is a definite fact therefore the ind. (Plummer; s. also RG, 967). εὐπρόσδεκτος acceptable, well-received. (For the

13 same principle in Judaism, s. SB III, 523.) ■ ἄνεσις relief, s. 2 Cor. 2:13. ἰσότης equality. Used here w. the prep. "according

14 to equality" (s. Hughes; s. also v. 11). ■ περίσσευμα abundance. εἰς for. The expression γίνεσθαι εἰς means "to be extended to" (Hughes). γένηται aor. mid. subj. used w. the parti-

15 cle to express purpose. ■ τὸ πολύ one must supply either "have"; i.e. "the one who has much" (s. RG, 1202), or supply the word "gathered"; i.e. "he who has gathered much." This arises from the context of the quotation from Exod. 16:18 (Hughes). ἐπλεόνασεν aor. ind. act. πλεονάζω to have an abundance, to have more than enough. ἠλαττόνησεν aor. ind. act. ἐλαττονέω to have little, to lack, to not have enough.

16   ■ δόντι aor. act. part. dat. sing. δίδωμι (variant reading διδόντι pres. act. part. dat. sing.). αὐτήν "same"; i.e., the same zeal that I have myself, and have now described (Barrett).

17 σπουδή encouragement, exhortation. ■ ἐδέξατο aor. ind. mid. δέχομαι to receive, to welcome. σπουδαιότερος comp. σπουδαῖος zealous, the elative comp. "very zealous" (BD, 127;

s. also MT, 30). ὑπάρχων pres. act. part. ὑπαρχω to exist, to be. αὐθαίρετος of one's own accord, s.v.3. ἐξῆλθεν aor. ind. act. ἐξέρχομαι to go out, to depart, epistolary aor. which views the action as past at the time the letter is read and refers to Titus' present trip (s. MT, 72f.). πρός to, unto. ■ συνεπέμψαμεν aor. 18 ind. act. συμπέμπω to send together, epistolary aor. "we are now sending" (Barrett). ἔπαινος praise. ἐν "in," "in the matter of." The prep. gives the sphere in which the praise occurs and gives in reality the reason for the praise. ■ χειροτονηθείς aor. 19 pass. part. χειροτονέω to stretch out the hand, to vote by holding up the hand, to elect, to appoint (s. MM). The verb may indicate that the churches elected by voting (Lenski) or it may simply point to the selection and appointment but it does not refer to ordination (Hughes). (For the use of the part. as continuing the construction begun w. the finite verb, s. BD, 245.) συνέκδημος traveling companion, one who goes out w. another. (For a discussion of the identity of the person and his identification as Tychicus, s. Hughes.) διακονουμένη pres. pass. part. διακονέω to minister (s. TDNT). πρός. The prep. can refer either to "the brother appointed to promote the glory" or to "the fund being ministered to promote the glory" (s. Plummer). προθυμία readiness, s.v.11. ■ στελλόμενοι pres. mid. 20 part. στέλλομαι to avoid, to take precautions. Perhaps the word is used here as a nautical metaphor w. the meaning "to furl or shorten the sail, when coming to shore or in order to avoid danger in navigation" (s. Hughes). (For the use of the part. as an example of anacoluthon, s. RG, 431.) μωμήσηται aor. mid. subj. μωμάομαι to blame. The subj. is used to express neg. purpose "lest anyone blame us" (RWP). ἁδρότης that which is thick or bulky, abundant, wealth (Hughes). Here it refers to a large sum of money (Barrett). ■ προνοοῦμεν pres. ind. act. to 21 plan beforehand, to think of beforehand, to care for, to take into consideration. καλός good, that which suits the occasion, that which is fitted to the purpose (s. TDNT). ἐνώπιον in the presence of, before ■ συνεπέμψαμεν aor. ind. act., s.v.18. 22 ἐδοκιμάσαμεν aor. ind. act. δοκιμάζω to approve after testing (s. TDNT; CBB). σπουδαῖος zealous, s.v.17. πολύ n. of the adj. used as an adv. "more." πεποίθησις confidence. εἰς in, into, toward. ■ ὑπέρ for, concerning, about. (For the prep. w. this 23 meaning, s. BD, 121; M, 105.) κοινωνός partner. συνέργος fellow-worker. ἀπόστολος official messenger, envoy. The word was used in Jewish writings to denote the official messenger who brought or delivered the collection (s. SB III, 316f.; s. also CBB; TDNT). δόξα Χριστοῦ "glory of Christ"; i.e., the glory belong-

24 ing to Him or the glory designed for Him. ■ ἔνδειξις demonstration, evidence, proof. καύχησις boasting. ἐνδεικνύμενοι pres. pass. part. ἐνδείκνυμι to demonstrate, to show proof, to give visible proof. εἰς πρόσωπον. A Semitic expression meaning "in the presence of" (Hughes).

Ch. 9

1   ■ περισσός superfluous. τὸ γράφειν pres. act. inf. w. the article. The inf. explains that which is superfluous and the article indicates that chapters 8 and 9 belong together. The pres. tense points to the act of writing, "it is superfluous for me to go on

2 writing to you like this" (Barrett). ■ προθυμία readiness (s. 2 Cor. 8:11). καυχῶμαι pres. ind. mid. to boast, to glory. The pres. tense emphasizes Paul's continual boasting on their behalf (s. Plummer). παρέσκεύασται perf. ind. pass. παρασκευάζω to prepare, to make preparations, to make ready. The perf. emphasizes the past completed action w. the pres. continuing state; i.e., "stands prepared" (RWP). ἀπὸ πέρυσι "last year" (s. 2 Cor. 8:10). ζῆλος zeal. ἠρέθισεν aor. ind. act. ἐρεθίζω to stir up, to stimulate, to excite. πλείονες comp. "the majority" (s. 2

3 Cor. 2:6). ■ ἔπεμψα aor. ind. act. epistolary aor. "I am sending." ἀδέλφους "the brothers." The article indicates those who were previously mentioned. τὸ ὑπὲρ ὑμῶν. The article is repeated here in order to avoid misunderstanding (BD, 141). κενωθῇ aor. pass. subj. κενόω to empty, to make void, effective use of the aor. "to be proven empty" (Barrett; s. also DM, 196f.). καθὼς ἔλεγον impf. ind. act. The impf. emphasizes the repeated action "just as I repeatedly said" (Plummer). παρεσκευασμένοι perf. pass. part., s.v.2. The part. is used w. the subj. of the verb to be to express the perf. pass. subj. in a final clause "that you may

4 really be prepared" (RWP). ■ ἔλθωσιν aor. subj. ἔρχομαι. εὕρωσιν aor. subj. εὑρίσκω. ἀπαρασκευάστους unprepared. καταισχυνθῶμεν aor. pass. subj. καταισχύνω to put to shame, pass. to be put to shame. ὑπόστασις basis, foundation, support, ground of hope or confidence, assurance (Hughes;

5 s. also Heb. 11:1). ■ ἀναγκαῖος necessary, compelling. ἡγησάμην aor. ind. mid. ἡγέομαι to consider. παρακαλέσαι aor. act. inf. παρακαλέω to ask, to urge, to encourage. προέλθωσιν aor. act. subj. προέρχομαι to go ahead, to go before. προκαταρτίσωσιν aor. act. subj. προκαταρτίζω to arrange beforehand, to organize beforehand. προεπηγγελμένην perf. pass. part. προεπαγγέλλω to promise before. The perf. part. emphasizes the continuing state; i.e., "that which was promised before and the promise remains val-

id." ἕτοιμος ready. Used w. the inf. to express purpose.
πλεονεξία selfishness, greed. The word indicates the greedy,
grasping for more at the expense of others (s. NTW, 97–99; CBB;
TDNT). The idea here is "ready as a gift and not as something
wrung from you" (Barrett).

■ σπείρων pres. act. part. σπείρω to sow, to sow seed. 6
φειδομένως. An adv. developed from a part. from φείδομαι to
spare, to be miserly, adv. sparingly, "in a miserly manner"
(BAG; Hughes). θερίσει fut. ind. act. θερίζω to reap, to gather
a harvest. ἐπὶ εὐλογίας. The prep. has an adverbial force and
the noun means a gift freely and spontaneously bestowed and
thus constituting a blessing to the recipient. The total phrase is
used as an adv. w. the meaning "generously," "bountifully"
(Hughes). ■ προῄρηται aor. mid. subj. προαιρέω mid. to deter- 7
mine beforehand, to decide. The word refers to the deliberate
choosing (Plummer). ἀνάγκη necessity, compulsion. ἱλαρός
cheerful. δότης one who gives, giver. Paul evidently alludes to
Prov. 22:9. ■ δυνατεῖ pres. ind. act. δυνατέω to make able, to 8
enable, to be able. The pres. tense emphasizes the continual
ability of God. περισσεῦσαι aor. act. inf. περισσεύω to
abound, to have more than enough, to overflow. αὐτάρκεια
sufficiency, self-sufficiency. The word indicates being independent of external circumstances, especially of the services of other
people (Plummer). (For the use of the word in the ancient world
both among the Stoic philosophers and also the common people,
s. Windisch; Barrett; TDNT; MM.) περισσεύητε pres. subj.
Subjunctive used to express purpose. πᾶν ἔργον "every good
work." The meaning here is that the less a man requires for
himself, the greater means he will have for relieving the wants
of others (Plummer). ■ ἐσκόρπισεν aor. ind. act. σκορπίζω to 9
scatter, to disperse, to distribute. ἔδωκεν aor. ind. act. δίδωμι
to give, gnomic aor. used in a proverb-like expression (Barrett).
πένης poor. The word describes the man for whom life and
living is a struggle, the man who is the reverse of the man who
lives in affluence (NTW, 110). ■ ἐπιχορηγῶν pres. act. part. 10
ἐπιχωρέω to supply, to furnish, to provide. βρῶσις eating.
χορηγήσει fut. ind. act. χορηγέω "to lead chorus," "to supply
the chorus" for a drama. A service which cost the persons who
undertook it a large outlay; "to supply anything plentifully"
(Plummer). πληθυνεῖ fut. πληθύνω increase, to multiply.
αὐξήσει fut. αὐξάνω increase, to cause to grow. γένημα produce, the yield of a harvest, particularly the fruit or juice of the
grape vine (Hughes). δικαιοσύνη righteousness, perhaps in the
sense of "almsgiving," "benevolence" (SB III, 525; MRT, 161)

or it is used to connote righteousness of life of which charity is
11 an expression (GW, 154). ■ πλουτιζόμενοι pres. pass. part.
πλουτίζω to make rich, to enrich. (For the construction w. the
part., s. BD, 245f.) ἁπλότης liberality (s. 2 Cor. 8:2).
κατεργάζεται pres. ind. mid. to produce. εὐχαριστία thanks-
12 giving. ■ διακονία ministry, service. The meaning here is
"ministration," "execution" (Barrett). λειτουργία ministry,
service. In classical Gr. the word was used of wealthy citizens
who rendered to the public service in financing choruses for
dramas. In Jewish in koine usage it indicated religious service or
freewill service (s. Plummer; MM; TDNT; Lietzmann).
προσαναπληροῦσα   pres.   act.   part.   fem   sing.
προσαναπληρόω to fill, to fill up. The prep. in compound
means "to fill up by adding to" (RWP). ὑστέρημα that which
lacks, deficiency, shortcoming, need, want. περισσεύουσα
pres. act. part. fem. sing., περισσεύω s.v.8. The collection has
a twofold effect: it fills up what is lacking to their poorer brethren
of the necessities of life as well as causing an overflow of praise
13 and gratitude to God (Hughes). ■ δοκιμή approval, proven, that
which has been tested and approved (s. 2 Cor. 2:9). δοξάζοντες
pres. act. part. δοξάζω to glorify, to cause one to think well of
someone. (For the construction of the part., s.v.13.) ὑποταγή
obedience, subordination of one's self. ὁμολογία confession.
The word is used specifically to introduce or express a conviction; i.e., the obj. *confession* which especially has reference to
"confessing Christ or the teaching of His church" (ECC, 17).
ἁπλότης liberality. The word indicates singleness of purpose
leading to liberality in giving to others (Hughes). κοιωνία fellowship. Here it is used in the sense of "participation in the
14 collection" (Barrett; s. also 2 Cor. 8:4). ■ δέησις request, petition. The word implies special petition for the supply of wants
(Plummer; s. also Trench; *Synonyms*, 189). The dat. indicates
accompanying circumstances; i.e., the intercession accompanies
their longing (Plummer). ἐπιποθούντων pres. act. part.
ἐπιποθέω to long for someone, to earnestly desire (s. Hering).
The part. is used in a gen. abs. (RWP). ὑπερβάλλουσα pres.
act. part. ὑπερβάλλω to throw beyond, to surpass. Here it refers
15 to the surpassing grace or generosity (Barrett). ■ ἀνεκδιήγητος
verbal adj. indescribable, not able to recount or to describe or to
set forth in detail (Lenski). God's exquisite working cannot be
fully described w. human words (Windisch). (For the neg. prefix,
s. Moorhouse, 47ff.) δωρέα gift, that which is freely given.

Ch. 10

■ αὐτὸς δὲ ἐγώ "now I myself." Paul is now calling atten- 1
tion to a specially personal matter (EGT). (For a defense of the
authenticity of chapters 10 through 13, s. Hughes.) πραΰτης
meekness. It denotes the humble and gentle attitude which expresses itself in particular in a patient submissiveness to offense,
free from malice and desire for revenge (R. Leivestad, "The
Meekness and Gentleness of Christ, II Cor. 10:1," NTS, 12
[January, 1966], 159; s. also NTW, 103f.; TDNT; Windisch).
ἐπιείκεια fitting, suitable, reasonable, fair. When applied to
authorities it denotes indulgence, equity, lenience. It also
denotes a humble, patient steadfastness, which is able to submit
to injustice, disgrace, and maltreatment without hatred and malice, trusting in God in spite of it all (Leivestad, 157, 158; s. also
TDNT; Trench; Synonyms, 153-157; NTW, 38f.). These words
indicate that Paul knew of the historical Jesus and refers to His
character (s. JNP, 108f.). κατὰ πρόσωπον "face to face," "present in person" (s. Hughes). ταπεινός low, humble. Used here
in the bad sense meaning "downcast" and expresses depression
when it is the effect of the want of courage (Hodge). θαρρέω
pres. ind. act. to be confident, to be courageous. ■ δέομαι to ask, 2
to beg. θαρρῆσαι aor. act. inf. The article is used w. the inf. and
the neg. expressing the direct object of the verb (s. RWP; BD,
105). The aor. inf. is the ingressive aor. "to become courageous."
παρών pres. part. πάρειμι to be present, adverbial use of the
inf. "when I am present." πεποίθησις having been persuaded,
confidence. ᾗ rel. pron. dat. sing. instrumental use "with which,"
"by which." λογίζομαι to judge, to reckon, to think. τολμῆσαι
aor. act. inf. τολμάω to be bold, to dare. κατὰ σάρκα "according to flesh"; i.e., according to fleshly principles.
περιπατοῦντας pres. act. part. περιπατέω to walk, to walk
about, to conduct one's life. ■ ἐν σαρκί "in the flesh"; i.e., in 3
the element of flesh, living his life, like every other man, subject
to the laws and limitations which are common to human flesh
(Hughes). (For Paul's style of using the same word or word stem
in close proximity, s. BD, 258.) ■ ὅπλα (pl.) weapons, instru- 4
ments of warfare. A general word used for both defensive and
offensive weapons (s. TDNT; Windisch). (For a brief description
of the weapons of the Roman army, s. ELR, 106; OCD, 121f.)
σαρκικός fleshly, pertaining to the flesh. The ending of the
word indicates "like the flesh" (s. MH, 378). δυνατός powerful.
θεῷ dat. The dat. indicates either personal interest "to or for
God"; i.e., employed on God's behalf (Barrett; BG, 20) or it may
be viewed as an intensive dat. corresponding to the Hebraic

485

construction indicating a superl. force; i.e., "divinely powerful" (s. Hughes; IBG, 184; MH, 443). καθαίρεσις tearing down, pulling down, destroying. ὀχύρωμα stronghold, fortress. In the papyri the word also had the meaning "prison" (MM). Paul may have had Prov. 21:22 in mind (Hughes). λογισμός calculation, reasoning, reflection, thought (BAG). καθαιροῦντες pres. act.
5 part. to tear down, to destroy. ■ ὕψωμα that which is lifted up, high, exalted. ἐπαιρόμενον pres. mid. part. ἐπαίρω to lift up, mid. to exalt one's self. The metaphor here is from walls and towers standing defiantly and the verb may be pass.; i.e., "erected" (Plummer). αἰχμαλωτίζοντες pres. act. part. αἰχμαλωτίζω to take one captive w. a spear, to bring into captivity, to bring into subjection. The pres. tense points to the continual struggle and warfare. νόημα thought, purpose, design (s. 2 Cor. 3:14). ὑπακοή obedience. τοῦ Χριστοῦ obj. gen.
6 "obedience to Christ." ■ ἕτοιμος ready. Used w. ἔχοντες pres. act. part. w. the meaning "to be ready," "to be prepared." ἐκδικῆσαι aor. act. inf. ἐκδικέω to punish, to avenge (s. BAG; TDNT). παρακοή disobedience. ὅταν used w. subj. "when," "whenever." πληρωθῇ aor. pass. subj. πληρόω to fill, pass. to be filled, the effective aor. "to reach completion" (Barrett).

7   ■ κατὰ πρόσωπον "according to the face"; i.e., "before your face." βλέπετε pres. ind. act. or better pres. act. imp. βλέπω "look at what is before your eyes," "face the obvious facts" (Hughes). εἴ τις used w. ind. to introduce a condition which is assumed to be true "if anyone." πέποιθα perf. ind. act. w. a pres. meaning to have confidence, to have been persuaded, to trust. ἑαυτῷ dat. of reflex. pron.; i.e., 'to have confidence or trust in one's self." Χριστοῦ εἶναι pred. gen. used w. the inf. in indirect discourse "confidence that he belongs to Christ" (s. RWP). λογιζέσθω pres. mid. imp. λογίζομαι to think, to consider, to reckon. ἑαυτοῦ "for himself," let him then consider once more for himself (Meyer). (For a study of Paul's opponents at Corinth, s. Hughes; C.K. Barrett, "Paul's Opponents in Sec-
8 ond Corinthians," NTS, 17 [April, 1971], 233–254.) ■ ἐάν τε γάρ "for if." (For the use of the particles here, s. Thrall, 96; BD, 229f.; Barrett.) περισσότερον comp. περισσόν abundant, comp. "somewhat more abundantly." καυχήσωμαι aor. mid. subj. καυχάομαι to boast, to glory. ἐξουσία authority. ἧς rel. pron. gen. sing. gen. by attraction. ἔδωκεν aor. ind. act. δίδωμι. οἰκοδομή building up, edification. καθαίρεσις tearing down, s.v.4. (cf. Jer. 1:10). αἰσχυνθήσομαι fut. ind. pass. αἰσχύνω
9 to put to shame, pass. to be put to shame. ■ δόξω aor. act. subj. δοκέω to appear, to seem to be. ὡσάν = ὡς ἄν "as it were" (M,

167). ἐκφοβεῖν pres. act. inf. ἐκφοβέω to terrify, to frighten, to distraction. The prep. in compound is intensive (Hughes). ■ ὅτι 10 equivalent to quotation marks introducing a direct quotation. φησίν pres. ind. act. 3rd sing. φημί to say; i.e., "one says." It may be however that Paul is quoting a particular person (Barrett). βαρύς heavy, weighty. παρουσία presence. Followed by the gen. τοῦ σώματος it emphasizes the external presence; i.e., the visible and tangible presence in the physical body (s. SBT, 48). ἀσθενής weak. ἐξουθενημένος perf. pass. part. ἐξουθενέω to despise, to consider one of no account. The perf. emphasizes the state or condition; i.e., "despised," "counted as nothing." ■ λογιζέσθω pres. mid. imp. 3rd sing., s.v.7. οἷος such a one. 11 τοιοῦτος "what sort of." The pron. is qualitive (RWP). παρόντες pres. act. part. s.v.2.

■ τολμῶμεν pres. ind. act. τολμάω to be bold, to dare, 12 s.v.2. ἐγκρῖναι aor. act. inf. ἐγκρίνω to judge among, to class or categorize. συγκρῖναι aor. act. inf. συνκρίνω to judge together, to compare. συνιστανόντων pres. act. part. συνίστημι to commend, to recommend (s. 2 Cor. 3:1). αὐτοί "they themselves." μετροῦντες pres. act. part. μετρέω to measure. The part. is used in the role of a pred. "they do not realize that they are measuring themselves by their own standards" (MT, 160). συνιᾶσιν pres. ind. act. συνίημι to understand, to comprehend, to realize. ■ ἄμετρος unmeasured, immeasurable. 13 The phrase here means "we shall not boast excessively" (Barrett; s. also IBG, 71). καυχησόμεθα aor. mid. subj., s.v.8. μέτρον measure. κανών, όνος rule, measuring rod, the fixed bounds of a territory (s. TDNT; Plummer). It may be that Paul has in mind the marked out lanes as used by runners in athletic contests (Hughes). οὗ rel. pron. gen. sing. gen. by attraction (s. RG, 719). The repetition of μέτρον in the gen. may be due to attraction and the word may be considered as in apposition to the rel. pron. (Hughes). ἐμέρισεν aor. ind. act. μερίζω to measure out, to distribute, to deal out, to assign. ἐφικέσθαι aor. mid. inf. ἐφικνέομαι to reach, to come to. The inf. is used to express result (Windisch). ἄχρι w. the gen. unto, as far as. ■ 14 ἐφικνούμενοι pres. mid. part. ὑπερεκτείνομεν pres. ind. act. to stretch out beyond, to overstretch, "we are not overextending ourselves beyond the limits set by God" (BAG). ἐφθάσαμεν aor. ind. act. φθάνω to arrive first, to come before others, to precede (s. Hughes). ἐν τῷ εὐαγγελίῳ "in the gospel"; i.e., in preaching the gospel as its ministers and envoys (Barrett). ■ 15 ἄμετρον without measure, s.v.13. καυχώμενοι pres. mid. part., s.v.8. ἀλλότριος another, belonging to another (RWP). κόπος

work. αὐξανομένης pres. pass. part. αὐξάνω to cause to grow, pass. to grow, to increase gen. abs. "as your faith increases" (Barrett). μεγαλυνθῆναι aor. pass. inf. μεγαλύνω to make large, to magnify, to enlarge. The inf. is used in indirect discourse, explaining what the "hope" is (RWP). κανών s.v.13. εἰς περισσείαν "unto abundance"; i.e., "in the highest degree possible" (Lietzmann). Paul expected a brilliant and glorious tri-
16 umph in Corinth (Windisch). ■ ὑπερέκεινα beyond; i.e., "the lands that lie beyond you" (BAG; s. also RG, 297). εὐαγγελίσασθαι aor. mid. inf. εὐαγγελίζομαι to proclaim the good news, to preach the gospel, to evangelize. ἕτοιμος ready, prepared, s.v.6. καυχήσασθαι aor. mid. inf., s.v.8. The idea is "without boasting of work already done in another's field" (s.
17/18 Hughes). ■ καυχάσθω aor. mid. imp., s.v.8. ■ συνιστάνων pres. act. part., s.v.12. δόκιμος approved, approved after a test.

Ch. 11
1 ■ ὄφελον "oh that," "would that" (BAG; for the form, s. RG, 1003; BD, 37). The word has become a particle w. the impf. or aor. ind. used to express an unattainable wish (BD, 181). ἀνείχεσθε impf. ind. mid. ἀνέχω to endure, to put up w. μου "w. me" gen. following the verb. μικρόν τι a little, adv. acc.; i.e., acc. of general reference "in reference to a little foolishness" (RG, 486). ἀφροσύνη lack of sense, foolishness. ἀλλὰ καί "but indeed." ἀνέχεσθε pres. ind. act. or pres. act. imp. The ind. appears to be better "but indeed you do already bear w. me"
2 (Hughes). ■ ζηλόω pres. ind. act. to be jealous. ζῆλος jealously. The word is taken up in a metaphor drawn from marriage (Barrett). ἡρμοσάμην aor. ind. mid. ἁρμόζω to fit together, to join, to harmonize, to give in marriage, to betroth (BAG). The mid. is probably used purposely to bring out the apostle's personal interest (MM). ἑνὶ ἀνδρί "to one man." The emphasis is on the fact that there is one person, and only one, to whom the Corinthians owe their allegiance (Barrett). παρθένος virgin. ἁγνός pure, chaste, undefiled. παραστῆσαι aor. act. inf. παρίστημι
3 to present, inf. used to express purpose. ■ φοβέομαι to fear, to be afraid. μή followed by the subj. "lest by any means" (RWP). ὄφις snake. ἐξηπάτησεν aor. ind. act. ἐξαπατάω to deceive. The prep. in compound is perfective "to completely deceive" (s. 1 Tim. 2:14). πανουργία craftiness (s. 2 Cor. 4:2). φθαρῇ aor. pass. subj. φθείρω to corrupt. νόημα thought, purpose, design.
4 ἁπλότης simplicity, sincerity. ἁγνότης purity. ■ εἰ w. the ind. introduces a condition which is assumed to be true. ἐρχόμενος pres. mid. part. ἐκηρύξαμεν aor. ind. act. κηρύσσω to pro-

claim, to proclaim as a herald (s. TDNT; CBB). ἐλάβετε aor. ind. act. λαμβάνω. ἐδέξασθε aor. ind. mid. δέχομαι to receive, to welcome. ἀνέχεσθε pres. ind. mid., s.v.1. ■ λογίζομαι to 5 consider, to judge, to reckon. μηδέν = οὐδέν acc., acc. of reference; i.e., "in reference to nothing," "in no way at all" (Barrett). ὑστερηκέναι perf. act. inf. ὑστερέω to come behind, to lack. ὑπερλίαν exceedingly, beyond measure, super. Paul's description is vibrant w. sarcasm "extra-super-apostles" (Hughes). ■ εἰ δὲ καί "but even if." ἰδιώτης a private person, 6 distinction to one who holds an office or to one who has special ability or knowledge, a layman, one who is unskilled (s. TDNT; Barrett; RWP). The word is followed by the dat. of reference. ἀλλ᾽ οὐ τῇ γνώσει "but not really in knowledge." ἐν παντί "in every respect." φανερώσαντες aor. act. part. φανερόω to make clear, to manifest.

■ ἤ "or." ταπεινῶν pres. act. part. ταπεινόω to make low, 7 to bring low, to make humble. ὑψωθῆτε aor. pass. subj. ὑψόω to lift up, to exalt. The subj. is used to express purpose. ὅτι because. δωρεάν adv. "freely," "without charge," emphatic juxtaposition; "God's gospel," that most precious thing—for nothing!" (Plummer). εὐηγγελισάμην aor. ind. mid. εὐαγγελίζω to proclaim good news, to preach the gospel, to evangelize (s. TDNT; CBB). ■ ἄλλος "other"; i.e., in distinction to the churches in 8 Corinth. ἐσύλησα aor. ind. act. συλάω to plunder. The word was used either for the robbing of temples or for the plundering of soldiers (s. Hughes; Barrett). λαβών aor. act. part. λαμβάνω. ὀψώνιον wages, pay. ὑμῶν διακονίαν (s. Rom. 6:23). ■ παρών 9 pres. part. πάρειμι to be present. ὑστερηθείς aor. pass. part., s.v.5. κατενάρκησα aor. ind. act. καταναρκάω to make or become numb, to be a burden. A noun based on the simplex of the verb was used for an electric eel which numbed its victims by an electric shock (s. Lenski; LS). The prep. in compound is perfective (s. MH, 316). ὑστέρημα need, lack, want. προσανεπλήρωσαν aor. ind. act. προσαναπληρόω to fill up, to fill up in addition. The prep. in compound signifies the adding of something and may indicate that the gift from Macedonia supplemented the amount which Paul earned (Hughes). ἀβαρής free from weight, not burdensome. ἐτήρησα aor. ind. act. τηρέω to guard, to keep. The aor. summarizes the past ministry of Paul. τηρήσω fut. ind. act. ■ ἔστιν. The verb is emphatic by 10 its position in the sentence. ἀλήθεια Χριστοῦ "the truth of Christ." The expression here reveals the intensity of Paul's feelings and is to be taken as a solemn assertion (Bruce). (See also IBG, 112.) καύχησις boasting. φραγήσεται fut. ind. pass.

φράσσω to fence in, to stop, to block in. The figure may be that of blocking or barricading a road or damming a river but in each case the central idea is that of blockage (Hughes; RWP). κλίμα

11 province, district, region (s. BAG). ■ διὰ τί "why?" οἶδα defective perf. w. the pres. meaning "to know." (For this word, s. ND, 344-356.)

12 ■ ποιήσω fut. ind. act. ἐκκόψω aor. act. subj. ἐκκόπτω to cut off, subj. used to express purpose. ἀφορμή opportunity, base of operation (s. 2 Cor. 5:12). θελόντων pres. act. part. θέλω to wish, to desire, to want to. καυχῶνται pres. ind. mid. to boast, to glory. εὑρεθῶσιν aor. pass. subj. εὑρίσκω to find, pass. to be

13 found. ■ τοιοῦτοι such ones. ψευδαπόστολοι false apostles, pseudo-apostles. ἐργάτης one who works. δόλιος deceitful, tricky, cunning, treacherous. The basic meaning of the word is "bait for fish" then "any cunning contrivance for deceiving or catching" (s. LS). μετασχηματίζεται pres. ind. mid. to transform one's outward appearance, to disguise (s. Barrett; TDNT; s. also 1 Cor. 4:6). The pres. tense points to that which Satan

14 habitually does (Plummer). ■ θαῦμα wonder, marvel. ἄγγελος φωτός angel of light. The term may have been used to indicate

15 "a messenger of God" (s. Lietzmann; Schlatter). ■ διάκονοι αὐτοῦ "his ministers" obj. gen. i.e. "those who serve Satan." ἔσται fut. εἰμί.

16 ■ μή used w. aor. subj. in a neg. prohibition (s. RG, 933). δόξῃ aor. act. subj. δοκέω to suppose, to think. The prohibitive aor. subj. could be used to prevent an action from arising without involving the notion "immediately" (MKG, 273). The aor. tense implies that no one did (s. RG, 853). ἄφρων fool, one who does not think. εἶναι inf. used in indirect discourse. εἰ δὲ μή γε "and even if," "otherwise" (s. Barrett; BD, 191, 226). δέξασθε aor. mid. imp. δέχομαι to accept, to receive, to welcome. κἀγώ = καὶ ἐγώ "I also," "I too." μικρόν τι s. 2 Cor. 11:1. καυχήσωμαι aor. mid. subj., s.v.12, subj. used to express pur-

17 pose. ■ κατά w. the acc. "according to," "according to the standard." Paul is not claiming to be uninspired but the expression means "in accordance w. the character or example of Christ" (Hughes). ὑπόστασις basis, confidence, followed by the descriptive or adjectival gen. "boastful confidence" (Barrett;

18 for this word, s. also Heb. 11:1). ■ καυχήσομαι fut. ind. mid.,

19 s.v.12. ■ ἡδέως adv. ἡδύς glad, adv. gladly, joyously. Paul is using irony of the sharpest kind (BD, 262). ἀνέχεσθε pres. ind. mid. to endure, to bear w. someone, followed by the gen. (s.v.1.). φρόνιμος wise, understanding. ὄντες pres. part. εἰμί. The part. could be concessive "although" or causal "because you are sensi-

ble." ■ καταδουλοῖ pres. ind. act. to enslave. Used in a condi- 20
tional clause which assumes the reality of the condition.
κατεσθίω to eat up, to devour. The prep. in compound is perfective. The reference may be to one who takes advantage of the
privilege of receiving maintenance, "if anyone eats you out of
house and home" (Barrett). λαμβάνει pres. ind. act. to take, to
receive, i.e. "catch you" as birds in a snare, or fish w. bait
(Plummer). ἐπαίρεται pres. ind. mid. to lift one's self up, to
exalt one's self. The exaltation is essentially self-exaltation, carnal, and worldly in character (Hughes). δέρει pres. ind. act. to
skin, to strike. The reference may be to physical violence or it
may be used to express verbal affronts (s. Windisch; Hughes).
The pres. tenses of the verb here may be explained as conative
or tendential and picture an action which is an attempt and
represents the idea of that which is intended, that which tends
toward realization (s. DM, 186; BD, 167; RG, 880). The prep.
used w. the verb "strike" often directs to a part of the body to,
or on, which an act is done (MT, 256). ■ κατὰ ἀτιμίαν "ac- 21
cording to dishonor." Here Paul used intense irony (RWP). ὡς
ὅτι "as that," i.e. "as people have been saying, that" (Hughes).
ἠσθενήκαμεν perf. ind. act. ἀσθενέω to be weak, to be powerless. The charge here may be of weakness caused by fear or
caution (BAG). ἐν ᾧ "in whatever." In whatever matter any
person exhibits real courage, the apostle does not fear comparison (Plummer). κἀγώ = καὶ ἐγώ "I also," "I too." The personal
pron. is strongly emphasized. ■ Ἑβραῖοι "Hebrews." The term 22
emphasizes the pure-blooded Jew and sometimes it can emphasize a Hebrew-speaking Jew or a Jew of Palestine (s. TDNT;
Lietzmann; Windisch; Barrett). Ἰσραηλίτης "Israelite." The
term emphasizes the social and religious character as well as the
national promises and blessings from God (s. Windisch; TDNT).
σπέρμα seed, descendant. The emphasis here may be from a
theological point of view (Barrett), particularly emphasizing the
promises made by God (Windisch). ■ διάκονοι Χριστοῦ "min- 23
isters of Christ." The gen. is obj. gen.; i.e., those who minister
or serve Christ. παραφρονῶν pres. act. part. to be beside one's
self, to be mentally deranged, "I am talking like a mad man" (s.
MM). ὑπέρ over, beyond. Here used as an adv. "more," "to a
higher degree, better" (BD, 121; s. also MT, 250). κόπος work,
toil. The word emphasizes the weariness which follows on the
straining of all of his powers to the utmost (Trench; *Synonyms*,
378). περισσοτέρως adv. comp. of περισσός abundant. Used
here in the superl. sense as elative "very abundantly." It may
mean "more abundantly than most men" or "than you would

believe" (Plummer). φυλακή prison, guarding. Places of confinement both public and private were used during the investigation as the accused awaited his trial. Most of the prisons were dark w. very little room, no sanitary facilities and inadequate food. (For prisons in the ancient world, s. RAC IX, 318–345; DGRA, 240f.; KP I, 1053, 1496; OCD, 879, 1099; TDNT.) πληγή strike, blow, wound, or bruise as the result of a blow (s. BAG). ὑπερβαλλόντως adv. built from the part. beyond measure, very exceedingly. θάνατοι pl. "deaths," i.e. "situations in which I was in danger of death" (Barrett). πολλάκις often.

24 ■ πεντάκις five times. τεσσεράκοντα forty. παρὰ μίαν "except one." This was the Jewish method of punishment based on Deut. 25:2f. The person had his two hands bound to a pillow on either side and his garments were removed so that his chest was bare. With a whip made of a strap of calf hide and two other straps of donkey hide connected to a long hand piece, the person received one-third of the thirty-nine stripes in front and two-thirds behind while he was bending low. During this time the reader reads over and again Deut. 28:58 (s. M Makkoth; SB III,

25 527–530). ■ τρίς three times. ἐρραβδίσθην aor. ind. pass. ῥαβδίζω to beat w. rods. This refers to the Roman method of beating or punishment which was often used as police coercion (s. Acts 16:22; TDNT; RAC IX, 469–490). In Paul's case it was probably a punishment prescribed by city magistrates (BAG). ἅπαξ once, one time. ἐλιθάσθην aor. ind. pass. λιθάζω to stone (s. Acts 14:19). ἐναυάγησα aor. ind. act. ναυαγέω to suffer shipwreck. (For the possible voyages during which Paul may have been involved in shipwrecks, s. Hughes.) νυχθήμερον "night-day." This refers to the Heb. custom of reckoning the day of 24 hours from evening to evening. The word may be viewed as adverbial or as the direct object of the verb (Hughes). βυθός deep. πεποίηκα perf. ind. act. The perf. shows that the dreadful experience is vividly before the apostle's mind, and possibly indicates that the occurence was recent (Plummer; s. also M,

26 144). ■ ὁδοιπορία walking journey, journey. κίνδυνος danger. The following gens. tell where the danger comes from. ποταμός river. The rivers were sometimes difficult to cross, some changed in a moment from half-dry riverbeds to rushing torrents (Barrett). λῃστής robber, bandit, one who uses weapons and violence in robbing others. (For a good description of bandits and robbers in the ancient world, s. Martin Hengel, *Die Zeloten* [Leiden: E.J. Brill, 1976] 25–47; TDNT.) γένος generation, contemporary, those descendant from a common ancestor (BAG). Here it refers to the Jews. ἐρημία desert, an isolated place.

ψευδάδελφος false brother. ■ κόπος work, s.v.23. μόχθος toil, 27
labor. The word is active indicating struggle and toil (Plummer).
ἀγρυπνία wakefulness. It refers evidently to the sleepless nights
Paul spent in work and ministry (Windisch). λιμός hunger.
δίψος thirst. νηστεία fasting. The word refers to the foregoing
of meals in order that Paul's work as a minister of Christ might
not be interrupted (Hughes). ψῦχος cold. γυμνότης nakedness.
Perhaps the last two descriptions recall when Paul was thrown
into prison, or drenched by rain, or stripped by brigands (Plummer). ■ χωρίς apart, besides. παρεκτός external, i.e. the out- 28
ward suffering or it may imply an exception, i.e., "apart from the
things that I have not mentioned" (s. Hughes). ἐπίστασις pressure, stress. The word here probably refers to the "daily pressure
of responsibility" (Hughes). μέριμνα concern, care. ■ ἀσθενέω 29
to be weak, s.v.21. σκανδαλίζεται pres. ind. pass. to cause to
stumble. The word means rather "to catch in a death trap," pass.
"to be caught." It refers to the moral offense that kills spiritually
(s. Lenski). πυροῦμαι pres. ind. pass. to set on fire, to enflame.
When a brother stumbles, Paul is set on fire w. grief (RWP).

■ καυχᾶσθαι pres. mid. inf. καυχάομαι to boast, to glory. 30
τὰ τῆς ἀσθενείας "things belonging to my weakness."
καυχήσομαι fut. ind. mid. ■ εὐλογητός blessed (s. 2 Cor. 1:3). 31
ψεύδομαι to lie. ■ ἐθνάρχης ethnarch. (For a discussion of 32
aretas in this passage, s. Hughes.) ἐφρούρει impf. ind. act.
φρουρέω to watch, to guard, to guard by posting sentries. The
impf. pictures the continual action in the past πιάσαι aor. act.
inf. πιάζω to seize, to arrest. The inf. is used to express purpose
(Barrett). Perhaps Paul escaped from Damascus in A.D. 37 which
would make his conversion around A.D. 34 (s. Hughes; Windisch). ■ θυρίς window. A small opening in the wall is still 33
shown as the "little door" through which St. Paul was let down
(Plummer). σαργάνη basket, rope basket. ἐχαλάσθην aor. ind.
pass. χαλάω to let down. διά through. τεῖχος wall. ἐξέφυγον
aor. ind. act. ἐκφεύγω to escape. The prep. in compound is
perfective indicating that the escape was successful.

Ch. 12

■ καυχᾶσθαι pres. mid. inf. δεῖ it is necessary. συμφέρον 1
pres. act. part. συμφέρω expedient. In Paul's usage the word
points to the welfare not of the individual but of the Christian
society (Barrett). The part. is used as an acc. abs. (s. RG, 1130).
ἐλεύσομαι fut. ind. mid. ἔρχομαι to come. ὀπτασία vision.
ἀποκάλυψις unveiling, revelation. κυρίου. The gen. could be
subj. gen., i.e. "visions and revelations from the Lord" (Barrett)

or it could be the obj. gen., i.e. visions and revelations which
2 have the Lord as their object (Hughes). ■ ἄνθρωπος man. It was
part of rabbinic style to substitute an impersonal word, e.g.,
"man" for the 1st and 2nd person when one talked of himself (SB
III, 530f.). ἔτος year. δεκατέσσαρες fourteen. ἐκτός w. gen.
"out of." The possibility of separability of the inner man from the
body is presented in this verse (s. SBT, 146f.). ἁρπαγέντα aor.
pass. part. ἁρπάζω to seize, to snatch, to take by force, to catch
up. (For various parallels to Paul's experience, s. Barrett; Windisch.) τρίτου οὐρανοῦ "the third heaven." Perhaps the expression means into the highest heaven where the presence of
God is. Paul was granted the sight of the glory that lies ahead
and was thereby fortified to enter patiently all the suffering
4 which awaited him (s. Hughes; SB V, 531f.). ■ ἡρπάγη aor. ind.
pass., s.v.2. παράδεισος paradise. The word refers to a blissful
abode within the very courts of heaven itself (s. Hughes; Luke
23:43). ἤκουσεν aor. ind. act. ἀκούω. ἄρρητος verbal adj. "un-
speakable," "unutterable." The word was often used of divine
secrets which were not intended for human beings (s. Windisch;
Barrett). ῥῆμα word. ἐξόν pres. part. n. sing. ἔξεστιν "it is
allowed." The word is to be taken in connection w. ἀνθρώπῳ,
5 i.e., "which it is not lawful for a man to speak" (Plummer). ■
ὑπέρ on behalf of, for the benefit of. καυχήσομαι fut. ind. mid.
6 καυχάομαι to glory. εἰ μή except. ἀσθένεια weakness. ■ ἐάν.
Used to introduce a conditional clause in which the condition is
considered to be probable. θελήσω aor. act. subj. θέλω to wish,
to will, to choose. The verb properly carries w. it an element of
deliberate preference (Barrett). ἔσομαι fut. εἰμί. ἄφρων foolish, senseless, without reason. It expresses a want of mental
sanity and sobriety, a reckless and inconsiderate habit of mind
(AS). ἐρῶ fut. ind. act. λέγω. φείδομαι pres. ind. mid. to spare,
to refrain from doing something. The inf. as object is to be
supplied, i.e. "refrain from boasting" (BAG). The pres. tense
could be taken as conative "but I am trying to spare you" (Barrett). εἰς ἐμέ "unto me." Used w. the verb in the sense "to
reckon to my account." The expression occurs often in commercial language (s. Lietzmann). λογίσηται aor. mid. subj.
λογίζομαι to reckon, to put to one's account. ὑπέρ beyond,
7 more than. ἐξ ἐμοῦ "from me." ■ ὑπερβολή excess, extraordinary quality or character, instrumental dat. ὑπεραίρωμαι pres.
mid. subj. ὑπεραίρω to lift up beyond, mid. to lift one's self up
beyond, to exalt one's self. The prep. in compound has the sense
of "excess" (MH, 326). The subj. is used to express purpose and
the clause is placed first for emphasis (s. MT, Style, 94). ἐδόθη

aor. ind. pass. δίδωμι to give. σκόλοψ stake, a stake used for impaling or torturing someone, a sharpened wooden staff, thorn, or splinter (s. Windisch, Barrett, Hughes). (For a discussion as to what the thorn was, s. Hughes; Windisch; T.Y. Mullens, "The Thorn in the Flesh," JBL, 76 [1957], 299f.) τῇ σαρκί The dat. is either dat. of advantage "for my flesh" or locative "in my flesh" (s. RG, 538). κολαφίζῃ pres. act. subj. to strike w. the fist, to beat (s. Mark 14:65). (For a listing of the various interpretations given to this phrase, s. BAG.) The pres. tense refers to either a constant buffeting or a reoccurring (Hughes). ■ τρίς 8 three times. παρακάλεσα aor. ind. act. παρακαλέω to ask, to entreat. ἀποστῇ aor. act. subj. ἀφίστημι to depart, to go away. The verb is generally used of persons not things (Hughes). ■ 9 εἴρηκεν perf. ind. act. λέγω. The perf. implies that the words remain w. Paul as an abiding source of assurance and comfort (Bruce; s. also IBG, 15). ἀρκεῖ pres. ind. act. to be sufficient, to be enough. τελεῖται pres. ind. pass. to bring to completion, to bring to perfection. The pres. tense emphasizes the continuous action "my power is being perfected in weakness" (M, 130). ἥδιστα superl. of the adv. ἡδύς gladly, elative use of the superl. "very gladly." μᾶλλον rather. The comp. is not to be connected w. the previous adv. (s. BD, 129). καυχήσομαι fut. ind. mid., s.v.1. ἐπισκηνώσῃ aor. subj. ἐπισκηνόω to take up one's residence, to abide, to dwell. There may be a reference to the shechina glory of God dwelling in a tent or tabernacle. Paul may mean that the power of God descends upon him and makes its abode in the frail tabernacle of his earthly body (Hughes). ἐπ'ἐμέ "upon me," "by me." ■ διό therefore. εὐδοκῶ pres. ind. act. to 10 take pleasure in. ὕβρις insulting injury. It refers to treatment which is calculated publicly to insult and openly to humiliate the person who suffers from it (MNTW, 83; s. also TDNT; Plummer). διωγμός persecution. στενοχωρία distress (s. 2 Cor. 6:4; 4:8). ὑπὲρ Χριστοῦ "on behalf of Christ." ὅταν whenever. δυνατός strong, powerful.

■ γέγονα perf. ind. act. γίνομαι to become. The verb is 11 emphatic and means that which was expected or predicted has come to pass (Plummer). ἄφρων fool, s.v.6. ἠναγκάσατε aor. ind. act. ἀναγκάζω to compel. ὤφειλον impf. ind. act. ὀφείλω to be obligated, to be under moral obligation, to ought. The impf. expresses an unfulfilled obligation (RWP; BD, 181). συνίστασθαι pres. pass. inf. to commend (s. 2 Cor. 3:1). ὑστέρησα aor. ind. act. ὑστερέω to lack, to come behind. ὑπερλίαν exceedingly, beyond measure, super (s. 2 Cor. 11:5). εἰ καί "if also," "although." The condition is treated as a matter

of indifference and something which makes no real difficulty
12 (RG, 1026). ■ σημεῖον sign. κατειργάσθη aor. ind. pass.
κατεργάζω to produce, to bring about. σημείοις instrumental
13 dat. τέρας to wonder. ■ ὅ acc. of reference "in regard to what?"
"wherein?" ἡσσώθητε aor. ind. pass. ἐσσόομαι to make less,
to make inferior, pass. to be defeated, to be weaker than or
inferior to, here "in what respect, then, are you worse off than
the other churches?" (BAG). ὑπέρ w. acc. "than." The prep. is
used to express the comp. κατενάρκησα aor. ind. act.
καταναρκάω to burden, to be a burden (s. 2 Cor. 11:9).
χαρίσασθε aor. mid. imp. χαρίζομαι to show grace, to forgive.
14 ἀδικία wrong, a wrong act. ■ ἰδού behold, look. τρίτον τοῦτο
"This is the third time." ἑτοίμως adv. ἕτοιμος ready. Used w.
the verb ἔχειν "to have readiness"; i.e., "to be ready to do
something." ἐλθεῖν aor. act. inf. ἔρχομαι. (For a discussion of
Paul's third visit to Corinth, s. Hughes.) καταναρκήσω fut. ind.
act., s. 2 Cor. 11:9. ζηῶ pres. ind. act. to seek followed by the
pl. article w. the gen. "to seek after your possessions." The pres.
tense indicates the continual and habitual action. ὀφείλει pres.
ind. act. s.v.11. The pres. tense is gnomic and is used to express
customary actions and general truths (SMT, 8). γονεῖς parents.
θησαυρίζειν pres. act. inf. to store up treasures, to accumulate
15 money. ■ ἥδιστα superl. adv. ἡδύς gladly, elative use of the
superl. "most gladly." δαπανήσω fut. ind. act. δαπανάω to
spend money, to spend money freely. (For the use of the word
in the papyri, s. MM; Preisigke.) ἐκδαπανηθήσομαι fut. ind.
pass. ἐκδαπανάω pass. "to be spent out," "to be utterly spent."
The prep. in compound is perfective (RG, 596). περισσοτέρως
adv. comp. περισσός abundantly, comp. "more abundantly."
ἧσσον adv. comp. ὀλίγον little, comp. "less." ἀγαπῶμαι pres.
16 ind. pass. ἀγαπάω to love. ■ ἔστω imp. εἰμί "let it be." The
previous sentence is to be considered as the subject of the imp.
(RG, 596). κατεβάρησα aor. ind. act. καταβαρέω to put
weight on someone, to be burdensome, to put a burden on someone. ὑπάρχων pres. act. part. ὑπάρχω to be, to exist, to be by
constitution (Hughes). πανοῦργος (πᾶν, ἔργον) "every work,"
"up to every trick," "crafty and unscrupulous" (Hughes). δόλος
guile, craftiness, trickery (s. 2 Cor. 4:2). ἔλαβον aor. ind. act.
λαμβάνω to take, to catch. The metaphor is from hunting or
fishing; he entrapped or caught them in his wiliness (Plummer).
17 ■ μή introduces a question expecting the answer no. τίνα any,
anyone. The anacolouthon is resumed by the personal pron. in
the prep. phrase "through him," i.e. "any one of whom I sent—I
did not defraud you through him, did I?" (For the construction,

s. RG, 436; IBG, 176; BG, 10; BD, 234.) ἀπέσταλκα perf. ind. act. ἀποστέλλω to send, to send as an authoritative representative. The perf. indicates that Paul had sent someone "from time to time" (M, 144) and is a perf. of repeated action or of broken continuity (RG, 893, 896). ἐπλεονέκτησα aor. ind. act. πλεονεκτέω to take advantage of someone often out of selfish, greedy arrogance (s. NTW, 97–99). ■ παρεκάλεσα aor. ind. 18 act. παρακαλέω to ask, to beseech, to exhort. συναπέστειλα aor. ind. act. συναποστέλλω to send someone w. another. to send together. μήτι interrogative particle used in questions expecting the answer no or "certainly not" (s. BD, 220). οὐ used in questions which expect the answer yes. περιεπατήσαμεν aor. ind. act. περιπατέω to walk, to conduct one's life. ἴχνος step, footstep. Used here in the pl. "in the same footsteps."

■ πάλαι long ago, in the past time. Used w. the pres. tense 19 which gathers up past and pres. into one phrase "you have been thinking this all the time" or as a question "have you been thinking all this time?" (M, 119; s. also RG, 879). δοκεῖτε pres. ind. act. to suppose, to think. (For the pres. tense, s. the previous word.) ἀπολογούμεθα pres. ind. mid. to defend one's self. This was a term used in law courts (Hughes). κατέναντι over against, before. ἀγαπητός verbal adj. beloved. οἰκοδομή building up, edification. ■ φοβέομαι pres. mid. ind. to fear, to be afraid. μή 20 πως lest, lest by any means. (For the use of these words w. verbs of fearing, s. RG, 995; SMT, 95.) When followed by the subj. it indicates fear of an uncertain thing in the fut. (MT, 99). ἐλθών aor. act. part. ἔρχομαι temporal or conditional use of the part. οὐχ οἵους = οὐ τοιούτους, οἵους = "not such ones as." εὕρω aor. subj. εὑρίσκω to find. ἔρις strife, quarreling. ζῆλος jealous, envying. θύμος anger, sudden flare up of burning anger (s. Trench; Synonyms, 130). ἐριθεία selfishness, intrigue (s. Phil. 2:3). καταλαλιά speaking against someone, backbiting. ψιθυρισμός whispering (s. Rom. 1:29). φυσίωσις inflated opinion (Barrett). ἀκαταστασία disorder. ■ πάλιν again. The 21 word could refer either to the part. or to the main verb (s. Barrett; Hughes). ἐλθόντος aor. act. part. ἔρχομαι to come. The part. is used as a gen. abs. "when I come" (s. BD, 218). ταπεινώσῃ aor. act. subj. ταπεινόω to make low, to humiliate. The subj. is used in a neg. purpose clause which goes back to the verb in v. 20 "I fear" (RWP). πενθήσω aor. act. subj. πενθέω to express sorrow for one who has died, to mourn. προημαρτηκότων perf. act. part. προαμαρτάνω to sin previously. The perf. tense of the part. indicates that the sinning began early and continued and refers to persistence in sexual sin by the

members of the Corinthian church during a previous period
(Barrett; Hughes). μετανοησάντων aor. act. part. μετανοέω to
change one's thinking, to repent. The aor. tense in contrast to the
previous perf. indicates that the repentence which might have
ended the sinning did not take place (Barrett). ἀκαθαρσία
uncleanness. The word refers to sexual sins of impurity. πορνεία
fornication, illicit sexual activity (s. TDNT). ἀσέλγεια not bri-
dled, unrestrained, lawless insolence, sheer animal lust. It is the
vice of a man who has no more shame than an animal in the
gratification of his physical desires (NTW, 27; s. also Trench;
Synonyms, 53f.).

Ch. 13

1 ■ τρίτον τοῦτο "this third time" (s. Hughes; Hodge). ἐπί
w. the gen. "upon," "on the basis of"; i.e. "on the basis of the
testimony." δύο καὶ τρεῖς "two or three." σταθήσεται fut.
ind. pass. ἵστημι to stand, pass. to be established. ῥῆμα word,
matter. The matter between Paul and the Corinthians is to be
brought in order by the third visit which would be in line w. this
2 statement from Deut. 19:15 (s. Windisch). ■ προείρηκα perf.
ind. act. προλογέω to say previously, to say beforehand, to tell
in advance. It is possible that the idea of the word is "to warn"
(Barrett). παρών pres. part. πάρειμι to be present, temporal use
of the part. δεύτερον second, the second time. ἀπών pres. part.
ἄπειμι to be absent. προημαρτηκόσιν perf. act. part.
προαμαρτάνω to sin beforehand (s. 2 Cor. 12:21). ἔλθω aor.
act. subj. ἔρχομαι. εἰς τὸ πάλιν "again," "for another visit"
(IBG, 69). φείσομαι fut. ind. mid. φείδομαι to spare. It
primarily means "to spare in battle—not to kill when the opportunity to do so exists." It then comes to mean "to have mercy
3 upon" (Barrett). ■ ἐπεί "since." Used in a causal sense "because." δοκιμή proof, that which passes an examination (s. 2
Cor. 2:9). ζητεῖτε pres. ind. act. to seek. τοῦ ἐν ἐμοὶ λαλοῦντος
Χριστοῦ. The gen. indicates that which was to be proven: "proof
that Christ is speaking in me." ἀσθενεῖ pres. ind. act. ἀσθενέω
to be weak. δυνατεῖ pres. ind. act. δυνατέω to be strong, to be
4 mighty. ■ καὶ γάρ "for even" (Hughes). ἐσταυρώθη aor. ind.
pass. σταυρόω to crucify. ἐκ "out of." The prep. here is used
in the causal sense (MT, 259f.). καὶ γάρ "for also" (Hughes),
"for indeed" (Barrett). εἰς ὑμᾶς "toward you." It is probably to
be taken w. the verb "we shall live" (Hughes).

5 ■ ἑαυτούς "yourselves." πειράζετε pres. act. imp. to try,
to examine (s. Trench; Synonyms, 280). δοκιμάζω pres. act.
imp. to test, to prove, to approve after examination. In the NT

the word almost always implies that the proof is victorously surmounted, the proven is also approved (Trench; *Synonyms*, 278; s. also Hughes). ἐπιγινώσκετε pres. ind. act. to recognize, to know. The prep. in compound is directive and directs the knowledge to the specific object (s. MH, 312). εἰ μήτι "if perhaps," "unless indeed." ἀδόκιμος disapproved, rejected after examination, not usable. ■ γνώσεσθε fut. ind. mid. γινώσκω 6 to recognize. ■ εὐχόμεθα pres. ind. mid. to pray, followed by 7 the gen. indicating the contents of the prayer. μὴ ποιῆσαι aor. act. inf. used w. the neg. The subject of the inf. is not clear either "that you may do no evil thing" or "that God may do no harm" (s. Barrett). δόκιμος approved, approved after testing. φανῶμεν aor. act. subj. φαίνομαι to appear. ὦμεν pres. subj. εἰμί. ■ ἀλήθεια truth. The word may be used here in a general 8 sense (Barrett). ■ ὅταν when, whenever. ἀσθενῶμεν pres. act. 9 subj. ἀσθενέω s.v.3. ἦτε pres. subj. εἰμί. κατάρτισις perfecting, fitting together. It is used in the sense of setting bones or reconciling parties and refers here to the growth in holiness (Plummer). ■ ἀποτόμως adv. cut off, curt, sharply, severely (s. 10 RWP; BAG). χρήσωμαι aor. mid. subj. χράομαι to use. οἰκοδομή building up, edification. καθαίρεσις tearing down, destroying.

■ λοιπόν acc. of the adj. used as an adv. "finally." χαίρετε 11 pres. act. imp. rejoice. καταρτίζεσθε pres. pass. imp. καταρτίζω to restore, pass. to be restored. παρακαλεῖσθε pres. imp. pass. παρακαλέω to exhort, to encourage (s. TDNT; MNTW, 134). φρονεῖτε pres. act imp. φρονέω to think, here "be of the same mind," "be harmonious in thought and aim" (Plummer). εἰρηνεύετε pres. act. imp. to be peaceable, to live in peace. ἔσται fut. εἰμί. ■ ἀσπάσασθε aor. mid. imp. 12 ἀσπάζομαι to greet. φίλημα kiss (s. 1 Cor. 16:10).

13 ■ κοινωνία τοῦ ἁγίου πνεύματος "the fellowship of the Holy Spirit." The gen. could be obj. gen., i.e., the fellowship or participation which has the Holy Spirit as its object or it could be subj. gen., i.e. the fellowship or participation which comes from the Holy Spirit (s. TDNT; Barrett).

GALATIANS

Ch. 1

1   ἀπό "from." The prep. indicates source and Paul states that his apostleship did not have a group of men (pl.) as its source. (For the term "apostle," s. 1 Cor. 1:1.) διά "through." The prep. denotes the means or agency. It points to the medium through which one would have conveyed the office of his apostleship. ἐγείραντος aor. act. part. ἐγείρω to raise up. The context indicates that the resurrection of Christ has a special bearing on Paul's apostleship: "I was commissioned by the risen and glorified Lord: I am in all respects an apostle, a qualified witness of His resurrection, and a signal instance of His power" (Lightfoot).

4   ■ δόντος aor. act. part. δίδωμι to give, to bestow (s. Gal. 2:20). The idea involved is a delivering up of one's self for a specific purpose (Guthrie). ἐξέληται aor. mid. subj. ἐξαιρέω to take out, to remove, to deliver. It denotes a rescue from the power of (Burton). The subj. is used to express purpose. ἐνεστῶτος perf. act. part. ἐνίσταμι to have come, to be present. The word points
5   to the pres. transitory age (Lightfoot; s. also Eadie). ■ ἀμήν truly. Used to emphasize and substantiate a statement (s. TDNT; CBB; Matt. 5:18).

6   ■ θαυμάζω pres. act. ind. to marvel, to wonder, to be astonished. The pres. tense points to the pres. continual attitude of Paul. οὕτως ταχέως "so quickly." Paul was astonished at the ταχέως w. which the Galatians were responding to a counterfeit gospel (Guthrie; Mussner). μετατίθεσθε pres. mid. ind. to transfer, to remove, to desert, to change one's opinion. The word was used of desertion or revolt in a military or political defection and it frequently had the idea of a change in religion, philosophy, or morals (Lightfoot; TDNT). καλέσαντος aor. act. part. The aor. points to the time when the Galatians received the gospel (Mussner). ἕτερον another. It expresses a difference in kind (Guthrie; TDNT; Lightfoot; Burton). The rabbis used a similar term for those who had rejected to receive traditions (Mussner).

7   ■ εἰ μή "except." The words limit that which went before (Ridderbos). ταράσσοντες pres. act. part. ταράσσω to shake back and forth, to trouble, to disturb. θέλοντες pres. act. part. to wish,

to desire. μεταστρέψαι aor. act. inf. μεταστρέφω to turn
about, to change from one thing to another, to change to the
opposite, to pervert (Burton; Lightfoot). The aor. tense would
indicate a complete and thorough change. ■ εὐαγγελίζηται 8
aor. mid. subj. εὐαγγελίζω to proclaim good news, to preach the
gospel. The aor. points to the act of one time preaching the
gospel. εὐηγγελισάμεθα aor. mid. ind. ἀνάθεμα accursed,
dedicated for destruction (s. TDNT). ἔστω pres. imp. εἰμί. ■ 9
προειρήκαμεν perf. ind. act. προλέγω to say beforehand, to
say previously. The perf. points to the abiding authority of that
which was said. παρελάβετε aor. ind. act. παραλαμβάνω to
receive from someone. The verb expresses the communication
of authorized Christian teaching (Guthrie).

■ πείθω pres. ind. act. to persuade, to win the favor of 10
someone (Burton). The pres. tense is conative indicating the
trying or attempting (BD, 167; RG, 880). ζητέω pres. ind. act.
to seek. ἀρέσκω pres. act. inf. to please, to cause pleasure. The
inf. gives the content of the verb "seek." ἤρεσκον impf. ind. act.
ἀρέσκω. The verb is used in a contrary to fact conditional
clause and the impf. indicates an incompleted action. ἤμην impf.
εἰμί.

■ γνωρίζω to make known, to make clear, to certify. It has 11
the effect of suggesting a somewhat formal statement to follow
(EBC, Vol. 10). εὐαγγελισθέν aor. pass. part., s.v.8. ■ οὐδέ not, 12
not even. The word indicates either "even I who so naturally
might have been taught of men did not . . ." or it might mean "I
as little as the other apostles," i.e., "I (distinctly emphatic)—as
little as any others did not . . ." (Ellicott; s. also Burton).
παρέλαβον aor. ind. act., s.v.9. ἐδιδάχθην aor. pass. ind.
ἀποκάλυψις unveiling, revelation. The word indicates that it
was an opening up of what was previously secret. The following
gen. is best taken as obj. gen. indicating that Christ was the
object of the revelation (Guthrie).

■ ἠκούσατε aor. ind. act. ἀκούω. ἀναστροφή manner of 13
life. It refers to Paul's ethical conduct (Ridderbos). ὑπερβολή
throwing beyond, beyond measure, in excess. ἐδίωκον impf. ind.
act. διώκω to pursue, to hunt, to persecute. The impf. pictures
the persistent and continual action in the past. ἐπόρθουν impf.
ind. act. πορθέω to ravage, to destroy. It was used of soldiers
ravaging a city (Burton). The impf. is conative "I was trying to
devastate it." ■ προέκοπτον impf. ind. act. προκόπτω to cut 14
forward (as in a forest), to blaze a way, to go ahead, to advance
(RWP). Saul of Tarsus was so intent in his ambition to further
the cause of Judaism that he did not hesitate to cut down all

opposition and in this respect he outstripped his contemporaries
(Guthrie). ὑπέρ beyond, over, above. The prep. used w. the acc.
designates that which excels or surpasses and is a type of comp.
(BD, 121). συνηλικιώτης one of the same age, contemporary.
γένος. Here it has the connotation "of my people" (Ridderbos).
περισσοτέρως adv. comp. περισσός abundantly, extremely.
ζηλωτής enthusiast, one who is zealous for a cause, followed by
the gen. indicating that which one is zealous of. (For a study of
the word, s. TDNT; Hengel, *Zeloten*, 67–78.) ὑπάρχων pres.
act. part. ὑπάρχω to be, to exist, to be by constitution (s. 2 Cor.
12:16). πατρικός pertaining to a father, fatherly. (For the meaning of the suf., s. MH, 378.) παράδοσις passing on from one to
another, tradition. In connection w. Judaism it refers to that
body of oral teaching which was complementary to the written
law and in fact possessed equal authority to the law (Guthrie).

15   ■ εὐδόκησεν aor. ind. act. εὐδοκέω to please, to be well-
pleased, followed by the inf. ἀφορίσας aor. act. part. ἀφορίζω
to divide w. a boundary, to mark off from others w. a boundary,
to set apart. The idea here is "to set aside for special purpose"
(Ridderbos). κοιλία body cavity, womb, i.e., "from before my
birth," "before I had any impulses, any principles of my own"

16   (Lightfoot). καλέσας aor. act. part. ■ ἀποκαλύψαι aor. act.
inf. ἀποκαλύπτω to unveil, to reveal. Infinitive used to express
purpose. ἐν ἐμοὶ "in me" or simply "to me," "me." With verbs
of knowing and making known, the prep. designates not only the
person through whom the communication comes, but also the
one who receives it (Ridderbos; BD, 118). εὐαγγελίζωμαι pres.
mid. subj. Subjunctive used in a purpose clause. ἔθνος nation, pl.
Gentiles. εὐθέως adv. immediately. προσανεθέμην aor. mid.
ind. προσανατίθεμι lit. "to lay on one's self in addition."
When used w. the gen. it suggests the gaining of information by
communicating w. others (Guthrie; Lightfoot; s. also Mussner).

17   ■ ἀνῆλθον aor. ind. act. ἀνέρχομαι to go up. ἀπῆλθον aor.
ind. act. ἀπέρχομαι to go away. ὑπέστρεψα aor. ind. act.
ὑποστρέφω to return. The prep. in compound has the sense of
"back" (s. MH, 327).

18   ■ ἔπειτα "then." The word draws particular attention to
the next event in order of sequence (Guthrie). ἔτος year.
ἱστορῆσαι aor. act. inf. ἱστορέω to inquire, to visit places or
persons (Burton; s. also MM; Preisigke). ἐπέμεινα aor. ind. act.
ἐπιμένω to remain. (For the prep. in compound, s. MH, 312.)

19   ■ εἰ μή "except." (For the possible ways of understanding these
words, s. L. Paul Trudinger, "A Note on Galatians 1:19," Nov
T, 17 [July, 1975], 200–202.) (For a discussion of the various

interpretations related to James, the brother of the Lord, s. Eadie; Lightfoot, 252–291.) ■ ψεύδομαι pres. mid. ind. to lie. (For 20
a comparison of Paul's statement to the oaths offered during
Roman court procedures, s. J.P. Sampley, " 'Before God, I Do
Not Lie' [Gal. 1:20]," NTS, 23 [July, 1977], 477–482.) ■ κλῖμα 21
region, area. ■ ἀγνοούμενος pres. pass. part. ἀγνοέω to be 22
ignorant, not to know, pass. to be unknown. The pres. tense
stresses the continuity of the state of not knowing (Guthrie).
■ ἀκούοντες pres. act. part. διώκων pres. act. part., s.v.13. ■ 23/24
ἐδόξαζον impf. ind. act. δοξάζω to glorify, to cause one to think
highly of another. The impf. indicates "they began to glorify."
ἐν ἐμοί "in me." The prep. constitutes the ground or basis of the
action "they found in me occasion and reason for praising God"
(Burton).

Ch. 2

■ ἔπειτα then (s. Gal. 1:18). ἔτος year. ἀνέβην aor. ind. 1
act. ἀναβαίνω to go up. μετά w. the gen. "with," "accompanied
by." It suggests that Paul was the leader (Guthrie).
συμπαραλαβών aor. act. part. συμπαραλαμβάνω to take
along w., to take someone along as a traveling companion, to
take someone along as a helper. The word is applied to a private
companion or minister, who is not sent forth on the mission of
an envoy, but is taken by the envoy on their authority (Ramsey;
s. also MM). ■ ἀποκάλυψις unveiling, revelation, used w. the 2
prep. "in obedience to such a revelation" (Burton). ἀνέθεμην
aor. mid. inf. ἀνατίθημι to lay something before someone for
consideration, to relate w. a view to consulting (BAG; Lightfoot). ἴδιος one's own, used in the idiomatic construction κατ'
ἰδίαν "privately." δοκοῦσιν pres. act. part. δοκέω to seem to
be, to appear. Used in this construction "οἱ δοκοῦντες εἶναί τι"
"those who seem to be something." It is used in the sense of "the
authorities" and the word itself implies position of honor (Meyer; Guthrie). μή "lest." Used w. the subj. to express a neg.
purpose or to prohibit that which is feared (s. 2 Cor. 12:20).
τρέχω pres. act. subj. to run. The preaching of the gospel is
pictured as a runner of a race and his concern about his eventual
success or failure in the race. The pres. subj. expresses the fear
of continuous fruitless effort into the fut. (s. PAM, 100f.).
ἔδραμον aor. ind. act. τρέχω. The ind. is used of that which has
already taken place or is entirely independent of the will. The
fact of having run in the past is no longer dependent of the will
of him who fears (BD, 188; PAM, 101; Schlier). ■ ὤν pres. act. 3
part. εἰμί. The part. is concessive "although . . ." ἠναγκάσθη

503

aor. pass. ind. ἀναγκάζω to exert pressure on someone, to compel, to coerce. The aor. is effective or resultative affirming that an action attempted in the past was accomplished (SMT, 42). περιτμηθῆναι aor. pass. inf. περιτέμνω to circumcise (s. Rom. 2:25; Neil J. McEleney, "Conversion, Circumcision and

4 the Law," NTS, 20 [April, 1974], 319–341). ■ δέ "but." The structure and grammatical connection of this verse is not clear. (For a discussion of the various possibilities, s. Lightfoot; Burton; Mussner.) παρείσακτος secretly brought in, smuggled in along side of, sneaked in (BAG). The word could also simply mean "alien," "foreign" (s. Eadie; MM). ψευδάδελφος false brother. ὅστις "who," "one who." The word specifies the class to which one belongs (Ellicott; RG, 727). παρεισῆλθον aor. ind. act. παρεισέρχομαι to come in along side of, to slip into. The word usually implies "stealth" (Burton). The metaphor is that of spies or traitors introducing themselves by stealth into the enemy's camp (Lightfoot). κατασκοπῆσαι aor. act. inf. κατασκοπέω to spy out, to examine carefully. The form is used most frequently where the notion of treachery is prominent (Lightfoot). (See Josh. 2:2, 3.) The aor. may refer to the act as done before they were detected (Eadie). The inf. is used to express purpose. ἐλευθερία freedom. καταδουλώσουσιν fut. ind. act. καταδουλόω to enslave, to bring down to bondage, to completely enslave. The prep. in compound is perfective (MH, 316).

5 ■ εἴξαμεν aor. ind. act. εἴκω to yield, to give into, to give way, to allow. ὑποταγή submission, dat. of reference or respect, i.e., "we did not yield w. respect to the submission." The definite article refers to the matter under discussion; i.e., circumcision (Guthrie). διαμείνῃ aor. act. subj. διαμένω to remain permanently, to continue throughout. The idea of "firm possession" is enforced by the compound verb, by the past tense, and by the

6 prep. (Lightfoot). ■ ὁποῖός ποτε "what kind of people they were." The general rel. pron. refers to quality (s. BD, 159; Schlier). διαφέρει "it makes a difference," "it matters." Used here w. the neg. "it makes no difference to me." προσανέθεντο aor. mid. ind. προσανατίθημι to add something in addition, here it has the sense "to teach in addition to what I have already learned" (s. Burton). Paul means that no restrictions were set to, no further and extraneous requirements were laid upon, the fundamental proclamation of the gospel (PAA, 146). (For Paul's view of his apostleship and authoritative message in relation to the other apostles, s. David M. Hay, "Paul's Indifference to

7 Authority," JBL, 88 [March, 1969], 36–44.) ■ τοὐναντίον "on the contrary." πεπίστευμαι perf. pass. ind. πιστεύομαι pass.

to be entrusted w. something. ἀκροβυστία foreskin, uncircum-
cised. περιτομή circumcised. ▪ ἐνεργήσας aor. act. part. 8
ἐνεργέω to be at work, to be active, to effect, to produce results
(Burton; Mussner). The verb is followed by the dat. of advantage. εἰς. The prep. points to the goal of the active working of
God (Mussner). ἀποστολή apostleship. The word is the act of
fulfilling the commission, i.e., the establishment of Christian
communities (PAA, 148; Robert Duncan Culver, "Apostles and
the Apostolate in the New Testament," Bib Sac, 134 [April,
1977], 131–143). ἐνήργησεν aor. act. ind. ἐνεργέω. γνόντες
aor. act. part. γινώσκω to know, to recognize. δοθεῖσαν aor.
pass. part. δίδωμι. στῦλος pillar. The metaphor was used by the
Jews in speaking of the great teachers of the law (Lightfoot; s.
also SB III, 537). δεξιά right. ἔδωκαν aor. act. ind. δίδωμι.
κοινωνία fellowship. In modern parlance this means that they
all shook hands to signify agreement (Guthrie). (For the term
"fellowship," s. CBB; TDNT; RAC IX, 1100–1145.) ▪ 10
μνημονεύωμεν pres. act. subj. μνημονεύω to remember.
ἐσπούδασα aor. ind. act. σπουδάζω to be diligent, to be eager.
αὐτὸ τοῦτο "this very thing." ποιῆσαι aor. act. inf. to do.

▪ ἀντέστην aor. act. ind. ἀνίστημι to stand against, to 11
oppose. κατεγνωσμένος perf. pass. part. καταγινώσκω to
condemn, pass. to be condemned. Peter was condemned either
by his own contradictory actions (Lightfoot) or by his own conscience. (For this view as well as examples from the papyri, s.
MM; Schlier.) ▪ ἐλθεῖν aor. act. inf. ἔρχομαι. The inf. is used 12
w. the prep. to express previous or antecedent time "before . . ."
(MT, 144). συνήσθιεν impf. ind. act. συνεσθίω to eat together. The impf. expresses the habitual action of the past "he
used to eat regularly w. Gentiles." ὑπέστελλεν impf. ind. act.
ὑποστέλλω to withdraw. The impf. is inceptive "he began to
withdraw." ἀφώριζεν impf. act. ind. ἀφορίζω to separate (s.
Gal. 1:14). The impf. is inceptive. φοβούμενος pres. mid. part.
φοβέομαι to fear, to be afraid. The part. is causal. ▪ 13
συνυπεκρίθησαν aor. pass. ind. συνυποκρίνομαι to act as a
hypocrite w. another. The basic meaning of the word is "to
answer from under" and refers to actors who spoke under a mask
in playing a part. The actors hid their true selves behind the role
they were playing. The word indicates the concealing of wrong
feelings, character, etc. under the pretense of better ones (Burton; Guthrie; TDNT). συναπήχθη aor. pass. ind. συναπάγω
to lead away together. The pass. of the word suggests that Barnabas did not play an active part in the hypocrisy and the meaning of the verb implies that Barnabas was swept off his balance

14 (Guthrie). ■ ὀρθοποδοῦσιν pres. act. ind. to walk correctly, to walk straight or upright. Followed by the prep. the verb means "they were not walking on the straight path towards the truth of the gospel" (Mussner). ὑπάρχων pres. act. part. ὑπάρχω to exist, to be. ἐθνικῶς adv. "in the manner of a heathen." ζῇς pres. ind. act. ζάω to live. The ind. is used in a conditional clause which assumes the reality of the condition. Ἰουδαΐζειν pres. act. inf. to live as a Jew, to adopt Jewish customs (Lightfoot).

15   ■ φύσις nature, here in the dat. "by nature," "by birth." The verb to be supplied is to be taken as concessive "though we are Jews by nature and not sinners of Gentile origin" (Burton;

16 Mussner). ἁμαρτωλός sinner. ■ εἰδότες perf. act. part. οἶδα defective perf. w. the pres. meaning "to know." (For a study of this verb, s. ND, 344ff.) δικαιοῦται pres. pass. ind. δικαιόω to declare righteous. (For the meaning of this term, s. Rom. 2:13.) The pres. tense indicates that which is always true. The pass. points to the fact that one does not justify himself but is declared righteous by another. The neg. w. the pres. tense indicates that justification can never at any time be achieved by works of the law. ἐάν μή "if not," "except." The expression is properly exceptive and introduces an exception related to the main verb. Here it can be translated "but only" (Burton). ἐπιστεύσαμεν aor. ind. act. The aor. could be ingressive aor. "we have come to believe" (Ridderbos). δικαιωθῶμεν aor. pass. subj.

17 δικαιωθήσεται fut. pass. ind. ■ δικαιωθῆναι aor. pass. inf. εὑρέθημεν aor. pass. ind. ἆρα here to be taken as the interrogative particle rather than an inferential particle. It expresses bewilderment as to a possible conclusion "is Christ then a minister of sin?" (s. Lightfoot; Mussner). γένοιτο aor. mid. opt. γίνομαι "let it not be," "certainly not!" This represents a characteristic Pauline reputation of an unthinkable suggestion

18 (Guthrie). ■ κατέλυσα aor. ind. act. καταλύω to tear down, to destroy, to annul, to abrogate. οἰκοδομέω pres. ind. act. to build up. The pres. tense suggests a maxim which would always be true (s. Eadie). παραβάτης one who goes beyond the boundary, transgressor. συνιστάνω pres. ind. act. to constitute, to prove. Used w. the double acc. Used w. the reflex. pron. as one of the accs. it means "to prove one's self something or someone," "to

19 recommend or present one's self as such" (Ridderbos). ■ ἐγώ. The idea here is "I Paul, the natural man, the slave of the old covenant" (Lightfoot). γάρ for. This explicative shows how this rehabilitation of the law actually amounts to a transgression of its true principles (Ellicott). ἀπέθανον aor. ind. act. ἀποθνήσκω to die, followed by the dat. of reference. ζήσω aor.

506

act. subj. ζάω followed by the dat. of advantage "to live for God." συνεσταύρωμαι perf. pass. ind. συνσταυρόω to crucify together. The perf. tense suggests that Paul is thinking of that specific completed event which marked his identification w. Christ and which has had an enduring effect upon his life (Guthrie). ■ οὐκέτι no longer. ἀγαπήσαντος aor. act. part. ἀγαπάω 20 to love. παραδόντος aor. act. part. παραδίδωμι to give over, to give. Christ's self-giving upon the cross was a definite act of love. ■ ἀθετέω pres. ind. act. to set aside, to reject. In the papyri 21 it was used of loans which were repaid and cancelled and for the rejection of certain officials who were described as inefficient and incapable of doing their duty. It was also used of grain which was rejected by the inspector as unfit for food (MM). δωρέαν gratuitously, i.e. "without (giving or receiving) pay" (Burton).

Ch. 3

■ ἀνόητος foolish, without thinking. It describes the acting 1 in a spirit which manifests the absence of wisdom (Eadie). ἐβάσκανεν aor. ind. act. βασκαίνω to bewitch, to cast a magic spell, to seek to bring damage to a person through an evil eye or through a spoken word (s. Lightfoot; TDNT; MM). One ancient writer felt that one could ward off the evil spell by spitting three times (BAG). προεγράφη aor. pass. ind. προγράφω to write before, to write up in public. The word was used to describe all public notices or proclamations and indicates a public announcement in which the validity of a particular fact or a particular condition is proclaimed (Lightfoot; Ridderbos; TDNT). ἐσταυρωμένος perf. pass. part. σταυρόω to crucify. The perf. tense indicates a state or condition and stresses the abiding significance of the event (Guthrie; s. also McKay). The lack of the article stresses the character; i.e. "a crucified one." (For a description of crucifixion in the ancient world, s. Martin Hengel, *Crucifixion in the Ancient World and the Folly of the Message of the Cross* [Philadelphia: Fortress Press, 1977].) ■ μαθεῖν aor. 2 act. inf. μανθάνω to learn. ἐλάβετε aor. act. ind. λαμβάνω to receive. ἀκόη hearing. ■ ἐναρξάμενοι aor. mid. part. ἐνάρχω 3 to begin. πνεύματι and σαρκί are dats. of instrument. ἐπιτελεῖσθε pres. mid. ind. ἐπιτελέω to accomplish, to complete, to finish, to come to the intended goal. ■ τοσοῦτος so 4 great, pl. "so great things." ἐπάθετε aor. ind. act. πάσχω to experience. The word may mean "to experience evil," i.e. "to suffer" or it may be used in a neutral sense "to experience" (s. Burton; Mussner). εἰκῆ in vain. εἴ γε καί "if it be really." The phrase leaves a loophole for doubt implying an unwillingness to

5 believe on the part of the speaker (Lightfoot). ■ ἐπιχορηγῶν pres. act. part. ἐπιχορηγέω to supply. The simple verb means "to defray the expense of providing a 'chorus' at the public feast" and the prep. expresses strongly the idea "to supply abundantly" (Burton; s. also 2 Cor. 9:10). The pres. tense implies the permanency of the action (Ellicott). ἐνεργῶν pres. act. part. ἐνεργέω

6 to be energetic, to work. ■ καθώς "just as." The word indicates that Paul is drawing a parallel between Abraham's justification and present-day justification (Mussner). ἐπίστευσεν aor. ind. act. ἐλογίσθη aor. ind. pass. λογίζομαι to place to one's account, to account, to reckon.

7 ■ γινώσκετε pres. ind. or imp. ἄρα so, therefore. It is used
8 as a particle of inference. ■ προϊδοῦσα aor. act. part. προοράω to see beforehand, to foresee. The word indicates that the faith element in God's method of justification is timeless (Guthrie). δικαιοῖ pres. ind. act. to justify, to declare righteous. ἔθνος nation, Gentile. προευηγγελίσατο aor. mid. ind. προευαγγελίζομαι to proclaim the good news beforehand. ὅτι recitative use introducing a direct quotation and is equivalent to quotation marks. ἐνευλογηθήσονται fut. ind. pass. ἐνευλογέω to bless. (For the term "blessing," "to bless," s. Cleon Rogers, "The Covenant with Abraham and Its Historical Setting," Bib

9 Sac, 127 [April, 1970], 241–256.) ■ ὥστε therefore. The word draws a conclusion from the previous material. εὐλογοῦνται
10 pres. ind. pass. εὐλογέω to bless. ■ ὅσοι as many as. κατάρα curse. This was the covenant curse for disobedience to the conditions of the Mosaic covenant (s. CBB; TDNT). γέγραπται pres. pass. ind. "it stands written." The perf. indicates that the authority of the document is binding (s. MM). ἐπικατάρατος curst, cursed. (For a discussion of the Heb. word "curst" as used here in the quotation from Deut. 27:26, s. TDOT, H.C. Brichto, *The Problem of "Curse" in the Hebrew Bible* [Philadelphia: Society of Biblical Literature, 1968].) ἐμμένει pres. ind. act. to remain in, to continue in. The pres. tense indicates the need for unbroken and continual observance of the whole law. γεγραμμένοις perf. pass. part. ποιῆσαι aor. act. inf. The inf. is used to express

11 purpose. ■ δικαιοῦται pres. pass. ind. δῆλος clear, evident.
12 ζήσεται fut. ind. mid. ζάω to live. ■ ποιήσας aor. act. part.
13 ■ ἐξηγόρασεν aor. ind. act. ἐξαγοράζω to buy out of the market place, to redeem, to randsom from slavery (s. APC; TDNT). γενόμενος aor. mid. part. γίνομαι. The part. gives the means or way in which the action of the main verb was accomplished. κρεμάμενος pres. mid. part. κρέμαμαι to hang. ξύλον wood, tree (s. Acts 10:39). (For the view that Paul combines

Deut. 21:22–23 w. a reference to Isaac in Gen. 22, s. Max Wilcox, " 'Upon the Tree'—Deut. 21:22–23 in the New Testament," JBL, 96 [March, 1977], 85–99.) ■ γένηται aor. mid. subj. 14 γίνομαι. The subj. is used to express purpose. ἐπαγγελία promise. The gen. ἐπαγγελίαν τοῦ πνεύματος is obj. gen., i.e. the promise which has the Spirit for its object (Eadie). λάβωμεν aor. act. subj. λαμβάνω to receive.

■ ὅμως even though, nevertheless, w. the possible transla- 15 tion "even though it is only a man's will, nevertheless." However it may be used to introduce a comparison and have the translation "also," "likewise" (s. BD, 234). κεκυρωμένην perf. pass. part. κυρόω to validate, to ratify. διαθήκη agreement, treaty, covenant. However it may have the meaning "will," "testament" (s. Guthrie; APC; TDNT). ἀθετεῖ pres. ind. act. to annul (s. Gal. 2:21). ἐπιδιατάσσεται pres. mid. ind. to add on to. The prep. in compound indicates "to make additional prescriptions" (Burton). The pres. tenses here are gnomic indicating that which is always true. ■ ἐρρέθησαν aor. pass. ind. λέγω. ■ τοῦτο δὲ 16/17 λέγω "now this I say." Paul comes to his real purpose and proceeds to apply the figure of v. 15 arguing from the lesser to the greater; i.e., if this is true among human beings and their agreements, it is even more true in respect to God and His promises (s. Ridderbos). προκεκυρωμένην perf. pass. part. προκυρόω to ratify beforehand, to confirm previously. The perf. tense points to the lasting authority of the legal ratification. ἔτος year. γεγονώς perf. act. part. γίνομαι. ἀκυρόω pres. act. ind. to make invalid, to annul either by rescinding or overriding or otherwise (Burton; s. also MM; BS, 228). καταργῆσαι aor. act. inf. καταργέω to render inoperative, to make of no effect. The inf. is used w. the prep. to express either purpose or result (s. MT, 143). ■ κληρονομία inheritance. οὐκέτι no longer. 18 κεχάρισται perf. mid. ind. χαρίζομαι to give graciously (s. TDNT). ■ παράβασις stepping over the boundary, transgres- 19 sion. χάριν used w. gen. "on account of," "because of." προσετέθη aor. pass. ind. προστίθημι to add to. ἄχρις until. ἔλθῃ aor. act. subj. ἔρχομαι. τὸ σπέρμα "the seed," "the offspring" has already been identified as Christ in v. 16 (Guthrie). ἐπήγγελται perf. pass. ind. ἐπαγγέλλω to promise. διαταγείς aor. pass. part. διατάσσω to enact "a law." It is a technical term for the carrying out of laws and ordinances (Ridderbos). (For the Jewish view concerning the activity of angels in the giving of the law, s. SB III, 554–556.) ■ μεσίτης mediator, one who stands 20 between two parties. ἑνός one. (For a discussion of the meaning of this passage, s. EBC, Vol. 10; Burton; Guthrie; Mussner; U.

Mauser, "Galater III 20: Die Universalität des Heils," NTS, 18 [April, 1967], 258–270.)

21 ■ γένοιτο aor. mid. opt. γίνομαι (s. Gal. 2:17). ἐδόθη aor. pass. ind. δίδωμι. The ind. is used in a contrary to fact conditional clause. δυνάμενος pres. mid. part. to be able. ζῳοποιῆσαι aor. act. inf. ζωοποιέω to make alive. The purpose of the law was not to make alive but to give Israel a rule of life

22 in the promised land. ■ συνέκλεισεν aor. ind. act. συγκλείω to lock up together, to shut in on all sides. The verb indicates there is no possibility of escape (Guthrie). δοθῇ aor. pass. subj. δίδωμι. The subj. is used in a purpose clause. πιστεύουσιν pres. act. part. The dat. is the indirect object.

23 ■ ἐλθεῖν aor. act. inf. ἔρχομαι. The inf. is used w. the prep. to express antecedent time "before" (s. MT, 144). πίστις "the faith," i.e. before the salvation given in Christ was revealed as the object of faith (Ridderbos). ἐφρουρούμεθα impf. pass. ind. φρουρέω to guard. The verb carries the idea of setting a guard to protect (Guthrie). It has the idea of a garrison keeping ward over a town (MM; s. also Preisigke). συγκλειόμενοι pres. pass. part. μέλλουσαν pres. act. part. μέλλω to be, about to be. It is used w. the inf. to express the fut. ἀποκαλυφθῆναι aor. pass.

24 inf. ἀποκαλύπτω to unveil, to reveal. ■ παιδαγωγός custodian, male nursemaid. He was a slave employed in Gr. and Roman families to have general charge of a boy in the years from about 6 to 16, watching over his outward behavior and attending him whenever he went home, as for example to school (Burton; s. also Mussner; TDNT; CC, 144f.; DGRA, 847). γέγονεν perf. ind. act. γίνομαι. δικαιωθῶμεν aor. pass. subj. The subj. is used

25 in a purpose clause. ■ ἐλθούσης aor. act. part. ἔρχομαι.

27 ■ ἐβαπτίσθητε aor. pass. ind. βαπτίζω to baptize. Baptism was the sign of an entry into a new kind of life (Guthrie). ἐνεδύσασθε aor. mid. ind. ἐνδύομαι to put on, to put on a garment. Just as a garment which one puts on envelops the person wearing it and identifies his appearance in his life, so the person baptized in Christ is entirely taken up in Christ and in the

28 salvation brought by Him (Ridderbos). ■ ἔνι. Used w. the neg. it means "there is not" and is a statement of a fact rather than a possibility (RWP). ἐλεύθερος free. ἄρσην male. θῆλυς

29 female. ■ κατ᾿ ἐπαγγελίαν "according to promise." κληρονόμος heir. It does not mean that the believer receives the land promises of Abraham but rather that he partakes of the spiritual blessing of justification which is through faith.

Ch. 4

■ λέγω δέ "I mean that." Paul begins w. an explanation of 1
his reference to the heirs (Guthrie). ἐθ᾽ ὅσον χρόνον "for as
long a time as," "as long as." κληρονόμος heir. The term was
uscd in the inscriptions of Asia Minor to indicate "a son after
he has succeeded to the inheritance" as the representative of his
father, undertaking all the duties and obligations of his father
(Ramsey). νήπιός infant, properly "one without understanding"
(Burton). Here it describes "a minor" in any stage of his minority
(Lightfoot). διαφέρει pres. ind. act. to ditter. ὤν pres. part. act.
εἰμί. The part. is concessive "although he is lord over all." ■ 2
ἐπίτροπος guardian, a general term referring to someone to
whom the whole care of the underaged boy is entrusted (Ridderbos). οἰκονόμος steward, trustee. The word usually denotes a
slave acting as a house steward for his master, or an employed
steward acting as an agent for his principal, or a treasurer (Burton). προθεσμία appointed day, fixed time. It was customary
in the ancient world for the father to set a fixed time or day on
which the son entered manhood (s. Lightfoot; Burton; Ramsey;
DGRA, 462, 630f.). ■ οὕτως "so," "thus." Paul now applies the 3
illustration. ἦμεν impf. εἰμί. στοχεῖα τοῦ κόσμου rudimentary
elements. It may mean the elementary teaching referring to the
elementary truths of natural religion or the elementary rules and
regulations or it may refer to elementary spirits; i.e., the spiritual
forces behind the world (Guthrie; s. also TDNT; Burton; Col.
2:8). ἤμεθα impf. εἰμί. δεδουλωμένοι perf. pass. part. The perf.
indicates the state of slavery. The part. is used in a past perf.
periphrastic construction (s. RWP). ■ πλήρωμα that which is 4
filled up, fullness. It refers here to the appointed time of the
father (s.v.2.). God had prepared thc whole world for the coming
of His Son at this particular time in history (s. Guthrie).
ἐξαπέστειλεν aor. ind. act. ἐξαποστέλλω to send out from, to
send forth. The word indicates to send someone as an authoritative representative w. a specific task (s. TDNT; CBB).
γενόμενον aor. mid. part. γίνομαι. The part. is used to define
the principle clause (Ellicott). ■ ἐξαγοράσῃ aor. act. subj. 5
ἐξαγοράζω to buy out of the marketplace, to redeem (s. Gal.
3:13). υἱοθεσία adoption (s. Rom. 8:15). ἀπολάβωμεν aor. act.
subj. ἀπολαμβάνω to receive from someone, to receive. ■ 6
κράζον pres. act. part. κράζω to cry out. ἀββά (Aramaic)
father. This was the language of the children and a daily but
polite form of address to the father (Mussner; TDNT; CBB).
■ ὥστε therefore. It is used to draw a conclusion from the 7
previous "it becomes apparent" (Ridderbos). οὐκέτι no longer.

8　■ εἰδότες perf. act. part. οἶδα (s. Gal. 2:16). ἐδουλεύσατε aor. ind. act. to be enslaved. οὖσιν pres. part. εἰμί. The dat.

9　indicates the one to whom they were enslaved. ■ γνωσθέντες aor. act. part. γινώσκω. The part. could be temporal "after you have come to know" or it could be causal "because you have come to know." ἐπιστρέφετε pres. ind. act. to turn to someone or something. The prep. in compound is directive. The pres. tense points to an action which is in progress. ἀσθενής weak, without strength. πτωχός poor, beggarly. The heathen religions were feeble and poor as beggars for they bring no rich endowment of spiritual treasures (Lightfoot). ἄνωθεν anew, again. Used in the expression "once more" which strongly expresses the completeness of their reversion (Guthrie). δουλεύσαι aor.

10　act. inf. ■ παρατηρεῖσθε pres. mid. ind. παρατηρέω to observe, to observe closely, to watch carefully (s. Eadie; for the prep. in compound, s. MH, 319). μήν month. The pl. "months" may be used for monthly reoccurring events (Burton). ἐνιαυτός year. (For a detailed discussion of these religious elements, s.

11　Mussner.) ■ φοβέομαι pres. mid. ind. to be afraid, to fear. μή lest, used here w. the ind. following a verb of fearing. The ind. indicates that the anxiety is directed toward something which has already taken place (BD, 188). εἰκῇ in vain. κεκοπίακα perf. ind. act. κοπιάω to labor, to toil, to work to exhaustion. The pres. tense draws attention to what Paul fears may be the permanent result of his past effort (Guthrie).

12　■ γίνεσθε pres. mid. imp. Paul appeals to the Galatians to become as he is in reference to freedom from the law and to the freedom which they have as sons of God (Schlier). δέομαι pres. mid. ind. to beseech, to beg. ἠδικήσατε aor. ind. act. ἀδικέω

13　to wrong someone, to injure someone. ■ ἀσθένεια weakness, disease, sickness, ailment. (For the various views regarding Paul's sickness, s. 2 Cor. 12:7; Lightfoot; Ramsey, 422f.) εὐηγγελισάμην aor. mid. ind. εὐαγγελίζομαι to preach the good news, to preach the gospel. τὸ πρότερον "the first time."

14　The word can mean "at first" or "formerly" (Guthrie). ■ πειρασμός temptation, trial (s. Trench; Synonyms, 280). ἐξουθενήσατε aor. act. ind. ἐξουθενέω to consider as nothing, to despise. ἐξεπτύσατε aor. act. ind. ἐκπτύω to spit out. The spitting out may refer to contempt and scorn or it may have referred to an attempt to ward off evil spirits (BAG) or it may refer to the fact that they did not spit out the message which Paul preached (Mussner; s. also MM). ἐδέξασθε aor. mid. ind.

15　δέχομαι to receive, to welcome. ■ ποῦ where. Used to state a question. μακαρισμός happiness, blessedness (s. Matt. 5:3).

μαρτυρέω pres. ind. act. to testify, to bear witness. ἐξορύξαντες aor. act. part. ἐξορύσσω to dig out, to tear out. ἐδώκατε aor. ind. act. δίδωμι. Used in a contrary to fact conditional clause (RWP). ■ ὥστε "therefore," "so then." Used here 16 w. a question "can it be that I have become your enemy?" (Lightfoot). γέγονα perf. ind. act. γίνομαι. ἀληθεύων pres. act. part. ἀληθεύω to speak the truth. The part. indicates the means "by speaking the truth." ■ ζηλοῦσιν pres. ind. act. to be 17 zealous, to busy one's self about someone, to take interest in, "they pay court to" (Lightfoot; s. also Gal. 1:14). καλῶς well, "in no honorable way" (Eadie). ἐκκλεῖσαι aor. act. inf. ἐκκλείω to shut out, to exclude. ζηλοῦτε pres. act. subj. (For the subj. form of this verb, s. BD, 46.) ■ ζηλοῦσθαι pres. pass. inf. 18 πάντοτε always, "but it is good to be courted fairly at all times" (Eadie). παρεῖναί pres. inf. πάρειμι to be present. The inf. is used w. the prep. to express contemporaneous time "when I am present w. you" (s. MT, 144f.). ■ πάλιν again. ὠδίνω to have 19 birth pains. (For childbearing and the figure of childbearing in the ancient world, s. RAC IX, 37–217.) μέχρις οὗ until. μορφωθῇ aor. pass. subj. μορφόω to form, pass. to take on form, to be formed. The form means the essential form rather than outward shape. The idea is therefore of real Christlike character (Guthrie; s. also TDNT). ■ ἤθελον impf. ind. act. 20 θέλω. The impf. is used to express an unfulfilled desire "I could wish" (RG, 886). ἀλλάξαι aor. act. inf. ἀλλάσσω to change. ἀπορέομαι pres. mid. ind. to be at a loss, to be at one's wits end, to be perplexed (s. Guthrie). ἐν "in respect to you" (Burton).

■ λέγετε pres. act. imp. θέλοντες pres. act. part. ■ 21/22 γέγραπται perf. pass. ind. The form was used to express an authoritative document (s. MM). ἔσχεν aor. act. ind. ἔχω to have. παιδίσκη maidservant. ἐλεύθερος free. ■ γεγέννηται 23 perf. pass. ind. γεννάω to bear, to bear a child. ἐπαγγελία promise. ■ ἀλληγορούμενα pres. pass. part. ἀλληγορέω to 24 allegorize, to use an allegory. Paul is using a historical event as an example. (For the allegorical interpretation in Paul's time, s. BE, 126ff.; Eadie; TDNT.) δουλεία bondage. slavery. γεννῶσα pres. act. part. The part. is adj. in force and timeless (Burton). ἥτις. The indefinite rel. pron. denotes an attribute which essentially belongs to the nature of the antecedent (Ellicott). ■ τό. 25 The article is n. and refers to the word Hagar as applied to the mountain (RWP). συστοιχεῖ pres. act. ind. to line up in the same rank in a military sense), here, to correspond to (Guthrie). δουλεύει pres. act. ind. to be in bondage, to be in slavery, i.e. in spiritual bondage w. her children just as Hagar was in social

26 bondage w. her child Ishmael (Lightfoot). ▪ ἥτις which (s.v.24).
27 ▪ εὐφράνθητι aor. pass. imp. εὐφραίνομαι to rejoice. στεῖρα
   sterile, barren. τικτοῦσα pres. act. part. τίκτω to bear a child.
   ῥῆξον aor. act. imp. ῥηγνυμι to break, to burst, to break loose,
   here "to break forth and shout." βόησον aor. act. imp. βοάω to
   cry aloud. ὠδίνουσα pres. act. part. to have labor pains, s.v.19.
   ἔρημος desolate. μᾶλλον more, more than. ἐχούσης pres. act.
   part. (For Isa. 54:1 in the rabbinical literature, s. SB III, 574.)
29 ▪ γεννηθείς aor. pass. part. ἐδίωκεν impf. act. ind. διώκω to
   hunt, to persecute. The impf. pictures the continual action in the
30 past. ▪ κληρονομήσει fut. ind. act. κληρονομέω to inherit.
31 ▪ διό therefore. It draws a conclusion from the previous discussion and summarizes the section. (For a discussion of this allegory in relation to the argument of Galatians, s. C.K. Barrett, "The
   Allegory of Abraham, Sarah, and Hagar in the Argument of
 1 Galatians," R, 1–16.) ▪ ἐλευθερία freedom. (For the meaning
   of this word, s. CBB; TDNT; RAC VIII, 269-306.) The dat.
   could be instrumental or it may be a dat. of purpose or designation (Ridderbos). ἠλευθέρωσεν aor. act. ind. ἐλευθερόω to
   free, to free from slavery. A slave was free under Gr. law for he
   had freedom to act as his own legal person, freedom from seizure
   of property, freedom to earn his own living as he might choose,
   and freedom to dwell where he wished (FCS, 115; for a discussion of the ways in which a slave could be freed, s. FCS, 88–120).
   στήκετε pres. act. imp. στήκω to stand fast. The pres. tense
   indicates a continual and habitual action. ζυγός yoke. δουλεία
   slavery, bondage. ἐνέχεσθε pres. mid. imp. ἐνέχομαι to be had
   in, to be ensnared. The pres. tense calls for the stopping of an
   action in progress "cease to be entangled" (Burton). The mid.
   voice could be permissive "stop allowing yourselves to be entangled."

Ch. 5

 2 ▪ ἴδε aor. act. imp. ὁράω "look!" "see." ἐγὼ παῦλος "I
    Paul," very emphatic emphasizing Paul's authority (Schlier).
    περιτέμνησθε pres. mid. subj. περιτέμνω to circumcise, here
    the mid. is permissive to allow one's self to be circumcised.
    ὠφελήσει fut. ind. act. ὠφελέω to be of value, to profit, to be
    an advantage, followed by the acc. of respect, i.e. "Christ will be
 3 an advantage to you in respect to nothing." ▪ περιτεμνομένῳ
    pres. mid. part. permissive mid. ὀφειλέτης one who is morally
 4 obligated to fulfill a debt, debtor. ποιῆσαι aor. act. inf. ▪
    κατηργήθητε aor. pass. ind. καταργέω to make idle or inac-
    tive, to render invalid, followed by the prep. "to be separated

from," "to be loosed from" (AS). δικαιοῦσθε pres. pass. ind. δικαιόω to declare righteous, to justify. The pres. tense is connative indicating an attempt "you are trying to be justified" (s. DM, 186). ἐξεπέσατε aor. act. ind. ἐκπίπτω to fall out of. Originally used for the falling out of a flower, then "to be loosened from something," "to loose one's grasp of" (Ridderbos). To attempt to be justified by the law is to reject the way of grace—justification by faith. ■ ἀπεκδεχόμεθα pres. mid. ind. to wait 5 expectingly, earnestly but patiently for someone or something. The first prep. in compound intensifies the verb and the second prep. in compound indicates "to be receiving from a distance" i.e. "to be intently awaiting" (Burton; s. also MM). ■ ἰσχύει 6 pres. ind. act. to be strong, to have power. When used of things it means "to be serviceable" (Guthrie). ἀκροβυστία foreskin, uncircumcision. ἐνεργουμένη pres. mid. part. ἐνεργέω to be act., mid. to demonstrate activity, to work, to work effectually.

■ ἐτρέχετε impf. ind. act. τρέχω to run, to run a race (s. 7 Gal. 2:2). καλῶς well. ἐνέκοψεν aor. ind. act. ἐγκόπτω to cut in, to hinder. The word suggests a breaking into or obstruction of the Galatian Christians in their course of following the truth. The picture is that of the runner who has allowed his progress to be blocked or who is still running, but is on the wrong course (PAM, 136f.). πείθεσθαι pres. mid. inf. to obey. The prep. is used to express results. ■ πεισμονή persuasion. The word can 8 have an act. or pass. sense (Mussner). καλοῦντος pres. act. part. "the one who does the calling" is obviously God (EBC, Vol 10). ■ ζύμη yeast, leaven (s. Matt. 13:33). φύραμα that which is 9 mixed, a lump or batch of dough (BAG). ζυμοῖ pres. ind. act. to leaven, to ferment (s. 1 Cor. 5:6f.). The pres. tense is gnomic to express the continuing truth of a proverb or saying. ■ 10 πέποιθα perf. ind. act. to be persuaded, to have confidence. (For the instructions employed by Paul after this verb, s. Burton.) φρονήσετε fut. ind. act. φρονέω to think, to hold an opinion, to set one's mind on something, to have an attitude or thought. ταράσσων pres. act. part. ταράσσω to shake back and forth, to disturb, to trouble. βαστάσει fut. ind. act. βαστάζω to carry, to bear. Paul thinks of the heavy weight which will press down upon those seeking to impose a load of Judaism on these Christians (Guthrie). κρίμα judgment. ᾖ pres. subj. εἰμί. ■ διώκομαι pres. pass. ind. διώκω to hunt, to hunt 11 down, to persecute. ἄρα then, "so it appears!" The word introduces a false statement or inference which is here used ironically (Lightfoot). διώκομαι perf. pass. ind. διώκω s.v.4. σκάνδαλον. The arm or stick on which bait was fixed in a trap,

515

that which trips one up, offense, cause of stumbling (s. NTW, 111–114; TDNT). σταυρός cross. The gen. can be either gen. of explanation, i.e., the "cause of offense which is the cross," or it could be causal "the offense which the cross causes" (Muss-
12 ner). ■ ὄφελον "I would," "oh, that," "would that," a fixed form functioning as a particle to introduce unobtainable wishes (BAG; BD, 181f.). Here it is used w. the fut. ind. for an obtainable wish even though strictly speaking fulfillment is inconceivable and this impossibility is forgotten only for the moment (BD, 181, 194). ἀποκόψονται fut. mid. ind. ἀποκόπτω to cut off. Here to castrate. Paul expresses the wish that his opponents would not stop w. circumcision, but would go on to emasculation (Burton). Perhaps there is also a reference to the practices of the ancient cult of cybele (s. TDNT; BAG *De Dea Syria—The Syrian God-dess*, 51 [Edited by Harold W. Attridge and Robert A. Oden, Missoula, Mont.: Scholars Press, 1976]; Strabo XIII, 4, 14). ἀναστατοῦντες pres. act. part. ἀναστατόω to upset, to trouble, to disturb. It was used in the papyri in the sense of upsetting or disturbing one's mind (RWP; MM).

13 ■ ἐκλήθητε aor. pass. ind. καλέω. τὴν ἐλευθερίαν object of a verb to be supplied ἔχετε. ἀφορμή properly it refers to the place from which an attack is made, i.e. "a base of operation," "opportunity," "occasion" (Burton; Guthrie). δουλεύετε pres. act. imp. to perform the duties of a slave. ἀλλήλοις (dat.) one
14 another, dat. of advantage. ■ πεπλήρωται perf. ind. pass. πληρόω to fulfill. ἀγαπήσεις fut. ind. act. ἀγαπάω to love. ὁ
15 πλησίον neighbor. ■ δάκνω pres. ind. to bite. κατεσθίω pres. ind. to eat up. The two presents are connative indicating the attempt (Burton) and the indicatives are used in a conditional clause which assumes the condition as true. βλέπετε pres. act. imp. μή used w. the subj. to express a neg. purpose. ἀναλωθῆτε aor. pass. subj. ἀναλίσκω to consume, to devour. These verbs suggest wild animals engaged in deadly struggle (Burton). Strength of soul, health of body, character and resources are consumed by broils and struggles (Bengel).

16 ■ περιπατεῖτε pres. act. imp. περιπατέω to walk, to walk about, to conduct one's life. The pres. tense indicates a continual habitual action. ἐπιθυμία desire, lust. The prep. in compound is directive. οὐ μή used w. the subj. as a strong neg. "not at all" (s. M, 188ff.). τελέσητε aor. act. subj. τελέω to fulfill, to bring
17 to the goal, to perform. ■ ἐπιθυμεῖ pres. act. ind. to desire, to yearn, to long for. The use of the verb brings the more act. side of the lust of the flesh (Guthrie). ἀντίκειται pres. mid. ind. to lie opposite, to oppose. The pres. tense indicates continual oppo-

sition. θέλητε pres. act. subj. ποιῆτε pres. act. subj. The subj. is used to express purpose or result. (For a discussion, s. Mussner.) ■ ἄγεσθε pres. pass. ind. ἄγω to lead, pass. to be lead. Here 18 the Spirit is regarded as a guide, to whom the believer is expected to submit himself (Guthrie). ■ φανερός clear, manifest. 19 πορνεία illicit sexual activity (s. TDNT). ἀκαθαρσία uncleanness, impurity. ἀσέλγεια unrestrained living, unbridled acts of indecency which shock the public (Lightfoot; TDNT; s. also 2 Cor. 12:21). ■ εἰδωλολατρία worship of idols, idolatry. 20 φαρμακεία the use of medicine or drugs, the use of drugs for magical purposes, magic, sorcery (Burton; Guthrie; Rev. 9:21). ἔχθρα hostility. ἔρις strife. ζῆλος jealousy. θύμος anger, a terrible flair up of temper (s. Trench; Synonyms, 130; TDNT; CBB). ἐριθεία selfishness, self-seeking ambition (s. 2 Cor. 12:20; Phil. 2:3). διχοστασία dissension. αἵρεσις faction. It is the result of the former—divisions organized into factions (Eadie), cliques. ■ φθόνος envy, the desire to appropriate what another pos- 21 sesses. The word "jealousy" in v. 20 refers to the desire of being as well off as another and the word "envy" refers to the desire to deprive another of what he has (s. Lightfoot; Eadie; CBB). μέθη drunkenness (s. Rom. 13:13). κῶμος carousing, drinking party (s. Rom. 13:13). ὅμοιος that which is like another. προλέγω to say beforehand, to tell forth, to tell publicly, to warn. The meaning here may be "to predict" (Burton). προεῖπον aor. act. ind. προλέγω. τοιοῦτος of such a kind, such as this. πράσσοντες pres. act. part. πράσσω to do, to practice. κληρονομήσουσιν fut. ind. act. κληρονομέω to inherit.

■ καρπός fruit, that which is produced by growth (s. CBB; 22 TDNT). The gen. "of the Spirit" indicates the source or cause of the fruit. ἀγάπη love. The word includes both love for God and love for fellowman. χαρά joy. It is joy grounded in conscience relationship to God (Burton). εἰρήνη peace. μακροθυμία longsuffering, patient endurance under injuries inflicted by others (Lightfoot; CBB; TDNT; s. Rom. 2:4). χρηστότης kindness, gentleness. It refers to a kindly disposition toward one's neighbors (Lightfoot). ἀγαθωσύνη goodness. It refers to active goodness as an energetic principle (Lightfoot; s. also Trench; Synonyms, 231f.; TDNT; CBB). πίστις faith, faithfulness. ■ πραΰτης meekness, gentle submissiveness (s. 23 Burton; 2 Cor. 10:1). ἐγκράτεια self-control, the holding in of passions and appetites (Eadie; Burton). ■ ἐσταύρωσαν aor. act. 24 ind. σταυρόω to crucify. The aor. points to a completed action in the past and might most naturally refer to conversion (Guthrie). πάθημα passion, affections (s. Trench; Synonyms, 323).

25 ■ ζῶμεν pres. act. ind. ζάω to live. The ind. is used in a conditional sentence which views the condition as real. στοιχῶμεν
pres. act. subj. στοιχέω to stand in a row, to walk in a straight
line, to behave properly. The word was used for movement in a
definite line, as in military formation or in dancing (Ridderbos).
Here it means "to walk (in a straight line)," "to conduct one's
self (rightly)" (Burton). The pres. tense points to the continual
26 and habitual action. The subj. is cohortatory "let us walk." ■
γινώμεθα pres. mid. subj. to become, hortatory subj. used w. the
neg. κενόδοξος empty glorying, vain glory, vain-minded. It refers to one who knows how or who attempts to achieve unfound-
ed respect and by his actions demonstrates big talk, boasting, and
ambition (Mussner; Burton). προκαλούμενοι pres. mid. part.
προκαλέω to invite or challenge to combat, to provoke (Eadie).
φθονοῦντες pres. act. part. φθονέω to be envious (s.v.21). The
two parts. describe the means or manner of the action in the
main verb.

Ch. 6

1   ■ προλημφθῇ aor. pass. subj. προλαμβάνω to overtake
by surprise, to overpower before one can escape (Lightfoot; Eadie). παράπτωμα the results of stepping aside, trespass. The
aspect of stepping aside may have been chosen because of its
appropriateness to the Christian life as a walk by the Spirit
(Guthrie). καταρτίζετε pres. act. imp. καταρτίζω to restore, to
correct. It is used especially as a surgical term, of setting a bone
or joint (Lightfoot). πραΰτης meekness, gentleness, submissiveness (s.v.23; s. also 2 Cor. 10:1). σκόπων pres. act. part.
σκοπέω to look at, to observe, to consider, to give heed to. The
verb indicates being sharply attentive, very diligent and the pres.
tense indicates continually doing so (Ridderbos). πειρασθῇς
aor. pass. subj. πειράζω to try, to attempt. The subj. may be used
to express purpose or it may be used after a verb of fearing, i.e.
2 "consider or give heed lest you be tempted" (Burton). ■
ἀλλήλων (gen.) one another. βάρος burden, that which is
heavy. βαστάζετε pres. act. imp. βαστάζω to carry, to bear,
to carry away, to endure (s. MM). ἀναπληρώσετε fut. act. ind.
ἀναπληρόω to fill, to fill up, to fulfill. The prep. in compound
3 gives the idea of a complete filling, of a filling up (Eadie). ■
δοκεῖ pres. act. ind. to think, to suppose. ὤν pres. part. εἰμί. The
part. is temporal or "temporal—concessive," i.e., "when, although he is nothing" (s. Ellicott). φρεναπατᾷ pres. act. inf. to
lead one's mind astray, to deceive. The word brings out the idea
4 of "subjective fantasies" which deceive (Lightfoot; RWP). ■

δοκιμαζέτω pres. act. imp. δοκιμάζω to examine, to approve after testing or examination. The word was used for testing of metals to see whether they were pure (Guthrie). καύχημα the ground or reason for boasting. ■ φορτίον burden, a load which 5 one is expected to bear. It was used as a military term for a man's pack or a soldier's kit (Lightfoot). βαστάσει fut. act. ind. ■ 6 κοινωνείτω pres. act. imp. κοινωνέω to share w. someone, to exercise fellowship. The apostle is thinking here especially of material things (Ridderbos). κατηχούμενος pres. pass. part. κατηχέω to instruct, pass. to be instructed, to be taught. κατηχοῦντι pres. act. part. The dat. is dat. of advantage and is used w. the main verb "to share w. someone." ■ πλανᾶσθε pres. 7 pass. imp. πλανάομαι to deceive, to lead astray. μυκτηρίζεται pres. pass. ind. μυκτηρίζω to turn up the nose at, to treat w. contempt, to ridicule. The idea is to make God ridiculous by outwitting Him and evading His laws (Burton). ἐάν used to make the rel. pron. general "whatever." σπείρῃ pres. act. subj. σπείρω to sow, to sow seeds. The pres. tenses are gnomic indicating that which is always true. θερίσει fut. ind. act. θερίζω to harvest, to gather. ■ σπείρων pres. act. part. φθόρα corruption, rottenness, no one would bother to harvest a field of decay- 8 ing matter. The "corruption" stands for that which results in death (Guthrie). αἰώνιος eternal. ■ ποιοῦντες pres. act. part. 9 The "doing the good" describes what the action of the main verb is. ἐγκακῶμεν pres. act. subj. ἐγκακέω to grow weary, to give into evil, to lose heart and become a coward (Lightfoot; s. also Luke 18:1). καιρός season, time, dat. of time "in its own sea- son," "at the time of harvest." It indicates there is an appointed time for the spiritual reaping (Guthrie). ἐκλυόμενοι pres. pass. part. ἐκλύω to loosen out, to relax, to faint, to be exhausted as a result of giving in to evil (RWP). ■ ἄρα so, then. It is used to 10 draw a conclusion from the previous. ἐργαζώμεθα pres. mid. subj. ἐργάζομαι to be active, to work effectively. The subj. is hortatory "let us work." οἰκεῖος household, members of a household.

■ ἴδετε aor. act. imp. ὁράω. πηλίκος how large. ἔγραψα 11 aor. act. ind. At this point Paul may have taken the pen from the amanuensis and have added his concluding remarks in his own handwriting which consisted of larger letters than the smaller and neater script of the amanuensis (Guthrie; s. also Richard N. Longenecker, "Ancient Amanuenses," ND, 281–297). ■ ὅσοι 12 "as many as." εὐπροσωπῆσαι aor. act. inf. εὐπροσωπέω to play a good role, to please, to make a fair appearance (s. Burton). ἐν σαρκί "in the flesh." ἀναγκάζω pres. act. ind. to compel, to

coerce (s. Gal. 2:3). The pres. tense is conative "they are trying
to coerce." περιτέμνεσθαι pres. pass. inf. περιτέμνω to circumcise. σταυρός cross. The dat. is causal "because of the
cross" (s. BD, 105). διώκωνται pres. pass. subj. διώκω to hunt,
to persecute, pass. to suffer persecution. The subj. is used in
13 a purpose clause. ■ περιτεμνόμενοι pres. pass. part.
φυλάσσουσιν pres. act. ind. to guard, to observe.
καυχήσωνται aor. mid. subj. καυχάομαι to glory. The subj. is
14 used in a purpose clause. ■ γένοιτο aor. mid. opt. γίνομαι,
followed by the inf. εἰ μή "except." δι' οὗ "through which."
ἐσταύρωται perf. ind. pass. σταυρόω to crucify, to put to
death by crucifixion. The perf. tense indicates the continuing
15 and lasting state or condition. ■ περιτομή circumcision.
16 ἀκροβυστία foreskin, uncircumcision. κτίσις creation. ■
κάνων rod, measuring rule, standard. (For this word, s. 2 Cor.
10:13.) στοιχήσουσιν fut. act. ind. to walk the line, to walk
according to a standard (s. Gal. 5:25). ἔλεος mercy. καὶ ἐπὶ τὸν
Ἰσραήλ "and upon the Israel of God." The phrase is not to be
taken as an explanation of the preceding but as a separate entity
or group. His thoughts turn to his own brethren after the flesh
and he pauses to specify those who were once Israelites according to the flesh but now are the Israel of God (Ellicott).
17 ■ τοῦ λοιποῦ. The gen. means "in respect of remaining
time" (RWP). κόπος trouble. παρεχέτω pres. act. imp.
παρέχω to furnish, to provide, to cause. στίγμα mark, brand.
It was the custom to mark slaves by scars (Ramsey) and religious
tattooing also played a great role in antiquity (BAG; The Assyrian Goddess, 59). Paul is speaking of the permanent marks which
he bore of persecution undergone in the service of Christ (Lightfoot; s. also TDNT). βαστάζω to carry, to bear. The pres. tense
18 indicates the continual bearing. ■ ἀμήν "so let it be." A Hebraic
word used to emphasize and confirm a statement. Paul means to
add weight to his conclusion (Guthrie).

EPHESIANS

οὖσιν pres. part. εἰμί. τοῖς ἁγίοις τοῖς οὖσιν "to the 1
saints who are ..." The dat. indicates to whom this letter was
written. The term "saints" are those who are cleansed by the
blood of Christ, and by the renewing of the Holy Ghost, and thus
separated from the world and consecrated to God (Hodge; s. also
TDNT). ■ χάρις grace, the undeserved and unmerited favor of 2
God (s. TDNT; CBB). εἰρήνη peace. Probably to be understood
in the term of the Heb. concept of "shalom" indicating "spiritual
prosperity" (Barth; TDNT; CBB).

■ εὐλογητός blessed. Verbal adjs. w. this ending indicate 3
one who is worthy, i.e. "worthy of blessing" (Abbott; s. also 2
Cor. 1:3). εὐλογήσας aor. act. part. εὐλογέω to bless, to endow
one w. the ability to succeed (s. TDOT; TDNT). ἐπουράνιος
"in the heavenlies." The term is to be understood in a local sense
indicating the sphere of the blessings which are related to the
Spirit. The term refers to heaven as seen in perspective of the
new age brought about in Christ and for this reason it is so
closely linked w. the Spirit of that age (A.T. Lincoln, "A Re-
examination of 'The Heavenlies' in Ephesians," NTS, 19 [July,
1973], 471; s. also Barth). ■ καθώς just as, because. Here the 4
word combines the comp. and causal idea (Schlier; BD, 236).
ἐξελέξατο aor. mid. ind. ἐκλέγω to choose out, to select. The
word involves three ideas: the stem of the word indicates "the
telling over"; the prep. in compound indicates the rejection of
some and acceptance of others; and the mid. voice indicates "the
talking to (for) Himself" (Lightfoot, Notes). καταβολή throwing down, foundation. (For the various usages of the word, s.
Barth; TDNT.) The meaning of the phrase "before the foundation of the world" means "from all eternity" (Abbott). εἶναι
pres. inf. Infinitive used to express purpose. ἄμωμος without
blame, unblemished, used of the absence of defects in sacrificial
animals (BAG). κατενώπιον prep. used w. a gen. "in the presence of" (s. RG, 644). ἀγάπη "in love." The phrase is best
understood as being joined w. the part. in v. 5 (s. Eadie). ■ 5
προορίσας aor. act. part. προορίζω to mark out w. a boundary

521

beforehand, to foreordain, to predestinate (s. TDNT; L.C. Allen, "The Old Testament Background of (πρό) ὁρίζειν in the New Testament," NTS, 17 [October, 1970], 104–108). The part. is causal giving the reason for the election (Abbott). υἱοθεσία adoption (s. Rom. 8:15). εὐδοκία good pleasure, satisfaction. The election and predestination is God's absolute act of free love which is grounded totally in Himself and there was nothing apart
6 from Him which gave His will direction (Gaugler). ■ ἔπαινος praise. δόξα glory (s. TDNT). ἧς rel. pron. The gen. is by attraction to its antecedent. ἐχαρίτωσεν aor. act. ind. χαριτόω to bestow grace, to give grace. The word means "begracing w. grace" and indicates exclusive and abundant demonstration of grace (Barth; s. also TDNT; Robinson; Luke 1:28). ἠγαπημένῳ perf. pass. part. ἀγαπάω to love. The pass. part. indicates the one who is in the state or condition of being loved, "the be-
7 loved." ■ ἀπολύτρωσις purchasing w. a price, redemption (s. Rom. 3:24; Abbott; Lightfoot; Notes). ἄφεσις releasing, forgiveness. παράπτωμα falling aside, transgression. The word signifies the actual and numerous results and manifestations of our
8 sinful nature (Eadie). ■ ἧς rel. pron. gen. by attraction rather than acc. ἐπερίσσευσεν aor. act. ind. περισσεύω to cause to overflow, to cause to abound. φρόνησις understanding. It refers to the display of wisdom in operation (Simpson). It is the ability to discern modes of action w. a view to their results (Lightfoot;
9 Notes). ■ γνωρίσας aor. act. part. γνωρίζω to make known. προέθετο aor. mid. ind. προτίθημι to place before. The prep. in compound can be local, i.e. "to set before one's self," i.e. "to
10 purpose" (Abbott). ■ οἰκονομία household management, administration (s. TDNT; BAG). πλήρωμα fullness. ἀνακεφαλαιώσασθαι aor. mid. inf. ἀνακεφαλαιόω to gather again under one head, to sum up, to gather up into one. (For this word, s. Barth; Robinson; Abbott.) The prep. in compound refers to the prior dispersion of the elements and the substitutive of the verb describes the ultimate aggregation in one; thus the whole compound involves the idea of "unity" effected out of diversity (Lightfoot; Notes). The inf. is used to explain the preceding.
11 ■ ἐκληρώθημεν aor. pass. ind. κληρόω to appoint by lot, pass. to be appointed by lot, to be destined, to be chosen (BAG). προορισθέντες aor. pass. part. s.v.5. πρόθεσις purpose, s.v.9. ἐνεργοῦντος pres. act. part. ἐνεργέω to be effective, to be energetic, to work, to accomplish (s. Robinson). βουλή counsel, will. It expresses counsel w. reference to action (Westcott). The word solemnly represents the almighty Will as displaying itself in action (Ellicott). θέλημα will. It denotes the will in general

(Westcott). ■ προηλπικότας perf. act. part. προελπίζω to 12 hope before, to hope beforehand. The prep. in compound is temporal but its significance is not clear. It could indicate the hope before the event (EGT) or the hope of the Jewish Christians prior to the conversion of the heathen (Abbott; Barth) or it could refer to the hope or belief "before Christ actually came" (Westcott). The perf. tense indicates that the hope continues. The part. is in apposition to the subject of the inf. "we." ■ 13 ἀκούσαντες and πιστεύσαντες aor. act. part. The parts. are temporal and express contemporaneous time "when you believed," "at the time you believed" (Simpson). ἐσφραγίσθητε aor. pass. ind. σφραγίζω to seal. Seals were used as a guarantee indicating not only ownership but also to guarantee the correctness of the contents (s. 2 Cor. 1:22). ἐπαγγελία promise. ■ 14 ἀρραβών down payment, pledge. It indicates a deposit which is in itself a guarantee that the full amount will be paid. The down payment is of the same kind as the full payment (s. 2 Cor. 1:22; Abbott; Lightfoot; *Notes*). κληρονομία inheritance. περιποίησις possessing, possession, that which is one's own (CBB).

■ ἀκούσας aor. act. part., temporal use of the part. ■ 15/16 εὐχαριστῶν pres. act. part. εὐχαριστέω to give thanks. The part. is used supplementary to complete the main verb. μνεία remembrance. ποιούμενος pres. mid. part. used w. the previous noun w. the sense to make mention of, esp. in the sense of mentioning someone in prayer (BAG). ■ δῴη aor. opt. δίδωμι. 17 The volitive opt. is used to express a wish or desire in prayer (s. RG, 939f.). (For the view that the form is subj. rather than opt., s. BD, 187.) ἀποκάλυψις unveiling, revelation. ἐπίγνωσις recognition, knowledge. The word means knowledge directed toward a particular object "perceiving, discerning, recognizing." The gen. following the word denotes the object of the knowledge (s. Robinson, 254). ■ πεφωτισμένους perf. pass. part. φωτίζω 18 to enlighten, to illuminate, to give light. It refers to the ministry of the Holy Spirit who continually illuminates spiritual truths (s. 1QS 2, 3; s. also Gnilka). The perf. tense points to the continuous process (Barth). The grammatical structure of the part. could be an anacoluthon or a third predicate of the main verb or an acc. abs. (s. RWP). εἰδέναι perf. act. inf. οἶδα (s. ND, 344ff.). κλῆσις calling. ■ ὑπερβάλλον pres. act. part. ὑπερβάλλω to 19 throw beyond, to exceed, to surpass. μέγεθος greatness. πιστεύοντας pres. act. part. ἐνεργία working, the effectual working of ability (Schlier; Robinson; TDNT). κράτος might, power. The word refers to strength regarded as abundantly effec-

tive in relation to an end to be gained or dominion to be exercised (Westcott; TDNT). ἰσχύς strength, strength which one has, power in possession, ability, or latent power (Eadie;
20 Schlier). ■ ἐνήργηκεν perf. ind. act. ἐνεργέω to be at work, to work effectually. ἐγείρας aor. act. part. ἐγείρω to raise. καθίσας aor. act. part. καθίζω to cause to sit, to seat. δεξιά right, right hand. Christ seated at the right hand pictures His place of honor and authority (s. David M. Hay, *Glory at the Right Hand: Psalm 110 in Early Christianity* [Nashville: Abingdon Press, 1973]; for a critical approach of this theme, s. W.R.G. Loader, "Christ at the Right Hand—Ps. CX. 1 in the New Testament," NTS, 24 [January, 1978], 199–217). ἐπουράνιος heav-
21 en, heavenly place. s.v.3. ■ ὑπεράνω high above, far above. ἀρχή rule, ruler. κυριότης lordship, dominions. In Jewish writings the terms were used to designate angelic powers and their ranks (s. SB III, 581; Abbott; Barth). ὀνομαζομένου pres. pass. part. ὀνομάζω to name. μέλλοντι pres. act. part. dat. sing.
22 masc. μέλλω to be about to, coming. ■ ὑπέταξεν aor. act. ind. ὑποτάσσω to subject. ἔδωκεν aor. act. ind. δίδωμι to give. The verb is followed by the indirect object, i.e., "he gave Him as head over all things to the church." Rather than speaking only of Christ as being "the Head of the church," Paul refers to the cosmic rule of Christ and implies that Christ is the sovereign head of all things (George Howard, "The Head-Body Metaphors
23 of Ephesians," NTS, 20 [April, 1974], 353f.). ■ πληρουμένου pres. mid.-pass. part. πληρόω to fill. The part. could be pass. (Robinson) or it could also be mid., i.e., "the one who fills for himself" (Howard, 351; s. also Abbott).

Ch. 2

1   ■ ὄντας pres. part. εἰμί. παράπτωμα transgression (s.
2 Eph. 1:7). ■ ἐν αἷς strictly speaking the antecedent of the rel. pron. is ταῖς ἁμαρτίαις but logically it refers to both "sins" and "transgressions." ποτέ at that time, formerly. περιεπατήσατε aor. act. ind. περιπατέω to walk about, to conduct one's life. The aor. views the total past life in summary fashion as a point. ἀήρ air, atmosphere, the realm in which the evil powers operate (s. Abbott; Barth; Hodge). τοῦ πνεύματος. The gen. is best understood as being in apposition to the words τῆς ἐξουσίας τοῦ ἀέρος (s. Ellicott). ἀπείθεια disobedience. The phrase "sons of disobedience" is a Hebraic expression indicating that their chief characteristic is that of "disobedience" (s. BG, 16).
3   ■ ἀνεστράφημεν aor. pass. ind. ἀναστρέφομαι to conduct one's life. The word refers to the social action whereas the verb

"walk" in v. 2 is used more of personal action (Westcott). ἐπιθυμία desires, strong lust. σαρκός gen., subjective gen. indicating the source of the desires. ποιοῦντες pres. act. part. διάνοια understanding, intelligence, mind, disposition, thought (BAG). ἤμεθα impf. εἰμί. φύσις nature. ὀργή wrath, anger (s. Rom. 1:18). ■ πλούσιος rich. ἔλεος mercy, compassion, pity. 4 The word indicates the emotion aroused by someone in need and the attempt to relieve the person and remove his trouble (CBB; TDNT; Trench; *Synonyms*, 166f.). ἠγάπησεν aor. act. ind. ἀγαπάω to love. ■ συνεζωοποίησεν aor. act. ind. 5 συζωοποιέω to make alive together w. The word is a synonym for the verb "to raise" but it can also have the meaning "to keep alive" or "to preserve life" (Barth). σεσωσμένοι perf. pass. part. σῴζω to rescue, to save. The perf. tense points to the completed action w. a continuing result thus emphasizing the continual state or condition. ■ συνήγειρεν aor. act. ind. 6 συνεγείρω to raise together w. Believers not only receive life, but they experience a resurrection (Eadie). συνεκάθισεν aor. act. ind. συνκαθίζω to cause to sit down together w. another. ἐπουράνιος heavenly (s. Eph. 1:3). ■ ἐνδείξηται aor. pass. 7 subj. ἐκδείκνυμι to demonstrate, to display, to show, to prove. ἐπερχομένοις pres. mid. part. ἐπέρχομαι to come upon, approaching. The times after the coming of the Lord are viewed as being already "on the approach" (Meyer). ὑπερβάλλον pres. act. part. ὑπερβάλλω to throw beyond, to exceed, to surpass. The part. is used in the sense "surpassing, extraordinary, outstanding" (BAG). χρηστότης usefulness, goodness, kindness. The word involves the idea of the exercise of kindness toward another (Abbott; s. also Trench; *Synonyms*, 232f.; TDNT). ■ τῇ 8 χάριτι instrumental dat. "by grace." The definite article appears w. the word because it is the grace already mentioned (Abbott). διὰ πίστεως "through faith." The prep. indicates the channel through which salvation comes (s. Ellicott). Faith is not viewed as a positive work or accomplishment of the individual (s. Gaugler). θεοῦ the gen. is emphasized by its position before the substitutive and stands in emphatic contrast w. the personal pron. "from you" (Abbott). ■ καυχήσηται aor. mid. subj. 9 καυχάομαι to boast, to glory. The subj. is used in a neg. purpose clause. ■ ποίημα that which is made, work. The word can also 10 have connation of a "work of art," esp. a poetic product, including fiction (Barth). κτισθέντες aor. pass. part. κτίζω to create. The word points to God's new creation in Christ. (For this aspect of Paul's teaching against its Jewish background, s. PRJ, 119ff.) ἐπί w. the dat. "for." The prep. indicates the goal or purpose. It primarily designates movement ending in a definite spot (IBG, 50). προητοίμασεν aor. act. ind. προετοιμάζω to prepare beforehand. The prep. refers to a period before the action described in the part. "created" and describes the means by which the end is secured according to divine arrangement (s. Eadie). περιπατήσωμεν aor. subj. The subj. is used in a purpose clause.

11   ■ διό therefore. μνημονεύετε pres. act. imp. μνημονεύω to remember. The word calls for repentence, decision, and gratitude (Barth). ποτέ formerly. ἔθνος nation, pl. Gentile, the non-Jewish world. ἐν σαρκί "in the flesh." The words suggest the external and temporary nature of the distinction (Robinson). λεγόμενοι pres. pass. part. ἀκροβυστία foreskin, uncircumcision. περιτομή circumcision (s. TDNT; Barth; CBB).

12 χειροποίητος verbal adj. handmade. ■ ἦτε impf., s.v.3. καιρός time, season, dat. of time. ἀπηλλοτριωμένοι perf. pass. part. ἀπαλλοτριόω to estrange, to alienate. The perf. tense indicates the state or condition. πολιτεία citizenship, state, commonwealth. It indicates the government of Israel framed by God in which religion and polity were co-joined (Eadie). ξένος stranger followed by the gen. of separation "strange to something" (BD, 98). διαθήκη covenant, treaty. ἐπαγγελία promise. ἔχοντες pres. act. part. ἄθεος without God, godless, atheist. The perf.

13 negates the stem of the word (s. Moorhouse, 47ff.). ■ ὄντες pres. act. part., s.v.1. μακράν adv. far, far off. ἐγενήθητε aor. pass. ind. ἐγγύς near. The terms "far" and "near" were used in rabbinical writings and indicated among other things non-Jews (far) and Jews (near) or those who were righteous and near God or those who were godless and far away (s. SB III, 585–587).

14   ■ ἡ εἰρήνη. The article used w. the pred. noun presents the pred. as something well known or as that which alone merits the designation, i.e., the only thing to be considered (BD, 143). ποιήσας aor. act. part. ἀμφότερος both, i.e., both Jews and Gentiles (Abbott). The n. is used if it is not the individual but a general quality that is to be emphasized (BD, 76). μεσότοιχον middle wall, dividing wall. (For a discussion of the various views concerning the "middle wall," s. Barth.) The context identifies the "wall" in four ways: it is the fact of separation between Israel and the nations; it has to do w. the law and its statutes and interpretations; it is experienced in the enmity between Jews and Gentiles; it also consists of the enmity of both Jews and Gentiles against God (Barth). φραγμός fence, partition. It signified originally a fence or railing erected for protection rather than separation (Barth). λύσας aor. act. part. λύω to loose, to destroy, to break down. The aor. tense points to the completed action.

ἔχθρα enmity, hostility. ■ ἐντόλη command. δόγμα decree. 15
The law consisted of, i.e. was "in decrees." καταργήσας aor.
act. part. καταργέω to invalidate, to nullify, to annul, to make
of no effect (Simpson). κτίσῃ aor. act. subj. κτίζω to create. The
subj. is used to express purpose. ποιῶν pres. act. part. ■ 16
ἀποκαταλλάξῃ aor. act. subj. ἀποκαταλλάσσω to change,
to exchange, to turn from hostility to friendship, to reconcile.
The double prep. in compound may be intensive (Abbott; s. also
Barth) or there may be a hint at a restoration to a primal unity
(Ellicott; s. also Col. 1:20). σταύρος cross. The term reveals two
things: Christ's death is shameful among men, not honorable; it
corresponds to death on the gallows. Also, it is an execution in
which God's curse was borne (Barth). ἀποκτείνας aor. act. part.
ἀποκτείνω to put to death, to kill. The part. is used to express
means. ■ ἐλθών aor. act. part. ἔρχομαι. εὐηγγελίσατο aor. 17
mid. ind. εὐαγγελίζομαι to proclaim good news. ■ 18
προσαγωγή entrance, access. The word was used of a solemn
approach to a deity and of access to a king's presence (Simpson).
■ ἄρα therefore. The word marks the progress in the argument 19
and has a connective sense implying a consequence. The double
particles (ἄρα οὖν) in combination are intended to imply logical
connection, the one simply reinforcing the other and both are
used to sum up the argument of the whole section (Thrall, 11;
Eadie). οὐκέτι no longer. πάροικος one living along side, alien.
A resident alien was subject to only a part of the law of the land
and enjoyed only corresponding legal protection according to
the OT meaning (Barth; s. also TDOT under "ger").
συμπολίτης fellow citizen. οἰκεῖος one's own household,
family. When used of persons it means "of one's family," strictly
of kinsmen, sometimes loosely of familiar friends (Robinson).
■ ἐποικοδομηθέντες aor. pass. part. ἐποικοδομέω to build 20
upon. θεμέλιος foundation. ἀκρογωνιαῖς foundation stone,
cornerstone, keystone. The word could refer either to the cornerstone or to the keystone in an archway (s. TDNT; 1 Peter
2:6). ■ οἰκοδομή building. συναρμολογουμένη pres. pass. 21
part. συναρμολογέω to fit together. In construction terms it
represents the whole of the elaborate process by which stones are
fitted together: the preparation of the surfaces, including the
cutting, rubbing, and testing; the preparation of the dowels and
the dowel holes, and finally the fitting of the dowels w. molten
lead (Robinson, 262). αὔξω pres. ind. act. to increase, to grow.
The pres. tense indicates the continual development. ναός temple. ■ συνοικοδομεῖσθε pres. pass. ind. συνοικοδομέω to 22
build together, pass. to be built together, i.e., together w. the

527

others. The pres. tense is used because the building is still going on (Abbott). κατοικητήριον place of dwelling, a place of settling down. (For the suf. indicating place or locality, s. MH, 343.) The prep. indicates the goal or intention.

Ch. 3

1   ■ τούτου χάριν "because of this," "on account of this," "for this reason." The illusion is not only to building God's house on a firm foundation, but also to the unification of Jews and Gentiles (Barth). δέσμιος prisoner. ἔθνος people, nation, pl.
2   "Gentile." ■ εἴ γε "if indeed," "surely." The particles here are used to express assurance (s. Thrall, 87f.). ἠκούσατε aor. act. ind. ἀκούω. οἰκονομία administration, responsibility. The term was used of the administrative responsibility given to a servant over a household (s. Eph. 1:10; TDNT). δοθείσης aor. pass.
3   part. δίδωμι. εἰς ὑμᾶς "for you"; i.e. for your benefit. ■ κατά w. the acc. according to. Used here in an adverbial sense "by way of revelation" and expresses the mode of the making known (Meyer). ἀποκάλυψις unveiling, revealing, revelation. ἐγνωρίσθη aor. ind. pass. γνωρίζω to make known. μυστήριον mystery, that which a human being cannot know but which is revealed by God (s. TDNT; ZPEB IV, 327–330). προέγραψα aor. act. ind. προγράφω to write beforehand. It refers to the previous part of this letter (Schlier). ἐν ὀλίγῳ "in
4   a few words," "in brief." ■ πρὸς ὅ "to that which," "w. reference to," i.e., "w. reference to what I have said" (s. Abbott; Barth). ἀναγινώσκοντες pres. act. part. ἀναγινώσκω to read, temporal use of the part. "when you read." νοῆσαι aor. act. inf. νοέω to perceive, to come to the knowledge of, to apprehend, to understand, to gain an insight into (BAG). σύνεσις understand-
5   ing, insight. ■ γενεά generation. The dat. could be dat. of time "in other generations" (Robinson) or it could be dat. of indirect object "to other generations" (Barth). ἀπεκαλύφθη aor. pass
6   ind. ἀποκαλύπτω to unveil, to reveal. ■ εἶναι pres. inf. εἰμί. The inf. is used to explain the content of the divine revelation. συγκληρονόμος fellow-heir. σύσσωμος fellow members of a body, belonging to the same body. συμμέτοχος fellow partaker, co-sharer. The word was used in the papyri of those who were
7   "joint possessors" of a house (MM). ἐπαγγελία promise. ■ ἐγενήθη aor. pass. ind. γίνομαι. κατά w. the acc., s.v.3. δωρέα gift, followed by the gen. of apposition (Eadie) or the gen. of
8   source. ἐνέργεια working, effectual working (s. Robinson). ■ ἐλαχιστότερος (comp. of the superl. ἐλάχιστος), less than the least, "the smallester," "leaster" (Barth). The form was used to

designate the deepest self-abasement (Eadie). Paul may be making an allusion to his own name (Simpson). (For the form, s. BD, 34.) ἐδόθη aor. pass. ind. δίδωμι. εὐαγγελίσασθαι aor. mid. inf. εὐαγγελίζω to proclaim the good news, to preach the gospel. ἀνεξιχνίατος not able to track out, untraceable (s. Rom 11:33). ▪ φωτίσαι aor. act. inf. φωτίζω to illuminate, to bring 9 into light, to shed light upon. ἀποκεκρυμμένον perf. pass. part. ἀποκρύπτω to hide. The perf. part. indicates the state or condition "that which was hidden." κτίσαντι aor. act. part. κτίζω to create. ▪ γνωρισθῇ aor. pass. subj., s.v.3. ἐπουράνιος heavenly 10 (s. Eph. 1:3). πολυποίκιλος many sided, variegated, very-varied. The word was used to describe robes or hems (Robinson). ▪ πρόθεσις purpose, design (s. Eph. 1:11). The gen. following 11 the word could be descriptive gen. "eternal purpose" or poss. gen. "the purpose that runs through the ages" (Abbott) or it could be obj. gen. "purpose about the ages," "the design concerning the ages." (For this view and a discussion of other views, s. Barth.) ἐποίησεν aor. ind. act. ▪ παρρησία speaking freely, 12 confidence, boldness. προσαγωγή entrance, access (s. Eph. 2:18). πεποίθησις having been persuaded, confidence. ▪ διό 13 therefore. αἰτέομαι pres. mid. ind. to ask, to request. ἐγκακεῖν pres. act. inf. to give in to evil, to be a coward, to be discouraged, to grow weary (s. Gal. 6:9; Luke 18:1). θλῖψις pressure, tribulation, trouble.

▪ κάμπτω to bow. γόνυ knee. (For a discussion of the 14 position of kneeling in prayer, s. Barth.) ▪ πατρία family, de- 15 scendant from a common father. It always refers to a concrete group of people. (For a discussion of the meaning of the term in this passage, s. Barth; SB III, 594.) ὀνομάζεται pres. pass. ind. ὀνομάζω to name, to give a name to a thing. ▪ δῶ aor. act. subj. 16 δίδωμι. The subj. is used w. the particle to give the content of Paul's prayer. δυνάμει "w. power," "w. infused strength," dat. of instrument (Ellicott; Abbott). κραταιωθῆναι aor. pass. inf. κραταιόομαι to strengthen, to fortify, to brace, to invigorate (Simpson; s. also Eph. 1:19). ἔσω inner. ▪ κατοικῆσαι aor. act. 17 inf. κατοικέω to dwell, to live in, to settle down. The verb denotes permanent habitation as opposed to sojourning or an occasional visit (Barth). The inf. could be used as a type of apposition explaining the previous inf. (Schlier). ἐρριζωμένοι perf. pass. part. ῥιζόω to cause to take root, pass. to be or to become firmly rooted or fixed (BAG). The perf. looks at the continuing state or condition. τεθεμελιωμένοι perf. pass. part. θεμελιόω to lay a foundation, to establish, to strengthen. The illusion is to the solid basement of the spiritual temple described

18 in chapter 2 (Eadie). ■ ἐξισχύσητε aor. act. subj. ἐξισχύω to be able, to be fully able, to be strong enough. The prep. in compound is perfective and indicates a strength exerted till its object is attained (MH, 310). καταλαβέσθαι aor. mid. inf. καταλαμβάνω to grasp mentally, to comprehend (s. Abbott).

19 πλάτος breath. μῆκος length. ὕψος height. βάθος depth. ■ γνῶναι aor. act. inf. γινώσκω. ὑπερβάλλουσαν pres. act. part. ὑπερβάλλω to throw beyond, to excel, to surpass (s. Eph. 1:19). πληρωθῆτε aor. pass. subj. πληρόω to fill (s. Eph. 1:23).

20 ■ δυναμένῳ pres. mid. part. dat. of advantage. ποιῆσαι aor. act. inf. ὑπερεκπερισσοῦ superabundantly, quite beyond all measure. The form is used as the highest form of comparison imaginable (BAG). αἰτούμεθα pres. mid. ind. to ask, s.v.13. νοέω pres. act. ind. to understand, s.v.4. ἐνεργουμένη pres. mid. part. ἐνεργέομαι to be active, to be effective (s. Robinson).

21 ■ γενεά s.v.5. ἀμήν truly. Used after a statement to add confirmation (s. TDNT).

Ch. 4

1 ■ παρακαλέω pres. act. ind. to beseech, to exhort, to encourage. The word signifies a will of the writer that is at the same time warm, personal, and urgent (Barth; TDNT; NTW). δέσμιος prisoner. ἀξίως adv. worthily. The adj. has the basic meaning "that which balances the scales," "equivalent" (TDNT). περιπατῆσαι aor. act. inf. περιπατέω to walk about, to conduct one's life. The inf. is used to express the content of Paul's urging. ἧς rel. pron. gen. sing. gen. by attraction to its

2 antecedent (RWP). ἐκλήθητε aor. pass. ind. καλέω to call. ■ ταπεινοφροσύνη lowly thinking, humility. The word refers to the quality of esteeming ourselves as small but at the same time recognizing the power and ability of God (s. TDNT; Trench; Synonyms, 148; CBB; RAC III, 735ff.). πραΰτης meek, gentle. The humble and gentle attitude which expresses itself in a patient submissiveness to offense, free from malice and desire for revenge (s. Matt. 5:5; TDNT; CBB). μακροθυμία longsuffering (s. Gal. 5:22). ἀνεχόμενοι pres. mid. part. ἀνέχομαι to bear, to bear up, to hold one's self up. The word indicates to have patience w. someone till the provocation is past (Eadie). ἀλλήλων

3 (gen. pl.) one another. ■ σπουδάζοντες pres. act. part. σπουδάζω to give diligence, to be eager, to make every effort. τηρεῖν pres. act. inf. to guard, to keep, to maintain (Schlier). ἑνότης unity. σύνδεσμος that which binds together, a bond. The word denotes that which keeps something together (Barth).

4/5 ■ καθώς just as. ἐλπίς hope. ■ βάπτισμα baptism.

■ ἕκαστος each, dat. of the indirect object. ἐδόθη aor. pass. 7 ind. δίδωμι. μέτρον measure. δωρέα gift. Unity is not uniformity, for it is quite consistent w. variety of gifts and offices in the church (Eadie). ■ διὸ λέγει "therefore he says." This formula 8 introduces a citation from the OT and is characterized by the absence of a legalistic and polemic undertone. It is an urgent invitation to listen attentively (Barth; s. also BE, 107ff.). ἀναβάς aor. act. part. ἀναβαίνω to ascend, to go up. ὕψος height. ἠχμαλώτευσεν aor. act. ind. αἰχμαλωτεύω to lead captive. The allusion is to a triumphal possession in which marched the persons taken in war (Eadie; s. also 2 Cor. 2:14). ■ ἀνέβη aor. act. ind. ἀναβαίνω to go up, to ascend. κατέβη 9 aor. act. ind. καταβαίνω to go down, to descend. τὰ κατώτερα μέρη the lower parts, the lower regions. The following gen. "of the earth" could be gen. of apposition and the reference could be to the Incarnation and Christ's coming to earth (RWP; s. also Barth; Hodge). ■ καταβάς aor. act. part. καταβαίνω. 10 ὑπεράνω w. the gen. "high above." πληρώσῃ aor. act. subj. πληρόω to fill (s. Eph. 1:23). ■ ὁ μέν ... ὁ δέ "the one ... the 11 other." εὐαγγελιστής one who proclaims the good news, evangelist. An evangelist was one who proclaimed the gospel which he had received from the apostle. He was particularly a missionary who brought the gospel into new regions (s. Schlier; Barth; TDNT; CBB). ποιμήν shepherd, pastor. The image of a shepherd w. his flock pictures the relation of a spiritual leader to those committed to his charge (Eadie). καί "and." Often the word has the meaning "that is" or "in particular" and indicates that the "shepherds" and "teachers" are viewed as one common group, i.e., "teaching shepherds" (Barth). ■ καταρτισμός 12 equipping. The word was a medical technical term for "the setting of a bone" (BAG). The noun describes the dynamic act by which persons or things are properly conditioned (Barth). οἰκοδομή building, building up, edify. The word is an expression of development (Meyer). ■ μέχρι until. καταντήσωμεν aor. 13 act. subj. καταντάω to come to, to arrive at, to reach, to attain to, to come down to the goal. The subj. is used in a temporal clause w. a purpose idea (RWP). ἐπίγνωσις knowledge, knowledge directed toward a particular object (s. Robinson). τέλειος that which has reached the set goal, perfect, mature. (For a discussion of the various views regarding the "perfect man," s. Barth.) ἡλικία age, full age, ripeness of full age. The word can also mean development in stature but is best understood as "mature age" (s. Eadie; Abbott). ■ μηκέτι no longer. ὦμεν pres. 14 subj. εἰμί. νήπιος baby, immature. It refers to the immaturity

of children in opposition to the perfection of the perfect man
(Barth). κλυδωνιζόμενοι pres. pass. part. κλυδωνίζομαι
driven by waves, to be agitated by waves (RWP).
περιφερόμενοι pres. pass. part. περιφέρω to carry about, to
carry around, to be borne to and fro. (For this figure of speech,
s. Abbott.) ἄνεμος wind. διδασκαλία teaching. κυβεία dice
playing. It means "wicked dice playing" and refers to intentional
fraud (BAG; Barth; Ellicott). πανουργία cleverness, trickery.
μεθοδεία following after, deceit, scheming (RWP; Barth).
πλάνη wandering, roaming. Used figuratively of wandering
from the path of truth: "error," "delusion," "deceit" (BAG).

15 ■ ἀληθεύοντες pres. act. part. ἀληθεύω to be truthful, to tell
the truth, to deal truly. Verbs ending in the suf. express the doing
of an action which is signified by the corresponding noun (Abbott). With this verb the relationship of quality passes to that of
action (MH, 399). αὐξήσωμεν aor. act. subj. αὐξάνω to grow,
to increase (s. Eph. 2:21). τὰ πάντα acc. of general reference
"in respect to all things." It may, however, be viewed adverbially

16 "in every way," "totally" (Barth). ■ συναρμολογούμενον pres.
pass. part. συναρμολογέω to join together, to fit together (s.
Eph. 2:21). συμβιβαζόμενον pres. pass. part. συμβιβάζω to
bring together, to unite, pass. to be held together. It refers to a
body which is held together by sinews, ligaments, joints (BAG).
It refers to a correlation as of a functioning organism (Simpson).
ἀφή joint, contact, touching, i.e., "contact w., the supply" (s.
Abbott). ἐπιχορηγία supply. The simple noun originally indicated a payment for the cost of bringing out a chorus at a public
festival. Then it signified provisions for an army or expedition.
The word w. the prep. in compound was a technical term describing the provision of food, clothing, etc., which a husband is
obligated to make for his wife. Here it indicates that the body
receives from the head what nourishment, life, and direction it
needs (Barth; s. also Robinson). ἐνέργειαν function. It refers to
the working process (Robinson). αὔξησιν part. αὐξάνω growing, pres. mid. ind. The mid. is used of the body promoting its
own growth (Abbott).

17 ■ μαρτύρομαι pres. mid. ind. to testify, to bear witness.
περιπατεῖν pres. act. inf. to walk about, to conduct one's life.
The inf. is used either to express a command or as obj. of the
verb. The pres. tense points to a habitual action. καθὼς just as.
ἔθνος people, nation, pl. Gentiles, heathen, those who were not
Jews. ματαιότης vanity, emptiness, vain. The word contains the
idea of aimlessness, the leading to no object or end, vanity (s.
Trench; Synonyms, 180–184; s. also TDNT). (For the Jewish

indictment of the Gentiles, s. Barth; SB III, 600; JPFC II, 1065ff.) νοῦς mind, thinking facility, reasoning capacity. ■ 18 ἐσκοτωμένοι perf. pass. part. σκοτόω to darken. The perf. part. is used in a periphrastic construction indicating the continuing darkened condition. διάνοια thinking through, understanding, intelligence, the mind as the organ of thinking (BAG). ὄντες pres. part. εἰμί. ἀπηλλοτριωμένοι perf. pass. part. ἀπαλλοτριόω to estrange, to alienate. The perf. tense emphasizes the continuing state or existence "being alienated from the life of God." It does not imply that they had at one time enjoyed that life: it means simply "being aliens" from it (Robinson). ἄγνοια ignorance, lack of knowledge. It refers to the inability to comprehend and see the light (Barth). πώρωσις hardening. The word could be used in a medical sense for callous hardening (RWP; CBB; Barth). ■ ἀπηλγηκότες perf. act. part. ἀπαλγέω 19 to cease to feel pain or grief, to become callous, insensible to pain (T). The translation "past feeling" expresses the sense accurately (Abbott). παρέδωκαν aor. act. ind. παραδίδωμι to deliver over to, to hand over to. ἀσέλγεια unrestrained living (s. Gal. 5:19). ἐργασία working, producing, performance, practice (Robinson). ἀκαθαρσία uncleanness, filthiness, impurity (Barth; s. also Gal. 5:19). πλεονεξία insatiable craving, greed, giving rein to appetites and desires which are against the laws of God and man (NTW, 99; Barth; s. also Rom. 1:29). ■ ἐμάθετε 20 aor. act. ind. μανθάνω to learn. ■ ἠκούσατε aor. act. ind. 21 ἀκούω. ἐδιδάχθητε aor. pass. ind. διδάσκω to teach, pass. to be taught. ■ ἀποθέσθαι aor. mid. inf. ἀποτίθημι to put off, to 22 remove as one puts off clothes. The inf. is used to denote the substance of what they had been taught (Eadie). The aor. tense denotes a once and for all, definite, concluding action: the stripping off is to be done at once, and for good (Barth). ἀναστροφή manner of life (s. Eph. 2:3). παλαιός old. φθειρόμενον pres. pass. part. φθείρω to corrupt. The whole character representing the former self was not only corrupt but ever growing more and more corrupt. This is indicated by the pres. tense (s. Westcott). Every trait of the Old Man's behavior is putrid, crumbling, or inflated like rottening waste or cadavers, stinking, ripe for being disposed of and forgotten (Barth). ἐπιθυμία strong desire, lust. ἀπάτη deceit. ■ ἀνανεοῦσθαι pres. pass. inf. ἀνανεόω to 23 make new again, to renew. The pres. tense emphasizes the continuing renewing. ■ ἐνδύσασθαι aor. mid. inf. ἐνδύομαι to put 24 on. Often used in the sense of putting on a garment. The inf. gives the positive side of v. 22. κτισθέντα aor. pass. part. κτίζω to create. ὁσιότης piety, holiness. It indicates fulfilling the divine demands which God places upon men (CBB; TDNT; Ellicott).

25   ■ ἀποθέμενος aor. mid. part., s.v.22. ψεῦδος lie. λαλεῖτε pres. act. imp. The pres. imp. points to a habitual action which is to characterize the life. πλησίον one who is close by, neigh-

26 bor. ἀλλήλων one another, s.v.2. μέλος member. ■ ὀργίζεσθε pres. mid. imp. ὀργίζω to be angry. A quotation from Ps. 4:5 (LXX). ἁρμαρτάνετε pres. act. imp. to sin. ἐπιδυέτω pres. act. imp. ἐπιδύω to go down, to set. The day of the anger should be the day of reconciliation (Barth). παροργισμός anger, angry mood, a violent irritation is meant, expressed by either hiding one's self from others or by flaming looks, harmful words, incon-

27 siderate actions (Barth). ■ δίδοτε pres. act. imp. τόπος place.

28 διάβολος slanderer, devil. ■ κλέπτων pres. act. part. κλέπτω to steal. The pres. part. indicates the continuous action, i.e., "the one stealing." μηκέτι no longer. κλεπτέτω pres. act. imp. The pres. imp. w. the neg. calls for the stopping of an action in progress. κοπιάτω pres. act. imp. κοπιάω to grow weary, to work w. effort, to labor (AS). ἐργαζόμενος pres. mid. part. to work. ἔχῃ pres. act. subj. Subjunctive used in a purpose clause. μεταδίδωμι pres. act. inf. to give w., to share. The inf. could express purpose or result. χρεία need, necessity. ἔχοντι pres. act. part. (For the sharing among the Dead Sea community, s.

29 CD, 14:12f.) ■ σαπρός rank, foul, putrid, rotten, worthless, disgusting (Simpson; Abbott). ἐκπορευέσθω pres. mid. imp. ἐκπορεύομαι to go out, to come out. οἰκοδομή building, edify. δῷ aor. act. subj. δίδωμι. The subj. is used in a purpose clause. χάρις grace. Used w. this verb it means "to confer a favor," i.e., to give pleasure or profit. The meaning is, "that it may benefit

30 the hearers" (Hodge). ἀκούουσιν pres. act. part. dat. pl. ■ λυπεῖτε pres. act. imp. λυπέω to cause sorrow, to grieve. The pres. imp. w. the neg. is used to forbid a continual and habitual action. The Spirit who makes men attest to the truth is put to shame when the saints "lie" to one another and utter "foul talk" (Barth). ἐσφραγίσθητε aor. pass. ind. σφραγίζω to seal (s. Eph. 1:13; 2 Cor. 1:22). ἀπολύτρωσις release through the pay-

31 ment of a price, redemption (s. Rom. 3:24). ■ πικρία bitterness. It is a figurative term denoting that fretted and irritable state of mind that keeps a man in perpetual animosity—that inclines him to harsh and uncharitable opinions of men and things—that makes him sour, crabby and repulsive in his general demeanor— that brings a scowl over his face and infuses venom into the words of his tongue (Eadie). θυμός anger. It expresses the temporary excitement or passion (Abbott; Trench; Synonyms,

130f.). ὀργή wrath. It refers to the more subtle and deep-flowing anger (Abbott; s. also Trench; *Synonyms*, 130f.; TDNT). κραυγή clamor, outcry, shouting. It is the cry of strife (Ellicott). βλασφημία slander, speaking evil of someone. It is a more enduring manifestation of inward anger, that shows itself in reviling. These two words are the outward manifestation of the foregoing vices (Ellicott). ἀρθήτω aor. pass. imp. αἴρω to pick up and carry away, to take away, to make a clean sweep (RWP). κακία malice, badness. It is a generic term and seems to signify "badhardiness," the root of all those vices (Eadie). ■ γίνεσθε 32 pres. mid. imp. χρηστός useful, worthy, good, kind, benevolent (BAG; TDNT; CBB; Gal. 5:22). εὔσπλαγχνος in the lit. and physical sense "having healthy bowels." The inward organs were considered the seat of emotion and intention. The word then means "compassionate," "tender-hearted" (Barth; TDNT; s. also 1 Peter 3:8). χαριζόμενοι pres. mid. part. χαρίζομαι to forgive, to exercise grace in freely forgiving. καθώς just as. ἐχαρίσατο aor. mid. ind.

Ch. 5

■ γίνεσθε pres. mid. imp. μιμητής imitator. ἀγαπητός 1 beloved. ■ περιπατεῖτε pres. act. imp. περιπατέω to walk 2 about, to conduct one's life. καθώς just as. ἠγάπησεν aor. act. ind. ἀγαπάω to love (s. John 3:16). παρέδωκεν aor. act. ind. παραδίδωμι to deliver over. The verb expresses wherein his love was shown (Abbott). προσφορά offering. The word generally denotes offerings which consist of products from the field and trees (Barth). θυσία sacrifice. The word describes the offering of animals from the flock or stable which were killed at the holy place and portions of which were burned upon the altar (Barth). ὀσμή smell. εὐωδία sweet odor, fragrance. The phrase "odor of fragrance" is a fig. designation for the acceptableness of the offering (Meyer). ■ πορνεία illicit sex activity (s. TDNT). 3 ἀκαθαρσία uncleanness, impurity, filthiness (s. Eph. 4:19; Gal. 5:19). πλεονεξία greediness (s. Rom. 1:29; Eph. 4:19). μηδέ emphatic neg. "not even." ὀνομαζέσθω pres. pass. imp. ὀνομάζω to name, pass. to be named. Here "let it not be even mentioned by name" (Ellicott). πρέπει pres. act. ind. to be fitting, to be suitable, to be proper. ■ αἰσχρότης shameful, filthy 4 or obscene speech, perhaps also w. the idea of "shameful conduct" (Abbott; Barth). μωρολογία foolish talk, silly talk. It is that "talk of fools," which is foolishness and sin together (Trench; *Synonyms*, 121). It is where a mere laugh is aimed at even without wit (Bengel). εὐτραπελία coarse jesting. It implies

the dexterity of turning a discourse to wit or humor; and lastly deceptive speech, so formed that the speaker easily contrives to wriggle out of its meaning or engagements (Eadie). Ephesus was especially known for producing facetious orators (Barth). ἀνῆκεν impf. act. ind. ἀνῆκει impersonal, it is proper, it is fitting. The impf. is used of necessity, obligation, duty and is used here in the sense "what is (really) not proper" (but yet happens) (BD, 181). μᾶλλον rather. εὐχαριστία thanksgiving. Gratitude is here singled out as the basic structural feature of the
5 Christian's ethic (Barth). ■ ἴστε pres. act. ind. or imp. οἶδα. The form is probably best understood as imp. and perhaps a Hebraism used w. the following part. w. the meaning "know of a surity" (s. M, 245; MH, 222; ND, 352; Barth). γινώσκοντες pres. act. part. πόρνος one who practices sexual immorality, fornicator. πλεονέκτης one who is greedy (s. Rom. 1:29). ὅ ἐστίν "that is to say." A formulaic phrase used without reference to the gender of the word explained or to that of the word which explains (BD, 73). εἰδωλολάτρης one who serves an idol, idolator. κληρονομία inheritance.
6   ■ ἀπατάτω pres. act. imp. ἀπατάω to lead astray, to mislead, to deceive. κενός empty, without content, "empty words" or words which have not inner substance and kernel of truth, hollow sophistries and apologies for sin (Trench; Synonyms, 180). διὰ ταῦτα γάρ refers not only to v. 6, but also to the previous verses. ὀργή wrath. ἀπείθεια disobedience, "sons of disobedience" is a Semitic expression indicating that the chief
7 characteristic of the per. is disobedience (s. BG, 15f.). ■ συμμέτοχος fellow partaker, partner, one who shares together
8/9 w. another. ■ ἦτε impf. εἰμί. ποτέ formerly. ■ ἀγαθωσύνη
10 goodness (s. Gal. 5:22). ■ δοκιμάζοντες pres. act. part. δοκιμάζω to approve after examination, to arrange and execute a test, to accept and heed the results of a test, to carry out a careful examination, to find out by experience (s. Barth). εὐάρεστος well-pleasing, acceptable, followed by the dat. of
11 advantage. ■ συγκοινωνεῖτε pres. act. imp. συγκοινωνέω to join in fellowship w. someone, to have part in a thing (Abbott). The pres. imp. w. the neg. forbids a continual and habitual act (MKG, 272f.). ἄκαρπος unfruitful. ἐλέγχετε pres. act. imp. ἐλέγχω to bring to light, to expose, to reveal hidden things, to convict or convince, to reprove, to correct, to punish, to discipline. (For the variant meanings, s. Barth; TDNT; Robinson.)
12/13 ■ κρυφῇ hidden, secret. γινόμενα pres. mid. part. ■ ἐλεγχόμενα pres. pass. part., s.v.11. φῶς light. φανεροῦται pres. pass. ind. φανερόω to make clear, to make known, pass.

to become visible or known, to be revealed (BAG). ■ 14
φανερούμενον pres. pass. part. διὸ λέγει (s. Eph. 4:8). Paul
evidently uses a free adaptation of Isa. 26:19 and 61:1 (RWP; s.
also Eadie). ἔγειρε pres. act. imp. ἐγείρω to rise, to wake up.
καθεύδων pres. act. part. καθεύδω to sleep, to be asleep.
ἀνάστα aor. act. imp. ἀνίσταμαι to stand up, to get up.
ἐπιφαύσει fut. act. ind. ἐπιφαύσκω to shine upon. The means
employed by the Messiah are compared to the rays of the rising
sun. God's glory or light appearing over Israel exerted the life-
giving power (Barth).

■ βλέπετε pres. act. inf. to watch, to give heed. ἀκριβῶς 15
accurately, carefully. περιπατέω pres. act. ind. to walk about,
to conduct one's life. The pres. tense points to the continual
action. ἄσοφος unwise. σοφός wise. The applying of acquired
knowledge (s. TDNT). ■ ἐξαγοραζόμενοι pres. mid. part. 16
ἐξαγοράζομαι to buy up at the market place. Either w. the
meaning "seizing the opportunity," "making your market to the
full from the opportunity of this life" (Abbott) or w. the meaning
"buying back (at the expense of personal watchfulness and self-
denial) the pres. time, which is now being used for evil and
godless purposes" (MM). καιρός time, opportunity. πονηρός
evil, active evil. ■ γίνεσθε pres. mid. imp. ἄφρων without 17
understanding, senseless. The word refers to imprudence or folly
in action (Abbott). συνίετε pres. act. imp. συνίημι to understand, the ability to bring things together and see them in relation to one another. The saints are encouraged to make use of
their reasoning power (Barth). ■ μεθύσκεσθε pres. mid. imp. 18
μεθύσκομαι to get drunk, to be drunk. In Philo's treatise entitled "On Drunkenness" he characterizes drunkenness generally
as a mark of the blind and foolish man who is a slave to the
material world (CBB). Others describe drunkenness as producing inability to preserve one's self-control and forcing one to
commit many distasteful acts (DC XXXVII, 55). The religious
aspects of drunkenness were seen in the Bacchus festivals in the
worship of Dionysus (s. Barth; KP II, 77–85; OCD 352f.;
DGRA, 410–414; Cleon Rogers, "The Dionysian Background of
Ephesians 5:18," Bib Sac 136 [July, 1979], 249–257). The neg.
w. the pres. imp. calls for a discontinuation of an action in
progress or is used to prohibit a habitual action. ἀσωτία excess.
The word indicated one who himself cannot save or spare thus
one who extravagantly squanders his means, and then it chiefly
denoted a dissolute, debauched, profligate manner of living
(Trench; Synonyms, 54f.; s. also Josephus; Jewish War, IV, 651f.;
MM; TDNT). The excesses and the flagrant and senseless activi-

ties connected w. the religious celebrations to Dionysus were well-known to the ancient world. The worshipers felt that they were united, indwelled, and controlled by Dionysus who gave them special powers and abilities (s. the references by the previous word; s. also H.J. Rose, *Religion in Greece and Rome*, 60f. [New York: Harper and Brothers, 1959]; Rogers, Bib Sac 136 [July, 1979], 249–257). πληροῦσθε pres. pass. imp. πληρόω to fill, pass. to be filled. The idea of the word is "control." The indwelling Spirit of God is the One who should continually control and dominate the life of the believer. This stands in marked contrast to the worshipers of Dionysus. The pres. tense calls for a habitual and continuing action. The pass. could be

19 permissive pass. "allow yourselves to be . . ." (s. BD, 165). ■ λαλοῦντες pres. act. part. The following parts. indicate the outworking or practice of being filled w. the Spirit (s. Schlier). ψαλμός song of praise, psalm. The verb meant primarily the plucking of the strings and the noun was used of sacred songs chanted to the accompaniment of instrumental music (Abbott; Eadie; Barth). ὕμνος hymn. It refers to sacred poetical compositions whose primary purpose is to praise (Eadie). ᾠδή song. This was the general word which originally meant any kind of song but was specially used of lyric poetry (Abbott). ᾄδοντες pres. act. part. ᾄδω to sing. ψάλλοντες pres. act. part. ψάλλω to play on strings, to sing to the accompaniment of a harp, to sing praise

20 (BAG). ■ εὐχαριστοῦντες pres. act. part. εὐχαριστέω to be
21 thankful, to give thanks. πάντοτε always. ■ ὑποτασσάμενοι pres. mid. part. ὑποτάσσομαι to line one's self up under, to submit. Used in a military sense of soldiers submitting to their superior or slaves submitting to their masters. The word has primarily the idea of giving up one's own right or will, i.e., "to subordinate one's self" (s. RWP; TDNT; Barth). ἀλλήλοις dat. pl. "to one another." φόβος fear, reverence.

22/23 ■ ἴδιος one's own. ■ κεφαλή head. The word speaks of
24 authority and direction (s. Eadie). σωτήρ savior, protector. ■ ὑποτάσσεται pres. mid. ind., s.v.21. The pres. tense points to
25 the continual action or state. οὕτως so. ■ οἱ ἄνδρες voc. "you men." The Attic Gr. used the nom. w. the article only in addressing inferiors in a rather harsh manner. However, the NT does not follow this practice and uses the nom. w. the article as the voc. sometimes under Semitic influence (s. BD, 81f.; MT, 31f.). ἀγαπᾶτε pres. act. imp. ἀγαπάω to love. The pres. imp. calls for a continual habitual action. καθώς just as. ἠγάπησεν aor. act. ind. παρέδωκεν aor. act. ind., s.v.2. In a time when marriages were arranged and morals were so loose, to fulfill the

commands of subordination and love was not an easy task. (For marriage and the home in the ancient world, including both Jewish and Gentile, s. SB III, 610–613; JPFC II, 748–769; Barth 655–662, 700–720; W.K. Lacey, *The Family in Classical Greek* [London: Thames & Hudson, 1972]; Heinrich Greeven, "Ehe nach dem Neuen Testament," NTS, 15 [July, 1969], 365–388.)

■ ἁγιάσῃ aor. act. subj. ἁγιάζω to sanctify, to make holy, to 26 set apart. (For the relation of this word to the marriage ceremony, s. Barth.) καθαρίσας aor. act. part. καθαρίζω to cleanse. λουτρόν bath. Since a bridal bath was the practice both among Jews and Gentiles, Paul may be making allusions to this custom (s. SB I, 506; DGRA, 737). Barth's objection that such an allusion would mean that the bridegroom would be said to have given the bride a bath is to press the allusion too far (s. Barth, 694). The case is either locative or instrumental. ῥῆμα word, spoken word. Perhaps the reference is to the gospel which is proclaimed. ■ παραστήσῃ aor. act. subj. παρίστημι to 27 present. ἔνδοξος glorious. ἔχουσαν pres. act. part. acc. fem. sing. σπίλος spot, speck, fleck, stain. ῥυτίς wrinkle, fold. The word referred to a wrinkle or fold on the face. The terms used here are taken from physical beauty, health, and symmetry, to denote spiritual perfection (Eadie). τοιοῦτος such a thing. ᾖ pres. subj. εἰμί. Subjunctive used in a purpose clause. ἄμωμος blameless. ■ ὀφείλω pres. act. ind. to owe someone a debt, to 28 be obligated, to ought to. The word indicates moral obligation (s. TDNT). The pres. tense indicates the continual existence of the obligation. ἀγαπῶν pres. act. part. ■ ἐμίσησεν aor. act. ind. 29 μισέω to hate. The aor. is gnomic and expresses something which is always true. ἐκτρέφει pres. act. ind. to nourish, to nourish children to maturity (T). The prep. in compound is perfective. The pres. tense of a linear verb denotes the whole process leading up to an attained goal (M, 114). θάλπει pres. act. ind. to cherish, to show affection and tender love. ■ μέλος 30 member. ■ ἀντὶ τούτου because of this, for this reason. 31 καταλείψει fut act. ind. καταλείπω to leave behind. προσκολληθήσεται fut. pass. ind. προσκολλάομαι to be glued to, to be joined to. The previous word suggests the complete separation from all former ties and this word gives the forming of a new relation. ἔσονται fut. mid. ind. εἰμί. ■ 32 μυστήριον (s. Eph. 3:3). The word refers to that which is incapable of being discovered by human being but also that which is revealed by God. Here it has to do w. the mystical union of Christ and His church. ■ πλήν in any case, however. The word 33 is used for breaking off discussion and emphasizing what is important (BAG). ἀγαπάτω pres. act. imp. φοβῆται pres. mid. subj. φοβέομαι to reverence, to show respect.

Ch. 6

1 ■ ὑπακούετε pres. act. imp. ὑπακούω to listen to, to obey.
2 γονεῖς parent. ■ τίμα pres. act. imp. τιμάω to count as valuable, to value, to honor, to revere (BAG; TDNT). ἐντολή commandment. ἐπαγγελία promise. (For the Jewish teaching regarding this commandment and the position of children in the
3 family, s. SB I, 705–717, III, 614; JPFC II, 769f.) ■ εὖ adv. well. γένηται aor. mid. subj. γίνομαι. ἔσῃ fut. mid. ind. 2nd per. sing. εἰμί. It is possible that the fut. is used here because there was no aor. subj. of the verb (Abbott). μακροχρόνιος long-
4 lived, long-timed (s. Eadie). ■ παροργίζετε pres. act. imp. παροργίζομαι to anger, to make angry, to bring one along to a deep-seated anger. The prep. in compound indicates an "onward motion" (MH, 320; s. also Schlier; TDNT; Eph. 4:26). The neg. w. the pres. imp. is used to prevent a habitual action. ἐκτρέφετε pres. act. imp. ἐκτρέφω to nourish, to provide for w. tender care (s. Eph. 5:29). (For the responsibility of the father for the children in a Jewish family, s. JPFC II, 769f.) παιδείᾳ education, child training, discipline. The word indicates the discipline used to correct the transgression of the laws and ordinances of the Christian household (Trench; *Synonyms*, 112; s. also TDNT). νουθεσίᾳ admonition. It refers to the training by word—by the word of encouragement, when this is sufficient, but also that of remonstrance, of reproof, of blame, where these may be required (Trench; *Synonyms*, 112; s. also TDNT).
5 ■ φόβος fear, reverence. τρόμος tremble. The words only express anxious solicitude about the performance of duty, so that there is no allusion to the hardness of the service (Abbott).
6 ἁπλότης simplicity, sincerity, uprightness (BAG). ■ ὀφθαλμοδουλία eyeservice. It is labor when the master is present, but relaxation and laziness as soon as he is gone (Eadie). ἀνθρωπάρεσκος men pleaser, one who tries to please men at
7 the sacrifice of principle (BAG). ποιοῦντες pres. act. part. ■ εὔνοια good will. It suggests the ready good will, which does not wait to be compelled (Robinson). δουλεύοντες pres. act. part.
8 ■ εἰδότες perf. act. part. οἶδα. ἕκαστος each. ποιήσῃ aor. act. subj. κομίσεται fut. mid. ind. κομίζομαι to receive, to receive back, i.e., to receive as a deposit; hence here it implies an adequate return (Abbott). εἴτε ... εἴτε whether ... or. ἐλεύθερος
9 free. ■ ποιεῖτε pres. act. ind. ἀνιέτες pres. act. part. ἀνίημι to loosen up, to relax, "to let up on" (RWP). ἀπειλή threatening.

προσωπολημψία the accepting of one's person, partiality.

■ τοῦ λοιποῦ finally, for the remaining. ἐνδυναμοῦσθε 10
pres. pass. imp. ἐνδυναμόω to empower, pass. to be
strengthened. κράτος strength. ἰσχύς might. (For these two
words, s. Eph. 1:19.) ■ ἐνδύσασθε aor. mid. imp. ἐνδύομαι to 11
put on, to clothe one's self. πανοπλία full armor, complete
armor. This included such things as a shield, sword, lance, helmet, greaves, and breastplate (T; for a description of a Roman
soldier and his armor, s. CC, 207f.; Josephus; *Jewish Wars*, III,
93ff.). Since armor of a soldier was often a display of splendor,
Barth prefers the translation "the splendid armor" (s. Barth,
793–795). τοῦ θεοῦ gen. of source or origin indicating that God
provides the armor (Eadie). στῆναι aor. act. inf. ἵσταμι to
stand. The word could be used in a military sense indicating
either "to take over," "to hold a watch post," or it could also
mean "to stand and hold out in a critical position on a battle-
field" (Barth). μεθοδεία scheming, craftiness. διάβολος slanderer, devil. ■ πάλη struggle, wrestling. The word refers partic- 12
ularly to a "hand-to-hand fight" (Barth). Wrestling was a fight
characterized by trickery, cunningness, and strategy (DGRA,
817; KP IV, 1436; CC, 143f.). κοσμοκράτωρ world ruler. (For
a discussion of the spiritual warfare in the DSS, s. 1QM.) ■ 13
ἀναλάβετε aor. act. imp. ἀναλαμβάνω to take up. The word
was used as a military technical term describing the last preparation and final step necessary before the actual battle begins
(Barth). The aor. imp. demands an immediate action. δυνηθῆτε
aor. pass. subj. Subjunctive used in a purpose clause. ἀνιστῆναι
aor. act. inf. ἀνθίσταμι to spend against, to resist.
κατεργασάμενοι aor. mid. part. κατεργάζομαι to accomplish, to carry out. Although the word may mean "to carry to
victory," it here means not only "having made all necessary
preparations," but indicates having done everything which the
crisis demands, in order to quail the foe and maintain the position (Eadie; s. also Barth). ■ στῆτε aor. act. imp. ἵσταμι ingres- 14
sive aor. "take your stand" (RWP). περιζωσάμενοι aor. mid.
part. περιζώννυμι to bind around one's self, to gird one's self.
The Roman soldiers wore one of at least three wide belts or
girdles. The breech-like leather apron worn to protect the lower
abdomen or the sword-belt which was buckled on together w. the
sword as the decisive step in the process of preparing one's self
for battle and the special belt or sash designating an officer or
high official (Barth; TDNT). ὀσφῦς hips. ἐνδυσάμενοι aor.
mid. part. θώραξ breastplate. The word denotes a piece of armor
that can mean everything that was worn at different periods to

protect the body between the shoulders and the loins. The average Roman soldier wore a piece of metal, but those who could afford it used the very best available: a scale or chain mail
15 that covered chest and hips (Barth; DGRA, 711f.). ■ ὑποδησάμενοι aor. mid. part. ὑποδέομαι to bind under, to strap on. It may refer to the *caliga*, the strong and heavy shoe worn by the Roman soldiers. This shoe was thickly studded w. hobnails or it may refer to the more elegant shoe, the *calceus*, which was worn by men of higher rank (s. DGRA, 233f.). τοὺς πόδας acc. of general reference. ἑτοιμασία preparation, readiness. The word may however in this context have the meaning "firmly" and express solidity, firmness, solid foundation (Barth).
16 ■ ἀναλαβόντες aor. act. part. ἀναλαμβάνω to take up, s.v.13. θυρεός shield. It refers to the large door-shaped shield in contrast to the small round convex shield. The reference is to the Roman soldiers *scutum* which had an iron frame and sometimes a metal boss in the center at the front. Often the several layers of leather were soaked in water before the battle in order to put out the incendiary missiles of the enemy (Barth). δυνήσεσθε fut. mid. ind. βέλος dart, arrow. The term could be used of any type of missile (Barth). πεπυρωμένα perf. pass. part. πυρόω to set on fire. The perf. pass. part. indicates that the arrows were set on fire and are burning. These were arrows or spears tipped w. tow and dipped in pitch (Barth; s. also Josephus; *Jewish Wars*, III, 173). σβέσαι aor. act. inf. σβέννυμι to put out, to quench.
17 ■ περικεφαλαία a protection around the head, helmet. The Roman soldier wore a bronze helmet equipped w. cheek pieces. The helmet was a heavy decorative and expensive item which had an inside lining of felt or sponge which made the weight bearable. Nothing short of an axe or hammer could pierce a heavy helmet (Barth; TDNT). σωτήριον salvation, gen. of apposition. δέξασθε aor. mid. imp. δέχομαι to take, to receive. μάχαιρα sword. It signifies the short, straight sword used by the
18 Roman soldier (Barth; DGRA, 577; TDNT). ■ δέησις request, prayer, petition. It is generally a petition for particular benefits or a petition arising from a particular need (s. Trench; *Synonyms*, 189; CBB; TDNT). προσευχόμενοι pres. mid. part. προσεύχομαι to pray. This is the general word which was used for making a petition to a divine being, i.e., to pray (s. CBB; TDNT; Trench; *Synonyms*, 188f.). καιρός time, occasion, opportunity. εἰς αὐτό "for this." ἀγρυπνοῦντες pres. act. part. ἀγρυπνέω to stay awake, to lie sleepless, to pass a sleepless night, to suffer from insomnia, to be watchful, to be vigilant (Barth). προσκαρτέρησις perseverance, constancy (s. LAE,

102). The verb was used in the papyri in the sense of holding out or waiting, e.g., waiting until one's trial came before the court or diligently remaining at one's work (s. Preisigke). ■ δόθῇ aor. 19 pass. subj. δίδωμι. ἄνοιξις opening. στόμα mouth. παρρησία speaking everything, speaking openly, boldness (s. TDNT). γνωρίσαι aor. act. inf. γνωρίζω to make known. μυστήριον mystery (s. Eph. 3:3). ■ πρεσβεύω to be an ambassador or 20 envoy, to travel or work as an ambassador (BAG; s. also 2 Cor. 5:20). ἄλυσις chain. The description of an ambassador in chains could be a paradox in three aspects. The term "chain" could indicate a necklace worn by ambassadors to reveal the riches, power, and dignity of the government they represent, but Paul's chain is one of an iron prison chain. The word could also refer to imprisonment, and because an ambassador normally would not be arrested, Paul indicates the wrong he is suffering. Finally, a delegate who is in prison knows that the end of his mission is near (Barth). παρρησιάσωμαι aor. mid. subj. παρρησιάζομαι to speak everything, to speak openly and frankly, to speak boldly, to be bold. δεῖ it is necessary. λαλῆσαι aor. act. inf.

■ εἰδῆτε perf. act. subj. οἶδα. γνωρίσει fut. act. ind. s.v.19. 21 ἀγαπητός beloved. ■ ἔπεμψα aor. act. ind. πέμπω to send. εἰς 22 αὐτὸ τοῦτο for this very reason. γνῶτε aor. act. subj. γινώσκω. Subjunctive used in a purpose clause. παρακαλέσῃ aor. act. subj. παρακαλέω to comfort, to encourage (TDNT; MNTW, 134).

■ ἀγαπώντων pres. act. part. ἀγαπάω to love. ἀφθαρσία 24 not corruptible, incorruption. The word does not point merely to time but to character (Abbott; s. also Rom. 2:7; 1 Cor. 15:52).

PHILIPPIANS

Ch. 1

1   οὖσιν pres. part. masc. dat. pl. εἰμί. σύν w. dat. The prep. implies close fellowship or cooperation (DM, 111). ἐπίσκοπος overseer, superintendent, bishop. The word was used for one who had the responsibility of oversight. It is important to note that Paul here uses the pl. and that elsewhere the term is used interchangeably w. "elder" (s. CBB; TDNT; Lightfoot, 95–99; Gnilka; ZPEB I, 617–620; Vincent).

3   ■ εὐχαριστέω pres. act. ind. to give thanks. μνεία remembrance, mention. Used w. the prep. to express the thought "as
4   often as I make mention of you (in prayer)" (BAG). ■ πάντοτε every time, always. δέησις request, petition, generally a specific petition arising from a need (s. Eph. 6:18). ποιούμενος pres. mid. part. The mid. voice of this verb is used where it has for object a noun denoting action, w. which it forms a periphrasis
5   equivalent to a simple verb, i.e., "to pray" (BG, 72f.). ■ κοινωνία fellowship, sharing. The word signifies "your cooperation toward, in aid of the gospel." The word refers not only to financial contributions but also denotes cooperation in the widest sense, their participation w. the apostle whether in sympathy or in suffering or in active labor (Lightfoot; s. also TDNT; CBB;
6   RAC IX, 1100–1145). ■ πεποιθώς perf. act. part. πέποιθα to persuade, perf. to be convinced, to be sure, to be certain. (For the construction of the verb followed by a noun clause, s. BD, 204.) The part. may have a faint causal force (Ellicott). αὐτὸ τοῦτο "this very thing," "just this (and nothing else)" (BD, 151). ἐναρξάμενος aor. mid. part. ἐνάρχομαι to begin. The prep. in compound represents the action of the verb as more directly concentrated on the object (Ellicott). ἐπιτελέσει fut. act. ind. ἐπιτελέω to complete, to bring to the goal. The prep. in compound is directive and the verb indicates "will carry it on
7   towards completion, and finally complete" (Vincent). ■ καθώς just as. The word has a slight causal sense and is often used to introduce new ideas (Gnilka). ἐστὶν δίκαιον ἐμοί "it is right for me." Although the expression may have been a daily figure of speech (Lohmeyer) the word does contain an ethical and general

544

moral sense which has its foundation in the moral relation of
man to God (Vincent; MRP, 148). φρονεῖν pres. act. inf. to be
minded. The word denotes a general disposition of mind (Vincent). ἔχειν pres. act. inf. used w. the prep. in a causal sense. The
words form an expression of heartfelt love on the part of the
apostle toward his readers (Meyer). δέσμος bond. ἀπολογία
defense, defense against a legal accusation. The word may be
more general including all of Paul's efforts, whatever put forth,
to defend the gospel (Vincent). βεβαίωσις confirmation, a legal
technical term for guaranteeing or furnishing security (BAG; s.
also BS, 104–109; MM). συγκοινωνός sharers together w.
someone, fellow partakers. ὄντας pres. part. εἰμί. Causal use of
the part. ■ ἐπιποθέω pres. act. ind. to long for, to yearn after. 8
The prep. in compound signifies direction; but the idea of straining after the object being thereby suggested, the idea implied is
"eagerness" (Lightfoot). σπλάγχνον the inward parts, i.e., the
heart, liver, lungs which were collectively regarded as the seat
of feeling and is the strongest word in Gr. for the feeling of
compassion (s. Vincent; MNTW, 156f.; TDNT; CBB). ■ 9
προσεύχομαι to pray. (For the prayer words and syntactical
constructions, s. PIP, 173f.) ἔτι yet. μᾶλλον more. The phrase
"more and more" accentuates their need for unremitting
progress (PIP, 209). περισσεύῃ pres. act. subj. περισσεύω to
overflow, to abound. The pres. tense is progressive and expresses
the desire "may continue to abound" (Vincent). ἐπίγνωσις
knowledge, recognition. The prep. in compound indicates a
knowledge directed toward an object. Here the word indicates
a firm conception of those spiritual principles which would guide
them in their relations w. one another and the world (EGT).
αἴσθησις insight, perception, discernment. The word was originally used of sense perception but is applicable to the inner
world of sensibility and refers to moral and spiritual perception
related to practical applications (EGT; Lightfoot). ■ 10
δοκιμάζειν pres. act. inf. to approve after testing (s. TDNT).
The inf. w. the prep. could express either purpose or result (MT,
143). διαφέροντα pres. act. part. διαφέρω to differ. Here it
refers to what is worthwhile, excellent, vital (PIP, 209).
εἰλικρινής pure, genuine, sincere. The etymology "tested by
sunlight" is possible but uncertain (s. GEW I, 459; Vincent;
Lohmeyer; TDNT). ἀπρόσκοπος without stumbling, without
offense. The word means either "not stumbling" or "not causing
others to stumble" (Vincent). ■ πεπληρωμένοι perf. pass. part. 11
πληρόω to fill. The perf. views the completed state or condition.
ἔπαινος praise.

12   ■ γινώσκειν pres. act. inf. to know, to realize. μᾶλλον
rather, i.e., rather than the reverse, as might have been anticipated (Lightfoot). προκοπή cutting forward, advance, progress,
furtherance. (For the verb, s. Gal. 1:14.) ἐλήλυθεν perf. ind.
13 ἔρχομαι. ■ φανερός clear, manifest. γενέσθαι aor. mid. inf.
γίνομαι. Infinitive used w. a particle to express actual result (s.
BD, 197f.). πραιτώριον praetorian guard, praetorium. The
word refers either to the elite troops or to the headquarters used
by such troops (s. Vincent; Lightfoot; Gnilka; ZPEB IV, 832–
14 834; CC, 198f.; KP IV, 1116–1117). ■ πλείονες "the majority"
(s. BD, 127). πεποιθότας perf. act. part., s.v.6. περισσοτέρως
adv. comp. περισσός abundantly. Here it denotes the "increased zeal" of the brethren, when stimulated by St. Paul's
endurance (Lightfoot). τολμᾶν pres. act. inf. to dare. Infinitive
used to express actual results (s.v.13). ἀφόβως adv. fearless.
15   ■ καί. Used here in a contrasting force and introduces
another and a different class (Vincent). φθόνος envy. εὐδοκία
goodwill. The word refers to the good motives and well wishes
16 from which an action comes (s. TDNT; Gnilka). ■ οἱ μέν ... οἱ
δέ "the ones ... the others." εἰδότες perf. act. part. οἶδα.
ἀπολογία defense (s.v.7). κεῖμαι to lie, to recline. Figuratively
17 to be appointed, to be destined (BAG). ■ ἐριθεία selfishness.
Originally, the character of a worker for pay. A hired worker was
looked down upon because his laboring was wholly for his own
interest (EGT; s. also Phil. 2:3). καταγγέλλουσιν pres. act. ind.
to proclaim, to proclaim w. authority. The prep. in compound is
perhaps intensive "making fully known" (Ellicott; Vincent;
CBB). ἀγνῶς adv. purely w. the neg. "w. mixed" impure motives
(Lightfoot). οἰόμενοι pres. mid. part. οἴομαι to suppose, to
imagine. It denotes a belief or judgment based principally upon
one's own feelings, or the peculiar relations of outward circumstances to one's self (Vincent). θλῖψις pressure, tribulation.
ἐγειρεῖν pres. act. inf. to raise up. Used in the context "to make
18 my chains gaul me" (Lightfoot). ■ γάρ then, assuredly (s. Thrall,
44). πλήν except, but, nevertheless. The particle is used in an
adversitive sense (s. Blomqvist, 75–100; Thrall, 20f.). τρόπος
manner, fashion. εἴτε whether. πρόφασις pretense, pretext,
excuse. The word indicates the "ostensible reason" for which a
thing is done, and generally points to a false reason as opposed
to the truth (MM; BAG). Here it is using the name of Christ as
a cover or mask for personal and selfish ends (Vincent). The dat.
expresses the manner (Ellicott). καταγγέλλεται pres. pass. ind.
ἀλλὰ καί. The two particles are combined in a progressive sense
"further," "what is more," "moreover" (s. Thrall, 14ff.).

χαρήσομαι fut. mid. (BD, 42) ind. χαίρω to be glad, to rejoice. The fut. is volitive indicating a decision of the will (s. RG, 889) and is a progressive fut. which affirms that an action will be in progress in fut. time (SMT, 32). ■ οἶδα defective perf. w. a pres. 19 meaning to know. The word speaks of the possession of knowledge which is grasped directly or intuitively by the mind (s. ND, 344f.). τοῦτο this, i.e., "this state of things," these perplexities and annoyances (Lightfoot). ἀποβήσεται fut. mid. ind. ἀποβαίνω to come from, to come back, to turn out (RWP). ἐπιχορηγία supply (s. Eph. 4:16; Gal. 3:5). ■ ἀποκαραδοκία 20 intense expectation, earnest watching. The word is composed of the prep. "away," the noun "head" and the verb "to watch" and indicates watching something w. the head turned away from other objects (Vincent). It indicates the concentrated intense hope which ignores other interests and strains forward as w. outstretched head (EGT; s. also Rom. 8:19; Gnilka). αἰσχυνθήσομαι fut. pass. ind. αἰσχύνομαι to be ashamed, to be put to shame. παρρησία speaking all things, forthrightness of speech then more broadly "boldness," esp. the courage appropriate to the free man, which acts openly even in a hostile atmosphere (Beare). μεγαλυνθήσεται fut. pass. ind. μεγαλύνω to make large, to magnify. ■ ζῆν pres. act. inf. ζάω to live. The 21 articular inf. is used as the subject of the sentence "the act of living." The pres. tense is continuous (Vincent). ἀποθανεῖν aor. act. inf. ἀποθνήσκω to die. The articular inf. is used as the subject. κέρδος gain, profit. The word was used of something advantageous and in the pl. sometimes refers to money (BAG; MM; for other examples, s. Lohmeyer). (For a discussion of this verse, s. D.W. Palmer, " 'To Die Is Gain.' Philippians 1:21," Nov T, 18 [July, 1975], 203–218.) ■ αἱρήσομαι fut. mid. ind. 22 αἱρέομαι to take, to pick, mid. to choose. γνωρίζω to understand, to know, to declare, to make known. The latter meaning is better in this context (s. Lightfoot; Vincent). ■ συνέχομαι 23 pres. pass. ind. συνέχω to hold together, to hem in on both sides. The idea is that of a strong pressure bearing upon him from two sides and keeping him motionless (EGT; Lightfoot). δέ and, now. It introduces an explanation and at the same time separates it from that which is to be explained (Vincent). ἐπιθυμία desire. ἔχων prcs. act. part. ἀναλῦσαι aor. act. inf. ἀναλύω to break up, to unloose, to undo. It is used of loosening a ship from its moorings, of breaking camp, and of death (Vincent; cf. 2 Cor. 5:1). The inf. w. the prep. is used to supply the limits of the noun "desire" (MT, 143). κρείσσων comp. stronger, better. ■ 24 ἐπιμένειν pres. act. inf. to remain, to stay. The prep. in compound implies rest in a place and hence at a more protracted stay (Ellicott). ἀναγκαιότερος comp. ἀναγκαῖος necessary, comp.

25 more necessary. ■ μενῶ fut. act. ind. μένω to remain. παραμενῶ fut. act. ind. παραμένω to remain w. someone, to stand by. In the koine the word often had the idea of "service"

26 (MM; Preisigke; Lohmeyer). ■ καύχημα ground or reason for boasting. Here it is their knowledge and possession of the gospel (EGT). περισσεύῃ pres. act. subj. to overflow, to abound. The subj. is used to express purpose. παρουσία arrival, presence.

27 ■ ἀξίως adv. worthily (s. Eph. 4:1). πολιτεύεσθε pres. mid. imp. πολιτεύομαι to be a citizen, to conduct one's self as a citizen. Paul may be alluding to the fact that the city of Philippi had the Roman status of "colonia," which meant that the city was a "mini-Rome" (s. DGRA, 315–320; IDB I, 657; s. also A.N. Sherwin White, *The Roman Citizenship* [Oxford: At the Clarendon Press, 1973]). (For verbs w. this suf. meaning "to play the part of," "to act as," s. MH, 398–400.) The pres. imp. calls for a continual and habitual action. ἐλθών aor. act. part. ἔρχομαι. ἰδών aor. act. part. ὁράω. The parts. could be conditional or translated as a main verb (s. Vincent). ἀπών pres. part. ἄπειμι to be away from, to be absent. στήκετε pres. ind. act. στήκω to stand, to stand firm, to hold one's ground. The word indicates the determination of a soldier who does not budge one inch from his post (Lohmeyer). ψυχή soul. It indicates the mind as the seat of sensation and desire (Vincent; TDNT; PAT). συναθλοῦντες pres. act. part. συναθλέω to contend or strug-

28 gle along w. someone (BAG). ■ πτυρόμενοι pres. pass. part. πτύρω to frighten, to startle, to terrify. The metaphor is from a timid horse (Lightfoot). Perhaps an allusion to Cassius who at the battle of Philippi committed suicide at the fear of defeat (CAH X, 24). ἀντικειμένων pres. mid. part. ἀντίκειμαι to line up against, to oppose, to be an adversary. ἥτις which, "seeing it is." The rel. has an explanatory force and takes its gender from the predicate but agrees logically w. the part. in the nom. (Vincent). ἔνδειξις evidence, proof. The word was used as an Attic law term (EGT). ἀπώλεια destruction. Here it is the destruction which consists in the loss of eternal life (Vincent; s. also

29 TDNT). ■ ἐχαρίσθη aor. pass. ind. χαρίζω to give graciously, "God has granted you the high privilege of suffering for Christ; this is the surest sign, that He looks upon you w. favor" (Lightfoot). πάσχειν pres. act. inf. to suffer. The articular inf. is used

30 as the subject of the verb. ■ ἀγών conflict, struggle. The word pictures Paul's apostolic life of service (PAM, 183). ἔχοντες pres. act. part. οἷος which kind of. εἴδετε aor. act. ind. ὁράω.

Ch. 2

■ παράκλησις comfort, consolation, exhortation, encour- 1
agement (s. TDNT; MNTW, 128ff.). παραμύθιον encouragement, esp. as consolation or alleviation (BAG). The prep. in
compound may have the force of "aside," i.e., "the converse
which draws the mind aside from care" (MM). κοινωνία fellowship. σπλάγχνα tender affection, mercy (s. Phil. 1:8).
οἰκτιρμός compassion. It signifies the manifestation of tender
feelings in compassionate yearnings and actions (Lightfoot). ■ 2
πληρώσατε aor. act. imp. πληρόω to fill. The particle ἵνα
"that" is used to introduce the object of the request and blends
in the purpose of making it (Ellicott; s. also BD, 199f.). φρονῆτε
pres. act. subj. φρονέω to think, to hold an opinion, to have
thoughts or an attitude, to be minded or disposed (BAG). The
pres. tense implies a continual habitual attitude. ἔχοντες pres.
act. part. σύμψυχος harmonious, united in spirit (BAG). The
following words appear on the grave stone of a man and his wife:
"we spoke the same things, we thought the same things and we
go the inseparable way in Hades" (s. Lohmeyer; BS, 256).
φρονοῦντες pres. act. part. ■ ἐριθεία selfishness, selfish ambi- 3
tion. The word is related to a noun which originally meant "a day
laborer" and was used esp. of those cutting and binding wheat
or of those who were spinners or weavers. The word later
denotes the attitude of those who worked for wages and particularly it denoted a self-seeking pursuit of political office by unfair
means. It then came to be used of "party squabbles," of the
jockeying for position and the intriguing for place and power.
Finally, it meant "selfish ambition," the ambition which has no
conception of service and whose only aims are profit and power
(s. BAG; TDNT; GEW I, 558; NTW, 39ff.). κενοδοξία empty
praise, vainglory. It refers to personal vanity (Lightfoot; s. also
Gal. 5:26). ταπεινοφροσύνη lowly thinking, humility. The
word indicates the recognition of personal insufficiency of one's
self but the powerful sufficiency of God (TDNT; CBB; Gnilka).
ἀλλήλους one another. ἡγούμενοι pres. mid. part. ἡγέομαι to
consider, to count as. The word implies a conscious sure judgment resting on a careful weighing of the facts (Vincent).
ὑπερέχοντας pres. act. part. ὑπερέχω w. the gen. to have over
and beyond, to excel or surpass, to be superior (RWP; Ellicott).
■ τὰ ἑαυτῶν "the things of others," i.e., "others, different from 4
those named." (For the contrast, s. BD, 161.) ἕκαστος each,
each one. σκοποῦντες pres. act. part. σκοπέω to look at, to
consider, to regard as one's aim. Used w. the article and the
reflex. pron. it means "to consult one's own interest" (Light-

549

5 foot). ■ φρονεῖτε pres. act. imp., s.v.2. ἐν ὑμῖν "in you," i.e., "in your community (of faith and love)," "in your common life"
6 (Beare). ■ μορφή form. The outward display of the inner reality or substance. Here it refers to the outward display of the divine substance, i.e., divinity of the preexistent Christ in the display of His glory as being in the image of the Father. (For a study of this word, s. Martin, 99–133; Lightfoot, esp. 127–133; TDNT; CBB; T.F. Glasson, "Two Notes on the Philippians' Hymn: II.6–11," NTS, 21 [October, 1974], 133–139; Vincent, 78ff.) ὑπάρχων pres. act. part. ὑπάρχω to be, to exist. The word expresses continuance of an antecedent state or condition (AS; s. also 2 Cor. 12:16). ἁρπαγμός. The word has either an active sense "robbing" or a pass. sense "prize gained through robbery." Perhaps the meaning is that Christ did not use His equality w. God in order to snatch or gain power and dominion, riches, pleasure, worldly glory. He did not reach out of His favored place and grasp at authority (s. Meyer; Martin, 152). (For detailed studies on this difficult word, s. Martin, 134–164; Lightfoot, 133–138; Glasson, 133–137; TDNT; Lampe.) ἡγήσατο aor. mid. ind. ἡγέομαι to consider. (For the view that the verb in connection w. the previous noun means "to treat as a piece of good fortune," "to regard as a lucky find," "to prize highly," "to welcome eagerly," s. Martin, 143f.; Lightfoot, 138.) ἴσος equal, exactly equal, equal in number, size, quality. The n. pl. can be used of an adv. which in turn is used here as an adj. w. the verb "to be" (s. BAG; BD, 224; s. also TDNT). The acc. is used w. the articular inf., "to be equal w. God," to form the acc. of object in a double acc. construction; "He did not regard the being equal w. God (acc. of object) as a robbing (pred. acc.)."
7 (For this construction, s. BD, 86; RG, 479ff.) ■ ἑαυτόν Himself. The word is emphasized by its position in the sentence. ἐκένωσεν aor. act. ind. κενόω to empty, to make empty, to make of no effect. The word does not mean He emptied Himself of His deity, but rather He emptied Himself of the display of His deity for personal gain. The word is a graphic expression of the completeness of His self-renunciation and His refusal to use what He had to His own advantage (Vincent; Martin, 195; for a study of the word, s. TDNT; Martin, 165–196; CBB). δοῦλος slave. λαβών aor. act. part. λαμβάνω. ὁμοίωμα likeness. The phrase expresses the fact that His mode of manifestation resembled what men are. The apostle views Him solely as He could appear to men (Vincent). This, however, does not deny His true humanity. γενόμενος aor. mid. part. γίνομαι. σχῆμα outward appearance. The word was used of a king who exchanges his

kingly robe for sackcloth (BAG; s. also Lightfoot, 127–133;
CBB; TDNT; Martin, 207f.). εὑρεθείς aor. pass. part. The parts.
are manner and indicate how Christ emptied Himself. ■ 8
ἐτάπείνωσεν aor. act. ind. ταπεινόω to make low, to humble.
ὑπήκοος obedient. μέχρι until, unto, "even unto death," i.e., to
the extent of death (Vincent). δέ and, even, yea. It introduces
another and more striking detail of the humiliation, and leads on
to a climax not only death but a death of suffering shameful and
accursed, the most ignominious of deaths (Vincent; Ellicott).
(For the horrors and the attitude of the ancient world toward the
despicable death by crucifixion which was a form of punishment
reserved for slaves, rebels and the lowest criminals, s. Blinzler;
Martin Hengel, *Crucifixion in the Ancient World and the Folly
of the Message of the Cross* [Philadelphia: Fortress Press, 1978].)
■ διό wherefore, in consequence of this voluntary humiliation, 9
in fulfillment of divine law which He Himself enuniciated
(Lightfoot; s. also Martin, 231ff.). ὑπερύψωσεν aor. act. ind.
ὑπερυψόω to exalt, to exalt above and beyond, to highly exalt.
The force of the prep. in compound is not to describe a different
stage in Christ's existence in a comp. sense, but to contrast His
exaltation w. the claim of other high powers, and thereby to
proclaim His uniqueness and absoluteness (Martin, 241; s. also
Beare). ἐχαρίσατο aor. mid. ind. χαρίζομαι to give out of
grace, to grant graciously. Now after a career of self-humbling
and obedience there comes to Him in the Father's good pleasure
the very thing He might have grasped (Martin, 236; s. also Phil.
1:29). ■ γόνυ knee. κάμψῃ aor. act. subj. κάπτω to bend, to 10
bow. The subj. is used to express purpose. ἐπουράνιος heavenly,
heaven (s. Eph. 1:3). ἐπίγειος earthly, on the earth.
καταχθόνιος under the earth. Christ is acknowledged as Lord
of all angelic forces, esp. malevolent demons and they are compelled to admit that He is victor; and they show their submission
by their prostration before Him (Martin, 261; for a discussion
of this threefold division of the universe, s. Martin 257–265).
■ γλῶσσα tongue. ἐξομολογήσεται aor. mid. subj. 11
ἐξομολογέομαι to admit openly, to acknowledge, to recognize,
to acclaim (s. Martin, 263; TDNT; Beare). The subj. is used to
express purpose. εἰς δόξαν θεοῦ πατρός "for the glory of God
the Father." The Lord Jesus was neither selfish nor did He seek
vainglory but even in His exaltation all praise, honor, and power
finally belonged to God the Father (s. Martin, 273).
■ ὥστε wherefore, so then, consequently. The particle 12
draws a conclusion from the preceding as Christ was perfectly
obedient, therefore, w. like subjection to Him the readers are to

carry out their own salvation (Vincent). ἀγαπητός beloved. καθώς just as. πάντοτε always. ὑπηκούσατε aor. act. ind. ὑπακούω to answer the door, to obey as a result of listening, to obey, to be obedient. The prep. in compound contains the idea of "submission" (MH, 327; Vincent). παρουσία presence. πολλῷ μᾶλλον much more. ἀπουσία absence. τρόμος trembling. The expression "w. fear and trembling" indicates a nervous and trembling anxiety to do right (Lightfoot). κατεργάζεσθε pres. mid. imp. κατεργάζομαι to work out, to work on to the finish. The prep. in compound is perfective and views the linear progress down to the goal "work on to the
13 finish" (RWP; M 114ff.). ■ θεός. The word is placed first as the subject not as the pred.: God is the agent (Meyer). γάρ for. It gives the reason for the entire previous verse and supplies at once the stimulus to and the corrective of the precept in the preceding (Vincent; Lightfoot). ἐνεργῶν pres. act. part. ἐνεργέω to work effectually and productively, to put forth power. The word describes the energy and the effective power of God Himself in action (Vincent; MNTW, 46–54). εὐδοκία good pleasure, satisfaction, "in fulfillment of His benevolent
14 purpose" (Lightfoot; s. also Phil. 1:15). ■ ποιεῖτε pres. act. imp. γογγυσμός murmuring, an expression of dissatisfaction, grumbling, muttering in a low voice. The word was used in the LXX for the murmuring of Israel against God (T; TDNT). διαλογισμός inward questionings, dispute, discussion, skeptical questioning or criticism (Vincent). It refers to the intellectual
15 rebellion against God (Lightfoot). ■ γένησθε aor. mid. subj. γίνομαι. ἄμεμπτος unblamed, without blame (s. Eph. 1:4; 5:-27; Trench; Synonyms, 379). ἀκέραιος unmixed, unadulterated, pure, sincere. The word was used of pure wine and of unalloyed metal (Lightfoot). ἄμωμος without spot, without blemish (Trench; Synonyms, 380). μέσον in the midst of, in the middle of. The n. as an adv. was used as a prep. w. the gen. (RG, 644). γενέα generation. σκολιός curved, crooked. διεστραμμένης perf. pass. part. διαστρέφω twisted, distorted, to twist in two. It denotes an abnormal moral condition. The perf. expresses a state or condition consequent to an action (s. Vincent; Matt. 17:17). φαίνομαι pres. mid. ind. φαίνω act. to shine, to give light, to be bright, mid. to appear, to be visible, to make one's appearance, to show one's self (s. BAG). The pres. tense points to the continual action. φωστήρ luminary, the light given off by heavenly bodies, mainly the sun and moon, the "lights," or "great lights" (Trench; Synonyms, 164; TDNT; s. also Gen. 1:14, 16; s. also 1QS 10:3; 1QM 10:11; 1QH 1:11; 7:25; 9:26).

(For the Jewish teaching regarding those who shine as luminaries, s. SB I, 236; III, 621.) ■ λόγον ζωῆς word of life, i.e., the 16 word which brings life and which is life. ἐπέχοντες pres. act. part. ἐπέχω to hold fast, to hold forth. The latter sense would be "to hold out" and the metaphor may be that of offering food or wine (Lightfoot; s. also MM). The part. would express means. καύχημα reason for boasting, ground of glorying. It is not a boasting in meritorious effort but the sign of the completion of a divinely assigned commission (PAM, 104; Lohmeyer). κένος empty, in vain. The word fits well into the picture of the runner and his eventual success or failure in the race (PAM, 100). ἔδραμον aor. act. ind. τρέχω to run. The word pictures Paul's work as an apostle spreading the gospel under the figure of a runner. The word indicates the strenuous effort and exertion involved. Paul's fear is that his own interest might impede the gospel or the threat of the introduction of the law as a condition for salvation or the possibility of unfaithfulness on the part of the Philippians might make his efforts fruitless or in vain (PAM, 107). ἐκοπίασα aor. act. ind. κοπιάω to work hard, to labor. This verb is qualified by the first and both verbs designate the intense labor and efforts of Paul toward the one goal (PAM, 109f.). ■ καί even. The word refers to the whole clause (Vin- 17 cent). σπένδομαι pres. pass. ind. σπένδω to pour out as a drink offering. A drink offering, usually a cup of wine, was poured out on the ground to honor deity. Paul is again referring to the prospect of martyrdom which he faces, and thinks of himself, his life's blood, as a libation poured forth to God (Beare). θυσία sacrifice. The prep. can mean "upon the sacrifice" or "in addition to the sacrifice" (s. Vincent). λειτουργία service, religious or sacred service. (For the development of this word, s. Lightfoot; s. also BS, 140f.; TDNT.) συγχαίρω pres. act. ind. to rejoice together, to rejoice w. someone. ■ χαίρετε and 18 συγχαίρετε pres. act. imp.

■ ταχέως quickly, soon. πέμψαι aor. act. inf. πέμπω to 19 send. The inf. explains the content of Paul's hope. εὐψυχέω pres. act. subj. to be glad, to have courage. The word is found in the papyri in the salutation of a letter of condolence (MM). γνούς aor. act. part. γινώσκω. The part. is used temporally "when I know," "after I know." ■ ἰσόψυχος likeminded, having the 20 same mind, having equal power, confident (s. Gnilka). The word may have the meaning "precious as life" (s. GELS, 75). γνησίως adv. genuinely, legitimate birth, not spurious (RWP). μεριμνήσει fut. act. ind. μεριμνάω to give one's thoughts to a matter, to be concerned (EGT). The fut. points to the time

21 when Timothy would come to them (Ellicott). ■ οἱ πάντες all.
The article w. the adj. excludes every exception (Lohmeyer; s.
22 also RG, 773f.). ζητοῦσιν pres. act. ind. to seek. ■ δοκιμή
approval, acceptance after being tested (s. TDNT). ἐδούλευσεν
23 aor. act. ind. to serve as a slave, to serve. ■ ὡς w. ἄν = ὅταν
"whenever," "as soon as." The construction is temporal and
indicates the uncertainty which surrounds the whole prospect
(EGT; s. also BD, 237f.). ἀφίδω aor. act. subj. ἀφοράω to look
away, to see. The prep. in compound implies looking away from
the pres. circumstances to what is going to happen, which will
decide the question of his sending Timothy (Vincent). ἐξαυτῆς
24 at once, immediately, soon thereafter. ■ πέποιθα perf. ind. act.
πείθω to persuade, perf. w. the pres. meaning to be convinced,
to be sure, to be certain (BAG). The perf. expresses a state or
condition "I am convinced" (s. BD, 176). ἐλεύσομαι fut. mid.
ind. ἔρχομαι.
25   ■ ἀναγκαῖος compelling, necessary. ἡγησάμην aor. mid.
ind., s.v.6. συνεργός fellow worker. συστρατιώτης fellow soldier. ἀπόστολος missionary, not apostle in the official sense,
but a messenger sent on a special commission (Vincent).
λειτουργός minister. The word was used of a public official in
civil service, then it was also used for one ministering in religious
26 ceremonies (s.v.17; s. also TDNT; CBB). χρεία need. ■ ἐπείδη
since, since then, because. It presents the reason for Paul feeling
compelled to send Epaphroditus (s. Ellicott). ἐπιποθῶν pres.
act. part. ἐπιποθέω to yearn after, to long for (s. Phil. 1:8). The
part. is used in a periphrastic impf. construction "he was yearning after" (RWP). ἀδημονῶν pres. act. part. ἀδημονέω to be
distressed. Although the root meaning of the word is not clear
(s. GEW I, 20), the word describes the confused, restless, half-
distracted state which is produced by physical derangement, or
by mental distress, as grief, shame, disappointment, etc. (Lightfoot). ἠκούσατε aor. act. ind. ἀκούω. ἠσθένησεν aor. act. ind.
27 ἀσθενέω to be without strength, to be weak, to be sick. ■ καὶ
γάρ "for even," "—yes, even" (BD, 236). παραπλήσιον w. the
dat. near to. ἠλέησεν aor. act. ind. ἐλεέω to have mercy, to
show mercy. λύπη sorrow. σχῶ aor. act. subj. ἔχω to have, aor.
to get, to receive (s. M, 110). The subj. is used in a neg. purpose
28 clause. ■ σπουδαιοτέρως adv. comp. of σπουδαῖος w. haste,
comp. w. special urgency (BAG), "w. increased eagerness," on
account of this circumstance (Lightfoot). ἔπεμψα aor. act. ind.
epistolary aor. (EGT). πάλιν again. The word is to be taken w.
the main verb "rejoice" rather than w. the part. (Vincent).
ἀλυπότερος comp. ἄλυπος without grief, free from sorrow.

(For the neg. character of the alpha privative, s. Moorhouse, 47ff.) Comparative "less sorrowful." The joy felt by the Philippians will mitigate the sorrow (in his confinement) of the sympathizing apostle (Ellicott). ὦ pres. subj. εἰμί. Subjunctive used in a purpose clause. ■ προσδέχεσθε pres. mid. imp. 29 προσδέχομαι to receive, to receive favorably, to welcome. τοιοῦτος such a one, one w. such characteristics. ἔντιμος in honor, prized, precious, pred. acc. in a double acc. construction "hold such ones in honor" (s. RWP). ■ ἤγγισεν aor. act. 30 ind. ἐγγίζω to come near, to draw near, to be near. παραβολευσάμενος aor. mid. part. παραβολεύομαι to gamble, to play the gambler, to expose one's self to danger. The word has connotations of gambling or playing dice by which high sums were often at stake (s. OCD, 338f.). The word was used in the papyri of one who in the interest of friendship had exposed himself to dangers as an advocate in legal strife by taking his clients' causes even up to emperors (MM; LAE, 88). The word was later used of merchants who for the sake of gain exposed themselves to death (PGL, 1008). The word was used of a fighter in the arena who exposed himself to the dangers of the arena (PGL, 1009). In the post-apostolic church a group called the "paraboloni" risked their lives by nursing the sick and burying the dead (Lightfoot; Vincent). (For the use of the dat. w. this verb, s. M, 64.) ἀναπληρώσῃ aor. act. subj. ἀναπληρόω to fill up, to make complete, to fill a gap, to replace. Used w. the gen. of a per. it means "to make up for someone's absence or lack," "to represent one who is absent" (BAG). ὑστέρημα that which is lacking, deficiency. There is no rebuke in the word for the only "deficiency" is that they could not be w. him themselves, to do him service (Beare). λειτουργίας service, ministry (s.v.17).

Ch. 3

■ τὸ λοιπόν finally. With this Paul probably intends to 1 draw to a close the general admonitions and then takes up specific matters in the latter part of the letter (s. Victor Paul Furnish, "The Place and Purpose of Philippians 3," NTS, 10 [October, 1963], 80–88). τὰ αὐτά "the same things." Paul perhaps means the same warnings and directives Epaphroditus and Timothy would orally communicate when they visit the Philippians in per. (Furnish, 86). ὀκνηρός causing fear or reluctance, troublesome (BAG). ἀσφαλής. The word is taken from a verb meaning "to trip up," "to overthrow," "to cause to fall or stumble." With the neg. prefix the adj. is used to describe anything which has stability and firmness enough not to be overthrown. It carries then the idea of "certain, dependable knowledge" (s. Furnish, 83ff.; s. also Luke 1:4).

2　■ βλέπετε pres. act. inf. "continually be on the lookout for" (s. Vincent). κύων dog. The Jews considered dogs to be the most despised and miserable of all creatures and used this to describe Gentiles. Perhaps it was because of the herds of dogs which prowled about eastern cities, without a home and without an owner, feeding on the refuge and filth of the streets, quarreling among themselves and attacking the passerby, that the Jews used this designation (Lightfoot; s. also SB III, 621; I, 722–726; TDNT; OCD, 358; KP II, 1245–1249). Paul uses the term here of those who prowl around the Christian congregations, seeking to win converts (s. Beare). ἐργάτης worker. κατατομή inci-
3　sion, mutilation. Used in contrast to circumcision (RWP). ■ περιτομή circumcision (s. Gal. 2:3). λατρεύοντες pres. act. part. λατρεύω to minister, to serve (s. TDNT; Phil. 2:17). καυχώμενοι pres. mid. part. καυχάομαι to boast, to glory. πεποιθότες perf. act. part. πείθω to persuade, perf. to be per-
4　suaded, to be confident, to have confidence (s. Phil. 2:24). ■ καίπερ "even though," "although." It is used to clarify the concessive sense of the part. (BD, 219; s. also Blomqvist, 47). ἔχων pres. act. part. concessive use of the part. πεποίθησις trusting, confidence. δοκέω pres. act. ind. to suppose, to seem, to think. Here "if anyone is disposed to think" (Vincent). πεποιθέναι perf. act. inf., s.v.3. μᾶλλον more, to a higher
5　degree. ■ περιτομή dat. of respect, "w. respect to circumcision an eighth-day one" (BD, 105; often called "dat. of reference," e.g. DM, 85; MT, 238). ὀκταήμερος eighth day, on the eighth day. The normal procedure was circumcision on the eighth day after birth, but under certain circumstances the circumcision could be on the ninth, tenth, eleventh or twelfth day (s. SB IV, 23ff.; M Shabbath, 19.5). φύλη tribe. Ἑβραῖος Hebrew. The term emphasized not only the rights and privileges belonging to the Jewish nation, but also emphasized that those who lived in the Diaspora, i.e., outside of Palestine, had remained true to the religious practices and especially regarding the language. Paul was trained in the use of the Heb. tongue by Heb.-speaking parents (Vincent; s. also Lightfoot; JPFC I, 184–225; s. also MM). νόμος law. Used here without the article. It emphasizes
6　law in the abstract, as a principle of action (Lightfoot). ■ ζῆλος zeal (s. Gal. 1:14). διώκων pres. act. part. διώκω to pursue, to persecute. γενόμενος aor. mid. part. γίνομαι. ἄμεμπτος with-
7　out blame (s. Phil. 2:15). ■ κέρδος profit, gain (s. Phil. 1:21). ἥγημαι perf. mid. ind. ἡγέομαι to consider, to reckon, to count

as (s. Phil. 2:6). The perf. indicates a completed action w. continuing results "I have counted (and they are now to me)" (Ellicott). ζημία loss. Used for a loss at sea (Acts 27:10) and used in the papyri of a commercial or business loss (MM). ■ μενοῦν 8 γε. The presence of so many particles is clearly for the purpose of emphasis (DM, 255) and could be translated "yes the previous is true but more than that I also. . . ." ὑπερέχον pres. act. part. n. sing. ὑπερέχω. The n. sing. is used as an abstract noun followed by the gen. "the surpassing greatness" (BAG; BD, 138; s. also Phil. 2:3). γνῶσις knowledge. It is the personal knowledge and acquaintance w. Christ. It is the knowledge of one who loves and knows himself beloved (s. Beare). ἐζημιώθην aor. pass. ind. ζημιόω pass. to suffer loss. The aor. points to the definite period of his conversion. In that great crisis all his legal possessions were lost (Vincent). σκύβαλον refuse. It refers either to human excrement, the portion of food rejected by the body as not being nutritive or it refers to the refuse or leavings of a feast, the food thrown away from the table (Lightfoot; s. also TDNT; MM). κερδήσω aor. act. subj. κερδαίνω to gain, to win. The subj. is used in a purpose clause. ■ εὑρεθῶ aor. pass. subj. εὑρίσκω to 9 find, pass. to be found. The idea involved is a revelation of true character (EGT). The subj. is used in a purpose clause. διὰ πίστεως Χριστοῦ "through faith in Christ," obj. gen. ἐπὶ τῇ πίστει "on the basis of faith," "resting upon faith" (Vincent). ■ γνῶναι aor. act. inf. γινώσκω to know, to recognize, to know 10 personally through experience, to appropriate. The word often implies a personal relation between the knower and the known, involving the influence of the object of knowledge upon the knower (Vincent; s. also TDNT; ND, 344ff.; CBB). The inf. is used to express purpose or perhaps intended results (s. Funk, 706). κοινωνία fellowship. πάθημα suffering. συμμορφιζόμενος pres. pass. part. συμμορφίζω to grant or invest w. the same form, pass. to be conformed to, to take on the same form as. This seems to be a reference to the kind of death Paul was to die (BAG; Meyer). ■ εἴ πως if perhaps. The word 11 introduces a clause expressing a possibility which is the object of hope or desire (SMT, 111; s. also BD, 191). καταντήσω aor. act. subj. καταντάω to reach, to arrive at a destination. ἐξανάστασις resurrection, rising up.

   ■ οὐχ ὅτι "not that." The words serve to correct a false 12 impression that might have arisen from his preceding words. ἔλαβον aor. act. ind. λαμβάνω (s. RWP), to receive, to obtain. The aor. points to the time of Paul's conversion "not as though by my conversion I did once attain" (Lightfoot). τετελείωμαι perf. pass. ind. τελειόω to reach the goal, to perfect, pass. to be perfect. The perfection referred to is moral and spiritual perfection (Vincent). The perf. tense describes his pres. state "not as though I were now already perfected" (Lightfoot). καταλάβω aor. act. subj. καταλαμβάνω to seize, to grasp, to lay hold of. The subj. is used w. the particle in a 3rd-class conditional clause which is a sort of purpose clause or aim (RWP; s. also RG, 1017). ἐφ᾽ ᾧ "for which," "for the reason that, because" (BD, 123). The phrase can also express purpose "whereunto" (Lightfoot).

13 κατελήμφθην aor. pass. ind. καταλαμβάνω. ■ οὔπω not yet. λογίζομαι pres. mid. ind. to reckon, to consider. κατειληφέναι perf. act. inf. καταλαμβάνω. The prep. in compound is perfective "to grant completely" (RWP). ἕν δέ "but one thing." The verb "I say" could be supplied (Lohmeyer) or the verb "I do" is to be understood (Vincent). ὀπίσω behind. ἐπιλανθανόμενος pres. mid. part. ἐπιλανθάνομαι to forget. The prep. in compound is directive (s. MH, 312). ἐπεκτεινόμενος pres. mid. part. ἐπεκτείνομαι to stretch one's self out for, to stretch one's self out toward. The metaphor is from the foot race and the word pictures the body of the racer bent forward, his hand outstretched toward the goal, and his eye fastened upon it (Vincent). The word is followed by the dat.

14 ■ σκοπός a mark on which to fix the eye, goal. Paul is evidently referring to the goal of a foot race. (For a description of the stadium and the foot race, s. DGRA, 1055f.; Oscar Broneer, "The Apostle Paul and the Isthmian Games," BA, 25 [February, 1962], 1–31.) The prep. has the sense of "down," i.e., "bearing down upon" (Vincent). Paul's picture is of a runner who has just turned the curve or gone around the post and is now in the home stretch where he can see the goal (s. Lohmeyer; PAM, 141). βραβεῖον prize, a prize awarded the winner at the games. ἄνω above, upward. The word could be an adv. telling where the calling comes from or it could point to the direction in which the calling leads "upward," "heavenward" (s. PAM, 149). κλῆσις

15 calling. ■ ὅσοι "as many as," "those who." τέλειος perfect, mature. The word refers to "grown men" as opposed to children (Lightfoot). φρονῶμεν pres. act. subj. φρονέω to think, to have an attitude (s. Phil. 2:2, 5), co-hortative subj. ἑτέρως adv. "otherwise." ἀποκαλύψει fut. act. ind. ἀποκαλύπτω to unveil, to

16 reveal. ■ πλήν nevertheless. The word is used at the conclusion of a section in order to bring out the main point of discussion "just one thing more" (s. RG, 1187; Blomqvist, 75ff.). ἐφθάσαμεν aor. act. ind. φθάνω to come to, to arrive at, to attain, dramatic aor. used to express what has just taken place

(RG, 842). στοιχεῖν pres. act. inf. to walk in line, to march in battle order. The word refers to walking according to principles of a system (s. Vincent; TDNT). The inf. is used in the sense of an imp. This construction generally follows an imp. and the command is carried on by the inf. (RG, 943; s. also BD, 196f.; IBG, 126).

■ συμμιμητής fellow imitator. γίνεσθε pres. mid. imp. 17 σκοπεῖτε pres. act. imp. σκοπέω to look at, to fix one's attention upon, to mark. Here "to mark and follow" (Lightfoot; s. also Rom. 16:17). περιπατουντας pres. act. part. περιπατέω to walk, to conduct one's life. κάθως just as. τύπος that which is formed by a blow or impression, pattern, type, example (T; s. also TDNT). ■ κλαίων pres. act. part. κλαίω to cry, to weep, 18 to weep audibly. The stress of St. Paul's grief would lie in the fact that they degraded the true doctrine of liberty (Lightfoot). σταυρός cross. ■ ἀπώλεια ruin, destruction. κοιλία stomach. 19 (For a description of the luxury of Roman eating, s. DGRA, 303–309; s. also LAE, 164f.) The word may be used as a general term to include all that belongs most essentially to the bodily, fleshly life of man and therefore inevitably perishes (EGT). αἰσχύνη shame. ἐπίγειος earthly, upon the earth. φρονοῦντες pres. act. part., s. Phil. 2:5. ■ πολίτευμα citizenship. The word 20 means either "the state, the constitution, to which as citizens we belong" or "the functions which as citizens we perform" (Lightfoot; s. also Vincent; TDNT; Phil. 1:27). ὑπάρχει pres. act. ind. to exist, to be (s. 2 Cor. 12:16). ἀπεκδέχομεθα pres. mid. ind. to expect anxiously, to await eagerly. The preps. in compound indicate the eager but patient waiting (s. Gal. 5:5). ■ 21 μετασχηματίσει fut. act. ind. μετασχηματίζω to refashion, to change, to change the outward form or appearance. The meaning of the word would be illustrated not merely by changing a Dutch garden into an Italian garden, but by transforming a garden into something wholly different, as into a city (Trench; Synonyms, 263; s. also Lightfoot, 130f.; Phil. 2:6). ταπείνωσις lowliness, humble, insignificant. σύμμορφος conformed, the changing of the inward and outward substance, conforming to or w. something (s. Phil. 2:6). ἐνέργεια working. The act. and productive power of God at work (s. Phil. 2:13; MNTW, 46–54). ὑποτάξαι aor. act. inf. ὑποτάσσω to place under, to subdue, to subject, to place under one's authority. αὐτός himself. The pron. is used here in a reflex. sense (BD, 148).

Ch. 4

1 ■ *ὥστε* wherefore, therefore. It draws a conclusion from chapter 3 verses 17–21 (EGT). *ἀγαπητός* beloved. *ἐπιπόθητος* longed for, desired (s. Phil. 1:8). The word is a verbal adj. (RWP; M, 221; MH, 370). *στήκετε* pres. act. imp. *στήκω* to stand, to stand firm (s. Phil. 1:27).

2   ■ *παρακαλέω* to beseech, to urge, to encourage (s. TDNT; MNTW, 128ff.). *φρονεῖν* pres. act. inf. to be minded, to have

3 an attitude or disposition, to think (s. Phil. 2:2). ■ *ναί* yes, yea. The particle is a confirmation of an assertion (s. Ellicott; RG, 1150). *ἐρωτάω* pres. act. ind. to ask, to request, to ask something of someone. (For examples in the papyri, s. BS, 276ff.; MM.) *γνήσιος* legitimately born, genuine, true, sincere (s. Phil. 2:20). *σύζυγος* yoked together, yokefellow, voc. masc. sing. Some view this as a proper name, i.e., "Synzygus" (s. Vincent). *συλλαμβάνον* pres. mid. imp. *συλλαμβάνομαι* to take and bring together, to lay hold of, to help, to assist (s. MM). *συνήθλησαν* aor. act. ind. *συναθλέω* to fight alongside, to contend w. someone against a common enemy, to labor together (s. Phil. 1:27). *καί* also. The word may be retrospective referring to the "true yokefellow" (Lightfoot) or it may be pleonastic, i.e., superfluous (BD, 228). *λοιπός* rest. *συνεργός* fellow worker.

4 ■ *χαίρετε* pres. act. imp. rejoice. The pres. imp. calls for a continual and habitual action. *πάντοτε* always. *ἐρῶ* fut. act. ind.

5 *λέγω*. ■ *τὸ ἐπιεικές* reasonableness in judging. The word signifies a humble, patient stedfastness, which is able to submit to injustice, disgrace, and maltreatment without hatred and malice, trusting in God in spite of all of it (Leivestad, 158; s. 2 Cor. 10:1; Trench; *Synonyms*, 154). *γνωσθήτω* aor. pass. imp. *γινώσκω*. *ἐγγύς* near. The word could imply "near in space" or "near in time." Here the phrase probably expresses general expectation

6 of the speedy second coming of Christ (Vincent). ■ *μεριμνᾶτε* pres. act. imp. *μεριμνάω* to be anxious, to be troubled, to care for something, to be fretful (Beare). *δέησις* request, generally a request arising from a specific need (s. Eph. 6:18). *εὐχαριστία* thanksgiving. It expresses that which ought never to be absent from any of our devotions; namely, the grateful acknowledgment of past mercies, as distinguished from the earnest seeking of fut. (Trench; *Synonyms*, 191). *αἴτημα* request, a thing asked for. The word in the pl. indicates the several objects of the request (Lightfoot; s. also Trench; *Synonyms*, 191). *γνωριζέσθω* pres.

7 pass. imp. *γνωρίζω* to make known. ■ *ὑπερέχουσα* pres. act. part. *ὑπερέχω* to rise above, to be superior, to surpass (Vincent; s. also Phil. 2:3; 3:8). *φρουρήσει* fut. act. ind. *φρουρέω* to

guard. The word is a military term picturing soldiers standing on guard duty and refers to the guarding of the city gate from within, as a control on all who went out (BAG; EGT). The fut. preceded by an imp. and joined by "and" has the character of a result clause in a Semitic type of conditional sentence, i.e., "make your request known, then the peace of God will guard your hearts" (s. Beyer, 238–255; BD, 227). καρδία heart. The heart is the center of each per. from which thoughts and affections flow (PAT, 326). νόημα thought, act of the will which issues from the heart (Vincent; PAT, 327).

■ τὸ λοιπόν "finally" (s. Phil. 3:1). ὅσος whatever. 8 ἀληθής truth. σεμνός worthy of respect or honor, noble, dignified, reverent. The word implies that which is majestic and awe-inspiring (BAG; Trench; *Synonyms*, 347; Lohmeyer). ἀγνός pure, morally pure, undefiled. In the LXX it signifies ceremonial purification (s. Vincent; Lohmeyer; Trench; *Synonyms*, 333). προσφιλής acceptable, pleasing, lovely. It refers to "those things whose grace attracts" (EGT). εὔφημος well-sounding, praiseworthy, attractive, appealing (BAG). ἀρετή virtue, the most comprehensive Gr. term for moral excellence and the central theme of Gr. ethics (Beare; s. also TDNT; CBB; Cremer; PS, 152ff.). (For a comparison of Paul and Stoicism, and esp. w. Seneca, s. Lightfoot, 270–333; PS; Beare, 42f.) ἔπαινος praise. λογίζεσθε pres. mid. imp. λογίζομαι to consider, to reckon, to take into account, to think on, "use your facilities upon them" (Ellicott; s. also Vincent). The pres. tense calls for a continual or habitual action. ■ καί "also." The word here is ascensive but its 9 other occurences in this v. are copulative, i.e., "and" (Ellicott). ἐμάθετε aor. act. ind. μανθάνω to learn. παρελάβετε aor. act. ind. παραλαμβάνω to receive, to receive tradition or that which is passed on (s. TDNT). ἠκούσατε aor. act. ind. ἀκούω. εἴδετε aor. act. ind. ὁράω. The last two verbs "heard and saw" refer to Paul's personal contact w. the Philippians (Vincent). πράσσετε pres. act. imp. πράσσω to do, to practice. The verb contains the idea of continuity and repetition of action (Trench; *Synonyms*, 361). The pres. tense calls for a continual practicing. ἔσται fut. εἰμί. (For the construction of the imp. plus "and" plus the fut. forming a type of conditional sentence w. the fut. used in a result clause, s.v.7.)

■ ἐχάρην aor. pass. ind. χαίρω to rejoice, to be glad (s. 10 Phil. 1:18). The aor. is epistolary aor. (Vincent). μεγάλως adv. "greatly." ἤδη ποτέ "now at last." The word indicates that there was an indefinite interval of delay but has more the notion of culmination rather than time (RG, 1147). ἀνεθάλετε aor. act.

ind. ἀναθάλλω to sprout again, to shoot up, to blossom again, to put forth new shoots (RWP; Lightfoot). The prep. in compound probably contains a causative idea (MH, 295). φρονεῖν pres. act. inf. (s. Phil. 2:2). The inf. is used as the obj. of the verb "you caused your thought for me to sprout and bloom afresh, like a tree putting out fresh shoots after the winter" (Vincent). ἐφ᾽ ᾧ "upon which," "upon whom." The phrase could indicate the object of their thinking (Ellicott) or it could be taken as causal (BD, 123). ἐφρονεῖτε impf. act. ind. The impf. emphasizes the continual action in the past "you were all along taking thought" (Vincent). ἠκαιρεῖσθε impf. mid. ind. ἀναιρέομαι to have no opportunity, to lack opportunity, to lack a convenient
11 time. ■ οὐχ ὅτι "not that." It is used to avoid a misunderstanding "my meaning is not . . ." (Meyer). ὑστέρησις coming short, lack. ἐγώ "I" strongly emphatic. ἔμαθον aor. act. ind., s.v.9. The aor. is effective aor. pointing to the completion of the process. αὐτάρκης content, being self-sufficient, having enough. The word indicates independence of external circumstances and often means the state of one who supports himself without aid from others (Lightfoot; BAG). The word indicates an inward self-sufficiency, as opposed to the lack or the desire of outward
12 things (Vincent). ■ ταπεινοῦσθαι pres. pass. inf. ταπεινόω to make low, pass. to be brought low. Here it has to do w. the physical rather than the moral or spiritual and is used in respect to the needs of daily life (EGT). The inf. is used as the object of the verb. περισσεύειν pres. act. inf. to overflow, to abound. μεμύημαι perf. pass. ind. μυέω to initiate, pass. to be initiated, to be instructed, a t.t. of the mystery religions (BAG). The perf. emphasizes the completed action w. a continuing state or result. χορτάζεσθαι pass. inf. χορτάζω to fill, pass. to be full. The word was used primarily of feeding and fattening animals in a stall (Vincent). πεινᾶν pres. act. inf. πεινάω to be hungry. ὑστερεῖσθαι pres. mid. inf. ὑστερέομαι to come short, to fall
13 behind, to lack, to suffer need. ■ ἰσχύω pres. act. ind. to be strong, to have strength, to be able (s. Eph. 1:19). ἐνδυναμοῦντι pres. act. part. ἐνδυναμόω to empower, to give strength, to
14 infuse strength into someone (Vincent). ■ πλήν "nevertheless," "however" (s. Phil. 3:16). καλῶς well. ἐποιήσατε aor. act. ind. συγκοινωνήσαντές pres. act. part. συγκοινωνέω to participate in something w. someone, to share together w. someone (s. Phil. 1:7). θλῖψις pressure, trouble, tribulation.
15 ■ δέ "and." It marks the transition to his first experience of their generosity (EGT). ἀρχή beginning. ἐξῆλθον aor. act. ind. ἐξέρχομαι to go out. ἐκοινώνησεν aor. act. ind. κοινωνέω to

have fellowship, to share, to be a partner. εἰς λόγον "as to an account." He used a metaphor from the business world. The Philippians by their contributions had "opened an account" w. him (Vincent; for the commercial t.t., s. also BAG; LAE, 117; MM). δόσις giving. The word is very common in financial transactions and is used for a payment or an installment (s. MM; Preisigke). λῆμψις receiving. This was also a t.t. in the business world meaning the receiving of a payment and was used in connection w. the word "giving" in the sense of "credit and debit" (s. Vincent; MM; Lohmeyer). ■ ἅπαξ once. δίς twice. 16 Used together in the sense of "not merely once but twice" (Vincent). χρεία need. ἐπέμψατε aor. act. ind. πέμπω to send. ■ ἐπιζητῶ pres. act. ind. to seek after. The prep. in compound 17 is directive indicating the concentration of the action upon some object (MH, 312). δόμα that which is given, gift. πλεονάζοντα pres. act. part. πλεονάζω to increase, to become more, to multiply. The commercial or business metaphor is continued and their earthly investment accrues heavenly dividends. ■ ἀπέχω pres. 18 act. ind. to have in full, to receive in full. The word was also a commercial t.t. meaning "to receive a sum in full and give a receipt for it." (For examples, s. BAG; MM; BS, 229; LAE, 111.) πεπλήρωμαι perf. pass. ind. πληρόω to fill, pass. to be filled. The perf. emphasizes the continuing state. δεξάμενος aor. mid. part. δέχομαι to receive. The part. expresses contemporaneous action "when I receive." ὀσμή smell. εὐωδία aroma, fragrance, "a scent of sweet savor" was a t.t. indicating the acceptance and pleasantness of a sacrifice (s. Gnilka). δεκτός acceptable. εὐάρεστος pleasing. ■ πληρώσει fut. act. ind. ἐν δόξῃ "in 19 glory." Used here as an adv. indicating the mode or manner of the fulfillment "gloriously," i.e. in such wise that His glory will be manifested (Vincent).

■ ἀσπάσασθε aor. mid. imp. ἀσπάζομαι to greet, to give 21 greetings. ■ μάλιστα especially. οἱ ἐκ τῆς Καίσαρος "the 22 members of Caesar's household." Probably slave and freedmen attached to the palace (Lightfoot, esp. 171–178).

COLOSSIANS

Ch. 1

2   *οἱ ἅγιοι*. The adjs. can be taken w. the substitutive "the holy brothers" or it can be taken as a substitutive indicating a definite class of people "the holy ones" (s. Moule; Martin, NCB). *πίστος*. The adjs. can mean "believing" or "faithful." The latter sense is perhaps preferable and has the idea "trustworthy, stedfast, unswerving" (Lightfoot).

3   ■ *εὐχαριστοῦμεν* pres. act. ind. to give thanks. The pl. could be epistolary pl., i.e. "I thank" or a real pl., i.e. "Timothy and I thank" (s. Moule). *πάντοτε* always. It could be taken either w. the part. or w. the main verb. The latter is probably more accurate (s. Lohse). *προσευχόμενοι* pres. mid. part. *προσεύχομαι* to pray. The pres. tense points to a repeated

4 action. ■ *ἀκούσαντες* aor. act. part. The part. could be temporal "after we heard" or causal "because we heard" (Martin, NCB). He heard from Epaphras for the apostle had no direct personal

5 knowledge of the Colossian church (Lightfoot). ■ *διά* w. acc. because. *ἐλπίς* hope. The prep. phrase can be taken either w. the main verb as the ground of thanksgiving or w. the words faith and love indicating the reason for these (s. Abbott; Eadie; Moule). (For the psychological necessity of hope in one's life, s. Basil Jackson, "Psychology, Psychiatry and the Pastor: Relationships Between Psychiatry, Psychology, and Religion," Bib Sac, 132 [January, 1975], 3–15.) *ἀποκειμένην* pres. mid. part. *ἀπόκειμαι* to put up, to store up, to put away for one's use. As an extension of a royal Persian custom Hellenistic rulers would lay up in store goods for faithful servants (Lohse; s. also TDNT). *προηκούσατε* aor. act. ind. *προακούω* to hear beforehand, to hear previously, i.e. they had heard the gospel before they had heard the false teaching (Moule). *ἀληθείας* gen. of quality belonging to logos followed by the gen. *λόγος* which explains the

6 words "the word of truth" (Abbott). ■ *παρόντος* pres. act. part. *πάρειμι* to arrive and be present (Lohmeyer). The prep. combines the idea of the gospel being present w. the idea of the gospel coming to them (s. Abbott; Lightfoot). *κάθως* just as. *καρποφορούμενον* pres. mid. part. *καρποφορέω* to bear fruit.

The mid. emphasizes that the gospel bears fruit of itself. The part. is used in a periphrastic construction emphasizing the continuity of the process (RWP). αὐξανόμενον pres. mid. part. αὐξάνομαι to grow, to increase, to develop. The word refers to the outward expansion as the previous part. refers to the personal inner working (Abbott). ἀφ᾽ ἧς ἡμέρας "from which day." The fruitfulness and growing started on the day they received the grace of God (s. Lohse). ἠκούσατε aor. act. ind. ἀκούω. ἐπέγνωτε aor. act. ind. ἐπιγινώσκω to know, to recognize. It implies not so much developed knowledge as active conscience recognition, of taking knowledge of (Abbott). The aor. is ingressive "you came to know." χάρις grace. It refers to God's unmerited and undeserved help to someone in need and here indicates the message of salvation in the gospel (s. TDNT; CBB). ἐν ἀληθείᾳ "in truth," i.e., the grace of God "as it truly is" (Moule). ■ ἐμάθετε aor. act. ind. μανθάνω to learn. 7 ἀγαπητός one who is loved, beloved. σύνδουλος fellow slave. πιστός faithful. διάκονος minister, one who ministers to the needs of another (s. TDNT) ■ δηλώσας aor. act. part. δηλόω 8 to make plain, to make clear. ἐν πνεύματι "in the Spirit." It is to be connected w. agape and expresses the ground of their love, which was not individual sympathy, personal acquaintance, or the like, but belonged to the sphere of the Holy Spirit's influence (Abbott).

■ καί "also." The word is to be taken w. the main verb 9 (Lohse). ἠκούσαμεν aor. act. ind., s.v.6. παυόμεθα pres. mid. ind. to cease. (For the 1st per. pl., s.v.3.) προσευχόμενοι pres. mid. part., s.v.3. αἰτούμενοι pres. mid. part. αἰτέω to ask, to request. The mid. indicates that one is asking something for himself. The mid. was often used in a commercial sense and was also used of requests addressed to God (s. BD, 165f.; M, 160f.). ἵνα "that." The particle is used to introduce the content of the prayer (s. Lohse). πληρωθῆτε aor. pass. subj. πληρόω to fill. The pass. is used as a substitute for God's name "may God fill you" (Lohse). The pass. is followed here by the acc. (s. BD, 87). ἐπίγνωσις knowledge. The knowledge here is not of other worlds but of the will of God (Lohse). The concept of knowledge in Colossians is related more to the concept of knowledge found in the DSS rather than that in the gnostic philosophy (s. Edwin Yamauchi, "Qumran and Colosse," Bib Sac, 121 [April, 1964], 141–152; for specific references in the DSS and other literature, s. Lohse; s. also CBC; Eph. 1:17). σοφία wisdom. The word indicated for the Gr. the mental excellency in its highest and fullest sense (Lightfoot; Abbott). The OT concept was that of

applying the knowledge of God's will to life's situations (s. TDNT; Lohse). σύνεσις understanding, insight. The word refers to the putting together the facts and information and drawing conclusions and seeing relationships. πνευματικῇ spiritual. The prevailing meaning of the word in the NT is "of, or belonging to the Holy Spirit" (Eadie; for the suf. of the adj., s. MH,
10 378). ■ περιπατῆσαι aor. act. inf. περιπατέω to walk about, to conduct one's life. The inf. is used to express intended or potential results (s. IBG, 141; BD, 197f.; S. Lewis Johnson, Jr., "Spiritual Knowledge and Walking Worthily of the Lord," Bib Sac, 118 [October, 1961], 342). According to the teaching of the Dead Sea community, those who walked according to the spirit of truth will walk pleasing before God. (For this teaching and the references in the DSS, s. Lohse.) ἀρεσκεία pleasing. The word was often used in a neg. sense of trying to gain favor from someone and describes that cringing subservient attitude which one has who would do anything to please a benefactor (Abbott; Johnson, 342; s. also MM; TDNT). καρποφοροῦντες pres. act. part., s.v.6. The pres. tense indicates that fruit-bearing for believers is to be a continuous thing and the act. voice may point to external diffusion or it may simply direct attention away from the inherent energy of the fruit-bearing instrument, the Christian (Johnson, 342). αὐξανόμενοι pres. mid. part., s.v.6. τῇ ἐπιγνώσει. The dat. could be either locative, i.e. "growing in knowledge," or it could be instrumental, i.e. "growing by knowledge." The simple instrumental dat. represents the knowledge of God as the dew or the rain which nurtures the growth of the
11 plant (Lightfoot). ■ δύναμις power, might. δυναμούμενοι pres. pass. part. δυναμόω to make powerful, to strengthen. κράτος strength, might. It refers to the inherent strength which displays itself in the rule over others (s. TDNT; GEW II, 8; s. also Eph. 1:19). Here it refers to the might which is characteristic of His glory (Eadie; s. also Moule). μακροθυμία patience, longsuffering. It refers to the self-restraint which does not hastily retaliate a wrong (Lightfoot; s. also TDNT; NTW, 83–85; s. also Gal.
12 5:22; Rom 2:4). ■ εὐχαριστοῦντες pres. act. part., s.v.3. ἱκανώσαντι aor. act. part. ἱκανόω to make sufficient, to qualify, to authorize. This is a qualification for inheritance due solely to the grace of God (Johnson, 344). μερίς part, portion. κλῆρος lot. The phrase is not exactly equivalent to the word "inheritance" since it designates only the allotted part. The gen. is either apposition "the portion which consists in the lot" or it is partitive "to have a share in the lot" (Abbott). (For the teaching of inheritance in the DSS, s. Lohse.) φῶς light. The inheri-

tance is "in the light" because He who is the Light dwells there
and fills heaven w. His marvelous light (Johnson, 344). ■ 13
ἐρρύσατο aor. mid. act. ῥύομαι to rescue, to deliver. (For the
relation of rescuing or deliverance w. the OT and the Dead Sea
community, s. Lohse.) ἐξουσία. The word properly means "liberty of action," i.e., freedom to do something without any hindrance. In relation to others it means "authority" and here refers
to the characteristic and ruling principle of the region in which
they dwelled before conversion to Christ (Abbott; TDNT)
μετέστησεν aor. act. ind. μεθίστημι to remove from one place
to another, to transfer. The word was often used to signify deportation of a body of men or the removal of them to form a colony
(Eadie). βασιλεία kingdom. τῆς ἀγάπης objective gen. "the
Son who is the object of His love" (Abbott). ■ ἐν ᾧ "in whom." 14
The reference is to Christ and the rel. sentence speaks of the new
life which we have received in Christ (Lohse). ἀπολύτρωσις
redemption, complete release based on the payment of a price
(s. Rom. 3:24; LAE, 327; s. also the references to the DSS listed
by Lohse). ■ εἰκων image, copy. In Gr. thought an image shares 15
in reality what it represents. Christ is the perfect likeness of God.
The word contains the idea of representation and manifestation
(s. CBB; Moule; Lightfoot; TDNT; Lohse). ἀόρατος not capable of being seen, invisible. πρωτότοκος firstborn. The word
emphasizes the preexistence and uniqueness of Christ as well as
His superiority over creation. The term does not indicate that
Christ was a creation or a created being. (For this important
word, s. Lohse; Lightfoot; Abbott; Moule; Martin; PJR, 150f.;
SB III, 626; TDNT; CBB; GI, 122–126; CEJC, 53f.) κτίσις
creation. ■ ἐν αὐτῷ "in Him." The prep. denotes Christ as the 16
"sphere" within which the work of creation takes place (Bruce).
All the laws and purposes which guide the creation and government of the universe reside in Him (Lightfoot). The prep. is
possibly both instrumental and local (Moule). He is not in all
things but all things are in Him and this difference is not insignificant (s. Fred B. Craddock, " 'All Things in Him': A Critical
Note on Col. I.15–20," NTS, 12 [October, 1965], 78–80).
ἐκτίσθη aor. pass. ind. κτίζω to create. ὁρατός visible. εἴτε
whether. κυριότης lordship. ἀρχή beginning, ruler. δι' αὐτοῦ
"through Him." The prep. w. the gen. describes Christ as the
immediate instrument of creation (Abbott; s. also Lightfoot). εἰς
αὐτόν "for Him, unto Him." The prep. indicates that Christ is
the goal of creation (Lohse). The rabbis taught that the world
was created for the Messiah (SB III, 626). ἔκτισται perf. pass.
ind. The perf. tense emphasizes the duration and persistence of

17 the act of creation (Ellicott). ■ αὐτός. The pron. is used emphatically "He Himself" in contrast to the created things (Abbott). Here it means "*He* and no other" (MT, 40). πρό before. The prep. could refer to priority in time or in rank but the idea of time is here more suitable. Used w. the pres. tense of the verb, the idea expresses immutability of existence, i.e., "His existence is before all things" (Abbott; s. also Moule, Lightfoot). συνέστηκεν perf. act. ind. συνίσταμι to place together, to stand together, to hold together, to cohere. He is the principal of cohesion in the universe (Lightfoot). God Himself is the unifying band which encompasses everything and holds it together. This applies not only to the largest things of the universe, but
18 also to the smallest things of the universe (Lohse). ■ ἀρχή beginning, origin. The word refers to priority in time and to originating power (Lightfoot; s. also Moule). γένηται aor. mid. subj. γίνομαι. The purpose clause indicates "that He Himself in all things (material and spiritual) may come to hold the first place" (RWP). πρωτεύων pres. act. part. πρωτεύω to be first, to have first place, to hold the chief place. (For the quotation from Meander—"Never does a house fail to come to grief, where
19 woman takes the lead in everything"—, s. MM.) ■ εὐδόκησεν aor. act. ind. εὐδοκέω to be pleased. The subject here is "God." πλήρωμα fullness. It could refer either to the totality of the divine powers and attributes (Lightfoot) or perhaps better it refers to the fullness of saving grace and power which belongs to one constituted as "savior" (Eadie; s. also S. Lewis Johnson, "From Enmity to Amity," Bib Sac, 119 [April, 1962], 141–142). κατοικῆσαι aor. act. inf. κατοικέω to live, to dwell, to settle down. The word indicates "permanent abode" (Lightfoot). The aor. could be ingressive aor. "to take up one's permanent
20 abode" (Johnson, 142). ■ ἀποκαταλλάξαι aor. act. inf. ἀποκαταλλάσσω to exchange hostility for friendship, to reconcile. (For this word, s. Johnson, 143; TDNT; CBB; APC, 186–223; MNTW, 101ff.) The prep. in compound has the meaning "back" and implies a restitution to a state from which one has fallen. The meaning is "to effect a thorough change back" (MH, 298; Lightfoot). εἰρηνοποιήσας aor. act. part. εἰρηνοποιέω to make peace. The part. describes the means of the reconciliation. The insertion of the part. indicates that reconciliation is not to be thought of as a cosmic miracle which merely changed the state of the universe outside of man but shows that reconciliation is primarily concerned w. the restoration of relationships (R.P. Martin, "Reconciliation and Forgiveness in Colossians," RH, 113). Peace is more than an end to hostilities.

It has a positive content and points to the presence of positive blessings and is concerned w. spiritual blessings and prosperity of the whole man (CNT, 251). σταυρός cross.

■ καί and, also. The word indicates that this message of 21 reconciliation is also applicable to those at the church of Colossae (Lohse). ποτέ once, formerly. ὄντας pres. act. part. εἰμί. ἀπηλλοτριωμένους pres. pass. part. ἀπαλλοτριόω to estrange, to alienate. The part. is used in a periphrastic construction and w. the perf. tense it expresses more forcibly the settleness of the alienation (Abbott; s. also Eph. 2:12). ἐχθρός hostility. The adj. is act. rather than pass. (Lightfoot). διάνοια mind. The hostile minds of the Colossian Christians have turned into a willing and glad subservience; and the ultimate result of this interchange of attitude toward God will be perfection in sanctification (Ladd, 455). ■ νύνι now. ἀποκατήλλαξεν aor. act. ind. 22 ἀποκαταλλάσσω s.v.20. The verb has a soteriological meaning, which embraces both the "overcoming of the cosmic hostility through the lordship of Christ" and the restoration of sinful men to God's favor and family (Martin, RH, 114). (For a discussion of the pass. as a variant reading, s. TC, 621f.; Lohsc.) παραστῆσαι aor. act. inf. παρίστημι to present. The inf. can be used to express either purpose or result. The picture here may be a sacrificial metaphor (Moule) or it may be a legal word indicating that one is placed before a court of justice (s. Lohse). ἄμωμος without spot, without blemish. In the LXX the word was used as a t.t. to designate the absence of anything amiss in a sacrifice, of anything which would render it unworthy to be offered (Trench; Synonyms, 379). ἀνέγκλητος without accusation, unaccused, free from any charge at all. It is a legal word indicating that there is no legal or judicial accusation which can be brought against a person (Trench; Synonyms, 381; TDNT; s. also Abbott; Lohse). κατενώπιον before, "right down in the eye of" (RWP). ■ εἴ γε "if," "assuming that" (Abbott). The particle 23 introduces a conditional clause which the author assumes to be true. ἐπιμένετε pres. act. ind. to remain, to continue. The prep. in compound adds to the force of the linear action of the pres. tense "to continue and then some" (RWP). τεθεμελιωμένοι perf. pass. part. θεμελιόω to lay the foundation of something, pass. to be founded. The word refers to the sure foundation (Abbott; s. also TDNT). The perf. emphasizes the completed state or condition. ἑδραῖος firm. This word refers to the firmness of the structure (Abbott). (For DSS parallels to the figure of a building used to describe the people of God, s. Lohse.) μετακινούμενοι pres. mid. or pass. part. μετακινέω to move from one place to another, to shift from one place to another. The pres. tense stresses the "not constantly shifting" (Abbott). κηρυχθέντος aor. pass. part. κηρύσσω to preach, to proclaim, to herald, to proclaim as a herald (TDNT; CBB). ἐγενόμην aor. mid. ind. γίνομαι.

24 ■ πάθημα that which is suffered, suffering. (The suf. in the word indicates a pass. idea or the result of an action; MH, 355.) ὑπὲρ ὑμῶν "on behalf of you," "for you." The prepositional phrase is to be connected w. the word "suffering" (Eadie). ἀνταναπληρόω pres. act. ind. to fill up. The idea of the prep. in compound may be reciprocal or it may signify that the supply comes "from an opposite quarter" or it may contain the idea of substituting for that which is lacking (s. MH, 297; Lightfoot; Lohse; S. Lewis Johnson, "The Minister of the Mystery," Bib Sac, 119 [July, 1962], 228ff.). ὑστέρημα lacking, that which is lacking. θλῖψις pressure, tribulation, affliction. The sufferings of Paul were the afflictions of Christ because He suffered in and w. Paul because of his identification w. Christ in mystical union (Johnson, 231; for a discussion of the various interpretations, s.

25 Moule). σάρξ flesh. ■ οἰκονομία stewardship. The word indicated the responsibility, authority, and obligation given to a household slave (s. Eph. 1:10; Lohse; J. Reumann, "OIKO-NOMIA—Terms in Paul in Comparison with Lukian Heilsges-chichte," NTS, 13 [January, 1967], 147–167). δοθεῖσαν aor. pass. part. δίδωμι. πληρῶσαι aor. act. inf. πληρόω to fill, to fulfill. The word has the sense of "doing fully," "carrying to

26 completion" (Moule). ■ μυστήριον mystery, that which is hidden and undiscoverable by human means, but that which has been revealed by God (s. Eph. 3:3; Johnson, 231f.; Lohse; Moule). ἀποκεκρυμμένον perf. pass. part. ἀποκρύπτω to hide, to veil, to conceal. The perf. part. emphasizes the state or condition. ἀπό from. The prep. is doubtless temporal (Lightfoot). αἰῶνες age. The pl. indicates successive periods of time (s. TDNT). γενεά generation, an age includes many generations (Abbott). ἐφανερώθη aor. pass. ind. φανερόω to make clear, to

27 manifest. ■ ἠθέλησεν aor. act. ind. θέλω. γνωρίσαι aor. act. inf. γνωρίζω to make known. δόξης glory. The word became a comprehensive word for God's glorious presence (Moule; s. also CBB; TDNT). ἔθνος folk, Gentile. ἐν ὑμῖν "in you," "among you." For Christ to be "among" the Gentiles involved being "in"

28 those who believed (Johnson, 232). ■ καταγγέλλω pres. act. ind. to proclaim. The word indicates an official proclamation (Lohmeyer; CBB). The pres. tense emphasizes the continual and habitual action. νουθετοῦντες pres. act. part. νουθετέω to ad-

monish, to correct through instruction and warning (s. TDNT).
The part. is a part. of manner defining more nearly the manner
or accompaniments of the proclamation (Ellicott).
διδάσκοντες pres. act. part. παραστήσωμεν aor. act. subj.,
s.v.22. The subj. is used in a purpose clause. τέλειος perfect,
mature (s. Lohse). ■ κοπιάω pres. act. ind. to work, to labor, to 29
labor w. wearisome effort, to work to exhaustion (T; TDNT).
ἀγωνιζόμενος pres. mid. part. ἀγωνίζομαι to strive, to exert
effort. The athletic picture behind this word emphasizes Paul's
missionary work, w. all its attendant toil, its tireless exertion, and
its struggles against all manner of setbacks and opposition
(PAM, 175). ἐνέργεια working, effectual working. The word is
used of the effective working of God's power (MNTW, 46–54).
ἐνεργουμένην pres. mid. part. ἐνεργέω to work effectively, to
be effectual (TDNT).

Ch. 2

■ εἰδέναι perf. act. inf. οἶδα defective perf. w. a pres. 1
meaning to know. ἡλίκος how great. ἀγών struggle. The picture
is that of an athletic contest which is strenuous and demanding.
The struggle here is not the struggle against God but pictures the
intense effort of the one praying as he struggles within himself
and against those who oppose the gospel (s. PAM, 113f.; 123f.).
ἑόρακαν perf. act. ind. ὁράω to see. (For the form of this verb,
s. BD, 44.) ἐν σαρκί "in the flesh." This is to be taken w. the
noun "my face" and implies that they had a knowledge of Him,
though not personal (Abbott). ■ ἵνα "that." The word in- 2
troduces the purpose of the struggle. παρακληθῶσιν aor. pass.
subj. παρακαλέω to comfort, to encourage (s. Phil. 2:1).
συμβιβασθέντες aor. pass. part. συμβιβάζω to bring together, to unite, to knit together. The meaning here could be "to
instruct," "to teach" (s. Dibelius; Lohse; TDNT). The part. is a
part. of manner. πληροφορία full assurance, firm conviction,
confidence. The gen. is descriptive, i.e. "the wealth consists" of
conviction (Moule). σύνεσις understanding, insight.
ἐπίγνωσις knowledge (s. Col. 1:9). μυστήριον mystery (s. Col.
2:26). The gen. τοῦ θεοῦ is possessive and the next gen.
Χριστοῦ "Christ" is in apposition to the word "mystery"
(Moule; Lightfoot). ■ θησαυρός storehouse, treasure. γνῶσις 3
knowledge. ἀπόκρυφος hidden. It is in Christ that all the treasures of divine wisdom and knowledge have been stored up—
stored up in hiding formerly, but now displayed to those who
have come to know Christ (Bruce). ■ ἵνα "that," "in order that." 4
The particle may be used to express purpose "I say this in order

that . . ." or it is equally possible that it has an imperatival sense: "Let no one . . ." (MT, 102). παραλογίζηται pres. mid. subj. παραλογίζομαι to reckon wrong, to cheat by false reckoning, to deceive by false reasoning (T). The word was used in the papyri of a keeper of a state library who had shown a willingness to "make a wrong use of" certain documents. Paul uses the word here to point to drawing an erroneous conclusion from the reasoning submitted (MM). The prep. in compound has the idea of counting "beside" or counting "aside" w. the idea of "miscalculating" (s. MH, 319; RWP). πιθανολογία "persuasive speech." The word was used by classical writers for probable reasoning and opposed to demonstration (Abbott). The word is used in the papyri in a court case of those who sought persuasive words to keep the things obtained by robbery (Lohse; MM). The terminology used here is practically equivalent to our English expression, "to talk someone into something" (S. Lewis Johnson, "Beware of Philosophy," Bib Sac, 119 [October, 1962],

5   304). ■ γάρ "for." The particle gives the reason how Paul who was unknown to the Colossians and not present w. them can give such a warning. Through the Holy Spirit he is so bound to them as though he were w. them (Dibelius). ἄπειμι to be away from someone, to be absent. χαίρων and βλέπων pres. act. parts. τάξις an orderly arrangement used in the military sense of a rank or orderly array (Lightfoot; s. also Lohse). στερέωμα that which is firm, hard, solid. (For the root meaning, s. GEW II, 790f.) Firmness, solidity. Here it is probably a continuation of the military metaphor and means "a solid front," "a closed phalanx" (Lightfoot).

6   ■ παρελάβετε aor. act. ind. παραλαμβάνω to receive, to receive through transmission, to receive through teaching and is equivalent to the rabbinical terms for receiving and passing on tradition (Johnson, 305f.; Lohse; TDNT). περιπατεῖτε pres. act. imp. περιπατέω to walk about, to walk, to conduct one's life. The command is for the Colossians to conduct their life in accord w. the truth of Paul's preaching and not in accord w. enticing words of the heretics (Johnson, 306). The pres. tense

7   calls for a continual and habitual action. ■ ἐρριζωμένοι perf. pass. part. ῥιζόω to cause to take root, pass. to be or to become firmly rooted or fixed. The word was also used in the metaphor of the building and pictured the firm and solid foundation (s. BAG; Lohse; TDNT; Eph. 3:17). The perf. tense points to the past completed action w. the continuing results or condition. The tense pictures the settled state brought about by conversion. The following parts. in the pres. tense emphasize the continuing

development which is always advancing (Abbott). ἐποικοδομούμενοι pres. pass. part. ἐποικοδομέω to build up, to build up upon. βεβαιούμενοι pres. pass. part. βεβαιόω to make firm, to establish, to strengthen (BAG; TDNT). The pres. tense gives the idea "being more and more established" (Abbott). πίστις faith. The word could be used in the subjective sense and the dat. would be instrumental "by your faith." Faith would be as it were the cement of the building (Lightfoot). It is, however, more probable that faith is to be taken in its objective sense referring to the doctrines of the Christian faith (Eadie; Johnson, 303). ἐδιδάχθητε aor. pass. ind. περισσεύοντες pres. act. part. περισσεύω to overflow, to abound. εὐχαριστία thanksgiving. ■ βλέπετε pres. act. imp. beware. The word is 8 normally followed by the subj. but the ind. in this case shows that the danger is real (Lightfoot). ἔσται fut. ind. συλαγωγῶν pres. act. part. συλαγωγέω to carry off as booty or as a captive. The word was used in the sense of "to kidnap" (Dibelius; Johnson, 306) and here is the figure of carrying someone away from the truth into the slavery of error (BAG). κενός empty. ἀπάτη deceit. παράδοσις tradition, that which is given over from one to another. ἄνθρωπος man, i.e., "man-made tradition which is to be contrasted w. the true, living, divine 'tradition' just alluded to" (Moule). στοιχεῖον component parts of a series, elementary things. The word could refer to elemental powers, i.e., "cosmic spirits" or more probably to "elementary teaching" (Johnson, 308; Moule; Dibelius; Lohse; TDNT). (For studies regarding the heresy at Colossae, s. Martin, 12ff.; Martin, NCB, 9–19; Andrew J. Bandstra, "Did the Colossian Errorists Need a Mediator?" ND, 329–343; s. also the various articles in CC.) ■ κατοικέω 9 pres. act. ind. to settle down, to be at home (s. Col. 1:19). The pres. tense indicates the continual state and points to the pres. reality (Lohse). πλήρωμα fullness (s. Col. 1:19). θεότης divine nature, deity. The word differs from the expression "Godhead" in Rom. 1:20 in that it emphasizes not so much divine attributes but divine nature or essence. They were no mere ways of divine glory which gilded Him lighting up His person for a season and w. a splendor not His own; but He was and is absolute and perfect God (Trench; *Synonyms*, 8; TDNT; Lightfoot). σωματικῶς adv. bodily. The word refers to the human body of Christ (Johnson, 310) indicating also the full humanity of Jesus which was not a humanity which was simply a covering for His deity (s. Lohse; TDNT; Moule; Lohmeyer). ■ πεπληρωμένοι 10 perf. pass. part. πληρόω to fill, to make full. The perf. is used in a periphrastic construction and accentuates the abiding results of believers' completeness through union w. the exalted Lord. In Him they find their needs fully met (Johnson, 310). κεφαλή head. The word here probably notes primarily supremacy but it also emphasizes that the head is the center of vital force, the source of all energy and life (Lightfoot). ἀρχή beginning, princi-

11 pality. ■ περιετμήθητε aor. pass. ind. περιτέμνω to circumcise (s. Gal. 2:3). περιτομή circumcision. ἀχειροποίητος not made w. hands. ἀπέκδυσις putting off. The prep. in compound express a complete putting off and laying aside (Abbott). σάρξ flesh. The reference here could be to the putting off of the fleshly nature of man, i.e., the crucifixion of the old man (S. Lewis Johnson, "The Sufficiency of Union with Christ," Bib Sac, 120 [January, 1963], 15) or it could be a reference to the physical

12 death of Christ, i.e., His crucifixion (s. Moule; SBT, 41f.). ■ συνταφέντες aor. pass. part. συνθάπτω to bury together. συνηγέρθητε aor. pass. ind. συγεγείρω to raise up together w. someone, to be co-resurrected. ἐνέργεια effective working, divine working (s. Col. 1:29). ἐγείραντος aor. act. part. ἐγείρω to raise up, to resurrect. The rite of baptism typified the reality of death and resurrection. Death is the neg. side and the resur-

13 rection is the positive (Johnson, 16). ■ ὄντας pres. part. εἰμί. παράπτωμα transgression (s. Eph. 2:1). The dat. could be locative or instrumental describing either the circumstances (Moule) or the reason for them being dead (Lightfoot). ἀκροβυστία foreskin, uncircumcision. συνεζωοποίησεν aor. act. ind. συζωοποιέω to make alive together (s. Eph. 2:5). χαρισάμενος aor. mid. part. χαρίζομαι to grant as a favor, to give graciously, to forgive out of grace (Abbott; s. also TDNT;

14 CBB). ■ ἐξαλείψας aor. act. part. ἐξαλείφω to wash over, to wipe out. The word was used for wiping out a memory of an experience or for cancelling a vote or annulling a law or cancelling a charge or debt. It was also used for "the washing out" the writing on a papyrus (s. NTW, 46–48; MM; Preisigke I, 507; Moule). κατά w. the gen. "against." χειρόγραπον handwriting. It was used as a t.t. for a written acknowledgment of debt. It is an "I.O.U.," a statement of indebtedness, personally signed by the debtor (Abbott; Moule; LAE, 334). (For a description of the Jewish certificate of indebtedness, s. SB III, 628; Lohse.) δόγμα decree. The word referred to a legal obligation which was a binding law or edict which was placed on a public place for all to see (s. TDNT; Lohmeyer; Lohse; Martin, NCB). The dat. is a dat. of description, i.e., a document containing or consisting of "decrees" (IBG, 45; s. also MT, 219). ὑπεναντίος opposed, against, hostile, directly opposed. It described the act. hostility

(Lightfoot). ἦρκεν perf. act. ind. αἴρω to take away. The perf. tense stands in contrast to the aor. in this section and fixes attention on the pres. state of freedom resulting from the action which was esp. before the apostle's mind (Abbott). μέσον middle, combined w. the verb is a strong expression meaning "and put out of sight" (Lightfoot). προσηλώσας aor. act. part. προσηλόω to nail to. The part. is modal and describes the manner in which Christ removed the handwriting. He nailed the Mosaic law with all its decrees to His cross and it died w. Him (Ellicott). σταυρός cross. ■ ἀπεκδυσάμενος aor. mid. part. 15 ἀπεκδύομαι to strip off, to put off as one puts off a garment. Christ divested Himself at the cross of the evil powers which had struggled w. Him so strongly during His ministry in attempts to force Him to abandon the pathway of the cross (Johnson, 20). ἐδειγμάτισεν aor. act. ind. δειγματίζω to display, to expose, to display as a victor displays his captives or trophies in a triumphal procession (Lightfoot). παρρησία openness, boldness, confidence (s. Abbott; Lightfoot). θριαμβεύσας aor. act. part. θριαμβεύω to lead in a triumph. It pictures a victorious general leading his prisoners in a triumphal procession (Moule; s. also 2 Cor. 2:14). See also Rory B. Egan, "Lexical Evidence of Two Pauline Passages," Nov T, 19 [January, 1977], 34–62). (For a study of these verses, s. Ralph P. Martin, "Reconciliation and Forgiveness in Colossians," RH, 116–124.)

■ κρίνετω pres. act. imp. κρίνω to judge, to take one to 16 task (Abbott). The pres. imp. w. the neg. calls for the stopping of an action in progress or indicates that an action should not be a habitual one (s. MKG, 272f.). βρῶσις eating. πόσις drinking. Here it refers to indulgence in wine (Dibelius). The idea that man could serve deity or draw near to deity or prepare one's self for the reception of a revelation through ascetic living and fasting was widespread in the ancient world (Lohse). μέρος part. Used in the construction in ἐν μέρει w. the meaning "in respect to," "in the matter of" (Abbott). ἑορτή festival. Here it refers chiefly to the annual festival like the Passover, Pentecost, etc. (Lightfoot). νεομηνία new moon. This describes the monthly festival and the following word "sabbath" refers to the weekly holy day (Lightfoot). ■ σκία shadow. The word indicates either 17 a "shadow" which in itself has no substance but indicates the existence of a body which casts the shadow (Abbott), or it indicates a dim outline, a sketch of an object in contrast w. the object itself. This would mean that the OT ritual observances were dim outlines of the NT redemptive truths (S. Lewis Johnson, "The Paralysis of Legalism," Bib Sac, 120 [April, 1963], 112). (For the

use of the figure of a shadow in Josephus and rabbinical writings, s. SB III, 628.) μελλόντων pres. act. part. μέλλω to be about
18 to. Here it has the meaning "things coming." ■ καταβραβευέτω pres. act. imp. καταβραβεύω to decide against someone, to give judgment against someone (Abbott; Lohse; s. also Preisigke I, 744; Lohmeyer). θέλων pres. act. part. The verb here followed by the prep. could be taken as a septuagintism and translated "being bent upon" (Fred O. Francis, "Humility and Angelic Worship in Colossians 2:18," CAC, 167). ταπεινοφροσύνη lowliness, humility. The word was often used in connection w. the fasting and several Jewish Christian writings specify that the consequence of this ascetic practice is entrance into the heavenly realm (Francis; CAC, 168ff.). θρησκεία worship. The word can be used in a variety of ways but stands for the act of worship (Francis, CAC, 180). τῶν ἀγγέλων gen. pl. The word is normally taken as obj. gen., i.e., "the worship given to angels," but it is also possible and more probable that the gen. is subj. gen. and refers to the worship the angels performed (Francis; CAC, 177–180). ἑόρακεν perf. act. ind., s.v.1. ἐμβατεύων pres. act. part. ἐμβατεύω to enter into, to penetrate. Perhaps the meaning here is the entering into heavenly spheres as a sort of superspiritual experience. (For various contexts in which this word appears and a discussion of this interpretation, s. CAC, 171–176; cf. also PGL, 453; for other views s. also Abbott; Lohse; Johnson, 111.) φυσιούμενος pres. pass. part. φυσιόω to puff up, to blow up, pass. to be puffed up. Their profession of humility was a cloak for excessive pride
19 (Lightfoot). νοῦς mind, thinking facility. ■ κρατῶν pres. act. part. κρατέω to hold fast to someone, to remain closely united w. someone (BAG; s. also Lohse). κεφαλή head, "the Head" regarded as a title, so that a person is at once suggested, and the rel. which follows is masc. (Lightfoot). σῶμα body. Here it refers to the church as the "body of Christ" consisting of the saints and deriving its unity and growth from Christ (s. SBT, 224). ἁφή ligament. The word could refer to the "nerves" (Meyer) or to the "joints" of the body as contacts between the members (Lightfoot). (For a study of the words, s. Robinson, Eph. 4:16; Lightfoot.) σύνδεσμος band, that which binds together. In relation to the figure of the church being the body of Christ, these words refer to believers in the body of Christ, who are to exercise their spiritual gift in the church for the edification of the whole body (Johnson, 115). ἐπιχορηγούμενοι pres. pass. part. ἐπιχορηγέω to furnish or provide, to support, pass. to be supported, to receive help (BAG). συμβιβαζόμενον pres. pass.

part., s.v.2. αὔξει pres. act. ind. to grow. The pres. tense emphasizes the continual growth. αὔξησις growth. The acc. is cognate acc. here being the acc. of the inner content and is used for emphasis (s. BD, 84f.; RG, 478; DM, 94). Growth does not come through a denial of certain foods but rather growth comes from God.

■ ἀπεθάνετε aor. act. ind. ἀποθνήσκω to die. The ind. is 20 used in a conditional clause which assumes the reality of the condition. στοιχεῖον elementary teachings, s.v.8. ζῶντες pres. act. part. The part. used w. the particle is concessive. The particle here gives the subj. motivation of the subject or action, i.e., "w. the assertion that, on the pretext that, w. the thought that" (BD, 219). δογματίζεσθε pres. mid. ind. to issue a decree, mid. to subject one's self to decrees. The mid. is permissive mid. "why are you allowing yourselves to be subjected to authoritative decrees?" (s. RG, 808; MT, 57) ■ ἅψῃ aor. mid. subj. ἅπτομαι to 21 touch, to take hold of, to grasp. γεύσῃ aor. mid. subj. γεύομαι to taste, to partake of, to enjoy. θίγῃς aor. act. subj. θιγγάνω to touch. (For a comparison of the words for "touch" and that the first word may be used in a sexual sense, s. Lightfoot; Abbott; Schweizer.) ■ ἀπόχρησις consuming, consumption, using up. 22 The prep. in compound is perfective, completely using up (MH, 299; Ellicott). ἔνταλμα commandment. διδασκαλία teaching, doctrine. ■ ἔχοντα pres. act. part. The part. is used w. ἐστίν to 23 form a periphrastic pres. ind. (RWP) and this points out that the character of the precepts is such that a word of wisdom belongs to them (Abbott). ἐθελοθρησκία. The word could mean "self-chosen worship" (Hendriksen; Martin; Lohse) or it could mean "would-be worship" (Francis; CAC, 181f.; MH, 290; s. also BD, 64). ταπεινοφροσύνη s.v.18. ἀφειδία unsparing, severity, hard treatment (S. Lewis Johnson, "Human Taboos and Divine Redemption," Bib Sac, 120 [September, 1963], 210). πλησμονή filling up, satisfaction, gratification, but it may be used in the bad sense "indulgence of the flesh" (s. BAG; Lightfoot; Abbott).

Ch. 3

■ συνηγέρθητε aor. pass. ind. συνεγείρω to raise up to- 1 gether, pass. to be coresurrected. The ind. is used in a conditional clause which assumes the reality "if then (as is the case) you were raised together w. Christ" (EGT). The aor. looks at the completed action. ἄνω above, "the things above." The words are used to mean "the heavenly world" (Lohse; s. also TDNT). (For a contrast of "things above and things below" in Jewish writings,

s. SB I, 395, 977; II, 116, 133, 430; III, 630.) ζητεῖτε pres. act. imp. ζητέω to seek. The pres. tense calls for a continual and habitual action. δεξία right, right hand (s. Eph. 1:20). καθήμενος pres. mid. part. κάθημαι to sit. The sitting at the right hand was considered to be a place of honor (s. Schweizer).

2 ■ φρονεῖτε pres. act. imp. φρονέω to think, to be minded. The verb in this v. differs so far from that employed in the preceding, that it refers more to an inner disposition, while the former is

3 rather practical pursuit (Eadie; s. also Phil. 2:2, 5). ■ ἀπεθάνετε aor. act. ind. ἀποθνῄσκω to die. κέκρυπται perf. pass. ind. κρύπτω to hide. The idea of life being hidden in God suggests three thoughts, i.e., secrecy where the believer's life is nurtured by secret springs; safety, "w. Christ in God" marks a double protection; identity, the believer is identified w. the risen Lord (Johnson, 212). The perf. tense views the completed state arising

4 from a past action. ■ ὅταν w. the subj. "whenever." φανερωθῇ aor. pass. subj. φανερόω to make plain, clear, to manifest. Here it refers to the coming of the Lord at which time the veil will be removed so that the things which are now hidden from our eyes will be illuminated in a bright light (Lohse). φανερωθήσεσθε fut. pass. ind.

5   ■ νεκρώσατε aor. act. imp. νεκρόω to put to death. The meaning here is to be compared to Rom. 6:11 and contains the idea "reckon as dead" (Bruce). μέλος member. The members of the body were used to carry out the desires. According to the rabbis there are as many commandments and restraints in the law as the body has members and the "Evil Impulse" is said to be king over 248 members (s. Schweizer) and the two great passions which the "Evil Inclination" plays the most upon are the passions of idolatry and adultery (s. S. Schechter, Some Aspects of Rabbinic Theology, 250). πορνεία illicit sex, sexual activity apart from marriage. Sexual activity was often connected w. the idolatrous worship of false gods (s. TDNT; Gal. 5:19). ἀκαθαρσία uncleanness, filthiness (s. Gal. 5:19). πάθος passion. The word indicates a drive or force which does not rest until it is satisfied (s. Trench; Synonyms, 324). ἐπιθυμία desire, lust. The word is wider than the previous word and reaches to all evil longing (Lightfoot). πλεονεξία insatiable selfishness, greed (s. NTW, 97; TDNT). εἰδωλολατρία idolatry. The accs. in this v. are accs. of general reference, i.e. "put to death the

6 members in reference to ..." (s. DM, 93; RG, 486). ■ ὀργή wrath, anger. It refers to the deep-seated anger of God which displays itself in eternal punishment which will come upon those who practice sexual sins, uncontrolled greed and service to idols

(s. TDNT; CBB; Lohse). ■ περιπατήσατε aor. act. ind. 7
περιπατέω to walk about, to conduct one's life. The verb used
w. the prep. indicates "to take part in" (BAG). The aor. is
constative summing up their whole life of thc past (RWP; DM,
196; Funk, 620f.). ἐζῆτε impf. ind. act. ζάω to live. The impf.
is customary impf. indicating the continual action of the past
time "you used to live." ■ ἀπόθεσθε aor. mid. imp. ἀποτίθημι 8
to take off from one's self, to change one's clothes, to remove
one's clothes from one's self, to put off. θυμός anger. It refers
to a burning anger which flares up and burns w. the intensity of
a fire (s. Trench; *Synonyms*, 130f.; TDNT). κακία malice. It
refers to the vicious nature which is bent on "doing harm to
others" (Lightfoot; s. also Trench; *Synonyms*, 37ff.; TDNT).
βλασφημία slander. It indicates the attempt to belittle and
cause someone to fall into disrepute or to receive a bad reputation (s. TDNT; for examples from the DSS, s. Lohse).
αἰσχρολογία filthy talk, dirty speech, abusive language (s.
Lightfoot; MM). ■ ψεύδεσθε pres. mid. imp. to lie. The pres. 9
imp. w. the neg. forbids a manner of life. ἀπεκδυσάμενοι aor.
mid. part. ἀπεκδύομαι to take off completely, to strip off of
one's self. The part. is causal and contains the motive for the
preceding exhortation (Abbott). Paul means: if the old man really has been put off, one must not at a critical moment revert to
the way one acted before his conversion. (For this and a discussion of the origin of Paul's metaphor along w. various parallel
usages, s. P.W. van der Horst, "Observations on a Pauline Expression," NTS, 19 [January, 1973], 185; 181–187.) παλαιός
old. πρᾶξις deed. The pl. describes the individual deeds which
characterized the former life. ■ ἐνδυσάμενοι aor. mid. part. 10
ἐνδύομαι to put on one's self, to cloth one's self. The part. is
causal (Hendriksen). νέος new. The word only expresses newness in point of time (Abbott; Lightfoot; Trench; *Synonyms*,
219f.). ἀνακαινούμενον pres. pass. part. ἀνακαιόω to make
new again, to renew. The idea of "new" is that of newness in
quality (s. Rom. 12:2; TDNT). The prep. in compound does not
suggest the restoration of the original state, but the contrast to
that which has lately existed (Abbott). The pres. tense points to
the continual action "which is ever being renewed" (Lightfoot).
The pass. indicates that the action is performed by another.
ἐπίγνωσις knowledge, "thorough knowledge" (Abbott; s. also
Col. 1:9). εἰκών image (s. TDNT; CBB). κτίσαντος aor. act.
part. κτίζω to create. αὐτόν "him." The reference is to the "new
man" rather than "man" in general (Ellicott). ■ ὅπου where. 11
περιτομή circumcision. ἀκροβυστία foreskin, uncircumci-

sion. βάρβαρος barbarian. The word properly denoted one who spoke an inarticulate, stammering, unintelligible language and was adopted by Gr. exclusiveness and pride to stigmatize the rest of mankind and denoted one who was not a Gr. (s. Lightfoot; Lohse; TDNT). ἐλεύθερος free, one who had been freed from slavery.

12 ■ ἐνδύσασθε aor. mid. imp., s.v.10. ἐκλεκτός chosen, elect. If God chose them as members of His new creation, they must fulfill the command to conduct themselves accordingly. ἠγαπημένοι perf. pass. part. ἀγαπάω to love. The perf. tense points to a past completed action w. a continuing state or results. σπλάγχνα heart. It denotes esp. the nobler inward parts, heart, liver, and lungs and figuratively it refers to the seat of the emotion (Abbott; s. also MNTW, 156; TDNT; Phil. 2:1). οἰκτιρμός compassion (s. Phil. 2:1). χρηστότης kindness. It is kindness expressed in attitude and deed. It is the friendly and helpful spirit which seeks to meet the needs of others through kind deeds (s. TDNT; Gal. 5:22). ταπεινοφροσύνη lowliness in thinking, humility. It is the recognizing of one's own weakness but also the recognition of the power of God (TDNT; CBB). πραΰτης meekness. The word indicates an obedient submissiveness to God and His will w. unwavering faith and enduring patience which displays itself in a gentle attitude and in kind acts toward others, and this often in the face of opposition. It is the restrained and obedient powers of the personality brought into subjection and submission to God's will by the Holy Spirit (s. Gal. 5:23). μακροθυμία longsuffering. It is a long holding out of the mind before it gives room to action or passion. It indicates the patient longsuffering in bearing injustices or unpleasant circumstances without revenge or retaliation but w. a view or hope for a final goal or betterment (s. Trench; Synonyms, 196; TDNT; Gal.

13 5:23). ■ ἀνεχόμενοι pres. mid. part. ἀνέχομαι to endure, to bear w., to put up w. someone (BAG). The part. describes the manner or means. The pres. tense emphasizes the continual action. χαριζόμενοι pres. mid. part. χαρίζομαι to be gracious, to forgive. ἑαυτοῖς = ἀλλήλοις. (For the reflex. pron. used instead of the reciprocal pron., s. BD, 150; MT, 37f.) The reflex. pron. here may suggest the performance of an act faintly resembling that of Christ, namely, of each one toward all, —yea even to themselves included, Christians being members one of another (Ellicott). ἔχῃ pres. act. subj. The pres. tense has the idea of "having" rather than the idea of "getting" as expressed by the aor. (s. M, 110). The subj. is used in a conditional clause where the condition is viewed as possible. μόμφη blame, cause for

complaint. The verb from which this noun is taken means "to find fault w. someone," "to be dissatisfied w. someone," and refers most commonly to errors of omission so the noun here is regarded as a debt which needs to be remitted (Lightfoot; s. also TDNT). ἐχαρίσατο aor. mid. ind. The aor. points to the completed action. ■ ἐπί w. the dat. the prep. could mean "in addition 14 to" or "on the top of all the others" or it may have an elative force and mean "above all," i.e., love is the most important moral quality in the believer's life (s. Moule; S. Lewis Johnson, "Christian Apparel," Bib Sac, 121 [January, 1964], 30). σύνδεσμος that which binds or holds something together, bond. τελειότης perfection, complete maturity. The gen. could be an obj. gen., i.e. "the bond producing perfection" (s. MT, 212; Lohse), or it could be a type of descriptive gen. indicating the bond which signifies or indicates perfection. The word here is the full expression of the divine life in the community, devoid of bitter words and angry feelings, and freed from the ugly defects of immorality and dishonesty (Bruce). ■ βραβενέτω pres. act. imp. 3rd per. sing. 15 βραβεύω to referee, to be an umpire, to call a decision, to decide between (s. TDNT; Lohse; Lightfoot). ἐκλήθητε aor. pass. ind. καλέω to call. εὐχάριστος thankful. The word indicates the obligation of being thankful to someone for a favor done. The thankfulness arises out of the grace of God and that which He has done (s. TDNT). γίνεσθε pres. mid. imp. The pres. tense indicates a continual action pointing to a habit of life. ■ 16 ἐνοικείτω pres. act. imp. 3rd per. sing. ἐνοικέω to live in, to dwell in, to take up one's residence in, to make one's home among (Moule; s. also Preisigke I, 493). πλουσίως adv. πλούσιος extravagantly rich, richly. διδάσκοντες pres. act. part. νουθετοῦντες pres. act. part. νουθετέω to admonish, to correct one who is at fault through admonition (s. Col. 1:28). ψαλμός psalm. It was often used of the psalms in the OT and has the idea of a song w. musical accompaniment (s. Trench; Synonyms, 296; Lightfoot; Lohse). ὕμνος hymn. The word is used of a song which is a praise to God (s. Trench; Synonyms, 297f.; Lightfoot). ᾠδή song. This is the general word for any kind of a song (Trench; Synonyms, 300f.; Lightfoot). ᾄδοντες pres. act. part. ᾄδω to sing. ■ ἐάν used w. the subj. and generalizes 17 the object "whatever," "everything whatever" (s. RWP). ποιῆτε pres. act. subj. εὐχαριστοῦντες pres. act. part. εὐχαριστέω to give thanks.

■ ὑποτάσσεσθε pres. mid. imp. ὑποτάσσω mid. to be in 18 subjection, to subject one's self. Submission for Paul is a voluntary submission based on one's own recognition of God's order

(Crouch, 110; s. also Eph. 5:21). (For references to the position of women in the ancient world, s. Crouch, 107.) ἀνῆκεν impf. ind. act. ἀνῆκει it is fitting, it is proper. The impf. is used w. a pres. meaning in an expression of necessity, obligation, or duty

19 (BD, 181; s. also RG, 919f.; MT, 90f.). ■ ἀγαπᾶτε pres. act. imp. The pres. imp. calls for a continual attitude and positive expression. πικραίνεσθε pres. mid.-pass. imp. πικραίνω to make bitter, to embitter, to become bitter. The verb has the idea of being sharp, harsh, and bitter. It speaks of friction caused by impatience and thoughtless "nagging." If love is absent, such obedience will not be secured by perpetual irritation and fault-finding (s. TDNT; Moule; Eadie). The pres. imp. w. the neg. forbids a habitual action.

20 ■ ὑπακούετε pres. act. imp. ὑπακούω to listen to, to obey. γονεῖς (pl.) parents. εὐάρεστος well-pleasing, commendable. The word is generally used in the Bible to mean "pleasing to

21 God" (Moule). ■ ἐρεθίζετε pres. act. imp. ἐρεθίζω to excite, to provoke, to irritate (Abbott). ἀθυμῶσιν pres. act. subj. ἀθυμέω to be without courage or spirit, to lose heart, to become spiritless, i.e., "to go about their task in a listless, moody, sullen frame of mind" (Lightfoot). A child frequently irritated by overseverity or injustice, to which, nevertheless, it must submit, acquires a spirit of sullen resignation, leading to despair (Abbott).

22 ■ ὀφθαλμοδουλία eye service. It might mean "merely such service as can be seen," i.e., superficial work—not dusting behind the ornaments, not sweeping under the wardrobe but the context suggests rather going through the outward movements of the work "without a corresponding keenness of will behind them" (Moule). The word could also have the idea of "when the master's eye is upon you" (S. Lewis Johnson, "The New Man in the Old," Bib Sac, 121 [April, 1964], 113). ἀνθρωπάρεσκος men-pleaser, one who tries to please men at the sacrifice of principle (BAG). ἁπλότης singleness. The phrase used here means "w. undivided service" (Lightfoot). φοβούμενοι pres. mid. part. φοβέομαι to be afraid, to fear, to fear the Lord (Christ) is the leading principle of Christian conduct (Lohse).

23 ■ ἐάν. Used w. the subj. and the rel. pron. w. the meaning "whatever" (s.v.17). ποιῆτε pres. act. subj., s.v.17. ἐργάζεσθε pres. mid. imp. ἐργάζομαι to work, to work energetically, to

24 work diligently (Lightfoot). ■ εἰδότες perf. act. part. οἶδα. ἀπολήμψεσθε fut. mid. ind. ἀπολαμβάνω to receive from someone. The prep. denotes that the recompense comes immediately from Christ, its possessor (Eadie). ἀνταπόδοσις receiving from another in return, recompensing, requittal. The prep. in

compound expresses the idea of full, complete return (Hendriksen). κληρονομία inheritance, gen. of apposition, the reward which consists in the inheritance. There is a special point in the word, inasmuch as slaves could not be inheritors of an earthly possession (Abbott). δουλεύετε pres. act. imp. or ind. to serve as a slave. The form could be either imp. (Lohse; Moule) or ind. (Lightfoot). ■ ἀδικῶν pres. act. part. ἀδικέω to commit an 25 unrighteous act, to wrong (s. TDNT). The sentence is an explanation and gives a general law applicable to all. κομίσεται fut. mid. ind. κομίζω to carry off safe, mid. to bear for one's self, to receive (AS). ἠδίκησεν aor. act. ind. ἀδικέω. προσωπολημψία the accepting of one's face or person, partiality (s. Moule; TDNT).

Ch. 4

■ ἰσότης equality, fairness. παρέχεσθε pres. mid. imp. 1 παρέχω to give, to grant, mid. to show one's self to be something, here "exhibit on your part fairness to the slaves." The idea is "reciprocation." The master's duty as corresponding to the slaves (Lightfoot; s. also BAG; BD, 166).

■ προσκαρτερεῖτε pres. act. imp. προσκαρτερέω to ad- 2 here to, to persist in, to busy one's self w., to busily engage in, to be devoted to (BAG; s. also TDNT). γρηγοροῦντες pres. act. part. γρηγορέω to be awake, to stay awake, to be watchful, to be vigilant. Perhaps Paul was reminded of the literal sleep which he had heard about in the story of the passion or of the Transfiguration (Moule). εὐχαριστία thanksgiving (s. Col. 3:17). ■ 3 προσευχόμενοι pres. mid. part. προσεύχομαι to pray. ἅμα to gather at the same time, "praying at the same time also for us" (BD, 220). ἀνοίξῃ aor. act. subj. ἀνοίγω to open. The picture of an open door stood for "opportunity." (For rabbinical examples, s. SB III, 631; TDNT.) λόγον "the word," obj. gen. "a door for preaching" (RWP). λαλῆσαι aor. act. inf. μυστήριον mystery (s. Col. 1:26; Eph. 3:3). δέδεμαι perf. pass. ind. δέω to bind. The perf. emphasizes the continuing state or condition. ■ 4 φανερώσω aor. act. subj. φανερόω to make clear, to manifest. δεῖ. Used w. the acc. and the inf. "it is necessary." The word denotes the logical necessity (s. AS; for the root meaning of the word, s. GEW I, 375). ■ περιπατεῖτε pres. act. imp. 5 περιπατέω to walk about, to walk, to conduct one's life. ἔξω outside. The expression "those outside" is equivalent to the rabbinical term denoting those who belong to another religious group and is used here to denote those who are "non Christians" (s. SB III, 362; TDNT; Lohse). καιρός time, opportunity. The

583

word does not emphasize a point of time but rather a time space filled w. all kinds of possibilities (s. TDNT; Lohse). ἐξαγοραζόμενοι pres. mid. part. ἐξαγοράζω to buy at the market place. The prep. in compound is probably intensive and the object of the verb is viewed as a commodity to be eagerly

6 bought (s. Eph. 5:16; Moule; Lightfoot). ■ πάντοτε always. ἅλας salt. ἠρτυμένος perf. pass. part. ἀρτύω to season. The figure of speech such as salt was used in the ancient world of sparkling conversation, speech dotted w. witty or clever remarks (Hendriksen; Moule; Lohse; SB III, 631). Here it indicates speech which gives a flavor to the discourse and recommends it to the pallet as well as speech which preserves from corruption and renders wholesome (Lightfoot). εἰδέναι perf. act. inf. οἶδα. The inf. is used to express results. πῶς how. The conversation must not only be opportune in regards to time; it must also be appropriate as regards the person (Lightfoot). ἀποκρίνεσθαι pres. mid. inf. to answer.

7 ■ τὰ κατ'ἐμέ "the things related to me," "my affairs." γνωρίσει fut. act. ind. γνωρίζω to make known. ἀγαπητός beloved. πίστος true, faithful. διάκονος minister (s. Col. 1:23).

8 σύνδουλος fellow servant. ■ ἔπεμψα aor. act. ind. πέμπω to send. γνῶτε aor. act. subj. γινώσκω. The subj. is used in a purpose clause. παρακαλέσῃ aor. act. subj. παρακαλέω to exhort, to encourage, to comfort (s. TDNT; MNTW, 128ff.).

9 ■ ὧδε here.

10 ■ ἀσπάζεται pres. mid. ind. to greet. συναιχμάλωτος fellow prisoner. The term denotes properly "a prisoner of war" but it also occurs in the general sense (s. TDNT; Moule). ἀνεψιός cousin (s. Lightfoot). ἐλάβετε aor. act. ind. λαμβάνω to receive. ἐντολή command. ἔλθῃ aor. act. subj. ἔρχομαι.

11 δέξασθε aor. mid. imp. δέχομαι to receive, to welcome. ■ λεγόμενος pres. pass. part. ὄντες pres. part. εἰμί. περιτομή circumcision. συνεργός fellow worker. ἐγενήθησαν aor. pass. ind. γίνομαι. παρηγορία encouragement, comfort. The word appears on gravestones and in a letter of condolence w. the meaning "comfort" (s. MM; Lohse; Lightfoot). ■ ἐξ ὑμῶν "one

12 who belongs to you," "who is one of you," i.e., a native or at least an inhabitant of Colossae (Lightfoot). ἀγωνιζόμενος pres. mid. part. ἀγωνίζομαι to struggle, to agonize. It is the zeal and intensity of prayer which is emphasized (PAM, 123). σταθῆτε aor. pass. subj. ἵστημι to place, pass. to stand. The word conveys the idea of standing firm (Abbott). τέλειος perf., mature. πεπληροφορημένοι perf. pass. part. πληροφορέω to fill completely, pass. to be fully convinced, to be assured through, rich,

gratifying insight into all spiritual matters is meant; understanding which not only penetrates the mind but also fills the heart w. satisfying conviction (Hendriksen; BAG). ■ μαρτυρέω pres. 13 act. ind. to witness, to testify. πόνος labor, strenuous work. It is labor such as does not stop short of demanding the soul strength of a man; and this exerted to the uttermost, if he is to accomplish the task which is set before him. It is the standing word by which the laborers of Hercules are expressed (Trench; *Synonyms*, 378). ■ ἰατρος doctor, physician. (For information 14 concerning physicians and medicine in the ancient world, s. RAC I, 720–724; OCB, 660–664; DGRA, 747–748; Preisigke III, 123; ZPEB IV, 788f.) ἀγαπητός beloved. ■ ἀσπάσασθε 15 aor. mid. imp. Νύμφαν. The manuscript evidence is divided as to whether the name refers to a woman or a man (s. TC, 627; Lightfoot). κατ᾿οἶκον at home, at one's house. The use of the home for Christian assembly is well attested in the NT period (s. Martin; Lightfoot). ■ ὅταν w. the subj. "when," "whenever." 16 ἀναγνωσθῇ aor. pass. subj. ἀναγιγνώσκω to read. ποιήσατε aor. act. imp. τὴν ἐκ Λαοδικείας "the letter that is at Laodicea" (s. BD, 225). (For the suggestion that the Laodicean letter was written by Epaphras, s. C.P. Anderson, "Who Wrote the 'Epistle From Laodicea'?" JBL, 85 [December, 1966], 436–440.) ἀναγνῶτε aor. act. subj. ἀναγιγνώσκω. ■ εἴπατε aor. act. 17 imp. λέγω. βλέπε pres. act. imp. to see, to take heed, to keep an eye on (RWP). διακονία ministry, service (s. Col. 1:23; TDNT). παρέλαβες aor. act. ind. παραλαμβάνω to receive, to receive from someone. The word suggests a mediate rather than a direct reception; Archippus received the charge immediately from St. Paul, though ultimately from Christ (Lightfoot). πληροῖς pres. act. subj. The pres. tense points to a continual action. It refers to a lifetime job (RWP).

■ ἀσπασμός greeting. μνημονεύετε pres. act. imp. 18 μνημονεύω to remember. The verb is followed by the gen. δέσμος bond. The chain clanked afresh as Paul took the pen to sign the salutation (RWP).

1 THESSALONIANS

Ch. 1

1 &ec~ &ver;. The prep. could be local and emphasizes that the church
is in the atmosphere of the divine (Frame). They live "in" Him
day by day. All their deeds are done in Him (Morris). The prep.
could also be taken in an instrumental sense which means that
for the believer salvation lies "in" what God accomplished by
Christ's life, death, and resurrection (Best).

2 ■ εὐχαριστοῦμεν pres. act. ind. to give thanks, to thank.
The pres. tense stresses the continual action. πάντοτε always.
μνεία remembrance, mention. The word indicates "remembrance" in a special case, i.e., "the direction of the memory to
some particular object" (Lightfoot, *Notes*). ποιούμενοι pres.
mid. part. used in connection w. the previous noun w. the meaning "making mention," "remembering." (For examples in the
papyri and inscriptions, s. Milligan.) This is the first of three
modal parts. describing the nature of the perpetual thanksgiving
(Milligan). ἀδιαλείπτως constantly, without interruption, un-
3 ceasingly (s. Rom. 1:9; 1 Thess. 5:17). ■ μνημονεύοντες pres.
act. part. μνημονεύω to remember. The verb regularly means
"to call something to mind," or "to make mention of it"
(Moore). ὑμῶν your. The word is placed emphatically at the
head of three phrases and should be taken w. each (Best). ἔργον
work. The word refers to active work (Lightfoot). The word
could also involve the results of the activity, i.e., "achievement"
(Best). The word comprehends the whole Christian life work, as
it is ruled and energized by faith (Milligan). κόπος labor. The
word denotes arduous, wearying toil involving sweat and fatigue
(Moore). The word emphasizes the weariness which follows on
this straining of all of one's powers to the utmost (Trench; *Synonyms*, 378). ὑπομονή endurance. It is the spirit which bears
things, not simply w. resignation, but w. blazing hope. It is the
spirit which bears things because it knows that these things are
leading to a goal of glory (NTW, 60; s. also TDNT; CBB). The
gens. "faith, love and hope" are subj. gens. (MT, 211).
4 ἔμπροσθεν in the presence of. ■ εἰδότες perf. act. part. οἶδα.
(For the meaning of this word, s. ND, 344-356.) ἠγαπημένοι

perf. pass. part. ἀγαπάω. The perf. pass. part. stresses continuing love which God shows to men (Morris). ἐκλογή choosing, election. ■ ἐγενήθη aor. pass. ind. γίνομαι to become, to come. 5 The word is significant as pointing to a result reached through the working of an outside force (Milligan). εἰς ὑμᾶς "unto you," "to you." The prep. w. the acc. is used here as an equivalent to the dat. (s. RG, 594). οὐκ ... ἐν λόγῳ μόνον "not in word alone," i.e., "our preaching was not merely declamation, a hollow and heartless rhetoric" (Lightfoot; Notes). δύναμις power. The word is generally used by Paul of divine energy (Moore). πληροφορία full assurance, conviction, confidence (Lightfoot; Notes; s. also Col. 4:12). οἷος what sort of, what kind of, what manner of. The qualitative pron. brings out the interest and advantage of those for whom that power was exercised (Milligan). ἐγενήθημεν aor. pass. ind. γίνομαι to become. The sense here is "came to be," "proven to be" (Ellicott). ἐν ὑμῖν "in your midst." δι᾿ ὑμᾶς "because of you," "for your sake." ■ μιμητής 6 imitator, one who imitates another particularly by following one's example or one's teaching (s. TDNT; von Dobschütz). ἐγενήθητε aor. pass. ind., s.v.5. δεξάμενοι aor. mid. part. δέχομαι to receive, to welcome. The part. expresses contemporaneous or identical action "in that you welcomed" (Frame). θλῖψις pressure, tribulation (s. TDNT). χαρά joy. The gen. following this word is a gen. of originating cause "joy inspired by, preceding from the Holy Spirit" (Milligan). ■ ὥστε w. the 7 inf. used here to introduce a result clause which expresses actual results rather than merely contemplated results (Milligan; s. also Funk, 707). τύπος example, type. Originally the word denoted the mark left by a blow. Then it was used in the ethical sense of a pattern of conduct but more usually, as here, of an example to be followed (Morris). ■ ἐξήχηται perf. pass. ind. ἐξηχέομαι to 8 sound forth, to sound out. The word suggests an echoing like thunder or sounding out as a trumpet (Moore; s. also Lightfoot; Milligan). Although the metaphor is not clear, the word indicates that a sound is made and it is heard spreading out from a center over an area (Best). The perf. denotes the continuing activity (Morris). τόπος place. The definite article w. θεόν indicates their faith in the true God and contrasts their present attitude to God w. their past pagan attitude to idols (Frame). ἐξελήλυθεν perf. act. ind. ἐξέρχομαι to go out. The perf. indicates the continuing result. χρεία need, necessity. λαλεῖν pres. act. inf. to speak. The inf. is used to explain the need. ■ αὐτοί 9 "they themselves," i.e. people generally (Moore). ἀπαγγέλλω pres. act. ind. to report. The pres. tense indicates a continuous

and repeated action. ὁποῖος what sort of. εἴσοδος entrance. The word indicates here the "act of entering" rather than the "means of entering" and points to the nature of the entrance, how happy and successful it was (Milligan). ἔσχομεν aor. act. ind. ἔχω. ἐπεστρέψατε aor. act. ind. ἐπιστρέφω to turn one's self to or toward. The prep. in compound is directive. εἴδωλον idol (cf. Acts. 17:16). ζῶντι pres. act. part. ζάω to live. The living God is not merely one who is alive but one who gives life, both the life of creation and the new life of redemption (Best). ἀληθινός genuine, true, real. The adj. w. this ending express the material out of which anything is made, therefore the word signifies "genuine" made up of that which is true and is used to distinguish the true God from idols and all other false gods (Trench;
10 Synonyms, 27). ■ ἀναμένειν pres. act. inf. to wait, to wait for. The leading thought here seems to be to wait for one whose coming is expected, perhaps w. the added idea of patience and confidence (Milligan). The pres. tense points to the continual waiting. The inf. is used to express purpose. ἤγειρεν aor. act. ind. ἐγείρω to raise. ῥυόμενον pres. mid. part. ῥύομαι to rescue, to deliver. The word indicates a deliverance and the avoidance of great danger (Moore). ὀργή wrath, deep-seated anger (s. TDNT; Morris). ἐρχομένης pres. mid. part. The part. is emphatic by position and emphasizes the approaching anger (Best).

Ch. 2

1 ■ οἴδατε perf. ind. act. defective perf. w. a pres. meaning "you yourselves know." εἴσοδος entrance (s. 1 Thess. 1:9). κενός empty, vain. The reference is to the essential content of the apostle's preaching rather than to its results (Milligan). The word refers to "hollow, empty, wanting in purpose and earnestness" (Lightfoot; Notes; s. also Trench; Synonyms, 180). γέγονεν perf. act. ind. γίνομαι. The perf. tense indicates the lasting effects of Paul's preaching (Lightfoot; Notes; s. also Best).

2 ■ προπαθόντες aor. act. part. προπάσχω to suffer beforehand, to suffer previously. ὑβρισθέντες aor. pass. part. ὑβρίζω to abuse, to treat shamefully. The word expresses insulting and outrageous treatment and esp. treatment which is calculated publicly to insult and openly to humiliate the person who suffers from it (MNTW, 83; s. also TDNT). Both parts. are to be taken w. the main verb and are either temporal, i.e. "after having suffered previously and having been shamefully treated" or they could be concessive "although ..." (Frame). ἐπαρρησιασάμεθα aor. mid. ind. παρρησιάζομαι to speak freely, to speak all things, to be bold and courageous. The word

588

was used in classical Gr. to signify freedom of speech or expression, often w. a political connotation (Moore). λαλῆσαι aor. act. inf. λαλέω. ἀγών conflict, effort. The word implies the intense effort and strenuous exertion in Paul's preaching the gospel esp. in the fact of hostility and conflict which he had w. the Jews at Thessalonia (PAM, 112–114). ■ παράκλησις exhortation, encouragement, appeal. The word implies an appeal, having for its object the direct benefit of those addressed, and which may be either hortatory or conciliatory according to circumstances. The word was used to encourage soldiers before going into battle and it was said that "encouragement" was necessary for hired soldiers but for those who fight for life and country no exhortation is required (Milligan; s. also MNTW, 128f.; TDNT). ἐκ πλάνης "out of error." The word is used either in the active sense of "deceit," "the leading astray," or in a pass. sense "error" (Lightfoot; Notes; s. also Best). ἐξ ἀκαθαρσίας "out of impurity." The word could refer to sexual or moral impurity but here it is more general and means that Paul does not preach from any impure motives, e.g. ambition, pride, greed, popularity (Best). ἐν δόλῳ "in guile." The word meant a bait or trap and then any form of trick or strategy (s. Moore; Milligan). ■ The word is to be taken in connection w. οὕτως w. the meaning "just as … so …" δεδοκιμάσμεθα perf. pass. ind. δοκιμάζω to prove, to approve after examination or testing. The word was used in classical Gr. w. the technical sense to describe the passing as fit for election to a public office (Milligan; s. also TDNT). The perf. tense indicates a lasting approval and not something over and done w. (Moore). πιστευθῆναι aor. pass. inf. πιστεύομαι to entrust. The inf. is explanatory serving to define more nearly that to which the approval was directed (Ellicott). ἀρέσκοντες pres. act. part. ἀρέσκω to please someone. The word is found in inscriptions of people who have served their fellow citizens and it conveys the sense of service and obedience (Moore). δοκιμάζοντι pres. act. part. δοκιμάζω to approve after testing. Here is is Paul's inner life in its totality of thought and intention which God scrutinizes (Best). ■ ποτέ ever, used w. the neg. "never." κολακεία flattery. The word contains the idea of deception for selfish ends. It is flattery not merely for the sake of giving pleasure to others but for the sake of self-interest. It is deception by slick eloquence, the idea being to win over the hearts in order to exploit them (Lightfoot; Notes; Moore; s. also Frame; Milligan). (For the use of the word in Dio Chrysostom, s. DCNT, 200f.) ἐγενήθημεν aor. pass. ind. γίνομαι to demonstrate one's self as (s. 1 Thess. 1:5). πρόφασις cloak, pretense.

589

The word denotes that which one puts on for appearance and w. the definite design to color or to cloak something else. It therefore denotes pretext, the outward show (Lünemann). πλεονεξία greed, selfishness. It is the disregard for the rights of others in order to meet one's own selfish desires to have more and more
6 (s. TDNT; NTW, 97f.). ■ ζητοῦντες pres. act. part. ζητέω to seek. The pres. tense points to a continual and habitual action.
7 ■ δυνάμενοι pres. mid. part. concessive use of the part. which qualifies the fact, "we never came requiring honor," by asserting the principle that the authority demand for honor inheres in their place of preponderance of Christ's apostles (Frame). βάρος weight, burden. Here the word is used in the sense of honor, authority, dignity, importance. The aspect of the word is closely related to the Heb. root kbd (Milligan; Best). ἤπιος gentle. (For the variant reading νήπιος "infants" and the textual problem, s. TC, 629f.) ὡς used w. the comparative particle and the subj. implying "a standing contingency," i.e. "as it may be at any time" (Milligan). τρόφος one who nourishes or feeds, nurse, wet nurse, nursing mother (s. Best; for a parallel in the DSS, s. 1QH 7.20f.; 9.29–32). A wet nurse in the ancient world not only had strict contractual stipulations, but often came to be a very trusted person whose influence lasted a lifetime (s. RAC I, 381–385; "Engagement of a Wet Nurse" No. 146, CPJ II, 15–19). θάλπῃ pres. act. subj. θάλπω to warm, to foster, to nourish, to cherish. In Deut. 22:6 it is used of a bird warming her
8 eggs (Moore; s. also Milligan; GEW I, 651). ■ ὁμειρόμενοι pres. mid. part. ὁμείρομαι to have a kindly feeling, to long for someone. The derivation of the word is uncertain (s. Lightfoot; Notes; Morris; MH, 251). It is used on a grave inscription describing the parents' sad yearning for their dead child and seems to indicate deep affection and great attraction (Moore; s. also MM). εὐδοκοῦμεν pres. act. ind. εὐδοκέω to be well-pleased, to be gladly determined. The word draws attention to the hearty good will attending the writer's attitude (Milligan). Although the form is pres. ind. it is probably a case where the impf. is used without the augment (s. Best; BD, 37). μεταδοῦναι aor. act. inf. μεταδίδωμι to share. It is the giving of something by which the giver retains a part and the receiver has a part so that they both share in the matter (von Dobschütz). ψύχη soul, life. The word signifies here the life of the individual person which is shared w. another. It is the life of the individual as it is manifested in behavior and refers to the observable totality of Paul's earthly existence (PAT, 346f.). διότι therefore, because. The word apparently always has a causal force in the NT (Milligan).

ἀγαπητός beloved. ▪ μνημονεύετε pres. act. ind. or imp. 9
μνημονεύω to remember. κόπος exhausting labor (s. 1 Thess.
1:3). μόχθος toil. The word refers to the trouble and pain of
arduous work and the leading notion is that of struggling to
overcome difficulties (Moore; Lightfoot; Notes). ἐργαζόμενοι
pres. mid. part. ἐργάζομαι to work. There were no paid teachers
in Palestine. It was necessary therefore for a rabbi to have some
other means of income than the gifts that might now and then
be made to him (Morris; s. also the rabbinical examples quoted
by Morris; Best). πρός. The prep. is used w. the inf. to indicate
purpose (s. MT, 144; BG, 135). ἐπιβαρῆσαι aor. act. inf.
ἐπιβαρέω to place a weight on someone, to be burdensome, to
make demands (Moore; s. also Milligan). ἐκηρύξαμεν aor. act.
ind. ▪ ὁσίως adv. piously, holy. The word describes one's duty 10
toward God (Lightfoot; Notes; Trench; Synonyms, 328f.; TDNT;
CBB). δικαίως adv. righteously. The word indicates one's duties
toward men but it also stresses a righteous life before God
(Lightfoot; Notes; Best). ἀμέμπτως adv. blamelessly.
πιστεύουσιν pres. act. part. The dat. could be dat. of reference
"in reference to you believers" or it could be dat. of advantage
"to the benefit of you believers" or it could be locative "among
you believers." (For the various views, s. Best.) ▪ καθάπερ just 11
as, in accordance w. The first part of the word marks comparison
and the last part the latitude of the application. It introduces a
confirmatory appeal to the individual experience of the hearers
(Ellicott; s. also Milligan). ▪ παρακαλοῦντες pres. act. part. 12
παρακαλέω to exhort, to encourage, to console. The word indicates "to exhort to a particular line of conduct" (Lightfoot;
Notes; TDNT; s. also v. 3). παραμυθούμενοι pres. mid. part.
παραμυθέομαι to encourage. The word indicates "to encourage to continue in a course" (Lightfoot; Notes). The word is
addressed to the feelings rather than to the will (Milligan).
μαρτυρόμενοι pres. mid. part. μαρτύρομαι to summon to witness, to solemnly charge (Milligan). περιπατεῖν pres. act. inf.
to walk, to conduct one's life. The inf. is used w. the prep. to
express either purpose (Morris) or to express the content of the
command or entreaty (M, 219). ἀξίως adv. worthily (s. Eph.
4:1). καλοῦντος pres. act. part. (For the variant reading of the
aor. part., s. TC, 630; Best.)

▪ The second καί in the expression "we also" indicates a 13
reciprocal relation between writers and readers (Frame) and
does not necessarily indicate that Paul was answering a letter
from the Thessalonians (s. Morris; Moore). εὐχαριστοῦμεν
pres. act. ind. to give thanks. ἀδιαλείπτως without interrup-

tion, continually, regularly (s. Rom. 1:9; 1 Thess. 1:2).
παραλάβοντες pres. act. part. παραλαμβάνω to receive, to
receive from another, a t.t. used for the reception of tradition
which was conveyed (s. Col. 2:6). ἀκοή hearing, report, message
(Best). παρ᾽ ἡμῶν "from us." The phrase is to be connected w.
the part. and indicates the immediate source of the message
delivered and received, while the emphatic τοῦ θεοῦ "from
God" is added to point to its real source (Milligan). The gen.
"from God" is therefore a subj. gen. "preceding from God, having God as its author," as its emphatic position requires (Lightfoot; Notes). ἐδέξασθε aor. mid. ind. δέχομαι to receive, to
welcome. καθὼς just as. ἀληθῶς adv. truly. ἐνεργεῖται pres.
mid. ind. to work effectually, to work efficiently and productively. The word is used to describe the energy and effective power
of God Himself (s. MNTW, 46–54; TDNT). πιστεύουσιν pres.
14 act. part. ■ μιμητής imitator (s. 1 Thess. 1:6). ἐγενήθητε aor.
pass. ind., s.v.5. οὐσῶν pres. part. εἰμί. ἐπάθετε aor. act. ind.
πάσχω to suffer. The word is used regularly to indicate good
fortune (Moore). ἴδιος one's own. συμφυλέτης countryman.
This expression may be in part geographical and include Thessalonian Jews, but it points to a large Gentile element in the
15 opposition (Morris). ■ ἀποκτεινάντων aor. act. part.
ἀποκτείνω to kill. ἐκδιωξάντων aor. act. part. ἐκδιώκω to
hunt down, to hunt out, to persecute. The prep. in compound
may indicate "to drive out w. the intention of persecuting"
(Moore). ἀρεσκόντων pres. act. part., s.v.4. ἐναντίος oppos-
16 ing, contrary to, hostile toward. ■ κωλυόντων pres. act. part.
κωλύω to hinder, to prevent, to forbid. The pres. tense would
be conative as well as indicating a continual action "they are
continually trying to hinder." ἔθνος nation, Gentile. λαλῆσαι
aor. act. inf. σωθῶσιν aor. act. pass. subj. σῴζω to rescue, to save.
The subj. is used in a purpose clause. εἰς. The prep. is used w.
the articular inf. to express purpose (Ellicott; Morris; MT, 143).
ἀναπληρῶσαι aor. act. inf. ἀναπληρόω to fill up, to fill up to
the full. The word indicates "to fill up the measure" of their sins,
implying that the process of filling had already begun, drop after
drop being poured into the cup of their guilt (Lightfoot; Notes).
πάντοτε always. ἔφθασεν aor. ind. act. φθάνω to arrive, to
reach. The word could have two meanings here. It could mean
"anger hangs over them and is just about to fall on them" or it
could mean "anger has fallen on them and they now experience
it." (For a discussion of these two meanings as well as the meaning of the aor., s. Best.) ὀργή wrath, anger (s. TDNT; CBB). εἰς

τέλος. The phrase means either "at last" or "to the end" (Morris).

■ ἀπορφανισθέντες aor. pass. part. ἀπορφανίζομαι to 17 make one an orphan by separation. The word could be used of a parentless child, or of childless parents, and even in a general sense of any severe deprivation or desolation (Moore), i.e. "we are like children who have lost their parents" (Lightfoot; Notes; s. also TDNT). The pass. voice points out that the situation was forced (von Dobschütz) and the aor. tense implies a single action and not a continued state (Best). καιρός time, period of time, space of time. προσώπῳ οὐ καρδίᾳ dat. of reference marking the true limiting power of the case, the metaphorical place to which the action is restricted (Ellicott). πρόσωπον "face," "person" indicates that which the outward connection or relationship is. καρδία "heart" indicates the place of the affections and of the inner connection in love (von Dobschütz). περισσοτέρως comp. adv. περισσός "more abundantly." The adv. could have the true comp. force "the more fervently" or it could be elative "excessively" (s. Frame). ἐσπουδάσαμεν aor. act. ind. σπουδάζω to make haste, to endeavor. ἰδεῖν aor. act. inf. ὁράω to see. ἐπιθυμία desire, longing. ■ διότι "because" 18 (s.v.8.). ἠθελήσαμεν aor. act. ind. θέλω to wish, to desire. The word probably points to the will which precedes from inclination (T; Morris). ἐγώ "I." This is the first of a number of instances where Paul speaks for himself alone in these letters (Moore). Paul's name is used to guarantee the correctness of the "we desired" (von Dobschütz; for a discussion of the "we" sections in the Thessalonian letters, s. von Dobschütz, 67f.; Milligan, 131f.). ἅπαξ once. δίς twice. The two words used together form an idiomatic expression meaning "and that more than once," "several times" (Morris; Best). ἐνέκοψεν aor. act. ind. ἐγκόπτω to cut in. The word was originally used of breaking up a road to render it impassable and later it was used in a military sense of making a break through the enemy's line. It was also used in the athletic sense of cutting in on someone during a race. The general meaning of the word is "to hinder" (s. Milligan; Moore; TDNT; Gal. 5:7). ■ καύχησις boasting. οὐχί strengthened 19 form of οὐ used in questions expecting the answer "yes" (s. BD, 220f.). The words "it is certainly you, isn't it?" form a rhetorical parenthesis interjected into the main sentence to draw special attention to the position of the Thessalonians (Milligan). παρουσία coming, presence. ■ γάρ "yes, indeed." The particle 20 is used to introduce the answer to a rhetorical question and in such cases it affirms what was asked, i.e. giving the reason for a tacit "yes" (BD, 236).

Ch. 3

1 ■ διό therefore, on which account, i.e. "on account of this very fervent desire, which I was unable to gratify" (Lightfoot; *Notes*). μηκέτι no longer. στέγοντες pres. act. part. στέγω to cover, to ward off by covering (e.g., a roof covering a house both conceals and wards off), to endure, to bear up under (s. Milligan; Morris; Best). The part. is either temporal or causal. εὐδοκήσαμεν aor. act. ind. εὐδοκέω to be well pleased, to willingly determine, to consider it good (s. 1 Thess. 2:8). καταλειφθῆναι aor. pass. inf. καταλείπω to leave behind, to

2 forsake. The idea here is "willing to be forsaken" (Moore). ■ ἐπέμψαμεν aor. act. ind. πέμπω to send. The verb is used w. the prep. εἰς and the articular inf. to express purpose (Frame). τοῦ Χριστοῦ. The gen. is either subjective or obj. gen. or could indicate both, i.e. Christ is the author and the content of the gospel (Best). στηρίξαι aor. act. inf. στηρίζω to support, to strengthen, to establish. The word has the idea of putting in a buttress as a support (Morris). The inf. is used to express purpose. παρακαλέσαι aor. act. inf. παρακαλέω to exhort, to encourage (s. 1 Thess. 2:11). ὑπέρ on behalf of, for the advan-

3 tage of (Morris). ■ σαίνεσθαι pres. pass. inf. σαίνω to shake or wag, used esp. of a dog wagging the tail to allure, to fascinate, to flatter, to beguile, to draw aside from the right path (Lightfoot; *Notes;* Best; Milligan). θλῖψις pressure, tribulation (s. TDNT). κείμεθα pres. mid. ind. κεῖμαι to lie, to place, used as a perf. pass. of τίθημι w. the meaning "to be appointed," "to be des-

4 tined" (s. Best; Milligan; Moore). ■ ἦμεν impf. εἰμί. προελέγομεν impf. ind. act. προλέγω to say beforehand, to foretell. The prep. in compound is predictive and the impf. denotes repeated action (Frame). μέλλομεν pres. act. ind. to be about to. The word is used w. the pres. inf. to denote a durative fut. ind. "we are going to . . ." (s. MKG, 307f.). θλίβεσθαι pres. pass. inf. θλίβω to put under pressure, pass. to suffer tribulation. καθώς just as. ἐγένετο aor. mid. ind. γίνομαι to happen, to

5 come to pass. ■ κἀγώ "I also" (Morris). It could also mean "I actually sent . . . ," or "that is in fact why I sent . . ." (IBG, 167). εἰς used w. the articular inf. to express purpose. γνῶναι aor. act. inf. γινώσκω ingressive aor. "to come to know" (RWP; s. also ND, 344f.). μή πως "lest." Used to express neg. purpose particularly in an expression of apprehension. It is used w. the subj. if the anxiety is directed toward warding off something still dependent on the will and w. the ind. if directed toward something which is entirely independent of the will. With the subj. it expresses feared results (s. BD, 188; RG, 988; s. also Gal. 2:2).

ἐπείρασεν aor. ind. act. πειράζω to test, to try, to tempt (s. Trench; *Synonyms*, 278–281). The ind. is used to express fear regarding a pres. inevitable reality (MT, 99). πειράζων pres. act. part. κένος empty (s. 1 Thess. 2:1). γένηται aor. act. subj. γίνομαι. The subj. expresses a fear of an uncertain thing in the fut. (MT, 99). κόπος labor, wearying work (s. 1 Thess. 4:3).

■ ἄρτι now, just now. ἐλθόντος aor. act. part. ἔρχομαι 6 gen. abs. εὐαγγελισαμένου aor. mid. part. εὐαγγελίζομαι to bring good news. This is the only place in the NT where the verb is used without a full and direct reference to the gospel which is Jesus Christ (Best; s. also Milligan, 141–144; TDNT). μνεία mention, remembrance. Used w. the main verb in the sense of "to hold, to maintain a recollection." Here it indicates a "kindly remembrance" toward their former teachers (Milligan). ἐπιποθοῦντες pres. act. part. ἐπιποθέω to long for, to yearn after. The prep. in compound is directive (s. Lightfoot; *Notes;* Phil. 1:8; 2:26). The part. further expands the preceding words and gives an example of their kindly remembrance (Ellicott; von Dobschütz). ἰδεῖν aor. act. inf. ὁράω. καθάπερ just as (s. 1 Thess. 2:11). ■ διὰ τοῦτο "because of this," "for that reason." 7 This is a transitional phrase taking up what precedes, i.e., the whole of v. 6 (Best). ἐφ᾽= ἐπί w. the dat. "because," "because of." The prep. frequently denotes the basis for a state of being, action, or result, esp. w. verbs of emotion (BD, 123). ἀνάγκη necessity, distress, affliction. The word is used of outward calamities or distresses (Milligan). ■ ζῶμεν pres. act. ind. to live, 8 "we live once more," i.e., in spite of this distress and affliction (Lightfoot; *Notes*). στήκετε pres. act. ind. to stand, to stand firm, to stand fast. ■ εὐχαριστία thanksgiving, thanks. 9 ἀνταποδοῦναι aor. act. inf. ἀνταποδίδωμι to render, to give back as an equivalent. The prep. in compound implies the adequacy of the return (Lightfoot; *Notes;* s. also Moore). ἔμπροσθεν before, in the presence of. ■ ὑπερεκπερισσοῦ adv. 10 more than out of bounds, overflowing all bounds, exceedingly, super abundantly (RWP; Best; s. also Eph. 3:20). δεόμενοι pres. mid. part. δέομαι to make a request, to pray. The word embodies a sense of personal need and is very common in petitions addressed to ruling sovereigns as distinguished form those addressed to magistrates (Milligan; s. also PIP, 19f.). καταρτίσαι aor. act. inf. καταρτίζω to fit together, to join together, to restore, to repair, to equip. The word had a variety of usages depending upon the context. It was used to reconcile political factions. It was a surgical term for "setting bones." It was used for repairing nets (Mark 1:19). It was used of making military and naval preparations (s. Best; Lightfoot; *Notes;* TDNT). ὑστέρημα that which is lacking, deficiency.

11 ■ (For a discussion of the background and form of intercessory wish prayers, s. PIP, 22–44.) αὐτὸς δέ ... "now God Himself." Although this was a conventional liturgical form of address, Paul adds a new depth of meaning and invokes the august majesty and unique power of almighty God, the original Creator and direct Controller of events (PIP, 54). κατευθύναι aor. act. opt. κατευθύνω to make straight. The word refers to the leveling or removal of those obstacles which Satan has used to obscure the path (Lightfoot; *Notes;* s. also Milligan). The opt. was often used to express a wish in prayers (PIP, 32f.; s. also M,

12 165f.; RG, 939f.; BD, 194). ■ πλεονάσαι aor. act. opt. πλεονάζω to make more, to increase. περισσεύσαι aor. act. opt. περισσεύω to cause to overflow. τῇ ἀγάπῃ. The dat. could be dat. of reference or locative or perhaps instrumental

13 (Ellicott). ■ εἰς τό στηρίξαι. The prep. and the aor. inf. w. the article expresses purpose. (For the meaning of the word "establish," s.v.2.) ἄμεμπτος blameless. The prayer gains sublimity in that they must be prepared to stand unblamable in holiness before God as judge, the searcher of the inward motives of men, who tests and tries the hearts of men (PIP, 62; s. also Frame). ἁγιωσύνη holiness. The word indicates the state or condition of holiness (Lightfoot; *Notes*). παρουσία coming, arrival. The word was used as a semi-t.t. for the visit of a king or emperor or for the appearance of a god (MM; LAE, 370ff.; s. also TDNT).

Ch. 4

1 ■ λοίπον finally, "as our last matter" (Best; s. also Phil. 3:1). ἐρωτῶμεν pres. act. ind. to ask, to request. The word lays stress on the person asked rather than on the thing asked for and it conceives the request in a question form (Milligan; Morris). παρακαλοῦμεν pres. act. ind. to beseech, to exhort. ἵνα "that." The word introduces the content of the request. καθώς just as. παρελάβετε aor. act. ind. παραλαμβάνω to receive, to receive from another, to receive tradition or teaching (s. Col. 2:6). δεῖ it is necessary. περιπατεῖν pres. act. inf. to walk, to walk about, to conduct one's life. ἀρέσκειν pres. act. inf. to please. The pres. inf. emphasizes the continual or habitual action (s. 1 Thess. 2:4). περισσεύητε pres. act. subj. περισσεύω to overflow, to abound. μᾶλλον more, still more. It is the intensive use of the

2 word (Milligan; s. also Moore). ■ παραγγελία order, command, instruction. The word often denotes a "word of command" received from a superior officer that it may be passed on

to others. Here the pl. points to special precepts or rules of living, which the writers had laid down when in Thessalonica, and in which they had referred to the Lord Jesus as the medium through whom alone they could be carried into effect (Milligan). ἐδώκαμεν aor. act. ind. δίδωμι to give. ■ ἁγιασμός sanctifica- 3 tion. The process of becoming holy (Moore). ἀπέχεσθαι pres. mid. inf. to hold one's self from, to abstain. The inf. is explanatory defining the neg. side of sanctification (Ellicott). πορνεία sexual sin, illicit sexual activity. Sex was often linked to pagan religious practice (Best; s. also TDNT; Lightfoot; Notes). ■ 4 εἰδέναι perf. act. inf. οἶδα to know. The verb was often used to describe "know how," the possession of knowledge or skill necessary to accomplish a desired goal (ND, 347). The word might mean in this context "to respect" (Frame). σκεῦος vessel. In this context the word could mean either "body" or more likely "life" (s. Best; Morris; TDNT; T). κτᾶσθαι pres. mid. inf. to acquire. Although the perf. generally means "to possess" some examples from the papyri indicate the word could also mean "possess" in the pres. (MM; Milligan; TDNT; Morris). It is possible that the word reflects a Heb. idiom and has the sense "to possess a woman sexually" (Best; TDNT). ■ πάθος passion. 5 ἐπιθυμία lust, desire. Paul does not forbid desire as a natural impulse but a "passion of lust," "lustful passion," i.e., a condition where sense has been converted into the ruling principle or into passion (Lünemann). καθάπερ just as (s. 1 Thess. 2:11). ἔθνος Gentile. εἰδότα perf. act. part. οἶδα. ■ ὑπερβαίνειν to go 6 beyond, to exceed the proper limits, to transgress. With the acc. of a person the verb has the sense of "to get the better of, to override" (Lightfoot; Notes). The inf. may be used to express results or purpose or it may be used parallel to the other inf. in the section (s. Frame; Best). πλεονεκτεῖν pres. act. inf. to claim more, to have more than one's due, to defraud, to selfishly attempt to gain more at all costs and w. all means disregarding others and their rights (Moore; TDNT; NTW, 97ff.; CBB). πρᾶγμα matter. In this case it could mean "in matters of sex" (TDNT; Best). ἔκδικος one who carries out that which is right, avenger. The word was used in the papyri for the office of an official legal representative (MM; Preisigke I, 443; III, 110; Milligan). The word may be a compound developed from a prep. phrase which had the meaning "just as *after* a legal decision" and the word would thus be one who carries out a sentence (MH, 311). προείπαμεν aor. act. ind. προλέγω to say previously, to say beforehand. The word is not used here in the sense of "prophesy, predict" (Best). διεμαρτυράμεθα aor. mid. ind.

διαμαρτύρομαι to solemnly declare. The prep. in compound
7 has the idea of "thoroughly" (MH, 302). ■ ἐκάλεσεν aor. act.
ind. καλέω to call. ἀκαθαρσία uncleanness, filthiness, impurity. The prep. used. w. the noun has the meaning "for the purpose
of" (Moore). ἐν. The prep. indicates the state of holiness result-
8 ing from the calling (Frame). ■ τοιγαροῦν for that very reason
then, therefore (BAG; for its position in usage, s. Blomqvist,
130). ἀθετῶν pres. act. part. ἀθετέω lit. "to do away w. what
has been laid down," to reject, to set aside, to spurn, to despise
(Milligan; Frame). διδόντα pres. act. part. The pres. tense describes the continual or the continually repeated action.
9   ■ χρεία need. θεοδίδακτος taught of God. The word
points not so much to "one divine communication" as to "a
divine relationship" established between believers and God:
hence, it is as those who have been born of God, and whose
hearts are in consequence filled by God's Spirit that the Thessalonians on their part can no longer help loving (Milligan). (For
the verbal adj. w. this ending, s. M 221; MH, 370; and for the
compound having an instrumental sense "God-taught," s. MH,
10 271.) ἀλλήλους reciprocal pron. "one another." ■ καὶ γάρ "for
also, for indeed." The phrase marks this statement as an advance
upon the preceding one. "You are not only taught the lesson, but
you also practice it" (Lightfoot; Notes). μᾶλλον more (s.v.1).
11 ■ φιλοτιμεῖσθαι pres. mid. inf. to make it one's ambition, to be
zealous, to strive eagerly (Milligan). ἡσυχάζειν pres. act. inf. to
be at rest, to be quiet, to remain silent, i.e., "to live quietly." The
context suggests that Paul is speaking to those whose brotherly
love expressed itself in busybodying and he directs that these
people should learn to behave and quietly get on w. their own
work (Moore). πράσσειν pres. act. inf. to do, to practice. ἴδιος
private, one's own. ἐργάζεσθαι pres. mid. inf. to work. Although the Gr. generally looked down on manual labor as the
work of slaves and others, the Jews did not have this attitude.
The emphasis here, however, is not on manual labor as opposed
to some other form but upon working as opposed to idling
(Moore; s. also RAC I, 585–590; KP I, 490–494).
παρηγγείλαμεν aor. act. ind. παραγγέλλω to charge, to order, to instruct. In classical writers the word was used of the
orders of military commanders and here brings out the authority
12 w. which the apostle spoke (Milligan). ■ περιπατῆτε pres. act.
subj. The subj. is used in a purpose clause. εὐσχημόνως decently, becomingly. πρός "toward," "w. an eye to" (Frame). ἔξω
outside, "those outside" reflects a rabbinic expression and means
anyone and everyone not within the Christian community

(Moore). ἔχητε pres. act. subj.

■ ἀγνοεῖν pres. act. inf. not to know, to be ignorant. 13 κοιμωμένων pres. mid. part. κοιμάομαι to sleep, to fall asleep. The pres. tense is probably timeless and denotes a class, "the sleepers" (Framc; Morris). λυπῆσθε pres. pass. subj. λυπέω to grieve, to pain, pass. to become sad, to be sorrowful, to be distressed. The pres. tense signifies a continuing sorrow (Morris). λοιπός remaining, here "the others." ἔχοντες pres. act. part. The general hopelessness of the pagan world in the presence of death is almost too well known to require illustration (Milligan; s. also Lightfoot; *Notes*; Morris; LAE, 176–178; s. also Gerhard Pfohl, *Römische Grabinschriften* [Munich: Ernst Heimeran, 1969]; G. Pfohl, *Griechische Inschriften*, 11–42). ■ εἰ "if." The 14 word introduces a condition of the first class, assuming the death and resurrection of Jesus to be true (RWP). ἀπέθανεν aor. act. ind. ἀποθνῄσκω to die. ἀνέστη aor. act. ind. ἀνίστημι to rise. κοιμηθέντας aor. pass. part., s.v.13. ἄξει fut. act. ind. ἄγω to lead, to bring. The prep. phrase is to be taken w. this verb, "God will bring through Jesus those who have fallen asleep" (Moore).

■ ζῶντες pres. act. part. ζάω to live. περιλειπόμενοι pres. 15 pass. part. περιλείπω to leave, to leave behind. The pres. tense indicates that the action is viewed as going on to the limit of time designated by the prep. "until" (Frame). παρουσία arrival, coming (s. 1 Thess. 3:13). οὐ μή "not in anywise." φθάσωμεν aor. act. subj. φθάνω to precede, to go before. The aor. subj. used w. the emphatic neg. has the sense of an emphatic fut. ind. (SMT, 78; RG, 929f.). ■ κέλευμα command, shout. The word was used 16 in a variety of ways, e.g., it is the cry made by the ship's master to its rowers, or by a military officer to his soldiers, or by a hunter to his hounds, or by a charioteer to his horses. When used to military or naval personnel, it was a battle cry. In most places it denotes a loud, authoritative cry, often one uttered in a thick of a great excitement (Morris; s. also Lightfoot; *Notes*). ἀρχάγγελος archangel. It was a term for those of the uppermost rank (Best). σάλπιγξ trumpet. The trumpet was used by the Jews in their festival and was also associated w. theophanies and w. the End and is again linked w. the resurrection of the dead (Best; s. also TDNT). καταβήσεται fut. mid. ind. καταβαίνω to come down. ἀναστήσονται fut. mid. ind. ἀνίστημι to rise. ■ ἔπειτα then, following. The word denotes the speedy follow- 17 ing of the event specified upon what has gone before (Milligan; Ellicott). ἁρπαγησόμεθα fut. pass. ind. ἁρπάζω to snatch up, to seize, to carry off by force, to rapture. The word often denotes the emotion of a sudden swoop, and usually that of a force which cannot be resisted (Morris). ἀνάντησις meeting. The word had a technical meaning in the Hellenistic world in relation to the visits of dignitaries to cities where the visitor would be formally met by the citizens, or a deputation of them, who had gone out from the city for this purpose and would then be ceremonially escorted back into the city (Best). ἀήρ air. πάντοτε always.

18 ἐσόμεθα fut. εἰμί. ■ ὥστε therefore. παρακαλεῖτε pres. act. imp. s.v.1.

Ch. 5

1   ■ χρόνος time. The word expresses simply duration, time viewed in its extension (Milligan; s. also Best; Morris; TDNT). καιρός originally, "the fit measure," time. It refers to "the right moment," "the opportunity for doing, or avoiding to do, anything." It is time w. reference to both its extent and character and refers to the kind of events that are taking place (s. Lightfoot; Notes; Milligan; Morris; TDNT). γράφεσθαι pres. pass.

2 inf. ■ ἀκριβῶς accurately, precisely, well (Moore; s. also Luke

3 1:3). ■ ὅταν used. w. the subj. "when," "whenever." λέγωσιν pres. act. subj. ἀσφάλεια safety. The word occurs in the papyri as a law term "bond," "security" (Milligan; MM). αἰφνίδιος sudden, suddenly. The word could be an adj., i.e. "sudden destruction comes upon them" or it could be used as an adv. "all of a sudden" (Frame). ἐφίσταται pres. mid. ind. ἐφίστημι to approach, to appear, to come upon. It is used of misfortunes which suddenly come upon someone (BAG). ὄλεθρος destruction, disaster, ruin. The word is used in the LXX particularly in the prophets w. the meaning "an eschatological destruction" (TDNT; CBB). ὠδίν birth pain. γαστήρ stomach. ἐχούσῃ pres. act. part. used in the expression "to have something in the stomach" w. the meaning "to be pregnant." οὐ μή "certainly not." ἐκφύγωσιν aor. act. subj. ἐκφεύγω to escape, to escape completely. (For the subj. w. the emphatic neg., s. 1 Thess. 4:15; s.

4 also Luke 21:34-36.) ■ ἵνα. Used w. the subj. to express result (s. IBG, 142; BD, 198; RG, 998; MT, 103f.; BG, 122). καταλάβῃ aor. act. subj. καταλαμβάνω to seize, to seize w. hostile intent, to overtake, to come upon. Used of the coming of the "day," unexpected by the "sons of darkness" and fraught w.

5 danger for them (BAG). ■ υἱοί φωτός "sons of light." The expression "son" followed by the gen. is a Semitic construction meaning "to be characterized by that thing" (Morris; s. also BG, 15ff.; BS, 161-166). (For the use of the term "sons of light" in the DSS, s. 1QM; 1QS I, 9; II, 16; III, 13, 24, 25; John 1:5.)

νυκτός and σκότους "of night," "of darkness." The gen. points to the sphere to which the subjects belong (Milligan). (For the term "sons of darkness" in the DSS, s. 1QM; 1QS I, 10; John 1:5.) ■ ἄρα "therefore," "then." Paul uses this to introduce a 6 new stage in the argument (Best). καθεύδωμεν pres. act. subj. καθεύδω to sleep, cohortative subj. used w. the neg. indicating a prohibition. γρηγορῶμεν pres. act. subj. γρηγορέω to stay away, to watch, to be vigilant. The word signifies the proper attitude of the Christian (Moore). The subj. is cohortative and the pres. tense indicates a continuing attitude. νήφωμεν pres. act. subj. νήφω to be sober, not to be under the influence of drink. The word points to a condition or moral alertness, the sense of being so exercised and disciplined that all fear of sleeping again is removed (Milligan; s. also TDNT; Best). ■ 7 καθεύδοντες pres. act. part. νυκτός gen. of time "during the night." The gen. specifies the time within which something occurs, "nighttime action" (MT, 235; DM, 77; BD, 99f.; RG, 494f.). μεθυσκόμενοι pres. mid. part. μεθύσκομαι to get drunk, to make drunk (s. Gal. 5:21; Eph. 5:18). μεθύω pres. act. ind. to be drunk. The pres. tense points to that which generally happens. ■ ὄντες pres. part. εἰμί. ἐνδυσάμενοι aor. mid. part. 8 ἐνδύομαι to clothe one's self, to put on. The aor. part. expresses identical or contemporaneous action in relation to the main verb (Ellicott; Frame). θώραξ breastplate (s. Eph. 6:14). πίστεως and ἀγάπης are epexegetical gens. explaining the breastplate (von Dobschütz; Best). περικεφαλαία that which goes around the head, helmet (s. Eph. 6:17). ἐλπίδα hope, appositional to "helmet" (von Dobschütz). ■ ἔθετο aor. mid. ind. τίθημι to 9 place, to destine (s. Best; MT, 55; BD, 165). ὀργή wrath, anger. περιποίησις obtaining, acquiring (Morris; Moorc). διά w. the gen. "through." The phrase is to be taken w. "the obtaining of salvation" (von Dobschütz). ■ ἀποθανόντος aor. act. part. 10 ἀποθνήσκω to die. περί for. (For the prep. in relation to the death of Christ as compared to other prep., s. IBG, 63; M, 105; BG, 96.) εἴτε whether. It is used as an alternative condition of a 3rd-class conditional clause w. the pres. subj. (s. RWP; RG, 1017; BD, 187). ζήσωμεν aor. act. subj. ζάω to live. The aor. points to this "life" as a definite fact secured to us by the equally definite death of our Lord (Milligan). ■ διό therefore. 11 παρακαλεῖτε pres. act. imp. παρακαλέω to encourage, to comfort (s. 1 Thess. 2:12). ἀλλήλους one another. οἰκοδομεῖτε pres. act. imp. οἰκοδομέω to build up, to edify. καθώς just as.

■ ἐρωτῶμεν pres. act. ind. to ask, to request (s. 1 Thess. 12 4:1). εἰδέναι perf. act. inf. οἶδα (s. ND, 344ff.). κοπιῶντας pres. act. part. κοπιάω to grow weary, to work w. effort. The word refers to both bodily and mental labor (Milligan; s. also 1 Thess. 1:3). προϊσταμένους pres. mid. part. προΐστημι to stand before someone. The word has two possible meanings either "to preside, to lead, to direct"; or "to protect, to care for" (s. Best; TDNT; MM). νουθετοῦντας pres. act. part. νουθετέω to put one in mind, to advise, to warn, to admonish. The word is used for the admonition and correction of those who are in

13 error (Moore; TDNT; s. also Col. 1:28). ▪ ἡγεῖσθαι pres. mid. inf. to consider, to esteem (Morris; for examples in the papyri, s. MM). ὑπερεκπερρισσῶς adv. exceedingly, very highly (Moore; s. also 1 Thess. 3:10). εἰρηνεύετε pres. act. imp. εἰρηνεύω to exercise peace, to be at peace. Verbs w. this suf. are often causative or connote the possession of a quality and this

14 quality sometimes passes to that of action (s. MH, 399f.). ▪ παρακαλέω pres. act. ind. (s. 1 Thess. 2:12). νουθετεῖτε pres. act. imp. s.v.12. ἄτακτος without rank, out of rank, disorderly. The word was primarily a military term used of the soldier who is out of step or out of rank or the army moving in disarray. It then was used more generally of whatever is out of order. In the pres. passage the special reference would seem to be to the idleness and neglect of duty which characterized certain members of the Thessalonian church in view of the shortly expected *parousia* (Milligan, esp. 152–154; Morris; Best). παραμυθεῖσθε pres. mid. imp. παραμυθέομαι to encourage (s. 1 Thess. 2:12). ὀλιγόψυχος fainthearted, worried, discouraged, fearful (Best). ἀντέχεσθε pres. mid. imp. ἀντέχομαι to lay hold of, to hold firmly to. (For this as well as examples from the papyri, s. Milligan; MM.) ἀσθενής without strength, weak. The word probably refers to those who are morally or spiritually weak (Best). μακροθυμεῖτε pres. act. imp. μακροθυμέω to be longsuffering. It indicates not giving way to a short or quick temper toward those who fail, but being patient and considerate of them (Milli-

15 gan; s. also TDNT; NTW, 83ff.; Trench; *Synonyms*, 195). ▪ ὁρᾶτε pres. act. imp. to see, to see to it. The combination of 2nd and 3rd per. in this construction conveys the idea that the whole group is being held responsible for the conduct of each individual. They are not only to abstain from retaliation, but to see that none of their number retaliates (Morris; s. also Frame). μὴ "that," "lest." The neg. is used in an expression of apprehension and the subj. indicates that anxiety is directed toward warding off something still dependent on the will (BD, 188; s. also MT, 98). ἀντί w. the gen. "instead of," "in return for." ἀποδῷ aor. act. subj. ἀποδίδωμι to give back, to pay back. πάντοτε always.

διώκετε pres. act. imp. διώκω to hunt, to pursue, to seek eagerly (Best).

■ χαίρετε pres. act. imp. χαίρω to rejoice. The pres. tense 16 calls for a continual attitude of rejoicing. ■ ἀδιαλείπτως adv. 17 without interruption, unceasingly, constantly. The word was used of that which was continually and repeatedly done; e.g., the uninterrupted necessary payment of hard taxes; the continual service or ministry of an official; a continual uninterrupted cough (Preisigke; MM); repeated military attacks (Josephus, Jewish Wars I, 252), the continual falling of a military effort (Josephus, Jewish Wars III, 241); the regular and consistent production of fruit (Josephus, Jewish Wars III, 519). προσεύχεσθε pres. mid. imp. προσεύχομαι to pray. This is the more comprehensive term for prayer and can include the other words for prayer (Morris; s. also TDNT). ■ ἐν παντί "in 18 every circumstance." This includes even in persecutions and trials (Milligan). εὐχαριστεῖτε pres. act. imp. εὐχαριστέω to give thanks (s. Col. 3:17). τοῦτο "this." Grammatically it could refer to the last injunction only but it is more likely that Paul means all three commands to be regarded as a unity (Moore). ■ σβέννυτε prcs. act. imp. σβέννυμι to put out (a fire), to 19 quench. ■ προφητεία prophecy. The gift of speaking for God. 20 ἐξουθενεῖτε pres. act. imp. ἐξουθενέω to consider as nothing, to make absolutely nothing of, to downgrade, to despise (s. Morris). ■ πάντα "all things." Here it is unlimited and refers to "all 21 things whatsoever" (Lightfoot; Notes). δοκιμάζετε pres. act. imp. δοκιμάζω to approve after testing (s. 1 Thess. 2:4). κατέχετε pres. act. imp. κατέχω to hold fast, to lay hold of, to take possession of (s. MM; Milligan, 155–157). ■ εἶδος visible 22 form, outward show. The word could also be used in the sense of "kind," "species," "class" (Milligan). πονηροῦ evil. The word could be taken either as an adj. or as a noun (s. Ellicott; Morris). ἀπέχεσθε pres. mid. imp. ἀπέχομαι to hold one's self from, to abstain (s. 1 Thess. 4:3).

■ ἁγιάσαι aor. act. opt. ἁγιάζω to sanctify. (For the use 23 of the opt. in prayers to express a wish, s. PIP, 32f.) ὁλοτελής wholly, entirely, "quite completely." The word not only implies entirety, but involves the further idea of completion (Lightfoot; Notes; s. also Moore). ὁλόκληρος whole, complete, undamaged, intact (BAG). The point is that no part of the Christian personality should be lacking in consecration (Frame). (For the possible construction of the entire v., s. PIP, 39ff.; Best.) ἀμέμπτως adv. blamelessly. παρουσία arrival, coming (s. 1 Thess. 3:13). τηρηθείη aor. pass. opt. τηρέω to keep. The word has a sense

24 of protecting, watching over, and guarding (Moore). ■ καλῶν
   pres. act. part. ποιήσει fut. act. ind.
25   ■ προσεύχεσθε pres. mid. imp., s.v.17.
26   ■ ἀσπάσασθε aor. mid. imp. ἀσπάζομαι to greet.
   φίλημα kiss. The kiss was used in the ancient world as a form
27 of greeting (s. Best; Moore; TDNT; 1 Cor. 16:20). ■ ἐνορκίζω
   to adjure, to cause someone to swear by something, to put someone on their oath (BAG; Morris). The verb is followed by the inf.
   (s. BD, 199f.) and the one by whom the oath is sworn is in the
   acc. (BD, 83; RG, 483f.). ἀναγνωσθῆναι aor. pass. inf.
   ἀναγινώσκω to read. From the context it is clear that it is a
   "public" reading or a reading "aloud" (Milligan). ἐπιστολή
   letter.

2 THESSALONIANS

εὐχαριστεῖν pres. act. inf. to give thanks (s. Col. 3:17; s. 3 also P.T. O'Brien, "Thanksgiving and the Gospel in Paul," NTS, 21 [October, 1974], 144–155). ὀφείλομεν pres. act. ind. to be obligated, ought. The word implies a special, personal obligation rather than one arising out of the nature of things (Best); "we owe it to God" (Moore). (For parallels to the necessity and propriety of giving thanks esp. in the midst of persecution, s. Roger D. Aus, "The Liturgical Background of the Necessity and Propriety of Giving Thanks According to II Thess. 1:3," JBL, 92 [September, 1973], 432–438.) πάντοτε always. καθώς just as. The word is slightly causal and resumes and explains the obligation to give thanks (Frame). ἄξιον fitting. The word indicates that this thanksgiving is also appropriate in the circumstances (Moore). ὑπεραυξάνει pres. act. ind. to grow abundantly, to grow over and beyond. It is a figure of the tree of faith growing above measure (RWP). The prep. in compound intensifies and magnifies the normal meaning of the word (Best; MH, 326). πλεονάζει pres. act. ind. to increase (s. 1 Thess. 3:12). ἑκάστου each one. ■ ὥστε used w. the inf. to express results. αὐτοὺς 4 ἡμᾶς "we ourselves." The words are emphatic and may form a contrast. (For the various interpretations, s. Best.) ἐγκαυχᾶσθαι pres. mid. inf. to boast. The inf. is used to express results. ἐν ταῖς ἐκκλησίαις. The prep. may be used for the normal dat.; i.e., "to the churches" but it is also possible that it has its normal local meaning "within the churches," "among the churches" (s. MT, 264). ὑπέρ concerning. ὑπομονή patience, endurance. The word indicates a "remaining under"; i.e., "bearing up under" difficult circumstances. It is the Spirit which can bear things, not simply w. resignation, but w. blazing hope. It is not the patience which grimly waits for the end, but the patience which radiantly hopes for the dawn (NTW, 60; s. also TDNT; CBB). δωγμός persecution. θλῖψις pressure, tribulation. The former is a special term for external persecutions inflicted by the enemies of the gospel; the latter is more general, and denotes tribulation of any kind (Lightfoot; Notes). ἀνέχεσθε pres. mid.

ind. to hold one's self up, to endure (MH, 295). The pres. tense
indicates that trouble did not end for the converts w. the expul-
5 sion of the missionaries (Moore). ■ ἔνδειγμα evidence, proof.
The ending of the word denotes strictly a result which has been
reached, "a thing proved," but frequently in similar cases where
the abstract gives place to the concrete the word can hardly be
distinguished from "evidence," the actual proof by an appeal to
facts (Milligan; but s. Lightfoot; *Notes*). κρίσις judging, judgment. καταξιωθῆναι aor. pass. inf. καταξιόω to consider or
declare worthy. The strengthened form of the verb means "to
declare to be worthy," "to deem worthy" (Morris). ὑπέρ for,
"for the sake of which," "in the name of which," "in the interest
of which" (Moore; Morris). πάσχειν pres. act. ind. to suffer.
The pres. tense denotes the sufferings are still going on (Frame).
6 ■ εἴπερ "if on the whole, provided that." The word introduces
a conditional clause which assumes the reality of the condition
(RWP; s. also von Dobschütz). παρά w. dat. The reference is to
the righteous judgment of God. ἀνταποδοῦναι aor. act. inf.
ἀνταποδίδωμι to pay back again, to recompense. The prep. in
compound conveys the thought of a full and due requittal (Morris). θλίβουσιν pres. act. part. θλίβω to put one under pressure,
to cause tribulation, to persecute. The pres. tense indicates that
7 the affliction was in process. ■ θλιβομένοις pres. pass. part.
ἄνεσις loosening, relaxing. In classical Gr. it could refer to the
release of a bow string and so comes to mean relaxation and
recreation generally. It is the relaxing of the cords of endurance
now tightly drawn (Moore; Milligan). ἀποκάλυψις unveiling,
8 revelation (s. Milligan, 149f.; TDNT). ■ πῦρ fire. φλόξ flame.
The flaming fire emphasizes the glory of the appearance of the
Lord and it may be a reference to judgment (Best; Lightfoot;
Notes; von Dobschütz). διδόντος pres. act. part. ἐκδίκησις
vengeance. The word indicates full, complete punishment (Milligan). εἰδόσιν perf. act. part. dat. pl. οἶδα (s. ND, 344f.).
ὑπακούουσιν pres. act. part. dat. pl. ὑπακούω to listen to, to
obey. The prep. in compound has the idea of "submission" (MH,
9 327). ■ οἵτινες who. The rel. pron. is generic indicating ones
who belong to such a class, "such people" (Best; s. also MT, 47f.;
IBG, 123f.; MKG, 174f.). δίκη the standard to which a thing is
to conform, right, law, judicial hearing. It then came to express
the results of the law suit, "execution of a sentence," "punishment" (s. Milligan; TDNT; GW, 99; CBB; Preisigke). τίσουσιν
fut. act. ind. τίνω to suffer, to pay a penalty. The word means
"to pay a price by way of recompense" (Moore). ὄλεθρος destruction, ruination. The word does not mean annihilation, but

implies the loss of all things that give worth to existence (s. MM;
Best; TDNT; 1 Thess. 5:3). The acc. case is in apposition to the
word "penalty" (RWP). αἰώνιος eternal. The adj. lit. means
"age long" and everything depends on the length of the age. In
the NT there is never a hint that the coming age has an end
(Morris; GW, 186–189; CBB; TDNT). ἰσχύς strength, might,
power (s. Eph. 1:19). ■ ὅταν w. the subj. "when," "whenever." 10
ἔλθῃ aor. act. subj. ἔρχομαι. ἐνδοξασθῆναι aor. pass. inf.
ἐνδοξάζω to glorify. The prep. in compound is repeated after
the verb and could have either a local meaning "in" or an instrumental meaning "by means of" or a causal meaning "because of"
(Best). The prep. is used to express purpose. θαυμασθῆναι aor.
pass. inf. θαυμάζω to marvel, to wonder, pass. to be marveled
at. The inf. is used to express purpose. πιστεύσασιν aor. act.
part. 3rd per. pl. The aor. part. focuses attention on the past act
of belief (Best). ἐπιστεύθη aor. pass. ind. μαρτύριον witness.
■ εἰς ὅ "to this end," "w. this in mind." The expression conveys 11
the idea of purpose (Morris; s. also Moore). προσευχόμεθα
pres. mid. ind. to pray (s. 1 Thess. 5:17). ἵνα "that." The particle
introduces the content of the prayer. ἀξιώσῃ aor. act. subj.
ἀξιόω to consider worthy, to reckon as worthy. κλῆσις calling.
The gen. is used after the verb "to consider worthy of."
πληρώσῃ aor. act. subj. πληρόω to fill. Here it has the sense
of "accomplishing" (Moore). εὐδοκία good pleasure, resolve,
consent, desire (BAG; TDNT). ἀγαθωσύνη goodness, obj. gen.
"delight in well doing" (Lightfoot; Notes; s. also Gal. 5:22). ■ 12
ἐνδοξασθῇ aor. pass. subj., s.v.10. The subj. is used to express
purpose.

Ch. 2

■ ἐρωτῶμεν pres. act. ind. to ask, to request (s. 1 Thess. 1
4:1). παρουσία arrival, coming (s. 1 Thess. 3:13).
ἐπισυναγωγή meeting, assembling, gathering together, collection, collecting together (s. LAE, 103f.). The prep. in compound
is directive (MH, 312). The word is used in 2 Maccabees 2:7
indicating a fut. time when God shall gather His people together.
■ εἰς τό w. the inf. is used either to express purpose (RWP) or 2
to introduce the object of the verb (Best; s. also MT, 143).
ταχέως quickly, hastily (Lightfoot; Notes). σαλενθῆναι aor.
pass. inf. σαλεύω to shake, to cause to move to and fro, to cause
to waiver, pass. to be shaken, to be made to waiver or totter
(BAG). By the aor. tense, the suddenness of the shock is emphasized (Moore). νοῦς mind, understanding, the reasoning faculty,
man's power of judgment (Best; s. also TDNT). θροεῖσθαι pres.

pass. inf. θροέω pass. to be inwardly aroused, to be disturbed, to be frightened (BAG). The pres. tense points to a continued state of agitation following upon a definite shock received and describes a state of "jumpiness" (Milligan; Morris). πνεῦμα spirit. It could refer here to some type of spiritual revelation (Lightfoot; Notes). λόγος word. A general expression which could refer to prophecy or sermon or any verbal communication (Moore). ὡς (before ὅτι) "to the effect that" (MT, 137). ἐνέστηκεν perf. act. ind. ἐνίστημι to place in, to stand in, perf. to be at hand, to be pres. The word could be translated "is now pres." and the verb is sometimes contrasted w. verbs expressing
3 the fut. idea (Morris; s. also RWP). ■ ἐξαπατήσῃ aor. act. subj. ἐξαπατάω to deceive, to deceive completely, to deceive successfully (MH, 311). The subj. is used w. the neg. to express a prohibition. The subj. of prohibition occurs in the 3rd per., esp. in clauses of fear or warning (DM, 171; s. also SMT, 76). τρόπος manner. Used in the expression "in no way" (Milligan). ἔλθῃ aor. act. subj. ἔρχομαι. ἀποστασία falling away, rebellion, revolt, apostasy (s. Best; Moore; TDNT). ἀποκαλυφθῇ aor. pass. subj. ἀποκαλύπτω to unveil, to reveal. The word is very significant, not only as marking the "superhuman" character of the one spoken of, but as placing it in mocking counterpart to the revelation of the Lord Jesus Himself (Milligan). ἀνομία lawlessness. The word describes the condition not of one living without law, but of one who acts contrary to law (Milligan; s. also Best; for a discussion of the antichrist, s. ZPEB I, 179–181; for the Jewish teaching regarding the antichrist named Armilos who was identified w. the Christ of Christianity, s. SB III, 637–640). The gen. is of Semitic influence and is used as an adj. describing the main quality or character (s. BG, 14f.; MT, 208; Best). υἱός son. Used in a Semitic construction followed by the gen. describing the character or quality (BG, 15f.; MH, 441). ἀπωλεία ruin, doom, destruction. The Semitic construction means "he who is
4 destined to be destroyed" (Moore; Best). ■ ἀντικείμενος pres. mid. part. ἀντίκειμαι to lie against, to oppose. The pres. part. indicates a constant opposing as habitual or as a life style. ὑπεραιρόμενος pres. mid. part. ὑπεραίρω to lift up, mid. to lift one's self up, to exalt one's self, to exalt one's self exceedingly, to exalt one's self above measure (Lightfoot; Notes). λεγόμενον pres. pass. part. σέβασμα an object of worship. The ending of the noun indicates a pass. idea; i.e., "something which is reverenced," "something which is worshiped" and the word includes anything at all that could be worshiped (s. MH, 355; Morris; TDNT). ὥστε. Used w. the inf. to express results. αὐτόν him-

self. ναός temple, sanctuary, the innermost part of the temple (Best). καθίσαι aor. act. inf. καθίζω to sit, to take one's seat. The inf. is used to express result. ἀποδεικνύντα pres. act. part. ἀποδείκνυμι to show off, to exhibit, to display, to prove, to nominate or proclaim to an office. Here "proclaiming himself that he is God" (Milligan; s. also Best). ἑαυτόν himself. ■ 5 μημονεύετε pres. act. ind. to remember, to call to remembrance (s. 1 Thess. 1:3). The verb is used in a question introduced by the neg. particle which expects the answer yes, "you remember don't you?" ὤν pres. part. εἰμί. ■ νῦν now. The word can be 6 logical introducing a new point, but it is almost certainly temporal in the pres. context (Best). κατέχον pres. act. part. κατέχω to hold down, to restrain. Though many explanations for "the restrainer" have been offered (s. Morris; Best; Milligan, 155–157) in light of the supernatural character of "the one holding back," the use of the masc. article in v. 7 (the n. article here is because the Gr. word for "spirit" is n.), it is best to understand "the restrainer" as the Holy Spirit (s. TDNT; and for ancient interpretations in this regard, s. PGL, 731; Milligan). ἀποκαλυφθῆναι aor. pass. inf. to reveal, s.v.3. The inf. is used to express purpose. καίρος time, opportunity, the moment appointed by God (Moore; s. also 1 Thess. 2:17). ■ μύστηριον 7 mystery, that which was unknown and incapable of being known by man except through a revelation of God (s. TDNT; ZPED IV, 327–330; Best; s. also Eph. 3:3). ἐνεργεῖται pres. mid. ind. to work, to work effectively. The word is often used of supernatural working (s. Best). μόνον only. ὁ κατέχων ἄρτι pres. act. part. The masc. article refers to the pers. of the Holy Spirit (s.v.6). ἕως until. μέσον mid. midst. γένηται aor. mid. subj. γίνομαι. The phrase means "to be removed," "to be taken away." (For this meaning as well as a discussion of the passage relating the "restrainer" to God, s. Roger D. Aus, "God's Plan and God's Power: Isaiah 66 and the Restraining Factors of 2 Thess. 2:6–7," JBL, 96 [December, 1977], 537–553.) ■ καὶ τότε "and then." 8 ἀποκαλυφθῆναι fut. pass. ind. to unveil, to reveal, s.v.3. ἄνομος lawless, s.v.3. ἀνελεῖ fut. act. ind. ἀναιρέω to take away, to do away w., to destroy (s. BAG). στόμα mouth. καταργήσει fut. act. ind. καταργέω to render inactive, to abolish, to bring to naught, to put out of commission. ἐπιφάνεια manifestation, glorious appearance. The word usually has some idea of striking splendor and was often used by the Greeks of a glorious manifestation of the gods (Morris; T; s. also LAE, 373; Milligan, 148f.). ■ κατά according to. The prep. not only refers 9 to the norm, but indicates the source or cause of the miracle (von

Dobschütz). ἐνέργεια work, effective work. The word was often
10 used of supernatural work (s. TDNT). τέρας wonder. ■ ἀπάτη
deception, deceitfulness. ἀδικία unrighteousness, wrongdoing.
The combination of the words "deceit" and "unrighteousness"
is evidently thought of here as an active, aggressive power (Milligan). ἀπολλυμένοις pres. mid. part. ἀπόλλυμι to destroy, to
ruin. The pres. tense of the verb perfectized by the prep. has the
sense of inevitable doom and indicates the fact that the goal is
ideally reached and a complete transformation of its subjects is
required to bring them out of the ruin implicit in their state (M,
114f.). ἀνθ᾿ ὧν "because" (s. Lightfoot; *Notes*). ἐδέξαντο aor.
mid. ind. δέχομαι to receive, to receive gladly, to welcome.
11 σωθῆναι aor. pass. inf. σῴζω to rescue, to save. ■ πέμπει pres.
act. ind. to send. πλάνη delusion, error. εἰς τό used w. the inf.
to express purpose (von Dobschütz; Milligan). πιστεῦσαι aor.
12 act. inf. The inf. is used to express purpose. ■ κριθῶσιν aor.
pass. subj. κρίνω to judge. Here "to be judged," "to be condemned" (Best). πιστεύσαντες aor. act. part. εὐδοκήσαντες
aor. act. part. εὐδοκέω to have pleasure in, to delight in.
13   ■ ὀφείλομεν pres. act. ind. to be obligated, to owe a debt,
ought to (s. 2 Thess. 1:3). εὐχαριστεῖν pres. act. inf. to give
thanks (s. 2 Thess. 1:3). ἠγαπημένοι perf. pass. part. ἀγαπάω.
The perf. tense emphasizes the continual state. εἵλατο aor. mid.
ind. αἱρέομαι to choose, to elect, mid. to choose for one's self.
14 ἀπαρχή firstfruits. ἁγιασμός sanctification. ■ εἰς ὅ "unto
which," "whereunto." The phrase is to be taken w. the whole of
the previous expression "salvation ... truth" (Morris).
ἐκάλεσεν aor. act. ind. περιποίησις possessing, obtaining (s.
15 1 Thess. 5:9). τοῦ κυρίου possessive gen. ■ ἄρα "therefore."
The practical conclusion is drawn from what has just been said
(Milligan). στήκετε pres. act. imp. στήκω to stand, to stand
fast. κρατεῖτε pres. act. inf. κρατέω to hold, to hold fast.
παράδοσις tradition, that which is passed on. Here it refers to
the teaching of the apostle (s. TDNT; Moore; Best). ἐδιδάχθητε
16 aor. pass. ind. ■ ἀγαπήσας aor. act. part. δούς aor. act. part.
δίδωμι to give. παράκλησις encouragement, comfort. Here it
refers to consolation and encouragement in the present (Light-
17 foot; *Notes*). ■ παρακαλέσαι aor. act. opt. παρακαλέω to
encourage, to comfort (s. TDNT; MNTW; 128). στηρίξαι aor.
act. opt. στηρίζω to strengthen, to support (s. 1 Thess. 3:2).

Ch. 3

1   ■ τὸ λοιπόν "finally," "as our last matter" (Best; s. also
Phil. 3:1). προσεύχεσθε pres. mid. imp. προσεύχομαι to pray.

The pres. tense means "pray continually" (Morris). ὁ λόγος the
word. Here "the word of the Lord." τρέχῃ pres. act. subj. τρέχω
to run. The word was used in the LXX of the running of a warrior
in battle and the picture of the word as the authorized messenger
of the Lord is then further applied to the prophets as His "runners" (PAM, 49). Paul uses the word here to express his dominating concern for the free course of the gospel. The important
thing here is the swift progress of the Word—if any image is
intended it is that of the herald in his urgency (PAM, 108).
δοξάζηται pres. pass. subj. δοξάζω to think well of, to have a
good opinion of, to glorify, pass. to be glorified. The
triumphant onrush of the gospel brings glory to God, and in its success His
glory is seen because it is God who spreads the gospel and brings
it to success or glory (Best). καθώς just as. πρὸς ὑμᾶς "w. you,"
"as in your case" (Frame). ■ ῥυσθῶμεν aor. pass. subj. ῥύομαι 2
to rescue, to deliver. Paul uses this term to express his second
request and the word often has the idea of deliverance w. power;
however, the use of the prep. here lays stress perhaps on the
deliverance rather than on the power from which it is granted
(Milligan; s. also Morris). ἄτοπος out of place, odd, unbecom-
ing, outrageous. The word was used in the papyri in one instance
to describe those who had pulled to pieces a farmer's sheaves of
wheat and thrown them to the pigs, and in another incidence it
was used of parents who publicly announced their prodigal son's
misdeeds "lest he should insult us, or do anything else amiss"
(that is outrageous) (MM; s. also Preisigke). ἡ πίστις "the
faith." The word w. the article may signify "the body of Christian teaching" or it may be used in the sense of "trust" (Morris).
■ στηρίξει fut. act. ind. στηρίζω to establish, to support, to 3
make firm (s. 1 Thess. 3:2). φυλάξει fut. act. ind. φυλάσσω to
guard, to protect. The Lord will also protect them from external
assaults (Milligan). ■ πέποιθα perf. ind. act. πείθω to persuade, 4
to have been persuaded, to trust. The perf. tense emphasizes a
state of trust (RWP; s. also Phil. 1:6). παραγγέλλω pres. act.
ind. to command, to charge, to instruct. (For the noun, s. 1
Thess. 4:2.) ποιήσετε fut. ind. act. ■ κατευθύναι pres. act. opt. 5
κατευθύνω to make straight, to guide (s. 1 Thess. 3:11).

■ στέλλεσθαι pres. mid. inf. The word originally meant 6
"to get ready," "to equip," esp. referring to equipping an army
for an expedition or for sailing. Then it came to mean "to bring
together" or "to gather up"—as for instance one gathers or tucks
up clothes and from this comes the sense of an inner gathering
up or withdrawl, and so of "flinching" and "avoiding." Here it
is withdrawl from brethren who are out of step (Moore; s. also

Milligan). περιπατοῦντος pres. act. part. περιπατέω to walk about, to conduct one's life. παράδοσις tradition, teachings that were passed down. It refers to the authoritative teaching of the apostle (s. 2 Thess. 2:15). παρελάβετε aor. act. ind. παράλαμβάνω to receive, to receive that which is passed on (s.
7 Col. 2:6; 1 Cor. 11:23; 15:1). ■ δεῖ "it is necessary." The word indicates a logical necessity arising from the circumstances (s. AS). μιμεῖσθαι pres. mid. inf. to imitate, to mimic (s. 1 Thess. 1:6). ἠτακτήσαμεν aor. act. ind. ἀτακτέω to be out of rank, to be out of order, to be disorderly, to be idle, to be a loafer (s. 1
8 Thess. 5:14; Best). ■ δωρέαν freely, "without paying," "gratis." One example in the papyri speaks of labor or work as "gratis or at reduced wages" (s. Milligan; MM; Moore). ἐφάγομεν aor. act. ind. ἐσθίω to eat. The phrase "to eat bread" is evidently a semitism and means "to get a living" (Morris). κόπος toil, working until one is weary. μόχθος labor, toil, hardship in working. (For these two words, s. 1 Thess. 2:9; AS.) ἐργαζόμενοι pres. mid. part. ἐργάζομαι to work, to work energetically. ἐπιβαρῆσαι aor. act. inf. ἐπιβαρέω to be heavy, to be burden-
9 some (s. 1 Thess. 2:9). ■ τύπος type, example (s. 1 Thess. 1:7; TDNT). δῶμεν aor. act. subj. δίδωμι. Subjunctive used to ex-
10 press purpose. ■ καί "also"; i.e., "not only did we set before you our own example, but we gave you a positive precept to this effect, when at Thessalonica" (Lightfoot; Notes). ἦμεν impf. act. ind. εἰμί. The impf. indicates continuing action in the past time for Paul had repeatedly used this injunction in his preaching (Morris). ὅτι recitative use and equivalent to quotation marks in a direct quote (RWP). ἐσθιέτω pres. act. imp. 3rd-per. sing. (s.
11 Best; Moore). ■ περιεργαζομένους pres. mid. part. περιεργάζομαι to work around, to waste one's energy, to be a busybody. Paul uses here a play on words "busybodies instead of busy." These people were not simply idle, they were meddling
12 in the affairs of others (Morris; Best; Moore). ■ τοιοῦτος "such ones." παρακαλέω pres. act. ind. to urge, to exhort. ἡσυχία quietness, calmness. The expression suggests a manner of life which is to characterize an activity and signifies the calm and contentment which are the opposite of busybodying (Moore).
13 ἐσθίωσιν pres. act. subj. ■ ἐγκακήσητε aor. act. subj. ἐγκακέω to behave badly in, to be cowardly, to lose courage, to faint (RWP; s. also Luke 18:1; Gal. 6:9). The aor. subj. is used w. the neg. in a prohibition in which the aor. is ingressive and the prohibition is used to forbid a thing not yet done (RG, 852). καλοποιοῦντες pres. act. part. καλαποιέω to do good, to do the noble thing. The word "good" carries w. it the thought not

only of what is right in itself, but of what is perceived to be right and consequently exercises an attractive power (Milligan). ■ 14 ὑπακούω pres. act. ind. to listen to, to obey. σημειοῦσθε pres. mid. imp. σημειόω to mark, to signify, to mark out, to take note of, "put a tag on that man" (RWP; s. also Lightfoot; *Notes;* Moore; MM). συναναμίγννσθαι pres. mid. inf. συναναμίγνυμι to mix up together, to associate w. someone. The first prep. in compound denotes "combination," and the second prep. denotes "interchange" (Lightfoot; *Notes*). The inf. is used as an indirect command (RWP). ἐντραπῇ aor. pass. subj. ἐντρέπω to turn about, to make one turn about, pass. to put someone to shame (Moore). ■ ἡγεῖσθε pres. mid. imp. ἡγέομαι 15 to consider, to reckon. νουθετεῖτε pres. act. imp. νουθετέω to admonish, to correct (s. 1 Thess. 5:12).

■ δώῃ aor. act. opt. δίδωμι. The opt. is used to express a 16 wish or desire. τρόπος manner, way.

■ ἀσπασμός greeting. Paul's greeting in his own hand 17 suggests that the autographs of these letters exhibited two hands, one in the body and the other in the subscription. Paul may have used an amanuensis (Richard N. Longenecker, "Ancient Amanuensis," ND, 290f.). σημεῖον sign, mark, token, signification; i.e., the means of authentication. This is the way he indicates that his letters are genuine (Morris).

613

1 TIMOTHY

Ch. 1

1   ἐπιταγή command, commission. The word connotes an
order and is used of royal commands which must be obeyed
2 (Kelly; s. also CBB). ■ γνήσιος genuine, legitimate, born in
lawful wedlock, true. Since Timothy's father was a Gentile and
his mother a Jewess, his birth according to Jewish teaching
would be illegitimate but his child-relation to Paul was genuine
(Schlatter; s. also Kelly). ἐν πίστει "in faith," "in the sphere of
Christian faith." The stress is on spiritual character, faith in and
loyalty to Christ (Lock; Ellicott). ἔλεος mercy, compassion,
pity. It is the emotion roused by contact w. an affliction which
comes undeservedly on someone else. It has special and immediate regard to the misery which is the consequence of sin and is
the tender sense of this misery displaying itself in the effort,
which only the continued perverseness of man can hinder or
defeat, to assuage and entirely remove it (TDNT; CBB; Trench,
Synonyms, 169).

3   ■ καθώς "just as." Used in an elliptical construction in
which the act of writing is understood as the last part of the
construction; i.e., "as I urged, so now I write" (Lock; s. also
MM). παρεκάλεσα aor. act. ind. παρακαλέω to urge, to exhort. προσμεῖναι aor. act. inf. προσμένω to remain, to stay
on. The prep. in compound could have a locative sense; i.e., "to
remain w. someone" (MH, 324). The inf. is used as the object
of the verb "to exhort." πορευόμενος pres. mid. part.
πορεύομαι to journey, to travel. The part. is temporal "when I
was going" and may indicate that he left Timothy enroute for
Ephesus and charged him to abide there (Guthrie).
παραγγείλῃς aor. act. subj. παραγγέλλω to command, to
charge, to instruct, to pass on commands from one to another.
It is a military term meaning "to give strict orders" and emphasizes that the commanding was to be done authoritatively (Guthrie; Kelly; Ellicott). ἑτεροδιδασκαλεῖν pres. act. inf. to teach
another doctrine, to teach something totally different (Ellicott).
The opponents in the pastoral epistles were not gnostic but
rather Jews or Jewish Christians who were teachers of the law,

who taught Jewish myths and genealogies, who forbade marriage and enjoined abstinence from food, who taught that the Resurrection had already occurred and who may have had significant success among the women, esp. because of their teaching about emancipation (s. Robert J. Karris, "The Background and Significance of the Polemic of the Pastoral Epistles," JBL 92 [December, 1973], 549–564; Guthrie, 32–38; PCG, 49ff.; s. also J. M. Ford, "A Note on Proto-Montanism in the Pastoral Epistles," NTS 17 [April, 1971], 338–346.) ■ προσέχειν pres. act. inf. to 4 turn one's mind to, to pay attention to, to give heed to, to be concerned about, to occupy one's self w. (BAG). μῦθος myth, fable, legendary stories, fiction (s. particularly the article by F.F. Bruce in the English edition of CBB; s. also TDNT; Dibelius). γενεαλογία genealogy, the tracing of one's ancestors, family tree. In postexilic Judaism there was a keen interest in family trees, and this played a part in controversies between Jews and Jewish Christians (Kelly; s. also Jastrow I, 575; for a lengthy discussion of genealogies in the ancient world, s. RAC IX, 1145–1268). ἀπέραντος endless, unrestrained (Guthrie). ἐκζήτησις seeking out, speculation, "out-of-the-way researches" (Lock). παρέχουσιν pres. act. ind. to cause, to bring about, to give rise to (BAG). μᾶλλον rather. οἰκονομία administration, office of stewardship; i.e., they do not help them carry out the stewardship entrusted to them by God (Lock; s. also Kelly; TDNT; Eph. 1:10). ■ παραγγελία instruction, command, s.v.3. συνείδησις 5 conscience. The word indicates "self-judgment" (Guthrie; s. also Rom. 2:15; PAT, 458f.). ἀνυπόκριτος without hypocrisy (s. 2 Cor. 6:6). ■ ἀστοχήσαντες aor. act. part. ἀστοχέω to miss the 6 mark, to swerve, to fail to aim at. The word indicates "taking no pains to aim at the right path" (Lock; Kelly). ἐξετράπησαν aor. pass. ind. ἐκτρέπομαι to turn or twist aside, to turn away. The word was used as a medical t.t. "to be dislocated" (BAG; s. also MM). ματαιολογία vain or useless talk, idle chatter, empty argument (Kelly; MM). ■ θέλοντες pres. act. part. The part. 7 could be concessive "although they desire." νομοδιδάσκαλος law teachers, a term from Judaism (s. Luke 5:17; Acts 5:34). They sought popularity not only in their subtle and detailed exegesis, but also in a strict legalism and ascetic demands (Jeremias). νοοῦντες pres. act. part. νοέω to understand, to comprehend. The pres. tense w. the neg. stresses their continuing inability to understand. The part. has a slight antithetical or perhaps even concessive force (Ellicott). διαβεβαιοῦνται pres. mid. ind. to confidently affirm, to strongly affirm, to speak confidently, to insist. The verb means "to make asseveration, or to

give one's opinion in a firm, dogmatic tone" (BAG; Fairbairn).
The prep. in compound has the meaning "thoroughly" (MH,
302).

8　　■ καλός good, suitable, useful (s. CBB; TDNT). νομίμως
lawfully; i.e., agreeably to the design of the law (Ellicott).
χρῆται pres. mid. subj. χράομαι to use, to make use of, fol-
9　lowed by the dat. as the object. ■ εἰδώς perf. act. part. οἶδα to
know. Used to express knowledge grasped directly by the mind
(ND, 344). κεῖται perf. pass. ind. τίθημι to place. Here used for
the introduction or enactment of a law "to establish" (Fairbairn).
ἀνυπότακτος not made subject, independent, undisciplined,
disobedient, rebellious (BAG). ἀσεβής ungodly, irreverent, irreligious. ἁμαρτωλός sinful. ἀνόσιος unholy. It speaks of one's
lack of inner purity (Ellicott; CBB; TDNT). βέβηλος profane.
It speaks of irreverent and contemptuous behavior toward the
things more particularly associated w. the name of God (Fairbairn). πατρολῴας one who kills one's father, one who smites
his father. μητρολῴας one who smites or strikes his mother.
The words speak of a most unnatural and shameful violation of
the honor due to the parents whether or not it might issue in fatal
consequences and was considered a transgression of the fifth
10　commandment (Fairbairn). ἀνδροφόνος murderer. ■ πόρνος
one who practices sexual immorality, an immoral person (BAG;
s. also TDNT; CBB). ἀρσενοκοίτης homosexual (s. 1 Cor. 6:9).
ἀνδραποδιστής one who catches the man by the foot, man
stealer, kidnapper. It includes all who exploit other men and
women for their own selfish ends (RWP; EGT). ψεύστης liar.
ἐπίορκος one who commits perjury, perjurer. The force of the
prep. in compound may be "against"; i.e., one goes against his
oath (s. MH, 314f.). ὑγιαινούσῃ pres. act. part. ὑγιαίνω to be
healthy, to be sound. The word denotes the wholesomeness or
healthiness of true Christian teaching (Guthrie; s. also Kelly).
διδασκαλία teaching. ἀντίκειται pres. mid. ind. to sit against,
11　to be contrary, to be opposite. ■ μακάριος blessed. It describes
God as containing all happiness in Himself and bestowing it on
men (Lock). ἐπιστεύθην aor. pass. ind. πιστεύω to believe,
pass. to be entrusted w.

12　　■ ἐνδυναμώσαντι aor. act. part. ἐνδυναμόω to empower,
to give strength, to enable (s. Phil. 4:13). The aor. is used because
the writer's thoughts pass back to the particular time when he
received inward strength increasingly (EGT). ἡγήσατο aor.
mid. ind. ἡγέομαι to consider, to reckon, to count. θέμενος aor.
mid. part. τίθημι to place, to appoint. διακονία ministry, ser-
13　vice (s. TDNT; CBB). ■ τὸ πρότερον formerly, previously, acc.

of general reference of the articular comp., "as to the former time" (RWP). ὄντα pres. part. εἰμί. The part. could be temporal or concessive "though I was" (Ellicott). βλάσφημος blasphemer, one who slanders God. διώκτης one who pursues as a hunter, persecutor. ὑβριστής sadist, a violent person. The word indicates one who in pride and insolence deliberately and contemptuously mistreats and wrongs and hurts another person just for hurting sake and to deliberately humiliate the person. It speaks of treatment which is calculated publicly to insult and openly to humiliate the person who suffers it. The word is used in Romans 1:30 to describe a man of arrogant insolence, and pictures one of the characteristic sins of the pagan world (MNTW, 77–85; s. also TDNT; CBB). ἠλεήθην aor. pass. ind. ἐλεέω to show mercy, to show compassion and pity, pass. to obtain mercy, to be shown pity (s. 1 Tim. 1:3). ἀγνοῶν pres. act. part. ἀγνοέω to be ignorant. Paul is availing himself of the distinction, conventional in Judaism (Lev. 22:14; Num. 15:22–31) and also in the Qumran sect, between "unwitting" and "presumptuous" sins, linking unbelief w. his ignorance. He does not claim that as a result he was without guilt, but mentions the fact as explaining how his career prior to his conversion became the object of God's compassion rather than His wrath (Kelly). ἐποίησα aor. act. ind. ■ ὑπερεπλεόνασεν aor. act. ind. ὑπερπλεονάζω to 14 abound over and beyond, to be present in great abundance, to abound exceedingly. The prep. in compound means "above its usual measure" and is an attempt to express the superabundance of divine grace (Lock; Guthrie). ■ ἀποδοχή reception, accep- 15 tance, approval. In the koine the word indicates the acceptance and recognition which someone or something has found (Dibelius; s. also MM). σῶσαι aor. act. inf. σῴζω to rescue, to save. The inf. is used to express purpose. πρῶτος first, foremost, chief. Here the word is used in the sense of "greatest" (Fairbairn). The verb used in pres. "I am," not "I was." The sinner remains a sinner even if forgiven; the past is always there as a stimulus to deeper penitence and service (Lock; s. also Kelly). (Cf. 1 Cor. 15:9; Eph. 3:8.) ■ ἐνδείξηται aor. mid. subj. ἐνδείκνυμι to 16 point out, to demonstrate. The prep. in compound suggest a more complete demonstration than the simple verb. It is the laying of the "index" finger, as it were, "on" the object (MH, 305). The subj. is used to express purpose. μακροθυμία longsuffering, patience (s. Gal. 5:22). μελλόντων pres. act. part. μέλλω to be about to. Use w. the inf. to express the durative fut. (s. MKG, 307). πιστεύειν pres. act. inf. Used w. the prep. w. the dat. to mean "to repose one's trust upon" and suggests more of

the state whereas the acc. emphasizes more the initial act of faith (M, 68; s. also Lock). αἰώνιος eternal, everlasting. The term "everlasting life" emphasizes "life of the age to come" and contains a temporal reference, but stresses the qualitative character. Although Paul regards eternal life as predominately eschatological, he also sees it as a pres. possession of the believer. It is the
17 result of the indwelling Spirit (s. GW, 188ff.). ■ ἄφθαρτος incorruptible; i.e., immune from decay, immortal (Kelly). ἀόρατος not able to be seen, invisible.

18   ■ παρατίθεμαι pres. mid. ind. to place beside, mid. to entrust, to pledge, to deposit w. another. The term here is a banking figure (RWP; MM). προαγούσας pres. act. part. προάγω to go before, to lead before. The phrase may be translated "relying on the prophecies once made about you," or it could mean "the prophecies which pointed me to you" (s. Kelly; Lock). στρατεύῃ pres. act. subj. στρατεύω to fight as a soldier, to war as a soldier. στρατεία military expedition or campaign, warfare. The cognate acc. or acc. of content; i.e., "to fight a
19 fight" (s. MT, 245; BD, 84f.; RG, 477f.). ■ ἔχων pres. act. part. to have, to possess (s. M, 110). ἀπωσάμενοι aor. mid. part. ἀπωθέομαι to push away from one's self, to push aside, to reject, to repudiate. The word implies a violent and deliberate rejection (Guthrie). ἐναυάγησαν aor. act. ind. ναυαγέω to make shipwreck, to suffer shipwreck. Paul himself had suffered shipwreck at least four times when he wrote this epistle. He had
20 on each occasion lost everything except himself (EGT). ■ παρέδωκα aor. act. ind. παραδίδωμι to deliver over to (s. 1 Cor. 5:5). παιδευθῶσιν aor. pass. subj. παιδεύω to train through discipline. The word conveys the idea of stern punishment rather then instruction (Kelly). The subj. is used to express purpose. βλασφημεῖν pres. act. inf. to ridicule, to slander, to slander God, to blaspheme.

Ch. 2

1   ■ παρακαλῶ pres. act. ind. to urge, to exhort (s. Rom. 12:1). πρῶτον πάντων "first of all." The words relate not to primacy of time but to primacy of importance (Guthrie). ποιεῖσθαι pres. mid. inf. to make, to do. The word is used in a causative sense (s. 1 Thess. 1:2). δέησις intercession, petition. The verb from which the noun is derived had the meaning "to chance upon," then "to have an audience w. a king," to have the good fortune to be admitted to an audience, so to present a petition. The word was a regular term for a petition to a superior and in the papyri it was constantly used of any writing addressed

to the king (Lock; Guthrie; MM; BS, 121f.; Preisigke; TDNT).
ἔντευξις thanksgiving (s. Col. 3:17). ■ ὑπεροχή prominence, a 2
place of prominence or authority, used of prominent officials.
The word was used in Hellenistic Gr. to indicate the prominent
position of a person (BAG; MM; Dibelius). ὄντων pres. part.
εἰμί. ἵνα introduces the result or purpose of the prayer (Lock).
(For references to Jewish prayers for those in authority, s.
Dibelius.) ἤρεμος quiet, tranquil. ἡσύχιος still, quiet.
διάγωμεν pres. act. subj. διάγω to lead, to conduct. εὐσέβεια
godliness, religious devotion. It refers to the true reverence
toward God which comes from knowledge. It is the right attitude
to God and to the holiness, the majesty, and the love of God
(Lock; MNTW, 66–77; Trench, Synonyms, 172ff.; TDNT; CBB;
RAC VI, 985–1052). σεμνότης gravity. The word denotes moral earnestness, affecting outward demeanor as well as interior
intention (Kelly; Trench, Synonyms, 347f.). ■ τοῦτο "this." The 3
word refers to the idea of universal prayer for all men (Guthrie;
EGT). καλόν good (s. 1 Tim. 1:8; Lock, 22f.). ἀπόδεκτος acceptable. ■ σωθῆναι aor. pass. inf. σῴζω to rescue, to save. 4
Used w. the verb meaning "to wish, to desire" (s. Guthrie).
ἐπίγνωσις recognition, knowledge, knowledge directed to a
particular object. ἐλθεῖν aor. act. inf. ἔρχομαι. ■ μεσίτης 5
mediator, go between (s. Gal. 3:19). ἄνθρωπος human being,
man. The lack of the article emphasizes the character; i.e., "one
possessing the nature, and in his work manifesting the attributes,
of humanity" (Fairbairn). ■ δούς aor. act. part. δίδωμι. 6
ἀντίλυτρον ransom, the price paid for the release of a slave. The
prep. in compound implies an exchange (EGT; s. also Matt.
20:28; Mark 10:45; TDNT; I. Howard Marshall, "The Development of the Concept of Redemption in the New Testament,"
RH, 153–169; Dibelius). μαρτύριον witness, testimony.
καιρός time, opportunity, season. The dat. is locative "in its due
seasons" (RWP). ■ ἐτέθην aor. pass. ind. τίθημι to place, to 7
appoint, to commission. κῆρυξ herald, preacher. The herald was
someone who had important news to bring. He often announced
an athletic event or religious festival, or functioned as a political
messenger, the bringer of some news or command from the
king's court. He was to have a strong voice and proclaim his
message w. vigor without lingering to discuss it. The herald's
most important qualification was that he faithfully represent or
report the word of the one by whom he had been sent. He was
not to be "original" but his message was to be that of another
(Victor Paul Furnish, "Prophets, Apostles, and Preachers: A
Study of the Biblical Concept of Preaching," Interpretation 17

[Jan., 1963], 55; s. also TDNT; CBB). (For the use of the nom. in this construction "to appoint as . . . ," s. RG, 401.) ψεύδομαι pres. mid. ind. to lie. (For the import of Paul's statement, s. Gal. 1:20.) ἐθνῶν pl. Gentiles, non-Jews. The gen. is obj. gen. ἐν. The prep. indicates the sphere in which the apostle performs his mission (Ellicott).

8 ■ βούλομαι pres. mid. ind. to purpose, to determine, to will. The apostolic authority is represented in this expression (Bengel). προσεύχεσθαι pres. mid. inf. to pray. τοὺς ἄνδρας acc. pl. ἀνήρ man, male. The word is used here to emphasize the responsibilities of the male members of the congregation. τόπος place. The expression is used for public worship (RWP). ἐπαίροντας pres. act. part. ἐπαίρω to lift toward, to raise up. The most general attitude for prayer in antiquity, for pagans, Jews, and Christians alike, was to stand w. hands outstretched and lifted up, the palms turned upward (Kelly; s. also SB II, 261; IV, 645; DGRA, 16; MM). ὅσιος holy. The word stood for that which was in accordance w. divine direction and providence. The word describes the pious, pure, and clean action which is in accordance w. God's command. The hands are holy which have not been given over to deeds of wicked lust (Huther; CBB; Trench, *Synonyms*, 328; TDNT). ὀργή anger, wrath. διαλογισμός a thinking back and forth, deliberation. The word then took on the meaning doubting or disputing. In relation to prayer in this section the meaning "doubting" is possible (Guthrie) or in relation to the idea of "holy hands" it could have the

9 meaning "disputing," "quarrelsomeness" (Kelly). ■ ὡσαύτως just as, likewise. καταστολή clothing, apparel. The word could be understood in a wider sense; i.e., "demeanour," "deportment" (MM; Ellicott). κόσμιος well-arranged, well-ordered, moderate, modest. αἰδώς modesty. The word connotes fem. reserve in matters of sex. In the word is involved an innate moral repugnance to the doing of the dishonorable. It is "shamefastness" which shrinks from overpassing the limits of womanly reserve and modesty, as well as from dishonor which would justly attach thereto (Kelly; Trench, *Synonyms*, 68, 71f.). σωφροσύνη sobriety, self-control. It stands basically for perfect self-mastery in the physical appetites and as applied to women it too had a definitely sexually nuance. It is that habitual inner self government, w. its constant reign on all the passions and desires (Kelly; Trench, *Synonyms*, 72; s. also TDNT). κοσμεῖν pres. act. inf. to put in order, to arrange, to adorn. πλέγμα that which is woven or plaited. Here it refers to "hair styles"; i.e., "plaited hair." Both Jewish and Gentile women were noted for

their elaborate hair styles (s. SB III, 428ff.; DGRA, 328-330). In Philo's description of pleasure coming in the guise of a prostitute, he describes such a woman as having her hair dressed in curious and elaborate plaits, her eyes w. pencil lines, her eyebrows smothered w. paint and her costly raiment broided lavishly w. flowers, and w. bracelets, necklaces of gold and jewels hanging around her (Philo, "The Sacrifices of Abel and Cain," 21) μαργαρίτης pearl. Pearls were considered to have had the topmost rank among valuables and were considered to be three times more valuable than gold. Pearls were esp. prized by women who used them to adorn their hair, to hang them on their fingers, to use them as earrings, or to use them to decorate their garments and even their sandals (s. Pliny, *Natural History*, IX, 106-123; KP III, 1020-1021; TDNT). ἱματισμός garment, clothing. πολυτελής very costly, very expensive. The best garments could cost as much as seven thousand denarii and those of inferior quality for commoners and slaves the cost would be between eight hundred and five hundred denarii (the average wage of the working man was one denarius a day). Tarsus was an important weaving center and its garments were classified as some of the best in the ancient world. (For information regarding clothes and the cloth industry under the Roman Empire, s. Jones, 350-364.) ■ πρέπει pres. act. ind. to be clearly seen, to resemble, to be 10 fitting or becoming, to suit (AS). ἐπαγγελλομέναις pres. mid. part. ἐπαγγέλλω to announce, to proclaim, to profess, to lay claim to, to give one's self out as an expert in something (BAG). The pres. tense emphasizes continual action. θεοσέβεια religious, godliness, reverence toward God. The emphasis in this section does not lie on the use of jewelry or clothing, but rather on the fact that true beauty and beautification is not in the outward appearance (Dibelius). ■ ἡσυχία quietness, silence. 11 The word expresses quietness in general (T). (For the relation of this command to the commands of Paul in 1 Cor., s. PWC, 74ff.) μανθανέτω pres. act. imp. 3rd per. sing. ὑποταγή submission (s. PWC, 72f.). ■ ἐπιτρέπω pres. act. ind. to allow, to permit. 12 The pres. tense emphasizes the continual action and points to an abiding attitude. αὐθεντεῖν pres. act. inf. to act on one's own authority, to exercise authority, to have mastery, to be an autocrat, to be dominating (s. AS; MM; Preisigke; Dibelius; LAE, 88f.). εἶναι pres. inf. "to be." ■ ἐπλάσθη aor. pass. ind. 13 πλάσσω to form, to fashion, to mold, to create. ■ ἠπατήθη 14 aor. pass. ind. ἀπατάω to deceive, to trick, to mislead. ἐξαπατηθεῖσα aor. pass. part. ἐξαπατάω to deceive completely, to deceive successfully (s. MH, 311). παράβασις stepping

over the boundary, transgression (s. Eph. 2:1). γέγονεν perf. act.
ind. γίνομαι. The perf. tense expresses an abiding state (Guth-
15 rie). ■ σωθήσεται fut. pass. ind. σώζω to save, to rescue.
τεκνογονία childbearing. The use of the definite article, "the
childbearing," may be a reference to the birth of the Savior
(Ellicott; but also s. Guthrie). ἁγιασμός sanctification. The
word is used here in the act. sense and would refer to the living
of a godly life.

Ch. 3

1   ■ ἐπισκοπή the office of one who oversees a work, the
office of bishop (s. CBB; TDNT; ZPEB I, 617–620). ὀρέγεται
pres. mid. ind. to stretch one's self out, to aspire to (Guthrie).
The verb takes its object in the dat. ἐπιθυμεῖ to set one's heart
2 upon, to desire (Guthrie). ■ δεῖ "it is necessary." The word
speaks of logical necessity according to the binding needs of the
circumstances (s. TDNT; AS). Plutarch used the word to describe the character of one who teaches children (*Moralia, The
Education of Children,* 7). ἐπίσκοπος overseer, bishop, pastor.
ἀνεπίλημπτος not able to be taken hold of, irreproachable,
beyond reproach. The word implies not only that the man is of
good report, but that he is deservedly so (AS; MM; Preisigke).
ἄνδρα acc. sing. "a husband of one wife," "one woman man."
The difficult phrase probably means that he is to have only one
wife at a time (s. Robert L. Saucy, "The Husband of One Wife,"
Bib Sac, 131 [July, 1974], 229–240; s. also SB III, 647–650).
νηφάλιος sober, sober-minded, clearheaded. The word originally connotes abstinence from alcohol, but here it has a wider,
metaphorical sense (Kelly). σώφρων self-controlled, thoughtful
(s. MM; TDNT). κόσμιος orderly. It implies well-ordered demeanor, but also the orderly fulfillment of all duties and the
ordering of the inner life from which these spring (Lock).
φιλόξενος hospitable. In his official capacity he has the duty of
keeping open house both for delegates traveling from church to
church and for ordinary needy members of the congregation
(Kelly). διδακτικός able to teach, skillful in teaching (BAG; s.
3 also MH, 379). ■ πάροινος one who sits long at his wine, one
who is a slave of drink (RWP; Kelly). πλήκτης not a giver of
blows, not given to violence (Kelly). ἐπιεικής equity, lenient,
kindly, forbearing (s. 2 Cor. 10:1). ἄμαχος without fighting, not
a fighter, not contentious (RWP; Guthrie). ἀφιλάργυρος not a
4 lover of money. ■ ἴδιος one's own. καλῶς well. προϊστάμενον
pres. mid. part. προΐστημι to stand before, to rule over, to
manage. ἔχοντα pres. act. part. ὑποταγή submission.

σεμνότης dignity, stateliness. It describes the characteristic of the man who carries himself w. the perfect blend of dignity and courtesy, independence and humility to his fellowmen (MNTW, 144; s. also Trench, *Synonyms*, 344f.). The word avoids the suggestion of sternness yet retains the idea of natural respect (Guthrie). ■ προστῆναι aor. act. inf. προΐστημι to rule, to 5 manage, to govern. ἐπιμελήσεται fut. mid. ind. ἐπιμελέομαι to care for, to exercise concern for. The prep. in compound is directive (RWP). ■ νεόφυτος newly planted, recent convert. 6 The word was used in a literal sense of newly planted trees (BS, 220f.). τυφωθείς aor. pass. part. τυφόω to wrap in smoke, to puff up, pass. to be beclouded w. pride (AS). The part. could be causal or temporal. κρίμα judgment. ἐμπέσῃ aor. act. subj. ἐμπίπτω to fall into. διάβολος slanderer, devil. The gen. could be obj. gen.; i.e., condemnation reserved for the devil; the judgment meeted out for the sin of pride or the gen. could be subj. gen.; i.e., condemnation wrought by the devil; the condemnation brought about by the further intrigues of the devil when a man is once lured into his grasp through pride (Guthrie; s. also Kelly). ■ ἔξωθεν outside, "those outside," is a term used for unbelievers 7 (s. 1 Thess. 4:12; Col. 4:5). ὀνειδισμός reproach, disgrace, insult. παγίς trap, snare. Here the gen. is subj. gen. "the snare made by the devil" (Ellicott).

■ ὡσαύτως likewise. σεμνός serious, dignified, stately 8 (s.v.4.). δίλογος double-tongued. The word could mean "talebearer," suggesting the idea of gossipers (Guthrie; Lock), or it could be "consistent in what one says," i.e., "not saying one thing while thinking another," or "not saying one thing to one man and a different thing to the next" (Kelly). προσέχοντας pres. act. part. προσέχω. Used w. the dat. to turn one's mind to, to occupy one's self w. Here "to be addicted to much wine" (BAG). The pres. tense points to an habitual action. αἰσχροκερδής greedy of gain. The gain may become shameful when a man makes the acquisition of it, rather than the glory of God, his prime object (EGT; s. also Plutarch, *Moralia*, *On Love of Wealth*). ■ τῆς πίστεως. The gen. gives the content or sub- 9 stance of "the mystery"; i.e., "the mystery, the substance of which is Christian faith" (Guthrie; Schlatter). συνείδησις conscience (s. Rom. 2:15; TDNT; PAT, 402ff.; 458f.). ■ 10 δοκιμαζέσθωσιν pres. pass. imp. 3rd per. pl. δοκιμάζω to approve after testing or examining (s. TDNT; MM). εἶτα then. διακονείτωσαν pres. act. imp. 3rd per. pl. to serve as a deacon, to minister. ἀνέγκλητος without charge, blameless, without accusation, irreproachable. (For examples of this word in the

papyri, s. MM; Preisigke.) ὄντες pres. part. εἰμί. The part. could
12/13 be conditional. ■ ἔστωσαν pres. imp. 3rd per. pl. εἰμί. ■
διακονήσαντες aor. act. part. to serve, to minister. βαθμός
step, base, foundation (for example of a pedestal). The word is
used in a fig. sense and may refer to "standing in the sight of
God" or it may refer to the repute and influence of the deacons
which they would have w. the congregation (s. Guthrie; Kelly).
περιποιοῦνται pres. mid. ind. περιποιέω to make besides,
mid. to achieve, to gain for one's self, to acquire for one's self
(s. RWP). παρρησία speaking all, confidence, assurance, boldness (s. TDNT).

14   ■ ἐλπίζων pres. act. part. The part. may be concessive
"although I hoped" (Ellicott). ἐλθεῖν aor. act. inf. ἔρχομαι.
τάχιον adv. comp. ταχύς fast, quickly, comp. "more quickly,"
15 "sooner," i.e., "than I at one time thought" (Fairbairn). ■
βραδύνω pres. act. subj. to hesitate, to delay. The subj. is used
in a third-class conditional clause expressing that which may be
possible (s. RWP). εἰδῇς perf. act. subj. οἶδα. The word was used
to describe "know how"; i.e., the possession of knowledge or
skill necessary to accomplish a desired goal (ND, 347f.).
ἀναστρέφεσθαι pres. mid. inf. to conduct one's self, to behave.
The word could well apply to the discharge of official duties and
aptly covers conduct expected from, and the mutual relations of,
all the groups discussed (Guthrie; Kelly; s. also Lock; MM). ἥτις
"which indeed," the explanatory use of the indef. rel. (Ellicott;
s. also RG, 960). ζῶντος pres. act. part. gen. sing. ζάω to live.
στῦλος pillar. ἑδραίωμα foundation, buttress, bulwark. (For
16 various views related to this v., s. Guthrie; Kelly; Lock.) ■
ὁμολογουμένως adv. confessedly, by common consent. The
word expresses the unanimous conviction of Christians (Kelly;
s. also ECC, 129f.). εὐσέβεια godliness, piety, religion. The
word may perhaps include the thought of doctrine as well as of
life (Lock; s. also Kelly). ἐφανερώθη aor. pass. ind. φανερόω
to make visible, to manifest. σάρξ flesh; i.e., He appeared on
earth as a real man (Kelly). The word does not indicate the
nature of natural man which is opposed to God, but in connection w. the OT use of the word it indicates the earthly existence
of Jesus (Jeremias). ἐδικαιώθη aor. pass. ind. δικαιόω to justify, to declare righteous, to vindicate. If the word "spirit" is taken
to be parallel to "flesh" the meaning is "declared righteous and
shown to be in fact Son of God, in respect to his spiritual nature"
and a reference to the Resurrection is implied. If the word "spirit" denotes the Holy Spirit, it means "he was declared righteous
through, or by means of, the Holy Spirit" (Kelly; s. also MRP,

154f.). ὤφθη aor. pass. ind. ὁράω to see, pass. to be seen, to appear. ἐκηρύχθη aor. pass. ind. κηρύσσω to preach, to proclaim as a herald. ἐπιστεύθη aor. pass. ind. ἀνελήμφθη aor. pass. ind. ἀναλαμβάνω to receive up. The verb is used of the Ascension (s. Acts 1:2, 11, 22).

Ch. 4

■ ῥητῶς adv. expressly, clearly, unmistakably, "in express 1 terms." The word indicates that these elements of fut. events have been distinctly made known (Guthrie; Lock). ὕστερος later, latter, last. καιρός period of time, season (s. TDNT; Trench, Synonyms, 209; CBB). ἀποστήσονται fut. mid. ind. ἀφίστημι to go away, to withdraw, to fall away, to become apostate. The gen. "from the faith" indicates that which they leave and is used in the obj. sense; i.e., "Christian doctrine, sound teaching" (s. Kelly). προσέχοντες pres. act. part. προσέχω. Used w. the dat. to give one's attention to, to devote one's self to, to give heed to (s. 1 Tim. 1:4). πνεύμασιν dat. pl. "spirits." These are evidently supernatural evil spirits who work through individuals and they stand in contrast to "the Spirit" mentioned immediately before (Guthrie; EGT; Fairbairn). πλάνος leading astray, deceptive, deceiving, seducing. διδασκαλία teaching. δαιμόνια demons, s. 1 Corinthians 10:-20. ■ ὑπόκρισις hypocrisy (s. Gal. 2:13). ψευδολόγος false 2 speakers, a speaker of that which is not true. This word expresses perhaps more than "liar," the notion of definite false statements (EGT). κεκαυστηριασμένων perf. pass. part. καυστηριάζω to brand w. a red hot iron, to sear. The idea of the word may be that these are people who are in the service of Satan and in consequence have their conscience stamped w. the brand mark which indicates his ownership. Another possible alternative interpretation is that their conscience has been "cauterized"; i.e., made insensible to the distinction between right and wrong (Kelly). The perf. tense looks at the completed and continuing state or condition. συνείδησις conscience. ■ κωλυόντων pres. act. 3 part. κωλύω to hinder, to forbid. γαμεῖν pres. act. inf. to marry. ἀπέχεσθαι pres. mid. inf. to hold one's self apart from, to abstain. These people may have been those who insisted that the new age had already been introduced by Christ and they failed to distinguish the pres. times of refreshing, which the resurrection of Jesus had initiated, from the consummation to be inaugurated by the yet fut. resurrection (s. William L. Lane, "First Timothy IV.1–3. An Early Instance of Over-Realized Eschatology," NTS 11 [Jan., 1965], 164–169). βρῶμα that which

is eaten, food. ἔκτισεν aor. act. ind. κτίζω to create.
μετάλημψις receiving, reception, sharing. The prep. in compound has the idea of "sharing" (s. MH, 318). εὐχαριστία
thanksgiving. ἐπεγνωκόσι perf. act. part. dat. pl. ἐπιγινώσκω
to recognize, to know, to know thoroughly. The prep. in com-
4 pound is directive (s. Col. 1:9). ■ κτίσμα that which is created,
creation, creature. ἀπόβλητος to be thrown away, rejected,
refused. The verbal adj. here has a pass. sense (RWP).
5 λαμβανόμενον pres. pass. part. ■ ἁγιάζεται pres. pass. ind.
ἁγιάζω to cause to be set apart, to remove from profane or
common use, to sanctify (s. TDNT; CBB). ἔντευξις prayer,
request (s. 1 Tim. 2:1).
6   ■ ὑποτιθέμενος pres. mid. part. ὑποτίθημι to place under,
to subject (Guthrie). The part. could have a conditional force "if
you suggest" (s. Ellicott), or the part. could be modal. ἔσῃ fut.
εἰμί. ἐντρεφόμενος pres. pass. part. ἐντρέφω to nourish in. The
metaphor is that of feeding w. the idea of reading and inwardly
digesting and the pres. part. suggests a continual process (Lock;
Guthrie). διδασκαλία teaching. παρηκολούθηκας perf. act.
ind. παρακολουθέω to follow, to follow beside. The word combines the ideas of "understanding" w. that of "practicing persev-
7 eringly" (Lock). ■ βέβηλος permitted to be trodden, accessible,
profane, unhallowed (AS; s. also 1 Tim. 1:9). γραώδης characteristic of old women. It is the sarcastic epithet which was
frequent in philosophical polemic and conveys the idea of limit-
less credulity (Kelly). μῦθος myth, fable, tale (s. 1 Tim. 1:4). The
"tale" here are such as old women tell to children quite unfit for
strong young men who have been trained to discipline themselves (Lock). παραιτοῦ pres. mid. imp. παραιτέομαι to
refuse, to turn away from, to decline, to have nothing to do w.
The word suggests a strong refusal (s. Ellicott; Guthrie).
γύμναζε pres. act. imp. γυμνάζω to exercise. It is not the
self-centered ascetic struggle of the individual for his own moral
and religious perfection, but the training necessary for the unhindered pursuit of God's purposes. Enemies may have accused
Paul of moral laxity since he refused to follow their demands of
abstention, but his exercise was a vigorous development and
application of all his strength and ability that he may serve the
glory of God w. every thought and action (PAM, 174f.).
εὐσέβεια godliness, piety (s. TDNT; CBB; MNTW, 66–77; 1
8 Tim. 2:2). ■ σωματικός bodily, that which pertains to the body.
γυμνασία exercise. The "bodily exercise" is a metaphor which
refers back to the errors of the heretics against which the author
has been warning. It is best to see in this phrase not the Hellenis-

tic culture of the body, but an external dualistic asceticism as propounded by the heretics and reflected in the warnings contained in v. 3 (PAM, 173; s. also TDNT; Jeremias). ὀλίγος little, that which is numerically small and lasts only a short time (Schlatter). ὠφέλιμος useful, profitable. ἐπαγγελία promise. The struggle of Paul and Timothy is not to gain eternal life, but has as its goal the honor and glory of God, the proclamation and demonstration of His faithfulness to this promise of life. The promise of life to all men is the basis and motive for their life's task (s. PAM, 175ff.). ἔχουσα pres. act. part. μελλούσης pres. act. part. μέλλω to be about to, "the coming age" (s. Lane, NTS, 11 [Jan., 1965], 166). ■ ἀποδοχή reception, acceptance. ■ 9/10 κοπιῶμεν pres. act. ind. to work hard, to work until one is weary. ἀγωνιζόμεθα pres. mid. ind. to struggle, to exert one's self. The two words speak of Paul's tremendous efforts and exertions in the proclamation of the gospel (s. PAM, 171-177). The pres. tense describes the continual action. ἠλπίκαμεν perf. act. ind. ἐλπίζω to hope. The perf. tense implies a continuous state of hope, i.e., "because we have fixed our hope" (Guthrie). ζῶντι pres. act. part. dat. sing. ζάω to live. The pres. tense indicates that God is living, and therefore able to give life now and hereafter (Lock). μάλιστα especially.

■ παράγγελλε pres. act. imp. παραγγέλλω to transmit a 11 message, to order, to command (s. 1 Tim. 1:3). δίδασκε pres. act. imp. The pres. tense indicates the continuation of an action and the continual habitual carrying out of the command (s. Bakker; MKG, 271ff.). ■ νεότης youth. καταφρονείτω pres. 12 act. imp. 3rd per. sing. καταφρονέω to think down, to despise, to underrate. In the ancient world a person between 30 and 40 years old could be considered young (Kelly). One rabbi said that a person at 30 was fit for authority and at 40 he was fit for discernment (M, Aboth V, 21). τύπος type, example. γίνου pres. mid. imp. ἀναστροφή behavior. ἁγνεία purity. The word covers not only chastity in matters of sex, but also the innocence and integrity of heart which are denoted by the related noun in 2 Cor. 6:6 (Kelly). The word refers to purity of act and thought (Lock). ■ πρόσεχε pres. act. imp. s.v.1. The pres. tense calls for 13 a continual action. The verb "to give attendance" implies previous preparation in private (Guthrie). ἀνάγνωσις reading. Used w. the verb it implies a wise choice of the passages to be read; audible reading; a power of correct exposition (Lock). παράκλησις exhortation, encouragement (s. TDNT; CBB). διδασκαλία teaching, doctrine. ■ ἀμέλει pres. act. imp. 14 ἀμελέω to be unconcerned about something, to neglect. (For the pref. as a neg., s. Moorhouse, 47ff.) The pres. imp. w. the neg. could mean "do not immediately ... ," "do not always ... ," and "do not continue ..." (s. MKG, 272). χάρισμα that which is a result of grace, free gift, grace gift. It denotes a special endowment of the Spirit enabling the recipient to carry out some function in the community (Kelly; s. also TDNT; CBB). ἐδόθη aor. pass. ind. δίδωμι. προφητεία speaking for someone, prophecy. μετά "with." The prep. does not express instrument or means but merely accompaniment (RWP; EGT). ἐπίθεσις placing upon, laying on. πρεσβυτέριον assembly of the elders, presbytery. This may be the rendering of a Heb. t.t. which meant "the leaning, or pressing on of elders," which in effect meant, "the leaning or pressing of hands upon someone w. the object of making him an elder or rabbi." In a Christian context it would mean "elder ordination" or "formal ordination to office" (Kel-

15 ly). ■ μελέτα pres. act. imp. μελετάω to take care, to practice, to cultivate, to take pains w. something, to think about, to meditate upon (BAG). ἴσθι pres. imp. εἰμί "be in them." It is a construction expressing absorption in anything. The mind is to be as immersed in these pursuits as the body in the air it breathes (Guthrie). προκοπή advance, progress (s. Phil. 1:12; Gal. 1:14). The expression is a favorite word in Stoic writers of a pupil's progress in philosophy (Lock). φανερός clear, obvious, manifest. ᾖ pres. subj. εἰμί. The subj. is used to express purpose.

16 ■ ἔπεχε pres. act. imp. ἐπέχω to hold upon, to give heed to, to give attention to, to fix attention upon. (For examples from the papyri, s. MM; Preisigke.) ἐπίμενε pres. act. imp. ἐπιμένω to remain upon, to continue. The prep. in compound is directive indicating the concentration of the verb's action upon some object (MH, 312). ποιῶν pres. act. part. ποιέω. σώσεις fut. act. ind. σώζω to rescue, to save. ἀκούοντας pres. act. part.

Ch. 5

1　　　■ ἐπιπλήξῃς aor. act. subj. ἐπιπλήσσω to strike upon, to strike at, to rebuke sharply. The word contains a note of severity, "to censure severely" (s. MM; Guthrie). The aor. subj. is used w. the neg. in a prohibition and implies that an action is not yet existent and should not arise (MKG, 273). παρακάλει pres. act. imp. παρακαλέω to encourage, to exhort. νεώτερος comp.

2 νέος young, comp. younger; i.e., "the younger men." ■ ἀδελφή sister. ἁγνεία purity, chastity (s. 1 Tim. 4:12).

3　　　■ χήρα widow. τίμα pres. act. imp. τιμάω to honor, to show respect. The word would also carry the idea of support in this context (EGT; Schlatter). ὄντως adv. from the part. of εἰμί actually, really. Paul means widows who have no other means of support, who have no opportunity for marriage and who have given themselves to the service of the Lord (Jeremias; Guthrie). ■ ἔκγονος descendant, grandchild (Guthrie). μανθανέτωσαν 4 pres. act. imp. 3rd per. pl. The subject of the pl. verb is "such children and grandchildren" (Lock). ἴδιος one's own. εὐσεβεῖν pres. act. inf. to show piety, to show reverence, to fulfill one's religious obligation (s. 1 Tim. 2:2; MM). ἀμοιβή return, recompense (s. MM). ἀποδιδόναι pres. act. inf. to give back, to return, to render. Used w. the noun it means "to make a worthy requittal" (Guthrie). πρόγονος one born early or before, parents, forefather, ancestor (s. BAG). ἀπόδεκτος acceptable (s. 1 Tim. 2:3). ■ μεμονωμένη perf. pass. part. μονόω to leave alone, 5 pass. to be left alone. The perf. tense looks at the continual condition or state. ἤλπικεν perf. act. ind. ἐλπίζω to hope. The perf. tense and the prep. convey the meaning "has fixed her hope and keeps it in the direction of God" (RWP; Guthrie). προσμένει to remain w. something, to continue, to remain w., to abide in. The pres. tense emphasizes the continual action. δέησις request. ■ σπαταλῶσα pres. act. part. σπαταλάω to 6 live a luxurious life, to give one's self to pleasure. The word connotes abandonment to pleasure and comfort (Kelly; s. also James 5:5). ζῶσα pres. act. part. ζάω to live. The part. expresses contemporaneous action. τέθνηκεν perf. act. ind. ἀποθνήσκω to die, perf. to be dead. ■ παράγγελλε pres. act. imp. 7 παραγγέλλω to command, to instruct (s. 1 Tim. 1:3). ἀνεπίλημπτος without reproach, irreproachable (s. 1 Tim. 3:2). ὦσιν pres. subj. εἰμί. ■ ἰδίων one's own; i.e., the near relatives 8 (EGT). μάλιστα especially. οἰκεῖος household. It refers to the members of one's household and refers to one's immediate family circle (Guthrie; EGT). προνοεῖ pres. act. ind. προνοέω to think of beforehand, to provide for. The object of the verb is in the gen. (For examples in the papyri, s. MM; Preisigke.) ἤρνηται perf. mid. ind. ἀρνέομαι to deny. ἄπιστος unbeliever, gen. of comparison. χείρων comp. κακός bad, comp. worse. He is worse than an unbeliever because unbelievers perform the duty (both Jew and Gentile) and because he not only has the law of nature but the law of Christ to guide him (Lock; s. also JPFC II, 761; M, Ketuboth V, 8–9; Epictetus III, 18f.). ■ 9 καταλεγέσθω pres. pass imp. καταλέγω to write down in a list, to enroll. It is a t.t. for being placed on a recognized list or "catalogue" (Kelly). ἔλαττον adv. comp. "less than." ἔτος year. The gen. is gen. of comparison or gen. of quality (s. RG, 516; BD, 99). γεγονυῖα perf. act. part. fem. γίνομαι. The Jews con-

sider that becoming old began w. the 60th year and Orientals
regarded it as the time for retiring from the world for quiet
10 contemplation (SB, III, 653; Lock). ■ μαρτυρουμένη pres. pass.
part. μαρτυρέω to witness, to testify. ἐτεκνοτρόφησεν aor. act.
ind. τεκνοτροφέω to rear children. ἐξενοδόχησεν aor. act. ind.
ξενοδοχέω to welcome strangers, to show hospitality. ἔνιψεν
aor. act. ind. νίπτω to wash. The washing of the feet was a
service to visitors which occupied a great place in eastern hospitality. The mistress of the house would act as a servant to the
servants of God (Kelly; EGT). θλιβομένοις pres. pass. part.
θλίβω to put under pressure, to bring about distress, pass. to be
under pressure, to be in distress. ἐπήρκεσεν aor. act. ind.
ἐπαρκέω to help, to aid, to assist, to relieve. ἐπηκολούθησεν
aor. act. ind. ἐπακολουθέω to follow after. The prep. in compound is directive (MH, 312). The verbs in this v. are used in
first-class conditional clauses which assume the reality of the
11 condition. ■ παραιτοῦ pres. mid. imp. παραιτέομαι to decline, to refuse; i.e., to refuse to put on the list of widows entitled
to special guardianship and sustenance on the part of the
church (Fairbairn). ὅταν w. the subj. "when," "whenever."
καταστρηνιάσωσιν aor. act. subj. καταστρηνιάω to feel the
impulse of sexual desire, here "to feel sensuous impulses that
alienate from Christ" (RWP; BAG). γαμεῖν pres. act. inf. to
12 marry. ■ ἔχουσαι pres. act. part. κρίμα judgment. The meaning
is that the widows who forsook their sacred obligation in order
to marry would be deserving of censure, for such action would
amount to casting aside their first faith, i.e., their pledge of
service (Guthrie). ἠθέτησαν aor. act. ind. ἀθετέω to set aside,
13 to regard as void, to annul (s. Gal. 2:21). ■ ἅμα at the same time.
Used here in the phrase "but at the same time also" (BAG).
ἀργός not working, idle. μανθάνουσιν pres. act. ind. to learn.
The verb w. a substitutive denoting a profession or occupation
was an idiomatic construction signifying "to qualify as such and
such" (for example a doctor, wrestler, etc.) (Kelly).
περιερχόμεναι pres. mid. part. περιέρχομαι to go about, to go
around. The word may mean that the younger widows were
misusing their opportunities in visitation (Guthrie; s. also EGT).
φλύαρος gossipy, loose talkers; i.e., babbling out whatever
might come into their mind (Fairbairn). περίεργος over careful,
taking needless trouble, busybodies (Kelly). The word marks a
meddling habit, a perverted activity that will not content itself
w. minding its own concerns, but must busy itself about those of
others (Ellicott; s. also 2 Thess. 3:11). λαλοῦσαι pres. act. part.
δέοντα pres. act. part. τὰ δέοντα "things which are necessary"

w. the neg. "things which are not proper" (s. EGT). ■ βούλομαι 14
pres. mid. ind. to will, to desire. Jewish formal law and accepted
Jewish custom beyond any doubt agree that a widow's remarriage was both permissible and desirable and she was only required to wait long enough for it to be ascertained that she was
not already pregnant at the time of the second marriage. There
were, however, in Judaism some groups which considered a
widow's abstinence from remarriage to be a pious and proper act
(JPFC II, 787–788f.). τεκνογονεῖν pres. act. inf. to bear children. οἰκοδεσποτεῖν pres. act. inf. to rule over the house, to
manage the household, to be master of a house. ἀφορμή a
starting point, a base of operations, an occasion, opportunity
(AS; s. 2 Cor. 5:12). ἀντικειμένῳ pres. mid. part. ἀντίκειμαι
to lie against, to oppose, to be an adversary. λοιδορία abuse,
reproach, railing. χάριν prep. w. the gen. "on account of,"
"because of." ■ ἐξετράπησαν aor. pass. ind. ἐκτρέπομαι to 15
turn from, to go astray, to turn out of the true path (Lock).
ὀπίσω w. the gen. "after," "behind"; i.e., they follow behind or
after Satan (EGT). ■ ἐπαρκείτω pres. act. imp. 3rd per. sing. 16
to help, to assist, s.v.10. βαρείσθω pres. pass. imp. βαρέω to
burden, pass. to be burdened. The word is used of financial
burdens and refers here to financial support (Kelly). ἐπαρκέσῃ
aor. act. subj. to help, to assist, s.v.10.

■ καλῶς adv. "well." προεστῶτες perf. act. part. 17
προΐστημι to stand first, to rule. The word means general
superintendence, and describes the duties allotted to all presby-
ters (Guthrie). διπλοῦς double. τιμή honor (Schlatter), remu-
neration (Kelly; EGT). ἀξιούσθωσαν pres. pass. imp. ἀξιόω to
consider worthy, to hold as worthy. κοπιῶντες pres. act. part.
κοπιάω to work, to labor, to work until one is exhausted. λόγος
word; i.e., those who preach and teach (Guthrie). διδασκαλία
teaching, doctrine. ■ γραφή writing, Scripture (s. TDNT). βοῦς 18
ox, cow. ἀλοῶντα pres. act. part. ἀλοάω to thrash. φιμώσεις
fut. act. ind. φιμόω to muzzle (s. 1 Cor. 9:9). The fut. is used to
express a prohibition and is used in the legal language of the OT
almost always as a categorical imp. (BG, 94; s. also RWP).
ἐργάτης worker. μισθός wage, salary. ■ κατηγορία that 19
which is brought against someone, charge, legal accusation (s.
MM; Preisigke). παραδέχου pres. mid. imp. παραδέχομαι to
entertain. ἐκτὸς εἰ μή "except when" (s. BS, 118). ■ 20
ἁμαρτάνοντας pres. act. part. ἁμαρτάνω to miss the mark, to
sin. ἔλεγχε pres. act. imp. ἐλέγχω to bring to light, to expose,
to demonstrate or prove, to convince or convict someone, to
reprove, to correct. Here it may have connotation of refuting

(BAG). λοιπός remaining, rest. ἔχωσιν pres. act. subj. The subj.
21 is used in a purpose clause. ■ διαμαρτύρομαι to charge, to
charge solemnly, to declare solemnly. The prep. in compound
has the idea of "thoroughly" (MH, 302; s. also 1 Thess. 4:6).
ἐκλεκτός chosen, elect. ἵνα "that." It introduces the content of
Paul's charge to Timothy. φυλάξῃς aor. act. subj. φυλάσσω to
guard, to observe, to keep. πρόκριμα a judgment beforehand,
prejudice. ποιῶν pres. act. part. πρόσκλισις inclining toward,
22 partiality (RWP). ■ ταχέως quickly. ἐπιτίθει pres. act. imp.
ἐπιτίθημι to place upon, to lay "hands" upon. κοινώνει pres.
act. imp. κοινωνέω to have fellowship w., to participate.
ἀλλότριος belonging to another, not one's own. ἁγνός pure (s.
23 1 Tim. 4:12). τήρει pres. act. imp. τηρέω to keep. ■ μηκέτι no
longer. ὑδροπότει pres. act. imp. ὑδροποτέω to drink water.
The command to abstain from drinking water exclusively may
have been that contaminated water contributed to Timothy's
indigestion (Guthrie). Epictetus used the word in a positive command "drink only water" to show one's ability in restraint (Epictetus III, 13, 21). χρῶ pres. mid. imp. χράομαι to use.
στόμαχος stomach. πυκνός often, frequent, numerous.
ἀσθένεια sickness, weakness. (For the text of a memorandum
requesting the purchase of a jar of wine according to doctor's
orders, s. SP I, 396–397.)
24   ■ πρόδηλος clear, evident, openly plain, plain before all
(RWP). προάγουσαι pres. act. part. fem. προάγω to go before,
25 to go ahead. κρίσις judgment. ■ ὡσαύτως likewise. ἄλλως
otherwise. ἔχοντα pres. act. part.; i.e., "those having it otherwise" (RWP). κρυβῆναι aor. pass. inf. κρύπτω to hide.

Ch. 6

1   ■ ὅσοι as many as. The pron. indicates those who belong
to a particular class or group. ζυγός yoke. (For ancient discourses on slavery, s. DC X, XIV, XV; Seneca, *Epistle* 47; s. also
1 Cor. 7:21; Philemon 21.) δεσπότης master. ἡγείσθωσαν
pres. mid. imp. ἡγέομαι to consider, to reckon, to deem.
διδασκαλία teaching, doctrine. βλασφημῆται pres. pass.
2 subj. βλασφημέω to slander, to blaspheme. ■ ἔχοντες pres. act.
part. καταφρονείτωσαν pres. act. imp. καταφρονέω to think
down upon, to despise. The word means "to treat without the full
consideration due to the other man's station" (Kelly). The pres.
imp. w. the neg. is to prohibit a continual or habitual action (s.
MKG, 272f.). μᾶλλον comp. "rather," "more." The word is
intensive and indicates that the Christian master should be
served more; i.e., better (Ellicott; RWP). δουλευέτωσαν pres.

act. imp. ἀγαπητός beloved. εὐεργεσία working well, good service, good deed, benefit. The word refers to the human kindness not of the masters but of the slaves as shown by their better service (Lock). ἀντιλαμβανόμενοι pres. mid. part. ἀντιλαμβάνομαι to take part in, to devote one's self to, to practice. Here "those who devote themselves to kindness" (BAG).

διδάσκε pres. act. imp. παρακάλει pres. act. imp. παρακαλέω to encourage, to exhort. ■ ἐτεροδιδασκαλεῖ pres. 3 act. ind. to teach another doctrine, to teach a completely different doctrine, to teach a false or heretical doctrine (s. Fairbairn). προσέρχεται pres. mid. ind. to come to, to approach, to attach one's self to, to consent (Guthrie). The verbs in the ind. are used in a first-class conditional clause which assumes the reality of the condition. ὑγιαίνουσιν pres. act. part. ὑγιαίνω to be in good health, to be healthy, to be sound (s. 3 John 2). εὐσέβεια godliness (s. 1 Tim. 2:2; 4:7). ■ τετύφωται perf. pass. ind. τυφόω to 4 be puffed up, to be proud (s. 1 Tim. 3:6). ἐπιστάμενος pres. mid. part. ἐπίσταμαι to know, to understand. νοσῶν pres. act. part. νοσέω to be sick, to be ailing w., to have a morbid craving for something (BAG). The disease is intellectual curiosity about trifles (EGT). ζήτησις seeking, speculation. It denotes the preoccupation w. pseudo-intellectual theorizing (Kelly; s. also 1 Tim. 1:4). λογομαχία word war, strife of words. φθόνος envy. ἔρις strife. βλασφημία slander, blasphemy. ὑπόνοια suspicion, conjecture. The prep. in compound suggests the idea of thoughts making their way up into the mind (MH, 327). ■ 5 διαπαρατριβή a mutual rubbing or irritation alongside, protracted quarreling, persistent wrangling (RWP; EGT; Kelly; MH, 303). διεφθαρμένων perf. pass. part. διαφθείρω to corrupt. The perf. tense emphasizes the completed state or condition. νοῦς mind, understanding. ἀπεστερημένων perf. pass. part. ἀποστερέω to steal, to rob, to deprive. νομιζόντων pres. act. part. νομίζω to suppose. πορισμός means of gain. ■ 6 αὐτάρκεια contentment, self-sufficiency. The word was a t.t. in Gr. philosophy used to denote the wise man's independence of circumstances (Kelly; Dibelius; s. also Phil. 4:11). ■ 7 εἰσηνέγκαμεν aor. act. ind. εἰσφέρω to bring into. ἐξενεγκεῖν aor. act. inf. ἐκφέρω to carry out of. (For Jewish and Gentile parallels, s. Kelly; SB III, 655.) ■ ἔχοντες pres. act. part. 8 διατροφή food, nourishment. σκέπασμα that which covers, clothing. ἀρκεσθησόμεθα fut. pass. ind. ἀρκέω pass. = to be content, to be satisfied. The fut. probably has an imp. sense as used in the legal language of the OT (s. BG, 94; EGT). ■ 9 βουλόμενοι pres. mid. part. βούλομαι to will, to purpose. πλουτεῖν pres. act. inf. to be rich, to be wealthy, ἐμπίπτουσιν pres. act. ind. to fall into. The pres. tense indicates that which always or normally happens. πειρασμός temptation. παγίς snare, trap. ἐπιθυμία strong desire. ἀνόητος irrational (s. Gal. 3:1). βλαβερός harmful, injuring. βυθίζουσιν pres. act. ind. to drag to the bottom, to submerge, to drown. The verb is the image of drowning someone in the sea (Kelly; RWP). ὄλεθρος destruction. ἀπώλεια ruin. The two words are used in the sense of ruin and suggest irretrievable loss (Guthrie). ▪ ῥίζα root. The pred. nom. without the article emphasizes the character or quality (s. John 1:1). κακά evil. The pl. emphasizes evils of all kinds (Kelly). φιλαργυρία love of money. (For parallels to this proverbial saying, s. Lock; Kelly; Dibelius; 1 Tim. 3:8). ὀρεγόμενοι pres. mid. part. ὀρέγομαι to reach out after something, to desire something. The object is in the gen. (s. 1 Tim. 3:1). ἀπεπλανήθησαν aor. act. ind. ἀποπλανάω to lead astray. περιέπειραν aor. act. ind. περιπείρω to pierce completely (RWP).

11   ▪ φεῦγε pres. act. imp. φεύγω to flee. δίωκε pres. act. imp. διώκω to hunt, to pursue. ὑπομονή patience, endurance (s. 2 Thess. 1:4). πραϋπαθία gentleness, meekness (s. 2 Cor. 10:1;

12 Gal. 5:22). ▪ ἀγωνίζου pres. mid. imp. ἀγωνίζομαι to carry on a contest, to strive, to struggle, to fight. The word includes the effort put forth in the proclamation of the gospel (s. PAM, 178f.). ἀγών struggle, contest. In opposition to those who crave material riches, Timothy is to strive after righteousness, godliness, faith, love, patience, and meekness (PAM, 178). ἐπιλαβοῦ aor. mid. imp. ἐπιλαμβάνομαι to lay hold on, to get a good grip on (RWP). This does not appear as a fut. prize lying at the end of the Agon, but as that which is to be grasped and retained in the pres. Agon of faith (PAM, 179f.). ἐκλήθης aor. pass. ind. καλέω. ὡμολόγησας aor. act. ind. ὁμολογέω to agree to, to confess. ὁμολογία agreement, confession. It is the acknowledg-

13 ing of Jesus as the Messiah (ECC, 133). ▪ παραγγέλλω to instruct, to command, to charge (s. 1 Tim. 1:3). ζωογονοῦντος pres. act. part. ζωογονέω to give life to, to make alive. μαρτυρήσαντος aor. act. part. μαρτυρέω to give witness to, to

14 testify. ▪ τηρῆσαι aor. act. inf. τηρέω to keep. The inf. is used to express the object of the verb "charge" and is used in an indirect command (RWP). ἄσπιλος without spot. ἀνεπίλημπτος irreproachable (s. 1 Tim. 3:2). ἐπιφάνεια manifestation, appearance. The word was a t.t. in the language of contemporary Hellenistic religion for the self-disclosure of a god

or king (Kelly; s. also 2 Thess. 2:8). ■ καιρός time, season, 15 opportune time. δείξει fut. act. ind. δείκνυμι to show. μακάριος happy, blessed. δυνάστης potentate. The word was used of one who exercised sovereignty in his own power (Guthrie). βασιλευόντων pres. act. part. βασιλεύω to be a king, to rule as king. κυριευόντων pres. act. part. κυριεύω to be a lord, to rule as a lord. ■ ἀθανασία not able to die, immortality (s. BS, 16 293). οἰκῶν pres. act. part. οἰκέω to dwell. ἀπρόσιτος unapproachable (s. SB, III, 656). εἶδεν aor. act. ind. ὁράω. ἰδεῖν aor. act. inf. ὁράω. κράτος power (s. Eph. 1:19).

■ πλούσιος rich, wealthy. παράγγελλε pres. act. imp. (s. 17 1 Tim. 1:3). ὑψηλοφρονεῖν pres. act. inf. to think exalted, to think highly, to be proud and haughty. ἠλπικέναι perf. act. inf. ἐλπίζω to hope, perf. to place one's hope upon something or someone and rest there; i.e., "to have hope and continue to hope" (Ellicott). ἀδηλότης uncertainty. From the adj. meaning "unseen, unobserved, not manifest," "indistinct" (AS). παρέχοντι pres. act. part. παρέχω to give, to grant, to cause, to bring about something for someone (BAG). πλουσίως adv. richly. ἀπόλαυσις enjoying, enjoyment, pleasure. ■ 18 ἀγαθοεργεῖν pres. act. inf. to do that which is good, to do good works, to do deeds inherently noble and praiseworthy (Fairbairn). εὐμετάδοτος sharing well, generous, ready to impart (MM). κοινωνικός ready to share, giving or sharing generously (BAG; s. also MH, 378). ■ ἀποθησαυρίζοντας pres. act. part. 19 ἀποθησαυρίζω to store up, to amass a treasure. The prep. in compound indicates that the rich are exhorted to take "from" their own plenty, and by devoting it to the service of God and the relief of the poor actually to "treasure" it up as a good foundation for the future (Ellicott; s. also Kelly). θεμέλιος foundation. μέλλον pres. act. part. μέλλω to be about to. Here "for that which is coming," "for the future." ἐπιλάβωνται aor. mid. subj. ὄντως adv. (from the part. of εἰμί) truly (s. 1 Tim. 5:4).

■ παραθήκη that which is placed beside, deposit, trust. It 20 is a legal term connoting something which is placed on trust in another man's keeping (Kelly; s. also MM). φύλαξον aor. act. imp. φυλάσσω to guard. ἐκτρεπόμενος pres. mid. part. ἐκτρέπομαι to go out of the way, to turn away from. The part. describes the manner or means. βέβηλος that which is accessible to all, profane (s. 1 Tim. 4:7). κενοφωνία empty talking, uttering emptiness (RWP). ἀντίθεσις opposition, objection, contradiction. ψευδώνυμος falsely named. γνῶσις knowing, knowledge. ■ ἐπαγγελλόμενοι pres. mid. part. 21 ἐπαγγέλλομαι to announce, to proclaim, to profess (s. 1 Tim.

2:10). *ἠστόχησαν* aor. act. ind. *ἀστοχέω* to miss the mark, to fail, to deviate (s. 1 Tim. 1:6).

2 TIMOTHY

κατά "according to." It gives the standard by which God 1 chose him and to which his apostleship must be true (Lock). The prep. also denotes the object and intention of the appointment, "to further, to make known, the promise of eternal life" (Ellicott). ἐπαγγελία promise. ζωή life. The gen. gives the content of the promise. (For a study of the concept of eternal life, s. GW, 163–201; TDNT; CBB.) ἐν "in." The prep. indicates that the source and sphere of life is "in Christ Jesus." ■ ἀγαπητός 2 beloved. τέκνον child. ἔλεος mercy (s. 1 Tim. 1:2).

■ λατρεύω to serve. The word was used esp. of carrying out 3 religious duties particularly of a cultic nature and was used in the sense of worship (BAG; TDNT). The prcs. tense emphasizes the continual unbroken habit of life "I have been serving" (RWP). πρόγονος forcbearer. The statement must be understood to mean that Paul thought of Judaism in such close connection w. Christianity that his present worship of God is in a sense a continuation of his own Jewish worship (Guthrie). ἐν "in." The prep. is local and gives the spiritual sphere in which the worship was offered (Ellicott). συνείδησις conscience (s. Rom. 2:15; 1 Tim. 3:9). ἀδιάλειπτος without interruption, unceasing (s. 1 Thess. 1:2; 5:17; Josephus, *Wars*, V, 71; 279; 298). μνεία remembrance, mention (s. 1 Thess. 1:2). δέησις request, prayer. ■ ἐπιποθῶν pres. act. part. ἐπιποθέω to have a strong desire 4 for, to yearn after. The prep. in compound is directive (s. Phil. 1:8; 1 Thess. 3:6). ἰδεῖν aor. act. inf. ὁράω. μεμνημένος perf. mid. part. μιμνήσκομαι to remind one's self, to recall to mind, to remember. The perf. tense emphasizes the continuing state. δάκρυον tear. ἵνα "that." Introduces the purpose of Paul wanting to see Timothy (s. Kelly). πληρωθῶ aor. pass. subj. πληρόω to fill, pass. to be filled. ■ ὑπόμνησις remembering, reminder. 5 The word is used properly of an external reminder (Lock). λαβών aor. act. part. λαμβάνω. The phrase "having received a reminder" may suggest that Paul had just had news of Timothy (s. Guthrie). ἀνυπόκριτος without hypocrisy, genuine. It was a genuine principle, the opposite of a hypocritical or wavering

637

profession (Fairbairn). ἐνῴκησεν aor. act. ind. ἐνοικέω to live in, to dwell in (s. Col. 3:16). μάμμη grandmother. πέπεισμαι perf. pass. ind. πείθω to persuade, to be persuaded, perf. "I stand
6 persuaded" (RWP). ■ αἰτία cause, reason. ἀναμιμνήσκω pres. act. ind. to remind, to cause to remember. The prep. in compound is causative (MH, 295). ἀναζωπυρεῖν pres. act. inf. to stir up smoldering embers into a living flame, to keep at white heat (Lock). The word means either "to kindle afresh" or "to keep a full flame" (AS; s. also MH, 296; RWP). Paul's statement does not necessarily contain a censure since fire in the ancient world was never kept at a continual blaze but rather kept alive through glowing coals which were then rekindled to a flame by a bellows whenever the situation demanded flame (s. Schlatter; TDNT; OCD, 439; Lev. 6:9). χάρισμα gift, grace gift.
7 ἐπίθεσις laying on. ■ ἔδωκεν aor. act. ind. δίδωμι to give. δειλία cowardice, timidity. σωφρονισμός self-discipline, the power to keep one's self in hand, free from all excitement or
8 hesitation (Lock; s. also TDNT). ■ ἐπαισχυνθῇς aor. pass. subj. ἐπαισχύνομαι to be ashamed of. The aor. subj. is used w. a neg. to form a prohibition which is designed to prevent an action from arising (MKG, 273). μαρτύριον witness. δέσμιος prisoner. συγκακοπάθησον aor. act. imp. συγκακοπαθέω to suffer evil together, to take one's share of evil treatment (AS). The aor. imp. indicates that the action is to be done immediately (s.
9 MKG, 272). ■ σώσαντος aor. act. part. σῴζω to rescue, to save. καλέσαντος aor. act. part. καλέω. κλῆσις calling. ἴδιος one's own. πρόθεσις facing before, purpose (s. Eph. 1:11). δοθεῖσαν aor. pass. part. δίδωμι. αἰώνιος eternal. This may be a reference to the earliest promise of triumph to the woman's seed (Gen. 3:15), or to the grace of the preexistent Christ (Guth-
10 rie). ■ φανερωθεῖσαν aor. pass. part. φανερόω to make visible, to make clear, to manifest. ἐπιφάνεια manifestation, appearing (s. 1 Tim. 6:14; 2 Thess. 2:8; TDNT; Dibelius). Here are two thoughts of the divine intervention of a Savior in an hour of need and of the drawing of a new light (Lock). καταργήσαντος aor. act. part. καταργέω to render inoperative, to make inactive, to annul (s. Rom. 3:3; 1 Cor. 1:28; Gal. 3:17). μέν ... δέ "on the one hand ... on the other hand." The particles are ind. at one of connection and contrast (Fairbairn). φωτίσαντος aor. act. part. φωτίζω to illuminate, to flood w. light, to bring to light (Kelly). The two part. indicate the meaning or manner in which the manifestation was accomplished. ἀφθαρσία incorruptibili-
11 ty, immortality. ■ ἐτέθην aor. pass. ind. τίθημι to place, to appoint, to commission (s. 1 Tim. 2:7). κῆρυξ proclaimer, her-

ald, preacher (s. 1 Tim. 2:7). ■ καί "also." πάσχω pres. act. ind. 12
to suffer. The pres. tense indicates a continual action which was
going on at the pres. time. ᾧ "whom," dat. case of the rel. pron.
used as object of the verb but the antecedent is not expressed.
Paul knows Jesus Christ whom he has trusted (RWP).
πεπίστευκα perf. act. ind. to believe, to trust in. The word
literally means "to whom I have given my trust" and the perf.
tense indicates "in whom I have put my trust, and still do put
it" (Ellicott). παραθήκη that which is committed to another,
deposit. It is a legal term connoting something which one person
places on trust in another's keeping (Kelly; Lock, 90f.; s. also 1
Tim. 6:20). The word is best understood as that which God
entrusted to Paul and the present v. focuses attention on God's
ability to guard (Guthrie; Kelly). φυλάξαι aor. act. inf.
φυλάσσω to guard, to protect, to keep watch over, to keep
guard. (For references, s. LS; TDNT.) ■ ὑποτύπωσις model, 13
example. The word denotes an outline sketch or ground plan
used by an artist or in literature the rough draft forming the basis
of a fuller exposition (Kelly). ἔχε pres. act. imp. to have, to hold.
ὑγιαινόντων pres. act. part. ὑγιαίνω to be healthy, to be sound.
ἤκουσας aor. act. ind. ἀκούω to hear. ἐν "in." The prep. specifies the principles in which the example is to be held (Ellicott).
■ φύλαξον aor. act. imp. (s.v.12). ἐνοικοῦντος pres. act. part. 14
to dwell in.

■ ἀπεστράφησαν aor. pass. ind. ἀποστρέφομαι to turn 15
away from, to desert. The verb is a pass. deponent and has its
object in the acc. (s. RG, 484f.). ■ δῴη aor. act. opt. δίδωμι to 16
give, to grant. ἔλεος mercy (s.v.2). ἀνέψυξεν aor. act. ind.
ἀναψύχω to cool again, to refresh. The idea is that the presence
of his friend provided a special tonic (Guthrie; s. also RWP).
ἅλυσις chain. (For prisons and prison conditions in the ancient
world, s. RAC IX, 318–345.) ἐπαισχύνθη aor. pass. ind. (s.v.8).
■ γενόμενος aor. mid. part. γίνομαι to become, to be, to arrive. 17
The part. is temporal and means "when he arrived and was
there" (Ellicott). σπουδαίως adv. diligently, eagerly. ἐξήτησέν
aor. act. ind. ζητέω to seek, effective aor. (RWP). εὗρεν aor. act.
ind. ■ εὑρεῖν aor. act. inf. ὅσος as many as, which one, those 18
belonging to this class or group. διηκόνησεν aor. act. ind.
διακονέω to minister, to serve. βέλτιον adv. comp. ἀγαθός.
The word could be taken as a true comp. "better than I" (RG,
665) or it could have the meaning "very well" (s. BAG; BD,
127).

Ch. 2

1   ■ ἐνδυναμοῦ pres. pass. imp. ἐνδυναμόω to enpower,
pass. to be strong (s. Eph. 6:10). ἐν "in." The prep. is probably
2 instrumental "by means of" or "in the power of" (Kelly). ■
ἤκουσας aor. act. ind. ἀκούω. παράθου aor. mid. imp.
παρατίθημι to place to another's trust, to entrust, to deposit,
to commit for safe keeping (s. MM; for the noun, s. 1 Tim. 1:12).
ἱκανός that which reaches or arrives at a certain standard, sufficient, capable (s. GEW I, 719f.; TDNT; LS). ἔσονται fut. εἰμί.
3 διδάξαι aor. act. inf. to teach. ■ συγκακοπάθησον aor. act.
imp. συγκακοπαθέω to suffer evil together, to endure affliction
together, to take one's share of rough treatment (Kelly; s. also
4 2 Tim. 1:8). ■ στρατευόμενος pres. mid. part. στρατεύομαι
to be a soldier. (For a description of the life, training, and discipline of Roman soldiers, s. Josephus, *Jewish Wars*, III, 70–109.)
ἐμπλέκεται pres. mid. ind. ἐμπλέκω to entangle, mid. to entangle one's self. The word pictures a soldier's weapon entram-
melled in his cloak (Guthrie). πραγματεία affairs, pursuits. The
soldier does not let himself get involved in the preoccupation
of civil life (Kelly). As applied to ministers this command
requires wholehearted devotion to their work (Lock).
στρατολογήσαντι aor. act. part. to enlist soldiers. It was the
general's duty to see that his soldiers were well equipped and
provided w. food and shelter (s. DC III, 67f.). ἀρέσῃ aor. act.
subj. ἀρέσκω to please. The Christian "soldier" has only one
goal and purpose—wholehearted devotion to the given task in
the effort to please his Lord (PAM, 169). The subj. is used in a
5 purpose clause. ■ ἀθλῇ pres. act. subj. ἀθλέω to compete in a
contest. στεφανοῦται pres. pass. ind. στεφανόω to crown one
w. a victor's crown. νομίμως adv. lawfully. There was need for
the athlete's adherence to the laws of the contest and he was not
allowed to lighten his struggle by bypassing the rules. When
applied to Timothy this meant that he as an athlete of Christ
must also be prepared to suffer. The word also contains rejection
of the heretics who do not "contend lawfully" (PAM, 170f.).
6 ἀθλήσῃ aor. act. subj. ■ κοπιῶντα pres. act. part. κοπιάω to
work, to work until one is exhausted. γεωργός farmer (s. 1 Cor.
9:7). δεῖ (w. the acc. and the inf.) it is necessary.
7 μεταλαμβάνειν pres. act. inf. to partake, to share. ■ νόει pres.
act. imp. νοέω to understand, to think over, to consider; i.e.,
"work out what I am getting at" (Kelly). δώσει fut. act. ind.
δίδωμι. σύνεσις insight, understanding.
8   ■ μνημόνευε pres. act. imp. μνημονεύω to remember, to
call to memory. ἐγηγερμένον perf. pass. part. ἐγείρω to rise,

pass. to be raised. The perf. tense points to the continual state; i.e., he was raised and continues to live. Timothy was to remember not just the mere fact of the Resurrection, but was to keep Him in mind as a living, risen Lord who is able to give His life to the believer (s. Lock). ■ κακοπαθῶ pres. act. ind. to suffer 9 trouble. The pres. tense emphasizes that which is continually taking place. δεσμῶν bond. κακοῦργος evil worker, criminal. The word is used for the criminals who were crucified alongside Jesus (Luke 23:32f.), and in technical legal parlance it was reserved for burglars, murderers, traitors, and the like (Kelly). δέδεται perf. pass. ind. δέω to bind. The perf. emphasizes that the Word of God is not bound; i.e., "has not been and is not now bound" (Ellicott). ■ ὑπομένω pres. act. ind. to remain under, to 10 endure, to endure patiently (s. 1 Thess. 1:3). ἐκλεκτός elected, chosen. τύχωσιν aor. act. subj. τυγχάνω followed by the gen. to reach, to obtain. The subj. is used in a purpose clause. ■ 11 πιστός faithful, trustworthy. συναπεθάνομεν aor. act. ind. συναποθνήσκω to die together. The ind. is used in a first-class conditional clause which accepts the condition as a reality. συζήσομεν fut. act. ind. συζάω to live together, to live w. someonc. ■ συμβασιλεύσομεν fut. act. ind. συμβασιλεύω to 12 be king together, to rule w. someone. ἀρνησόμεθα fut. mid. ind. ἀρνέομαι to deny. ■ ἀπιστοῦμεν pres. act. ind. ἀπιστέω to 13 be unfaithful, to be untrustworthy. (For the alpha pref., s. Moorhouse, 47ff.) μένει pres. act. ind. to remain. ἀρνήσασθαι aor. act. inf.

■ ὑπομίμνησκε pres. act. imp. ὑπομιμνήσκω to call to 14 remembrance, to remind someone of something. διαμαρτυρόμενος pres. mid. part. διαμαρτύρομαι to solemnly charge someone (s. 1 Tim. 5:21). λογομαχεῖν pres. act. inf. to wage a word war. The inf. is used to give the content of the charge and the pres. tense w. the neg. could indicate the stopping of an action in progress or it could prohibit the carrying on of such an action. χρήσιμος useful. καταστροφή turning against, overturning, subverting, demoralizing (Kelly). ἀκουόντων pres. act. part. The gen. is objective gen. ■ 15 σπούδασον aor. act. imp. σπουδάζω to give diligence. The word contains the notion of persistent "zeal" (Guthrie). δόκιμος approved after examination or testing (s. TDNT; BS, 259–262; MM; Preisigke). παραστῆσαι aor. act. inf. παρίστημι to stand alongside of, to present. ἐργάτης worker. ἀνεπαίσχυντος not being ashamed, having no occasion to be ashamed of (Fairbairn). ὀρθοτομοῦντα pres. act. part. ὀρθοτομέω to cut along a straight line, to cut a straight road.

The metaphor could be that of plowing a straight furrow or of a road maker driving his road straight or of a mason squaring and cutting a stone to fit in its proper place or the cutting of a sacrifice or food for household use (s. Lock; EGT; Kelly; MM).

16 ▪ βέβηλος available for everyone, profane (s. 1 Tim. 4:7). κενοφωνία empty or vain talking. In the ancient world useless talking was considered to be caused from a sickness of the soul and demonstrated itself either in the quantity or quality of the speech (s. RAC X, 829–837). περιῖστασο pres. act. imp. περιῖστημι to shift around, to avoid, to shun (s. MH, 231). ἐπὶ πλεῖον "fair the more"; i.e., "they will arrive at an ever greater measure of godlessness"; i.e., become more and more deeply involved in godlessness (BAG). προκόψουσιν fut. act. ind. προκόπτω to set before, to advance, to make progress (s. Gal.

17 1:14). ἀσέβεια godlessness (s. TDNT). ▪ γάγγραινα gangrene, cancer, spreading ulcer. It is a disease by which any part of the body suffering from inflammation becomes so corrupted that unless a remedy be seasonably applied, the evil continually spreads, attacks other parts, and at last eats away at the bones (T). The metaphor illustrates insidiousness and nothing could more suitably describe the manner of advancement of most false teachings, whether ancient or modern (Guthrie). νομή pasture, grazing, feeding. It is used of a spreading sore (AS). ἕξει fut. act. ind. ἔχω. The true thought is "will spread further into the church

18 and corrupt others" (Lock). ▪ ἠστόχησαν aor. act. ind. ἀστοχέω to miss the mark, to go astray (s. 1 Tim. 1:6; 6:21). γεγονέναι perf. act. inf. γίνομαι. The inf. is used in indirect discourse. ἀνατρέπουσιν pres. act. ind. to over turn, to upset,

19 to break down, to ruin (s. MM). ▪ μέντοι however. The particle gives a strong adversitive sense (RWP; Blomqvist, 27). στερεός solid, hard, firm, steadfast, strong (s. BAG). θεμέλιος foundation. ἕστηκεν perf. act. ind. ἵστημι to stand, perf. to remain standing. ἔχων pres. act. part. σφραγίς seal. The illusion is to the practice of placing on a building, or its foundation stone, an inscription or other sign to indicate its owner's purpose (Kelly). ἔγνω aor. act. ind. γινώσκω (s. ND, 344ff.). ὄντας pres. part. εἰμί. ἀποστήτω aor. act. imp. 3rd per. sing. ἀφίστημι to depart, to leave, "let everyone stand off from" (RWP). The aor. tense calls for a definite break. ἀδικία unrighteousness.

20 ὀνομάζων pres. act. part. ὀνομάζω to name. ▪ σκεῦος vessel. χρυσοῦς golden. ἀργυροῦς silver. ξύλινος wooden. The suf. of the adj. signifies material (MH, 359; s. also MH, 378). ὀστράκινος made out of clay, earthenware, pottery. ἀτιμία

21 dishonor. ▪ ἐκκαθάρῃ aor. act. subj. ἐκκαθαίρω to clean out,

to cleanse completely. The purging out relates either to the false teachers or it denotes inward purification (Guthrie). ἔσται fut. εἰμί. ἡγιασμένον perf. pass. part. ἁγιάζω to separate, to sanctify, to set apart for holy use (s. TDNT; CBB). The perf. tense looks at the completed state or condition. εὔχρηστος for good use, useful. δεσπότης master, ruler, lord. The term denotes absolute ownership and uncontrolled power (T). ἡτοιμασμένον perf. pass. part. ἑτοιμάζω to prepare. ■ 22 νεωτερικός youthful, that which pertains to youth. (For the suf., s. MH, 378.) ἐπιθυμία strong desire, passion. φεῦγε pres. act. imp. φεύγω to flee. The pres. imp. calls for a continuous action which indicates a habit of life and could have an interat. force. δίωκε pres. act. imp. διώκω to pursue. εἰρήνη peace. ἐπικαλουμένων pres. mid. part. ἐπικαλέω to call upon. ■ 23 μωρός foolish, stupid. ἀπαίδευτος without discipline, without training, uninstructed, uneducated (s. BAG). ζήτησις questioning, speculation. παραιτοῦ pres. mid. imp. παραιτέομαι to refuse, to reject. εἰδώς perf. act. part. οἶδα. γεννῶσιν pres. act. ind. to give birth to, to produce. The pres. tense points to that which happens continually. μάχη fight, strife. ■ μάχεσθαι 24 pres. mid. inf. to fight. The word was generally used of armed combatants, or those who engage in hand-to-hand struggle. It was then used of those who engage in a war of words, i.e., "to quarrel, to wrangle, to dispute" (T). ἤπιος gentle. διδακτικός skillful in teaching (s. 1 Tim. 3:2). ἀνεξίκακος bearing up w. evil, ready to put up w. evil, patient of wrong. The word denotes an attitude of patient forbearance toward those who are in opposition (Guthrie; Kelly; Ellicott; RWP). ■ πραΰτης meekness, 25 gentle, submissiveness. It denotes the humble and gentle attitude which expresses itself in particular in a patient submissiveness to offense, free from malice and desire for revenge (s. 2 Cor. 10:1). παιδεύοντα pres. act. part. παιδεύω to train, to train by discipline, to instruct. ἀντιδιατιθεμένους pres. mid. part. ἀντιδιατίθημι to place one's self in opposition, to oppose (s. MH, 297). μήποτε "if perhaps," "in the hope that" (Ellicott; s. also BD, 188). δώῃ aor. act. opt. δίδωμι. The problematic construction may mean "it may be that he will give" (IBG, 157; s. also MT, 129; BD, 118; RWP). μετάνοια change of mind, change of attitude, repentance (Kelly; s. also TDNT; CBB). ἐπίγνωσις recognition, acknowledgment, knowledge. ■ 26 ἀνανήψωσιν aor. act. subj. ἀνανήφω to sober up, to return to sobriety, to return to one's senses. The metaphor implies some previous duping by evil influences as in the case of intoxication; the devil's method is "to numb the conscience, confuse the

senses and paralyze the will" (Guthrie; s. also Kelly). παγίς
snare, trap. ἐζωγρημένοι perf. pass. part. ζωγρέω to capture
alive, to make captive.

Ch. 3

1 ■ γίνωσκε pres. act. imp. i.e., "recognize," "realize"
(Lock). ἔσχατος last. ἐνστήσονται fut. mid. ind. ἐνίστημι to
stand on, to be at hand, to set in (RWP; Ellicott). καιρός period
of time, season, a particular time. χαλεπός difficult, dangerous.
It is not merely the outward dangers that might be involved, but
the evils that mark them (Ellicott; for the Jewish teaching and
description of the difficulties of the last times, s. SB IV, 977–
2 1015.) ■ ἔσονται fut. εἰμί. φίλαυτος lover of one's self, self-
loving. φιλάργυρος money loving. ἀλαζών bragger, boaster. It
is one who brags and boasts about his accomplishments and in
his boasting he overpasses the limits of truth and stresses the fact
to magnify himself in his attempt to impress men (s. MNTW,
38–42; Trench, *Synonyms*, 98–102; TDNT). ὑπερήφανος
haughty, arrogant, one who shows himself above his fellow
(Trench, *Synonyms*, 101f.; TDNT). βλάσφημος abusive
speech, slanderer. γονεῖς parents. ἀπειθής disobedient.
ἀχάριστος not thankful, ungrateful. ἀνόσιος unholy, wicked
3 (s. 1 Tim. 1:9). ■ ἄστοργος unloving, without family affection,
without love of kindred, destitute of love toward those for whom
nature herself claims it. The verb without the neg. pref. denotes
primarily and properly the love between parents and children
(Ellicott; s. also AS). ἄσπονδος without a truth, irreconcilable.
It denotes a hostility that admits of no truce (Guthrie). The word
denotes a man who cannot bring himself to come to terms w.
other people (Kelly; s. also Trench, *Synonyms*, 193f.). διάβολος
slanderer, "setters at variant." These are those who promote
quarrels in hope that they may gain from them (Lock). ἀκρατής
without power, without self-control; i.e., w. respect to both their
tongue and to their appetite and everything else (EGT).
ἀνήμερος not tamed, uncivilized, fear, savage. ἀφιλάγαθος
4 without laws for good, haters of good. ■ προδότης traitor, betrayer. The word was used of one who betrays his country or one
who is a traitor to his oath or one who abandons another in
danger (LS; s. also MH, 323). προπετής one who falls before
or ahead, hasty, reckless, one who is ready to precipitate matters
by hasty speech or action (Fairbairn; s. also Lock).
τετυφωμένοι perf. pass. part. τυφόω to fill w. smoke, to be
conceited (s. 1 Tim. 3:6; 6:4). φιλήδονος pleasure lover.
5 μᾶλλον rather. φιλόθεος God lover. ■ ἔχοντες pres. act. part.

μόρφωσις shaping, bringing into shape, embodiment, outline, outward form, resemblance (LS; BAG). εὐσέβεια reverence of God, godliness (s. 1 Tim. 2:2). ἠρνημένοι perf. mid. part. ἀρνέομαι to deny. The word involves always more than an act of the mind; it means carrying the ligation into practice (EGT). καί. The word seems here to retain its proper force by specifying those particularly who were to be avoided (Ellicott). ἀποτρέπου pres. mid. imp. ἀποτρέπομαι to turn from, to turn one's self away from. The verb is a strong one, implying that Timothy is to avoid them w. horror (Kelly). ■ ἐνδύνοντες pres. 6 act. part. ἐνδύνω to enter in, to creep in, to run one's way in. The word implies insidious method (Guthrie). αἰχμαλωτίζοντες pres. act. part. αἰχμαλωτίζω to take captive at spear point, to make a prisoner of war, to capture. The word denotes here "getting complete possession of" (Huther). γυναικάριον little woman, silly or idle woman. The word is a diminutive and expresses contempt (Fairbairn). σεσωρευμένα perf. pass. part. σωρεύω to heap or pile up, to overwhelm. The perf. tense emphasizes the continual state or condition. ἀγόμενα pres. pass. part. ἄγω to lead, to drive. ἐπιθυμία strong desire, lust. The dat. is instrumental used w. the pass. ποικίλος many-colored, variegated, various, diversified. ■ πάντοτε always. 7 μανθάνοντα pres. act. part. The part. refers to the women who apparently desired to listen to other people's advice, but their mind had become so fickle and warped that they had become incapable of obtaining the knowledge of the truth (Guthrie). μηδέποτε never. ἐπίγνωσις recognition, knowledge (s. Col. 1:9; Eph. 1:17). ἐλθεῖν aor. act. inf. ἔρχομαι. δυνάμενα pres. mid. part. ■ τρόπος manner, adverbial acc. "in which manner" 8 (RWP). ἀντέστησαν aor. act. ind. ἀνθίστημι to stand against, to withstand, to oppose (s. Acts 13:8). οὕτως so. It refers rather to the degree of their hostility than to the manner in which it was expressed (EGT). κατεφθαρμένοι perf. pass. part. καταφθείρω to corrupt, to corrupt completely, to ruin, pass. to be perverted, to be depraved (BAG; for examples in the papyri, s. also MM). νοῦς mind, understanding. ἀδόκιμος rejected after trial, disqualified (s. 1 Cor. 9:27). πίστις faith. (For Jewish references concerning Jannes and Jambres, s. SB III, 660–664; s. also CD 5:18; ZPEB III, 403–405.) ■ προκόψουσιν fut act. 9 ind. προκόπτω to cut before, to make progress, to advance (s. 2 Tim. 2:16). ἐπὶ πλεῖον "farther, very far" (Lock; s. also 2 Tim. 2:16). ἄνοια without understanding, foolishness, faithlessness. ἔκδηλος clear, evident, very clear. The prep. in compound is defective (s. MH, 311). ἔσται fut. εἰμί. ἐγένετο aor. mid. ind. γίνομαι.

10 ■ παρηκολούθησας aor. act. ind. παρακολουθέω to follow along, to follow closely, to accompany. The word is also a t.t. defining the relation of a disciple to his master; i.e., "study at close quarter," "follow in spirit," "carefully note w. a view to reproducing," and so "take as an example" (Kelly). διδασκαλία teaching, doctrine. ἀγωγή the way one leads his life, manner of life, the word denotes general behavior, which a man's closest associate can never fail to know in all its aspects (Guthrie). πρόθεσις purpose; i.e., the guiding motive of his life and work (Kelly). μακροθυμία longsuffering, patient endurance (s. Gal. 5:22; Rom. 2:4). ὑπομονή bearing under, patience, patient and hopeful endurance (s. 2 Thess. 1:4; RAC IX, 243–

11 294). ■ διωγμός persecution. πάθημα that which is suffered, suffering. οἷος which kind, which sort of. ὑπήνεγκα aor. act. ind. ὑποφέρω to bear by being under, to carry or be under a heavy load, to hold out, to endure. (For examples, s. LS; 1 Cor.

12 10:13.) ἐρρύσατο aor. mid. ind. ῥύομαι to rescue. ■ καί ... δέ "but even," "yea and" (Ellicott). θέλοντες pres. act. part. to desire, to want to, to wish. ζῆν pres. act. inf. to live. εὐσεβῶς adv. godly, Godfearingly. It denotes living in the right attitude to God and to things divine. It can sometimes have the meaning of loyalty or true religion (s. MNTW, 66–76; 1 Tim. 2:2). διωχθήσονται fut. pass. ind. διώκω to hunt, to follow after, to

13 persecute. ■ γόης one who gives incantations by howling, one who practices magic art, sorcerer, swindler, cheat (Ellicott; BAG). χείρων comp. worse. πλανῶντες pres. act. part. πλανάω to lead astray, to deceive. πλανώμενοι pres. pass.

14 part. ■ μένε pres. act. imp. μένω to remain. The pres. imp. calls for a constant and continual habit of life. ἔμαθες aor. act. ind. μανθάνω to learn. ἐπιστώθης aor. pass. ind. πιστόω to make reliable, pass. to be assured of, to be convinced of (s. RWP).

15 εἰδώς perf. act. part. οἶδα (s. ND, 344ff.). ■ ὅτι "that." It introduces the object of the verb "to know" and presents a second fact which Timothy was to take into consideration (Ellicott). βρέφος child. The Jewish parents' duty was to teach their children the law when in their fifth year (Lock; s. also M, Aboth 5:21; SB III, 664–666). ἱερός sacred. The term τὰ ἱερὰ γράμματα is the name for the Holy Scriptures of the OT which was used among Gr.-speaking Jews (Dibelius; but s. also Guthrie; Lock). τὰ δυνάμενα pres. mid. part. to be able "which are able." σοφίσαι aor. act. inf. σοφίζω to impart wisdom, to make

16 wise. ■ γραφή writing, Scripture (s. TDNT; Schlatter; Guthrie).

θεόπνευστος God-breathed, breathed into by God, inspired. The rabbinical teaching was that the Spirit of God rested on and in the prophets and spoke through them so that their words did not come from themselves, but from the mouth of God and they spoke and wrote in the Holy Spirit. The early church was in entire agreement with this view (s. Kelly; SB IV, 435–451; ZPEB III, 286–293; TDNT; Schlatter; Gerhard Delling, "Die biblische Prophetie bei Josephus," JS 109–121). ὠφέλιμος profitable. ἐλεγμός proving, convicting, reproof; i.e., for refuting error and rebuking sin (Kelly; Lock). ἐπανόρθωσις setting up straight in addition, setting right, correction. It is the setting upright on their feet (Lock; for example in the papyri, s. MM; Preisigke). παιδεία training, instruction, discipline. ■ ἄρτιος fit, complete, 17 capable, sufficient; i.e., able to meet all demands (BAG). ᾖ subj. εἰμί. The subj. is used in a purpose clause. ἐξηρτισμένος perf. pass. part. ἐξαρτίζω completely outfitted, fully furnished, fully equipped, fully supplied. The word was used of documents which were completely outfitted or of a wagon which was completely outfitted or of a completely outfitted rescue boat. (For these and other examples, s. MM; Preisigke; LS.) The prep. in compound is effective (s. MH, 308ff.).

Ch. 4

■ διαμαρτύρομαι pres. mid. ind. to solemnly charge (s. 1 1 Tim. 5:21). μέλλοντος pres. act. part. μέλλω to be about to. The word was used w. the inf. to express a durative fut. (s. MKG, 307). κρίνειν pres. act. inf. ζῶντας pres. act. part. ζάω to live. ἐπιφάνεια appearance, manifestation. The word was used in reference to the appearance of a god (s. 1 Tim. 6:14; 2 Thess. 2:8). ■ κήρυξον aor. act. imp. to proclaim as a herald, to preach 2 (s. 1 Tim. 2:7). ἐπίστηθι aor. pass. imp. ἐφίστημι to take one's stand, to stand by, to be at hand. The word was also used in a military sense; i.e., "to stay at one's post," but here it means "to be at one's task" and indicates that the Christian minister must always be on duty (Kelly; Guthrie). εὐκαίρως adv. well-timed, suitably, conveniently; i.e., when it is convenient (BAG). ἀκαίρως not well-timed, inconveniently; i.e., when it is inconvenient (BAG). ἔλεγξον aor. act. imp. ἐλέγχω to prove w. demonstrative evidence, to convict, to reprove. It is so to rebuke another, w. such effectual feeling of the victorious arms of the truth, as to bring one, if not always to a confession, yet at least to a conviction, of sin (Trench, Synonyms, 13; s. also TDNT). ἐπιτίμησον aor. act. imp. ἐπιτιμάω to rebuke. The word denotes in the NT usage the idea of censure and sharp rebuke (Guthrie; Trench, Synonyms, 13; TDNT; s. also Matt. 17:18).

παρακάλεσον aor. act. imp. *παρακαλέω* to urge, to encourage, to exhort, to admonish (s. 1 Thess. 4:1; Rom. 12:1). *μακροθυμία* longsuffering, patient endurance (s. Gal. 5:22).

3 ■ *ἔσται* fut. *εἰμί*. *καιρός* season, period of time. *ὑγιαινούσης* pres. act. part. *ὑγιαίνω* to be well, to be in good health, to be sound. *διδασκαλία* teaching, doctrine. *ἀνέξονται* fut. mid. ind. *ἀνέχομαι* to bear up, to endure, to put up w. *ἐπιθυμία* strong desire, lust. *ἐπισωρεύσουσιν* fut. act. ind. *ἐπισωρεύω* to pile upon, to heap upon (s. 2 Tim. 3:7). *κνηθόμενοι* pres. mid. part. *κνήθομαι* to tickle, to scratch, to itch, pass. to feel an itching. It is used fig. of curiosity that looks for interesting and spicy bits of information. This itching is relieved by the messages of the new teachers (BAG; s. also MM). *ἀκοή* hearing, ear, acc. of general reference; i.e., "being tickled in reference to their

4 hearing" (Kelly). ■ *ἀποστρέψουσιν* fut. act. ind. *ἀποστρέφω* to turn away from. *μῦθος* myth (s. 1 Tim. 1:4). *ἐκτραπήσονται* fut. pass. ind. *ἐκτρέπομαι* to turn away from, to turn aside from

5 (s. 1 Tim. 1:6). ■ *νῆφε* pres. act. imp. *νήφω* to be sober; i.e., to be in a vigilant, wakeful considerate frame of mind taking good heed to what is proceeding around and pursuing its course w. calm and steady aim (Fairbairn). *κακοπάθησον* aor. act. imp. *κακοπαθέω* to suffer evil, to suffer hardship (s. 2 Tim. 1:8; 2:3). *ἔργον* work, activity. *ποίησον* aor. act. imp. *εὐαγγελιστής* one who proclaims the good news, evangelist. The word was found on a non-Christian inscription w. the meaning "a proclaimer of oracle" (TDNT). The word, however, occurs primarily of those who preach the gospel (TDNT; s. also PGL). *διακονία* ministry, service. *πληροφόρησον* aor. act. imp. *πληροφορέω* to carry full, to make full, to fulfill, to accomplish (s. LAE, 86f.).

6 ■ *σπένδομαι* pres. pass. ind. to offer, to pour out as a drink offering (s. Phil. 2:17; Kelly). *ἀνάλυσις* lifting up, departure. The word is used as a euphemism for death and evokes the picture of a ship weighing anchor or of a soldier or traveler striking camp (Kelly). *ἐφέστηκεν* perf. act. ind. *ἐφίστημι* to be

7 present, to be at hand (s.v.2). ■ *ἀγών* struggle, fight. *ἠγώνισμαι* perf. mid. ind. *ἀγωνίζομαι* to struggle, to exert effort (s. PAM, 182ff.). The perf. tense conveys a sense of finality (Guthrie). *δρόμος* foot race, race (s. PAM, 183f.). *τετέλεκα* perf. act. ind. *τελέω* to finish, to complete, to arrive at the goal. *τετήρηκα* pres. act. ind. *τηρέω* to keep. The expression indi-

8 cates "to remain faithful or true" (PAM, 183.). ■ *λοιπόν* finally. *ἀπόκειται* pres. pass. ind. to be laid away (RWP). The word appeared not only in an athletic context, but was also used of the

award made to loyal subjects by oriental sovereigns for services rendered (Guthrie; s. also Dibelius; Kelly). This, however, is not the certainty of the man who now looks forward to the reward which he has merited. It is rather the certainty of faith and hope (PAM, 184). ἀπόδωσει fut. act. ind. ἀποδίδωμι to give, to give back, to recompense. The prep. in compound does not necessarily convey any sense of due. Here the prep. only seems to allude to the reward as having been laid up and being taken, so to say, out of some reserve treasure (Ellicott). ἠγαπηκόσι perf. act. part. ἀγαπάω to love.

■ σπούδασον aor. act. imp. σπουδάζω to make haste, to 9 be zealous or eager, to give diligence, to do one's best (AS; Kelly; s. also 2 Tim. 2:15). ἐλθεῖν aor. act. inf. ἔρχομαι. ταχέως adv. quickly. ■ ἐγκατέλιπεν aor. act. ind. ἐγκαταλείπω to aban- 10 don, to desert, to leave one in lurch, to forsake. ἀγαπήσας aor. act. part. ἐπορεύθη aor. pass. ind. πορεύομαι to travel. ■ 11 ἀναλαβών aor. act. part. ἀναλαμβάνω to take up, to pick up (RWP). ἄγε pres. act. imp. ἄγω to lead, to take, to bring. εὔχρηστος useful, serviceable (Guthrie). ■ ἀπέστειλα aor. act. 12 ind. ἀποστέλλω to send. ■ φαιλόνης cloak. It was a large, 13 sleeveless outer garment made of a single piece of heavy material w. a hole in the middle through which the head was passed. It was used for protection against cold and rain, particularly in traveling. It may have been that Paul felt the need of it because winter was at hand and his dungeon was cold (Kelly; s. also DGRA, 848). ἀπέλιπον aor. act. ind. ἀπολείπω to leave behind. φέρε pres. act. imp. φέρω to carry, to bring. βιβλίον book. μάλιστα especially. μεμβράνα parchment, pergamena. The word denotes a piece of skin or vellum prepared for writing purposes and was a t.t. for a codex or leaf book made of parchment (Kelly). Paul mave have been referring to OT Scriptures (s. Charles C. Ryrie, "Especially the Parchments," Bib Sac 117 [July, 1960], 246f.). ■ χαλκεύς one who works w. copper, cop- 14 persmith, smith. The word does not mean that he only worked in copper. The term came also to be used of workers in any kind of metal (EGT). ἐνεδείξατο aor. mid. ind. ἐνδείκνυμι to show, to demonstrate, to do something to someone. ἀποδώσει fut. act. ind. ἀποδίδωμι to give back. ■ φυλάσσου pres. mid. imp. 15 φυλάσσω to guard, mid. to guard one's self, to be on one's guard. λίαν greatly, violently. ἀντέστη aor. act. ind. ἀνθίστημι to stand against, to oppose.

■ ἀπολογία legal defense. παρεγένετο aor. mid. ind. 16 παραγίνομαι to be alongside of, to stand by, to support. The verb is technical for a witness or advocate standing forward in

court on a prisoner's behalf (Kelly). λογισθείη aor. pass. opt.
λογίζομαι to reckon, to place to one's account. The opt. is used
17 to express a wish. ■ παρέστη aor. act. ind. παρίστημι to stand
by one's side. ἐνεδυνάμωσεν aor. act. ind. ἐνδυναμόω to empower, to strengthen. κήρυγμα proclamation, that which is proclaimed or preached. πληροφορηθῇ aor. pass. subj. (s.v.5).
ἀκούσωσιν aor. act. subj. ἐρρύσθην aor. pass. ind. ῥύομαι to
rescue. στόμα mouth. λέων lion. (For a discussion of the prob-
18 lems involved in the words of Paul, s. Guthrie.) ■ ῥύσεται fut.
mid. πονηρός evil, active evil. σώσει fut. act. ind. σῴζω to
save, to rescue. ἐπουράνιος heavenly (s. Eph. 1:3).
19/20   ■ ἄσπασαι aor. mid. imp. ἀσπάζομαι to greet. ■ ἔμεινεν
aor. act. ind. μένω to remain. ἀπέλιπον aor. act. ind. (s.v.13).
ἀσθενοῦντα pres. act. part. ἀσθενέω to be weak, to be sick.
21 ■ σπούδασον aor. act. imp. (s.v.9). χειμών winter. ἐλθεῖν aor.
act. inf.

TITUS

κατά "according to," i.e., "for (the furtherance of) the faith 1 of God's elect" (Ellicott). ἐκλεκτός chosen, elect. ἐπίγνωσις recognition, knowledge (s. Col. 1:9; Eph. 1:17). εὐσέβεια godliness, reverence for God (s. 1 Tim. 2:2). ■ ἐπί for, based upon. 2 The prep. suggests that such hope is the basis on which the superstructure of Christian service is built (Guthrie). ἐπηγγείλατο aor. mid. ind. ἐπαγγέλλω mid. to promise. ἀψευδής not a liar, one who does not lie. (For the negating pref., s. Moorhouse, 47ff.) ■ ἐφανέρωσεν aor. act. ind. φανερόω to 3 make clear, to manifest. καιρός time, season of time, opportune time. ἴδιος one's own. κήρυγμα that which is proclaimed, proclamation. ἐπιστεύθην aor. pass. ind., pass. to entrust. ἐπιταγή command (s. 1 Tim. 1:1). ■ γνήσιος legitimate, true (s. 1 Tim. 4 1:2). κοινός common, that which all share in.

■ χάριν prep. w. the gen. "because of," "on account of." 5 ἀπέλιπόν aor. act. ind. ἀπολείπω to leave behind. λείποντα pres. act. part. λείπω to leave; i.e., "the things remaining," "the things that are lacking." ἐπιδιορθώσῃ aor. mid. subj. ἐπιδιορθόω to set straight thoroughly in addition to, to set in order. (For the prep. in compound, s. RWP; MH, 313.) καταστήσῃς aor. act. subj. καθίστημι to appoint (s. Acts 6:3). πρεσβυτέρους elder. διεταξάμην aor. mid. ind. διατάσσομαι to give orders to, to appoint, to arrange, to ordain (s. 1 Cor. 11:34). ■ ἀνέγκλητος without indictment, un- 6 chargeable, above reproach (s. 1 Tim. 3:10). ἔχων pres. act. part. κατηγορία accusation. ἀσωτία inability to save, one who wastes his money often w. the implication of wasting it on pleasures, and so ruining himself; luxurious living, extravagant squandering of means (Lock; Trench, *Synonyms*, 53f.; TDNT; s. also Eph. 5:18). ἀννπότακτος independent, unruly, insubordinate. ■ δεῖ "it is necessary," it is a logical necessity. ἐπίσκοπος 7 overseer, bishop (s. 1 Tim. 3:1, 2). οἰκονόμος manager of a household or family, steward. The word emphasizes the commitment of a task to someone and the responsibility involved. It is a metaphor drawn from contemporary life and pictures the manager of a household or estate (Guthrie; TDNT; s. also 1 Cor. 4:1; Gal. 4:2). αὐθάδης self-willed, obstinate in one's own opinion, arrogant, refusing to listen to others. It is the man who obstinately maintains his own opinion or asserts his own rights and is reckless of the rights, feelings and interests of others (Lock; Trench, *Synonyms*, 349f.; MM; TDNT). ὀργίλος inclined to anger, quick-tempered (BAG). Words w. this ending often denote "habit," "custom" (Ellicott). πάροινος given to drink, heavy drinker (Kelly; s. also 1 Tim. 3:3). πλήκτης one who strikes, fighter. The word could be quite literal "not hasty to strike an opponent" (Lock; s. also 1 Tim. 3:3). αἰσχροκερδής greedy of shameful gain; i.e., making money discreditably, adopting one's teaching to the hearers in hope of getting money from them, or perhaps it refers to engaging in discreditable trade

8 (Lock; s. also 1 Tim. 3:8). ■ φιλόξενος lover of strangers, hospitable. φιλάγαθος lover of that which is good. It denotes devotion to all that is best (Kelly). ὅσιος devout, holy (s. 1 Tim. 2:8). ἐγκρατής control over one's self. It means complete self-mastery, which controls all passionate impulses and keeps the will loyal to the will of God (Lock; s. also Lock, 148; Gal. 5:23).

9 ■ ἀντεχόμενον pres. mid. part. ἀντέχομαι to hold on to, to hold fast. The prep. in compound appears to involve a faint idea of holding out against something hostile or opposing. This, however, passes into that of "steadfast application" (Ellicott). πιστός reliable, trustworthy (Guthrie). δυνατός able. ᾖ pres. subj. εἰμί. The subj. is used in a purpose clause. παρακαλεῖν pres. act. inf. to exhort, to urge (s. Rom. 12:1; 1 Thess. 4:1). διδασκαλία teaching, doctrine. The dat. is instrumental. ὑγιαινούσῃ pres. act. part. ὑγιαίνω to be well, to be healthy, to be sound. ἀντιλέγοντας pres. act. part. ἀντιλέγω to speak against, to oppose, to object. ἐλέγχειν pres. act. inf. to convict, to reprove (s. 2 Tim. 4:2).

10 ■ ματαιολόγος worthless words, evil talkers; i.e., using impressive language w. little or no solid content of truth (Kelly; s. also 2 Tim. 2:16). φρεναπάτης deceivers of the mind, deceivers of thinking, deceiver, subducer. μάλιστα especially.

11 περιτομή circumcision. ■ ἐπιστομίζειν pres. act. inf. to put something on the mouth, to muzzle, to silence. ἀνατρέπουσιν pres. act. ind. to turn upside down, to upset (s. 2 Tim. 2:18). διδάσκοντες pres. act. part. The part. gives the means or manner. αἰσχρός shameful, ugly, dishonest (BAG). κέρδος gain,

12 profit. ■ ἐξ αὐτῶν "from them." Paul quotes from Epimenides of Cnossus, in Crete, a religious teacher and worker of wonders of the sixth century B.C. (Kelly; s. also Lock; Dibelius; OCD,

399; KP II, 319). ἴδιος αὐτῶν προφήτης "one of their own prophets." Epimenides was a famous figure of Crete and was considered to be a prophet. Because a well-known Cretian condemns his own people, the apostle cannot be charged w. censoriousness for his exposures (Guthrie).

ψεύστης liar. θηρίον wild animal, beast. γαστήρ stomach. ἀργός inactive, lazy. The expression "lazy belly" describes their uncontrolled greed (Guthrie; for gluttony in the ancient world, s. RAC IX, 345–390). ■ αἰτία reason, cause. ἔλεγχε pres. act. 13 imp. (s. 2 Tim. 4:2). ἀποτόμως adv. severely, sharply. ὑγιαίνωσιν pres. act. subj. to be well, to be healthy, to be sound. The subj. is used in a purpose clause. ■ προσέχοντες pres. act. 14 part. προσέχω to give heed to, to devote one's self to (s. 1 Tim. 1:4). μῦθος myth (s. 1 Tim. 1:4). ἐντολή command, rule. ἀποστρεφομένων pres. mid. part. ἀποστρέφομαι to turn one's self from something, to reject. ■ μεμιαμμένοις perf. pass. 15 part. μιαίνω to stain, to defile, to pollute. The perf. points to a past completed action w. a continuing result or state or condition. νοῦς mind, understanding. συνείδησις conscience. ■ 16 ὁμολογοῦσιν pres. act. ind. to confess, to profess. εἰδέναι perf. act. inf. οἶδα to know. ἀρνοῦται pres. mid. ind. to deny. βδελυκτός detestable, abominable. It is an expression of disgust at their hypocrisy (Guthrie). ὄντες pres. part. εἰμί. ἀπειθής disobedient. ἀδόκιμος rejected after trial, disqualified (s. 2 Tim. 3:8).

Ch. 2

■ λάλει pres. act. imp. ἅ "the things," "the things which." 1 πρέπει pres. act. ind. "it is fitting." The word indicates that which is fitting or suitable to a particular context. ὑγιαινούσῃ pres. act. part. ὑγιαίνω to be well, to be healthy, to be sound. διδασκαλία teaching, doctrine, dat. of respect. ■ πρεσβύτης 2 one who is older, an older man. νηφάλιος sober. It refers here to general restraint in indulging desires (Kelly; s. also 1 Tim. 3:2). σεμνός dignified (s. 1 Tim. 2:2; 3:8). ■ πρεσβύτης older 3 woman. ὡσαύτως likewise. κατάστημα demeanor, deportment, behavior. The word describes a state of mind (Guthrie). ἱεροπρεπής that which is suitable to holiness, reverence, temple-like, like people engaged in sacred duties, "like those employed in sacred service." They are to carry into daily life the demeanor of priestesses in a temple (Lock; MM; Dibelius). διάβολος slanderer (s. 2 Tim. 3:3). δεδουλωμένας perf. pass. part. to be enslaved. The perf. tense emphasizes the completed state or condition. καλοδιδάσκαλος teacher in good. The word

does not refer to formal instruction, but rather the advice and
encouragement they can give privately, by word and example
4 (Kelly). ■ σωφρονίζωσιν pres. act. subj. σωφρονίζω to teach
someone self-control, to train someone in self-control (s. Lock,
148f.; TDNT). νέος young. φίλανδρος husband-loving.
5 φιλότεκνος children-loving. ■ ἁγνός chaste (s. 1 Tim. 5:22).
οἰκουργός working at home, housekeeping. In a Jewish
household the married woman had to grind flour, bake, launder,
cook, nurse children, make the beds, spin wool, keep the house,
and was also responsible for hospitality and the care of guests
(s. M, Ketuboth, 5:5; JPFC II, 761ff.; SB III, 667).
ὑποτασσομένας pres. mid. part. ὑποτάσσομαι to be in subjection (s. Eph. 5:22). βλασφημῆται pres. pass. subj.
βλασφημέω to slander, to speak lightly of sacred things, to
6 blaspheme (s. AS; TDNT). ■ νεώτερος comp. νέος younger.
παρακάλει pres. act. imp. παρακαλέω to urge, to exhort (s.
Rom. 12:1; 1 Thess. 4:1). σωφρονεῖν pres. act. inf. to be of a
sound mind, to exercise self-control, to have one's total life
7 under control of the mind (s. Lock, 148ff.; TDNT). ■
παρεχόμενος pres. mid. part. παρέχομαι to show one's self to
be something (BAG). τύπος example, type, model.
διδασκαλία teaching, doctrine. ἀφθορία uncorruptness, sincerity, untaintedness. It is purity of motive, without desire of
gain or respect of persons and purity of doctrine (Lock; Guthrie;
8 MM). σεμνότης dignity (s. 1 Tim. 2:2; 3:8, 11). ■ λόγος word,
speech. The word denotes the content of what is said (Guthrie).
ὑγιής healthy, sound. ἀκατάγνωστος without accusation, unable to be accused, that which cannot be condemned. ὁ "he that
is on the contrary part" (Lock). ἐντραπῇ aor. pass. subj.
ἐντρέπομαι mid. to turn one on himself and so be ashamed (i.e.,
to blush) (RWP; s. also 2 Thess. 3:14). ἔχων pres. act. part.
9 φαῦλος bad, worthless. ■ δεσπότης master. εὐάρεστος well-
pleasing. ἀντιλέγοντας pres. act. part. ἀντιλέγω to speak
10 against, to answer back, to talk back. ■ νοσφιζομένους pres.
mid. part. νοσφίζομαι to set apart for one's self, to separate or
lay on one's side, to embezzle (RWP; Kelly). ἐνδεικνυμένους
pres. mid. part. ἐνδείκνυμι to show one's self, to demonstrate,
to show forth. κοσμῶσιν pres. act. subj. κοσμέω to put in
order, to adorn. The word is used of the arrangement of jewels
in a manner to set off their full beauty (Guthrie).
11 ■ ἐπεφάνη aor. pass. ind. ἐπιφαίνομαι to appear, pass. to
be made clear, to be made manifest. The essential meaning of the
word is to appear suddenly upon a scene and it is used particularly of divine interposition, especially to aid, and of the dawning

of light upon darkness (Lock; s. also MM). σωτήριος saving,
delivering, bringing salvation. Followed by the dat. the word
means "bringing deliverance to" and the phrase "to all men"
belongs to the noun showing the universal scope of Christian
salvation (Guthrie; s. also BAG). ■ παιδένουσα pres. act. part. 12
παιδεύω to train by discipline, to train a child, to instruct. ἵνα
that. The particle introduces the purpose of the training.
ἀρνησάμενοι aor. mid. part. ἀρνέομαι to deny, to say no to.
ἀσέβεια godlessness, the rejection of all that is reverent and of
all that has to do with God (s. TDNT). ἐπιθυμία strong desire,
lust. σωφρόνως adv. w. self-control (s.v.6). δικαίως adv. righteously. εὐσεβῶς adv. godly, reverently (s. 1 Tim. 2:2). ζήσωμεν
aor. act. subj. ζάω to live. The subj. is cohortative "let us live."
■ προσδεχόμενοι pres. mid. part. προσδέχομαι to expect, to 13
wait for, to eagerly wait for. μακάριος blessed, happy.
ἐπιφανεία appearance (s. 2 Thess. 2:8). ■ ἔδωκεν aor. act. ind. 14
δίδωμι to give. λυτρώσηται aor. mid. subj. λυτρόομαι to obtain release by the payment of a price, to redeem, to ransom (s.
Matt. 20:28; RAC VI, 54–219). ἀνομία lawlessness. καθαρίσῃ
aor. act. subj. καθαρίζω to cleanse. The subj. are used in purpose
clauses. περιούσιος chosen, special; i.e., something that belongs
in a special sense to one's self (Guthrie). ζηλωτής zealous (s.
Gal. 1:14). ■ ἔλεγχε pres. act. imp. ἐλέγχω to convince, to 15
convict, to reprove (s. 2 Tim. 4:2). ἐπιταγή command, order,
here "w. all impressiveness" (BAG). περιφρονείτω pres. act.
imp. περιφρονέω to think around someone, to despise someone, to overlook, to disregard (s. MH, 321).

Ch. 3

■ ὑπομίμνησκε pres. act. imp. ὑπομιμνῆσκω to call to 1
remembrance, to remind someone of something. ἀρχή ruler.
ἐξουσία authority. ὑποτάσσεσθαι pres. mid. inf. to be in subjection. πείθαρχεῖν pres. act. inf. to be obedient. The inf. are
used in indirect discourse after the verb "to remind." ἔτοιμος
prepared, ready. ■ βλασφημεῖν pres. act. inf. to slander, to 2
treat w. contempt, to blaspheme. ἄμαχος without fighting.
ἐπιεικής forbearing, reasonable, fair (s. 2 Cor. 10:1).
ἐνδεικνυμένους pres. mid. part. ἐνδείκνυμι to demonstrate, to
display. πραΰτης meekness, mildness, patient trust in the midst
of difficult circumstances (s. 2 Cor. 10:1). ■ ἦμεν impf. εἰμί. 3
ποτέ formerly. ἀνόητος without understanding, foolish.
ἀπειθής disobedient. πλανώμενοι pres. pass. part.
πλανάομαι to deceive, to lead astray. The word suggests a false
guide leading astray (Guthrie). δουλεύοντες pres. act. part. to

be in slavery to. ἐπιθυμία strong desire, lust. ἡδονή pleasure. ποικίλος many-colored, variegated, various (s. 2 Tim. 3:6). κακία evil (s. TDNT; CBB). φθόνος envy. διάγοντες pres. act. part. διάγω to live, to spend time. στυγητός hated, hateful, detestable. μισοῦντες pres. act. part. μισέω to hate. ἀλλήλους
4 kindness, goodness (s. Gal. 5:22). ■ χρηστότης love of mankind, love toward men, generosity. While generosity was sometimes attributed to God, inscriptions show that in the Hellenistic age it was the most prized of the stock virtues acclaimed in rulers
5 (Kelly). ■ τῶν. The definite article is used here as a rel.; i.e., "not as a result of works, *those* in righteousness which we did" (RWP). ἐποιήσαμεν aor. act. ind. ἔλεος mercy (s. 1 Tim. 1:2). ἔσωσεν aor. act. ind. σῴζω to rescue, to save. λουτρόν bath, washing (s. Eph. 5:26; Fairbairn). παλιγγενεσία a birth again, regeneration, new birth. The term was current in Stoicism for periodic restorations of the natural world. It was also used in an eschatalogical sense especially by the Jews of the renewing of the world in the time of the Messiah, but here the word takes on a new meaning in view of the Christian new birth which is applied not cosmically but personally (Guthrie; BAG; Lock; Dibelius; s. also TDNT; CBB; RAC IX, 43–171; s. also Matt. 19:28). ἀνακαίνωσις renewing, making new (s. Rom. 12:2; Col. 3:10).
6 ■ ἐξέχεεν aor. act. ind. ἐκχέω to pour out. πλουσίως adv.
7 richly. ■ δικαιωθέντες aor. pass. part. δικαιόω to declare righteous, to justify (s. Rom. 2:13; 5:1). The part. is either temporal "after having been justified" or it could be causal "because we have been justified." κληρονόμος heir. γενηθῶμεν aor. pass. subj. (For an attempt to explain the teaching in light of Philo, s. Stephen Charles Mott, "Greek Ethics and Christian Conversion: The Philonic Background of Titus II 10–14 and III 3–7," Nov T 20 [Jan., 1978], 22–48.)
8   ■ τούτων "these things," refers to all that has been included in the previous part of the letter (Guthrie). βούλομαι to determine, to will. διαβεβαιοῦσθαι pres. mid. inf. to speak confidently, to insist, to confirm, to make a point of (Lock; s. also 1 Tim. 1:7). The pres. tense calls for a continual action. φροντίζωσιν pres. act. subj. φροντίζω to take thought of, to give heed to. προΐστασθαι pres. mid. inf. προΐσταμι to stand before, to take the lead in, to be careful to busy one's self w. The word has a technical meaning "to practice a profession" (s. RWP; Kelly). πεπιστευκότες perf. act. part. ὠφέλιμος useful,
9 profitable, serviceable. ■ μωρός dull, stupid, foolish (AS). ζήτησις questioning, speculation (s. 1 Tim. 1:4). γενεαλογία genealogy (s. 1 Tim. 1:4). ἔρις strife. μάχη fight, controversy.

νομικός pertaining to law, legal. The word here refers to the Mosaic law (Guthrie). περίστασο pres. mid. imp. περιΐσταμι to step around, to stand aside, to turn one's self about, to avoid, to shun (RWP; MM; s. also 2 Tim. 2:16). ἀνωφελής useless, unprofitable. μάταιος futile. ■ αἱρετικός having the power of 10 choice, a self-chosen party or sect or it could mean "a self-chosen teaching," i.e., "heresy," "heretical" (s. Lock). δεύτερος second. νουθεσία admonition, warning. It is the attempt to cause a person to correct his wrong by warning or counseling w. him (s. TDNT; 1 Cor. 10:11; Eph. 6:4). παραιτοῦ pres. mid. imp. παραιτέομαι to ask from, to beg off, to avoid (RWP; s. also 1 Tim. 4:7; 5:11). ■ εἰδώς perf. act. part. οἶδα. ἐξέστραπται 11 perf. mid. or pass. ἐκστρέφω to turn from, to turn inside out, to twist, to divert (s. RWP). τοιοῦτος such a one. ἁμαρτάνει pres. act. ind. to sin. ὤν pres. part. εἰμί. αὐτοκατάκριτος condemnation of one's self, self-condemned; i.e., he is condemned "by his own action" (Lock).

■ ὅταν used w. the subj. "when," "whenever." πέμψω aor. 12 act. subj. πέμπω to send. σπούδασον aor. act. imp. σπουδάζω to hurry, to endeavor, to do one's best (Kelly). ἐλθεῖν aor. act. inf. ἔρχομαι. κέκρικα perf. act. ind. κρίνω to judge, to determine, to decide. The perf. tense looks at the settled decision which had been reached. παραχειμάσαι aor. mid. inf. παραχειμάζω to spend the winter. ■ νομικός pertaining to 13 law, lawyer. The word may be used of an expert in either Heb. or Roman law. Here it probably refers to a Roman lawyer. If one did not know the laws of a city, he consulted w. a lawyer (s. Guthrie; TDNT; MM; Preisigke). σπουδαίως speedily, hurriedly, earnestly, diligently. πρόπεμψον aor. act. imp. προπέμπω to send forth, to send on. The word often had the idea of supplying one w. money for material needs for a trip (s. Rom. 15:24; 1 Cor. 16:6). λείπῃ pres. act. subj. λείπω to leave behind, to lack. The word suggests that Titus was in a position to provide material assistance (Guthrie). ■ μανθανέτωσαν 14 pres. act. imp. προΐστασθαι pres. mid. inf. (s.v.8). ἀναγκαῖος necessary. ὦσιν pres. subj. εἰμί. ἄκαρπος fruitless.

■ ἀσπάζονται pres. mid. ind. to greet. ἄσπασαι aor. mid. 15 imp. φιλοῦντας pres. act. part. φιλέω to love.

PHILEMON

Ch. 1

1 Δέσμιος prisoner (s. 2 Tim. 1:8, 16). Χριστοῦ Ἰησοῦ. The gen. expresses to whom Paul belonged and indicates that the writing is not simply to be looked at as a private letter but contains a message which those who receive it are obligated to obey (Lohse). ἀγαπητός beloved. συνεργός fellow worker. The term is a frequent name given to Paul's colleagues in the "work" of the gospel. Just how Philemon had labored w. Paul in
2 missionary service is not clear (Martin; NCB). ■ ἀδελφή sister. Since the women at that time had to do w. the business of the house, it was important for her what Paul had to say about the slave Onesimus (Stuhlmacher; Lohse; s. also Titus 2:5). συστρατιώτης fellow soldier. This was one who engaged in the same conflicts, faced the same dangers, and fought for the same goals (s. TDNT).

4 ■ εὐχαριστῶ pres. act. ind. to give thanks. It was a common feature of Hellenistic letters that the sender praised the gods for the health and well-being of his addressees, and assured them of his prayers on their behalf. Paul gives a distinctly Christian content to the formula by the way in which he goes on to describe the reason for his thankfulness (Martin, NCB; Lohse; s. also LAE, 184f.; P.T. O'Brien, *Introductory Thanksgivings in the Letters of Paul* [Leiden: E.J. Brill, 1977]). πάντοτε always. μνεία mention, remembrance. ποιούμενος pres. mid. part. The construction means "to make mention in prayer" (Moule; s. also
5 1 Thess. 1:2). ■ ἀκούων pres. act. part. The part. could be causal "because I hear" and indicates the cause of Paul's giving thanks (Vincent). πρός. The prep. signifies direction "forward to," "toward." Here it is used of faith which aspires toward Christ (Lightfoot; s. also Vincent; Ellicott). εἰς πάντας τοὺς ἁγίους "unto all saints." The prep. denotes "arrival" and so "contact," i.e., "into," "unto" and is used of love which is exerted upon men
6 (Lightfoot; but s. also MT, 256). ■ ὅπως "that," "in order that." The particle introduces either the aim and purport of Paul's prayer (Lightfoot) or it simply gives the content of Paul's prayer (Lohse). κοινωνία fellowship, sharing. The word could mean

generosity or participation and the main idea is that Philemon's
faith is to show itself in loving service (Martin, NCB; s. also
TDNT; CBB; RAC IX, 1100–1145). πίστεώς. The gen. can be
the obj. gen. (For a discussion of the various problems and interpretations, s. Moule; Stuhlmacher.) ἐνεργής active, effective,
productive (s. TDNT; MNTW, 46–54). γένηται aor. mid. subj.
γίνομαι. ἐπίγνωσις recognition, acknowledgment, knowledge
(s. Col. 1:9). παντὸς ἀγαθοῦ "of every good." The words may
refer to that which is God's will and generally refers to something which is done or performed (s. Moule; s. also Stuhlmacher). ■ ἔσχον aor. act. ind. ἔχω to have, aor. to get, to receive 7
(s. M, 110). The aor. tense expresses forcibly the moment of joy
which Paul experienced when he heard this good news about
Philemon (EGT). παράκλησις encouragement, comfort.
σπλάγχον the inner organs, heart. The term is used here to
denote the total person and his personality at the deepest level
(Martin, NCB; Lohse; TDNT). ἀναπέπαυται perf. mid. ind.
ἀναπαύω to cause to rest, to refresh. The word implies "relaxation, refreshment," as a preparation for the renewal of labor or
suffering (Lightfoot). ἀδελφέ vocative. The place of the word
here makes it emphatic (EGT).

■ διό therefore. παρρησία speaking all things, openness, 8
boldness (s. TDNT). ἔχων pres. act. part. The part. is concessive
(IBG, 102). ἐπιτάσσειν pres. act. inf. to command. When a
slave ran away, he could be searched for through a wanted list
and if anyone recognized him and caught him, he was to bring
him back to his owner who could punish the slave as he wished.
In such a case it was also possible for one to intercede w. the
master for the slave. (For examples and references, s. Lohse; for
the text of the description of two runaway slaves, s. Moule, 34ff.)
ἀνῆκον that which is required, that which is fitting; i.e. one's
duty (Martin, NCB). ■ μᾶλλον rather. παρακαλέω pres. act. 9
ind. to urge, to beseech. The verb contains the idea of a request
(s. TDNT; Lohse). τοιοῦτος such a one. (For the construction
of this section, s. Lightfoot.) ὤν pres. part. εἰμί. πρεσβύτης old
man, ambassador. The sense requires Paul's invoking his authority as an ambassador (Martin, NCB). νυνί now. δέσμιος prisoner (s.v.1). ■ παρακαλῶ pres. act. ind. Used w. the prep. here 10
in the sense of "making a request on behalf of someone" (s.
Lohse; Stuhlmacher). ἐγέννησα aor. act. ind. γεννάω to bear,
to give birth. Here it is the metaphor of fatherhood "of whose
conversion I was the instrument" (Vincent; Moule). (For references to the DSS and rabbinical literature concerning the metaphor of spiritual parenthood, s. Stuhlmacher; SB, III, 340f.;

11 TDNT.) δεσμός bond. ■ ποτέ formerly. ἄχρηστος useless,
12 unserviceable. εὔχρηστος useful, serviceable, profitable. ■
ἀνέπεμψα aor. act. ind. ἀναπέμπω to send again, to send back
(s. BAG; Moule). The aor. is an epistolary aor. which is translated by the pres. tense in English. It indicates that Onesimus
carried the letter (Lightfoot; Stuhlmacher; s. also BD, 172).
σπλάγχνα inward organs, heart, "my very heart" (Lightfoot; s.
13 also v. 7; Phil. 1:8; 2:1). ■ ἐβουλόμην impf. mid. ind. βούλομαι
to desire, to wish. The word involves the idea of "purpose, deliberation, desire, mind" (Lightfoot; s. also TDNT). The impf. is
either an epistolary tense which is rendered in English "I wish"
or "I would like" (Moule) or it could be used of a wish which
was either impossible to fulfill; i.e., "I could have desired" (s.
BD, 181f.; Lightfoot). κατέχειν pres. act. inf. to retain, to keep.
Although the word is capable of several meanings, the idea here
in this construction is "to keep w. me" (Lohse). ὑπὲρ σοῦ "instead of you." The idea of substitution is in the word and the
prep. was used of one who wrote "for" another who could not
write (s. Lohse; LAE, 331; TDNT; Stuhlmacher). διακονῇ pres.
act. subj. to wait on, to minister to, to minister (s. TDNT).
εὐαγγέλιον good news, gospel. The gen. may be subjective
indicating that his bonds arise from the gospel (Lohmeyer) or it
14 may mean "my imprisonment for the gospel" (Moule). ■ χωρίς
w. the gen. without. γνώμη opinion, consent. The word was
used often in the papyri in this sense (s. Stuhlmacher; Dibelius;
Preisigke; MM). ἠθέλησα aor. act. ind. θέλω to wish, to desire.
The aor. tense describes a definite completed action (s. Lightfoot; EGT). ποιῆσαι aor. act. inf. ἀνάγκη pressure, necessity,
complusion. τὸ ἀγαθόν σου "the benefit arising from you," i.e.,
"the good which I should get from the continued presence of
Onesimus and which would be oweing to you" (Lightfoot).
ἑκουσίος voluntary. Used here w. the prep. "of one's own free
15 will" (BAG). ■ τάχα perhaps. ἐχωρίσθη aor. pass. ind. χωρίζω
to separate, to depart; i.e. by escaping. The pass. may contain a
conviction of the divine overruling and would be parallel to the
"divine pass." in Heb. which was a mode of expression to denote
the hidden action of God as an agent responsible for what is done
(Martin, NCB). αἰώνιος eternal. In this context it appears to
mean "for good," "permanently" (Moule). ἀπέχῃς pres. act.
subj. ἀπέχω to have. The word was a commercial t.t. meaning
"to receive a sum in full and give a receipt for it." Here the idea
16 is to keep, to keep for one's self (s. BAG; Ellicott). ■ οὐκέτι no
longer. ὑπὲρ δοῦλον "beyond a slave," "more than a slave"
(RWP). ἀγαπητός beloved (s.v.1). μάλιστα especially. πόσῳ

μᾶλλον "how much rather," having first said "most of all to me," he goes a step further, "more than most of all to thee" (Lightfoot). ἐν σαρκί "in the flesh," i.e., "as a man" (Martin, NCB).

■ ἔχεις pres. act. ind. The ind. is used in a first-class condi- 17 tional clause which accepts the condition as a reality. κοινωνιός sharer, partner. The word denotes those who have common interest, common feelings, and common work (Lightfoot; s. also v. 6). προσλαβοῦ aor. mid. imp. προσλαμβάνω mid. to take to one's self, to receive or accept in one's society or into one's home or circle of acquaintances (BAG). ■ ἠδίκησεν aor. ind. 18 act. ἀδικέω to act unjustly, to wrong someone, to injure. ὀφείλει pres. act. ind. to owe someone a debt. ἐλλόγα pres. act. imp. ἐλλογάω to place on someone's account. The word was a commercial t.t. meaning "to charge to someone's account" (s. MM; Preisigke; BAG; Dibelius; Lohse). ■ ἔγραψα aor. act. ind. 19 epistolary aor. (s.v.12). ἀποτίσω fut. act. ind. ἀποτίνω to repay, to pay back. The word is a legal t.t. and appears in promissory notes (s. Lohse; LAE, 331f.). λέγω pres. act. subj. προσοφείλω pres. act. ind. to owe a debt besides, to owe in addition to (s. Ellicott). ■ ναί yes. ὀναίμην aor. mid. opt. to 20 benefit, to profit. The opt. is used to express a wish and was used in the formula "may I have joy, profit or benefit" and was used w. the gen. of the person or thing that is the source of the joy or profit (s. BAG). ἀνάπαυσον pres. act. imp. (s.v.7).

■ πεποιθώς perf. act. part. πέποιθα to persuade, perf. to 21 be persuaded, to have confidence (s. Phil. 1:6). ὑπακοή listening to, obedient. ἔγραψα aor. act. ind. εἰδώς perf. act. part. οἶδα. ποιήσεις fut. act. ind. (For general discussions of slavery in the ancient world and esp. of slaves obtaining their freedom, s. FCS; Lohse; Stuhlmacher, 42–48; DC XIV-XV; Seneca, Letters to Lucilus, 47: DGRA, 1034–1042; KP V, 230–234; CC, 109–112; 1 Cor. 7:21; Rom. 1:1). ■ ἅμα at the same time, besides. 22 ἐτοίμαζε pres. act. imp. ἑτοιμάζω to prepare, to prepare a guest room (s. Stuhlmacher). ξενία lodging, a place of entertainment. It may denote quarters in an inn or a room in a private house (Lightfoot). χαρισθήσομαι fut. pass. ind. χαρίζομαι to give graciously, to grant somebody to someone (s. Lightfoot; Moule). The pass. voice suggests that it is God who alone can secure Paul's release, though Paul relies on the prayers of the community to entreat God for this favor (Martin, NCB).

■ ἀσπάζομαι pres. mid. ind. to greet. συναιχμάλωτος 23 fellow captive. ■ συνεργός fellow worker (s.v.1). (For a discus- 24 sion of churches in homes in the ancient Christian world, s. Stuhlmacher, 70–75.)

HEBREWS

πολυμερῶς adv. in many ways, in many parts. The word ¹ points to the fragmentary character of former revelations. The revelation of God was essentially progressive (EGT). πολυτρόπως adv. in many ways, in various manners. It could refer both to the various geographical locations of the revelation as well as to the various methods of disclosure; i.e., direct revelation, dreams, visions, etc. (Buchanan; s. also Westcott; Michel). πάλαι formerly, of old time. The word describes something completed in the past. Here the thought is of the ancient teachings now long since sealed (Westcott). λαλήσας aor. act. part. λαλέω to speak, w. the dat. to speak to. The aor. tense points to the completed action. The part. is used temporally indicating antecedent time; i.e., "after he had spoken." πατράσιν dat. pl. "to the fathers." ἐν "in," "through." The prep. could refer to the teaching of inspiration which viewed the prophets as being indwelled by the Holy Spirit (Michel; s. also Westcott). ■ ἐπ' ² ἐσχάτου at the end. ἐπ᾽ ἐσχάτου τῶν ἡμερῶν "the last of these days." The rabbinic term indicated the time of the Messiah (SB III, 617; s. also Buchanan; Hughes). ἐλάλησεν aor. act. ind. λαλέω to speak. The aor. tense used both of God speaking by the prophets and also His speaking by Christ indicates that God has finished speaking in both cases (Hughes). ἐν υἱῷ "in one who is a son." The absence of the article fixes attention upon the nature and not upon the personality of the mediator of a new revelation. God spake to us in one who has this character that He is Son (Westcott). ἔθηκεν aor. act. ind. τίθημι to place, to appoint. κληρονόμος heir. The word is derived from the term "lot" and referred to a situation in which lots were drawn to divide property or select a winner; the one who drew the lot was the heir. The word came to be used for dividing the property that a father left to his children when he died. When there was only one son, there would only be one heir. Christ is the heir of all things precisely because God has only one Son and only one heir (Buchanan; Hughes; s. also TDNT). ἐποίησεν aor. act. ind. ποιέω to make, to create. τοὺς αἰῶνας acc. pl. the ages. According to rabbinical use, the word refers not only to the periods of time, but also to the content of the world (Michel; s. also SB

3 III, 671f.; Bruce). ■ ὤν pres. part. εἰμί. The word refers to the absolute and timeless existence (RWP). ἀπαύγασμα radiance. The active meaning has the idea of emitting brightness and the meaning is that the shekinah glory of God radiated from Him. The pass. idea is not so much that of reflection, but rather the radiation through the source of the light. It is as the sun radiates its rays of light (s. RWP; Hughes; Michel; Westcott; TDNT). δόξα glory. It refers to the brilliant radiancy from the person of God (s. TDNT; s. also CBB). χαρακτήρ impression, stamp. It refers to an engraved character or impress made by a die or a seal. It also indicates the characteristic trait or distinctive mark. It was used w. special reference to any distinguishing pecularity and hence indicated "an exact reproduction" (Hughes; BAG; MM; TDNT). ὑπόστασις essence, substance, nature (s. Heb. 11:1). φέρων pres. act. part. φέρω to carry. The concept is dynamic and not static. The Son's work of upholding involves not only support, but also movement. He is the One who carries all things forward on their appointed course (Hughes; Bruce; s. also Michel). τὰ πάντα "all things." τῷ ῥήματι dat. of instrument. καθαρισμός cleansing, purification. ποιησάμενος aor. mid. part. ποιέω to make. The use of the mid. suggests the thought that Christ Himself, in His own person made the purification (Westcott). The aor. tense points to the completed action and the temporal part. expresses action which occurred before the main verb. ἐκάθισεν aor. act. ind. καθίζω to sit down, to take one's seat. ἐν δεξιᾷ (on the right hand). (For the concept of Christ sitting at the right hand, s. Eph. 1:20.) μεγαλωσύνη majesty. ὑψηλός high, pl. equivalent to the term "in heaven" (s.

4 Michel). ■ τοσούτῳ dat. of instrument used w. the comp. "by how much more" (RWP). κρείττων comp. κρατός strong comp. better, superior. The word is characteristic of the epistle (thirteen times) and the idea is that of superiority in dignity or worth or advantage, the fundamental idea being power and not goodness (Westcott). τοσούτῳ as great, how great, as much, how much. Used as a correlative w. the comp. in the sense "by as much ... as" (s. BAG; RWP). διαφορώτερος comp. διάφορος different, comp. excellent, more excellent. παρά "than." The prep. is used w. the acc. after a comp. (s. MT, 251; IBG, 51). κεκληρονόμηκεν perf. act. ind. κληρονομέω to inherit, perf. to have inherited, to be an heir (s. Buchanan; Michel; TDNT).

5   ■ ποτέ ever. εἶ 2nd per. sing. εἰμί. σήμερον today. The

day spoken of here is the day of His glorious victory and vindication. The Resurrection, Ascension and glorification should be
viewed as forming a unity, each one contributing to the exaltation of the Son to transcendental heights of power and dignity
(Hughes). γεγέννηκα perf. act. ind. γεννάω to give birth to, to
bear. This begetting is the begetting of the incarnate Son and it
marks the completion and the acceptance of His redeeming
mission to our world (Hughes). ἔσομαι fut. εἰμί. ἔσται fut.
■ ὅταν when, whenever. εἰσαγάγῃ aor. act. subj. εἰσάγω to   6
lead into. The word is probably a Hebraism w. the meaning "to
bring something into the world" and referred either to a birth or
to the entrance into the fut. world. Here it refers either to the
Incarnation or to the enthronement (Michel; s. also Riggenbach). πρωτότοκος firstborn (s. Col. 1:18; Michel; TDNT;
Hughes). οἰκουμένη world, inhabited world. προσκυνησάτω
aor. act. imp. προσκυνέω w. the dat. to fall on the knees before
someone, to worship (s. TDNT; CBB). ■ πρός used w. the acc. 7
"to." ποιῶν pres. act. part. πνεῦμα wind. λειτουργός minister.
The description here may be understood in two ways, either as
a personification as when the wind storm and fire do His word,
or as referring to real persons; i.e., the angels can take the form
of wind or fire (Delitzsch; s. also Hughes). φλόξ flame. ■ ὁ θεός 8
voc. "O God." The article used w. the voc. is due to Semitic
influence (BG, 11; s. also MT, 34). αἰών age. Used here in the
expression to mean "eternal" (s. TDNT). ῥάβδος scepter.
εὐθύτης strictness, uprightness. ■ ἠγάπησας aor. act. ind. 2nd 9
per. sing. ἀγαπάω. ἐμίσησας aor. act. ind. 2nd per. sing.
μισέω to hate. The aor. tense could apply to the life and ministry of the incarnate Son on earth (Westcott; s. also Hughes;
Riggenbach). ἀνομία lawlessness. διὰ τοῦτο because of this.
ἔχρισέν aor. act. ind. χρίω to anoint. The idea is the crowning
of the sovereign w. joy as at the royal banquet (Westcott; s. also
TDNT). ἔλαιον oil. ἀγαλλίασις joy, gladness. The gen. would
be gen. of description indicating the oil which was used on
occasions of gladness. παρά. Used in a comp. "more than,"
"above." μέτοχος partner, comrade, colleague. The reference
here is not to angels but to believers who will share His reign in
the age to come (Kent). ■ κατ᾽ ἀρχάς "at the beginning," "in   10
the beginning." ἐθεμελίωσας aor. act. ind. 2nd per. sing.
θεμελιόω to lay a foundation. ■ ἀπολοῦνται fut. mid. ind. 11
ἀπόλλυμι to perish. διαμένει pres. act. ind. to remain, to continue throughout. The pres. tense plus the prep. in compound
emphasize the permanent continual existence (s. MH, 301f.).
ἱμάτιον garment. παλαιωθήσονται fut. pass. ind. παλαιόω

12 pass. to grow old, to become old, ingressive aor. ■ ὡσεί as.
περιβόλαιον that which one wraps around himself, cloak. The
word suggests a costly robe (Westcott). ἐλίξεις fut. act. ind.
ἐλίσσω to roll up, to fold together. ἀλλαγήσονται fut. pass.
ind. ἀλλάσσω to change, to change clothes. εἶ 2nd per. sing.
εἰμί. Used in the sense of "remain," i.e., "but you remain (are)
the same." ἔτη nom. pl. ἔτος year. ἐκλείψουσιν fut. act. ind.
ἐκλείπω to leave off, to fail. (For the prep. in compound, s. MH,
13 309.) ■ εἴρηκεν perf. act. ind. λέγω. κάθου pres. mid. imp.,
s.v.3. ἐκ δεξιῶν "on the right (hand)." θῶ aor. act. subj. τίθημι
to set, to place. ἐχθρός one who actively hates, enemy.
ὑποπόδιον footstool, double acc. used w. the verb (Michel).
ποδῶν gen. pl. πούς foot. The figure arose from the oriental
custom of the victor putting his foot on the neck of the defeated
14 enemy (N. Lightfoot). ■ λειτουργικός ministering. The suf. of
the word has the idea of "belonging to," "pertaining to," "w. the
characteristic of" (s. MH, 378). διακονία service (s. TDNT).
The rabbinical term "angel of service or ministry" was used of
angels who protected or accompanied a person (s. SB III, 680f.).
ἀποστελλόμενα pres. pass. part. ἀποστέλλω to send out, to
commission, to send as an authoritative representative (s.
TDNT; CBB). διά w. the acc. "because of." μέλλοντας pres.
act. part. μέλλω to be about to. The word is used w. the inf. to
express the fut. (s. MKG, 307f.). κληρονομεῖν pres. act. inf. to
inherit. σωτηρία salvation. Here it is salvation in its ultimate
and broadest term (s. Michel; TDNT; CBB; NTW, 114f.). (For
the use of the OT by the author of Hebrews, s. N. Lightfoot, 63f.;
BE.)

Ch. 2

1   ■ δεῖ impersonal used w. the acc. and the inf. "it is binding,"
"it is necessary." The word marks the logical necessity "we
must" (Westcott). περισσοτέρως comp. adv. "more abundantly," "more earnestly" (s. BD, 33). The word here could have
almost an elative sense "w. extreme care" (Moffatt). προσέχειν
pres. act. inf. to give heed to, to give attention to. The word is
commonly used of bringing a ship to land (EGT). The verb is
followed by the dat. ἀκουσθεῖσιν aor. pass. part. ἀκούω to
hear. παραρυῶμεν aor. pass. subj. παραρρέω to flow by. The
word was used to describe a river that flows by a place or flows
aside from its normal channel in the sense of flooding or escaping
its channel. It was used of something slipping from one's memory or of a ring slipping from one's finger or of a crumb going
down the wrong way. It also indicated a ship drifting away (s.

Hughes; Buchanan; Moffatt; Michel; Westcott). The pass. signifies to get or to find one's self in a state of flowing or passing by;
i.e., in reference to an object which requires close attention
(Delitzsch). ■ λαληθείς aor. pass. part. λαλέω. ἐγένετο aor. 2
mid. ind. γίνομαι. βέβαιος firm, dependable, reliable, guaranteed. The word was used in the papyri in a technical sense for
a legal guarantee (BS, 107; s. also BAG; TDNT; s. also 1 Cor.
1:6). παράβασις stepping beside, transgression. παρακοή
hearing beside, disobedience. Both expressions here involve an
expressed rejection of the divine will (Riggenbach). ἔλαβεν aor.
act. ind. λαμβάνω to receive. ἔνδικος just, that which conforms
to right. The prep. in compound indicates that the word stands
in antithesis to the term "unrighteous" (s. MH, 307).
μισθαποδοσία giving back w. payment, a paying back, recompense, retribution. The word indicates a full recompense as punishment (s. Riggenbach). ■ ἐκφευξόμεθα fut. mid. ind. 3
ἐκφεύγω to flee from, to escape. τηλικοῦτος so great, so large,
so important. ἀμελήσαντες aor. act. part. ἀμελέω w. the gen.
to be unconcerned about, to neglect. The part. is used condition-
ally "if we neglect." λαβοῦσα aor. act. part. fem. sing.
λαμβάνω. ἀρχὴν λαβοῦσα lit. "having received a beginning
to be spoken," "having begun to be spoken" (RWP). λαλεῖσθαι
pres. pass. inf. epexegetical describing the "beginning." The
pass. used here is the "divine pass." implying that it is God who
spoke (Hughes). ἀκουσάντων aor. act. part. ἀκούω. This came
to the author and his contemporaries from "those who heard"
and probably means that they received it from the ear and eyewitnesses—those who saw and heard the very words of Jesus
(Buchanan). This information plainly rules out the admissibility
of any "first-hand" apostle or disciple as the writer of our epistle
(Hughes). ἐβεβαιώθη aor. pass. ind. βεβαιόω to make firm, to
confirm, to guarantee. A t.t. indicating legal security and validity
(s.v.2; s. also MM). ■ συνεπιμαρτυροῦντος pres. act. part. 4
συνεπιμαρτυρέω to witness together w. someone, to join in
giving additional testimony. The part. is used in a gen. abs.
construction (s. RWP). τέρας wonder. σημεῖον sign. The word
indicates that the event is not an empty ostentation of power, but
it is significant in that it points beyond itself to the reality of the
mighty hand of God in operation (Hughes). ποικίλος various,
variegated, manifold. δύναμις power, miracle. The word emphasizes the dynamic character of the event w. particular regard
to its outcome or effect (Hughes). μερισμός dividing, distribution. The following gen. could be subjective gen.; i.e., "distribution which the Holy Spirit gives" or perhaps better obj. gen.

"distribution of the Holy Spirit," i.e., the reference is God's distribution of spiritual gifts to His people (Bruce). κατά w. the acc. "according to," "in accordance w." θέλησις will, willing. The word describes the active exercise of will (Westcott).

5 ■ ὑπέταξεν aor. act. ind. ὑποτάσσω to subordinate, to subject to one's authority. μέλλουσαν pres. act. part. μέλλω to be about to, fut. The phrase "the world to come" was considered by the rabbis to be the age of Messiah, the time when the Messiah would rule as king from His throne at Jerusalem (Buchanan; s. also SB IV, Michel). The term refers to the coming age when Christ at His return shall establish His rule as the promised

6 Davidic king (Kent). ■ διεμαρτύρατο aor. mid. ind. διαμαρτύρομαι to testify, to solemnly testify, to solemnly declare (s. MH, 302). πού where, somewhere. It is characteristic of the author that he is not concerned to provide a precise identification of the sources from which he quotes. It is sufficient for him that he is quoting from Holy Scripture, whose inspiration and authority he accepts without question (Hughes). τις someone. μιμνήσκῃ pres. mid. ind. 2nd per. sing. to remember. ἐπισκέπτῃ pres. mid. ind. 2nd per. sing. to look upon, to visit. The word is used almost exclusively in the LXX, as in the NT,

7 of a visitation for good (Westcott). ■ ἠλάττωσας aor. act. ind. ἐλαττόω to make less, to make lower, to reduce in rank (Buchanan). βραχύ a little. The word could have a temporal force "for a little while" (Bruce). παρά w. the acc. "than." (For the prep. used in a comp. construction, s. Heb. 1:4, 9.) δόξα glory.

8 ἐστεφάνωσας aor. act. ind. στεφανόω to crown. ■ ὑπέταξας aor. act. ind., s.v.5. ὑποκάτω under. ὑποτάξαι aor. act. inf., s.v.5. The articular inf. is used w. a prep. to express time "when." Although the aor. inf. w. the prep. generally expresses antecedent time while the pres. inf. expresses contemporaneous time, the context must decide and here it could be translated "putting everything in subjection" (MT, 145). ἀφῆκεν aor. act. ind. ἀφίημι to leave out, to omit. ἀνυπότακτος unsubjected. The verbal adj. here has a pass. sense (RWP). οὔπω not yet. ὁρῶμεν pres. act. ind. ὁράω to see. ὑποτεταγμένα perf. pass. part. ὑποτάσσω s.v.5. The perf. tense indicates the completed state

9 or condition. ■ βραχύ temporal "a little while." παρά than, s.v.7. ἠλαττωμένον perf. pass. part., s.v.7. The perf. emphasizes the completed state or condition and indicates that the human nature which Christ assumed He still retains (Westcott). πάθημα suffering. δόξα glory (s. Heb. 1:3). ἐστεφανωμένον perf. pass. part., s.v.7. ὅπως in order that. The particle introduces a purpose clause which is to be taken w. the idea of

"suffering" (s. Moffatt; Bruce). χάριτι θεοῦ instrumental "by the grace of God." (For a discussion of the textual variant "without God," s. Michel; TC.) ὑπέρ w. the gen. "for," "for the benefit of." γεύσηται aor. mid. subj. γεύομαι (w. the gen.) to taste, to taste of. The verb is used in this common idiomatic sense and means "to experience something to the full" (Hughes).

■ ἔπρεπεν impf. ind. act. πρέπει used impersonally "it is 10 fitting," "it is appropriate." It was appropriate that action taken to help man should include suffering, since suffering is mankind's common lot (Montefiore; s. also Westcott). διά w. the acc. "because of." διά w. the gen. "through." The phrases indicate that the sufferings and death of Jesus are not accidental; they form part of the eternal world purpose of God (Moffatt). ἀγαγόντα aor. act. part. ἄγω to lead. The part. could refer to Christ who leads sons into glory or it could refer to the subject of the inf.; i.e., God the Father who leads sons into glory (s. Hughes, 101f.; Michel). The aor. part. could express coincident action "by bringing in" (MT, 80) or it could be explained as a proleptic aor. which envisages the work of Christ and its consequences for mankind as a unit (Hughes, 102). ἀρχηγός leader, pioneer. In Gr. writings it was used of a "hero" who founded a city, gave it its name, and became its guardian. It also denoted one who was "head" of a family or "founder" of a philosophic school. The term also had a distinct military connotation referring to a commander of an army who went ahead of his men and blazed the trail for them. The idea here is of a leader who opens up a new way (N. Lightfoot; s. also TDNT; MM; Preisigke; Michel). The acc. is to be taken as the object of the inf. τελειῶσαι aor. act. inf. τελειόω to complete, to initiate, to perfect, to qualify. To make Jesus fully qualified as "the pioneer of their salvation," the training required involved passing "through suffering" (Buchanan; s. also Michel; TDNT). ■ 11 ἁγιάζων pres. act. part. ἁγιάζω to sanctify, to consecrate (s. TDNT; CBB). ἁγιαζόμενοι pres. pass. part. ἑνός gen. of εἷς, ἐξ ἑνός "from one," "from one source." The "one" could refer to God indicating that He is the source (s. Bruce) or it could refer to Abraham or Adam indicating the humanity of Christ (s. Hughes). αἰτία cause, reason. δι᾽ ἣν αἰτίαν "for this reason," "because." ἐπαισχύνεται pres. mid. ind. to be ashamed. ■ 12 ἀπαγγελῶ fut. act. ind. ἀπαγγέλλω to proclaim, to announce (s. CBB). μέσον middle. ὑμνήσω fut. act. ind. ὑμνέω to praise, to sing the praise of someone (AS). ■ ἔσομαι fut. εἰμί. 13 πεποιθώς perf. act. part. πέποιθα to persuade, perf. to be persuaded, to be convinced (s. Phil. 1:6). The perf. part. is used in

a periphrastic fut. perf. construction (RWP). παιδίον child, lit-
14 tle child. ἔδωκεν aor. act. ind. δίδωμι. ■ ἐπεί since. τὰ παιδία
children. It refers to men and women, creatures of flesh and
blood (Bruce). κεκοινώνηκεν perf. act. ind. κοινωνέω followed
by the gen. to share in. The perf. tense describes the constant
human situation (Hughes; s. also Westcott). αἷμα blood. σάρξ
flesh. The expression "flesh and blood" was the postbiblical Heb.
designation for "men" or "human beings" (Delitzsch).
παραπλησίως adv. coming near, nearly, resembling, in like
manner. μετέσχεν aor. act. ind. μετέχω to have a part in, to
share. The aor. tense points to the historical event of the Incarnation when the Son of God assumed this same human nature and
thus Himself became truly man and accordingly truly one w.
mankind (Hughes). αὐτῶν gen. used as object of the verb and
refers to "flesh and blood"; i.e., "the human beings."
καταργήσῃ aor. act. subj. καταργέω to render inoperative, to
nullify, to make idle or ineffective, to render impotent as though
no longer existing (Hewitt). κράτος power, control (s. TDNT;
Eph. 1:19). ἔχοντα pres. act. part. (For rabbinical teaching regarding Satan and his angels and their power over death, s.
Michel; SB I, 144f.; Buchanan.) Here is a paradox. Jesus suffered
and overcame death; the devil, willing death, succumbed (Ben-
15 gel). ■ ἀπαλλάξῃ aor. act. subj. ἀπαλλάσσω to change from,
to set free from. The word was used in the papyri for the release
from a place of responsibility; e.g., a marriage contract; the superintendence of land under lease or the release from a munici-
pal office. (For these and other examples, s. MM; Preisigke.) ζῆν
pres. act. inf. ζάω to live. διὰ παντὸς τοῦ ζῆν "through the
whole of life," "all through the living." (For the use of the prep.
and the inf. here, s. IBG, 56; RWP; MT, 144.) ἔνοχος held in,
16 subject to. δουλεία slavery, bondage. ■ δήπου certainly, surely.
ἐπιλαμβάνεται pres. mid. ind. to take hold of, to seize, to take
to one's self. The word may have in this context the sense of "to
help," "to assist," "to draw someone to one's self to help." (For
this interpretation, s. Bruce; Moffatt; TDNT; for a discussion of
the various meanings and implications of the word, s. Hughes.)
17 ■ ὅθεν "from there," "therefore," "wherefore." This seems to be
a favorite word of the writer of this epistle (Riggenbach).
ὤφειλεν impf. act. ind. ὀφείλω to be obligated; i.e., "one must."
The word often implies moral necessity (s. AS; TDNT). κατὰ
πάντα "in every respect." ὁμοιωθῆναι aor. pass. inf. ὁμοιόω
to make like, pass. to become like. This likeness is nothing less
than complete identification: assimilation, not simulation
(Hughes). ἐλεήμων merciful, sympathetic (s. TDNT; CBB).

γένηται aor. mid. subj. γίνομαι. The verb suggests the notion of a result reached through the action of that which we regard as a law (Westcott). ἀρχιερεύς high priest. (For the term high priest in Judaism, s. Michel, 165f.; Westcott, 137–141; SB III, 696–700; TDNT; CBB.) τὰ πρὸς τὸν θεόν acc. of reference; i.e., "w. reference to the things that pertain to God." The expression points to "all man's relations towards God" (Westcott; s. also Riggenbach). εἰς used w. the prep. to express purpose. ἱλάσκεσθαι pres. mid. inf. to satisfy, to render well disposed, to conciliate, to propitiate (s. Hughes; APC, 125–185; TDNT; CBB; Riggenbach). ■ πέπονθεν perf. act. ind. πάσχω to suffer. 18 The perf. tense serves to emphasize that, though the temptation Christ suffered in the flesh is a thing of the past, yet its effect is permanent, the effect of compassion and understanding as He aids us in the hour of our temptation (Hughes). πειρασθείς aor. pass. part. πειράζω to test, to tempt. The part. describes the manner in which the suffering took place (s. Moffatt). The aor. tense points to the completion of the action. πειραζομένοις pres. pass. part. The pres. tense of the part. points to the continuous action that was at that time taking place. βονθῆσαι aor. act. inf. βοηθέω to help, to help someone in need (s. Michel).

Ch. 3

■ ὅθεν wherefore, therefore, lit. "from which," meaning 1 that the following arguments could be deduced from the conclusion reached above (Buchanan). κλῆσις calling. ἐπουράνιος heavenly (s. Eph. 1:3). μέτοχος one who shares, partner. κατανοήσατε aor. act. imp. κατανοέω to put the mind down on a thing, to fix the mind on something, to consider. The word expresses attention and continuous observation and regard (s. RWP; Westcott). ἀπόστολος one who is commissioned as an authoritative representative, apostle (s. 1 Cor. 1:1; TDNT; Hughes; Michel; CBB). ὁμολογία agreement, confession (s. ECC; TDNT). ■ ὄντα pres. part. masc. acc. sing. εἰμί. 2 ποιήσαντι aor. act. part. Here the word has the idea "to appoint." The word could be used of actions that one undertakes or states of being that one brings about (BAG; Hughes; Moffatt). ■ πλείων comp. "greater" followed by the gen. of comparison. 3 δόξα glory. παρά "than." (For the prep. used in a comp. construction, s. Heb. 1:4.) ἠξίωται perf. pass. ind. ἀξιόω to consider worthy. The perf. tense looks at the state or condition. ὅσος how much, as much as. Used in a comp. expression denoting measure and degree (s. AS). κατά according to. Used in the comp. construction w. the meaning "as much more . . . as" (s.

BAG). τιμή honor. τοῦ οἴκου gen. of comparison "than the house." κατασκευάσας aor. act. part. κατασκευάζω to equip, to make ready, to construct, to furnish. The word expresses more than the mere construction of the house. It includes the supply of all necessary furniture and equipment (Westcott; s. also Mich-
4 el; MM). ■ κατασκευάζεται pres. pass. ind. The pres. is a gnomic pres. indicating that which always occurs as a general rule (s. SMT, 8). θεός pres. nom. "is God." The lack of the article w. the pred. nom. emphasizes character or quality (s. John
5 1:1). ■ θεράπων server, minister. The word suggests a personal service freely rendered. It denotes both the willing service rendered as well as the relationship between the one serving and the one he serves. It also emphasizes an office which was honorable and dignified. In this case it may have been taken over from the LXX as a translation of the Heb. word (TDNT; EGT; Hughes; Riggenbach). λαληθησομένων fut. pass. part. λαλέω. The word indicates that the position of Moses was one which pointed beyond itself to a fut. and higher revelation (Moffatt; s. also
6 Michel). ■ χρίστος subject of the unexpressed pred. "is faithful" (Westcott). ἐσμέν 1st per. pl. εἰμί. παρρησία boldness, confident (s. Michel; TDNT). καύχημα boasting, ground of boasting. The following gen. "hope" may be described as a gen. of content or definition: the Christian's hope is the theme of our boasting or glorying (Hughes). μέχρι until. βέβαιος firm, adverbial acc. "firmly." (For the variant readings and textual problem here, s. TC.) κατάσχωμεν aor. act. subj. κατέχω to hold down, to hold fast to.
7   ■ διό wherefore, therefore. The particle introducing the quotation looks backward as well as forward (Michel). ἀκούσητε aor. act. subj. The subj. is used in a conditional clause.
8 ■ σκληρύνητε pres. act. subj. σκληρύνω to dry out, to dry up, to make hard, to harden (Michel). παραπικρασμός embittering, exasperation, rebellion. The word is a translation of the Heb. proper name Meribah which means in Heb. "conflict" or "rebellion" (s. Montefiore; Buchanan; Hughes). κατά w. the acc. used in a temporal sense "at" (s. IBG, 58). πειρασμός tempting, temptation. It is a translation of the Heb. name Massah meaning
9 "tempting" or "testing" (s. Buchanan; Montefiore; Hughes). ■ οὗ adv. of place "where." ἐπείρασαν aor. act. ind. πειράζω to try, to test, to tempt. instrumental use of the prep. "by." δοκιμασία proof, testing. The word implies a testing which is intended to
10 bring out the good (s. TDNT). εἶδον aor. act. ind. ὁράω. ■ τεσσεράκοντα forty. ἔτα acc. pl. ἔτος year, acc. of time. The words "forty years" could be taken either w. that which pre-

cedes; i.e., "your fathers put me to the test and saw my works for forty years," or it could be taken w. what follows; i.e., "for forty years I was provoked" (Hughes). προσώχθισα aor. act. ind. προσοχθίζω to loath, to be burdened down, to be laden w. grief, to be exhausted, to be indignant (s. Buchanan). The verb is followed by the dat. πλανῶνται pres. pass. ind. πλανάω to lead astray, pass. to go astray, to wander astray. ἔγνωσαν aor. act. ind. γινώσκω τὰς ὁδοὺς τοῦ θεοῦ. The word here is not so much the understanding of the revelatory acts of God and His leading as it is obedience to God's command (s. Riggenbach). ■ ὡς as, according as. ὤμοσα aor. act. ind. ὄμνυμι to swear. 11 ὀργή wrath, anger. εἰ "if." The word is the translation of the Heb. particle and is the equivalent of a strong neg. (s. MT, 333; MH, 468). This construction is in accord w. the Semitic idiom used in the taking of an oath (s. Buchanan; Michel). εἰσελεύσονται fut. mid. ind. εἰσέρχομαι to go into. κατάπαυσις rest (s. TDNT; Michel, 183f.; O. Hofius, *Katapausis. Die Vorstellung vom endzeitlichen Ruheort im Hebräerbrief* [Tübingen, 1970]).

■ βλέπετε pres. act. imp. βλέπω to see, to see to it, to 12 beware. When the word is followed by the neg. and the ind., it expresses a warning and fear regarding a pres. inevitable reality and indicates the warning should be taken very seriously (MT, 99; Riggenbach). ἔσται fut. εἰμί. ἀπιστίας unbelief, gen. of quality indicating that unbelief characterizes the "evil heart" (Westcott). ἀποστῆναι aor. act. inf. ἀφίσταμι to fall away, to depart, to leave, to step aside from. The inf. w. the prep. is used here epexegetically indicating the content of an evil heart (s. MT, 146; RG, 1073). ζῶντος pres. act. part. ζάω to live. The construction without the article fixes attention upon the character (Westcott). ■ παρακαλεῖτε pres. act. imp. παρακαλέω 13 to encourage, to beseech. ἑαυτούς yourselves. The reflex. pron. is deliberately used here instead of the reciprocal pron. "each other," w. the purpose of emphasizing the close unity of the Christian body (Westcott), but it may be that the two pron. are used interchangeably (Hughes). κατά w. the acc. used distributively "at each day," i.e., "every day," "daily" (s. IBG, 59; Westcott; Hughes). ἄχρις οὗ "as long as," "while" (RWP). καλεῖται pres. pass. ind. σκληρυνθῇ aor. pass. subj., s.v.8. The subj. is used in a neg. purpose clause. The pass. could perhaps be understood as a pass. of permission; i.e., "allow or permit one's self to be hardened." ἀπάτη deceitfulness, dat. of means used w. a pass. verb. ■ μέτοχος partner, sharer, partaker. (For 14 a discussion of this phrase, s. Hughes; Michel.) γεγόναμεν perf.

act. ind. γίνομαι. The perf. tense signifies that the readers have
become and consequently now are partakers of Christ (Hughes).
ἐάνπερ "if at least" (s. Westcott). ὑπόστασις that which
underlies, ground, basis. The word then means "confidence,"
"assurance," "conviction" and refers to the reality, essence, or
nature of something, or the ground work or basis of hope (Bruce;
Buchanan). κατάσχωμεν aor. act. subj. κατέχω to hold down,
15 to hold fast. ■ λέγεσθαι pres. pass. inf. The inf. used w. the prep.
16 could be temporal or it could also be causal (s. MT, 146). ■
ἀκούσαντες aor. act. part. The part. could be concessive "although they had heard." παρεπίκραναν aor. act. ind.
παραπικραίνω to provoke, to exasperate. ἐξελθόντες aor. act.
17 part. ἐξέρχομαι. ■ προσώχθισεν aor. act. ind., s.v.10.
ἁμαρτήσασιν aor. act. part. masc. pl. dat. κῶλον body, corpse.
18 ἔπεσεν aor. act. ind. πίπτω to fall. ■ ὤμοσεν aor. act. ind.,
s.v.11. ἀπειθήσασιν aor. act. part. ἀπειθέω to be disobedient,
19 unbelief passed into action (Westcott). ■ ἠδυνήθησαν aor. pass.
ind. δύναμαι. Their exclusion from Canaan was not only a fact,
but a moral necessity (Westcott). εἰσελθεῖν aor. act. inf.
εἰσέρχομαι. ἀπιστία unbelief. Used w. the prep. and the acc.
"because of disbelief."

Ch. 4

1 ■ φοβηθῶμεν aor. pass. subj. φοβέομαι to be afraid, to
fear. The cohortative subj. is used to express a command or
excitation in the 1st per.; i.e., "let us fear." μήποτε lest. Used
after a verb of fear expressing anxiety. Its use w. the subj. indicates that it is a fear of an uncertain thing (MT, 99).
καταλειπομένης pres. pass. part. καταλείπομαι to leave behind, pass. to be left behind. Here the sense is of being "left
open" (Bruce). The part. is used in a gen. abs. and could express
cause or it could be concessive (s. Riggenbach). ἐπαγγελία
promise (s. TDNT; CBB; Michel). εἰσελθεῖν aor. act. inf.
εἰσέρχομαι. The inf. is epexegetical and explains what the
promise is. κατάπαυσις rest (s. Heb. 3:11). δοκῇ pres. act. subj.
δοκέω to appear, to seem, to suppose. The word could also have
a forensic idea "to be found" (Michel; Riggenbach).
ὑστερηκέναι perf. act. inf. ὑστερέω to fall short, to be late, to
come behind, to fall behind. The verb pictures someone in a
company marching together w. others who march faster than he
can. He cannot keep up, so he falls behind. Falling behind in
religious matters means not being able to fulfill all the demands
or commandments; being negligent failing to qualify or measure
up (Buchanan). The perf. tense marks not only a present or past

defeat, but an abiding failure (Westcott). ■ εὐηγγελισμένοι 2
perf. pass. part. εὐαγγελίζομαι to proclaim good news, pass. to
have good news proclaimed to someone. The part. is used to
build the periphrastic perf. pass, ind. and the perf. emphasizes
the completeness of the evangelization that has taken place, and
thus leaves no room for any excuse to the effect that evangelization had been inadequate or deficient (Hughes). καθάπερ just
as. κακεῖνοι = καί ἐκεῖνοι "those also." ἀκοή hearing. The
gen. is descriptive gen. and emphasizes that the word or message
is associated w. hearing, the implication being that the message
is intended for people to hear and so must be proclaimed
(Hughes). ὠφέλησεν aor. act. ind. ὠφελέω to profit, to be profitable. συγκεκερασμένος perf. pass. part. συγκεράννυμι to
mix together, to blend, to unite. (For the textual problem here,
s. PC; Hughes.) ■ εἰσερχόμεθα pres. mid. ind. Although the 3
pres. tense could be used as a futuristic pres., it is better to take
it as an expression of a pres. fact (Westcott). The pres. tense
could express the idea "we are already in process of entering"
(Montefiore). πιστεύσαντες aor. act. part. εἴρηκεν perf. act.
ind. λέγω. ὤμοσα aor. act. ind. ὄμνυμι to swear, to take an
oath. ὀργή anger, wrath. εἰσελεύσονται fut. mid. ind.
εἰσέρχομαι. (For the Semitic expression of the oath implying
a strong negative, s. Heb. 3:11.) καίτοι used w. the part. expressing a concessive idea "although." καταβολή laying down, foundation. γενηθέντων aor. pass. part. γίνομαι to become, here
the pass. sense in the perf. "to be completed," "to be finished."
■ εἴρηκεν perf. act. ind., s.v.3. πού where, somewhere. 4
ἑβδόμης seventh. κατέπαυσεν aor. act. ind. καταπαύω to
rest. ■ ἐν τούτῳ "in this," "here." ■ ἐπεί since, because. 5/6
ἀπολείπεται pres. pass. ind. ἀπολείπω to remain over, to
leave behind, pass. to be left over. εἰσελθεῖν aor. act. inf. The
inf. explains what remains to be done. πρότερον formerly.
εὐαγγελισθέντες aor. pass. part., s.v.2. εἰσῆλθον aor. act. ind.
διά w. the acc. "because," "because of." ἀπείθεια unpersuaded,
disobedient. The act. expression of unbelief is manifested in
disobedience (Westcott). ■ ὁρίζει to mark out w. a boundary, to 7
appoint, to designate. σήμερον today. τοσοῦτος so long. Used
in the temporal expression "after so long a time." προείρηται
perf. pass. ind. προλέγω to say before, to say previously.
ἀκούσητε aor. act. subj. σκληρύνετε aor. act. subj. σκληρύνω
to harden. The aor. subj. is used w. the neg. to express a prohibition. ■ Ἰησοῦς Joshua. κατέπαυσεν aor. act. ind. καταπαύω 8
to give rest. The ind. is used here in a second-class conditional
clause expressing that which is contrary to fact. ἐλάλει impf.

act. ind. λαλέω "he would not speak," "he would not be speak-
9 ing" (RWP). ■ ἄρα "so then." The word draws a conclusion
from the preceding argument. ἀπολείπεται pres. pass. ind.,
10 s.v.6. σαββατισμός sabbath rest. ■ εἰσελθών aor. act. part.
εἰσέρχομαι. κατέπαυσεν aor. act. ind. to rest, to cease. ἴδιος
11 one's own. ■ σπουδάσωμεν aor. act. subj. σπουδάζω to be in
a hurry, to make haste, to be in earnest, to concentrate one's
energies on the achievement of a goal, to endeavor (Hughes).
The subj. is hortatory expressing a command "let us . . . ."
εἰσελθεῖν aor. act. inf. ἵνα "that." ὑπόδειγμα example. The
word is used here in the sense of a warning sign (Michel). The
word refers not to an example of disobedience, but to an example
of falling into destruction as a result of disobedience (BAG).
ἀπείθεια disobedience, s.v.6.

12   ■ ζῶν pres. act. part. ζάω to be alive, living. ἐνεργής energetic, active, productive. The word is used of activity which
produces results and is used often for divine activity which produces effective results (s. MNTW, 46ff.; TDNT). τομώτερος
comp. τομός sharp, comp. sharper. ὑπέρ than. The word is used
in a comp. construction; i.e., "sharper beyond," "sharper than."
μάχαιρα sword (s. Eph. 6:17). δίστομος double-edged, two
edged. διϊκνούμενος pres. mid. part. διϊκνέομαι to pass
through, to pierce, to penetrate (cf. Exod. 26:28, LXX).
μερισμός dividing. ἁρμός joint. μυελός marrow. The expressions serve to convey effectively the notion of the extreme
power of penetration of the word of God, to the very core of
man's being (Hughes). ἐνθύμησις capable of making a decision,
discerning, able to judge, followed by the objective gen. ἐννοιῶν
thought, reflection, feelings. The word refers to the action of the
affections and is related to the will (Westcott; Michel). ἔννοια
thought, intent. The word refers to the action of reason (West-
13 cott). ■ κτίσις creature. ἀφανής hidden, not manifest. γυμνός
naked, open. τετραχηλισμένα perf. pass. part. τραχηλίζω to
lay bear, to expose. The figure of speech behind the word is not
clear. It has been suggested that it refers to the bending back the
neck of a sacrificial victim making ready for the final stroke or
it may refer to the wrestler's art of seizing one by the throat
rendering him limp and powerless. (For these suggestions w.
references to usage, s. Riggenbach; Michel; Hughes; Bruce; Delitzsch.) πρὸς ὅν ἡμῖν ὁ λόγος "w. whom our matter is," "w.
whom our account is," i.e., "w. whom we have to deal," "w.
whom our final reckoning has to be made" (Bruce). (For the
meaning "w. reference to which our message applies," "which

word applies to us" as well as a discussion of other interpretations, s. Buchanan.)

■ ἔχοντες pres. act. part. to have, to possess. The part. 14 could be causal. ἀρχιερεύς high priest. διεληλυθότα perf. act. part. διέρχομαι to pass through, to go through. The perf. tense indicates that he has passed through the heavens and is still there. κρατῶμεν pres. act. subj. κρατέω to be in control of, to exercise power over, to hold to, to hold fast, followed by the gen. ὁμολογία confession, profession ■ δυνάμενον pres. mid. part. 15 συμπαθῆσαι aor. pass. inf. συμπαθέω to share the experience of someone, to sympathize w. someone. The word is not to be understood in a psychological sense, but rather in an existential sense. The exalted one suffers together w. the weakness of the one tempted (Michel). ἀσθένεια weakness. πεπειρασμένον perf. pass. part. πειράζω to tempt, to test, to try. The perf. tense emphasizes the completed state and continuing results. ὁμοιότης likeness. The word emphasizes exact correspondence (s. Michel; TDNT). ■ προσερχώμεθα pres. mid. subj. 16 προσέρχομαι to come to, to draw near. The word was used in the LXX for the priestly approach to God in service (Westcott). The subj. is cohortative "let us come near." The pres. tense emphasizes that the privilege is always available. θρόνος τῆς χάριτος "throne of grace," i.e., a throne characterized by grace. παρρησία speaking all things, boldness, confidence, assurance (s. Heb. 3:6). λάβωμεν aor. act. subj. λαμβάνω to receive. Subjunctive used in a purpose clause. ἔλεος mercy (s. 1 Tim. 1:2). εὕρωμεν aor. act. subj. εὕκαιρος convenient, good time, well timed; i.e., at the right time (Delitzsch; s. also Michel; Preisigke; MM). βοήθεια help, help given to one in need (s. Heb. 2:18).

Ch. 5

■ λαμβανόμενος pres. pass. part. καθίσταται pres. pass. 1 ind. καθίστημι to constitute, to appoint. The pass. voice implies that he does not appoint himself (Hughes). The pres. tense is gnomic referring to that which is always true. τὰ πρὸς τὸν θεόν "in reference to things pertaining to God," "in reference to things in relation to God." προσφέρῃ pres. act. subj. προσφέρω to carry to, to offer. The word was used in a religious sense of bringing an offering or sacrifice to God. δῶρον gift. θυσία sacrifice. The expressions are best understood here as a general description of the offerings over which the high priest officiated (Hughes). ■ μετριοπαθεῖν pres. act. inf. 2 μετριοπαθέω to moderate one's feelings, to have feelings in the right measure. The word was used in Aristotelian philosophical tradition in the sense of moderating one's feelings or passions so as to avoid excesses either of enthusiasm or impassivity. The word indicates that an earthly high priest is not to pass over the sin of his fellow man without any regard at all; however, on the other hand he is not to allow himself to be caught up in his passion and pity for the sinner but he is rather to have a controlled feeling of sympathy (s. Michel; Buchanan; Hughes). δυνάμενος pres. mid. part. The part. is used to describe the character of one who is taken or appointed to be a high priest. ἀγνοοῦσιν pres. act. part. dat. pl. ἀγνοέω to be without understanding, to be ignorant. πλανωμένος pres. mid. part. πλανάω to go astray, to wander. The two part. used w. a single article refer to a single class or category of those sinning; i.e., those who erred through ignorance (N. Lightfoot; Montefiore; Westcott). περίκειται pres. pass. ind. περίκειμαι to be surrounded by, to be encompassed by. It is like a millstone around his neck (Mark 9:42; Luke 17:2) or like a chain lying around him (Acts 28:20)

3 (RWP). ἀσθένεια weakness. ■ ὀφείλει pres. act. ind. to be obligated "he must." The word speaks of moral obligation; i.e., "he is bound" in the very nature of things, in virtue of his constitution and of his office (Westcott). The pres. tense is gnomic indicating that which is always true (s. SMT, 8). καθώς

4 just as, as. προσφέρειν pres. act. inf., s.v.1. ■ τιμή honor. The word was used in Josephus to describe the "honor" of the office of high priest (Josephus, *Antiquities* III, 188f.; s. also Michel). καλούμενος pres. pass. part. καλέω. καθώσπερ just as. The author may have had in mind the leading sacerdotal families of Jerusalem in his day, who were not descendants of Aaron, but had sought for themselves the high priestly office and been elevated to it by Herod the Great. Such men, though approved by the state, were not approved by God (Hughes).

5 ■ ἐδόξασεν aor. act. ind. δοξάζω to glorify. γενηθῆναι aor. pass. inf. γίνομαι. The inf. may be epexegetical explaining the main verb; i.e., "Christ did not take for Himself the honor of becoming high priest" or it may be used to express result (s. IBG, 127). ὁ λαλήσας aor. act. part. λαλέω. εἶ pres. ind. 2nd per. sing. εἰμί. γεγέννηκα perf. act. ind. γεννάω to beget, to

6 become the father of. ■ ἐν ἑτέρῳ "in another place." τάξις rank,

7 order. ■ δέησις prayer. ἱκετηρία supplication, petition. The word properly denotes an olive branch entwined w. wool borne by suppliants. The olive branch was the sign of the suppliant (Westcott; BAG; for the use of the word in the papyri, s. MM). δάκρυον tear. Later rabbinic piety laid stress on tears in regard to the three kinds of prayers; i.e., entreaty, crying, and tears. It

is said that entreaty is offered in a quiet voice, crying w. a raised voice, but tears are higher than all (Moffatt). προσενέγκας aor. act. part. προσφέρω to offer, s.v.1. εἰσακουσθείς aor. pass. part. εἰσακούω to hear, to answer, pass. to be heard. ἀπό "from." It is to be understood here in the sense of "arising from," "as the result of" (Hughes). εὐλάβεια godly fear. The word marks that careful and watchful reverence which pays regard to every circumstance in that which it has to deal (Westcott; s. also Michel; for various interpretations of the passage, s. Hughes; s. also Bruce). ■ καίπερ. Used w. the part. "although." ἔμαθεν 8 aor. act. ind. μανθάνω to learn. ἀφ᾿ ὧν = ἀπὸ τούτων ἅ "from these things which." ἔπαθεν aor. act. ind. πάσχω to suffer. ὑπακοή obedience. The article indicates the "particular obedience" which was required of him in the days of his flesh (EGT). ■ τελειωθείς aor. pass. part. τελειόω to complete, to perfect. 9 The part. could be temporal or causal. His perfection consisted in the retention of his integrity, in the face of every kind of assault on his integrity, and thereby the establishment of his integrity (Hughes; for a study of this word and its possible contextual backgrounds, s. Michel; TDNT; A. Wikgren, "Patterns of Perfection in the Epistle to the Hebrews," NTS, 6 [1960], 159–167). ὑπακούουσιν pres. act. part. ὑπακούω to obey, to be obedient. αἴτιος cause, reason, author. (For various examples of the word esp. from Philo, s. Bruce; N. Lightfoot; Westcott.) ■ προσαγορευθείς aor. pass. part. προσαγορεύω to desig- 10 nate, to greet, to salute, to hail. The word contains the idea of a formal and solemn ascription of a title (s. BAG; MM; EGT; Westcott).

■ περὶ οὗ "concerning whom," "concerning which." The 11 author refers to the priesthood of Christ; i.e., the order of Melchisedck (Hughes). ἡμῖν dat. pl. The dat. indicates the obligation signifying "the exposition which it is incumbent on us to undertake" (EGT). δυσερμήνευτος difficult to explain, difficult to interpret, hard to explain (s. Moffatt; Michel; EGT). λέγειν pres. act. inf. The inf. is used epexegetically to explain the adj. νωθρός dull, slow, sluggish. The word was used of the numbed limbs of a sick lion (EGT). In the papyri the corresponding verb is used of "sickness" (MM). γεγόνατε perf. act. ind. γίνομαι to become. It is not a question of what they are by nature, but of what they have become by default, the implication being that this was not the case w. them originally (Hughes). The perf. tense signifies the state or condition. ταῖς ἀκοαῖς dat. pl. dat. of reference "in reference to hearing." ■ ὀφείλοντες pres. act. 12 part. to be obligated, one must. The part. is concessive "although

679

you are obligated." χρείαν ἔχετε "you have a need." It is followed by the gen. of the inf. indicating what is needful. στοιχεῖα pl. basic elements (s. Michel; TDNT). ἀρχή beginning. The gen. can be gen. of definition (Bruce) or descriptive gen.; i.e., "original elements." Here it denotes the foundational teaching (Spicq; s. also EGT). τὰ λόγια τοῦ θεοῦ "the oracles of God." The phrase might refer to the new revelation given by Christ to His apostles; but is seems more natural to refer it to the collected writings of the OT (Westcott). γάλα milk. The word can be compared to the rabbinical term "suckling" referring to young

13 students (EGT; Spicq; TDNT). στερεός solid. τροφή food. ■ μετέχων pres. act. part. to partake of, to partake, followed by the gen. ἄπειρος unskilled. It describes a person who lacks experience, is untried, or ignorant (Buchanan). λόγος δικαιοσύνης "word of righteousness." The phrase has been taken to refer to an infant's inability to speak correctly (Riggenbach) or to instruction concerning ethical righteousness (Westcott) or it is taken in the sense of the righteousness of Christ which is imputed to the believer (s. Hughes). νήπιος lit. "not

14 able to speak or talk," "infant" (RWP; Hughes). ■ τέλειος perfect, mature. It would refer to those who should assume adult responsibilities. The author is using terms of human development to describe the readers' development in faith (Buchanan; s. also v.6; for a parallel in the DSS, s. 1QS 1:10–11). ἕξις habit. It refers to a habit of body or mind indicating not the process but the result; i.e., the condition has been produced by past exercise and is then the habitual or normal condition, the disposition or character (EGT; Westcott; Spicq). αἰσθητήριον faculty. It means the faculties or senses of perception and is used here of spiritual sensitivity (Hughes). γεγυμνασμένα perf. pass. part. γυμνάζω to exercise, to train by exercise. διάκρισις distinguishing, deciding, making a judgment between two things. (For the force of the prep. in compound, s. MH, 303.)

Ch. 6

1   ■ διό therefore. ἀφέντες aor. act. part. ἀφίημι to leave. The part. could be means; i.e., "in that we leave." The "leaving" does not mean to despise or abandon the elementary doctrines. The point is that the beginning is not a stopping place; it is the door to progress and the spring board to achievement (Hughes). τὸν ... Χριστοῦ λόγον "the word of the beginning of Christ." The gen. "of Christ" could be obj. gen.; i.e., the beginning teaching about Christ; or it could be subjective gen.; i.e., Christ's initial teachings (s. Buchanan; Hughes; J.C. Adams, "Exegesis of He-

brews 6:1f," NTS, 13 [July, 1967], 378–385). τελειότης perfection, maturity (s. Heb. 5:6, 14). φερώμεθα pres. pass. subj. φέρω
to carry, pass. to be carried. The subj. is cohortative "let us be
carried," and the pass. gives the thought of personal surrender
to an active influence (Westcott). It is not a matter of the learn-
ers being carried by their instructors, but of both being carried
forward together by God. It is a "divine pass." implying the
agency of God (Hughes; s. also BG, 76). θεμέλιον foundation,
basis. καταβαλλόμενοι pres. mid. part. καταβάλλω to cast
down, mid. to lay a foundation. μετάνοια change of mind,
repentence. νεκρός dead. ■ βάπτισμα washing. The pl. evi- 2
dently refers to the various washings to be found in Judaism.
(For this as well as evidence that the matters here refer primarily
to Judaism, s. J.C. Adams cited in v. 1; for various interpretations of the pl. of the word "baptisms," s. Hughes.) διδαχῆς
teaching. ἐπίθεσις placing upon, laying on. (For the Jewish
teaching regarding the laying on the hands, s. SB II, 647f.;
TDNT.) ἀνάστασις resurrection. κρίμα judgment. ■ 3
ποιήσομεν fut. act. ind. ἐάνπερ "if." The 2nd particle used w.
the conditional particle emphasizes that the action is in spite of
opposition; i.e., "if in spite of opposition God permits," "if indeed, if after all" (s. RG, 1154; BD, 237). ἐπιτρέπῃ pres. act.
subj. ἐπιτρέπω to allow, to permit. ■ ἀδύνατος impossible. 4
(For a study of this word in this connection, s. Spicq.) The adj.
is used w. the inf. which occurs in v.6. ἅπαξ once, once for all.
φωτισθέντας aor. pass. part. φωτίζω to enlighten, to illuminate. Illumination indicates that God gives the understanding
and the eyes of the person spiritual light (s. Michel; Hughes).
γευσαμένους aor. act. part. γεύομαι w. the gen. to taste of, to
taste. The verb expresses a real and conscious enjoyment of the
blessings apprehended in its true character (Westcott; s. also
Hughes). δωρεά gift. ἐπουράνιος heavenly (s. Eph. 1:3).
μέτοχος sharer, participant. γενηθέντας aor pass. part.
γίνομαι. ■ ῥῆμα that which is spoken, word. μέλλοντος pres. 5
act. part. μέλλω to be about to, coming (s. Heb. 1:5). ■ 6
παραπεσόντας aor. act. part. παραπίπτω to fall beside, to go
astray, to fall away. The part. could be conditional (s. Hughes).
ἀνακαινίζειν pres. act. inf. to renew again, to make new again.
εἰς "unto." The prep. gives the direction or the goal.
ἀνασταυροῦντας pres. act. part. ἀνασταυρόω to crucify
again. The part. is causal and indicates why it is impossible for
such people to repent and make a new beginning (Hughes;
Bruce). (For the force of the prep. in compound meaning
"again," s. MH, 295.) ἑαυτοῖς dat. pl., dat. of advantage "for

themselves." παραδειγματίζοντας pres. act. part.
παραδειγματίζω to expose publicly, to make a public example
of, to expose to disgrace (RWP; BAG). If the readers were to
return again to Judaism, there would be no possibility for them
to begin their spiritual life anew. This would require a recrucifix-
ion of Christ and a putting Him to open shame. For this reason
they must continue toward maturity despite the difficulties,
7 problems, and persecutions which attend their walk. ■ πιοῦσα
aor. act. part. πίνω to drink. ἐρχόμενον pres. mid. part.
ἔρχομαι. ὑετός rain. τίκτουσα pres. act. part. τίκτω to bear,
to bring forth, to produce. βοτάνη vegetation, green plants.
εὔθετος well-suited, conveniently placed, suitable, useable (s.
BAG). διά w. the acc. "because of," "on whose account." The
owners are intended or it refers to those whom the owners meant
to supply (EGT). γεωργεῖται pres. pass. ind. γεωργέω to cultivate. μεταλαμβάνει pres. act. ind. to receive w. someone, to
8 partake, to share in. ■ ἐκφέρουσα pres. act. part. ἐκφέρω to
carry out, to bring forth, to produce. The part. could be conditional "if it produces." ἄκανθα thorn. τρίβολος thistle, lit.
"three-pointed." (For the use of these terms in the LXX, s.
EGT.) ἀδόκιμος disapproved, rejected after examination (s. 1
Cor. 9:27). κατάρα curse. ἐγγύς near, "nigh unto a curse," for
in Gen. 3:17f. thorns and thistles are a consequent of the cursing
of the land for man's sake (Bruce). καῦσις burning.
9   ■ πεπείσμεθα perf. pass. ind. πείθω to persuade, pass. to
be persuaded, perf. to have confidence (s. Phil. 1:6). κρείσσονα
comp. pl. "better things." ἐχόμενα pres. mid. part. ἔχω to have,
mid. to hold one's self fast, to belong to, to accompany. The mid.
is used of inner belonging and close association; the "to" of
belonging and the "w." of association are expressed by the gen.
(BAG). εἰ καί "if also," "although." The words introduce a
10 concessive condition of the 1st class (RWP). ■ ἐπιλαθέσθαι
aor. mid. inf. ἐπιλανθάνομαι w. the gen. to forget. The inf. is
epexegetical explaining the word "unrighteous." ἐνεδείξασθε
aor. mid. ind. ἐκδείκνυμι to demonstrate. The prep. in compound suggests more complete demonstration than the simplest
—laying the "index" finger, as it were, on the object (MH, 305).
εἰς "for." This implies that their coming to the assistance of their
brethren is evidence of their willingness to identify themselves
w. the stigma attached to the name of Jesus, and thus of the
genuineness of their love for Him (Hughes). διακονήσαντες
aor. act. part. διακονοῦντες pres. act. part. to minister, to serve.
The pres. part. emphasizes the continuous action which was at
11 the pres. time going on. ■ ἐπιθυμοῦμεν pres. act. ind. to long

for, to yearn for, to have a strong desire (s. 1 Tim. 3:1). ἕκαστος each one. αὐτός "the same." σπούδη earnestness, endeavor. ἐκδείκνυσθαι pres. mid. inf., s.v.10. The inf. expresses the object of that which is desired. πληροφορία fullness, full assurance (s. Col. 2:2; 1 Thess. 1:5; MM; Michel). ■ νωθρός dull (s. 12 Heb. 5:11). γένησθε aor. mid. subj. γίνομαι. The subj. is used in a neg. purpose clause. μιμητής imitator. διά w. the gen. "through." μακροθυμία longsuffering, patience, patient endurance (s. Gal. 5:22; Rom. 2:4). κληρονομούντων pres. act. part. κληρονομέω to inherit. ἐπαγγελία promise.

■ ἐπαγγειλάμενος aor. mid. part. ἐπαγγέλλομαι to 13 promise, to make a promise. The part. is temporal expressing contemporaneous action "when God promised." ἐπεί since, because. μείζων greater. ὀμόσαι aor. act. inf. ὄμνυμι followed by the prep. κατά w. the gen. to swear by (s. Heb. 3:11). The fact that God swore by Himself indicates that He binds Himself to His word by His eternal person (s. Cleon Rogers, "The Covenant with Abraham and Its Historical Setting," Bib Sac, 127 [1970], 214–256; Michel; Buchanan). ■ μήν surely. εὐλογῶν πρεσ. 14 αξτ. παρτ. εὐλογέω to bless. εὐλογήσω fut. act. ind. The part. and the finite verb are used as a translation of the Heb. inf. abs. giving emphasis and certainty to the expression; i.e., "I shall certainly bless you" (s. BG, 128; BD, 218). πληθύνων pres. act. part. πληθυνῶ fut. act. ind. πληθύνω to increase, to multiply. ■ μακροθυμήσας aor. act. part. μακροθυμέω to endure pa- 15 tiently, to be longsuffering (s. Gal. 5:22). ἐπέτυχεν aor. act. ind. ἐπιτυγχάνω w. the gen. to arrive at, to obtain. ■ ἀντιλογία 16 controversy, dispute, contradiction (s. EGT). πέρας confirming, confirmation, legal guarantee. The word was a technical expression for a legal guarantee (s. BS, 104–109; TDNT; MM; Hughes). ■ ἐν ᾧ "in which," "wherefore," "wherein," i.e., in this 17 method of appeal to remove all doubt and gainsaying (Westcott; s. also EGT). περισσότερον adv. more abundantly, more convincingly. It is probably best to take the adv. in its emphatic and elative sense; i.e., "especially" (Hughes). βουλόμενος pres. mid. part. βούλομαι to purpose, to will. ἐπιδεῖξαι aor. act. inf. ἐπιδείκνυμι to point out, to demonstrate. The prep. in compound may be directive (MH, 312) or it may have the force of "to show in addition" (RWP). κληρονόμος heir. ἀμετάθετος not able to be removed, unchangeable, immutable, The word belongs to the legal terminology of the time and signifies a ruling or contract which is incapable of being set aside or annulled. Here it indicates the irrevocability of God's purpose as expressed in the promise and confirmed by the oath (Hughes).

ἐμεσίτευσεν aor. act. ind. μεσιτεύω to intervene, to act as a mediator or sponsor or surety. Intransitively it is used to pledge one's self as surety (RWP; s. also Riggenbach; Michel). ὅρκος
18 oath. ■ πρᾶγμα thing, matter. ἀδύνατος impossible. ψεύσασθαι aor. mid. inf. ψεύδομαι to lie. ἔχωμεν pres. act. subj. dependent on ἵνα. The subj. is used in a purpose clause. καταφυγόντες aor. act. part. καταφεύγω to flee, to flee for refuge. In the LXX (Deut. 4:42; 19:5; Josh. 20:9) for fleeing from the avenger to the asylum of the cities of refuge (EGT). κρατῆσαι aor. act. inf. κρατέω to hold fast, seize. The idea is "to lay hold on and cling to that which has been taken" (Westcott). The inf. could express either purpose or result. The object of the verb is in the gen. προκειμένης pres. mid. part.
19 πρόκειμαι to set before, to lie before. ■ ἄγκυρα anchor. The term anchor was used in the Gr. Hellenistic world as the picture for hope (s. Moffatt; EGT; Michel; RAC I, 440–443). ἀσφαλής safe. The word indicates that which is outwardly safe (Michel). βέβαιος firm, established, steadfast. The word indicates that which is firm within itself (Michel). εἰσερχομένην pres. mid. part. εἰσέρχομαι to go into. ἐσώτερον within, inside of. καταπέτασμα curtain, veil. The reference is to the Holy of
20 Holies (Hughes; Michel). ■ ὅπου where. πρόδρομος one who runs before, forerunner. The word was used esp. of the men or troops which were sent to explore before the advance of an army (Westcott; s. also Bruce; Spicq). εἰσῆλθεν aor. act. ind. εἰσέρχομαι to go into. τάξις order. (For literature and a discussion of the priesthood of Melchisedek, s. Hughes; Bruce Demarest, *A History of Interpretation of Hebrews 7:1–10 from the Reformation to the Present* [Tübingen: Mohr, 1976].)

Ch. 7

1 ■ οὗτος this one. ὕψιστος superl. highest, most high. "The most high God" was not the title of some heathen deity, but the same sovereign God whom Abraham worshiped (Hughes). συναντήσας aor. act. part. συναντάω to meet. ὑποστρέφοντι pres. act. part. ὑποστρέφω to return. The dat. is used because the verb "to meet" takes its object in the dat. κοπή slaughter, defeat (s. Bruce; EGT). εὐλογήσας aor. act.
2 part. εὐλογέω to bless (s. Eph. 1:3). ■ ᾧ καί "to whom also." δεκάτη tenth. The offering of a tithe of the spoils to the gods was a custom of antiquity (EGT). ἐμέρισεν aor. act. ind. μερίζω to divide. ἑρμηνευόμενος pres. pass. part. ἑρμηνεύω to interpret. ἔπειτα then. Σαλήμ Salem. The word refers to the
3 city of Jerusalem (s. Riggenbach; Bruce). ■ ἀπάτωρ without a

father. ἀμήτωρ without a mother. The words indicate that the father and mother were unknown (Riggenbach). In rabbinical writings such expressions could mean that the father and mother had died and the child was an orphan (SB III, 693). ἀγενεαλόγητος without genealogy. This would indicate that his genealogy was not known, which fact would have disqualified him for a Levitical priesthood (SB III, 693). The argument from silence plays an important part in rabbinical interpretation of Scripture where (for exegetical purposes) nothing must be regarded as having existed before the time of its first biblical mention (Bruce; SB III, 694). μήτε ... μήτε "neither ... nor." ἀρχή beginning. ἔχων pres. act. part. ἀφωμοιωμένος perf. pass. part. ἀφομοιάω to make like, to produce a facsimile or copy. The likeness is in the picture drawn in Genesis, not in the man himself (RWP). μένει pres. act. ind. to remain, to continue. διηνεκής without interruption, continually. In referring to a dynasty this word means that the family would never fail to have a male heir to rule (Buchanan).

■ θεωρεῖτε pres. act. imp. θεωρέω to see, to observe, to 4 consider. The word expresses the regard of attentive contemplation (Westcott). Although the form of the verb can be ind. or imp., the imp. would be stronger in this context (s. Hughes). πηλίκος how great. δεκάτη tenth, s.v.2. ἔδωκεν aor. act. ind. δίδωμι. ἀκροθίνιον (n. pl.) the top of the heap, spoils, the best part of the spoils. The Greeks after a victory gathered the spoils in a heap and the top or the best part of the heap was presented to the gods (EGT; s. also Riggenbach). πατριάρχης the one who ruled a tribe, patriarch. The definite article used w. the word contains the sense of "the great patriarch" or "our great patriarch" (Hughes). ■ ἱερατεία priesthood. The word emphasizes 5 the priestly office and service. The word ἱερωσύνη in v. 11 is originally more abstract and could be used to emphasize the worth or honor of the office (s. Michel; TDNT). λαμβάνοντες pres. act. part. to receive. ἐντολή command, commandment. ἀποδεκατοῦν pres. act. inf. to take a tenth from someone, to receive a tithe. The inf. is used epexegetically to explain the content of the command. κατά w. the acc. according to, in accordance w. the standard of. νόμος law. καίπερ although. ἐξεληλυθότας perf. act. part. ἐξέρχομαι to go out, to descend from. ὀσφύς waist, hip, loins. The Hebrews considered this to be the place of the reproductive organs and the expression "to go forth from someone's loins" means "to be someone's son or descendant" (BAG; T). ■ γενεαλογούμενος pres. mid. part. 6 γενεαλογέομαι to trace one's genealogical descent, to have one's genealogical descent from someone, to count or reckon someone's genealogy from another (s. EGT). δεδεκάτωκεν perf. act. ind. δεκατόω to take or receive the tithe. ἔχοντα pres. act. part. ἐπαγγελία promise. εὐλόγηκεν perf. act. ind., s.v.1. That this higher status is permanent may be indicated by the two perf. tenses here in v. 6 (Bruce). (For the so-called "perfect of allegory" used of a past but still relevant event, s. IBG, 15ff.)

7 ■ χωρίς w. the gen. "without." ἀντιλογία contradiction, opposition, quarrel (s. MM). ἔλαττον comp. lesser, inferior. κρεῖττον comp. better, superior. εὐλογεῖται pres. pass. ind.,

8 s.v.1. ■ ἀποθνήσκοντες pres. act. part. ἀποθνήσκω to die. The anarthrous part. is used as an attributive and emphasizes the character; i.e., "dying men," i.e., "mortal men" (s. RG, 1105f.; Hughes). μαρτυρούμενος pres. pass. part. μαρτυρέω to witness, pass. to be witnessed, to be reported (BS, 265; s. also BD,

9 164). ζῇ pres. act. ind. ζάω to live. ■ ὡς ἔπος εἰπεῖν "so to speak," an idiomatic expression found often in Philo. Here it could have the meaning "one might almost say" or "to use just the right word" (BAG). The phrase is used to limit a startling statement and the inf. could express conceived result (RWP) or it could be an example of the so-called "inf. abs." (MT, 136). λαμβάνων pres. act. part. λαμβάνω perf. pass. ind., pass. to

10 pay a tenth. ■ ἦν impf. εἰμί. συνήντησεν aor. act. ind. s.v.1.

11   ■ τελείωσις perfection, reaching the goal. The OT law and the Levitical system could not produce forgiveness or an eschatological completion or the holiness of heart demanded by God (s. Michel; TDNT). ἱερωσύνη priesthood, s.v.5. αὐτῆς "on the basis of it," i.e., "the Levitical priesthood," "in association w. it" (Hughes). νενομοθέτηται perf. pass. ind. νομοθετέομαι to enact a law, to furnish w. law (s. RWP; BAG). ἀνίστασθαι pres. mid. inf. ἀνίστημι to rise up. The mid. is used intransitively (RWP). If the form is taken as pass., the meaning of the verb is trans., i.e., "to be raised up" (s. BAG).

12 λέγεσθαι pres. pass. inf. ■ μετατιθεμένης pres. pass. part. μετατίθημι to change, to transfer. (For the idea of change involved in the prep. in compound, s. MH, 318.) The part. is used in a gen. abs. expressing either a conditional or temporal idea. ἀνάγκη necessity. καί also. μετάθεσις changing, transfer,

13 change. ■ ἐπί upon, concerning, w. reference to (EGT). φύλη tribe. μετέσχηκεν perf. act. ind. μετέχω w. the gen. to share w., to be a partaker of, to belong to. The choice of this word points to the voluntary assumption of humanity by the Lord. It is not said simply that He was born of another tribe: He was of His own will so born (Westcott; s. also Heb. 2:14). The perf. expresses a

condition of fact, both historic and official; beyond doubt it is intended to accentuate the abs. incompatibility, resulting from His birth, between Christ and the priesthood in terms of the conditions of the validity prescribed by the old legislation (Spicq; s. also Hughes). προσέσκεν perf. act. ind. προσέχω w. the dat. to give attention to, to attend to, to serve at. θυσιαστήριον the place of sacrifice, altar. ■ πρόδηλος before 14 all, obvious. It is an intensified adj. which means "it is perfectly obvious" (Hughes). ἀνατέταλκεν perf. act. ind. ἀνατέλλω to spring up, to arise. The word refers to rising as the sun, moon, and stars arise, and is also used to describe the sprouting or growing of plants, hair, and disease, and was used metaphorically where the imagery reflects the rising or growth of stellar bodies or planets; the idea being that the subjects would arise or had arisen to prominence or prosperity, and would increase in prominence. For this reason the word easily applied to a king or to the expected Messiah (Buchanan; s. also Michel). εἰς to, unto, concerning. The prep. is applied to the direction of the thought (EGT). ἐλάλησεν aor. act. ind. λαλέω to speak. ■ 15 περισσότερον comp. "more," especially." κατάδηλος quite clear, evident. The prep. in compound is perfective. ὁμοιότης likeness. ἀνίσταται pres. mid. or pass., s.v.11. ■ σάρκινος 16 fleshly. Adjectives w. this ending signify material, origin, or kind (MH, 359). The enactment was fleshly inasmuch as it took to do only w. the flesh. It caused the priesthood to be implicated w. and dependent on fleshly descent (EGT; s. also Michel). γέγονεν perf. act. ind. γίνομαι. ἀκατάλυτος not able to be destroyed, indestructible. ■ μαρτυρεῖται pres. pass. ind. 17 μαρτυρέομαι to bear witness, to testify. The pass. may be the divine or "theological pass." used to imply God as the subject (s. BG, 76). ὅτι used to introduce direct discourse. ■ ἀθέτησις 18 setting aside, annulling, cancellation. The word was a legal term used in the papyri for the cancellation or annulment of a legal enactment. Here it has the idea "cancellation has taken place" (s. BS, 228f.; Preisigke; MM; Hughes; Bruce). προαγούσης pres. act. part. προάγω to go before, to precede. The part. is used in an adjectival sense w. the meaning "former." ἐντολή commandment. ἀνωφελής uselessness, profitlessness. The commandment was useless in that it had no ability to aid men to draw near to God and was unable to effect the justification of sinners before God (EGT; Hughes). ■ ἐτελείωσιν aor. act. ind. 19 τελειόω to perfect. to bring to perfection, to bring to the goal. ἐπεισαγωγή bring in. The word was used in Josephus w. the idea of "replacement" (Moffatt). The prep. in compound has the idea of "in addition to," "over and beyond," i.e., "a bringing in in addition to" (Bruce). κρείττων comp. "better." The gen. "better hope" is obj. gen. ἐγγίζομεν pres. act. ind. to come near, to draw near. The pres. tense indicates that which is continually possible.

20 ■ καθ᾽ ὅσον "according to how much," i.e., "inasmuch as." ὁρκωμοσία taking of an oath. εἰσίν ... γεγονόντες. The perf. act. part. of γίνομαι is used in a periphrastic perf. act. construction. The periphrasis marks the possession as well as the impartment of the office: they have been made priests and they act as
21 priests (Westcott). ■ διὰ τοῦ λέγοντος "through the one who said." ὤμοσεν aor. act. ind. ὄμνυμι to swear, to take an oath (s. Heb. 6:13). μεταμεληθήσεται fut. pass. ind. μεταμέλομαι to be sorry, to repent out of sorrow, to have an "after" care (s.
22 EGT; Trench, Synonyms, 241; TDNT). ■ κατὰ τοῦτο "according to so much," "by so much." κρείττονος comp. "better." ἔγγυος surety, guarantee. The word means a bond, bail, collateral, or some kind of guarantee that a promise will be fulfilled. The word was used in the papyri in legal and promissory documents meaning "a guarantor" or "one who stands security." Jesus Himself is our security that there will be no annulment of this new and better covenant (s. Buchanan; Bruce; TDNT; Spicq; Michel; MM). διαθήκη contract, covenant, agreement, testament (s.
23 Michel; TDNT; CBB). ■ πλείονες comp. pl. of πολύς "many," "many in number," not many at one and the same time but many in succession (EGT). εἰσίν ... γεγονότες (s.v.20). διά used w. the acc. of the inf. to express cause. θανάτῳ dat. sing., instrumental use of the dat. "by death." κωλύεσθαι pres. pass. inf. κωλύω to hinder, to prevent. The inf. is used w. the prep. to express cause "because they were prevented by death." παραμένειν pres. act. inf. to remain along side of, to continue, to remain in office or serve (Moffatt; for its use in the papyri, s. MM). The inf. is used epexegetically to explain that which was
24 prevented. ■ μένειν pres. act. inf. to remain, to continue. The pres. tense indicates the unending and continuing action or state. The inf. is used w. the prep. to express cause or reason. ἀπαράβατος not able to be passed on to another, intransmittable, nontransferable. The priesthood of Christ does not pass to another precisely because it is a perpetual priesthood (Hughes;
25 s. also Bruce; Moffatt). ἱερωσύνη priesthood. ■ ὅθεν therefore. καί also. παντελής complete. The phrase εἰς τὸ παντελές "unto completeness," can have a temporal sense "for all time" or it can have a qualitative sense and emphasize full completeness, i.e., "fully and completely," or it may be that both ideas are

contained and expressed in the phrase (s. Hughes; Michel).
προσερχομένους pres. mid. part. προσέρχομαι w. the dat. to
come to. The pres. tense emphasizes the continual activity.
πάντοτε always. ζῶν pres. act. part. ζάω to live. The part. is
causal "because He continually lives." εἰς w. the inf. is used to
express purpose. ἐντυγχάνειν pres. act. inf. to make intercession, to intercede for another. It was sometimes used of bringing
a petition before a king on behalf of another (s. 1 Tim. 2:1; EGT;
Hughes; TDNT, MNTW, 54–56). Since rabbinical scholars assigned an intercessory function to the angels, it may be that the
readers were tempted to worship angels as intercessors and
therefore the writer makes it perfectly plain that Christ is the
sole mediator and intercessor. To rely upon angels or saints or
any other finite being for intercession is not only futile, but it also
betrays a failure of confidence in the adequacy of Christ as our
intercessor (Hughes).

■ τοιοῦτος such a one, "such a high priest." The word 26
refers to the previous indicating the one who is absolute in power
and eternal in being (Westcott). καί indeed. The word emphasizes the thought; i.e., "such a high priest exactly befitted us"
(Hughes; s. also Westcott). ἔπρεπεν impf. ind. act. πρέπω w.
the dat. to be suited for, to be fit for. ἀρχιερεύς high priest.
ὅσιος holy, pious (s. TDNT; CBB). ἄκακος without evil. The
word describes the absence of all that is bad and wrong
(Hughes). ἀμίαντος without defilement, stainless, untainted.
The word implies not merely ritual purity, but real ethical cleanliness (RWP). κεχωρισμένος perf. pass. part. χωρίζω to separate. The separation is due to His perfect qualities; i.e., He is
separated in that He is in a class separate from sinners. The perf.
tense suggests that He is permanently separated from them (Hewitt). ὑψηλότερος comp. of ὑψηλός "higher," followed by the
gen. of comparison. γενόμενος aor. mid. part. γίνομαι. The
part could express means or manner. ■ καθ᾽ἡμέραν "daily." 27
ἀνάγκη necessity. πρότερον first, first of all. The adv. is used
for comparison between two things (RWP). ἴδιος one's own.
ἀναφέρειν pres. act. inf. to bring up, to offer. The inf. is epexegetical explaining the necessity. ἔπειτα then; i.e., "after that."
ἐποίησεν aor. act. ind. The aor. points here to the one time
completed action. ἐφάπαξ once for all. ἀνενέγκας aor. act.
part. ἀναφέρω to offer up, to sacrifice. The part could be temporal. ■ καθίστησιν pres. act. ind. to constitute, to appoint. The 28
pres. tense indicates that at the time when this epistle was being
written the Levitical priesthood was still functioning, w. the
implication that the Jerusalem temple was still standing

(Hughes). ἀρχιερεῖς acc. pl. in a double acc. construction; i.e., "appoint men as high priests." ἔχοντας pres. act. part. ἀσθένεια weakness. ὁρκωμοσία oath, taking of an oath, "oath taking" (Westcott). μετά w. the acc. "after." υἱός son. The lack of the article emphasizes the character or quality; i.e., one who is a son. τετελειωμένον perf. pass. part. τελειόω to perfect, to make perfect, to bring to the goal (s. Heb. 5:9).

Ch. 8

1 ■ κεφάλαιον pertaining to the head. The word can refer to the "sum" as of numbers added up from below to the head of the column where the result is set down and would have the meaning "summary," "synopsis" which is limited to the main points. The word however could also mean "the chief point" as of a copestone or capital of a pillar and thus have the meaning "main thing," "main point" (s. Buchanan; EGT; Michel; BAG; Westcott). ἐπί w. the dat. "in the matter of" (RWP). λεγομένος pres. pass. part. "that which is being discussed," "the things being talked about." τοιοῦτος such a one. ἐκάθισεν aor. act. ind. καθίζω to take one's seat, to sit down. (For the concept of sitting at the right hand, s. Heb. 1:4; Eph. 1:20.) ἐν δεξίᾳ "on the right hand"; i.e., the place of honor. μεγαλωσύνη majesty.

2 ■ τὰ ἅγια n. gen. pl. "the holy things"; i.e., "the sanctuary" (s. Hughes; Michel). λειτουργός minister, one who ministers in religious matters (s. TDNT; Heb. 1:14). σκηνή tent, tabernacle. ἀληθινός true, genuine; i.e., the ideal or antitypical tabernacle. The word is used in the fourth gospel in contrast not to what is false, but to what is symbolical (EGT; for an extended discussion of this verse in relation to Heb. 9:11, s. Hughes 283–290). ἔπηξεν aor. act. ind. πήγνυμι to fix, to fasten as the pegs of a

3 tent, to pitch a tent (s. RWP). κύριος lord. ■ εἰς used w. the inf. to express purpose. προσφέρειν pres. act. inf. to bring to, to offer. The pres. tense emphasizes an action which was repeatedly done. καθίσταται pres. pass. ind. καθίστημι to appoint. ὅθεν wherefore. ἀναγκαῖος necessity, necessary. ἔχειν pres. act. inf. The so-called subject of the inf. in the acc. case is τοῦτον "this one," "this priest," and refers to Christ. καί "also." προσενέγκῃ aor. act. subj. προσφέρω The aor. tense emphasizes that Christ's offering was once for all and is consistent w. the author's repeated emphasis on the singularity of the sacrifice

4 which Christ offered (Bruce; Spicq; Hughes). ■ ἦν impf. ind. The ind. is used in a 2nd-class conditional sentence which expresses a contrary to fact statement. ὄντων pres. part. εἰμί. The part. is used in a gen. abs. construction and is causal. προσφερόντων

pres. act. part. s.v.3. κατά w. the acc. "according to," "according to the standard of." It was the law which regulated all that concerns the earthly priesthood and by this law He is excluded from priestly office, not being of the tribe of Levi (EGT). ■ 5 οἵτινες "which one," i.e., those belonging to this class. The qualitative relative emphasizes the character of the Levitical priesthood (Westcott). ὑπόδειγμα pattern, copy. σκιά shadow. λατρεύουσιν pres. act. ind. to minister, to perform religious service. τὰ ἐπουράνια "the heavenly things" (s. Eph. 1:3). κεχρημάταισται perf. pass. ind. χρηματίζομαι to warn, to instruct. The word was used in the papyri of official pronouncements by magistrates and of a royal reply to a petition as well as an answer of an oracle. In the NT it is used of divine communications (AS; s. also BS, 122; MM). μέλλων pres. act. part. to be about to. The part. is used temporarily; i.e., "as he was about to." ἐπιτελεῖν pres. act. inf. to bring to completion. ὅρα pres. act. imp. to see. ὁράω pres. act. ind. to speak, to say. ποιήσεις fut. act. ind. The fut. used to express an imp. It's a fut. under Semitic influence and is a translation of the Heb. imp. (s. BG, 94). τύπος type, pattern. This was the stamp or impression struck from a die or seal; hence, a figure, draft, sketch, or pattern (EGT; s. also TDNT). δειχθέντα aor. pass. part. δείκνυμι to show. The pass. is the divine or theological pass. indicating God as the One who did the action (s. Hughes; BG, 76). ■ νῦν now. 6 The particle is logical rather than temporal but the temporal factor is inevitably involved in the argument (Hughes). διαφορώτερος comp. διάφορος differing, excellent, comp. more excellent. τέτυχεν perf. act. ind. τυγχάνω to attain, to obtain. The perf. tense emphasizes the continual possession. The verb is followed by the gen. λειτουργία service, ministry, religious or sacred service (s. TDNT). ὅσῳ "by how much," instrumental case of the relat. (RWP). καί also. κρείττων better. μεσίτης mediator, arbitrator, go between (s. Michel; Bruce). ἥτις which. The antecedent of the relat. pron. is διαθήκη. This relat. properly indicates the class or kind to which an object belongs (RG, 727). ἐπαγγελία promise. νενομοθέτηται perf. pass. ind. νομοθετέω to legislate, to enact by law, to ordain by law. The perf. tense looks at the continuing result. (For this word, s. Hughes.)

■ πρώτη first; i.e., the first covenant. ἄμεμπτος blameless, 7 faultless. δεύτερος second. ἐζητεῖτο impf. pass. ind. ζητέω to seek. The verb is used in the second part of a contrary to fact conditional clause. τόπος place, room, occasion, followed by the gen.; i.e., "room for . . . ," "occasion for . . . ." ■ μεμφόμενος 8 pres. mid. part. μέμφομαι to blame, to find fault w. αὐτούς acc. pl. "them"; i.e., the Israelites. συντελέσω fut. act. ind. συντελέω to bring to completion, to accomplish, to establish.

9 ἐπί upon, w. ■ κατά according to. The second covenant was not only to be a second one, but one of a different type (Westcott). ἐπόιησα aor. act. ind. ποιέω. ἐπιλαβομένου aor. mid. part. ἐπιλαμβάνομαι w. the gen. indicating the part affected (RWP) to grasp, to take hold of. The part. is used in a gen. abs. construction indicating the time (BD, 218). ἐξαγαγεῖν aor. act. inf. ἐξάγω to lead out. The inf. is used to express purpose. ἐνέμειναν aor. act. ind. ἐμμένω to remain in, to continue in. ἠμέλησα aor. act. ind. ἀμελέω to have no concern for, to

10 neglect (s. Heb. 2:3). ■ αὕτη "this." The pron. is used as the subject of the verb to be supplied ἐστίν "this is ...." διαθήσομαι fut. mid. ind. διατίθημι to make a covenant. Used w. the dat. διδούς pres. act. part. δίδωμι. The part. could be used temporarily or it could express the manner or means of making the covenant; i.e., "I will make a covenant even by putting ..." (Westcott). διάνοια mind, understanding, intellect (s. EGT; RWP). ἐπί w. the acc. "upon." ἐπιγράψω fut. act. ind. ἐπιγράφω to write upon. ἔσομαι fut. mid. εἰς "to." The prep. is used w. the verb "to be" to indicate the thought "to serve as." Although this is a Hebraic use of the prep., there are also examples in Koine apart from a Semitic influence (s. LAE, 120f.; M,

11 71f.). ■ διδάξωσιν aor. act. subj. διδάσκω to teach. πολίτης citizen, fellow citizen. γνῶθι aor. act. imp. γινώσκω to know. ὅτι because. εἰδήσουσιν fut. perf. act. ind. οἶδα to know. (For the fut. perf. form, s. RG, 361.) μικρός small. μέγας great. The two adjectives are used in the superl. sense; i.e., "from the least

12 to the greatest." ■ ἵλεως gracious, merciful. ἔσομαι fut. mid. ἀδικία unrighteousness. μνησθῶ aor. pass. subj.

13 μιμνήσκομαι to remember. ■ πεπαλαίωκεν perf. act. ind. παλαιόω to declare or treat as old or obsolete, pass. to become old or obsolete. The word was used in the papyri for a temple and a wall which had become old and obsolete and needed repairing (s. Preisigke II, 224; MM). καινήν new. παλαιούμενον pres. pass. part. γηράσκον pres. act. part. γηράσκω to grow old. The word refers to the decay of old age (RWP). ἐγγύς near. ἀφανισμός disappearing, vanishing away. The word is suggestive of utter destruction and abolition (EGT).

Ch. 9

1   ■ εἶχε impf. act. ind. ἔχω. πρώτη first. The word is to be understood as modifying the unexpressed word "covenant"

(Hughes). δικαίωμα that which is demanded by righteousness, regulation, ordinance (s. Westcott; Michel). λατρεία worship, ministry, religious service. The word is to be understood as a gen. sing. modifying the word "ordinance" rather than the acc. pl. (s. Hughes; Riggenbach). ἅγιον holy place, sanctuary. κοσμικός pertaining to the world, earthly. Here the word could mean "mundane" or "material" (Bruce). ■ σκηνή tent, tabernacle. 2 κατεσκευάσθη aor. pass. ind. κατασκευάζω to outfit w. vessels, to equip, to prepare, to furnish (s. Heb. 3:3). ᾗ rel. pron. fem. dat. sing. "in which." λυχνία lampstand. It refers to the menorah which was placed at the south side of the holy place; it was made of gold, w. three branches springing from either side of the main stem; the main stem and all six branches each supported a flower-shaped lamp holder (Exod. 25:31ff.; 37:17ff.) (Bruce; s. also ND III, 707–718). πρόθεσις placing before, setting out. τῶν ἄρτων bread. The expression lit. means "the setting out of the bread (loaves)" i.e., "the bread set forth in two rows" (Lightfoot; s. also SB III, 719–728). ἅγια n. pl. The Holy Place (s. Hughes). ■ μετά w. the acc. "after," "behind." δεύτερος sec- 3 ond. καταπέτασμα curtain, veil. λέγομένη pres. pass. part. ἅγια ἁγίων The Holy of Holies. The translation of the Heb. idiom which is equivalent to a superl. (EGT). ■ χρυσοῦς golden. 4 ἔχουσα pres. act. part. θυμιατήριον altar of incense. The word has also been understood as being the "censer," or "incense shovel," and some have thought to connect the altar of incense to the Holy Place in a theological sense and point out a special doctrinal association between the altar of incense and the Holy of Holies. (For a discussion of this problem, s. Hughes; s. also SB III, 728ff.) κιβωτός box, chest, ark (s. EGT). περικεκαλυμμένην perf. pass. part. περικαλύπτω to cover, to cover on all sides. πάντοθεν all around. χρυσίον gold. στάμνος pitcher, jar. The rabbis believed that in the fut. Elijah would restore to Israel the container of manna, the flask of sprinkling water, and the jar of anointing oil (Buchanan). ῥάβδος stick, staff. βλαστήσασα aor. act. part. βλαστάνω to sprout, to bud. πλάξ flat stone, tablet. ■ ὑπεράνω w. the gen. 5 "above." χερουβίν cherubim. The cherubim are the carriers of the divine glory and shekinah (Michel; s. also SB III, 168f.; TDNT). The cherubim were two figures, made of beaten gold, standing at either end of the mercy seat with which they were integrally connected, and facing inward toward each other, their wings stretched out and overarching the mercy seat (Exod. 25:17ff.) (Hughes). κατασκιάζοντα pres. act. part. κατασκιάζω to overshadow. ἱλαστήριον place of propitiation

(s. Rom. 3:25); mercy seat. The mercy seat was a slab of pure gold, two and one-half cubics long by one and a half cubics wide, which fit exactly over the top of the ark of the covenant (Hughes; s. also Bruce). περὶ ὧν "concerning which things." κατὰ μέρος "in detail," the distributive use of the prep. (RWP).

6 ■ κατεσκευασμένων perf. pass. part. gen. abs. used temporarily (s.v.2). διὰ παντός "through all," i.e., "continually." The phrase seems to express the continuous, unbroken permanence of a characteristic habit (Westcott). εἰσίασιν pres. act. ind. 3rd per. pl. εἴσειμι to go into. λατρεία religious service (s.v.1; s. also TDNT). ἐπιτελοῦντες pres. act. part. ἐπιτελέω to bring to conclusion, to complete, to fulfill, to perform. The verb is used by various writers for the accomplishing of religious services (EGT).

7 ■ δευτέραν second; i.e., the second tent or the "Holy of Holies." ἅπαξ once. ἐνιαυτός year, gen. of time; i.e., "once for each year" (RWP). χωρίς w. the gen. "without." ὅ rel. pron. n. sing. referring to the word "blood." προσφέρει pres. act. ind. to bring to, to offer, to offer a sacrifice, to sacrifice. The pres. tense is customary or iterat. indicating that which continually happened year after year. ὑπέρ w. the gen. "on behalf of." ἀγνόημα ignorances, sin of ignorance, error. The word refers to those sins which are committed inadvertently or in ignorance; i.e., unintentionally or through human frailty (Lev. 4:1f.; 5:17ff.), as distinct from those who sin in deliberate and rebellious defiance of God and His law (Hughes; s. also Michel; Moffatt; SB III, 177f.).

8 ■ δηλοῦντος pres. act. part. δηλόω to make clear. The part. is used as a gen. abs. μήπω not yet. πεφανερῶσθαι perf. pass. inf. φανερόω to make plain, to manifest. The inf. is used in indirect discourse explaining the part. of the gen. abs. τῶν ἁγίων sanctuary. Here the word is used to comprise the Holy Place and the Holy of Holies together (Bruce). ἐχούσης pres. part. gen. abs. στάσις standing. Used w. the previous part., the phrase means "retaining its status" (Bruce; s. also Westcott).

9 ■ παραβολή parable, symbol, figure (s. TDNT). εἰς "unto" (s. Riggenbach). καιρός time, time period. ἐνεστηκότα perf. act. part. ἐνίστημι to be present (s. Gal. 1:4). καθ᾽ ἥν "according to which." The rel. pron. refers to the word "parable." It is in accordance w. the parabolic significance of the tabernacle and its arrangements, that gifts and sacrifices were offered which could purge only the flesh, not the conscience (EGT). προσφέρονται pres. pass. ind., s.v.7. The pres. tense implies that the temple ritual has not yet been discontinued (Hughes). δυνάμεναι pres. mid. part. συνείδησις conscience (s. Rom. 2:15; 1 Cor. 8:7). τελειῶσαι aor. act. inf. τελειόω to perfect (s. Heb. 5:9).

λατρεύοντα pres. act. part. λατρεύω to worship, to perform
religious services (s. TDNT). ■ μόνον only. ἐπί w. the dat. "in   10
the matter of" (RWP). βρῶμα food. πόμα drink. διάφορος
different. The expression "meats and drink" denotes food laws
in general (Bruce; s. also Moffatt). βαπτισμός washing (s. Heb.
6:2). δικαίωμα regulation, s.v.1. μέχρι w. the gen. "until."
διόρθωσις setting straight, restoring that which is out of line,
improvement, reformation, new order (Hughes; BAG).
ἐπικείμενα pres. mid. or pass. part. ἐπιτίθημι to lay upon, to
impose (RWP).

■ παραγενόμενος aor. mid. part. παραγίνομαι to come,   11
to appear (s. Hughes; s. also Westcott). γενομένων aor. mid.
part. γίνομαι to become, to be. ἀγαθόν good. διά w. the gen.
"through." The prep. is best understood not in the local sense,
but in the instrumental sense "by means of" (EGT). μείζων
(comp.) greater. τελειότερος (comp.) more perfect.
χειροποίητος made w. hands. κτίσις creation. The gen. is gen.
of source or origin. ■ τράγος goat, male goat, he goat. μόσχος   12
calf. The goat was used for the sacrifice for the people and the
calf was used for the sacrifice for the high priest and his house
(s. Michel). δέ adversative "but." ἴδιος one's own, own.
εἰσῆλθεν aor. act. ind. εἰσέρχομαι to go in. ἐφάπαξ once for
all. The prep. in compound gives a directive strengthening (MH,
315). ἅγια sanctuary (s.v.8). αἰώνιος eternal. λύτρωσις redeeming, releasing by the payment of a price (s. Rom. 3:24;
Bruce; Hughes). εὑράμενος aor. mid. part. εὑρίσκω to find, to
obtain, to secure. The aor. part. means that Christ entered into
the heavenly sanctuary "after He had secured" an eternal redemption: the securing of our eternal redemption took place at
the cross and was followed by His entry into heaven (Hughes).

■ ταῦρος steer, young bull. σποδός ashes. δάμαλις young   13
female calf, heifer. ῥαντίζουσα pres. act. part. ῥαντίζω to
sprinkle. The "ashes of a heifer" were those obtained by burning
a red heifer outside the camp according to a specially prescribed
process. The ashes were used to mix w. water, as necessity arose,
to be sprinkled on persons who had become defiled by touching
a corpse or being in a tent where there was a corpse, or by
touching the slain in battle, or a bone from a corpse (Num. 19).
This ceremonial impurity was regarded as a disqualification for
intercourse w. men or God (Buchanan; Moffatt).
κεκοινωμένους perf. pass. part. κοινόω to make common, to
defile. The perf. part. looks at the state or condition. ἁγιάζει
pres. act. ind. to sanctify, to set apart, to remove from the "common" or "profane" thus qualifying the person for again worship-

ing God (EGT). πρός w. the acc. "w. a view to," "for."
14 καθαριεῖ purity, cleanliness. ■ πόσῳ "by how much." μᾶλλον
more. (For this type of rabbinical argument, s. Rom. 5:9.)
προσήνεγειν aor. act. ind. προσφέρω s.v.7. ἄμωμος unblemished, without blemish (s. Hughes; Eph. 1:4; Col. 1:22). The
word was used of the Leviticus sacrifices but now it has an
ethical significance and explains how the blood of Christ should
not merely furnish ceremonial cleansing (EGT). καθαριεῖ fut.
act. ind. καθαρίζω to cleanse. The word marks what the object
is itself; i.e., "clean" ceremonially or morally (Westcott). The
fut. tense is the logical fut. used in this type argument (Riggenbach; s. also Buchanan). The word was used in the papyri for
religious cleansing (s. BS, 216f.). λατρεύειν pres. act. inf. to
serve, to do religious service, to minister (s. AS, 226). The inf.
is used w. the prep. and article to express purpose. ζῶντι pres.
act. part. ζάω to live. The part. is used adjectivally and the dat.
follows the verb "to serve." (For the use of the "ashes of a heifer"
in relation to the death of Christ, s. Hughes 362ff.)
15   ■ διὰ τοῦτο "because of this." It refers to Christ's effective-
ness in offering sacrifice and cleansing from sin so that the
believer might worship the living God (Buchanan). μεσίτης
mediator. ὅπως used w. the subj. to express purpose (s. MT,
105). γενομένου aor. mid. part. The part. is a gen. abs. expressing cause. ἀπολύτρωσις a releasing by the payment of a price,
redemption (s. Rom. 3:25). ἐπί used w. the dat. "upon," here
"by," "under." παράβασις transgression. The gen. case (ablative) expresses the idea of separation (s. Riggenbach). λάβωσιν
aor. act. subj. λαμβάνω to receive. κεκλημένοι perf. pass. part.
καλέω to call. The perf. tense indicates the completed state or
condition. κληρονομία inheritance. The gen. is to be taken w.
the word "promise" giving a further definition or content of the
16 promise (Westcott). ■ ἀνάγκη necessity. φέρεσθαι pres. pass.
inf., pass. to be brought. The word is probably used here in the
legal technical sense of "to be registered" or "to be publicly
known" (s. Bruce; Michel; MM; TDNT). διαθέμενος pres. mid.
part. διατίθημι to make a covenant, to make a testament. (For
a detailed discussion of the meaning of the word "covenant"
17 here, s. Hughes; Bruce.) ■ βέβαιος firm, guaranteed. Used here
in the legal sense "valid" (s. BAG; Riggenbach). ἐπεί since,
because. μήποτε never. ἰσχύει pres. act. ind. to have strength,
to be in force. (For the legal term, s. Michel; Riggenbach;
Hughes.) ζῇ pres. act. ind., s.v.14. The pres. tenses here are
18 gnomic indicating that which is always true. ■ ὅθεν wherefore. χωρίς w. the gen. without. ἐγκεκαίνισται perf. pass. ind.

ἐγκαινίζω to renew, to inaugurate. The idea of the word is "to introduce something new," "to initiate" w. the concepts of "inauguration" and "dedication" being closely related (Hughes). The perf. is used not in an aoristic sense, but rather to describe what "stands written" in Scripture and is a marked feature of the author's style (M, 142; s. also Michel; Riggenbach). ■ 19 λαληθείσης aor. pass. part. λαλέω. The part. is used as a gen. abs. expressing time "after . . . ." ἐντόλη commandment. κατά w. the acc. "according to." λάβων aor. act. part. λαμβάνω. μόσχος calf. The Heb. term "oxen" used in Exod. 24:5 is applicable to bovine animals of any age (Hughes). The related word is used in the Ugaritic language w. the meaning "young cow" (s. Joseph Aistleitner, Wörterbuch der Ugaritischen Sprache, 259f.). τράγος goat. The text here is unclear and many manuscripts omit this word and the omission is probably the best reading (s. Hughes; Bruce; s. also TC). μετά w. the gen. "with." ἔριον wool. κόκκινος scarlet. ὕσσωπος hyssop, marjoram. The hyssop was apparently tied w. the scarlet wool to a cedar wood stick, thus forming a sprinkling implement which was dipped in the blood diluted w. water. Although "water and scarlet wool and hyssop" are not mentioned in the Exodus account, there is no reason why this common method of sprinkling should not have been used by Moses in the procedure described in Exod. 24 (Hughes; s. also Delitzsch). ἐρράντισεν aor. act. ind. ῥαντίζω to sprinkle. ■ 20 ἐνετείλατο aor. mid. ind. ἐντέλλομαι to command. ■ σκεῦος 21 vessel. λειτουργία ministry, worship service. τῷ αἵματι dat. of instrument "w. the blood." ὁμοίως adv. "likewise." ἐρράντισεν cf. vs. 19. ■ σχεδόν almost. καθαρίζεται pres. 22 pass. ind., s.v.14. The pres. tense is gnomic indicating that which is always true. αἱματεκχυσία blood shedding, shedding of blood. The word may have been coined by the author, but is related to the expression ἐκχεῖν αἷμα "to pour out blood" and ἔκχυσις αἵματος "the pouring out of blood" which appear in the LXX (s. Bruce; Michel). γίνεται pres. mid. ind. The pres. tense is gnomic indicating that which is always true. ἄφεσις releasing, forgiving, forgiveness. The expression here may have been a proverbial expression since it occurs in the rabbinical writings; i.e., "does not atonement come through the blood?" or "surely atonement can be made only w. the blood" (Bruce; Buchanan).

■ ἀνάγκη necessity, necessary. ὑποδείγμα pattern, copy 23 (s. Heb. 8:5). τούτοις instrumental dat. "by these things," i.e., by these rites or by the different materials of cleansing depicted from Heb. 9:19ff. (Hughes; Michel). καθαρίζεσθαι pres. pass.

inf. The inf. is epexegetical describing the "necessity." τὰ
ἐπουράνια "the heavenly things." κρείττων comp. dat. pl.
24 "better." παρά used in the comp. sense "than." ■
χειροποίητος s.v.11. εἰσῆλθεν aor. act. ind., s.v.12. ἁγιά
sanctuary, s.v.3. ἀντίτυπον copy, antitype. The word lit. means
"answering to the type" and means here a counterpart of reality
(Moffatt). ἀληθινός true, genuine. ἐμφανισθῆναι aor. pass.
inf. ἐμφανίζω to make visible, pass. to become visible, to appear
to someone. The prep. in compound is local; i.e., "to appear in
the presence of." The inf. is used to express purpose. πρόσωπον
face, presence. ὑπὲρ ἡμῶν "for us," "on our behalf." (For
Christ's appearing in the presence of God, s. Hughes, 329–354,
25 esp. 349f.) ■ προσφέρῃ pres. act. subj., s.v.7. The subj. is used
in a neg. purpose clause. The pres. tense emphasizes the continuous action and may be viewed here as iterat.; i.e., "to offer
Himself over and over again." ὥσπερ as, just as. κατ'ἐνιαυτόν
"yearly," the distributive use of the prep.; i.e., "year after year,"
"every year the same thing." ἀλλότριος belonging to another,
not one's own. The blood provided by our High Priest for the
atonement of mankind was human blood, and, moreover, His
26 own blood (Hughes). ■ ἐπεί since, since in that case (Westcott).
The word is used to introduce causal clauses (s. MT, 318). ἔδει
impf. act. ind. δεῖ it is necessary, impf. "it would have been
necessary." The construction is a 2nd-class conditional clause
(contrary to fact) w. the condition omitted in an eliptical construction; i.e., "since, if that were true, it would be necessary for
Him to suffer often" (RWP; s. also RG, 963). παθεῖν aor. act.
inf. πάσχω to suffer. The inf. is used to explain the necessity.
καταβολή foundation. ἅπαξ once for all. συντέλεια completion, consummation (s. Heb. 5:9). ἀθέτησις putting away (s.
Heb. 7:18). The prep. used w. the word indicates the aim, goal,
or purpose. πεφανέρωται perf. pass. ind. φανερόω to appear.
The verb indicates a public manifestation and appearance of
Christ before the world (Michel). The perf. emphasizes the com-
27 pleted action w. continuing results. ■ καθ' "according to so
much," i.e., "inasmuch as," "just as." ἀπόκειται pres. mid.-
pass. ind. ἀπόκειμαι to lay away, to appoint. The pres. tense
indicates a truth which is continually true. ἀποθανεῖν aor. act.
inf. ἀποθνήσκω to die. The inf. is used epexegetically explaining that which is appointed. The aor. tense points to the fact of
death as a conclusive act. μετά w. the acc. "after." κρίσις
judging, judgment. The rabbis taught that those born are appointed to die and those who die to live again and those who live
again to be judged (s. Michel; Buchanan; M Aboth 4:11, 22).

■ οὕτως so. The comparison extends to both terms, the once 28
dying and the judgment. The results of Christ's life are settled.
In Christ's case the result is that He appears a second time
without sin unto salvation, the sin having been destroyed by His
death (EGT). προσενεχθείς aor. pass. part., s.v.7. The part. is
used temporarily "after . . . ." ἀνενεγκεῖν aor. act. inf.
ἀναφέρω to take up and carry away, to take away. The inf. is
used to express purpose. ἐκ δευτέρου "a second time." The
prep. is used temporarily (s. IBG, 72f.). χωρίς without; i.e.,
"without any further sin being laid upon Him," or "unburdened
further by any sin" (Delitzsch). ὀφθήσεται fut. pass. ind. ὁράω
to see, pass. to appear. ἀπεκδεχομένοις pres. mid. part.
ἀπεκδέχομαι to eagerly but patiently expect or await (s. Phil.
3:20). The word is used in the NT w. reference to a fut. manifestation of the glory of Christ (Westcott).

Ch. 10

■ σκία shadow. It refers to the outline or shadow cast by 1
the object which is the reality (s. Riggenbach; Michel). ἔχων
pres. act. part. The part. could be taken as causal. μέλλων pres.
act. part. to be about to. The part. is used as a substitutive "the
fut. things," "the things about to come." εἰκών image. The image is the real object which cast the shadow that the law has
(Buchanan; s. also Hughes; Michel). πρᾶγμα that which is
done, matter, thing; i.e., "the real object." It expresses the "good
things which are coming" so far as they were embodied (Westcott). κατ᾽ἐνιαυτόν "yearly" (s. Heb. 9:25). προσφέρουσιν
pres. act. ind. to bring a sacrifice, to offer. The pres. tense points
to the continual repeated sacrifices. εἰς τὸ διηνεκές "continually," "without interruption" (s. Heb. 7:3). προσερχομένους
pres. mid. part. προσέρχομαι to come to, to approach. The
part. is used as a substitutive "those approaching," "those who
continually draw near." τελειῶσαι aor. act. inf. τελειόω to
perfect, to complete, to bring to the goal (s. Heb. 5:9). ■ ἐπεί 2
"since," "for otherwise." Used in an elliptical construction of a
contrary to fact conditional clause (s. Heb. 9:26; BD, 238f.).
ἐπαύσαντο aor. mid. ind. παύομαι to cease. προσφερόμεναι
pres. pass. part. The part. is used supplementarily to complete
the action of the verb "to cease." This sentence should be taken
as a question; i.e., "for if it were otherwise, would they have not
ceased to be offered?" (s. Bruce). διά used w. the acc. of the
articular inf. to express cause. μηδείς "not one," "no." The word
is to be taken as negating the noun "conscience." ἔτι yet, any
longer. Used in the neg. expression meaning "more," i.e., "no

more." συνείδησις conscience, consciousness. λατρεύοντας
pres. act. part. λατρεύω to worship. The part. is used as a substitutive and is the so-called "subject" of the inf. ἅπαξ once for
all. κεκαθαρισμένους perf. pass. part. καθαρίζω to cleanse.
The part. could be conditional or causal. The perf. tense suggests
3 a cleansing that is permanent (Hughes). ■ ἐν αὐταῖς "in these,"
i.e., "in the sacrifices." ἀνάμνησις remembering, reminder.
The word means "a calling to mind of sins" whereby men are put
4 in remembrance of them by a divine institution (Westcott). ■
ἀδύνατος impossible. ταῦρος steer, bull. τράγος goat, male
goat. ἀφαιρεῖν pres. act. inf. ἀφαιρέω to take away from, to
take away, to remove. The pres. tense points to a continual
action and emphasizes that which is always true.
5   ■ διό wherefore. εἰσερχόμενος pres. mid. part. The part.
is temporal "when He came." The words are considered prophetic, depicting beforehand the mind of Christ regarding OT
sacrifice, and His own mission (EGT). λέγει pres. act. ind.
Christ Himself speaks from Ps. 40:16–18 (Hewitt). προσφορά
offering. It refers to the Heb. "non-bloody offering" i.e., the
"meal offering" (EGT). ἠθέλησας aor. act. ind. θέλω.
κατηρτίσω aor. mid. ind. 2nd per. sing. καταρτίζω to prepare.
The words "a body you have prepared for me" were evidently
taken from the LXX and are an interpretative paraphrase of the
Heb. text. It could have been that the Gr. translators regarded
the Heb. words as an instance of "a part for the whole," i.e., the
"digging" or hollowing out of the ears is part of the total work
of fashioning a human body (Bruce). It may also have been that
the "ears" were taken as a symbol of obedience in that they were
the organ of reception of the divine will and the body was considered the organ of the fulfillment of the divine will (Riggenbach).
Perhaps there is an illusion to the custom of piercing a slave's
ears showing that he had voluntarily refused his liberty (s. Exod.
6 21:1–6; Deut. 15:17; but s. Hughes). ■ ὁλοκαύτωμα total or
whole offering, burnt offering. περὶ ἁμαρτίας "concerning
sin," i.e., sin offering. The phrase occurs frequently in Lev. to
denote sin offering (EGT). εὐδόκησας aor. act. ind. 2nd per.
7 sing. εὐδοκέω w. the acc. to be pleased w. ■ ἥκω. The verb has
the meaning of a perfect "I have come," "I am present" (s. BAG;
Westcott). κεφαλίς diminuative of the word "head" and is used
here w. the meaning "roll." (For various interpretations regarding the literal meaning of the word, s. Hughes; Michel.) The
words "the roll of the book" signify the books of Moses in which
the will of God and the way of obedience were written (Hughes).
γέγραπται perf. pass. ind. γράφω to write, perf. "it stands

written." The perf. signifies the legal binding authority of a document (s. MM). περὶ ἐμοῦ "concerning me." ποιῆσαι aor. act.
inf. The inf. is used to express the purpose of His coming. Perhaps the gen. of the article used w. the inf. to express purpose
indicates that which is closely connected w. the action as its
motive (s. Westcott, 342). θέλημα will. ■ ἀνώτερον adv. higher 8
up. Here it has the meaning "in the former part of the quotation"
(EGT). ὅτι. Used to introduce a direct quotation and is the
equivalent of quotation marks. κατά w. the acc. according to,
according to the standard of. ■ εἴρηκεν perf. act. ind. λέγω. The 9
perf. expresses completed action indicating what the speaker
said stands henceforth on permanent record (Bruce). ἀναιρεῖ
pres. act. ind. to lift up, to take away, to remove, to abolish. The
word was used in classical Gr. of the destruction or abolition or
repeal of laws, governments, customs, etc. (EGT; s. also Westcott; Michel). πρῶτον first. δεύτερον second. στήσῃ aor. act.
subj. ἵστημι to place, to establish. ■ ἐν "in," "by." The instru- 10
mental use of the prep. can also have a causal coloring (s. BD,
118). ᾧ rel. pron. "by which will," means "by the will of God
thus fulfilled by Christ" (Bruce). ἡγιασμένοι perf. pass. part.
ἁγιάζω to set apart, to sanctify. The part. is used in a perf. pass.
periphrastic construction emphasizing the completed state or
condition (s. RWP). προσφορά offering, s.v.5. ἐφάπαξ once
for all. The prep. in compound gives a directive strengthening
force (MH, 315). The word is found in the papyri where the
context may suggest the meaning "at one time" (MM; s. also
Preisigke).

■ ἕστηκεν perf. act. ind. ἵσταμι perf. to stand. The idea 11
of "standing" is that of a work still to be done, of service still to
be rendered (Westcott). καθ᾿ ἡμέραν daily. λειτουργῶν pres.
act. part. λειτουργέω to perform religious service. The word
was used in classical Gr. at Athens w. the meaning "to supply
public offices at one's own cost," then generally "to serve the
state," "to do a service." It was then used of service done by a
priest and indicated the fulfillment of an office. The word has a
definite representative character and corresponds to the function to be discharged (s. AS; NTW, 74f.; BS, 140; TDNT; Westcott, 230–233). The part. is used as a part. of manner. αὐτός "the
same." προσφέρων pres. act. part., s.v.1. αἵτινες which, which
one. The rel. pron. properly indicates the class or kind to which
an object belongs (s. RG, 727). οὐδέποτε never. περιελεῖν aor.
act. inf. περιαιρέω to take from around, to remove utterly (s.
RWP; Acts 27:20). The aor. tense expresses the finality. ■ 12
προσενέγκας aor. act. part. προσφέρω to sacrifice (s.v.1). The

part. is temporal "after ...." εἰς τὸ δηνεκές continually, un-broken, perpetually, forever (s. Heb. 7:3; AS). ἐκάθισεν aor. act. ind. καθίζω to take one's seat. ἐν δεξιᾷ "on the right" (s.

13 Eph. 1:20). ■ τὸ λοιπόν henceforth; i.e., "for the rest," "for the future"; i.e., all the remaining time till the end of the pres. world. The acc. is the acc. of the extent of time (Delitzsch; RWP). ἐκδέχομενος pres. mid. part. to await, to wait for. The prep. in compound has a perfective idea indicating that one is ready and prepared to deal with the situation when it arrives. It pictures the "going on w. the acc. of receiving till it comes" (MH, 310). τεθῶσιν aor. pass. subj. τίθημι to place, to put. The subj. is used

14 in a purpose and temporal clause (RWP). ■ μιᾷ προσφορᾷ "by one offering," dat. of instrument. τετελείωκεν perf. act. ind. τελειόω to complete, to perfect (s. Heb. 5:9). The perf. indicates a one time event w. a continuing result which is completed in the continual process depicted by the part. (s. Michel). ἁγιαζομένους pres. pass. part., s.v.10.

15   ■ μαρτυρεῖ pres. act. ind. to witness, to bear witness. For the writer of Heb. the truth of one kind of testimony required confirmation by another, in this case, by the testimony of the Scriptures. The testimony of the Scripture is the testimony of God (NTCW, 218, 221). εἰρηκέναι perf. act. inf. λέγω. The inf. is used w. the prep. expressing time "after ...." (For the signifi-

16 cance of the perf. tense, s.v.9.) ■ αὕτη this. The verb "is" must be supplied; i.e., "this is the covenant.'' διαθήσομαι fut. mid. ind. διατίθημι to make an agreement, to make a treaty, to make a covenant. πρός w. the acc. "with." μετά w. the acc. after. διδούς pres. act. part. δίδωμι. The part. could be temporal or it could express means or manner. ἐπί w. the acc. upon. διανοια mind (s. Heb. 8:10). ἐπιγράψω fut. act. ind. ἐπιγράφω to write

17 upon. αὐτούς them; i.e., the laws. ■ ἀνομία lawlessness, iniqui-ty. μνησθήσομαι fut. pass. ind. μιμνήσκω w. the gen. to remember. The fut. is used here instead of the subj. of the LXX and of 8:12, because the writer emphasizes the extension of the forgetting to all futurity (EGT). οὐ ....ἐτί "no longer," "no

18 more." ■ ὅπου where. ἄφεσις forgiveness. οὐκέτι no longer. περί w. the gen. concerning, for.

19   ■ ἔχοντες pres. act. part. The part. is causal. παρρησία boldness, confidence, assurance (s. Heb. 3:6). εἴσοδος entrance. τῶν ἁγίων sanctuary. The expression designates the innermost sanctuary of the Holy of Holies into which, under the old dispen-sation, the people were forbidden to enter (Hughes). ἐν "by."

20 ■ ἥν rel. pron. "which" referring to the "entrance." ἐνεκαίνισεν aor. act. ind. ἐγκαινίζω to inaugurate, to dedicate.

The word is used in the LXX of the inauguration (dedication) of the altar, the temple, the kingdom (1 Sam. 11:14), a house (Deut. 20:5) (Westcott; s. also Heb. 9:18). πρόσφατος freshly slaughtered, fresh, new, recent. The word indicates "fresh" not only in the sense that it is a way which was before unknown, but also as one that retains its freshness and cannot grow old (Westcott; Buchanan). ζῶσαν pres. act. part. ζάω to live. It is "living" as a way which consists in fellowship w. a Person (Westcott; s. also Michel). καταπέτασμα that which falls down, curtain, veil. ■ ἐπί w. the acc. "over." ■ προσερχώμεθα pres. mid. subj. 21/22 προσέρχομαι to come to, to draw near (s. Heb. 4:16). The subj. is cohortatory, "let us draw near." πληροφορία full assurance. ρεραντισμένοι perf. pass. part. ραντίζω to sprinkle, to cleanse. The perf. tense indicates a completed state or condition. λελουσμένοι perf. pass. part. λούω to wash. The part. express not conditions of approach to God which are yet to be achieved, but conditions already possessed (EGT). ■ κατέχωμεν pres. 23 act. subj. κατέχω to hold down, to hold fast. The subj. is cohortatory. ὁμολογία confession, agreement (s. ECC; TDNT). ἀκλινῆ unwavering, not leaning (RWP). ἐπαγγειλάμενος aor. mid. part. ἐπαγγέλλομαι to promise. ■ κατανοῶμεν pres. act. 24 subj. κατανοέω to place the mind down upon, to consider, to consider thoughtfully (s. Heb. 3:1). The subj. is hortatory, "let us . . . ." παροξυσμός irritating, inciting, stimulation (s. EGT; RWP; Michel). ■ ἐγκαταλείποντες pres. act. part. to leave in 25 the lurch, to forsake. The part. is manner describing the main verb "consider thoughtfully." ἐπισυναγωγή a gathering together, assembly. The pres. in compound indicates the common responsibility (s. Michel). The term here should be understood as simply the regular gathering together of Christian believers for worship and exhortation in a particular place (Hughes). ἔθος custom. τισίν dat. pl. The dat. may be possession "the custom of some" or dat. of reference "the custom in reference to some." παρακαλοῦντες pres. act. part. παρακαλέω to encourage, to entreat. τοσούτῳ so much. Used in the expression μᾶλλον ὅσῳ meaning "by so much more." It is a dat. or instrumental of measure or degree, "by so much the more as" (RWP). βλέπετε pres. act. ind. ἐγγίζουσαν pres. act. part. ἐγγίζω to draw near, to come near.

■ ἑκουσίως adv. from ἑκούσιος willingly, voluntarily, de- 26 liberately, intentionally. ἁμαρτανόντων pres. act. part. gen. abs. used to express a condition. λαβεῖν aor. act. inf. λαμβάνω. The inf. is used w. the prep. in a temporal sense; i.e., "after . . . ." ἐπίγνωσις knowledge, recognition. ἀπολείπεται pres. pass.

ind. ἀπολείπω to leave off, to leave behind, pass. to be left
behind, to remain. The concept of a "willful sin" without a
sacrifice is an OT teaching also reflected in Judaism (s. Num.
27 15:31; Michel; Moffatt; Hughes). ■ φοβερός fearful. ἐκδοχή
expectation. ζῆλος zeal. The phrase may be translated "zeal of
fire" or "fiery zeal" (Hughes). ἐσθίειν pres. act. inf. The inf. is
used w. the following part. to express the fut. μέλλοντος pres.
act. part. μέλλω to be about to. ὑπεναντίος one who opposes,
28 adversary. ■ ἀθετήσας pres. act. part. ἀθετέω to place aside,
to reject, to annul. τίς anyone. χωρίς without. οἰκτιρμός compassionate mercy, heartfelt mercy (s. Phil. 2:1; s. also TDNT).
δυσίν dat. "two." τρίσιν dat. "three." ἀποθνήσκει pres. act.
ind. The pres. tense is gnomic indicating that which is generally
29 true. ■ πύσῳ how much. The argument from the less to the
greater was common in rabbinical arguments (s. Moffatt; s. also
Rom. 5:9). δοκεῖτε pres. act. ind. to suppose. χείρων gen. of
comp. "worse." ἀξιωθήσεται fut. pass. ind. ἀξιόω to consider
worthy, to consider worthy of, followed by the gen. τιμωρία
punishment. καταπατήσας aor. act. part. καταπατέω to trample, to stomp upon. The word indicates to treat w. the utmost
contempt (Hughes). κοινός common, profane. It denotes the
opposite of "holy" (s. Michel). ἡγησάμενος aor. mid. part.
ἡγέομαι to consider, to count as. ἡγιάσθη aor. pass. ind.
ἁγιάζω to separate, to set apart for divine use, to sanctify.
ἐνυβρίσας aor. act. part. ἐνυβρίζω to treat w. utter contempt,
30 to arrogantly insult (s. TDNT; MNTW, 77–85). ■ εἰπόντα aor.
act. part. λέγω. ἐκδίκησις avenging, revenge. ἀνταποδώσω
fut. act. ind. ἀνταποδίδωμι to pay back. The prep. in compound indicates to pay back w. the same thing. κρινεῖ fut. act.
31 ind. κρίνω to judge. ■ φοβερός fearful. ἐμπεσεῖν aor. act. inf.
ἐμπίπτω to fall in, to fall into. The inf. is used as the subject of
the verb "to be" which is understood. ζῶντος pres. act. part.
ζάω to live.
32   ■ ἀνμιμνήσκεσθε pres. mid. imp. to remind one's self, to
remember. πρότερον former, first. Since the distinction between comp. and superl. had been weakened in Koine, the
phrase may be translated "the first days," i.e., the time when
they first responded to the message of the gospel (Hughes).
φωτισθέντες aor. pass. part. φωτίζω to make light, to enlight-
en. ἄθλησις fighting, conflict, struggle. ὑπεμείνατε aor. act.
ind. ὑπομένω to remain under, to patiently bear, to patiently
33 and hopefully endure (s.v.36). πάθημα suffering. ■ τοῦτο μέν
... τοῦτο δέ "partly so" ... "and partly so." The acc. w. gen.
reference is used w. the particles for contrast (RWP).

ὀνειδισμός reproach, revile, insult. θλῖψις pressure, trouble,
affliction. θεατριζόμενοι pres. pass. part. θεατρίζω to bring
upon the stage, to hold up to derision, to put to shame, to dispose
publicly. The meaning is that they had been held up to public
derision, scoffed and sneered at, accused of crime and vice,
unjustly suspected and denounced (s. RWP; BAG; Moffatt;
Michel). κοινωνός partner, sharer. ἀναστρεφομένων pres.
mid. part. ἀναστρέφομαι to conduct one's life, to be treated.
γενηθέντες aor. pass part. γίνομαι. ■ δέσμιος prisoner. 34
συνεπαθήσατε aor. act. ind. συμπαθέω to suffer together, to
suffer w. someone. ἁρπαγή seizing, plundering. The word implies that their own property had been either confiscated by the
authorities or plundered in some mob riot (Moffatt).
ὑπάρχοντα possessions. χαρά joy. προσεδέξασθε aor. mid.
ind. προσδέχομαι to accept. γινώσκοντες pres. act. part.
ἔχειν pres. act. inf. The inf. is used in indirect discourse, i.e., the
object of the part. "knowing." κρείττων better. ὕπαρξις possession. μένουσαν pres. act. part. μένω to remain, to abide. ■ 35
ἀποβάλητε aor. act. subj. ἀποβάλλω to throw away. The aor.
subj. is used w. the neg. in a prohibitive sense implying that the
action is not yet existent and should not arise (MKG, 273).
παρρησία boldness, confidence (s. Heb. 3:6). μισθαποδοσία
payment, reward, recompense. ■ ὑπομόνη patient endurance. It 36
is the spirit which can bear things, not simply w. resignation, but
w. blazing hope; it is not the spirit which sits statically enduring
in one place, but the spirit which bears things because it knows
that these things are leading to a goal of glory (NTW, 60; s. also
TDNT; CBB). ἔχω χρείαν followed by the gen. "to have need
of something." ποιήσαντες aor. act. part. The part. is used
temporally, i.e., "after ...." κομίσησθε aor. mid. subj.
κομίζομαι to receive. The word indicates "to receive the fulfillment of promise" (Hughes). ■ μικρόν ὅσον ὅσον a very little, 37
i.e., "only for a very little while" (BD, 160). ἐρχόμενος pres.
mid. part. ἥξει fut. act. ind. ἥκω to come. χρονίσει fut. act. ind.
χρονίζω to delay. ■ ζήσεται fut. mid. ind. ζάω to live. 38
ὑποστείληται aor. mid. subj. ὑποστέλλομαι to draw one's
self back, to withdraw one's self, to shrink back. εὐδοκεῖ pres.
act. ind. to delight in, to have pleasure in. ■ ὑποστολή shrink- 39
ing, timidity. Used here in the expression "we do not belong to
those who are timid" (BAG). ἀπώλεια ruin, destruction.
περιποίησις possession. The term indicates what one makes
one's own, either by keeping or by gaining it (Hughes; s. also
Eph. 1:4).

Ch. 11

1 ■ ἔστιν pres. ind. The emphatic position of the word may suggest a "definition style" (s. Michel). ἐλπιζομένων pres. pass. part. ὑπόστασις assurance. The word has a number of connotations and usages, e.g., "essence," "substance" or "foundation," or "confident assurance" or "guarantee," "attestation," i.e., documents which attest or provide evidence of ownership. (For these meanings as well as other references, s. Hughes; Michel; TDNT; MM.) πρᾶγμα matter, thing. ἔλεγχος evidence, proof. The word was used in the papyri of legal proofs of an accusation
2 (s. MM; Preisigke; TDNT). βλεπομένων pres. pass. part. ■ ἐν "by." The prep. is used instrumentally. ταύτῃ "this," i.e., "face." ἐμαρτυρήθησαν aor. pass. ind. μαρτυρέω to bear witness. The pass. may be the so-called "theological passives" indicating that it is God who bears witness concerning the elders (s. BG, 76). πρεσβύτερος comp. πρέσβυς old, elder. These were the men and women of old who received the divine commendation for faith of this kind (Bruce).

3 ■ πίστει dat. sing. dat. of instrument "by faith." νοοῦμεν pres. act. ind. to understand. The word expresses a mental as distinguished from a sensuous perception (Westcott). κατηρτίσθαι perf. pass. inf. καταρτίζω to outfit, to perfect. The word expresses the manifoldness and the unity of all creation. The tense marks that the original lesson of creation remains for abiding use and application (Westcott). The word was used in Hellenistic literature to describe the act of creation and in this sense it has a solemn tone (Michel). The inf. is used in indirect discourse. αἰών age, world (s. TDNT). ῥήματι dat. sing. ῥῆμα that which is spoken, word. The dat. is instrumental dat. φαινομένων pres. mid. part. φαίνομαι to appear, to be visible. βλεπόμενον pres. pass. part. γεγονέναι perf. mid. inf. γίνομαι. The inf. is used here to express results (s. RG, 1003; BD, 207f.). The neg. should be taken w. the inf. and the translation would be "so that what is seen has not come into being from things which appear" (Hughes).

4 ■ πλείων better. παρά than. (For the prep. used in a comp. construction, s. Heb. 1:4.) προσήνεγκεν aor. act. ind. προσφέρω to bring to, to offer, to sacrifice. ἐμαρτυρήθη aor. pass. ind., s.v.2. μαρτυροῦντος pres. act. part. gen. sing. μαρτυρέω to testify, to bear witness. The part. is used in a gen. abs. construction. ἐπί concerning, w. respect to. (For the textual variation here, s. Bruce.) ἀποθανών aor. act. part. ἀποθνήσκω
5 to die. The part. could be concessive "although He died." ■ μετετέθη aor. pass. ind. μετατίθημι to change, to transpose, to

706

transfer, to remove from one place to another, to translate (s. EGT). μεμαρτύρηται perf. pass. ind., s.v.2. εὐαρεστηκέναι perf. act. inf. εὐαρεστέω to be well pleasing to. The inf. is used in indirect discourse. ■ χωρίς without. ἀδύνατος impossible. 6 εὐαρεστῆσαι aor. act. inf., s.v.5. The inf. is used to explain what is impossible. πιστεῦσαι aor. act. inf. The inf. is used to explain that which is necessary. δεῖ pres. act. ind. "it is necessary." The word speaks of the binding and logical necessity. προσερχόμενον pres. mid. part. προσέρχομαι to come to, to approach. ἐκζητοῦσιν pres. act. part. ἐκζητέω to search out, to seek after. The prep. in compound always seems to denote that the seeker "finds," or at least exhausts his powers of seeking (MH, 310). μισθαποδότης one who gives a reward, one who pays back a reward. ■ χρηματισθείς aor. pass. part. 7 χρηματίζομαι to give divine instruction, to warn (s. Heb. 8:5). μηδέπω not yet. βλεπομένων pres. pass. part., s.v.1. εὐλαβηθείς aor. pass. part. εὐλαβέομαι to take hold well or carefully, to act circumspectly or w. reverence, to beware, to reverence (RWP; AS; s. also Michel). κατεσκεύασεν aor. act. ind. κατασκευάζω to construct, to outfit. κιβωτός ark. κατέκρινεν aor. act. ind. κατακρίνω to pass. judgment against, to condemn. κατὰ πίστιν "according to the standard of faith." The prep. can also have the idea of "by virtue of," "on the ground of," "in consequence of" (s. IBG, 59; EGT). κληρονόμος heir.

■ καλούμενος pres. pass. part. καλέω to call. The part. 8 could be temporal "when he was called." ὑπήκουσεν aor. act. ind. ὑπακούω to listen to, to obey. ἐξελθεῖν aor. act. inf. ἐξέρχομαι to go out, to go forth from. The inf. is used to explain the obedience. ἤμελλεν impf. act. ind. μέλλω to be about to. The word is used w. the inf. to express the future and the impf. w. the inf. expresses futurity or intention reckoned from a moment in the past (s. MKG, 307). εἰς "for." κληρονομία inheritance. ἐξῆλθεν aor. act. ind. ἐπιστάμενος pres. mid. part. ἐπίσταμαι to know, to understand. ποῦ where. ■ παρῴκησεν 9 aor. act. ind. παροικέω to dwell alongside of, to be a foreigner residing in a foreign country. Such foreigners had certain legal rights even though they were considered to be only temporary or foreign residents (s. TDNT; Michel; Eph. 2:19). ἀλλότριος foreigner, stranger. κατοικήσας aor. act. part. κατοικέω to reside, to dwell, to be at home. συγκληρονόμος fellow heir. ■ ἐξεδέχετο impf. mid. ind. ἐκδέχομαι to await expectantly. 10 The prep. in compound indicates "to be ready," "to be prepared to deal w. the situation" (EGT). θεμέλιος foundation. ἔχουσαν pres. act. part. ἔχω. τεχνίτης craftsman, artificer, designer, maker (s. Bruce; Michel; Hughes). δημιουργός public workman, constructer, maker. The first word refers to the plan and this word refers to the execution of it (s. Westcott; Bruce; Michel). ■ αὕτη fem. sing. "herself." καταβολή casting down. Used as a t.t. for the sowing of a seed and used here in the idiom "to receive the sowing of the seed" to mean "to conceive." σπέρμα seed, sperm. ἔλαβεν aor. act. ind. λαμβάνω to receive. παρά beyond, past. ἡλικία age, i.e., "beyond the season of age" (s. RWP). ἡγήσατο aor. mid. ind. ἡγέομαι to consider, to reckon as, to count as. ἐπαγγειλάμενον aor. mid. part. ἐπαγγέλλω to promise. The part. is used here substitutively, i.e., "the one who promised." ■ διό therefore. ἑνός gen. of εἷς "one." The idea is one who stands at the beginning of a long series. Abraham was known as "the One" (s. Michel; Delitzsch). ἐγεννήθησαν aor. pass. ind. γεννάω to bear, pass. to be born. (For the variant reading ἐγενήθησαν aor. pass. ind. γίνομαι to be, to become, s. Delitzsch; Bruce.) νενεκρωμένον perf. pass. part. νεκρόομαι to make dead, to treat as dead, to consider dead, "as good as dead" (RWP; Bruce). καθώς just as. ἄστρον star. πλῆθος quantity, number. The dat. is either locative "in number" or dat. of reference "in reference to quantity." ἄμμος sand. παρά w. the acc. "along," "along side of." χεῖλος lip, shore. ἀναρίθμητος unable to be counted, innumerable.

13   ■ κατά w. the acc. "according to," i.e., "in accordance w. the principle of faith" (Hughes). ἀπέθανον aor. act. ind. ἀποθνήσκω to die. κομισάμενοι aor. mid. part. κομίζω to receive, to obtain; i.e., "to obtain the fulfillment of the promise" (Michel). πόρρωθεν from afar, from a long distance away. ἰδόντες aor. act. part. ὁράω to see. ἀσπασάμενοι aor. mid. part. ἀσπάζομαι to greet. They hailed them from afar, as those on board ship descry friends on shore and wave a recognition (EGT), or they greet the fulfillment which is still far off as a wanderer who sees his home city arising on the horizon (Riggenbach). ὁμολογήσαντες aor. act. part. ὁμολογέω to agree, to confess. ξένος foreigner. παρεπίδημος one who makes his home alongside of, one from another country, pilgrim, one who stays for a while in a strange place. The word was used in the LXX and in the papyri for those who settled in a particular district only for a time (s. MM; BS, 149; Preisigke; BAG). ■ τοιοῦτος such a one. λέγοντες pres. act. part. ἐμφανίζω pres. act. ind. to manifest, to show, to make clear. πατρίδα acc. sing. fatherland. ἐπιζητοῦσιν to seek after. The prep. in compound indicates direction (EGT). ■ ἐκείνης gen. sing. "that one," i.e.,

the earthly country. The gen. is used after the verb. ἐμνημόνευσον impf. ind. act. μνημονεύω to remember, to be mindful of something. The ind. is used in a contrary to fact conditional clause. ἐξέβησαν aor. act. ind. ἐκβαίνω to go out. ἀνακάμψαι aor. act. inf. ἀνακάμπτω to bind back, to turn back again. The inf. is used to explain the word "time," "opportunity." ■ νῦν now; i.e., "the truth is," "as it is" (Bruce). 16 ὀρέγονται pres. mid. ind. to desire, to stretch one's self out for, to yearn for (RWP; s. also 1 Tim. 3:1). The verbs in the pres. tense in this context indicate the continual habitual attitude of life. ἐπουράνιος heavenly (s. Eph. 1:3). ἐπαισχύνεται pres. mid. ind. to be ashamed. ἐπικαλεῖσθαι pres. mid.-pass. inf. ἐπικαλέω to call upon, to name. If the verb is taken as mid., the meaning is "God is not ashamed of them to call Himself their God." If pass. "God is not ashamed of them to be called their God." The inf. is epexegetical explaining the main verb. ἡτοίμασεν aor. act. ind. ἑτοιμάζω to prepare, to make ready.

■ προσενήνοχεν perf. act. ind. προσφέρω to offer, to 17 offer as a sacrifice. The perf. indicates that this was an abiding example (BD, 177). πειραζόμενος pres. pass. part. πειράζω to try, to examine, to test. The pass. is "divine" pass. indicating that "God tested Abraham" (Hughes; BG, 76). μονογενής unique, only one of the kind, only (s. TDNT; CBB). ἀναδεξάμενος aor. mid. part. ἀναδέχομαι to receive, to gladly receive. The idea suggested here seems to be that of welcoming and cherishing a divine charge which involves a noble responsibility (Westcott). ■ ἐλαλήθη aor. pass. ind. λαλέω. κληθήσεται fut. pass. ind. 18 καλέω. σπέρμα seed. ■ λογισάμενος aor. mid. part. 19 λογίζομαι to consider, to reckon. The verb is used by Paul in the sense of to calculate or reckon up on the basis of firm evidence. The word denotes the inward conviction, persuasion, not a more or less reliable opinion (Hughes). The part. could be used to express the cause or reason and explains why Abraham had the courage to sacrifice Isaac, although the action seemed certain to ruin the fulfillment of what God had promised him (Moffatt). ἐγείρειν pres. act. inf. δυνατός capable, able. ὅθεν wherefore. παραβολή parable, analogy, used here adverbially "figuratively speaking" (s. Hughes; s. also Michel; Westcott). ἐκομίσατο aor. mid. ind., s.v.13. ■ περί concerning. μέλλοντα 20 pres. act. part. The part. is used as a substitutive; i.e., "future, coming things." εὐλόγησεν aor. act. ind. ■ ἀποθνήσκων pres. 21 act. part. The part. is used temporally and the pres. tense indicates that he was in the process of dying. ἕκαστος each one. προσεκύνησεν aor. act. ind. προσκυνέω to worship. ἐπί w.

22 the acc. on, upon. ἄκρον top. ῥάβδος stick, staff. ■ τελευτῶν
   pres. act. part. τελευτάω to come to the end, to expire, to die.
   The part. is temporal and the pres. tense indicates that he was
   in the process of dying. ἔξοδος way out, departure.
   ἐμνημόνευσεν aor. act. ind., s.v.15. ὀστοῦν bones. ἐνετείλατο
   aor. mid. ind. ἐντέλλομαι to instruct, to command.

23 ■ γεννηθείς aor. pass. part. γεννάω to bear, pass. to be
   born. ἐκρύβη aor. pass. ind. κρύπτω to hide. τρίμηνον three
   months, acc. of time "for three months." πατέρες fathers, parents. διότι because. εἶδον aor. act. ind. ὁράω to see. ἀστεῖος
   beautiful. It describes an attractive comeliness that is uncom-
   monly striking (Hughes; s. also Bruce). ἐφοβήθησαν aor. pass.
   ind. φοβέομαι to be afraid, to fear. διάταγμα command, order.

24 ■ γενόμενος aor. mid. part. γίνομαι. ἠρνήσατο aor. mid. ind.

25 ἀρνέομαι to say no to, to deny, to refuse. ■ μᾶλλον rather.
   ἑλόμενος aor. mid. part. αἱρέω to lift up, mid. to choose.
   συγκακουχεῖσθαι pres. pass. inf. to suffer evil together, to
   suffer w. someone. The inf. is used to explain the choosing.
   πρόσκαιρος for a time, temporary, fleeting. ἀπόλαυσις enjoyment, pleasure. (For the use of the word in the papyri and in-

26 scriptions, s. MM; Preisigke.) ■ μείζων greater. ἡγησάμενος
   aor. mid. part. ἡγέομαι to consider, to reckon. θησαυρός treasure, gen. of comparison. ὀνειδισμός reproach. ἀπέβλεπεν
   impf. ind. act. ἀποβλέπω to look away from. Used w. the prep.
   "to," to look to. The impf. emphasizes the continuous action in
   the past time. The word was used of keeping one's attention
   fixed upon something, as an artist fixes his attention on the
   object or model that he is reproducing in painting or sculpture

27 (Bruce). μισθαποδοσία recompense, reward. ■ κατέλιπεν
   aor. act. ind. καταλείπω to leave behind, to leave. φοβηθείς
   aor. pass. part. φοβέομαι to be afraid, to fear. θυμός anger,
   wrath (s. TDNT). ὁ ἀόρατος the one not able to be seen, "the
   invisible one," i.e., God. ὁρῶν pres. act. part. to see.
   ἐκαρτέρησεν aor. act. ind. καρτερέω to be strong, to hold out,

28 to endure. ■ πεποίηκεν perf. act. ind. ποιέω. The perf. tense
   indicates that the celebration was the inauguration of a divine
   institute (Spicq; s. also Westcott; Bruce). πρόσχυσις pouring,
   sprinkling, followed by the obj. gen. ὀλοθρεύων pres. act. part.
   ὀλοθρεύω to destroy. πρωτότοκος firstborn. θίγῃ aor. act.
   subj. θιγγάνω to touch. The object of the verb is in the gen. The

29 subj. is used in a neg. purpose clause. ■ διέβησαν aor. act. ind.
   διαβαίνω to go through, to pass through. ἐρυθρός red. ξηρός
   dry. πεῖρα attempt, try. λαβόντες aor. act. part. λαμβάνω.
   The part. is used temporally "when the Egyptians made an at-

tempt." κατεπόθησαν aor. pass. ind. καταπίνω to swallow down, to engulf. The prep. in compound is intensive, i.e., "they were totally engulfed," "overwhelmed" (Hughes). ■ τεῖχος 30 wall. ἔπεσαν aor. act. ind. πίπτω to fall. κυκλωθέντα aor. pass. part. κυκλόω to encircle. ■ πόρνη prostitute, whore. 31 συναπώλετο aor. mid. ind. συναπόλλυμι to destroy together, to be destroyed together. ἀπειθήσσιν aor. act. part. ἀπειθέω to be disobedient. δεξαμένη aor. mid. part. δέχομαι to welcome, to receive κατάσκοπος spy.

■ ἐπιλείψει fut. act. ind. ἐπιλείπω to fall upon, to fail. 32 διηγούμενον pres. mid. part. διηγέομαι to narrate, to tell about, to carry a discussion through. The words are lit. "will leave me telling about" (RWP). ■ κατηγωνίσατο aor. mid. ind. 33 κατηγωνίζομαι to struggle against, to overcome, to subdue. The prep. in compound not only indicates the idea of "against," but indicates that the action is unfavorable to an object (MH, 316). ἠργάσαντο aor. mid. ind. ἐργάζομαι to work effectively. The verb is used w. the noun "righteousness" in the LXX w. the meaning "to practice justice" (Ps. 15:2) and is used of doing that which is right in reference to personal integrity (Hughes). ἐπέτυχον aor. act. ind. ἐπιτυγχάνω followed by the object in the gen. to obtain, to receive. ἔφραξαν aor. act. ind. φράσσω to fence in, to block up, to stop (s. RWP). ■ ἔσβεσαν aor. act. 34 ind. σβέννυμι to quench, to put out a fire. ἔφυγον aor. act. ind. φεύγω to flee. The aor. is perfective indicating the success in fleeing; i.e., "to escape." στόμα mouth, edge. μάχαιρα sword. ἐδυναμώθησαν aor. pass. ind. δυναμόομαι to make strong, to be strong. The aor. is ingressive; i.e., "to become strong," "they became mighty." ἀσθένεια weakness. ἐγενήθησαν aor. pass. ind. γίνομαι. πόλεμος war. παρεμβολή encampment, barracks, armies in a battle line, army (RWP). ἔκλιναν aor. act. ind. κλίνω to make to bend, to bow, to turn to flight (AS). ἀλλότριος foreign. ■ ἔλαβον aor. act. ind. λαμβάνω. 35 ἀνάστασις resurrection. ἐτυμπανίσθησαν aor. pass. ind. τυμπανίζω to torture. The root meaning of the word is "to beat," "to strike," or "to pound." A related noun means a kettle drum which has a skin stretched taut for striking. Those who were tortured by some such means as this might either be beaten directly or stretched over a wheel and whirled while being afflicted w. rods to break their limbs until they died (Buchanan; s. also Westcott; Michel; BAG). προσδεξάμενοι aor. mid. part. προσδέχομαι to accept, to receive. ἀπολύτρωσις release by the payment of a price, release (s. Rom. 3:24). κρείττων better. τύχωσιν aor. act. subj. τυγχάνω to receive, to obtain. ■ ἕτερος 36

other. ἐμπαιγμός mocking, heaping derision upon a person by
sarcastically imitating him. μάστιξ scourging, whipping w. a
scourge. πεῖραν ἔλαβον s.v.29. The expression "received the
trial" is the same idiom used in the LXX Deut. 28:56 to describe
a woman so delicate that she would not "risk" setting her foot
on ground. These "others" were not that delicate (Buchanan).
ἔτι δέ yea, moreover. The expression is commonly used to indi-
37 cate a climax (EGT). δεσμός bonds. φυλακή prison. ■
ἐλιθάσθησαν aor. pass. ind. λιθάζω to stone. ἐπειράσθησαν
aor. pass. ind. πειράζω to try, to tempt. (For the suspected
textual variation, s. Hughes; Riggenbach.) ἐπρίσθησαν aor.
pass. ind. πρίω to saw into. The tradition that the prophet Isaiah
suffered death by being sawed in two w. a wooden saw is also
found in writings as well as the Talmudic books and in the
pseudepigraphic Jewish work, *The Martyrdom of Isaiah*, in
which it is recounted that during this terrible ordeal "Isaiah
neither cried aloud nor wept, but his lips spoke w. the Holy Spirit
until he was sawn in two" (Hughes; s. also SB III, 747). φόνος
murder. The prep. is used here instrumentally, i.e., "by murder
of the sword." ἀπέθανον aor. act. ind. ἀποθνήσκω to die.
περιῆλθον aor. act. ind. περιέρχομαι to go about. μηλωτή
sheepskin, used of the cloak worn by prophets (BAG). αἴγειος
of a goat. Adjectives w. this suf. have the meaning "of, or belonging to" (MH, 336). δέρμα skin; i.e., animal hide which was
processed. ὑστερούμενοι pres. mid. part. ὑστερέομαι to lack,
to suffer need. θλιβόμενοι pres. pass. part. θλίβω to put under
pressure, to cause distress, to afflict. κακουχούμενοι pres. pass.
38 part. κακουχέω to mishandle, to treat evilly, to ill treat. ■ ἦν
impf. εἰμί. πλανώμενοι pres. mid. part. πλανάομαι to wander,
to wander aimlessly, they wandered like lost sheep hunted by
wolves (RWP). σπήλαιον cave. ὀπή opening, hole, den. They
were outlawed as people who were unfit for civilized society; the
truth was that civilized society was unfit for them (Bruce). (For
an account of those who were persecuted who lived in caves and
dens and wandered about the mountains, s. I Maccabees 2:29–
38.)
39   ■ μαρτυρηθέντες aor. pass. part. μαρτυρέομαι to witness, pass. to be witnessed, to be attested by witness (s. Hughes;
Westcott). The part. is used concessively, i.e., "although . . . ."
40 ἐκομίσαντο aor.mid. ind., s.v.13. ■ προβλεψαμένου aor. mid.
part. προβλέπομαι to see before, to exercise forethought, to
foresee, to provide. The part. is used in a gen. abs. construction.
χωρίς without. τελειωθῶσιν aor. pass. subj. τελειόω to bring
to the goal, to complete, to perfect (s. Heb. 5:9).

Ch. 12

■ *τοιγαροῦν* therefore then, a triple compound inferential 1
particle to draw a conclusion of emphasis making Heb. 12:1-3
the climax of the whole argument about the better promises
(RWP). *τοσοῦτος* such a one, so great. *ἔχοντες* pres. act. part.
ἔχω. The part. is used to express cause. *περικείμενον* pres. mid.
part. *περίκειμαι* to lie around, to spread around, to surround.
The competitors feel the crowd towering about above them
(Westcott). *νέφος* cloud. The picture of a cloud describing a
crowded group of people is a common classical figure and expresses not only the great number of people, but also the unity
of the crowd in their witness (Michel). *μάρτυς* witness. The
witness was to confirm and to attest to the truth of a matter (s.
NTCW; TDNT). *ὄγκος* bulk, mass, weight. An athlete would
strip for action both by the removal of superfluous flesh through
rigorous training and by the removal of all his clothes (Hughes).
ἀποθέμενοι pres. mid. part. *ἀποτίθημι* to lay aside from one's
self, to lay aside one's clothing. *εὐπερίστατος*. The word could
have a variety of meanings; e.g., (1) "easily avoided," (2) "ad-
mired"; lit. "well-surrounded," (3) "easily surrounding," "beset-
ting," (4) "dangerous"; lit. "having easy distress." The picture
here may be that of putting off a long heavy robe which would
be a hindrance in running. (For this word, s. MH, 282; Michel;
Westcott; MM; Hughes.) *ὑπομονή* patient endurance (s. Heb.
10:36). *τρέχωμεν* pres. act. subj. *τρέχω* to run, cohortative subj.
"let us run." *προκείμενον* pres. mid. part. *πρόκειμαι* to lie
before (s. Heb. 6:18). *ἀγών* struggle, contest, race. ■ 2
ἀφορῶντες pres. act. part. *ἀφοράω* to look away from one
thing and to concentrate on another, to look away to (cf. Heb.
10:36). *ἀρχηγός* pioneer, author (s. Heb. 2:10; s. also Michel;
Westcott). *τελειωτής* perfecter, one who brings to the goal (s.
Heb. 5:9). *ἀντί* for the sake of, because of. The prep. can also
have the idea of "exchange" or "substitution." (For a discussion
of the meaning of the prep. here, s. Hughes.) *προκειμένης* pres.
mid. part., s.v.1. *ὑπέμεινεν* aor. act. ind. *ὑπομένω* to patiently
endure (s. Heb. 11:26). *σταυρός* cross. *αἰσχύνη* shame, disgrace. *καταφρονήσας* aor. act. part. *καταφρονέω* followed by
the gen. to think down on something, to despise, to treat as
contemptible. *ἐν δέξιᾳ* on the right. *κεκάθικεν* perf. act. ind.
καθίζω to take one's seat, to sit down. The perf. tense indicates
that He is still there (s. Heb. 1:3; Eph. 1:20). ■ *ἀναλογίσασθε* 3
aor. mid. imp. *ἀναλογίζομαι* to reckon up, to count up, to
consider. The verb can also include the idea of meditation
(Michel). *τοιοῦτος* such a one. *ὑπομεμενηκότα* perf. act. part.,

s.v.2. The perf. part. suggests the abiding effect of Christ's redemptive suffering (Hughes). ἁμαρτωλός sinner. εἰς against. ἀντιλογία speaking against, hostility (s. Hughes). κάμητε aor. act. subj. κάμνω to grow weary, ingressive aor. to become weary. The subj. is used in a neg. purpose clause. ἐκλυόμενοι pres. pass. part. ἐκλύομαι to release, pass. to become weary or slack, to give out (s. BAG). The part. further describes the "weariness" of the main verb.

4   ■ οὔπω not yet. μέχρις w. the gen. unto, unto the point of. ἀντικατέστητε aor. act. ind. ἀντικαθίστημι to stand in opposition against, in line of battle (RWP). πρός against. ἀνταγωνιζόμενοι pres. mid. part. ἀνταγωνίζομαι to struggle against. The metaphor is still that of the athletic contest, but now
5 shifts from the race track to the boxing ring (Hughes). ■ ἐκλέλησθε perf. mid. ind. ἐκλανθάνω to cause to forget, mid. to forget, to forget completely. The prep. in compound is perfective (s. MH, 311). παράκλησις encouragement, exhortation (s. Phil. 2:1). διαλέγεται pres. mid. ind. followed by the dat. to reason w., to converse w. The utterance of Scripture is treated as the voice of God conversing w. men (Westcott). ὀλιγώρει pres. act. imp. ὀλιγωρέω to think little of, to think lightly, to make light of something, to neglect (BAG; MM; Preisigke). παιδεία discipline, instructive discipline. In Judaism a father was required to provide for the instruction of his sons and daughters and to teach them good behavior. Whipping was accepted, along w. other disciplinary measures (JPFC II, 770f.; s. also TDNT). ἐκλύου pres. pass. imp., s.v.3. ἐλεγχόμενος pres. pass.
6 part. ἐλέγχω to reprove. ■ παιδεύει pres. act. ind. μαστιγοῖ to beat w. a whip, to scourge. (For the concept of suffering being the chastisement or discipline from God, s. Michel; TDNT.)
7 παραδέχεται pres. mid. ind. to accept, to receive. ■ ὑπομένετε pres. act. ind. to patiently endure (s. Heb. 10:36). προσφέρομαι pres. mid. ind. to carry one's self toward, to deal w. someone.
8 ■ μέτοχος participant, partner. γεγόνασιν perf. act. ind. γίνομαι. The perf. shows that the chastisement was personally accepted and permanent in its effects (Westcott). ἄρα therefore. νόθος illegitimate. The word not only indicates that the father is not sufficiently interested in them to inflict on them the discipline that fits his legitimate children (Moffatt), but it is also to be taken in the legal sense in which an illegitimate child does not enjoy the inheritance rights and the rights to participate in
9 family worship (s. Spicq; Hughes). ■ εἶτα then, besides this (Hughes). εἴχομεν impf. act. ind. ἔχω to have. The impf. is the customary impf. "we used to have" (RWP). παιδευτής one who

exercises discipline, one who instructs through discipline. The acc. is a double acc., i.e., "fathers as ones who discipline." ἐνετρεπόμεθα impf. mid. ind. ἐντρέπομαι to fear, to reverence. The impf. is customary impf. ὑποταγησόμεθα fut. mid. ind. ὑποτάσσομαι to subject, to be in subjection, to be in submission, to submit one's self. ζήσομεν fut. act. ind. ζάω to live. ■ ἐπί w. the acc. for. The prep. indicates the purpose of a 10 few days and is a description for the whole earthly life (Michel). δοκοῦν pres. act. part. acc. n. sing. to seem, to seem to be good, "according to the thing seeming good to them" (RWP). ἐπαίδευον impf. act. ind. συμφέρον pres. act. part. συμφέρω to differ, to be better. The part. is used as a substitutive "that which is best," "for our advantage" (EGT). μεταλαβεῖν aor. act. inf. μεταλαμβάνω followed by the gen. to partake of, to have a share in. The inf. is used w. the prep. to express purpose. ἁγιότης holiness. ■ πρὸς τὸ παρόν "for the present." δοκεῖ 11 s.v.10. λύπη pain, sorrow. ὕστερον afterwards. καρπός fruit. εἰρηνικός pertaining to peace, peaceful. γεγυμνασμένοις perf. pass. part. γυμνάζω to exercise, to train. The perf. part. indicates the completed state or condition. ἀποδίδωσιν pres. act. ind. to give back, to repay, to yield. (For rabbinical parallels regarding the results of suffering, s. Bruce.)

■ παρειμένας perf. pass. part. παρίημι to let fall at the 12 side, to slacken, to weaken, pass. to be listless, drooping (BAG). παραλελυμένα perf. pass. part. παραλύω to loosen on the side, to dissolve, to paralyze, to undo, pass. to be weak, to be lame (s. RWP; BAG). γόνυ knee. ἀνορθώσατε aor. act. imp. ἀνορθόω to set up straight, to set upright or straighten again, to revive (EGT). ■ τροχία track of a wheel, track made by the 13 feet of the runners. Here it could have the meaning "running lane" and develop the athletic imagery (Hughes). ὀρθός straight. ποιεῖτε pres. act. imp. πούς foot, dat. of advantage "for your feet." χωλός lame. ἐκτραπῇ aor. mid. subj. ἐκτρέπομαι to turn from, to turn aside. The word could have the idea of turning aside in a race or it could be a medical figure of putting a limb out of joint (Hughes; Westcott; Michel). ἰαθῇ aor. pass. subj. ἰάομαι to heal, pass. to be healed. The subjs. are used here to express purpose.

■ διώκετε pres. act. imp. διώκω to hunt, to follow after, to 14 pursue. ἁγιασμός holiness. In this epistle it is explained as a drawing near to God w. a cleansed conscience (10:14, 22), a true acceptance of Christ's sacrifice as bringing the worshiper into fellowship w. God (EGT). ὄψεται fut. mid. ind. ὁράω to see. ■ ἐπισκοποῦντες pres. act. part. ἐπισκοπέω to watch over, to 15

watch out for. The word expresses the careful regard of those
who occupy a position of responsibility (as a physician, or a
superintendent) (Westcott). ὑστερῶν pres. act. part. ὑστερέω
to lack, to come short, to fail. ῥίζα root. πικρία bitterness. The
"root of bitterness" in Deut. 29:18 probably referred to anything
that lead to idolatry and apostasy (Buchanan). ἄνω up. φύουσα
pres. act. part. φύω to sprout, to spring up. ἐνοχλῇ pres. act.
subj. ἐνοχλέω to trouble, to trouble w. a crowd, to annoy, to
harass (s. Acts 15:19; RWP; Hughes). μιανθῶσιν aor. pass.
16 subj. μιαίνω to stain, to defile. ■ πόρνος immoral. βέβηλος
profane, irreligious. βρῶσις food. ἀπέδοτο aor. mid. ind.
ἀποδίδωμι to sell. τὰ πρωτοτόκια birthright, the privilege of
17 the firstborn son (s. TDNT). ■ ἴστε perf. act. ind. 2nd per. pl.
οἶδα defective perf. w. a pres. meaning to know. μετέπειτα
afterwards. θέλων pres. act. part. The part. is concessive.
κληρονομῆσαι aor. act. inf. κληρονομέω to inherit.
ἀπεδοκιμάσθη aor. pass. ind. ἀποδοκιμάζω to reject after
examination, to reject completely. μετάνοια change of mind,
repentance. τόπος room, place, opportunity. εὗρεν aor. act. ind.
εὑρίσκω to find. καίπερ although. The particle is used in a
clause of concession. δάκρυον tear. ἐκζητήσας aor. act. part.
ἐκζητέω to seek out, to look for.
18   ■ προσελήλυθατε perf. act. ind. προσέρχομαι to come
to, to draw near. ψηλαφωμένῳ pres. pass. part. ψηλαφάω to
handle, to touch, i.e., to the mountain which may be touched (s.
Hughes). κεκαυμένῳ perf. pass. part. καίω to burn. πῦρ fire.
γνόφος darkness, blackness, thick darkness (Westcott). ζόφος
darkness, deep gloom (AS). θύελλα storm, hurricane (RWP).
19 ■ σάλπιγξ trumpet. ἦχος sound. ῥῆμα word. ἀκούσαντες
aor. act. part. παρῃτήσαντο aor. mid. ind. παραιτέομαι to
beg, to ask for, to request. προστεθῆναι aor. pass. inf.
προστίθημι to place to, to add to. The inf. is used in indirect
20 discourse. ■ ἔφερον impf. ind. act. φέρω to carry, to bear, to
endure. διαστελλόμενον pres. act. part. διαστέλλω to command, to order. The pres. tense presents the command as ringing
constantly in their ears (Westcott). κἄν = καὶ ἄν "if even."
θηρίον animal. θίγῃ aor. act. subj. θιγγάνω to touch, followed
by the gen. λιθοβοληθήσεται fut. pass. ind. λιθοβολέω to
21 throw stones at, to stone. ■ φοβερός terrible, fearful. ἦν impf.
εἰμί. φανταζόμενον pres. mid. part. φαντάζομαι to appear.
ἔκφοβος terrified. The prep. in compound is perfective.
22 ἔντρομος trembling. ■ προσελήλυθατε perf. act. ind., s.v.18.
ζῶντος pres. act. part. ζάω to live. μυριάς myriad, ten thousand. It indicates a number that cannot be counted, i.e., "tens of

thousands" (Hughes). πανήγυρις festive gathering. The word
indicated the great gathering for a festival occasion. In the OT
it was for the religious festivals. In the Gr. world it was a gathering for large athletic contests (Michel). ■ πρωτότοκος firstborn 23
(s. Heb. 11:28; TDNT; Col. 1:18). They are "firstborn ones"
enjoying the rights of firstborn sons, because of their union w.
Christ, the firstborn (Kent). ἀπογεγραμμένων perf. pass. part.
ἀπογράφω to write off, to enroll. τετελειωμένων perf. pass.
part. τελειόω to bring to the goal, to perfect (s. Heb. 5:9). ■ 24
μεσίτης mediator. ῥαντισμός sprinkling. κρεῖττυν better.
λαλοῦντι pres. act. part. παρά used in a comparison "than."

■ βλέπετε pres. act. imp. βλέπω to see, to beware, to take 25
heed. παραιτήσησθε aor. mid. subj. to ask, to request, to
refuse, s.v.19. λαλοῦντα pres. act. part. ἐξέφυγον aor. act. ind.
ἐκφεύγω to flee from, to flee from successfully, to escape. The
prep. in compound is perfective and the aor. is complexive emphasizing the completion of the action. παραιτησάμενοι aor.
mid. part., s.v.19. χρηματίζοντα pres. act. part. to give divine
instruction, to warn (s. Heb. 8:5; 11:7). ἀποστρέφομενοι pres.
mid. part. to turn away from, to turn from. ■ ἐσάλευσεν aor. 26
act. ind. σαλεύω to shake. τότε formerly, at that time.
ἐπήγγελται perf. mid. ind. ἐπαγγέλλομαι to promise. The
perf. tense indicates that the promise is still valid. ἅπαξ once,
"yet once more." σείσω fut. act. ind. σείω to shake, to cause
to tremble (s. Matt. 21:10). μόνον alone. ■ δηλοῖ pres. act. ind. 27
to make clear. σαλευομένων pres. pass. part., s.v.26.
μετάθεσις removing (s. Heb. 7:12). πεποιημένων perf. pass.
part. ποιέω. μείνῃ aor. act. subj. μένω to remain. ■ ἀσάλευτος 28
not able to be shaken, unshakeable. παραλαμβάνοντες pres.
act. part. παραλαμβάνω to receive. ἔχωμεν pres. act. subj.
used in the expression ἔχω χάριν to be grateful. The subj. is
hortatory "let us be grateful." λατρεύωμεν pres. act. subj.
λατρεύω to worship, to serve. εὐαρέστως well-pleasing.
εὐλάβεια reverence (s. Heb. 5:7). δέος awe. It is the apprehension of danger as in a forest (RWP). ■ καταναλίσκον pres. act. 29
part. καταναλίσκω to consume completely. The prep. in compound is perfective.

Ch. 13

■ μενέτω pres. act. imp. μένω to remain. The use of the 1
verb suggests that the bond had been in danger of being severed
(Westcott). ■ φιλοξενία entertaining of strangers, hospitality. 2
Since there were very few inns, the entertainment and showing
of hospitality to travelers was an important part of Jewish home

life (s. JPFC II, 762). ἐπιλανθάνομαι pres. mid. imp. followed
by the gen. to forget. The pres. imp. w. the neg. means "do not
go on being unmindful" of hospitality (Hughes). ἔλαθόν aor.
act. ind. λανθάνω to escape notice, to do something without
knowing it (s. BAG). ξενίσαντες aor. act. part. ξενίζω to entertain strangers, to show hospitality. The part. is used supplementary to the main verb giving the meaning "some escaped notice
3 when entertaining angels" (RWP). ■ μιμνήσκεσθε pres. mid.
imp. to remember followed by the gen. συνδεδεμένοι perf. pass.
part. συνδέω to bind together, pass. to be bound w. another, to
be a fellow prisoner. The perf. tense views the completed state
or condition. κακουχουμένων pres. pass. part. κακουχέω to
mishandle, to treat evilly (s. Heb. 11:37). ὄντες pres. part. εἰμί.
4 The part. is causal. ■ τίμιος ἐν honorable. γάμος marriage.
κοίτη bed, marriage bed, sexual intercourse. ἀμίαντος undefiled. πόρνος immoral. The word designates those persons
who indulge in sexual relationships outside the marriage bond,
both heterosexual and homosexual (Hughes). μοῖχος adulter-
ous. This word indicates those who are unfaithful to their marriage vows; thus, the two adjs. cover all who licentiously engage
in forbidden practices (Hughes). κρινεῖ fut. act. ind. to judge.
5 ■ ἀφιλάργυρος without a love for money. τρόπος manner,
manner of life, disposition, "let your turn of mind be free from
love of money, content w. what you have" (EGT). ἀρκούμενοι
pres. pass. part. ἀρκέομαι to have enough, pass. to be content.
παροῦσιν pres. part. πάρειμι to be present, to be at hand.
εἴρηκεν perf. act. ind. λέγω. The perf. indicates that the statement has been made and its authority continues. ἀνῶ aor. act.
subj. ἀνίημι to send up, to send back, to let go, to leave without
support (AS). ἐγκαταλίπω aor. subj. ἐγκαταλείπω to leave
6 someone in distress, to leave in the lurch, to desert. ■ ὥστε used
w. the inf. to introduce a result clause. θαρροῦντας pres. act.
part. θαρρέω to be courageous, to be bold, to be confident.
βοηθός helper, one who brings help in the time of need.
φοβηθήσομαι fut. mid. ind. φοβέομαι to be afraid. ποιήσει
fut. act. ind.
7   ■ μνημονεύετε pres. act. imp. to remember, to be mindful
of, followed by the gen. ἡγουμένων pres. mid. part. ἡγέομαι to
lead. ἐλάλησαν aor. act. ind. λαλέω. ἀναθεωροῦντες pres.
act. part. ἀναθεωρέω to look back upon, to scan closely (Moffatt), to look back carefully on (Hughes). ἔκβασις going out,
away out, end. The phrase can mean either "the end of one's life"
or more probably "the successful outcome or result of one's way
of life" (BAG). ἀναστροφή manner of life. μιμεῖσθε pres. mid.

imp. μεμέομαι to imitate. ■ ἐχθές yesterday. ■ ποικίλος vary- 8/9
ing, diverse. ξένος foreign, strange. παραφέρεσθε pres. pass.
imp. παραφέρομαι to carry along, to lead away. The pass.
would be permissive pass. καλός good. The words "it is" are to
be supplied. βεβαιοῦσθαι pres. pass. inf. βεβαιόομαι to make
firm, to confirm, to make stable. βρῶμα food. ὠφελήθησαν
aor. pass. ind. ὠφελέομαι to be profitable, to be useful.
περιπατοῦντες pres. act. part. περιπατέω to walk about, to
conduct one's life. ■ θυσιαστήριον altar, place of sacrifice. 10
φαγεῖν aor. act. inf. ἐσθίω to eat. The inf. is used epexegetically
explaining what is lawful. ἐξουσία that which is legal, lawful,
authority, prerogative. σκηνή tent, tabernacle. λατρεύοντες
pres. act. part. λατρεύω to serve religiously, to perform religious
service. ■ εἰσφέρεται pres. pass. ind. εἰσφέρω to bring in. ζῷον 11
living creature, animal. κατακαίεται pres. pass. ind. to burn, to
burn completely, to burn up. ἔξω outside. παρεμβολή camp.
■ διό therefore, wherefore. ἁγιάσῃ aor. act. subj. ἁγιάζω to set 12
apart, to sanctify. ἴδιος one's own. πύλη gate. He refers to the
gate of the city of Jerusalem which, bounded by its walls, corresponds to the holy ground of the wilderness camp (Hughes).
ἔπαθεν aor. act. ind. πάσχω to suffer. The purpose of Christ's
suffering outside of the city gates is the sanctification of His
people. ■ τοίνυν therefore. The inferential particle draws a con- 13
clusion from the preceding. ἐξερχώμεθα pres. mid. subj.
ἐξέρχομαι. The subj. is hortatory "let us go out." The pres.
tense expresses vividly the immediate effort (Westcott). This
could be a call for the readers to refuse to go back into Judaism
(s. Hughes; Westcott). ὀνειδισμός reproach, insult. φέροντες
pres. act. part. φέρω to bear. ■ μένουσαν pres. act. part. μένω 14
to remain. μέλλων pres. act. part. to be about to, here "coming."
ἐπιζητοῦμεν pres. act. ind. to search for. ■ ἀναφέρωμεν pres. 15
act. subj. ἀναφέρω to bring up, to offer up. The subj. is cohortative "let us offer up." αἴνεσις praise. διὰ παντός "through all,"
"continually." A rabbinical tradition teaches that all the Mosaic
sacrifices would have an end except the thank offering, and all
prayers would cease except the prayer of thanksgiving (s.
Hughes; Michel; SB I, 246). χεῖλος lip. ὁμολογούντων pres.
act. part. ὁμολογέω to confess, to profess. The word carries the
idea of a proclamation (Michel) as well as the idea of praise (s.
MM). ■ εὐποιΐα good deed, doing good. κοινωνία fellowship, 16
sharing (s. Phil. 1:5). ἐπιλανθάνεσθε pres. mid. imp. to forget
something, followed by the gen. The pres. imp. w. the neg. is
used to forbid a habitual action. εὐαρεστεῖται pres. mid. ind.

to be well pleased w. The pres. tense indicates that which is always true.

17 ■ **πείθεσθε** pres. mid. imp. to obey. **ἡγουμένοις** pres. mid. part., s.v.7. **ὑπείκετε** pres. act. imp. to give in, to yield, to submit. **ἀγρυπνοῦσιν** to be without sleep, to seek after sleep, to be watchful (RWP). **ἀποδώσοντος.** The part. is fut. act. part. and the expression means "to give an account," "to render account." **ποιῶσιν** pres. act. subj. **ποιοῦσιν. στενάζοντες** pres. act. part. **στενάζω** to groan. **ἀλυσιτελής** unprofitable, harmful.

18 ■ **προσεύχεσθε** pres. mid. imp. to pray. **πείθομεθα** pres. mid. ind. to be persuaded, to have confidence, to be confident. **συνείδησις** conscience (s. Rom. 2:15). **καλῶς** adv. good, clear. **θέλοντες** pres. act. part. **ἀναστρέφεσθαι** pres. mid. inf. to

19 conduct one's life. ■ **περισσοτέρως** adv. more earnestly. **ποιῆσαι** aor. act. inf. **τάχιον** comp. n. sing. The adj. is used as an adv. "sooner." **ἀποκατασταθῶ** aor. pass. subj. **ἀποκαθίστημι** to restore back again.

20 ■ **ἀναγαγών** aor. act. part. **ἀνάγω** to lead up, to bring
21 again. **ποιμήν** shepherd. **αἰώνιος** eternal. ■ **καταρτίσαι** aor. act. opt. **καταρτίζω** to equip. The word includes the thoughts of the harmonious combination of different powers, of the supply of that which is defective, and of the amendment of that which is faulty (Westcott). The opt. is used to express a wish for the future (RWP). **ποιῆσαι** aor. act. inf. The inf. is used w. the prep. to express purpose. **ποιῶν** pres. act. part. **εὐάρεστος** well-pleasing. **ἐνώπιον** before, in the presence of.

22 ■ **ἀνέχεσθε** pres. mid. imp. to hold one's self back from (RWP), to endure, to bear w. **βραχύς** short. Used w. the prep. w. the meaning "in few words" (Westcott). **ἐπέστειλα** aor. act.
23 ind. **ἐπιστέλλω** to send a letter to, to write. ■ **ἀπολελυμένον** perf. pass. part. **ἀπολύω** to release. Although the word has a variety of meanings, its most frequent sense in the NT is that of releasing from custody persons who were under arrest or in prison (Hughes). **τάχιον** soon. **ἔρχηται** pres. mid. subj. **ἔρχομαι. ὄψομαι** fut. mid. ind. **ὁράω.**

24 ■ **ἀσπάσασθε** aor. mid. imp. **ἀσπάζομαι** to greet. **ἡγουμένους** pres. mid. part., s.v.7.

JAMES

φυλή tribe. διασπορά scattering, dispersion, diaspora. 1 The term indicates one who is living in a foreign country (Mussner; Dibelius; s. 1 Peter 1:1). The term could refer to Jewish Christians living outside of Palestine (Mayor; for a discussion of the word, s. also Ropes).

■ ἡγήσασθε aor. mid. imp. ἡγέομαι to consider, to deem 2 as, to reckon as. The object of the verb is placed first for emphasis (Mussner). The aor. is perhaps used because the writer is thinking of each special case of temptation (Ropes; Mayor). ὅταν w. the subj. "whenever." πειρασμός trial, temptation. The word is used sometimes regarding outward trials and inward temptations (Tasker; s. also Mayor; TDNT; CBB). ποικίλος many colored, variegated, various, varied (s. 2 Tim. 3:6; Titus 3:2). ■ γινώσκοντες pres. act. part. The part. could be causal. 3 δοκίμιον trying, testing, proving. (For this active sense, s. Mayor.) The pass. sense has the idea of "approved after testing," "tested and approved," "the genuine part" (s. BS, 259ff.; IBG, 96; Ropes; Dibelius). ■ τέλειον perfection. Here James contin- 4 ues the OT idea of perfection as a right relationship to God expressed in undivided obedience and unblemished life (Adamson). ἐχέτω pres. act. imp. ἦτε pres. subj. εἰμί. The subj. is used to express purpose. ὁλόκληρος complete in all its parts, entire. The word indicates the entirety of all of the Christian virtues (s. Mussner). λειπόμενοι pres. mid. part. λείπομαι to be left behind, to lack. ■ αἰτείτω pres. act. imp. third-person sing. αἰτέω 5 to ask. διδόντος pres. act. part. ἁπλῶς adv. simply, unconditionally, without bargaining. The word could possibly have the meaning here "generously," which would be derived from the noun meaning "liberality," which comes from the idea of frankness and openheartedness (Mayor). Perhaps the best translation here is "freely" (Adamson). ὀνειδίζοντος pres. act. part. ὀνειδίζω to rebuke, to reprove, to reproach, to insult. δοθήσεται fut. pass. ind. δίδωμι. The pass. would be the "divine pass." indicating that God is the giver (BG, 236). ■ πίστις 6 faith. Here it does not denote "constancy in the Christian reli-

gion" as in v.3. Here it means "confidence in prayer." It means
the petitioner's faith, his belief and trust, that God will heed his
prayer, and grant it or only in His superior wisdom deny it
(Adamson; s. also Ropes). (For the grammatical structure of the
conditional clause followed by the imp., s. Mussner; Beyer, 238.)
διακρινόμενος pres. mid. part. διακρίνομαι to divide, to be at
variance w. one's self, to waver, to doubt (Ropes). ἔοικεν pres.
act. ind. to be like, to resemble. κλύδων wave; i.e., "the surge
of the sea," "the billowing sea" (Ropes). ἀνεμιζομένῳ pres.
pass. part. ἀνεμίζω to drive w. the wind (Dibelius). ῥιπιζομένῳ
pres. pass. part. ῥιπίζω to fan, most often used of fanning a
7 flame (Mayor), here "to toss" (Dibelius). ■ οἰέσθω pres. mid.
imp. 3rd sing. οἴομαι to suppose. The word is often used in a
neg. sense indicating wrong judgment or conceit (Ropes).
8 λήμψεται fut. mid. ind. λαμβάνω to receive. ■ ἀνήρ male,
man. The word is used here in the sense of a "person" (Dibelius).
δίψυχος double-souled, double-minded, i.e., "w. soul divided
between faith and the world" (Ropes; s. also Adamson).
ἀκατάστατος not having stability, unsettled, unstable. Polybi-
us uses it both of political disturbance and of individual character
(Mayor). The word refers to "vacillating in all his activity and
conduct" (Dibelius).
9   ■ καυχάσθω pres. mid. imp. καυχάομαι to boast, to boast
over a privilege or possession. The word is used in the OT of
"any proud and exulting joy" (Ropes). ταπεινός low, low degree, humble position. The word is used in the LXX to translate
the Heb. word for "poor," "without possessions" (Dibelius).
ὕψος high, exaltation. It refers to the pres. spiritual status which,
by virtue of his relation to Christ, the Christian now enjoys
10 (Adamson). ■ πλούσιος rich. ταπείνωσις lowliness, humiliation. ἄνθος flower. χόρτος grass. παρελεύσεται fut. mid. ind.
παρέχομαι to pass along the side of, to pass away, to disappear
11 (Ropes). ■ ἀνέτειλεν aor. act. ind. ἀνατέλλω to rise up, to rise.
The aor. is gnomic indicating that which generally happens
(Ropes). καύσων burning heat. The word may refer to the blistering east wind called Sirocco (Mayor; Ropes; Adamson).
ἐξήρανεν aor. act. ind. ξηραίνω to dry, to dry out, to wither.
ἐξέπεσεν aor. act. ind. ἐκπίπτω to fall off. The word was used
in the LXX of flowers falling from the stem (Mayor). εὐπρέπεια
outward beauty. The word is used w. a suggestion of fitness to
the object and its relations, and so sometimes gains a notion of
stateliness or majesty (Ropes). ἀπώλετο aor. mid. ind.
ἀπόλλυμι to ruin, to come to ruin, to be destroyed. πορεία
way. The word could be used in the sense of "a business journey"

but here it is to be taken as a reference to the rich man's "whole" way of life (Dibelius). μαρανθήσεται fut. pass. ind. μαραίνω to wither, to waste away. The picture of the rich "withering" continues the simile of the fading flower: the verb is picturesque and may be used of the dying of a flower or the decaying of plants like roses as well as ears of corn (Adamson; Ropes). The reference is to the loss of riches and earthly prosperity, not to eternal destiny (Ropes).

■ μακάριος blessed, happy (s. TDNT). The idea expressed 12 here is familiar in Judaism: "Happy is the man who can withstand the test, for there is none whom God does not prove" (Adamson). ὑπομένει pres. act. ind. to endure, to patiently and triumphantly endure, to show constancy under (Ropes). It is not the patience which can sit down and bow its head and let things descend upon it and passively endure until the storm is passed. It is the spirit which can bear things, not simply w. resignation, but w. blazing hope (NTW, 60). δόκιμος approved after testing (s.v.3). γενόμενος aor. mid. part. γίνομαι. The part. is temporal "after being approved" and not conditional (Dibelius; Ropes). τῆς ζωῆς "of life." The crown spoken of here was a head wreath or circlet which was the victor's prize in the Gr. games; it might also be given to a man the public wished to honor and it was worn in religious and secular feasts (Adamson; s. also Ropes; TDNT). The gen. could be descriptive; i.e., "a living crown" in contrast to the perishable crown or it could be an appositional gen.; i.e., the crown is life. (For a discussion of the various possibilities, s. Dibelius; s. also Mayor.) ἐπηγγείλατο aor. mid. ind. ἐπαγγέλλομαι to promise. ἀγαπῶσιν pres. act. part. ἀγαπάω to love. ■ πειραζόμενος pres. pass. part. πειράζω to 13 try, to tempt. Here the word is used meaning "temptation to sin" (Ropes). λεγέτω pres. mid. imp. ὅτι. Used as quotation marks to introduce a direct quotation. ἀπὸ θεοῦ "from God." The prep. expresses the remoter rather than the nearer cause (Mayor). ἀπείραστος not able to be tempted, "invincible to assault of evils" (Ropes; s. also Peter H. Davis, "The Meaning of Apeirastos in James I.13," NTS, 24 [March, 1978], 386–392). ■ 14 ἕκαστος each. ἴδιος one's own. ἐπιθυμία desire, strong desire directed toward an object, lust. ἐξελκόμενος pres. pass. part. ἐξέλκω to draw out, to draw away, to lure. δελεαζόμενος pres. mid. part. δελεάζω to entice or catch by the use of bait. These words were applied to the hunter or, esp., the fisherman who lures his prey from its retreat and entices it by bait to his trap, hook, or net (Ropes; s. also Adamson). In like manner the first effect of lust is to draw the man out of his original repose, the

second to allure him to a definite bait (Mayor). (For the comparison of James' teaching regarding "lust," "desire" w. the Jewish teaching regarding the "Evil Inclination," s. Mussner; s. also SB
15 IV, 466–483; PRJ, 17–35.) ∎ εἶτα then. The word introduces the practical result of the temptation arising from lust (Ropes). συλλαβοῦσα aor. act. part. συλλαμβάνω to become pregnant, to conceive. If the previous words refer to the enticement of a prostitute, then these words would picture the result of yielding to her seductive temptations (s. Mussner). The part. is temporal. τίκτει pres. act. ind. to give birth, to bear. ἀποτελεσθεῖσα aor. pass. part. ἀποτελέω to come to completion, to come to maturity, to be fully grown. The word connotes "completeness of parts and function . . . accompanying full growth as opposed to a rudimentary or otherwise incomplete state" (Adamson; Ropes). ἀποκύει pres. act. ind. to cease being pregnant, to give birth to. The word is frequently used of animals; otherwise it is a medical rather than literary word (Ropes). The prep. in compound denotes cessation (Mayor; s. also MH, 298).

16   ∎ πλανᾶσθε pres. mid.-pass. imp. πλανάω to lead astray, to deceive. The mid. or pass. could be permissive; i.e., "don't
17 allow yourselves to be deceived." ἀγαπητός beloved. ∎ δόσις giving. δώρημα that which is given, gift. ἄνωθεν from above. καταβαῖνον pres. act. part. καταβαίνω to come down. πατήρ father. φῶτα lights. The word generally refers to the light given to heavenly bodies and it describes God as the cosmic Father and Creator of the heavenly bodies (Mayor; Ropes; Dibelius). ἔνι = ἔνεστι pres. ind. ἔνειμι to be in, to be present (on this contracted form which may also be considered to be a strengthened form of the prep., s. BAG; BD, 49; MH, 306; RG, 313). It is not just the fact only which is negated but also the possibility (Mayor). παραλλαγή variation. It is used in Gr. for the setting of the teeth in a saw, or for stones set alternately, for a sequence of beacons or seasons and generally denotes some regularity or system in change (Adamson). τροπή turning. The gen. is a gen. of definition, "a variation consisting in turning." ἀποσκίασμα shadow. The word can mean the shadow cast by an object, as in an eclipse, or it can mean the act of overshadowing or it can have the meaning of a reflected image (Adamson; s. also Dibelius; Mayor; Ropes). God's benevolence is like a light which cannot be extinguished, eclipsed, or "shadowed out" in any way at all. Nothing can block God's light, interrupt the flow of His goodness, or put us "in shadow," so that we are out of the
18 reach of His "radiance" (Adamson). ∎ βουληθείς aor. pass.

724

part. βούλομαι to counsel, to decide after counsel, to will. Here
it refers to the free sovereign, creative will, decision, decree of
God (Mussner; s. also TDNT). The part. is either temporal
"after deciding" or causal "because he decided." ἀπεκύησεν
aor. act. ind. ἀποκνέω = ἀποκύω to give birth, to bear (s.v.15).
Although the contract verb generally refers to the birth through
a woman, it is used here in reference to God giving birth (s.
Mussner; Adamson). ἀπαρχή first fruit. κτίσμα creation.

■ ἴστε 2nd per. pl. οἶδα defective perf. w. a pres. meaning. 19
ἔστω pres. imp. εἰμί. ταχύς quick, swift, fast. ἀκοῦσαι aor. act.
inf. The inf. w. the prep. can express purpose or result or it can
have the meaning "w. reference to hearing" (Ropes). βραδύς
slow. λαλῆσαι aor. act. inf. The inf. used w. the prep. and article
in the sense of "w. reference to" (Ropes). ὀργή anger, wrath. It
refers to the deep-seated anger (s. TDNT). ■ θεοῦ. Here the 20
gen., "God's righteousness," refers not to the righteousness that
is part of His character, but to the way of life, in deed and
thought, that He requires in us (Adamson; s. also Lenski).
ἐργάζεται pres. mid. ind. to work, to do, to practice (s. Ropes).
The pres. tense indicates that which is continually true. ■ διό 21
therefore. ἀποθέμενοι aor. mid. part. ἀποτίθημι to put off, to
strip off. It is a metaphor from the putting off of clothes (Mayor).
ῥυπαρία dirtiness, filthiness. The word was used of dirty clothes
and also referred to moral defilement (Mayor; Ropes).
περισσεία overabundance, excess. κακία evil, wickedness,
gen. of apposition. The phrase calls attention to the fact that
wickedness is in reality an excrescence on character, not a normal part of it (Ropes). πραΰτης meekness, mildness, gentleness.
It is the humble and gentle attitude which expresses itself in a
patient submissiveness to offense, free from malice and desire for
revenge. The word stands in contrast to the term "wrath" (s.
Mussner; Gal. 5:22; 2 Cor. 10:1; Matt. 5:5). δέξασθε aor. mid.
imp. δέχομαι to receive, to accept. ἔμφυτος implanted. It is the
word for an "implanting" not at birth but later in life. It is used
metaphorically to mean "sent into a man to be, or grow to be,
a part of his nature" (Adamson, 98–100). δυνάμενον pres. mid.
part. σῶσαι aor. act. inf. σῴζω to rescue, to save.

■ γίνεσθε pres. mid. imp. The pres. tense indicating con- 22
tinual action calls for a habit of life. ποιητής one who performs
an action, one who does something, doer. The expression would
be the same as the Semitic phrase "to do the law" meaning "to
observe the law" or "to fulfill the law." (For examples, s. Dibelius.) ἀκροατής one who hears. Both in the Jewish home as well
as in the education process and the synagogue worship, the

hearing of the law which was read aloud played an important
part in Jewish life (s. JPFC II, 800f.; 945–977; Dibelius). The
rabbis also stressed very strongly the necessity of keeping the
law (s. e.g. M Aboth 1, 17; for other examples, s. Mussner; SB
III, 84–88; 753). παραλογιζόμενοι pres. mid. part.
παραλογίζομαι to reason beside the point, to misjudge, to
miscalculate, to deceive one's self, to cheat in reckoning, to
23 deceive through fallacious reasoning (s. MM; MH, 319). ∎
ἔοικεν pres. act. ind., s.v.6. κατανοοῦντι pres. act. part.
κατανοέω to put the mind down upon, to consider attentively,
to take note of, to look at (RWP; Ropes). γένεσις birth, origin,
natural, mortal. The word indicates the face which one received
at birth and the gen. is either gen. of attribute or perhaps of
source (s. Mussner; Adamson; Ropes). ἔσοπτρον mirror. Mirrors were generally highly polished metal (s. 1 Cor. 13:12; May-
24 or). ∎ κατενόησεν aor. act. ind. κατανοέω (s.v.23).
ἀπελήλυθεν perf. act. ind. ἀπέρχομαι to go away. The force
of the perf. tense here is to express an immediate sequel, e.g., a
swift result (s. Adamson; Ropes). εὐθέως adv. immediately.
ἐπελάθετο aor. mid. ind. ἐπιλανθανομαι to forget. ὁποῖος
25 what sort of, what kind of. ∎ παρακύψας aor. act. part.
παρακύπτω to stoop down and look into in order to see something exactly and to recognize (Mussner). Here it means "binding over the mirror in order to examine it more minutely,"
"hearing into it" (Mayor). ἐλευθερία freedom (s. Adams, 33f.).
The gen. is gen. of attribute (Mussner). παραμείνας pres. act.
part. παραμένω to stay beside, to remain, to continue (s. Phil.
1:25). ἐπιλησμονή forgetfulness. γενόμενος aor. mid. part.
s.v.12. ἔργον work. The gen. is a certain emphasis, "a doer who
does" (Ropes). ποίησις doing. ἔσται fut. εἰμί.

26   ∎ θρησκός religious, pious. The word denotes the scrupulous observance of religious exercise—in action or words—sin-
cerely or hypocritically performed in the guise of devout religion. The word describes one who stands in awe of the gods, and
is tremendously scrupulous in what regards them (Adamson; s.
also Mayor; Ropes; TDNT). χαλιναγωγῶν pres. act. part.
χαλιναγωγέω to lead w. a bridle, to bridle. The picture is that
of a man putting the bridle in his own mouth, not in that of
another (RWP). ἀπατῶν pres. act. part. ἀπατάω to deceive.
μάταιος vain, empty, nonproductive, useless, dead (Mussner; s.
also TDNT). θρησκεία piety, religious worship. The word expresses the worship of God, religion, especially as it expresses
itself in religious service or cult (BAG; s. also MM; s. also the
27 adj. in this verse). ∎ ἀμίαντος without defilement, undefiled,

free from contamination (AS). ἐπισκέπτεσθαι pres. mid. inf.
to look upon, to visit, to provide help for. The word often was
used for the visiting of the sick (Mayor; Ropes). ὀρφανός orphan. χήρα widow. (For the needs of the orphans and widows
particularly in Judaism, s. Mussner; Mayor; JPFC II, 787ff.)
θλῖψις stress, pressure, affliction. ἄσπιλος without a spot, unstained. τηρεῖν pres. act. inf. to observe, to keep, to guard. The
inf. used in this v. are epexegetical explaining the nature of true
piety or worship. κόσμος world, world system (s. TDNT; CBB).

Ch. 2

■ προσωπολημψία the receiving of one's face, partiality 1
(s. Rom. 2:11; Mayor). ἔχετε pres. act. imp. to have, to possess.
δόξα glory. The gen. has been variously interpreted as having an
objective, a subjective, or a qualitative force and has been connected to the various substitutives in the sentence. (For various
interpretations, s. Mayor; Adamson; Dibelius; Ropes.) ■ 2
εἰσέλθη aor. act. subj. εἰσέρχομαι to come into.
χρυσοδακτύλιος w. a golden ring on the finger. It was common
to wear rings in the ancient world either as a signet ring or as
a piece of jewelry for adornment. Sometimes more than one ring
was worn and the social status of a person could be noted by the
quality of his ring (s. DGRA, 95–97; M, Kelim 11:8, 12:1).
ἐσθής garment, clothes. λαμπρός shining. Some robes were
said to have been made from silver which would glisten in the
sunlight (s. Acts 12:21). The word here could refer to elegant and
luxurious clothes or it may be used of fresh and clean clothes
without reference to costliness (Ropes). πτωχός poor, abject
poverty, poor as a beggar (s. NTW, 109–111; TDNT). ῥυπαρός
filthy, dirty. The normal toga of the Romans was white, as was
the robe of the Jews, and political candidates wore a brighter
white which was produced by rubbing it with chalk. The white
toga had to be cleaned, and when this was neglected, the Romans called it *sordida* and those who wore such garments were
called *sordidati* (s. DGRA, 1137; Mayor; Mussner). ■ 3
ἐπιβλέψητε aor. act. subj. ἐπιβλέπω to look upon, to direct
one's attention to, to look w. attention or interest or respect or
favor (Adamson). φοροῦντα pres. act. part. φορέω to carry, to
wear, to wear clothes. εἴπητε aor. act. subj. λέγω. The subj. in
this section are used in a third-class conditional clause assuming
the possibility of the condition. κάθου pres. mid. imp. κάθημαι
to sit. It has been supposed that the type of synagogue referred
to here was one in which the cultic center was located close to
the entrance and therefore the distinguished person is immedi-

ately provided w. a seat "here," while the poor man must either
also take his seat near the sanctuary or else be satisfied w. a place
to stand over "there" in that part of the building which is further
from the entrance and the cultic center (s. Dibelius). καλῶς adv.
"please," or it has the meaning "in a good place" (Adamson; s.
also Matt. 23:6). στῆθι aor. act. imp. ἵστημι to stand, ingressive aor. "to take one's stand" (RWP). ὑπό w. the acc. under,
down against, down beside (RWP). ὑποπόδιον footstool. This
could have been something like that which was found in a synagogue of the 2nd or 3rd century. There was a stone bench running along the walls, w. a lower tier for the feet of those sitting
4 on the bench (s. Adamson). ■ διεκρίθητε aor. pass. ind.
διακρίνομαι to judge between two, to face both ways, to be
divided against one's self, to waiver, to distinguish. The verb has
numerous meanings, here the best seems to be that of "to make
a distinction," "to make differences." The neg. used in the question expects the answer yes and the words could be translated
"You have made differences, haven't you?" w. the phrase "in
(among) yourselves" meaning either distinctions between
church members or the subjective opinion which one makes
within himself (s. Mussner; Adamson; Dibelius; MM). ἐγένεσθε
aor. mid. ind. γίνομαι. διαλογισμός reasoning. The word includes "purpose" as well as "deliberation" and the gen. is gen.
of quality, "judges w. evil thoughts" (Ropes).

5   ■ ἀκούσατε aor. act. imp. ἐξελέξατο aor. mid. ind.
ἐκλέγω to pick out, to choose out, mid. to choose for one's self.
τῷ κόσμῳ. The dat. could be locative indicating the place "in
the world" or it could be dat. of respect "those poor in respect
to worldly goods" (Dibelius) or it could be an ethical dat. "poor
in the opinion of the world"; i.e., "in the world's judgment"
(Mayor; s. also BD, 103; MT, 239). πλούσιος rich, wealthy. ἐν
πίστει "in faith." The phrase could mean "abounding in faith"
(Mayor) or "in virtue of faith" or better "in the realm of faith"
(Ropes; Adamson). κληρονόμος heir. ἐπηγγείλατο aor. mid.
ind. ἐπαγγέλλομαι to promise. ἀγαπῶσιν pres. act. part.
6 ἀγαπάω to love. ■ ἠτιμάσατε aor. act. ind. ἀτιμάζω to treat
without honor, to dishonor. τὸν πτωχόν "the poor." The article
could point to a specific person or it is simply generic (Ropes).
καταδυναστεύουσιν pres. act. ind. to exercise power against
someone, to oppress. (For a description of the wealthy class as
well as the middle class and poor class—to which the teachers
of the law or the scribes often belonged—in Jerusalem at this
time, s. JTJ, 87–119.) ἕλκουσιν pres. act. ind. to drag.
κριτήριον place where cases are judged, tribunal, law court,

court of justice. ■ βλασφημοῦσιν pres. act. ind. to slander, to 7
blaspheme. ἐπικληθέν aor. pass. part. ἐπικαλέω to call upon,
pass. to be called upon, to be named. ■ μέντοι indeed. The 8
particle has both an adversative meaning "but," "nevertheless,"
"however," and an affirmative meaning "verily," "really" (s.
Ropes; Adamson). τελεῖτε pres. act. ind. to fulfill. βασιλικός
pertaining to a king, royal, sovereign, excellent, supreme. (For
various interpretations of this word, s. Adamson; Mayor; Ropes;
Dibelius.) ἀγπήσεις fut. act. ind. The fut. under Semitic influence is used as a "categorical imp." (BG, 94). πλησίον neighbor. ■ προσωπολημπτεῖτε pres. act. ind. to show partiality 9
(s.v.1). The ind. is used in a first-class condition assuming the
reality of the condition. ἐργάζεσθε pres. mid. ind. to work, to
do (s. James 1:20). ἐλεγχόμενοι pres. pass. part. ἐλέγχω to
convict, to convince w. overwhelming evidence. παραβάτης
transgressor, one who steps across a boundary (s. TDNT). ■ 10
ὅστις w. the subj. "whoever." (For this use w. the subj., s. RG,
956f.; BD, 192.) τηρήσῃ aor. act. subj. τηρέω to quard, to keep.
πταίσῃ aor. act. subj. πταίω to stumble, to trip. The "stumbling" means "to make a mistake, to go astray, to sin" (BAG).
ἐν ἑνί "in one point." The word is n. since "law" is not used of
single precepts (Ropes). γέγονεν perf. act. ind. γίνομαι. The
perf. tense indicates the continuing results of the action "he has
become guilty of all points" and ever remains so (Lenski).
ἔνοχος in the power of, guilty. Here the following gen. indicates
the authority or law against which one has transgressed (Dibelius; s. also Mayor). Stricter rabbis taught that the Torah even in
its separate statutes was immutable and indivisible (Adamson; s.
also SB III, 755). ■ εἰπών aor. act. part. λέγω. μοιχεύσῃς aor. 11
act. subj. μοιχεύω to commit adultery. φονεύσῃς aor. act. subj.
φονεύω to murder. (For εἰ ... οὐ, s. M, 171. The sense of the
expression may be concessive; i.e., "although ..." SMT, 179f.)
■ λαλεῖτε pres. act. imp. ποιεῖτε pres. act. imp. ἐλευθερία 12
freedom, liberty. The prep. here indicates the "state or condition
in which one does or suffers something"; i.e., "under the law of
liberty" (Ropes). μέλλοντες pres. act. part. μέλλω to be about
to. κρίνεσθαι pres. pass. inf. The part. w. the inf. has the meaning "those who are going to be judged by the law of liberty,"
signifying not just a fut. event, but a deliberate choice of the law
of liberty (and mercy) in preference to the old ruthless rigor of
the "Law" (Adamson). ■ κρίσις judgment. ἀνέλεος without 13
mercy, merciless (on the form s. Mayor; MM). ποιήσαντι aor.
act. part. ἔλεος mercy, pity. κατακαυχᾶται pres. mid. ind. to
boast against someone, to triumph over (s. Mayor; Dibelius;

Mussner). (For rabbinical parallels and Jewish emphasis on mercy and pity, s. Adamson; SB I, 203; Matt. 5:7.)

14 ■ ὄφελος profit. λέγῃ pres. act. subj. It is used in presenting this one's claim to be approved of men and of God (Ropes). ἔργα works. The word seems here to be a recognized term for "good works" (Ropes; s. also Mayor; Adamson, 34–38). ἔχῃ pres. act. subj. ἡ πίστις "the faith." The article could be the article of previous reference meaning "the previously mentioned faith," "*that* faith" (Mussner; BD, 131f.). The article could also be used to emphasize the particular faith of the one speaking; i.e., "*his* faith" (IBG, 111). σῶσαι aor. act. inf. σῴζω to rescue, to save. The aor. signifies "achieve salvation for him" (Adamson).

15 ■ ἀδελφή sister. γυμνός naked. The term does not necessarily imply absolute nakedness; it was used of a person wearing only an undertunic and means that someone was poorly clad (Mayor). ὑπάρχωσιν pres. act. subj. ὑπάρχω to exist, to be (s. 2 Cor. 12:16). λειπόμενοι pres. pass. part. λείπω to lack, pass. to be lacking (followed by the gen.). ἐφήμερος for the day. The phrase implies "food for the day" or "the day's supply of food"

16 (MM; for examples, s. also Dibelius). ■ ὑπάγετε pres. act. imp. ὑπάγω to go away, to depart. The expression "go in peace" is a Jewish expression meaning "good-by" and as an address to beggars; it may still be heard today in the streets of Jerusalem and it has the same effect. It signals the end of the encounter (s. Ropes; Adamson). θερμαίνεσθε pres. mid.-pass. imp. θερμαίνομαι to warm one' self, to be warm. The word was commonly used of the effect of warm clothes (Ropes). χορτάζεσθε pres. pass. imp. χορτάζω to feed until one is full, pass. to be filled. The word has the general meaning of satisfying hunger (Mayor; MM). δῶτε aor. act. subj. δίδωμι. ἐπιτήδεια pl. necessities, the necessities of the body, the necessities of life

17 (RWP). ■ οὕτως likewise. This is used in making the application (Ropes). καθ᾿ ἑαυτήν "in itself, in reference to itself, inwardly" (Dibelius; s. also Mayor; Adamson).

18 ■ ἐρεῖ fut. act. ind. λέγω. δεῖξον aor. act. imp. δείκνυμι to show. (For a discussion concerning the ones referred to here by the personal pron., s. Ropes; Adamson.) δείξω fut. act. ind.

19 ■ δαιμόνιον demon, evil spirits. φρίσσουσιν pres. act. ind. to bristle. It was used of the physical signs of terror, esp. of the hair standing on end. The word often expresses only a high degree of awe or terror (Mayor). The pres. tense indicates that which

20 is always true. ■ γνῶναι aor. act. inf. γινώσκω. ἄνθρωπος man. The term is used here in a derogatory sense. κενός empty, deficient. The word is used of a man who cannot be depended

upon, whose deeds do not correspond to his words; hence, of
boasters and imposters (Mayor). ἀργός inactive, barren, unprofitable, unproductive of salvation (Ropes). ■ ἐδικαιώθη aor. 21
pass. ind. δικαιόω to declare righteous, to pronounce to be in
the right, to justify (s. TDNT; Rom. 2:13; Bengel; Lenski).
ἀνενέγκας aor. act. part. ἀναφέρω to offer up, to sacrifice.
θυσιαστήριον place of sacrifice, altar. ■ συνήργει impf. ind. 22
act. συνεργέω to cooperate, to work together. ἐτελειώθη aor.
pass. ind. τελειόω to bring to completion, to bring to maturity,
to perfect, to consummate. As the tree is perfected by its fruits,
so faith by its works (Mayor). Works do not animate faith; but
faith produces works, and works perfect faith. Faith itself "is
perfected," i.e., is shown to be true, by works (Bengel). ■ 23
ἐπληρώθη aor. pass. ind. πληρόω to make full, to fulfill.
λέγουσα pres. act. part. ἐπίστευσεν aor. act. ind. ἐλογίσθη
aor. pass. ind. λογίζομαι to place to one's account, to reckon.
ἐκλήθη aor. pass. ind. καλέω. ■ ἐξ ἔργων "from works." 24
Though neither ignored nor belittled, faith is regarded as com-
plementing works, w. which it must be combined. The contrast
is between faith minus works, and works minus faith—not between faith and works (Adamson). δικαιοῦται pres. pass. ind.
■ ὁμοίως adv. "in like manner." πόρνη whore, prostitute. (For 25
the view that Rahab was one who provided lodging for strangers
or travelers, s. D.J. Wiseman, "Rahab of Jericho," TB, 14 [June,
1964], 8–11; for the Jewish views on Rahab, s. Adamson; SB I,
20–23.) ὑποδεξαμένη aor. mid. part. ὑποδέχομαι to receive,
to welcome. ἐκβαλοῦσα aor. act. part. ἐκβάλλω to throw out,
to send forth. The word is not used here in a bad sense, but it
simply emphasizes the difficulties of escape (Adamson). ■ γάρ 26
"for." The particle is used to introduce the supporting argument.
The relationship between vv. 25 and 26 is this: Rahab was justified by works; she could not have been justified in any other way,
for without works faith is dead. Therefore, the faith of Rahab is
presupposed (Dibelius). πνεύματος spirit, breath. The word refers to the "vital principle by which the body is animated"
(Ropes). A dead faith is like a corpse and therefore cannot save
(Mussner).

Ch. 3

■ γίνεσθε pres. mid. imp. γίνομαι to become. 1
διδάσκαλος teacher. The word is used perhaps in the rabbinical
sense of "rabbi" indicating one who had studied the law and its
application to life and was engaged in teaching others (s. TDNT;
Adamson; Herschel Shanks, "Is the Title 'Rabbi' Anachronistic

in the Gospels?" *Jewish Quarterly Review*, 53 [1963], 337–345). εἰδότες perf. act. part. οἶδα defective perf. w. the pres. meaning "to know." The part. is causal. μείζων comp. μέγας great, comp. greater. κρίμα judgment, results of a judicial decision, condemnation, sentence of punishment (Dibelius). The teacher's condemnation is greater than that of others because having, or professing to have, clear and full knowledge of duty, he is the more bound to obey it (Ropes). λημψόμεθα fut. mid. ind. λαμβάνω. James uses the first-per. pl. because he himself is a teacher in the church and knows that he must some day give
2 account to the divine Judge for his teaching (Mussner). ■ πολλά. The acc. can be acc. of general reference "in reference to many things" (s. RWP). πταίομεν pres. act. ind. to stumble, to offend (s. James 1:10). The pres. tense could be interat. indicating an action that occurs over and again. οὗτος this one. χαλιναγωγῆσαι aor. act. inf. χαλιναγωγέω to bridle (s.
3 James 1:26). ■ ἵππος horse. The gen. is dependent on the word "bits" but is put first because it contains the new emphatic idea (Ropes). χαλινός bridle, bit. The word is used of the "bridle" proper (or "reins"), of the "bit," and, as perhaps here, of the whole bridle, including both (Ropes). (For a description of bridles and bits in the ancient world, s. DGRA, 548.) The word used here was also used of a particular type of rope connected w. sails of a ship (s. DGRA, 790). πείθεσθαι pres. mid. inf. to obey. The inf. is used w. the prep. to express purpose. μετάγομεν pres. act. ind. to change the direction, to guide (RWP). The pres. tense is used to express that which is always
4 true. ■ τηλικοῦτος so great. ὄντα pres. part. εἰμί. ὑπό w. the gen. "by." The frequent use of the prep. in connection w. the word "wind" and similar words suggest that here it retains something of its local force, not simply "by," but "under" (Mayor). ἄνεμος wind. σκληρός harsh, stiff, strong (Ropes). ἐλαυνόμενα pres. pass. part. ἐλαύνω to drive. The word is used of wind or of sailors rowing or sailing a boat (AS). μετάγεται pres. pass. ind., s.v.3. ἐλάχιστος. The superl. of the adj. is used in an elative sense "very small" (BAG; s. also BD, 33). πηδάλιον rudder. The rudder of an ancient ship was like an oar w. a very broad blade and ships generally had two rudders which were placed on each side of the stern, not at the ship's extremity. Both rudders were managed by the same steersman to prevent confusion (s. DGRA, 788–789; Pliny, *Natural History*, VII, 57). ὁρμή. The word was used of the origin of motion either moral or physical. The word could mean here either the "pressure," or "touch" of the steersman or it could refer to the "impulse" of the

steersman (s. Mayor; TDNT; MM). εὐθύνοντος pres. act. part. εὐθύνω to direct, to guide, to steer. βούλεται pres. mid. ind. to decide, to will. (For examples of the use of the two figures of the control of a horse and a ship, s. Dibelius; Ropes.) ■ οὕτως so, 5 thus. The word introduces the application of the examples. γλῶσσα tongue. μέλος member. μέγαλα great, great things. Sometimes the adj. is written in connection w. the following verb: αὐχεῖ pres. act. ind. to boast. The phrase is used here in the sense not of an empty boast, but of a justified, though haughty, sense of importance (Ropes, Dibelius; Mussner).

ἡλίκος what size. In this context the n. has the meaning "how small" and the fem. the meaning "how much," "how large" (s. Ropes; Mayor). ὕλη woods, forest. It has been suggested that the word means "thicket" or "brush" (s. L.E. Elliott-Binns, "The Meaning of ὕλη in James III.5," NTS 2 [1956], 48–50; s. also Dibelius). (For examples paralleling James' illustration of fire, s. Dibelius; Ropes.) ἀνάπτει pres. act. ind. ἀνάπτω to set on fire, to ignite. ■ κόσμος world, here followed 6 by the gen. "world of injustice." (For the various interpretations of this phrase, s. Mayor; Ropes; Dibelius.) καθίσταται pres. mid. or pass. The pass. has the meaning "is constituted" and the mid. the meaning "presents itself" (RWP; s. also Mayor). σπιλοῦσα pres. act. part. σπιλόω to stain, to defile. φλογίζουσα pres. act. part. φλογίζω to set in flames, to inflame, to set on fire. τροχός wheel, cycle, circle. γενέσεως gen. sing. γένεσις origin, birth. The phrase has been variously interpreted; e.g., "the cycle of the coming" signifying little more than "life" (Dibelius); i.e., "the whole circle of life" (Mussner). Others see the phrase as eschatological signifying the course (of time) ordained by God for the present era, now in its last days, and the phrase is translated "sets afire all that revolving time brings to birth" (Adamson). (For examples, s. Ropes; Mayor; Dibelius; SB I, 820.) φλογιζομένη pres. pass. part. γέεννα (Heb.) the valley of Henna, Gehenna, hell. The valley of Henna just outside of Jerusalem was the city garbage dump and is used as a picture of hell, the place of punishment for the wicked (s. TDNT). ■ φύσις 7 nature. θηρίον wild animal. πετεινά (pl.) birds. ἑρπετά (pl.) crawling animals, reptiles. ἐνάλιον sea creatures (s. Adamson). δαμάζεται pres. pass. ind. δαμάζω to tame, gnomic pres. The pres. points to the continual possibility of taming wild animals. δεδάμασται perf. pass. ind. The perf. tense points to the completed action and the two tenses could be translated "is from time to time, and has actually been, tamed" (Ropes). τῇ φύσει. The dat. is used in the sense of "in subjection to" and the term itself means "human kind" (Ropes). Both pagan and Heb. were proud of man's lordship over the animal world (Adamson).

8 ἀνθρώπινος human. ■ δαμάσαι aor. act. inf. ἀκατάστατος restless, unquiet, like the least tameable beasts (Mayor). μεστός

9 full. ἰός poison. θανατηφόρος death bearing. ■ εὐλογοῦμεν pres. act. ind. to bless. The pres. tense is customary indicating that which one usually does (s. Eph. 1:3). καταρώμεθα pres. mid. ind. to curse. ὁμοίωσις likeness. γεγονότας perf. act. part. The perf. tense looks at the completed action or state of man

10 being in the image of God. ■ ἐξέρχεται pres. mid. ind. to go out. κατάρα curse. χρή impersonal verb "it is necessary," "it ought to be." The necessity expressed by this word signifies a need or necessity resulting from time or circumstances or from the fitness of things (AS; T; Mayor). Here it denotes the incongruity for blessing and cursing to come out of the same mouth (RWP).

11 ■ μήτι. Used in a question which expects the answer "no" (s. Mussner). πηγή spring, fountain, well. The word is used w. the definite article and it is suggested that among country folk "the spring" or "the well" has a prominent individuality (Adamson). ὀπή opening. The word is used elsewhere of "a cleft in a rock" (Mayor; s. also Heb. 11:38). βρύω to gush forth. The word means "teem," "the full of bursting," and is ordinarily used of the swelling buds of plants and so figuratively of various kinds of fullness. Here the thought is of the gushing forth of the water (Ropes; s. also Mayor). γλυκύς sweet. πικρός bitter. The word here may denote a case where above the outlet good water has

12 suffered contamination from a salty source (Adamson). ■ συκῆ fig, fig tree. ἐλαία olive. ποιῆσαι aor. act. inf. to produce. ἄμπελος vine, grape vine. These three fruits, fig, olive, and grape, found in all the Near East, are particularly associated w. Palestine (Adamson). ἁλυκός salty.

13 ■ σοφός wise. The t.t. for the Teacher; in Jewish usage one who has a knowledge of practical, moral wisdom, resting on a knowledge of God (Ropes). In contrast the Gr. philosophical term meant "theoretical wisdom" (s. GPT, 179). ἐπιστήμων understanding. The word implies expert or professional knowledge (Tasker). The use of the interrogative is a Semitic construction which takes the place of a condition (s. Mayor; Mussner; Byer, 167). δειξάτω aor. act. imp. δείκνυμι to show, to demonstrate. ἀναστροφή manner of life, conduct. πραΰτης meekness, gentleness. It is the opposite of arrogance and indicates the humble and gentle attitude which expresses itself in a patient submissiveness to offense, free from malice and desire for re-

14 venge (s. Matt. 5:5; 2 Cor. 10:1; Gal. 5:6). ■ ζῆλος zeal. The idea

is of a fierce desire to promote one's own opinion to the exclusion of others (Ropes). ἐριθεία selfish ambition. The word really means the vice of a leader of a party created for his own pride: It is partly ambition, partly rivalry (Dibelius; s. also NTW, 39f.; TDNT; Phil. 2:3). κατακαυχᾶσθε pres. mid. imp. κατακαυχάομαι to boast against, to boast arrogantly. The word is used sometimes w. the gen. to denote the triumph of one principle over another. The prep. in compound is either intensive or indicates an unfavorable action (Mayor; MH, 316). The pres. imp. w. the neg. indicates either the stopping of an action in progress or prohibits the habitual action. ψεύδεσθε pres. mid. imp. ψεύδομαι to lie. ■ σοφία wisdom. ἄνωθεν from above. 15 κατερχομένη pres. mid. part. κατέρχομαι to come down. ἐπίγειος earthly, on the earth (s. Adamson). ψυχικός natural; i.e., pertaining to the natural life which men and animals alike have, unspiritual (s. Ropes; Adamson). δαιμονιώδης demonic (s. Adamson). ■ ἀκαταστασία disorder, disturbance, trouble, 16 instability. The word sometimes had political associations and had the meaning "anarchy." Here it would refer to the "disorder" caused by those who w. their "false wisdom" trouble the group of believers by demanding their own rights and exercising a party spirit (s. Ropes; Adamson; Mussner). φαῦλος bad, foul, vile. πρᾶγμα matter, thing. ■ ἁγνός pure. The word implies 17 sincere, moral and spiritual integrity (Adamson). εἰρηνικός peaceable, loving, and promoting peace. ἐπιεικής gentle, reasonable in judging. The word signifies a humble patience, steadfastness which is able to submit to injustice, disgrace, and maltreatment without hatred and malice, trusting in God in spite of all of it (s. Phil. 4:5; 2 Cor. 10:1; NTW, 38f.). εὐπειθής easily persuaded, willing to yield, compliant. The opposite of the word is "disobedient." The word is used of submission to military discipline and for observance of legal and moral standards in ordinary life; e.g., one who willingly submits to a fatherly will (s. MM; Adamson; Mayor). ἔλεος merciful. ἀδιάκριτος undivided, unwavering, wholehearted w. reference to the evil situation described in verses 9 and 10 (Ropes). ἀνυπόκριτος without hypocrisy, unhypocritical. ■ δικαιοσύνης. The gen. could be 18 gen. of definition or apposition indicating that the fruit is righteousness (s. Mayor). Some view it as a subjective gen. or gen. of source indicating that fruit is the product of righteousness and the source of the fruit (Ropes). σπείρεται pres. pass. ind. σπείρω to sow (s. Dibelius). ποιοῦσιν pres. act. part. dat. pl. The dat. is either dat. of agency; i.e., "sown by those who do

peace" (Mussner) or it is dat. of advantage; i.e., "for peaceable
people" (Dibelius; s. also Mayor).

Ch. 4

1 ■ πόθεν where, from where. πόλεμος war. μάχη battle,
fight. The first word pictures the chronic state or campaign of
war while the second word presents the separate conflicts or
battles of the war (RWP). ἐνετεῦθεν from here. It is used to
indicate the reason or source (BAG). ἡδονή lust, pleasure. Although the word has a strong philosophical flavor (s. GPT, 75–
78; TDNT), it is to be taken here in a practical and bad sense
(Adamson; Mussner). στρατευομένων pres. mid. part.
στρατεύομαι to carry on a campaign, to fight a military battle.
μέλος member. Here the word "members" is used collectively
2 as the abode of the passions (Adamson). ■ ἐπιθυμεῖτε pres. act.
ind. to desire, to long for. φονεύετε pres. act. ind. to murder.
ζηλοῦτε pres. act. ind. to be zealous, to hotly desire, to possess,
to covet (Ropes; s. also James 3:14). ἐπιτυχεῖν aor. act. inf.
ἐπιτυγχάνω to obtain (s. Mayor). μάχεσθε pres. mid. ind. to
fight a battle. πολεμεῖτε pres. act. ind. to wage war. αἰτεῖσθαι
pres. mid. inf. to ask, to ask for one's self. (For a discussion of
the significance of the mid. voice, s. Mayor; M, 160.) The inf.
3 is used w. the prep. to express cause. ■ κακῶς adv. evilly,
wrongly. δαπανήσητε aor. act. subj. δαπανάω to spend, to
spend freely. The object of the verb "to spend" is the means of
securing enjoyment for which they pray; throughout the passage
money is esp. in mind (Ropes). The subj. is used to express the
purpose of the asking and at the same time indicates the reason
4 or cause for asking (Mussner). ■ μοιχαλίς adulteress, one who
is unfaithful to the marriage vows. The term was a figure of
speech particularly in the OT to indicate unfaithfulness to God
and the practice of idolatry, here the false god being "world"
(Adamson). φιλία friendship. The word involves the idea of
loving as well as of being loved (Mayor). ἔχθρα enmity, active
hostility. τοῦ θεοῦ obj. gen.; i.e., "hostility against God."
βουληθῇ aor. pass. subj. βούλομαι to will, to want, to desire.
The word has the connotation of preference or choosing one
thing before another (Mussner; s. also TDNT). καθίσταται
pres. pass. ind. to be constituted, to be rendered (s. RWP; James
5 3:6). ■ δοκεῖτε pres. act. ind. to suppose, to think. κενῶς adv.
emptily; i.e., "without meaning all that it says" (Ropes). γραφή
writing, Scripture. (For a discussion of the source of the quotation, s. Mayor; Ropes; Adamson.) φθόνος envy, malice, or envy
arising out of ill will, jealousy (s. Mayor; Adamson; Trench,
Synonyms, 34). ἐπιποθεῖ pres. act. ind. to strongly desire.

κατῴκισεν aor. act. ind. κατοικίζω to cause to dwell, to take up one's dwelling. (For a discussion of the difficulties of this v., s. Adamson; S.S. Laws, "The Scripture Speaks in Vain; A Reconsideration of James IV. 5," NTS, 20 [1973–74], 220ff.) ■ 6 μείζων comp. μέγας greater. ὑπερήφανος haughty, one who thinks above and beyond that which is proper, arrogant. The word sometimes signifies the arrogant rich (Adamson; s. James 4:16; 5:1; s. also 1QH VI, 36; CD I, 15). ἀντιτάσσεται pres. mid. ind. to stand against, to oppose. The pres. tense indicates that which is always true. ταπεινός low, humble. ■ ὑποτάγητε 7 aor. pass. imp. ὑποτάσσομαι to submit, to align one's self under the authority of another. ἀντίστητε aor. act. imp. ἀνθίστημι to oppose, ingressive aor. to take one's stand against. The aor. imp. call for urgent action (RWP). διάβολος slanderer, devil. φεύξεται fut. mid. ind. φεύγω to flee. The use of the imp. followed by the fut. forms a Semitical conditional sentence; i.e., "when you take your stand against the devil, then he will flee from you" (s. Byer, 253; Mussner). ■ ἐγγίσατε aor. 8 act. imp. ἐγγίζω to come near, to draw near. ἐγγίσει fut. act. ind. (For the construction of an imp. followed by the fut. building a type of conditional clause, s.v.7.) καθαρίσατε aor. act. imp. καθαρίζω to cleanse, to purify. ἁμαρτωλός sinful, sinner. ἁγνίσατε aor. act. imp. ἁγνίζω to purify, to make pure. δίψυχος doubleminded (s. James 1:8). ■ ταλαιπωρήσατε aor. 9 act. imp. ταλαιπωρέω to undergo hardship, to endure misery. Here it is used intransitively "be miserable, feel miserable" and refers to the inner attitude of repentance (s. Mayor; Dibelius; Mussner; Adamson). πενθήσατε aor. act. imp. πενθέω to mourn. The word expresses a self-contained grief, never violent in its manifestation (Ropes). The word is often connected w. the term "weep" and it describes the mourning which cannot be hidden. It describes not only a grief which brings an ache to the heart, but also a grief which brings tears to the eyes (MNTW, 137; s. also Mussner). κλαύσατε aor. act. imp. κλαίω to cry, to weep. γέλως laughter. The word indicates the leisurely laughter of gods and men in their pleasures. It is the laughter of a fool who rejects God as the One who determines reality and believes man to be an autonomous being (Mussner; s. also TDNT). πένθος sorrow, mourning. μετατραπήτω aor. pass. imp. third-per. sing. μετατρέπω to turn about, to turn into. The prep. in compound has the idea of change (MH, 318). κατήφεια dejection, downcast, dismay. It describes the condition of one w. eyes cast down like the publican in Luke 18:13 (Mayor; Adamson). ■ ταπεινώθητε aor. pass. imp. ταπεινόω to make low, to hum- 10

ble. The form is pass. but the meaning is reflex. "to humble one's
self" (Adamson). ὑψώσει fut. act. ind. ὑψόω to exalt, to make
high, to lift up. The use of the imp. followed by the fut. is a
Semitic conditional construction (s. Beyer, 252f.).

11 ■ καταλαλεῖτε pres. act. imp. καταλαλέω to talk against,
to defame, to speak evil of. It usually is applied to harsh words
about the per. who is absent (Ropes). καταλαλῶν pres. act.
part. κρίνων pres. act. part. κρίνω to judge. ποιητής one who
performs an act, doer. The construction "doer of the law" means
12 "lawgiver" (Ropes). ■ νομοθέτης lawgiver, one who makes a
law. δυνάμενος pres. mid. part. σῶσαι aor. act. inf. σῴζω to
rescue, to save. ἀπολέσαι aor. act. inf. ἀπόλλυμι to destroy,
to ruin. ὁ πλησίον the next one, neighbor.

13 ■ ἄγε pres. act. imp. ἄγω. The imp. is used as an interjection w. the meaning "come now," "see here" and is usually an
insistent, here a somewhat brusque address (Mayor; Ropes).
λέγοντες pres. act. part. ἤ "or." The word indicates the choice
in planning. αὔριον tomorrow. πορευσόμεθα fut. mid. ind.
πορεύομαι to travel, to go on a journey. The fut. tense indicates
the certainty in the minds of those planning. There were three
kinds of merchants, the old Hellenistic mariners; sea and cara-
van traders; and those who combined domestic w. foreign trade
(Adamson). εἰς τήνδε τὴν πόλιν "into this city." The old
demonstrative form "this" has the force of the particular as
opposed to the general "we will go to this city," pointing it out
on the map (Mayor). ποιήσομεν fut. act. ind. to do, to spend
time. ἐνιαυτός year. ἐμπορευσόμεθα fut. mid. ind.
ἐμπορεύομαι to conduct business, to carry on business as a
merchant. κερδήσομεν fut. act. ind. κερδαίνω to make a profit,
14 to profit, to gain. ■ ἐπίστασθε pres. mid. ind. to know, to
understand. ποῖος of what character; i.e., "is it secure or precari-
ous?" (Ropes). ἀτμίς vapor, steam, smoke. The word was used
of steam from a kettle or smoke which the wind carried away and
graphically depicts the transience of life (Adamson; Mussner;
Mayor). φαινομένη pres. mid. part. φαίνομαι to appear, to
appear visible. ἔπειτα then. ἀφανιζομένη pres. pass. part.
ἀφανίζω to cause to vanish, to make to disappear, pass. to
vanish, to disappear. Aristotle used the word of the migration of
15 birds (Mayor). ■ ἀντὶ τοῦ λέγειν "instead of you saying." The
thought of v. 13 is resumed (Adamson; s. also Dibelius). θελήσῃ
aor. act. subj. θέλω to will. ζήσομεν fut. act. ind. ζάω to live.
16 ■ νῦν δέ "but now," "but actually, in point of fact," in contrast
to what they ought to do (Ropes). καυχᾶσθε pres. mid. ind. to
boast, to glory. ἀλαζονεία bragging, pretentious, arrogant, arro-

738

gant words. The word refers to empty boasting which seeks to
impress men. It is extravagant claims which one cannot fulfill
(BAG; MNTW, 38–42; TDNT). καύχησις boasting. ■ εἰδότι 17
perf. act. part. οἶδα. ποιοῦντι pres. act. part. The dat. is dat. of
disadvantage and indicates that such a one is guilty of sin (May-
or).

Ch. 5

■ ἄγε "come now" (s. James 4:13). πλούσιος rich. 1
κλαύσατε aor. act. imp. κλαίω to cry, to weep. ὀλολύζοντες
pres. act. part. ὀλολύζω howl, to cry aloud. The word is used in
the LXX as the expression of violent grief (Mayor; Joel 1:5, 13;
Isa. 13:6; 14:31; 15:3; 16:7; Jer. 4:8; s. also Mussner; TDNT).
The part. is manner describing the crying. ταλαιπωρία misery.
ἐπερχομέναις pres. mid. part. ἐπέρχομαι to come upon. ■ 2
σέσηπεν perf. act. ind. σήπω to be rotten. The perf. tense
indicates the state or condition "is rotten" (Ropes). ἱμάτιον
garment. σητόβρωτος moth eaten. γέγονεν perf. act. ind.
γίνομαι. The perf. tenses are of prophetic anticipation rather
than "historical record" (Adamson). ■ ἄργυρος silver. 3
κατίωται perf. pass. ind. κατιόομαι to rust, to rust out, to rust
through. The prep. in compound is perfective "to rust through
down to the bottom" (RWP). ἰός poison, rust (s. Mayor). ἔσται
fut. εἰμί. φάγεται fut. mid. ind. ἐσθίω to eat. πῦρ fire.
ἐθησαυρίσατε aor. act. ind. θησαυρίζω to treasure up, to store
up. (For rabbinical and DSS parallels of fire being God's judgment, s. Mussner; SB IV, 866f.) ■ μισθός wage, pay. ἐργάτης 4
one who works, worker. ἀμησάντων aor. act. part. ἀμάω to
reap, to mow. χώραι (pl.) fields. ἀφυστερημένος perf. pass.
part. ἀφυστερέω to be behind from, to fail of, to cause to
withdraw, to withhold. The verb indicates not just delay, but
complete default (Adamson; RWP). The perf. tense looks at the
completed state or condition. ἀφ᾽ ὑμῶν "from you," "by you."
κράζει pres. act. ind. to cry out. The pres. tense indicates the
continual crying out. Both the OT (Lev. 19:13; Deut. 24:14) and
rabbinic teaching required that the workers be paid at the end
of the day and the withholding of wages is one of the four sins
which are said to cry to heaven (Mayor; s. also Adamson). βοή
cry. θερισάντων aor. act. part. θερίζω to reap, to harvest. οὖς,
ὠτός ear. σαβαώθ (Heb.) armies, hosts. εἰσελήλυθαν perf.
act. ind. εἰσέρχομαι to come into. The perf. emphasizes that
the cries that come to the ears of the Lord remain, so that He
does not forget and they are not in vain. ■ ἐτρυφήσατε aor. act. 5
ind. τρυφάω to live in luxury. The word literally means "to

break down" and denotes soft luxury, not necessarily wanton vice (Ropes). The aor. is constantive and summarizes their total life (s. M, 109). ἐσπαταλήσατε aor. act. ind. σπαταλάω to give one's self to pleasure. The prominent idea is that of self-indulgence without distinct reference to squandering (Mayor; s. also 1 Tim. 5:6). ἐθρέψατε aor. act. ind. τρέφω to feed, to fatten,
6 to nourish. σφαγή slaughter. ■ κατεδικάσατε aor. act. ind. καταδικάζω to give a sentence against someone, to condemn. ἐφονεύσατε aor. act. ind. φονεύω to kill, to murder. ἀντιτάσσεται pres. mid. ind. to stand against, to oppose. The pres. tense brings the action before our eyes and makes us dwell upon this, as the central point, in contrast w. the accompanying circumstances (Mayor).

7   ■ μακροθυμήσατε aor. act. imp. μακροθυμέω to patient-ly endure. The word describes the attitude which can endure delay and bear suffering and never give in (NTW, 84; s. also TDNT; Gal. 5:22). παρουσία arrival, coming. γεωργός farmer. ἐκδέχεται pres. mid. ind. to wait for something. The pres. tense is gnomic indicating that which is common to farmers. τίμιος precious, valuable. μακροθυμῶν pres. act. part. λάβη aor. act. subj. λαμβάνω. πρόϊμος early. ὄψιμος late. The "early rain" normally begins in Palestine late October or early November, and is anxiously awaited because, being necessary for the germi-nation of the seed, it is the signal for sowing. In the spring the maturing of the grain depends on the "late rain," light showers falling in April and May. Without these even heavy winter rains will not prevent failure of crops (Ropes; s. also Mussner; Mayor).
8 ■ στηρίξατε aor. act. imp. στηρίζω to strengthen, to make stable. ἤγγικεν perf. act. ind. ἐγγίζω to come near, to draw
9 near. ■ στενάζετε pres. act. imp. στενάζω to groan. The word denotes feeling which is internal and unexpressed (Mayor). The pres. imp. w. the neg. calls for the discontinuing of an action in progress or prohibits habitual action. κριθῆτε aor. act. subj. κρίνω to judge. The subj. is used in a neg. purpose clause.
10 ἕστηκεν perf. act. ind. ἵστημι to stand. ■ ὑπόδειγμα example. λάβετε aor. act. imp. λαμβάνω to take. κακοπαθία suffering hardship, suffering evil. μακροθυμία patient endurance (s.v.7).
11 ἐλάλησαν aor. act. ind. ■ μακαρίζομεν pres. act. ind. to con-sider happy, to consider blessed. The word refers to the preve-lant habitual estimate of the worth of constancy (Ropes). ὑπομείναντας aor. act. part. ὑπομένω to remain under, to be patient in adverse circumstances (s. NTW, 60; TDNT; CBB; Heb. 10:36). ἠκούσατε aor. act. ind. ἀκούω to hear. τέλος κυριόυ goal, purpose, outcome, result; i.e., "the conclusion

wrought by the Lord to his trouble" (Ropes; s. also Adamson).
εἴδετε aor. act. ind. ὁράω to see. πολύσπλαγχος very kind,
very pitiful, very sympathetic, extremely compassionate (s.
Mayor; MNTW, 156f.; TDNT). οἰκτίρμων compassion.

■ ὀμνύετε pres. act. imp. ὀμνύω to swear. ὅρκος oath (s. 12
Matt. 5:33). ἤτω pres. imp. εἰμί. πέσητε aor. act. subj. πίπτω.

■ κακοπαθεῖ pres. act. ind. to suffer misfortune, to suffer 13
trouble. προσευχέσθω pres. mid. imp. προσεύχομαι to pray.
εὐθυμεῖ to be happy, to feel good. ψαλλέτω pres. act. imp.
ψάλλω to sing, to sing praises, to play on a harp (s. Adamson).

■ ἀσθενέω to be weak, to be sick. προσκαλεσάσθω aor. mid. 14
imp. προσκαλέω to call one along side, to summon.
προσευξάσθωσαν aor. mid. imp. to pray. ἀλείψαντες aor. act.
part. ἀλείφω to anoint. The word is used basically for an outward anointing of the body (s. TDNT). The aor. part. can express
antecedent time; i.e., "after anointing pray," or contemporaneous time; i.e., "while anointing pray," or it can be used in the
sense of an imp.; i.e., "anoint and pray" (Mussner; s. also BG,
129f.). ἔλαιον oil, olive oil. Oil was used as a curative by the
ancients generally, including the rabbis (s. Adamson; TDNT;
Mayor; Ropes; SB IV, 533f.). ■ εὐχή prayer. σώσει fut. act. ind. 15
σῴζω to rescue, to save, to heal. Here the word has the idea "to
restore to health" (Ropes). ἐγερεῖ fut. act. ind. ἐγείρω to raise.
The word means "raise from the bed of sickness to health"
(Ropes). κἂν = καὶ ἐάν. ᾖ pres. subj. εἰμί. πεποιηκώς perf.
act. part. The perf. part. is used in a periphrastic perf. act. subj.
in a condition of 3rd class which indicates the possibility of sin
being related to the sickness (s. RWP). ἀφεθήσεται fut. pass.
ind. ἀφίημι to forgive. The pass. is the so-called "theological or
divine" pass. indicating that God is the One who forgives (s. BG,
76). ■ ἐξομολογεῖσθε pres. mid. imp. ἐξομολογέω to openly 16
agree to, to confess. The confession is to be not only to the elders
but to "one another," i.e., probably to those they have wronged
(Adamson). προσεύχεσθε pres. mid. imp. to pray. ἰαθῆτε aor.
pass. subj. ἰάομαι to heal. The pass. is the theological pass.
indicating that God is the One who heals (s.v.15). ἰσχύει pres.
act. ind. to be strong, to be powerful, to have power, to be
competent, to be able (BAG; s. also Phil. 4:13). δέησις request,
prayer. ἐνεργουμένη pres. mid.-pass. part. ἐνεργέω to be effective, to produce (s. MNTW, 46; TDNT). (For a discussion of
whether the form is mid. or pass. and the suggested translation,
"the prayer of a righteous man is very powerful in its operation,"
s. Adamson 205–210; s. also Mayor; Ropes.) ■ ὁμοιοπαθής like 17
feelings, of similar feelings, circumstances, experiences w. the

741

same nature as someone (BAG). The word indicates that the power of Elijah's prayer did not lie in his supernatural greatness, but rather in his humanity and the prophet was only a human being like we are (s. Mussner). βρέξαι aor. act. inf. βρέχω to rain. The inf. is used in indirect discourse indicating the content of the prayer. ἔβρεξεν aor. act. ind. ἐνιαυτός year. μήν month.

18 ■ ὑετός rain. ἔδωκεν aor. act. ind. δίδωμι. ἐβλάστησεν aor. act. ind. βλαστάνω to sprout, to bring forth.

19   ■ πλανηθῇ aor. pass. subj. πλανάω to go astray. ἐπιστρέψῃ aor. act. subj. ἐπιστρέφω to turn around, to turn,

20 to convert. ■ γινώσκετε pres. act. imp. to know, to recognize. ἐπιστρέψας aor. act. part. πλάνη error. καλύψει fut. act. ind. καλύπτω to cover, to hide, to veil. πλῆθος a great number, multitude, many.

1 PETER

ἀπόστολος apostle, an official representative who was 1
appointed and authorized by the one sending (s. TDNT; Best;
CBB; 1 Cor. 1:1). (For the omission of the article w. all of the
substitutives in this v. indicating a stereotype epistolary introduction, s. BD, 137.) ἐκλεκτός elect. Verbal adj. from the verb
meaning "to pick out, to select" (RWP). The word was used in
the papyri in our sense of the word "select" or "choice" (Beare).
παρεπίδημος one who lives alongside of, sojourner. The word
is used of those who are temporary residents, not permanent
settlers in the land; who have a deep attachment and a higher
allegiance in another sphere (Beare). The word emphasizes both
alien nationality and temporary residents (Stibbs; s. also Hort,
154–156; BS, 149; CBB; TDNT; TDOT under "Ger").
διασπορά dispersion, scattering, diaspora. The Jewish "diaspora" came about through deportation and through voluntary
moving to a foreign land. The people generally lived in their own
settlement or quarters in a foreign land and were still vitally
joined to the land of Palestine and the city of Jerusalem w. her
temple. There was always the hope for the eschatological regath-
ering of those who had been scattered. Peter uses the term for
believers who are scattered throughout the world yet have a
heavenly fatherland and a hope of one day being gathered into
this land (s. Goppelt; SB II, 490; TDNT; RAC III, 972–982;
JPFC I, 117–215). ■ πρόγνωσις knowing beforehand, fore- 2
knowledge. God's foreknowledge is much more than knowing
what will happen in the future; it includes, as it does in the
language of the LXX (e.g. Num. 16:5; Judges 9:6; Amos 3:2), His
effective choice (Kelly). ἁγιασμός holiness, sanctification.
πνεύματος gen. sing. The word could refer to the human spirit
but by the analogy of the other clauses, it refers to the Holy Spirit
(Hort). The gen. is subjective gen. indicating that the Spirit
produces the sanctification. ὑπακοή obedience. ῥαντισμός
sprinkling. It is probably a reference to Exodus 24:3–8 (Best).
πληθυνθείη aor. pass. opt. πληθύνω to multiply. The opt. is
used to express a wish or desire (s. MT, 120f.). Peter prays for

743

the multiplication of grace and peace that the trials through which the Asiatic Christians are about to pass may result in a manifold increase of grace and peace (Hort).

3 ■ εὐλογητός blessed (s. Eph. 1:3). ἔλεος mercy, pity, compassion (s. CBB; TDNT). ἀναγεννήσας aor. act. part. ἀναγεννάω to regenerate, to cause to be born again. The idea of a new beginning through a new birth w. the infusion of divine life is an idea which was widespread in the ancient world. It was an idea present in the mystery religions and also in Judaism. A proselyte to Judaism was regarded as a newborn baby (s. Best; RAC IX, 153–155; Schelkle; Goppelt; SB III, 763; for a parallel in the DSS, s. 1QH3, 19–23). The part. gives the reason why God is blessed (Schelkle). ζῶσαν pres. act. part. ζάω to live. Life is a quality or characteristic of the hope here spoken of, not the obj. of it (Hort). A living hope is one that is never extinguished by untold circumstances, just as "living waters" are waters flow-

4 ing fresh from a perennial spring (Selwyn). ■ κληρονομία inheritance. The word can mean a property already received as well as one that is expected. But in the present passage the "inheritance" is kept for the believer, not on earth, but in heaven, and is another name for that salvation which is ready to be revealed (Bigg; s. also Hort; Kelly). ἄφθαρτος imperishable, not corruptible, not liable to pass away (Beare). It has been suggested that the main idea of the word is "to injure, to spoil" and the chief idea in mind is the ravaging of a land by a hostile army (Hort). ἀμίαντος unstained, undefiled. The thought here is being unstained by evil (Beare). ἀμάραντος unfading. The word was used of flowers and suggests a supernatural beauty which time does not impair. The three verbal adjectives indicate that the inheritance is "untouched by death," "unstained by evil," "unimpaired by time"; it is compounded of immortality, purity, and beauty (Beare). τετηρημένην perf. pass. part. τηρέω to guard, to keep, to take care of, to reserve. The perf. tense indicates the state or condition and underlines the fact that the inheritance already exists and is being preserved for those who

5 are now being "guarded" (v.5) (Best). ■ φρουρουμένους pres. pass. part. φρουρέω to guard, to watch over. The term is a military term indicating the guarding done by soldiers and the pres. tense emphasizes our need for continual protection in the unending struggle of the soul. They are being guarded by God's power and this is the guarantee of the final victory (Beare; s. also Stibbs). σωτηρία salvation. The word indicates deliverance or preservation bestowed by God, more specifically deliverance from His wrath at the final judgment (Kelly). The term here

744

indicates "salvation" in its broadest sense (s. TDNT; CBB).
ἕτοιμος ready, prepared. ἀποκαλυφθῆναι aor. pass. inf.
ἀποκαλύπτω to unveil, to reveal. The pass. would be the "theological" or "divine" pass. indicating that God is the One who
does the action. The inf. is used to express purpose (s. BAG). ἐν
καιρῷ ἐσχάτῳ "in the last time." The word "time" indicates
the fit or appointed time or season for some particular thing,
whether it be a period or a moment (Bigg). The word "last"
means simply "last in order of time" (Bigg). ■ ἐν ᾧ "in which," 6
"in which circumstance," "wherefore." (For a discussion of the
antecedent of the rel. pron., s. Selwyn.) ἀγαλλιᾶσθε pres.
mid. ind. to rejoice, to be glad. This verb appears to be used
always w. the connotation of a "religious" joy, a joy which
springs from the contemplation of God or of the salvation which
comes from God (Beare; s. also TDNT; Hort; Kelly). ὀλίγον a
little, a little while, a short while (Kelly). δέον pres. act. part. δεῖ
it is necessary. The part. is used w. the conditional particle which
can be taken as a concessive sentence "although" (Beare), or it
can be taken as a first-class conditional clause which borders on
a causal sentence "since" (BD, 189; Kelly). λυπηθέντες aor.
pass. part. λυπέω to cause pain, to cause sorrow, to put to grief.
The word expresses not suffering but mental effect of suffering
(Hort). ποικίλος various, diversified, manifold, different kinds.
πειρασμός trial. The word here could mean the undeserved
sufferings from without (Bigg). ■ δοκίμιον tried, approved after 7
trial, genuineness. The genuine element in their faith was proven
by a process similar to that of metal refining and is found to be
something more precious than these precious metals (Selwyn; s.
also James 1:3; BS, 259f.). πολυτιμότερος comp. πολύτιμος
more precious, of greater price. ἀπολλυμένου pres. mid. part.
ἀπόλλυμι to destroy, to ruin, to perish. πῦρ fire.
δοκιμαζομένου pres. pass. part. δοκιμάζω to approve after
examination. εὑρεθῇ aor. pass. subj. εὑρίσκω. The subj. is used
to express purpose. ἀποκάλυψις unveiling, revelation. ■ 8
ἰδόντες aor. act. part. ὁράω to see. The part. is concessive
"although." The word here refers to physical sight or eye sight
(Selwyn). ἀγαπᾶτε pres. act. ind. The pres. tense indicates the
continual action. ὁρῶντες pres. act. part. The neg. used w. the
part. here is introduced as it were hypothetical, merely to bring
out the full force of "believing" (Hort; s. also Selwyn).
πιστεύοντες pres. act. part. ἀνεκλάλητος verbal adj. unspeak-
able, inexpressible, ineffable. The word contains the sense of a
divine mystery exceeding the powers of speech and thought
(Beare). δεδοξασμένη perf. pass. part. δοξάζω to glorify, pass.

to be glorified. Here the idea is "to be endowed w. glory from above" (Selwyn; for a study of the word s. esp. Selwyn, 253–258;
9 s. also TDNT; CBB). ■ κομιζόμενοι pres. mid. part. κομίζω mid. = to receive, to obtain. ψυχαί souls. This is not a special part of man's structure but is man as a whole; it is a Jewish rather than a Gr. or modern usage of the word (Best).
10 ■ ἐξεζήτησαν aor. act. ind. ἐκζητέω to seek out. The prep. in compound is intensive. ἐξηρεύνησαν aor. act. ind. ἐξερευνάω to search out. The prep. in compound is intensive. "Seeking out" is the more general term, "searching out" the minute and sedulous process of thought and investigation which subserve the seeking (Hort). The two verbs taken together give emphatic expression to the earnestness w. which enlightenment was sought (Beare; s. also MH, 310). προφητεύσαντες aor. act.
11 part. προφητεύω to speak for, to speak forth, to prophesy. ■ ἐρευνῶτες pres. act. part. ἐρευνάω to search. ποῖος what sort of. The indefinite pron. suggests a definite period, almost a date to be fixed, while this word suggests the general outward circumstances to be expected (Beare; s. also BD, 155). ἐδήλου impf. ind. act. δηλόω to make clear, to make plain. Though the word is often used of declarations through articulate language, it is still more often used of any indirect kind of communication (Hort). The impf. indicates continual action in the past time. προμαρτυρόμενον pres. mid. part. προμαρτύρομαι to testify beforehand (s. Selwyn). τὰ εἰς Χριστὸν "the sufferings to Christ," i.e., "the sufferings in store for Christ" (Kelly). It is quite possible that we have a reference to the words recorded in Luke 24:26–27 (Bigg). (For a discussion of the passages in 1 Peter which point to the words of Christ and support Petrine authorship of the epistle and the authenticity of the gospel passages, s. Robert H. Gundry, " 'Verba Christi' in I Peter: Their Implications Concerning the Authorship of I Peter and the Authenticity of the Gospel Tradition," NTS, 13 [July, 1967], 336–350; R.H. Gundry, "Further Verba on 'Verba Christi' in I Peter," Biblica, 55 [1974], 211–232.) πάθημα suffering. δόξαι glories, glorious
12 deeds, triumphs (Selwyn). ■ ἀπεκαλύφθη aor. pass. ind. ἀποκαλύπτω to reveal, to unveil (s. Selwyn, 250ff.). διηκόνουν impf. act. ind. διακονέω to serve, to minister to. The impf. tense points to the continual or customary action in the past. ἀνηγγέλη aor. act. ind. ἀναγγέλλω to report, to set forth, to tell, to declare, to proclaim (s. Selwyn; CBB). εὐαγγελισαμένων pres. mid. part. εὐαγγελίζομαι to proclaim good news, to evangelize, to preach the gospel. ἀποσταλέντι aor. pass. part. ἀποστέλλω to send, to send as an official au-

thoritative representative of the one sending (s. TDNT; CBB). ἐπιθυμοῦσιν pres. act. ind. to desire, to long for, to eagerly desire. The verb is fairly strong and consistent w. a longing not yet fulfilled (Kelly). The pres. tense indicates the continual action which did not reach a fulfillment. ἄγγελοι angels, heavenly messengers, heavenly beings. παρακύψαι aor. act. inf. παρακρύπτω to stretch forward the head, as esp. through a window or door, sometimes inward, more often outward. When used figuratively, it commonly implies a rapid and cursory glance. The word means "to bend down to look" and often suggests a fleeting glance; i.e., "to peep," "to catch a glimpse of" (Hort; Kelly).

■ διό therefore. This is the usual particle when an author 13 passes from statement to inference (Selwyn). ἀναζωσάμενοι aor. mid. part. ἀναζώννυμι to bind up, to gather up, to gird up. The word refers to the habit of the Orientals, who quickly gather up their loose robes w. a girdle or belt when in a hurry or starting on a journey. This is because the easterners' long flowing robes would impede physical activity unless tucked under the belt (RWP; Best). One writer describes tavern keepers who worked in front of their taverns w. their tunics belted high (DC, LXXII, 2). ὀσφῦς hip. διάνοια mind. The word refers to more than the mere intellectual faculties and indicates that which guides and directs conduct (Best). This is a call for the readers to be alert and ready in their whole spiritual and mental attitude (Kelly). νήφοντες pres. act. part. νήφω to be sober. In the NT the word generally denotes self-control and the clarity of mind which goes w. it (Kelly; s. also 2 Tim. 4:5; 1 Thess. 5:6, 8). τελείως adv. perfectly, unreservedly. The adv. is best taken w. the main verb "hope" (Selwyn). ἐλπίσατε aor. act. imp. to hope, to set one's hope upon something. φερομένη pres. pass. part. φέρω to carry, to bear, to bring. The pres. part. pictures the process, "that is being brought" (RWP). Although a pres. part. can have a fut. force, it is used here in keeping w. the writer's conviction that the object of their hope is already virtually within his readers' grasp (Kelly). χάρις grace. The word is used here in a concrete sense of the eschatological consummation (Beare). ἀποκάλυψις s.v.7. ■ ὑπακοή obedience, s.v.2. 14 συσχηματιζόμενοι pres. mid. part. to form together, to conform (s. Rom. 12:2). The mid. voice is a direct mid. i.e., "do not fashion yourselves" (RWP). The mid. could also be a permissive mid., i.e., "do not allow yourselves to be fashioned." The part. is used to convey a command and conforms to the rabbinic Heb. practice of using part. to express rules of conduct and even religious precepts (Kelly; for this use of the part., s. further David Daube in Selwyn, 467–488; s. also GI, 165–168; MT Style, 128f.). πρότερον former, previous. ἄγνοια ignorance. (For a discussion of this word, s. Hort.) ἐπιθυμία strong desire, lust.

15 ■ καλέσαντα aor. act. part. ἅγιος separate, marked off, holy. The word indicates the display of the character of God whose perfect attributes cause Him to be separated from His creation (s. Kelly; CBB; TDNT). The adj. is a pred. adj. used in the clause "just as the one who called you is holy." ἀναστροφή conduct, active life. The word is used of public activity, life in relation to others. Being holy as members of a holy people, they were to show themselves holy in every kind of dealing w. other men (Beare; Hort; s. also BS, 194). γενήθητε aor. pass. imp. γίνομαι. The aor. may be taken as ingressive "began to be,"

16 "become" (Beare; RWP). ■ διότι therefore. γέγραπται perf. pass. ind. "it stands written." The word was used of legal documents whose validity continued (s. MM). ἔσεσθε fut. ind. εἰμί. The fut. here is volitive and is used like an imp. (RWP; s. also BG, 94).

17 ■ ἐπικαλεῖσθε pres. mid. ind. to call, to call upon, to invoke, to appeal to (s. Selwyn). ἀπροσωπολήμπτως adv. impartially, without showing respect or favoritism (s. Bigg). κρίνοντα pres. act. part. παροικία temporary residency, temporary stay. The word denotes residence in a place without taking out or being granted citizen rights (Kelly; s. also Hort; 1 Peter 1:1; TDNT). ἀναστράφητε aor. pass. imp. ἀναστρέφω

18 to conduct one's life (s.v.15). ■ εἰδότες perf. act. part. οἶδα. The part. could be causal. Christian reverence rests upon the knowledge of redemption, four aspects of which are now enumerated: (1) its cost in the death of Christ, (2) its transcendent origin, (3) its certification in Christ's resurrection, (4) its fruit in the church's faith and hope in God (Selwyn). φθαρτός subject to decay, corruptible. ἀργύριον silver, instrumental dat. or dat. of means (Beare). Silver and gold were used as money and slaves were set free by silver and gold (BAG; RWP). ἐλυτρώθητε aor. pass. ind. λυτρόω to release, to procure a release by a ransom, to deliver by the payment of a price, to redeem. For the Jews the picture of redemption would be God's deliverence from Egypt. For the Gentiles it would be the picture of a slave whose freedom was purchased w. a price (s. Hort; Beare; TDNT; CBB; GWHM, 70f.; APC; NTW, 76–83; LAE, 319–327; NTRJ, 268–284). μάταιος vain, vanity. The idea is that which is lacking reality (Beare). πατροπαράδοτος that which is passed on from fa-

19 thers, inherited. ■ ἀμνός lamb. ἄμωμος blameless. ἄσπιλος

spotless, without stain. Perhaps Peter has the Passover lamb in mind (s. Hort). ■ προεγνωσμένου perf. pass. part. 20 προγινώσκω to know beforehand, to foreknow (s. 1 Peter 1:2). καταβολή foundation. φανερωθέντος aor. pass. part. φανερόω to make clear, to make plain, to manifest. δι᾽ὑμᾶς "because of you," "for your sake." ■ ἐγείραντα aor. act. part. 21 ἐγείρω to raise up. δόντα aor. act. part. δίδωμι to give, to grant that. The particle w. the inf. can express intended or contemplated results (Selwyn; s. also BD, 197). Since the book deals w. the believer's pilgrim life on the earth and persecution w. emphasis on faith and eschatological hope, it is felt that this clause is a sort of climax to the whole passage (s. William J. Dalton, " 'So That Your Faith May also Be Your Hope'," RH, 262–274; s. esp. 272f.). ἡ πίστις ὑμῶν καὶ ἐλπίς could be taken as the subject, "so that your faith and hope may be in God," or the word "hope" may be considered as the pred., "so that your faith may also be your hope in God" (Dalton, 272). εἶναι pres. inf. The inf. is used to express intended results.

■ ἡγνικότες perf. act. part. ἁγνίζω to make pure, to purify, 22 to cleanse. In the LXX the word generally has a ceremonial reference but it can also have the sense of moral purification. The perf. tense emphasizes the completed state or condition (s. Selwyn; Beare). ὑπακοή obedient. τῆς ἀληθείας obj. gen. ἀνυπόκριτος unhypocritical, without hypocrisy. ἀγαπήσατε aor. act. imp. ἐκτενῶς adv. earnestly. The fundamental idea is that of earnestness, zealousness (doing a thing not lightly and perfunctorily, but as it were, w. straining) (Hort). ■ 23 ἀναγεγεννημένοι perf. pass. part. (s.v.3). σπορά seed. The contrast is between human seed which produces mortal human life and divine seed which produces eternal life (Best). ἄφθαρτος incorruptible (s.v.4). ζῶντος pres. act. part. (s.v.3). μένοντος pres. act. part. μένω to remain. ■ χόρτος grass. 24 ἄνθος flower (s. James 1:10). ἐξηράνθη aor. pass. ind. ξηραίνω to dry up, pass. to be withered. ἐξέπεσεν aor. act. ind. ἐκπίπτω to fall off. The aor. vividly expresses the rapid blooming and fading of herbage (Kelly). ■ εὐαγγελισθέν aor. pass. part. 25 (s.v.12).

Ch. 2

■ ἀποθέμενοι aor. mid. part. ἀποτίθημι to put off, to put 1 away. The part. shares the imp. force of the governing verb (Beare). The word is applied to any kind of rejection, esp. of what is in any way connected w. the person, body, or mind, whether clothing or hair (Hort). κακία wickedness. The word is an all-inclusive term (Kelly). δόλος deceit. It comes from a verb meaning "to catch w. bait" (RWP). ὑπόκρισις hyprocrisy, pretense. φθόνος envy. The verb was used often in secular Gr. to express the envy which makes one man grudge another something which he himself desires, but does not possess (CBB). καταλαλιά speaking against someone. The verb means "to run down," "to disparage," and was used by Aristophanes of a slave who "blabs" his master's secrets (Selwyn; Bigg). ■ ἀρτιγέννητος recently born, newborn. βρέφος baby, infant. The word is used of a baby as long as it nurses at its mother's breast (Goppelt). λογικός that which pertains to a word. There are three possible renderings of this word: (1) "of the word," (2) "reasonable," "rational," (3) "spiritual" (s. Best; TDNT). However, it seems hardly creditable that he is not also consciously referring back to God's "word," about which he was so concerned in 1:22–25 (Kelly). ἄδολος without deceit, pure, unadulterated, uncontaminated. The word is commonly used in this sense of corn, wheat, barley, oil, wine, and farm products (Beare; Kelly; s. also MM). γάλα milk. The many-breasted goddesses of the heathen religions who were to sustain and nourish life were widespread in the ancient world. The rabbis also compared the law to milk (s. Goppelt; Beare; TDNT; Montefiore, 163f.; Selwyn; esp. 308; RAC II, 657–664). ἐπιποθήσατε aor. act. imp. ἐπιποθέω to long for, to desire, to crave. The prep. in compound indicates intensive desire directed toward an object (cf. Ps. 42:1). αὐξηθῆτε aor. pass. subj. αὐξάνω to cause to grow, pass. to grow. ■ 3 ἐγεύσασθε aor. mid. ind. γεύομαι to taste. The ind. is used in a conditional sentence of the 1st class which accepts the reality of the condition. χρηστός useful, good, gracious. ■ 4 προσερχόμενοι pres. mid. part. προσέρχομαι to come to. The pres. part. is used because stones keep coming one after another (Bigg). ζῶντα pres. act. part. ζάω to live. (For the figure of a "living stone," s. Beare; Selwyn.) ἀποδεδοκιμασμένον perf. pass. part. ἀποδοκιμάζω to reject after examination, to examine and deem useless. παρὰ θεῷ "by the side of God," and He looks at it, in contrast w. the rejection "by men" (RWP). ἐκλεκτός chosen, choice, select, elect (s. 1 Peter 1:1; Hort). ἔντιμος precious, costly, expensive (s. Hort). ■ αὐτοὶ ὡς λίθοι 5 ζῶντες "you also are yourselves, like living stones" (s. Kelly; Hort). οἰκοδομεῖσθε pres. pass. ind. οἰκοδομέω to build, to erect a building. πνευματικός spiritual, pertaining to the Spirit, "suited for the Spirit." ἱεράτευμα priesthood. ἀνενέγκαι aor. act. inf. ἀναφέρω to bring up, to offer, to offer sacrifice. πνευματικὰς θυσίας "spiritual sacrifices." These are sacrifices

which consist of praise and thanksgiving, charity and mutual
sharing, and which are inspired by the Spirit (Kelly).
εὐπρόσδεκτος acceptable (s. Rom. 15:16). ■ διότι therefore. 6
περιέχει (impersonal) pres. act. ind. "it is included." The word
was used in the papyri concerning a will in the sense "in the will
as it stands written" (MM; s. also Beare). γραφή writing, Scripture. τίθημι pres. act. ind. to lay. ἀκρογωνιαῖος λίθος foundation stone, cornerstone, chief cornerstone. The word refers
either to a massive cornerstone placed at the upper corner of the
building in order to bind the walls firmly together, or it refers to
the key stone in the middle of an archway (Beare; s. also TDNT;
Eph. 2:20). οὐ μή "not at all." The two negatives form a strong
denial (s. M, 187ff.). καταισχυνθῇ aor. pass. subj. καταισχύνω
to put to shame. ■ ἡ τιμή "the honor." This honor includes their 7
privileged status here and now and also their triumph over their
mocking assailants and their salvation on the last day (Kelly).
(For a discussion of the grammatical difficulties and various
interpretations, s. Hort.) τοῖς πιστεύουσιν pres. act. part. "to
you who are believing." The part. is in apposition to the personal
pron. "you." The dat. is personal advantage or possession.
ἀπιστοῦσιν pres. act. part. ἀπιστέω to be unbelieving.
ἀπεδοκίμασαν aor. act. ind. ἀποδοκιμάζω to reject after examination (s.v.4). οἰκοδομοῦντες pres. act. part. ἐγενήθη aor.
pass. ind. γίνομαι. γωνία corner. ■ πρόσκομμα stumbling. 8
The "stone of stumbling" is the loose stone lying in the way,
against which the traveler "strikes" his foot (Hort).
προσκόπτουσιν pres. act. ind. to cut against, to stumble.
ἀπειθοῦντες pres. act. part. ἀπείθω to disobey. The word carries a strong sense of "to refuse to believe" (Kelly). εἰς ὅ "unto
which." ἐτέθησαν aor. pass. ind. τίθημι to place, to put, to
appoint.

■ γένος generation, race. βασίλειος kingly, royal. The 9
word could be taken as an adj. modifying "priesthood" or it can
be taken as a substitutive either w. the meaning "royal house,"
"palace," or "a group of kings" (Best; s. also Kelly; Goppelt; J.H.
Elliott, *The Elect and Holy. An Exegetical Examination of I
Peter 2:4–10* [Leiden: Brill, 1966]). ἱεράτευμα priesthood (s. E.
Best, "Spiritual Sacrifice: General Priesthood in the New Testament," *Interpretation* 14 [July, 1960], 273–299). περιποίησις
possession, private possession (s. Eph. 1:14). ἀρετή virtue, the
ability to do heroic deeds. When the word is applied to deity it
does not denote His virtues or intrinsic qualities but the manifestations of His power; i.e., His mighty and glorious deeds (s.
TDNT; Goppelt; Kelly; Hort; Beare; BS, 95f.; MM).

ἐξαγγείλητε aor. act. subj. ἐξαγγέλλω to tell out, to tell forth.
The word often has the additional force of declaring things unknown (Hort). In the LXX the word is used w. the sense of cultic
proclamation, or the rehearsal in adoring language of God's
righteousness and praises (Kelly). The subj. is used w. the particle to express purpose. καλέσαντος aor. act. part. The word
refers to the affective call of God. θαυμαστός wonderful, mar-
10 velous. ■ ποτέ then, at that time, formerly. ἠλεημένοι perf.
pass. part. ἐλεέω to be merciful, pass. to obtain mercy, to have
mercy and pity showed upon one. The perf. tense emphasizes the
completed state or condition. The contrast of the perf. tense w.
the following aor. tense stresses the contrast between the long
antecedent state and the single event of conversion which ended
it (Hort). ἐλεηθέντες aor. pass. part.

11   ■ ἀγπητός verbal adj. "love one," "beloved." παρακαλῶ
pres. act. ind. to urge, to encourage, to beseech (s. Rom. 12:1).
πάροικος alien. It denotes a man who lives in a foreign country
(Kelly; s. also 1 Peter 1:1). παρεπίδημος foreigner, stranger,
temporary sojourner. This word suggests a visitor making a brief
stay (Kelly; s. also 1 Peter 1:1). As long as we are in this world,
there should be in our lives as Christians a certain detachment
(Stibbs). ἀπέχεσθαι pres. mid. inf. to hold one's self away from,
to abstain. The inf. is used in indirect discourse after the main
verb. The object of the verb is in gen. indicating what one is not
to indulge in (s. Beare). σαρκικός fleshly, that which pertains
to the flesh; i.e., the impulses which belong to the selfish and
lower side of man's nature (Selwyn). (For the significance of the
suf., s. MH, 378f.) ἐπιθυμία strong desires, lust. στρατεύονται
pres. mid ind. to fight, to carry on a military campaign, to wage
12 war. The pres. tense emphasizes the continual warfare. ■
ἀναστροφή manner of life, conduct, behavior (s. 1 Peter 1:15).
ἔθνος nation, pl. heathen; i.e., those who have no knowledge of
the true God, "Gentiles." ἔχοντες pres. act. part. The pres. tense
indicates the continual possession and could have an imp. force
(Beare). καταλαλοῦσιν pres. act. ind. to speak against, to speak
evil of (s. Hort). κακοποιός evildoer. It denotes the doing of
mischief or injury, either to a specific person or other object, or
else absolutely. It is a wicked man who does evil in such a way
that he is liable to punishment from the magistrate (Hort; Bigg).
ἐποπτεύοντες pres. act. part. ἐποπτεύω to look upon, to observe, to be a spectator, to view carefully, to watch over a period
of time. The pres. tense indicates the covering of a longer period
of time and includes the observer's memory and reflection upon
the deeds. The thought is of spiritual insight which is to be

gained in the future "through the influence of" the "good works" (RWP; Selwyn; Beare). The part. could be temporal "when" or causal "because they observe." δοξάσωσιν aor. act. subj. δοξάζω to hold a high opinion of, to glorify. The subj. is used to express purpose. ἐπισκοπή visitation. The word is used in the OT either in the sense of a "visit" or in the sense of a visitation for blessing but here the visitation must be one of judgment (Hort; Best).

■ ὑποτάγητε aor. pass. imp. ὑποτάσσω to be in subjec- 13 tion, to submit one's self, to be subject to. ἀνθρώπινος human, that which is made by human beings, that which proceeds from men. (For the suf. of the word, s. MH, 378f.) κτίσις creation, institution. The word may refer to institutions which men have created (s. Best) or the word may refer to creations by God w. the previous adj. having the force "among men," so that the phrase means "to every (divine) institution among men" (Hort). διὰ τὸν κύριον "because of the Lord," "for the Lord's sake" (Kelly). βασιλεύς king, emperor (Beare). ὑπερέχοντι pres. act. part. ὑπερέχω to send out above, to have it over, to be supreme. The word refers to the head of public administration, not as a deity (Beare). ■ ἡγεμών governor. The word has various appli- 14 cations but was specially applied about this time to governors of provinces whether appointed by the emperor or appointed by the senate (Hort; Best). πεμπομένοις pres. pass. part. πέμπω to send. ἐκδίκησις punishment, legal punishment, avenging (s. Bigg). ἀγαθοποιός doing good, upright, one who does right as opposed to an evildoer (BAG). ■ ἀγαθοποιοῦντας pres. act. 15 part. ἀγαθοποιέω to do good, to do right. The part. further defines the will of God and gives the manner or means "by showing yourselves to be good subjects," "by active benefi- cence" (Beare). φιμοῦν pres. act. inf. φιμόω to muzzle, to put to silence, to gag, to restrain (Hort). ἄφρων foolish, without reason, those who are senseless in what they are prone to say about Christianity (Stibbs). ἀγνωσία ignorant. The word sug- gests culpable ignorance rather than mere lack of knowledge (Best). ■ ἐλεύθερος free, freedman. To describe the ideal life in 16 terms of freedom meant much for the ancient world because of its clear distinction between the slave and the free man (Best). ἐπικάλυμμα that which covers over, veil, cloak. Here it has the significance of "pretext" (Hort). ἔχοντες pres. act. part. ἐλευθερία freedom, liberty. ■ τιμήσατε aor. act. imp. τιμάω 17 to honor, constantive use of the imp. (RWP). ἀδελφότης broth- erhood. The word has the concrete sense of a band of brothers (Hort; s. also RAC II, 631–640; TDNT; CBB). ἀγαπᾶτε pres.

act. imp. **φοβεῖσθε** pres. mid. imp. to fear, be afraid.

18   ■ **οἰκέτης** household servant. The word denotes household slaves, many of whom might be well-educated and hold responsible positions in their households (Best; s. also Goppelt; Philemon). The nom. w. the article is used as a voc. (Beare; s. also M, 70). **ὑποτασσόμενοι** pres. mid. part. The part. is used as an imp. (Selwyn; s. also Daube in Selwyn, 467–488). **παντί** used w. **φόβῳ** "in all fear." Not fear of the masters to whom they are subject, but fear of God. It is the spirit of reverence toward Him that induces respect and faithfulness to duty in the sphere of human relationships (Beare). **δεσπότης** master, ruler, one who has complete authority. **ἐπιεικής** mild, gentle (s. Phil. 4:5). **σκολιός** bent, crooked, severe, hard to deal w., harsh (Kelly;

19 Selwyn; s. also Phil. 2:15). ■ **χάρις** grace, thanks, excellence. The word is used here in the sense of that which is admirable, enhancing the esteem in which those who display it are held (Beare; s. also TDNT). **συνείδησις** conscience (s. Rom. 2:15; RAC X, 1025–1107). **ὑποφέρει** pres. act. ind. to bear up under, to endure, to put up w. (Kelly; s. also Goppelt). **λύπη** pain, sorrow. **πάσχων** pres. act. part. **πάσχω** to suffer. The part. could be temporal. Mere endurance is no cause for pride. Slaves, like school boys, sometimes vied w. one another in demonstrating the ability to endure corporal punishment without flinching. If the beating is deserved, there is no glory in bearing it; but to show patience in the face of injustice is true evidence of Chris-

20 tian character (Beare). **ἀδίκως** adv. unjustly. ■ **ποῖος** what kind of, what sort of. **κλέος** reputation, prestige, glory, credit (s. Kelly; Selwyn). **ἁμαρτάνοντες** pres. act. part. to sin, to do wrong (s. Bigg). **κολαφιζόμενοι** pres. pass. part. **κολαφίζω** to strike w. the fist, to beat, to treat roughly. Since the word was used of Christ and His suffering (s. Matt. 26:67; Mark 14:65), it could be that Peter is comparing the beating of a slave to the suffering which Christ endured (s. Selwyn; Schelkle; TDNT). **ὑπομενεῖτε** fut. act. ind. **ὑπομένω** to endure, to patiently endure. **ἀγαθοποιοῦντες** pres. act. part. to do good, to do that which is right. **πάσχοντες** pres. act. part. to suffer. The part. are

21 used temporally. ■ **τοῦτο** "this," i.e., the patient and cheerful endurance of maltreatment when you least deserve it (Kelly). **ἐκλήθητε** aor. pass. ind. **καλέω** to call. The pass. is the divine pass. indicating that it is God who calls. In calling us "to his eternal glory" (5:10), "out of darkness into his marvelous light" (2:9), God also calls us to do the exercise of this patient endurance of suffering that we have done nothing to deserve. In this very respect, Christ has given us a model of Christian conduct

(Beare). ἔπαθεν aor. act. ind. πάσχω to suffer. ὑπολιμπάνων
pres. act. part. ὑπολιμπάνω to leave behind. ὑπογραμμός
copy, example. The word is used in 2 Maccabees 2:28 of the
"outlines" of a sketch which the artist fills in w. details. It is also
used as the model of handwriting to be copied by the school boy,
then fig. of a model of conduct for imitation (Bigg; Beare).
ἐπακολουθήσητε aor. act. subj. ἐπακολουθέω to follow after,
to follow upon, to follow closely (RWP). The subj. is used to
express purpose (RWP) or the clause is epexegetical explaining
the "pattern" or "example" (Beare). ἴχνος footprint. In the pl.
it means the line of footprints. To follow a man's footprints is to
move in the direction he is going (Kelly). ■ ἐποίησεν aor. act. 22
ind. εὑρέθη aor. pass. ind. δόλος deceit (s.v.1). στόμα mouth.
■ λοιδορούμενος pres. pass. part. λοιδορέω to abuse, to revile, 23
to use vile and abusive language against someone, to heap abuse
upon someone (s. TDNT; T). The pres. part. indicates that this
was done over and over. ἀντελοιδόρει impf. act. ind.
ἀντιλοιδορέω to return abuse, to give back abusive language in
return. (For the prep. in compound indicating reciprocal action,
s. MH, 297.) The impf. is used for repeated incidences (RWP).
πάσχων pres. act. part. ἠπείλει impf. act. ind. ἀπειλέω to
threaten. The impf. is either inchoative; i.e., "he did not begin
to threaten," or it emphasizes the repeated action (RWP).
παρεδίδου impf. ind. act. παραδίδωμι to deliver over, to give
over to, to entrust, to commit. κρίνοντι pres. act. part. to judge.
δικαίως adv. righteously, according to justice. Christ accepted
without rebellion the unjust treatment meted out to Him, confident of vindication before God (Beare). ■ αὐτός Himself. 24
ἀνήνεγκεν aor. act. ind. ἀναφέρω to bear up, to bear away.
Peter stresses the redemptive significance of Jesus' death by his
use of OT sacrificial language (s. Best; Selwyn; Heb. 9:28; John
1:29). ξύλον wood, tree (s. TDNT; Gal. 3:13). ἀπογενόμενοι
aor. mid. part. ἀπογίνομαι to get away from, to die, to depart.
The word is followed by the dat. of reference; i.e., "to die in
reference to sin" (s. Selwyn; RWP). ζήσωμεν aor. act. subj. ζάω
to live. μώλωψ whelp, bruise, wound caused by blows. The word
denotes the weal or discolored swelling left by a blow from a fist
or whip. The word strictly means a cut which bleeds; he thinks
here of the lashing which draws blood (s. BAG; Kelly; Beare).
ἰάθητε aor. pass. ind. ἰάομαι to heal. ■ ἦτε impf. εἰμί. 25
πρόβατον sheep. πλανώμενοι pres. mid. part. πλανάω to
wander, to wander away, to go astray. The part. is used in periphrastic construction emphasizing the continual action in the
past "you were going astray" (s. Beare). ἐπεστράφητε aor. pass.

ind. ἐπιστρέφω to turn, to return. ποιμήν shepherd (s. TDNT). ἐπίσκοπος overseer, guardian, bishop (s. Best; Kelly; TDNT; CBB).

Ch. 3

1 ■ ὁμοίως adv. likewise, in like manner. ὑποτασσόμεναι pres. mid. part. ὑποτάσσομαι to be in subjection, to subject one's self. ἴδιος one's own. ἴνα used w. the fut. (s. BD, 186–187). ἀπειθοῦσιν pres. act. ind. ἀπειθέω to be disobedient, to disobey (s. 1 Peter 2:8). The ind. is used in a first-class conditional clause which assumes the reality of the condition. ἀναστροφή conduct, behavior (s. 1 Peter 1:15). κερδηθήσονται fut. pass. ind. κερδαίνω to win, to gain. Here the verb means "to win over to a point of view" (Selwyn; s. also TDNT; Goppelt; David Daube, "Κερδαίνω As a Missionary Term," Harvard Theologi-
2 cal Review 40 [1947], 109–120). ■ ἐποπτεύσαντες aor. act. part. ἐποπτεύω to look at, to observe (s. 1 Peter 2:12). ἁγνός pure, clean, chaste. Here it indicates the irreproachable conduct
3 of the wife (Kelly). ■ ἔστω pres. imp. εἰμί. ἔξωθεν outward. ἐμπλοκή plaited, braiding. θρίξ, τριχός hair (s. 2 Tim. 2:4). περίθεσις placing around, wearing. χρυσίον gold, gold jewelry. (For references of writers in the ancient world who also spoke against the superficial preoccupation of women w. dress, jewelry, etc., s. Kelly; Goppelt; Selwyn, 432–439.) ἔνδυσις putting on.
4 ἱμάτιον garment, clothes. ■ κρυπτός hidden. ἄφθαρτος incorruptible (s. 1 Peter 1:4). πραΰς meek, gentle. The word refers to the humble and gentle attitude which expresses itself in a patient submissiveness (s. Matt. 5:5; 2 Cor. 10:1; Gal. 5:23). ἡσύχιος quiet. πνεῦμα spirit, disposition (Selwyn). The gen. is
5 gen. of definition (Beare). πολυτελής very valuable, costly. ■ οὕτως so, thus, in this way. ποτέ at that time, formerly. ἅγιαι holy. ἐλπίζουσαι pres. act. part. fem. pl. to hope. ἐκόσμουν impf. act. ind. κοσμέω to adorn. The impf. indicates customary
6 action "they used to adorn themselves" (RWP). ■ ὑπήκουσεν aor. act. ind. ὑπακούω to listen to, to obey. καλοῦσα pres. act. part. ἐγενήθητε aor. pass. ind. γίνομαι to become. The verb "become" insinuates that they were formerly pagans (Kelly). The aor. tense points to a one-time act (Goppelt). ἀγαθοποιοῦσαι pres. act. part. ἀγαθοποιέω to do good. φοβούμεναι pres. mid. part. φοβέομαι to be afraid, to have fear. The part. provide proof that they have become Sarah's children "in that you do good and are not a prey to terror" (Beare; Goppelt). πτόησις frightening, terrifying. The word means fluttering, excitement, perturbation of spirit, caused by

any passion, but more esp. by fear (Bigg). The acc. seems to be used as a cognate acc. (Beare).

■ συνοικοῦντες pres. act. part. συνοικέω to live together. 7 The part. is used as an imp. (s. Selwyn). γνῶσις understanding. Here it means Christian insight and tact, a conscious sensitivity to God's will (Kelly; s. also Beare). ἀσθενέτερος comp. ἀσθενής weak, comp. weaker. Here it may be "weaker" in the physical sense (s. Selwyn; Best; Beare). σκεῦος vessel, jar, instrument. The word may refer to the physical body (Selwyn; Schelkle). γυναικεῖος fem. female, woman. The n. adj. is used w. the article to denote an abstract noun (Selwyn). ἀπονέμοντες pres. act. part. ἀπονέμω to assign, to show, to pay. Used here in the sense of "to show honor to someone" (BAG). συγκληρονόμος fellow heir, joint heir, followed by the obj. gen. "fellow heirs of the grace of life," i.e., God's gracious gift of eternal life (Bigg). ἐγκόπτεσθαι pres. pass. inf. ἐγκόπτω to cut in on, to hinder (s. Rom. 15:22; Gal. 5:7; 1 Thess. 2:18; s. also TDNT; CBB). The inf. is used w. the prep. to express purpose (RWP). προσευχαί prayers.

■ τὸ τέλος used adverbially "finally." In this adverbial 8 sense the word always seems to introduce a fresh point and not simply to summarize what has gone before. Here it affects the transition from specific ethical duties to a general statement of Christian character (Selwyn). ὁμόφρων like-minded, i.e., of that inward unity of attitude in spiritual things which makes schism unthinkable (Beare). συμπαθής full of sympathy, sharing in feeling. The word denotes a readiness to enter into and share the feelings of others and to unite alike in sorrow and in joy (Kelly; Beare). φιλάδελφος love of brother, brotherly love (s. 1 Peter 1:22). εὔσπλαγχνος compassionate, compassionate tenderness (s. Eph. 4:32; TDNT; MNTW, 156f.). ταπεινόφρων humble minded (s. Phil. 2:3; TDNT). ■ ἀποδιδόντες pres. act. part. 9 ἀποδίδωμι to give back, to pay back. The part. is used as an imp. λοιδορία railing, abuse (s. 1 Peter 2:23). τοὐναντίον = τὸ ἐναντίον on the contrary (s. RWP). εὐλογοῦντες pres. act. part. ἐκλήθητε aor. pass. ind. καλέω (s. 1 Peter 2:21). κληρονομήσητε aor. act. subj. κληρονομέω to inherit. The idea of an inheritance as a free gift which comes to the recipient without his having to merit it remains present (Kelly). ■ θέλων 10 pres. act. part. ἰδεῖν aor. act. inf. ὁράω. παυσάτω aor. act. imp. παύω to cease, to stop. (For the change from the 2nd pers. imp. of the LXX to the 3rd pers., s. Selwyn.) λαλῆσαι aor. act. inf. δόλος deceit, trickery (s. 1 Peter 2:1). ■ ἐκκλινάτω aor. act. 11 imp. 3rd pers. sing. ἐκκλίνω to turn from, to turn away from.

ποιησάτω aor. act. imp. ζητησάτω aor. act. imp. ζητέω to
seek. διωξάτω aor. act. imp. διώκω to hunt, to pursue. The
words enjoin the same active and persistent effort on behalf of
peace as enjoined in the beatitude in Matthew 5:9 (Selwyn).

12 ■ οὕς, ὡτός ear. δέησις request, prayer. ποιοῦντας pres. act.
part. The pres. tense emphasizes the continual doing of something.

13   ■ καί besides. The resumption is rapid after the quotation
from Psalm 34 and effects a swift and easy entrance into the new
theme (Selwyn). κακώσων fut. act. part. κακόω to do evil to
someone, to harm someone. The fut. part. has the idea "who is
going to harm you?" (s. Kelly). ζηλωτής zealot, enthusiast, one
who exercises zeal for an object (s. Selwyn; Best; Titus 2:14; Gal.

14 1:14). γένησθε aor. mid. subj. γίνομαι. ■ πάσχοιτε pres. act.
opt. πάσχω to suffer. The opt. is used in a condition of the 4th
class which implies that there is no certainty of fulfillment of the
condition "if perchance" (s. RWP; Best; BD, 195; BG, 111).
There is no contradiction w. this statement and 1 Peter 4:12ff.
and there is no evidence that the letter should be divided into
different writings. (For arguments against viewing 1 Peter 4:12ff.
as a separate writing, s. Kelly.) μακάριος happy, blessed, fortunate (s. TDNT; BAG; CBB). φοβηθῆτε aor. pass. subj.
φοβέομαι to be afraid, to fear. The subj. w. the neg. is used to
form a prohibition. ταραχθῆτε aor. pass. subj. ταράσσω to

15 shake, to disturb, to trouble. ■ ἁγιάσατε aor. act. imp. ἁγιάζω
to sanctify; i.e., "to venerate and adore Him," thus dispelling all
fear of man (Beare). ἕτοιμος ready, prepared. ἀεί always.
ἀπολογία defense. The word was often used of the argument
for the defense in a court of law and though the word may have
the idea of a judicial interrogation in which one is called to
answer for the manner in which he has exercised his responsibility (Beare), the word can also mean an informal explanation or
defense of one's position (s. 1 Cor. 9:3; 2 Cor. 7:11) and the word
would aptly describe giving an answer to the skeptical, abusive,
or derisive inquiries of ill-disposed neighbors (Kelly). αἰτοῦντι
pres. act. part. αἰτέω to ask. The pres. tense would be interat.;
i.e., "every time someone asks." λόγος account, a rational account of (Selwyn). ἐλπίς hope. In this letter "hope" is used

16 almost as an equivalent for "faith" (s. 1 Peter 1:21; Best). ■
ἀλλά but, however. πραΰτης meekness, gentleness (s.v.4).
συνείδησις conscience (s. 1 Peter 2:19). ἔχοντες pres. act. part.
to have. The pres. tense can have the meaning "to possess," "to
maintain," and the part. is used as an imp. (Beare).
καταλαλεῖσθε pres. pass. ind. καταλαλέω to speak evil

against (s. 1 Peter 2:12). καταισχυνθῶσιν aor. pass. subj.
καταισχύνω to put to shame. Perhaps Peter was thinking of his
personal experience at Pentecost, when the Jews first scoffed
and were then pierced to the heart (Acts 2:13, 37) (Hart). The
subj. is used in a purpose clause. ἐπηρεάζοντες pres. act. part.
ἐπηρεάζω to threaten, to mistreat, to abuse, to insult, to treat
wrongfully, to deal despitefully w. someone. (For examples from
the papyri, s. MM.) ἀναστροφή behavior, conduct (s. 1 Peter
1:15). ■ κρεῖττον n. comp. ἀγαθός "better." ἀγαθοποιοῦντας 17
pres. act. part. to do good (s.v.6). The part. is acc. pl. agreeing
w. the subject of the inf. and is causal giving the reason for
suffering. θέλοι pres. act. opt. The opt. is used in a fourth-class
conditional clause (s.v.14). κακοποιοῦντας pres. act. part.
κακοποιέω to do evil, to do wrong. The part. is causal. (For
eschatological interpretation of this v. which views this v. as
referring to eschatological judgment, s. J.R. Michaels, "Eschatology in I Peter 3:17," NTS 13 [July, 1967], 394–401.) ■ ὅτι 18
καὶ Χριστός "because Christ also." This introduces a new
application of the imitation of Christ: we pass from the patient
Christ to the victorious Christ (Selwyn). ἀπέθανεν aor. act. ind.
ἀποθνήσκω to die. (For the variant reading ἔπαθεν aor. act.
ind. πάσχω to suffer, s. TC, 692f.; Selwyn; Kelly; Goppelt.)
προσαγάγῃ aor. act. subj. προσάγω to lead or bring to, to
introduce, to provide access for, to bring about a right relationship. The word had various usages and could denote the bringing
of a person before a tribunal or presenting him at a royal court
or the ritual act of bringing sacrifice to God or the consecration
of persons to God's service (s. Kelly; TDNT; Eph. 2:18).
θανατωθείς aor. pass. part. θανατόω to put to death. σαρκί
dat. sing. "flesh." The expression refers to the reality of Christ's
physical death and the dat. is dat. of reference (Selwyn).
ζωοποιηθείς aor. pass. part. ζωοποιέω to make alive. The expression "in reference to spirit" could refer either to the Holy
Spirit or to the spirit of Christ (s. Best). ■ ἐν ᾧ "in which." The 19
rel. pron. could refer to the word "spirit" or it can refer to the
state or circumstances; i.e., "in which state or circumstances"
(Selwyn; s. esp. Selwyn, 315f.; Reicke, 138; Best). φυλακή prison. πορευθείς aor. pass. part. πορεύομαι to go. ἐκήρυξεν aor.
act. ind. κηρύσσω to proclaim, to preach. (For various discussions and literature on this difficult passage, s. Goppelt; Best;
Selwyn, 314–362; Sherman E. Johnson, "The Preaching to the
Dead," JBL 79 [March, 1960], 48–51; Bo Reicke, *The Disobedient Spirits and Christian Baptism* [Copenhagen, 1946]; W.J.
Dalton, *Christ's Proclamation to the Spirits* [Rome, 1965].) ■ 20

ἀπειθήσασιν aor. act. part. to be disobedient (s. 1 Peter 2:8).
ἀπεξεδέχετο impf. mid. ind. ἀπεκδέχομαι to earnestly and
eagerly await w. expectancy, to wait out the time (Beare; s. also
1 Cor. 1:7; Gal. 5:5; Phil. 3:20). μακροθυμία longsuffering,
patience (s. Rom. 2:4; Gal. 5:22). κατασκευαζομένης pres.
pass. part. κατασκευάζω to make ready, to build, to construct.
The part. is used as a gen. abs. expressing contemporaneous
time. κιβωτός box, ark. διεσώθησαν aor. pass. ind. διασώζω
to save through, to bring safe through (RWP; s. also Acts 27:44).
δι᾽ ὕδατος "through water." The prep. could be taken in a local
sense; i.e., "they were brought to safety by passing through
water" or it could be taken in an instrumental sense (s. Kelly).

21 ■ ἀντίτυπος n. adj. used as a noun (s. Goppelt), antitype. The
word connotes the exactness of correspondence between the
stamp and the die (Selwyn; MM; s. also Heb. 9:24). σῴζει pres.
act. ind. to save, to rescue. The saving by baptism which Peter
here mentions is only symbolic, not actual as Peter hastens to
explain (RWP). Baptism is the occasion and sign of transition
from an old way of life to another that is marked by a new ethic.
In accepting baptism the person is affirming willingness to share
in the known experience of baptized persons; i.e., the experience
of suffering and being treated w. suspicion and hostility. This
indicates that the main theme of 1 Peter is not baptism but rather
suffering (s. David Hill, "On Suffering and Baptism in I Peter,"
Nov T 17 [July, 1976], 181–189; for those who would seek to
make this v. the key to 1 Peter and view the book as a baptismal
instructional sermon, s. Oscar S. Brooks, "I Peter 3:21—The
Clue to the Literary Structure of the Epistle," Nov T 16 [Octo-
ber, 1974], 290–305; for Jewish parallels related to baptismal
catechism for Jewish proselytes, s. NTRJ, 106–140.) ἀπόθεσις
putting off, putting away. ῥύπος filth, dirt. ἐπερώτημα question, inquiry, pledge. In the papyri there is evidence that this
word was a t.t. in making a contract and denotes the "pledge"
or "undertaking" given by one of the parties in answer to formal
questions addressed to him. The word then implies the register-
ing of agreement to conditions or demands. Here the pledge is
an expression of accent to certain conditions; i.e., it may imply
a confession of faith as well as the willingness to accept the new
duties (s. David Hill, "On Suffering and Baptism in I Peter,"
187f.; Reicke; Kelly; MM). δι᾽ ἀναστάσεως "through the resurrection." Baptism is a symbolic picture of the resurrection of

22 Christ as well as our own spiritual renewal (RWP). ■ δεξιά right
hand. (For the meaning of being "on the right hand," s. Eph.
1:20.) ὑποταγέντων aor. pass. part. ὑποτάσσω to subject, to

be in subjection. ἐξουσίαι authorities, powers. The designations
"angels and principalities and powers" embrace all ranks of spiritual beings (Beare; s. also TDNT).

Ch. 4

■ οὖν therefore. This word introduces the main lesson to be 1
drawn from 1 Peter 3:18–22 (Bigg). παθόντος aor. act. part.
πάσχω to suffer. The part. is used in a gen. abs. ἔννοια thought,
principle, counsel, mind, resolve. The principle of thought and
feeling here referred to is that of the dying life voluntarily accepted and put on as armor, and finding expression in the meek
and courageous pursuit of the spiritual life (Selwyn; s. also Bigg;
for the philosophical meaning of the word, s. GPT, 57).
ὁπλίσασθε aor. mid. imp. ὁπλίζω to arm one's self w. weapons. The idea of the word is "put on as your armor" (Selwyn),
"arm yourselves w. the same insight" (Goppelt). ὁ παθών aor.
act. part. used here as a noun "the one who has suffered."
πέπαυται perf. mid. ind. παύομαι to cease. The words seem to
have been a proverbial expression related to Romans 6:7 and the
suffering is taken to mean "dying" in the sense of "dying to sin"
(Best; Beare; Stibbs). The perf. tense stresses the condition or
state. ■ εἰς τό "in order that." The words introduce a purpose 2
clause (RWP). μηκέτι no longer. ἐπιθυμία strong desire, lust,
passion. θελήματι dat., sing. dat. of advantage indicating personal interest. These dat. could also express the rule by which
man shapes his life (Bigg). ἐπίλοιπος remaining. βιῶσαι aor.
act. inf. βιόω to live. ■ ἀρκετός sufficient. The sense of the 3
word is "more than sufficient," "far too much" (Beare). The
word may be used ironically w. the meaning "more than
enough" (Kelly; s. also Goppelt). παρεληλυθώς perf. act. part.
παρέρχομαι to go by, to pass by. One after another, the three
perf. in this v. emphasize the thought that this past of theirs is
a closed chapter; that part of the story is over and done w.
(Beare). βούλημα will, wish. κατειργάσθαι perf. mid. inf.
κατεργάζομαι to produce, to work, to accomplish.
πεπορευμένους perf. mid. part. πορεύομαι to go. The word is
used here in the Hebraic sense of "to walk," "to conduct one's
life" (s. Bigg; Selwyn). ἀσέλγεια unbridled and unrestrained
living. The word describes "the spirit which knows no restraints
and which dares whatever caprice and wanton insolence suggest" (NTW 26; s. also TDNT; Gal. 5:19; Eph. 4:19). ἐπιθυμία
lust, passion. οἰνοφλυγία wine bubbling up, drunkenness. The
context shows that the word means "habitual drunkards" (s.
RWP; Selwyn). κῶμος drunken party, reveling. The word orig-

761

inally referred to a band of friends who accompanied a victor in
the games on his way home. They sang the rejoicings and his
praises. But the word degenerated until it came to mean a "ca-
rousal," a band of drunken revellers, swaying and singing their
way through the streets (NTW, 27). The public parties and revel-
ings were associated w. the cult of certain gods, esp. Dionysus
(Selwyn; s. also Eph. 5:18). πότος drinking, drinking parties.
ἀθέμιτος abominable, unrighteous, lawless. εἰδωλολατρία
worship of idols, idolatry. The prominence here is on sexual and
4 alcoholic excess w. the stress on idolatry (Kelly). ■ ἐν ᾧ "in
which thing," "wherein," "in which manner of life" (Bigg).
ξενίζονται pres. pass. ind. ξενίζω to entertain, to entertain
strangers, to astonish, to surprise. The word has the idea of being
surprised or entertained by the novelty of a thing or being surprised or upset at a new turn of events (Selwyn). The word also
includes the thought of "take offense," as ignorant people often
feel an unreasonable resentment at anything that does not fit into
the pattern of life familiar to them. The matter of this resentful
astonishment is expressed by the gen. abs. which follows (Beare).
συντρεχόντων pres. act. part. συντρέχω to run together. The
metaphor suggests the thought of joining in a mad race (Beare).
The gen. abs. describes that which is considered to be thought
strange. ἀσωτία wasteful, riotous living, dissipation (s. TDNT;
Eph. 5:18). ἀνάχυσις pouring forth. The word was used of the
rock pools filled up by the sea at high tide (Selwyn) or of a
swamp which was formed by the pouring forth of waters. Here
it has the act. verbal sense followed by the obj. gen.—"outpouring of profligacy"; w. the thought of the life of paganism as a
feverish pursuit of evil, wherein men vie w. one another in pouring forth profligate living (Beare). βλασφημοῦντες pres. act.
part. βλασφημέω to defame someone, to injure the reputation
5 of someone, to blaspheme (BAG). ■ ἀποδώσουσιν fut. act. ind.
ἀποδίδωμι to pay back, to give account. ἑτοίμως adv. ready.
ἔχοντι pres. act. part. The dat. indicates to whom account is
rendered; i.e., "to the one who stands ready." (For this construction, s. Kelly; RWP; Acts 21:13.) κρῖναι aor. act. inf. κρίνω to
judge. The inf. is epexegetical explaining the readiness. ζῶντας
pres. act. part. ζάω to live. The phrase "the living and the dead"
6 means "all men" (Best). ■ νεκροῖς "to the dead." The reference
may be to those who are spiritually dead, but it seems better to
understand the term as referring to those to whom the gospel
was preached during their earthly life and they have since died
physically (Stibbs). εὐηγγελίσθη aor. pass. ind.
εὐαγγελίζομαι to proclaim the good news, to evangelize, to

preach the gospel. κριθῶσι aor. pass. subj. The subj. is used in a purpose clause. ζῶσι pres. act. subj. ζάω to live. (For the omission of the moveable nu, s. Francis Thomas Gignac, *A Grammar of the Greek Papyri of the Roman and Byzantine Periods.* Vol. I Phonology [Milan, Italy: Cisalpano-Goliardica, 1976], 114f.) κατὰ θεόν "according to God." The phrase could mean either "in the eyes of God" (Kelly) or "in God's likeness," "as God lives," i.e., eternally (Selwyn).

■ ἤγγικεν perf. act. ind. ἐγγίζω to come near, perf. "to be 7 at hand." σωφρονήσατε aor. act. imp. σωφρονέω to be sound in mind. The word connotes the cool head and balanced mind to exercise self-control or moderation (Beare; Selwyn; GPT, 179f.; TDNT). νήψατε aor. act. imp. νήφω to be sober, to keep a clear head (Kelly). ■ πρὸ πάντων "before all things," "above 8 all." ἐκτενής strenuous, intense (s. 1 Peter 1:22). ἔχοντες pres. act. part. καλύπτει pres. act. ind. to cover, to hide. The proverbial expression may be a quotation or adaptation of Proverbs 10:12 (Best; s. also Beare). The pres. tense is gnomic indicating that which is constantly true. πλῆθος multitude. ■ φιλόξενος 9 hospitality, entertaining of strangers. The lack of a network of decent hotels for ordinary people had the results that readiness to provide board and lodging for friends and other suitably sponsored travelers was even more highly esteemed than it is today (Kelly; s. also 1 Tim. 3:2; and for Jewish parallels, s. SB III, 297; and in general RAC VIII, 1061–1123; TDNT). γογγυσμός murmuring, complaining, grumbling. The addition of these words has a sharp twang of realism about it. Then as now guests could overstay or otherwise abuse their host's welcome and a reminder that hospitality can be an exasperating chore, to be shouldered cheerfully if it is to be worthwhile, is in place (Kelly). ■ ἕκαστος each one. καθώς just as. ἔλαβεν aor. act. ind. 10 λαμβάνω to receive. χάρισμα gift, gracious gift, grace gift (s. 1 Cor. 1:7; TDNT; CBB). διακονοῦντες pres. act. part. to minister, to serve. οἰκονόμος steward. The word denotes a slave who was responsible for managing a man's property or household and for distributing their wages, food, etc. to its members (Kelly; s. also 1 Cor. 4:1; TDNT). ποικίλος many colored, manifold, variegated (s. James 1:2; 1 Peter 1:6). ■ λόγιον utter- 11 ance, oracle. The word sometimes means "Scripture" and in classical Gr. it means any divine utterance (Selwyn). ἰσχύς strength, might. χορηγεῖ pres. act. ind. to supply. The word originally meant "to be in a chorus." Then it meant "to supply a chorus" and so produce a play at one's own risk. Finally it simply meant to furnish or supply anything (Selwyn; s. also Eph.

4:16). δοξάζηται pres. pass. subj. δοξάζω to glorify. The subj. is used to express purpose.

12   ■ ἀγαπητός one loved, beloved. ξενίζεσθε pres. pass. imp. (s.v.4). πύρωσις burning, fiery. The word was often used in the sense of a purifying or refining fire (s. Goppelt). πειρασμός trial, ordeal. γινομένη pres. mid. part. ξένος strange, foreign. συμβαίνοντος pres. act. part. συμβαίνω to happen, to occur.

13   ■ καθό "insofar; far as," "according to which thing" (RWP). κοινωνεῖτε pres. act. ind. to share in, to have fellowship. πάθημα suffering. χαίρετε pres. act. imp. χαίρω to be happy, to rejoice. The pres. tense calls for continual rejoicing. χαρῆτε aor. act. subj. χαίρω to rejoice. The subj. is used in a purpose clause. ἀγαλλιώμενοι pres. mid. part. ἀγαλλιάομαι to be exuberantly happy (s. 1 Peter 1:8). The part. w. the imp. is emphatic,

14   i.e., "rejoice w. rapture" (Selwyn). ■ ὀνειδίζεσθε pres. pass. ind. ὀνειδίζω to revile, to insult. The word is used in the LXX for reproaches heaped on God and His saints by the wicked and in the NT becomes associated w. the indignities and maltreatment which Christ had to endure (Kelly). ἀναπαύεται pres. mid.

15   ind. to give rest, to refresh. ■ πασχέτω pres. act. imp. 3rd sing. to suffer. φονεύς murderer. κακοποιός evildoer. ἀλλοτριεπίσκοπος one who looks after the affairs of another, agitator, mischief maker. (For this unusual word, s. Kelly; Best.)

16   ■ αἰσχυνέσθω pres. pass. imp. αἰσχύνομαι to put to shame,

17   pass. to be put to shame. δοξαζέτω pres. act. imp. (s.v.11). ■ ἄρξασθαι pres. mid. imp. ἄρχομαι to begin. The construction of the inf. is unusual and may be in apposition or epexegetical (RWP). ἀπειθούντων pres. act. part. ἀπειθέω to be disobedient

18   (s. 1 Peter 2:8). ■ μόλις w. difficulty, scarcely. The words do not imply doubt about the salvation of Christians, but emphasize the greatness of God's effort in saving them (Best). σώζεται pres. pass. ind. ἀσεβής ungodly. φανεῖται fut. mid. ind. φαίνομαι

19   to appear. ■ ὥστε therefore, wherefore. The word sums up the thought of the entire paragraph (Beare). καί also. The word introduces a new thought: the certainty of divine justice being exercised is a call to a complete serenity of faith in God (Selwyn). πάσχοντες pres. act. part. κτίστης creator. παρατιθέσθωσαν pres. mid. imp. παρατίθημι to deliver over to, to entrust, to entrust for safe keeping. ἀγαθοποιΐα active well-doing (Kelly).

Ch. 5

1   ■ παρακαλῶ pres. act. ind. to beseech, to encourage (s. Rom. 12:1). συμπρεσβύτερος fellow elder. Here the word el-

der denotes the officials who acted as pastoral leaders of the
congregations (Kelly; s. also TDNT). πάθημα suffering.
μελλούσης pres. act. part. μέλλω to be about to.
ἀποκαλύπτεσθαι pres. pass. inf. ἀποκαλύπτω to reveal.
κοινωνός partner, sharer. ■ ποιμάνατε aor. act. imp. 2
ποιμαίνω to shepherd. The aor. may be ingressive "take up the
task of shepherding" (Beare). ἀναγκαστῶς forced, constrained. ἑκουσίως willingly. αἰσχροκερδῶς adv. shameful
gain. προθύμως zealously, eagerly. The word is extremely
strong and expresses enthusiasm and devoted zeal (Kelly). ■ 3
κατακυριεύοντες pres. act. part. κατακυριεύω to lord it over
someone, to domineer, to exercise complete control. The prep.
in compound indicates that the action is unfavorable to an object
(MH, 316). κλῆρος lot, charge. The word probably refers to the
flock or those who were put in charge of the flock (s. Best;
Beare). τύπος pattern, example. γινόμενοι pres. mid. part. ■ 4
φανερωθέντος aor. pass. part. φανερόομαι to appear.
ἀρχιποίμην chief shepherd, master shepherd. (For the use of
this term in the papyri, s. LAE, 100f.) κομιεῖσθε fut. mid. ind.
κομίζω to receive, to obtain. ἀμαράντινος unfading (s. 1 Peter
1:4).

■ ὁμοίως adv. likewise. νεώτερος comp. νέος new, young. 5
ὑποτάγητε aor. pass. imp. ὑποτάσσομαι to submit, to be in
subjection. ταπεινοφροσύνη lowly thinking, humility (s.
TDNT). ἐγκομβώσασθε aor. mid. imp. ἐγκομβόομαι to tie or
fasten something on one's self firmly w. a clasp, knot, or bow.
The word was also used of a slave who tied on an apron so that
the idea may be that of wearing humility as a slave's apron
(Selwyn; Beare). ὑπερήφανος showing one's self above others,
proud, arrogant (AS). ἀντιτάσσεται pres. mid. ind. to line up
against, to oppose, to resist. ταπεινός lowly, humble.

■ ταπεινώθητε aor. pass. imp. ταπεινόω to make low, to 6
humble, pass. to humble one's self, to be humble. κραταιός
strong, mighty (s. Eph. 1:19). ὑψώσῃ aor. act. subj. ὑψόω to
exalt, to lift up, to make high. ■ ἐπιρίψαντες aor. act. part. 7
ἐπιρρίπτω to throw something upon something else, e.g., to
throw clothes on an animal for riding (Luke 19:35) (BAG). The
part. is to be closely connected w. the imp. "humble yourselves"
showing that the true Christian attitude is not neg. self-abandon-
ment or resignation, but involves as the expression of one's
self-humbling the positive and trusting of one's self and one's
troubles to God (Kelly; s. also Ps. 45:22). μέλει pres. act. ind.
to have concern, to have care. Used impersonally w. the dat.
"there is constant care and concern to Him."

8   ■ νήψατε aor. act. imp. νήφω to be sober (s. 1 Peter 4:7).
γρηγορήσατε aor. act. imp. γρηγορέω to stay awake, to be
watchful, to be on the alert. The aor. imp. ring sharply: "be
alert!" "be awake!" Confidence in God must not lead to slack-
ness; the spiritual warfare which they wage demands vigilance
(Beare). ἀντίδικος legal adversary, opponent in a law suit. The
word then denotes an enemy in general (Kelly). διάβολος slanderer, devil. λέων lion. ὡρύομενος pres. mid. part. ὡρύομαι
roar. The pres. tense pictures the continual roaring of Satan as
a lion. περιπατεῖ pres. act. ind. to walk about, to prowl around
(Kelly). ζητῶν pres. act. part. ζητέω to seek, to look for.
καταπιεῖν aor. act. inf. καταπίνω to swallow down, to eat up,
to devour. The word lit. means "to drink down" but it can be
9 used of an animal swallowing its prey (Jonah 2:1) (Kelly). ■
ἀντίστητε aor. act. imp. ἀνθίστημι to stand up against, to
withstand, to resist. The aor. could be ingressive, i.e., "take your
stand against" (s. James 4:7). στερεός compact, solid, firm,
stedfast (Selwyn; Kelly). εἰδότες perf. act. part. οἶδα.
ἀδελφότης brotherhood (s. 1 Peter 2:17; MM). ἐπιτελεῖσθαι
pres. mid. or pass. inf. ἐπιτελέω to complete, to perform, to lay
something upon someone (BAG), mid. the meaning can be "is
required," "to pay in full" (MT, 55) w. the idea of "knowing how
to pay the same tax of suffering" (Bigg). The mid. could also
have the meaning "to fulfill a religious duty," "to perform the
obligations of piety." The gen. "sufferings" would be a gen. of
definition and the meaning would be "to make the same fulfillment (of duty toward God) of sufferings" (Beare). If the pass. is
adopted the verb might be translated "knowing that the same tax
of suffering will be paid by your brotherhood" (s. Best). The inf.
10 is used as the object of the verb "to know." ■ καλέσας aor. act.
part. καλέω to call. παθόντος aor. act. part. πάσχω to suffer.
The part. is used temporally "after you have suffered."
καταρτίσει fut. act. ind. καταρτίζω to put in order, to mend,
to reestablish, to make whole. The word could be used in a
medical sense of "settling a broken bone" or of repairing and
refitting a damaged vessel (s. Selwyn; Beare; TDNT; Gal. 6:1).
στηρίξει fut. act. ind. στηρίξω to set up, to fix firmly, to
establish, to strengthen (s. BAG; MM). σθενώσει fut. act. ind.
σθενόω to strengthen, to make strong (s. Kelly; BAG).
θεμελιώσει fut. act. ind. θεμελιόω to make a foundation, to
provide a solid foundation, to ground firmly (Goppelt; Eph.
3:17).
12   ■ λογίζομαι to reckon, to count as, to regard. This does not
imply that others have doubted the ability of Silvanus but em-

phasizes Peter's confidence in his fidelity (Best). ἔγραψα aor.
act. ind. γράφω epistolary aor. "I am writing" (Beare).
παρακαλῶν pres. act. part. (s.v.1). ἐπιμαρτυρῶν pres. act.
part. ἐπιμαρτυρέω to testify, to affirm, to supply evidence that,
to confirm that fact by evidence (Selwyn; s. also Goppelt).
στῆτε aor. act. imp. ἵστημι to stand, ingressive aor. "take your
stand" (RWP). ∎ ἀσπάζεται pres. mid. ind. to greet. 13
συνεκλεκτή fem. adj. "fellow elect." The fem. could refer to the
local church from which the letter was written (Kelly). Μάρκος
John Mark is intended who was not the real son but rather the
spiritual son of Peter (s. Best). ∎ ἀσπάσασθε aor. mid. imp. 14
φίλημα kiss (s. 1 Cor. 16:20).

2 PETER

Ch. 1

1   ἰσότιμος w. the same honor. Here the word has the meaning "equal privilege" or "equally privileged," i.e., a faith which carries equal privileges (Mayor). ἡμῖν "w. us." The contrast could be between Jews and Gentiles who have equal privileges but the contrast is almost certainly between the apostles who had been eyewitnesses of the original revelation (cf. 1:16), and the Christians of the second or even third generation (Kelly; s. also Bigg). λαχοῦσιν aor. act. part. λαγχάνω to obtain by lot, to obtain. The word implies a gift of favor and God gives to all Christians equal privileges in His city (Bigg). πίστις faith. Here it is not the faith as a body of doctrine, but the faith or trust which brings a man salvation and is the God-given capacity to trust Him (Green). ■ πληθυνθείη aor. pass. opt. πληθύνω to
2 multiply, to increase, pass. to be multiplied, to grow, to increase as "may grace and peace be yours in ever greater measure" (BAG). The opt. is used to express a wish or desire (RWP; s. also 1 Peter 1:2). ἐπίγνωσις knowledge, knowledge which is directed toward a particular object which can imply a more detailed or fuller knowledge (s. Col. 1:9; Mayor, 171–174).

3   ■ θεῖος godly, divine. The term "divine power" in the gen. is the subject of the part. and was a phrase used for the term "God." A parallel expression is found in the decree of Stratonicea, an inscription in honor of Zeus and Hekate. (For this and its importance in relation to 2 Peter, s. BS, 360–368.) εὐσέβεια godliness, true religion which displays itself in reverence in the presence of that which is majestic and divine in worship and in a life of active obedience which befits that reverence (MNTW, 67ff.; TDNT; CBB; s. also 1 Tim. 2:2; 3:16). δεδωρημένης perf. mid. part. δωρέω to give as a gift, to grant, to bestow. The part. is used as a gen. abs. The perf. tense emphasizes the continuing nature of that which was given. καλέσαντος aor. act. part. καλέω to call. ἀρετή virtue, excellence, the display of divine power and divine acts (s. 1 Peter 2:9). The dat. case could be either instrumental "by" or dat. of advantage "to," "for" (s.
4 RWP). ■ δι' ὧν "through which things." The antecedent of the

768

rel. pron. would be the words "glory and virtue" (Bigg). τίμιος honorable, precious, valuable. μέγιστος magnificent, elative superl. "very great." ἐπάγγελμα that which was promised, promised. δεδώρηται perf. mid. ind. (s.v.3). γένησθε aor. mid. subj. γίνομαι. The subj. is used to express purpose. κοινωνός partner, sharer, partaker (s. TDNT). φύσις nature. Peter does not mean that man is absorbed into deity but rather those who are partakers of Christ will be partakers of the glory that shall be revealed (s. Green; Kelly). ἀποφυγόντες aor. act. part. ἀποφεύγω to escape, to escape completely. ἐπιθυμία strong desire, lust, passion. φθορά corruption. The basic meaning of the word denotes primarily not a sudden destruction owing to external violence, but a dissolution brought on by means of internal decay, i.e., "rottenness" (s. Mayor, 175–179). ■ 5 σπουδή haste, effort. παρεισενέγκαντες aor. act. part. παρεισφέρω to bring in alongside of. Used idiomatically w. the word "effort" to express the idea of bringing in every effort. We are to bring "into" this relationship "alongside" what God has done every ounce of determination we can muster (Green; s. also Bigg; Kelly; Mayor; BS, 361). ἐπιχορηγήσατε aor. act. imp. ἐπιχορηγέω to supply in addition to, to outfit the chorus w. additional (complete) supplies (RWP). The prep. in compound seems to have an accumulative force, "to add further supplies," "to provide more than was expected or could be demanded" (Mayor), "to give lavishly, w. generosity" (Kelly; for this graphic word, s. also 2 Cor. 9:10; Gal. 3:5; Col. 2:19; 1 Peter 4:11; Green; Bigg). ἐν "in." The since is: since you have faith, let it not be wanting in virtue, etc. (Huther). πίστις faith. Here it is to be understood subjectively of loyal adhesion to Christian teaching rather than of that teaching itself (Kelly). ἀρετή virtue, moral energy. In classical times the word meant the god-given power or ability to perform heroic deeds whether military deeds or athletic or artistic accomplishments or the conducting of one's life. The basic meaning of the word indicated the quality by which one stands out as being excellent. In respect to ethics Aristotle held that it was the right behavior or mean between two extremes. The Stoics connected it w. nature and taught that the essence of virtue was "living harmoniously w. nature" (s. Mayor; TDNT; GPT, 25; KP I, 530–531). γνῶσις knowing, knowledge. ■ ἐγκράτεια self-control, lit. "holding himself in" (RWP; s. also 6 Gal. 5:23). ■ ταῦτα "these things," i.e., "the possession of these 8 qualities and their continued increase" (Mayor). πλεονάζοντα pres. act. part. πλεονάζω to abound, to increase. In the classical writers the word is a term of disparagement, implying excess, to be or to have more than enough, to exaggerate. But to fervent Christianity there can be no excess of good (Mayor). The pres. tense emphasizes the continual action. ἀργός not active, inactive, idle. ἄκαρπος not fruitful, unfruitful. καθίστησιν pres.

9 act. ind. to bring a person to a place, to make (s. Bigg). ■ πάρεστιν pres. act. ind. to be by, to be present. τυφλός blind. μυωπάζων pres. act. part. μυωπάζω to be short-sighted. The word refers to the involuntary contraction of the half-closed eyes of a short-sighted man and the word may be a correction or limitation of the idea of being blind (Mayor). On the other hand the meaning may be "shutting the eyes to the truth," the intention being to emphasize the responsibility of the believer (Kelly). λήθη forgetfulness. λαβών aor. act. part. λαμβάνω to take, to receive. Used in the expression "having received forgetfulness," i.e., "to forget." The part. could be causal "because he has forgot-

10 ten" (Bigg). καθαρισμός cleansing, purifying. πάλαι old. ■ διό μᾶλλον "wherefore the more" (Bigg). σπουδάσατε aor. act. imp. σπουδάζω to be in a hurry, to give diligence, to exert effort. The word stresses the urgency of his plea that they should determine to live for God (Green). βέβαιος firm, secure. Used w. the inf. in the sense of "to make firm," "to certify," "to confirm," "to attest." In the papyri the word was a t.t. for a legal guarantee (s. Mayor; BS, 107; TDNT; s. also 1 Cor. 1:6; Heb. 3:6). κλῆσις calling. ἐκλογή selection, election, choosing. ποιεῖσθαι pres. mid. inf. to do, to make. Used w. the adj. in the sense of "to make certain," "to give a guarantee." The holy life is the guarantee demonstrating the calling and election to others. The inf. is epexegetical or complementary explaining the verb "give diligence." ποιοῦντες pres. act. part. οὐ μή "never in any wise." πταίσητε aor. act. subj. πταίω to stumble. ποτέ ever,

11 never. ■ πλουσίως adv. richly. ἐπιχορηγηθήσεται fut. pass. ind. (s.v.5). εἴσοδος the way in, entrance.

12 　　■ μελλήσω fut. act. ind. μέλλω to be about to, to be on the point of doing something. The verb is used w. the inf. to express the idea "I shall take care to remind you." This thought of the duty of reminding his readers appears again in verses 13 and 15, and in 3:1 (Mayor; s. also RWP). ἀεί always, ever. The word implies a prospect of frequent communication between him and them (Mayor). καίπερ "although." Used w. the part. to express concession. εἰδότας perf. act. part. οἶδα to know (s. ND, 344ff.). ἐστηριγμένους perf. pass. part. στηρίζω to set up, to formally establish, to strengthen. The perf. tense indicates the settled state or condition. The part. is used to express conces-

13 sion. παρούσῃ pres. act. part. (s.v.9). ■ ἡγοῦμαι pres. mid. ind.

to consider, to think. ἐφ᾽ὅσον "for as long as." σκήνωμα tent. (For the concept of the "tent" picturing the body, s. 2 Cor. 5:1; Mayor.) διεγείρειν pres. act. inf. to wake out of sleep, to stir up. The prep. in compound is perfective "to stir up or wake up thoroughly" (RWP; s. also Mayor). The inf. is used epexegetically to explain that which Peter considers to be "right." ὑπόμνησις remembering, reminder. ■ ταχινός speedy, soon, 14 swiftly. The word here could mean either "suddenly" or "soon" (Bigg). ἀπόθεσις putting off. The word could be used for the idea of putting off clothing (s. Bigg; 1 Peter 3:21). ἐδήλωσεν aor. act. ind. δηλόω to make clear, to make plain, to inform, to reveal. The word is sometimes used of special revelations (1 Cor. 3:13; 1 Peter 1:11; s. also Kelly; TDNT). ■ σπουδάσω fut. act. 15 ind. (s.v.10). καί "even." Here he speaks of making provision for them after his death (Mayor). ἑκάστοτε every time, on each occasion, i.e., whenever there is need (Mayor). ἔξοδος departure, exodus. The word is used to indicate death (Bigg; s. also Green). ποιεῖσθαι pres. mid. inf. to do, to make. Used w. the noun "remembering" w. the meaning "to recall, to remember." The inf. is used to complete the idea of the main verb "to make an effort."

■ σεσοφισμένοις perf. pass. part. σοφίζω to make wise, 16 to be wise, to behave wisely, to cleverly contrive, to concoct subtly, to reason out subtly (s. Mayor; Kelly; BAG). μῦθος myth, fable. The word stood for mythical stories about gods, the creation of the world, miraculous happenings, etc. (Kelly; s. also CBB; TDNT; Bigg; Mayor; GPT, 120f.). Apparently the mockers of 3:3 spoke of the Christian hope of the glories to come as resting on factitious prophecies (Mayor). ἐξακολουθήσαντες aor. act. part. ἐξακολουθέω to follow after, to follow out, to rest upon. (For the use of the verb in the papyri, s. MM.) ἐγνωρίσαμεν aor. act. ind. γνωρίζω to make known. παρουσία coming. The word was often used as a term for the appearance of a god or the arrival of a king or ruler (s. Schelkle; TDNT; 1 Thess. 2:19; 3:13). ἐπόπτης one who sees w. his eyes, eyewitness. γενηθέντες aor. act. part. γίνομαι to become, to be. μεγαλειότης majesty. The word means the majesty of the divine and is used here to express the divine majesty as revealed in the transfiguration of Jesus (Green). ■ λαβών aor. act. part. 17 (s.v.9). τιμή honor. Here the word denotes the exalted status which the proclamation of sonship implies, while "glory" points to the ethereal radiance of the transfigured Jesus, a radiance which is a participation in that splendor of light which, according to OT conceptions, belongs to God's very being (Kelly; s. also

Mayor). ἐνεχθείσης aor. pass. part. φέρω to bring, to bear. The word is used in the sense of "to make a word, speech, announcement, charge," and it is used of a divine proclamation, whether direct or indirect (BAG). τοιόσδε such, such as this, of this kind. The word refers to what follows and in the sense "so unique" (BAG). μεγαλοπρεπής magnificent, sublime, majestic. The word was used in the papyri as a term of honor and respect for political personalities. As preparations were made for the reception of a Roman senator in Egypt the instructions were "let him be received w. special magnificence" (MM; s. also Mayor). It was common for the Jews to use such statements when referring to God Himself (Schelkle). ἀγαπητός one who is loved, beloved. εὐδόκησα aor. act. ind. εὐδοκέω to be well-pleased, to be satisfied w. The word suggests the good pleasure of the Father

18 alighting and remaining on Jesus (Green). ■ ἠκούσαμεν aor. act. ind. ἀκούω to hear. ὄντες pres. part. εἰμί. The part. is used

19 temporally "when we were on the holy mountain." ■ βεβαιότερος comp. "certain," "more certain," "more sure." (For this word, s.v.10.) Peter is saying that the holy Scriptures are more certain than experience. He is saying "if you don't believe me, go to the scriptures" (Green). προφητικός prophetical, that which pertains to the message of a prophet. The term "the prophetic word" was a current expression embracing the OT as a whole and not simply the prophets proper (Kelly). καλῶς adv. "well." προσέχοντες pres. act. part. προσέχω to hold the mind on something, to give heed to (RWP). The part. could be understood either as conditional "if you give heed" or it could express the manner or means of doing well "by giving heed to." λύχνος lamp. φαίνοντι pres. act. part. φαίνω to shine. The pres. tense emphasizes the continual shining. αὐχμηρός dry and parched, dirty, dark, murky. The word does not seem to imply absolute darkness, but dingy and dusky obscurity as contrasted w. "the brightness of Messiah's rising" (Isa. 60:3; Rom. 13:12) (Mayor; s. also RWP; MM). The word may also have the idea of dirty since that which is dirty is destitute of brightness and the thought may be that light shows up the dirt, and makes possible its removal (T; Green). τόπος place. The "darksome place" is the world as it at present exists, which in the NT is regularly characterized as darkness (Kelly). ἕως οὗ who "until," "until which time." The temporal conjuction w. the subj. is a usual construction for future time (RWP; s. also Mayor). διαυγάσῃ aor. act. subj. διαυγάζω to shine through, to dawn. The word is used of the first streaks of dawn breaking through the darkness (Mayor). φωσφόρος light bringing, light

bringer, the morning star, i.e., the planet Venus. The imagery lay
ready at hand, for the famous prophecy in Numbers 24:17 "there
shall come a star out of Jacob," was understood in Judaism as
pointing to the Messiah (Kelly) and the coming of the Messiah
is also compared to the dawn in Malachi 4:2 (Mayor). (For the
eschatological and messianic interpretation of Num. 24:17 in the
DDS, s. 1QM11, 6–7f.) In Greek and Roman times the term was
applied not only to the morning star (Venus), but also to royal
and divine persons (Green; s. also KP V, 1179–1180; MM).
ἀνατείλῃ aor. act. subj. ἀνατέλλω to rise, to arise (s. Matt.
5:45; James 1:11). ἐν ταῖς καρδίαις ὑμῶν "in your hearts."
This phrase could possibly be connected w. the part. of v. 20 w.
the meaning "knowing this first and foremost in your hearts . . ."
or the rising of the morning star in Christian hearts at the dawning of the day may mean the glow of anticipation in Christian
hearts when "the finds of the approaching Day are manifest to
Christians" (Green; s. also Mayor). ■ γινώσκοντες pres. act. 20
part. The part. could be causal or it continues the construction
of "you do well giving heed," and defines the spirit and feeling
w. which the Scriptures should be read, "recognizing this truth
first of all" (Mayor). πᾶσα all. Used w. the neg. in the sense of
"not even one" (BG, 151; s. also RG, 753). In the sing. the word
"all" without the article means "every" in a distributive sense,
i.e., "every single one" (s. BG, 61). προφητεία the message of
a prophet, prophecy (s.v. 19). γραφή writing, Scripture. Normally in the NT the word denotes the OT (Kelly). ἴδιος one's
own. It was the mark of a false prophet to speak "his own thing"
or "from himself" (Mayor). ἐπίλυσις releasing, solving, explaining, interpreting. The word almost comes to mean "inspiration" (Green; s. also Mayor; MM). The gen. (ablative) indicates
source. Peter is talking about the divine origin of Scripture, not
about its proper interpretation (Green). γίνεται pres. mid. ind.
to become. ■ ἠνέχθη aor. pass. ind. φέρω to bear. The word was 21
used of bearing or conveying or uttering a divine proclamation
and it could also have the sense of "to produce," "to bring forth"
(s. BAG; T). φερόμενοι pres. pass. part., pass. to be carried, to
be borne along. The word was used of a ship carried along by the
wind (s. Acts 27:15, 17) and the metaphor here is that the
prophets raised their sails and the Holy Spirit filled them and
carried their craft along in the direction He wished. Men spoke:
God spoke (Green). The part. expresses contemporaneous time.
ἐλάλησαν aor. act. ind. (For references to the inspiration of the
Scripture, s. 2 Tim. 3:16.)

Ch. 2

1 ■ ἐγένοντο aor. mid. ind. γίνομαι to become, to appear, to arise. καί "also," "too," i.e., in addition to the holy men who spoke the inspired Word of God there were also some in Israel and now history was repeating itself (Green). ψευδοπροφήτης false prophets. The compound in the word may either mean falsely named, a "sham" or "counterfeit," or it may mean falsely doing the work implied, i.e., "to speak falsely," and either meaning would suit the word, for to prophesy falsely in the narrow sense was at any rate one of the marks of a pretended prophet (Mayor). ἔσονται fut. εἰμί. ψευδοδάσκαλος false teacher (s. the discussion in Mayor, CLXVII-CLXXX). οἵτινες who, i.e., who belong to a particular class or group. παρεισάξουσιν fut. act. ind. παρεισάγω to bring into alongside of, to smuggle in. The word may signify to bring in secretly w. the 1st prep. in compound giving the idea of creeping along under some sort of cover (Bigg; s. also Gal. 2:4). αἵρεσις heresy, false teaching. ἀπώλεια destruction. ἀγοράσοντα aor. act. part. ἀγοράζω to buy at the market place, to buy. δεσπότης lord, master, one who holds authority over another. ἀρνούμενοι pres. mid. part. ἀρνέομαι to say no to, to deny. The heretics were professing Christians (RWP). ἐπάγοντες pres. act. part. ἐπάγω to bring 2 upon. ταχινός quick, sudden, soon. ■ ἐξακολουθήσουσιν fut. act. ind. ἐξακολουθέω to follow, to follow after (s. 2 Peter 1:16). αὐτῶν "their." The pron. refers to the false teachers, whose bad example will be largely followed (Mayor). ἀσέλγεια unbridled living. The pl. may denote either different forms, or repeated habitual acts of lasciviousness (Bigg; s. also 1 Peter 4:3). δι᾽οὕς "because of whom." The reference is clearly to the many backsliders (Kelly). ὁδὸς τῆς ἀληθείας "the way of truth." The phrase refers to the teaching of the truth, the correct teaching, the correct religion (Schelkle). Here the expression denotes the Christian message and way of life which are inevitably brought into discredit when their adherents identify themselves w. patently immoral courses (Kelly). βλασφημηθήσεται fut. pass. ind. βλασφημέω to injure the reputation of someone, to 3 defame, to blaspheme. ■ πλεονεξία uncontrolled greed, insatiable greed (s. TDNT; NTW, 97; Rom. 1:29; 2 Cor. 9:5; Col. 3:5; 1 Thess. 2:5). πλαστός made up, factitious. The word was used in the papyri of a "forged" contract (MM; s. also Mayor). ἐμπορεύσονται fut. mid. ind. ἐμπορεύομαι to travel as a merchant, to travel on business, to carry on business, to trade in, to cheat, to make a gain of, to exploit (Kelly; s. also Mayor). κρίμα the decision of a judgment, verdict, condemnation, judgment.

ἔκπαλαι for a long time, from of old. ἀργεῖ pres. act. ind. not working, to be idle. The judgment is not idle, but already active in the punishment of other offenders, and gathering up for these false teachers (Mayor). νυστάζει pres. act. ind. to nod, to sleep (s. Matt. 25:5).

■ ἁμαρτησάντων aor. act. part. ἐφείσατο aor. mid. ind. 4 φείδομαι w. the gen. to spare. The ind. is used in a first-class conditional clause which assumes the reality of the condition. σιρός underground pit. The word is properly a pit for the storage of grain but was used for a large bin for holding edible roots or of a pit made for trapping a wolf (Mayor). ζόφος dark, darkness. ταρταρώσας aor. act. part. ταρταρόω to confine in Tartarus. Tartarus was the name in classical mythology for the subterranean abyss in which rebellious gods and other such beings as the Titans were punished. The word was, however, taken over into Hellenistic Judaism and used in the book of Enoch (Enoch 20:2) in connection w. fallen angels. It is the angel Uriel who is the rule of Tartarus (s. Kelly; Mayor; Bigg; KP V, 530–531). παρέδωκεν aor. act. ind. παραδίδωμι to deliver over, to hand over, to confine. κρίσις judging. τηρουμένους pres. pass. part. τηρέω to keep, to guard. ■ ἀρχαῖος ancient. The gen. is used 5 as the object of the verb "to spare." ὄγδοος eighth, i.e., "Noah w. seven others," "he being the eighth" (BD, 130). δικαιοσύνη righteousness. The word denotes here the just or upright moral behavior (Kelly). κῆρυξ preacher, herald (s. 1 Tim. 2:7). ἐφύλαξεν aor. act. ind. φυλάσσω to guard, to watch over, to protect. κατακλυσμός flood, deluge. ἀσεβής ungodly, impious (s. Rom. 4:5; 1 Tim. 1:9). ἐπάξας aor. act. part. ἐπάγω to bring upon. The part. is used temporally expressing contemporaneous action. ■ Σοδόμων καὶ Γομόρρας gen. of apposition 6 (s. BD, 92; Mayor). τεφρώσας aor. act. part. τεφρόω to reduce to ashes, or perhaps here better "to cover w. ashes" (s. Mayor). The Roman historian Dio Cassius used the word to describe the inner part of Mount Vesuvius which was constantly growing brittle and "being reduced to ashes" so that the center section in the course of time settled and became concave (Dio Cassius, *Roman History*, LXVI, 21, 2). καταστροφή overturning, destruction, instrumental dat. κατέκρινεν aor. act. ind. κατακρίνω to pronounce a verdict against someone, to sentence to punishment, to condemn. The verb continues the condition found in the first-class conditional clause beginning w. v. 4 (s. RWP). ὑπόδειγμα pattern, example. μελλόντων pres. act. part. μέλλω to be about to. Used w. the inf. to form the fut. ἀσεβεῖν pres. act. inf. to live ungodly, to be impious (s.v.5). (For

the variant reading "ungodly men" which would give the sense
"unto ungodly men of things about to be," i.e., "of things in store
for them," s. RWP; TC, 702.) τεθεικώς perf. act. part. τίθημι
to place, to make, to constitute. The perf. tense emphasizes that
7 the example still has lasting validity. ■ καταπονούμενον pres.
pass. part. καταπονέω to wear down through exhausting work,
to trouble greatly. ἄθεσμος lawless. It pictures them as being
rebels against the law not of Moses, but of nature and conscience
(Bigg). ἐν ἀσελγείᾳ "in unbridled living" (s.v.2). The prepositional phrase indicates the sphere in which their conduct displayed itself. ἀναστροφή behavior, conduct (s. 1 Peter 1:15).
8 ἐρρύσατο aor. mid. ind. ῥύομαι to rescue. ■ βλέμμα sight.
The word is generally subjective, where the eye reveals to outsid-
ers the inner feeling of man. The idea would be "the righteousness of man showed itself in his shrinking from the sights and
sounds which met him on every side": lit. "righteous in look and
in hearing he tortured himself at their lawless deeds while he
lived among them" (Mayor). ἀκοή hearing. ἐγκατοικῶν pres.
act. part. ἐγκατοικέω to live or dwell among. The part. is used
temporally describing contemporary action. ἄνομος lawless.
ἐβασάνιζεν impf. ind. act. βασανίζω to torture, to torment.
The impf. pictures the continual action of the past time. The
rabbis generally viewed Lot as one who despised God and was
given over to immorality (s. SB III, 769–771). Compare however
the statements recorded in "the Genesis Apocryphon"
(1QGENAP, XXI 5–7) "pasturing his herds he (Lot) reached
Sodom and he bought himself a house in Sodom and settled in
it. But I remained in the hill country of Bethel, and it grieved me
that my nephew Lot had parted from me" (s. *Aramaic Text from
Qumran* w. translations and annotations by B. Jongeling, C.J.
Labuschagne, A.S. Van Der Voude [Leiden: E.J. Brill, 1976],
9 105). ■ εὐσεβής God-fearing, godly, devout (s. 2 Peter 1:3).
κολαζομένους pres. pass. part. κολάζω to punish. The original
sense of the word was "to cut short" and was used of "pruning"
a tree and later took on the meaning "to correct" and then "to
punish" and was also used of the punishment of slaves as well
as divine punishment (s. BAG; MM; Kelly; s. also Acts 4:21).
10 ■ μάλιστα especially. ὀπίσω w. the gen. "after." The phrase
"them that walk after the flesh" suggests sodomy (Green).
ἐπιθυμία strong desire, lust, passion. μιασμός pollution. The
gen. could be obj. gen. in the sense of "in their hankering after
pollution," but if it is subjective, it would mean "in lust which
pollutes" (Kelly). πορευομένους pres. mid. part. πορεύομαι to
walk, to go. κυριότης lordship. καταφρονοῦντας pres. act.

part. καταφρονέω to think down upon, to despise. The false
teachers despised the power and majesty of the Lord (Bigg).

ὁ τολμητής one who dares, one who is brazen, "headstrong
daredevils," "shameless and headstrong." The word smacks of
the reckless daring that defies God and man (Mayor; Green).
αὐθάδης self-pleasing, arrogant. The word is used for an obstinate fellow who is determined to please himself at all costs
(Green; RWP; s. also Titus 1:7). δόξαι "glorious ones." The
word could refer to angelic beings, either those heavenly beings
in God's service, or celestial beings, probably the fallen angels
(Kelly). τρέμουσιν pres. act. ind. to tremble, to be afraid to. The
verb is completed by the complementary part. rather than by an
inf. (RWP). βλασφημοῦντες pres. act. part. to defame, to blaspheme. ■ ὅπου "where," "in a case in which," "whereas," "see- 11
ing that" (Mayor). ἰσχύς strength, indwelling strength (RWP;
s. also Eph. 1:19). μείζων comp. μέγας great, comp. greater,
superior. ὄντες pres. part. εἰμί. The part. is used concessively,
i.e., "although." φέρουσιν pres. act. ind. to bear, to bring. The
pres. tense emphasizes a continual attitude which is negated by
the neg. particle. βλάσφημος defamation, railing, blaspheming.
■ ἄλογος without reason, irrational. They have physical, but not 12
intellectual life; they are no better than the brutes that perish
(Bigg). ζῷον living creature, animal, beast. γεγεννημένα perf.
pass. part. γεννάω to bear, pass. to be born. φυσικός natural,
pertaining to nature, in accordance w. nature, here used in the
sense of "mere creatures of instinct, born to be caught and
killed" (BAG). ἅλωσις capture. φθορά corruption, destruction.
The combination of the verb w. the noun makes it almost certain
that destruction is meant (Bigg). ἀγνοοῦσιν to be without
knowledge, to be ignorant. These have no more knowledge than
brute beasts would have (Kelly). φθαρήσονται fut. pass. ind.
φθείρω to corrupt, to decay, to destroy, to devastate (s. Mayor,
175ff.; s. also 2 Peter 1:4). ■ ἀδικούμενοι pres. mid. or pass. 13
part. ἀδικέω to commit injustice, to do wrong, mid. or pass. to
suffer injustice, to be damaged, to be harmed (s. Kelly). The
phrase "being defrauded of the wages of fraud" has been vindicated by an example from the papyri which reads "when this
has been done [in the context, 'when a receipt has been given'],
we shall not be defrauded" (Green). μισθός wage, recompense.
ἀδικία unrighteousness, fraud. ἡδονή pleasure. In the NT the
word always means sensual gratification (Bigg). ἡγούμενοι pres.
mid. part. ἡγέομαι to consider, to reckon, to count. τρυφή
indulgence, reveling. Daylight debauchery was frowned on even
in degenerate Roman society (Green; s. also Kelly). Dio

Chrysostom represents Alexander the Great as feeling that other
men "had all been well-nigh ruined in soul by luxury and idleness
and were slaves of money and pleasure" (DC IV, 6). σπίλος
spot, blot, a disfiguring spot (Bigg; s. also Eph. 5:27). μῶμος
blemish. The accusation is one of riotous misbehavior at banquets, and since the correspondents participated in these, it
would seem to be some kind of community celebration (Kelly).
ἐντρυφῶντες pres. act. part. ἐντρυφάω to live in luxury, to
revel. ἀπάτη deception. Perhaps the meaning here is in the
sense of "dissipations" and the transition from "guile" or
"deception" to "sinful pleasure" was natural and easy (Kelly).
συνευωχούμενοι pres. mid. part. συνευωχέομαι to feed well,
to feed abundantly, to eat together, to feast w. (s. RWP). The
part. denotes the circumstances of the preceding action (Mayor).
14 ■ ἔχοντες pres. act. part. μεστός full. μοιχαλίς adultress. The
connotation is probably more general and the meaning is "loose
woman" (Kelly). ἀκατάπαυστος without succession, not paus-
ing, "unable to stop" (RWP). δελεάζοντες pres. act. part.
δελεάζω to trap by using bait, to ensnare. ἀστήρικτος without
firmness, unstable. They lack a firm foundation in faith and
discipline, and so are liable to be unsettled by scandalous conduct or erroneous teaching (Kelly; s. also Green).
γεγυμνασμένην perf. pass. part. γυμνάζω to exercise, to do
bodily exercise, to be familiar w. The gen. used after the part.
denotes familiarity w. anything (Bigg). κατάρα curse. The Hebraic expression "children of curse" means "accursed creatures"
(Kelly; s. also Bigg), i.e., "God's curse on them." These men rest
under the curse of God, as do all who fail to trust in Christ who
15 bore man's curse (Green). ■ καταλείποντες pres. act. part.
καταλείπω to leave off, to abandon. εὐθύς straight. Upright
conduct is pictured in the Bible as a "straight path" (Kelly).
ἐπλανήθησαν aor. pass. ind. παλανάω to go astray, to follow
the wrong path. ἐξακολουθήσαντες aor. act. part.
ἐξακολουθέω to follow after (s. 2 Peter 1:16). ἀδικίας unrighteousness, fraud. The gen. could be subjective or obj. gen., i.e.,
either reward prompted by fraud or reward which has fraud or
unrighteousness as its object. ἠγάπησεν aor. act. ind. ἀγαπάω.
16 ■ ἔλεγξις rebuke. ἔσχεν aor. act. ind. ἔχω to have, to get.
παρανομία beyond the law, transgression. The word indicates
not a general defiance of law, but rather a breech of a particular
law (Mayor). ὑποζύγιον "being under a yoke." The term was
used for a beast of burden, then specifically for a donkey (s. BS,
160f.). ἄφωνος not having a sound, speechless, dumb.
φθεγξάμενον aor. mid. part. φθέγγομαι to make a sound, to

speak. The verb is esp. used of a portentous prophetic utterance (Bigg). ἐκώλυσεν aor. act. ind. κωλύω to hinder. παραφρονία beyond understanding, madness. It is being beside one's wits (RWP). The idea of the v. is "he who was bribed by Balak to curse Israel was rebuked for his own disobedience by the disobedience of the ass and thus hindered from receiving the promised reward" (Mayor).

■ πηγή spring. ἄννδρος waterless. ὁμίχλη fog, mist. 17 λαῖλαψ storm, squall (s. Mark 4:37; Luke 8:23). ἐλαυνόμεναι perf. pass. part. ἐλαύνω to drive, to blow. τετήρηται perf. pass. ind. ■ ὑπέρογκος swelling, inflated. The word means "unnatu- 18 rally swollen." They used big, ponderous words in their discourses. Ostentatious verbosity was their weapon to ensnare the unwary and licentiousness was the bait on their hook (Green). ματαιότης vanity, futility. Their words amount to nothing of significance w. the gen. being a descriptive gen. (Green). φθεγγόμενοι pres. mid. part. (s.v. 16). ὀλίγως adv. The word can mean either "very recently" or "in a small degree," i.e., "slightly," "a little" (Kelly; Mayor). ἀποφεύγοντας pres. act. part. ἀποφεύγω to escape from. πλάνη error. The word stands specifically for idolatry or paganism (Kelly; s. also TDNT). ἀναστρεφομένους pres. mid. part. ἀναστρέφομαι to conduct one's life, to live. ■ ἐλευθερία freedom, liberty. 19 ἐπαγγελλόμενοι pres. mid. part. ἐπαγγέλομαι to promise. ὑπάρχοντες pres. act. part. ὑπάρχω to be, to exist. The word denotes continuance of an antecedent state or condition (AS; s. also 2 Cor. 12:16). φθορά corruption, destruction (s.v. 12). ἥττηται perf. pass. ind. ἡττάομαι to be inferior, to be defeated, to be overcome. δεδούλωται perf. pass. ind. to enslave. The imagery derived directly from the ancient practice of enslaving an enemy defeated in battle and so made prisoner (Kelly). ■ 20 ἀποφυγόντες aor. act. part. ἀποφεύγω to escape from. μίασμα pollution. ἐπίγνωσις recognition, knowledge. ἐμπλακέντες aor. pass. part. ἐμπλέκω to enweave, to entangle. γέγονεν perf. act. ind. γίνομαι. χείρων (comp.) worse. ■ 21 κρείττων (comp.) better. ἐπεγνωκέναι perf. act. inf. ἐπιγινώσκω to know (s. 2 Peter 1:3). The inf. is used epexegetically to explain that which is "better." ἐπιγνοῦσιν aor. act. part. ἐπιγινώσκω. The dat. pl. agrees w. the pron. "for them" (RWP). ὑποστρέψαι fut. act. inf. ὑποστρέφω to turn back. παραδοθείσης aor. pass. part. παραδίδωμι to deliver over, to commit. The word was almost a t.t. for the passing on of tradition (s. TDNT). ■ συμβέβηκεν perf. act. ind. συμβαίνω to happen. 22 The dramatic perf. treats what is certain to befall as already

accomplished (Kelly). παροιμία proverb. κύων dog.
ἐπιστρέψας aor. act. part. ἐπιστρέφω to turn to. ἐξέραμα
that which is thrown out, vomit (s. Prov. 26:11). ὗς pig, hog.
λουσαμένη aor. mid. part. λούομαι to wash one's self. The
word means "having bathed itself in mud" (Bigg). κυλισμός
wallowing. βόρβορος mud, mire, filth, slime (BAG). Epictetus
says of those who refuse to keep themselves clean "go and talk
to a pig, that he may wallow no more in mud!" (Epictetus, IV.
XI. 29).

Ch. 3

1   ■ δεύτερος second. διεγείρω pres. act. ind. to awaken, to
stir up (s. 2 Peter 1:13). ὑπόμνησις remembering, reminder.
εἰλικρινής pure, unmixed, sincere. The word was used of things
unmixed, e.g., air as well as ethical purity (Mayor; s. Phil. 1:10).
διάνοια thinking, understanding. The phrase was used by Plato
to mean "pure reason," uncontaminated by the seductive influ-
2 ence of the senses (Green; s. also GPT, 37). ■ μνησθῆναι aor.
pass. inf. μιμνήσκομαι to remind. The inf. is used to express
purpose, i.e., it states the purpose of his writing. The inf. could
also be taken as epexegetical defining the verb "to stir up" (May-
or). προειρημένων perf. pass. part. προλέγω to say before.
ἐντολή commandment. The construction of the gen. is not entirely clear, but probably could be translated "of the command-
3 ment of the Lord transmitted by the apostles" (BD, 93). ■
γινώσκοντες pres. act. part. The part. could be understood here
as having the force of an imp. (s. Mayor). ἐλεύσονται fut. mid.
ind. ἔρχομαι to come. ἐμπαιγμονή scoffing, making fun of
through mockery. ἐμπαίκτης one who makes fun through
mockery, mocker, scoffer. The phrase "mockers w. (in) mockery," i.e., "scoffers shall come w. scoffing" is a strong Hebraic
influence on the analogy of the Heb. inf. abs. (s. Bigg; MT, Style,
142f.). ἐπιθυμία strong desire, lust, passion. πορευόμενοι pres.
4 mid. part. πορεύομαι to walk, to come. ■ λέγοντες pres. act.
part. ποῦ "where?"; i.e., "what has become of?" This is a tradi-
tional formula for expressing skepticism (Kelly). ἐπαγγελία
promise. παρουσία coming (s. 2 Peter 1:16). ἐκοιμήθησαν
aor. pass. ind. κοιμάομαι to sleep, to fall asleep. The term is
used as a metaphor for dying (Kelly). διαμένει pres. act. ind. to
remain, to remain through, to continue. The pres. tense emphasizes the continual unbroken action. ἀρχή beginning. κτίσις
creation. They maintain that God's promise is unreliable, and
that God's universe is a stable, unchanging system where events
5 like the parousia just do not happen (Green). ■ λανθάνει pres.

act. ind. to escape notice of, to be hidden from, i.e., "for they shut their eyes to this fact that" (Mayor; s. RWP; Kelly). θέλοντας pres. act. part. The part. has here almost an adverbial sense (RWP). ἦσαν impf. εἰμί. ἔκπαλαι for a long time, long ago (s. 2 Peter 2:3). συνεστῶσα perf. act. part. συνίστημι to consist (s. Col. 1:17). ■ κατακλυσθείς aor. pass. part. 6 κατακλύζω to surge over completely, to inundate, to flood (s. 2 Peter 2:5). ἀπώλετο aor. mid. ind. ἀπόλλυμι to ruin, to destroy. ■ νῦν "now," "present." τεθησαυρισμένοι perf. pass. 7 part. θησαυρίζω to treasure up, to store up, to reserve. The sense of the metaphor here is "to set apart for," "destined for" (Mayor). The perf. tense emphasizes the completed state or condition. πῦρ fire. τηρούμενοι pres. pass. part. τηρέω to guard, to watch. κρίσις judging. ἀπώλεια ruin, destruction. ἀσεβής ungodly, impious (s. 2 Peter 2:5; Rom. 4:5; 1 Tim. 1:9).

■ λανθανέτω pres. act. imp. 3rd pers. sing. (s.v.5). ἔτος 8 year. ■ βραδύνει to be slow, to delay. (For examples in the 9 papyri, s. MM.) βραδύτης slowness, delay. ἡγοῦνται pres. mid. ind. to consider, to think, to count, i.e., as if delay sprang from impotence or unwillingness to perform (Bigg). μακροθυμεῖ pres. act. ind. to be longsuffering and patient. It is the Spirit which could take revenge if He liked, but utterly refuses to do so (s. NTW, 84; TDNT; Rom. 2:4). βουλόμενος pres. mid. part. βούλομαι to wish, to desire, to want. ἀπολέσθαι aor. mid. inf. ἀπόλλυμι to perish. μετάνοια change of thinking, repentence (s. Matt. 3:2). χωρῆσαι aor. act. inf. χωρέω to make room, to have room for. The apparent delay of God is rooted in the fact that His desire is that all have room, i.e., have opportunity for repentence. ■ ἥξει fut. act. ind. ἥκω to come. The verb is placed 10 for strong emphasis at the beginning of the sentence (Kelly). ῥοιζηδόν adv. w. a hissing or crackling sound. The word is onomatopoeic, expressing the whizzing sound produced by rapid motion through the air and was used of shrill rushing sounds, the hissing of a snake, the whirr of a bird's wings, the hurtling of an arrow and is then used for the rushing movement itself or the accompanying crash or roar. Here probably the roaring of flame is meant (Bigg; Mayor). παρελεύσονται fut. mid. ind. παρέρχομαι to pass by, to go away, to pass away. στοιχεῖον "things arranged in a row," e.g., the letters of the alphabet, or the elements of nature. Here it clearly means physical elements (Bigg). It could refer to the elements of earth, air, fire, and water or the heavenly bodies such as sun, moon, and stars (Green), or it may refer to the atomic particles which are the basic structure of nature. καυσούμενα pres. mid. part. καυσόομαι to burn, to

melt. The word was employed by medical writers to express
feverish heat. It may be intended to denote a conflagration arising from internal heat, such as a volcano (Mayor). λυθήσεται
fut. pass. ind. λύω to loosen, to disintegrate. The word is used
of breaking up a structure as in John 2:44, as well as of dissolving
a compound into its elements (Mayor). εὑρεθήσεται fut. pass.
ind. "will be found." The meaning here may be that the earth and
man's achievements will be discovered and exposed to divine

11 judgment (s. Kelly; Mayor). ■ λυομένων pres. pass. part. The
part. is used in a gen. abs. construction w. a causal meaning. The
pres. tense is either the futuristic pres. or the process of dissolution is pictured (RWP). ποταπός what sort of, what kind of. In
the context the word hints that great things are expected of the
readers; "how outstandingly excellent" (Kelly). δεῖ used w. the
acc. and the inf. "it is necessary." ὑπάρχειν pres. act. inf. to be,
to exist as (s. 2 Peter 2:19). ἀναστροφή walk, life's practice,
manner of living, way of life. εὐσέβεια godliness, a life of piety,

12 respect, and reverence (s. 1 Peter 1:3). ■ προσδοκῶντας pres.
act. part. προσδοκάω to await expectantly, to look forward to.
σπεύδοντας pres. act. part. σπεύδω to hasten, to accelerate, to
desire, to be eager for (Mayor; s. also Kelly; Bigg). δι᾽ ἥν
"because of which." The destruction takes place because God's
"day" has arrived (Green). πυρούμενοι pres. pass. part. πυρόω
to set on fire, pass. to be on fire, to burn. τήκεται pres. pass. ind.
τήκω to melt, to make liquid, pass. to be melted. The pres. tense

13 is futuristic (Bigg). ■ ἐπάγγελμα that which was promised,
promise. κατοικεῖ pres. act. ind. to settle down, to dwell, to be
at home at (s. Rev. 21:1).

14   ■ ταῦτα "these things," i.e., a freshly created heaven and
earth where God's will is paramount (Kelly). προσδοκῶντες
pres. act. part. to earnestly await, to expect (s.v.12).
σπουδάσατε aor. act. imp. σπουδάζω to give diligence, to
make an effort (s. 1 Peter 1:10). ἄσπιλος spotless. ἀμώμητος
blameless. αὐτῷ "him." The dat. may be taken w. the adj.,
"spotless and blameless in His sight," or w. the inf. "to be found
by Him" (Bigg). εὑρεθῆναι aor. pass. inf. The inf. is used to
complete the verb "make an effort," "give diligence." ἐν εἰρήνῃ
"in peace." This describes the state of reconciliation w. God

15 which the restored sinner enjoys (Kelly). ■ μακροθυμία longsuffering, patient endurance (s. Gal. 5:22; RAC IX, 254f.).
ἡγεῖσθε pres. mid. imp. to consider, to count, followed by the
double acc. ὁ ἀγαπητὸς ἡμῶν ἀδελφός "our beloved brother."
The phrase refers not simply to a fellow Christian but in this case
to a fellow apostle (Kelly). δοθεῖσαν aor. pass. part. δίδωμι to

give. The pass. is a theological or divine pass. indicating that God is the subject (s. BG, 76). ἔγραψεν aor. act. ind. Peter may be referring to Paul's letter to the Romans or he may be alluding simply to Paul's constant teaching in all his letters (Green). ■ 16 λαλῶν pres. act. part. δυσνόητος difficult to understand, hard to understand. ἀμαθής untaught. The word brings out the moral value of teaching, of trained habits of reflection, of disciplined good sense (Bigg). ἀστήρικτος unstable (s. 2 Peter 2:14). στρεβλοῦσιν pres. act. ind. to twist, to torture. The fig. sense seems to flow from the notion of twisting or warping rather than that of torturing on the rack (Mayor). λοιπός rest. γραφή Scripture. Peter gives a very high place to Paul's writings. They are placed alongside "the other scriptures" (Green). ■ 17 προγινώσκοντες pres. act. part. προγινώσκω to know beforehand, to know in advance. The part. could be causal. φυλάσσεσθε pres. mid. imp. φυλάσσω to guard, to keep watch, mid. to guard one's self. ἄθεσμος lawless (s. 2 Peter 2:7). πλάνη error. συναπαχθέντες aor. pass. part. συναπάγω to lead away together, to carry away together. ἐκπέσητε aor. act. subj. ἐκπίπτω to fall out of, to dislodge. The subj. is used in a neg. purpose clause. στηριγμός fixedness, firmness, steadfastness, firm stance. It connotes fixity as opposed to movement, and is used in conscience contrast to "unstable" above, to characteristic of the heretics and their dupes (II.14). Stability, or being firmly established in the faith, is clearly a quality which he greatly esteems (Kelly). ■ αὐξάνετε pres. act. imp. αὐξάνω to 18 grow, to advance. ἐν "in." The prep. could express either the sphere of growth or the means by which one grows. γνῶσις knowledge.

1 JOHN

Ch. 1

1 ἦν impf. εἰμί. ἀρχή beginning. The "beginning" here could refer to the beginning of creation or better, beginning in the abs. sense and emphasizes the preexistence and divine character (Schnackenburg; s. also Marshall). ἀκηκόαμεν perf. act. ind. ἀκούω to hear. ἑωράκαμεν perf. act. ind. ὁράω to see. The perf. tenses express an act in the past w. lasting results. It indicates that a revelation has been made in terms which men can understand and the results are abiding (Marshall; Brooke; s. also Abbott, 344). The 1st pers. pl. "we" could mean the writer of the epistle and his companions, but it more probably means "we all," "we disciples of Christ" (Abbott, 311; s. esp. Schnackenburg, 52–58). ἐθεασάμεθα aor. mid. ind. θεάομαι to look at, to behold. The verb expresses the calm, intent, continuous contemplation of an object which remains before the spectator (Westcott; s. also John 1:14). ἐψηλάφησαν aor. act. ind. ψηλαφάω to grope or feel after in order to find, like a blind man or one who is in the dark; hence, "to handle, to touch." The idea of searching sometimes disappears altogether. Here it naturally suggests all the evidence available for sense perception other than hearing and sight (Brooke). ζωή life. The gen. could indicate the content of the word or it could be gen. of quality and indicate "the living word" or it could indicate the object; i.e., "the life-giving word"

2 (s. Stott; Marshall). ■ ἐφανερώθη aor. pass. ind. φανερόω to make clear, to manifest, pass. to be revealed. The verb is used of the revelation of the Lord at His first coming and indicates the Incarnation (Westcott; Schnackenburg). μαρτυροῦμεν pres. act. ind. μαρτυρέω to be a witness, to testify. The pres. tense indicates the continuing abiding action or state. ἀπαγγέλλομεν to report, to declare, to report w. reference to the source from which a message comes (Brooke). The word "to witness, to testify" is a word of experience and this word "to declare" indicates the authority of commission (Stott) and both words emphasize that the message rests on eyewitnesses (Bultmann). Verse 2 forms a parenthesis which the writer inserted to make clear beyond all possibility of mistake that the life to which

John bears witness was revealed by God in the historical person of Jesus (Marshall). ■ ἀπαγγέλλομεν pres. act. ind. This is the 3 main verb of the sentence which was started in v.1. κοινωνία fellowship. The word indicates the setting aside of private interest and desires and the joining in w. another or others for common purposes (s. TDNT; CBB; RAC IX, 1100–1145). ἔχητε 4 pres. act. subj. The subj. is used to express purpose. ■ ταῦτα "these things." The reference could be to the entire contents of the letter (Brooke; Marshall) or it refers to the apostolic message in vv. 1 3 (Westcott). ᾖ subj. εἰμί. πεπληρωμένη perf. pass. part. πληρόω to fill, to fulfill, to make full. The part. is used as a periphrastic perf. pass. subj. stressing the state of completion in the purpose clause (RWP).

■ ἀγγελία report, message. The word may suggest that the 5 message contains a conception of God which men could not have formed for themselves without His help. It is a "revelation and not a discovery" (Brooke). ἀναγγέλλομεν pres. act. ind. to announce. The prep. in compound has the additional idea of bringing the tidings "up to" or "back" to the person receiving them. It is the recipient who is prominent in this verb (Westcott). ■ ἐάν "if." The five conditional clauses introduced by this word 6 are followed by the aor. subj. or the pres. subj. In each case the condition is a supposition which is possible "if this should happen" (s. Abbott, 371–374; Marshall). εἴπωμεν aor. act. subj. λέγω "if we should say." In vv. 6, 8, 10, the phrase introduces three statements of false doctrine (Abbott, 372). περιπατῶμεν pres. act. subj. to walk about, to conduct one's life. The word is comparable to the Heb. word "to walk" (s. TDOT) and is used in the sense of the practical, ethical dealing (Schnackenburg). ■ περιπατῶμεν pres. act. subj. The conditional clauses in vv. 7 7, 9 introduce the hypothesis of pres. and continuous Christian life, "on the supposition that we are walking or confessing" (Abbott, 372). "Walking in the light" is the conscious and sustained endeavor to live a life in conformity w. the revelation of God, who is "light," esp. as that revelation has been made finally and completely in Jesus Christ, and this is the necessary condition of fellowship (Brooke). κοινωνία fellowship (s.v.3). ἀλλήλων (gen.) "w. one another." Although the phrase could mean fellowship between God and man, John's general use indicates that he takes the fellowship of Christians as the visible sign correlative of fellowship w. God (Westcott; Schnackenburg). καθαρίζει pres. act. ind. to cleanse. The verbs suggest that God does more than forgive; He erases the stain of sin and the pres. tense shows that it is a continuous process (Stott). (For a study

of the term "blood" in the Scripture, s. APC, 108–124; A.M.
Stibbs, *The Meaning of the Word "Blood" in Scripture* [London:
9 The Tyndale Press, 1962].) ■ ὁμολογῶμεν pres. act. subj.
ὁμολογέω to say the same thing, to agree, to concede, to admit,
to confess. (For a study of the word, s. ECC, 13–20; TDNT.)
δίκαιος righteous, just. ἀφῇ aor. act. subj. ἀφίημι to release, to
forgive (s. TDNT; CBB). The subj. clause expresses the way in
which God expresses His faithfulness and justice and it is equivalent to an inf. of result (Marshall; s. also BD, 198). καθαρίσῃ
10 aor. act. subj. ἀδικία unrighteousness. ■ ἡμαρτήκαμεν perf.
act. ind. ἁμαρτάνω to sin. ψεύστης one who lies, liar.

Ch. 2

1   ■ τεκνίον little child, small child. The dim. form is used
expressing affection "dear child" (Marshall). ἁμάρτητε aor.
act. subj. The aor. tense indicates the thought of a single act, not
that of a state (Westcott). The subj. is used in a neg. purpose
clause. παράκλητος helper. In rabbinical literature the word
could indicate one who offers legal aid or one who intercedes on
behalf of someone else. In the pres. context the word undoubtedly signifies an "advocate" or "counsel for the defense" in a legal
context (Marshall; s. also Schnackenburg; Brooke; John 14:16).
2 ■ ἱλασμός satisfaction, propitiation. The idea is placating the
wrath of God and the pres. passage would then be that Jesus
propitiates God w. respect to our sins (Marshall; s. also Stott;
3 Rom. 3:25). ■ ἐγνώκαμεν perf. act. ind. γινώσκω. The tenses
here are significant as we learn to perceive more and more
clearly that our knowledge is genuine through its abiding results
in a growing willingness to obey (Brooke). ἐντολή commandment. τηρῶμεν pres. act. subj. τηρέω to guard, to keep. The
word has the idea of observing or holding something fast in
memory (Schnackenburg). The subj. is used in a third-class con-
4 ditional clause which views the condition as a possibility. ■
5 λέγων pres. act. part. ψεύστης one who lies, liar. ■ τηρῇ pres.
act. subj. The subj. is used w. the generalized rel. pron. w. the
meaning "whoever keeps." ἀληθῶς adv. truly. ἡ ἀγάπη τοῦ
θεοῦ "the love of God." The gen. could be subjective gen., i.e.,
"God's love for man" or it could be obj. gen., i.e., "man's love
for God" or the gen. could be gen. of quality, i.e., "God's kind
of love" (s. Marshall). (For the meaning of the term "love," s.
1 Cor. 13:1; Oda Wischmeyer, "Agape in der ausserchristlichen
Antike," ZNW, 69 [1978], 212–238.) τετελείωται perf. pass.
ind. τελειόω to bring to the goal, to perfect. True love for God
is expressed not in sentimental language or mystical experience,

but in moral obedience. The proof of love is loyalty. Such love
is "perfected" (Stott). ■ μένειν pres. act. inf. to remain. The 6
pres. tense and the meaning of the verb indicate a continual
being in Him. (For a study of this word, s. John 15:4; Schnackenburg, 105–110.) The inf. is used as indirect discourse after the
part. "the one who says." ὀφείλει pres. act. ind. to be morally
obligated "he ought to." καθώς just as. ἐκεῖνος "that one," i.e.,
Christ. περιεπάτησεν aor. act. ind. περιπατέω to walk, to
conduct one's life (s. 1 John 1:6). The aor. tense sums up the total
life of Jesus. οὕτως so, in like manner.

■ ἀγαπητός one who is loved, beloved. καινός new, novel, 7
new in kind (RWP; s. also Trench, *Synonyms*, 219–225;
Schnackenburg). παλαιός old, ancient; i.e., old in time.
ἠκούσατε aor. act. ind. ἀκούω. ■ ἀληθής true, genuine. The 8
word expresses not only the truth of the logical content but it
says that the newness of the commandment to love was actually
manifested in Christ and in those who received the letter
(Schnackenburg). παράγεται pres. mid. ind. παράγω to pass
away. The pres. tense indicates that the process has already
begun and the darkness is passing away (Brooke). φῶς light.
ἀληθινός true, genuine. ■ μισῶν pres. act. part. to hate. ἄρτι 9
now, at the pres. time. ■ ἀγαπῶν pres. act. part. "the one who 10
loves." μένει pres. act. ind. (s.v.6). ■ περιπατεῖ pres. act. ind. 11
to walk about, to conduct one's life. The pres. tense pictures the
pres. continual action "he is walking about." ὑπάγει pres. act.
ind. to go. The idea is not that of preceding to a definite point,
but of leaving the pres. scene (Westcott). ἐτύφλωσεν aor. act.
ind. τυφλόω to make blind, to cause to be blind, to blind. ■ 12
γράφω pres. act. ind. The pres. tense could indicate the letter
that John is now writing. (For a discussion of the views regarding
the tenses of the verbs "to write," s. Marshall; Schnackenburg.)
ὅτι. This particle used six times in vv. 12–14 could be causal
"because," or they could indicate the content of that which John
is writing, i.e., "that" (s. Schnackenburg; Marshall; Plummer).
ἀφέωνται perf. pass. ind. ἀφίημι to release, to forgive. The
perf. tense indicates that the sins have been and remain forgiven
(Stott). The pass. could be the theological pass. indicating that
God is the one who forgives the sins. διά w. the acc. "because
of." ■ ἐγνώκατε perf. act. ind. to know. The perf. indicates the 13
continuing results of the knowledge. τόν ἀπ᾽ ἀρχῆς "the one
who was from the beginning." νεανίσκος "young man." The
word could indicate either one who is young in the faith or one
who is physically young. νενικήκατε perf. act. ind. νικάω to
bring about a victory, to achieve the victory, to conquer. The

perf. tense indicates the pres. consequence of a past event
14 (Stott). ▪ ἔγραψα aor. act. ind. γράφω. The aor. could be epistolary aor. referring to the pres. letter or it could indicate a
previous writing (s.v.12). μένει pres. act. ind. to remain (s.v.6).
15   ▪ ἀγαπᾶτε pres. act. imp. κόσμος world, world system.
The word can signify mankind organized in rebellion against
God (Marshall; s. also Schnackenburg, 133–137; TDNT). ἡ
ἀγάπη τοῦ πατρός "the love of the Father." The gen. could be
subj. gen., i.e., "the love from the Father" or it could be obj. gen.,
16 i.e., "the love for the Father." ▪ ἐπιθυμία strong desire, lust,
passion. ἀλαζονεία pride, boasting arrogance. It means the
braggadocio which exaggerates what it possesses in order to
impress other people (Marshall; s. also MNTW, 38–42; Trench,
17 Synonyms, 98–102f.). ▪ παράγεται pres. mid. ind. to pass
away, pres. tense "it is in the process of passing away" (s.v.8).
ποιῶν pres. act. part.
18   ▪ παιδίον little child, dear child (s.v.1). ἀντίχριστος
Antichrist. The prep. could refer either to one who comes "instead of Christ" or one who "opposes" Christ. The lack of the
article stresses the category or quality (Schnackenburg; s. also
MT, 132). ἔρχεται pres. mid. ind. "he is coming." γεγόνασιν
perf. act. ind. γίνομαι, perf. "to have come to be," "to have
19 arisen" (Brooke). ▪ ἐξῆλθαν aor. act. ind. ἐξέρχομαι.
μεμενήκεισαν plperf. ind. act. μένω to remain (s.v.6). The
plperf. expresses the continuance of the contingent results to the
time of speaking (M, 148). The plperf. often lacks the augment
in koine (BD, 36). The ind. is used in a contrary to fact conditional clause. φανερωθῶσιν aor. pass. subj. φανερόω to manifest, to bring to light, to reveal. The subj. is used in a purpose
clause. John not only relates the fact of their departure from the
fellowship, but discerns a purpose in it. The heretics went out of
their own volition, but behind the secession was the divine purpose that they should be "made manifest." Their departing was
their "unmasking." What is counterfeit cannot remain forever
20 hidden (Stott). ▪ καί "and yet." The word has here an adversative force "but" (Marshall; BD, 227; Abbott, 135f.). χρῖσμα
anointing. The word, which expresses not the act of anointing
but that w. which it is performed, marks the connection of Chris-
21 tians w. their Head (Westcott; s. also TDNT; Marshall). ▪
ἔγραψα aor. act. ind. epistolary aor. "I am writing." ὅτι "that."
22 ▪ ψεύστης liar. εἰ μή "if not," "except." ἀρνούμενος pres. mid.
23 part. ἀρνέομαι to say no to, to deny. ▪ ὁμολογῶν pres. mid.
24 part. ὁμολογέω to agree, to confess (s. 1 John 1:9). ▪ ἠκούσατε
aor. act. ind. ἀκούω to hear, to hear and accept what has been

heard. μενέτω pres. act. imp. 3rd pers. sing. (s.v.6). μείνη aor.
act. subj. μένω. The subj. is used in a third-class conditional
clause which views the condition as possible (s. 1 John 1:6).
μενεῖτε fut. act. ind. It is significant that "remain" expresses a
continuing relationship (Marshall). ■ ἐπαγγελία announce- 25
ment, promise, pledge (s. BAG; Schnackenburg). ἐπηγγείλατο
aor. mid. ind. ἐπαγγέλλω to promise, to pledge, to pledge one's
self to do something.

■ πλανώντων pres. act. part. πλανάω to lead astray, to 26
deceive. The particle has a conative force, i.e., "trying to deceive" (Marshall). ■ ἐλάβετε aor. act. ind. λαμβάνω to receive, 27
to accept. διδάσκη pres. act. subj. The clause is used epexegetically to explain what the "need is." ἐδίδαξεν aor. act. ind.
μένετε pres. act. imp.

■ φανερωθῇ aor. pass. subj. (s.v.19). The subj. is used in a 28
third-class conditional clause and is a clear reference to the
second coming of Christ which may be at any time (RWP).
σχῶμεν aor. act. subj. ἔχω to have. The subj. is used in a
purpose clause. παρρησία speaking everything, openness, boldness, confidence. The word originally meant openness in speaking and came from the political scene. It was soon taken over
into the ethical area and was closely connected w. the concept
of friendship. Philo used the word regarding a slave who had
"openness," "confidence" w. his master when he had a good
conscience. The person who has been cleansed from sin and
continues in love also has "freedom of speech" w. his master
who is also the ruler of the whole world (Schnackenburg; s. also
TDNT; Heb. 3:6). αἰσχυνθῶμεν aor. pass. subj. αἰσχύνω to
shame, pass. to be put to shame, to be made ashamed. παρουσία
presence, coming (s. 1 Thess. 1:19; 3:13). ■ εἰδῆτε perf. act. subj. 29
οἶδα. γεγέννηται perf. pass. ind. γεννάω to bear, pass. to be
borne. The child exhibits the parents' character because he
shares the parents' nature (Stott).

Ch. 3

■ ἴδετε aor. act. imp. ὁράω to see. The verb is followed by 1
an indirect statement as a means of arousing the readers' attention (Marshall). He invites his readers to contemplate the same
truth as presented before them in an intelligent shape (Westcott). ποταπός what kind of. The word is used often of something of an admirable character (Brooke). The word means originally "of what country" and seems always to imply astonishment (Stott; Plummer). δέδωκεν perf. act. ind. δίδωμι to give.
The word signifies an unearned gift. The perf. indicates that what

they had received is permanent and abiding (Brooke; s. also Schnackenburg). **κληθῶμεν** aor. pass. subj. **καλέω** to call, pass. to be named. The subj. could be used here to express either purpose (Westcott) or results (RWP). **ἔγνω** aor. act. ind.

2 **γινώσκω**. ■ **οὔπω** not yet. **ἐφανερώγη** aor. pass. ind. **φανερόω** to make clear, to manifest, to reveal. **ἐσόμεθα** fut. **εἰμί**. **φανερωθῇ** aor. pass. subj. The subject of the verb could be either Jesus Himself or it could refer to "what we shall be" (s. Marshall; Schnackenburg; Westcott). **ὅμοιοι** like. This likeness of man redeemed and perfected to God is the likeness of the creature reflecting the glory of the Creator (Westcott). **ὀψόμεθα** fut. mid. ind. **ὁράω** to see. (For the ambiguous construction, s. Marshall.) ■ **ἔχων** pres. act. part. to have, to possess. **ἁγνίζει**

3 pres. act. ind. to purify. The word originally had a cultic meaning indicating to withdraw from the profane and to dedicate to God, i.e., "to make ceremonially ready." The term, however, also took on an ethical character (Schnackenburg; s. also TDNT). The hope of appearing before the presence of God, and of seeing Christ as He is, necessarily inspires its possessors w. the desire of putting away every defilement which clouds the vision of God (Brooke).

4   ■ **ποιῶν** pres. act. part. to do, to continue to do, to practice.
5 **ἀνομία** that which is without the law, lawlessness. ■ **ἄρη** aor. act. subj. **αἴρω** to lift up, to take away, to remove completely.
6 The subj. is used in a purpose clause (s. John 1:29). ■ **μένων** pres. act. part. **μένω**. **ἐώρακεν** perf. act. ind. **ὁράω**. The perf. would indicate to see and to experience the continual results of having seen. **ἔγνωκεν** perf. act. ind. **γινώσκω** to know. The verb "to see" lays stress on the object, which appears and is grasped by the mental vision; the verb "to know" stresses the subsequent subjective apprehension of what is grasped in the vision, or it is
7 unfolded gradually in experience (Brooke). ■ **πλανάτω** pres.
8 act. imp. **πλανάω** to lead astray, to deceive. ■ **διάβολος** devil. **ἁμαρτάνει** pres. act. ind. to sin. The pres. tense indicates continual, habitual action. **λύσῃ** aor. act. subj. **λύω** to loose, to destroy. The word suggests destruction by undoing or dissolving that which forms the bond of cohesion (Brooke). The subj. is
9 used in a purpose clause. ■ **γεγεννημένος** perf. pass. part. **γεννάω** to bear, pass. to be borne (s. 1 John 2:29). **γεγέννηται** perf. pass. ind. The perf. tense marks not only the single act of birth, but the continuous presence of its efficacy (Westcott). The v. indicates that it is the abiding influence of "His seed" within everyone who is "born of God," which enables John to affirm without fear of contradiction that "he cannot" go on living in

"sin." Indeed, "if he should thus continue in sin, it would indicate that he has never been born again" (Stott; for a discussion of this v. w. various viewpoints presented, s. Marshall). ■ 10 φανερός clear, manifest, evident, conspicuous (s. MM).

■ ἀγγελία report, message (s. 1 John 1:5). ἠκούσατε aor. 11 act. ind. ἀκούω. ἀγαπῶμεν pres. act. subj. The subj. is used in a clause explaining the "message" (s. RWP). The pres. tense would indicate a continual, habitual attitude of love. ἀλλήλους (acc. pl.) "one another." ■ χάριν τίνος "for the sake of what?" 12 "wherefore?" (RWP). ἔσφαξεν aor. act. ind. σφάζω to slaughter, to kill, to butcher, to murder. Although the word was used often of the slaying of animals particularly for sacrifice, this is not the sense here. It is used here of violent killing (s. Schnackenburg; Marshall; RWP). ■ θαυμάζετε pres. act. imp. θαυμάζω 13 to be amazed, to wonder, to marvel. The aor. tense would emphasize the immediate feeling aroused by a particular thought, or action (s. John 3:7). Here the pres. tense is used of the continuous feeling stirred up by the whole temper of men (Westcott; s. also Brooke). The verb is followed by the particle "if," "that" (s. BD, 237). μισεῖ pres. act. ind. μισέω to hate. ■ 14 μεταβεβήκαμεν perf. act. ind. μεταβαίνω to pass over from one place to another, to transfer, to migrate (RWP). The perf. tense indicates the permanency of the step of salvation (Schnackenburg). ■ μισῶν pres. act. part. ἀνθρωποκτόνος one 15 who kills a human being, murderer. μένουσαν pres. act. part. fem. sing. ■ ἐγνώκαμεν perf. act. ind. (s.v.6). ἔθηκεν aor. act. 16 ind. τίθημι to place. Used here in the Semitic sense of "to lay down one's life," "to give one's life" (s. Marshall; Brooke; Bultmann; Gaugler). ὀφείλομεν pres. act. ind. to be morally obligated (s. 1 John 2:6). θεῖναι aor. act. inf. τίθημι. ■ ἔχῃ pres. act. 17 subj. to have, to possess. βίος life, i.e., things pertaining to life, "possessions," "wealth" (Houlden; s. also Schnackenburg). θεωρῇ pres. act. subj. θεωρέω to see. ἔχοντα pres. act. part. κλείσῃ aor. act. subj. κλείω to shut up, to lock. The word perhaps suggests that a barrier has been raised against the natural human feelings which the contemplation of such cases calls out (Brooke). σπλάγχνον the inward organs, tender mercy, strong compassion (s. Phil 2:1; TDNT; MNTW, 156). ἡ ἀγάπη τοῦ θεοῦ "the love of God," i.e., God's own love—which comes and dwells in the genuine believer, and is the source of the love in the believing community (Houlden). μένει pres. act. ind. ■ 18 γλῶσσα tongue, language, speech, i.e., w. mere outward expression as opposed to the genuine movement of our whole being (Westcott).

19   ■ γνωσόμεθα fut. mid. ind. γινώσκω. ἐκ τῆς ἀληθείας
      ἐσμέν "we are from the truth," i.e., "we draw the power of our
      being from the Truth as its source" (Westcott). πείσομεν fut.
      act. ind. πείθω to persuade, to convince, to reassure, to set at
      rest, to appease (s. Marshall; Stott). καρδία heart. The word is
20   used here in the sense of "conscience" (s. Marshall). ■
      καταγινώσκῃ pres. act. subj. καταγινώσκω to know some-
      thing against someone, to condemn. μείζων comp. μέγας w. the
      gen. "greater than." Our conscience is by no means infallible; its
      condemnation may often be unjust. We can, therefore, appeal
      from our conscience to God who is greater and more knowledge-
      able. Indeed, He knows all things, including our secret motives
      and deepest resolves, and it is implied, will be more merciful
21   toward us than our own heart (Stott). ■ παρρησία openness,
22   confidence, assurance (s. 1 John 2:28). ■ αἰτῶμεν pres. act. subj.
      αἰτέω to ask, to request. τηροῦμεν pres. act. ind. to guard, to
      keep, to obey. ἀρεστός verbal adj. pleasing, here "the things
23   pleasing." ■ πιστεύσωμεν aor. act. subj. The subj. is used in a
      clause explaining what His commandment is. ἔδωκεν aor. act.
24   ind. δίδωμι to give. ■ τηρῶν pres. act. part. to observe, to hold,
      to obey. οὗ rel. pron. gen. sing. The pron. is gen. because it is
      attracted to the case of πνεύματος.

Ch. 4

1   ■ ἀλλά "but," "rather." δοκιμάζετε pres. act. imp.
      δοκιμάζω to prove by trial, to test. τὰ πνεύματα "the spirits"
      (s. 1 Cor. 12:10). (For a treatment of the word "spirit" in 1 John,
      s. Schnackenburg, 209–215.) ἐξεληλύθασιν perf. act. ind.
      ἐξέρχομαι to go out from. The perf. tense expresses the continu-
      ance of their agency as distinguished from the single fact of their
2   departure (Westcott). ■ γίνώσκετε pres. act. ind. The verb is to
      be taken as ind. rather than imp. (Marshall). ὁμολογεῖ pres. act.
      ind. to agree, to confess (s. 1 John 1:9; 2:22). ἐληλυθότα perf.
      act. part. ἔρχομαι predicate acc. of the part. used after the verb
      "to confess" (RWP; for this construction, s. also Stott; Mar-
      shall). The perf. tense indicates that the coming of Christ in the
      flesh was well-known and that the effects of the Incarnation were
3   abiding (Schnackenburg; Brooke; McKay). ■ ἀκηκόατε perf.
      act. ind. ἀκούω. ἔρχεται pres. mid. ind. The pres. tense here
4   also has a fut. implication. ■ νενικήκατε perf. act. ind. νικάω
      to conquer, to be victorious. μείζων comp. μέγας "greater."
      κόσμος world. In v. 3 the word means more the area inhabited
      by man, but in v. 4 it refers rather to sinful mankind, while in
      v. 5 the stress is more on the sinful principle found in such people

(Marshall; s. also TDNT). ■ διὰ τοῦτο "because of this." 5
ἀκούει pres. act. ind. followed by the gen. "to listen to," "to
hear." The world recognizes its own people and listens to a
message which originates in its own circle. This explains their
popularity (Stott). ■ γινώσκων pres. act. part. πλάνη error. 6
The word here can have the meaning "cause of error." (For this
and other parallels to the "spirits of truth and perversity" (s.
Marshall; Schnackenburg, 211f.; TDNT; CBB).

■ ἀγαπῶμεν pres. act. subj. cohortatory subj. "let us love." 7
ἀγαπῶν pres. act. part. γεγέννηται perf. pass. ind. γεννάω to
bear, pass. to be born. The perf. tense emphasizes the continuing
results of the new birth. ■ ἔγνω aor. act. ind. γινώσκω. (For the 8
term love and its relation to the person and nature of God, s.
Schnackenburg, 231–239; Marshall; 1 John 2:5.) ■ ἐφανερώθη 9
aor. pass. ind. to make clear, to make evident, to reveal. The
word conveys the thought of the manifestation of what was
previously hidden (Marshall). μονογενής only one of its kind,
single one, only, unique (s. Marshall; John 3:16). ἀπέσταλκεν
perf. act. ind. ἀποστέλλω to send, to send an official authoritative representative to do a specific task (s. TDNT). The perf.
indicates that God the Father sent Him and we now enjoy the
blessings of the mission (Westcott). ζήσωμεν aor. act. subj. ζάω
to live. The subj. is used in a purpose clause. ■ ἀγάπη love, i.e., 10
the quality of true love. True love is selfless (Brooke).
ἠγαπήκαμεν perf. act. ind. ἀγαπάω. The use of the perf. perhaps stresses that it is not our continuing love for God which
should be central, but the love which He revealed historically to
us in Jesus (Marshall). ἀπέστειλεν aor. act. ind. ἀποστέλλω.
The change from the perf. to the aor. stresses the historic manifestation of the love rather than the continuing effect of God's act
(Marshall). ἱλασμός satisfaction, propitiation (s. 1 John 2:2).
■ ὀφείλομεν pres. act. ind. to be morally obligated, to owe a 11
debt which must be paid, to have to do something, "we must,
ought" (s. 1 John 2:6). ■ πώποτε at any time, ever. τεθέαται 12
perf. mid. ind. θεάομαι to see, to behold (s. 1 John 1:1). Here
the thought is of the continuous beholding which answers to
abiding fellowship (Westcott). ἀγαπῶμεν pres. act. subj. The
subj. is used in a third-class conditional clause which views the
condition possible. τετελειωμένη perf. pass. part. τελειόω to
bring to completion, to bring to the goal, to perfect (s. 1 John
2:5).

■ δέδωκεν perf. act. ind. δίδωμι. The perf. emphasizes the 13
completed action w. the continuing results. ■ τεθεάμεθα perf. 14
mid. ind. (s.v.12). ἀπέσταλκεν perf. act. ind. (s.v.9). ■ 15

16 ὁμολογήσῃ aor. act. subj. (s.v.2). ■ ἐγνώκαμεν perf. act. ind. γινώσκω. The perf. tense indicates "we have come to know and still know" (Marshall). πεπιστεύκαμεν perf. act. ind. The perf. indicates that the recognition of the love of God is considered to be a lasting and settled conviction (Schnackenburg).

17 μένων pres. act. part. ■ τετελείωται perf. pass. ind. (s.v.12). παρρησία openness, confidence, assurance (s. 1 John 2:28). ἔχωμεν pres. act. subj. The subj. is used either as in a purpose clause or in apposition w. "in this" or w. the clause "because," the latter of which would make this clause a paren-

18 thesis (RWP; s. also Westcott). κρίσις judging, judgment. ■ φόβος fear. ἔξω outside, out. βάλλει pres. act. ind. to cast out, to drive out, to turn out of doors (RWP). κόλασις punishment. The word indicates the disciplinary chastisement of the wrong-doer (Westcott; s. also 2 Peter 2:9). φοβούμενος pres. mid. part.

19 φοβέομαι to be afraid, to have fear. ■ ἀγαπῶμεν pres. act. subj. cohortatory subj. "let us love." ἠγάπησεν aor. act. ind. (s.v.10).

20 ■ εἴπῃ aor. act. subj. λέγω to say. The subj. is used in a third-class conditional clause viewing the condition as a possibility. μισῇ pres. act. subj. μισέω to hate. ψεύστης liar. ἑώρακεν

21 perf. act. ind. ὁράω to see. ■ ἐντολή command.

Ch. 5

1   ■ ὅτι "that." The particle introduces the content of what is believed. γεγέννηται perf. pass. ind. γεννάω to bear, pass. to be born (s. 1 John 2:29; RAC IX, 43–171). ἀγαπῶν pres. act. part. γεννήσαντα aor. act. part. γεννάω. γεγεννημένον perf. pass. part. This new birth, which brings us into believing recognition of the eternal Son, also involves us in a loving relationship w. the Father and His other children and the part. here refers to

2 every child of God (Stott). ■ ὅταν used w. the subj. "whenever." ἀγαπῶμεν pres. act. subj. ποιῶμεν pres. act. subj. The subj. are used in an indefinite temporal clause (RWP; s. also Schnacken-

3 burg). ■ τηρῶμεν pres. act. subj. τηρέω to keep, to observe, to obey. The subj. is used in an explanatory clause which defines our love for God. βαρύς heavy, burdensome. The word suggests

4 the idea of a heavy and oppressive burden (Brooke). ■ πᾶν τὸ γεγεννημένον "everyone who has been born" perf. pass. part. n. sing. The n. phrase is possibly meant in a generalizing sense or it is possible that the use is influenced by the fact that the Gr. words for "child" are n. (Marshall). νικᾷ pres. act. ind. to con-quer, to gain a victory, to overcome. νικήσασα aor. act. part. The aor. could point to a definite act or fact (Brooke). πίστις faith. "Our faith enables us to overcome the world." It acts as

a weapon of war, and its force consists in the fact that its content
is the true nature of Jesus (Houlden). ■ νικῶν pres. act. part. εἰ 5
μή "except," "if not."

■ ἐλθών aor. act. part. ἔρχομαι. αἷμα blood. Perhaps the 6
best explanation of the meaning of the term here is that it refers
to the bloody death upon the cross (s. Plummer; Westcott; Marshall; Brooke). μαρτυροῦν pres. act. part. μαρτυρέω to be a
witness, to testify. ■ τρεῖς three. μαρτυροῦντες pres. act. part. 7
(For a discussion of the textual problem in vv. 7 and 8, s. TC,
716–718.) ■ μείζων comp. μέγας "greater." In John 5:36 the 9
word indicates the greater credence, in 1 John 5:9 it indicates the
stronger, obligating power of the divine witness (Schnackenburg). μεμαρτύρηκεν perf. act. ind. μαρτυρέω to be a witness,
to bear witness, to testify. ■ πιστεύων pres. act. part. The verb 10
constructed w. the dat. usually expresses acceptance of the statement rather than surrender to the person (Brooke). πεποίηκεν
perf. act. ind. πεπίστευκεν perf. act. ind. The perf. tenses indicate the abiding affects. ■ ἔδωκεν aor. act. ind. δίδωμι. ■ ἔχων 11/12
pres. act. part. to have, to possess. The pres. tense of the verb
indicates continual possession (s. M, 110). The word is used to
describe our personal possession of the Father through confessing the Son (Stott).

■ ἔγραψα aor. act. ind. γράφω to write. The word could 13
be epistolary aor. referring to the whole epistle or it could refer
to the immediately preceding section either vv. 1–12 or vv. 5–12
(s. Marshall). εἰδῆτε perf. act. subj. οἶδα to know. The subj. is
used in a purpose clause. ■ παρρησία openness, confidence (s. 14
1 John 2:28). ἐάν τι "whatever," "if we ask anything." The
particle introduces a third-class conditional clause (RWP).
αἰτώμεθα pres. mid. ind. αἰτέω to ask, to request. ἀκούει pres.
act. ind. ■ ἐάν "if." The particle is used w. the ind. in a first-class 15
conditional clause and has almost a causal sense (s. BD, 189; MT
115f.; RWP). αἴτημα that which is asked, request. ᾐτήκαμεν
perf. act. ind. αἰτέω to ask, to request.

■ ἴδῃ aor. act. subj. ὁράω. The subj. is used in a third-class 16
conditional clause which views the condition as a possibility.
ἁμαρτάνοντα pres. act. part. (For a discussion of the "sin unto
death," s. Stott; Westcott; Marshall.) αἰτήσει fut. act. ind.
δώσει fut. act. ind. δίδωμι to give. ἁμαρτάνουσιν pres. act.
part. dat. pl. ἐρωτήσῃ aor. act. subj. ἐρωτάω to ask about, to
request information about (s. Westcott). ■ ἀδικία unrighteous- 17
ness.

■ γεγεννημένος perf. pass. part. (s.v.1). γεννηθείς aor. 18
pass. part. γεννάω (s.v.1). πονηρός evil, mean. The word refers

to active evil (s. TDNT; Trench, *Synonyms*, 315f.). ἅπτεται
pres. mid. ind. ἅπτω w. the gen. to touch. The verb means to
19 lay hold of someone in order to harm him (Marshall). ■ ὅλος
whole, total. κεῖται pres. mid. ind. of the defective verb κεῖμαι
20 to lie (RWP). ■ ἥκει pres. act. ind. "to have come." δέδωκεν
perf. act. ind. (s.v.11). διάνοια knowing, understanding. The
faculty of knowing or discerning seems to be what it expresses.
It is the ability to reason correctly and was used in Gr. philosophy of syllogistic reasoning (Brooke; Westcott; GPT, 37).
γινώσκωνεν pres. act. subj. The subj. is used in a purpose clause.
ἀληθινός true, genuine. οὗτος "this one." The pron. clearly
21 refers to Jesus (s. Marshall). ■ φυλάξατε aor. act. imp.
φυλάσσω to guard, to keep. The use of the act. w. the reflex.
may be regarded as emphasizing the duty of personal effort
(Westcott). εἴδωλον image, idol, false god. The presence of idols
in the ancient world is witnessed to not only by the geographical
description of Strabo and Pausanias, but also in literature, art,
theater, music, and the various archeological discoveries (s. Acts
17:16).

2 JOHN

ἐκλεκτός verbal adj. ἐκλέγω to choose out, to select, elect, 1 chosen, choice (s. 1 Peter 1:1). The phrase "to the elect lady" could refer to a specific person or it could be a personification indicating some local church (Stott; s. also Westcott; Marshall). τοῖς τέκνοις αὐτῆς "to her children." This would refer to the members of the church (Marshall). ἐγνωκότες perf. act. part. γινώσκω. The perf. tense emphasizes the continuing results of having known. ■ ἀλήθεια truth. Here the word refers to the 2 divine reality and signifies what is ultimately real, namely, God Himself. Hence, it can refer to the expression of God in His incarnate Son and in the Christian message (Schnackenburg; Marshall). μένουσαν pres. act. part. μένω to remain. ἔσται fut. εἰμί. ■ ἔλεος mercy (s. 1 Tim. 1:2). 3

■ ἐχάρην aor. pass. ind. χαίρω to rejoice, to be glad. The 4 aor. is not epistolary, but refers back to the time when the elder met the members of the church (Marshall). λίαν greatly, very much, very. ὅτι "that." The word introduces not only the content of the rejoicing but also gives the reason for rejoicing (Bultman). εὕρηκα perf. act. ind. εὑρίσκω to find. The perf. tense strongly suggests personal experience (Marshall). περιπατοῦντας pres. act. part. περιπατέω to walk about, to conduct one's life. καθώς just as. The sentence introduced by this word explains how the walk of these church members can be called a "walk in the truth" (Schnackenburg). ἐλάβομεν aor. act. ind. λαμβάνω to receive. ■ ἐρωτῶ pres. act. ind. to ask, to 5 request. γράφων pres. act. part. καινός new, new in quality (s. 1 John 2:7). εἴχομεν perf. act. ind. ἔχω to have. ἀγαπῶμεν pres. act. subj. The subj. is used in a clause describing the content of the request. ■ ἀγάπη love. Love means living according to 6 the Father's commands (Marshall). περιπατῶμεν pres. act. subj. (s.v.4). The subj. is used in a clause explaining what the "commandment" is. ἠκούσατε aor. act. ind. ἀκούω. ■ πλάνος 7 deceiver, one who leads to wrong action and not only to wrong opinion (Westcott). ἐξῆλθον aor. act. ind. ἐξέρχομαι to go out. ὁμολογοῦντες pres. act. part. ὁμολογέω to agree to, to profess.

The verb is used w. the double acc. and has to do w. the messianic character of Jesus, and John uses the words in order to correct faulty or inadequate messianic ideas current in his time (ECC,
8　105). ἐρχόμενον pres. mid. part. ■ βλέπετε pres. act. imp. to see, to beware, to watch out. ἀπολέσητε aor. act. subj. ἀπόλλυμι to lose, to suffer loss. ἠργασάμεθα aor. mid. ind. ἐργάζομαι to work. μισθός pay. The metaphor seems to be taken from the payment of labor since this word refers to a workman's wage (Stott). πλήρης full, complete. ἀπολάβητε aor. act. subj. ἀπολαμβάνω to take away, to receive. The word
9　was used in the papyri of "receiving" what is due (MM). ■ προάγων pres. act. part. προάγω to go before, to run ahead. Perhaps this is a sarcastic reference to the way in which the false teachers themselves proudly claim to be offering "advanced" teaching; the elder claims that they have "advanced" beyond the
10　boundaries of true Christian belief (Marshall). ■ λαμβάνετε pres. act. imp. to receive, to show hospitality to. It was common in the ancient world to receive traveling teachers in the home and offer them shelter and lodging. χαίρειν pres. act. inf. to give greeting. The giving of greetings indicates entering in to fellowship w. the one greeted and to welcome a false teacher was to express solidarity w. them (Schnackenburg; Marshall). The inf. is used in indirect discourse as the object of the verb "to say." λέγετε pres. act. ind. to speak, to say. Used here in connection w. the inf. to mean "to give greeting." John's instruction may relate not only to an official visit of false teachers, but to the extending to them of an official welcome rather than merely
11　private hospitality (Stott). ■ ὁ λέγων pres. act. part. "the one saying," "the one who says." κοινωνεῖ pres. act. ind. to have fellowship, to share in (s. 1 John 1:3).
12　　■ ἔχων pres. act. part. The part. is used in a concessive sense "although I have." ἐβουλήθην aor. pass. ind. βούλομαι to will, to want to. χάρτης paper. The word was a leaf of papyrus prepared for writing by cutting the pith into stripes and pasting together (RWP). μέλας black, black ink. γενέσθαι aor. mid. inf. γίνομαι. The inf. is used to present the content of the hope. λαλῆσαι aor. act. inf. λαλέω. πεπληρωμένη perf. pass. part. πληρόω to make full, to fulfill, to complete (s. 1 John 1:4).
13　　■ ἀσπάζεται pres. mid. ind. to greet.

3 JOHN

ἀγαπητός verbal adj. one who is loved, beloved. The name 1
"Gaius" was a very prominent name in the Roman Empire and
occurs several times in the NT (e.g., Acts 19:29; 1 Cor. 1:4) (s.
Plummer; Brooke). We do not know who this Gaius was but it
is clear from the terms in which John writes that he occupied a
position of responsibility and leadership in the local church
(Stott).

■ ἀγαπητέ voc. περὶ πάντων "in all respects" (Marshall). 2
The phrase is to be taken w. the inf. "to prosper." The writer
prays for the prosperity of Gaius in all respects and the thought
may be of the public and social work of Gaius as well as his
personal health (Brooke; Westcott). εὔχομαι pres. mid. ind. to
pray, to wish (s. Marshall). σέ "you" acc. sing. used as the
"subject" or the inf. εὐδοδῦσθαι pres. pass. inf., pass. "to be lead
along a good road," i.e., "to get along well," "to prosper," "to
succeed" (BAG; s. also MM). The inf. is used in indirect discourse as object of the verb "to pray," "to wish." ὑγιαίνειν pres.
act. inf. to be well, to be in good health. It was a common
greeting and desire expressed in letters for the recipient to be in
good health (s. LAE, 187f.; Schnackenburg; MM; CBB; TDNT;
for the general concept of health and well-being in the ancient
world, s. RAC X, 902–945). καθώς "just as." The wish is that
Gaius' outward prosperity may correspond to the condition of
his soul (Schnackenburg). ■ ἐχάρην aor. pass. ind. χαίρω to be 3
happy, to rejoice, to be glad. λίαν very, exceedingly.
ἐρχομένων pres. mid. part. μαρτυρούντων pres. act. part. The
part. are causal but the temporal element of concurrent action
is also present. The pres. part. indicate repetition and show that
several visits had been paid to the elder, possibly by different
groups of Christians (Marshall). ἀλήθεια truth (s. 2 John 2).
περιπατεῖς pres. act. ind. to walk about, to conduct one's life.
The pres. tense indicates continual action. ■ μειζότερος comp. 4
of the comp. μείζων from μέγας. Used w. the gen. w. the
meaning "greater than." The koine has a number of the popular
new formations of double comp. and double superl. (s. BD, 33f.).

περιπατοῦντα pres. act. part. The pres. tense indicates the continual habitual conducting of one's life.

5   ■ ἀγαπητέ voc. ἐργάσῃ aor. mid. subj. 2nd pers. sing. ἐργάζομαι to work. The use of the rel. pron. "whatever" w. the subj. is indefinite and implies an unspecified number of ways or occasions of helping the brothers (Marshall; s. also Gal. 6:10; Col. 3:23). ξένος stranger. The fact that brethren who were strangers were helped is emphasized by the use of the acc. of general reference "and that too" (RWP; Westcott; Plummer).

6   ■ ἐμαρτύρησαν aor. act. ind. (s.v.3). The dat. is used to express the object of the witness, i.e., the thing to which one testifies. ἐνώπιον in the presence of. The absence of the article w. the word "church" denotes a meeting of the church at which the witness was borne (Brooke). καλῶς adv. well. ποιήσεις fut. act. ind. The expression "you will do well" is an idiom that means "please," "kindly," and was used often in the papyri to express a polite request (MM; Marshall). προπέμψας aor. act. part. προπέμπω to send forth, to send someone on their way. The sending of missionaries on their way involved providing for their journey—supplying them w. food and money to pay for their expenses, washing their clothes and generally helping them to travel as comfortably as possible (Marshall; s. also BAG; Acts 15:3; 1 Cor. 16:6, 11; 2 Cor. 1:16; Titus 3:13). (For a study regarding the support of wandering ministers and missionaries in the early church, s. Gerd Theissen, "Legitimation und Leben-sunterhalt: Ein Beitrag zur Soziologie Urchristlicher Missionäre," NTS 21 [Jan., 1975], 192–221.) ἀξίως adv. followed by the gen. "worthily," "worthily of God," i.e., "worthily of their

7   dedication to the service of God" (Westcott). ■ ἐξῆλθαν aor. act. ind. ἐξέρχομαι to go out, i.e., to go out from the church (or from God) into the world, regarded as a field for evangelism (Marshall). λαμβάνοντες pres. act. part. The pres. tense indi- cates habitual and customary action. It was their custom to carry out the spirit of the commission to the Twelve and to the tradi- tion established by Paul. They had, therefore, a special claim on hospitality and help of the churches in places through which they had to pass (Brooke; s. also Westcott). ἐθνικός pagan, heathen. That these missionaries were supported by fellow Christians stands in marked contrast both to the wandering philosophers of the day as well as the beggar priests of the Syrian goddess who went out on behalf of the goddess and returned triumphantly boasting that "each journey brought in seventy

8   bags" (LAE, 109; s. also Bultmann; Schnackenburg). ■ ὀφείλομεν pres. act. ind. to be morally obligated, to owe a debt.

ὑπολαμβάνειν pres. act. inf. to take up under in order to raise, to bear on high, to take up and carry away, to receive hospitality, to welcome, to support. The word is often used in the sense of "receiving" w. hospitality, and esp. of "supporting" (T; Brooke). Christians should finance Christian enterprises which the world will not, or should not be asked to, support. Indeed, Christians have an obligation to do so. They "must" support their brethren to whom the world should not be asked to contribute (Stott). τοιοῦτος such ones. συνεργός fellow-worker. As sharers in the truth themselves, they must prove to be fellow-workers in practice and are to work together w. the missionaries for the benefit of the truth (Marshall). ἀλήθεια truth. The dat. could mean either "fellow-workers w. the truth" or "on behalf of, for the truth" (s. Schnackenburg).

■ ἔγραψα aor. act. ind. γράφω. φιλοπρωτεύων pres. act. 9 part. φιλοπρωτεύω to be fond of the first position, to wish to be first, to like to be the leader. The word expresses ambition, the desire to have the first place in everything (BAG; Brooke). The pres. tense indicates the continual and habitual attitude. ἐπιδέχεται pres. mid. ind. to accept, to receive gladly. The word can mean either "to accept the authority of" or "to welcome." The pl. "us" will refer to the elder and his associates (Marshall). The pres. tense again indicates a continuing attitude. ■ 10 ὑπομνήσω fut. act. ind. ὑπομιμνῄσκω to call to memory, to remind. φλυαρῶν pres. act. part. φλυαρέω to talk nonsense (about), to bring unjustified charges against. The word emphasizes the emptiness of the charges (s. BAG; MM; Brooke; 1 Tim. 5:13). ἀρκούμενος pres. mid. part. ἀρκέω to be enough, to be satisfied. βουλομένους pres. mid. part. βούλομαι to want to, to desire to. κωλύει pres. act. ind. to forbid. ἐκβάλλει pres. act. ind. to throw out, to put out. The verbs in the pres. tense here may be conative i.e., "he is trying to" (Westcott; but s. also Marshall; Schnackenburg).

■ μιμοῦ pres. mid. imp. μιμέομαι to mimic, to imitate. 11 ἀγαθοποιῶν pres. act. part. to do good. κακοποιῶν pres. act. part. to do evil. ἑώρακεν perf. act. ind. ὁράω to see. ■ 12 μεμαρτύρηται perf. pass. ind. (s.v.3).

■ γράψαι aor. act. inf. The aor. expresses the writing of a 13 single letter containing what the writer felt obliged to say. The pres. inf. indicates the continuation of the pres. letter (Marshall). μέλας black, ink. The ink used was a writing fluid whose chief ingredient was soot or black carbon. It was mixed w. gum or oil for use on parchment, or w. a metallic substance for use on papyrus (ZPEB II, 279). κάλαμος reed, reed pen used for writ-

14 ing (Marshall; Brooke). ■ εὐθέως immediately, soon. ἰδεῖν aor.
   act. inf. ὁράω to see. στόμα mouth. Here used in the expression
15 "face to face." λαλήσομεν fut. act. ind. λαλέω. ■ ἀσπάζονται
   pres. mid. ind. ἀσπάζου pres. mid. imp. ἀσπάζομαι to greet.
   (For the form of 2 and 3 John in relation to ancient letter writing,
   s. Robert W. Funk, "The Form and Structure of Second and
   Third John," JBL 86 [Dec., 1967], 424–430; s. also Joseph A.
   Fitzmyer, "Some Notes on Aramaic Epistolography," JBL 93
   [June, 1974], 201–225.)

JUDE

ἠγαπημένοις perf. pass. part. ἀγαπάω to love. The perf. 1
tense suggests that they were not only once but continued to be
the objects of God's love and care (Kelly). τετηρημένοις perf.
pass. part. τηρέω to keep safe, to guard, to watch over. The verb
used in a friendly sense means "to keep safe from harm," "to
preserve." The word expresses the watchful care given to someone (Mayor; T). The perf. tense emphasizes the continuing
watch care. κλητός verbal adj. "called." ■ ἔλεος mercy, pity (s. 2
1 Tim. 1:2). πληθυνθείη aor. pass. opt. πληθύνω to multiply,
to increase. The opt. is used to express a wish (s. 1 Peter 1:2).

■ σπουδή haste, diligence, effort, earnestness. ποιούμενος 3
pres. mid. part. to make, to do. The verb was used in connection
w. a noun to build the verbal idea found in the noun (s. M, 159).
κοινός common, that which all believers share commonly (s. 1
John 1:3). ἀνάγκη compulsion, necessity. ἔσχον aor. act. ind.
ἔχω to have, aor. "to receive." (For the distinction between the
pres. tense "to have" and the aor. tense "to get, to receive," s.
M, 110; Kelly.) γράψαι aor. act. inf. The aor. contrasted w. the
preceding pres. inf. implies that the new epistle had to be written
at once and could not be prepared for at leisure, like the one he
had previously contemplated (Mayor). The inf. is used epexegetically to explain the "necessity." παρακαλῶν pres. act.
part. παρακαλέω to urge, to encourage, to beseech. It is the
word used of speeches of leaders and of soldiers who urge each
other on. It is the word used of words which sent fearful and
timorous and hesitant soldiers and sailors courageously into battle (MNTW, 134; s. also Rom. 12:1). ἐπαγωνίζεσθαι pres. mid.
inf. to struggle for, to contend for, to exercise great effort and
exertion for something. The word was used of athletic contests
and the struggle and effort of the athletes in their games (s. Kelly;
1 Cor. 9:24–27). The prep. in compound denotes direction (MH,
312) and the word following in the dat. denotes the cause on
behalf of which one fights (Kelly). The inf. is used as the object
of the verb "to exhort." ἅπαξ "once for all" (s. Mayor).
παραδοθείσῃ aor. pass. part. παραδίδωμι to deliver over, to

803

hand down, to commit and entrust. The word is used for handing down authorized tradition in Israel (s. 1 Cor. 15:1-3; 2 Thess. 3:6), and Jude is therefore saying that the Christian apostolic tradition is normative for the people of God (Green). πίστει dat. sing. faith. The word here indicates the body of truth and the dat. is to be related to the verb "to struggle for" (s. Kelly).

4 ■ παρεισεδύησαν aor. act. ind. παρεισδύομαι to slip in along side of, secretly. (For this sinister and secretive word, s. Green; Gal. 2:4; 2 Peter 2:1.) πάλαι long ago. προγεγραμμένοι perf. pass. part. προγράφω to write down beforehand, to write down previously, i.e., "written before in God's book of judgment." The word is intended to show that they are already doomed to punishment as enemies of God (Mayor; s. also Kelly; SB II, 173). The perf. tense indicates the continuing authority of that which was written (s. MM). κρίμα that which was decided upon, judgment. ἀσεβής ungodly, impious (s. 2 Peter 2:5; 3:7). μετατιθέντες pres. act. part. to transpose, to change from one place to another, to transfer. The pres. tense could be conative, i.e., "they are trying to change." ἀσέλγεια unbridled living (s. 1 Peter 2:16; 2 Peter 2:19). ἀρνούμενοι pres. mid. part. ἀρνέομαι to say no to, to deny.

5 ■ ὑπομνῆσαι aor. act. inf. ὑπομιμνήσκω to cause someone to remember, to remind. εἰδότας perf. act. part. οἶδα to know. The part. could be concessive "although you know" and this justifies the reminder. They only need to be reminded of truths already known, so that it is unnecessary to write at length (Mayor; s. also Schelkle). λαός people. The word is used without the article, i.e., "a people" indicating that not all the ones who left Egypt were believers (s. Green). σώσας aor. act. part. σῴζω to rescue, to deliver, to save. The part. is used temporally "after he saved." τὸ δεύτερον "the second time." The phrase could mean "the next time" or as an adverbial acc. "afterwards." Here the word marks a strong contrast and sharpens the point of the warning (Bigg; s. also Green; RWP; Kelly). πιστεύσαντας aor. act. part. ἀπώλεσεν aor. act. ind. ἀπόλλυμι to ruin, to destroy.

6 ■ τηρήσαντας aor. act. part. to keep, to guard. (s.v.1). ἀρχή dominion, office, authority. The word could indicate either the office of the angels or their domain, i.e., sphere of rule, or it could indicate the spiritual state in which they were created, i.e., they were made different from humanity but did not maintain this original state, rather they left their own habitation (s. Kelly; Mayor; Green). ἀπολιπόντας aor. act. part. ἀπολείπω to leave, to desert, to leave behind, to forsake. οἰκητήριον place of living, dwelling place. The ending of the word indicates the

place of action (s. MH, 343; RG, 154). κρίσις judging. δεσμός
band, bond, chain. ἀΐδιος eternal, everlasting. ζόφος darkness,
gloom (s. 2 Peter 2:7). τετήρηκεν perf. act. ind. to guard, to
keep. The word is used here in a neg. sense w. a punitive meaning, i.e., "to keep in custody" (s.v.1; Mayor). ■ ὅμοιος like, 7
similar. τρόπος manner. The phrase is a verbal acc. meaning
"likewise," "in like manner." τούτοις masc. dat. pl. "to these,"
"w. these." Since the word is masc., it cannot refer to the cities
"Sodom and Gomorrah" (Kelly) and evidently refers to the
"angels" of v. 6. It was a common understanding among many
of the Jewish rabbis that the beings referred to in Gen. 6 were
angelic beings (s. SB III, 780). ἐκπορνεύσασαι aor. act. part.
ἐκπορνεύω to indulge in excessive immorality. The prep. in
compound may be intensive (s. T) or it may suggest that this
immorality was "against the course of nature" (Green).
ἀπελθοῦσαι aor. act. part. ἀπέρχομαι to go after. ὀπίσω
behind, after. The participial phrase would emphasize their bent
and determination for unnatural sexual acts and the prep. in
compound indicates the turning aside from the right way (Huther). πρόκεινται pres. mid. ind. to lie before, to be exposed to
public view. The word was used of a corpse lying in state (BAG).
δεῖγμα example, sample. The word was used in the papyri of
samples of corn or wheat (MM). These are laid out before all as
a sample or warning of judgment (s. Bigg). πῦρ fire. αἰώνιος
eternal, everlasting. The pres. tense of the verb and the adj.
"everlasting" are intended to impress on readers that the appall-
ing effects of the catastrophe are still visible for all to see and
note w. dread (Kelly). δίκη punishment. Here it would indicate
a judicial sentence passed by a judge (s. MM). ὑπέχουσαι pres.
act. part. ὑπέχω to undergo, to suffer. The word was a legal t.t.
meaning "to undergo punishment" (BAG; s. also MM).
   ■ ὁμοίως adv. "likewise." This introduces the comparison 8
between examples that they knew about and the spiritual spies
about whom he is writing. μέντοι "notwithstanding," i.e., "in
spite of the dreadful fate of the three groups just mentioned"
(Kelly). ἐνυπνιαζόμενοι pres. mid. part. ἐνυπνιάζω to dream.
The word may indicate that in the false teachers' delusion and
their blindness, they take the real for the unreal and the unreal
for the real (Mayor) which would emphasize their false source
of revelation, but the word may also stress the fact that they are
asleep to God's judgment and entertained by the temporal allu-
sive and imaginary character of the pleasures of their lusts.
μιαίνουσιν pres. act. ind. to stain, to defile. The word often is
used of moral defilement or pollution (s. Kelly). The pres. tense

of the part. indicates a continual habitual action. κυριότης lordship, authority. The word indicates the majestic power that a lord uses in ruling (s. BAG). ἀθετοῦσιν pres. act. ind. to set aside, to do away w., to nullify, to not recognize as valid, to despise (s. Mayor; Gal. 2:21). δόξαι "glorious ones." The word refers here to angelic beings. They are the angels, whom they blaspheme by supposing that they had created the world in opposition to the will of the true God (Mayor; s. also Kelly). βλασφημοῦσιν pres. act. ind. to revile, to defame, to blaspheme. ▪ ἀρχάγγελος archangel. The Jews considered Michael to be the highest among the angels and to be the representative of God (s. SB III, 831). διάβολος devil. διακρινόμενος pres. mid. part. διακρίνομαι to take issue w., to dispute (s. Acts 11:2; James 1:6). διελέγετο impf. mid. ind. διαλέγομαι to argue, to dispute. The impf. pictures the continuous action in the past time. ἐτόλμησεν aor. act. ind. τολμάω to dare. ἐπενεγκεῖν aor. act. inf. ἐπιφέρω to bring upon, to pronounce. βλασφημιά railing, blasphemy. Michael did not dare to pronounce a judgment of reproach upon Satan. ἐπιτιμήσαι aor. act. opt. ἐπιτιμάω to rebuke. This was a word of command used by Jesus that brought the hostile powers under control (s. Matt. 17:18). The opt. is used in a wish. ▪ ὅσος how much, how great, which things. φυσικῶς naturally, by instinct (s. 2 Peter 2:12). ἄλογος without reason, without rationality (s. 2 Peter 2:12). ζῷον living creature, animal (s. 2 Peter 2:12). ἐπίστανται pres. mid. ind. ἐπίσταμαι to understand. φθείρονται pres. pass. ind. φθείρω to corrupt, to ruin, to destroy. The natural antithesis here would have been "these things they admire and delight in." For this Jude substitutes by a stern irony "these things are their ruin" (Mayor; for this word, s. 2 Peter 1:4; 2:12). ▪ οὐαί "woe." The word is an imprecation of doom which is found in 1 Corinthians 9:16, frequently in the gospels, and repeatedly in 1 Enoch (esp. XCIV-C) (Kelly). ἐπορεύθησαν aor. pass. ind. πορεύομαι to go, to travel along. The word is used to indicate a manner of life. πλάνη error, wandering (s. 1 John 1:8). μισθός wage, reward, pay. The gen. is gen of price "for pay or gain." They were like Balaam greedy for money (Green). ἐξεχύθησαν aor. pass. ind. ἐκχέω to pour out. The pass. is used to express either the outward sweeping movement of a great crowd, or the surrender to an overwhelming motive on the part of an individual (Mayor). ἀντιλογία speaking against, hostility, rebellion. ἀπώλοντο aor. mid. ind. ἀπόλλυμι to perish. The aor. tense is a dramatic way of saying that their fate is already settled (Kelly). So in these three pen pictures from the OT we see three leading characteristics of the errorists. Like Cain, they were devoid of love. Like Balaam, they were prepared in return for money to teach others that sin did not matter. Like Korah, they were careless of the ordinances of God and insubordinate to church leaders (Green). ■ οὗτοι εἰσιν "these are." The same phrase 12 reoccurs in vv. 16 and 19 and begins an independent description of the false teachers in which sections of each statement is balanced by something said on the other side, which is introduced w. a conj. "but" (s. Green; Alford). σπιλάς spot (s. 2 Peter 2:13). The better meaning here is "hidden rocks." The word was used to denote rocks in the sea close to shore and covered w. water and so were dangerous to vessels (Kelly; s. also Mayor). συνευωχούμενοι pres. mid. part. συνευωχέομαι to come together to have a feast, to eat a feast together (s. 2 Peter 2:13). The meaning here is that at these meals the false teachers are liable to undermine the faith and decent comportment of their fellow Christians much as submerged reefs can wreck shipping (Kelly). ἀφόβως adv. without fear, fearless, without respect. ποιμαίνοντες pres. act. part. ποιμαίνω to shepherd, to care for as a shepherd. Here the sense is "to fatten, to indulge" (Mayor). νεφέλη cloud. ἄνυδρος waterless, without water. παραφερόμεναι pres. pass. part. παραφέρω to carry-by. The picture here is that of clouds being blown by and passing on without bringing the long hoped for and refreshing rains. The suggestion is that the errorists are all show and no substance; they have nothing to give to those who are so foolish as to listen to them (Kelly). φθινοπωρινός belonging to late autumn. The word describes trees such as they are at the close of autumn, dry, leafless, w. bare branches w. all growth sapped at the approach of winter and without fruit (T; Kelly). ἄκαρπος without fruit, fruitless. Late autumn would be toward the end of the harvest and the picture here is that harvest had come and was almost gone but these trees had no fruit on them. They were worthless and disappointing. δίς twice. ἀποθανόντα aor. act. part. ἀποθνήσκω to die, to be dead. The trees were "twice dead" in the sense of being sterile and then of being actually lifeless (Kelly). ἐκριζωθέντα aor. pass. part. ἐκριζόω to uproot. Such trees were commonly torn up by the roots and disposed of by burning, and the uprooting of trees is a favorite OT metaphor of judgment (Ps. 53:5; Prov. 2:22) (Kelly; Green). ■ κῦμα wave. 13 ἄγριος untamed, wild. ἐπαφρίζοντα pres. act. part. ἐπαφρίζω to foam up, to cause to splash like foam. The word refers to the seaweed and other refuse borne on the crest of the waves and thrown up on the beach, to which are compared the overflowings

of ungodliness (Mayor; s. also Isa. 57:20). αἰσχύνη shame.
ἀστήρ star. πλανήτης wandering. The figure of the "wandering star" is used in the Book of Enoch (s. Enoch 43, 44, 18, etc.)
and describes shooting stars which fall out of the sky and are
engulfed in darkness (Mayor; Green). τετήρηται perf. pass. ind.
τηρέω (s.v.6).

14   ■ ἐπροφήτευσεν aor. act. ind. προφητεύω to deliver the
message of a prophet, to speak forth, to prophesy. ἕβδομός the
seventh. In Genesis 5:21 Enoch is listed as the seventh after
Adam and is designated as the seventh from Adam in Enoch
60:8; 93:3; Jubilees 7:39 (s. Mayor; Green). μυριάς myriad, ten
thousand. This refers to the angels who accompany God, esp. in
15   judgment (Kelly). ■ ποιῆσαι aor. act. inf. This verb is used w.
the noun to form a verbal idea contained in the noun, i.e., lit. "to
make judgment," "to do judgment" (s.v.3). The inf. is used to
express purpose. ἐλέγξαι aor. act. inf. ἐλέγχω to convict. The
inf. is used to express purpose. ἀσέβεια godless, irreverence
(s.v.4). ἠσέβησαν aor. act. ind. ἀσεβέω to conduct an irreligious life, to be ungodly. σκληρός hard, harsh. The word conveys always a reproach and a grave one, it indicates a character
of harsh inhumane and uncivil (Trench, Synonyms, 48).
ἐλάλησαν aor. act. ind. ἁμαρτωλός sinful sinner. Jude's quotation from Enoch (Enoch 1:9) does not mean that the Book of
Enoch was regarded as inspired or equal w. Scripture. An inspired man might well use contemporary ideas which were not
contrary to revelation (Green, 49; for a study of the comparison
between Enoch 1:9 and the quotation in Jude, s. Carroll D.
Osborne, "The Christological Use of I Enoch I.9 in Jude 14, 15,"
16   NTS 23 [April, 1977], 334–341). ■ γογγυστής one who grum-
bles, one who murmurs and complains (s. 1 Cor. 10:10; Phil.
2:14). μεμψίμοιρος complaining of one's lot, to grumble about
one's condition in life. The word was used to describe a standard
Gr. character: "You're satisfied by nothing that befalls you; you
complain at everything. You don't want what you have got; you
long for what you haven't got. In winter you wish it were summer, and in summer that it were winter. You are like the sick
folk, hard to please, and one who complains about his lot in life"
(s. Green's quotation from Lucian, Cynic, XVII). The word indicates one who complained against God who has appointed each
man his fate (TDNT; s. also MM). ἐπιθυμία strong desire, lust,
passion. πορευόμενοι pres. mid. part. (s.v.11). ὑπέρογκος
excessive size, puffed up, swollen. The word is generally used of
great or even excessive size, and in later writers it is also used
of "big" words, arrogant speech and demeanor (Mayor).

θαυμάζοντες pres. act. part. θαυμάζω to marvel, to wonder, to admire. The expression is used to translate the Heb. idiom "to take, or raise, a man's countenance," i.e., do honor or show favor to him. The formula had its origin in the oriental custom of making one to rise from the ground in token of welcome. This imagery soon disappeared and the expression meant "to show favoritism toward" or "to curry favor w." (Kelly). ὠφέλεια profit, gain, advantage. χάριν w. the gen. "on account of," "for the sake of."

■ μνήσθητε aor. pass. imp. μιμνήσκομαι to remember, 17 to recall to memory. προειρημένων perf. pass. part. προλέγω to say beforehand, to speak prior, to the events predicted, to foretell (Kelly). The perf. tense indicates the lasting result of the prediction. ■ ἔλεγον impf. ind. act. The impf. is customary 18 "they used to say," or it pictures the interat. action, i.e., "they continued to say from time to time." ἔσονται fut. εἰμί. ἐμπαίκτης one who makes fun by mocking, mocker, scoffer (s. 2 Peter 3:3). ἀσέβεια godlessness (s.v.4). ■ ἀποδιορίζοντες 19 pres. act. part. ἀποδιορίζω to make a boundary between someone and to separate from this one, to make a distinction, to make a division, to cause division. The word would indicate to make divisive distinctions between themselves and other people (Green). It could also mean that by their ungodly living they divide those in the assembly and some were being or about to be taken by their error. ψυχικός worldly minded. The word implies that these men follow their natural lusts and appetites without restraint or control. ἔχοντες pres. act. part. ἔχω to have, to possess. These do not have the Spirit of God and therefore live unrestrained lives. ■ ἐποικοδομοῦντες pres. act. part. 20 ἐποικοδομέω to build up, to edify. The part. could express the means or the manner of "guarding one's self" and expresses contemporaneous time. ἁγιώτατος superl. most holy, holiest. The superl. is used w. an elative force "very holy" (s. MT, 31). The "most holy faith" would be the body of truth or faith which has been once delivered to the saints (s.v.3) upon which one is to build his life. προσευχόμενοι pres. mid. part. προσεύχομαι to pray. The Christian must not only study the Scriptures if he is to grow in the faith and be of use to others, but he must also "pray in the Spirit" for the battle against false teaching is not won by argument (Green). ■ τηρήσατε aor. act. imp. (s.v.1). 21 προσδεχόμενοι pres. mid. part. προσδέχομαι to earnestly expect, to look forward to, to wait for. The part. expresses contemporary action and could be temporal, i.e., "while you are awaiting." τὸ ἔλεος "the mercy." ■ ἐλεᾶτε pres. act. imp. 22

ἐλεάω to show pity, to be merciful. (For the textual problems in vv. 22 and 23, s. TC, 727ff.) διακρινομένους pres. mid. part. to dispute (s.v.9). The word may also have the meaning "to doubt," "to waiver," and the meaning might be "show pity on the waiv-
23 erers" (Green). ■ σῴζετε pres. act. imp. to rescue, to save. ἁρπάζοντες pres. act. part. ἁρπάζω to seize, to snatch. The figure of snatching them from fire may have been suggested by the allusion to the punishment of Sodom and Gomorrah (Mayor). μισοῦντες pres. act. part. μισέω to hate. ἐσπιλωμένον perf. pass. part. σπιλόω to stain, to defile, to contaminate. The perf. tense emphasizes the state or result. χιτών the garment which was worn next to the body, i.e., undergarment. Then it referred to any garment. The idea seems to be that they are so corrupt that their very clothes are defiled (Green).
24   ■ δυναμένῳ pres. mid. part. "to the one who is able." φυλάξαι aor. act. inf. φυλάσσω to guard, to protect w. guards. The idea of protection and safety seems to be prominent here (s. T). ἄπταιστος without stumbling, not falling. The word is used of a horse which is sure-footed and does not stumble or of a good man who does not make moral lapses (Green). This would be the stumbling into the grievous sins of the spiritual spies. στῆσαι aor. act. inf. ἵστημι to place, to present. κατενώπιον "before the face of," i.e., "in the presence of." ἄμωμος without blame. ἀγαλλίασις rejoicing, exaltation. The word has special eschatological overtones denoting the jubilation of God's chosen people at His manifestation at the end (Kelly; s. also 1 Peter 1:6).
25   ■ μεγαλωσύνη greatness, majesty. ἀμήν truly, amen. The word regularly closes doxologies and sets a seal on this confident attribution of glory to the One to whom it belongs—the God who is able! (Green). (For general remarks regarding the Book of Jude, s. D.J. Rowston, "The Most Neglected Book in the New Testament," NTS 21 [July, 1975], 554–563.)

REVELATION

ἀποκάλυψις unveiling, revealing, revelation (s. Hort; 1
Swete; 2 Thess. 1:7). The following gen. could be either obj., i.e.,
"a revelation of Jesus Christ" w. Him as the object or it could
be subjective gen. which fits better here, i.e., Jesus Christ is the
One who originates the revelation (s. Charles; Bousset). ἔδωκεν
aor. act. ind. δίδωμι to give. δεῖξαι aor. act. inf. δείκνυμι to
show. This word is characteristic of our author when it means
to communicate a divine revelation by means of visions
(Charles). δεῖ it is binding, it is necessary. The word denotes the
sure fulfillment of the purpose of God revealed by the prophets
(Swete). γενέσθαι aor. mid. inf. γίνομαι to happen, to come to
pass. τάχος quickly, suddenly, soon. The word indicates rapidi-
ty of execution (Walvoord). ἐσήμανεν aor. act. ind. σημαίνω
to signify. The word properly means strictly to show by some
sort of sign and it is esp. used of any intimation given by the gods
to men, particularly w. reference to the fut. (Hort). ἀποστείλας
aor. act. part. ἀποστέλλω to send, to send a commissioned
authoritative representative on a specific mission (s. TDNT).
■ ἐμαρτύρησεν aor. act. ind. μαρτυρέω to testify, to bear 2
witness. ■ μακάριος happy, blessed (s. Matt. 5:3). 3
ἀναγινώσκων pres. act. part. ἀναγινώσκω to read, to read
aloud. This is not the private student but the public reader
(Charles; s. also Swete). ἀκούοντες pres. act. part. nom. pl. "the
ones who hear." The public reading of Scripture was taken over
from Jewish practice (Mounce). προφητεία the message of a
prophet, prophecy. τηροῦντες pres. act. part. τηρέω to keep, to
observe. γεγραμμένα perf. pass. part. γράφω. The perf. tense
stresses the state or condition and often the authority of a legal
document (s. MM). ἐγγύς near.
■ ἀπό "from." The prep. is normally followed by the gen. 4
Here the names of God are to be treated as an indeclinable noun
and as an indeclinable noun are probably intended to be treated
as a paraphrase of the tetragrammaton, Y-H-W-H, "He who is"
(Ford; s. also Mounce; Swete). ὤν pres. act. part. εἰμί. ἦν impf.
εἰμί. ἐρχόμενος pres. mid. part. In the Gr. world similar titles

for the gods are found. In the song of the doves at Dodona we read of "Zeus who was, Zeus who is, and Zeus who will be"

5 (Mounce). ■ πρωτότοκος firstborn (s. Col. 1:15). ἄρχων pres. act. part. ἄρχω to be at the beginning, ruler, prince. The Resurrection carried w. it the potential lordship over all humanity and the words "the ruler of the kings of the earth" stand appropriately at the head of a book which represents the glorified Christ as presiding over the destinies of nations (Swete).

ἀγαπῶντι pres. act. part. λύσαντι aor. act. part. λύω to loose, to release. The aor. tense points to the completed act. ἐν τῷ αἵματι "by His blood." The prep. is instrumental (Ford) and the blood speaks of the sacrificed life which was the ransom or

6 payment for release (Swete; s. also 1 Peter 1:18-19). ■ ἐποίησεν aor. act. ind. ἀμήν "amen." The word is acknowledgement of that which is valid. In the synagogue it is the response of the community to the prayers uttered by the leader (Ford).

7 ■ νεφέλη cloud. Not simply that He has a surrounding of clouds, but that He compels all the clouds into His retinue (Hort). It may be that the clouds are not the ordinary clouds of nature, but clouds in heaven seen in the vision around the throne of God. In any case the cloud in Heb. thought is commonly associated w. the divine presence (Exod. 13:21; 16:10; Matt. 17:5; Acts 1:9) (Mounce; s. also Dan. 7:13; Jastrow II, 1095; s. also 1QM 12:9). ὄψεται fut. mid. ind. ὁράω to see. ἐξεκέντησαν aor. act. ind. ἐκκεντέω to pierce. The word is used in John 19:37 and there they looked to Him in amazement; they will look to Him for forgiveness and salvation (Abbott, 247). In the gospel the main reference is to the crucifixion: whereas here it is eschatological (Charles). κόψονται fut. mid. ind. κόπτομαι to smite the chest in sorrow. φυλή tribe. ναί yes.

8 ■ ἄλφα "alpha," the first letter of the Gr. alphabet. ὦ "omega," the last letter of the Gr. alphabet. The phrase is seen to express not eternity only, but infinitude, the boundless life which embraces all while it transcends all (Swete). ὤν pres. act. part. ἦν impf. ἐρχόμενος pres. mid. part. (s.v.4). παντοκράτωρ the almighty, the omnipotent. The reference is more to God's supremacy over all things than to the related idea of divine omnipotence. The word was used in secular literature to describe the attributes of the gods and is probably used here in contrast to the Roman emperor's self-designation as *autokrator* (s. Mounce; Ford; TDNT).

9 ■ συγκοινωνός fellow partaker, one who shares together. θλίψις pressure, trouble, tribulation (s. TDNT; Trench, *Synonyms*, 202). ἐγενόμην aor. mid. ind. γίνομαι. νῆσος island.

καλουμένη pres. pass. part. καλέω to call, to name. The island
of Patmos was a small, rocky island about 16 sq. miles in the
Aegean Sea some 40 miles southwest of Miletus. It was a penal
settlement to which the Roman authorities sent offenders
(Mounce; s. also LSC, 82–92; KP IV, 549; IBD III, 677; Caird).
■ ἐν πνεύματι "in the Spirit." The phrase denotes the prophet 10
under inspiration (Swete). κυριακός pertaining to the Lord, the
Lord's Day. This could be a reference to "Sunday or it could be
an eschatological reference to 'the Day of the Lord' so that the
prophet was stationed as a spectator amid the very scenes of the
great judgment itself" (Seiss; s. also W. Stott, "A Note on the
Word KURIAKE in Revelation I.10," NTS 12 [Oct., 1965],
70–75; K.A. Strand, "Another Look at 'Lord's Day' in the Early
Church and in Revelation I.10," NTS 13 [Jan., 1967], 174–181).
ἤκουσα aor. act. ind. ἀκούω. ὀπίσω behind. ■ λεγούσης pres. 11
act. part. fem. sing. The part. agrees w. the dependent gen.
"trumpet," rather than the noun "voice," "sound" (Mounce).
γράψον aor. act. imp. πέμψον aor. act. imp. πέμπω to send.
(For writing and the sending of letters in the ancient world, s.
LSC 1–49; RAC II, 564–585; KP II, 324–327; for Roman roads
in the province of Asia, s. GAM 164–179.)
    ■ ἐπέστρεψα aor. act. ind. ἐπιστρέφω to turn around, to 12
turn toward. ἔλαλει impf. act. ind. λαλέω. The impf. emphasizes the continual action in the past time. ἐπιστρέψας aor. act.
part. The part. is used temporally expressing either antecedent
or contemporaneous action. λυχνία lampstand. The Mosaic
lampstand for the Tabernacle, that which stood (one or more) in
the later temples and in the vision of Zech. 6:2, had seven
branches, but here we have seven distinct lampstands each w. its
one light. Of course, it has nothing to do w. candlesticks but was
a kind of lamp w. a wick and oil (Hort; s. also Mounce; Swete).
■ μέσον middle. ὅμοιος like. ἐνδεδυμένον perf. pass. part. 13
ἐνδύω to put on, pass. to be clothed. ποδήρης reaching to the
foot. The word is used in Exodus 28:4 for the blue-purple outward robe of the high priest which reached down to his feet
(Bousset; Mounce). The word is also used in Ezra 9:2 where it
is applied to the man charged w. setting a mark upon some of
the Jerusalemites before the destruction of the city. Of the two
possible emphases, a priestly ministry and one of mercy in the
face of impending judgment, the latter is more likely the choice
since nowhere else in the book does Christ appear in a priestly
capacity (Robert L. Thomas, "The Glorified Christ on Patmos,"
Bib Sac 122 [July, 1965], 243). περιεζωσμένον perf. pass. part.
περιζώννυμι to be girded round about, to wear a wide belt

around one's self. μαστός breast. The ordinary girding for one
actively engaged was "at the loins," but Josephus (Antiq. III.7.2)
expressly tells us that the Levitical priests were girded higher up,
about the breast—favoring a calmer more majestic movement. In
like manner the angels who carry out the judgments of God have
their breasts girded w. golden girdles (Rev. 15:6). ζώνη girdle.
The girdle or wide belt is often contemplated as the symbol of
14 strength and activity (SCA; Swete). ■ θρίξ, τριχός hair. λευκός
white. ἔριον wool. χιών snow. In Daniel 7:9 the Ancient of
Days is described as having hair "like pure wool" and raiment
"white as snow." The ascriptions of the titles and attributes of
God to Christ is an indication of the exalted Christology of the
Apocalypse. The hoary head was worthy of honor and conveyed
the idea of wisdom and dignity (Lev. 19:32; Prov. 16:31)
(Mounce). φλόξ flame. πῦρ fire. The "eyes as a flame of fire"
indicated the penetrating glance which flashed w. quick intelligence and when need arose w. righteous wrath (Swete; s. also
15 SCA). ■ χαλκολίβανον gold ore, fine brass or bronze. The
meaning of the word is somewhat uncertain but it is best understood as an alloy of gold or fine brass. In any case the shining
bronze like feet portray strength and stability (Mounce; Swete;
s. also BAG; Ford). κάμινος oven. πεπυρωμένης perf. pass.
part. πυρόω to set on fire, to burn. The perf. tense emphasizes
the completed state or results, i.e., "having been burned," "having been refined." The idea may be "glowing" and it would
indicate that the metal is not only the finest and brightest, but
16 it is aglow as if still in the crucible (Swete). ■ ἔχων pres. act. part.
δεξιός right. ἀστήρ star. στόμα mouth. ῥομφαία sword. This
word is properly the long and heavy broad sword w. which the
Thracians and other barbarous nations were armed and symbolizes the irresistible power of divine judgment (SCA; Mounce).
δίστομος two-edged. ὀξύς sharp. ἐκπορευομένη pres. mid.
part. ἐκπορεύομαι to go out. ὄψις appearance, outward appearance, face. In the context its primary reference is to the face but
should not be limited to that alone (Mounce). φαίνει pres. act.
ind. to shine "as the sun shines in His might" (Swete).
17   ■ ἔπεσα aor. act. ind. πίπτω to fall. ἔθηκεν aor. act. ind.
τίθημι to place. φοβοῦ pres. mid. imp. φοβέομαι to be afraid.
The pres. imp. w. the neg. indicates the stopping of an action in
progress: "stop being afraid." ἔσχατος last. The expression "I
am the first and the last" is the expression of absolute Godhead
18 (s. Isa. 41:4; 44:6; 48:12) (SCA; Ford). ■ ζῶν pres. act. part. ζάω
to live. κλείς key. ᾅδης Hades, death, the place of the dead
(TDNT; CBB; s. also SB IV, 1016–1065). To "have the keys of

death and of Hades" is to possess authority over their domain.
The claim to possess potentially the key of death is made by
Christ Himself in John 5:28; the Apocalypse connects the actual
possession of the keys w. His victory over death. They are from
that moment in His keeping (Swete). ■ εἶδες aor. act. ind. ὁράω 19
to see. εἰσίν pres. ind. εἰμί to be. μέλλει pres. act. ind. to be
about to. Used w. the inf. to express the fut. γενέσθαι aor. mid.
inf. γίνομαι to become, to happen. This v. gives the threefold
division of the Book of Revelation: "the things which you saw"
refer to the vision of the glorified Christ, esp. vv. 11–18, "the
things which are" refer to the letters to the churches in chapters
2 and 3; and "the things which will happen, come to pass after
these things" refer to the events described in 4–22 (s. Lohse;
Walvoord; Govett; Scott; Bousset; Robert L. Thomas, "John's
Apocalyptic Outline," Bib Sac 123 [Oct., 1966], 334–341). ■ 20
μυστήριον mystery.

Ch. 2

■ γράψον aor. act. imp. γράφω. κρατῶν pres. act. part. 1
κρατέω to have power over, to hold, to grasp, to hold fast (s.
Ford). ἀστήρ star. δεξιά right. περιπατῶν pres. act. part.
περιπατέω to walk about. The Lord patrols the ground and is
ever on the spot when He is needed; His presence is not localized
but coextensive w. the church (Swete). μέσον middle. λυχνία
lampstand (s. Rev. 1:12). χρυσοῦς golden. ■ κόπος laborious 2
work, toil. The word signifies not merely labor, but labor "unto
weariness" (s. Hort; SCA; Trench, Synonyms, 378; s. also 1
Thess. 2:9). βαστάσαι aor. act. inf. βαστάζω to carry, to bear.
ἐπείρασας aor. act. ind. πειράζω to try, to examine. καὶ οὐκ
εἰσίν "and they are not." The words are a Hebraism for "not
being" (Charles). εὗρες aor. act. ind. εὑρίσκω. ψευδής lying,
liars. ■ ἐβάστασας aor. act. ind. κεκοπίακας perf. act. ind. 3
κοπιάω to be weary, to work and labor to the point of weariness.
The word implies strenuous and exhausting labor. Here it could
be weary morally, i.e., to allow one's self to become weary (Hort;
s. also SCA). The perf. tense looks at the continuing results of
the labor. ■ ἀφῆκας aor. act. ind. ἀφίημι to leave, to forsake. 4
■ μνημόνευε pres. act. imp. μνημονεύω to remember, to call 5
to remembrance. πόθεν from where. πέπτωκας perf. act. ind.
πίπτω to fall. μετανόησον aor. act. imp. μετανοέω to change
one's thinking, to think differently, to repent. The pres. imp.,
"repent," stands in contrast to the aor. imp., "repent," and suggests a continuing attitude over against a decisive break. "Bear
in mind the loving relationships you once enjoyed and make a

clean break w. your present manner of life!" (Mounce).
ποίησον aor. act. imp. σοί "to you." The dat. could be taken
as dat. of disadvantage (Swete). κινήσω fut. act. ind. κινέω to
move. τόπος place. μετανοήσῃς aor. act. subj. μετανοέω The
subj. is used in a third-class conditional clause which assumes
6 that the condition is possible. ■ μισεῖς pres. act. ind. to hate.
(For a discussion of the identity of the Nicolaitans, s. Mounce;
7 Ford; Swete.) ■ ἔχων pres. act. part. οὕς ear. ἀκουσάτω aor.
act. imp. νικῶντι pres. act. part. νικάω to be victor, to gain a
victory, to be victorious. δώσω fut. act. ind. δίδωμι. φαγεῖν
aor. act. inf. ἐσθίω to eat. ξύλον tree. παράδεισος paradise, a
Persian word meaning a park or enclosed garden. According to
rabbinical teaching there was a threefold paradise, i.e., the paradise of Adam where the tree of life stood; the paradise of the
souls in heaven which was the abode of the redeemed between
death and the Resurrection; the eschatological paradise where
the souls of the righteous would be. The eschatological paradise
was considered to be the paradise of Adam restored w. the tree
of life (s. SB III, 792f.; IV, 1144–1165; Ford; s. also Luke 23:43).
8   ■ ἔσχατος last (s. Rev. 1:17). ἐγένετο aor. mid. ind.
γίνομαι. ἔζησεν aor. act. ind. ζάω to live. The purpose of this
statement is to fix attention upon the fact of the Resurrection.
As the Lord rose, so will His martyrs triumph over death
9 (Swete). ■ θλῖψις pressure, trouble, tribulation (s. Rev. 1:9).
πτωχεία poverty, extreme and abject poverty (s. 2 Cor. 8:9;
NTW, 109–111). πλούσιος rich, wealthy. βλασφημία slan-
10 der, railing, blasphemy. ■ φοβοῦ pres. mid. imp. φοβέομαι to
be afraid. μέλλεις pres. act. ind. to be about to. The word is used
w. the inf. to express the fut. πάσχειν pres. act. inf. to suffer.
βάλλειν pres. act. inf. to throw, to cast. διάβολος devil.
πειρασθῆτε aor. pass. subj. The prisons in the ancient world
were a place where the accused awaited sentencing which resulted either in execution or banishment (s. Mounce). ἔξετε fut.
act. ind. ἔχω. γίνου pres. mid. imp. γίνομαι to become, to
"prove thyself loyal and true, to the extent of being ready to die
11 for my sake" (Swete). δώσω fut. act. ind. (s.v.7). ■ ἔχων pres.
act. part. ἀκουσάτω aor. act. imp. (s.v.7). ἀδικηθῇ aor. pass.
subj. ἀδικέω to harm, to injure.
12   ■ ἔχων pres. act. part. ρομφαία sword (s. Rev. 1:16).
13 δίστομος two-edged. ὀξύς sharp. ■ κατοικεῖς pres. act. ind. to
settle down, to live. κρατεῖς pres. act. ind. to hold, to grasp, to
hold fast (s.v.1). ἠρνήσω aor. act. ind. ἀρνέομαι to say no, to
14 deny. ἀπεκτάνθη aor. pass. ind. ἀποκτείνω to kill. ■
κρατοῦντας pres. act. part. to hold to. ἐδίδασκεν impf. ind.

act. βαλεῖν aor. act. inf. (s.v.10). φαγεῖν aor. act. inf. (s.v.7).
εἰδωλόθυτον sacrifices offered to idols, that which is slain for
a sacrifice (s. SCA). πορνεῦσαι aor. act. inf. πορνεύω to engage in sexual activities. The inf. are used after the verb "to
teach." ■ οὕτως so, thus. The application and parallel is now 15
drawn. The city of Pergamum was a stronghold of idolatry. It
was famous for the great altar of Zeus which had a frieze around
the base of the altar depicting the gods of Greece in victorious
combat against the giants of the earth (symbolizing the triumph
of civilization over barbarianism). The shrine of Asklepios, the
god of healing, attracted people from all over the world. Of
greatest import for the Christians living in Pergamum was the
fact that it was the official center in Asia for the imperial cult
(Mounce; s. also Charles; LSC, 281–315). ὁμοίως adv. in like
manner. ■ μετανόησον aor. act. imp. (s.v.5). ταχύ adv. quickly, 16
soon. πολεμήσω fut. act. ind. πολεμέω to wage war, to fight
against. ■ ἀκουσάτω aor. act. imp. νικῶντι pres. act. part. 17
δώσω fut. act. ind. (s.v.7). μάννα manna. κεκρυμμένου perf.
pass. part. κρύπτω to hide. It was a Jewish teaching that in the
messianic time the Messiah would send manna from heaven and
in the fut. age, manna would be the food of the righteous (SB,
793; s. also Mounce). In the context here the hidden manna
alludes to the proper and heavenly food in contrast to the unclean food supplied by the Balaamites. While the promise is
primarily eschatological, it is not without immediate application
for a persecuted people (Mounce). ψῆφος stone. λευκός white.
γεγραμμένον perf. pass. part. γράφω. λαμβάνων pres. act.
part. There were various usages of "a white stone" in the ancient
world. Perhaps in the context it is best to take the white stone
as a token which served for admission to a banquet. Many of
such tokens were little tablets of wood, metal, or stone and these
were distributed to the poor in Rome by the emperors to insure
a regular supply of corn. Or they were given to the victor at
games and to gladiators who won the admiration of the public
and had been allowed to retire from further combat. Here the
white stone as symbol of the triumph of faith would be considered to be a token for admission to the messianic feast (s.
Mounce; LSC, 303ff.).

■ ἔχων pres. act. part. φλόξ flame. πῦρ fire. 18
χαλκολίβανον (s. Rev. 1:15). ■ διακονία ministry. πλείων 19
comp. πολύς more than. τῶν πρώτων gen. of comparison "than
the first one." ■ ἀφεῖς pres. act. ind. ἄφημι to allow, to tolerate. 20
προφῆτις prophetess. πλανᾷ pres. act. ind. to lead astray, to
deceive. πορνεῦσαι aor. act. inf. (s.v.14). φαγεῖν aor. act. inf.

(s.v.7). εἰδωλόθυτον sacrifice offered to an idol (s.v.14). (For a good discussion of the woman "Jezebel" and an identification of her and her teachings, s. Mounce. She is viewed as a prominent woman claiming the gift of divine prophecy and leading many in pagan worship and pagan feasts which often led to sexual
21 promiscuity.) ■ ἔδωκα aor. act. ind. δίδωμι. μετανοήσῃ aor. act. subj. The subj. is used in a purpose clause. μετανοῆσαι aor. act. inf. πορνεία immorality. The word here means wanton behavior including fornication (s. Joseph Jensen, "Does *Porneia* Mean Fornication? A Critique of Bruce Malina," Nov T 20
22 [July, 1978], 168–184). ■ κλίνη bed. The bed is not a "funeral-bier" or a "dining couch" of the guild feast, but a bed of sickness or pain. Disease as a punishment for sin was an accepted view (Mounce). μοιχεύοντας pres. act. part. μοιχεύω to commit
23 adultery. μετανοήσουσιν fut. act. ind. ■ ἀποκτενῶ fut. act. ind. (s.v.13). γνώσονται fut. mid. ind. γινώσκω. ἐρευνῶν pres. act. part. ἐρευνάω to search. The pres. tense indicates habitual and continual action. νεφρός kidney. Kidneys were regarded as the seat of the emotions, just as the heart was the seat of the intelligence or the will. Hence, the speaker w. divine omniscience will prove that no deceit or sophistry of any kind
24 can escape him (Ford). δώσω fut. act. ind. (s.v.7). ■ λοιπός rest, remaining. ἔγνωσαν aor. act. ind. γινώσκω. βάθος deep,
25 depth. βάρος burden (s. Acts 15:28, 29). ■ πλήν except, only. κρατήσατε aor. act. imp. (s.v.1). ἄρχι οὗ "until, until which time." ἥξω fut. act. ind. ἥκω to come. Used in an indefinite temporal clause and the form can be either fut. act. ind. or aor.
26 act. subj. (RWP). ■ νικῶν pres. act. part. (s.v.7). τηρῶν pres.
27 act. part. τηρέω to keep, to guard, to observe. ■ ποιμανεῖ fut. act. ind. ποιμαίνω to shepherd. The word should be taken here in the sense of wheeling the shepherd's staff or club to ward off attacks of marauding beasts (Mounce). ῥάβδος stick, staff. σιδηροῦς, ᾶ, οῦν iron. σκεῦος vessel. κεραμικός pottery, earthenware. συντρίβεται pres. pass. ind. συντρίβω to crush
28 together, to smash. ■ εἴληφα perf. act. ind. λαμβάνω. πρωϊνός morning, "morning star." In addition to authority over the nations the overcomer is promised the morning star. No complete-ly satisfactory answer for this symbol has been offered (Mounce;
29 s. also his listing of various possibilities). ■ ἀκουσάτω aor. act. imp. (s.v.7).

Ch. 3

1   ■ γράψον aor. act. imp. γράφω
         ἔχων pres. act. part. ἀστήρ star. ζῇς pres. act. ind. to live.

As the city was rebuilt in the time of Alexander the Great, it was dedicated to a local Asiatic goddess usually referred to as Cybele, who was identified w. the Gr. Artemis. This patron deity was believed to possess the special power of restoring the dead to life (Mounce; s. also LSC, 363–365f.). ∎ γίνου pres. mid. imp. 2 γρηγορῶν pres. act. part. γρηγορέω to be awake, to be watchful. Although the city of Sardis was considered to be a natural citadel and incapable of capture, there were several times in the city's history that the city fell because of self-confidence and failure to watch. Perhaps the most famous incidence was when Cyrus, king of Persia, captured the city as Croesus was king of Sardis (s. Herodotus I, 84; LSC, 354–362; Mounce; C.J. Hemer, "The Sardis Letter and the Croesus Tradition," NTS 19 [Oct., 1972], 94–97). στήρισον aor. act. imp. στηρίζω to make firm, to strengthen, to establish. ἔμελλον impf. act. ind. Used w. the inf. to express the fut. The impf. w. the inf. expresses futurity or intention reckoned from a moment in the past (MKG, 307). ἀποθανεῖν aor. act. inf. ἀποθνήσκω to die. εὕρηκα perf. act. ind. πεπληρωμένα perf. pass. part. πληρόω to fill, to be filled; their works have not measured up to God's standard (RWP). ∎ μνημόνευε pres. act. imp. μνημονεύω to remember. 3 εἴληφας perf. act. ind. λαμβάνω to receive. The word represents the faith as a trust and the perf. tense calls attention to the abiding responsibility of the trust then received (Swete). ἤκουσας aor. act. ind. ἀκούω to hear. The aor. looks back to the moment when faith came by hearing (Swete). τήρει pres. act. imp. τηρέω to keep, to watch, to guard. The pres. tense calls for a continual watchful attitude. μετανόησον aor. act. imp. μετανοέω to change one's thinking, to repent (s. Rev. 2:5). γρηγορήσῃς aor. act. subj. The subj. is used in a third-class conditional clause which views the condition as a possibility. ἥξω fut. act. ind. ἥκω to come (note the history of the city alluded to in v. 2). οὐ μή "not in any wise." γνῷς aor. act. subj. γινώσκω. ποῖος what kind of. The acc. here is acc. of time but looks more at a point of time rather than a long duration (s. RG, 470f.; RWP; Mounce). ∎ ἐμόλυναν aor. act. ind. μολύνω to 4 soil. The language recalls the inscription found in Asia Minor which announced that soiled garments disqualified the worshiper and dishonored the god (Ford). It is also often noted that since the manufacture and dying of woolen goods was a principle trade in Sardis, an allusion to defiled garments would be immediately recognized. It is unlikely, however, that any more than a general reference to the danger of contaminating the Christian witness by accommodation to the prevailing standards of a pagan city is

in mind (Mounce). περιπατήσουσιν fut. act. ind. περιπατέω to walk about. λευκός white. The raiment here spoken of is the heavenly raiment or it is the symbol of inner purity (Charles; 5 Ford). ■ νικῶν pres. act. part. νικάω to win a victory, to be victorious, to overcome. περιβαλεῖται fut. mid. ind. περιβάλλω to throw clothes around one's self, to clothe one's self. ἐξαλείψω fut. act. ind. ἐξαλείφω to wipe out, to blot out. In the OT the book of life was a register of all who held citizenship in the theocratic community of Israel. The idea was also common in the secular world and all Gr. and Roman cities of that time kept a list of citizens according to their class or tribe in which new citizens were entered and from which degraded citizens were expunged (Mounce; Ford; LSC, 385f.). The promise here is positive that these will not in any way have their names blotted out. ὁμολογήσω fut. act. ind. ὁμολογέω to con-
6 fess, to acknowledge, to profess. ■ ἀκουσάτω aor. act. imp.
7   ■ γράψον aor. act. imp.
    ἀληθινός true, genuine. ἔχων pres. act. part. κλείς key. The "key of David" is a metaphorical expression indicating complete control over the royal household (Mounce; s. also Swete). ἀνοίγων pres. act. part. ἀνοίγω to open. κλείσει fut. act. ind. κλείω to shut, to lock. κλείων pres. act. part. (For a description of keys and locks in the ancient world and how they worked and how they were used as a symbol of power, s. OCD, 573; KP V,
8 18f.; TDNT.) ■ δέδωκα perf. act. ind. δίδωμι to give. ἠνεῳγμένην perf. pass. part. ἀνοίγω to open. The perf. tense indicates the continuing condition, i.e., "a door standing open." The metaphor of the "open door" indicated the opportunity for preaching the gospel (Swete; SCA; s. also 1 Cor. 16:9). κλεῖσαι aor. act. inf. ἐτήρησας aor. act. ind. (s.v.3). ἠρνήσω aor. mid. ind. ἀρνέομαι to say no, to deny. The aor. refer to some distinct occasions in the past when, being put to the test, they had proved
9 themselves faithful to Him (SCA). ■ διδῶ pres. act. ind. A late omega form for δίδωμι to give (s. RWP). ποιήσω fut. act. ind. ἥξουσιν fut. act. ind. (s.v.3). ἠγάπησα aor. act. ind. ἀγαπάω.
10 ■ ὑπομενή remaining under, patient endurance. It is the spirit which can bear things not simply w. resignation, but w. blazing hope (NTW, 60; s. also TDNT; CBB; RAC IX, 255ff.). τηρήσω fut. act. ind. πειρασμός testing, temptation. μελλούσης pres. act. part. to be about to. The word is used w. the inf. to express the fut. tense οἰκουμένη pres. pass. part. οἰκέω to live. The word is used for the inhabited earth. πειράσαι aor. act. inf.
11 πειράζω to try. κατοικοῦντας pres. act. part. κατοικέω. ■ ταχύ quickly, soon. κράτει pres. act. imp. κρατέω to hold fast,

to grasp. λάβῃ aor. act. subj. λαμβάνω. The subj. is used in a
neg. purpose clause. ■ νικῶν pres. act. part. (s.v.5). στῦλος 12
pillar. The metaphor of being a pillar in a temple is current in
most languages and conveys the idea of stability and permanence (Mounce). ἐξέλθῃ aor. act. subj. ἐξέρχομαι to go out. To
a city that had experienced devastating earthquakes which
caused people to flee into the countryside and to establish temporary dwellings there, the promise of permanence within the
New Jerusalem would have a special meaning (Mounce; s. also
LSC, 396f.). γράψω fut. act. ind. καταβαίνουσα pres. act. part.
καταβαίνω to come down. ■ ἀκουσάτω aor. act. imp. (s.v.6). 13
■ γράψον aor. act. imp.   14
     ἀρχή beginning, first (s. Col. 1:18). ■ ψυχρός cold. ζεστός 15
boiling, hot. ὄφελον. Used to express a wish about the pres. "I
would that you were" (RWP). ■ χλιαρός warm, lukewarm. The 16
contrast here is between the hot medicinal waters of Hierapolis
and the cold, pure waters of Colossae. Thus, the church in Laodicea was providing neither refreshment for its spiritual weary nor
healing for the spiritual sick. It was totally ineffective and thus
distasteful to the Lord (Mounce; s. also Ford). μέλλω pres. act.
ind. to be about to. ἐμέσαι aor. act. inf. ἐμέω to vomit, to reject
w. disgust (s. RWP; SCA). ■ ὅτι. Used after the verb "you say" 17
to introduce direct speech and is equivalent to quotation marks.
πλούσιος rich, wealthy. πεπλούτηκα perf. act. ind. πλουτέω
to become rich, to be rich, i.e., my wealth is due to my own
exertion (Swete). The city of Laodicea was known for its wealth
(Ford; s. also LSC, 416ff.; Mounce). ταλαίπωρος miserable,
wretched. ἐλεεινός pitiable, miserable. The word indicates one
who is set forth as an object of extremest pity (SCA). πτωχός
poor, extremely poor, poor as a beggar. τυφλός blind. Laodicea
was widely known for its medical school and particularly famous
for an eye salve made from "phrygian powder" mixed w. oil
(Mounce; s. also LSC, 419f.; Ford). γυμνός naked. The city was
famous for its garments of glossy black wool (Ford; LSC, 416).
■ συμβουλεύω pres. act. ind. to give counsel, to advise. 18
ἀγοράσαι aor. act. inf. ἀγυράζω to buy. πεπυρωμένον perf.
pass. part. πυρόω to burn, pass. to be refined. πλουτήσῃς aor.
act. subj. (s.v.17). περιβάλῃ aor. mid. subj. (s.v.5). φανερωθῇ
aor. pass. subj. φανερόω to make known, to make clear, pass.
to be manifest, to be revealed. αἰσχύνη shame. γυμνότης
nakedness. In the biblical world nakedness was a symbol of
judgment and humiliation (Mounce). κολλύριον eye salve. The
phrygian powder was apparently applied to the eyes in the form
of a doughy paste (Mounce). ἐγχρῖσαι aor. act. inf. ἐγχρίζω to

19 anoint w. salve. βλέπῃς pres. act. subj. ■ φιλῶ pres. act. subj.
φιλέω to be fond of, to love. ζήλευε pres. act. imp. to be zealous.
20 μετανόησον aor. act. imp. (s.v.3). ■ ἕστηκα perf. act. ind.
ἵστημι to place, perf. to stand. κρούω pres. act. ind. to knock.
The pres. tense indicates the continual knocking. ἀκούσῃ aor.
act. subj. The subj. is used in a third-class conditional clause
which assumes the condition to be possible. ἀνοίξῃ aor. act.
subj. (s.v.7). εἰσελεύσομαι fut. mid. ind. εἰσέρχομαι to come
in. δειπνήσω fut. act. ind. δειπνέω to eat, to eat a meal. The
word refers to the meal which came at the end of the day and
was the principal meal and the usual occasion for hospitality
21 (Swete). ■ νικῶν pres. act. part. (s.v.5). δώσω fut. act. ind.
δίδωμι to give. καθίσαι aor. act. inf. καθίζω to sit, to cause to
22 sit. ἐνίκησα aor. act. ind. ἐκάθισα aor. act. ind. ■ ἔχων pres.
act. part. ἀκουσάτω aor. act. imp. (s.v.6).

Ch. 4

1   ■ εἶδον καὶ ἰδού "I saw and behold." The words serve to
introduce a new vision of special importance (Swete; Charles).
ἠνεῳγμένη perf. pass. part. ἀνοίγω to open. The perf. tense
could suggest that the door had been opened and left that way
for John's arrival (Mounce). ἤκουσα aor. act. ind. ἀκούω.
λαλούσης pres. act. part. ἀνάβα aor. act. imp. ἀναβαίνω to
go up. δείξω fut. act. ind. δείκνυμι to show, to exhibit. δεῖ "it
is binding," "it is necessary." The vision that follows is an anticipation of a fut. which is yet to find its accomplishment and is a
prophecy of the things which will take place after "the things
which are" at the present time as described in Revelation 2–3
2 (s. Swete; Bousset; Rev. 1:19). ■ εὐθέως adv. "immediately."
ἐγενόμην aor. mid. ind. γίνομαι (s. Rev. 1:10). ἔκειτο impf.
mid. ind. κεῖμαι to lie, to stand. The verb is used as the pass.
of the verb "to place" (RWP; s. also Swete). καθήμενος pres.
mid. part. κάθημαι to sit. John is allowed to see the throne room
of the heavenly palace and his eye falls at first on the ruler's
throne, which kind was used by kings and judges as they presid-
ed. The one enthroned in heaven can then only be the king of
3 all kings who rules and judges the whole world (Lohse). ■
ὅμοιος like. ὅρασις appearance. ἴασπις jasper stone. Perhaps
this ancient stone was a translucent rock crystal or perhaps a
diamond, and it may suggest such qualities as majesty, holiness,
or purity (Mounce). σάρδιον sardius stone. This was a blood-
red stone named after Sardis near which it was found. The stone
may be interpreted as wrath or judgment (Mounce). ἶρις rainbow, rainbow colored. The word may indicate the halo of em-

erald which encircled the throne (Swete). κυκλόθεν w. the gen. "encircling." σμαράγδινος made of emerald. If the rainbow which surrounded the throne was a halo, then the emerald is usually pictured as green; otherwise it is a colorless crystal which would refract a rainbow of prismatic colors and would speak of God's mercy (Mounce; s. also Ford). ■ περιβεβλημένους perf. 4 pass. part. περιβάλλω to throw around, pass. to be clothed. λευκός white. χρυσοῦς golden. The 24 elders clothed in white robes w. golden crowns could represent the church (Seiss; s. also Walvoord; Scott). Others would interpret them as being an exalted angelic order who serve and adore God as an angelic priesthood (Mounce; Govett). ■ ἐκπορεύονται pres. mid. ind. to go 5 out from, to proceed from. ἀστραπή lightning. βροντή thunder. The thunderstorm is in Heb. poetry a familiar symbol of the divine power and glory (Swete). λαμπάς torch. πῦρ fire. καιόμεναι pres. pass. part. καίω to burn, pass. to be burning. ■ ὑάλινος made of glass. κρύσταλλος crystal. It was a pave- 6 ment of glass resembling an expanse of water which was clear as rock crystal (Swete).

μέσον middle. κύκλος circle, encircling, around. It is an adv. in the locative case used here as a prep. This seems to mean that one of the four living creatures was on each of the four sides of the throne, either stationary or moving rapidly around (RWP). The exact location is a bit uncertain but "in the midst" apparently means "in the immediate vicinity." Thus, they surround the throne as an inner circle (Mounce). ζῷον living creature. γέμοντα pres. act. part. γέμω to be full of. ἔμπροσθεν in front. ὄπισθεν behind, in back of. ■ λέων lion. μόσχος a young 7 steer, calf. ἔχων pres. act. part. ἀετός eagle. The four forms suggest whatever is noblest, strongest, wisest, and swiftest in the animate nature (Swete). The beings here are heavenly creatures which serve and worship God. πετομένῳ pres. mid. part. πέτομαι to fly. ■ ἀνά each one, one by one, the distributive use 8 of the prep. (s. BAG). πτέρυξ wing. ἔσωθεν within. ἀνάπαυσις ceasing, pause, rest. παντοκράτωρ almighty (s. Rev. 1:8). ἦν impf. εἰμί. ὤν pres. part. εἰμί. ἐρχόμενος pres. mid. part. ἔρχομαι. ■ ὅταν when, whenever. δώσουσιν fut. act. 9 ind. δίδωμι. εὐχαριστία thanksgiving. ζῶντι pres. act. part. dat. sing. ζάω to live. ■ πεσοῦνται fut. mid. ind. πίπτω to fall, 10 to fall down. προσκυνήσουσιν fut. act. ind. προσκυνέω to worship. βαλοῦσιν fut. act. ind. βάλλω to throw. ■ λαβεῖν aor. 11 act. inf. λαμβάνω. The inf. is used in explaining the adj. "worthy." ἔκτισας aor. act. ind. κτίζω to create. ἐκτίσθησαν aor. pass. ind.

Ch. 5

1   ■ δεξιά right. καθημένον pres. mid. part. κάθημαι to sit.
βιβλίον book, scroll, document. This is a term used for writing
material of papyrus, leather, skin, or parchment (Ford).
γεγραμμένον perf. pass. part. The perf. tense indicates the
completed action and was often used of legal authoritative documents whose authority continued (s. MM; TDNT). ἔσωθεν
within. ὄπισθεν on the back. That the scroll is also written on
the back indicates how extensive and comprehensive are the
decrees of God (Mounce). κατεσφραγισμένον perf. pass. part.
κατασφραγίζω to seal, to seal up, to seal completely and se-
curely (Swete). σφραγίς seal. Seals were used as a stamping
device in place of signatures to make a document valid. The
impression was normally made on clay, wax, or some other soft
material (Ford; s. also TDNT). According to Roman law a testament or will was sealed w. seven seals by seven witnesses (Bousset; s. also Emmet Russell, "A Roman Law Parallel to Rev. V,"
Bib Sac 115 [July, 1958], 258–264; s. also Buckland, 238f.). The
book spoken of here seems to be the book of God's decrees and
contains the full account of what God in His sovereign will has
2 determined as the destiny of the world (Mounce; Bousset). ■
κηρύσσοντα pres. act. part. proclaiming. ἀνοῖξαι aor. act. inf.
ἀνοίγω to open. λῦσαι aor. act. inf. λύω to loose, to remove.
3   ■ ἐδύνατο impf. mid. ind. ὑποκάτω down under, underneath.
4   ■ ἔκλαιον impf. act. ind. κλαίω to cry, to weep aloud, to wail.
The word is frequently used to mean professional mourning
5 (Ford). εὑρέθη aor. pass. ind. ■ εἷς one. ἐνίκησεν aor. act. ind.
νικάω to win a victory, to be victor, to overcome. λέων lion.
The lion was an emblem of strength, majesty, courage, and menace as well as symbolic of intellectual excellence (Ford). φυλή
tribe. ῥίζα root (s. Isa. 11:1). ἀνοῖξαι aor. act. inf. to open. The
word is used of unrolling a book (Charles).
6   ■ μέσον in the middle (s. Rev. 4:6). ζῷον living creature.
ἀρνίον lamb (s. John 1:29). This word for lamb is used exclusively of the resurrected and victorious Christ (Mounce).
ἑστηκός perf. act. part. ἵστημι to stand. ἐσφαγμένον perf.
pass. part. σφάζω to slaughter, to slaughter a sacrifice. The perf.
indicates the lasting effects. The lamb has been offered, yet it
stands erect and alive in the sight of heaven (Swete). ἔχων pres.
act. part. κέρας horn. The horn is proverbially a symbol of
courage, strength, and might (Ford). John sees a lamb w. seven
horns and seven eyes, bearing the wounds of sacrificial slaughter,
yet standing in readiness for action. In one brilliant stroke John
portrays his central theme of NT revelation—victory through

sacrifice (Mounce). ἀπεσταλμένοι perf. pass. part.
ἀποστέλλω to send, to send as an official representative. The
verb has reference to the mission of the Spirit (Swete). ■ 7
εἴληφεν perf. act. ind. λαμβάνω to receive, to take. Rather than
being an aroistic perf. the perf. tense here is like a highly dramatic historical pres. (s. K.L. McKay, "Syntax in Exegesis," TB 23
[1972], 54). ■ ἔλαβεν aor. act. ind. λαμβάνω. ἔπεσαν aor. act. 8
ind. πίπτω to fall. κιθάρα harp. This is the general term for a
kind of harp or lyre (Ford; s. also 1 Cor. 14:7). φιάλη bowl. This
was a flat, shallow cup or bowl for drinking or libations
(Mounce). χρυσοῦς golden. γεμούσας aor. act. part. γέμω to
be full of. θυμίαμα incense. In Judaism the angels were considered to be the carrier of the prayers of men (s. SB III, 807f.).
Incense was used to produce fragrant perfumes and was used
both in secular life and liturgical life (Ford; s. also Matt. 2:11).
■ ᾄδουσιν pres. act. ind. to sing. ᾠδή song. The idea of a "new 9
song" grows out of the use of the expression in the Psalms. Every
new act of mercy calls forth a new song of gratitude and praise
(Mounce). In Judaism it was taught that Israel will first sing a
new song in the days of the Messiah as a song of praise for the
miracle of deliverance (SB III, 801). ἄξιος worthy. λαβεῖν aor.
act. inf. λαμβάνω to receive. The inf. is used to explain the adj.
"worthy." ἐσφάγης aor. pass. ind. σφάζω to slaughter (s.v.6).
ἠγόρασας aor. act. ind. ἀγοράζω to buy at the market place,
to redeem. γλῶσσα tongue, language. ■ ἐποίησας aor. act. ind. 10
βασιλεύσουσιν fut. act. ind. βασιλεύω to be a king, to rule
as king, to reign.

■ ἤκουσα aor. act. ind. ἀκούω. κύκλῳ dat. encircling, 11
round about. ἦν impf. ind. εἰμί. ἀριθμός number. Now it is the
innumerable host of angels who lift their voices in a great dox-
ology of praise. Their number is an apocalyptic symbol for
countless thousands (Mounce). ■ ἰσχύς strength, might (s. Eph. 12
1:19). εὐλογία praise (s. Bousset). ■ κτίσμα that which is 13
created, creation. λέγοντας pres. act. part. ■ προσεκύνησαν 14
aor. act. ind. προσκυνέω to worship.

Ch. 6

■ ἤνοιξεν aor. act. ind. ἀνοίγω to open, to break the seal. 1
With the opening of the first seal, the beginning of the seven-year
tribulation period is described. The Jews considered this to be a
time of unprecedented trouble and judgment which was to precede the messianic salvation. This was a time of judgment for
Israel and for the whole world (s. Matt. 24:8; esp. SB IV, 858ff.).
ἀρνίον lamb (s. Rev. 5:6). σφραγίς seal (s. Rev. 5:1). ἤκουσα

aor. act. ind. ἀκούω to hear. ζῷον living creature. βροντή thunder. ἔρχου pres. mid. imp. ■ ἵππος horse. The rabbis felt that
2 the appearance of a white horse was a favorable sign. In the later
rabbinic writings the coming of the Messiah was associated w.
the sight of a horse. Perhaps war horses were associated w. the
messianic woes, i.e., the suffering which would precede the advent of the Messiah (Ford). λευκός white. καθήμενος pres.
mid. part. κάθημαι to sit. ἔχων pres. act. part. τόξον bow. The
bow is not only the weapon of the Parthians, but, in general, a
feared weapon of attack for all nations. It is a part of the typical
cavalry equipment of all Oriental armies and the particular
weapon of the king (s. Mathias Rissi, "The Rider on the White
Horse," *Interpretation* 18 [Oct., 1964], 414). ἐδόθη aor. pass.
ind. δίδωμι to give. ἐξῆλθεν aor. act. ind. ἐξέρχομαι to go out.
νικῶν pres. act. part. νικάω to conquer. The part. is the manner
of his going out and the pres. tense may be conative, i.e., "trying
to conquer." νικήσῃ aor. act. subj. νικάω to be the victor, to
overcome, to conquer. The subj. is used in a purpose clause.
Although some have felt that the rider on the white horse is
Christ Himself (Zane Hodges, "The First Horseman of the
Apocalypse," Bib Sac 119 [Oct., 1962], 324–334), it is better to
view this one as the Antichrist, i.e., the "man of sin" (s. Rissi,
407–418; s. also the discussion by Mounce; Walvoord; Ford).
4   ■ πυρρός fiery, red. The color represents bloodshed and sin
(Ford). λαβεῖν aor. act. inf. λαμβάνω. The inf. is epexegetical
explaining that which was given. σφάξουσιν fut. act. ind.
σφάζω to slaughter. The fut. ind. is used here in an epexegetical
explanatory purpose clause (RWP). (For the use here of the ind.
rather than the subj., s. MT, 100.) μάχαιρα sword. This was the
short Roman sword and is symbolic of violent death, war, and
the power of the authorities to punish evildoers (Mounce; Ford).
5   ■ μέλας black. This color is symbolic of mourning or affliction or famine (Ford; Mounce). ζυγός scales. The beam of a pair
6 of scales (Swete). ■ χοῖνιξ quart. This was a dry measure of
about a quart, i.e., approximately 1.92 pints. One of these rations
was the daily ration of one man (Ford). δηνάριον denarius. This
was a Roman silver coin equivalent to one day's wages. This
indicated that enough wheat to feed one man for one day cost
a full day's wages. The cost of wheat here is five to twelve times
its normal price. Famine is indicated (Ford; s. also Mounce).
κριθή barley. Barley was largely the food of the poor and was
relatively cheaper than wheat (Swete). ἔλαιον oil, olive oil.
ἀδικήσῃς aor. act. subj. ἀδικέω to injure, to do harm to. The

subj. w. the neg. is used to express a prohibition or neg. command.

■ χλωρός green, pale. The word means a yellowish green 8 but refers here to the color of a corpse or the blanched appearance of a person struck w. terror (Ford; Mounce). ἐπάνω upon, on. ᾅδης Hades, the place of the dead, the underworld (s. Rev. 1:18). ἠκολούθει impf. ind. act. ἀκολουθέω to follow after, to follow. ἀποκτεῖναι aor. act. inf. ἀποκτείνω to kill. The inf. is used epexegetically to explain that which was given. ρομφαία sword. This was the sword w. the large blade (s. Rev. 1:16). The word is used w. the prep. in an instrumental sense "w. the sword." λιμός hunger. θηρίον wild animal, wild beast. Death by wild beasts would be expected in a land decimated by war and famine (Mounce).

■ ὑποκάτω under, underneath. θυσιαστήριον place of 9 offering, altar. ἐσφαγμένων perf. pass. part. σφάζω to slaughter, to slay. The souls of the slaughtered ones are seen "under the altar" because in the Levitical rite the blood was poured out at the foot of the altar (Swete). ■ ἔκραξαν aor. act. ind. κράζω 10 to scream out, to cry. δεσπότης lord, master, ruler, one who exercises absolute authority. ἀληθινός true, genuine. ἐκδικεῖς pres. act. ind. to avenge, to revenge, to execute vengeance. κατοικούντων pres. act. part. κατοικέω to reside, to dwell. ■ στολή robe. The word refers to any stately robe and as long, 11 sweeping garments would have eminently this stateliness about them, always or almost always it refers to a garment reaching to the feet, or one train-like, sweeping the ground (Trench, Synonyms, 186). ἐρρέθη aor. pass. ind. λέγω. The pass. is the divine or theological pass. indicating that God is the One who does the action (s. BG, 76). ἀναπαύσωνται fut. mid. ind. ἀναπαύομαι to cease, to pause, to rest. The fut. mid. used in the subfinal clause is to be preferred rather than the aor. mid. subj. (RWP). πληρωθῶσιν aor. pass. subj. πληρόω to fill, to fulfill. σύνδουλος fellow slave. μέλλοντες pres. act. part. to be about to. The verb is used w. the inf. to form the fut. tense. ἀποκτέννεσθαι pres. pass. inf. ἀποκτέννω to kill.

■ σεισμός earthquake. Earthquakes were often used to 12 introduce God's judgment (s. Richard Buckham, "The Eschatological Earthquake in the Apocalypse of John," Nov T 19 [July, 1977], 224–233). ἐγένετο aor. mid. ind. γίνομαι to happen, to occur, to be. σάκκος sackcloth. The was the rough cloth made from the hair of a black goat and worn in times of mourning (Mounce). τρίχινος made of hair. σελήνη moon. ■ ἀστήρ star. 13 ἔπεσαν aor. act. ind. πίπτω to fall. συκῆ fig tree. βάλλει pres.

act. ind. to throw, to cast. The pres. tense is gnomic picturing
that which is always true. ὄλυνθος fig, unripe fig. The word
means the green figs which appear in winter and of which, while
some ripen, many fall off in the spring (Swete). ἄνεμος wind.
σειομένη pres. pass. part. σείω to shake. The world and its well
being depend on the faithfulness w. which the luminaries of
heaven fulfill their parts. When the sun and moon and stars
forsake this order, the end of the world is at hand (Charles).

14 ■ ἀπεχωρίσθη aor. pass. ind. ἀποχωρίζω to tear apart, to rip
apart. βιβλίον book, scroll, roll. ἑλισσόμενον pres. pass. part.
ἑλίσσω to roll up. The figure is that of a papyrus rent into,
whereupon the divided portions curl and form a roll on either
side (Charles). νῆσος island. ἐκινήθησαν aor. pass. ind. κινέω

15 to move. ■ μεγιστᾶνες (pl.) magistrates, the civil officials in
authority (Swete). χιλίαρχος leaders of a thousand soldiers,
tribune. The term was commonly used of the military tribune no
matter how many he commanded. The word refers to the military authorities (Ford; Swete). πλούσιος rich, wealthy.
ἐλεύθερος free, those who were no longer slaves. The seven
conditions of life are named, covering the whole fabric of society
from the emperor down to the meanest slave (Swete). ἔκρυψαν

16 aor. act. ind. κρύπτω to hide. σπήλαιον cave. ■ πέσετε aor.
act. imp. πίπτω to fall. κρύψατε aor. act. imp. ὀργή wrath,
anger. The "wrath of the lamb" is a deliberate paradox by which
John intends to goad his readers into theological alertness

17 (Caird). ■ σταθῆναι aor. pass. inf. ἵστημι to stand, to hold
one's ground (Swete).

Ch. 7

1   ■ μετὰ τοῦτο εἶδον "after this I saw." The phrase introduces another part of the vision (s. Rev. 4:1). ἑστῶτας perf.
act. part. ἵστημι perf. to stand. γωνία corner. κρατοῦντα pres.
act. part. κρατέω to hold, to grasp, to have power over. ἄνεμος
wind. πνέῃ pres. act. subj. πνέω to blow. The subj. is used in a
neg. purpose clause (RWP). μήτε neither. The four winds as
destructive agents of God are a regular feature in apocalyptic

2 literature (s. Mounce). ■ ἀναβαίνοντα pres. act. part.
ἀναβαίνω to come down. ἀνατολή rising, "the rising of the
sun" indicates the east. ἔχοντα pres. act. part. σφραγίς seal. To
the prophet's contemporaries "seal" would have connoted the
branding of cattle and the tattooing of slaves and soldiers, esp.
those in the service of the emperor who could be recognized by
this mark if they deserted; the marking of a soldier or the member of a guild on the hand, brow, or neck to seal him as a religious
devotee, i.e., a member of a sacred militia. The mark in this case

was a sign of consecration to the deity; it could refer to the mark prophets might have worn on their forehead, either painted or tattooed; or it could refer to the phylactery worn on the forehead and hand (s. Ford). The idea of the sealing would be to mark one's property and show ownership (Swete). ζῶντος pres. act. part. ζάω to live. ἔκραξεν aor. act. ind. κράζω to scream, to cry out. οἷς ἐδόθη αὐτοῖς "to whom it was given to them." This may reflect the Hebraic construction of the resumptive pron. (s. MH, 434f.; s. also W.F. Bakker, *Pronomen Abundans and Pronomen Coniunctum*, 41). ἐδόθη aor. pass. ind. δίδωμι. The theological or divine pass. indicating that God is the subject of the action. ἀδικῆσαι aor. act. inf. ἀδικέω to harm, to injure. The inf. is used to explain that which was given. ■ ἀδικήσητε 3 aor. act. subj. The subj. is used w. the neg. to form a prohibition or neg. command. σφραγίσωμεν aor. act. subj. σφραγίζω to seal. The aor. subj. is used in a temporal clause of indefinite action for the fut. (RWP). μέτωπον between the eyes, forehead. ■ ἤκουσα aor. act. ind. ἀκούω to hear. ἀριθμός number. 4 ἐσφραγισμένων perf. pass. part. σφραγίζω. φυλή tribe.

■ ἀριθμῆσαι aor. act. inf. ἀριθμέω to count, pass. to be 9 counted. ἐδύνατο impf. ind. γλῶσσα tongue, speech. ἀρνίον lamb. περιβεβλημένους perf. pass. part. περιβάλλω to cast around, pass. to be clothed. στολή robe (s. Rev. 6:11). λευκός white. φοῖνιξ palm branch. The palm is a sign of festive joy. One inscription describes how the inhabitants of a city out of gratitude to the gods prescribed that thirty boys should daily sing prescribed hymns as they were "clothed in white and crowned w. a twig, likewise holding a twig in their hands" (BS, 370). ■ καθημένῳ pres. mid. part. κάθημαι to sit. ■ εἱστήκεισαν 10/11 plperf. act. ind. ἵστημι. The plperf. is used like an imperf. (RWP). κύκλῳ (dat.) encircling, in a circle, round about. ζῷον living creature. ἔπεσαν aor. act. ind. πίπτω to fall, to fall down. προσεκύνησαν aor. act. ind προσκυνέω to worship. ■ 12 εὐχαριστία thanksgiving. ἰσχύς strength, might (s. Eph. 1:19).

■ ἀπεκρίθη aor. pass. ind. ἀποκρίνομαι to answer. πόθεν 13 from where, "where have they come from?" ■ εἴρηκα perf. act. 14 ind. λέγω. ἐρχόμενοι pres. mid. part. θλῖψις tribulation (s. Rev. 6:1). ἔπλυναν aor. act. ind. πλύνω to wash. ἐλεύκαναν aor. act. ind. λευκαίνω to whiten, to make white. The idea of making robes white by washing them in blood is a striking paradox. It is the sacrifice of the lamb upon the cross which supplies white garments for the saints (Mounce). ■ λατρεύουσιν pres. 15 act. ind. to perform worshipful service (s. TDNT). ναός temple, sanctuary. σκηνώσει fut. act. ind. σκηνόω to live in a tent, to

16 tabernacle (s. John 1:14). ■ πεινάσουσιν fut. act. ind. πεινάω to be hungry. διψήσουσιν fut. act. ind. διψάω to be thirsty. πέσῃ aor. act. subj. πίπτω to fall. καῦμα burning, scorching.

17 ■ μέσον middle. Used in the phrase ἀνὰ μέσον w. the meaning "between," "amongst" (Swete). ποιμανεῖ fut. act. ind. ποιμαίνω to shepherd. ὁδηγήσει fut. act. ind. ὁδηγέω to lead along the way, to guide, to lead. πηγή spring. The order in the phrase emphasizes "life"—"to Life's water springs" (Swete). ἐξαλείψει fut. act. ind. ἐξαλείφω to wipe away. δάκρυον tear, i.e., "every single tear."

Ch. 8

1   ■ ὅταν "when." The temporal particle is not used here in the indefinite sense "whenever" but as was common in the Koine, writers used this particle w. the aor. ind. for a definite occurrence (RG, 973). ἤνοιξεν aor. act. ind. ἀνοίγω to open, to break a seal. σφραγίς seal. ἐγένετο aor. mid. ind. γίνομαι to be. σιγή silence. ἡμίωρον half an hour. The silence is a dramatic pause which makes even more impressive the judgment about to fall upon the earth. Although a thirty-minute period is a relatively short period, it would form an impressive break in
2 such a rapidly moving drama (Mounce; s. also Seiss). ■ ἑστήκασιν aor. act. ind. ἵστημι to stand. ἐδόθησαν aor. pass. ind. δίδωμι to give. The theological pass. indicating that God is the one who gives.

3   ■ ἐστάθη aor. pass. ind. ἵστημι to stand, ingressive aor. "he took his place" (RWP). θυσιαστήριον place where sacrifices are made, altar. ἔχων pres. act. part. λιβανωτός golden censer or fire pan. The word usually means incense but here it appears to signify censer (Ford). χρυσοῦς golden. ἐδόθη aor. pass. ind. (s.v.2). θυμίαμα incense (s. Rev. 5:8). δώσει fut. act. ind. δίδωμι to give, to add. The fut. is used in a purpose clause
4 (s. MT, 100). ■ ἀνέβη aor. act. ind. ἀναβαίνω to go up. καπνός smoke. The meeting of the incense and the hot coals produces the fragrant smoke cloud, the symbol of divine accep-
5 tance (Swete). ■ εἴληφεν perf. act. ind. λαμβάνω. (For the use of the perf., s. Rev. 5:7.) ἐγέμισεν aor. act. ind. γεμίζω to fill, to make full of, to fill up. πῦρ fire. ἔβαλεν aor. act. ind. βάλλω to throw. ἐγένοντο aor. mid. ind. (s.v.1). βροντή thunder. ἀστραπή lightning. σεισμός earthquake (s. Rev. 6:12).

6   ■ ἔχοντες pres. act. part. ἡτοίμασαν aor. act. ind. ἑτοιμάζω to prepare. σαλπίσωσιν aor. act. subj. σαλπίζω to blow the trumpet. (For various uses of trumpets in the OT and

in an eschatological sense, s. Ford.) The subj. is used to express purpose.

■ ἐσάλπισεν aor. act. ind. ἐγένετο aor. mid. ind. (s.v.1). 7 χάλαζα hail. μεμιγμένα perf. pass. part. μείγνυμι to mix. ἐβλήθη aor. pass. ind. βάλλω (s.v.5). The syntax of the v. suggests that the blood-red storm appeared in heaven before it was cast upon the earth (Mounce). κατεκάη aor. pass. ind. κατακαίω to burn down, to burn up. The prep. in compound is perfective. χόρτος grass. χλωρός green. It is only one-third of the land and its vegetation that is devastated by fire. The fraction would indicate that although God is bringing punishment upon the earth, it is not as yet complete and final (Mounce).

■ καιόμενον pres. pass. part. καίω to set on fire, pass. to 8 be burning, to burn. ■ ἀπέθανεν aor. act. ind. ἀποθνήσκω to 9 die. διεφθάρησαν aor. pass. ind. διαφθείρω to corrupt, to destroy. The prep. in compound is perfective.

■ ἔπεσεν aor. act. ind. πίπτω to fall. ἀστήρ star. λαμπάς 10 torch. ποταμός river. πηγή spring. Now the fresh water supply is smitten (Swete). ■ λέγεται pres. pass. ind., pass. to be called. 11 ἄψινθος wormwood. It is called wormwood after the strong bitter taste of the plant of that name. Wormwood symbolizes God's punishment or bitterness, suffering and sorrow (Mounce; s. also FFB, 198; ZPEB V, 969). ἐπικράνθησαν aor. pass. ind. πικραίνω to make bitter, to cause to be bitter.

■ ἐπλήγη aor. pass. ind. πλήσσω to strike, to smite. 12 σελήνη moon. σκοτισθῇ aor. pass. subj. σκοτίζω to blacken, to darken. φάνῃ aor. act. subj. φαίνομαι to shine. The subj. moods are used in purpose clauses.

■ ἤκουσα aor. act. ind. ἀκούω to hear. ἀετός eagle. The 13 word may also be used for a vulture as well as an eagle which in this context would symbolize impending doom. The vulture hovers in mid heaven so as to be seen by all, and cries out in a great voice so that none will fail to hear (Mounce). πετομένου pres. mid. part. πέτομαι to fly. μεσουράνημα at the zenith, in the meridian, i.e., "in mid heaven" (Ford; Swete). κατοικοῦντας pres. act. part. κατοικέω to dwell, to inhabit, to live. μελλόντων pres. mid. part. μέλλω to be about to. It is used w. the inf. to express the fut. σαλπίζειν pres. act. inf. to blow a trumpet.

Ch. 9

■ ἐσάλπισεν aor. act. ind. σαλπίζω to blow the trumpet. 1 ἀστήρ star. πεπτωκότα perf. act. part. πίπτω to fall. The perf. is the dramatic perf. (s. Rev. 5:7; DM, 204; Mounce). ἐδόθη aor. pass. ind. δίδωμι. The theological or divine pass. indicating that

God is the One who gives. κλείς key (s. Rev. 1:18; 3:7). φρέαρ pit, well, shaft (s. Ford and esp. the references to the DSS; 1QS 9:16, 22; 10:19). ἄβυσσος bottomless, abyss, lit. "unfathomably deep." It is a place of imprisonment for disobedient spirits (Ford;

2 s. also Swete; Charles). ■ ἤνοιξεν aor. act. ind. ἀνοίγω to open. ἀνέβη aor. act. ind. ἀναβαίνω to go up, to ascend. καπνός smoke. κάμινος furnace. ἐσκοτώθη aor. pass. ind. σκοτόω to darken. As the smoke rises it blots out the sun and darkens the

3 atmosphere of the earth (Mounce). ■ ἐξῆλθον aor. act. ind. ἐξέρχομαι to come out. ἀκρίς locust, grasshopper. Throughout the OT the locust is a symbol of destruction. Bred in the desert, they invade cultivated areas in search of food. They may travel in a column of a hundred feet deep and up to four miles in length leaving the land stripped bare of all vegetation (Mounce; s. also FFB, 53; ZPEB III, 948–950). σκορπίος scorpion, a lobster-like vermin some four or five inches long, it had a claw on the end of the tail that secreted a poison when it struck. It should be noted that the demonic locusts of the first Woe have the power rather than the appearance of scorpions (Mounce; s. also FFB,

4 70; ZPEB V, 297). ■ ἐρρέθη aor. pass. ind. λέγω. ἀδικήσουσιν fut. act. ind. ἀδικέω to injure, to harm. χόρτος grass. χλωρός green. εἰ μή "except." σφραγίς seal. μέτωπον forehead (s.

5 Rev. 7:3f.). ■ ἀποκτείνωσιν pres. or aor. act. subj. ἀποκτείνω to kill. βασανισθήσονται fut. pass. ind. βασανίζω to torment, to torture. μήν month. βασανισμός torturing, torture. The word has the idea of punishment (Mounce). ὅταν w. the

6 subj. "whenever." παίσῃ aor. act. subj. παίω to strike. ■ ζητήσουσιν fut. act. ind. ζητέω to seek, to look for. εὑρήσουσιν fut. act. ind. ἐπιθυμήσουσιν fut. act. ind. ἐπιθυμέω to long for, to yearn after. ἀποθανεῖν aor. act. inf. ἀποθνήσκω to die. The inf. is used as the obj. of the verb "to long for," "to desire." φεύγει pres. act. ind. The pres. tense could perhaps be designated a "historical pres." in the fut., i.e., "death keeps fleeing from them."

7			■ ὁμοίωμα likeness, shape (s. Swete). ἵππος horse. ἡτοιμασμένοις perf. pass. part. ἑτοιμάζω to prepare, perf. to

8 be made ready. πόλεμος war. ■ θρίξ, τριχός hair. ὀδούς teeth.

9 λέων lion. ἦσαν impf. εἰμί. ■ θώραξ chest, breastplate. σιδηροῦς iron, of iron, made of iron. The scaly backs and flanks of the insects resembled coats of mail made of iron. The word "of iron" points to the material of which such armor was ordinarily made, and at the same time indicates the hopelessness of any effort to destroy assailants who were so protected (Swete). πτέρυξ wing. ἅρμα wagon, chariot. τρεχόντων pres.

act. part. τρέχω to run. Pliny wrote "this plague (of locusts) is
interpreted as a sign of the wrath of the gods; for they are seen
of exceptional size, and also they fly w. such a noise of wings that
they are believed to be birds, and they obscure the sun, making
the nations gaze upward in anxiety lest they should settle over
all their lands" (Pliny, *Natural History*, XI.xxv.104). ■ οὐρά tail. 10
κέντρον goad for an ox, sting. ἀδικῆσαι aor. act. inf. to injure,
to harm. In Italy the swarms of locusts were so bad that a law
was passed that war should be made upon them three times a
year by crushing the eggs, then the grubs, and at last the fully
grown insects. The law had the penalty of a deserter for the man
who held back (Pliny, *Natural History*, XI.xxxv.105).

　　■ ἀπῆλθεν aor. act. ind. ἀπέρχομαι to go out, to go forth, 12
to go away.

　　■ ἐσάλπισεν aor. act. ind. (s.v.1). ἤκουσα aor. act. ind. 13
ἀκούω to hear. μίαν "one." Here it means a "single or solitary
voice" (Mounce). κέρας horn. The horns on the altar were the
symbol of God's power (Ford). θυσιαστήριον place where sacrifices are made, altar. χρυσοῦς golden. ■ ἔχων pres. act. part. 14
λῆσον aor. act. imp. λύω to loose, to release. δεδεμένους perf.
pass. part. δέω to bind. The perf. tense emphasizes the state or
condition. ποταμός river. ■ ἐλύθησαν aor. pass. ind. to release. 15
ἡτοιμασμένοι perf. pass. part. (s.v.7). μήν month. ἐνιαυτός
year. ἀποκτείνωσιν pres. or aor. subj. ἀποκτείνω to kill
(s.v.5). ■ ἀριθμός number. στράτευμα army. ἱππικόν per- 16
taining to a horse, horseman. The army consisted of cavalry
(Swete). ■ ἵππος horse. ὅρασις appearance, vision. 17
καθημένους pres. mid. part. κάθημαι to sit. θώραξ breastplate
(s.v.9). πύρινος fiery, made of fire (s. Swete). ὑακίνθινος hya-
cinth-colored, i.e., dark blue, a dusky blue color as of sulphurous
smoke (BAG; MM). θειώδης sulphur, sulphur-colored. Brimstone is what is known today as sulphur; hence, yellow. It is
difficult to determine whether the breastplates were of three
colors each or whether each breastplate was of a single color; i.e.,
some red, some blue, some yellow (Mounce). λέων lion. στόμα
mouth. ἐκπορεύεται pres. mid. ind. to go out, to come out. πῦρ
fire. καπνός smoke. θεῖον brimstone, sulphur. ■ πληγή stripe, 18
wound, calamity, plague (AS). ἀπεκτάνθησαν aor. pass. ind.
ἀποκτείνω to kill. ἐκπορευομένου pres. mid. part. ■ οὐρά tail. 19
ὄφις snake. ἀδικοῦσιν pres. act. ind. to injure, to harm.

　　■ λοιπός rest. μετενόησαν aor. act. ind. μετανοέω to 20
change one's mind, to change one's thinking, to repent,
προσκυνήσουσιν fut. act. ind. προσκυνέω to worship. The
fut. ind. could be used here to express result rather than purpose

(s. RG, 992). **εἴδωλον** idol, false god. **ἀργυροῦς** silver. **χαλκοῦς** brass. **λίθινος** made of stone. **ξύλινος** wooden, made
21 of wood. **περιπατεῖν** pres. act. inf. to walk about. ■ **φόνος** murder. **φαρμακεία** magic art, sorcery. The use of drugs either for divination or for healing (s. BAG; MM; Ford; Gal. 5:20). It is suggested that here the word has the special sense of magic spells inciting to illicit lust (EGT). Pliny describes the use of many superstitious and magical practices to bring about healing (*Natural History*, XXVIII) one being "that snake bites and scorpion stings are relieved by intercourse" (*Natural History*, XXVIII.x.44; for further remedies against snake bites and scorpion stings, s. XXVII.xlii. 149–155). **πορνεία** unlawful sexual intercourse, immorality (s. Rev. 2:21). **κλέμμα** stealing theft.

Ch. 10

1 ■ **καταβαίνοντα** pres. act. part. **καταβαίνω** to come down, to descend. **περιβεβλημένον** perf. pass. part. **περιβάλλω** to cast about, to be clothed, to be enveloped. This word is used of encircling or throwing an embankment around a city, or clothing someone, and in the context it indicates that the angel is encircled by a cloud (Ford). **νεφέλη** cloud (s. Rev. 1:7). **ἶρις** rainbow (s. Rev. 4:3). Here the word refers to the ordinary rainbow of many colors connected w. the cloud and due in this instance to the shining of the angel's face (Swete). **στῦλος** pillar. **πῦρ** fire. Some have taken "the other angel" described here as being Christ Himself (Seiss; Scott) but others see him as
2 an angelic being rather than Christ Himself (s. Mounce). ■ **ἔχων** pres. act. part. **βιβλαρίδιον** little book, a very small book. **ἠνεῳγμένον** perf. pass. part. **ἀνοίγω** to open. The perf. pass. part. indicates "having been opened and remaining so," i.e., "standing open." **ἔθηκεν** aor. act. ind. **τίθημι** to place, to put.
3 **δεξιός** right. **εὔθηκεν** left. ■ **ἔκραξεν** aor. act. ind. **κράζω** to scream, to cry out in a loud voice. **λέων** lion. **μυκᾶται** pres. mid. ind. **μυκάομαι** to roar. The word is used of a low, deep sound like the lowing of an ox or the growl of thunder and the word may have been preferred here to indicate that the voice of the angel had not only volume but depth, at once compelling attention and inspiring awe (Swete). **ἐλάλησαν** aor. act. ind. to
4 speak. **βροντή** thunder. ■ **ἤμελλον** impf. act. ind. **μέλλω** to be about to. The word is used w. the inf. to express fut. The impf. here is inchoative w. the meaning "I was on the point of beginning to write" (RWP). **ἤκουσα** aor. act. ind. **ἀκούω** to hear. **σφράγισον** aor. act. imp. **σφραγίζω** to seal, to seal up (s. Rev. 5:1). **γράψῃς** aor. act. subj. The subj. used w. the neg. is a

834

prohibition or a neg. command "do not start to write." ■ 5
ἐστῶτα perf. act. part. ἵστημι perf. to stand. ἦρεν aor. act. ind.
αἴρω to lift up. ■ ὤμοσεν aor. act. ind. ὄμνυμι to take an oath, 6
to swear. ζῶντι pres. act. part. ζάω to live. ἔκτισεν aor. act. ind.
κτίζω to create. χρόνος time. The word here means "delay,"
i.e., "there shall be delay no longer." Now nothing stands in the
way of the final dramatic period of human history (Mounce).
οὐκέτι no longer. ἔσται fut. εἰμί. ■ ὅταν w. the subj. "when- 7
ever." μέλλῃ pres. act. subj. The subj. is used in an indefinite
temporal clause. σαλπίζειν pres. act. inf. to blow the trumpet.
ἐτελέσθη aor. pass. ind. τελέω to bring to the goal, to complete,
to bring to completion. The proleptic use of the aor. This use of
the aor. occurs in vivacious speech of that which is annunicated
as a consequence of a condition, and is expressed as if it had
already come to pass, the condition being regarded as fulfilled.
The condition here would be the indefinite temporal clause
"whenever he sounds the trumpet" (s. BG, 84f.). εὐηγγέλισεν
aor. act. ind. εὐαγγελίζω to proclaim the good news, to deliver
good news (s. TDNT).

■ λαλοῦσαν pres. act. part. ὕπαγε pres. act. imp. "go 8
now." This is a Hebraic construction (s. Charles). λάβε aor. act.
imp. λαμβάνω. βιβλίον book, small book. ■ ἀπῆλθα aor. act. 9
ind. ἀπέρχομαι to go out, to go away from. John left his position by the door and went to the angel (RWP). δοῦναι aor. act.
inf. δίδωμι to give. The inf. is used in indirect discourse after the
verb "saying" and is used to express a command (s. RWP).
κατάφαγε aor. act. imp. κατεσθίω to eat down, to eat up
completely. πικρανεῖ fut. act. ind. πικραίνω to make bitter.
The imp. followed by the fut. tense is a Hebraic form of a conditional clause in which the fut. expresses the result of having filled
the command. (For this construction, s. Phil. 4:7; Beyer, 238–
255.) κοιλία stomach. γλυκύς sweet. μέλι honey. ■ ἔλαβον 10
aor. act. ind. λαμβάνω. κατέφαγον aor. act. ind. κατεσθίω.
ἦν impf. εἰμί. ἔφαγον aor. act. ind. ἐσθίω to eat. The effective
use of the aor., i.e., "after I had finished eating." ἐπικράνθη aor.
pass. ind., ingressive aor. "my stomach became bitter." The Seer,
if he would be admitted into a part of God's secret, must be
prepared for very mixed sensations; the first joy of fuller knowledge would be followed by sorrow deeper and more bitter than
those of ordinary men (Swete). ■ λέγουσίν μοι pres. act. ind. 11
"they say unto me." It is best to take the expression as an
indefinite pl. or the equivalent of the pass. "it was said"
(Mounce). δεῖ (followed by the acc. and the inf.) "it is binding,"
"it is necessary." προφητεῦσαι aor. act. inf. προφητεύω to

seek forth, to prophesy. The inf. is used to explain "what is necessary." ἐπί "about," "concerning" (Mounce; s. also John 12:16). ἔθνος nations. γλῶσσα tongue, speech, language.

Ch. 11

1 ■ ἐδόθη aor. pass. ind. δίδωμι. κάλαμος reed. This served for a surveyor's rule or measuring rod and it might have been the cane which grows along the Jordan valley and was known as the "giant reed" of Mediterranean lands. It grows in swampy areas and sometimes it may reach the height of twelve or even fifteen or twenty feet (Ford; s. also FFB, 171). ῥάβδος staff. ἔγειρε pres. act. imp. ἐγείρω to rise, to get up. μέτρησον aor. act. imp. μετρέω to measure. ναός temple, sanctuary. θυσιαστήριον place where offerings or sacrifices are made, altar.

2 προσκυνοῦντας pres. act. part. προσκυνέω to worship. ■ αὐλή court. ἔξωθεν outside. The outer court of the temple in Jerusalem is called the Court of the Gentiles (Ford). ἔκβαλε aor. act. imp. βάλλω to throw out, to cast out. The word is used here in the sense of "to exclude," i.e., exclude it from the sanctuary though the other courts are included (Swete). μετρήσῃς aor. act. subj. The neg. used w. the subj. indicates a prohibition or neg. command. πατήσουσιν fut. act. ind. πατέω to walk upon, to tread down, to trample. μήν month. The designation "forty-two months" is equal to three and one half years which is the half

3 of the seven-year tribulation period. ■ δώσω fut. act. ind. δίδωμι. προφητεύσουσιν fut. act. ind. προφητεύω to prophe-sy. The construction "I shall give and they shall prophesy" is a Hebraic construction meaning "I will commission (or give per-mission to) my two witnesses to prophesy" (Charles). περιβεβλημένοι perf. pass. part. περιβάλλω to throw about, to clothe. σάκκος sack, sackcloth. The fabric from which a sack is made is usually dark in color; hence, it is especially suited to be worn as a mourning garment (BAG). As latter-day prophets the two witnesses wear the rough garb of their ancient predeces-sors (Zech. 13:4). Their message is to call to repentance

4 (Mounce). ■ ἐλαία olive tree. λυχνία lampstand. ἑστῶτες

5 perf. act. part. ἵστημι to stand. ■ ἀδικῆσαι aor. act. inf. ἀδικέω to injure, to harm. ἐκπορεύεται pres. mid. ind. to go out, to come out of. The pres. tense would be interat. indicating that fire would come out of their mouth every time someone would seek to harm them. κατεσθίει pres. act. ind. to eat up, to consume completely. θελήσῃ aor. act. subj. οὕτως so, thus. δεῖ (w. the acc. and the inf.) "it is binding," "it is necessary."

6 ἀποκτανθῆναι aor. pass. inf. ἀποκτείνω to kill. ■ κλεῖσαι

aor. act. inf. κλείω to close, to shut up. The inf. is epexegetical explaining the authority. ὑετός rain. βρέχῃ pres. act. subj. βρέχω to rain. The subj. is used in a neg. purpose clause which may also be considered a result clause. στρέφειν pres. act. inf. to turn, to change. The inf. is used epexegetically explaining the authority. πατάξαι aor. act. inf. πατάσσω to strike, to hit. πληγή blow, plague. ὁσάκις as often as. Used w. the particle ἐάν and the subj. to express an indefinite temporal clause "as often as they will" (RWP). ■ ὅταν w. the subj. "whenever." 7 τελέσωσιν aor. act. subj. τελέω to complete, to finish. θηρίον animal, wild animal. ἀναβαῖνον pres. mid. part. ἀναβαίνω to go up, to ascend. ἄβυσσος bottomless pit, abyss (s. Rev. 9:1). ποιήσει fut. act. ind. πόλεμος war. νικήσει fut. act. ind. νικάω to gain the victory, to be victor, to overcome. ἀποκτενεῖ fut. act. ind. ἀποκτείνω to kill. ■ πτῶμα that which is fallen, 8 corpse, dead body. πλατεῖα wide street, open street. καλεῖται pres. pass. ind. πνευματικῶς spiritually, pertaining to the Spirit. Perhaps the idea here is not "allegorically," but rather how the Spirit of God interprets. ὅπου where. Here the word is used as a pron. "the place where." ἐσταυρώθη aor. pass. ind. σταυρόω to crucify. ■ βλέπουσιν pres. act. ind. ἐκ τῶν λαῶν "some of 9 the peoples." The expression is to be taken as a partitive gen. (Mounce). ἥμισυ half. ἀφίουσιν pres. act. ind. to leave, to allow. τεθῆναι aor. pass. inf. τίθημι to place, to put. μνῆμα grave. ■ κατοικοῦντες pres. act. part. κατοικέω to reside, to 10 dwell. εὐφραίνονται pres. mid. ind. to rejoice, to be happy. πέμψουσιν fut. act. ind. πέμπω to send. ἀλλήλοις dat. pl. "to one another." ἐβασάνισαν aor. act. ind. βασανίζω to torment, to torture. ■ εἰσῆλθεν aor. act. ind. εἰσέρχομαι to come 11 into, to enter. ἔστησαν aor. act. ind. ἵστημι to stand. ἐπέπεσεν aor. act. ind. ἐπιπίπτω to fall upon. θεωροῦντας pres. act. part. θεωρέω to see, to behold, to watch. ■ ἤκουσαν 12 aor. act. ind. ἀκούω. ἀνάβατε aor. act. imp. ἀναβαίνω to come up. ἀνέβησαν aor. act. ind. ἀναβαίνω to go up, to ascend. νεφέλη cloud. ἐθεώρησαν aor. act. ind. ■ ἐγένετο aor. mid. 13 ind. γίνομαι to be, to become, to happen, to come about. σεισμός earthquake. ἔπεσεν aor. act. ind. πίπτω. ἀπεκτάνθησαν aor. pass. ind. ἀποκτείνω to kill. ὀνόματα names, i.e., "people," "person." (For the use of the word in this sense, s. BS, 196f.) ἔμφοβος afraid, scared. ἔδωκαν aor. act. ind. δίδωμι to give. ■ ἀπῆλθεν aor. act. ind. ἀπέρχομαι to go away, to pass. 14 ταχύ quickly, soon. ■ ἐσάλπισεν aor. act. ind. σαλπίζω to blow the trumpet. 15

ἐγένοντο aor. mid. ind. (s.v.13). χριστός anointed, Messiah, Christ. βασιλεύσει fut. act. ind. βασιλεύω to be king, to rule
16 as a king, to reign. ■ καθήμενοι pres. mid. part. κάθημαι to sit. ἔπεσαν aor. act. ind. (s.v.13). προσεκύνησαν aor. act. ind.
17 προσκυνέω to worship. ■ παντοκράτωρ almighty (s. Rev. 1:8). ὤν pres. part. εἰμί. ἦν impf. εἰμί. εἴληφας perf. act. ind. λαμβάνω. The perf. may indicate that God has taken the power permanently (s. Mounce). ἐβασίλευσας aor. act. ind.
18 βασιλεύω. ■ ὠργίσθησαν aor. pass. ind. ὀργίζω to make angry, pass. to be angry. ὀργή wrath, anger. κριθῆναι aor. pass. inf. κρίνω to judge. δοῦναι aor. act. inf. δίδωμι. The inf. are used to explain the word "time," "season." μισθός reward, wage, pay. φοβουμένοις pres. mid. part. φοβέομαι to fear, to have reverence for. διαφθεῖραι aor. act. inf. διαφθείρω to destroy, to corrupt. The prep. in compound is perfective, i.e., to
19 utterly destroy. ■ ἠνοίγη aor. pass. ind. ἀνοίγω to open. ναός temple, sanctuary. ὤφθη aor. pass. ind. ὁράω to see, pass. to be seen, to appear. κιβωτός box, ark. διαθήκη covenant. In the OT the ark of the covenant was a symbol of the abiding presence of God (Mounce). ἀστραπή lightning. βροντή thunder. σεισμός earthquake (s. Rev. 6:12). χάλαζα hail.

Ch. 12

1 ■ ὤφθη aor. pass. ind. ὁράω to see, pass. to be seen, to appear. περιβεβλημένη perf. pass. part. περιβάλλω to cast about, to clothe, pass. to be clothed. σελήνη moon. ὑποκάτω w. the gen. "under." ἀστήρ star. Of all the various interpretations of the woman here the most fitting is to view the woman as representing the nation Israel. In the OT the image of a woman is a classical symbol for Zion, Jerusalem, and Israel (Ford; Scott; Bousset). The twelve stars may be an allusion to the
2 twelve tribes of Israel (s. Mounce). ■ ἐν γαστρὶ ἔχουσα "to have something in the stomach," i.e., "to be pregnant." κράζει pres. act. ind. to scream, to cry out w. a loud voice. ὠδίνουσα pres. act. part. ὠδίνω to have birth pains, to be in labor. βασανιζομένη pres. pass. part. βασανίζω to torment, to be in pain. τεκεῖν aor. act. inf. τίκτω to bear a child, to give birth. The
3 inf. is used epexegetically explaining the pain. ■ δράκων dragon. John does not leave us in doubt as to the identity of this monster: he is "the old serpent, he that is called the devil and Satan" (v. 9; cf. 20:2) (Mounce). πυρρός fiery, red. κέρας horn. The horn was a symbol of strength. διάδημα diadem, a royal crown. The royal crown was a symbol of political authority and denotes
4 sovereignty (Swete). ■ οὐρά tail. σύρει pres. act. ind. to drag,

to sweep. ἔβαλεν aor. act. ind. βάλλω to throw. ἔστηκεν perf.
act. ind. ἵστημι to stand. μελλούσης pres. act. part. μέλλω to
be about to. Used w. the inf. to express the fut. tense. ὅταν w.
the subj. whenever. τέκη aor. act. subj. τίκτω to give birth.
καταφάγη aor. act. subj. κατεσθίω to eat up, to consume.
■ ἔτεκεν aor. act. ind. τίκτω. ἄρσεν male. ποιμαίνειν pres. 5
act. inf. to shepherd, to lead, to rulc. Thc inf. is used in the
construction expressing the fut. ῥάβδος staff. σιδηροῦς made
of iron. ἡρπάσθη aor. pass. ind. ἁρπάζω to seize, to snatch, to
take away. ■ ἔφυγεν aor. act. ind. φεύγω to flee. 6
ἡτοιμασμένον perf. pass. part. ἑτοιμάζω to prepare. The perf.
pass. indicates "to stand prepared," i.e., "that which has been
prepared and now stands ready." τρέφωσιν pres. act. subj.
τρέφω to nourish. The subj. is used in a purpose clause. The pl.
may be impersonal and equivalent to a pass.

■ ἐγένετο aor. mid. ind. γίνομαι. πόλεμος war. 7
πολεμῆσαι aor. act. inf. πολεμέω to conduct war, to fight. The
nom. used w. the inf. may be the result of a Hebraic construction
(s. Charles). ἐπολέμησεν aor. act. ind. ■ ἴσχυσεν aor. act. ind. 8
ἰσχύω to be strong, to be strong enough, to be able. The Dragon's supreme effort was not only a failure, but it resulted in his
final expulsion from heaven (Swete). εὑρέθη aor. pass. ind. ■ 9
ἐβλήθη aor. pass. ind. βάλλω. ὄφις snake. ἀρχαῖος old, ancient. καλούμενος pres. pass. part. πλανῶν pres. act. part.
πλανάω to lead astray, to deceive. The pres. part. indicates a
continuous action which has become a habitual character. ■ 10
ἤκουσα aor. act. ind. ἀκούω. κατήγωρ one who brings a legal
charge against another, accuser. κατηγορῶν pres. act. part.
κατηγορέω to bring a legal accusation, to accuse. ■ ἐνίκησαν 11
aor. act. ind. νικάω to be a victor, to overcome. διά w. the acc.
"because of." The prep. here gives the ground, not the means of
their victory (Mounce). ἀρνίον lamb. ἠγάπησαν aor. act. ind.
ἀγαπάω. Their non-attachment to life was carried to the extent
of being ready to die for their faith (Swete). ■ εὐφραίνεσθε 12
pres. mid. imp. εὐφραίνομαι to rejoice, to be happy.
σκηνοῦντες pres. act. part. σκηνόω to tabernacle, to live in a
tent, to dwell. Here the word does not indicate a temporary
residence, but emphasizes the presence of God (Mounce). οὐαί
woe. The acc. which follows may be acc. of general reference
instead of the normal dat. κατέβη aor. act. ind. καταβαίνω to
go down, effective aor. "he did go down" (RWP). ἔχων pres. act.
part. θυμός anger, burning anger (s. Trench, Synonyms, 131f.).
εἰδώς perf. act. part. οἶδα. The part. is causal. ■ ἐδίωξεν aor. 13
act. ind. διώκω to hunt, to pursue, to persecute. This would

839

indicate the tremendous persecution to be suffered by Israel in
14 the tribulation period. ■ ἐδόθησαν aor. pass. ind. δίδωμι. The
pass. would be the theological or divine pass. indicating that God
is the One who gives. πτέρυξ wing. ἀετός eagle. πέτηται pres.
mid. subj. πέτομαι to fly. The subj. is used in a purpose clause.
ἥμισυ half. The words indicate that the nation Israel will be
protected from total destruction for the last three and one half
15 years of the Tribulation. ■ στόμα mouth. ὀπίσω behind, after.
ποταμός river. ποταμοφόρητος to be carried by the river, to
be swept away by the river. ποιήσῃ aor. act. subj. The verb is
used in connection w. the noun to express the verbal action
contained in the noun. The subj. is used in a purpose clause.
ἐβοήθησεν aor. act. ind. βοηθέω to help. ἤνοιξεν aor. act. ind.
ἀνοίγω to open. κατέπιεν aor. act. ind. καταπίνω to swallow
17 down, to swallow up completely. ■ ὠργίσθη aor. pass. ind.
ὀργίζω to make angry, ingressive aor. "to become angry."
ἀπῆλθεν aor. act. ind. ἀπέρχομαι to go out, to go away from,
to depart. ποιῆσαι aor. act. inf. The inf. is used to express intent
or purpose. λοιπός rest. σπέρμα seed. τηρούντων pres. act.
18 part. τηρέω to watch, to keep, to observe. ■ ἐστάθη aor. pass.
ind. ἵστημι to stand. ἄμμος sand, beach.

Ch. 13

1   ■ θάλασσα sea. The sea is an apt symbol of the agitated
surface of unregenerated humanity and esp. of the seething caul-
dron of national and social life, out of which the great historical
movements of the world arise (Swete). θηρίον beast, monster.
This is the monstrous person in whom the political power of the
world is finally concentrated and represented and who is spoken
of in Daniel 7 and called "the man of sin" in 2 Thessalonians 2:3
(s. Walvoord; Seiss, ZPEB I, 180f.). ἀναβαῖνον pres. act. part.
ἀναβαίνω to go up, to arise, to ascend. ἔχον pres. act. part.
κέρας horn. διάδημα diadem, royal crown. These two figures
represent the mighty political power and also stand for kings and
their kingdom as in Daniel 7 (s. Walvoord). βλασφημία blas-
2 phemy. ■ πάρδαλις leopard. ἄρκος bear. λέων lion. This beast
combines the characteristics of Daniel's beasts in which the
leopard (or panther) indicates agility, cat-like vigilance, craft,
and fierce cruelty, and the feet of the bear indicate the slow
strength and power to crush. The lion blends massive strength
w. feline dexterity, following up a stealthy and perhaps unobserved policy of repression w. the sudden terrors of a hostile
edict (Swete). ἔδωκεν aor. act. ind. δίδωμι. δράκων dragon.
The great political leader receives his power directly from Satan.

■ μίαν ἐκ τῶν κεφαλῶν "one of his heads." This takes up the 3
narrative of v. 1 and the verb to be supplied is "and I saw"
(Swete). ἐσφαγμένην perf. pass. part. σφάζω to slay, to slaughter, to kill. The use of this word indicates that the deadly wound
was like the slaying of the Lamb (s. Bousset; Swete). πληγή
blow, wound. The following gen. is descriptive "death wound,"
"lethal wound" (Ford). ἐθεραπεύθη aor. pass. ind. θεραπεύω
to heal. Here we have the political death and resurrection of the
beast (Scott). ἐθαυμάσθη aor. pass. ind. θαυμάζω to cause
someone to wonder, to cause to marvel. ὀπίσω behind, after.
The pregnant use of the prep. means "all the earth wondered at
and followed after the beast" (RWP). ■ προσεκύνησαν aor. 4
act. ind. προσκυνέω to worship. πολεμῆσαι aor. act. inf.
πολεμέω to wage war, to fight against.

■ ἐδόθη aor. pass. ind. δίδωμι. λαλοῦν pres. act. part. 5
ποιῆσαι aor. act. inf. to do, i.e., to carry out his work. During
the forty-two months the beast actively carries out the will of the
dragon (Mounce; Swete). μήν month, acc. of time "for forty-two
months." ■ ἤνοιξεν aor. act. ind. ἀνοίγω to open. 6
βλασφημῆσαι aor. act. inf. βλασφημέω to ridicule, to slander, to blaspheme. σκηνή tent, habitation, dwelling place, tabernacle. To blaspheme the name of God is to speak evil of all that
He is and stands for. The name sums up the person. His tabernacle is His dwelling place (Mounce). σκηνοῦντας pres. act.
part. σκηνόω to live in a tent, to tabernacle, to dwell. ■ 7
πόλεμος war. νικῆσαι aor. act. inf. νικάω to win a victory, to
conquer, to overcome. ■ προσκυνήσουσιν fut. act. ind. to 8
worship. αὐτόν "him" The masc. pron. indicates that the beast
is a person. κατοικοῦντες pres. act. part. κατοικέω to live, to
dwell, to reside. γέγραπται perf. pass. ind. The perf. tense
indicates the continuing results and binding authority of that
which was written (s. MM). βιβλίον book, little book. ἀρνίον
lamb. καταβολή foundation, laying of a foundation. The "foundation of the world" refers to the creation of the visible order
(Mounce; s. also Eph. 1:4; 1 Peter 1:20).

■ ἀκουσάτω aor. act. imp. ■ αἰχμαλωσία one taken cap- 9/10
tive at spear point, captivity. ὑπάγει pres. act. ind. to go forth.
The pres. tense is gnomic indicating the statement of a general
truth. The proverbial style of the v. could be translated "if any
man leads into captivity, into captivity he goes." Thus, the v.
would stress that the enemies of God's people will be requited
for their persecution of believers in the same form they employed (captivity for captivity, sword for sword) (Mounce).
μάχαιρα sword. ἀποκτενεῖ fut. act. ind. ἀποκτείνω to kill. δεῖ

(w. the acc. and inf.) "it is binding," "it is necessary."
ἀποκτανθῆναι aor. pass. inf. ἀποκτείνω to kill.

11   ■ θηρίον wild animal, beast, monster. The second beast
introduced is the religious leader or false prophet. ἀναβαῖνον
pres. act. part. to come up, to ascend (s.v.1). κέρας horn. ὅμοιος
like. ἀρνίον lamb. The second beast is a pseudochrist (Swete).
ἐλάλει impf. act. ind. The impf. pictures the customary action.

12   δράκων dragon (s.v.2). ■ προσκυνήσουσιν fut. act. ind.
(s.v.8). The false prophet who is a religious leader also inspired
of Satan causes the world to worship the man of sin who has set
himself up as God (s. 2 Thess. 2:4f.). ἐθεραπεύθη aor. pass. ind.

13   to heal (s.v.3). ■ ποιῇ pres. act. subj. to make, to cause. The subj.
could either be a purpose or result clause (RWP). καταβαίνειν
pres. act. inf. to come down. The inf. is used to complete the verb

14   "to make, to cause." ■ πλανᾷ pres. act. ind. to lead astray, to
deceive. ἐδόθη aor. pass. ind. (s.v.5). ποιῆσαι aor. act. inf.

15   (s.v.5). εἰκων image. ἔζησεν aor. act. ind. ζάω to live. ■ δοῦναι
aor. act. inf. δίδωμι. λαλήσῃ aor. act. subj. ποιήσῃ aor. act.
subj. The subj. are used in a purpose or result clause. The second
beast is given the power to animate the image of the first beast.
He gives to it the breath of life and the image speaks (Mounce).
προσκυνήσωσιν aor. act. subj. προσκυνέω. The subj. is used
in a third-class conditional clause which views the condition as

16   a possibility. ἀποκτανθῶσιν aor. pass. subj. (s.v.10). ■
πλούσιος rich, wealthy. πτωχός poor, poor as a beggar.
ἐλεύθερος free. δῶσιν aor. act. subj. δίδωμι. χάραγμα brand,
mark. (For various usages of the brand in the ancient world, s.
Mounce; BS, 242; LAE, 341f.; Ford; TDNT.) δεξιός right.

17   μέτωπον forehead. ■ δύνηται pres. act. subj. The subj. is in a
purpose clause or the clause is the obj. of the verb. ἀγοράσαι
aor. act. inf. ἀγοράζω to buy. πωλῆσαι aor. act. inf. πωλέω to

18   sell. ἔχων pres. act. part. ἀριθμός number. ■ νοῦς understanding, comprehension. ψηφισάτω aor. act. imp. ψηφίζω to count
up, to calculate, lit. to count w. pebbles, to reckon (s. MM; Luke
14:28).

Ch. 14

1   ■ καὶ εἶδον, καὶ ἰδού "and I saw and behold." The words
introduce a new and dramatic part of the vision (s. Rev. 4:1; 6:2;
Mounce). ἀρνίον lamb (s. Rev. 5:6). ἑστός perf. act. part.
ἵστημι to stand. That the lamb is standing forms a contrast w.
the beasts who are rising and indicates "being established,"
"standing firm," "holding one's own ground" (Ford). ἔχουσαι
pres. act. part. γεγραμμένον perf. pass. part. to write, to in-

scribe. The perf. tense indicates the continuing result of the authoritative writing. The seal consists in the name of God inscribed on the brow. This inscription declares that the person so inscribed is God's own possession (Charles). The scene is an obvious contrast to the beast of chapter 13 whose followers are stamped w. his mark on the right hand or forehead (Mounce). μέτωπον forehead, brow. ■ ἤκουσα aor. act. ind. ἀκούω. 2 βροντή thunder. κιθαρῳδός one who plays on a harp, harpist. κιθαριζόντων pres. act. part. κιθαρίζω to play the harp. κιθάρα harp (s. Rev. 5:8; 1 Cor. 14:7). ■ ᾄδουσιν pres. act. ind. 3 to sing. ᾠδή song (s. Rev. 5:9). ζῷον living creature. ἐδύνατο impf. mid. ind. The impf. is used of unfulfilled action. μαθεῖν aor. act. inf. μανθάνω to learn. εἰ μή "except." ἠγορασμένοι perf. pass. part. ἀγοράζω to buy, to redeem, to purchase (s. APC, 50f.; TDNT). ■ ἐμολύνθησαν aor. pass. ind. μολύνω to 4 defile, to soil, to stain. παρθένος virgin. It seems best to take this description of chastity in a figurative sense indicating that they have kept themselves pure from all defiling relationships w. the pagan world system. They have resisted the seduction of the great harlot, Rome, w. whom the kings of the earth have committed fornication (Mounce). ἀκολουθοῦντες pres. act. part. to follow, to follow after, to be a disciple of someone. ἀκολουθέω w. the subj. "wherever." ὅπου ἄν pres. act. subj. ὑπάγῃ to go forth, to go. ἠγοράσθησαν aor. pass. ind. ἀγοράζω to buy at the market place, to purchase, to redeem. ἀπὸ ἀνθρώπων "from men," "from among men." The part. here denotes not "separation," but "extraction" (Swete). ἀπαρχή firstfruit. In the OT until the firstfruit of harvest or flock were offered to God the rest of the crop could not be put to profane or secular use (Ford; s. also Rom. 16:5; 1 Cor. 16:15). ■ στόμα mouth. εὑρέθη 5 aor. pass. ind. ἄμωμος unblemished. This is a Levitical sacrificial term meaning not spoiled by any flaw. If "unblemished" continues the metaphor of the "firstfruit" it would refer to "flock" rather than "crop," and Lamb (Ford).

■ πετόμενον pres. mid. part. πέτομαι to fly. 6 μεσουράνημα mid-heaven (s. Rev. 8:13). ἔχοντα pres. act. part. εὐαγγέλιον good news, good tidings. It is not the gospel of God's redeeming grace in Christ Jesus, but as the following vv. show a summons to fear, honor, and worship the Creator (Mounce). εὐαγγελίσαι aor. act. inf. εὐαγγελίζω to proclaim good news. The inf. is used to express purpose or it could be also epexegetical explaining that which the angel has (s. RWP; Swete). καθημένους pres. mid. part. κάθημαι to sit. (For the variant reading "the ones dwelling on the earth" rather than "the ones sitting on the earth," s. Charles.) ἔθνος nation. φυλή tribe.

7 γλῶσσα tongue, language. ■ λέγων pres. act. part. φοβήθητε aor. pass. imp. φοβέομαι to fear, to show reverence. δότε aor. act. imp. δίδωμι to give. κρίσις judging, judgment. προσκυνήσατε aor. act. imp. προσκυνέω to worship. The eternal gospel calls upon men to fear and honor the Creator, for the hour of judgment is at hand. God has revealed Himself in nature so that men are without excuse (Mounce). ποιήσαντι aor. act. part. to make, to create. πηγή spring.

8   ■ ἠκολούθησεν aor. act. ind. ἀκολουθέω to follow. ἔπεσεν aor. act. ind. πίπτω to fall. The ancient Mesopotamian city of Babylon had become the political and religious capital of a world empire, renowned for its luxury and moral corruption. Above all it was the great enemy of the people of God. For the early church the city of Rome was a contemporary Babylon (Mounce). θυμός anger, burning anger (s. Rev. 12:12). πορνεία immorality, illicit sexual activity. πεπότικεν perf. act. ind. ποτίζω to give to drink, to cause to drink. The drinking of the wine indicates the intoxicating influence of Babylon's vices (Ford).

9   ■ θηρίον wild beast, monster. εἰκών image. χάραγμα
10 brand, mark. ■ πίεται fut. mid. ind. πίνω to drink. The pron. "he" in Gr. indicates that the pron. is there to emphasize "man," not to indicate another person. The author probably means that one cannot drink one cup and not the other for both are linked; the consequence of drinking Babylon's cup is the inescapable necessity to receive the Lord's (Ford). κεκερασμένου perf. pass. part. καρέννυμι to mix. The word was used of the preparation of wine by the addition of various spices and the word later came to mean "properly prepared" (Mounce; s. also Charles). ἄκρατος unmixed, undiluted, not diluted w. water. The words mean that those who worship the image will drink the wine of God's wrath poured out in full strength, untempered by the mercy and grace of God (Mounce). ποτήριον cup. ὀργή wrath, anger. This word refers more to the settled feeling of righteous indignation whereas the word in v.8 and the first part of v. 10 refers to the white heat of God's anger (s. Mounce; Swete; Trench, Synonyms, 131ff.). βασανισθήσεται fut. pass. ind.

11 βασανίζω to torment, to torture. ■ καπνός smoke. βασανισμός torturing, pain, suffering. ἀναβαίνει pres. act. ind. to go up, to ascend. The pres. tense connected w. the temporal designation "forever" indicates a continual unbroken action. ἀνάπαυσις stopping, resting, ceasing, relief. The word was used in the papyri w. the idea of relief from public duties and the word

contains the idea of temporary rest as a preparation for fut. toil (MM). The time indicator "day and night" is gen. of time indicating the kind of time within which something takes place (s. RG, 495; MT, 235; DM, 77; BD, 99f.). προσκυνοῦντες pres. act. part. προσκυνέω. ■ τηροῦντες pres. act. part. τηρέω to 12 keep, to observe. πίστις Ἰησοῦ "faith of Jesus." The gen. is obj. gen., i.e., "faith in Jesus."

■ ἤκουσα aor. act. ind. γράψον aor. act. imp. μακάριος 13 happy, blessed. ἀποθνήσκοντες pres. act. part. ἀποθνήσκω to die. ἵνα. The word here passes into the meaning "in that" rather than "in order that" (Swete). ἀναπαήσονται fut. mid. ind. ἀναπαύομαι to have relief, to cease, to rest. κόπος toil, labor, hard work which produces weariness (s. Rev. 2:2).

■ καὶ εἶδον, καὶ ἰδού "and I saw and behold" (s.v.1). 14 νεφέλη cloud (s. Rev. 1:7). λευκός white. καθήμενον pres. mid. part. to sit. This is none other than the risen Christ (Mounce). ἔχων pres. act. part. χρυσοῦς golden. The golden crown or wreath indicated the type of crown or wreath given to a victor and this designates the Messiah as the One who has conquered and thereby won the right to act in judgment (Mounce; s. also Trench, Synonyms, 78–81; esp. CBB). δρέπανον sickle. ὀξύς sharp. ■ ἐξῆλθεν aor. act. ind. 15 ἐξέρχομαι to come out. ναός temple, sanctuary. The angel that delivers the divine command to commence the harvest comes out from within the temple, that most holy place of the presence of God. Judgment upon sin is a necessary function of righteousness (Mounce). κράζων pres. act. part. κράζω to scream, to cry out w. a loud voice. πέμψον aor. act. imp. πέμπω to send, ingressive aor. "start at once." θέρισον aor. act. imp. θερίζω to harvest, ingressive aor. "begin at once." θερίσαι aor. act. inf. The inf. is epexegetical explaining the word "hour." The classical use of reaping to symbolize death and destruction is very common (s. EGT). ἐξηράνθη aor. pass. ind. ξηραίνω to dry, to be dry. Here the word indicates perfect ripeness (Swete). θερισμός harvest. ■ ἔβαλεν aor. act. ind. βάλλω to cast. ἐθερίσθη aor. 16 pass. ind.

■ θυσιαστήριον altar. ἐφώνησεν aor. act. ind. φωνέω to 18 make a sound, to call out. τρύγησον aor. act. imp. τρυγάω to gather ripe fruit, esp. to pick grapes (BAG). βότρυς grapes, bunch of grapes. ἄμπελος grape vine. ἤκμασαν aor. act. ind. ἀκμάζω to be ripe, to be in the prime, to be at the peak (s. GEW I, 53; Mounce). σταφυλή the ripe grape cluster (Swete). ■ 19 ἐτρύγησεν aor. act. ind. (s.v. 18). ληνός trough, vat, wine press (AS; s. also Matt. 21:33). ■ ἐπατήθη aor. pass. ind. πατέω to 20

walk, to walk on, to trample. In biblical days grapes were tram-
pled by foot in a trough which had a duct leading to a lower basin
where the juice collected. The treading of grapes was a familiar
figure for the execution of divine wrath upon the enemies of God
(Mounce; Isa. 63:3). ἔξωθεν w. the gen. "outside." χαλινός
bridle. ἵππος horse. στάδιον stadion. A stadion measures about
670 feet so that the distance here would be approximately 184
miles (s. Mounce). When Jerusalem was taken by Titus, Josephus says that the Roman soldiers slew all they met w. and made
the whole city run down w. blood to such a degree that the fire
of many houses was quenched w. these men's blood (Govett;
Josephus, *Jewish War*, VI, 406).

Ch. 15

1   ■ ἄλλο "another." The words "another sign" look back to
12:1 and 3 (Swete). θαυμαστός amazing, that which causes
wonder. ἔχοντας pres. act. part. πληγή blow, wound, plague.
ἐτελέσθη aor. pass. ind. τελέω to bring to conclusion, to complete.

2   ■ ὑάλινος glassy, crystal (s. Rev. 4:6). μεμιγμένην perf.
pass. part. μείγνυμι to mix. πῦρ fire. νικῶντας pres. act. part.
νικάω to gain a victory, to be victor, to overcome. θηρίον wild
beast, monster. εἰκών image. ἀριθμός number. ἑστῶτας perf.
act. part. ἵστημι to stand. This phrase could mean "standing
on" or "standing by." This scene of the victors standing on the
heavenly sea w. harps in their hands and praising God recalls
Israel's song of triumph over Egypt on the shore of the Red Sea
3   (Charles). κιθάρα harp, lyre. ■ ᾄδουσιν pres. act. ind. to sing.
ᾠδή song. ἀρνίον lamb. παντοκράτωρ almighty (s. Rev. 1:8).
4   ■ φοβηθῇ aor. pass. subj. φοβέομαι to fear, to show respect, to
reverence. δοξάσει fut. act. ind. δοξάζω to glorify. ὅσιος undefiled by sin, free from wickedness, pure, holy (T; CBB; Trench,
Synonyms, 328f.; TDNT). ἥξουσιν fut. act. ind. ἥκω to come.
προσκυνήσουσιν fut. act. ind. προσκυνέω to worship.
δικαίωμα righteous deed. This refers to the acts of God which
meet His standards of faithfulness and loyalty to His person and
word. It could refer also to God's judgments in a judicial sense
(s. TDNT; Ford; Charles). ἐφανερώθησαν aor. pass. ind.
φανερόω to make clear, to manifest, to reveal.

5   ■ ἠνοίγη aor. pass. ind. ἀνοίγω to open. ναός temple,
sanctuary. σκηνή tent, tabernacle. The word refers to the dwell-
6   ing place of God. ■ ἐξῆλθον aor. act. ind. ἐξέρχομαι to go out,
to come out. ἐνδεδυμένοι perf. pass. part. ἐνδύω to dress, to put
on clothes, to be clothed. λίνον linen. λαμπρός shining. The

robes of linen, pure and shining, denote the noble and sacred nature of their office (Mounce). περιεζωσμένοι perf. pass. part. περιζώννυμι to be girded around, to wear a wide belt which held up the long flowing garments. στῆθος breast, chest. ζώνη wide belt, girdle. χρυσοῦς. The golden girdles are symbolic of royal and priestly functions (Mounce; s. also Rev. 1:13). ■ ζῷον 7 living creature. ἔδωκεν aor. act. ind. δίδωμι. φιάλη bowl. This was a wide shallow bowl like a deep saucer (Mounce; T; NBD, 1310). γεμούσας pres. act. part. γέμω to be full, to be full of. ζῶντος pres. act. part. ζάω to live. ■ ἐγεμίσθη aor. pass. ind. 8 γεμίζω to fill up, to make full. καπνός smoke. ἐδύνατο impf. mid. ind. εἰσελθεῖν aor. act. inf. εἰσέρχομαι to go into. τελεσθῶσιν aor. pass. subj. to complete. The subj. is used in an indefinite temporal clause.

Ch. 16

■ ἤκουσα aor. act. ind. ἀκούω to hear. ναός temple, sanc- 1 tuary. ὑπάγετε pres. act. imp. ὑπάγω to go forth. ἐκχέετε impf. act. ind. ἐκχέω to pour out, to empty out. φιάλη bowl. (s. Rev. 15:7). θυμός anger, burning, blistering anger (s. Rev. 14:8, 10).

■ ἀπῆλθεν aor. act. ind. ἀπέρχομαι to go forth, to go out. 2 ἐξέχεεν aor. act. ind. ἐκχέω. ἐγένετο aor. mid. ind. γίνομαι to become, to happen, to come to pass. ἕλκος sore, abscess, boil. This is the word used in the LXX of the boils w. which God smote the Egyptians (Ford; s. also Mounce). (For Pliny's description of the treatment of boils and carbuncles, s. Pliny, Natural History, XXX, 107–108.) ἔχοντες pres. act. part. χάραγμα brand, mark. θηρίον beast, monster. εἰκών image.

■ ἀπέθανεν aor. act. ind. ἀποθνήσκω to die. 3

■ ποταμός river. πηγή spring. ■ ὤν pres. part. εἰμί. ἦν 4/5 impf. εἰμί. ὅσιος pure, holy (s. Rev. 15:4). ἔκρινας aor. act. ind. κρίνω to judge. ■ δέδωκας perf. act. ind. δίδωμι. πεῖν aor. act. 6 inf. πίνω to drink. The inf. is epexegetical after the verb "to give" (s. RWP). ἄξιοί εἰσιν "they are worthy," i.e., "it is what they deserve" (Mounce). ■ θυσιαστήριον place of sacrifice, 7 altar. ναί "yes," "Yea." παντοκράτωρ almighty (s. Rev. 1:8). ἀληθινός true, genuine. κρίσις judging, judgment.

■ ἐδόθη aor. pass. ind. δίδωμι. The verb is used in the sense 8 of "he was given authority," "he was allowed." καυματίσαι aor. act. inf. καυματίζω to burn, to scorch (s. Ford; Swete). ἐκαυματίσθησαν aor. pass. ind. καῦμα heat, scorching. The cognate acc. retained w. a pass. verb (RWP). ἐβλασφήμησαν aor. act. ind. βλασφημέω to blaspheme. πληγή blow, wound, plague. μετενόησαν aor. act. ind. μετανοέω to change one's mind, to change one's thinking, to repent. δοῦναι aor. act. inf. δίδωμι. The inf. is used to express actual or realized results.

10 ■ ἐσκοτωμένη perf. pass. part. σκοτόω to make dark, to darken. ἐμασῶντο perf. mid. ind. μασάομαι to chew, to gnaw. The word indicates that the pain caused by the scorching heat of the fourth plague and the malignant sores of the first was such that men chewed their tongues in agony. The phrase was used as an indication of intolerable pain (Swete; s. also Matt. 8:12). γλῶσσα tongue. πόνος pain, agony.

12 ■ ἐξηράνθη aor. pass. ind. ξηραίνω to dry, to dry up. ἐτοιμασθῇ aor. pass. subj. ἐτοιμάζω to prepare, to make ready. Subj. used in purpose clause. ἀνατολή rising, "rising of the sun,"
13 i.e., "the east" (s. Matt. 2:1). ■ δράκων dragon. ψευδοπροφήτης false prophet. ἀκάθαρτος impure, unclean. βάτραχος frog. The frog was classified as an unclean animal, an abomination (Lev. 11:10, 41) (Ford; s. also FFB, 33). The unclean spirits proceed from the "mouths" of the unholy triumvirate, suggesting the persuasive and deceptive propaganda which in the last days will lead men to an unconditional commitment
14 to the cause of evil (Mounce). ■ ποιοῦντα pres. act. part. to do, to perform. ἐκπορεύεται pres. mid. ind. to go out, to proceed from. συναγαγεῖν aor. act. inf. συνάγω to lead together, to gather together, to assemble. The inf. is used to express purpose.
15 πόλεμος war. ■ κλέπτης thief. μακάριος blessed, happy. γρηγορῶν pres. act. part. γρηγορέω to be awake, to watch. τηρῶν pres. act. part. to keep, to protect. γυμνός naked. περιπατῇ pres. act. subj. περιπατέω to walk about. As the priest kept watch in the temple an officer of the temple used to go around every watch w. a lighted torch before him and if any watch did not stand up and say to him "O officer of the Temple Mount, peace be to thee!" and it was manifest that he was asleep, he would beat him w. his staff, and he had the right to burn his raiment (M. Middoth 1:2). βλέπωσιν pres. act. subj. The pl. is used impersonally which gives the verb the force of a pass. "his shame is seen." ἀσχημοσύνη shamefulness, indecency. The word is probably a euphemism for "private parts" (Mounce;
16 BAG). ■ συνήγαγεν aor. act. ind. συνάγω to gather together, to lead together, to assemble. καλούμενον pres. pass. part.
17 ■ ἀήρ air. ἐξῆλθεν aor. act. ind. ἐξέρχομαι to go out, to come out of. γέγονεν perf. act. ind. γίνομαι. The perf. tense could be translated "it is done," "it has come to pass." The voice is esp. appropriate in this connection, since these plagues are "the last"; there remain no further manifestations of this kind
18 (Swete). ■ ἀστραπή lightning. βροντή thunder. σεισμός

earthquake. οἶος of such a kind. ἀφ᾿ οὗ "from when."
τηλικοῦτος so large, so great (s. Rev. 6:12). ▪ μέρος part, 19
section. ἔπεσαν aor. act. ind. πίπτω to fall. ἐμνήσθη aor. pass.
ind. μιμνήσκω to remember, pass. to be remembered.
ποτήριον cup. ὀργή wrath, anger (s. Rev. 14:10). ▪ νῆσος 20
island. ἔφυγεν aor. act. ind. φεύγω to flee. εὑρέθησαν aor.
pass. ind. ▪ χάλαζα hail. ταλαντιαῖος talent. The talent varied 21
in weight among different peoples at different times. The range
seems to be from about sixty pounds to something over a hundred (Mounce). καταβαίνει pres. act. ind. to go down, to descend. σφόδρα very much, extremely, greatly, very.

Ch. 17

▪ ἐχόντων pres. act. part. φιάλη bowl (s. Rev. 15:7). 1
ἐλάλησεν aor. act. ind. δεῦρο "come here." δείξω fut. act. ind.
δείκνυμι to show. κρίμα sentence, judgment. πόρνη prostitute, whore. In the OT and prophetic language prostitution or
adultery was equal to idolatry and denoted religious apostasy
(Ford; Mounce). The harlot here is Rome and denotes the corrupt apostate religious system headed by the false prophet who
is the second beast of Revelation 13. καθημένης pres. mid. part.
κάθημαι to sit. ἐπὶ ὑδάτων πολλῶν "upon many waters" (s.
Rev. 13:1). ▪ ἐπόρνευσαν aor. act. ind. πορνεύω to engage in 2
immoral acts, to engage in unlawful sex. Again the picture is one
of religious apostasy. ἐμεθύσθησαν aor. pass. ind. μεθύσκω to
be drunk, pass. to be made drunk. The aor. could be ingressive,
i.e., "to enter in the state of drunkenness," "get drunk." The
figure indicates the intoxicating and controlling aspects of the
false religion. κατοικοῦντες pres. act. part. κατοικέω to live,
to reside, to dwell. πορνεία immorality, unlawful sexual activity
(s. Rev. 2:21). ▪ ἀπήνεγκεν aor. act. ind. ἀποφέρω to carry 3
away. θηρίον wild animal, beast. κόκκινος scarlet, crimson.
The color was popular in the Roman Empire and indicated luxurious and haughty splendor (EGT; TDNT). γέμοντα pres. act.
part. γέμω to be full. βλασφημία blasphemy. κέρας horn. The
picture is the close union of the political and religious powers of
the last days. ▪ ἦν impf. εἰμί. περιβεβλημένη perf. pass. part. 4
περιβάλλω to cast about, to be clothed. πορφυροῦς purple.
Purple was often used of royal garments and scarlet was a color
of magnificence (Mounce). κεχρυσωμένη perf. pass. part.
χρυσόω to inlay w. gold, to cover w. gold. μαργαρίτης pearl
(s. 1 Tim. 2:9). ποτήριον cup. χρυσοῦς golden. βδέλυγμα that
which stinks, abomination, that which is detestable. The word is
used in the LXX of the moral and ceremonial impurity connect-

ed w. idolatrous practices (Mounce). ἀκάθαρτος impure, un-
5 clean. ■ μέτωπον forehead, brow. γεγραμμένον perf. pass.
6 part. to write, to inscribe. ■ μεθύουσαν pres. act. part. μεθύω
to get drunk. The metaphor of getting drunk on the blood of the
saints and the blood of the witnesses of Jesus portrays the wanton slaughter of a great number of believers along w. the intoxicating effect it produced upon the murderous harlot (Mounce).
This depicts the tremendous persecution of true believers by the
apostate religion of the last days.

  ἐθαύμασσα aor. act. ind. θαυμάζω to be amazed, to won-
7 der. θαῦμα wonderment. ■ ἐρῶ fut. act. ind. λέγω to tell.
8 βαστάζοντος pres. act. part. βαστάζω to carry, to bear. ■ ἦν
καὶ οὐκ ἔστιν καὶ μέλλει ἀναβαίνειν "who was and is not
and is about to arise . . ." is perhaps an intentional antithesis to
Revelation 1:4: "the one who was and is" (Swete). μέλλει pres.
act. ind. to be about to. Used w. the inf. to express the fut. tense.
ἀναβαίνειν pres. act. inf. to go up, to ascend. ἄβυσσος bottomless pit, abyss (s. Rev. 9:1; 11:7). ἀπώλεια destruction, ruin.
ὑπάγει pres. act. ind. to go forth. θναμασθήσονται fut. pass.
ind. to be amazed, to wonder w. the amazement of a horrible
surprise; the world will still wonder and admire (Swete).
γέγραπται perf. pass. ind. καταβολή foundation (s. Eph. 1:4;
Rev. 13:8). βλεπόντων pres. act. part. The part. is used temporarily "when they see." The gen. pl. agrees w. the gen. pl. of
the rel. pron. (RWP). παρέσται fut. act. ind. πάρειμι to be
9 present. ■ νοῦς mind, understanding. The formula is a call to
vigilance and close attention (Swete). ὅπου where. βασιλεύς
king. The reference is either to seven world empires (Seiss) or
it refers to seven emperors of the Roman Empire (s. Govett; s.
also a discussion by Mounce; Ford). Others have viewed this as
10 various forms of government of the Roman Empire (Scott). ■
ἔπεσαν aor. act. ind. πίπτω to fall. οὔπω not yet. ὅταν w. the
subj. "whenever." ἔλθῃ aor. act. subj. ἔρχομαι. The subj. is used
in an indefinite temporal clause. δεῖ (w. the acc. and an inf.) "it
is binding," "it is necessary." μεῖναι aor. act. inf. μένω to re-
11 main. ■ ὄγδοός eighth. The beast himself is an eighth king who
is at the same time one of the seven. He is Antichrist, not simply
another Roman emperor. His period of hegemony is the Great
12 Tribulation preceding the return of the Messiah (Mounce). ■
ἔλαβον aor. act. ind. λαμβάνω. The ten kings who are yet to
receive their power refer to ten European kingdoms of a revived
Roman Empire. The political beast of Revelation 13 will be one
13 of these leaders (s. Scott). ■ γνώμη opinion, purpose. The unity
14 of the ten appears in their support of the beast (Swete). ■ ἀρνίον

lamb. πολεμήσουσιν fut. act. ind. πολεμέω to wage war. νικήσει fut. act. ind. νικάω to gain the victory, to be victor, to overcome, to conquer. κλητός called. ἐκλεκτός chosen, elect. ■ οὗ where. ὄχλος crowd, multitudes. ἔθνος nation. 15 γλῶσσα tongue, language. The fourfold grouping stresses universality (Mounce). (For the figure of the "sea" representing people and nations, s. Rev. 13:1.) ■ μισήσουσιν fut. act. ind. 16 μισέω to hate. ἠρημωμένην perf. pass. part. ἐρημόω to desolate, to make into a desert or desolate place. ποιήσουσιν fut. act. ind. γυμνος naked. φάγονται fut. mid. ind. ἐσθίω to eat. κατακαύσουσιν fut. act. ind. κατακαίω to burn down, to burn up, to completely destroy by fire. The political forces will turn against the false religious system and completely destroy it. ■ 17 ἔδωκεν aor. act. ind. δίδωμι. ποιῆσαι aor. act. inf. δοῦναι aor. act. inf. δίδωμι. τελεσθήσονται fut. pass. ind. τελέω to bring to the goal, to complete.

Ch. 18

■ μετὰ ταῦτα "after these things." καταβαίνοντα pres. 1 act. part. καταβαίνω to come down, to descend. ἔχοντα pres. act. part. ἐφωτίσθη aor. pass. ind. φωτίζω to light up, to illuminate. So recently has he come from the Presence that in passing he flings a broad belt of light across the dark earth (Swete). ■ 2 ἔκραξεν aor. act. ind. κράζω to scream, to cry out w. a loud voice. ἔπεσεν aor. act. ind. πίπτω to fall (s. Rev. 14:8; cf. also Isa. 21:9). The proleptic aor. are repeated like a solemn dirge or lament of the damned (RWP). ἐγένετο aor. mid. ind. γίνομαι. κατοικητήριον place of living, habitation. φυλακή prison, place of banishment. ἀκάθαρτος unclean. ὄρνεον bird. μεμισημένον perf. pass. part. μισέω to hate. ■ θυμός anger, 3 wrath, burning anger (s. Rev. 14:8, 10). πορνεία immorality, unlawful sexual acts. The figure is also used for apostasy and idolatry (s. Rev. 17:1). πέπωκαν perf. act. ind. πίνω to drink. The perf. tense would indicate the continuing results. ἐπόρνευσαν aor. act. ind. πορνεύω to commit immorality. ἔμπορος merchant. στρῆνος strong, mighty, arrogant, complacent luxury. The noun along w. the verb contains the idea of "excessive luxury and self-indulgence w. accompanying arrogance and wanton exercise of strength" (Mounce; s. also GEW II, 890f.; Swete). ἐπλούτησαν aor. act. ind. πλουτέω to be wealthy, ingressive aor. "they became wealthy."

■ ἤκουσα aor. act. ind. ἀκούω. ἐξέλθατε aor. act. imp. 4 ἐξέρχομαι to come out, to depart from. συγκοινωνήσητε aor. act. subj. συγκοινωνέω to be a partner w., to be a copartner w.

(s. 1 John 1:3; 2 John 11). πληγή blow, wound, plague. λάβητε aor. act. subj. λαμβάνω. The subj. here are used in a neg. purpose clause. The neg. in an expression of apprehension is combined in classical Gr. w. the subj. if the anxiety is directed toward warding off something still dependent on the will (BD, 188).

5 ■ ἐκολλήθησαν aor. pass. ind. κολλάω to stick to, to join to. The idea here is "joined to one another till they reach heaven, till the ever growing mass rose sky high" (Swete). ἐμνημόνευσεν aor. act. ind. μνημονεύω to remember.

6 ἀδίκημα unrighteous act, injustice. ■ ἀπόδοτε aor. act. imp. ἀποδίδωμι to pay back. διπλώσατε aor. act. imp. διπλόω to double, to make double. διπλοῦς double. In this v. there is precise compensation: double punishment for double crimes (Ford). ποτήριον cup. ἐκέρασεν aor. act. ind. κεράννυμι to mix. κεράσατε aor. act. imp. κεράννυμι to mix a drink in

7 preparation for drinking (s. Rev. 14:10). ■ ὅσος "how much," "as much as" (s. AS). ἐδόξασεν aor. act. ind. δοξάζω to glorify. ἐστρηνίασεν aor. act. ind. στρηνιάω to live a proud and luxurious life (s.v.2). τοσοῦτος "so much," "so great." δότε aor. act. imp. δίδωμι. βασανισμός torture, torment, pain. πένθος mourning. κάθημαι pres. mid. ind. to sit, to sit established. βασίλισσα queen. χήρα widow. οὐ μή w. the subj. "not ever,"

8 "never in any wise." ἴδω aor. act. subj. ὁράω. ■ ἥξουσιν fut. act. ind. ἥκω to come. θάνατος death. λιμός hunger. πῦρ fire. κατακαυθήσεται fut. pass. ind. κατακαίω to burn down, to consume completely w. fire, to burn up. κρίνας aor. act. part. κρίνω to judge.

9 ■ κλαύσουσιν fut. act. ind. κλαίω to weep, to cry aloud. κόψονται fut. mid. ind. κόπτω to beat, to cut, mid. to beat upon one's self, to beat one's breast as an act of mourning, to mourn for someone (BAG). πορνεύσαντες aor. act. part. πορνεύω (s.v.3). στρηνιάσαντες aor. act. part. (s.v.3, 7). ὅταν w. the subj. when, whenever. βλέπωσιν pres. act. subj. καπνός

10 smoke. πύρωσις burning. ■ μακρόθεν from afar off. ἑστηκότες perf. act. part. ἵστημι to stand. κρίσις judging, judgment.

11 ■ πενθοῦσιν pres. act. ind. to mourn, to lament. γόμος ship's cargo, merchandise (s. MM). ἀγοράζει pres. act. ind. to

12 buy, to purchase. οὐκέτι no longer. ■ ἄργυρος silver. τίμιος costly, expensive. μαργαρίτης pearl (s. 1 Tim. 2:9). βύσσινος linen. πορφύρα purple. σηρικόν silk. κόκκινον scarlet. ξύλον wood. θύϊνος wood of a citrus tree. This wood which was imported from North Africa, where it grew freely in the neighborhood of the Atlas, was much prized for its veining, which in the

best specimens simulated the eyes of the peacock's tail or the
stripes of the tiger and spots of the panther or the seeds of the
parsley. At Rome citrus wood was much sought after for dining
tables, but it was also used for veneering and for small works of
art which were made out of the hard roots of the tree (Swete; s.
also Pliny, *Natural History*, XIII, 96-102; for a description of the
citron tree, s. also FFB, 190f.). σκεῦος vessel. ἐλεφάντινος
ivory. τιμιώτατος superl. used in the elative sense, "extremely
expensive." χαλκός brass. σίδηρος iron. μάρμαρος marble.
■ κιννάμωμον cinnamon. ἄμωμον spice. This was a plant from 13
India which was used as perfume (s. Pliny, *Natural History*, XII,
48). θυμίαμα incense. μούρον myrrh. λίβανος frankincense
(s. Matt. 2:11). ἔλαιον olive oil. σεμίδαλις fine flour. The fine
flour imported for the use of the wealthy (Swete). κτῆνος cattle.
πρόβατον sheep. ἵππος horse. ῥέδη chariot. A chariot which
came from Gaul and had four wheels (Swete; RWP). σώματα
bodies, human beings, slaves. ■ ὀπώρα fruit, the autumn fruit 14
ripe for ingathering (Swete). ἐπιθυμία strong desire, lust, passion. ἀπῆλθεν aor. act. ind. ἀπέρχομαι to go away, to pass.
λιπαρός oily, fat, costly, rich, luxury, sleek (BAG; Ford). The
word may refer to the rich and dainty food (Swete). λαμπρός
bright, shining. This may refer to the gay attire and costly furniture which were the fruits of Roman conquest and policy
(Swete). ἀπώλετο aor. mid. ind. οὐκέτι "no longer." οὐ μή
"not at all." εὑρήσουσιν fut. act. ind. to find. The impersonal
3rd pl. is equal to a pass. ■ πλουτήσαντες aor. act. part. 15
πλουτέω to be rich, to become rich. στήσονται fut. act. ind.
ἵστημι to stand. κλαίοντες pres. act. part. to weep, to weep
aloud. πενθοῦντες pres. act. part. to lament. ■ περιβεβλημένη 16
perf. pass. part. περιβάλλω to cast about, to clothe. πορφυροῦν
purple, purple garment. κεχρυσωμένη perf. pass. part. χρυσόω
to cover w. gold, to overlay w. gold, to decorate w. gold. ■ 17
ἠρημώθη aor. pass. ind. ἐρημόω to turn into a desert, to make
desolate, to devastate. κυβερνήτης one who guides a ship,
steersman, pilot. τόπος place. πλέων pres. act. part. πλέω to
travel w. a ship, to sail. "He who sails for (any) part" is the
merchantman who goes w. his goods, or the chance passenger
(Swete). ναύτης sailor. ἐργάζονται pres. mid. ind. to work, i.e.,
"those who gain their living by the sea" and it may refer to all
those who earn their living in connection w. the maritime industry (Mounce). ἔστησαν aor. act. ind. ἵστημι to stand. ■ 18
ἔκραζον impf. act. ind. The impf. could be inceptive "they began to cry out." βλέποντες pres. act. part. The part. could be
temporal "when they see" or it could be causal "because they

19 see." ■ ἔβαλον aor. act. ind. βάλλω to throw. χοῦς dirt.
20 τιμιότης costliness. ■ εὐφραίνου pres. mid. imp. εὐφραίνομαι
to rejoice. ἔκρινεν aor. act. ind. κρίμα judgment.
21   ■ ἦρεν aor. act. ind. αἴρω to lift up. μύλινος millstone.
ὁρμήματι rushing, instrumental dat. "w. a rushing," "like a
stone whizzing through the air" (Swete). The great millstone
does not fall but is violently hurled into the sea. This stresses
how suddenly and spectacularly the judgment of God will be
executed, not only upon an ancient city but ultimately upon the
entire anti-Christian world in its opposition to God (Mounce).
22 βληθήσεται fut. pass. ind. βάλλω. εὑρεθῇ aor. pass. subj. ■
κιθαρῳδός harp player. μουσικός pertaining to music, musi-
cian. The word means skilled in music and here it may refer
either to instrumentalists or vocalists (Swete). αὐλήτης flute
player. σαλπιστής trumpet player. ἀκουσθῇ aor. pass. subj.
Music was used in various aspects of life both for entertainment
and religion (s. Mounce; Swete). τεχνίτης skilled worker. It
may refer to an artist in metal, in stone, or even in textile fabrics
(Swete). τέχνη craft, skill. μύλος mill. The word is here apparently the mill, i.e., the whole apparatus as distinguished from the
millstone. The "sound of the mill" is best explained as the sound
23 made by the mill (Swete). ■ λύχνος lamp. φάνῃ aor. mid. subj.
φαίνομαι. ἔμποροι merchants. The word may refer to merchants who deal in foreign exports and imports (s. Mounce).
μεγιστᾶνες "the great ones." φαρμακεία use of drugs either
as medicine, poison, or magic (s. Gal. 5:20; Rev. 9:21).
ἐπλανήθησαν aor. pass. ind. πλανάω to lead astray, to de-
24 ceive. ■ εὑρέθη aor. pass. ind. ἐσφαγμένων perf. pass. part.
σφάζω to slaughter, to kill.

Ch. 19

1   ■ ἤκουσα aor. act. ind. ἀλληλουϊά "Hallelujah," "praise
2 the Lord," "praise God" (Ford). ■ ἀληθινός true. κρίσις judging, judgment. ἔκρινεν aor. act. ind. κρίνω to judge. πόρνη
prostitute, whore. ἔφθειρεν aor. act. ind. φθείρω to corrupt.
πορνεία immorality, illicit sexual acts. ἐξεδίκησεν aor. act. ind.
3 ἐκδικέω to avenge. ■ δεύτερον a second time. εἴρηκαν perf.
act. ind. λέγω to say. ἀναβαίνει pres. act. ind. to go up, to
4 ascend. ■ ἔπεσαν aor. act. ind. πίπτω to fall, to fall down. ζῷον
living creature. προσεκύνησαν aor. act. ind. προσκυνέω to
worship. καθημένῳ pres. mid. part. κάθημαι to sit.
5   ■ ἐξῆλθεν aor. act. ind. ἐξέρχομαι to go out. αἰνεῖτε pres.
act. imp. αἰνέω to praise. φοβούμενοι pres. mid. part.
6 φοβέομαι to be afraid, to fear, to reverence (s. TDNT). ■

βροντή thunder. ἐβασίλευσεν aor. act. ind. βασιλεύω to be king, to reign as a king, to rule. παντοκράτωρ almighty (s. Rev. 1:8). ■ χαίρωμεν pres. act. subj., hortatory subj. χαίρω "let us 7 rejoice." ἀγαλλιῶμεν pres. act. subj. ἀγαλλιάω to be glad, to rejoice exuberantly (s. 1 Peter 1:8), hortatory subj. δώσομεν fut. act. ind. δίδωμι. The variant reading would be aor. subj. and would be grammatical parallel to the preceding subj. (s. TC, 762). ἦλθεν aor. act. ind. ἔρχομαι γάμος marriage. ἀρνίον lamb. ἡτοίμασεν aor. act. ind. ἐτοιμάζω to prepare, to make ready. (For references to wedding customs, s. Rev. 21:2.) ■ 8 ἐδόθη aor. pass. ind. δίδωωι to give, to allow. περιβάληται aor. mid. subj. περιβάλλω to throw around, to be clothed. βύσσινος linen. λαμπρός bright, shining. δικαίωμα righteous deeds, acts of righteousness. The expression here is the sum of the saintly acts of the members of Christ wrought in them by His Holy Spirit which are regarded as making up the clothing of His mystical body (Swete).

■ γράψον aor. act. imp. μακάριος happy, blessed. δεῖπον 9 banquet. (For an excellent description of both the preparation as well as the different parts of a Jewish banquet, s. SB IV, 611–639.) κεκλημένοι perf. pass. part. to call, to invite. It was not only an honor to be invited to a wedding feast, but it was also very impolite and discourteous to reject an invitation. ἀληθινός true, genuine. ■ προσκυνῆσαι aor. act. inf. The inf. is used to 10 express intended purpose. ὅρα pres. act. imp. ὁράω to see. An elliptical expression which understands the words "do not do it," i.e., "see that you do not do it" (s. RWP). ἐχόντων pres. act. part. Ἰησοῦ "of Jesus," subjective gen., i.e., the witness which was borne by Jesus. By His life and death Jesus has demonstrated to His followers what it means to bear a faithful witness to the message revealed by God (Mounce). προσκύνησον aor. act. imp. προσκυνέω. προφητεία prophecy. (For the meaning of this expression, s. Mounce; Swete.)

■ ἠνεῳγμένον perf. pass. part. ἀνοίγω to open. The perf. 11 tense of the part. indicates "to have been opened and now stands open." ἵππος horse. λευκός white. καθήμενος pres. mid. part. καλούμενος pres. pass. part. πολεμεῖ pres. act. ind. to wage war. The Messiah now returns to the earth as the conquering king. ■ φλόξ flame. πῦρ fire (s. Rev. 1:14). διάδημα diadem, 12 the crown of royalty, a kingly crown. ἔχων pres. act. part. ὄνομα name. The name was that which signified the character of the person as well as the character of His kingly rule (s. TDNT). Here the name no one knows would indicate the name that can be known only when the apocaplyse is fulfilled and the name or

character which will then be revealed is "Jesus Christ his Lord"
13 (Ford). γεγραμμένον perf. pass. part. εἰ μή "except." ■
περιβεβλημένος perf. pass. part. (s.v.8). βεβαμμένον perf.
pass. part. βάπτω to dip. The perf. tense indicates a past completed action w. the continuance of the results or state. The
blood which stains the garment of the conquering Messiah is not
His own, but the blood of the enemy shed in conflict (Mounce).
κέκληται perf. pass. ind. καλέω to call, pass. to be named.
14 ■ στράτευμα army. ἠκολούθει impf. act. ind. ἀκολουθέω to
follow, to follow after. ἐνδεδυμένοι perf. pass. part. ἐνδύω to
15 put on clothes, pass. to be clothed. βύσσινον linen (s.v.8). ■
ἐκπορεύεται pres. mid. ind. to go out, to come out. ῥομφαία
sword, a large broad sword (s. Rev. 1:16). ὀξύς sharp. πατάξῃ
aor. act. subj. πατάσσω to smite. The subj. is used in a purpose
clause (Charles). ποιμανεῖ fut. act. ind. ποιμαίνω to shepherd,
to rule, to govern. ῥάβδος stick, staff, scepter. σιδηροῦς iron.
The Messiah's rod is a rod of iron; i.e., it is strong and unyielding
in its mission of judgment (Mounce). πατεῖ pres. act. ind. to
tread. ληνός trough, wine press. θυμός anger, burning anger.
ὀργή wrath, deep-settled, righteous wrath (s. Rev. 16:19).
16 παντοκράτωρ almighty (s. Rev. 1:8). ■ μηρός thigh. The inscription "king of kings, and lord of lords" was probably the
name written on that part of the garment which fell open across
the thigh (Mounce).
17 ■ ἑστῶτα perf. act. part. ἵστημι to stand. ἔκραξεν aor.
act. ind. κράζω to scream, to cry out w. a loud voice. ὄρνεον
bird. πετομένοις pres. mid. part. πέτομαι to fly.
μεσουράνημα mid heaven (s. Rev. 8:13). δεῦτε "come here."
συνάχθητε aor. pass. imp. συνάγω to gather together, to lead
together, to assemble. δεῖπνον feast, banquet. It is the supper of
18 God in the sense that God will provide it (Mounce). ■ φάγητε
aor. act. subj. ἐσθίω to eat. The subj. is used in a purpose clause.
σάρκας flesh, pl. "pieces of flesh" (RWP). χιλίαρχος commander of a thousand (s. Rev. 6:15; Mark 6:21). καθημένων
19 pres. mid. part. ■ θηρίον animal, beast. στράτευμα army.
συνηγμένα perf. pass. part. συνάγω to gather together, to
assemble. The perf. pass. part. indicates "to be assembled," "to
stand assembled." ποιῆσαι aor. act. inf. The inf. is used to
express purpose. πόλεμος war. The political leader described in
Revelation 13 as the first beast assembles his forces for war and
20 the battle takes place at Armageddon. ■ ἐπιάσθη aor. pass. ind.
πιάζω to seize, to take hold of. The word was used of arresting
someone and taking him into custody and it was used of catching
animals (BAG). ψευδοπροφήτης false prophet. The religious

leader who is the second beast of Revelation 13. **ποιήσας** aor. act. part. **ἐπλάνησεν** aor. act. ind. **πλανάω** to lead in the wrong way, to lead astray, to deceive. **λαβόντας** aor. act. part. **λαμβάνω** to receive, to take. **χάραγμα** brand, mark. **προσκυνοῦντας** pres. act. part., to worship. **εἰκών** image. **ζῶντες** pres. act. part. **ζάω** to live. **ἐβλήθησαν** aor. pass. ind. **βάλλω** to throw, to cast. **λίμνη** lake. **πῦρ** fire. **καιομένης** pres. pass. part. **καίω** to burn, pass. to be burning. **θεῖον** brimstone, sulphur. ■ **ἀπεκτάνθησαν** aor. pass. ind. **ἀποκτείνω** to kill. 21 **ῥομφαία** sword (s.v.15; Rev. 1:16). **ἐξελθούσῃ** aor. act. part. **ἐξέρχομαι** to go out. **ἐχορτάσθησαν** aor. pass. ind. **χορτάζω** to feed, to fatten, pass. to be filled, to be satisfied. The supper of God is ready, and the vultures gorge themselves on the flesh of the wicked (Mounce).

Ch. 20

■ **καταβαίνοντα** pres. act. part. **καταβαίνω** to come 1 down, to descend. **ἔχοντα** pres. act. part. **κλείς** key. The key symbolized the authority over a place (s. Rev. 1:18; 3:7). **ἄβυσσος** bottomless pit, abyss (s. Rev. 9:1). The abyss stands here in sharp contrast w. the lake (19:20); the locked dungeon w. its black and bottomless depths form an antithesis to the open shallow pool of fire (Swete). **ἅλυσις** chain. ■ **ἐκράτησεν** aor. 2 act. ind. **κρατέω** to exercise power, to take into custody (Mounce). **δράκων** dragon. **ὄφις** snake. **ἀρχαῖος** old, ancient. **ἔδησεν** aor. act. ind. **δέω** to bind. **ἔτος** year. The acc. "a thousand years" is acc. of time indicating the extent of time. ■ 3 **ἔβαλεν** aor. act. ind. **βάλλω** to cast. **ἔκλεισεν** aor. act. ind. **κλείω** to shut up, to lock. **ἐσφράγισεν** aor. act. ind. **σφραγίζω** to seal. The sealing would indicate the authoritative placing of a seal so that no one is allowed in or out (s. Matt. 27:66). The purpose of sealing the entrance to a prison was to prevent any attempt at escape or rescue passing unobserved (Swete). The activity of Satan is completely removed from the earth for a thousand years (s. Walvoord). **πλανήσῃ** aor. act. subj. **πλανάω** to lead astray, to deceive. The subj. could be used either in a purpose or a result clause. **τελεσθῇ** aor. pass. subj. **τελέω** to complete. **δεῖ** (w. the acc. and the inf.) "it is binding," "it is necessary." **λυθῆναι** aor. pass. inf. **λύω** to loose, to release. The release will be brief in comparison w. the captivity (Swete).

■ **ἐκάθισαν** aor. act. ind. **καθίζω** to take one's seat, to sit. 4 **κρίμα** judgment. **ἐδόθη** aor. pass. ind. **δίδωμι** to give, to grant. **πεπελεκισμένων** perf. pass. part. **πελεκίζω** to cut one's head off w. a double-edge ax, to behead. This ax was the instrument of execution in the Roman republic (Mounce). προσεκύνησαν aor. act. ind. προσκυνέω to worship. θηρίον beast. εἰκών image. ἔλαβον aor. act. ind. λαμβάνω. χάραγμα brand, mark. μέτωπον forehead, brow. ἔζησαν aor. act. ind. ζάω to live. ἐβασίλευσαν aor. act. ind. βασιλεύω to be king, to rule, to reign. The aor. could be ingressive aor. "they began to reign."

5 ■ λοιπός rest. These were the wicked who did not have a part
6 in the first resurrection. ■ μακάριος happy, blessed. ἔσονται fut. εἰμί. βασιλεύσουσιν fut. act. ind.

7 ■ ὅταν w. the subj. "when." τελεσθῇ aor. pass. subj. (s.v.3).
8 λυθήσεται fut. pass. ind. (s.v.3). ■ ἐξελεύσεται fut. mid. ind. ἐξέρχομαι to go out. πλανῆσαι aor. act. inf. to lead astray, to deceive. The inf. is used to express purpose. γωνία corner. συναγαγεῖν aor. act. inf. συνάγω to lead together, to gather, to assemble. The inf. is used to express purpose. πόλεμος war.
9 ἀριθμός number. ἄμμος sand. ■ ἀνέβησαν aor. act. ind. ἀναβαίνω to go up, to ascend. πλάτος breadth. ἐκύκλευσαν aor. act. ind. κυκλεύω to encircle. παρεμβολή camp. The word signifies either a camp or an army on the march or engaged in battle (Swete). ἠγαπημένην perf. pass. part. ἀγαπάω. κατέβη aor. act. ind. καταβαίνω to come down. πῦρ fire. κατέφαγεν aor. act. ind. κατεσθίω to eat up, to consume completely. The
10 prep. in compound is perfective. ■ διάβολος devil. πλανῶν pres. act. part. The part. is used here as a noun "the deceiver," "the one who deceives them." ἐβλήθη aor. pass. ind. βάλλω to cast, to throw. λίμνη lake. θεῖον brimstone, sulphur. ὅπου where. Here it is used as a rel. pron. ψευδοπροφήτης false prophet. βασανισθήσονται fut. pass. ind. βασανίζω to torment, to torture, to cause pain.

11 ■ λευκός white. The great white throne is the final judgment of the unbeliever and takes place after the thousand year millennial reign of Christ and the judgment of Satan. The absolute purity of this supreme court is symbolized by the color of the throne (Swete). καθήμενον pres. mid. part. κάθημαι to sit. ἔφυγεν aor. act. ind. φεύγω to flee. Earth and heaven flee away before the awesome grandeur of God seated upon the throne of
12 judgment (Mounce). εὑρέθη aor. pass. ind. ■ ἑστῶτας perf. act. part. ἵστημι to stand. βιβλίον book. ἠνοίχθησαν aor. pass. ind. ἀνοίγω to open. ἐκρίθησαν aor. pass. ind. κρίνω to judge. γεγραμμένων perf. pass. part. The perf. tense indicates "that which stands written." The sentence of the judge is not arbitrary; it rests upon written evidence; the books which were opened contain, as it seems, a record of the deeds of every human being
13 who came up for judgment (Swete). ■ ἔδωκεν aor. act. ind.

δίδωμι. ᾅδης Hades, the grave, the underworld as the place of the dead. ἕκαστος each one. ■ ἐβλήθησαν aor. pass. ind. 14 (s.v.10). λίμνη lake. πῦρ fire.

Ch. 21

■ ἀπῆλθαν aor. act. ind. ἀπέρχομαι to go away, to depart, 1 to pass away. In rabbinical literature some taught that the world would be renovated and made new so that it would return to its original state after creation but would be cleansed from sin and evil. Others taught that the earth would return to the original chaos and would then be recreated w. a new cleansed existence and others taught that the world would be completely destroyed and the new heaven and new earth would be a totally new creation (s. SB III, 842–847; Moore, *Judaism*, II, 338ff.). ■ 2 καταβαίνουσαν pres. act. part. καταβαίνω to come down, to descend. ἡτοιμασμένη perf. pass. part. ἐτοιμάζω to make ready, to prepare. The perf. pass. part. indicates "to have been prepared and to stand ready." νύμφη bride. κεκοσμημένην perf. pass. part. κοσμέω to make orderly, to put in order, to adorn, to decorate, to make beautiful or attractive (BAG). In preparation for the marriage and the arrival of the groom the bride was bathed and oiled, perfumed, her hair fixed, and was adorned w. her wedding garment. (For marriage preparations, s. JPFC II, 752–760; SB I, 500–517; II, 373–399.) ■ ἤκουσα aor. 3 act. ind. ἀκούω. σκηνή tent, tabernacle. σκηνώσει fut. act. ind. σκηνόω to live in a tent, to tabernacle. The word indicates the abiding presence of God (s. Mounce). ἔσονται fut. εἰμί. ■ ἐξαλείψει fut. act. ind. ἐξαλείφω to wipe away, to wipe out. 4 δάκρυον tear, i.e., "every individual single tear." πένθος sorrow, mourning. κραυγή shouting, outcry, crying in grief or anxiety (MM). πόνος pain. ■ καθήμενος pres. mid. part. κάθημαι to sit. γράψον aor. 5 act. imp. ■ γέγοναν perf. act. ind. γίνομαι "they have come to 6 pass." Not only are the sayings mentioned in v. 5 faithful and true, but they have come to pass and their results continue on in the fut. ἀρχή beginning. διψῶντι pres. act. part. διψάω to thirst, to be thirsty. δώσω fut. act. ind. δίδωμι. πηγή spring, fountain. δωρεάν freely, without cost. In the arid climate of Palestine a spring of cool water would be a vivid symbol of refreshment and satisfaction (Mounce). ■ νικῶν pres. act. part. 7 νικάω to be a victor, to conquer, to overcome. κληρονομήσει fut. act. ind. κληρονομέω to inherit. ■ δειλός cowardly. 8 ἄπιστος unfaithful, unbelieving. ἐβδελυγμένοις perf. pass. part. βδελύσσω to pollute, to defile, to make detestable, to commit abomination, perf. pass. part. "to be detestable." The word indicates persons whose very natures have been saturated w. the abominations which they practiced in their lifetime and the context suggests that in this case the abominations are not merely idolatrous acts, but the monstrous and unnatural vices of heathendom (Swete). φονεύς murderer. πόρνος immoral person, one who practices sexual immorality. φαρμακός one who mixes and uses drugs which were used either in sorcery or magic practices (s. Rev. 9:21; 18:23; Gal. 5:20). εἰδωλολάτρης one who worships idols, idolater. μέρος part. λίμνη lake. καιομένη pres. pass. part. καίομαι to burn, pass. to be burning. πῦρ fire. θεῖον brimstone, sulphur.

9 ■ ἐχόντων pres. act. part. φιάλη bowl. γεμόντων pres. act. part. γέμω to be full of. πληγή blow, wound, plague. ἔσχατος last. ἐλάλησεν aor. act. ind. to speak. δεῦρο "come here." δείξω fut. act. ind. δείκνυμι to show. νύμφη bride. ἀρνίον

10 lamb. ■ ἀπήνεγκεν aor. act. ind. ἀποφέρω to carry away. ὑψηλός high. ἔδειξεν aor. act. ind. δείκνυμι. καταβαίνουσαν

11 pres. act. part. (s.v.2). ■ δόξα glory, brilliance. The word refers to the shining radiance which comes from the presence and glory of God (s. Mounce; TDNT; CBB). φωστήρ radiance, luminary. The word means something in which light is concentrated and thence radiates (Swete). τιμιώτατος superl. τίμιος precious, costly. The elative use of the superl., "extremely expensive," "very expensive." ἴασπις jasper. In antiquity the designation jasper was used for any opaque precious stone. The point of comparison is the brilliance and sparkle of a gem and the reference could be to a diamond (Mounce). κρυσταλλίζοντι pres. act. part. κρυσταλλίζω to sparkle and shimmer like a crystal.

12 ■ τεῖχος wall. μέγας great, mighty. ἐπιγεγραμμένα perf. pass. part. ἐπιγραφω to write upon, to inscribe upon. φυλή tribe.

13 ■ ἀνατολή rising, east (s. Matt. 2:1). βορρᾶς north wind, north.

14 νότος south wind, south. δυσμός going down, west. ■ θεμέλιος foundation. Each foundation was probably a stout oblong block like the stones which may still be seen in the lower rows of the Herodian masonry at Jerusalem (Ford).

15 ■ λαλῶν pres. act. part. μέτρον measure. κάλαμος reed, rod (s. Rev. 11:1). χρυσοῦς golden. μετρήσῃ aor. act. subj.

16 μετρέω to measure. ■ τετράγωνος square, four corners. κεῖται pres. mid. ind. to lie. μῆκος length. πλάτος width. ἐμέτρησεν aor. act. ind. στάδιον stadion, furlong. A stadion is about 607 English feet; thus, the city would be about 1,400 miles in each

17 direction (Mounce). ὕψος height. ἴσος equal. ■ πῆχυς cubit. A cubit is roughly the length of a man's forearm and 144 cubits

would be 14 miles in height (Mounce). ■ ἐνδώμησις the act of 18
building *into*, "structure," building (Ford; s. also Mounce).
καθαρός pure, clean. ὕαλος glass. ■ κεκοσμημένοι perf. pass. 19
part. (s.v.2). σάπφιρος sapphire. This is a blue transparent precious stone (Ford). χαλκηδών agate, chalcedony. This gem is
taken to be of a green color (Charles; Ford; BAG). σμάραγδος
emerald. This is a bright green transparent precious stone, the
most valued variety of beryl (Ford). ■ σαρδόνυξ onyx, sard- 20
onyx. This was a layered stone of red and white. It was prized
for use in making cameos (Mounce). σάρδιον sardus, carnelian.
This was a blood-red stone and was commonly used for engrav-
ing (Mounce; Ford). χρυσόλιθος "gold stone," topaz, chryso-
lite. The ancients seemed to have used this term for the yellow
topaz (Ford; s. also Charles). βήρυλλος beryl. This was a green
stone ranging from transparent sea green to opaque blue (Ford;
Mounce). τοπάζιον topaz, a greenish yellow or gold. In ancient
times it was often used in the making of seals and gems (Ford;
s. also Mounce). χρυσόπρασος chrysoprase. This is an apple
green, finely grained hornstone, a variety of quartz, highly translucent (Ford). ὑάκινθος jacinth. It was a bluish purple stone and
similar to the modern sapphire (Mounce; s. BAG). ἀμέθυστος
amethyst, a variety of quartz, in color clear transparent purple
or bluish violet. It got its name from being regarded an antidote
for drunkenness (Mounce; s. also Ford). (For a brief description
of these stones, s. NBD, 631–634; Pliny, *Natural History*,
XXXVII; N. Hillyer, "Precious Stones in the Apocalypse," CBB
[English], III, 395–398.) ■ μαργαρίτης pearl. ἀνά "each one," 21
distributive use of the prep. ἦν impf. εἰμί. πλατεῖα street,
broad street. διαυγής transparent, clear.

■ ναός temple, sanctuary. παντοκράτωρ almighty. Rev. 22
1:8). ■ σελήνη moon. φαίνωσιν aor. act. subj. fut. act. 24
ἐφώτισεν aor. act. ind. φωτίζω to give light. φέρουσιν
to give light. λύχνος lamp.
περιπατέω to walk
ind. to carry. (s.v.3).
κλεισθῶσι subj. εἰσέρχ
gates, profane. ποιῶ
part. βδέλυγμα

Ch. 22

1 ■ ἔδειξεν aor. act. ind. δείκνυμι to show. ποταμός river. λαμπρός brilliant, bright. κρύσταλλον crystal. ἐκπορευόμενον pres. mid. part. ἐκπορεύομαι to go out.

2 ἀρνίον lamb. ■ πλατεῖα wide street. Probably one is meant to think of one main broad street in contrast to the narrow streets in Eastern cities (Ford). ἐντεῦθεν "from here." ἐκεῖθεν "from there." ξύλον tree. ποιοῦν pres. act. part. to make, to bear. μήν month. ἕκαστος each. ἀποδιδοῦν pres. act. part. ἀποδίδωμι

3 to give, to render. φύλλον leaf. θεραπεία healing. ■ κατάθεμα curse. The word may refer to that which is cursed (Swete). ἔσται fut. εἰμί. λατρεύσουσιν fut. act. ind. λατρεύω to wor-

4 ship, to worship by serving. ■ ὄψονται fut. mid. ind. ὁράω to

5 see. μέτωπον forehead, brow. ■ λύχνος lamp. φωτίσει fut. act. ind. φωτίζω to illuminate, to shine, to give light. βασιλεύσουσιν fut. act. ind. βασιλεύω to be king, to rule as king, to reign.

6 ■ ἀληθινός true, genuine. ἀπέστειλεν aor. act. ind. ἀποστέλλω to send, to send as an official authoritative representative. δεῖξαι aor. act. inf. (s.v.1). The inf. is used to express purpose. δεῖ "it is binding," "it is necessary." γενέσθαι aor. mid. inf. γίνομαι to happen, be become, to come to pass. τάχος

7 quickly. The prepositional phrase is used adverbially. ■ ταχύ quickly. μακάριος happy, blessed. τηρῶν pres. act. part. τηρέω to keep, to observe. The pres. tense indicates a continual keeping. βιβλίον book.

8 ■ κἀγὼ Ἰωάννης "and I John." John now attests that he has actually heard and seen all the things that are recorded in the book (Mounce). ἀκούων pres. act. part. βλέπων pres. act. part. ἀκούσα aor. act. ind. ἀκούω. ἔβλεψα aor. act. ind. ἔπεσα aor. act. ind. πίπτω to fall down. προσκυνῆσαι aor. act. inf. δεικνύ... to ... worship. The inf. is used to express purpose. slav...

10 act. imp. ... part. ■ ὅρα pres. act. imp. (For this to seal. (For ... aor. subj. is used ... ng s. Rev. 9:10.) σύνδουλος fellow

11 prophe... ἐγγύς ... (s.v.7). προσκύνησον aor. injust... do unrigh... act. subj. σφραγίζω cates h... whose habit ... aor. act. ... ince perhaps ... special re... to make d... ρυπαίνω to ... ρυπαρός dirty ... tion. προφητεία ... 86... εύω to do ... indi... " w.

would be 14 miles in height (Mounce). ■ ἐνδώμησις the act of 18
building into, "structure," building (Ford; s. also Mounce).
καθαρός pure, clean. ὕαλος glass. ■ κεκοσμημένοι perf. pass. 19
part. (s.v.2). σάπφιρος sapphire. This is a blue transparent precious stone (Ford). χαλκηδών agate, chalcedony. This gem is
taken to be of a green color (Charles; Ford; BAG). σμάραγδος
emerald. This is a bright green transparent precious stone, the
most valued variety of beryl (Ford). ■ σαρδόνυξ onyx, sard- 20
onyx. This was a layered stone of red and white. It was prized
for use in making cameos (Mounce). σάρδιον sardus, carnelian.
This was a blood-red stone and was commonly used for engrav-
ing (Mounce; Ford). χρυσόλιθος "gold stone," topaz, chryso-
lite. The ancients seemed to have used this term for the yellow
topaz (Ford; s. also Charles). βήρυλλος beryl. This was a green
stone ranging from transparent sea green to opaque blue (Ford;
Mounce). τοπάζιον topaz, a greenish yellow or gold. In ancient
times it was often used in the making of seals and gems (Ford;
s. also Mounce). χρυσόπρασος chrysoprase. This is an apple
green, finely grained hornstone, a variety of quartz, highly translucent (Ford). ὑάκινθος jacinth. It was a bluish purple stone and
similar to the modern sapphire (Mounce; s. BAG). ἀμέθυστος
amethyst, a variety of quartz, in color clear transparent purple
or bluish violet. It got its name from being regarded an antidote
for drunkenness (Mounce; s. also Ford). (For a brief description
of these stones, s. NBD, 631-634; Pliny, *Natural History*,
XXXVII; N. Hillyer, "Precious Stones in the Apocalypse," CBB
[English], III, 395-398.) ■ μαργαρίτης pearl. ἀνά "each one," 21
distributive use of the prep. ἦν impf. εἰμί. πλαντεῖα street,
broad street. διαυγής transparent, clear.

■ ναός temple, sanctuary. παντοκράτωρ almighty (s. Rev. 22
1:8). ■ σελήνη moon. φαίνωσιν aor. act. subj. φαίνω to shine. 23
ἐφώτισεν aor. act. ind. φωτιζω to illuminate, to cause to shine,
to give light. λύχνος lamp. ■ περιπατήσουσιν fut. act. ind. 24
περιπατέω to walk about. ἔθνος nation. φέρουσιν pres. act.
ind. to carry, to bring. ■ οὐ μή "never in any wise." 25
κλεισθῶσιν aor. pass. subj. κλείω to close, to lock, to shut. The
gates would be closed for security at night (Ford). One is reminded of the Isaianic declaration concerning the restored
Jerusalem, "your gates shall be open continually" (Isa. 60:11)
(Mounce). ἔσται fut. (s.v.3). ■ οἴσουσιν fut. act. ind. φέρω. 26
■ εἰσέλθῃ aor. act. subj. εἰσέρχομαι to go in, to come in. 27
κοινός common, profane. ποιῶν pres. act. part. βδέλυγμα that
which is detestable, abomination. εἰ μή "except." γεγραμμένοι
perf. pass. part. βιβλίον book.

Ch. 22

1 ■ ἔδειξεν aor. act. ind. δείκνυμι to show. ποταμός river.
λαμπρός brilliant, bright. κρύσταλλον crystal.
ἐκπορευόμενον pres. mid. part. ἐκπορεύομαι to go out.
2 ἀρνίον lamb. ■ πλατεῖα wide street. Probably one is meant to
think of one main broad street in contrast to the narrow streets
in Eastern cities (Ford). ἐντεῦθεν "from here." ἐκεῖθεν "from
there." ξύλον tree. ποιοῦν pres. act. part. to make, to bear. μήν
month. ἕκαστος each. ἀποδιδοῦν pres. act. part. ἀποδίδωμι
3 to give, to render. φύλλον leaf. θεραπεία healing. ■ κατάθεμα
curse. The word may refer to that which is cursed (Swete).
ἔσται fut. εἰμί. λατρεύσουσιν fut. act. ind. λατρεύω to wor-
4 ship, to worship by serving. ■ ὄψονται fut. mid. ind. ὁράω to
5 see. μέτωπον forehead, brow. ■ λύχνος lamp. φωτίσει fut. act.
ind. φωτίζω to illuminate, to shine, to give light.
βασιλεύσουσιν fut. act. ind. βασιλεύω to be king, to rule as
king, to reign.
6 ■ ἀληθινός true, genuine. ἀπέστειλεν aor. act. ind.
ἀποστέλλω to send, to send as an official authoritative representative. δεῖξαι aor. act. inf. (s.v.1). The inf. is used to express
purpose. δεῖ "it is binding," "it is necessary." γενέσθαι aor.
mid. inf. γίνομαι to happen, be become, to come to pass. τάχος
7 quickly. The prepositional phrase is used adverbially. ■ ταχύ
quickly. μακάριος happy, blessed. τηρῶν pres. act. part. τηρέω
to keep, to observe. The pres. tense indicates a continual keeping. βιβλίον book.
8 ■ κἀγὼ Ἰωάννης "and I John." John now attests that he
has actually heard and seen all the things that are recorded in
the book (Mounce). ἀκούων pres. act. part. βλέπων pres. act.
part. ἤκουσα aor. act. ind. ἀκούω. ἔβλεψα aor. act. ind. ἔπεσα
aor. act. ind. πίπτω to fall down. προσκυνῆσαι aor. act. inf.
προσκυνέω to worship. The inf. is used to express purpose.
9 δεικνύοντος pres. act. part. ■ ὅρα pres. act. imp. (For this
construction and the meaning, s. Rev. 9:10.) σύνδουλος fellow
slave. τηρούντων pres. act. part. (s.v.7). προσκύνησον aor.
10 act. imp. προσκυνέω. ■ σφραγίσῃς aor. act. subj. σφραγίζω
to seal. (For the meaning of sealing, s. Rev. 5:1.) The neg. w. the
aor. subj. is used in a neg. command or a prohibition. προφητεία
11 prophecy. ἐγγύς near. ■ ἀδικῶν pres. act. part. ἀδικέω to do
injustice, to do unrighteousness. The part. used as a noun indicates he whose habit it is to do wrong, "the wrong doer," w.
special reference perhaps to the persecutor (Swete). ἀδικησάτω
aor. act. imp. ῥυπαρός dirty, filthy. ῥυπανθήτω aor. pass. imp.
ῥυπαίνω to soil, to make dirty, to defile (BAG). The filthy

disregard purity of life or even common decency. The aor. tenses here indicate the fixity of the state into which these have entered; there is henceforth no break in the downward course, which is indeed viewed as a single act (Swete). ποιησάτω aor. act. imp. ποιέω. ἁγιασθήτω aor. act. imp. ἁγιάζω to make holy, to sanctify, to set apart (s. CBB; TDNT, EWNT)

■ ταχύ adv. quickly. μισθός reward, wage, pay. 12 ἀποδοῦναι aor. act. inf. ἀποδίδωμι to give, to pay, to render. The inf. is used to express purpose. ■ ἔσχατος last. ἀρχή begin- 13 ning (s. Rev. 1:8).

■ πλύνοντες pres. act. part. πλύνω to wash. στολή robe. 14 The word refers to a long flowing stately robe (s. Trench, Synonyms, 186; TDNT). ἵνα "that," "in order that." The word is used to introduce a purpose clause which is expressed first by the fut. ind. then by the aor. subj. (s. RWP). ἔσται fut. (s.v.3). ξύλον tree. πυλών gate. εἰσέλθωσιν aor. act. subj. εἰσέρχομαι to go into. ■ ἔξω outside, without. κύων, κυνός dog (s. Phil. 3:2). 15 φαρμακός one who mixes drugs either for magic or for sorcery (s. Gal. 5:20; Rev. 9:21; 18:23). πόρνος immoral person, one who commits sexual acts of immorality. φονεύς murderer. εἰδωλολάτρης idol worshiper. φιλῶν pres. act. part. φιλέω to be fond of, to love. ποιῶν pres. act. part.

■ ἔπεμψα aor. act. ind. πέμπω to send. μαρτυρῆσαι aor. 16 act. inf. μαρτυρέω to witness, to testify (s. Trites). The inf. is used to express purpose. ῥίζα root (s. Rev. 5:5). ἀστήρ star. λαμπρός bright, shining, brilliant. πρωϊνός morning star, Venus (s. 2 Peter 1:19). ■ πνεῦμα spirit. νύμφη bride. The 17 Spirit is the Holy Spirit and the bride is the church. It is the testimony of the church empowered by the Holy Spirit that constitutes the great evangelizing force of this age (Mounce). ἔρχου pres. mid. imp. ἀκούων pres. act. part. εἰπάτω aor. act. imp. λέγω. διψῶν pres. act. part. διψάω to be thirsty, to thirst. ἐρχέσθω pres. mid. imp. θέλων pres. act. part. λαβέτω aor. act. imp. λαμβάνω to take, to receive. δωρεάν without cause, freely, without charge.

■ μαρτυρῶ pres. act. ind. to bear witness, to testify (s.v.16). 18 The Speaker is still surely Jesus. Jesus has borne testimony throughout the Book by His angel, and now He bears it in person (Swete). ἀκούοντι pres. act. part. dat. sing. προφητεία prophecy. βιβλίον book. ἐπιθῇ aor. act. subj. ἐπιτίθημι to place upon, to place in addition, to add to. (For the meaning of the prep. in compound, s. MH, 312f.) The subj. is used in a third-class conditional clause which views the condition as a possibility. ἐπιθήσει fut. act. ind. ἐπιτίθημι. πληγή blow, wound,

plague. γεγραμμένας perf. pass. part. The perf. tense indicates the continuing authority of that which was written (s. MM;
19 TDNT). ■ ἀφέλῃ aor. act. subj. ἀφαιρέω to take away, to take away from, to deduct from. (For examples in the papyri, s. MM; Preisigke.) ἀφελεῖ fut. act. ind. ἀφαιρέω. μέρος part. ξύλον tree.

20   ■ μαρτυρῶν pres. act. part. (s.v.18). ναί yes, yea (s. Rev. 1:7). ταχύ adv. quickly, soon. ἀμήν amen (s. Rev. 1:7; EWNT). ἔρχου pres. mid. imp.

21   ■ χάρις grace. The benediction is pronounced upon all who have listened to the book as it was read aloud in the churches of Asia (Mounce). Grace is the only ground on which any can stand for eternity (Govett). μετὰ πάντων "with all." Through clouds and sunshine, by night and by day, in all times and circumstances, His unfailing grace is their support and strength. It is grace from beginning to end, from otherwise hopeless ruin till complete redemption (Scott).